PUBLIC HEALTH LAW
Second Edition

PUBLIC HEALTH LAW

Second Edition

Wendy K. Mariner
Edward R. Utley Professor of Law
Boston University School of Public Health,
School of Medicine & School of Law

George J. Annas
William Fairfield Warren Distinguished Professor & Chair
Health Law, Bioethics & Human Rights Department
Boston University School of Public Health,
School of Medicine & School of Law

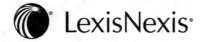

ISBN: 978-0-7698-6800-4
Looseleaf ISBN: 978-0-7698-6801-1
eBook ISBN: 978-0-3271-9159-9

Library of Congress Cataloging-in-Publication Data

Mariner, Wendy K., author.

Public health law / Wendy K. Mariner, Edward R. Utley Professor of Law, Boston University School of Public Health, School of Medicine & School of Law; George J. Annas, William Fairfield Warren Distinguished Professor & Chair, Health Law, Bioethics & Human Rights Department, Boston University School of Public Health, School of Medicine & School of Law. -- Second Edition.

pages cm

Includes index.

ISBN 978-0-7698-6800-4 (hardbound)

1. Public health laws--United States. I. Annas, George J., author. II. Title.

KF3775.M3736 2014

344.7304--dc23

2014041977

NOTE TO USERS

To ensure that you are using the latest materials available in this area, please be sure to periodically check the LexisNexis Law School web site for downloadable updates and supplements at www.lexisnexis.com/lawschool.

Editorial Offices

630 Central Ave., New Providence, NJ 07974 (908) 464-6800

201 Mission St., San Francisco, CA 94105-1831 (415) 908-3200

www.lexisnexis.com

MATTHEW⬥BENDER

With thanks to Benjamin Briggs, Michael Cannella, Christopher Kornak, Valerie Moore, Joshua C.L. Trein, and Ted Woo for their assistance with the second edition. With thanks to Nancy Ammons, Stephanie Wilson, Brook Assefa, Aaron Bass, Amy Condon, Julie Kamerrer, Hajung Lee, Angela Macey-Cushman, Sophia Palmer, Coreen Schnepf, Britnye Segraves, Jason D. Smith, and Aimee Welch for their assistance with the first edition. And particular thanks to Leonard Glantz for his original contributions to these materials.

Preface to the Second Edition

Why public health?

First, public health is vital to our lives and health. That's why public health is in the news every day: mass shootings; drug overdoses; new disease epidemics; school BMI "report cards"; data mining to evaluate health care quality and cost; religious objections to immunizations; access to contraceptives; drunk driving; contaminated food, water and drugs; electronic cigarette regulation; mental health treatment; and even hospital patient injuries. These examples and hundreds like them present legal and policy questions. The answers to those questions can make our lives better or worse.

Second, public health issues affect everyone — students, their families, the professionals they aspire to be, the people they will become responsible for as lawyers, legislators, managers, counselors, administrators, and other professionals. Public health measures have added almost 38 years to the life expectancy of Americans since 1900. While medical care receives the lion's share of public attention, especially since the Affordable Care Act took effect, some of the most dramatic improvements in health and longevity have occurred through mostly invisible public health programs. Public health law demonstrates how difficult it can be to make sure nothing bad happens.

Third, public health law offers students opportunities for real-world legal problem solving. Laws governing public health run the gamut — from constitutional to statutory to administrative to common law — and solving public health problems requires considering all of these. What law applies? Will it be effective? What alternative approaches would be suitable? These are the kinds of questions that graduates will face in their careers.

Organization of PUBLIC HEALTH LAW

Chapter 1. Introduction to Public Health in the United States. The first edition of PUBLIC HEALTH LAW began with the history of public health — a history rooted in 19th and early 20th century epidemics of contagious diseases. Today, the field of public health — and the laws that shape and respond to it — covers much richer ground. Chapter 1, therefore, begins with examples from the news to illustrate the range of topics within the field. These are by no means exhaustive. Indeed, as the materials explain, the very definition of public health law can be controversial. For some, public health can be seen as anything that affects the health of more than a handful of people. For others, it is limited to government laws and policies. It certainly has become entwined with the field of health law and the laws and policies that affect personal medical care. What is clear is that public health law is no longer primarily a matter for the states; the federal government is a major player in the field. And, although this text is focused on law in the United States, it recognizes and includes materials on global health issues, which increasingly affect domestic public health policy. Nonetheless, this book does not cover environmental or occupational law or, with a few exceptions, mental health law. Those subjects are typically well covered in dedicated separate courses. Furthermore, although many public health laws are criminal laws, this book only glancingly touches on criminal law where it most obviously intersects with non-criminal goals of public health protection, as in drug and alcohol use.

Chapter 2. Defining Risks to Public Health. Chapter 2 confronts the threshold question in public health law: what counts as a risk to public health? This can be a fraught question in many cases. Although public health scholars insist that identifying and preventing risks should be based on solid evidence, persistent disagreements over the existence or magnitude of specific risks make clear that one's answer often depends on something other than evidence. Even the most objective person can fall prey to mental short-cuts and cultural biases that distort perceptions of risks and benefits. Thus, this Chapter offers materials from experts in risk perception to introduce readers to methods of evaluating risk and recognizing the potential for error.

Chapter 3. State and Federal Power: Constitutional Principles Applicable to Public Health. Chapter 3 includes several classic United States Supreme Court decisions — and some recent ones — on the respective powers of the state and federal government in matters of public health. Although some cases may be familiar to students of constitutional law, a refresher should prove useful to identify which level of government can and should address particular public health issues. The first part includes cases attempting to distinguish state and federal jurisdiction. These are followed by an illustrative selection of early and contemporary cases concerning the state's police power. Federal powers to regulate commerce and to tax and spend revenue are covered in the last two parts, respectively, to illustrate the federal government's direct and indirect regulation of public health programs.

Chapter 4. Public Health, Morals, and Religion. In earlier centuries, the state's police power was often described as including the power to protect public morals, as well as public safety, welfare and good order. Today, the line between protecting public health and protecting public morals can sometimes seem rather blurred. This Chapter expands on the constitutional principles in Chapter 3, here focusing on the clash between the authority to protect the public health and morals and the limits that the constitution imposes on that authority when it touches intimate spheres of liberty and the free exercise of religion.

Chapter 5. Contagious Diseases. The field of public health arose to prevent or contain the spread of contagious diseases. While epidemics are no longer the source of terror they were long ago, disease outbreaks still occur, and new strains of influenza and other diseases could portend future epidemics. This Chapter considers public health responses to individuals with contagious diseases in the community. It compares the use of civil commitment for this purpose with its doctrinal predecessor, civil commitment of mentally ill, dangerous persons, as well as comparing civil detention with criminal detention. While the subject matter covers some well-trodden ground, unsettled issues remain, such as whether constitutional protections of liberty prevent the government from confining individuals not known to have a disease and requiring individuals to take medication to cure a contagious disease.

Chapter 6. Emergency Preparedness and Bioterrorism. Chapter 6 expands on the materials in Chapter 5 to examine responses to post 9/11 national disasters, examining how 9/11 has changed the nature of public health and preparedness planning to incorporate terrorism with epidemics and natural disasters. How closely should the public health community align its goals and workforce with the national security community? Since both public health and terrorist threats are global and national, the federal government plays the dominant role in both preparedness and response to disasters. Attempts at wide-spread smallpox vaccination in the run-up to the second Iraq war,

Preface to the Second Edition

responding to SARS and anthrax, and even planning for the detonation of an improvised nuclear device in a major American city, can all be used to identify public health issues that have not yet been adequately addressed.

Chapter 7. Privacy and Uses of Medical Information. Identifying and preventing health risks depend importantly on information, and some of the most useful information lies in medical records. Information technology increasingly allows that information to be accessed efficiently, linked with other databases, and analyzed for multiple purposes, from identifying the source of an epidemic to calculating the costs and outcomes of medical care. In this age of Big Data, however, not everyone is comfortable with sharing his or her personal health information with government agencies and researchers, no matter how benign or potentially useful the goal. This Chapter reviews the patchwork of laws governing privacy and confidentiality and further examines examples of ways in which health records can be used, both with and without patient consent.

Chapter 8. Chronic Diseases and Health Promotion. As the toll of contagious diseases declined, public health officials shifted their attention to reducing chronic diseases like heart disease, cancers and stroke, which are the major causes of death in the United States. Public health offers a population-based perspective distinct from the principle of autonomy underlying the physician-patient relationship. This Chapter offers an opportunity for comparing the rationales for intervening in personal medical care and personal behaviors for the purpose of improving the overall health and longevity of the population. In particular, it raises the question of paternalism, examining when government should — and should not — intervene with an individual to protect the individual's own health in order to improve the overall health of the population as a whole.

Chapter 9. Weight and Health. The federal public health agency, the Centers for Diseases Prevention and Control, once proclaimed an epidemic of obesity in the United States, giving new meaning to the concept of epidemic. Since then, the nation has become even more obsessed with weight than earlier generations. This Chapter considers the relationship between weight and health — especially chronic diseases — a relationship not without controversy. In so doing, it raises questions about the goals of public health interventions. The Chapter also reviews possible interventions, such as regulating the food supply, the built environment and schools, placing conditions on employment or the receipt of government benefits, and using litigation to induce food producers to alter their products.

Chapter 10. Tobacco and Health. At the end of the 20th century, tobacco use might have been considered the modern scourge of public health. This Chapter examines the ways in which governments have attempted to reduce tobacco use, both successfully and unsuccessfully. These measures include Food & Drug Administration regulation, advertising restrictions, geographic smoking bans, employment restrictions, and litigation against tobacco companies, as well as legislative reactions to many of these approaches. Because similar measures may be considered to reduce other threats to public health, the tobacco initiatives provide an opportunity to evaluate their application in other contexts.

Chapter 11. Drugs and Alcohol. Intoxication could be the eighth deadly sin, so often is it the subject of preventive — or punitive — legislation. Like tobacco, licit drugs and alcohol are lawful for adult use and are unlikely to be banned. Unlike tobacco, however, excessive use of alcohol or drugs can cause more immediate harm, both to the user and others. This Chapter considers how civil measures may discourage abuse of alcohol and drugs and how to distinguish permissible from impermissible criminalization and civil restrictions. The growing use of drug testing by government agencies is examined in light of Fourth Amendment protections against unreasonable searches and seizures. The Chapter concludes by examining responsibility for harm caused by intoxication.

Chapter 12. Injury Prevention. If a goal of public health is to prevent avoidable causes of death, then it must include injuries as well as illnesses. This Chapter examines two important causes of injury and death: medical care and firearms. These turn out not to be strange bedfellows: both have benign or beneficial uses; both contribute significantly to the nation's death toll; and effective policies to reduce deaths from either cause have not been implemented. The Chapter examines the major policy options and whether they can address the underlying cause of harm to the public. In the case of firearms, the Second Amendment places some limits on regulation, while legislation has restricted the causes of action available for litigation.

Chapter 13. Global Health. The final Chapter addresses the emerging topic of global health, and concentrates on global public health, a field that has spawned its own legal specialty: health and human rights. The human rights framework provides a theoretical framework to promote global health on the basis of universal human rights and dignity, as spelled out in the Universal Declaration of Human Rights and other post-World War II human rights instruments. Public health challenges routinely cross international boundaries, and it is not just contagious diseases that are of contemporary concern, but chronic diseases as well. The field of global health governance is in its infancy, and most law in this area can properly be described as "soft" law, including the expanding field of litigation designed to enforce the growing international "right to health." The most developed legal area is in the regulation of global research on human subjects, dating from the Nuremberg Doctors' Trial. While governments tend to dominate public health, global health will require the active participation of the private sector as well — nongovernmental organizations (NGOs), transnational corporations, and transnational professionals (especially physicians and lawyers).

Ways to Use PUBLIC HEALTH LAW

Courses in public health law have been offered as a stand-alone course and as a supplement or alternative to courses in health law or law and medicine or law and bioethics. This book can be used in any of such courses. The first four Chapters provide the foundation for examining government power and policies affecting public health, as well as constitutional limitations on policy options. The remaining Chapters serve as case studies of specific topics. Each of these Chapters provides examples of different laws and policies — such as mandates, prohibitions, regulatory standards, and litigation — to address each problem. Some Chapters include additional constitutional issues. For example, the First Amendment principles applicable to commercial speech generally are examined using the example of tobacco advertising in Chapter 10; and Fourth Amendment search and seizure principles applicable to some civil matters are discussed in the materials on drug screening in Chapter 11.

Much has changed since the first edition of Public Health Law was published and, therefore, a substantial portion of the materials in this second edition is new. The most recent Supreme Court decisions on public health issues are included. At the same time, we have retained many of the foundational decisions concerning the state's police power to protect public health and federal powers to regulate health-related matters.

Preface to the Second Edition

The Notes and Questions provide some background and explanation of many of the court decisions. They also include references to basic reference materials, which are hyperlinked in the electronic versions of this book. Perhaps more important, the Notes offer examples of current issues to which the materials may apply. We have grouped notes, commentary and questions to follow the material to which the Notes refer, instead of consolidating all notes at the end of a Chapter. To locate a specific topic, consult the Table of Contents, which lists each Note and its subject matter.

Our First Edition Co-Authors

Professor Ken Wing, of University School of Law, who inspired the Ken Wing Fun Run, held annually at the Health Law Professors Conference, led the writing of the first edition of PUBLIC HEALTH LAW. He greatly disappointed us by retiring, but was generous in encouraging us to go forward with a new edition.

Professor Dan Strouse was also taken from us too soon. We are pleased that the Center for the Study of Law, Science, & Technology, of which Dan was Director at Arizona State University Sandra Day O'Connor College of Law, established the Daniel Strouse Prize in his memory.

Wendy Mariner
George Annas
Boston University
Boston, Massachusetts
May 2014

Summary Table of Contents

Table of Contents

Table of Contents

Table of Contents

Table of Contents

Table of Contents

Table of Contents

Table of Contents

Table of Contents

Table of Contents

Table of Contents

Table of Contents

Table of Contents

Table of Contents

Table of Contents

Table of Contents

Table of Contents

Table of Contents

Table of Contents

Table of Contents

Acknowledgements

Annas, George J., Glantz, Leonard H. & Roche, Patricia A., *Drafting the Genetic Privacy Act: Science, Policy, and Practical Considerations*, 23 JOURNAL OF LAW, MEDICINE & ETHICS 360 (1995). Copyright © 1995. Reprinted with permission.

Annas, George J., *Global Health and Post-9/11 Human Rights, in* HEALTH AND HUMAN RIGHTS IN A CHANGING WORLD 102 (M. Grodin, D. Tarantola, G. Annas & S. Gruskin, eds., 2013). Copyright © 2013 Routledge. Reprinted with Permission.

Annas, George J., Mariner, Wendy K. & Parmet, Wendy, PANDEMIC PREPAREDNESS: PROTECTING PUBLIC HEALTH AND CIVIL LIBERTIES (A report prepared for the American Civil Liberties Union, 2008). Copyright © 2008. Reprinted with permission.

Annas, George J., Roche, Patricia A. & Green, Robert C., *GINA, Genism, and Civil Rights*, 22 BIOETHICS ii (2008). Copyright © 2008. Reprinted with permission.

Annas, George J., *The Patient's Right to Safety — Improving the Quality of Care through Litigation against Hospitals*, 354 NEW ENGLAND JOURNAL OF MEDICINE 2063 (2006). Copyright © 2006 by George J. Annas. Reprinted with permission.

Annas, George J., *The Statue of Security: Human Rights and Post-9/11 Epidemics*, 38 JOURNAL OF HEALTH LAW 319 (2005). Copyright © 2005 George J. Annas. Reprinted with permission.

BARRY, JOHN M., THE GREAT INFLUENZA: THE EPIC STORY OF THE DEADLIEST PLAGUE IN HISTORY 2 (2004). Copyright © 2004 John M. Barry. Reprinted with permission.

Berkelman, Ruth L., et al., *Public Health Surveillance, in* 2 OXFORD TEXTBOOK OF PUBLIC HEALTH 759 (R. Detels, et al., eds., 4th ed., 2002). Copyright © 2002 Oxford University Press. Reprinted with permission.

Brownell, Kelly, et al., *Personal Responsibility and Obesity: A Constructive Approach to a Controversial Issue*, 29 HEALTH AFFAIRS 379 (2010). Copyright © 2010. Reprinted with permission.

Campos, Paul, et al., *The Epidemiology of Overweight and Obesity: Public Health Crisis or Moral Panic?*, 35 INTERNATIONAL JOURNAL OF EPIDEMIOLOGY 55 (2006). Copyright © 2006. Reprinted with permission.

Daynard, Richard A., Howard, P. Tim & Wilking, Cara L., *Private Enforcement: Litigation as a Tool to Prevent Obesity*, 25 JOURNAL OF PUBLIC HEALTH POLICY 408 (2004). Copyright © 2004. Reprinted with permission.

Fainauru, Steve & Fainauru-Wada, Mark, *Study: New Cases of CTE in Players* ESPN/FRONTLINE, Dec. 3, 2012. Copyright © 2012. Reprinted with permission.

Fairchild, Amy L., *Dealing with Humpty Dumpty: Research, Practice, and the Ethics of Public Health Surveillance*, 31 JOURNAL OF LAW, MEDICINE & ETHICS 615 (2003). Copyright © 2003. Reprinted with permission.

Finkelstein Eric A. & Strombotne, Kiersten L., *The Economics of Obesity*, 91(suppl.) THE AMERICAN JOURNAL OF CLINICAL NUTRITION 1520s (2010). Copyright © 2010. Reprinted with permission.

GLANTZ, LEONARD H., CONTROL OF PERSONAL BEHAVIOR AND THE INFORMED

Acknowledgements

CONSENT MODEL (2006). Copyright © 2006. Reprinted with permission of the author.

Harris, Jennifer L., et al., *Fast Food FACTS 2013: Measuring Progress in Nutrition and Marketing to Children and Teens, Executive Summary*, Yale Rudd Center for Nutrition Policy and Obesity (2013). Copyright © 2013. Reprinted with permission.

Horton, Richard, et al., *From Public to Planetary Health: A Manifesto*, 383 THE LANCET 847 (2014). Copyright © 2014. Reprinted from *The Lancet* with permission from Elsevier.

Inglesby, Thomas V., et al., *A Plague on Your City: Observations from TOPOFF*, 32 CLINICAL INFECTIOUS DISEASES 436 (2001). Copyright © 2001 University of Chicago Press. Reprinted with permission.

INSTITUTE OF MEDICINE, TO ERR IS HUMAN: BUILDING A SAFER HEALTH SYSTEM 1 (2000). Copyright © 2000 by the National Academy of Sciences, courtesy of the National Academies Press, Washington, D.C. Reprinted with permission.

KAHNEMAN, DANIEL, THINKING, FAST AND SLOW 20 (2012). Copyright © 2012. Reprinted with permission.

Kirn, Walter, *I've Owned Six Guns; I've Drawn Them on Bad Guys; I Want to Be Understood*, THE NEW REPUBLIC, Feb. 11, 2013, at 31. Copyright © 2013. Reprinted with permission.

KLUGER, RICHARD, ASHES TO ASHES xiii (1996). Copyright © 1996 by Richard Kluger. Used by permission of Alfred A. Knopf, a division of Random House, Inc.

Mariner, Wendy K., *Medicine and Public Health: Crossing Legal Boundaries*, 10 JOURNAL OF HEALTH CARE LAW & POLICY 121 (2007). Copyright © 2007. Reprinted with permission.

Mariner, Wendy K., *Mission Creep: Public Health Surveillance and Medical Privacy*, 87 BOSTON UNIVERSITY LAW REVIEW 347 (2007). Copyright © 2007. Reprinted with permission.

Mariner, Wendy K., *Law and Public Health: Beyond Emergency Preparedness*, 38 JOURNAL OF HEALTH LAW 251 (2005). Copyright © 2005. Reprinted with permission.

Miller, Matthew, Azrael, Deborah & Hemenway, David, *Firearms and Violent Death in the United States, in* REDUCING GUN VIOLENCE IN AMERICA 3 (D. W. Webster & J. S. Vernick, eds., 2013). Copyright © 2013. Reprinted with permission.

Outterson, Kevin, *Regulating Compounding Pharmacies After NECC*, 367 NEW ENGLAND JOURNAL OF MEDICINE 1969 (2012). Copyright © 2012 Massachusetts Medical Society. Reprinted with permission.

Parmet, Wendy, *AIDS and Quarantine: The Revival of an Archaic Doctrine*, 14 HOFSTRA LAW REVIEW 53 (1985). Copyright © 1985. Reprinted with permission.

SAGUY, ABIGAIL C., WHAT'S WRONG WITH FAT? 10 (2013). Copyright © 2013 Abigail C. Saguy. Reprinted with permission.

Sweeney, Latanya, *DataMap*, Data Privacy Lab, Harvard University, 2010. Reprinted with permission.

TALEB, NASSIM N., THE BLACK SWAN — THE IMPACT OF THE HIGHLY IMPROBABLE xxi (2d ed., 2010). Copyright © 2010. Reprinted with permission.

Acknowledgements

Tarantola, Daniel & Gruskin, Sofia, *Human Rights Approach to Public Health Policy,* in HEALTH AND HUMAN RIGHTS IN A CHANGING WORLD 43 (M. Grodin, D. Tarantola, G. Annas & S. Gruskin, eds., 2013). Copyright © 2013 Routledge. Reprinted with permission.

Taubes, Gary, *Do We Really Know What Makes Us Healthy?*, NEW YORK TIMES MAGAZINE, Sept. 16, 2007. Copyright © 2007. Reprinted with permission.

Terry, Nicolas P., *What's Wrong with Health Privacy?*, 5 JOURNAL OF HEALTH & BIOMEDICAL LAW 1 (2009). Copyright © 2008 Nicolas P. Terry. Reprinted with permission.

The Lancet — University of Oslo Commission on Global Governance for Health, Ottersen, Ole Petter, et al., *The Political Origins of Health Inequity: Prospects for Change*, 383 THE LANCET 631 (2014). Copyright © 2014. Reprinted from *The Lancet* with permission from Elsevier.

WELCH, H. GILBERT, OVERDIAGNOSED — MAKING PEOPLE SICK IN THE PURSUIT OF HEALTH 11 (2011). Copyright © 2011 Dr. H. Gilbert Welch. Reprinted with permission.

Wikler, Daniel I., *Persuasion and Coercion for Health: Ethical Issues in Government Efforts to Change Life-Styles*, 56 MILBANK MEMORIAL FUND QUARTERLY 303 (1978). Copyright © 1978 Milbank Memorial Fund. Reprinted with permission.

Chapter 1

INTRODUCTION TO PUBLIC HEALTH IN THE UNITED STATES

A. WHAT IS PUBLIC HEALTH?

Perhaps the threshold question in undertaking the study of any area of law is how to define the subject matter. This chapter examines the meaning — or, rather, meanings — of public health. Public health has evolved from its early focus on epidemics of contagious diseases (described in Chapter 5). To see how far, consider the following sample of issues appearing in the media today. They illustrate the scope of problems that public heath encompasses — and the many laws that might address them — which are examined the remaining Chapters of this book.

Steve Fainauru and Mark Fainauru-Wada, *Study: New Cases of CTE in Players*
ESPN/Frontline (Dec. 3, 2012)
http://espn.go.com/espn/otl/story/_/id/8697286/boston-university-researchers-discover-28-new-cases-chronic-brain-damage-deceased-football-players

Researchers at Boston University have discovered 28 new cases of chronic brain damage in deceased football players — including 15 who played in the NFL — more than doubling the number of documented cases connecting football to long-term brain disease.

The NFL players include two Hall of Famers: running back Ollie Matson, who played 14 seasons in the 1950s and 1960s, and Colts tight end John Mackey, who played 10 seasons and once served as the head of the NFL players' union. Both died last year after suffering from dementia.

The study examined brain tissue from 85 people with a history of repetitive head trauma, including military veterans, boxers and football and hockey players . . . . Sixty-eight were found to have chronic traumatic encephalopathy — a degenerative brain disorder linked to memory loss, depression and dementia.

According to the study, the BU researchers now have 50 confirmed cases of former football players with CTE — 33 who played in the NFL, one in the CFL, one semi-professionally, nine through college and six who played only through high school. That included Nathan Stiles, 17, who died of a subdural hematoma after a hit in a 2010 high school homecoming game in Spring Hill, Kan.

1

. . . .

. . . Linemen made up 40 percent of those cases, supporting research that suggests repetitive head trauma occurring on every play — not concussions associated with violent collisions — may be the biggest risk. BU also reported CTE in four former NHL players.

The findings, published in the December issue of Brain, a medical journal affiliated with Oxford University, are certain to feed the growing debate about the risks of playing football . . . .

Note: In 2011, former NFL players sued the NFL claiming that the organization concealed any link between football and traumatic brain injury. In January 2014, U.S. District Court judge Anita Brody rejected a proposed $765 million settlement of the suit, on the ground that the amount might not be sufficient to compensate all former players with relevant diagnoses, including those who are not part of the suit. Further proceedings are expected.

Eric S. Blake et al., *Tropical Cyclone Report: 22–29 October 2012 — Hurricane Sandy*
National Hurricane Center 1, 14-15 (Feb. 12, 2013)
http://www.nhc.noaa.gov/data/tcr/AL182012_Sandy.pdf

Sandy was a classic late-season hurricane in the southwestern Caribbean Sea. . . . Sandy weakened somewhat and then made landfall as a post-tropical cyclone near Brigantine, New Jersey with 70-kt [knots] maximum sustained winds. Because of its tremendous size, however, Sandy drove a catastrophic storm surge into the New Jersey and New York coastlines . . . . There were at least 147 direct deaths recorded across the Atlantic basin due to Sandy, with 72 of these fatalities occurring in the mid-Atlantic and northeastern United States. This is the greatest number of U.S. direct fatalities related to a tropical cyclone outside of the southern states since Hurricane Agnes in 1972.

. . . .

At least 87 deaths, an even greater number than for direct [US] deaths, were indirectly associated with Sandy or its remnants in the United States. About 50 of these deaths were the result of extended power outages during cold weather, which led to deaths from hypothermia, falls in the dark by senior citizens, or carbon monoxide poisoning from improperly placed generators or cooking devices. The remaining deaths were mostly from storm cleanup efforts, including removing falling trees, and car accidents.

. . . . Sandy's impacts in the United States were widespread. At least 650,000 houses were either damaged or destroyed as a result of the cyclone, with the vast majority of the damage caused by storm surge and/or waves. About 8.5 million customers lost power as a result of Sandy or its remnants, with power out for weeks or even months in some areas. Preliminary estimates compiled from a variety of sources suggest that Sandy was responsible for at least 50 billion dollars in damage in the United States. . . . Sandy is expected to rank as the second-costliest cyclone on record, after Hurricane Katrina of 2005.

TUMMINO v. HAMBURG
936 F. Supp. 2d 162 (E.D.N.Y. 2013)

KORMAN, J.

Plan B and Plan B One-Step are emergency contraceptives that can be taken to reduce the risk of pregnancy after unprotected intercourse. In 1999, Plan B became the first emergency contraceptive drug approved for prescription-only use in the United States. In 2006, the Food and Drug Administration ("FDA") approved non-prescription access to Plan B for women 18 and older, and with a prescription to adolescents under the age of 18. Subsequently, the FDA was ordered to make it available without a prescription to adolescents aged 17. *Tummino v. Torti*, 603 F. Supp. 2d 519 (E.D.N.Y. 2009). Even for women 17 and older, Plan B can only be purchased at a pharmacy and requires government-issued proof of age. Plan B One-Step was approved by the FDA in 2009 and is available without a prescription subject to the same restrictions. Though Plan B itself is no longer marketed, generic versions are available.

Both contraceptives contain the same total dose of levonorgestrel, a synthetic hormone similar to the naturally occurring hormone progesterone; Plan B consists of two pills containing 0.75 mg each of levonorgestrel that are to be taken 12 hours apart, while Plan B One-Step consists of one pill containing 1.5 mg of levonorgestrel. Studies have shown that combining the two 0.75 mg doses of the hormone into one pill does not decrease its effectiveness; indeed, the two Plan B pills may be taken simultaneously, fewer than 12 hours apart, or up to 24 hours apart, without any adverse consequences. Both Plan B and Plan B One-Step are most effective when taken immediately after intercourse and preferably no later than 24 hours later, though they may retain some effectiveness if taken within 72 hours. Neither drug has any known serious or long-term side effects, though they may have some mild short-term side effects, such as nausea, fatigue, and headache.

Levonorgestrel-based emergency contraception "interferes with prefertilization events. It reduces the number of sperm cells in the uterine cavity, immobilizes sperm, and impedes further passage of sperm cells into the uterine cavity. In addition, levonorgestrel has the capacity to delay or prevent ovulation from occurring." . . . .

. . . This action was originally brought in January 2005 to challenge the FDA's denial of a Citizen Petition seeking over-the-counter ("OTC") access to Plan B for women of all ages. . . . In light of the overwhelming evidence of political pressure underlying the agency's actions, I vacated the FDA's denial of the Citizen Petition [as arbitrary and capricious] and remanded for the agency to exercise its discretion without impermissible political intrusion. [Tummino v. Torti, *supra*.]

. . . .

. . . This case has proven to be particularly controversial because it involves access to emergency contraception for adolescents who should not be engaging in conduct that necessitates the use of such drugs and because of the scientifically unsupported speculation that the drug could interfere with implantation of fertilized eggs. Nevertheless, the issue in this case involves the interpretation of a general statutory and regulatory scheme relating to the approval of drugs for over-the-counter sale. The standards are the same for aspirin and for contraceptives. . . .

. . . .

. . . [T]he obstructions in the path of those adolescents in obtaining levonorgestrel-based emergency contraceptives under the current behind-the-counter regime have the practical effect of making the contraceptives unavailable without a doctor's prescription. Consequently, the decision of the FDA denying the Citizen Petition is reversed, and the case is remanded to the FDA with the instruction to grant the Citizen Petition and make levonorgestrel-based emergency contraceptives available without a prescription and without point-of-sale or age restrictions within thirty days.

Penn State Faculty Protest New Wellness Program

Pennsylvania State University's 2013 announcement of a new wellness program sparked a protest among faculty and employees, who objected to financial penalties for nonparticipation. An art history professor obtained more than 2,000 signatures on a petition asking the university to cancel the program, and the university was forced to reconsider the program.

Like a growing number of health promotion or wellness programs adopted by employers, Penn State's program was intended to reduce health care costs by identifying ways for employees to improve their health, such as by quitting smoking, exercising and losing weight. It asked employees to complete a health assessment questionnaire and biometric screenings (measuring blood-sugar, cholesterol, and body-mass index), which are common in wellness programs. Employees who did not complete the assessments were to be charged up to $100 per month or $1,200 per year. According to a newspaper report, the health assessment asked questions about diet, the use of alcohol, tobacco and drugs, and emotional problems, as well as "whether they perform regular testicular self-exams." Anna Wilde Matthews & Timothy W. Martin, *Penn State Employees Protest Wellness Effort*, WALL ST. J., Aug. 15, 2013, http://online.wsj.com/article/SB10001424127887323455104579014653816536802.html.

Many members of the faculty expressed alarm at what they perceived to be a coercive invasion of their privacy. Others noted that experience with wellness programs has been mixed so far, with different employers saving and losing money, with similar variation in health effects. The program would be administered by an independent company that offers wellness programs to insurance companies and employers. While the university may have believed that a separate company isolated university personnel from employee information, it could not guarantee that the information would be used only to help individual employees.

The Penn State experience is somewhat unusual, because it attracted media attention; and perhaps also because the program affected employees like faculty members who were willing to object publicly.

Mass Shootings

Eric Harris and Dylan Kelbold horrified the nation in 1999 by shooting 12 students and a teacher to death at Columbine High School in Colorado, then killing themselves. Since then, mass shootings continue to cause a small but tragic and frightening number of deaths in the United States, raising questions about whether the availability of firearms or mental illness play a role in sparking these rampages.

April 2, 2014: After being denied leave, 34 year old army specialist Ivan Lopez shot and killed 3 people and himself with a .45 caliber handgun at Fort Hood, Texas.

September 16, 2013: Former Navy reservist Aaron Alexis killed 12 people in the Washington D.C. Navy Yard before being shot and killed in a gun battle with police.

December 14, 2012: Adam Lanza, 20 years old, first killed his mother at their home in Newtown, Connecticut, then took two automatic pistols and a semiautomatic rifle belonging to his mother and went to the Sandy Hook Elementary School. There, he shot up classroom after classroom, killing 20 students and 6 adults before killing himself at the site.

August 5, 2012: Wade Michael Page, 40 years old, killed 7 people at a Sikh Temple in Oak Creek, Wisconsin, perhaps mistaking it for a mosque. Page was killed by police responding to the scene.

July 20, 2012: James Holmes, 24 years old, used several firearms to kill 12 people in the audience at a movie theater in Aurora, Colorado. His criminal trial may begin in October 2014.

November 5, 2009: Army psychiatrist Nidal Malik Hasan killed 13 people at Fort Hood, Texas and injured more than 30. He was convicted and sentenced to death in 2014.

April 16, 2007: Cho Seung-Hui, a 23 year old student at Virginia Polytechnic Institute, bought a .22 caliber pistol over the internet and a .9.mm pistol at a local gun store. He marched into university dormitories and classrooms, chained doors shut and killed 27 students and 5 professors, then fatally shot himself in the face.

Agency for Toxic Substances & Disease Registry, Centers for Disease Control and Prevention, *Exposure to Contaminated Drinking Water and Specific Birth Defects and Childhood Cancers at Marine Corps Base Camp Lejeune, North Carolina* (2013)
http://www.atsdr.cdc.gov/sites/lejeune/birthdefectstudy.html

The purpose of this study was to determine if maternal exposures to the drinking water contaminants at Camp Lejeune increased the risk of neural tube defects (NTDs), oral clefts, and childhood hematopoietic cancers . . . . Drinking water at Camp Lejeune was contaminated with volatile organic compounds (VOCs) including trichloroethylene (TCE), tetrachloroethylene (PCE), benzene, 1,2-dichloroethylene (DCE) and vinyl chloride from the 1950s through 1985.

The Agency for Toxic Substances and Disease Registry (ATSDR) surveyed the parents of 12,598 children during 1999–2002 to identify potential cases of birth defects and childhood cancers. ATSDR asked parents if their child had a birth defect or developed a childhood cancer. To be eligible for the survey, the mother had to reside on base some time during her pregnancy and children had to be born between 1968–1985.

The survey's participation rate was approximately 76% . . . . ATSDR was able to confirm 15 NTDs, 24 oral clefts, and 13 cancers.

. . . .

ATSDR's study results suggested associations between TCE and benzene in Camp Lejeune drinking water and NTDs.

A. [T]hese effects were seen in children born from 1968–1985 whose mothers were exposed to contaminated drinking water in their residences at Camp Lejeune.

B. During the first trimester of pregnancy, the risk of a NTD increased with increasing levels of exposure to TCE.

. . . .

Investigators observed an association between NTDs and first trimester exposure to benzene. . . .

ATSDR's study results suggested weaker associations between 1st trimester exposure to PCE, vinyl chloride, and 1,2- DCE and childhood hematopoietic cancers such as leukemia.

. . . .

The study found no evidence suggesting any other associations between outcomes and exposures.

———

Kevin Outterson, *Regulating Compounding Pharmacies After NECC*
367 NEW ENGL. J. MED. 1969, 1970, 1972 (2012)

Today, compounding pharmacies are at the center of a controversy after a rare outbreak of fungal meningitis that was traced to several lots of the injectable glucocorticoid methylprednisolone acetate compounded by the New England Compounding Center (NECC). . . .

Since 1938, the FDA has had clear authority to regulate drug manufacturing, but compounding falls into a gray area between state and federal oversight. The FDA's authority here is generally limited to reacting to problems identified by others. Traditional compounding pharmacies are not registered with the FDA as drug manufacturers, the agency doesn't approve their prescriptions before marketing, and related adverse events need not be reported to the FDA. State law generally controls recordkeeping, certifications, and licensing for compounding pharmacies.

. . . .

Fungal contamination at NECC has sickened more than 400 patients and killed at least 29. . . . [M]any patients received these sterile injections for back and joint pain, a procedure that lacks high-quality evidence of efficacy.

———————

Kerry: Failure to Pass Disabilities Treaty is Evidence of a Broken Senate
United States Senate Committee on Foreign Relations, Dec. 4, 2012
www.foreign.senate.gov/press/chair/release/kerry_failure-to-pass-disabilities-treaty-is-evidence-of-a-broken-senate

Senator John Kerry (D-Mass.), Chairman of the Senate Foreign Relations Committee, issued the following statement today after Senate Republicans voted down the "Convention on the Rights of Persons with Disabilities," an international agreement for protecting the rights of individuals with disabilities, by a vote of 61 to 38. The Treaty required 66 votes to pass or two-thirds of the Senators who were present.

. . . .

After the Committee on Foreign Relations received the Convention on the Rights of Persons with Disabilities last May, Kerry held a hearing in which administration officials and advocacy group representatives voiced their strong support. He has emphasized the impact the convention would have on American service members. Testifying at the July hearing was John Lancaster, 1st LT., U.S. Marine Corps (ret.), who called it "unacceptable that many Americans with disabilities cannot leave the borders of the United States without the fear of stigma, barriers and denial of their rights" and urged passage on behalf of 21 veteran service organizations. Later that month, the resolution was amended and passed out of the Foreign Relations Committee by a bi-partisan vote of 13 to 6.

The Convention on the Rights of Persons with Disabilities had the bipartisan backing of President George H.W. Bush and former Republican Majority leader Bob Dole, who attended today's vote with his wife, former Senator Elizabeth Dole.

B.   AMERICAN PUBLIC HEALTH . . . PAST AND FUTURE

In 1988, the Institute of Medicine (IOM) issued a report entitled *The Future of Public Health*, strongly criticizing the nation's public health infrastructure, and the capacity of local, state, and federal agencies to respond to the nation's pressing health needs. The report also delineated a long list of public health issues and problems that needed to be addressed. The 1988 report spawned a number of reform efforts both within and without government (see Notes 7–9, following the readings below, for examples and references), and some public and political attention — but a questionable amount of progress or remediation.

In 2003, the IOM issued an updated report, THE FUTURE OF THE PUBLIC'S HEALTH IN THE TWENTY-FIRST CENTURY, largely echoing the original message of the 1988 report. The assessment of the readiness of local, state, and federal agencies to deal with the various public health problems facing the nation was no more flattering. But a new element in the analysis was the report's use of the terms "public health" and "health" virtually synonymously, at least when defining the health-related problems of Americans and in assessing their underlying causes. Another notable element was renewed attention to the social determinants of health — factors like the environment, conditions of employment, diet, and physical activity. Moreover, in assessing what needed to be done, the report attempted to bridge the distinction between medicine and public health and between the private and public sectors, projecting solutions that would require cooperative "partnerships" among not only the various public health agencies of government but also with private medical care providers and institutions, employers, even the media. Indeed, virtually everyone was given some responsibility for the problems and some role in their potential solution. The excerpts from the 2003 report below are illustrative of the tone as well as the content of that report. These excerpts are followed by materials and Notes that sometimes question the IOM's particular view.

INSTITUTE OF MEDICINE, THE FUTURE OF THE PUBLIC'S
HEALTH IN THE 21ST CENTURY
20, 21, 23–25, 47–48, 51, 53–54, 56–61, 63–64, 66, 68 (2003)

ACHIEVEMENT AND DISAPPOINTMENT

The health of the American people at the beginning of the 21st Century would astonish those living in 1900. By every measure, we are healthier, live longer, and enjoy lives that are less likely to be marked by injuries, ill health, or premature death. In the past century, infant mortality declined and life expectancy increased. Vaccines and antibiotics made once life-threatening ailments preventable or less serious; and homes, workplaces, roads, and automobiles became safer. In addition to the many health achievements facilitated by public health efforts such as sanitation and immunization, unparalleled medical advances and national investment in health care also have contributed to improvements in health outcomes . . .

[Nonetheless] despite the nation's wealth, expenditures for health care and research, and scientific and technical accomplishments, the United States is not fully meeting its potential in the area of population health. For years, the life expectancies of both men and women in the United States have lagged behind those of their counterparts in most other industrialized nations. . . . In 1998, the United States also ranked 28th in infant mortality among 39 industrialized nations. In the area of chronic disease, reported incidence rates in 1990 for all cancers in males and females were highest in the United States among a group of 30 industrialized nations. Some birth defects that appear to have links to environmental factors are increasing. The prevalence of obesity and chronic diseases like diabetes are increasing, and infectious disease constitutes a growing concern because of newly recognized or newly imported agents like West Nile virus, the emergence of drug-resistant pathogens, and the all-too-real threat of bioterrorism.

. . . .

ISSUES THAT MAY SHAPE THE NATION'S HEALTH

Because health is the result of many interacting factors, it stands in the balance between economic, political, and social priorities and is caught in the middle of necessary and important tensions between rights and responsibilities — individual freedoms and community or social needs, regulation, and free enterprise. These tensions pose complicated questions. How can the public's health be maintained in the face of infectious disease threats without compromising individual privacy and confidentiality? Or how can a vibrant, prosperous economy be supported without sacrificing health to pollutants or to occupational hazards? How can society balance the individual desire to pursue the pleasures of life (e.g., food) with scientific evidence about health risk? Alternatively, how are increased employment, better housing, health benefits, and an improved standard of living in a community achievable in the absence of economic development? . . .

. . . [H]ealth is part individual good served by medicine and part public good secured by public health activities. Instead of complementary and collaborating systems, however, the two disciplines, their institutional cultures, their agencies and organizations, and the public's opinion of them have often been deeply divergent; and the individual focus of one and population focus of the other have become further reinforced and polarized. Often it has been harder to motivate and accomplish the long-term changes needed in the broad environments that influence health status because of the potential of immediate "silver bullet" solutions that can address poor personal health once it occurs . . .

The personal health and health care agenda has dominated the nation's health concerns and policy for quite some time. In fact, the majority of funding in the health care delivery system is public, and there is a major public investment in biomedical research, yet the United States has failed to make the same level of commitment to population-based health promotion and disease prevention as it has to clinical care and research and biomedical technologies . . . . However, with the resurgence of infectious disease and the escalation of chronic diseases, as well as the new-found awareness of the multiple determinants of population health and the potential impact of macro-level and even global threats to health, the necessity of population-oriented approaches has become clearer. It has also been recognized that the infrastructure and capacity for such approaches must be permanent and sustained by resources equitably distributed between the governmental public health agencies and their partners and the biomedical and personal health care system.

*   *   *

UNDERSTANDING POPULATION HEALTH AND ITS DETERMINANTS

. . . .

Three realities are central to the development of effective population-based prevention strategies. First, disease risk is . . . a continuum rather than a dichotomy. There is no clear division between risk for disease and no risk for disease with regard to levels of blood pressure, cholesterol, alcohol consumption, tobacco consumption, physical activity, diet and weight, lead exposure, and other risk factors. . . . for many social and environmental conditions . . . Any population model of prevention should be built on the recognition that there are degrees of risk rather than just two extremes of exposure (i.e., risk and no risk).

The second reality is that most often only a small percentage of any population is at the extremes of high or low risk. The majority of people are in the middle of the distribution of risk. [Yet an] exposure of a large number of people to a small risk can yield a more absolute number of cases of a condition than exposure of a small number of people to a high risk. This relationship argues for the development of strategies that focus on the modification of risk for the entire population rather than for specific high-risk individuals. [The resulting approach is often termed] the "prevention paradox" because it brings large benefits to the community but offers little to each participating individual . . . [S]uch strategies would move the entire distribution of risk to lower levels to achieve maximal population gains [but are difficult to achieve based on appeals to individual self-interest.]

The third reality . . . is that an individual's risk of illness cannot be considered in isolation from the disease risk for the population to which he or she belongs. Thus, someone in the United States is more likely to die prematurely from a heart attack than someone living in Japan, because the population distribution of high cholesterol in the United States as a whole is higher than the distribution in Japan. Applying the population perspective to a health measure means asking why a population has the existing distribution of a particular risk, in addition to asking why a particular individual got sick. This is critical, because the greatest improvements in a population's health are likely to derive from interventions based on [answers to] the first question . . . American society experienced this approach to disease prevention and health promotion in the early 20th century, when measures were taken to promote sanitation and food and water safety, and in more recent policies on seat belt use, unleaded gasoline, vaccination, and water fluoridation. . . .

. . . .

Understanding and ultimately improving a population's health rests not only on understanding this population perspective, but also on understanding the ecology of health and the interconnectedness of the biological, behavioral, physical, and socio-environmental domains. . . . The last several decades of research have resulted in a deeper understanding, not only of the physical dimensions of the environment that are toxic, but also a broad range of related conditions in the social environment that are factors in creating poor health.

. . . .

THE PHYSICAL ENVIRONMENT AS A DETERMINANT OF HEALTH

. . . Improved water, food, and milk sanitation, reduced physical crowding, improved nutrition, and central heating with cleaner fuels were the developments most responsible for the great advances in public health achieved during the 20th Century. These advantages of a developed nation are taken for granted, but, in fact, could deteriorate without adequate support of the governmental public health infrastructure.

Environmental health problems, historically local in their effects and short in duration, have changed dramatically within the last 25 years. Today's problems are also persistent and global. Together, global warming, population growth, habitat destruction, loss of green space, and resource depletion have produced a widely acknowledged environmental crisis. These long-term environmental problems are not amenable to quick technical fixes, and their resolution will require community and societal engagement. . . .

The importance of "place" to health status became increasingly clear in the last decades of the 20th century. The places in which people work and live have an enormous impact on their health. The characteristics of place include the social and economic environments, as well as the natural environment (e.g., air, water) and the built environment, which may include transportation, buildings, green spaces, roads, and other infrastructure. Environmental hazards in workplaces and communities may range from tobacco smoke to pesticides to toxic housing. Rural areas may present increased health risks from pesticides and other environmental exposures. . . .

. . . Although rural Americans experience certain health-related disadvantages . . . some of the health effects of the inner city (*i.e.*, decay and crime) are often dramatic and may be related to broader social issues. The "urban health penalty" — the "greater prevalence of a large number of health problems and risk factors in cities than in suburbs and rural areas" — has been frequently discussed and studied. A variety of political, socioeconomic, and environmental factors shape the health status of cities and their residents by influencing health behaviors such as exercise, diet, sexual behavior, alcohol and substance use. The negative environmental aspects of urban living — toxic buildings, proximity to industrial parks, and a lack of parks or green spaces, among others — likely affect those who are already at an economic and social disadvantage because of the concentration of such negative aspects in specific pockets of poverty and deprivation. Urban dwellers may experience higher levels of air pollution, which is associated with higher levels of cardiovascular and respiratory disease. People who live in aging buildings and in crowded and unsanitary conditions may also experience increased levels of lead in their blood, as well as asthma and allergies. . . .

. . . .

THE SOCIAL DETERMINANTS OF HEALTH

. . . Among the greatest advances in understanding the factors that shape population health over the last two decades . . . has been the identification of social and behavioral conditions that influence morbidity, mortality, and functioning.

. . . .

A strong and consistent finding of epidemiological research is that there are health differences among socioeconomic groups. Lower mortality, morbidity, and disability rates among socio-economically advantaged people have been observed for hundreds of years; and in recent decades, these observations have been replicated using various indicators of socioeconomic status (SES) and multiple disease outcomes. . . . Furthermore, educational differentials in mortality have increased in the United States over the past three decades, leading to a growing inequality, even though mortality rates have dropped for all groups.

. . . .

A striking finding that emerges from analyses of occupation- and area-based income measures is the graded and continuous nature of the association between socioeconomic position and mortality, with differences persisting well into the middle socioeconomic ranges. . . .

Although many of the studies that focused on occupation — , education — or area-level SES showed a gradient that is virtually linear, studies that focus on income often show somewhat different results. For example, the association between (increasing) income and (decreasing) mortality is clearly curvilinear, with the decline in the mortality rate with increasing income greatest among those in groups earning less than $25,000 per year and with the decline with increasing income being much less among those earning between $25,000 and $60,000 per year. This curvilinear relationship suggests diminishing returns of income as one approaches the highest income categories, although some association may persist. This curvilinear association between income and health is what lays the framework for findings that more egalitarian societies (i.e., those with a less steep differential between the richest and the poorest) have better average health, because a dollar at the bottom "buys" more health than a dollar at the top. Whether SES has a linear or curvilinear relationship with health has enormous implications for understanding both the etiologic associations and the policy implications of this research. In either case, how-ever, it is important to note that a "threshold" model focused exclusively on the very poorest segments and ignoring others near the bottom and the working poor will not address the relatively poor population health outcomes for the U.S. population as a whole. The major reason for this is because there are groups in the moderate risk categories of working poor and working class who contribute disproportionately large numbers to death rates and poor health outcomes.

. . . There is ample evidence that SES is strongly related to access to and the quality of preventive care, ambulatory care, and high-technology procedures; but health care appears to account for a small percentage of variation in health status among different SES groups. . . .

Despite the past century's great advances in sanitation, which have contributed to the sharp increase in life expectancy observed among all socioeconomic groups, the socioeconomic gradient in health status persists. It has been proposed, and to some extent documented, that the gap in health status by SES may still be attributable to the effects of crowded and unsanitary housing, air and water pollution, environmental toxins, an inadequate food supply, poor working conditions, and other such deficits that have historically affected and that still disproportionately affect those in the lower socioeconomic strata. . . .

Considerable evidence links low SES to adverse psychosocial conditions. People in lower socioeconomic positions are not only more materially disadvantaged, but also have higher levels of job and financial insecurity; experience more unemployment, work injuries, lack of control, and other social and environmental stressors; report fewer social supports; and, more frequently, have a cynically hostile or fatalistic outlook.

There is more often, especially in the United States, a striking and consistent association between SES and risk-related health behaviors such as cigarette smoking, physical inactivity, a less nutritious diet, and heavy alcohol consumption. This patterned behavior response has led [some experts] to speak of situations that place people "at risk of risks." Understanding why "poor people behave poorly" requires recognition that specific behaviors formerly attributed exclusively to individual choice have been found to be influenced by the social context. . . . Both physical and social environments place constraints on individual choice. Over time, those with more economic and social resources have tended to adopt health-promoting behaviors and reduce risky behaviors at a faster rate than those with fewer economic resources.

Socioeconomic disparities in health in the United States are large, are persistent, and appear to be increasing over recent decades, despite the general improvements in many health outcomes. The most advantaged American men and women experience levels of longevity that are the highest in the world. However, less advantaged groups experience levels of health comparable to those of average men and women in developing nations of Africa and Asia or to Americans about half a century ago. Furthermore, these wide disparities coupled with the large numbers of people in these least-advantaged groups contribute to the low overall health ranking of the United States among developed, industrialized nations. A major opportunity for us to improve the health of the U.S. population rests on our capacity to either reduce the numbers of the most disadvantaged men, women, and children in the highest risk categories or to reduce their risks for poor health.

A substantial body of research documents the relationship between racial and ethnic disparities and differences in health status. Numerous studies have shown that minority populations may experience burdens of disease and health risk at disproportionate rates because of complex and poorly under-stood interactions among socioeconomic, psychosocial, behavioral, and health care-related factors.

Although Americans in general experienced substantial improvements in life expectancy at all ages throughout the 20th century, substantial gaps in life expectancy, morbidity and functional status remain between white and minority populations. Life expectancy at birth for African Americans in 1990 was the same as that for whites in 1950. Even after controlling for income, African-American men and women have lower life expectancies than white men and women at every income level. When indicators of SES are considered, these differences, which are often substantial across a diversity of health outcomes, are commonly reduced but remain significant. . . . This phenomenon has led researchers to investigate the health effects of discrimination itself. . . .

The association between social connectedness and health has received much attention in recent years. Concepts of social connectedness relate to social integration at the broadest level, social networks, social support, and loneliness. Social connectedness may be conceptualized as a social characteristic related to civic trust and social capital. . . .

[P]eople who are isolated or disconnected from others are at increased risk of dying prematurely from various causes, including heart disease, cerebrovascular disease, cancer, and respiratory and gastrointestinal conditions. Studies of large cohorts of people enrolled in health maintenance organizations or occupational cohorts of people also report that social integration is critical to survival, although it may not be as critical an influence on the onset of disease.

Powerful epidemiological evidence supports the notion that social support, especially intimate ties and the emotional support provided by them, is associated with increased survival and a better prognosis among people with serious cardiovascular disease. The lack of social support, expressed in terms of conflict or loss of intimate ties, is also associated with health outcomes and risk factors such as neuroendocrine changes in women, high blood pressure, elevated plasma catecholamine concentrations, and autonomic activation. . . .

. . . .

Two decades of research show that the workplace not only generates adverse health effects due to economic circumstances such as downsizing and unemployment or to work conditions such as job demands, control, latitude, and threatened job loss, but also generates protective health effects such as social ties that may help counteract the physical and mental adverse effects of work stressors. . . .

. . . .

Social characteristics of individuals are closely related to health. Among the most important findings to emerge from public health research over recent years is the extent to which characteristics of areas exert independent effects on health. This ecological approach has been rediscovered and is now embedded in a multilevel framework. The major idea is that characteristics of places — neighborhoods, schools, work sites, and even nations — carry with them health risks for the individuals who live in those environments. The health risk conferred by these places is above and beyond the risk that individuals carry with them. Thus, we might view characteristics of physical environments (*e.g.*, parks and buildings), as well as social environments (*e.g.*, levels of inequality and civic trust) as truly properties of places, not individuals. . . .

Wendy K. Mariner, *Law and Public Health: Beyond Emergency Preparedness*
38 J. HEALTH L. 251–68 (2005)

Public health has been both broadly and narrowly defined, usually as a function of its political influence. Broad definitions offer a more accurate description, as in the classic definition by C.E.A. Winslow:

Public Health is the science and art of preventing disease, prolonging life, and promoting physical health and efficiency through organized community effort for the sanitation of the environment, the control of communicable infections, the education of the individual in personal hygiene, the organization of medical and nursing services for the early diagnosis and preventive treatment of disease, and the development of the social machinery to insure everyone a standard of living adequate for the maintenance of health, so organizing these benefits as to enable every citizen to realize his birthright of health and longevity.

This broad description still accurately depicts the wide range of activities of people who work in the field of public health. It is also consistent with the broad range of laws enacted in the name of public health. Given such a broad scope, public health might be equated with any public policy that serves in any way to prevent physical or mental harm or to maintain or improve health. This may pose some definitional problems for those seeking a unifying vision of public health. But, the fact that different groups working within public health define their own territory more narrowly should not deter lawyers from recognizing the broad scope of issues relevant to health.

Six trends in public health demonstrate how the field of public health is changing today, in some ways going back to its roots, in others expanding well beyond them.

1. Social Determinants of Health

. . . The field of "social hygiene" began with the nineteenth century recognition that environmental hazards, as well as poor personal hygiene, could cause illness. Sanitary engineers, perhaps the first real public health workers, eliminated cholera and other water-borne diseases by creating systems for sewer-age and purifying the water supply; other infectious diseases by regulating waste at animal slaughter houses and dockyards and pasteurizing milk; and dramatically reduced tuberculosis by cleaning up slum housing. Many public health pioneers were social reformers, who sought to reduce the hazardous living and working conditions in nineteenth century cities and factories. Their motives varied, from genuine concern for the disadvantaged, to the economic benefits of hiring healthier workers, to forestalling class rebellion by the poorer classes.

. . . Today, empirical research offers growing evidence that socioeconomic factors, such as the distribution of wealth and income, political inequality, education, employment, and housing, can affect health. Known as the "social determinants of health," these factors recall the concerns of early public health reformers and remind us that contagious disease is not the sole threat to health in the United States. Attention to the social determinants of health poses a challenge to defining public health as a unified or recognizable field. On one hand, scholars in public health have made significant contributions to research identifying social and environmental factors affecting the health of populations. As a practical matter, it may be difficult, if not impossible, to improve health significantly in the future without addressing the social factors . . . . On the other hand, including housing, employment, and political inequality may spread the health sphere so thin that it ceases to have any discernible limits. Some critics argue that research on wealth as it affects health is still too crude to produce useful information for making policy and there are dangers in medicalizing so many social issues. Nonetheless, it is increasingly difficult to avoid recognizing how broad social policies, such as those concerning drug abuse and homelessness, affect health. It should be possible to study and identify the effect of factors external to individuals without necessarily making it the responsibility of health professionals to devise or implement solutions. Only if such factors are investigated can their effects be accurately understood.

2. Medicine and Public Health

People in public health have traditionally distinguished their field from medicine by emphasizing that physicians treat individual patients while public health practitioners "treat" entire populations. This distinction, however, is rapidly blurring. It is true that the population-based approach had as much or more success than physicians did with their patients until shortly after World War II, when federal support for hospital construction and medical research fueled the development of modern medical science. The growth of medical technology, beginning with new vaccines and drugs, enabled physicians to save patients' lives, and medicine was rewarded with the mantle of scientific and political superiority.

Nonetheless, medicine and public health have often worked in synergistic ways, both to identify opportunities for research and to translate new technologies into practice. Discovery of bacteria and the germ theory by researchers gave public health its first scientific credibility, as laboratories began to identify specific causes of disease. Medical research also produced the vaccines that enabled public health immunization programs to eradicate or control many infectious diseases, and physicians and nurses, in private practice as well as public clinics, administered the vaccines. Public health research on the distribution of HIV infection in the early 1980s helped academic scientists target their research to identify the virus and also helped practicing physicians counsel their patients about how to prevent transmission of the infection. Public health screening programs, like those for cholesterol or diabetes, are intended to encourage people to get medical care to control their condition. These are only a few examples of essential and productive links between medicine and public health.

Artificial separation of public health and medicine may have more to do with economics and political influence than substance. Until very recently, physicians have been the dominant professionals in health policy, and medicine (and medical research) has received the vast majority of public and private funding. Physicians still play most primary leadership roles in public health. Public attention to public health has waxed and waned, usually rising in response to a crisis, such as, recently, the September 11 attacks, the anthrax letters, severe acute respiratory syndrome (SARS), the recall of Vioxx, and possible avian influenza. Historically, public health has received only a tiny fraction of national expenditures for health, and its share has not risen substantially even with additional post-September 11 funding. Public health tends to be defined by its general goal, improving health, not by the methods it employs, which are legion. Physicians also pursue health as a goal, but the medical profession is defined by a universal method of training for physicians. Similarly, the legal profession is defined by a universal method of training for lawyers. Professions typically are identified by a common (if complex) methodology and knowledge base. These skills can be used to achieve many different goals. In contrast, people who work in public health are trained in many different skills that use very different methodologies. They are united only by the goal they use their skills to achieve — health.

A related distinction between public health and medicine lies in the difference between defining health goals in terms of an entire population (whether defined by geography, sex, or race, for example) as opposed to an individual patient. Success in public health depends on improving the health of the entire population, which can only be measured in aggregate statistics, such as life expectancy and rates of mortality, disease, and disability. Physicians deal with one patient at a time and measure success patient by patient. Although physicians want to save lives and prevent or cure disease, they have an obligation to do what the individual believes to be in her own best interest. Thus, physicians are also successful when their patients succeed in making their own decisions. This kind of individual "success" does not necessarily count as success in public health terms. Patients who refuse life-saving therapy because they find it too burdensome may adversely affect population mortality rates. Public health programs that focus on aggregate outcomes for a population cannot account for individual values in the same manner as medicine.

Nevertheless, some occupational groups within medicine and public health have greater affinity with each other than with other specialists in their own field. For example, academic researchers have similar research methods and values, whether they conduct laboratory experiments with cells or epidemiological studies using large databases. They may have more in common with each other than with practitioners who provide clinical services to patients. Physicians who treat patients in private practice and public health workers who offer substance abuse treatment use similar methods to help individuals, just as physicians and public health workers who offer preventive services share similar methods and concerns. Indeed, a substantial proportion of public health expenditures are for individual healthcare services.

It is difficult to disentangle these professions from one another simply by looking at what people do. This suggests that, whether they acknowledge it or not, public health and medicine are already integrated to a remarkable degree, primarily by the methodology they use, and that it would be both disingenuous and counterproductive to insist on separation.

3. Health Promotion: External and Internal Risks to Health

Public health successes in eradicating or controlling contagious diseases in the nineteenth and mid-twentieth centuries, coupled with research on the causes of disease may have combined to produce another trend — health pro-motion. In the past, public health programs were most successful at preventing or controlling infectious diseases. The goal was to protect the population from external sources of disease. Relatively straightforward measures, like purifying the water supply, creating sewage systems, monitoring the food supply, and encouraging immunization, dramatically reduced the threat of immediately life-threatening diseases. Ironically, perhaps, these important successes left public health programs with less to do and less public support and funding.

The top four leading causes of death today in the United States are heart disease, cancers, stroke, and chronic respiratory diseases, with accidental injuries in fifth place. Unlike infectious diseases, these problems lack a single viral or bacterial cause. Rather, they may result from multiple factors, including genetic predisposition, diet, personal behaviors, exposure to environmental or occupational hazards and dangerous products, as well as social, economic, and political factors. In addition, chronic diseases develop over a long period, often decades. There are few single interventions that completely prevent or cure a chronic disease comparable to those for an infectious disease. Prevention is multifaceted and success uncertain. The public is likely to think first of medicine, not public health, as the profession with the most expertise in chronic diseases and the most to offer, primarily in the form of curative medical therapies. At the same time, however, the many factors contributing to chronic disease, coupled with their increasing prevalence, may have encouraged the field of public health to characterize such diseases as public health problems.

As the types of diseases affecting Americans changed, the public health field shifted its attention to health promotion, encouraging public education about the causes of chronic diseases, as well as regulations that reduce environmental risks. Given the complex causes of many chronic diseases, one might expect public health programs to focus renewed attention on the full range of social determinants of health. There have been some attempts to educate the public about hazardous working conditions or housing. The mapping of the human genome increased awareness of genetic predispositions to certain diseases. So far, however, most public health campaigns, from education to advocacy for new laws, have focused on the risks to health that arise from personal behaviors, such as a high fat diet, lack of physical exercise, smoking cigarettes, and violence. This emphasis on personal risk behaviors lends support to those who wish to characterize the primary problems in public health as the personal responsibility of individuals themselves, rather than as problems that require societal solutions. Rather than making the world safer for people, it seeks to have people protect themselves from risks in the world as it exists.

The trend toward changing personal behavior coincides with renewed concern about the rising cost of healthcare and a political climate that emphasizes personal responsibility and discourages reliance on public benefit programs. If people change their behavior in ways that improve their health, they are less likely to need expensive medical care. Employers have adopted policies forbid-ding their employees from smoking or drinking at home as well as on the job. While such policies can be justified as encouraging healthy behavior, they are often initiated primarily to reduce health insurance costs.

Public awareness of how to improve one's health is usually a good thing. If health policy targets personal behavior to the exclusion of more influential causes of ill health, however, it may prove ineffective. Public education programs require a long-term commitment to public education. Moreover, programs that depend on individuals to change their behavior are typically less effective than programs that remove risks from the external environment. Health promotion programs increasingly target conditions that, unlike contagious diseases, affect only the individual. Both diabetes and obesity have been declared "epidemics," giving a new meaning to the term. It also moves the field of public health farther from any concentration on preventing the spread of disease (from one place or person to another person), and places it squarely beside medicine in the effort to improve the health of an individual for his own sake.

4. Federalization of Public Health

Public health practitioners often think of public health as primarily a local and state endeavor. The Institute of Medicine perpetuated this view in its influential 1988 report by defining public health activities as by and for the community and confining the community to the state, city, or town level, barely mentioning national or international activities. It is true that, when the country began, most governmental efforts to prevent disease were carried out by local officials, but the federal government was never entirely absent from the field. After all, it was the federal government that sent federal public health officials to try to control the spread of plague in San Francisco at the turn of the twentieth century. By the late twentieth century, the federal government had moved decisively into public health and medicine, with legislation such as Medicare and Medicaid, the Occupational Safety and Health Act of 1970, and the Clean Air and Clean Water Acts. Indeed, many of the most important public health achievements have come from federal legislation.

Today, countless public health programs are influenced, if not controlled, by a federal government agency. Despite recent Supreme Court decisions limiting the scope of congressional authority under the Commerce Clause, the federal government retains ample power. Even with block grants and decentralization, the federal government controls the shape and direction of many state and local public health programs through the power of its purse. Most states enacted laws requiring drivers to wear seatbelts when having those laws in place became a prerequisite for the state to receive certain federal highway funds. Similarly, most states enacted laws raising the minimum age for drinking alcoholic beverages to twenty-one years in order to qualify for federal highway funding. Title X funding for family planning programs is subject to specific requirements for how funds are spent. Many state disease-reporting systems might not exist without federal funding from the Centers for Disease Control and Prevention (CDC), and such funding is increasingly tied to legislative requirements. As states face declines in tax revenues and pressure for more services, they may have to rely on federal financial assistance to carry out many of their basic programs. Thus, today, it is often difficult to disentangle federal from state control over even, ostensibly, state public health programs.

After September 11, 2001, as part of the war on terror, the federal government has asserted even greater influence in matters that affect public health — as a matter of national security subject to federal jurisdiction. Even if the states remain primarily responsible for carrying out public health activities, they will often take their cue from Washington, DC.

5. Globalization of Health

Increasing interdependence among global economies is pushing the public health field more firmly into the international sphere. As companies expand their operations around the world, they are beginning to recognize the need for consistent international standards in product safety, environmental controls, and occupational hazards. Sales of goods over the internet raise questions about which product safety standards and marketing rules should apply. Climate change and natural disasters require a coordinated global response from many countries. Disasters like the December 2004 Tsunami create financial and logistical challenges, from identifying the dead to housing and feeding the displaced, that no single country can meet alone. Even war is increasingly recognized as an international public health concern, which requires multinational efforts to provide for the health and safety of civilians, who are often targets of military or terrorist violence. Here, especially, the international human rights movement has brought attention to the positive relationship between human health and respect for human rights.

People in public health are rightly paying more attention to these global issues. Research itself is increasingly international, with scientists in different countries sharing insights and techniques to study everything from genetic diseases to management. As in the United States, affinities tend to follow the subject matter rather than the professional category.

Infectious diseases that cross national borders no longer exhaust the subject matter of global health concerns, but they remain firmly on the radar. Global travel and migration make it relatively easy for viruses and parasites to become world travelers, as SARS' leap from Hong Kong to Toronto demonstrated. Although SARS proved to be less hardy than feared, with most deaths in Canada occurring among people infected before the disease was recognized and most infections occurring in the hospital, a new virus might be more lethal, especially if the population has no natural immunity and no vaccine or treatment is available. For example, if the avian influenza virus (H5N1), which has ravaged poultry stocks in Southeast Asia and killed forty-six people, became efficiently transmissible to humans and from person to person, it might cause a global pandemic affecting millions.

Although no one knows whether such a viral shift will occur, it would be prudent to pursue not simply an early warning system, but public education about contact with animals, research on possible vaccines, and organizing services to care for people who become ill. Perhaps the most effective preventive measure would be to create new job opportunities that make it unnecessary for people to rely on raising chickens and ducks to survive.

6. Bioterrorism

An image of the world as an incubator of dreadful diseases that can cause epidemics gained currency with the spread of HIV infection in the 1980s, reinforced by popular books like "The Hot Zone" and movies like "Outbreak." When letters containing (non-contagious) anthrax killed five people soon after September 11, 2001, federal officials warned that terrorists might bring smallpox into the country next. Concern for infectious diseases "imported" from abroad transmogrified from a manageable medical problem into a terrifying worldwide conspiracy against Americans. Not only might viruses and parasites accidentally board a ship or airplane and fall out in America, but a terrorist might deliberately attack the country with biological weapons.

The combination of terrorism and disease has simultaneously focused much needed attention on public health and perversely narrowed public appreciation of public health largely to bioterrorism. The most positive response has been new federal funding to shore up the perennially neglected "public health infrastructure," the collection of public and private programs that study, prevent, and treat health problems that affect communities large and small. Less positive has been the emphasis on emergency preparedness to the detriment — some would say exclusion — of the less glamorous, ordinary tasks of public health practitioners, which may offer better protection against illness and death.

The country already has some experience with what today would be called bioterrorists — from United States residents who used viruses or bacteria to frighten and make people sick. Only five deaths resulted, all from the anthrax letters mailed in 2001, while each year, influenza kills twenty to thirty thou-sand Americans. The federal government is spending millions of dollars to pre-pare for a terrorist attack using smallpox or other biological weapons, but still has not developed a plan to assure an adequate annual supply of influenza vaccine.

B. SUMMARY

These six trends suggest that, despite current public attention to bioterrorism, the field of public health is in fact wide-ranging and even expanding. It reaches around the world because both risks to health and ways to protect health are increasingly global, requiring more coordinated international attention. This global reach, coupled with concerns about bioterrorism and renewed constraints on state budgets, places the federal government in the forefront of public health today. A national view of public health may encourage recognition of its importance and the many social determinants of health. Indeed, as public health is increasingly tied to medicine, with internal special-ties crossing professional boundaries and public health professionals increasingly seeking individual health promotion instead of removing external threats to populations, it may be time to change our terminology. Instead of medicine and public health, the world sees a field of Health, writ large, with shared components of research, prevention, treatment, and care throughout.

NOTES AND QUESTIONS

1. **Defining public health.** As all of these materials demonstrate, the term "public health" has several different meanings and connotations.

As used in the IOM reports, it appears that "public health" is virtually anything that has to do with the health status of the American public. In this regard, there is little real difference between the terms "health" and "public health," other than the underlying assumption, espoused by most people who identify themselves as public health professionals, that they view "public health" in terms of the whole population and not just on an individual-by-individual basis. Other "public health" authorities make similar claims, referring to their thinking as "population-" or "community-based."

Is there real meaning here? What does it really mean to view a health problem in community-based, population-based, or public health terms? What does it add — or subtract — from the analysis of any particular problem? Is it a skill or discipline? Or is it better described as a perspective or goal? For a thoughtful examination of how to integrate a public health and population-based perspective into law, see WENDY E. PARMET, POPULATIONS, PUBLIC HEALTH AND THE LAW (2009).

Some public health authorities have attempted to refine the definition of public health more specifically, albeit somewhat more pedantically. *See, e.g.*, Roger Detels & Lester Breslou, *Current Scope and Concerns in Public Health*, I OXFORD TEXTBOOK OF PUBLIC HEALTH, 3-20 (R. Detels et al., eds., 4th ed. 2002). For a good effort to clarify all this and limit the scope of public health to manageable proportions, see Mark Rothstein, *The Limits of Public Health: A Response*, 2(1) PUBLIC HEALTH ETHICS 84 (2009) (finding three different variations in contemporary efforts to broadly define public health and rejecting them all in favor of a more narrow, legalistic definition).

2. **Government programs.** With all due respect to these more sophisticated definitions of public health, the most literal definition of the term "public health" may be the most useful. That is, the term "public health" can be used simply as a reference to the broad range of activities, primarily governmental ("public"), that attempt to maintain and protect "health." In this view, public health is what the government does. It includes the various activities of the state's department of public health (which may be one part of a larger department of health), as well as departments of health at the municipality level. At the federal level, public health is what is done by a number of agencies, most within the Department of Health and Human Services (DHHS). These include, most prominently, the Centers for Disease Control and Prevention, the Public Health Service, the Health Resources and Services Administration, the Agency for Healthcare Research and Quality, and, arguably, the Food and Drug Administration to the extent that it protects the safety and efficacy of drugs and medical devices. Other federal agencies, such as the Environmental Protection Agency, the Occupational Safety and Health Administration (in the Department of Labor), the Bureau of Alcohol, Tobacco, Firearms and Explosives (within the Department of Justice), the Department of Agriculture, the

Department of Housing and Urban Development and even the Department of Homeland Security (especially the Federal Emergency Management Agency or FEMA), conduct research, fund programs, and carry out direct-service activities that can be described as public health. This is, of course, somewhat of an oversimplification. Public health programs are often carried out by non-governmental (usually non-profit) private organizations, either independently or with governmental funding. Examples include disaster relief, domestic or international disease control initiatives, substance abuse programs, and family planning clinics. For a general description of public health activities and occupations, see BERNARD J. TURNOCK, PUBLIC HEALTH: WHAT IT IS AND HOW IT WORKS (2009).

So many federal, state, local, and tribal agencies have responsibility for public health programs — sometimes complementary, sometimes overlapping, and sometimes conflicting — that public health can appear quite fragmented. Laws applicable to public health problems come from both federal and state sources, as well as international laws and treaties. This makes the study of public health law both challenging and exciting. The federal government's influence on public health has grown significantly in recent decades, via both direct legislation and the use of federal funding to encourage states to adopt favored laws. For a discussion of federal and state jurisdiction in public health, see Chapter 3, *infra*.

     3. Public health and law. A 2011 IOM committee report recognized the importance of law to public health:

> Laws transform the underpinnings of the health system and also act at various points in and on the complex environments that generate the conditions for health. Those environments include the widely varied policy context of multiple government agencies, such as education, energy, and transportation agencies, as well as many statutes, regulations, and court cases intended to reshape the factors that improve or impede health. The measures range from national tobacco policy to local smoking bans and from national agricultural subsidies and school nutrition standards to local school-board decisions about the types of foods and beverages to be sold in school vending machines.

IOM, FOR THE PUBLIC'S HEALTH: REVITALIZING LAW AND POLICY TO MEET NEW CHALLENGES xii (2011).

This recognition led some public health organizations to advocate for changing specific laws to provide better protection for public health and, especially important from their perspective, more funding for public health agencies and services. The 2011 report concluded, "Many public health statutes have not been systematically updated in decades or more. They do not reflect current circumstances, provide insufficient mandates and powers, and guarantee human rights protections that might be interpreted judicially as overbroad." *Id.* at 33.

While current laws on almost any topic may not reflect current circumstances (think of the internet and social media), it is worth considering what laws the authors believed granted governments insufficient powers or overly protected human rights. For a discussion of early state police powers, see Chapter 3, *infra*. For a discussion of human rights and health, see Chapter 13, *infra*.

4. Public health activities. The 1988 IOM report classified what public health does into three "core functions" — assessment, policy development, and assurance. Assessment includes identifying and measuring health risks and evaluating the effectiveness of interventions. Lawyers may easily understand the concept of policy development, since it suggests creating, modifying and amending laws. Assurance includes both programs and policies intended to get appropriate services to the population.

In 1994, another committee of public health organizations and officials laid out what it called the ten "essential public health services," listed below. As the 2011 report noted, the list is "extremely broad and somewhat vague" in order "to illustrate the range of modern public health practice." IOM, For the Public's Health: Revitalizing Law and Policy to Meet New Challenges 31–32 (2011). Do all of these "essential" services sound like what you thought — or now think — public health does or should do? To what degree does — or should — a profession define its sphere of expertise for purposes of the law?

The 10 Essential Public Health Services

1. Monitor health status to identify and solve community health problems.
2. Diagnose and investigate health problems and health hazards in the community.
3. Inform, educate, and empower people about health issues.
4. Mobilize community partnerships and action to identify and solve health problems.
5. Develop policies and plans that support individual and community health efforts.
6. Enforce laws and regulations that protect health and ensure safety.
7. Link people to needed personal health services and assure the provision of health care when otherwise unavailable.
8. Assure a competent public and personal health care workforce.
9. Evaluate effectiveness, accessibility, and quality of personal and population-based health services.
10. Research for new insights and innovative solutions to health problems.

IOM, For the Public's Health: Revitalizing Law and Policy to Meet New Challenges (2011).

5. Taking care of populations. Whether public health is defined in terms of everything that affects our health or more narrowly in terms of government agencies and their activities, any use of the term "public health" carries with it another meaning: Whether inspired by "community-" or "population-based thinking," by the principles of good science, or simply by common sense, public health activities are usually designed to influence a whole range of the social, environmental, and other factors that have some causal role in health-related problems — as distinguished from individualized medical care, which typically attempts to remedy the impact of such factors on each individual affected. The distinction is not complete or even wholly accurate. In fact, government public health programs provide individual medical care (*e.g.*, clinics in some local health departments, state and local public hospitals, or the Indian Health Service); conversely, individual physicians and other medical care practitioners often attempt to prevent health problems and promote health in their communities as well as in each patient. But make no mistake about it: Most people who use the term "public health" to describe health-related activities do so in part as a reminder of what their activities are generally not: "medicine."

Public health is also *public* health and generally not *private* medicine. That is to say, in part we refer to public health to emphasize the population-based thinking and preventive orientation that characterizes public health practice; but we also do so to draw attention to the public — meaning governmental — nature of the great bulk of public health activities. American practitioners of medical care have struggled hard to maintain their private and autonomous nature. And while that struggle has not been completely successful, when government crosses the line from the public health arena and enters the area of individual medical practice (for example, when public health departments require preventive measures), it is often a controversial step.

6.   Public health and medicine. The distinction between what is called public health and what is called private medicine is much more than a parsing of terms or even a reminder of an underlying political battle. It has important implications for public policy. Public health activities — mass immunizations, improved water supplies and sanitation, and so on — have been responsible for many important improvements in the nation's health. Americans saw tremendous advances in health through the late 19th and early 20th century in the United States, measured even in the crudest of terms. The role of medicine in achieving these visible advances cannot be denied, but that role must be viewed in the context of the other social and economic improvements and in light of various *public health* initiatives. Sanitation, clean water, and decent housing saved more lives than the provision of individual medical care.

Others have argued that much the same could be said of the decades that followed. Americans in the 20th century witnessed wave after wave of biomedical advances, but the role of these advances in improving the health of Americans should not be exaggerated or overshadow that of other, *public health* measures, *e.g.*, health education and promotion programs, seat belts and other mandatory safety laws, and efforts to maintain water and air quality.

From the foregoing data, some reason that many health-related problems are more likely to be resolved by public health techniques than by medicine, and that we should transfer some of our public investment in medical care to a growing investment in public health. That has both a good side and a bad side. For example, such reasoning could be used to justify cutbacks in programs such as Medicaid and Medicare (at least if some of the resulting savings are used for other health-related programs or, if nothing more, that they are spared from budget cutbacks). For an attempt to illustrate this point, a further recounting of the data, and an analysis of the implications for health spending, see J. Michael McGinnis, Pamela Williams-

Russo & James R. Knickman, *The Case for More Active Policy Attention to Health Promotion*, 21 HEALTH AFF. 78 (2003).

7.   **New public health.** There was even an active school of criticism in the 1970s that argued that our focus on medicine and our tendency to overlook the role played by other influences was inhibiting advances in health and even harming us in some ways. *See* THOMAS MCKEOWN, THE ROLE OF MEDICINE: DREAM, MIRAGE, OR NEMESIS? (1976); IVAN ILLYCH, LIMITS TO MEDICINE (5th ed. 1976); RICK CARLSON, THE END OF MEDICINE (1975). One author described this school as initiating a "new public health".

> . . . The origins of the "new" public health movement are generally located by commentators in the 1970s, a time when the writings of critics calling into question the efficacy and social cost of medicine were attracting attention and when other social movements championing improved living conditions and human rights were under way. Proponents of the "new" public health . . . were also influential in constructing a vision of the "cultural crisis of modern medicine." As a result, public health reformers began to argue that resources should be directed away from curative technologies to the prevention of illness and disease.

> The "new" public health is typically represented as a reaction against both the individualistic and victim-blaming approach of health education and the curative model of biomedicine. It is heralded as a return to the concern with environmental factors that first generated the public health movement of the 19th century. Proponents of the "new" public health argue that during the early to mid-20th century the public health movement lost its direction in narrowing the focus on the individual, by championing preventive medicine rather than community health-oriented strategies to improve population health, and by being disease-focused rather than health-focused. They routinely refer to the time between the original public health movement of the mid- to late 19th century and the "renaissance" of public health in the 1970s, when therapeutic medical services took over and the emphasis on "holistic" and "preventive" health was lost. . . . Proponents often refer back to the original public health movement of the 19th century as an exemplar for remodeling the "new" public health, recalling its imputed interest in environmental and improved living standards, rather than the emphasis on the individual. . . .

DEBORAH LUPTON, THE IMPERATIVE OF HEALTH: PUBLIC HEALTH AND THE REGULATED BODY 49–50 (1995).

8.   **Social determinants of health.** Toward the end of the twentieth century, researchers picked up the holistic mantel, one might say, by investigating the broader influences on health, including environmental and social conditions, and political and income inequality, or what has become known as the social determinants of health. *See* World Health Organization (WHO) Commission on Social Determinants of Health, Closing the Gap in a Generation (final report, 2008), www.who.int/social_determinants/thecommission/finalreport/en/index.html   (last visited July 2013); MICHAEL MARMOT & RICHARD G. WILKINSON, SOCIAL DETERMINANTS

OF HEALTH (2d ed. 2006); Norman Daniels, et al., *Why Justice Is Good for Our Health: The Social Determinants of Health Inequalities*, 128 DAEDALUS 215 (1999). For a comprehensive review of one country's health status and recommendations to reduce inequalities, see FAIR SOCIETY, HEALTHY LIVES: A STRATEGIC REVIEW OF HEALTH INEQUALITIES IN ENGLAND POST-2010 (The Marmot Review), www.instituteofhealthequity.org/projects/fair-society-healthy-lives-the-marmot-review (last visited July 2013).

The public health community has begun to embrace the social determinants of health, because they have the greatest potential for health improvement with far less reliance on individual action than traditional public health measures. *See, e.g.,* Thomas R. Frieden, *A Framework for Public Health Action: The Health Impact Pyramid*, 100 AM. J. PUB. HEALTH 590 (2010).

This broader view of what is needed to protect health is reflected in international declarations and conventions, including the Universal Declaration of Human Rights, discussed in Chapter 13. In May 2012, the World Health Assembly endorsed a resolution committing WHO member states to take steps to eradicate hunger and poverty, ensure food security, enable access to healthcare, and improve daily living conditions through provision of safe drinking-water and sanitation, employment opportunities and social protection. Human rights advocates around the world recognized the ways in which human rights safeguards also protected both individual and population health and fostered the health and human rights movement. *See* HEALTH AND HUMAN RIGHTS IN A CHANGING WORLD (Michael A. Grodin et al., eds., 2013).

9.   **Political resources.** Advocates of the "new" public health were only the most eloquent of many voices from within and without the public health professions that were increasingly frustrated in the last several decades of the twentieth century by the lack of attention — and resources — directed towards public health activities. A 1988 IOM report, THE FUTURE OF THE PUBLIC'S HEALTH, attempted to document and publicize those frustrations. Despite the progress that could be traced to public health efforts, as the report argued, public health had captured neither the attention of the American public nor the support of its pocketbook. Most Americans looked to private medicine, not public health, for solutions to their health problems. "Public health is in disarray" became an oft-repeated quotation and the basis for a call to action.

What followed was a certain amount of political smoke but little direct political fire. For example, the CDC, with the help of various state and local public health officials and several health-related professional organizations, attempted to organize political efforts at both the state and federal levels to improve the status of the nation's public health infrastructure. One such effort was the "Healthy People 2000 initiative," sponsored by the Public Health Service, which attempted to define workable goals for improving public health programs and enhancing the health status of Americans.

By the end of the decade, however, most of these goals had not been met. The sponsors published a series of documents — Healthy People 2010: Understanding And Improving Health, Healthy People 2010 — tacitly admitting that most of their projected goals remained just that — goals. These documents, while excessive and excessively bureaucratic, nonetheless provide a detailed assessment of the health status of Americans, a specification of our unmet health needs, and techniques for measuring progress towards improvements. The initiative continues — the current iteration is Healthy People 2020 — with online information, available at www. healthy people.gov/ (last visited July 2013).

In the first decade of the 21st century, public health did receive renewed attention and resources, if perhaps only temporarily. Ironically, this resurgence had less to do with the efforts of the CDC, the IOM or anyone within the ranks of the public health professions, and more to do with the public's reaction to the events of September 11, 2001. For a description and discussion, see Chapter 6, *infra.*

10. Why does public health receive so little attention? Public health has always focused on prevention, but prevention gets little public attention and, thus, limited public support. Some reasons for this lack of celebrity are obvious. Public health succeeds when population rates of illness, injury and death decline. First, success means that harm does *not* happen — such as the epidemic that immunization prevented. "Nothing happened" does not grab headlines. Heroic medical achievements, like organ transplants or breakthrough drugs, attract far more public attention. Second, translating population-based measures to individual outcomes can be difficult. For example, although preventive behaviors like lowering one's blood pressure are correlated with lower rates of stroke and heart disease at the population level, how do we know whether there is a causal relationship for any particular individual? Third, while human beings can empathize with identifiable individuals, empathy with large populations (statistical lives) is rarer. *See* Thomas C. Schelling, *The Life You Save May Be Your Own,* in PROBLEMS IN PUBLIC EXPENDITURE ANALYSIS 127, 129–30 (Samuel B. Chase, Jr. ed., 1968); GUIDO CALABRESI & PHILIP BOBBITT, TRAGIC CHOICES 21 (1978) (discussing "why, for instance, the United States will spend a million dollars to rescue a single, downed balloonist but will not appropriate a similar sum to provide shore patrols").

Additional factors undermine public zeal for public health initiatives. Many preventive measures take years, even decades, to produce demonstrable results. Human beings already struggle to accept delayed gratification. Prevention often requires abstaining from something pleasurable for the promise of health in the future. And, that promise is not a guarantee. Moreover, prevention often requires long-term behavior change, which can be difficult to maintain. Finally, recommendations change in light of new evidence, which can undermine faith in public health recommendations and lead many to conclude that some measures are not worth the effort. *See* Harvey V. Fineberg, *The Paradox of Disease Prevention — Celebrated in Principle, Resisted in Practice,* 310 JAMA 85, 85–88 (2013)(summarizing these and similar insights into why public health goals, which tend to be widely accepted, have proved so difficult to achieve in practice).

11. Public health professions. At a somewhat more mundane level, "public health" is also a term used to describe various professional activities. There are schools and professional organizations of public health, just as there are agencies and departments that in part define their mission by reference to public health. Again, none of these lines of distinction is completely discrete. Medical schools teach preventive medicine to some of their future physicians, mirroring some of what is being taught by their colleagues in the schools of public health. Medical and health service researchers often apply the same techniques as their public health counterparts — and study similar if not identical problems.

There also are discrete areas of expertise that are typically, although not exclusively, used by public health professionals, most prominently epidemiology. Epidemiology is generally described as the study of the distribution of diseases or other health problems in a population and the attempt to ascertain their causes. Sometimes the term refers to the investigative work that typically follows an outbreak of an unknown disease or the sudden onset of a particular health problem — again, in a population. Accessible texts on epidemiology include KENNETH J. ROTHMAN, EPIDEMIOLOGY — AN INTRODUCTION, 2d ed. (2012); ANN ASCHENGRAU & GEORGE R. SEAGE, III, ESSENTIALS OF EPIDEMIOLOGY IN PUBLIC HEALTH, 3d ed. (2014). For a good description of epidemiology, epidemiologists, and what makes them different from other health-related researchers, see Alan Peterson & Deborah Lupton, *Epidemiology: Governing By Numbers*, in THE NEW PUBLIC HEALTH (1996). For a classic (even if somewhat outdated) illustration of what epidemiologists do in the field, see BERTON ROUECHE, ELEVEN BLUE MEN, AND OTHER NARRATIVES OF MEDICAL DETECTION (1953). *See also* KERR L. WHITE, HEALING THE SCHISM: EPIDEMI-OLOGY, MEDICINE, AND THE PUBLIC'S HEALTH (1991) (a good history of the development of the distinctive approach of epidemiology in studying public health problems and how epidemiology and its practitioners were often ignored in American medical education).

Chapter 2

DEFINING RISKS TO PUBLIC HEALTH

A. CAUSES OF DEATH

How many people die in the United States each year? What is your estimate?

Has the death rate been increasing or decreasing over the past decade or so?

If you made a guess, you can look at Figure 1 on the next page. (If you did not guess, do not look until after you guess.) How close to the answer is your estimate? Are you surprised? Why?

Figure 1 shows both the number of deaths between 1935 and 2010 and the death rate (the number of deaths for every 100,000 people). Note that the absolute number of deaths increased as the total population grew. At the same time, the death rate — the percentage of the population dying — declined. How would you explain that?

The primary mission of public health is to prevent disease and death — or what is often called "premature death," meaning death from a cause that could have been prevented. Those in the public health professions pay close attention to death rates. Declining death rates suggest success in prevention efforts, while increasing death rates signal a problem. The absolute number of deaths tells us how big a problem is. Of course, both the number of deaths and the death rate vary with the specific causes of death, as well as age, gender, race, income, and many other variables.

What causes death in the United States? Try to estimate again. Once you have a guess, look at Table 1, which shows the top 10 causes of death in 2010 (the latest year for which final data are available). Data on causes of death are updated annually and can be found at the National Center for Health Statistics website, www.cdc.gov/nchs/fastats/lcod.htm (last visited July 2013).

It may not surprise anyone to learn that heart disease and cancers cause most deaths in the United States. Indeed, they have been the first and second causes of death since 1935. But, what causes heart disease or cancer, or any other disease, for that matter? In the early 1990's, J. Michael McGinnis and William H. Foege reviewed published reports to identify the factors that were associated with the major causes of death. They estimated that the "actual" causes of almost half of all deaths in 1990 were tobacco (400,000 deaths), diet and activity patterns (300,000), alcohol (100,000), microbial agents (90,000), toxic agents (60,000), firearms (35,000), sexual behavior (30,000), motor vehicles (25,000), and illicit use of drugs (20,000). J. Michael McGinnis & William H. Foege, *Actual Causes of Death*, 270 JAMA 2207 (1993). Their work did not examine genetic or socioeconomic factors, but it did encourage more sustained attention to the risk factors underlying the reported causes of death and illness. Subsequent estimates of the actual causes of death parallel the original estimates, although the reference to diet and activity patterns has often been recast, somewhat controversially, simply as "obesity." See Chapter 9 for a discussion of obesity as a health risk, Chapter 10 for tobacco, Chapter 11 for alcohol and drugs, and Chapter 12 for firearms and other injuries.

Only a few epidemiologists dared to question the push to prevent heart disease, asking whether it would be preferable to die slowly and painfully from cancer than to die more suddenly from a heart attack. Of course, heart disease can also be debilitating for many years. Moreover, the goal of health promotion is to enable people to live longer *without* debilitating disease of any sort. The goal cannot be to avoid death entirely; in the long run, the probability of death is still 100%. Rather, the goal is to compress fatal illness into a very brief span at the end of a very long and healthy life.

Figure 1. Number of Deaths, Crude and Age-Adjusted Death Rates: United States, 1935–2010

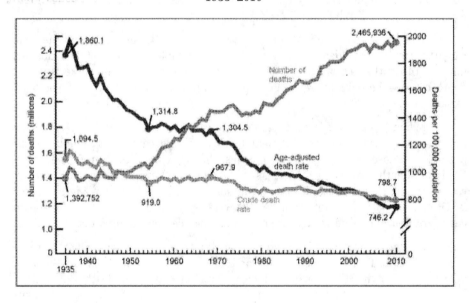

Source: Donna L. Hoyert, *75 Years of Mortality in the United States, 1935–2010*, NCHS Data Brief No. 88 (Mar. 2012)

Table 1. CAUSES OF DEATH — 2010

Cause of Death	Number of Deaths
1. Heart disease	597,689
2. Cancer	574,743
3. Chronic lower respiratory diseases	138,080
4. Stroke (cerebrovascular diseases)	129,476
5. Accidents (unintentional injuries)	120,859
6. Alzheimer's disease	83,494
7. Diabetes	69,071

Cause of Death	Number of Deaths
8. Nephritis, nephrotic syndrome, and nephrosis	50,470
9. Influenza and pneumonia	50,097
10. Intentional self-harm (suicide)	38,364
Other	640,593
Total Deaths	2,465,936

Source: National Center for Health Statistics, CDC, www.cdc.gov/nchs/fastats/lcod. htm

Gary Taubes, *Do We Really Know What Makes Us Healthy?*
NEW YORK TIMES MAGAZINE, Sept 16, 2007

Many explanations have been offered to make sense of the here-today-gone-tomorrow nature of medical wisdom — what we are advised with confidence one year is reversed the next — but the simplest one is that it is the natural rhythm of science. An observation leads to a hypothesis. The hypothesis (last year's advice) is tested, and it fails this year's test, which is always the most likely outcome in any scientific endeavor. There are, after all, an infinite number of wrong hypotheses for every right one, and so the odds are always against any particular hypothesis being true, no matter how obvious or vitally important it might seem.

In the case of H.R.T. [hormone replacement therapy], as with most issues of diet, lifestyle and disease, the hypotheses begin their transformation into public-health recommendations only after they've received the requisite support from a field of research known as epidemiology. This science evolved over the last 250 years to make sense of epidemics — hence the name — and infectious diseases. Since the 1950s, it has been used to identify, or at least to try to identify, the causes of the common chronic diseases that befall us, particularly heart disease and cancer. In the process, the perception of what epidemiologic research can legitimately accomplish — by the public, the press and perhaps by many epidemiologists themselves — may have run far ahead of the reality. . . .

. . . .

No one questions the value of these epidemiologic studies when they're used to identify the unexpected side effects of prescription drugs or to study the progression of diseases or their distribution between and within populations. One reason researchers believe that heart disease and many cancers can be prevented is because of observational evidence that the incidence of these diseases differ greatly in different populations and in the same populations over time. Breast cancer is not the scourge among Japanese women that it is among American women, but it takes only two generations in the United States before Japanese-Americans have the same breast cancer rates as any other ethnic group. This tells us that something about the American lifestyle or diet is a cause of breast cancer. Over the last 20 years, some two dozen large studies, the Nurses' Health Study included, have so far failed to identify what that factor is. They may be inherently incapable of doing so.

Nonetheless, we know that such a carcinogenic factor of diet or lifestyle exists, waiting to be identified.

These studies have also been invaluable for identifying predictors of disease — risk factors — and this information can then guide physicians in weighing the risks and benefits of putting a particular patient on a particular drug. The studies have repeatedly confirmed that high blood pressure is associated with an increased risk of heart disease and that obesity is associated with an increased risk of most of our common chronic diseases, but they have not told us what it is that raises blood pressure or causes obesity. Indeed, if you ask the more skeptical epidemiologists in the field what diet and lifestyle factors have been convincingly established as causes of common chronic diseases based on observational studies without clinical trials, you'll get a very short list: smoking as a cause of lung cancer and cardiovascular disease, sun exposure for skin cancer, sexual activity to spread the papilloma virus that causes cervical cancer and perhaps alcohol for a few different cancers as well.

Richard Peto, professor of medical statistics and epidemiology at Oxford University, phrases the nature of the conflict this way: "Epidemiology is so beautiful and provides such an important perspective on human life and death, but an incredible amount of rubbish is published," by which he means the results of observational studies that appear daily in the news media and often become the basis of public-health recommendations about what we should or should not do to promote our continued good health.

In January 2001, the British epidemiologists George Davey Smith and Shah Ebrahim, co-editors of The International Journal of Epidemiology, discussed this issue in an editorial titled "Epidemiology — Is It Time to Call It a Day?" They noted that those few times that a randomized trial had been financed to test a hypothesis supported by results from these large observational studies, the hypothesis either failed the test or, at the very least, the test failed to confirm the hypothesis: antioxidants like vitamins E and C and beta carotene did not prevent heart disease, nor did eating copious fiber protect against colon cancer.

The Nurses' Health Study is the most influential of these cohort studies, and in the six years since the Davey Smith and Ebrahim editorial, a series of new trials have chipped away at its credibility. The Women's Health Initiative hormone-therapy trial failed to confirm the proposition that H.R.T. prevented heart disease; a W.H.I. diet trial with 49,000 women failed to confirm the notion that fruits and vegetables protected against heart disease; a 40,000-woman trial failed to confirm that a daily regimen of low-dose aspirin prevented colorectal cancer and heart attacks in women under 65. And this June, yet another clinical trial — this one of 1,000 men and women with a high risk of colon cancer — contradicted the inference from the Nurses' study that folic acid supplements reduced the risk of colon cancer. Rather, if anything, they appear to increase risk.

The implication of this track record seems hard to avoid. "Even the Nurses' Health Study, one of the biggest and best of these studies, cannot be used to reliably test small-to-moderate risks or benefits," says Charles Hennekens, a principal investigator with the Nurses' study from 1976 to 2001. "None of them can. "

. . . .

While the tools of epidemiology — comparisons of populations with and without a disease — have proved effective over the centuries in establishing that a disease like cholera is caused by contaminated water, as the British physician John Snow demonstrated in the 1850s, it's a much more complicated endeavor when those same tools are employed to elucidate the more subtle causes of chronic disease.

And even the success stories taught in epidemiology classes to demonstrate the historical richness and potential of the field — that pellagra, a disease that can lead to dementia and death, is caused by a nutrient-deficient diet, for instance, as Joseph Goldberger demonstrated in the 1910s — are only known to be successes because the initial hypotheses were subjected to rigorous tests and happened to survive them. Goldberger tested the competing hypothesis, which posited that the disease was caused by an infectious agent, by holding what he called "filth parties," injecting himself and seven volunteers, his wife among them, with the blood of pellagra victims. They remained healthy, thus doing a compelling, if somewhat revolting, job of refuting the alternative hypothesis.

Smoking and lung cancer is the emblematic success story of chronic-disease epidemiology. But lung cancer was a rare disease before cigarettes became widespread, and the association between smoking and lung cancer was striking: heavy smokers had 2,000 to 3,000 percent the risk of those who had never smoked. This made smoking a "turkey shoot," says Greenland of U.C.L.A., compared with the associations epidemiologists have struggled with ever since, which fall into the tens of a percent range. The good news is that such small associations, even if causal, can be considered relatively meaningless for a single individual. If a 50-year-old woman with a small risk of breast cancer takes H.R.T. and increases her risk by 30 percent, it remains a small risk.

The compelling motivation for identifying these small effects is that their impact on the public health can be enormous if they're aggregated over an entire nation: if tens of millions of women decrease their breast cancer risk by 30 percent, tens of thousands of such cancers will be prevented each year. In fact, between 2002 and 2004, breast cancer incidence in the United States dropped by 12 percent, an effect that may have been caused by the coincident decline in the use of H.R.T. (And it may not have been. The coincident reduction in breast cancer incidence and H.R.T. use is only an association.)

Saving tens of thousands of lives each year constitutes a powerful reason to lower the standard of evidence needed to suggest a cause-and-effect relationship — to take a leap of faith. This is the crux of the issue. From a scientific perspective, epidemiologic studies may be incapable of distinguishing a small effect from no effect at all, and so caution dictates that the scientist refrain from making any claims in that situation. From the public-health perspective, a small effect can be a very dangerous or beneficial thing, at least when aggregated over an entire nation, and so caution dictates that action be taken, even if that small effect might not be real. Hence the public-health logic that it's better to err on the side of prudence even if it means persuading us all to engage in an activity, eat a food or take a pill that does nothing for us and ignoring, for the moment, the possibility that such an action could have unforeseen harmful consequences. As Greenland says, "The combination of data, statistical methodology and motivation seems a potent anesthetic for skepticism."

. . . .

Another thing that epidemiologic studies have established convincingly is that wealth associates with less heart disease and better health, at least in developed countries. The studies have been unable to establish why this is so, but this, too, is part of the healthy-user problem and a possible confounder of the hormone-therapy story and many of the other associations these epidemiologists try to study. George Davey Smith, who began his career studying how socioeconomic status associates with health, says one thing this research teaches is that misfortunes "cluster" together. Poverty is a misfortune, and the poor are less educated than the wealthy; they smoke more and weigh more; they're more likely to have hypertension and other heart-disease risk factors, to eat what's affordable rather than what the experts tell them is healthful, to have poor medical care and to live in environments with more pollutants, noise and stress. Ideally, epidemiologists will carefully measure the wealth and education of their subjects and then use statistical methods to adjust for the effect of these influences — multiple regression analysis, for instance, as one such method is called — but, as Avorn says, it "doesn't always work as well as we'd like it to."

. . . .

So how should we respond the next time we're asked to believe that an association implies a cause and effect, that some medication or some facet of our diet or lifestyle is either killing us or making us healthier? We can fall back on several guiding principles, these skeptical epidemiologists say. One is to assume that the first report of an association is incorrect or meaningless, no matter how big that association might be. After all, it's the first claim in any scientific endeavor that is most likely to be wrong. Only after that report is made public will the authors have the opportunity to be informed by their peers of all the many ways that they might have simply misinterpreted what they saw. The regrettable reality, of course, is that it's this first report that is most newsworthy. So be skeptical.

If the association appears consistently in study after study, population after population, but is small — in the range of tens of percent — then doubt it. For the individual, such small associations, even if real, will have only minor effects or no effect on overall health or risk of disease. They can have enormous public-health implications, but they're also small enough to be treated with suspicion until a clinical trial demonstrates their validity.

If the association involves some aspect of human behavior, which is, of course, the case with the great majority of the epidemiology that attracts our attention, then question its validity. If taking a pill, eating a diet or living in proximity to some potentially noxious aspect of the environment is associated with a particular risk of disease, then other factors of socioeconomic status, education, medical care and the whole gamut of healthy-user effects are as well. These will make the association, for all practical purposes, impossible to interpret reliably.

The exception to this rule is unexpected harm, what Avorn calls "bolt from the blue events," that no one, not the epidemiologists, the subjects or their physicians, could possibly have seen coming — higher rates of vaginal cancer, for example, among the children of women taking the drug DES to prevent miscarriage, or mesothelioma among workers exposed to asbestos. If the subjects are exposing themselves to a particular pill or a vitamin or eating a diet with the goal of promoting health, and, lo and behold, it has no effect or a negative effect — it's associated with an increased risk of some disorder, rather than a decreased risk — then that's a bad sign and worthy of our consideration, if not some anxiety. . . .

All of this suggests that the best advice is to keep in mind the law of unintended consequences. The reason clinicians test drugs with randomized trials is to establish whether the hoped-for benefits are real and, if so, whether there are unforeseen side effects that may outweigh the benefits. If the implication of an epidemiologist's study is that some drug or diet will bring us improved prosperity and health, then wonder about the unforeseen consequences. In these cases, it's never a bad idea to remain skeptical until somebody spends the time and the money to do a randomized trial and, contrary to much of the history of the endeavor to date, fails to refute it.

NOTES AND QUESTIONS

1. **Data and statistics.** Public health depends on data. It is, after all, focused on populations, not individuals. Data about everything from age at death to weight to the use of legal and illegal drugs are collected and analyzed to find clues about risks to health and how to avoid or mitigate them. (See Chapter 7 for ways in which data are collected and used.) Epidemiological studies are a primary, but hardly exclusive, source of public health data. The excerpt from Taube's article offers a concise summary of the strengths and limits of epidemiology in the search for causes of disease and death. In particular, epidemiological studies rarely purport to find causes of disease, although they are often reported as doing so in the media.

Public health uses statistical analysis of the data it collects in order to draw conclusions about risks to health in the general population (or a subset of the population, such as Medicare recipients, residents of Arkansas, or Hispanic youth). Thus, public health reports often present statistics expressing incidence, prevalence, probabilities, risks, and rates. *See* Box for definitions.

Definitions

Incidence: The proportion (or percentage) of a given population that is newly diagnosed with a disease or injury in a given year (or other time period).

Prevalence: The proportion (or percentage) of a given population that has a disease or injury in a given year, regardless of when the condition first occurred.

Risk: The probability that a specific harm will occur.

Absolute Risk: The probability that a specific harm will occur in a given population.

> **Relative Risk:** The ratio of the probability that a harm will occur to a person with a particular condition, to the probability that a harm will occur to a person without that condition.

Public health data are often presented in terms of relative risk. Relative risk is important in public health because it expresses how much a particular risk factor influences (or possibly causes) a health condition. Relative risk is a comparative statistical calculation of the probability of an outcome (*e.g.*, breast cancer) in a person with a particular risk factor (*e.g.*, having the BRCA1 gene) compared with a person without that risk factor (*e.g.*, no BRCA1 gene). Relative risk is used to describe how much the risk factor increases the probability of the outcome. It is typically expressed as a ratio. A relative risk of 1 means the probability is the same with or without the risk factor. A relative risk of 2 means that a person having the risk factor has twice the risk of a person without the risk factor. A relative risk of less than 1 means that the "risk factor" is protective; that is, the person with the risk factor is less likely to experience the outcome. Thus, a relative risk of 0.5 means that a person has half the risk of a person who does not have the "risk" (protective) factor.

Relative risks are useful for comparative purposes. In order to determine the overall magnitude of a possible harm, however, one needs to know the absolute risk. Absolute risk is the probability of experiencing the harm at all; this can vary from population to population. For example, suppose that the relative risk of getting kidney cancer is 5:1 for a person with high cholesterol compared to a person with low cholesterol. That sounds like another reason to lower your cholesterol. But what is the absolute risk of getting kidney cancer? If the absolute risk in the general population is 0.1% over a lifetime, then a person with high cholesterol may have only a 0.5% risk of kidney cancer. If the absolute risk is 5%, then high cholesterol increases the risk to 25%, a significant concern. Surprisingly few public health reports present risk in terms of absolute risk, despite their importance to making policy judgments about health priorities.

    2. Presenting information on risks. The American Cancer Society's statements that the risk of breast cancer in women is 1 in 8 generated some controversy in the 1990s. How Many Women Get Breast Cancer?, www.cancer.org/docroot/CRI/content/CRI_2_2_1X_How_many_people_get_breast_cancer_5.asp?sitearea= (last visited Jan. 2007; no longer available). The figure is derived from estimates that 12.3% of women born today (about 1 in 8) will be diagnosed with breast cancer during their lifetimes. Statistics from the National Cancer Institute below show that the incidence of breast cancer in women increases with age, so that the risk reaches 1 in 8 women only among women who live past age 70:

Age	Risk
30–39	0.44% (1 in 227)
40–49	1.47% (1 in 68)
50–59	2.38% (1 in 42)
60–69	3.56% (1 in 28)
70–	3.82% (1 in 26)

National Cancer Institute FactSheet, Breast Cancer Risk In American Women, http://www.cancer.gov/cancertopics/factsheet/detection/probability-breast-cancer (visited Oct. 2013).

When challenged on its use of the 1 in 8 figure, the Cancer Society responded that it was important to get women's attention to the need for prevention and screening. Is it ethical to use misleading statistics to encourage people to get preventive care? Compare the different opinions of the risk of breast cancer among women who had abortions in *Christ's Bride Ministries v. Southeastern Pennsylvania Transportation Authority*, in B. below. For a discussion of mammography and other screening programs, see Chapter 8, Part C, *infra*.

3. **Education and advocacy.** The American Cancer Society was involved in another controversy in 2007, this one over its public service advertisement showing a young woman (looking 15 to 25 years old) holding a photograph of her (also young) sister. The ad said, "My sister accidentally killed herself. She died of skin cancer. Most people think skin cancer happens to other people. But it's actually the most common of all cancers. Left unchecked, skin cancer can be fatal. The good news, it's almost always curable if you catch it early. Start now." Much of the controversy over the ad arose from its recommendation to use sunscreen, because a maker of sunscreen financed the ad campaign. For our purposes, the question is whether the ad accurately presents the risk of skin cancer. Read literally, the quoted statement above is almost correct. Skin cancer is the most common type of cancer that people get. However, skin cancer is rarely life threatening; it causes less than 2% of all cancer deaths, most of which are from melanoma. The fact that the model in the ad was so young left many observers with the mistaken impression that skin cancer kills many young people. Furthermore, it is not clear whether whether sunscreen can prevent melanoma or other skin cancers, or even whether screening for skin cancer can prevent deaths. Christie Aschwanden, *Doctors Balk at Cancer Ad, Citing Lack of Evidence*, NEW YORK TIMES (July 10, 2007). Is the ad overly simplistic, misleading, or a good way to get the public's attention? See the excerpt from Daniel Kahneman and Note 2 following the excerpt in C (Risk Perception), *infra*, for a discussion of how the way a risk is framed can affect individual responses.

4. **Correlation and causation.** As epidemiologists remind us, correlation is not causation. Nonetheless, studies showing the correlation of a toxin, product, or behavior sometimes catalyze research that can find a cause. An incidental finding in a study of violent behavior among Boston high school students might be an example. The study found that students who drank five or more cans of non-diet-soda a week were more likely to report engaging in violent behavior against other students than those who drank less soda (57% compared with 39%). Sara J. Solnick & David Hemenway, *'The Twinkie Defense:' The Relationship Between Carbonated Non-Diet Soft Drinks and Violence Perpetration Among Boston High School Students*, 18 INJURY PREVENTION 259 (2012), http://injuryprevention.bmj.com/content/18/4/259. full.pdf+html?sid=43d9bfe8-78c7-4472-8c26-3050368deeac. The "heavy drinkers" also reported carrying a gun or knife (40% v. 27%), violence against siblings (42% v. 27%), and violence against dates (26% v. 16%) significantly more than students who drank less soda. *Id.* The researchers were careful to note that there could be other reasons for the correlation. Teens who drank more soda also drank more alcohol (46% v. 34%). Could violent teens like soda (and alcohol) more than

non-violent teens? The study was conducted in inner-city public schools, where the student population is poorer than the general student population, and violence is more prevalent in poorer populations. What, if anything, should we conclude from this study? Should we be wary of teens drinking soda on the subway? Should we investigate the causes of violence in more depth? See Chapter 11 *infra* for discussions of injury prevention.

A more amusing study of correlation found that there was "a close, significant linear correlation (r=0.791, P<0.0001) between chocolate consumption per capita and the number of Nobel Laureates per 10 million persons in a total of 23 countries." Franz H. Messerli, *Chocolate Consumption, Cognitive Function, and Nobel Laureates*, 367 NEW ENGL. J. MED. 1562 (2012). The author's tongue-in-cheek conclusion was: "Chocolate consumption enhances cognitive function, which is a sine qua non for winning the Nobel Prize." He cautioned, however, that reverse causation could not be ruled out: "It is conceivable that enhanced cognitive function could stimulate countrywide chocolate consumption." *Id.*

B. DEFINING RISKS TO PUBLIC HEALTH

CHRIST'S BRIDE MINISTRIES, INC. v. SOUTHEASTERN PENNSYLVANIA TRANSPORTATION AUTHORITY
148 F.3d 242 (3d Cir. 1998)

ROTH, JUDGE.

Southeastern Pennsylvania Transportation Authority (SEPTA) refused to display an advertisement stating that "Women Who Choose Abortion Suffer More & Deadlier Breast Cancer." We must decide in this appeal whether, in doing so, SEPTA violated the First Amendment rights of the advertiser, Christ's Bride Ministries, Inc. (CBM) . . . .

SEPTA is an "agency and instrumentality" of the Commonwealth of Pennsylvania. It operates buses, subways, and regional rail lines in and around the City of Philadelphia. SEPTA contracts with a licensee, Transportation Display's Inc. (TDI), for the construction and sale of advertising space in its stations and in and on its vehicles. TDI and SEPTA are the defendants in this case.

The plaintiff, CBM, began a public service campaign in 1995 to inform the public of what it believes to be the increased risk of breast cancer for women who have had abortions . . . .

CBM contacted SEPTA in late November 1995 about placing posters in the Philadelphia area transit system . . . . In December 1995, [Bradley] Thomas [president of CBM] sent a draft poster to TDI for review by [TDI] and SEPTA. The poster stated "Women Who Choose Abortion Suffer More & Deadlier Breast Cancer." The district court described the poster as "graphically designed with bold white lettering on a background of black and bright red, except that the word 'deadlier' was written in red." The poster also included a 1-800 number for information which connected callers not with CBM but with an organization called the American Rights Coalition (ARC).

SEPTA requested that the poster better identify the sponsor, CBM. CBM complied and added a description of CBM: "Christ's Bride Ministries, Inc. is a charitable, religious, educational, non-profit 501(c)(3) organization. CBM, P.O. Box 22 Merrifield, VA 22116. (703) 598-2226." SEPTA then approved the posters for display.

On January 15, 1996, the posters went up. TDI put two of them next to overhead clocks in Suburban Station in Philadelphia, and 24 others in subway and railroad stations in Philadelphia and its suburbs. SEPTA immediately began receiving what it described as "numerous" complaints about the poster, which included "rider protest" and "criticism" by "women's health organizations" and "local government officials." . . .

After the posters were installed, TDI faxed to CBM a contract, which Thomas signed and returned to TDI, also via fax. The contract was signed by Robert Meara of TDI and dated January 22, 1996. The monthly charge for the signs on the clocks was $642.60, while the monthly charge for the 24 other posters was $2400. There were "terms and conditions" on the back of the contract, including one that stated "if the Transportation Facility concerned should deem such advertising objectionable for any reason, TDI shall have the right to terminate the contract and discontinue the service without notice."

In early February, SEPTA received a copy of a letter written by Dr. Philip Lee, Assistant Secretary of Health in the United States Department of Health and Human Services [which said:] "It has recently come to my attention that the Metro Transit System has posted more than 1,100 free public service ads from the Christ's Bride Ministries. The ad states: 'Women who choose abortion suffer more & deadlier breast cancer. Information: 1-800-634-2224.' This ad is unfortunately misleading, unduly alarming, and does not accurately reflect the weight of the scientific literature."

Dr. Lee went on to state that in his opinion the studies showing a link between breast cancer and abortion suffered from methodological weaknesses, that there was no consensus on the purported relationship between breast cancer and abortion, and that Dr. Lee knew of no evidence supporting the claim that abortion causes "deadlier" breast cancer. Dr. Lee also complained that callers to the 1–800 number were referred to an article in the Journal of the National Cancer Institute, describing a study that suggested a positive correlation between induced abortions and breast cancer. Dr. Lee noted that although the article did appear in the Journal, the Journal also published an editorial stating that the results were not "conclusive." . . .

Based on Dr. Lee's letter, SEPTA removed the posters on February 16, 1996. According to the testimony of Mr. Gambaccini, SEPTA's General Manager, the "heart" of the decision to remove them was the questions about their accuracy . . . . It is uncontested that no one at SEPTA or TDI conducted any other inquiry into the accuracy of the message on the poster, or contacted CBM for information that would support the claim made by the ad, or informed CBM of SEPTA's objections to the ad before removing the posters.

On March 13, 1996, Meara of TDI wrote to Thomas of CBM, explaining that the posters had been removed on February 16. Meara stated in his letter that the decision had been made by SEPTA as a result of "a letter from the U.S. Department of Health and Human Services in which it concluded that the ad was 'unfortunately misleading, unduly alarming and does not accurately reflect the weight of the scientific literature'."

TDI included a check to CBM for $3042.60 for the "unused portion" of the contract. CBM filed suit on May 10, 1996, alleg[ing] violations of CBM's rights under the First and Fourteenth Amendments and also breach of contract . . . . During the trial, three experts testified that the existing studies and research do not support the existence of a cause and effect relationship between abortion and breast cancer. These experts did, however, acknowledge that some studies show a weak "association" between induced abortions and breast cancer [a relative risk of 1.23]. One of SEPTA's experts testified that the better studies have not been consistent and that some studies show no link at all. CBM's expert, on the other hand, testified that he had analyzed 23 epidemiological studies, 12 of which, in his opinion, showed a statistically significant increase in breast cancer among women who had under-gone induced abortions [a relative risk of 1.3]. He argued that this risk could not be accounted for by the presence of other variables, such as age or family. The increased risk, CBM's expert noted, was greater than the relative risk associated with oral contraceptives [1.1]. Because manufacturers of contraceptives alert the public as to the possible link between their product and breast cancer, it should not be "unduly alarming" for CBM to report a slightly greater risk purportedly associated with induced abortions.

The district court issued an opinion on August 16, 1996, holding for the defendants on all counts. The court reasoned that public transit stations do not constitute traditional public fora and that SEPTA and TDI had not created a public forum because they maintained control over the use of the advertising space. The court also found that Dr. Lee's letter was a "reasonable" basis on which to remove the advertisement. The court did not decide whether either SEPTA's or CBM's experts were "right."

III. State Action

In this case, the parties agree that SEPTA is a state actor, as is its licensee, TDI, and that their actions are constrained by the First and Fourteenth Amendments.

. . . .

IV. Public Forum

The government may, as a general rule, limit speech that takes place on its own property without running afoul of the First Amendment. Where, however, the property in question is either a traditional public forum or a forum designated as public by the government, the government's ability to limit speech is impinged upon by the First Amendment. In either a traditional or a designated public forum, the government's content-based restrictions on private speech must survive strict scrutiny to pass constitutional muster. The government has, however, a far broader license to curtail speech if the forum has not been opened to the type of expression in question. In such a case, the government's restrictions need only be viewpoint neutral and "reasonable in light of the purpose served by the forum."

[The court concluded that "that the forum at issue is SEPTA's advertising space" and that it is "not a traditional public forum" like streets and parks. Nonetheless, it found that, although the "main function of the advertising space at issue is to earn a profit for SEPTA," SEPTA created a designated public forum by dedicating the space to the public for the purpose of promoting awareness of social issues and by accepting all advertising except "alcohol and tobacco advertising beyond a specified limit and ads deemed libelous or obscene."]

. . . .

B. SEPTA's Past Practice and the Suitability of the Forum for CBM's Ad

SEPTA has accepted a broad range of advertisements for display. These include religious messages, such as "Follow this bus to FREEDOM, Christian Bible Fellowship Church;" an ad criticizing a political candidate; and explicitly worded advertisements such as "Safe Sex Isn't" and an advertisement reminding viewer that "Virginity — It's cool to keep" and "Don't give it up to shut 'em up." Indeed, many ads address topics concerning sex, family planning, and related topics. Other examples include a controversial ad campaign on AIDS education and awareness, posters stating "The Face of Adoption" "Consider Adoption" and "Every child deserves a family," and another ad reading "Pregnant? Scared? Confused? A.R.C. Can Help Call 1-800-884-4004 or (215-844-1082.)"

On the topic of abortion, SEPTA has accepted two ads. One read "Choice Hotline, For Answers to Your Questions About: Birth Control * Pregnancy * Prenatal Care * Abortion * Adoption * HIV/AIDS * Sexually Transmitted Diseases (STDs) Abortion — Making A Decision, Call State Health Line 1-800-692-7254 For Free Booklet on Fetal Development, Fetus is Latin for Little one — A Little Human is a Baby, Confidential * Free." The other one addressed the health benefits of legalizing abortion: "When Abortion Was Illegal, Women Died. My Mother Was One of Them. Keep Abortion Legal and Safe. Support the Clara Bell Duvall Education Fund. 471-9110."

. . . .

We conclude then, based on SEPTA's written policies, which specifically provide for the exclusion of only a very narrow category of ads, based on SEPTA's goals of generating revenues through the sale of ad space, and based on SEPTA's practice of permitting virtually unlimited access to the forum, that SEPTA created a designated public forum. Moreover, it created a forum that is suitable for the speech in question, i.e., posters which presented messages concerning abortion and health issues . . . .

. . . .

Moreover, as to the subject of abortion specifically, and family planning issues generally, permission to post advertisements has been granted as a "matter of course." There is no policy, written or unwritten, pursuant to which CBM's ads were removed.

Because we find that SEPTA has created a designated public forum, content-based restrictions on speech that come within the forum must pass strict scrutiny to comport with the First Amendment. As the Supreme Court explained in *Police Dept. of the City of Chicago v. Mosley*, "above all else, the First Amendment means that government has no power to restrict expression because of its message, its ideas, its subject matter, or its content. " Thus the government "may not grant the use of a forum to people whose views it finds acceptable, but deny use to those wishing to express less favored or more controversial views. And it may not select which issues are worth discussing or debating in public facilities." The prohibited expression in this case, CBM's ad, falls within the scope of the forum created by SEPTA. Thus, SEPTA's restriction is subject to heightened review.

SEPTA has not argued that its actions survive strict scrutiny. Accordingly, we conclude that CBM's First Amendment rights were violated when SEPTA removed CBM's ads.

V. Reasonableness of SEPTA's Restrictions

Even if the speech in question had fallen outside the limited public forum created by SEPTA, we would nonetheless conclude that SEPTA's removal of the posters violated the First Amendment because the removal was not "reasonable."

[T]he reasonableness of the government's restriction on speech depends on the nature and purpose of the property from which it is barred. In this case, . . . [t] he subject of the speech, and the manner in which it was presented, were compatible with the purposes of the forum.

. . . SEPTA could have argued that based on Dr. Lee's letter, it viewed CBM's ad as "debated and dubious," and accordingly excluded it. A prohibition on "debated and dubious ads," put in place before, or because of the concerns about CBM's ad, might qualify as reasonable. We note, however, that SEPTA does not have a policy of protecting riders from "debated and dubious" speech generally. . . .

In any event, we need not reach that question. Gambaccini did not testify to such a policy, implemented either before or after the removal of CBM's ad. Instead, when questioned if he would post an ad saying "women who choose abortion live longer and have less breast cancer," he answered "Not unless there was some credible evidence to support it." This is a different standard — a debatable advertisement may well be supported by credible evidence. And if this standard controlled, SEPTA was unreasonable because it failed to give CBM an opportunity to produce such evidence . . . . SEPTA has left us to guess why, in terms of the purpose of the forum, it excluded CBM's ad, and why, and to what extent, other ads will also be excluded. This makes it difficult to evaluate the extent of the governmental interest in excluding the speech from SEPTA's property.

. . . .

We conclude, therefore, that under the facts presented SEPTA's actions were not reasonable. SEPTA acted as a censor, limiting speech because it found it to be "misleading." SEPTA argues that it cannot investigate the accuracy of medical claims in ads. For that reason, it relied on Dr. Lee's letter. We do not hold that SEPTA must hire its own cadre of experts to evaluate medical claims made in ads. It was SEPTA, however, which accepted advertising on a permitted topic, and then decided that CBM's ad was unacceptably misleading. Having decided to exclude the posters on this basis, SEPTA did not act reasonably when it failed to ask CBM to clarify the basis on which the claim was made. This is all the more true where SEPTA has failed to explain how its content-based distinctions are related to preserving the advertising space for its intended use, and where SEPTA has in place no policy, old or new, written or unwritten, governing the display of ads making contested claims.

NOTES AND QUESTIONS

1. **Relative risk perceptions.** *Christ's Bride* illustrates how different groups may view the same information and characterize similar levels of risk as negligible or significant. The decision in *Christ's Bride* turned on the reasonableness of the determination to exclude the advertising. Reasonableness depended upon the degree of relative risk found in epidemiological studies, which in turn depended on the credibility of the studies' methods and statistical analysis. (See the discussion of relative risk in Part A., Note 1, *supra*.) CMB's expert testified that his "metanalysis" of studies found a relative risk of breast cancer for women who had abortions of 1.3. One of SEPTA's experts had published a study finding a relative risk of 1.23. SEPTA's experts argued that a relative risk of 1.2 or 1.3 was too small to be persuasive evidence of any cause and effect relationship. They also argued that some of the breast cancer studies may have exaggerated the risk from abortion, because they did not use the standard 95% confidence intervals to calculate relative risk. CMB countered that the FDA required disclosure of relative risks of 1.1 for oral contraceptives. The testimony is reviewed in the district court decision, *Christ's Bride Ministries, Inc. v. Southeastern Pennsylvania Transportation Authority*, 937 F. Supp. 425 (E.D. Pa. 1996).

One's view of what counts as a high relative risk may vary, depending on one's view of the risk factor itself. Current estimates of the relative risk of death from heart disease among nonsmokers exposed to environmental tobacco smoke (ETS, also called secondhand smoke) are about 1.3 — the same as the relative risk of breast cancer for women who have had abortions, according to CBM in *Christ's Bride*. Do you believe one estimate, but not the other? Why? (See the discussion of Risk Perception in Part C, *infra*.)

2. **Tobacco and relative risks.** The Environmental Protection Agency's report on environmental tobacco smoke, *Respiratory Health Effects of Passive Smoking: Lung Cancer and Other Disorders* (Dec. 1992), provided evidence for the health risks of ETS in Surgeon Generals' reports, as well as legislative hearings on bills to ban smoking in public places. EPA produced the report as part of its statutory risk assessment of whether ETS should be classified and regulated as a Group A

carcinogen, meaning that there is evidence that it causes cancer in humans. The EPA concluded that the relative risk of cancer from ETS was 1.19 and that it should be deemed to be a Group A carcinogen. How does that compare with the risk of breast cancer claimed by CBM in *Christ's Bride*? Prior to its ETS analysis, the EPA had found that higher relative risks of 2.6 and 3.0 for other chemicals were not high enough to classify those chemicals as Group A carcinogens.

The EPA's methods were challenged by the tobacco industry. In *Flue-Cured Tobacco Cooperative Stabilization Corp. v. U.S. Environmental Protection Agency*, 4 F. Supp. 2d 435 (M.D. N.C. 1998), *vacated and remanded*, 313 F.3d 852 (4th Cir. 2002), the North Carolina district court found that the EPA had exceeded its statutory authority by basing its conclusion on faulty analyses that left "substantial holes in the administrative record." More specifically, the court concluded that: "EPA publicly committed to a conclusion before research had begun [that ETS caused cancer]; excluded industry by violating the Act's procedural requirements; adjusted established procedure and scientific norms to validate the Agency's public conclusion . . . EPA disregarded information and made findings on selective information; . . . failed to disclose important findings and reasoning; and left significant questions without answers." *Id.* at 465–66.

Regardless of one's views on smoking or this district court, the problems that the court identified in the EPA's research methods are unsettling: "EPA could not produce statistically significant results with its selected studies. Analysis conducted with a .05 significance level and 95% confidence level included relative risks of 1 . . . In order to confirm its hypothesis, EPA maintained its standard significance level but lowered the confidence interval to 90%. This allowed EPA to confirm its hypothesis by finding a relative risk of 1.19, albeit a very weak association." *Id.* at 462. The court rejected the EPA's report as credible evidence for a determination that ETS was a Class A carcinogen. The court's decision, however, did not prevent others from using the EPA's report as evidence of the risk of ETS among non-smokers. The Court of Appeals held that the district court lacked subject matter jurisdiction, because the EPA report was not final agency action.

Like the studies concerning abortion and breast cancer, studies of exposure to ETS have reported conflicting results, with one study reporting the implausible finding that children living with parents who smoked have a lower risk of cancer than children living with non-smokers. For our purposes, the question is to what degree can studies showing minimal risks be relied upon? Why is one set of studies believed to demonstrate no more than a negligible risk at best, while another set of studies are believed to demonstrate substantial risk? How would you characterize the responses of SEPTA and EPA to similar relative risks? To what degree is your attitude toward particular risks likely to affect your willingness to believe some studies and not others?

C. RISK PERCEPTION

Daniel Kahneman, Thinking, Fast and Slow
20–26, 28 (2012)

Two Systems

Psychologists have been intensely interested for several decades in the two modes of thinking evoked by [a] picture of an angry woman and by [a] multiplication problem and have offered many labels for them. I adopt terms originally proposed by Keith Stanovich and Richard West, and will refer to two systems in the mind, System 1 and System 2.

• *System* 1 operates automatically and quickly, with little or no effort and no sense of voluntary control.

• *System* 2 allocates attention to the effortful mental activities that demand it, including complex calculations. The operations of System 2 are often associated with the subjective experience of agency, choice, and concentration.

. . . .

When we think of ourselves, we identify with System 2, the conscious reasoning self that has beliefs, makes choices, and decides what to think about and what to do. Although System 2 believes itself to be where the action is, the automatic System 1 is the hero of this book. I describe System 1 as effortlessly originating impressions and feelings that are the main sources of the explicit beliefs and deliberate choices of System 2. The automatic operations of System 1 generate surprisingly complex patterns of ideas, but only the slower System 2 can construct thoughts in an orderly series of steps. . . .

. . . .

In rough order of complexity, here are some examples of the automatic activities that are attributed to System 1:

- Detect that one object is more distant than another.
- Orient to the source of a sudden sound.
- Complete the phrase "bread and . . . ."
- Make a "disgust face" when shown a horrible picture.
- Detect hostility in a voice.
- Answer to $2 + 2 = ?$
- Read words on large billboards.
- Drive a car on an empty road.
- Find a strong move in chess (if you are a chess master).
- Understand simple sentences.
- Recognize that a "meek and tidy soul with a passion for detail" resembles an occupational stereotype.

. . . The capabilities of System 1 include innate skills that we share with other animals. We are born prepared to perceive the world around us, recognize objects, orient attention, avoid losses, and fear spiders. Other mental activities become fast and automatic through prolonged practice. System 1 has learned associations between ideas (the capital of France?); it has also learned skills such as reading and understanding nuances of social situations . . . . The knowledge is stored in memory and accessed without intention and without effort.

. . . .

The highly diverse operations of System 2 have one feature in common: they require attention and are disrupted when attention is drawn away. Here are some examples:

- Brace for the starter gun in a race.
- Focus attention on the clowns in the circus.
- Focus on the voice of a particular person in a crowded and noisy room.
- Look for a woman with white hair.
- Search memory to identify a surprising sound.
- Maintain a faster walking speed than is natural for you.
- Monitor the appropriateness of your behavior in a social situation.
- Count the occurrences of the letter a in a page of text.
- Tell someone your phone number.
- Park in a narrow space (for most people except garage attendants).
- Compare two washing machines for value.
- Fill out a tax form.
- Check the validity of a complex logical argument.

In all these situations you must pay attention, and you will perform less well, or not at all, if you are not ready or if your attention is directed inappropriately. System 2 has some ability to change the way System 1 works, by programming the normally automatic functions of attention and memory . . . .

The often-used phrase "pay attention" is apt: you dispose of a limited budget of attention that you can allocate to activities, and if you try to go beyond your budget, you will fail. It is the mark of effortful activities that they interfere with each other, which is why it is difficult or impossible to conduct several at once. You could not compute the product of 17 x 24 while making a left turn into dense traffic, and you certainly should not try. You can do several things at once, but only if they are easy and undemanding . . . .

. . . .

Intense focusing on a task can make people effectively blind, even to stimuli that normally attract attention. The most dramatic demonstration was offered by Christopher Chabris and Daniel Simons in their book *The Invisible Gorilla.* They constructed a short film of two teams passing basketballs, one team wearing white shirts, the other wearing black. The viewers of the film are instructed to count the number of passes made by the white team, ignoring the black players. This task is difficult and completely absorbing. Halfway through the video, a woman wearing a gorilla suit appears, crosses the court, thumps her chest, and moves on. The gorilla is in view for 9 seconds. Many thousands of people have seen the video, and about half of them do not notice anything unusual. It is the counting task — and especially the instruction to ignore one of the teams — that causes the blindness. No one who watches the video without that task would miss the gorilla. Seeing and orienting are automatic functions of System 1, but they depend on the allocation of some attention to the relevant stimulus. The authors note that the most remarkable observation of their study is that people find its results very surprising. Indeed, the viewers who fail to see the gorilla are initially sure that it was not there — they cannot imagine missing such a striking event. The gorilla study illustrates two important facts about our minds: we can be blind to the obvious, and we are also blind to our blindness.

Plot Synopsis

. . . Systems 1 and 2 are both active when we are awake. System 1 runs automatically and System 2 is normally in a comfortable low-effort mode, in which only a fraction of its capacity is engaged. System 1 continuously generates suggestions for System 2: impressions, intuitions, intentions, and feelings. If endorsed by System 2, impressions and intuitions turn into beliefs, and impulses turn into voluntary actions. When all goes smoothly, which is most of the time, System 2 adopts the suggestions of System 1 with little or no modification. You generally believe your impressions and act on your desires, and that is fine — usually.

When System 1 runs into difficulty, it calls on System 2 to support more detailed and specific processing that may solve the problem of the moment. System 2 is mobilized when a question arises for which System 1 does not offer an answer, as probably happened to you when you encountered the multiplication problem 17 x 24. You can also feel a surge of conscious attention whenever you are surprised. System 2 is activated when an event is detected that violates the model of the world that System 1 maintains. In that world, lamps do not jump, cats do not bark, and gorillas do not cross basketball courts . . . . System 2 is also credited with the continuous monitoring of your own behavior — the control that keeps you polite when you are angry, and alert when you are driving at night . . . .

The division of labor between System 1 and System 2 is highly efficient: it minimizes effort and optimizes performance. The arrangement works well most of the time because System 1 is generally very good at what it does . . . . System 1 has biases, however, systematic errors that it is prone to make in specified circumstances. [I] t sometimes answers easier questions than the one asked, and it has little understanding of logic and statistics. One further limitation is that System 1 cannot be turned off. If you are shown a word on the screen in a language you know, you will read it — unless your attention is totally focused elsewhere.

Conflict

. . . .

. . . Conflict between an automatic reaction and intention to control it is common in our lives. We are all familiar with the experience of trying not to stare at the oddly dressed couple at the neighboring table in a restaurant . . . . One of the tasks of System 2 is to overcome the impulses of System 1. In other words, System 2 is in charge of self-control.

. . . .

. . . Because System 1 operates automatically and cannot be turned off at will, errors of intuitive thought are often difficult to prevent. Biases cannot always be avoided, because System 2 may have no clue as to the error. Even when cues to likely errors are available, errors can be prevented only by the enhanced monitoring and effortful activity of System 2. As a way to live your life, however, continuous vigilance is not necessarily good, and it is certainly impractical. Constantly questioning our own thinking would be impossibly tedious, and System 2 is much too slow and inefficient to serve as a substitute for System 1 in making routine decisions. The best we can do is a compromise: learn to recognize situations in which mistakes are likely and try harder to avoid significant mistakes when the stakes are high . . . .

———

NOTES AND QUESTIONS

1. **Analytic v. automatic thinking.** Kahneman's book collects a career's worth of theories and experiments analyzing how people think and make decisions. "System 1" and "System 2" are, of course, shorthand, but nicely capture the complex thought processes that they represent. Kahneman offers considerable evidence that we do not necessarily behave rationally, despite our own beliefs to the contrary. If his book were made into a movie (a highly unlikely event, as he himself notes), he says, "System 2 would be a supporting character who believes himself to be the hero." Yet, he concludes that we can "learn to recognize situations in which mistakes are likely" and try to avoid them. His book offers many examples of such situations and when to kick System 2 into gear to check our homework. It is especially important to be alert to such situations in analyzing risk and developing policy and laws to respond.

2. **Framing risk information.** In the 48th Super Bowl in 2014, the Seattle Seahawks played the Denver Broncos. To tell your friends the result, you could say "The Seahawks won" or "The Broncos lost." Does it matter which statement you make? Daniel Kahneman uses similar examples to explain the importance of "framing": "The fact that logically equivalent statements evoke different reactions makes it impossible for Humans to be as reliably rational as Econs [rational economic persons]." KAHNEMAN, THINKING, FAST AND SLOW, at 363. How matters are framed can affect our reactions. For example, people tend to view losses as worse than simply not gaining something. Discounts are more appealing than surcharges for this reason. A discount for paying cash sounds better than a surcharge for

paying with a credit or debit card, even when the resulting price is the same. System 1 responds to emotional words and how facts and choices are framed.

Even experts can fall prey to this type of thinking. Kahneman describes an experiment by Amos Tversky, who asked a group of physicians at Harvard Medical School whether they would recommend surgery or radiation to treat lung cancer. Half were told that the one-month survival rate after surgery was 90%. The others were told that the mortality rate at one-month was 10%. These are, of course, equivalent statements. Yet, 84% of physicians in the first group, who heard the data expressed as a survival rate, chose surgery over radiation, while only 50% of the second group, who heard mortality data, chose surgery. *Id.* at 367.

Tversky presented his "Asian disease" scenario to a public health audience. The audience was asked to choose between options A and B — two ways of preparing for the arrival of a new Asian disease expected to kill 600 people if nothing were done. Half the audience was presented with the following description of the options:

1-A Under Option A, 200 people will be saved.

1-B Option B has a 1/3 probability of saving 600 people and a 2/3 probability that no one will be saved.

The other half received the following description:

2-A Under Option A, 400 people will die.

2-B Option B has a 1/3 probability that no one will die and a 2/3 probability that 600 will die.

You will undoubtedly see that both descriptions say the same thing. Yet, public health professionals in group 1 chose option A, presented in terms of lives saved. Group 2 chose option B — a gamble — presented as a likelihood that people will die. *Id.* at 368–9. On the basis of these and other experiments, Tversky, Kahneman and others conclude that people tend to prefer a gamble when thinking in terms of losses, but a sure bet when thinking of positive gains, even when the odds are exactly the same.

Recognizing the equivalence of information framed in different terms requires some mental effort — System 2 — and most of us are lazy. Kahneman argues that we typically allow our System 1 emotional reactions to make choices for us. Both governments and businesses take advantage of our laziness by framing choices so that their desired result is the easiest option. Opt-out systems are good examples. Retailers know that people are not likely to make the effort to opt out of the default option. Unless limited by legislation, journal subscriptions and club memberships are automatically renewed unless the consumer affirmatively cancels, and only a minority bothers to do so. Similarly, it is no accident that organ donation rates are higher in countries like Sweden with opt-out systems and low in countries like the United States and Germany, with opt-in systems, which require people to take some action to become an organ donor. For a discussion of how similar choice architecture, such as default rules, can draw on psychology to encourage more rational choices, from savings to foods, see RICHARD H. THALER & CASS R. SUNSTEIN, NUDGE: IMPROVING DECISIONS ABOUT HEALTH, WEALTH AND HAPPINESS (2008).

NASSIM NICHOLAS TALEB, THE BLACK SWAN — THE IMPACT OF THE
HIGHLY IMPROBABLE
xxi—xxv, xxix-xxx (2d ed., 2010)

Before the discovery of Australia, people in the old World were convinced that *all* swans were white, an unassailable belief as it seemed completely confirmed by empirical evidence. The sighting of the first black swan might have been an interesting surprise for a few ornithologists . . . , but that is not where the significance of the story lies. It illustrates a severe limitation to our learning from observations or experience and the fragility of our knowledge. One single observation can invalidate a general statement derived from millennia of confirmatory sightings of millions of white swans . . . .

. . . What we call here a Black Swan (and capitalize it) is an event with the following three attributes.

First, it is an *outlier*, as it lies outside the realm of regular expectations, because nothing in the past can convincingly point to its possibility. Second, it carries an extreme impact (unlike the bird). Third, in spite of its outlier status, human nature makes us concoct explanations for its occurrence *after* the fact, making it explainable and predictable.

I stop and summarize the triplet: rarity, extreme impact, and retrospective (though not prospective) predictability. A small number of Black Swans explain almost everything in our world, from the success of ideas and religions, to the dynamics of historical events, to elements of our own personal lives . . . .

Just imagine how little your understanding of the world on the eve of the events of 1914 would have helped you guess what was to happen next. (Don't cheat by using the explanations . . . by your dull high school teacher.) How about the rise of Hitler and the subsequent war? . . . . How about the consequences of the rise of Islamic fundamentalism? . . . .

. . . .

. . . It is easy to see that life is the cumulative effect of a handful of significant shocks. It is not so hard to identify the role of Black Swans . . . . Count the significant events, the technological changes, and the inventions that have taken place in our environment since you were born and compare them to what was expected before their advent. How many of them came on schedule? Look into your own personal life, to your choice of profession, say, or meeting your mate, your exile from country of origin, the betrayals you faced, your sudden enrichment or impoverishment. How often did these things occur according to plan?

. . . .

Black Swan logic makes *what you don't know* far more relevant than what you do know. Consider that many Black Swans can be caused and exacerbated *by their being unexpected.*

Think of the terrorist attack of September 11, 2001: had the risk been reasonably conceivable on September 10, it would not have happened. If such a possibility were deemed worthy of attention, fighter planes would have circled the sky . . . , airplanes would have had locked bulletproof doors, and the attack would not have taken place, period. Something might have taken place. What? I don't know.

. . . .

The inability to predict outliers implies the inability to predict the course of history, given the share of these events in the dynamics of events.

But we act as though we are able to predict historical events . . . . We produce thirty-year projections of social security deficits and oil prices without realizing that we cannot even predict these for next summer . . . . What is surprising is not the magnitude of our forecast errors, but our absence of awareness of it . . . .

. . . .

Black Swans being unpredictable, we need to adjust to their existence (rather than naively try to predict them) . . . . There are so many things we can do if we focus on anti knowledge, or what we do not know . . . . Indeed, in some domains — such as scientific discovery and venture capital investments — there is a disproportionate payoff from the unknown, since you typically have little to lose and plenty to gain from a rare event . . . . So I disagree with the followers of Marx and those of Adam Smith: the reason free markets work is because they allow people to be lucky, thanks to aggressive trial and error, not by giving rewards or "incentives" for skill. The strategy is, then, to tinker as much as possible and try to collect as many Black Swan opportunities as you can.

. . . .

. . . There are two possible ways to approach phenomena. The first is to rule out the extraordinary and focus on the "normal." The examiner leaves aside "outliers" and studies ordinary cases. The second approach is to consider that in order to understand a phenomenon, one needs first to consider the extremes — particularly if, like the Black Swan, they carry an extraordinary cumulative effect.

. . . If you want to get an idea of a friend's temperament, ethics, and personal elegance, you need to look at him under the tests of severe circumstances, not under the regular rosy glow of daily life. Can you assess the danger a criminal poses by examining only what he does on an *ordinary* day? Can we understand health without considering wild diseases and epidemics? . . . .

. . . .

What I call Platonicity, after the ideas (and personality) of the philosopher Plato, is our tendency to mistake the map for the territory . . . .

Platonicity is what makes us think that we understand more than we actually do. But this does not happen everywhere. I am not saying that Platonic forms don't exist. Models and constructions, these intellectual maps of reality, are not always wrong: they are wrong only in some specific applications. The difficulty is that a) you do not know beforehand (only after the fact) *where* the map will be wrong, and b) the mistakes can lead to severe consequences. These models are like potentially helpful medicines that carry random but very severe side effects.

NOTES AND QUESTIONS

3. Risk perception. Risk perception has become an area of sophisticated research by psychologists, such as Kahneman and Tversky, behavioral economists, and other social scientists. For an introduction to risk perception and reviews of research results by another master of the field, see PAUL SLOVIC, PERCEPTION OF RISK (2000) and THE FEELING OF RISK (2010).

Aaron Wildavsky & Karl Dake warn against presuming that one trait can predict how a person will view a particular risk. Aaron Wildavsky & Karl Dake, *Theories of Risk Perception*, 119 DAEDALUS 41 (1990). They contrasted cultural theory with other theories of risk perception prevalent before 1990. Knowledge theory held that perceptions of risk were based on knowledge, so that people feared technologies that they knew to be dangerous. Economic theory held that the more affluent people were, the less risk they perceived in technology. However, post-materialist theory argued that the rich were more risk averse, perhaps in order to preserve what they had. Cultural theory has some similarities to political theory, which aligned risk perception along the political and ideological spectrum. However, cultural theory argues that people perceive risks according to how such risks affect their own values and social relationships, and that the perception is often a choice.

Wildavsky and Dake argue that the following three categories explain the differences in perceptions of risk, especially risks from technology, better than traditional theories:

- Hierarchical — "adherents of hierarchy perceive acts of social deviance to be dangerous, because such behaviors may disrupt their preferred (superior/subordinate) form of social relations." *Id.*

- Equality — adherents of equality reject hierarchical relationships and are not troubled by social deviance

- Individualist — Individualists resemble libertarians in the sense that they view social controls (favored by hierarchical groups) as threats to autonomy and tolerate social deviance as long as it does not disrupt voluntary market relationships.

Are these categories persuasive today? Do any of the categories describe you?

4. Factors affecting risk perception. Fischhoff et al. attempted to identify commonalities across populations and found that people's perceptions of the magnitude of risk are influenced by factors other than numerical risk calculations. They conclude:

- Risks perceived to be voluntary are more accepted than risks perceived to be imposed.

- Risks perceived to be under an individual's control are more accepted than risks perceived to be controlled by others.

- Risks perceived to have clear benefits are more accepted than risks perceived to have little or no benefit.

- Risks perceived to be fairly distributed are more accepted than risks perceived to be unfairly distributed.

- Risks perceived to be natural are more accepted than risks perceived to be manmade.

- Risks perceived to be statistical are more accepted than risks perceived to be catastrophic.

- Risks perceived to be generated by a trusted source are more accepted than risks perceived to be generated by an untrusted source.

- Risks perceived to be familiar are more accepted than risks perceived to be exotic.

- Risks perceived to affect adults are more accepted than risks perceived to affect children.

BARUCH FISCHHOFF ET AL., ACCEPTABLE RISK, 134–39 (1981).

Although this summary may appear logical, even obvious, it is not always easy to keep in mind when analyzing something that happens to be especially frightening or especially desirable to you. How would you characterize your own perceptions of risk? If you are especially afraid of a particular risk, such as a shark attack or a drive-by shooting, do you know how many people actually die from that risk each year? For detailed statistics on causes of death, see National Center for Health Statistics, www.cdc.gov/nchs/deaths.htm.

5. **Black swans, hedgehogs and foxes.** Taleb argues that life-changing events are often Black Swans, or what Jerry Avorn called "bolts from the blue events" — unexpected and unpredictable. His book challenges the efforts of public health researchers and social scientists to draw conclusions and make predictions from what currently exists. Taleb offers a highly skeptical view of experts, especially those in the financial and social fields. Another view of experts was offered by Philip E. Tetlock, who studied experts in political and economic trends and their forecasts over 20 years. Using Isaiah Berlin's essay, he characterized the experts as either hedgehogs or foxes. Hedgehogs were closeminded, relating everything to a central insight or theory and explaining away anything to the contrary. Foxes were openminded with knowledge of lots of things; they accepted ambiguity and contradictions and adjusted their conclusions in response to events. How would you categorize yourself?

6. **Regression to the mean.** John P. A. Ioannidis, a physician, critiques scientific research. His seminal article explained, as its title makes clear, *Why Most Published Research Findings Are False*, 2(8) PLoS MED. e124 (2005), www. plosmedicine.org/article/info:doi/10.1371/journal.pmed.0020124. His subsequent research also finds that an original study reporting success, such as an effective drug treatment, is often followed by later studies that refute the original study's findings. What are we to make of such research? Ioannidis suggests several reasons why follow-up studies may not replicate earlier, typically positive, results: the original study may have been too small; the effects of the factors being studied may be limited; there may be too many relevant relationships to study efficiently; different studies may have different designs; the field may be a hot topic attracting many

investigators; and the investigators may have financial or professional interests in reaching positive results, consciously or unconsciously. Finally, Ioannidis and colleagues suggest that original studies producing positive results, such as a successful cardiac intervention or diagnostic marker, are more likely to be published than those without positive results. These original studies may prove to be the apex of success, while follow-up studies follow the path of a regression to the mean, in which the rate or magnitude of positive results declines over time. *See, e.g.,* John P. A. Ioannidis & Orestis A. Panagiotou, *Comparison of Effect Sizes Associated With Biomarkers Reported in Highly Cited Individual Articles and in Subsequent Meta-Analyses,* 305 JAMA 2200 (2011); John P. Ioannidis, *Why Most Discovered True Associations Are Inflated,* 19 EPIDEMIOLOGY 640–648 (2008).

Chapter 3

STATE AND FEDERAL POWER: CONSTITUTIONAL PRINCIPLES APPLICABLE TO PUBLIC HEALTH

A. INTRODUCTION

This chapter is an introduction to the constitutional foundations of public health law. It reviews the basic constitutional principles describing the powers of the federal, state, and local governments in matters concerning the public's health. In doing so, it also reviews principles concerning the distribution of power between the state and federal governments and among branches of government. Most fundamentally, this chapter outlines the basic issues that must be addressed in judicial, legislative, and administrative decision making that attempts to strike a balance between individual rights and the power of the government when it acts to protect the public's health.

Part B surveys early cases attempting to define the boundaries between state and federal jurisdiction over matters of public health. Part C then presents a series of cases, both historical and contemporary, examining the scope of the police power in relation to the state's own residents. These involve fairly traditional exercises of the state's police powers, ranging from mandatory vaccination to prohibitions on owning potentially dangerous animals. In each case, the courts have to evaluate the importance of a perceived risk to public health against various claims of infringement on individual liberty, autonomy, or property interests. In cases where the law is directed towards eliminating a risk to a third party or to the public at large, the courts generally defer to the judgment of local and state legislative bodies as to the proper balance between the public's and the individual's interests. At the same time, as some of these cases illustrate, the courts also have been somewhat reluctant to defer to legislative discretion where the government's claimed interest has more to do with protecting the individual from his/her own behavior, and less to do with protecting others (or somewhat more abstractly, the polity). The state retains vast powers to protect individual health, but it reaches its limits when the state is attempting to force specific behaviors on individuals for the sake of their own health.

Part D picks up the examination, begun in Part B, of federal power in matters of public health and safety, focusing on Congress's power to regulate foreign and interstate commerce. Congress has always exercised authority over the health of immigrants and visitors, and the safety of cargo, arriving in the United States. In the twentieth century, as the nation's economy expanded, the federal government assumed increasing responsibility for protecting the health and safety of the products and services distributed in commerce, establishing regulatory agencies like the Food and Drug Administration that have become household terms. Most direct federal regulation of public health, safety, and welfare has been characterized as the regulation of commerce. This Part examines the scope and limits of that concept.

Part E reviews the power of the federal government to regulate indirectly under Congress's power to tax and spend for the general welfare. The power of the purse often persuades both states and private entities to abide by federal rules voluntarily. Examples of conditions on the use of federal funds include: The No Child Left Behind Act, 20 U.S.C. § 7906, which prohibits the use of funds under the act to provide sex education or HIV prevention education in schools unless that instruction is age appropriate and includes the health benefits of abstinence, or to operate a contraceptive distribution program in schools; and the Ryan White Care Act, which provides funding for AIDS treatment and HIV prevention and prohibits the use of its funds to provide individuals with hypodermic needles or syringes so that they can use illegal drugs, 42 U.S.C. § 300ff-1.

The principles in this chapter serve as the foundation for examining many different public health problems. The remaining chapters in this textbook present problems by subject matter, rather than by legal domain, to reflect the fact that there can be many different legal approaches to solving a public health problem. Some involve individual claims, such as those based on the right of privacy, religion, or speech, which have received closer judicial scrutiny and greater constitutional protection than the examples in this chapter. Many contemporary public health cases challenge the power to interfere with individual constitutional rights that were not fully recognized until the mid-twentieth century. Judicial opinions from the nineteenth century and the first half of the twentieth century noting that the constitution did not apply to exercises of the police power to protect public health and safety now seem quaintly anachronistic in their failure to address the importance of the individual's specific interest (or right). The state can, for example, require physicians to be licensed, but has much less authority to dictate actions physicians must, or must not, take with regard to their individual patients. Comparing these examples reminds us that the degree of deference that courts give legislative decisions varies with the importance of the right at stake.

B. DISTINGUISHING STATE AND FEDERAL JURISDICTION

COMPAGNIE FRANÇAISE DE NAVIGATION Á VAPEUR v. LOUISIANA STATE BOARD OF HEALTH
186 U.S. 380 (1902)

[T]he plaintiff, a corporation created by and existing under the laws of the Republic of France and a citizen of said republic, on or about September 2, 1898, caused its steamship Britannia to be cleared from the ports of Marseilles, France, and Palermo, Italy, for New Orleans with a cargo of merchandise and with about 408 passengers, some of whom were citizens of the United States returning home, and others who were seeking homes in the United States, and who intended to settle in the State of Louisiana or adjoining States, and that all the passengers referred to at the time of their sailing were free from infectious or contagious diseases. It was further averred that on September 29, 1898, the vessel arrived at the quarantine station some distance below the city of New Orleans, was there regularly inspected, and was found both as to the passengers and cargo to be free from any infectious or contagious disease, and accordingly was given a clean bill of health, whereby the ship became entitled to proceed to New Orleans and land her passengers and discharge her cargo. This, however, it was asserted she was not permitted to do, because, on the date last mentioned, at a meeting held by the Board of Health, the following resolution was adopted:

"*Resolved*, That hereafter in the case of any town, city or parish of Louisiana being declared in quarantine, no body or bodies of people, immigrants, soldiers or others shall be allowed to enter said town, city or parish so long as said quarantine shall exist, and that the president of the board shall enforce this resolution."

. . . .

It was averred that . . . the resolution of the Board of Health . . . was passed with the sole object of preventing the landing of the passengers from the Britannia, and this was demonstrated because no attempt was made by the Board of Health to enforce the provisions of the resolution against immigrants from Italy coming into the United States via the port of New York and thence reaching New Orleans by rail, and that after the promulgation of said resolution "more than 200 such persons, varying in groups of 30 to 100 in number, have from time to time been permitted to enter said city." It was averred that the action of the board was not authorized by the state law, and if it was, such law was void because repugnant to the provision of the Constitution of the United States conferring upon Congress power "to regulate commerce with foreign nations, and among the several States and with the Indian tribes."

[The trial court dismissed the suit and the Supreme Court of Louisiana affirmed the dismissal.]

MR. JUSTICE WHITE, after making the foregoing statement, delivered the opinion of the court.

The law of Louisiana, under which the Board of Health exerted the authority which is complained of, is found in section 8 of Act No. 192, enacted in 1898 . . . .

. . . .

The Supreme Court of the State of Louisiana, interpreting this statute, held that it empowered the board to exclude healthy persons from a locality infested with a contagious or infectious disease, and that this power was intended to apply as well to persons seeking to enter the infected place, whether they came from without or from within the State.

. . . .

That from an early day the power of the States to enact and enforce quarantine laws for the safety and the protection of the health of their inhabitants has been recognized by Congress, is beyond question. That until Congress has exercised its power on the subject, such state quarantine laws and state laws for the purpose of preventing, eradicating or controlling the spread of contagious or infectious diseases, are not repugnant to the Constitution of the United States, although their operation affects interstate or foreign commerce, is not an open question. The doctrine was elaborately examined and stated in *Morgan Steamship Company* v. *Louisiana Board of Health,* 118 U.S. 455. That case involved determining whether a quarantine law enacted by the State of Louisiana was repugnant to the commerce clause of the Constitution because of its necessary effect upon interstate and foreign commerce. The court said:

"Is the law under consideration void as a regulation of commerce? Undoubtedly it is in some sense a regulation of commerce. It arrests a vessel on a voyage which may have been a long one. It may affect commerce among the States when the vessel is coming from some other State of the Union than Louisiana, and it may affect commerce with foreign nations when the vessel arrested comes from a foreign port. This interruption of the voyage may be for days or for weeks. It extends to the vessel, the cargo, the officers and seamen, and the passengers. In so far as it provides a rule by which this power is exercised, it cannot be denied that it regulates commerce. We do not think it necessary to enter into the inquiry whether, notwithstanding this, it is to be classed among those police powers which were retained by the States as exclusively their own, and, therefore, not ceded to Congress. For, while it may be a police power in the sense that all provisions for the health, comfort and security of the citizens, are police regulations, and an exercise of the police power, it has been said more than once in this court that, even where such powers are so exercised as to come within the domain of Federal authority as defined by the Constitution, the latter must prevail." *Gibbons* v. *Ogden*, 9 Wheat. 1, 210; *Henderson* v. *The Mayor*, 92 U.S. 259, 272; *New Orleans Gas Co.* v. *Louisiana Light Co.*, 115 U.S. 650, 661.

"But it may be conceded that whenever Congress shall undertake to provide for the commercial cities of the United States a general system of quarantine, or shall confide the execution of the details of such a system to a National Board of Health, or to local boards, as may be found expedient, all state laws on the subject will be abrogated, at least so far as the two are inconsistent. But, until this is done, the laws of the State on the subject are valid. This follows for two reasons:"

"1. [The 1799 federal Act governing quarantine provided that] 'there shall be no interference [by federal officials] in any manner with any quarantine laws or regulations as they now exist or may hereafter be adopted under state laws,' showing very clearly the intention of Congress to adopt these laws or to recognize the power of the State to pass them. . . . "

"2. . . . [Q]uarantine laws belong to that class of state legislation which, whether passed with intent to regulate commerce or not, must be admitted to have that effect, and which are valid until displaced or contravened by some legislation of Congress."

. . . .

[H]ealth and quarantine laws of the several States are not repugnant to the

Constitution of the United States, although they affect foreign and domestic commerce, as in many cases they necessarily must do in order to be efficacious, because until Congress has acted under the authority conferred upon it by the Constitution, such state health and quarantine laws producing such effect on legitimate interstate commerce are not in conflict with the Constitution . . . .

   . . . .

   . . . And it is also to be borne in mine, as said by this court in *Louisiana* v. *Texas*, [176 U.S. 1], 22, if any [abuse by the state of its power] should be perpetrated "Congress could by affirmative action displace the local laws, substitute laws of its own, and thus correct any unjustifiable and oppressive exercise of power by state legislation. "

   . . . .

   . . . [T[he Supreme Court of Louisiana did not err in deciding that the act in question was not repugnant to the Constitution of the United States, and was not in conflict with the acts of Congress on the treaties made by the United States which were relied upon to show to the contrary and its judgment is, therefore,

Affirmed.

UNITED STATES v. WINDSOR
133 S. Ct. 2675 (2013)

JUSTICE KENNEDY delivered the opinion of the Court.

Two women then resident in New York were married in a lawful ceremony in Ontario, Canada, in 2007. Edith Windsor and Thea Spyer returned to their home in New York City. [New York recognizes their marriage as lawful.] When Spyer died in 2009, she left her entire estate to Windsor. Windsor sought to claim the estate tax exemption for surviving spouses. She was barred from doing so, however, by a federal law, the Defense of Marriage Act [110 Stat. 2419], which excludes a same-sex partner from the definition of "spouse" as that term is used in federal statutes. Windsor paid the taxes [$363,053] but filed suit [for a refund] to challenge the constitutionality of this provision. The United States District Court and the Court of Appeals ruled that this portion of the statute is unconstitutional and ordered the United States to pay Windsor a refund. This Court granted certiorari and now affirms the judgment in Windsor's favor.

   . . . DOMA contains two operative sections: Section 2, which has not been challenged here, allows States to refuse to recognize same-sex marriages performed under the laws of other States. See 28 U. S. C. § 1738C.

Section 3 is at issue here. It amends the Dictionary Act in Title 1, § 7, of the United States Code to provide a federal definition of "marriage" and "spouse." Section 3 of DOMA provides as follows:

"In determining the meaning of any Act of Congress, or of any ruling, regulation, or interpretation of the various administrative bureaus and agencies of the United States, the word 'marriage' means only a legal union between one man and one woman as husband and wife, and the word 'spouse' refers only to a person of the opposite sex who is a husband or a wife." 1 U. S. C. § 7.

The definitional provision does not by its terms forbid States from enacting laws permitting same-sex marriages or civil unions or providing state benefits to residents in that status. The enactment's comprehensive definition of marriage for purposes of all federal statutes and other regulations or directives covered by its terms, however, does control over 1,000 federal laws in which marital or spousal status is addressed as a matter of federal law.

. . . .

. . . By history and tradition the definition and regulation of marriage . . . has been treated as being within the authority and realm of the separate States. Yet it is further established that Congress, in enacting discrete statutes, can make determinations that bear on marital rights and privileges. . . . Congress has the power both to ensure efficiency in the administration of its programs and to choose what larger goals and policies to pursue.

Other precedents involving congressional statutes which affect marriages and family status further illustrate this point. In addressing the interaction of state domestic relations and federal immigration law Congress determined that marriages "entered into for the purpose of procuring an alien's admission [to the United States] as an immigrant" will not qualify the noncitizen for that status, even if the noncitizen's marriage is valid and proper, for state-law purposes. 8 U. S. C. § 1186a(b)(1) (2006 ed. and Supp. V). And in establishing income-based criteria for Social Security benefits, Congress decided that although state law would determine in general who qualifies as an applicant's spouse, common-law marriages also should be recognized, regardless of any particular State's view on these relationships. 42 U. S. C. § 1382c(d)(2).

Though these discrete examples establish the constitutionality of limited federal laws that regulate the meaning of marriage in order to further federal policy, DOMA has a far greater reach; for it enacts a directive applicable to over 1,000 federal statutes and the whole realm of federal regulations. And its operation is directed to a class of persons that the laws of New York, and of 11 other States, have sought to protect . . . .

In order to assess the validity of that intervention it is necessary to discuss the extent of the state power and authority over marriage as a matter of history and tradition. State laws defining and regulating marriage, of course, must respect the constitutional rights of persons, see, e.g., *Loving v. Virginia*, 388 U. S. 1 (1967); but, subject to those guarantees, "regulation of domestic relations" is "an area that has long been regarded as a virtually exclusive province of the States." *Sosna v. Iowa*, 419 U. S. 393, 404 (1975).

The recognition of civil marriages is central to state domestic relations law applicable to its residents and citizens . . . . The definition of marriage is the foundation of the State's broader authority to regulate the subject of domestic relations with respect to the "[p]rotection of offspring, property interests, and the enforcement of marital responsibilities." "[T]he states, at the time of the adoption of the Constitution, possessed full power over the subject of marriage and divorce . . . [and] the Constitution delegated no authority to the Government of the United States on the subject of marriage and divorce." *Haddock v. Haddock*, 201 U. S. 562, 575 (1906) . . . .

Consistent with this allocation of authority, the Federal Government, through our history, has deferred to state-law policy decisions with respect to domestic relations . . . .

. . . .

Against this background DOMA rejects the long-established precept that the incidents, benefits, and obligations of marriage are uniform for all married couples within each State, though they may vary, subject to constitutional guarantees, from one State to the next. Despite these considerations, it is unnecessary to decide whether this federal intrusion on state power is a violation of the Constitution because it disrupts the federal balance. The State's power in defining the marital relation is of central relevance in this case quite apart from principles of federalism. Here the State's decision to give this class of persons the right to marry conferred upon them a dignity and status of immense import. When the State used its historic and essential authority to define the marital relation in this way, its role and its power in making the decision enhanced the recognition, dignity, and protection of the class in their own community. DOMA, because of its reach and extent, departs from this history and tradition of reliance on state law to define marriage. " '[D] iscriminations of an unusual character especially suggest careful consideration to determine whether they are obnoxious to the constitutional provision.' " *Romer v. Evans*, 517 U. S. 620, 633 (1996) (quoting *Louisville Gas & Elec. Co. v. Coleman*, 277 U. S. 32, 37–38 (1928)).

The Federal Government uses this state-defined class for the opposite purpose — to impose restrictions and disabilities. That result requires this Court now to address whether the resulting injury and indignity is a deprivation of an essential part of the liberty protected by the Fifth Amendment. What the State of New York treats as alike the federal law deems unlike by a law designed to injure the same class the State seeks to protect.

. . . .

. . . Private, consensual sexual intimacy between two adult persons of the same sex may not be punished by the State, and it can form "but one element in a personal bond that is more enduring." *Lawrence v. Texas*, 539 U. S. 558, 567 (2003). By its recognition of the validity of same-sex marriages performed in other jurisdictions and then by authorizing same-sex unions and same-sex marriages, New York sought to give further protection and dignity to that bond. For same-sex couples who wished to be married, the State acted to give their lawful conduct a lawful status. This status is a far-reaching legal acknowledgment of the intimate relationship between two people, a relationship deemed by the State worthy of dignity in the community equal with all other marriages. It reflects both the community's considered perspective on the historical roots of the institution of marriage and its evolving understanding of the meaning of equality.

IV

DOMA seeks to injure the very class New York seeks to protect. By doing so it violates basic due process and equal protection principles applicable to the Federal Government. See U. S. Const., Amdt. 5; *Bolling v. Sharpe*, 347 U. S. 497 (1954). The Constitution's guarantee of equality "must at the very least mean that a bare congressional desire to harm a politically unpopular group cannot" justify disparate treatment of that group . . . . In determining whether a law is motived by an improper animus or purpose, " '[d] iscriminations of an unusual character' " especially require careful consideration . . . . DOMA cannot survive under these principles . . . . DOMA's unusual deviation from the usual tradition of recognizing and accepting state definitions of marriage here operates to deprive same-sex couples of the benefits and responsibilities that come with the federal recognition of their marriages. This is strong evidence of a law having the purpose and effect of disapproval of that class. The avowed purpose and practical effect of the law here in question are to impose a disadvantage, a separate status, and so a stigma upon all who enter into same-sex marriages made lawful by the unquestioned authority of the States.

The history of DOMA's enactment and its own text demonstrate that interference with the equal dignity of same-sex marriages, a dignity conferred by the States in the exercise of their sovereign power, was more than an incidental effect of the federal statute. It was its essence. The House Report announced its conclusion that "it is both appropriate and necessary for Congress to do what it can to defend the institution of traditional heterosexual marriage . . . ." H. R. Rep. No. 104–664, pp. 12–13 (1996). The House concluded that DOMA expresses "both moral disapproval of homosexuality, and a moral conviction that heterosexuality better comports with traditional (especially Judeo- Christian) morality." *Id.*, at 16 (footnote deleted). The stated purpose of the law was to promote an "interest in protecting the traditional moral teachings reflected in heterosexual-only marriage laws." *Ibid.* Were there any doubt of this far-reaching purpose, the title of the Act confirms it: The Defense of Marriage.

. . . The Act's demonstrated purpose is to ensure that if any State decides to recognize same-sex marriages, those unions will be treated as second-class marriages for purposes of federal law. This raises a most serious question under the Constitution's Fifth Amendment.

. . . .

DOMA's principal effect is to identify a subset of state-sanctioned marriages and make them unequal. The principal purpose is to impose inequality, not for other reasons like governmental efficiency. Responsibilities, as well as rights, enhance the dignity and integrity of the person. And DOMA contrives to deprive some couples married under the laws of their State, but not other couples, of both rights and responsibilities. By creating two contradictory marriage regimes within the same State, DOMA forces same-sex couples to live as married for the purpose of state law but unmarried for the purpose of federal law, thus diminishing the stability and predictability of basic personal relations the State has found it proper to acknowledge and protect. By this dynamic DOMA undermines both the public and private significance of state- sanctioned same-sex marriages; for it tells those couples, and all the world, that their otherwise valid marriages are unworthy of federal recognition. This places same-sex couples in an unstable position of being in a second-tier marriage. The differentiation demeans the couple, whose moral and sexual choices the Constitution protects and whose relationship the State has sought to dignify. And it humiliates tens of thousands of children now being raised by same-sex couples. The law in question makes it even more difficult for the children to understand the integrity and closeness of their own family and its concord with other families in their community and in their daily lives.

Under DOMA, same-sex married couples have their lives burdened, by reason of government decree, in visible and public ways . . . . It prevents same-sex married couples from obtaining government healthcare benefits they would otherwise receive . . . . It forces them to follow a complicated procedure to file their state and federal taxes jointly . . . . It prohibits them from being buried together in veterans' cemeteries.

. . . .

DOMA also brings financial harm to children of same-sex couples. It raises the cost of health care for families by taxing health benefits provided by employers to their workers' same-sex spouses . . . . And it denies or reduces benefits allowed to families upon the loss of a spouse and parent, benefits that are an integral part of family security . . . .

DOMA divests married same-sex couples of the duties and responsibilities that are an essential part of married life and that they in most cases would be honored to accept were DOMA not in force.

* * *

The power the Constitution grants it also restrains. And though Congress has great authority to design laws to fit its own conception of sound national policy, it cannot deny the liberty protected by the Due Process Clause of the Fifth Amendment.

What has been explained to this point should more than suffice to establish that the principal purpose and the necessary effect of this law are to demean those persons who are in a lawful same-sex marriage. This requires the Court to hold, as it now does, that DOMA is unconstitutional as a deprivation of the liberty of the person protected by the Fifth Amendment of the Constitution.

The liberty protected by the Fifth Amendment's Due Process Clause contains within it the prohibition against denying to any person the equal protection of the laws . . . . While the Fifth Amendment itself withdraws from Government the power to degrade or demean in the way this law does, the equal protection guarantee of the Fourteenth Amendment makes that Fifth Amendment right all the more specific and all the better understood and preserved.

The class to which DOMA directs its restrictions and restraints are those persons who are joined in same-sex marriages made lawful by the State. DOMA singles out a class of persons deemed by a State entitled to recognition and protection to enhance their own liberty. It imposes a disability on the class by refusing to acknowledge a status the State finds to be dignified and proper. DOMA instructs all federal officials, and indeed all persons with whom same-sex couples interact, including their own children, that their marriage is less worthy than the marriages of others. The federal statute is invalid, for no legitimate purpose overcomes the purpose and effect to disparage and to injure those whom the State, by its marriage laws, sought to protect in personhood and dignity. By seeking to displace this protection and treating those persons as living in marriages less respected than others, the federal statute is in violation of the Fifth Amendment. This opinion and its holding are confined to those lawful marriages.

NOTES AND QUESTIONS

1. **Federalism and boundaries between state and federal regulation.** *Compagnie Française* illustrates the type of conflict between state and federal authority that has arisen periodically since the U.S. Constitution was ratified. Quarantine to prevent people or cargo with contagious diseases from entering a state had long been seen as the archetypal subject of the police powers, which were reserved to the states. At the same time, the U.S. Constitution granted the federal government authority over matters of foreign and interstate commerce, as well as immigration. (The federal Marine Hospital Act of 1893, 27 Stat. 449, established a federal system of health inspections and quarantine at the nation's borders.) The Compagnie Française argued (among other claims) that the Louisiana statute vested authority in the Board of Health to interfere with foreign and interstate commerce in violation of the federal Constitution. The Supreme Court granted that Louisiana law did affect commerce, but because Congress had not yet adopted quarantine legislation that displaced state laws, the state law could stand.

The twenty-first century has seen its own high profile federalism disputes. *Gonzales v. Raich*, excerpted in Part D *infra*, pitted the federal Controlled Substances Act against California's decriminalization of marijuana possession for medical purposes. There, the Commerce Power trumped the state's authority. Most prominent, perhaps, was the constitutional challenge to the requirement that individuals obtain health insurance coverage in the Patient Protection and Affordable Care Act, Pub. L. No. 111-148, 124 Stat. 119 (2010). The U.S. Supreme Court concluded that Congress's authority under the Commerce Power did not include the power to require individuals to buy health insurance, but upheld the requirement as a constitutional exercise of the power to tax. *National Federation of Independent Business v. Sebelius*, 132 S. Ct. 2566 (2012), excerpted in D, *infra*. No one disputed the assumption that a state could impose the same requirement on its own residents, however, as Massachusetts did in 2006.

2. **The Negative or Dormant Commerce Clause.** State laws that appear to exercise the enumerated powers that the Article I of the Constitution grants to Congress pose difficult challenges for federalism. Although the Constitution does not expressly forbid the states from exercising similar powers — at least within its own borders — the text of the Commerce Clause impliedly negates any state power over foreign or interstate commerce.

Wendy Parmet provides succinct background on the development of dormant (or negative) commerce clause doctrine:

> The doctrine itself dates back to the early days of the nineteenth century, when the Constitution's grant to Congress of authority to regulate commerce was understood as depriving states of the same power. Under this exclusive powers approach, jurists assumed that because the Constitution vested the power to regulate interstate commerce with the Congress, it effectively took any such powers away from the states. Thus state regulations of interstate commerce were deemed to be unconstitutional, even though there is no language in the Constitution to that effect. (Hence, the negative commerce clause.) On the other hand, because courts deemed the protection of public health to be solidly within the core of the states' police powers, a state regulation would be held constitutional and not an impermissible regulation of interstate commerce if the law were viewed as a public health law . . . .

> By the mid-nineteenth century, however, . . . [c]ourts recognized that some state regulation of interstate commerce was desirable or at least inevitable. Moreover, courts perceived that states might use putative public health measures as a pretext for interfering with interstate commerce. As a result, alternative rationales were offered to justify federalism boundaries under the dormant commerce clause.

> One highly influential rationale explained the dormant commerce clause doctrine as embodying the Constitution's disdain for discrimination and favoritism between the states. Seeking to protect commerce from the evils of state protectionism and balkanization, this theory found state laws that appeared either facially or by their impact to discriminate against out-of-state economic interests as unconstitutional. . . .

>   . . . .

> This deference to the states' police power eroded after the Supreme Court settled on a two-tiered analysis for determining whether state laws, including those that purport to protect health or safety, violate the dormant commerce clause. Today, courts treat as per se unconstitutional those state laws that "directly regulate[] or discriminate[] against interstate commerce." [quoting Pike v. Bruce Church, Inc., 397 U.S. 137, 142 (1970)]. On the other hand, state laws that have a less direct or only an incidental impact upon commerce fall into the second tier and are usually subject to the so-called *Pike* balancing test that asks whether the state law is legitimate and whether the burdens it places on commerce outweigh its local benefits.

WENDY E. PARMET, POPULATIONS, PUBLIC HEALTH, AND THE LAW 82–84 (2009).

Supreme Court decisions addressing dormant commerce clause issues have not consistently sorted fact patterns into neat categories. Compare *City of Philadelphia v. New Jersey*, 437 U.S. 617 (1978) (finding a New Jersey law forbidding the importation into the state of most solid or liquid waste that was collected or originated outside the state to be unconstitutional protectionism, despite its goal of protecting the environment), with *United Haulers Assoc., Inc. v. Oneida-Herkimer Solid Waste Management Authority*, 550 U.S. 330 (2007)(upholding a county ordinance requiring private haulers to obtain permits to collect solid waste and deliver it to public waste transfer stations, even though out-of-state disposal would be cheaper without permit costs). The state of Maine created the "Maine Rx" program in 2000 to protect its residents — primarily the uninsured — from the high cost of prescription drugs. The program allowed the state to negotiate rebates with drug manufacturers to offset the cost to the state of providing the drugs at a reduced price. Without prior authorization, Maine's Medicaid program would not pay for drugs from pharmaceutical companies and distributors that did not enter into a rebate agreement. An association of nonresident pharmaceutical manufacturers successfully challenged the Maine Rx program on the ground that it violated the negative commerce clause. *Pharmaceutical Research & Manufacturers of America v. Walsh*, 538 U.S. 644 (2003).

Would the New Orleans Board of Health actions in *Compagnie Française* be viewed as discrimination against the French (or the particular ship) or as having only an incidental impact on commerce under modern doctrine? The court did not address the issue of protectionism or discrimination. The company argued that Louisiana was playing favorites by forbidding a French company to unload its passengers, while allowing Italian immigrants to enter the city by train from the port of New York City. The company's ship had been inspected at a quarantine station below New Orleans and found to have no contagious disease aboard. The Board of Health also threatened that if the ship attempted to unload at any other port in Louisiana, it would impose a quarantine on that port, too.

3. **Implications of *Windsor*.** Justice Kennedy's opinion for the 5 to 4 majority avoids answering the federalism question of whether the federal government intrudes on the state's power to define marriage, basing the decision on DOMA's violation of the Fifth Amendment. Can you identify the standard of review that Justice Kennedy used to find that DOMA violated the Fifth Amendment's due process guarantee? For that matter, is it clear whether DOMA violated the Amendment's protection of liberty or equal protection or both? Justice Kennedy's opinion frequently mentions inequality and unequal treatment as DOMA's intent, as well as effect. The opinion also included evidence of Congress's discriminatory intent in enacting DOMA, suggesting that heightened scrutiny would be appropriate, at least for "determining whether a law is motived by an improper animus or purpose: '[d]iscriminations of an unusual character' especially require careful consideration." The legislature's motive is not ordinarily relevant to an evaluation of a law's constitutionality. What was unusual about this discrimination? Certainly, discrimination against same-sex couples was not unusual, despite growing public acceptance. Was the federal government's refusal to defer to a state's definition of legal marriage considered discriminatory? What arguments could be made to support a consistent federal definition of marriage?

JUSTICE SCALIA wrote a feverish dissent, calling the majority's justifications "rootless and shifting." *Windsor*, 133 S.Ct. at 2705 (Scalia, J. dissenting):

Some might conclude that this loaf could have used a while longer in the oven. But that would be wrong; it is already overcooked. The most expert care in preparation cannot redeem a bad recipe. The sum of all the Court's nonspecific hand-waving is that this law is invalid (maybe on equal-protection grounds, maybe on substantive-due-process grounds, and perhaps with some amorphous federalism component playing a role) because it is motivated by a "'bare . . . desire to harm'" couples in same-sex marriages.

Id. at 2707.

JUSTICE SCALIA objected that legislation that has a rational basis has not and should not be overturned simply because the legislature's motive may have been impure — or even malicious. He worried that "the majority has declared open season on any law that . . . can be characterized as mean-spirited." *Id.* at 2707. Finally, he predicted that the majority's decision offers a blueprint for future litigants to challenge state laws that bar same-sex couples from lawful marriage, an issue the Court declined to decide during the same term in *Hollingsworth v. Perry*, 133 S. Ct. 1521 (2013). For an examination of morality as a basis for legislation, including same-sex marriage prohibitions, see Chapter 4, C, *infra*.

4.   **Federal preemption of state laws.** The *Windsor* case mentions examples of federal laws that might appear to conflict with the states' jurisdiction over marriage and domestic relations. The reverse is also possible — state laws that conflict with federal law.

Nine days before the Windsor decision, the Court struck down an Arizona law that required persons seeking to vote in federal elections to register by showing documentary proof of citizenship. *Arizona v. The Inter-Tribal Council of Arizona, Inc.*, 133 S. Ct. 2247 (2013). The National Voter Registration Act of 1993, 42 U. S. C. § 1973gg *et seq.*, requires states to "accept and use" a federal registration form, which does not require such documentary evidence. The Court found that the National Act preempted Arizona's law. Although states retain the authority to determine the qualifications for voters in their state, the Elections Clause in the federal Constitution's Article I, sec. 4, cl. 1, expressly authorizes Congress to supersede state laws governing federal election procedures: "The Times, Places and Manner of holding Elections for Senators and Representatives, shall be prescribed in each State by the Legislature thereof; but the Congress may at any time by Law make or alter such Regulations, except as to the places of chusing Senators."

C.   STATE REGULATION OF STATE RESIDENTS

JACOBSON v. MASSACHUSETTS
197 U.S. 11 (1905)

This case involves the validity, under the Constitution of the United States, of certain provisions in the statutes of Massachusetts relating to vaccination.

The Revised Laws of the Commonwealth, c. 75, § 137, provide that "the board of

Mass statute

health of a city or town if, in its opinion, it is necessary for the public health or safety shall require and enforce the vaccination and revaccination of all the inhabitants thereof and shall provide them with the means of free vaccination. Whoever, being over twenty-one years of age and not under guardianship, refuses or neglects to comply with such requirement shall forfeit five dollars."

An exception is made in favor of "children who present a certificate, signed by a registered physician that they are unfit subjects for vaccination." § 139.

Proceeding under the above statutes, the Board of Health of the city of Cambridge, Massachusetts, on the twenty-seventh day of February, 1902, adopted the following regulation: "Whereas, smallpox has been prevalent to some extent in the city of Cambridge and still continues to increase; and whereas, it is necessary for the speedy extermination of the disease, that all persons not protected by vaccination should be vaccinated; and whereas, in the opinion of the board, the public health and safety require the vaccination or revaccination of all the inhabitants of Cambridge; be it ordered, that all the inhabitants of the city who have not been successfully vaccinated since March 1, 1897, be vaccinated or revaccinated."

Subsequently, the Board adopted an additional regulation empowering a named physician to enforce the vaccination of persons as directed by the Board at its special meeting of February 27.

The above regulations being in force, the plaintiff in error, Jacobson, was proceeded against by a criminal complaint in one of the inferior courts of Massachusetts . . . .

. . . .

π refused to be vaccinated in accordance to statute & was fined

[Jacobson was convicted of refusing vaccination, sentenced to pay a fine of $5.00, and ordered to "stand committed until the fine was paid."]

MR. JUSTICE HARLAN, after making the foregoing statement, delivered the opinion of the court.

2.

. . . [W]e assume for the purposes of the present inquiry that . . . [the statute's] provisions require, at least as a general rule, that adults not under guardianship and remaining within the limits of the city of Cambridge must submit to the regulation adopted by the Board of Health. Is the statute, so construed, therefore, inconsistent with the liberty which the Constitution of the United States secures to every person against deprivation by the State? → is statute unlawful?

The authority of the State to enact this statute is to be referred to what is commonly called the police power — a power which the State did not surrender when becoming a member of the Union under the Constitution. Although this court has refrained from any attempt to define the limits of that power, yet it has distinctly recognized the authority of a State to enact quarantine laws and "health laws of every description;" indeed, all laws that relate to matters completely within its territory and which do not by their necessary operation affect the people of other States. According to settled principles the police power of a State must be held to embrace, at least, such reasonable regulations established directly by legislative enactment as will protect the public health and the public safety. It is equally true that the State may invest local bodies called into existence for purposes of local administration with authority in some appropriate way to safeguard the public health and the public safety. The mode or manner in which those results are to be accomplished is within the discretion of the State, subject, of course, so far as Federal power is concerned, only to the condition that no rule prescribed by a State, nor any regulation adopted by a local governmental agency acting under the sanction of state legislation, shall contravene the Constitution of the United States or infringe any right granted or secured by that instrument . . . .

We come, then, to inquire whether any right given, or secured by the Constitution, is invaded by the statute as interpreted by the state court. The defendant insists that his liberty is invaded when the State subjects him to fine or imprisonment for neglecting or refusing to submit to vaccination; that a compulsory vaccination law is unreasonable, arbitrary and oppressive, and, therefore, hostile to the inherent right of every freeman to care for his own body and health in such way as to him seems best; and that the execution of such a law against one who objects to vaccination, no matter for what reason, is nothing short of an assault upon his person. But the liberty secured by the Constitution of the United States to every person within its jurisdiction does not import an absolute right in each person to be, at all times and in all circumstances, wholly freed from restraint. There are manifold restraints to which every person is necessarily subject for the common good. On any other basis organized society could not exist with safety to its members. Society based on the rule that each one is a law unto himself would soon be confronted with disorder and anarchy. Real liberty for all could not exist under the operation of a principle which recognizes the right of each individual person to use his own, whether in respect of his person or his property, regardless of the injury that may be done to others. This court has more than once recognized it as a fundamental principle that "persons and property are subjected to all kinds of restraints and burdens, in order to secure the general comfort, health, and prosperity of the State . . . . In *Crowley v. Christensen*, 137 U.S. 86, 89, we said: "The possession and enjoyment of all rights are subject to such reasonable conditions as may be deemed by the governing authority of the country essential to the safety, health, peace, good order and morals of the community. Even liberty itself, the greatest of all rights, is not unrestricted license to act according to one's own will. It is only freedom from restraint under conditions essential to the equal enjoyment of the same right by others. It is then liberty regulated by law." . . . [A] fundamental principle of the social compact . . . [reflected in the Massachusetts Constitution of 1780 is that] the whole people covenants with each citizen, and each citizen with the whole people, that all shall be governed by certain laws for "the common good," and that government is instituted for "the common good, for the protection, safety, prosperity and happiness of the people, and not for the profit, honor or private interests of any one man . . . ."

Applying these principles to the present case, it is to be observed that the legislature of Massachusetts required the inhabitants of a city or town to be vaccinated only when, in the opinion of the Board of Health, that was necessary for the public health or the public safety. The authority to determine for all what ought to be done in such an emergency must have been lodged somewhere or in some body; and surely it was appropriate for the legislature to refer that question, in the first instance, to a Board of Health, composed of persons residing in the locality affected and appointed, presumably, because of their fitness to determine such questions. To invest such a body with authority over such matters was not an unusual nor an unreasonable or arbitrary requirement. Upon the principle of self-defense, of paramount necessity, a community has the right to protect itself against an epidemic of disease which threatens the safety of its members. It is to be observed that when the regulation in question was adopted, smallpox, according to the recitals in the regulation adopted by the Board of Health, was prevalent to some extent in the city of Cambridge and the disease was increasing. If such was the situation — and nothing is asserted or appears in the record to the contrary — if we are to attach any value whatever to the knowledge which, it is safe to affirm, is common to all civilized peoples touching smallpox and the methods most usually employed to eradicate that disease, it cannot be adjudged that the present regulation of the Board of Health was not necessary in order to protect the public health and secure the public safety. Smallpox being prevalent and increasing at Cambridge, the court would usurp the functions of another branch of government if it adjudged, as matter of law, that the mode adopted under the sanction of the State, to protect the people at large, was arbitrary and not justified by the necessities of the case. We say necessities of the case, because it might be that an acknowledged power of a local community to protect itself against an epidemic threatening the safety of all, might be exercised in particular circumstances and in reference to particular persons in such an arbitrary, unreasonable manner, or might go so far beyond what was reasonably required for the safety of the public, as to authorize or compel the courts to interfere for the protection of such persons . . . . There is, of course, a sphere within which the individual may assert the supremacy of his own will and rightfully dispute the authority of any human government, especially of any free government existing under a written constitution, to interfere with the exercise of that will. But it is equally true that in every well-ordered society charged with the duty of conserving the safety of its members the rights of the individual in respect of his liberty may at times, under the pressure of great dangers, be subjected to such restraint, to be enforced by reasonable regulations, as the safety of the general public may demand . . . .

Looking at the propositions embodied in the defendant's rejected offers of proof it is clear that they are more formidable by their number than by their inherent value. Those offers in the main seem to have had no purpose except to state the general theory of those of the medical profession who attach little or no value to vaccination as a means of preventing the spread of smallpox or who think that vaccination causes other diseases of the body. What everybody knows the court must know, and therefore the state court judicially knew, as this court knows, that an opposite theory accords with the common belief and is maintained by high medical authority. We must assume that when the statute in question was passed, the legislature of Massachusetts was not unaware of these opposing theories, and was compelled, of necessity, to choose between them. It was not compelled to commit a matter involving the public health and safety to the final decision of a court or jury. It is no part of the function of a court or a jury to determine which one of two modes was likely to be the most effective for the protection of the public against disease. That was for the legislative department to determine in the light of all the information it had or could obtain. It could not properly abdicate its function to guard the public health and safety. The state legislature proceeded upon the theory which recognized vaccination as at least an effective if not the best known way in which to meet and suppress the evils of a smallpox epidemic that imperiled an entire population. Upon what sound principles as to the relations existing between the different departments of government can the court review this action of the legislature? If there is any such power in the judiciary to review legislative action in respect of a matter affecting the general welfare, it can only be when that which the legislature has done comes within the rule that if a statute purporting to have been enacted to protect the public health, the public morals or the public safety, has no real or substantial relation to those objects, or is, beyond all question, a plain, palpable invasion of rights secured by the fundamental law, it is the duty of the courts to so adjudge, and thereby give effect to the Constitution.

Whatever may be thought of the expediency of this statute, it cannot be affirmed to be, beyond question, in palpable conflict with the Constitution. Nor, in view of the methods employed to stamp out the disease of smallpox, can anyone confidently assert that the means prescribed by the State to that end has no real or substantial relation to the protection of the public health and the public safety . . . .

. . . It must be conceded that some laymen, both learned and unlearned, and some physicians of great skill and repute, do not believe that vaccination is a preventive of smallpox. The common belief, however, is that it has a decided tendency to prevent the spread of this fearful disease and to render it less dangerous to those who contract it. While not accepted by all, it is accepted by the mass of people, as well as by most members of the medical profession. It has been general in our State and in most civilized nations for generations . . . . A common belief, like common knowledge, does not require evidence to establish its existence, but may be acted upon without proof by the legislature and the courts . . . . The fact that the belief is not universal is not controlling, for there is scarcely any belief that is accepted by everyone. The possibility that the belief may be wrong, and that science may yet show it to be wrong, is not conclusive; for the legislature has the right to pass laws which, according to the common belief of the people, are adapted to prevent the spread of contagious diseases. In a free country, where the government is by the people, through their chosen representatives, practical legislation admits of no other standard of action; for what the people believe is for the common welfare must be accepted as tending to promote the common welfare, whether it does in fact or not. Any other basis would conflict with the spirit of the Constitution, and would sanction measures opposed to a republican form of government. While we do not decide and cannot decide that vaccination is a preventive of smallpox, we take judicial notice of the fact that this is the common belief of the people of the State, and with this fact as a foundation we hold that the statute in question is a health law, enacted in a reasonable and proper exercise of the police power . . . .

Holding

. . . .

The defendant offered to prove that vaccination "quite often" caused serious and permanent injury to the health of the person vaccinated; that the operation "occasionally" resulted in death; that it was "impossible" to tell "in any particular case" what the results of vaccination would be or whether it would injure the health or result in death; that "quite often" one's blood is in a certain condition of impurity when it is not prudent or safe to vaccinate him; that there is no practical test by which to determine "with any degree of certainty" whether one's blood is in such condition of impurity as to render vaccination necessarily unsafe or dangerous; that vaccine matter is "quite often" impure and dangerous to be used, but whether impure or not cannot be ascertained by any known practical test; that the defendant refused to submit to vaccination for the reason that he had, "when a child," been caused great and extreme suffering for a long period by a disease produced by vaccination; and that he had witnessed a similar result of vaccination not only in the case of his son, but in the cases of others.

It's reason for not wanting vaccination

These offers, in effect, invited the court and jury to go over the whole ground gone over by the legislature when it enacted the statute in question. The legislature assumed that some children, by reason of their condition at the time, might not be fit subjects of vaccination; and it is suggested — and we will not say without reason — that such is the case with some adults. But the defendant did not offer to prove that, by reason of his then condition, he was in fact not a fit subject of vaccination at the time he was informed of the requirement of the regulation adopted by the Board of Health. It is entirely consistent with his offer of proof that, after reaching full age, he had become, so far as medical skill could discover, and when informed of the regulation of the Board of Health was, a fit subject of vaccination, and that the vaccine matter to be used in his case was such as any medical practitioner of good standing would regard as proper to be used. The matured opinions of medical men everywhere, and the experience of mankind, as all must know, negative the suggestion that it is not possible in any case to determine whether vaccination is safe. Was defendant exempted from the operation of the statute simply because of his dread of the same evil results experienced by him when a child and had observed in the cases of his son and other children? Could he reasonably claim such an exemption because "quite often" or "occasionally" injury had resulted from vaccination, or because it was impossible, in the opinion of some, by any practical test, to determine with absolute certainty whether a particular person could be safely vaccinated? — NO

It seems to the court that an affirmative answer to these questions would practically strip the legislative department of its function to care for the public health and the public safety when endangered by epidemics of disease. Such an answer would mean that compulsory vaccination could not, in any conceivable case, be legally enforced in a community, even at the command of the legislature, however widespread the epidemic of smallpox, and however deep and universal was the belief of the community and of its medical advisers, that a system of general vaccination was vital to the safety of all.

We are not prepared to hold that a minority, residing or remaining in any city or town where smallpox is prevalent, and enjoying the general protection afforded by an organized local government, may thus defy the will of its constituted authorities, acting in good faith for all, under the legislative sanction of the state. If such be the privilege of a minority then a like privilege would belong to each individual of the community, and the spectacle would be presented of the welfare and safety of an entire population being subordinated to the notions of a single individual who chooses to remain a part of that population. We are unwilling to hold . . . [this] to be an element in the liberty secured by the Constitution of the United States . . . . The safety and health of the people of Massachusetts are, in the first instance, for the Commonwealth to guard and protect. They are matters that do not ordinarily concern the National Government . . . . [W]e do not perceive that this legislation *Holding* has invaded any right secured by the Federal Constitution.

Before closing this opinion we deem it appropriate, in order to prevent misapprehension as to our views, to observe — perhaps to repeat a thought already sufficiently expressed — that the police power of a State, whether exercised by the legislature, or by a local body acting under its authority, may be exerted in such circumstances or by regulations so arbitrary and oppressive in particular cases as to justify the interference of the courts to prevent wrong and oppression. Extreme cases can be readily suggested. Ordinarily such cases are not safe guides in the administration of the law. It is easy, for instance, to suppose the case of an adult who is embraced by the mere words of the act, but yet to subject whom to vaccination in a particular condition of his health or body, would be cruel and inhuman in the last degree. We are not to be understood as holding that the statute was intended to be applied to such a case, or, if it was so intended, that the judiciary would not be competent to interfere and protect the health and life of the individual concerned. "All laws" this court has said, "should receive a sensible construction. General terms should be so limited in their application as not to lead to injustice, oppression or absurd consequence. It will always, therefore, be presumed that the legislature intended exceptions to its language which would avoid results of that character. The reason of the law in such cases should prevail over its letter." Until otherwise informed by the highest court of Massachusetts we are not inclined to hold that the statute establishes the absolute rule that an adult must be vaccinated if it be apparent or can be shown with reasonable certainty that he is not at the time a fit subject of vaccination or that vaccination, by reason of his then condition, would seriously impair his health or probably cause his death. No such case is here presented. It is the case of an adult who, for aught that appears, was himself in perfect health and a fit subject of vaccination, and yet, while remaining in the community, refused to obey the statute and the regulation adopted in execution of its provisions for the protection of the public health and the public safety, confessedly endangered by the presence of a dangerous disease.

. . . .

The judgment of the court below must be affirmed.

MR. JUSTICE BREWER and MR. JUSTICE PECKHAM dissent.

NOTES AND QUESTIONS

1. *Jacobson* in context. *Jacobson* was one of the first major decisions to examine the state's power to regulate individuals. Earlier Supreme Court decisions examined the state's police power in the context of a claim of conflicting federal

authority, as illustrated in *Compagnie Française*, in B, *supra*. The state's jurisdiction over its own residents was not questioned in *Jacobson*, because no federal entity claimed any authority to control a local epidemic. This placed the question of the scope of state power to regulate individuals squarely before the Court. *Jacobson* is widely regarded as a seminal decision in American public health law, because it recognizes that the Constitution protects individual liberty, but also upholds the constitutional validity of the state's curtailment of individual liberty in the interests of public health. Much has changed in both medicine and law since the 1905 decision, but the case raises several features of public health law that arise in contemporary public policy debates. For examples, see Wendy K. Mariner, George J. Annas & Leonard H. Glantz, *Jacobson v. Massachusetts: It's Not Your Great-Great Grandfather's Public Health Law*, 95 Am. J. Pub. Health. 581 (2005). These are explored in the following notes.

   2. **Defining the police power.** The court's opinion makes plain that the authority of a state to enact and enforce "health laws of every description" rests firmly within the "police power" that is an inherent artifact of the political sovereignty of each state. This was well established by 1905. *Gibbons v. Ogden*, 22 U.S. 1, 73 (1824). *See generally* Ernst Freund, The Police Power: Public Power and Constitutional Rights (1904) (police power is "the power of promoting the public welfare by restraining and regulating the use of liberty and property . . . ", *id.* at iii, 3; the "public welfare" referred to in the definition embraces "the primary social interests of safety [which includes health], order, and morals," which the Supreme Court "concedes on principle to the states . . . .", *id.* at 7). Professor Freund's lengthy 1904 treatise catalogs state exercises of the police power.

   Perhaps because the state's police power was so well understood, courts rarely bothered to define it. The *Jacobson* court expressly "refrained from any attempt to define the limits of that power." But what does it mean to have the power to promote public welfare? One set of theories, which most courts appear to accept, holds that the state has all the plenary powers of a sovereign, with only two limitations: (1) states cannot exercise the powers that they relinquished to the federal government as specified in the U.S. Constitution; and (2) states cannot infringe the rights of individuals to the extent that such rights are protected by the U.S. or state constitution. *See generally* T. M. Cooley, A Treatise on the Limitations of Police Power in the United States Considered from Both A Civil and Criminal Law Standpoint (1868). Another, less well-accepted set of theories holds that state sovereignty (and the police power) has inherent limits imposed by natural rights, as propounded by Enlightenment era political theorists like John Locke. The idea is that the purpose of a *legitimate* government is to protect the natural rights and liberty of all people. In those days, the idea of enforcing one's rights was sometimes described as policing one's rights. Hence, the government's police power was the power to enforce rights. For a more modern exposition of this theory, see Randy Barnett, Restoring The Lost Constitution: The Presumption of Liberty (2005). How would courts define the scope and limits of state power with inherent limits? Are there any theories of justice that could provide universally acceptable principles for deciding what a state government can and cannot do? If not, does that mean that states have the power to do anything that is not prohibited to them by the federal or state constitution? In other words, is the prevailing theory the only feasible judicial option?

Under either theory, the state's police power remains what it was when the U.S. Constitution was adopted. Judicial recognition of limits on that power, however, has changed somewhat, as conceptions of constitutional protections (and standards of judicial review) evolved over more than a century since the *Jacobson* decision. Thus, the question embedded in *Jacobson* continues to be asked in circumstances lofty and mundane today: What, if anything, constrains the state's power?

3. **Delegation of power.** Note the law's mechanism for triggering governmental action. The Massachusetts legislature did not directly require (though it surely could have) that persons in the state be vaccinated. Rather, the legislature empowered municipal boards of health to make that decision, if "in [the board's] . . . opinion" this was "necessary for the public health and safety. . . ." It was not until the Cambridge Board of Health adopted, and the authorities then attempted to enforce, the regulation calling for vaccination of Cambridge residents, that the coercive impact of law came into play.

This kind of delegation of formal legal power and discretion — common by the time *Jacobson* was decided and noted with approval by the Court — remains a common feature of public health regulation. Instead of making specific decisions about precisely what to do and when, legislatures at all levels (federal, state, and local) often enact rather general laws that state a policy goal and delegate to an administrative arm of government the authority to make important choices about how to achieve that goal, such as standard-setting authority. These are sometimes the more difficult (one is tempted to say the "real") decisions that must be made in order to implement a law. Massachusetts' delegation from the state to city boards of health to decide whether and when to impose vaccination was "vertical." More commonly, legislative bodies delegate power and discretion "horizontally" to an executive-branch agency, to flesh out, implement, and enforce the law. For example, contemporary immunization statutes in many states broadly establish immunization as a condition of school attendance, but delegate to state health departments (sometimes in conjunction with state education agencies) the authority to determine and periodically modify the specifics: which vaccines are required for school attendance, administration dosages and schedules, implementation of statutory exemptions, and other programmatic matters. The agencies thus "complete" and apply the law, through administrative rulemaking or other mechanisms.

Imagine yourself a Massachusetts legislator in the early 1900s. Based on what you know from the case, why might the approach actually taken — conferring broad discretion about vaccinating citizens in municipal boards of health — appeal to you? What considerations, more generally, support legislative delegations of authority to administrative bodies for legal and programmatic implementation in complex regulatory matters? What are some of the drawbacks of this approach? *See New York Statewide Coalition, infra.*

4. **Jacobson's claims.** Henning Jacobson may have objected to vaccination for several reasons argued in his brief, but not mentioned in the opinion, including religious beliefs and lack of confidence in vaccines. For more detailed discussion of

religious opposition to immunizations, as well as other public health measures, see Chapter 4, D, *infra*.

Jacobson pressed two vague constitutional theories which the Court rejected out of hand: (1) that the Massachusetts statute violated the Constitution's "Preamble," tending to defeat its "purposes"; and (2) that it violated the "spirit" of the Constitution. A third theory was that the law "was in derogation of . . . the clauses [of the Fourteenth Amendment] . . . providing that no State shall make or enforce any law abridging the privileges or immunities of citizens of the United States, nor deprive any person of life, *liberty* or property *without due process of law . . . .*" [emphasis added].

In substance, the Court took seriously Jacobson's claim that the "liberty" in the Fourteenth Amendment extended to freedom from compelled vaccination — even though no reference whatsoever can be found in the Constitution to medical dimensions of "liberty" (much less to "bodily integrity" or "vaccination"). The Court stated the question before it to be: "Is this statute . . . inconsistent with the liberty which the Constitution of the United States secures to every person against deprivation by the State?" Had the Court concluded that the Fourteenth Amendment did not protect any such liberty, it need not have considered, much less discussed, the merits of Jacobson's claim. Instead, the Court proceeded to balance that liberty against the counterweight of the state's interest in protecting public health and, further, to assess the "fit" between the state's interest and the chosen means of its expression. Indeed, in a modern case, Chief Justice Rehnquist — not an advocate of a broad judicial interpretation of "liberty" — recognized (somewhat begrudgingly) that it "may be inferred" that the *Jacobson* Court viewed freedom from state-imposed medical treatment as a constitutionally-protected dimension of "liberty." *Cruzan v. Director, Missouri Department of Health*, 497 U.S. 261, 278 (1990). (*Cruzan* and cases that have explicitly recognized Fourteenth Amendment due process protection for the liberty to refuse unwanted medical care are explored in Chapter 4,B., *infra*).

As the Court recognized, legislatures routinely impose manifold intrusions upon individuals' liberty. You can readily identify dozens of examples that you encounter in your daily life. What is it about coerced medical treatment that distinguishes it from many other such intrusions, and arguably lends special, even if here unavailing, credence to a claim of constitutional protection?

5. **State interests.** The outcome of the case tells us that the Court found the polity's interest in having Jacobson vaccinated, against his preferences, was sufficiently great to outweigh his constitutionally protected liberty interest. Can you determine, with confidence, the precise nature and content of the state's interest(s) on which the Court relied? Would courts rely on the same interest(s) today?

The Court's opinion suggests at least two possible interests or goals that a state might assert in having citizens vaccinated. (This note presents these interests in the specific context of vaccination, but they are of near-universal applicability in explorations of state "interests in public health" more generally.) One is protecting others from an external danger, such as smallpox. The more people in a group who enjoy immunity from a contagious disease, the less chance an epidemic will develop and spread to any who are susceptible. In this view, restraining an individual's liberty by vaccinating him may be justified primarily on the basis of protecting others from harm — the classic rationale advanced by John Stuart Mill in his book *On Liberty*. A second is protecting or advancing the interests of the polity itself — "the state," or the collective, as an organized entity, as distinguished from the interests and preferences of individual members. Consider the Court's opinion in light of each of these interests (or any others you might be able to think of). Is the Court's presentation of them persuasive? What is your own view of the strength of these interests? Do you subscribe to the result in *Jacobson*, either for the reasons given by the Court (as you understand them), or for your own reasons?

A third possible state interest — not mentioned in the opinion, formally eschewed by courts, but circulating in public debate today — is protecting people against the consequences of their own failure to be vaccinated — whether based on ignorance, misunderstanding, poverty, recalcitrance, or *bona fide* intellectual opposition. This is what might be thought of as the most "paternalistic" of state interests.

As you will see in progressing through these materials, courts frequently assert the state's "interest in public health" without actually exploring or explaining, with any great clarity, the underlying content of that interest in the particularized context of the case. Sometimes the nature and legitimacy of the state interest may appear self-evident to you. On the other hand, sometimes it may not seem so clear, or may not appear to withstand careful consideration. It is worth maintaining your critical judgment about such matters. To critically analyze the constitutional justification for legislation, as judges must, the legislature's specific concrete goal — beyond an "interest in public health" — needs identification.

6.   Standards of judicial review. By contemporary judicial standards, the precise constitutional framework under which the Court analyzed Jacobson's claim is a bit shadowy. The case recognizes that there are constitutional limitations on state legislative power, even though finding none applicable here. Using the language of earlier decisions, the Court notes that the law cannot be "arbitrary" or "oppressive." It also suggests that the state should use means to achieve its goal that have a "real or substantial relation" to that goal. These terms sound like precursors to what later became "substantive due process" analysis under the Fourteenth Amendment. What standard of review would the Supreme Court apply today? How would it differ from the analysis in *Jacobson*?

First, the *Jacobson* Court does not question the goal of preventing the spread of smallpox. It emphasizes the importance to its holding of the actual existence of the danger protected against — a threatened epidemic — which was both a condition the statute imposed on cities' exercise of the delegated power and a duly-made finding by the Cambridge Board of Health. Absent the finding of such "necessity," there is reason to think that, at the time, mandatory vaccination might not have passed constitutional muster.

Only the emergency of present danger can justify quarantine, isolation or removal to hospital and compulsory treatment, and it is at least doubtful whether vaccination can be made compulsory apart from such necessity, certainly not under a mere general delegation of authority to administrative bodies; but such general

delegation is sufficient to cover the most ample powers in case of an emergency
. . . ."

FREUND, *supra*, Note 2, at 116. According to one account, the actual threat of an epidemic — the "necessity" — may not have been as great as the opinion implies. *See* Michael R. Albert, Kristen G. Ostheimer & Joel G. Breman, *The Last Small Pox Epidemic in Boston and the Vaccination Controversy, 1901–1903*, 344 NEW ENG. J. MED. 375–79 (2001). It should not surprise us that the Court took the Board of Health's finding at face value. Is it wise for courts to do so?

Second, the Court declines to second-guess the Board of Health's determination that smallpox vaccination was a real and substantial means of achieving its intended aim — preventing a larger epidemic. For the Court, the existence of the medical debate over efficacy, taken up and reflected in the legislative deliberations, defeats any claim that the law is, in today's terminology, "irrational." The Court states that the law cannot impose what is "beyond all question, a plain, palpable invasion of a Constitutional right," but this formulation imposes a high burden of proof on the party seeking to establish a law's constitutional flaw, a burden that was unmet by Jacobson here.

Third, despite the Court's deference to the choices of the legislature and the determination of the Board of Health, its opinion indicates some limits to legislative and agency discretion. The Court suggests that any law that failed to accommodate persons for whom vaccination would create a grave health risk would be constitutionally infirm — arbitrary or oppressive (or irrational in contemporary formulations) — and courts would stay its application to such persons, even absent an express textual exemption in the law. If the Court, and Massachusetts' highest court, seem to have been a little quick to dismiss Jacobson's claim of potential medical unfitness, this may be because the claim was not really in issue: Massachusetts Supreme Judicial Court had ruled that forced immunization was not permissible under the law, and that the only sanction for noncompliance allowable was the statutory fine. *Commonwealth v. Pear*, 66 N.E. 719, 722 (Mass. 1903) ("If a person should deem it important that vaccination should not be performed in his case, and the authorities should think otherwise, it is not in their power to vaccinate him by force, and the worst that could happen to him under the statute would be the payment of the penalty of $5.").

Was this just an easy case? An epidemic of smallpox, spread casually from person to person (and by contact with infected items), with horrific and often fatal consequences, certainly presented "the pressure of great dangers" that justified reasonable preventive measures like immunization. Are immunizations equally justified for all contagious diseases? What would you want to know about each disease itself and the vaccine to prevent it?

Today, we do not demand the threat of a pending epidemic to require childhood immunizations for school, suggesting perhaps that the standard for "necessity" has relaxed considerably as the benefits and general safety of immunizations have become better established. In *Zucht v. King*, 260 U.S. 174 (1922), the only other Supreme Court decision involving immunization, the Court upheld a city ordinance requiring a certificate of smallpox immunization as a condition of school attendance over the claim of a student who objected, claiming (with plausibility at that time) that there was no evidence of smallpox in the area — hence, no great danger to prevent. The Court's three-paragraph opinion said simply that states can grant cities broad authority to establish health regulations, without further analysis or discussion.

7. Enforcement. The sanction authorized by the state statute for noncompliance with a Board of Health's vaccination order was a $5.00 fine (about $115 in 2013). On appeal, the Massachusetts Supreme Judicial Court ordered that Jacobson "stand committed [jailed] until the fine was paid." 197 U.S. at 14. That court concluded that the Massachusetts legislation did not grant the power to physically seize and vaccinate anyone against his will. *Commonwealth v. Pear, supra*, Note 6. (In the Massachusetts court's view, the absence of the power to forcibly vaccinate anyone refuted Jacobson's argument that his liberty would be invaded.) Do the sanctions imposed on Jacobson for noncompliance seem more, or less, draconian than vaccination itself would be?

According to one account, forcible vaccinations *did* happen, with the assistance of the police, to some homeless persons in Boston who objected to being vaccinated, even though Boston's smallpox ordinance forbade such conduct. *Albert* et al., *supra*, Note 6, at 375–376. If true, this suggests something about the relevance of socioeconomic status to equal legal treatment.

The means of enforcing modern immunization laws avoid are analogous: In most states, immunizations are required for school attendance, but are not physically imposed upon the children of unwilling parents. Yet since school attendance is required (up to a certain age), with non-attendance punished as truancy (unless a family opts for "home schooling"), there is surely a form of coercion at play here. Do such indirect sanctions suggest a general societal unease with truly mandatory medical treatment, and a preference for coercion over frank physical force? Are you more or less comfortable with one approach than with the other? Why?

MULLER v. OREGON
208 U.S. 412 (1908)

Mr. Justice Brewer delivered the opinion of the court:

On February 19, 1903, the legislature of the State of Oregon passed an act . . . the first section of which is in these words:

> SEC. 1. That no female [shall] be employed in any mechanical establish- *[Statute]* ment, or factory, or laundry in this State more than ten hours during any one day. The hours of work may be so arranged as to permit the employment of females at any time so that they shall not work more than ten hours during the twenty-four hours of any one day.

Sec. 3 made a violation of the provisions of the prior sections a misdemeanor subject to a fine of not less than $10 nor more than $25. — *consequence of violation*

[Curt Muller owned a laundry that required employees, including Mrs. Gotcher, to work more than ten hours per day. He was convicted of violating the law and fined $10. His conviction was affirmed by the Oregon Supreme Court and brought to the U.S. Supreme Court on writ of error.]

The single question is the constitutionality of the statute under which the defendant was convicted so far as it affects the work of a female in a laundry. That it does not conflict with any provisions of the state constitution is settled by the decision of the Supreme Court of the State . . . .

. . . .

It is the law of Oregon that women, whether married or single, have equal contractual and personal rights with men . . . .

It thus appears that, putting to one side the elective franchise, in the matter of personal and contractual rights, they stand on the same plane as the other sex. Their rights in these respects can no more be infringed than the equal rights of their brothers. We held in *Lochner v. New York*, 198 U.S. 45, that a law providing that no laborer shall be required or permitted to work in bakeries more than sixty hours in a week or ten hours in a day was not, as to men, a legitimate exercise of the police power of the State, but an unreasonable, unnecessary, and arbitrary interference with the right and liberty of the individual to contract in relation to his labor, and, as such, was in conflict with, and void under, the Federal Constitution. That decision is invoked by plaintiff in error as decisive of the question before us. But this assumes that the difference between the sexes does not justify a different rule respecting a restriction of the hours of labor.

. . . .

It is undoubtedly true, as more than once declared by this Court, that the general right to contract in relation to one's business is part of the liberty of the individual, protected by the Fourteenth Amendment to the Federal Constitution; yet it is equally well settled that this liberty is not absolute, and extending to all contracts, and that a State may, without conflicting with the provisions of the Fourteenth Amendment, restrict in many respects the individual's power of contract . . . . *Allgeyer v. Louisiana*, 165 U.S. 578; *Holden v. Hardy*, 169 U.S. 366; *Lochner v. New York*, 198 U.S. 45.

That woman's physical structure and the performance of maternal functions place her at a disadvantage in the struggle for subsistence is obvious. This is especially true when the burdens of motherhood are upon her. Even when they are not, by abundant testimony of the medical fraternity, continuance for a long time on her feet at work, repeating this from day to day, tends to injurious effects upon the body, and, as healthy mothers are essential to vigorous offspring, the physical wellbeing of woman becomes an object of public interest and care in order to preserve the strength and vigor of the race.

Still again, history discloses the fact that woman has always been dependent upon man. He established his control at the outset by superior physical strength, and this control in various forms, with diminishing intensity, has continued to the present. As minors, though not to the same extent, she has been looked upon in the courts as needing especial care that her rights may be preserved. Education was long denied her, and while now the doors of the schoolroom are opened and her opportunities for acquiring knowledge are great, yet, even with that and the consequent increase of capacity for business affairs, it is still true that, in the struggle for subsistence, she is not an equal competitor with her brother. Though limitations upon personal and contractual rights may be removed by legislation, there is that in her disposition and habits of life which will operate against a full assertion of those rights. She will still be where some legislation to protect her seems necessary to secure a real equality of right. Doubtless there are individual exceptions, and there are many respects in which she has an advantage over him; but, looking at it from the viewpoint of the effort to maintain an independent position in life, she is not upon an equality. Differentiated by these matters from the other sex, she is properly placed in a class by herself, and legislation designed for her protection may be sustained even when like legislation is not necessary for men, and could not be sustained. It is impossible to close one's eyes to the fact that she still looks to her brother, and depends upon him. Even though all restrictions on political, personal, and contractual rights were taken away, and she stood, so far as statutes are concerned, upon an absolutely equal plane with him, it would still be true that she is so constituted that she will rest upon and look to him for protection; that her physical structure and a proper discharge of her maternal functions — having in view not merely her own health, but the wellbeing of the race — justify legislation to protect her from the greed, as well as the passion, of man. The limitations which this statute places upon her contractual powers, upon her right to agree with her employer as to the time she shall labor, are not imposed solely for her benefit, but also largely for the benefit of all. Many words cannot make this plainer. The two sexes differ in structure of body, in the functions to be performed by each, in the amount of physical strength, in the capacity for long-continued labor, particularly when done standing, the influence of vigorous health upon the future wellbeing of the race, the self-reliance which enables one to assert full rights, and in the capacity to maintain the struggle for subsistence. This difference justifies a difference in legislation, and upholds that which is designed to compensate for some of the burdens which rest upon her.

We have not referred in this discussion to the denial of the elective franchise in the State of Oregon, for, while that may disclose a lack of political equality in all things with her brother, that is not of itself decisive. The reason runs deeper, and rests in the inherent difference between the two sexes and in the different functions in life which they perform.

For these reasons, and without questioning in any respect the decision in *Lochner v. New York*, we are of the opinion that it cannot be adjudged that the act in question is in conflict with the Federal Constitution so far as it respects the work of a female in a laundry, and the judgment of the Supreme Court of Oregon is affirmed.

NOTES AND QUESTIONS

8. **Historical notes.** The decisions in *Jacobson* and *Muller* looked like exceptions to the rule prevailing in the first decade of the twentieth century, but

foreshadowed decisions involving state and federal legislation to protect public health and safety after 1937. In that first decade, the state government's power to regulate matters of public health and safety was constrained by the Supreme Court Justices' protection of the so-called freedom of contract as an aspect of liberty in *Lochner v. New York*, 198 U.S. 45 (1905), cited in *Muller*. In *Lochner*, decided shortly after *Jacobson*, the Court struck down a New York labor law that prohibited employers from requiring or permitting employees to work more than ten hours a day. The *Lochner* Court found no particular danger in working in a bakery, thus viewing the law not as a "health law," but solely a labor law:

[handwritten margin note: Found no particular danger to working in a bakery]

> There is no reasonable ground for interfering with the liberty of person or the right of free contract, by determining the hours of labor, in the occupation of a baker. There is no contention that bakers as a class are not equal in intelligence and capacity to men in other trades or manual occupations, or that they are not able to assert their rights and care for themselves without the protecting arm of the State, interfering with their independence of judgment and of action.

[handwritten note: → this was a labor law issue.]

> We think the limit of the police power has been reached and passed in this case. There is, in our judgment, no reasonable foundation for holding this to be necessary or appropriate as a health law to safeguard the public health or the health of the individuals who are following the trade of a baker . . . .

Government interference with business practices that did not significantly affect an aspect of personal liberty, however, remained far less controversial. By 1900, several states had in place legislation and ordinances requiring businesses to provide ventilation, sanitation, safe entrances and exits, fire escapes, and heating equipment, for example. Early judicial interpretations of the police powers generally allowed ample discretion to the legislature in commercial matters that did not directly implicate personal liberty. *See, e.g., Dent v. West Virginia*, 129 U.S. 114 (1889) (examining the scope of the states' discretion to regulate the practice of medical care); *Lawton v. Steele*, 152 U.S. 133 (1892) (outlining the power of the state to abate nuisances under the police powers); *Austin v. Tennessee*, 179 U.S. 343 (1900) (upholding Tennessee's limits on the sale of cigarettes).

Lochner was overruled during the New Deal (*see West Coast Hotel Co. v. Parrish*, 300 U.S. 379 (1937)) and has been generally rejected ever since. References to *Lochner* since the 1930s are generally confined to illustrations of what the courts should *not* do in reviewing state regulatory legislation: In particular, judges should not (the critique goes) "read into" general constitutional phrases like the "liberty" clause of the Fourteenth Amendment their own personally-preferred values in order to enshrine those values against legislative erosion or regulation. While special constitutional protection for economic "rights" of the kind recognized in *Lochner* has long since been abandoned, a few other values affected by some types of public health laws do enjoy comparatively privileged constitutional treatment. These include laws affecting the constitutionally protected right of privacy, free exercise of religion, freedom of speech, and most recently, the right to bear arms, which are discussed in later chapters.

9. *Muller* and the Brandeis Brief. By the time *Muller* was decided, it appeared that the Court would be unsympathetic to the state's power to limit the hours of employment, absent a convincing demonstration that the law was necessary to protect the public health, or that a particular group of employees was vulnerable to health risks beyond those of ordinary employment. Louis Brandeis responded with his famous "factual" brief, which helped persuade the Justices in *Muller* that Oregon's law was warranted to protect public health — specifically the health of women — as a matter of public interest: "the physical well-being of woman becomes an object of public interest and care in order to preserve the strength and vigor of the race." 421 U.S. at 421.

Muller was rightly praised for breaking through the Court's resistance to health legislation regulating industry's labor practices, although that resistance had not been entirely uniform prior to *Lochner*. In 1898, the Court had upheld a Utah state law limiting to 8 hours the working day of miners and smelters in underground mines, finding that the underground environment posed a threat to their health not present in other occupations. *Holden v. Hardy*, 169 U.S. 366 (1898). That Court explained that "the law is, to a certain extent, a progressive science," evolving with the exigencies of the times:

> [I]n some of the States, methods of procedure, which at the time the Constitution was adopted were deemed essential to the protection and safety of the people or to the liberty of the citizen have been found to be no longer necessary; that restrictions which had formerly been laid upon the conduct of individuals or of classes of individuals had proved detrimental to their interests, while, upon the other hand, certain other classes of persons, particularly those engaged in dangerous or unhealthful employments, have been found to be in need of additional protection.

Id. at 385–6.

Since 1937, the Court's consideration of health and safety legislation, including labor laws, has evolved as something like a "progressive science." The Court has exhibited deference to legislative choices in matters not affecting what have come to be known as rights warranting heightened scrutiny. This deference to the legislature gave medical and public health experts considerable influence in determining what counts as a matter of public interest and how it should be handled. Yet *Muller* also illustrates how such expertise sometimes depends more on the culture of the times than scientific certainty. A more disturbing example is seen in *Buck v. Bell*, *infra*, Chapter Three.

ABATE OF GEORGIA v. GEORGIA
137. F. Supp. 2d 1349 (N.D. Ga. 2001)

THRASH, JUDGE.

This is an action challenging the constitutionality of Georgia's motorcycle helmet law. It is brought pursuant to 42 U.S.C. § 1983 and is before the Court on

Defendants' Motion to Dismiss . . . .

I. BACKGROUND

Plaintiff ABATE of Georgia, Inc. ("ABATE") brings this suit on behalf of itself and all others similarly situated. ABATE is an acronym for American Bikers Active Toward Education. Its main purposes are to promote motorcycling and the rights of motorcyclists. The named Defendants in this case are Roy E. Barnes, in his official capacity as Governor of Georgia, Commissioner Robert E. Hightower of the Georgia Department of Public Safety in his official and individual capacities, [and] the Georgia Board of Public Safety . . . .

The Georgia General Assembly has enacted a statute that requires all persons to wear "protective headgear" while operating or riding a motorcycle. At the time this action was filed, the statute, O.C.G.A.§ 40-6-315, provided:

(a) No person shall operate or ride upon a motorcycle unless he or she is wearing protective headgear which complies with standards established by the Board of Public Safety.

(b) No person shall operate or ride upon a motorcycle if the motorcycle is not equipped with a windshield unless he or she is wearing an eye-protective device of a type approved by the Board of Public Safety.

(c) This Code section shall not apply to persons riding within an enclosed cab or motorized cart. This Code section shall not apply to a person operating a three-wheeled motorcycle used only for agricultural purposes.

(d) The Board of Public Safety is authorized to approve or disapprove protective headgear and eye-protective devices required in this Code section and to issue and enforce regulations establishing standards and specifications for the approval thereof. The Board of Public Safety shall publish lists of all protective headgear and eye-protective devices by name and type which have been approved by it.

O.C.G.A. § 40-6-315 (Supp. 1999).

The statute was amended in the 2000 session of the Georgia General Assembly to substitute the newly created Commissioner of Motor Vehicle Safety as the applicable regulatory authority . . . .

Pursuant to the authority granted by the statute, the Board of Public Safety has promulgated rules and regulations that establish standards for headgear and eye-protective devices . . . . These regulations define technical standards that acceptable headgear and eye-protective devices must satisfy. The regulations also require that manufacturers affix a permanent label showing that the equipment complies with the applicable standard. Helmets are held to the standards set by the United States Department of Transportation . . . Compliance requirements for eye-protective devices are determined in accordance with those test methods . . . of the American Standards Institute Standard . . . . It is undisputed that the Board of Public Safety has not published lists of all protective headgear and eye-protective devices by name and type which have been approved by it.

. . . .

Many states have enacted statutes that require motorcyclists to wear protective headgear. Motorcycle helmet laws generally require motorcyclists to wear helmets or other protective devices that have been approved by a state agency . . . . The statutes "reflect a widespread effort to combat the rising death and injury toll of accidents that involve motorcyclists." Motorcyclists have mounted a variety of challenges to the constitutional validity of these statutes . . . . Plaintiffs in this case challenge the constitutionality of Georgia's statute, O.C.G.A. § 40-6-315. Defendants respond that the suit should be dismissed for failure to state a claim upon which relief can be granted.

. . . Plaintiffs' argument underlying all [their constitutional] claims is that O.C.G.A. § 40-6-315 and the regulations promulgated pursuant to it are unconstitutionally vague: "[the] statutory requirements as mandated by the Georgia Legislature [and interpreted by the state regulations] cannot be intelligently applied by the citizens of the State of Georgia so as to make an intelligent and knowledgeable determination of what does or does not meet the statutory requirements necessary to be in compliance with the instant statute in question."

Plaintiffs do not state explicitly whether they are making a facial challenge, an as-applied challenge, or both. Consequently, construing the Second Amended Complaint in the light most favorable to Plaintiffs, the Court will presume that they are making both. A facial challenge to a statute asserts that the statute is unconstitutional on its face. In other words, the challenge asserts that the statute is unconstitutional generally and without reference to any particular set of facts. An as-applied challenge, in contrast, asserts that the statute is unconstitutional because of the manner in which it was applied in the particular case.

A "facial challenge to a legislative act is, of course, the most difficult challenge to mount successfully, since the challenger generally must establish that no set of circumstances exists under which the challenged statute would be valid." The fact that an act "might conceivably operate unconstitutionally under some set of circumstances is insufficient to render it wholly invalid" since the Supreme Court does not recognize "an 'overbreadth' doctrine outside the limited context of the First Amendment." In other words, where a law does not implicate First Amendment rights, it can be challenged for vagueness only "as applied," unless the enactment is "impermissibly vague in all its applications." . . .

In this case, Plaintiffs have alleged a First Amendment violation, but they fail to specify the nature of the alleged violation. Plaintiffs have cited no cases that operating or riding a motorcycle without a helmet is an exercise of their rights of free speech, freedom of religion or their right to peaceably assemble and petition the government for redress of grievances. The Court on its own research has found no such cases. Without any case support whatsoever, the Court refuses to broaden the First Amendment by concluding that it is implicated in the enforcement of motorcycle helmet laws . . . . There is no First Amendment right to ride a motorcycle wearing a baseball cap, a bandana, or bareheaded.

. . . .

Additionally, there is no substantive due process privacy right implicated in this case. The Eleventh Circuit has explained in another motorcycle helmet case that "[t]here is little that could be termed private in the decision whether to wear safety equipment on the open road. " There is no right to be let alone that is implicated in this case. Accordingly, if Plaintiffs' Second Amended Complaint can be construed as including a substantive due process privacy challenge to O.C.G.A. § 40-6-315, that due process challenge must fail also. Finally, the Court notes that the applicable regulations merely require Plaintiffs to check to see if their headgear has affixed to it the applicable U.S. Department of Transportation certification. Such a requirement does not seem vague at all. As a matter of fact, it seems a simple way to tell if one's headgear meets the statutory requirements.

Plaintiffs also allege a violation of their equal protection rights protected by the Fourteenth Amendment. Motorcycle riders, however, are not a protected class. Requiring a person who rides a motorcycle to wear a helmet serves a rational purpose. An occupant of an automobile who is wearing a seatbelt is likely to remain in the vehicle in an accident. In contrast, a motorcyclist involved in an accident is much more likely to end up on the pavement with the chance of a serious head injury. Failure to require motorcyclists to wear appropriate headgear may increase costs to the taxpaying public, and the Georgia General Assembly's desire to limit such costs constitutes a rational purpose for O.C.G.A. § 40-6-315. As Justice Powell, sitting by designation with the Eleventh Circuit explained in *Picou v. Gillum*:

A motorcyclist without a helmet is more likely to suffer serious injury than one wearing the prescribed headgear. State and local governments provide police and ambulance services, and the injured cyclist may be hospitalized at public expense. If permanently disabled, the cyclist could require public assistance for many years. As Professor Tribe has expressed it, "[in] a society unwilling to abandon bleeding bodies on the highway, the motorcyclist or driver who endangers himself plainly imposes costs on others."

Motorcycle helmet laws are a permissible means of attempting to reduce this cost. "Legislatures and not courts have the primary responsibility for balancing conflicting interests in safety and individual autonomy." Plaintiffs' equal protection argument is without merit.

NOTES AND QUESTIONS

10. **Motorcycle helmet laws.** *ABATE of Georgia v. Georgia* raises some fairly novel theories, but the ultimate decision to uphold the Georgia law on the core issue — state power to compel helmet use — is only one example of what has been virtually a unanimous trend. Almost every court that has considered the constitutionality of motorcycle helmet legislation has come to the same conclusion: Such legislation is clearly within the state's police powers. *See, e.g., Benning v. Vermont,* 641 A.2d 757 (VT. 1994); *Buhl v. Hannigan,* 16 Cal. App. 4th 1612, 1620 Cal. Rptr. 2d 740 (1993).

Courts have not found that mandatory helmet laws involve or infringe on the type of important individual right that can require courts to closely scrutinize attempts by the state to impose restrictions. To the contrary, the courts have generally adopted a low level of scrutiny, asking only whether mandatory helmet laws are a legitimate exercise of the state's police powers in the more limited sense, requiring only that the state show that such legislation is reasonably related to the public's health, safety, welfare, or morals. As one court described what it considered its proper, deferential role:

> The legislature [under the police powers] has the power to control and regulate the use of the highways. Moreover, if the relation between the statute and the public welfare is debatable, the legislative judgment must be accepted, because of the presumption of constitutionality afforded a statute.

Adrian v. Poucher, 247 N.W.2d 798, 799 (Mich. 1976).

The fact that some oppose such legislation, and even argue that it (paradoxically) is actually counterproductive when it comes to safety (*e.g.*, by obscuring bikers' vision), does not change the judicial role: "Plaintiffs are not entitled to have the courts act as a super-legislature and retry legislative judgments based on evidence presented to the court . . . [t]he question before us is whether the link between safety for highway users and the helmet law is rational, not whether we agree [with the legislature] that the statute actually leads to safer highways." *Benning, supra*, 641 A.2d at 762. Arguments of opponents of such laws, therefore, are best directed at the legislature. Motorcyclists, although sometimes vocal advocates, represent only about three percent of vehicles on the road. How much influence do they have on legislation affecting their interests?

11. What is the state's interest? What is interesting about these cases, and where the courts have been somewhat inconsistent, has been their reasoning concerning the particular state interest or goal that helmet requirements serve. Specifically, the courts have not been able to decide whether helmet requirements should be characterized as an attempt to protect the health and safety of the public — meaning third parties affected by the cyclist or the passenger — or whether helmet laws are primarily attempts to protect the wearer from the risks he or she would otherwise choose to assume. Courts tend to shy away from characterizing a law as paternalistic — protecting only the person himself or herself. As discussed earlier, although the courts generally have given the legislatures great discretion in fashioning "public health laws," meaning laws that protect other members of the public from one individual's conduct, courts have at least suggested that truly paternalistic laws, those that protect the individual only from his or her own conduct, may not be so easily upheld. Some courts have reasoned that such legislation may fall within the reach of the police powers but should trigger a more demanding judicial review and therefore require the Court to review more closely the state's actual purposes, the effectiveness of the particular legislative scheme, and the actual impact on the individual's interest. On occasion, courts have gone farther and suggested that if the legislation is found to be truly paternalistic, it must be invalidated. As one judge argued (dissenting from his court's decision in *Poucher* to uphold the state's mandatory helmet law):

The protection of an individual from himself is not among the proper functions of government.

. . . [O]therwise there would be no restriction or limitation to this power, and the State could regulate an individual's life, his way of living, and even his way of thinking. The statute is not concerned with the preservation of public safety, health, order, morals, or welfare; and though the headgear requirement may be beneficent, nevertheless, it is unconstitutional because it attempts to infringe upon and stifle the fundamental personal right of liberty, under which each individual may act as he sees fit to preserve his own safety if he does not harm others in doing so . . . .

The fact that the general public may consider it foolhardy to ride a motorcycle without a safety helmet is alone insufficient basis or justification for defining the nonuse of a helmet a criminal offense. I believe that our State Constitution affords one the privilege of making a fool of himself . . . .

398 Mich. at 322; 247 N.W.2d at 801 (C.J. KAVANAGH, dissenting).

Somewhat understandably, most courts have labored to avoid addressing the question of the validity of truly paternalistic legislation. Instead they have attempted to find a public or third-party interest in helmet legislation and, therefore, they have limited their review to a more conservative judicial role. To do so, the courts have had to rely, at times, on some rather tortured judicial logic. Some courts have argued that third parties are affected by cyclists who ride without helmets because a serious motorcycle accident will cause a traffic hazard or cause harm to other motorists. Other courts have argued that protecting cyclists and their passengers from injury or death promotes society's interest in maintaining a strong and productive citizenry. One court went so far as to recognize the "well known fact" that cyclists ride near the center of the road and are therefore more likely to cross into oncoming traffic if injured. See Chapter 8 for further exploration of paternalism in public health law.

The majority of courts, however, have focused on what is perhaps the strongest argument to characterize mandatory helmet legislation as a "public health law:" that serious injuries resulting from a failure to wear protective helmets may result in an economic burden on the public, as well as on the families of the victims. Given the costs to the public of motorcycle injuries, most courts regard helmet legislation as well within the state's discretion and a matter over which the judiciary will exercise limited review. Consider the implications of this kind of economic argument. Does it authorize the state to require individuals to protect themselves from *any* harm that could result in costly (or perhaps not so costly) injuries? What costs should count? What if the costs are borne entirely by the individual or the individual's family? Should such persons be exempted from the requirement? If so, is the state's power limited to imposing regulations only on those who cannot afford medical care? Or does ascension to a more privileged economic status offer greater protection of certain aspects of liberty? If the majority of the United States population obtains health insurance as a result of the Affordable Care Act, will the cost argument provide justification for such laws any longer?

Current helmet requirements in Florida, Michigan and Texas exempt motorcyclists over the age of 21 who are covered by health insurance. Fla. Stat. Ann.

§ 316.211 (West); Mich. Comp. Laws Ann. § 257.658 (West); Tex. Transp. Code Ann. § 661.003 (West). The Insurance Institute for Highway Safety reported that, as of July 2013, nineteen states and the District of Columbia had helmet laws that cover all riders, twenty-eight states covered riders under a certain age, and three states did not require helmets at all. Motorcycle Helmet Laws History Table, http://www. iihs.org/laws/helmet_history.aspx (last visited July, 2013).

12.   **Perceptions of risk.** Recall the discussion of risk perception in Chapter 2. An example involving motorcycles and helmets and different perceptions of what risks are acceptable is that of Ben Roethlisberger, the Pittsburgh Steeler's quarterback, who was seriously injured in the face and head when a car hit the motorcycle he was riding without a helmet. One reporter noted two paradoxes in public reaction to the absence of a helmet. "As a champion N.F.L. quarterback, Roethlisberger is a brilliant risk/benefit analyst, making split-second decisions about probabilities and consequences even as linemen try to bury him. So how could a savvy risk manager ride without a helmet, a low-reward, high-risk activity that exposes a team, a city, and untold corporate interests to its consequences?" The second paradox noted was that "Roethlisberger became a football star and brought a championship to Pittsburgh by accepting physical risks that ordinary people would avoid. So how can these critics, who have benefited from his acceptance of physical risk, get all snippy that he took *this* one?" John Leland, *The Superstar Athlete Is Paid to Take Risks, Right?* N.Y. TIMES, June 18, 2006, at WK3 (emphasis in original). Paul Slovic noted that our past experience shapes our perception of a risk as manageable or too high. For example, if a rider has not had an accident after many miles on a motorcycle, he may not consider himself at risk for injury without a helmet. According to Leland's interview with Slovic, "Wearing a helmet is a cost, measured in comfort, and perhaps liberty, but provides a benefit only if there is a crash. After a number of safe rides, Dr. Slovic said, 'you feel you're rewarded for not wearing one and punished for wearing one.' " *Id.*

13.   **Seat belt requirements.** Mandatory seat belt legislation has generated far less litigation than the helmet legislation, but the same judicial response. *See, e.g., Atwater v. City of Lago Vista, 532 U.S. 318 (2001); State v. Hartog,* 440 N.W.2d 852 (Iowa), *cert. denied,* 493 U.S. 1005 (1989). As with the helmet cases, the courts have made efforts to characterize the underlying purpose of the legislation as protecting third parties from harm, not protecting the individual who is required to comply with the law.

In one case involving highway safety, the court both was unwilling to defer to legislative discretion and held, ultimately, that the state had exceeded its police powers. In 1989, the Minnesota Supreme Court reviewed the constitutionality of a state law that required all vehicles traveling on public roads to have specific warning devices. Members of the Amish community refused to attach such devices to their horse-drawn buggies, arguing that to do so would violate various Amish principles; nonetheless they were convicted on resulting criminal charges. The Minnesota Supreme Court ruled that the state law interfered with the freedom of the Amish to practice their religion as secured by the First Amendment to the U.S. Constitution. On appeal, the U.S. Supreme Court vacated the judgment of the state court, ruling that the state court had misinterpreted the demands of the First Amendment. On rehearing, the state court found that the state law interfered with the freedom of religion protected by the state constitution, and, once again, invalidated the prosecution. In doing so on state constitutional grounds, the state effectively prevented any subsequent appeal to the U.S. Supreme Court. *State v. Hershberger*, 462 N.W.2d 393 (Minn. 1990). A few other state courts have interpreted their constitutions similarly. *See State v. Miller*, 549 N.W.2d 235 (Wis. 1996). *Cf.* discussion of *Smith*, Chapter 4, Section B, *infra*.

14. Alternative regulatory measures. Seat belts differ from helmets in that they are attached to the vehicle, suggesting that automobile manufacturers might alter the vehicle itself to provide protection against injury in a crash, rather than rely on drivers and passengers to put on their seat belts. The federal Department of Transportation had encouraged the industry to do just that, but the industry had opposed a requirement to install airbags or passive restraints in cars since 1969. The Department of Transportation issued a final standard requiring passive restraints for all cars by 1984, but reopened the rulemaking process in 1981 and ultimately rescinded the standard, when it appeared that automobile makers were going to install passive seat belts instead of airbags in 99% of new cars. Some of the history of the regulatory battle between the automobile industry and the Department can be found in *Motor Vehicle Manufacturers Association of the United States v. State Farm Mutual Automobile Insurance Co.*, 463 U.S. 29 (1983). In that case, the Supreme Court overturned the Department's rescission of the so-called "air-bag" standard, because it was not "the product of reasoned decisionmaking." Although substantial evidence supported issuing the standard, the agency rescinded it primarily because of industry practice. The Court found this reasoning to be arbitrary and capricious: "If, under the standard, the agency should not defer to the industry's failure to develop safer cars, which it surely should not do, *a fortiori* it may not revoke a safety standard which can be satisfied by current technology simply because the industry has opted for an ineffective seatbelt design." 463 U.S. at 49. A presidential election resulted in a new Secretary of Transportation, however, who agreed with the industry that the airbag standard would not be issued as a final rule if two-thirds of the states enacted legislation requiring people to wear seatbelts. The effort to pass such laws was successful, although it prompted occasionally heated debates over whether laws were unjustifiably paternalistic or a safety-conscious condition on the privilege of obtaining a license to drive. Almost entirely ignored in the arguments was the reason for having the debate in the first place — rejection of effective safety standards for motor vehicles.

NEW YORK CITY FRIENDS OF FERRETS v. CITY OF NEW YORK
876 F. Supp. 529 (S.D.N.Y. 1995)

SCHWARTZ, JUDGE.

New York City Friends of Ferrets, an unincorporated association of individuals in New York City who own or wish to own ferrets as household pets, bring this action challenging the legality of the City of New York's (the "City") prohibition against the keeping of ferrets within the City limits and the requirement that in any case where a ferret is reported to have bitten a human being, the ferret be immediately surrendered to the New York City Department of Health ("DOH") and humanely destroyed in order to conduct a rabies examination.

Plaintiff seeks a judgment declaring that the City's regulation of ferret ownership denies plaintiff's members of liberty and property without due process of law and violates the Equal Protection Clause of the United States Constitution.

Webster's New World Dictionary of the American Language (College Ed.1968) defines a ferret as "a kind of weasel, easily tamed and used for hunting or killing of rabbits, rats . . . ." Two types of ferrets can be found in the United States: the black footed ferret (*Mustela nigripes*) and the domestic or common ferret (*Mustela putorius or Mustela putorious furo*). This action involves domestic ferrets and, hereinafter, the term "ferret" shall refer to common or domestic ferrets. Domestic ferrets have been bred in captivity, initially for the purposes of hunting, since the fourth century B.C., and have, more recently, become a popular household pet in the United States . . . .

The City moves to dismiss the Complaint . . . . The Court has determined to consider materials which the parties have submitted; therefore, we elect to convert this motion to dismiss into a motion for summary judgment, and interpret the expanded record accordingly.

Summary judgment is appropriate where "the pleadings, depositions, answers to interrogatories, and admissions on file, together with affidavits, if any, show that there is no genuine issue as to any material fact and that the moving party is entitled to a judgment as a matter of law." . . . The burden of proof, however, lies with the moving party and we must resolve all ambiguities and draw all inferences in favor of the party against whom summary judgment is sought . . . .

The Equal Protection Clause of the Fourteenth Amendment to the United States Constitution guarantees that classifications imposed by law will not be used to burden a group of people arbitrarily. As the challenged Municipal Code provisions regulating ferret ownership do not classify people based on "suspect" criteria, such as race or nationality, they are constitutionally permissible under equal protection analysis so long they bear a rational relationship to a legitimate state interest. Thus, "the Equal Protection Clause is satisfied so long as there is a plausible policy reason for the classification, . . . the legislative facts on which the classification is apparently based rationally may have been considered to be true by the governmental decisionmaker, . . . and the relationship of the classification to its goal is not so attenuated as to render the distinction arbitrary or irrational . . . ."

The courts, moreover, show great deference to legislatures' choices in creating classifications, even where those classifications seem imperfect. A law will not fail to pass constitutional muster under equal protection analysis merely because it contains classifications which are underinclusive — that is, which "do not include all who are similarly situated with respect to a rule, and thereby burden less than would be logical to achieve the intended government end."

     . . . .

In its exercise of the power to protect its citizens — to wit its police power — the

City is also limited by the constitutional requirement that the sovereign may not deprive citizens of property without due process of law . . . . Where, as here, the exercise of police power does not affect fundamental rights, such as voting or freedom of speech, we apply the same rational basis analysis used under the constitutional guarantee of equal protection. Thus, deprivation of private property pursuant to an exercise of police power is constitutionally permissible where the challenged legislative enactment bears a rational relationship to legitimate legislative goal or purpose . . . .

In applying the rational basis analysis to a health and welfare regulation, such as the portions of the Health Code at issue here, courts apply a basic test of reasonableness; that is, a police power regulation is to be upheld if the requirements of the law have a rational connection with the promotion and protection of public safety . . . . Moreover, courts have noted that:

> [t]he exceedingly strong presumption of constitutionality applies not only to enactments of the Legislature but to ordinances of municipalities as well. While this presumption is rebuttable . . . only as a last resort should courts strike down legislation on the ground of unconstitutionality. The ordinance may not be arbitrary. It must be reasonably related to some manifest evil which, however, need only be reasonably apprehended. It is also presumed that the legislative body has investigated and found the existence of a situation showing or indicating the need for or desirability of the ordinance, and, if any state of facts [that can be proven or] assumed justifies the disputed measure, this court's power of inquiry ends. Thus, as to reasonableness, plaintiffs in order to succeed have the burden of showing that "no reasonable basis at all" existed for the challenged provision of the ordinance.

. . . .

The City has submitted significant materials in support of its decision to classify ferrets as wild animals and to insist upon the immediate euthanasia and testing of any ferret reported to have bitten a human. This evidence includes the affidavits of [public health officials from around the country].

The City explains its decisions to classify ferrets as a species which is "wild, ferocious, fierce, dangerous or naturally inclined to do harm," to prohibit the keeping of ferrets in New York City, and to destroy and examine any ferret reported to have bitten a human being and suspected of having rabies as the product of several public health and safety concerns. First, the City contends that, despite their recent popularity as household pets, ferrets remain prone to vicious, unprovoked attacks on humans, particularly children and infants. In support of this assertion, the City has submitted various epidemiological studies and monographs . . . . [One of the researchers has also] received information on 452 ferret attacks from this period, with reports concentrated (425 episodes) in California and the neighboring states of Arizona and Oregon . . . .

The City has also submitted materials to illustrate the disturbing frequency among these documented ferret bitings of unprovoked attacks on infants and small children, characterized in some instances by a large number of bites covering the child's face and body. The California DHS *Pet European Ferrets* study catalogued among its data 63 unprovoked attacks on infants and small children less than three years of age . . . .

The City also furnishes evidentiary support for its second articulated public health concern underlying its decision to prohibit ownership of ferrets as pets and to euthanize and test immediately for rabies ferrets that bite humans, namely, that failure to take such measures risks an increase in the spread of rabies in the New York City area. As a threshold matter, the City points out that New York City is presently under a rabies alert and rabies has been declared endemic in the Metropolitan area . . . .

The City's motivating public health concern relating to ferrets and rabies centers on the lack of knowledge of the behavioral symptoms of the rabid ferret and the indeterminate viral shedding period in the animal. The clinical signs of rabies in dogs and cats are well-known. It has also been established, moreover, that the time from which a dog or cat has the rabies virus in its saliva (i.e., begins its viral shedding period) to the time that the animal will exhibit the clinical behavioral signs indicating rabies does not exceed ten days . . . . Accordingly, the World Health Organization and the Compendium of Animal Rabies Control . . . recommend that a healthy dog or cat that bites a person should be confined and observed for 10 days. If the dog or cat exhibits behavioral signs suggestive of rabies, the foregoing authorities recommend that the animal be humanely killed, its head removed, and the brain tissue examined for the rabies virus.

The viral shedding period in ferrets is unknown. In addition, the clinical behavioral signs of rabies in ferrets are not well established, and such data as exist suggest that the clinical signs of the disease may be less noticeable in ferrets than in dogs and cats . . . . Euthanasia and immediate testing remain the recommended course of action in biting incidents involving ferrets, the City points out, despite the approval by the United States Department of Agriculture of the IMRAB rabies vaccine for ferrets, because no vaccine is completely efficacious and the above discussed uncertainties regarding the etiology of rabies in ferrets persist.

The final public health risk posed by ownership of ferrets as pets, according to the City, is the potential for ferrets to escape and form feral populations, as have stray cats and dogs. Such a development may lead to the decimation of certain wildlife species as well as excessive competition with other wild natural predators . . . .

The City also emphasizes that the foregoing considerations have persuaded a number of states to prohibit or regulate the ownership of ferrets as pets in precisely the manner that the City has by means of its enactment of the Health Code regulations at issue here . . . .

Plaintiff offers two affidavits, those of Dr. Kent Marshall and Dr. Freddie Ann Hoffman in support of its position. We note as a threshold matter that certain issues confront this Court with respect to the disinterested, unbiased and expert status of these affiants. First, both suggest an actual or apparent conflict of interest. It is not disputed that Dr. Marshall maintains a veterinary practice in Wayne County, New York, site of Marshall Farms USA, Inc. — a large ferret breeding farm owned by

Dr. Marshall's parents. Dr. Hoffman is the Vice-President of the American Ferret Association, Inc., an organization whose purpose is to promote the keeping of ferrets as pets. Even more significant, Dr. Hoffman submits no proof of her professional training or expertise in the veterinary issues at the core of this case. She is a board certified pediatrician specializing in the study of blood and tumors, and is presently employed by the U.S. Food and Drug Administration.

A central tenet of plaintiff's constitutional claims is that pet ferrets pose no greater a danger to public health and safety — as measured by incidence of bites, severity of injury, and risk of rabies infection — than pet dogs. The City, however, offers unrefuted evidence in support of the proposition that comparisons between dogs and ferrets with respect to the foregoing public health parameter are inapposite. First, there is reason to suspect that ferret bites are underreported relative to dog bites because of the frequent public health policy requirement that pet ferrets be euthanized if they bite humans as well as the lack of the almost uniform public health requirement that dog bites be reported. Accordingly, any comparison of rate or frequency of bites as between dogs and ferrets is likely to be skewed in favor of ferrets. Second, the more recent experience of adoption of ferrets in somewhat more significant numbers as domestic pets — and the lack of sound estimates of the number of pet ferrets — as opposed to the longstanding and well documented presence of dogs in that role, renders statistical comparisons of biting and rabies incidents between the two species of limited usefulness.

. . . .

With respect to the pathogenesis of rabies in ferrets, plaintiff's own expert, Dr. Hoffman, has acknowledged in her writings on the subject of ferrets as pets that:

The duration of viral shedding following exposure to rabies has not yet been adequately determined in ferrets. Therefore, no quarantine period can be recommended. As a result, once a ferret has bitten a person, local health authorities may require that the ferret be euthanized for rabies testing regardless of immunization status. For this reason, ferret advocates consider the evaluation of the viral shedding time in the context of a well — controlled study to be the single most important issue impacting on the health and welfare of the pet ferret today.

. . . Plaintiff submits no such study to this Court, nor furnishes evidence that any of the foregoing national animal public health organizations have been made aware that such data exists and is reliable. . . . In short, plaintiff fails to dispute the City's evidence in connection with one of its most pressing articulated concerns in regulating ferret ownership — to wit, the uncertain viral shedding period in rabid ferrets — and makes no showing with respect to Dr. Hoffman's claims regarding the dangers posed by rabid ferrets.

Finally, plaintiff emphasizes that New York City does not regulate pit bull terriers, which have been shown to be dangerous in certain circumstances, and suggests that the absence of such regulation establishes a constitutional infirmity, under the Equal Protection Clause, of the Health Code regulations relating to ferrets. We disagree . . . [T]he Constitution does not prohibit underinclusive statutes *per se*. That the City has chosen, in the field of ownership of animals, to regulate ferrets and not pit bull terriers, simply embodies the permissible exercise of its discretion to address "[e]vils in the same field [which] may be of different dimensions and proportions, requiring different remedies . . . The [City] may select one phase of one field and apply a remedy there, neglecting the others." . . . Plaintiff's arguments with respect to regulation of pit bulls, and, in fact, plaintiff's appeal to the regulation of dogs and cats in general, betray its fundamental misconception of constitutional equal protection and due process analysis as such analysis applies to public safety laws. The Constitution simply does not guarantee owners of ferrets regulatory status precisely equal to the status of owners of other animals, even potentially dangerous animals, but rather mandates only that the decision of the sovereign to regulate them, as well as the nature of that regulation, have a rational basis and not be undertaken and applied arbitrarily and capriciously. Here, the undisputed evidence . . . establishes that the City's ban on ferrets and its summary euthanasia and testing of ferrets that bite humans has ample basis in public health concerns regarding the propensity of pet ferrets to bite, particularly infants and small children, and the uncertain pathogenesis of rabies in domestic ferrets; therefore, the City's regulation of ferret ownership cannot be deemed arbitrary or irrational.

NOTES AND QUESTIONS

15.   Dangerous animals. *New York City Friends of Ferrets* is another illustration of prototypical local public health and safety legislation. Here, again, in the absence of any fundamental right to own ferrets or to keep them alive, the court defers to legislative judgment concerning the importance of the risk of rabies and the proper remedial response. In this case, however, the government provided considerable evidence for its conclusion that ferrets posed a danger of biting people and transmitting rabies. Perhaps more importantly, the City was able to demonstrate the need for the seemingly extreme remedy of euthanizing any ferret reported to have bitten a human being. Plaintiffs failed to provide similarly persuasive evidence to meet their heavy burden of proving that the law was irrational.

The *Ferrets* decision is also an illustration of the application of equal protection analysis to what the plaintiffs claim is the arbitrary targeting of one group (ferrets) by the legislature (the City Council), to the exclusion of other similar groups (potentially dangerous or infected animals). The Friends of Ferrets were probably not alone in their frustration at being singled out for regulation. However, as the court notes, to be rational, a classification need not attack the most serious problem first or all problems of comparable merit. For a general discussion, *see New York City Transit Authority v. Beazer,* 440 U.S. 568 (1979); *Williamson v. Lee Optical,* 348 U.S. 483 (1955). The fact that some people think that the problem is less important or that some critics question whether the severe measures adopted by the city are really necessary, by themselves, do not render the city's choice irrational. Such choices are left to legislative discretion and limited only by political, not constitutional constraints.

16.   Dog bites. Dog bites occur about 4.5 million times a year in the United States, a number that has remained relatively constant in recent decades. Dog Bite

Prevention,   http://www.cdc.gov/HomeandRecreationalSafety/Dog-Bites/
biteprevention.html (last visited July 2013). About one-fifth of these bites require
medical attention, and account for about 1 percent of emergency department visits.
Annelise Adams et. al., *Emergency Department Visits and Hospitalizations
Associated with Animal Injuries, 2009*, May 2012, Agency for Healthcare Research
and Quality, Rockville, MD. According to the Agency for Healthcare Research and
Quality, hospital admissions for dog bites increased 86% between 1983 and 2008.
Hospital Admissions for Dog Bites Increase 86% Over a 16-Year Period: AHRQ
News and Numbers, December 1, 2010. December 2010. Agency for Healthcare
Research and Quality, Rockville, MD. http://www.ahrq.gov/news/newsroom/news-
and-numbers/120110.html (last visited July 2013).

Should states or cities take stronger measures to prevent dog bites — beyond
existing laws requiring dogs to be vaccinated against rabies and other diseases and
to be on leash in public? What kinds of measures are appropriate? Should owners
be required to confine their dogs in prescribed enclosures? Should pit bulls,
Doberman pinschers, or other specific breeds be singled out for regulation? Should
their ownership be banned entirely?

17.   Fluoridation of the water supply. From time to time, health or safety
regulations believed to be well settled resurface as a subject of renewed public
debate, perhaps as a result of new scientific information, perhaps for other or
politically expedient reasons. An example is efforts by state and local governments
to fluoridate drinking water. Virtually all courts that have considered the issue have
upheld the constitutionality of fluoridation. *See, e.g., City of Port Angeles v. Our
Water-Our Choice!* 239 P. 3d 589 (Wa. 2010); *City of Watsonville v. State Dept. of
Health Services*, 133 Cal. App. 4th 875 (2005); *Young v. Board of Health of
Somerville*, 293 A.2d 164 (N.J. 1972). The Supreme Court, however, has not
addressed the question of whether fluoridation of water is a valid exercise of the
police power.

In some respects, fluoridation tests the outer limits of government authority.
Fluoridating water is primarily an effort to prevent dental caries. Dental caries can
be related to other health conditions, can cause pain and discomfort, and may even
make eating and drinking more difficult, but they are clearly not a life-threatening
condition or even something that, in relative terms, necessarily threatens overall
health status. Fluoridation of the water supply is largely an effort to protect
individual people for their own benefit. Thus, it can be seen as largely a paternalistic
effort, not a protection of third parties. In theory, anyone who objects to fluoridated
water can buy water without fluoride, although the question of affordability may
limit the choices of the poor. How does this compare to the "freedom" of
motorcyclists to avoid having to wear a helmet by not riding motorcycles? The
major difference may be that helmet laws (for both motorcycles and bicycles)
regulate an individual's behavior, whereas fluoridation regulates a water supply —
a "thing," not a person.

Dental associations and most public health organizations argue that fluoridation
is a safe, cost-effective way to prevent dental caries. They emphasize the need for
protecting the developing teeth of children, who may not have access to dental care.
Opponents of fluoridation argue that it amounts to compulsory medication (through

the water supply). The U.S. Environmental Protection Agency (EPA) recently recognized that over-fluoridation may result in dental fluorosis resulting in stained, pitted teeth (dental fluorosis) or bone disease (skeletal fluorosis). 40 C.F.R. § 141.208 (2011). The Department of Health and Human Services followed by proposing a reduction in the recommended level of fluoride in drinking water from 0.7–1.2 mg/L to 0.7 mg/L. Proposed HHS Recommendation for Fluoride Concentration in Drinking Water for Prevention of Dental Caries, 76 Fed. Reg. 2383 (Jan. 13 2011). As of June 2013, the Department had neither changed nor finalized its recommendation.

For a rather provocative effort to document the claims that fluoridation is ineffective in preventing dental caries and causes cancer and other health problems, see John Remington Graham & Pierre *Morian, Highlights in North American Litigation During the Twentieth Century on Artificial Fluoridation of Public Water Supplies*, 14 J. Land use & Env't L. 195 (1999). For a more traditional view of the benefits of fluoridation, see CDC, *Achievements in Public Health 1900–1999: Fluoridation of Drinking Water to Prevent Dental Caries*, 48 Morbidity/Mortality Wkly Rep. 933–940 (1999).

To what degree are these divergent views susceptible to resolution by scientific evidence and to what degree are they rooted in beliefs about the value of public health measures and the role of government?

NEW YORK STATEWIDE COALITION OF HISPANIC CHAMBERS OF COMMERCE v. NEW YORK CITY DEPARTMENT OF HEALTH AND MENTAL HYGIENE
___ N.Y. 2d ___, 2014 N.Y. LEXIS 1442 (2014)

Pigott, Judge.

. . . .

I.

The New York City Board of Health is part of the City's Department of Health and Mental Hygiene and consists of the Commissioner of that Department, the Chairperson of the Department's Mental Hygiene Advisory Board, and nine other members, appointed by the Mayor. In June 2012, as part of its effort to combat obesity among City residents, the Department proposed that the Board amend Article 81 of the City Health Code so as to restrict the size of cups and containers used by food service establishments for the provision of sugary beverages. . . . On September 13, 2012, the Board voted, with one abstention, to adopt the Department's proposed rule — referred to as the "Portion Cap Rule" — to go into effect in March 2013.

The Portion Cap Rule provides in relevant part that "[a] food service establishment may not sell, offer, or provide a sugary drink in a cup or container that is able to contain more than 16 fluid ounces" and "may not sell, offer or provide to any customer a self-service cup or container that is able to contain more than 16 fluid ounces" (NY City Health Code § 81.53 [b], [c]). A "sugary drink" is defined as a non-alcoholic beverage that "is sweetened by the manufacturer or establishment with sugar or another calorie sweetener; . . . has greater than 25 calories per 8 fluid ounces of beverage; . . . [and] does not contain more than 50 percent of milk or milk substitute by volume as an ingredient" (NY City Health Code § 81.53 [a][1]). The Portion Cap Rule does not apply to establishments, such as supermarkets and convenience stores, that are subject to regulation and inspection by the New York State Department of Agriculture and Markets.

II.

In October 2012, petitioners, six national or statewide not-for-profit and labor organizations, commenced this . . . action seeking to invalidate the Portion Cap Rule. . . .

. . . .

The Appellate Division unanimously affirmed Supreme Court's order [declaring the Rule invalid and permanently enjoining its enforcement], . . . holding that "under the principles set forth in *Boreali* [*v Axelrod* (71 NY2d 1 [1987])], the Board of Health overstepped the boundaries of its lawfully delegated authority when it promulgated the Portion Cap Rule. . . . It therefore violated the state principle of separation of powers" (110 AD3d 1, 16 [1st Dept 2013]). . . .

. . . .

III

First, we address respondents' claim that the Board, having been created by the State Legislature, has legislative powers separate and apart from the City Council. The City Charter unequivocally provides for distinct legislative and executive branches of New York City government. The City Council is the sole legislative branch of City government; it is "*the* legislative body of the city. . . . vested with the legislative power of the city" (New York City Charter § 21 [emphasis added]. The New York State Constitution mandates that . . . "[e]very local government . . . shall have a legislative body elective by the people thereof" (NY Const Art IX, § 1 [a]; and that elective body in New York City is the City Council.

Respondents, however, contend that the Board of Health is a unique body that has inherent legislative authority. We disagree. The provision of the City Charter principally cited by respondents — setting out the authority of the Board to "add to and alter, amend or repeal any part of the health code, . . . [to] publish additional provisions for security of life and health in the city and [to] confer additional powers on the [Department of Health and Mental Hygiene] not inconsistent with the constitution, laws of this state or this charter" — reflects only a regulatory mandate, not legislative authority. It is true that the Board "may embrace in the health code all matters and subjects to which the power and authority of the [Department of Health and Mental Hygiene] extends" and that the Charter refers to the Board's supervision over "the reporting and control of communicable and chronic diseases and conditions hazardous to life and health" and "the abatement of nuisances affecting or likely to affect the public health". Nonetheless, the Charter contains no suggestion that the Board of Health has the authority to create laws. While the Charter empowers the City Council "to adopt local laws . . . for the preservation of the public health, comfort, peace and prosperity of the city and its inhabitants", the Charter restricts the Board's rule-making to the publication of a health code, an entirely different endeavor.

. . . .

Respondents offer no practical solution to the difficulties that would arise from treating the Board and the City Council as co-equal legislative bodies. On respondents' theory, it is unclear what the law in New York City would be were the Board to pass a health "law" that directly conflicted with a local law of the City Council. It is no solution to this difficulty that the State Legislature could step in to resolve such a conflict. In short, it is clear from the Charter that the Board's authority, like that of any other administrative agency, is restricted to promulgating "rules necessary to carry out the powers and duties delegated to it by or pursuant to federal, state or local law". A rule has the force of law, but it is not a law; rather, it "implements or applies law or policy".

. . . .

IV

Given our position that the Board's role is regulation, not legislation, the next issue raised in this appeal is whether the Board properly exercised its regulatory authority in adopting the Portion Cap Rule. . . . Because a doctrine of "separation of powers [is] delineated in the City Charter", *Boreali* provides the appropriate framework.

Boreali sets out four "coalescing circumstances" present in that case that convinced the Court "that the difficult-to-define line between administrative rule-making and legislative policy-making ha[d] been transgressed." . . .

[The court summarizes the *Boreali* circumstances or factors in an earlier passage as follows: (1) "whether the agency engaged in the balancing of competing concerns of public health and economic costs, thus acting on its own idea of sound public policy"; (2) "whether the agency created its own comprehensive set of rules without benefit of legislative guidance"; (3) "whether the challenged rule governs an area in which the Legislature has repeatedly tried to reach agreement in the face of substantial public debate and vigorous lobbying by interested factions"; and (4) "whether the development of the rule required expertise in the field of health".]

As the term "coalescing circumstances" suggests, we do not regard the four circumstances as discrete, necessary conditions that define improper policy-making by an agency, nor as criteria that should be rigidly applied in every case in which an agency is accused of crossing the line into legislative territory. Rather we treat the circumstances as overlapping, closely related factors that, taken together, support the conclusion that an agency has crossed that line. Consequently, respondents may not counter petitioners' argument merely by showing that one *Boreali* factor does not obtain.

1st factor

V

In *Boreali*, the Court initially pointed out that the Public Health Council's scheme for protecting nonsmokers indicated its "effort to weigh the goal of promoting health against its social cost and to reach a suitable compromise." We took this to violate the principle that "[s]triking the proper balance among health concerns, cost and privacy interests . . . is a uniquely legislative function". We reasoned that "to the extent that the agency has built a regulatory scheme on its own conclusions about the appropriate balance of trade-offs between health and cost to particular industries in the private sector, it was acting solely on its own ideas of sound public policy and was therefore operating outside of its proper sphere of authority". Here, similarly, the Appellate Division noted that the Board of Health included exemptions and other indicators of political compromise in its Portion Cap Rule, notably the exclusion of food service establishments subject to the State Department of Agriculture and Markets. The Appellate Division interpreted this as evidence that the Board was engaged in policy-making, rather than simply in protecting the health of New York City residents.

However, the promulgation of regulations necessarily involves an analysis of societal costs and benefits. . . . We stated as much in *Boreali*, noting that "many regulatory decisions involve weighing economic and social concerns against the specific values that the regulatory agency is mandated to promote". Therefore, *Boreali* should not be interpreted to prohibit an agency from attempting to balance costs and benefits. Rather, the *Boreali* court found that the Public Health Council had "not been given any legislative guidelines at all for determining how the competing concerns of public health and economic cost are to be weighed".

. . . By restricting portions, the Board necessarily chose between ends, including public health, the economic consequences associated with restricting profits by beverage companies and vendors, tax implications for small business owners, and personal autonomy with respect to the choices of New York City residents concerning what they consume. Most obviously, the Portion Cap Rule embodied a compromise that attempted to promote a healthy diet without significantly affecting the beverage industry. This necessarily implied a relative valuing of health considerations and economic ends, just as a complete prohibition of sugary beverages would have. Moreover, it involved more than simply balancing costs and benefits according to pre-existing guidelines; the value judgments entailed difficult and complex choices between broad policy goals — choices reserved to the legislative branch.

. . . .

By choosing between public policy ends in these ways, the Board of Health engaged in law-making beyond its regulatory authority, under the first *Boreali* factor. Notably, such policy-making would likely not be implicated in situations where the Board regulates by means of posted warnings (e.g. calorie content on menus) or by means of an outright ban of a toxic substance (e.g. lead paint). In such cases, it could be argued that personal autonomy issues related to the regulation are nonexistent and the economic costs either minimal or clearly outweighed by the benefits to society, so that no policy-making in the *Boreali* sense is involved.

To apply the distinction between policy-making and rule-making, a court is thus required to differentiate between levels of difficulty and complexity in the agency's task of weighing competing values. For example, when an agency regulates the purity of drinking water, or prohibits the use of interior lead paint, or requires guards in the windows of high-rise apartments housing children, it chooses among ends (e.g. a landowner's convenience and short-term profit versus the safety, health and well-being of tenants), but the choices are not very difficult or complex. This is because the connection of the regulation with the preservation of health and safety is very direct, there is minimal interference with the personal autonomy of those whose health is being protected, and value judgments concerning the underlying ends are widely shared.

. . . Few people would wish to risk the physical safety of their children who play near high-rise apartment windows for the sake of unobstructed views. However, the number of people who over-indulge in sugary drinks, at a risk to their health, is clearly significant. An agency that adopts a regulation, such as the Portion Cap Rule or an outright prohibition of sugary beverages, that interferes with commonplace daily activities preferred by large numbers of people must necessarily wrestle with complex value judgments concerning personal autonomy and economics. That is policy-making, not rule-making.

VI

2nd Factor

With respect to the second *Boreali* factor, respondents are unable to point to any legislation concerning the consumption of sugary beverages by the State Legislature or City Council that the Portion Cap Rule was designed to supplement. Although "[t]he Legislature is not required in its enactments to supply agencies with rigid marching orders" and the legislative branch may, while declaring "its policy in general terms by statute, endow administrative agencies with the power and flexibility to fill in details and interstices and to make subsidiary policy choices consistent with the enabling legislation", the policy choices made here were far from "subsidiary." Devising an entirely new rule that significantly changes the manner in which sugary beverages are provided to customers at eating establishments is not an auxiliary selection of means to an end; it reflects a new policy choice. . . .

Therefore, it is clear that the Board of Health wrote the Portion Cap Rule without benefit of legislative guidance, and did not simply fill in details guided by independent legislation. Because there was no legislative articulation of health policy goals associated with consumption of sugary beverages upon which to ground the Portion Cap Rule, the application of the second *Boreali* factor generates the same conclusion as the first factor: the adoption of the Rule involved the choosing of ends, or policy-making.

3rd Factor

VII

With regard to the third *Boreali* factor, little needs to be added to the Appellate Division's analysis. [In an earlier passage, the court states, "the Appellate Division noted that '[o]ver the past few years, both the City and State legislatures have attempted, albeit unsuccessfully, to target sugar sweetened beverages. For instance, the City Council has rejected several resolutions targeting sugar sweetened beverages (warning labels, prohibiting food stamp use for purchase, and taxes on such beverages). Moreover, the State Assembly introduced, but has not passed, bills prohibiting the sale of sugary drinks on government property and prohibiting stores with 10 or more employees from displaying candy or sugary drinks at the check out counter or aisle."]. . . . Here, inaction on the part of the State Legislature and City Council, in the face of plentiful opportunity to act if so desired, simply constitutes additional evidence that the Board's adoption of the Portion Cap Rule amounted to making new policy, rather than carrying out preexisting legislative policy.

In light of *Boreali's* central theme that an administrative agency exceeds its authority when it makes difficult choices between public policy ends, rather than finds means to an end chosen by the Legislature, we need not, in this appeal, address the fourth *Boreali* factor: whether special expertise or technical competence was involved in the development of the rule. We do not mean to imply that the fourth factor will always lack significance. A court might be alerted to the broad, policy-making intent of a regulation, and the absence of any perceived need for agency expertise, by the fact that the rule was adopted with very little technical discussion. Here, regardless of who or which arm of government first proposed or drafted the Portion Cap Rule, and regardless of whether the Board exercised its considerable professional expertise or merely rubber-stamped a rule drafted outside the agency, the Portion Cap Rule is invalid under *Boreali*.

VIII

In sum, the New York City Board of Health exceeded the scope of its regulatory authority by adopting the Portion Cap Rule. . . . .[T]he order of the Appellate Division should be affirmed, with costs.

NOTES AND QUESTIONS

18. **Separation of powers and administrative authority**. The *New York Statewide Coalition* decision above illustrates how laws often grant health departments their authority in brief, general language, such as "controlling disease." How would you interpret the New York City Charter's text? The City's health department and its board of health read the Charter as authorizing almost any rule that could "promote" or "protect" health. In contrast, the Appellate Division (the state's appellate level court) concluded that the board's power is limited to "protect[ing] the public from inherently harmful and inimical matters affecting the health of the City," like contamination and toxins, and that soda could not be considered

"inherently harmful."

The New York State Court of Appeals, the state's highest court, did not expressly interpret the operative text. Instead, the determinative issue was whether the board's action went beyond its permissible authority, usurping the legislature's power. The court (in a 4:2 decision) roundly dismissed the claim that the board of health had legislative authority, emphasizing that the board was an administrative agency, not a legislative body. Thus, the board could carry out statutes — "interstitial rule making" to fill in the gaps — but not establish policy, which is reserved to the City's legislative body, the City Council.

Does this decision nonetheless suggest anything about the meaning of the board's power to "control disease?" *See* Chapter 8, B, for another example of the health department's interpretation of its power — to require the reporting of individual blood sugar levels without patient consent to control Type 2 diabetes. Could such a rule be vulnerable to challenge under the *New York Statewide Coalition* reasoning?

Judge Pigott's decision was joined by three other judges. Judge Read wrote a lengthy dissent, joined by Judge Lippman, describing the history of the New York City Board of Health, which has enjoyed an unusual degree of discretionary authority not necessarily typical of public health agencies. Much of the disagreement between the majority and the dissent lies in how each interprets various amendments to the authorizing legislation — which should remind us always to pay close attention to statutory text and history. The dissent argues that state legislation granted the board its authority directly, so that the board could act without City Council authorization. Perhaps more interesting, Judge Read argues that the act of balancing health and economic costs — which the majority finds to be an exclusively legislative function — is what an agency should be doing: "And what is inherently wrong with a regulation that seeks to 'promote a healthy diet without significantly affecting the beverage industry'?" The dissent challenges the majority's ends-means test as "virtually inscrutable and certainly unworkable." Instead, Judge Read would simply have the court determine whether the regulation is "so lacking in reason that for its promulgation that it is essentially arbitrary." Would such a standard of review be preferable? Does it take into account the substantive subject matter over which the agency has authority?

19. Power and policy. Both the Portion Cap Rule and the *New York Statewide Coalition* decision generated substantial controversy, but that controversy focused almost entirely on the policy of limiting portion sizes and largely ignored the threshold legal question of the board of health's power. The Court of Appeals, of course, does not address the rule's merits. Rather, the court seems to suggest that the City Council, like any legislature, would have the power to enact something like the Portion Cap Rule. (It had not done so, partly because of business opposition. Note that the challengers include many small businesses in the City.) If the City Council enacted a Portion Cap Rule, would it be a valid exercise of the police power delegated to the City?

No one seriously disputed the idea that drinking too much soda can make you gain weight. The Board argued that it was compelled to take action in order to save lives. Supporters of the Rule, as well as the Board, relied on behavioral science concepts of "soft paternalism" to argue that people are less likely to drink excessive amounts of soda if the portions available are smaller. *See* RICHARD H. THALER & CASS R. SUNSTEIN, NUDGE: IMPROVING DECISIONS ABOUT HEALTH, WEALTH, AND HAPPINESS (2008). Opponents argued that the Rule was unlikely to be effective in reducing obesity among New Yorkers, because it did not apply to many food services establishments, such as grocery stores, or to other high calorie drinks, such as milk shakes and alcoholic beverages. These latter points had persuaded the trial judge that the Rule was not only a violation of separation of powers, but also arbitrary and capricious — an issue not reached by the Court of Appeals. *See* Chapter 9 for materials on alternative policies to reduce obesity.

20. Constitutional and legislative sources of administrative authority. Many legal disputes over the legitimacy of various public health programs focus not on the broad constitutional parameters within which the government must operate, but whether the particular measures under consideration have been authorized by state or, in some cases, city or county legislative bodies. As a result, in many cases, the legality of any public health measure taken at the local level may require some parsing of the various statutory schemes, and often raises interesting questions of administrative law and statutory preemption. For a good example, see *Parkland Light & Water Co. v. Tacoma-Pierce County Bd. of Health*, 151 Wash. 2d 428, 90 P.2d 37 (2004) (holding that the local health department could not require the fluorida-tion of the water supply because of a conflict with a statewide statute giving local water authorities discretionary authority to fluoridate the water). In some jurisdic-tions, such as Washington, there is also the possibility that a local jurisdiction may be acting under its own (state) constitutional authority, apart from any state authorizing legislation. A good illustration of these jurisdictional disputes can be found in *Spokane County Health Dist. v. Brockett*, 120 Wash. 2d 140, 839 P.2d 324 (1992).

21. Bans to protect health and safety. Legal bans intended to protect the public health often originate in California. The New York Times offered the following summary:

> Bonfires on the beach? Sorry, Gidget: Newport Beach is waiting for permission from the California Coastal Commission to remove its long-cherished fire pits, which it banned this summer as health hazards. Newport's fleet of diesel-burning yachts are still OK, but napping in the city's libraries? Forbidden, as of July [2012], along with any "use of perfume or fragrance" that interferes with librarians' "ability to perform duties."

> . . . .

> But that beach town really earned its bones in the ban business with smoking, which is outlawed almost everywhere, including the beach and at A.T.M.'s. Private apartments are one exception, and the city spent most of last summer embroiled in a battle over closing that loophole. Eventually, the push to forbid smoking in apartments was dropped, partly because it would complicate the smoking of medical marijuana.

Brooks Barnes & Michael Cieply, *At Least Fun in the Sun Isn't Banned. For Now*

. . . NEW YORK TIMES, Sept. 3, 2012, www.nytimes.com/2012/09/03/us/in-california-banning-bonfires-and-library-napping.html.

More positive legal initiatives include laws that enable people to stay healthy. For example, several states have enacted laws requiring private employers to provide paid sick days for their employees. New York City, which prides itself on public health promotion, finally passed such a bill in 2013, although few employees qualify for sick pay under its terms. Opposition to the law came from then Mayor Bloomberg, who has been a champion of public health measures like the Portion Cap Rule at issue in *New York Statewide Coalition, supra*, but the City Council overrode his veto of the sick leave law.

D.   FEDERAL REGULATION: THE POWER TO REGULATE COMMERCE

Generally speaking, "Congress does not exercise lightly" the "extraordinary power" to "legislate in areas traditionally regulated by the States." . . . *Gregory v. Ashcroft*, 501 U. S. 452, 460 (1991). The Supreme Court typically introduces its analysis of a federal preemption or Supremacy Clause question with a caveat like the following: "we start with the assumption that the historic police powers of the States were not to be superseded by the Federal Act unless that was the clear and manifest purpose of Congress." *Rice v. Santa Fe Elevator Corp.*, 331 U. S. 218, 230 (1947) . . . . These admonitions, however, have not posed a significant barrier to the expanding scope of federal legislation governing public health and safety.

GONZALES v. RAICH
545 U.S. 1 (2005)

JUSTICE STEVENS delivered the opinion of the Court.

California is one of at least nine States that authorize the use of marijuana for medicinal purposes. The question presented in this case is whether the power vested in Congress by Article I, § 8, of the Constitution "to make all Laws which shall be necessary and proper for carrying into Execution" its authority to " "regulate Commerce with foreign Nations, and among the several States" " includes the power to prohibit the local cultivation and use of marijuana in compliance with California law.

I

California has been a pioneer in the regulation of marijuana. In 1913, California was one of the first States to prohibit the sale and possession of marijuana, and at the end of the century, California became the first State to authorize limited use of the drug for medicinal purposes. In 1996, California voters passed Proposition 215, now codified as the Compassionate Use Act of 1996. The proposition was designed to ensure that "seriously ill" residents of the State have access to marijuana for medical purposes, and to encourage Federal and State Governments to take steps towards ensuring the safe and affordable distribution of the drug to patients in need. The Act creates an exemption from criminal prosecution for physicians, as well as for patients and primary caregivers who possess or cultivate marijuana for medicinal purposes with the recommendation or approval of a physician.

Respondents Angel Raich and Diane Monson are California residents who suffer from a variety of serious medical conditions and have sought to avail themselves of medical marijuana pursuant to the terms of the Compassionate Use Act. They are being treated by licensed, board-certified family practitioners, who have concluded, after prescribing a host of conventional medicines to treat respondents' conditions and to alleviate their associated symptoms, that marijuana is the only drug available that provides effective treatment. Both women have been using marijuana as a medication for several years pursuant to their doctors' recommendation, and both rely heavily on cannabis to function on a daily basis.

Respondent Monson cultivates her own marijuana, and ingests the drug in a variety of ways including smoking and using a vaporizer. Respondent Raich, by contrast, is unable to cultivate her own, and thus relies on two caregivers, litigating as "John Does," to provide her with locally grown marijuana at no charge. These caregivers also process the cannabis into hashish or keif, and Raich herself processes some of the marijuana into oils, balms, and foods for consumption.

On August 15, 2002, county deputy sheriffs and agents from the federal Drug Enforcement Administration (DEA) came to Monson's home. After a thorough investigation, the county officials concluded that her use of marijuana was entirely lawful as a matter of California law. Nevertheless, after a 3-hour standoff, the federal agents seized and destroyed all six of her cannabis plants.

Respondents thereafter brought this action against the Attorney General of the United States and the head of the DEA seeking injunctive and declaratory relief prohibiting the enforcement of the federal Controlled Substances Act (CSA) [84 Stat. 1242, 21 U. S. C. § 801 *et seq.*] to the extent it prevents them from possessing, obtaining, or manufacturing cannabis for their personal medical use . . . .

The case is made difficult by respondents' strong arguments that they will suffer irreparable harm because, despite a congressional finding to the contrary, marijuana does have valid therapeutic purposes. The question before us, however, is not whether it is wise to enforce the statute in these circumstances; rather, it is whether Congress' power to regulate interstate markets for medicinal substances encompasses the portions of those markets that are supplied with drugs produced and consumed locally. Well-settled law controls our answer. The CSA is a valid exercise of federal power, even as applied to the troubling facts of this case . . . .

II

[A]s early as 1906 Congress enacted federal legislation imposing labeling regulations on medications and prohibiting the manufacture or shipment of any adulterated or misbranded drug traveling in interstate commerce. Aside from these labeling restrictions, most domestic drug regulations prior to 1970 generally came in the guise of revenue laws, with the Department of the Treasury serving as the Federal Government's primary enforcer. For example, the primary drug control law, before being repealed by the passage of the CSA, was the Harrison Narcotics Act of 1914, 38 Stat. 785 (repealed 1970). The Harrison Act sought to exert control over the possession and sale of narcotics, specifically cocaine and opiates, by requiring producers, distributors, and purchasers to register with the Federal Government, by assessing taxes against parties so registered, and by regulating the issuance of prescriptions.

Marijuana itself was not significantly regulated by the Federal Government until 1937 when accounts of marijuana's addictive qualities and physiological effects, paired with dissatisfaction with enforcement efforts at state and local levels, prompted Congress to pass the Marihuana Tax Act . . . . Like the Harrison Act, the Marihuana Tax Act did not outlaw the possession or sale of marijuana outright. Rather, it imposed registration and reporting requirements for all individuals importing, producing, selling, or dealing in marijuana, and required the payment of annual taxes in addition to transfer taxes whenever the drug changed hands. Moreover, doctors wishing to prescribe marijuana for medical purposes were required to comply with rather burden-some administrative requirements. Non-compliance exposed traffickers to severe federal penalties, whereas compliance would often subject them to prosecution under state law. Thus, while the Marihuana Tax Act did not declare the drug illegal per se, the onerous administrative requirements, the prohibitively expensive taxes, and the risks attendant on compliance practically curtailed the marijuana trade.

Then in 1970, after declaration of the national "war on drugs," federal drug policy underwent a significant transformation. A number of noteworthy events precipitated this policy shift. First this Court held certain provisions of the Marihuana Tax Act and other narcotics legislation unconstitutional. Second, at the end of his term, President Johnson fundamentally reorganized the federal drug control agencies. . . . .Finally, prompted by a perceived need to consolidate the growing number of piecemeal drug laws and to enhance federal drug enforcement powers, Congress enacted the Comprehensive Drug Abuse Prevention and Control Act.

Title II of that Act, the CSA, repealed most of the earlier antidrug laws in favor of a comprehensive regime to combat the international and interstate traffic in illicit drugs. The main objectives of the CSA were to conquer drug abuse and to control the legitimate and illegitimate traffic in controlled substances. Congress was particularly concerned with the need to prevent the diversion of drugs from legitimate to illicit channels. To effectuate these goals, Congress devised a closed regulatory system making it unlawful to manufacture, distribute, dispense, or possess any controlled substance except in a manner authorized by the CSA. The CSA categorizes all controlled substances into five schedules. Each schedule is associated with a distinct set of controls regarding the manufacture, distribution, and use of the substances listed therein. The CSA and its implementing regulations set forth strict requirements regarding registration, labeling and packaging, production quotas, drug security, and recordkeeping.

In enacting the CSA, Congress classified marijuana as a Schedule I drug . . . . Schedule I drugs are categorized as such because of their high potential for abuse, lack of any accepted medical use, and absence of any accepted safety for use in medically supervised treatment. These three factors, in varying gradations, are also used in medically supervised treatment . . . . By classifying marijuana as a Schedule I drug, as opposed to listing it on a lesser schedule, the manufacture, distribution, or possession of marijuana became a criminal offense, with the sole exception being use of the drug as part of a Food and Drug Administration pre-approved research study.

The CSA provides for the periodic updating of schedules and delegates authority to the Attorney General, after consultation with the Secretary of Health and Human Services, to add, remove, or transfer substances to, from, or between schedules. Despite considerable efforts to reschedule marijuana, it remains a Schedule I drug.

III

Respondents in this case do not dispute that passage of the CSA, as part of the Comprehensive Drug Abuse Prevention and Control Act, was well within Congress' commerce power . . . . Rather, respondents' challenge is actually quite limited; they argue that the CSA's categorical prohibition of the manufacture and possession of marijuana as applied to the intrastate manufacture and possession of marijuana for medical purposes pursuant to California law exceeds Congress' authority under the Commerce Clause.

. . . As charted in considerable detail in *United States v. Lopez*, our understanding of the reach of the Commerce Clause, as well as Congress' assertion of authority thereunder, has evolved over time. For the first century of our history, the primary use of the Clause was to preclude the kind of discriminatory state legislation that had once been permissible. Then, in response to rapid industrial development and an increasingly interdependent national economy, Congress "ushered in a new era of federal regulation under the commerce power," "beginning with the enactment of the Interstate Commerce Act in 1887, and the Sherman Antitrust Act in 1890.

Cases decided during that "new era," which now spans more than a century, have identified three general categories of regulation in which Congress is authorized to engage under its commerce power. First, Congress can regulate the channels of interstate commerce. Second, Congress has authority to regulate and protect the instrumentalities of interstate commerce, and persons or things in interstate commerce. Third, Congress has the power to regulate activities that substantially affect interstate commerce. Only the third category is implicated in the case at hand.

Our case law firmly establishes Congress' power to regulate purely local activities that are part of an economic "class of activities" that have a substantial effect on interstate commerce. See, *e.g.*, *Wickard v. Filburn*, 317 U.S. 111, 128–129 (1942). As we stated in *Wickard*, "even if appellee's activity be local and though it may not be regarded as commerce, it may still, whatever its nature, be reached by Congress if it exerts a substantial economic effect on interstate commerce." We have never required Congress to legislate with scientific exactitude. When Congress decides that the " 'total incidence' " of a practice poses a threat to a national market, it may regulate the entire class . . . . In this vein, we have reiterated that when " 'a general regulatory statute bears a substantial relation to commerce, the *de minimis* character of individual instances arising under that statute is of no consequence.' "

In *Wickard*, we upheld the application of regulations promulgated under the Agricultural Adjustment Act of 1938, which were designed to control the volume of wheat moving in interstate and foreign commerce in order to avoid surpluses and consequent abnormally low prices. The regulations established an allotment of 11.1 acres for Filburn's 1941 wheat crop, but he sowed 23 acres, intending to use the excess by consuming it on his own farm. Filburn argued that Congress' power did not authorize "federal regulation [of] production not intended in any part for commerce but wholly for consumption on the farm." Justice Jackson's opinion for a unanimous Court rejected this submission. He wrote:

"The effect of the statute before us is to restrict the amount which may be produced for market and the extent as well to which one may forestall resort to the market by producing to meet his own needs. That appellee's own contribution to the demand for wheat may be trivial by itself is not enough to remove him from the scope of federal regulation where, as here, his contribution, taken together with that of many others similarly situated, is far from trivial."

. . . .*Wickard* thus establishes that Congress can regulate purely intrastate activity that is not itself "commercial," in that it is not produced for sale, if it concludes that failure to regulate that class of activity would undercut the regulation of the interstate market in that commodity.

The similarities between this case and *Wickard* are striking. Like the farmer in *Wickard*, respondents are cultivating, for home consumption, a fungible commodity for which there is an established, albeit illegal, interstate market. Just as the Agricultural Adjustment Act was designed "to control the volume [of wheat] moving in interstate and foreign commerce in order to avoid surpluses . . . " and consequently control the market price, a primary purpose of the CSA is to control the supply and demand of controlled substances in both lawful and unlawful drug markets. In *Wickard*, we had no difficulty concluding that Congress had a rational basis for believing that, when viewed in the aggregate, leaving home-consumed wheat outside the regulatory scheme would have a substantial influence on price and market conditions. Here too, Congress had a rational basis for concluding that leaving home-consumed marijuana outside federal control would similarly affect price and market conditions.

More concretely, one concern prompting inclusion of wheat grown for home consumption in the 1938 Act was that rising market prices could draw such wheat into the interstate market, resulting in lower market prices. The parallel concern making it appropriate to include marijuana grown for home consumption in the CSA is the likelihood that the high demand in the interstate market will draw such marijuana into that market. In both cases, the regulation is squarely within Congress' commerce power because production of the commodity meant for home consumption, be it wheat or marijuana, has a substantial effect on supply and demand in the national market for that commodity.

. . . .

In assessing the scope of Congress' authority under the Commerce Clause, we stress that the task before us is a modest one. We need not determine whether respondents' activities, taken in the aggregate, substantially affect interstate commerce in fact, but only whether a "rational basis" exists for so concluding. Given the enforcement difficulties that attend distinguishing between marijuana culti- vated locally and marijuana grown elsewhere, and concerns about diversion into illicit channels, we have no difficulty concluding that Congress had a rational basis for believing that failure to regulate the intrastate manufacture and possession of marijuana would leave a gaping hole in the CSA. That the regulation ensnares some purely intrastate activity is of no moment.

IV

. . . .

. . . The CSA designates marijuana as contraband for any purpose; in fact, by characterizing marijuana as a Schedule I drug, Congress expressly found that the drug has no acceptable medical uses. Moreover, the CSA is a comprehensive regulatory regime specifically designed to regulate which controlled substances can be utilized for medicinal purposes, and in what manner. Accordingly, the mere fact that marijuana — like virtually every other controlled substance regulated by the CSA — is used for medicinal purposes cannot possibly serve to distinguish it from the core activities regulated by the CSA.

First, the fact that marijuana is used "for personal medical purposes on the advice of a physician" cannot itself serve as a distinguishing factor. More funda- mentally, if, as the principal dissent contends, the personal cultivation, possession, and use of marijuana for medicinal purposes is beyond the " 'outer limits' of Congress' Commerce Clause authority," it must also be true that such personal use of marijuana (or any other homegrown drug) for recreational purposes is also beyond those " 'outer limits,' " whether or not a State elects to authorize or even regulate such use . . . . One need not have a degree in economics to understand why a nationwide exemption for the vast quantity of marijuana (or other drugs) locally cultivated for personal use (which presumably would include use by friends, neighbors, and family members) may have a substantial impact on the interstate market for this extraordinarily popular substance. The congressional judgment that an exemption for such a significant segment of the total market would undermine the orderly enforcement of the entire regulatory scheme is entitled to a strong presumption of validity.

Second, limiting the activity to marijuana possession and cultivation "in accor- dance with state law" cannot serve to place respondents' activities beyond congres- sional reach. The Supremacy Clause unambiguously provides that if there is any conflict between federal and state law, federal law shall prevail. It is beyond peradventure that federal power over commerce is " 'superior to that of the States to provide for the welfare or necessities of their inhabitants,' " however legitimate or dire those necessities may be. Just as state acquiescence to federal regulation cannot expand the bounds of the Commerce Clause, so too state action cannot circumscribe Congress' plenary commerce power.

Respondents acknowledge this proposition, but nonetheless contend that their activities were not "an essential part of a larger regulatory scheme" because they had been "isolated by the State of California, and [are] policed by the State of California," and thus remain "entirely separated from the market. " The notion that California law has surgically excised a discrete activity that is hermetically sealed off from the larger interstate marijuana market is a dubious proposition, and, more importantly, one that Congress could have rationally rejected.

Indeed, that the California exemptions will have a significant impact on both the supply and demand sides of the market for marijuana is not just "plausible" as the principal dissent concedes, it is readily apparent. The exemption for physicians provides them with an economic incentive to grant their patients permission to use the drug. In contrast to most prescriptions for legal drugs, which limit the dosage and duration of the usage, under California law the doctor's permission to recommend marijuana use is open-ended. The authority to grant permission whenever the doctor determines that a patient is afflicted with "any other illness for which marijuana provides relief, " is broad enough to allow even the most scrupulous doctor to conclude that some recreational uses would be therapeutic. And our cases have taught us that there are some unscrupulous physicians who overprescribe when it is sufficiently profitable to do so.

The exemption for cultivation by patients and caregivers can only increase the supply of marijuana in the California market. Congress could have rationally concluded that the aggregate impact on the national market of all the transactions exempted from federal supervision is unquestionably substantial.

V

We do note, however, the presence of another avenue of relief. [T]he statute authorizes procedures for the reclassification of Schedule I drugs. But perhaps even more important than these legal avenues is the democratic process, in which the voices of voters allied with these respondents may one day be heard in the halls of Congress. Under the present state of the law, however, the judgment of the Court of Appeals must be vacated.

NATIONAL FEDERATION OF INDEPENDENT BUSINESS, INC. v. SEBELIUS
132 S. Ct. 2566 (2012)

CHIEF JUSTICE ROBERTS announced the judgment of the Court and delivered the opinion of the Court with respect to Parts I, II, and III-C, in which Ginsburg, Breyer, Sotomayor, and Kagan, JJ., joined . . . .

. . . .

This case concerns two powers that the Constitution does grant the Federal Government, but which must be read carefully to avoid creating a general federal authority akin to the police power.

I

In 2010, Congress enacted the Patient Protection and Affordable Care Act, 124 Stat. 119. The Act aims to increase the number of Americans covered by health insurance and decrease the cost of health care . . . . This case concerns constitutional challenges to two key provisions, commonly referred to as the individual mandate and the Medicaid expansion.

The individual mandate requires most Americans to maintain "minimum essential" health insurance coverage. The mandate does not apply to some individuals, such as prisoners and undocumented aliens. Many individuals will receive the required coverage through their employer, or from a government program such as Medicaid or Medicare. But for individuals who are not exempt and do not receive health insurance through a third party, the means of satisfying the requirement is to purchase insurance from a private company.

. . . .

III. A.

. . . .

Given its expansive scope, it is no surprise that Congress has employed the commerce power in a wide variety of ways to address the pressing needs of the time. But Congress has never attempted to rely on that power to compel individuals not engaged in commerce to purchase an unwanted product . . . .

The Constitution grants Congress the power to "*regulate* Commerce." (emphasis added). The power to *regulate* commerce presupposes the existence of commercial activity to be regulated. If the power to "regulate" something included the power to create it, many of the provisions in the Constitution would be superfluous. For example, the Constitution gives Congress the power to "coin Money," in addition to the power to "regulate the Value thereof." And it gives Congress the power to "raise and support Armies" and to "provide and maintain a Navy," in addition to the power to "make Rules for the Government and Regulation of the land and naval Forces." If the power to regulate the armed forces or the value of money included the power to bring the subject of the regulation into existence, the specific grant of such powers would have been unnecessary. The language of the Constitution reflects the natural understanding that the power to regulate assumes there is already something to be regulated.

As expansive as our cases construing the scope of the commerce power have been, they all have one thing in common: They uniformly describe the power as reaching "activity." It is nearly impossible to avoid the word when quoting them . . . .

The individual mandate, however, does not regulate existing commercial activity. It instead compels individuals to *become* active in commerce by purchasing a product, on the ground that their failure to do so affects interstate commerce. Construing the Commerce Clause to permit Congress to regulate individuals precisely because they are doing nothing would open a new and potentially vast domain to congressional authority. Every day individuals do not do an infinite number of things. In some cases they decide not to do something; in others they simply fail to do it. Allowing Congress to justify federal regulation by pointing to the effect of inaction on commerce would bring countless decisions an individual could *potentially* make within the scope of federal regulation, and — under the Government's theory — empower Congress to make those decisions for him.

. . . .

Indeed, the Government's logic would justify a mandatory purchase to solve almost any problem. To consider a different example in the health care market, many Americans do not eat a balanced diet. That group makes up a larger percentage of the total population than those without health insurance. The failure of that group to have a healthy diet increases health care costs, to a greater extent than the failure of the uninsured to purchase insurance. Those increased costs are borne in part by other Americans who must pay more, just as the uninsured shift costs to the insured. Under the Government's theory, Congress could address the diet problem by ordering everyone to buy vegetables.

That is not the country the Framers of our Constitution envisioned. While Congress's authority under the Commerce Clause has of course expanded with the growth of the national economy, our cases have "always recognized that the power to regulate commerce, though broad indeed, has limits." The Government's theory would erode those limits, permitting Congress to reach beyond the natural extent of its authority, "everywhere extending the sphere of its activity and drawing all power into its impetuous vortex." Congress already enjoys vast power to regulate much of what we do. Accepting the Government's theory would give Congress the same license to regulate what we do not do, fundamentally changing the relation between the citizen and the Federal Government.

To an economist, perhaps, there is no difference between activity and inactivity; both have measurable economic effects on commerce. But the distinction between doing something and doing nothing would not have been lost on the Framers, who were "practical statesmen," not metaphysical philosophers. The Framers gave Congress the power to *regulate* commerce, not to *compel* it, and for over 200 years both our decisions and Congress's actions have reflected this understanding. There is no reason to depart from that understanding now.

. . . .

UNITED STATES v. GRAYDON EARL COMSTOCK, JR.
560 U.S. 126 (2010)

JUSTICE BREYER delivered the opinion of the Court.

A federal civil-commitment statute authorizes the Department of Justice to detain a mentally ill, sexually dangerous federal prisoner beyond the date the prisoner would otherwise be released. 18 U.S.C. § 4248 . . . .

I

The federal statute before us allows a district court to order the civil commitment of an individual who is currently " "in the custody of the [Federal] Bureau of Prisons," "§ 4248, if that individual (1) has previously "engaged or attempted to engage in sexually violent conduct or child molestation," (2) currently "suffers from a serious mental illness, abnormality, or disorder," and (3) "as a result of" that mental illness, abnormality, or disorder is "sexually dangerous to others," in that "he would have serious difficulty in refraining from sexually violent conduct or child molestation if released." §§ 4247(a)(5)-(6).

In order to detain such a person, the Government (acting through the Department of Justice) must certify to a federal district judge that the prisoner meets the conditions just described . . . . When such a certification is filed, the statute automatically stays the individual's release from prison, thereby giving the Government an opportunity to prove its claims at a hearing through psychiatric (or other) evidence. The statute provides that the prisoner " "shall be represented by counsel" and shall have "an opportunity" at the hearing "to testify, to present evidence, to subpoena witnesses on his behalf, and to confront and cross-examine" the Government's witnesses. §§ 4247(d), 4248(c).

If the Government proves its claims by "clear and convincing evidence," the court will order the prisoner's continued commitment in "the custody of the Attorney General," who must "make all reasonable efforts to cause" the State where that person was tried, or the State where he is domiciled, to "assume responsibility for his custody, care, and treatment." § 4248(d). If either State is willing to assume that responsibility, the Attorney General "shall release" the individual "to the appropriate official" of that State. § 4248(d). But if, "notwithstanding such efforts, neither such State will assume such responsibility," then "the Attorney General shall place the person for treatment in a suitable [federal] facility." *Ibid.*

Confinement in the federal facility will last until either (1) the person's mental condition improves to the point where he is no longer dangerous (with or without appropriate ongoing treatment), in which case he will be released; or (2) a State assumes responsibility for his custody, care, and treatment, in which case he will be transferred to the custody of that State. §§ 4248(d)(1)-(2) . . . .

In . . . 2006, the Government instituted proceedings in the Federal District Court for the Eastern District of North Carolina against the five respondents in this case. Three of the five had previously pleaded guilty in federal court to possession of child pornography, . . . and the fourth had pleaded guilty to sexual abuse of a minor, . . . [T]he fifth respondent, . . . was found mentally incompetent to stand trial.

[The five prisoners moved to dismiss the civil-commitment proceeding on constitutional grounds. . . . The Court of Appeals for the Fourth Circuit upheld the District Court's decision that], in enacting the statute, Congress exceeded its Article I legislative powers [without addressing other claims].

. . . .

II

The question presented is whether the Necessary and Proper Clause, Art. I, § 8, cl. 18, grants Congress authority sufficient to enact the statute before us . . . . [W]e conclude that the Constitution grants Congress legislative power sufficient to enact § 4248. We base this conclusion on five considerations, taken together.

First, the Necessary and Proper Clause grants Congress broad authority to enact federal legislation. Nearly 200 years ago, this Court stated that the Federal "[G]overnment is acknowledged by all to be one of enumerated powers," *McCulloch [v. Maryland]*, 17 U.S. 316, 4 Wheat. 316, at 405 (1819) . . . . But, at the same time, "a government, entrusted with such" powers "must also be entrusted with ample means for their execution." [*Id.*] Accordingly, the Necessary and Proper Clause makes clear that the Constitution's grants of specific federal legislative authority are accompanied by broad power to enact laws that are "convenient, or useful" or "conducive" to the authority's "beneficial exercise." . . . . Chief Justice Marshall emphasized that the word "necessary" "does not mean "absolutely necessary." *Id.* . . . . In language that has come to define the scope of the Necessary and Proper Clause, he wrote:

"Let the end be legitimate, let it be within the scope of the constitution, and all means which are appropriate, which are plainly adapted to that end, which are not prohibited, but consist with the letter and spirit of the constitution, are constitutional." *McCulloch, supra*, at 421, 17 U.S. 316.

We have since made clear that, in determining whether the Necessary and Proper Clause grants Congress the legislative authority to enact a particular federal statute, we look to see whether the statute constitutes a means that is rationally related to the implementation of a constitutionally enumerated power. *Sabri v. United States*, 541 U.S. 600, 605 (2004); . . . see *Gonzales v. Raich*, 545 U.S. 1, 22 (2005) . . . .

. . . .

Thus, the Constitution, which nowhere speaks explicitly about the creation of federal crimes beyond those related to "counterfeiting," " "treason," or "Piracies and Felonies committed on the high Seas" or "against the Law of Nations," Art. I, § 8, cls. 6, 10; Art. III, § 3, nonetheless grants Congress broad authority to create such crimes. . . . And Congress routinely exercises its authority to enact criminal laws in furtherance of, for example, its enumerated powers to regulate interstate and foreign commerce, to enforce civil rights, to spend funds for the general welfare, to establish federal courts, to establish post offices, to regulate bankruptcy, to regulate naturalization, and so forth. Art. I, § 8, cls. 1, 3, 4, 7, 9; Amdts. 13–15

. . . .

Similarly, Congress, in order to help ensure the enforcement of federal criminal laws enacted in furtherance of its enumerated powers, "can cause a prison to be erected at any place within the jurisdiction of the United States, and direct that all persons sentenced to imprisonment under the laws of the United States shall be confined there." *Ex parte Karstendick*, 93 U.S. 396, 400 (1876). Moreover, Congress, having established a prison system, can enact laws that seek to ensure that system's safe and responsible administration by, for example, requiring prisoners to receive medical care and educational training, . . . and can also ensure the safety of the prisoners, prison workers and visitors, and those in surrounding communities by, for example, creating further criminal laws governing entry, exit, and smuggling, and by employing prison guards to ensure discipline and security . . . .

Neither Congress' power to criminalize conduct, nor its power to imprison individuals who engage in that conduct, nor its power to enact laws governing prisons and prisoners, is explicitly mentioned in the Constitution. But Congress nonetheless possesses broad authority to do each of those things in the course of "carrying into Execution" the enumerated powers "vested by" the "Constitution in the Government of the United States," "Art. I, § 8, cl. 18 — authority granted by the Necessary and Proper Clause.

Second, the civil-commitment statute before us constitutes a modest addition to a set of federal prison-related mental-health statutes that have existed for many decades . . . .

Here, Congress has long been involved in the delivery of mental health care to federal prisoners, and has long provided for their civil commitment. In 1855 it established Saint Elizabeth's Hospital in the District of Columbia to provide treatment to "the insane of the army and navy . . . and of the District of Columbia." Act of Mar. 3, 1855, 10 Stat. 682; 39 Stat. 262. In 1857 it provided for confinement at Saint Elizabeth's of any person within the District of Columbia who had been "charged with [a] crime" and who was "insane" or later became "insane during the continuance of his or her sentence in the United States penitentiary. " Act of Feb. 7, 1857§§ 5–6, 11 Stat. 157. In 1874 . . . . Congress provided for civil commitment in federal facilities (or in state facilities if a State so agreed) of "*all* persons who have been or shall be convicted of any offense in any court of the United States" and who are or "shall become" insane "during the term of their imprisonment." . . . . And in 1882 Congress provided for similar commitment of those "*charged*" with federal offenses who become "insane" while in the "custody""of the United States. Act of Aug. 7, 1882 (emphasis added). Thus, over the span of three decades, Congress created a national, federal civil-commitment program under which any person who was either charged with or convicted of any federal offense in any federal court could be confined in a federal mental institution.

These statutes did not raise the question presented here, for they all provided that commitment in a federal hospital would end upon the completion of the relevant "terms" of federal "imprisonment" as set forth in the underlying criminal sentence or statute . . . . But in the mid-1940's that proviso was eliminated.

In 1945 the Judicial Conference of the United States proposed legislative reforms of the federal civil-commitment system. . . . [Its] committee studied . . . the "serious problem faced by the Bureau of Prisons, namely, what to do with insane criminals upon the expiration of their terms of confinement, where it would be dangerous to turn them loose upon society and where no state will assume responsibility for their custody." Judicial Conference, Report of Committee to Study Treatment Accorded by Federal Courts to Insane Persons Charged with Crime 11 (1945). [According to the federal Bureau of Prisons, States would not accept released federal prisoners who could be dangerous, because of their "lack of legal residence in any State." Congress modified its law to provide for the federal civil commitment of prisoners who were or became mentally incompetent before their federal prison sentence expired. Act of June 25, 1948, 62 Stat. 683, 18 U.S.C. §§ 4241–4243 (1952 ed.); Act of Sept. 7, 1949, 63 Stat. 686, 18 U.S.C. §§ 4244–4248. Congress further amended these statutes in 1984 to add the requirement that the prisoner's "release would create a substantial risk of bodily injury to another person or serious damage to the property of another." Insanity Defense Reform Act of 1984, 18 U.S.C. § 4246(d) (2006 ed.)]

. . . .

In 2006, Congress enacted the particular statute before us. It differs from earlier statutes in that it focuses directly upon persons who, due to a mental illness, are sexually dangerous. Notably, many of these individuals were likely already subject to civil commitment under § 4246, which, since 1949, has authorized the postsentence detention of federal prisoners who suffer from a mental illness and who are thereby dangerous (whether sexually or otherwise) . . . . In that respect, it is a modest addition to a longstanding federal statutory framework, which has been in place since 1855.

Third, Congress reasonably extended its longstanding civil-commitment system to cover mentally ill and sexually dangerous persons who are already in federal custody, even if doing so detains them beyond the termination of their criminal sentence. For one thing, the Federal Government is the custodian of its prisoners. As federal custodian, it has the constitutional power to act in order to protect nearby (and other) communities from the danger federal prisoners may pose . . . . If a federal prisoner is infected with a communicable disease that threatens others, surely it would be "necessary and proper" for the Federal Government to take action, pursuant to its role as federal custodian, to refuse (at least until the threat diminishes) to release that individual among the general public, where he might infect others (even if not threatening an interstate epidemic) . . . . And if confinement of such an individual is a "necessary and proper" "thing to do, then how could it not be similarly "necessary and proper" to confine an individual whose mental illness threatens others to the same degree?

Moreover, § 4248 is "reasonably adapted," . . . to Congress' power to act as a responsible federal custodian . . . . Congress could have reasonably concluded that federal inmates who suffer from a mental illness that causes them to "have serious difficulty in refraining from sexually violent conduct," would pose an especially high danger to the public if released. And Congress could also have reasonably concluded (as detailed in the Judicial Conference's report) that a reasonable number of such individuals would likely not be detained by the States if released from federal custody, in part because the Federal Government itself severed their claim to "legal residence in any State" by incarcerating them in remote federal prisons . . . . Here Congress' desire to address the specific challenges identified in the Reports cited above, taken together with its responsibilities as a federal custodian, supports the conclusion that § 4248 satisfies "review for means-end rationality," *i.e.*, that it satisfies the Constitution's insistence that a federal statute represent a rational means for implementing a constitutional grant of legislative authority . . . .

Fourth, the statute properly accounts for state interests. Respondents and the dissent contend that § 4248 violates the Tenth Amendment because it "invades the province of state sovereignty" in an area typically left to state control . . . . But the Tenth Amendment's text is clear: "The powers *not delegated to the United States* by the Constitution, nor prohibited by it to the States, are reserved to the States respectively, or to the people." (Emphasis added.) The powers "delegated to the United States by the Constitution" include those specifically enumerated powers listed in Article I along with the implementation authority granted by the Necessary and Proper Clause. Virtually by definition, these powers are not powers that the Constitution "reserved to the States." See New York, *supra*, at 156, 159 ("[I]f a power is delegated to Congress in the Constitution, the Tenth Amendment expressly disclaims any reservation of that power to the States . . . .") . . . .

Nor does this statute invade state sovereignty or otherwise improperly limit the scope of "powers that remain with the States." . . . To the contrary, it requires *accommodation* of state interests: The Attorney General must inform the State in which the federal prisoner "is domiciled or was tried" that he is detaining someone with respect to whom those States may wish to assert their authority, and he must encourage those States to assume custody of the individual. He must also immediately "release" that person "to the appropriate official of" either State "if such State will assume [such] responsibility." And either State has the right, at any time, to assert its authority over the individual, which will prompt the individual's immediate transfer to State custody. Respondents contend that the States are nonetheless "powerless to *prevent* the detention of their citizens under § 4248, even if detention is contrary to the States' policy choices." But that is not the most natural reading of the statute, and the Solicitor General acknowledges that "the Federal Government would have no appropriate role" with respect to an individual covered by the statute once "the transfer to State responsibility and State control has occurred."

. . . .

Fifth, the links between § 4248 and an enumerated Article I power are not too attenuated. Neither is the statutory provision too sweeping in its scope. Invoking the cautionary instruction that we may not "pile inference upon inference" in order to sustain congressional action under Article I, *Lopez,* 514 U.S., at 567, respondents argue that, when legislating pursuant to the Necessary and Proper Clause, Congress' authority can be no more than one step removed from a specifically enumerated power. But this argument is irreconcilable with our precedents . . . . In [*Greenwood v. United States*], we upheld the (likely indefinite) civil commitment of a mentally incompetent federal defendant who was accused of robbing a United States Post Office. 350 U.S., at 369, 375. The underlying enumerated Article I power was the power to "Establish Post Offices and Post Roads." Art. I, § 8, cl. 7. But, as Chief Justice Marshall recognized in *McCulloch,*

> "the power 'to establish post offices and post roads' . . . is executed by the single act of *making* the establishment . . . . [F]rom this has been inferred the power and duty of *carrying* the mail along the post road, from one post office to another. And, from this *implied* power, has *again* been inferred the right to *punish* those who steal letters from the post office, or rob the mail." 4 Wheat., at 417, 17 U.S. 316, 4 L. Ed. 579 (emphasis added).

And, as we have explained, from the implied power to punish we have further inferred both the power to imprison, and, in *Greenwood*, the federal civil-commitment power. Our necessary and proper jurisprudence contains multiple examples of similar reasoning. For example, in *Sabri* we observed that "Congress has authority under the Spending Clause to appropriate federal moneys" and that it therefore "has corresponding authority under the Necessary and Proper Clause to see to it that taxpayer dollars" are not "siphoned off" by "corrupt public officers. " We then further held that, in aid of that implied power to criminalize graft of "taxpayer dollars," Congress has the *additional* prophylactic power to criminalize bribes or kickbacks even when the stolen funds have not been "traceably skimmed from specific federal payments." . . . .

Indeed even the dissent acknowledges that Congress has the implied power to criminalize any conduct that might interfere with the exercise of an enumerated power, and also the additional power to imprison people who violate those (inferentially authorized) laws, and the additional power to provide for the safe and reasonable management of those prisons, and the additional power to regulate the prisoners' behavior even after their release . . . . And the same enumerated power that justifies the creation of a federal criminal statute, and that justifies the additional implied federal powers . . . , justifies civil commitment under § 4248 as well. Thus, we must reject respondents' argument that the Necessary and Proper Clause permits no more than a single step between an enumerated power and an Act of Congress.

Nor need we fear that our holding today confers on Congress a general "police power, which the Founders denied the National Government and reposed in the States. " *Morrison*, 529 U.S., at 618. [Section 4248] is narrow in scope. It has been applied to only a small fraction of federal prisoners . . . . (105 individuals have been subject to § 4248 out of over 188,000 federal inmates); . . .

. . . .

* * *

We take these five considerations together. They include: (1) the breadth of the Necessary and Proper Clause, (2) the long history of federal involvement in this arena, (3) the sound reasons for the statute's enactment in light of the Government's custodial interest in safeguarding the public from dangers posed by those in federal custody, (4) the statute's accommodation of state interests, and (5) the statute's narrow scope. Taken together, these considerations lead us to conclude that the statute is a "necessary and proper" means of exercising the federal authority that permits Congress to create federal criminal laws, to punish their violation, to imprison violators, to provide appropriately for those imprisoned, and to maintain the security of those who are not imprisoned but who may be affected by the federal imprisonment of others. The Constitution consequently authorizes Congress to enact the statute.

. . . .

The judgment of the Court of Appeals for the Fourth Circuit with respect to Congress' power to enact this statute is reversed, and the case is remanded for further proceedings consistent with this opinion.

It is so ordered.

Justices Kennedy and Alito filed concurring opinions. Justice Thomas filed a dissenting opinion, which Justice Scalia joined in part.

———

NOTES AND QUESTIONS

1. Federal regulation under the commerce clause. A glance through the United States Code reveals that Congress has created multiple federal agencies and regulatory systems for the purpose of protecting the health, safety and welfare of the country's population. The vast majority of these were created to "regulate commerce." One of the earliest federal initiatives was the Marine Hospital Service, created in 1798, which was ultimately transformed into the federal Public Health Service. Today, the federal government directly governs many sectors of public health and influences many others through federal funding, as discussed in Part D, *infra.*

2. Federal regulation of controlled substances. *Raich* is a good illustration of the primacy of federal laws where otherwise valid state and federal laws are in conflict. The individual patients [respondents in *Raich*] obtained their own marijuana in conformance with California's "Compassionate Use Act," a voter-approved initiative that permitted the individual use of marijuana for medical purposes recommended by a physician. (Note that the California law required only a physician's recommendation, not a formal prescription. The Controlled Substances Act precludes a physician from writing a prescription for a Schedule I drug.) Respondents argued that California's law offered sufficiently careful state regulation to escape ties to interstate commerce, because the law carved out a local, non-economic activity distinct from criminal drug use. However, the majority considers marijuana a fungible product, one that could be used in recreation or crime as well as patient care. They also do not exhibit much confidence in the state's ability to limit marijuana to medical uses. Moreover, if Congress did not have the power to reach medical marijuana use because it was *local*, then neither could it reach any other local use, including recreational use, whether regulated by the state or not.

JUSTICE O'CONNOR, dissenting, would require a factual analysis of the prohibited acts' actual effect on commerce, which she argues *Wickard* met and *Raich* did not, while the majority requires only a rational basis for Congress' assumption. Justice O'Connor writes:

> This case exemplifies the role of the States as laboratories. Today the Court sanctions an application of the federal [CSA] that extinguishes that experiment, without any proof that the personal cultivation, possession, and use of marijuana for medicinal purposes, if economic activity in the first place, has a substantial effect on inter-state commerce . . . .

545 U.S. at 35.

Perhaps acting as laboratories, more states have decriminalized marijuana since 2005. Federal prosecution, which remains lawful, depends primarily on prosecutorial discretion. Recent federal administrations did not give priority to prosecutions for medical marijuana. For more discussion of law and policies governing marijuana and other controlled substances, see Chapter 11, B. For a summary of the issues concerning potentially conflicting federal and state laws, federalism, and the Supremacy Clause, see Todd Garvey, *Medical Marijuana: The Supremacy Clause, Federalism, and the Interplay Between State and Federal Laws*, Congressional Research Service, R42398 (Nov. 9, 2012), http://fas.org/sgp/crs/misc/R42398.pdf (visited Mar. 2014).

3. ***NFIB v. Sebelius* and federalism.** *NFIB v. Sebelius* is one of the few Supreme Court decisions since 1937 in which a majority of the Justices find a federal statutory provision (the individual mandate) to be beyond the power of Congress under the Commerce Clause. Part III of Chief Justice Roberts' opinion addressing the Commerce Power, excerpted above, might be considered *dictum*, since the Affordable Care Act's individual mandate or minimum coverage requirement (whichever you prefer) was upheld as a constitutional exercise of the taxing power by five Justices. (The Court's preface to the decision does not describe any Justice's opinion as an "opinion of the Court" on the issue of the Commerce Power.) Whatever its precedential value, however, the Chief Justice's opinion makes clear his view that the power of Congress should be circumscribed so as not to replicate or overlap with the police powers of the States. Four dissenting Justices (Kennedy, Scalia, Thomas, and Alito) argued for limitations on the Commerce Power in even stronger language, suggesting that a majority of Justices were especially concerned to preserve a role for the States in regulating individual decisions. Are such views likely to dampen federal initiatives in the health arena, or is the federal horse out of the barn, so to speak?

Chief Justice Roberts' opinion drew a line in the sand — the Commerce Clause does not authorize Congress to require individuals to enter commerce. Somewhat surprisingly, however, his opinion did not further constrain Congress' power. It simply said that the Court would not recognize a larger scope for regulating commerce than the Court had approved in the past. Unless and until the Court revisits this issue, that leaves Congress ample authority.

4. **Limitations on the commerce power: *United States v. Lopez*.** Both *Raich* and *NFIB v. Sebelius* cite *United States v. Lopez*, 514 U.S. 549 (1995), which, when issued, was widely seen as an indication that a majority of Justices sought to rein in expanding federal regulation under the Commerce Clause. *Raich*, decided only five years later, therefore surprised many court observers.

The following excerpts from the Court's decision in *Lopez* indicate some limits on the definition of activities that affect interstate commerce:

> In the Gun-Free School Zones Act of 1990, Congress made it a federal offense "for any individual knowingly to possess a firearm at a place that the individual knows, or has reasonable cause to believe, is a school zone." 18 U.S.C. § 922 (q)(1)(A) (1988 ed., Supp. V). The Act neither regulates a commercial activity nor contains a requirement that the possession be connected in any way to interstate commerce . . . .

> . . . .

Section 922(q) is a criminal statute that by its terms has nothing to do with "commerce" or any sort of economic enterprise, however broadly one might define those terms. Section 922(q) is not an essential part of a larger regulation of economic activity, in which the regulatory scheme could be undercut unless the intrastate activity were regulated. It cannot, therefore, be sustained under our cases upholding regulations of activities that arise out of or are connected with a commercial transaction, which viewed in the aggregate, substantially affects interstate commerce . . . .

Second, § 922(q) contains no jurisdictional element which would ensure, through case-by-case inquiry, that the firearm possession in question affects interstate commerce . . . .

. . . .

. . . The Government argues that possession of a firearm in a school zone may result in violent crime and that violent crime can be expected to affect the functioning of the national economy in two ways. First, the costs of violent crime are substantial, and, through the mechanism of insurance, those costs are spread throughout the population. Second, violent crime reduces the willingness of individuals to travel to areas within the country that are perceived to be unsafe. The Government also argues that the presence of guns in schools poses a substantial threat to the educational process by threatening the learning environment. A handicapped educational process, in turn, will result in a less productive citizenry. That, in turn, would have an adverse effect on the Nation's economic well-being. As a result, the Government argues that Congress could rationally have concluded that § 922(q) substantially affects interstate commerce.

We pause to consider the implications of the Government's arguments. The Government admits, under its "costs of crime" reasoning, that Congress could regulate not only all violent crime, but all activities that might lead to violent crime, regardless of how tenuously they relate to interstate commerce. Similarly, under the Government's "national productivity" reasoning, Congress could regulate any activity that it found was related to the economic productivity of individual citizens: family law (including marriage, divorce, and child custody), for example. Under the theories that the Government presents in support of § 922(q), it is difficult to perceive any limitation on federal power, even in areas such as criminal law enforcement or education where States historically have been sovereign. Thus, if we were to accept the Government's arguments, we are hard-pressed to posit any activity by an individual that Congress is without power to regulate.

. . . .

. . . The possession of a gun in a local school zone is in no sense an economic activity that might, through repetition elsewhere, substantially affect any sort of interstate commerce. Respondent was a local student at a local school; there is no indication that he had recently moved in interstate commerce, and there is no requirement that his possession of the firearm have any concrete tie to interstate commerce.

To uphold the Government's contentions here, we would have to pile inference upon inference in a manner that would bid fair to convert congressional authority under the Commerce Clause to a general police power of the sort retained by the States. Admittedly, some of our prior cases have taken long steps down that road, giving great deference to congressional action. The broad language in these opinions has suggested the possibility of additional expansion, but we decline here to proceed any further. To do so would require us to conclude that the Constitution's enumeration of powers does not presuppose something not enumerated, and that there never will be a distinction between what is truly national and what is truly local. This we are unwilling to do.

. . . .

Both *Raich* and *Lopez* challenged the application of a federal criminal law to individuals within a locality (although *Raich* brought an "as applied" claim, while *Lopez* challenged the facial constitutionality of the statute). Can you identify distinguishing facts in *Raich* and *Lopez* that explain the different results in the two decisions? Could the fact that *Raich* concerned marijuana incline Justices whose views of federalism favored interpreting Congress' Article I powers more narrowly to favor a national scheme to restrict unlawful drug use?

5.   Preserving the states' police power. A key concern for a majority of the Justices in *Lopez* and *Sebelius* appeared to be preserving state jurisdiction over its own citizens. Consider the language concerning the police power in the opinions. Not long after *Lopez*, the Court struck down a provision of the Violence Against Women Act allowing victims of violence to bring suit in federal court. *United States v. Morrison*, 529 U.S. 598 (2000).

In *Sebelius*, Justice Ginsburg wrote a lengthy dissenting opinion (joined by Justices Breyer, Sotomayor and Kagan), arguing that the individual mandate was a necessary and proper addition to the ACA's comprehensive scheme of regulating health care financing. She compared the majority's view of Congress' power to that of the *Lochner* era:

> In the early twentieth century, this Court regularly struck down economic regulation enacted by the peoples' representatives in both the States and the Federal Government . . . . THE CHIEF JUSTICE's Commerce Clause opinion, and even more so the joint dissenters' reasoning, bear a disquieting resemblance to those long overruled decisions.

132 S.Ct. at 2628–9 (GINSBURG, J., dissenting).

What areas should remain the exclusive province of state regulation? The court mentions domestic relations, but Congress enacted the Defense of Marriage Act (DOMA), defining marriage for purposes of federal laws. The *Windsor* case, excerpted in Part B, *supra*, struck down a provision of DOMA. Did federalism issues influence the Court's decision in that case? The *Sebelius* court also mentioned violent crime as a subject reserved to the States' police power. Has Congress created any crimes of violence? Apart from formal recognition that Congress has no police power, what limits federal regulation of matters traditionally considered to be the subject of state jurisdiction?

6. Drugs and guns. The federal-state tension governing the use of marijuana also affects firearms. The federal Gun Control Act governing firearms (part of which was at issue in *United States v. Lopez*, Note 4, *supra*), prohibits anyone who is an "unlawful user of or addicted to any controlled substance" from transporting, receiving, or possessing firearms or ammunition. Marijuana remains a Schedule I controlled substance. Persons who use marijuana for medical purposes are deemed to be unlawful users under federal law, even if their use is lawful under state law. Therefore, according to a September 21, 2012 letter from the Department of Justice's Bureau of Alcohol, Tobacco, Firearms and Explosives to all federal firearms licensees, anyone who uses marijuana for medical purposes is forbidden from possessing firearms under federal law. For a discussion of laws governing firearms, see Chapter 12, C, *infra*.

7. Ernest Hemingway's cats. The Ernest Hemingway Home and Museum in Key West, Florida, found itself the subject of litigation under the Commerce Clause. *907 Whitehead Street v. Secretary of the U.S. Dep't of Agriculture*, 701 F. 3d 1345 (11th Cir. 2012). The Museum has been an attraction to admirers of not only the author's work, but also his cats. Between 40 and 50 descendants of Hemingway's polydactyl cat, Snowball, inhabit the house, cared for by Museum staff. (A polydactyl cat has an extra toe on some paws.) A U.S. Department of Agriculture (USDA) investigator, presumably acting upon a complaint, determined that the Museum was an animal "exhibitor" subject to regulation under the Animal Welfare Act (AWA), 7 U.S.C. § 2131 *et seq*. The Museum objected to AWA requirements, such as obtaining an exhibitor's license and caging each cat individually at night or constructing a fence higher than the existing brick wall surrounding the property. It sought a declaratory judgment that, *inter alia*, the Hemingway cats did not affect interstate commerce sufficiently to come within the constitutional scope of the AWA. Both the federal district court and the court of appeals disagreed.

The AWA defines an animal exhibitor as "any person (public or private) exhibiting any animals which were purchased in commerce or the *intended distribution of which affects commerce*, or will affect commerce, to the public for compensation, as determined by the Secretary." 7 U.S.C. § 2132(h)(emphasis added). The Museum charges for admission and tours, which includes seeing the cats, but does not allow the cats outside the Museum property in Key West. The federal court of appeals for the Eleventh Circuit noted that the AWA was intended to apply not only to traveling circuses and the like, but also to zoos, which are stationary and intrastate. It concluded that the USDA reasonably interpreted the term "distribution" (in the italicized statutory phrase above) to include a local display of cats for compensation (and was entitled to *Chevron* deference). The court concluded that the Museum "distributed" the cats by allowing visitors to see them, as well, perhaps, as by showing their photos on the Museum's website and in promotional materials. See www.hemingwayhome.com/.

On the question of Congress' constitutional authority to regulate such local displays, the Eleventh Circuit noted, "the Hemingway cats themselves are neither channels of interstate commerce nor things in interstate commerce." Nonetheless, the court found that the Museum's activities affected interstate commerce, citing both *Raich* and *NFIB v. Sebelius*, such that "Congress has the power to regulate the Museum and the exhibition of the Hemingway cats via the AWA." It explained:

> [I]t is well-settled that, when local businesses solicit out-of-state tourists, they engage in activity affecting interstate commerce . . . . The Museum invites and receives thousands of admission-paying visitors from beyond Florida, many of whom are drawn by the Museum's reputation for and purposeful marketing of the Hemingway cats. The exhibition of the Hemingway cats is integral to the Museum's commercial purpose, and thus, their exhibition affects interstate commerce.

The court expressed sympathy with the Museum's "unique situation" and its "frustration," but concluded, "it is not the court's role to evaluate the wisdom of federal regulations implemented according to the powers constitutionally vested in Congress."

8.   **What is necessary and proper?** *Comstock* reviews the importance of the Necessary and Proper Clause in implementing Congress' Article 1 powers. It also upholds federal power in an area — civil commitment — that has traditionally been believed to belong exclusively to the States. In a concurring opinion, Justice Kennedy said, "When the inquiry is whether a federal law has sufficient links to an enumerated power to be within the scope of federal authority, the analysis depends not on the number of links in the congressional-power chain but on the strength of the chain." How strong are the links in the chain described in Justice Breyer's opinion for the Court?

Note that the Court did not address the prisoners' claims that the federal civil commitment statute violated the Fifth Amendment to the Constitution: "We do not reach or decide any claim that the statute or its application denies equal protection of the laws, procedural or substantive due process, or any other rights guaranteed by the Constitution. Respondents are free to pursue those claims on remand, and any others they have preserved." The Court has considered some of those claims. See the discussion of *Kansas v. Hendricks* and later decisions in Chapter 5, B, Note 8, *infra*.

E.   FEDERAL REGULATION: THE POWER TO TAX AND SPEND

In the field of public health and health care, federal regulation is often achieved indirectly, by offering grants and other funding to states, localities, and private organizations — with strings attached. These strings — requirements or conditions that recipients must meet to qualify for funding — sometimes enable Congress to accomplish goals (through grant recipients) that are beyond the scope of its Article I enumerated powers. Some recipients depend so heavily on federal funding for their continued operation that they seem to regard conditions on funding as equivalent to direct federal regulation. This Section explores the question whether some conditions are beyond the power of Congress to impose. The following cases illustrate the variety of federal funding programs with conditions attached, as well as the Supreme Court's approach to evaluating Congress's power to impose conditions. As you read the cases below, consider the difference between conditions imposed on states and those imposed on private entities.

SOUTH DAKOTA v. DOLE
483 U.S. 203 (1987)

CHIEF JUSTICE REHNQUIST delivered the opinion of the Court.

. . . South Dakota permits persons 19 years of age or older to purchase beer containing up to 3.2% alcohol. S. D. Codified Laws § 35-6-27 (1986). In 1984 Congress enacted 23 U.S.C. § 158, which directs the Secretary of Transportation to withhold a percentage of federal highway funds otherwise allocable from States "in which the purchase or public possession . . . of any alcoholic beverage by a person who is less than twenty-one years of age is lawful." The State sued in United States District Court seeking a declaratory judgment that §158 violates the constitutional limitations on congressional exercise of the spending power and violates the Twenty-first Amendment to the United States Constitution. The District Court rejected the State's claims, and the Court of Appeals for the Eighth Circuit affirmed.

In this Court, the parties direct most of their efforts to defining the proper scope of the Twenty-first Amendment . . . . South Dakota asserts that the setting of minimum drinking ages is clearly within the "core powers" reserved to the States under § 2 of the Amendment . . . . [H]owever, we need not decide in this case whether that Amendment would prohibit an attempt by Congress to legislate directly a national minimum drinking age. Here, Congress has acted indirectly under its spending power to encourage uniformity in the States' drinking ages . . . . [W]e find this legislative effort within constitutional bounds even if Congress may not regulate drinking ages directly.

The Constitution empowers Congress to "lay and collect Taxes, Duties, Imposts, and Excises, to pay the Debts and provide for the common Defence and general Welfare of the United States." Art. I, § 8, cl.1. Incident to this power, Congress may attach conditions on the receipt of federal funds, and has repeatedly employed the power "to further broad policy objectives by conditioning receipt of federal moneys upon compliance by the recipient with federal statutory and administrative directives." . . . . The breadth of this power was made clear in *United States v. Butler*, 297 U.S. 1, 66 (1936), where the Court, resolving a longstanding debate over the scope of the Spending Clause, determined that "the power of Congress to authorize expenditure of public moneys for public purposes is not limited by the direct grants of legislative power found in the Constitution." Thus, objectives not thought to be within Article I's "enumerated legislative fields," may nevertheless be attained through the use of the spending power and the conditional grant of federal funds.

The spending power is of course not unlimited, but is instead subject to several general restrictions articulated in our cases. The first of these limitations is derived from the language of the Constitution itself: the exercise of the spending power must be in pursuit of "the general welfare." In considering whether a particular expenditure is intended to serve general public purposes, courts should defer substantially to the judgment of Congress. Second, we have required that if Congress desires to condition the States' receipt of federal funds, it "must do so unambiguously . . . , enabl[ing] the States to exercise their choice knowingly, cognizant of the consequences of their participation." Third, our cases have suggested (without significant elaboration) that conditions on federal grants might be illegitimate if they are unrelated "to the federal interest in particular national projects or programs." . . . . Finally, we have noted that other constitutional provisions may provide an independent bar to the conditional grant of federal funds.

We can readily conclude that the provision is designed to serve the general welfare, especially in light of the fact that "the concept of welfare or the opposite is shaped by Congress . . . ." Congress found that the differing drinking ages in the States created particular incentives for young persons to combine their desire to drink with their ability to drive, and that this interstate problem required a national solution. The means it chose to address this dangerous situation were reasonably calculated to advance the general welfare. The conditions upon which States receive the funds, moreover, could not be more clearly stated by Congress. And the State itself, rather than challenging the germaneness of the condition to federal purposes, admits that it "has never contended that the congressional action was . . . unrelated to a national concern in the absence of the Twenty-first Amendment." Indeed, the condition imposed by Congress is directly related to one of the main purposes for which highway funds are expended — safe interstate travel. This goal of the interstate highway system had been frustrated by varying drinking ages among the States. A Presidential commission appointed to study alcohol-related accidents and fatalities on the Nation's highways concluded that the lack of uniformity in the States' drinking ages created "an incentive to drink and drive" because "young persons commut[e] to border States where the drinking age is lower." By enacting §158, Congress conditioned the receipt of federal funds in a way reasonably calculated to address this particular impediment to a purpose for which the funds are expended.

The remaining question about the validity of § 158 — and the basic point of disagreement between the parties — is whether the Twenty-first Amendment constitutes an "independent constitutional bar" to the conditional grant of federal funds. Petitioner, relying on its view that the Twenty-first Amendment prohibits direct regulation of drinking ages by Congress, asserts that "Congress may not use the spending power to regulate that which it is prohibited from regulating directly under the Twenty-first Amendment." But our cases show that this "independent constitutional bar" limitation on the spending power is not of the kind petitioner suggests . . . .

. . . .

. . . Instead, we think that the language in our earlier opinions stands for the unexceptionable proposition that the power may not be used to induce the States to engage in activities that would themselves be unconstitutional. Thus, for example, a grant of federal funds conditioned on invidiously discriminatory state action or the infliction of cruel and unusual punishment would be an illegitimate exercise of the Congress' broad spending power. But no such claim can be or is made here. Were South Dakota to succumb to the blandishments offered by Congress and raise its drinking age to 21, the State's action in so doing would not violate the constitutional rights of anyone.

Our decisions have recognized that in some circumstances the financial inducement offered by Congress might be so coercive as to pass the point at which "pressure turns into compulsion." Here, however, Congress has directed only that a State desiring to establish a minimum drinking age lower than 21 lose a relatively small percentage of certain federal highway funds. Petitioner contends that the coercive nature of this program is evident from the degree of success it has achieved. We cannot conclude, however, that a conditional grant of federal money of this sort is unconstitutional simply by reason of its success in achieving the congressional objective.

When we consider, for a moment, that all South Dakota would lose if she adheres to her chosen course as to a suitable minimum drinking age is 5% of the funds otherwise obtainable under specified highway grant programs, the argument as to coercion is shown to be more rhetoric than fact . . . .

. . . .

Here Congress has offered relatively mild encouragement to the States to enact higher minimum drinking ages than they would otherwise choose. But the enactment of such laws remains the prerogative of the States not merely in theory but in fact. Even if Congress might lack the power to impose a national minimum drinking age directly, we conclude that encouragement to state action found in §158 is a valid use of the spending power. Accordingly, the judgment of the Court of Appeals is

Affirmed.

NATIONAL FEDERATION OF INDEPENDENT BUSINESS, INC. v. SEBELIUS
132 S. Ct. 2566 (2012)

CHIEF JUSTICE ROBERTS delivered . . . an opinion with respect to Part IV.

. . . .

IV

A

The States also contend that the Medicaid expansion exceeds Congress's authority under the Spending Clause. They claim that Congress is coercing the

States to adopt the changes it wants by threatening to withhold all of a State's Medicaid grants, unless the State accepts the new expanded funding and complies with the conditions that come with it. This, they argue, violates the basic principle that the "Federal Government may not compel the States to enact or administer a federal regulatory program." [citing *New York v. United States*, 505 U.S. 144, 188 (1992)]

There is no doubt that the Act dramatically increases state obligations under Medicaid. The current Medicaid program requires States to cover only certain discrete categories of needy individuals — pregnant women, children, needy families, the blind, the elderly, and the disabled. 42 U.S.C. § 1396a(a)(10). There is no mandatory coverage for most childless adults, and the States typically do not offer any such coverage. The States also enjoy considerable flexibility with respect to the coverage levels for parents of needy families. § 1396a(a)(10)(A)(ii). On average States cover only those unemployed parents who make less than 37 percent of the federal poverty level, and only those employed parents who make less than 63 percent of the poverty line.

The Medicaid provisions of the Affordable Care Act, in contrast, require States to expand their Medicaid programs by 2014 to cover all individuals under the age of 65 with incomes below 133 percent of the federal poverty line. §1396a(a)(10)(A)(i)(VIII). The Act also establishes a new "[e]ssential health benefits" package, which States must provide to all new Medicaid recipients — a level sufficient to satisfy a recipient's obligations under the individual mandate. §§ 1396a(k)(1), 1396u–7(b)(5), 18022(b). The Affordable Care Act provides that the Federal Government will pay 100 percent of the costs of covering these newly eligible individuals through 2016. § 1396d(y)(1). In the following years, the federal payment level gradually decreases, to a minimum of 90 percent. *Ibid.* In light of the expansion in coverage mandated by the Act, the Federal Government estimates that its Medicaid spending will increase by approximately $100 billion per year, nearly 40 percent above current levels.

. . . .

. . . "We have repeatedly characterized . . . Spending Clause legislation as 'much in the nature of a contract.' " [citations omitted] The legitimacy of Congress's exercise of the spending power "thus rests on whether the State voluntarily and knowingly accepts the terms of the 'contract.' " Respecting this limitation is critical to ensuring that Spending Clause legislation does not undermine the status of the States as independent sovereigns in our federal system. That system "rests on what might at first seem a counterintuitive insight, that 'freedom is enhanced by the creation of two governments, not one.' " [citations omitted] For this reason, "the Constitution has never been understood to confer upon Congress the ability to require the States to govern according to Congress' instructions." Otherwise the two-government system established by the Framers would give way to a system that vests power in one central government, and individual liberty would suffer.

That insight has led this Court to strike down federal legislation that commandeers a State's legislative or administrative apparatus for federal purposes. [citing, *e.g.*, *Printz v. United States*, 521 U.S. 898, 933 (1997) (striking down federal legislation compelling state law enforcement officers to perform federally mandated background checks on handgun purchasers); *New York, supra,* at 174–175 (invalidating provisions of an Act that would compel a State to either take title to nuclear waste or enact particular state waste regulations) . . . .

. . . .

. . . In the typical case we look to the States to defend their prerogatives by adopting "the simple expedient of not yielding" to federal blandishments when they do not want to embrace the federal policies as their own . . . . The States are separate and independent sovereigns. Sometimes they have to act like it.

. . . .

In this case, the financial "inducement" Congress has chosen is much more than "relatively mild encouragement" — it is a gun to the head. Section 1396c of the Medicaid Act provides that if a State's Medicaid plan does not comply with the Act's requirements, the Secretary of Health and Human Services may declare that "further payments will not be made to the State." 42 U.S.C. § 1396c . A State that opts out of the Affordable Care Act's expansion in health care coverage thus stands to lose not merely "a relatively small percentage" of its existing Medicaid funding, but all of it. [citing *Dole*]. Medicaid spending accounts for over 20 percent of the average State's total budget, with federal funds covering 50 to 83 percent of those costs . . . . It is easy to see how the *Dole* Court could conclude that the threatened loss of less than half of one percent of South Dakota's budget left that State with a "prerogative" to reject Congress's desired policy, "not merely in theory but in fact." . . . . The threatened loss of over 10 percent of a State's overall budget, in contrast, is economic dragooning that leaves the States with no real option but to acquiesce in the Medicaid expansion.

Justice GINSBURG claims that *Dole* is distinguishable because here "Congress has not threatened to withhold funds earmarked for any other program." But that begs the question: The States contend that the expansion is in reality a new program and that Congress is forcing them to accept it by threatening the funds for the existing Medicaid program. We cannot agree that existing Medicaid and the expansion dictated by the Affordable Care Act are all one program simply because "Congress styled" them as such. If the expansion is not properly viewed as a modification of the existing Medicaid program, Congress's decision to so title it is irrelevant.

Here, the Government claims that the Medicaid expansion is properly viewed merely as a modification of the existing program because the States agreed that Congress could change the terms of Medicaid when they signed on in the first place. The Government observes that the Social Security Act, which includes the original Medicaid provisions, contains a clause expressly reserving "[t]he right to alter, amend, or repeal any provision" of that statute. 42 U.S.C. § 1304. So it does . . . .

The Medicaid expansion, however, accomplishes a shift in kind, not merely degree. The original program was designed to cover medical services for four particular categories of the needy: the disabled, the blind, the elderly, and needy families with dependent children . . . . Previous amendments to Medicaid eligibility merely altered and expanded the boundaries of these categories. Under the Affordable Care Act, Medicaid is transformed into a program to meet the health care needs of the entire nonelderly population with income below 133 percent of the poverty level. It is no longer a program to care for the neediest among us, but rather an element of a comprehensive national plan to provide universal health insurance coverage.

Indeed, the manner in which the expansion is structured indicates that while Congress may have styled the expansion a mere alteration of existing Medicaid, it recognized it was enlisting the States in a new health care program . . . .

. . . As we have explained, "[t]hough Congress' power to legislate under the spending power is broad, it does not include surprising participating States with post-acceptance or 'retroactive' conditions." . . . . A State could hardly anticipate that Congress's reservation of the right to "alter" or "amend" the Medicaid program included the power to transform it so dramatically.

. . . .

B

Nothing in our opinion precludes Congress from offering funds under the Affordable Care Act to expand the availability of health care, and requiring that States accepting such funds comply with the conditions on their use. What Congress is not free to do is to penalize States that choose not to participate in that new program by taking away their existing Medicaid funding. Section 1396c gives the Secretary of Health and Human Services the authority to do just that. It allows her to withhold all "further [Medicaid] payments . . . to the State" if she determines that the State is out of compliance with any Medicaid requirement, including those contained in the expansion. 42 U.S.C. § 1396c. In light of the Court's holding, the Secretary cannot apply § 1396c to withdraw existing Medicaid funds for failure to comply with the requirements set out in the expansion.

. . . .

. . . The remedy for that constitutional violation is to preclude the Federal Government from imposing such a sanction. That remedy does not require striking down other portions of the Affordable Care Act.

RUST v. SULLIVAN
500 U.S. 173 (1991)

CHIEF JUSTICE REHNQUIST delivered the opinion of the Court.

. . . .

In 1970, Congress enacted Title X of the Public Health Service Act (Act), as amended, 42 U.S.C. §§ 300 to 300a-6, which provides federal funding for family-planning services. The Act authorizes the Secretary to "make grants to and enter into contracts with public or nonprofit private entities to assist in the establishment and operation of voluntary family planning projects which shall offer a broad range of acceptable and effective family planning methods and services." § 300(a). Grants and contracts under Title X must "be made in accordance with such regulations as the Secretary may promulgate." § 300a-4(a). Section 1008 of the Act, however, provides that "none of the funds appropriated under this subchapter shall be used in programs where abortion is a method of family planning." 42 U. S. C. § 300a-6 . . . .

In 1988, the Secretary [of Health and Human Services] promulgated new regulations designed to provide " 'clear and operational guidance' to grantees about how to preserve the distinction between Title X programs and abortion as a method of family planning." 53 Fed. Reg. 2923–2924 (1988). The regulations clarify, through the definition of the term "family planning," that Congress intended Title X funds "to be used only to support *preventive* family planning services." . . . .

The regulations attach three principal conditions on the grant of federal funds for Title X projects. First, the regulations specify that a "Title X project may not provide counseling concerning the use of abortion as a method of family planning or provide referral for abortion as a method of family planning." 42 CFR § 59.8(a)(1) (1989) . . . . Title X projects must refer every pregnant client "for appropriate prenatal and/or social services by furnishing a list of available providers that promote the welfare of mother and unborn child." *Id.* . . . The Title X project is expressly prohibited from referring a pregnant woman to an abortion provider, even upon specific request.

Second, the regulations broadly prohibit a Title X project from engaging in activities that "encourage, promote or advocate abortion as a method of family planning." " . . . .

Third, the regulations require that Title X projects be organized so that they are "physically and financially separate" "from prohibited abortion activities . . . .

Petitioners are Title X grantees and doctors who supervise Title X funds suing on behalf of themselves and their patients. Respondent is the Secretary of HHS . . . .

[The Court first found that the text and legislative history of Section 1008 of the Act, prohibiting funding abortion as a method of family planning, was ambiguous and that HHS's interpretation of that section as forbidding funding for counseling, referral, and advocacy for abortion was reasonable.]

. . . .

Petitioners contend that the regulations violate the First Amendment by impermissibly discriminating based on viewpoint because they prohibit "all discussion about abortion as a lawful option — including counseling, referral, and the provision of neutral and accurate information about ending a pregnancy — while compelling the clinic or counselor to provide information that promotes continuing a pregnancy to term." . . . .

There is no question but that the statutory prohibition contained in § 1008 is constitutional. In *Maher v. Roe*, 432 U.S. 464 (1977), we upheld a state welfare regulation under which Medicaid recipients received payments for services related to childbirth, but not for nontherapeutic abortions. The Court rejected the claim that this unequal subsidization worked a violation of the Constitution. We held that the government may "make a value judgment favoring childbirth over abortion, and . . . implement that judgment by the allocation of public funds." Here the Government is exercising the authority it possesses under *Maher* and *Harris v. McRae*, 448 U.S. 297 (1980), to subsidize family planning services which will lead to conception and childbirth, and declining to "promote or encourage abortion." The Government can, without violating the Constitution, selectively fund a program to encourage certain activities it believes to be in the public interest, without at the same time funding an alternative program which seeks to deal with the problem in another way. In so doing, the Government has not discriminated on the basis of viewpoint; it has merely chosen to fund one activity to the exclusion of the other. "[A] legislature's decision not to subsidize the exercise of a fundamental right does not infringe the right." . . . .

. . . This is not a case of the Government "suppressing a dangerous idea," but of a prohibition on a project grantee or its employees from engaging in activities outside of the project's scope.

. . . .

. . . The Secretary's regulations do not force the Title X grantee to give up abortion-related speech; they merely require that the grantee keep such activities separate and distinct from Title X activities . . . . The regulations govern the scope of the Title X *project's* activities, and leave the grantee unfettered in its other activities. The Title X *grantee* can continue to perform abortions, provide abortion-related services, and engage in abortion advocacy; it simply is required to conduct those activities through programs that are separate and independent from the project that receives Title X funds.

In contrast, our "unconstitutional conditions" cases involve situations in which the Government has placed a condition on the *recipient* of the subsidy rather than on a particular program or service, thus effectively prohibiting the recipient from engaging in the protected conduct outside the scope of the federally funded program . . . .

. . . .

. . . The [Title X grantee] employees remain free . . . to pursue abortion-related activities when they are not acting under the auspices of the Title X project. The regulations, which govern solely the scope of the Title X project's activities, do not in any way restrict the activities of those persons acting as private individuals. The employees' freedom of expression is limited during the time that they actually work for the project; but this limitation is a consequence of their decision to accept employment in a project, the scope of which is permissibly restricted by the funding authority.

. . . .

We turn now to petitioners' argument that the regulations violate a woman's Fifth Amendment right to choose whether to terminate her pregnancy. We recently reaffirmed the long-recognized principle that "'the Due Process Clauses generally confer no affirmative right to governmental aid, even where such aid may be necessary to secure life, liberty, or property interests of which the government itself may not deprive the individual.'} *Webster*, 492 U.S. at 507, quoting *DeShaney v. Winnebago County Dept. of Social Services*, 489 U.S. 189 (1989). The Government has no constitutional duty to subsidize an activity merely because the activity is constitutionally protected . . . .

. . . The difficulty that a woman encounters when a Title X project does not provide abortion counseling or referral leaves her in no different position than she would have been if the Government had not enacted Title X.

. . . .

Petitioners also argue that by impermissibly infringing on the doctor-patient relationship and depriving a Title X client of information concerning abortion as a method of family planning, the regulations violate a woman's Fifth Amendment right to medical self-determination and to make informed medical decisions free of government-imposed harm . . . .

In *Akron* [*v. Akron Center for Reproductive Health, Inc.*, 462 U.S. 416 (1983)], we invalidated a city ordinance requiring *all* physicians to make specified statements to the patient prior to performing an abortion in order to ensure that the woman's consent was "truly informed." Similarly, in *Thornburgh* [*v. American College of Obstetricians and Gynecologists*, 476 U.S. 747 (1986),] we struck down a state statute mandating that a list of agencies offering alternatives to abortion and a description of fetal development be provided to every woman considering terminating her pregnancy through an abortion. Critical to our decisions in *Akron* and *Thornburgh* to invalidate a governmental intrusion into the patient-doctor dialogue was the fact that the laws in both cases required *all* doctors within their respective jurisdictions to provide *all* pregnant patients contemplating an abortion a litany of information, regardless of whether the patient sought the information or whether the doctor thought the information necessary to the patient's decision. Under the Secretary's regulations, however, a doctor's ability to provide, and a woman's right to receive, information concerning abortion and abortion-related services outside the context of the Title X project remains unfettered. It would undoubtedly be easier for a woman seeking an abortion if she could receive information about abortion from a Title X project, but the Constitution does not require that the Government distort the scope of its mandated program in order to provide that information.

Petitioners contend, however, that most Title X clients are effectively precluded by indigency and poverty from seeing a health-care provider who will provide abortion-related services. But once again, even these Title X clients are in no worse position than if Congress had never enacted Title X. "The financial constraints that restrict an indigent woman's ability to enjoy the full range of constitutionally protected freedom of choice are the product not of governmental restrictions on access to abortion, but rather of her indigency." *McRae, supra,* at 316.

The Secretary's regulations are a permissible construction of Title X and do not violate either the First or Fifth Amendments to the Constitution.

UNITED STATES AGENCY FOR INTERNATIONAL DEVELOPMENT v. ALLIANCE FOR OPEN SOCIETY INTERNATIONAL, INC.

133 S.Ct. 2321 (2013)

CHIEF JUSTICE ROBERTS delivered the opinion of the Court.

The United States Leadership Against HIV/AIDS, Tuberculosis, and Malaria Act of 2003 (Leadership Act), 22 U. S. C. § 7601 et seq., outlined a comprehensive strategy to combat the spread of HIV/AIDS around the world. As part of that strategy, Congress authorized the appropriation of billions of dollars to fund efforts by nongovernmental organizations to assist in the fight. The Act imposes two related conditions on that funding: First, no funds made available by the Act "may be used to promote or advocate the legalization or practice of prostitution or sex trafficking." § 7631(e). And second, no funds may be used by an organization "that does not have a policy explicitly opposing prostitution and sex trafficking." § 7631(f). This case concerns the second of these conditions, referred to as the Policy Requirement. The question is whether that funding condition violates a recipient's First Amendment rights.

. . . .

. . . Congress found that the "sex industry, the trafficking of individuals into such industry, and sexual violence" were factors in the spread of the HIV/AIDS epidemic, and determined that "it should be the policy of the United States to eradicate" prostitution and "other sexual victimization."

. . . .

The Department of Health and Human Services (HHS) and the United States Agency for International Development (USAID) are the federal agencies primarily responsible for overseeing implementation of the Leadership Act. To enforce the Policy Requirement, the agencies have directed that the recipient of any funding under the Act agree in the award document that it is opposed to "prostitution and sex trafficking because of the psychological and physical risks they pose for women, men, and children." 45 CFR §89.1(b) (2012) . . . .

Respondents are a group of domestic organizations engaged in combating HIV/AIDS overseas . . . . Respondents fear that adopting a policy explicitly opposing prostitution may alienate certain host governments, and may diminish the effectiveness of some of their programs by making it more difficult to work with prostitutes in the fight against HIV/AIDS. They are also concerned that the Policy Requirement may require them to censor their privately funded discussions in publications, at conferences, and in other forums about how best to prevent the spread of HIV/AIDS among prostitutes.

. . . .

III.

The Policy Requirement mandates that recipients of Leadership Act funds explicitly agree with the Government's policy to oppose prostitution and sex trafficking. It is, however, a basic First Amendment principle that "freedom of speech prohibits the government from telling people what they must say." *Rumsfeld v. Forum for Academic and Institutional Rights, Inc.*, 547 U. S. 47, 61 (2006) . . . . Were it enacted as a direct regulation of speech, the Policy Requirement would plainly violate the First Amendment. The question is whether the Government may nonetheless impose that requirement as a condition on the receipt of federal funds.

As a general matter, if a party objects to a condition on the receipt of federal funding, its recourse is to decline the funds. This remains true when the objection is that a condition may affect the recipient's exercise of its First Amendment rights. See, e.g., *United States v. American Library Assn., Inc.*, 539 U. S. 194, 212 (2003) (plurality opinion) (rejecting a claim by public libraries that conditioning funds for Internet access on the libraries' installing filtering software violated their First Amendment rights, explaining that "[t]o the extent that libraries wish to offer unfiltered access, they are free to do so without federal assistance") ; . . . .

At the same time, however, we have held that the Government " 'may not deny a benefit to a person on a basis that infringes his constitutionally protected . . . freedom of speech even if he has no entitlement to that benefit.' " *Forum for Academic and Institutional Rights*, *supra*, at 59 (quoting *American Library Assn.*, *supra*, at 210).

The dissent thinks that can only be true when the condition is not relevant to the objectives of the program (although it has its doubts about that), or when the condition is actually coercive, in the sense of an offer that cannot be refused. See post, at 2–3 (opinion of SCALIA, J.). Our precedents, however, are not so limited. In the present context, the relevant distinction that has emerged from our cases is between conditions that define the limits of the government spending program — those that specify the activities Congress wants to subsidize — and conditions that seek to leverage funding to regulate speech outside the contours of the program itself. The line is hardly clear, in part because the definition of a particular program can always be manipulated to subsume the challenged condition. We have held, however, that "Congress cannot recast a condition on funding as a mere definition of its program in every case, lest the First Amendment be reduced to a simple semantic exercise." *Legal Services Corporation v. Velazquez*, 531 U. S. 533, 547 (2001).

. . . In *Rust* [*v. Sullivan*], we considered Title X of the Public Health Service Act, a Spending Clause program that issued grants to nonprofit health-care organizations "to assist in the establishment and operation of voluntary family planning projects [to] offer a broad range of acceptable and effective family planning methods and services." The organizations received funds from a variety of sources other than the Federal Government for a variety of purposes. The Act, however, prohibited the Title X federal funds from being "used in programs where abortion is a method of family planning." To enforce this provision, HHS regulations barred Title X projects from advocating abortion as a method of family planning, and required grantees to ensure that their Title X projects were " 'physically and financially separate'" from their other projects that engaged in the prohibited activities. A group of Title X funding recipients brought suit, claiming the regulations imposed an unconstitutional condition on their First Amendment rights. We rejected claim.

We explained that Congress can, without offending the Constitution, selectively fund certain programs to address an issue of public concern, without funding alternative ways of addressing the same problem. In Title X, Congress had defined the federal program to encourage only particular family planning methods. The challenged regulations were simply "designed to ensure that the limits of the federal program are observed," and "that public funds [are] spent for the purposes for which they were authorized."

In making this determination, the Court stressed that "Title X expressly distinguishes between a Title X grantee and a Title X project." The regulations governed only the scope of the grantee's Title X projects, leaving it "unfettered in its other activities." "The Title X grantee can continue to . . . engage in abortion advocacy; it simply is required to conduct those activities through programs that are separate and independent from the project that receives Title X funds." Because the regulations did not "prohibit the recipient from engaging in the protected conduct outside the scope of the federally funded program," they did not run afoul of the First Amendment.

As noted, the distinction drawn in these cases — between conditions that define the federal program and those that reach outside it — is not always self-evident . . . . Here, however, we are confident that the Policy Requirement falls on the unconstitutional side of the line.

The dissent views the Requirement as simply a selection criterion by which the Government identifies organizations "who believe in its ideas to carry them to fruition." As an initial matter, whatever purpose the Policy Requirement serves in selecting funding recipients, its effects go beyond selection. The Policy Requirement is an ongoing condition on recipients' speech and activities, a ground for terminating a grant after selection is complete. In any event, as the Government acknowledges, it is not simply seeking organizations that oppose prostitution. Rather, it explains, "Congress has expressed its purpose 'to eradicate' prostitution and sex trafficking, and it wants recipients to adopt a similar stance." This case is not about the Government's ability to enlist the assistance of those with whom it already agrees. It is about compelling a grant recipient to adopt a particular belief as a condition of funding.

By demanding that funding recipients adopt — as their own — the Government's view on an issue of public concern, the condition by its very nature affects "protected conduct outside the scope of the federally funded program." A recipient cannot avow the belief dictated by the Policy Requirement when spending Leadership Act funds, and then turn around and assert a contrary belief, or claim neutrality, when participating in activities on its own time and dime. By requiring recipients to profess a specific belief, the Policy Requirement goes beyond defining the limits of the federally funded program to defining the recipient. See [*Rust*, 500 U. S., at 197] ("our 'unconstitutional conditions' cases involve situations in which the Government has placed a condition on the recipient of the subsidy rather than on a particular program or service, thus effectively prohibiting the recipient from engaging in the protected conduct outside the scope of the federally funded program").

The Policy Requirement compels as a condition of federal funding the affirmation of a belief that by its nature cannot be confined within the scope of the Government program. In so doing, it violates the First Amendment and cannot be sustained.

Justice Scalia dissented, joined by Justice Thomas. Justice Kagan took no part in consideration or decision of this case.

NOTES AND QUESTIONS

1. *Dole's* **4-part test.** In *Dole*, the Court summarized "restrictions" on Congress's permissible exercise of the Spending Power. (These are often referred to as Dole's principles or 4-pronged test.) Consider how easy or hard it might be to satisfy each prong.

The first prong — that the exercise of the Spending Power itself must be for the general welfare, and not for a single state or favored group — is straightforward, especially since courts tend to defer to Congress's judgment of what counts as a general public purpose. This is really a threshold test of a valid exercise of the Spending Power. It goes to the purpose of the legislation that authorizes *spending* federal monies in the first place, and not any conditions on *receiving* the monies. Nonetheless, the Court discussed whether the condition itself served the general welfare.

The second prong — that the condition imposed on receiving federal monies be unambiguous — is similarly straightforward. Recipients should not have to guess at what they must do to qualify for funding.

It is the third prong that often raises questions. The conditions on receipt of federal grants must be related "to the federal interest in particular national projects or programs." What is the national project or program in *Dole*? It cannot be the requirement that states have minimum drinking age laws, because that is merely the condition on funding. (Moreover, the Court questioned, but did not decide, whether the Twenty-first Amendment allowed Congress to directly regulate alcohol within the states.) Rather, the national program must be the programs for which the money is spent. In this case, the spending statute authorized the Secretary to allocate federal funds to the states to build highways. The National Minimum Drinking Age Amendment, 23 U. S. C. § 158 (1982 ed., Supp. III), added the condition to the allocation of funds. How does the Court relate the drinking age condition to building and maintaining highways?

Justice Sandra Day O'Connor dissented in *Dole*, arguing that the majority had misapplied the third factor. She did not question the goal of safe interstate travel, but reasoned that if the condition is intended to deter drunk driving, it was both over-inclusive and under-inclusive, and therefore not adequately related to highway construction or maintenance:

"It is over-inclusive because it stops teenagers from drinking even when they are not about to drive on interstate highways. It is under-inclusive because teenagers pose only a small part of the drunken driving problem in this Nation. See, *e.g.*, 130 Cong. Rec. 18648 (1984) (remarks of Sen. Humphrey) ("Eighty-four percent of all highway fatalities involving alcohol occur among those whose ages exceed 21"); . . . *ibid.* (remarks of Sen. Symms) ("Most of the studies point out that the drivers of age 21–24 are the worst offenders").

"When Congress appropriates money to build a highway, . . . it is not entitled to insist as a condition of the use of highway funds that the State impose or change regulations in other areas of the State's social and economic life because of an attenuated or tangential relationship to highway use or safety. Indeed, if the rule were otherwise, the Congress could effectively regulate almost any area of a State's social, political, or economic life on the theory that use of the interstate transportation system is somehow enhanced. If, for example, the United States were to condition highway moneys upon moving the state capital, I suppose it might argue that interstate transportation is facilitated by locating local governments in places easily accessible to interstate highways — or, conversely, that highways might become overburdened if they had to carry traffic to and from the state capital. In my mind, such a relationship is hardly more attenuated than the one which the Court finds supports § 158."

South Dakota v. Dole, 483 U.S. at 214–15 (O'CONNOR, J., dissenting).

The fourth prong — that the condition cannot require anything the Constitution forbids — was the focus of *Rust v. Sullivan, supra* (discussed in Note 3, *infra*.) and *USAID v. Alliance for Open Society, supra* (discussed in Note 4, *infra*.) It played a minor role in *Dole*. Why? Note that the condition in *Dole* and in *NFIB* applied to the states, whereas the condition in *Rust* and *USAID* applied to *private entities*. How does that affect the analysis? Recall that the *Dole* condition required the states to enact a law. Thus, the question was whether the constitution prohibited the state from enacting minimum drinking age legislation. Did the state's police power include the power to limit the age for the purchase or consumption of alcoholic beverages? Can you think of laws that would be beyond the state's power? Suppose that Congress sought to reduce drunk driving in all age groups by withholding 5% of federal highway funding from states unless they had legislation in effect forbidding the purchase or consumption of alcoholic beverages entirely, regardless of age, in the state.

Of course, South Dakota already had legislation setting a minimum drinking age. South Dakota did not want to lower its minimum age, presumably because that would be politically unpopular. But, political opposition is a democratic or political hurdle, not a constitutional bar. The state had to choose between the federal money and the voters. (Most choose the money.)

2.   **Coercion and the power of the purse.** In *Dole*, the Court noted that there might be circumstances in which the condition "might be so coercive as to pass the point at which 'pressure turns into compulsion.'" Scholars came to consider this caveat as not only *dictum*, but of little practical relevance, since it had not been used

to strike down any condition on federal spending — until the Court's 2012 decision on the Affordable Care Act's Medicaid expansion provision in *NFIB v. Sebelius, supra*. (The cases cited as precedent in Chief Justice Roberts' opinion, *Printz v. United States* and *New York v. United States*, turned on the Court's conclusion that the federal government "commandeered" a state government agency, not that it used funding to coerce the state's compliance.)

The *Sebelius* decision caused some head scratching, since the federal government was not withholding funds, but instead would pay 100% (90% after 2016) of the cost of providing care to the newly eligible Medicaid beneficiaries (adults with income under 133% of the federal poverty level). How could such generosity be considered coercive?

The Court found that the loss of 5% of highway funding was not coercive in *Dole*, but the possible loss of 100% of federal Medicaid funding was coercive in *Sebelius*. How did the Court convert 100% federal funding for the newly eligible into a 100% loss of all federal Medicaid funding? The loss was one of several possible penalties listed in the statute for a state's noncompliance with any Medicaid requirement. As Justice Ginsburg noted in her dissenting opinion (joined by Justices Breyer, Sotomayor, and Kagan) on this issue, that penalty had never been used and is extremely unlikely to be used in the future. Can you think why?

What, if any, standards did the Court establish to determine what counts as a coercive condition on federal funding? Can you answer the following questions that Justice Ginsburg asks in her dissenting opinion?

> When future Spending Clause challenges arrive, as they likely will in the wake of today's decision, how will litigants and judges assess whether "a State has a legitimate choice whether to accept the federal conditions in exchange for federal funds"? Are courts to measure the number of dollars the Federal Government might withhold for noncompliance? The portion of the State's budget at stake? And which State's — or States' — budget is determinative: the lead plaintiff, all challenging States (26 in this case, many with quite different fiscal situations), or some national median? Does it matter that Florida, unlike most States, imposes no state income tax, and therefore might be able to replace foregone federal funds with new state revenue? Or that the coercion state officials in fact fear is punishment at the ballot box for turning down a politically popular federal grant?

132 S.Ct. at 2640–2641 (GINSBURG, J., dissenting).

Chief Justice Roberts' opinion is not reported as the opinion of the Court, but the result received grudging acquiesce from Justices Kennedy, Scalia, Thomas, and Alito, giving the Chief Justice a majority of five votes to render the Medicaid expanded eligibility provisions optional for the states. The latter four Justices wrote a dissenting opinion arguing for striking down the entire Affordable Care Act as unconstitutional. They agreed with the Chief Justice that the Medicaid expansion was coercive. How much of their argument depends on characterizing the Medicaid expansion as a "new" program, different from the original Medicaid? As Justice Ginsburg pointed out in her dissenting opinion, the Medicaid statute had been amended perhaps fifty times since its enactment in 1965, with many amendments adding new categories of eligibility, without protest by the states. What makes the ACA amendment to Medicaid different? Can you discern any principle in Justice Roberts' opinion that distinguishes an acceptable amendment to a federal program from the creation of a new program?

For a critique of the majority's analysis of this issue, see Nicole Huberfeld *et al., Plunging into Endless Difficulties: Medicaid and Coercion in National Federation of Independent Businesses v. Sebelius*, 93 B.U. L. Rev. 1 (2013).

3. **Private entities as grant recipients.** Grants to private entities obviously do not raise federalism concerns. No state is required to enact legislation to qualify for funding. Instead, Congress, or a federal agency acting pursuant to a federal statute, imposes a requirement directly on those who seek or obtain a grant or otherwise qualify for federal funding. For example, the National Institutes of Health now requires recipients of its grants for clinical research to post information about their studies on the federal website, www.clinicaltrials.gov. Some conditions on federal funding, however, are not perceived by the recipient to be so benign. *Rust v. Sullivan* and *USAID v. Alliance for Open Society International, supra,* are examples, with quite different outcomes. Which of the four *Dole* factors are most important in these cases?

Recall that, under *Dole's* analytic framework, conditions on funding should be unambiguous. How would you interpret the meaning of the prohibition using federal funds in "programs where abortion is a method of family planning" in Title X's section 1008? In *Rust*, the Court was quite deferential to the Department of Health and Human Services' interpretation, even though it reversed a long-standing department policy permitting family planning programs to provide neutral, non-directive counseling that included the subject of abortion. That policy was itself reversed by a subsequent administration, and is subject to repeated reversals as long as the statute remains open to interpretation.

The challengers in *Rust* argued that the new Title X regulations violated the First Amendment's protection of freedom of speech (both physicians' freedom to discuss abortion with their patients and patients' freedom to hear about abortion) and the Fifth Amendment's due process protection of the patients' liberty to make reproductive choices. The majority of Justices, however, viewed the condition as a valid Congressional decision to fund one activity and not another. Individuals within the Title X program could discuss only what the program paid for; elsewhere, they remained free to discuss abortion or anything else. How did the Court characterize the physician-patient relationship? Physicians, nurses and counselors in family planning programs often are full-time employees who do not see patients outside that program. Moreover, for many patients, the program was their primary source of medical care, at least for reproductive health. Should either fact matter to the rights or responsibilities of providers and patients within the program?

4. **Unconstitutional conditions.** The Court accepts the federal government's use of funding to promote the government's point of view on abortion in *Rust*, but not its point of view on prostitution in *USAID*. Are you persuaded by the Court's explanation of how the two differ?

Another, rare, example of the Court finding a condition unconstitutional is *Legal Services Corporation v. Velasquez*, 531 U.S. 533 (2001). Congress created the Legal Services Corporation (LSC) to distribute grants to hundreds of local organizations to provide (non-criminal) legal services to the indigent, including litigation concerning eligibility for welfare benefits. The Legal Services Corporation Act, 42 U.S.C. §§ 2996 *et seq.* Annual appropriations bills prohibited LSC from funding any organization "that initiates legal representation or participates in any other way, in litigation, lobbying, or rulemaking, involving an effort to reform a Federal or State welfare system, except that this paragraph shall not be construed to preclude a recipient from representing an individual eligible client who is seeking specific relief from a welfare agency *if such relief does not involve an effort to amend or otherwise challenge existing law in effect on the date of the initiation of the representation.*" Omnibus Consolidated Rescissions and Appropriations Act of 1996 (1996 Act), § 504(a) (16) (emphasis added).

The U.S. Supreme Court, in a five to four decision, struck down the italicized proviso. The dissenting Justices would have followed *Rust* in concluding that the condition did not discriminate on the basis of viewpoint, but merely ensured that the limits of the program's scope were observed by refusing to subsidize a certain class of litigation. Unlike the condition at issue in *Rust*, however, the Legal Services condition applied to all of the grantees' activities, including those paid for by non-federal sources.

Justice Kennedy's opinion for the Court reasoned that the limitation on LSC grants "forecloses advice or legal assistance to question the validity of statutes under the Constitution" or federal statutes. The Court emphasized the primary mission of the judiciary to interpret the law and the Constitution and the importance to the judiciary of an "informed, independent bar." Prohibiting lawyers from even raising constitutional questions in court was viewed as threatening the judicial function. Since welfare recipients could not be expected to obtain private attorneys, the LSC-funded legal services attorneys would be the only ones likely to bring constitutional questions before a court:

> The effect of the restriction . . . is to prohibit advice or argumentation that existing welfare laws are unconstitutional or unlawful. Congress cannot recast a condition on funding as a mere definition of its program in every case, lest the First Amendment be reduced to a simple semantic exercise.
>
> . . . .
>
> The attempted restriction is designed to insulate the Government's interpretation of the Constitution from judicial challenge. The Constitution does not permit the Government to confine litigants and their attorneys in this manner.

531 U.S. at 547, 548.

Compare the Court's characterization of the role of legal services attorneys with its earlier characterization of physicians in Title X family planning programs. Is one more important to its clientele than the other? If not, can *Rust* and *Velazquez* be reconciled?

Chapter 4

PUBLIC HEALTH, MORALS, AND RELIGION

A. INTRODUCTION

The constitutional principles explored in the cases in Chapter 3 apply to government protection of the health and safety of the public, primarily in connection with the risk of physical (and sometimes mental) harms. Health and safety, of course, are not the only interests that states protect under the police power: Many laws are designed to advance and protect property and other economic interests, regulate business and industry, address various kinds of inequalities, and countless other matters. See Freund, The Police Power, Chapter 3, *supra*. Generally, however, such examples share a common attribute: The particular harm sought to be prevented is a concrete and tangible (even if not always a physical) one.

This chapter explores less tangible harms. In some instances, the state seeks to prevent actions that offend the moral sensibilities of a community (often left undefined), while in others, individuals seek to prevent the state's imposition of a dignitary harm. More rigorous judicial scrutiny of public health legislation has been justified by the law's impact on family autonomy, religious practices, or other individual, constitutionally protected rights. In such circumstances, the courts may undertake to weigh independently the merits and impact of the legislation on the asserted constitutional interests. Part B includes salient U.S. Supreme Court decisions concerning the state's power to regulate decisions about health and medical care. Although often viewed from the perspective of constitutional protection of individuals' rights to make their own decisions about such care, these cases represent the Court's major contributions to a central issue in public health — the ways in which government can regulate the availability and use of medical care in order to protect life.

Part C further examines the scope of the right to privacy in intimate relationships. Using the example of same-sex relationships, Part C focuses on the state's power to protect public morality and whether public morals can be defined in a meaningful way in the twenty-first century. Part D considers claims that the state interferes with religious freedom when imposing requirements that are ostensibly intended to prevent more typical tangible harms to the public. In contrast to the large body of law regulating commercial businesses, products and practices, where courts have allowed the state substantial discretion in its choice of ends and means, the cases in this chapter highlight some of the most personal decisions that individuals make, where courts are particularly sensitive to the constitutionally protected rights of individual human beings.

B.   HEALTH CARE AND THE RIGHT TO PRIVACY

BUCK v. BELL
274 U.S. 200 (1927)

MR. JUSTICE HOLMES delivered the opinion of the Court.

This is a writ of error to review a judgment of the Supreme Court of Appeals of the State of Virginia, affirming a judgment of the Circuit Court of Amherst County, by which the defendant in error, the superintendent of the State Colony for Epileptics and Feeble Minded, was ordered to perform the operation of salpingectomy upon Carrie Buck, the plaintiff in error, for the purpose of making her sterile. 143 Va. 310. The case comes here upon the contention that the statute authorizing the judgment is void under the Fourteenth Amendment as denying to the plaintiff in error due process of law and the equal protection of the laws.

Carrie Buck is a feeble minded white woman who was committed to the State Colony above mentioned in due form. She is the daughter of a feeble minded mother in the same institution, and the mother of an illegitimate feeble minded child. She was eighteen years old at the time of the trial of her case in the Circuit Court, in the latter part of 1924. An Act of Virginia, approved March 20, 1924, recites that the health of the patient and the welfare of society may be promoted in certain cases by the sterilization of mental defectives, under careful safeguard, &c.; that the sterilization may be effected in males by vasectomy and in females by salpingectomy, without serious pain or substantial danger to life; that the Commonwealth is supporting in various institutions many defective persons who if now discharged would become a menace but if incapable of procreating might be discharged with safety and become self-supporting with benefit to themselves and to society; and that experience has shown that heredity plays an important part in the transmission of insanity, imbecility, &c. The statute then enacts that whenever the superintendent of certain institutions including the above named State Colony shall be of opinion that it is for the best interests of the patients and of society that an inmate under his care should be sexually sterilized, he may have the operation performed upon any patient afflicted with hereditary forms of insanity, imbecility, &c., on complying with the very careful provisions by which the act protects the patients from possible abuse.

The superintendent first presents a petition to the special board of directors of his hospital or colony, stating the facts and the grounds for his opinion, verified by affidavit. Notice of the petition and of the time and place of the hearing in the institution is to be served upon the inmate, and also upon his guardian, and if there is no guardian the superintendent is to apply to the Circuit Court of the County to appoint one. If the inmate is a minor notice also is to be given to his parents if any with a copy of the petition. The board is to see to it that the inmate may attend the hearings if desired by him or his guardian. The evidence is all to be reduced to writing, and after the board has made its order for or against the operation, the superintendent, or the inmate, or his guardian, may appeal to the Circuit Court of the County. The Circuit Court may consider the record of the board and the evidence before it and such other admissible evidence as may be offered, and may affirm, revise, or reverse the order of the board and enter such order as it deems just. Finally any party may apply to the Supreme Court of Appeals, which, if it grants the appeal, is to hear the case upon the record of the trial in the Circuit Court and may enter such order as it thinks the Circuit Court should have entered. There can be no doubt that so far as procedure is concerned the rights of the patient are most carefully considered, and as every step in this case was taken in scrupulous compliance with the statute and after months of observation, there is no doubt that in that respect the plaintiff in error has had due process of law.

The attack is not upon the procedure but upon the substantive law. It seems to be contended that in no circumstances could such an order be justified. It certainly is contended that the order cannot be justified upon the existing grounds. The judgment finds the facts that have been recited and that Carrie Buck "is the probable potential parent of socially inadequate offspring, likewise afflicted, that she may be sexually sterilized without detriment to her general health and that her welfare and that of society will be promoted by her sterilization," and thereupon makes the order. In view of the general declarations of the legislature and the specific findings of the Court, obviously we cannot say as matter of law that the grounds do not exist, and if they exist they justify the result. We have seen more than once that the public welfare may call upon the best citizens for their lives. It would be strange if it could not call upon those who already sap the strength of the State for these lesser sacrifices, often not felt to be such by those concerned, in order to prevent our being swamped with incompetence. It is better for all the world, if instead of waiting to execute degenerate offspring for crime, or to let them starve for their imbecility, society can prevent those who are manifestly unfit from continuing their kind. The principle that sustains compulsory vaccination is broad enough to cover cutting the Fallopian tubes. *Jacobson v. Massachusetts*, 197 U.S. 11. Three generations of imbeciles are enough.

But, it is said, however it might be if this reasoning were applied generally, it fails when it is confined to the small number who are in the institutions named and is not applied to the multitudes outside. It is the usual last resort of constitutional arguments to point out shortcomings of this sort. But the answer is that the law does all that is needed when it does all that it can, indicates a policy, applies it to all within the lines, and seeks to bring within the lines all similarly situated so far and so fast as its means allow. Of course so far as the operations enable those who otherwise must be kept confined to be returned to the world, and thus open the asylum to others, the equality aimed at will be more nearly reached.

Judgment affirmed.

Mr. Justice Butler dissents.

NOTES AND QUESTIONS

1. **Public welfare and involuntary medical procedures.** The entire opinion in *Buck v. Bell* is reproduced above. Justice Oliver Wendell Holmes had little difficulty

finding that a broad view of public welfare justified forcing surgery on a young woman against her will and ending her ability to have children. Note that Justice Holmes cites *Jacobson v. Massachusetts*, Chapter 3, *infra*, as support for a general principle that would permit both involuntary vaccination and involuntary surgery. What principle could that be? Can you define such a principle? What, if any, limitations might it entail? The opinion in *Buck* did not mention that the Massachusetts law in *Jacobson* did not permit involuntary vaccination, but rather imposed a monetary penalty (and, failing that, incarceration) for refusal, whereas the Virginia law required Buck to submit to surgery once she was found "feeble minded." The Court did not require the state to demonstrate that sterilization was necessary and not arbitrary or oppressive. This suggests that the Court did not view *Jacobson* as requiring any substantive standard of necessity or reasonableness that would prevent what today would be considered an indefensible assault. The Court focused on the state's justification for requiring the sterilization of "feeble minded," institutionalized people, apparently relying on eugenic theories that were popular in some medical and scientific communities in the 1920's and 1930's. Would mainstream medicine and science today hold the same views? What does this suggest about reliance on contemporary theories of public welfare? What alternative does the judiciary have?

The Court did not consider that Carrie Buck might have any substantive right to personal liberty. Thus, it appeared to expand the justifications for restrictions on personal liberty. But not for long. Neither *Jacobson* nor *Buck* could serve as precedent for requiring individuals to undergo surgical procedures against their will today. In particular, *Buck* is incompatible with *Cruzan v. Director, Missouri Dep't of Health, infra,* and the common law which it cites upholding an individual's right to refuse medical treatment.

2.   *Skinner v. Oklahoma.* Several decades after *Buck v. Bell*, the Court began a more searching inquiry into the state's reasons for intruding into matters of individual medical procedures, especially procedures affecting reproduction, as seen in *Griswold v. Connecticut*, 381 U.S. 479 (1965), and cases in the rest of Part C, *infra. Skinner v. Oklahoma*, 316 U.S. 535 (1942), examined another law that reflected eugenic theories, Oklahoma's Habitual Criminal Sterilization Act, which was enacted in 1935 and authorized sterilization for offenders convicted of three "felonies involving moral turpitude." Earl Skinner had been convicted of and sentenced for a theft of chickens and two robberies with firearms, in different years, and then further sentenced to have a vasectomy pursuant to the Act. The U.S. Supreme Court found that the Act violated the equal protection clause of the Fourteenth Amendment, because it exempted crimes like embezzlement. Noting that, in *Buck*, the Court had dismissed equal protection as "the usual last resort of constitutional arguments," it found that the use of sterilization required strict scrutiny of the classification of crimes, suggesting that reproductive choices are fundamental:

> . . . . We are dealing here with legislation which involves one of the basic civil rights of man. Marriage and procreation are fundamental to the very existence and survival of the race. The power to sterilize, if exercised, may have subtle, far-reaching and devastating effects. In evil or reckless hands, it can cause races or types which are inimical to the dominant group to

wither and disappear. There is no redemption for the individual whom the law touches. Any experiment which the State conducts is to his irreparable injury. He is forever deprived of a basic liberty. We mention these matters not to reexamine the scope of the police power of the States. We advert to them merely in emphasis of our view that strict scrutiny of the classification which a State makes in a sterilization law is essential, lest unwittingly, or otherwise, invidious discriminations are made against groups or types of individuals in violation of the constitutional guaranty of just and equal laws. The guaranty of "equal protection of the laws is a pledge of the protection of equal laws." *Yick Wo v. Hopkins*, 118 U.S. 356, 369. When the law lays an unequal hand on those who have committed intrinsically the same quality of offense and sterilizes one and not the other, it has made as invidious a discrimination as if it had selected a particular race or nationality for oppressive treatment.

316 U.S. at 541.

Compare the language concerning reproduction in *Skinner* with that used in *Buck v. Bell*. What happened between 1927 and 1942?

3.   The real Carrie Buck. For a fascinating history of the real Carrie Buck, who was not "feeble minded," see Paul A. Lombardo, *Three Generations, No Imbeciles: New Light on Buck v. Bell*, 60 N.Y. U. L. Rev. 30 (1985). Carrie Buck may have been chosen as a test case in which the state hoped to (and did) gain the U.S. Supreme Court's approval of laws authorizing involuntary medical procedures for eugenic purposes. Indiana was the first state to enact an involuntary sterilization law. With the Court's imprimatur on involuntary sterilization laws, more than 60,000 Americans, mostly poor women, were sterilized by 1978. *Buck v. Bell* was also used by the Nazis to help justify their own sterilization program and was cited by the defense at the Nuremberg Trials. Of course, it is no longer either good law or good genetics. *See* A Century of Eugenics in America: From the Indiana Experiment to the Human Genome (Paul A. Lombardo, ed., 2011). Carrie Buck Detamore died in 1983. Twenty years later, Virginia honored her memory with a historical marker and a legislative resolution to remind the state of "the most egregious outcome of the lamentable eugenics movement in the Commonwealth." www.hmdb.org/marker.asp?marker= 10128 (visited April 2014); Carlos Santos, *Historic Test Case — Wrong Done to Carrie Buck Remembered*, Times-Dispatch, Feb. 17, 2002.

CRUZAN v. DIRECTOR, MISSOURI DEPARTMENT OF HEALTH
497 U.S. 261 (1990)

Rehnquist, Chief Justice.

*   *   *

On the night of January 11, 1983, Nancy Cruzan lost control of her car as she traveled down Elm Road in Jasper County, Missouri. The vehicle overturned, and

Cruzan was discovered lying face down in a ditch without detectable respiratory or cardiac function. Paramedics were able to restore her breathing and heartbeat at the accident site, and she was transported to a hospital in an unconscious state. An attending neurosurgeon diagnosed her as having sustained probable cerebral contusions compounded by significant anoxia (lack of oxygen). The Missouri trial court in this case found that permanent brain damage generally results after 6 minutes in an anoxic state; it was estimated that Cruzan was deprived of oxygen from 12 to 14 minutes. She remained in a coma for approximately three weeks and then progressed to an unconscious state in which she was able to orally ingest some nutrition. In order to ease feeding and further the recovery, surgeons implanted a gastrostomy feeding and hydration tube in Cruzan with the consent of her then husband. Subsequent rehabilitative efforts proved unavailing. She now lies in a Missouri state hospital in what is commonly referred to as a persistent vegetative state: generally, a condition in which a person exhibits motor reflexes but evinces no indications of significant cognitive function. The State of Missouri is bearing the cost of her care.

After it had become apparent that Nancy Cruzan had virtually no chance of regaining her mental faculties, her parents asked hospital employees to terminate the artificial nutrition and hydration procedures. All agree that such a removal would cause her death. The employees refused to honor the request without court approval. The parents then sought and received authorization from the state trial court for termination. The court found that a person in Nancy's condition had a fundamental right under the State and Federal Constitutions to refuse or direct the withdrawal of "death prolonging procedures." The court also found that Nancy's "expressed thoughts at age twenty-five in somewhat serious conversation with a housemate friend that if sick or injured she would not wish to continue her life unless she could live at least halfway normally suggests that given her present condition she would not wish to continue on with her nutrition and hydration." The Supreme Court of Missouri reversed by a divided vote.

At common law, even the touching of one person by another without consent and without legal justification was a battery. Before the turn of the century, this Court observed that "no right is held more sacred, or is more carefully guarded, by the common law, than the right of every individual to the possession and control of his own person, free from all restraint or interference of others, unless by clear and unquestionable authority of law." *Union Pacific R. Co. v. Botsford*, 141 U.S. 250, 251 (1891). This notion of bodily integrity has been embodied in the requirement that informed consent is generally required for medical treatment. Justice Cardozo, while on the Court of Appeals of New York, aptly described this doctrine: "Every human being of adult years and sound mind has a right to determine what shall be done with his own body; and a surgeon who performs an operation without his patient's consent commits an assault, for which he is liable in damages." *Schloendorff v. Society of New York Hospital*, 211 N.Y. 125, 129–130, 105 N.E. 92, 93 (1914). The informed consent doctrine has become firmly entrenched in American tort law.

The logical corollary of the doctrine of informed consent is that the patient generally possesses the right not to consent, that is, to refuse treatment. Until about 15 years ago and the seminal decision in *In re Quinlan*, 70 N.J. 10, 355 A.2d 647, *cert. denied sub nom. Garger v. New Jersey*, 429 U.S. 922 (1976), the number of right-to-refuse-treatment decisions was relatively few. Most of the earlier cases involved patients who refused medical treatment forbidden by their religious beliefs, thus implicating First Amendment rights as well as common-law rights of self-determination. More recently, however, with the advance of medical technology capable of sustaining life well past the point where natural forces would have brought certain death in earlier times, cases involving the right to refuse life-sustaining treatment have burgeoned . . . .

As these cases demonstrate, the common-law doctrine of informed consent is viewed as generally encompassing the right of a competent individual to refuse medical treatment. Beyond that, these cases demonstrate both similarity and diversity in their approaches to what all agree is a perplexing question with unusually strong moral and ethical overtones. State courts have available to them for decision a number of sources — state constitutions, statutes, and common law — which are not available to us. In this Court, the question is simply and starkly whether the United States Constitution prohibits Missouri from choosing the rule of decision which it did. This is the first case in which we have been squarely presented with the issue whether the United States Constitution grants what is in common parlance referred to as a "right to die." . . .

The Fourteenth Amendment provides that no State shall "deprive any person of life, liberty, or property, without due process of law." The principle that a competent person has a constitutionally protected liberty interest in refusing unwanted medical treatment may be inferred from our prior decisions. In *Jacobson v. Massachusetts*, 197 U.S. 11 (1905), for instance, the Court balanced an individual's liberty interest in declining an unwanted smallpox vaccine against the State's interest in preventing disease. Decisions prior to the incorporation of the Fourth Amendment into the Fourteenth Amendment analyzed searches and seizures involving the body under the Due Process Clause and were thought to implicate substantial liberty interests. *See, e.g., Breithaupt v. Abram*, 352 U.S. 432, 439 (1957) ("As against the right of an individual that his person be held inviolable . . . must be set the interests of society . . . ").

Just this Term, in the course of holding that a State's procedures for administering antipsychotic medication to prisoners were sufficient to satisfy due process concerns, we recognized that prisoners possess "a significant liberty interest in avoiding the unwanted administration of antipsychotic drugs under the Due Process Clause of the Fourteenth Amendment." *Washington v. Harper*, 494 U.S. 210, 221–22 (1990) ("The forcible injection of medication into a non-consenting person's body represents a substantial interference with that person's liberty"). Still other cases support the recognition of a general liberty interest in refusing medical treatment. *Vitek v. Jones*, 445 U.S. 480, 494 (1980) (transfer to mental hospital coupled with mandatory behavior modification treatment implicated liberty interests); *Parham v. J. R.*, 442 U.S. 584, 600 (1979) ("[A] child, in common with adults, has a substantial liberty interest in not being confined unnecessarily for medical treatment"). But determining that a person has a "liberty interest" under the Due Process Clause does not end the inquiry; "whether respondent's constitutional rights have been violated must be determined by balancing his liberty interests against the relevant state interests." *Youngberg v. Romeo*, 457 U.S. 307, 321 (1982).

Petitioners insist that under the general holdings of our cases, the forced administration of life-sustaining medical treatment, and even of artificially delivered food and water essential to life, would implicate a competent person's liberty interest. Although we think the logic of the cases discussed above would embrace such a liberty interest, the dramatic consequences involved in refusal of such treatment would inform the inquiry as to whether the deprivation of that interest is constitutionally permissible. But for purposes of this case, we assume that the United States Constitution would grant a competent person a constitutionally protected right to refuse lifesaving hydration and nutrition.

Petitioners go on to assert that an incompetent person should possess the same right in this respect as is possessed by a competent person. They rely primarily on our decisions in *Parham v. J. R., supra*, and *Youngberg v. Romeo, supra*. In *Parham*, we held that a mentally disturbed minor child had a liberty interest in "not being confined unnecessarily for medical treatment," but we certainly did not intimate that such a minor child, after commitment, would have a liberty interest in refusing treatment. In *Youngberg*, we held that a seriously retarded adult had a liberty interest in safety and freedom from bodily restraint. *Youngberg*, however, did not deal with decisions to administer or withhold medical treatment.

The difficulty with petitioners' claim is that in a sense it begs the question: An incompetent person is not able to make an informed and voluntary choice to exercise a hypothetical right to refuse treatment or any other right. Such a "right" must be exercised for her, if at all, by some sort of surrogate. Here, Missouri has in effect recognized that under certain circumstances a surrogate may act for the patient in electing to have hydration and nutrition withdrawn in such a way as to cause death, but it has established a procedural safeguard to assure that the action of the surrogate conforms as best it may to the wishes expressed by the patient while competent. Missouri requires that evidence of the incompetent's wishes as to the withdrawal of treatment be proved by clear and convincing evidence. The question, then, is whether the United States Constitution forbids the establishment of this procedural requirement by the State. We hold that it does not.

Whether or not Missouri's clear and convincing evidence requirement comports with the United States Constitution depends in part on what interests the State may properly seek to protect in this situation. Missouri relies on its interest in the protection and preservation of human life, and there can be no gainsaying this interest. As a general matter, the States — indeed, all civilized nations — demonstrate their commitment to life by treating homicide as a serious crime. Moreover, the majority of States in this country have laws imposing criminal penalties on one who assists another to commit suicide. We do not think a State is required to remain neutral in the face of an informed and voluntary decision by a physically able adult to starve to death . . . .

But in the context presented here, a State has more particular interests at stake. The choice between life and death is a deeply personal decision of obvious and overwhelming finality. We believe Missouri may legitimately seek to safeguard the personal element of this choice through the imposition of heightened evidentiary requirements.

No doubt is engendered by anything in this record but that Nancy Cruzan's mother and father are loving and caring parents. If the State were required by the United States Constitution to repose a right of "substituted judgment" with anyone, the Cruzans would surely qualify. But we do not think the Due Process Clause requires the State to repose judgment on these matters with anyone but the patient herself. . . . the State may choose to defer only to those wishes, rather than confide the decision to close family members.

. . . .

The judgment of the Supreme Court of Missouri is *Affirmed.*

. . . .

O'CONNOR, JUSTICE, concurring.

I agree that a protected liberty interest in refusing unwanted medical treatment may be inferred from our prior decisions, and that the refusal of artificially delivered food and water is encompassed within that liberty interest . . . .

I write separately to emphasize that the Court does not today decide the issue whether a State must also give effect to the decisions of a surrogate decision-maker. In my view, such a duty may well be constitutionally required to protect the patient's liberty interest in refusing medical treatment . . . . Today's decision, holding only that the Constitution permits a State to require clear and convincing evidence of Nancy Cruzan's desire to have artificial hydration and nutrition withdrawn, does not preclude a future determination that the Constitution requires the States to implement the decisions of a patient's duly appointed surrogate.

BRENNAN, JUSTICE, with JUSTICES MARSHALL and BLACKMUN, dissenting.

The starting point for our legal analysis must be whether a competent person has a constitutional right to avoid unwanted medical care. Earlier this Term, this Court held that the Due Process Clause of the Fourteenth Amendment confers a significant liberty interest in avoiding unwanted medical treatment. *Washington v. Harper*, 494 U.S. 210, 221–22 (1990). Today, the Court concedes that our prior decisions "support the recognition of a general liberty interest in refusing medical treatment." . . . .

But if a competent person has a liberty interest to be free of unwanted medical treatment, as both the majority and Justice O'Connor concede, it must be fundamental. "We are dealing here with [a decision] which involves one of the basic civil rights of man." *Skinner v. Oklahoma ex rel. Williamson*, 316 U.S. 535, 541 (1942) (invalidating a statute authorizing sterilization of certain felons). Whatever other liberties protected by the Due Process Clause are fundamental, "those liberties that are 'deeply rooted in this Nation's history and tradition' " are among them. *Bowers v. Hardwick*, 478 U.S. 186, 192 (1986).

The right to be free from medical attention without consent, to determine what shall be done with one's own body, *is* deeply rooted in this Nation's traditions, as the majority acknowledges. This right has long been "firmly entrenched in American tort law" and is securely grounded in the earliest common law. *See also Mills v.*

Rogers, 457 U.S. 291, 294, n.4 (1982) ("The right to refuse any medical treatment emerged from the doctrines of trespass and battery, which were applied to unauthorized touchings by a physician"). "Anglo-American law starts with the premise of thorough-going self determination. It follows that each man is considered to be master of his own body, and he may, if he be of sound mind, expressly prohibit the performance of lifesaving surgery, or other medical treatment." *Natanson v. Kline*, 186 Kan. 393, 406–07, 350 P.2d 1093, 1104 (1960). "The inviolability of the person" has been held as "sacred" and "carefully guarded" as any common law right. *Union Pacific R. Co. v. Botsford*, 141 U.S. 250, 251–52 (1891). Thus, freedom from unwanted medical attention is unquestionably among those principles "so rooted in the traditions and conscience of our people as to be ranked as fundamental." *Snyder v. Massachusetts*, 291 U.S. 97, 105 (1934) . . . .

That there may be serious consequences involved in refusal of the medical treatment at issue here does not vitiate the right under our common-law tradition of medical self-determination. It is "a well-established rule of general law . . . that it is the patient, not the physician, who ultimately decides if treatment — any treatment — is to be given at all . . . . The rule has never been qualified in its application by either the nature or purpose of the treatment, or the gravity of the consequences of acceding to or foregoing it." *Tune v. Walter Reed Army Medical Hospital*, 602 F. Supp. 1452, 1455 (DC 1985). *See also Downer v. Veilleux*, 322 A.2d 82, 91 (Me. 1974) ("The rationale of this rule lies in the fact that every competent adult has the right to forego treatment, or even cure, if it entails what for him are intolerable consequences or risks, however unwise his sense of values may be to others") . I respectfully dissent.

NOTES AND QUESTIONS

4.   **The right to refuse treatment.** As both the majority and minority in *Cruzan* make clear, the right to refuse treatment has always been taken seriously by the common law, and now also has strong support from constitutional doctrine as well. The majority's opinion offers no case involving treatment against the will of a free living competent person other than *Jacobson*, and that case does not stand for such a proposition. Instead they point to cases involving children and mentally-impaired prisoners. There is no suggestion that treatment could ever be forced on a competent adult for the adult's own good, including saving the adult's life, by any of the justices. This is a difficult case for the majority only because Nancy Cruzan is incapable of expressing her own wishes. That controversy remains regarding what treatment to compel an incompetent person to undergo, over either the wishes of their next-of-kin, or contrary to what it is believed the person would want done, is well-illustrated by the interference by the U.S. Congress, the Legislature and Governor of Florida, and the President of the United States in the decision of Michael Schiavo, upheld by every court that reviewed it, that it would be his wife's decision not to continue tube-feeding if she was in a permanent vegetative state. *See, e.g.,* George J. Annas, *"I Want to Live": Medicine Betrayed by Ideology in the Political Debate Over Terri Schiavo*, 35 STETSON L. REV. 49 (2005); Norman L. Cantor, *The Relation Between Autonomy-Based Rights and Profoundly Mentally*

Disabled Persons, 13 ANNALS HEALTH L. 37 (2004).

ROE v. WADE
410 U.S. 113 (1973)

BLACKMUN, JUSTICE delivered the opinion of the Court.

This Texas federal appeal . . . presents constitutional challenges to state criminal abortion legislation. The Texas statutes under attack here are typical of those that have been in effect in many States for approximately a century . . . .

We forthwith acknowledge our awareness of the sensitive and emotional nature of the abortion controversy, of the vigorous opposing views, even among physicians, and of the deep and seemingly absolute convictions that the subject inspires. One's philosophy, one's experiences, one's exposure to the raw edges of human existence, one's religious training, one's attitudes toward life and family and their values, and the moral standards one establishes and seeks to observe, are all likely to influence and to color one's thinking and conclusions about abortion.

. . . .

Our task, of course, is to resolve the issue by constitutional measurement, free of emotion and of predilection. We seek earnestly to do this, and, because we do, we have inquired into, and in this opinion place some emphasis upon, medical and medical-legal history and what that history reveals about man's attitudes toward the abortion procedure over the centuries . . . .

I

The Texas statutes that concern us here . . . make it a crime to "procure an abortion," as therein defined, or to attempt one, except with respect to "an abortion procured or attempted by medical advice for the purpose of saving the life of the mother." Similar statutes are in existence in a majority of the States.

. . . .

II

Jane Roe, a single woman who was residing in Dallas County, Texas, instituted this federal action in March 1970 against the District Attorney of the county. She sought a declaratory judgment that the Texas criminal abortion statutes were unconstitutional on their face, and an injunction restraining the defendant from enforcing the statutes.

Roe alleged that she was unmarried and pregnant; that she wished to terminate her pregnancy by an abortion "performed by a competent, licensed physician, under safe, clinical conditions"; that she was unable to get a "legal" abortion in Texas because her life did not appear to be threatened by the continuation of her pregnancy; and that she could not afford to travel to another jurisdiction in order to secure a legal abortion under safe conditions. She claimed that the Texas statutes were unconstitutionally vague and that they abridged her right of personal privacy, protected by the First, Fourth, Fifth, Ninth, and Fourteenth Amendments. By an amendment to her complaint Roe purported to sue "on behalf of herself and all other women" similarly situated.

. . . .

V

The principal thrust of appellant's attack on the Texas statutes is that they improperly invade a right, said to be possessed by the pregnant woman, to choose to terminate her pregnancy. Appellant would discover this right in the concept of personal "liberty" embodied in the Fourteenth Amendment's Due Process Clause; or in personal, marital, familial, and sexual privacy said to be protected by the Bill of Rights or its penumbras, see *Griswold v. Connecticut*, 381 U.S. 479 (1965); *Eisenstadt v. Baird*, 405 U.S. 438 (1972); or among those rights reserved to the people by the Ninth Amendment, *Griswold v. Connecticut*, 381 U.S., at 486 (Goldberg, J., concurring). Before addressing this claim, we feel it desirable briefly to survey, in several aspects, the history of abortion, for such insight as that history may afford us, and then to examine the state purposes and interests behind the criminal abortion laws.

VI

It perhaps is not generally appreciated that the restrictive criminal abortion laws in effect in a majority of States today are of relatively recent vintage. Those laws, generally proscribing abortion or its attempt at any time during pregnancy except when necessary to preserve the pregnant woman's life, are not of ancient or even of common-law origin. Instead, they derive from statutory changes effected, for the most part, in the latter half of the 19th century.

1. *Ancient attitudes*. These are not capable of precise determination. We are told that at the time of the Persian Empire abortifacients were known and that criminal abortions were severely punished. We are also told, however, that abortion was practiced in Greek times as well as in the Roman Era, and that "it was resorted to without scruple." The Ephesian, Soranos, often described as the greatest of the ancient gynecologists, appears to have been generally opposed to Rome's prevailing free-abortion practices. He found it necessary to think first of the life of the mother, and he resorted to abortion when, upon this standard, he felt the procedure advisable. Greek and Roman law afforded little protection to the unborn. If abortion was prosecuted in some places, it seems to have been based on a concept of a violation of the father's right to his offspring. Ancient religion did not bar abortion.

2. *The Hippocratic Oath*. What then of the famous Oath that has stood so long as the ethical guide of the medical profession and that bears the name of the great Greek (460(?)-377(?) B.C.), who has been described as the Father of Medicine, the "wisest and the greatest practitioner of his art," and the "most important and most complete medical personality of antiquity," who dominated the medical schools of his time, and who typified the sum of the medical knowledge of the past? The Oath

varies somewhat according to the particular translation, but in any translation the content is clear: "I will give no deadly medicine to anyone if asked, nor suggest any such counsel; and in like manner I will not give to a woman a pessary to produce abortion," . . . .

Although the Oath is not mentioned in any of the principal briefs in this case . . . , it represents the apex of the development of strict ethical concepts in medicine, and its influence endures to this day. Why did not the authority of Hippocrates dissuade abortion practice in his time and that of Rome? The late Dr. Edelstein provides us with a theory: The Oath was not uncontested even in Hippocrates' day; only the Pythagorean school of philosophers frowned upon the related act of suicide. Most Greek thinkers, on the other hand, commended abortion, at least prior to viability. For the Pythagoreans, however, it was a matter of dogma. For them the embryo was animate from the moment of conception, and abortion meant destruction of a living being. The abortion clause of the Oath, therefore, "echoes Pythagorean doctrines," and "in no other stratum of Greek opinion were such views held or proposed in the same spirit of uncompromising austerity."

Dr. Edelstein then concludes that the Oath originated in a group representing only a small segment of Greek opinion and that it certainly was not accepted by all ancient physicians. He points out that medical writings down to Galen (A.D. 130–200) "give evidence of the violation of almost every one of its injunctions." But with the end of antiquity a decided change took place. Resistance against suicide and against abortion became common. The Oath came to be popular. The emerging teachings of Christianity were in agreement with the Pythagorean ethic. The Oath "became the nucleus of all medical ethics" and "was applauded as the embodiment of truth." Thus, suggests Dr. Edelstein, it is "a Pythagorean manifesto and not the expression of an absolute standard of medical conduct."

This, it seems to us, is a satisfactory and acceptable explanation of the Hippocratic Oath's apparent rigidity. It enables us to understand, in historical context, a long-accepted and revered statement of medical ethics.

3. *The common law.* It is undisputed that at common law, abortion performed before "quickening" — the first recognizable movement of the fetus *in utero*, appearing usually from the 16th to the 18th week of pregnancy — was not an indictable offense. The absence of a common-law crime for prequickening abortion appears to have developed from a confluence of earlier philosophical, theological, and civil and canon law concepts of when life begins. These disciplines variously approached the question in terms of the point at which the embryo or fetus became "formed" or recognizably human, or in terms of when a "person" came into being, that is, infused with a "soul" or "animated." A loose consensus evolved in early English law that these events occurred at some point between conception and live birth. This was "mediate animation." Although Christian theology and the canon law came to fix the point of animation at 40 days for a male and 80 days for a female, a view that persisted until the 19th century, there was otherwise little agreement about the precise time of formation or animation. There was agreement, however, that prior to this point the fetus was to be regarded as part of the mother, and its destruction, therefore, was not homicide. Due to continued uncertainty about the

precise time when animation occurred, to the lack of any empirical basis for the 40-80-day view, and perhaps to Aquinas' definition of movement as one of the two first principles of life, Bracton focused upon quickening as the critical point. The significance of quickening was echoed by later common-law scholars and found its way into the received common law in this country.

Whether abortion of a quick fetus was a felony at common law, or even a lesser crime, is still disputed. Bracton, writing early in the 13th century, thought it homicide. But the later and predominant view, following the great common-law scholars, has been that it was, at most, a lesser offense. In a frequently cited passage, Coke took the position that abortion of a woman "quick with child" is "a great misprision, and no murder." Blackstone followed, saying that while abortion after quickening had once been considered manslaughter (though not murder), "modern law" took a less severe view. A recent review of the common-law precedents argues, however, that those precedents contradict Coke and that even post-quickening abortion was never established as a common-law crime. This is of some importance because while most American courts ruled, in holding or *dictum*, that abortion of an unquickened fetus was not criminal under their received common law, others followed Coke in stating that abortion of a quick fetus was a "misprision," a term they translated to mean "misdemeanor." That their reliance on Coke on this aspect of the law was uncritical and, apparently in all the reported cases, *dictum* (due probably to the paucity of common-law prosecutions for post-quickening abortion), makes it now appear doubtful that abortion was ever firmly established as a common-law crime even with respect to the destruction of a quick fetus.

4. *The English statutory law.* England's first criminal abortion statute, Lord Ellenborough's Act, came in 1803. It made abortion of a quick fetus, § 1, a capital crime, but in § 2 it provided lesser penalties for the felony of abortion before quickening, and thus preserved the "quickening" distinction. . . . In 1929, the Infant Life (Preservation) Act, came into being. Its emphasis was upon the destruction of "the life of a child capable of being born alive." It made a willful act performed with the necessary intent a felony. It contained a proviso that one was not to be found guilty of the offense "unless it is proved that the act which caused the death of the child was not done in good faith for the purpose only of preserving the life of the mother."

. . . . Recently, Parliament enacted a new abortion law. This is the Abortion Act of 1967. The Act permits a licensed physician to perform an abortion where two other licensed physicians agree (a) "that the continuance of the pregnancy would involve risk to the life of the pregnant woman, or of injury to the physical or mental health of the pregnant woman or any existing children of her family, greater than if the pregnancy were terminated," or (b) "that there is a substantial risk that if the child were born it would suffer from such physical or mental abnormalities as to be seriously handicapped." . . .

5. *The American law.* In this country, the law in effect in all but a few States until mid-19th century was the pre-existing English common law. Connecticut, the first State to enact abortion legislation, adopted in 1821 that part of Lord Ellenborough's Act that related to a woman "quick with child." The death penalty was not imposed.

Abortion before quickening was made a crime in that State only in 1860. In 1828, New York enacted legislation that, in two respects, was to serve as a model for early anti-abortion statutes. First, while barring destruction of an unquickened fetus as well as a quick fetus, it made the former only a misdemeanor, but the latter second-degree manslaughter. Second, it incorporated a concept of therapeutic abortion by providing that an abortion was excused if it "shall have been necessary to preserve the life of such mother, or shall have been advised by two physicians to be necessary for such purpose." By 1840, when Texas had received the common law, only eight American States had statutes dealing with abortion. It was not until after the War Between the States that legislation began generally to replace the common law. Most of these initial statutes dealt severely with abortion after quickening but were lenient with it before quickening. Most punished attempts equally with completed abortions. While many statutes included the exception for an abortion thought by one or more physicians to be necessary to save the mother's life, that provision soon disappeared and the typical law required that the procedure actually be necessary for that purpose.

Gradually, in the middle and late 19th century the quickening distinction disappeared from the statutory law of most States and the degree of the offense and the penalties were increased. By the end of the 1950's, a large majority of the jurisdictions banned abortion, however and whenever performed, unless done to save or preserve the life of the mother. The exceptions, Alabama and the District of Columbia, permitted abortion to preserve the mother's health. Three States permitted abortions that were not "unlawfully" performed or that were not "without lawful justification," leaving interpretation of those standards to the courts. In the past several years, however, a trend toward liberalization of abortion statutes has resulted in adoption, by about one-third of the States, of less stringent laws.

It is thus apparent that at common law, at the time of the adoption of our Constitution, and throughout the major portion of the 19th century, abortion was viewed with less disfavor than under most American statutes currently in effect. Phrasing it another way, a woman enjoyed a substantially broader right to terminate a pregnancy than she does in most States today. At least with respect to the early stage of pregnancy, and very possibly without such a limitation, the opportunity to make this choice was present in this country well into the 19th century. Even later, the law continued for some time to treat less punitively an abortion procured in early pregnancy.

6. *The position of the American Medical Association.* The anti-abortion mood prevalent in this country in the late 19th century was shared by the medical profession. Indeed, the attitude of the profession may have played a significant role in the enactment of stringent criminal abortion legislation during that period.

An AMA Committee on Criminal Abortion was appointed in May 1857. It presented its report, 12 Trans. of the Am. Med. Assn. 73–78 (1859), to the Twelfth Annual Meeting. That report observed that the Committee had been appointed to investigate criminal abortion "with a view to its general suppression." It deplored abortion and its frequency and it listed three causes of "this general demoralization":

The first of these causes is a wide-spread popular ignorance of the true character of the crime — a belief, even among mothers themselves, that the foetus is not alive till after the period of quickening. The second of the agents alluded to is the fact that the professionals themselves are frequently supposed careless of foetal life . . . .

The third reason of the frightful extent of this crime is found in the grave defects of our laws, both common and statute, as regards the independent and actual existence of the child before birth, as a living being. These errors, which are sufficient in most instances to prevent conviction, are based, and only based, upon mistaken and exploded medical dogmas. With strange inconsistency, the law fully acknowledges the foetus *in utero* and its inherent rights, for civil purposes; while personally and as criminally affected, it fails to recognize it, and to its life as yet denies all protection.

The Committee then offered, and the Association adopted, resolutions protesting "against such unwarrantable destruction of human life," calling upon state legislatures to revise their abortion laws, and requesting the cooperation of state medical societies "in pressing the subject."

In 1871 a long and vivid report was submitted by the Committee on Criminal Abortion. It ended with the observation, "We had to deal with human life. In a matter of less importance we could entertain no compromise. An honest judge on the bench would call things by their proper names. We could do no less." 22 Trans. of the Am. Med. Assn. 258 (1871). It proffered resolutions, adopted by the Association, *id.*, at 38–39, recommending, among other things, that it "be unlawful and unprofessional for any physician to induce abortion or premature labor, without the concurrent opinion of at least one respectable consulting physician, and then always with a view to the safety of the child — if that be possible," and calling "the attention of the clergy of all denominations to the perverted views of morality entertained by a large class of females — aye, and men also, on this important question."

Except for periodic condemnation of the criminal abortionist, no further formal AMA action took place until 1967. In that year, the Committee on Human Reproduction urged the adoption of a stated policy of opposition to induced abortion, except when there is "documented medical evidence" of a threat to the health or life of the mother, or that the child "may be born with incapacitating physical deformity or mental deficiency," or that a pregnancy "resulting from legally established statutory or forcible rape or incest may constitute a threat to the mental or physical health of the patient," two other physicians "chosen because of their recognized professional competence have examined the patient and have concurred in writing," and the procedure "is performed in a hospital accredited by the Joint Commission on Accreditation of Hospitals." The providing of medical information by physicians to state legislatures in their consideration of legislation regarding therapeutic abortion was "to be considered consistent with the principles of ethics of the American Medical Association." This recommendation was adopted by the House of Delegates. Proceedings of the AMA House of Delegates 40–51 (June 1967).

In 1970, after the introduction of a variety of proposed resolutions, and of a report from its Board of Trustees, a reference committee noted "polarization of the medical profession on this controversial issue"; division among those who had testified; a difference of opinion among AMA councils and committees; "the remarkable shift in testimony" in six months, felt to be influenced "by the rapid changes in state laws and by the judicial decisions which tend to make abortion more freely available"; and a feeling "that this trend will continue." On June 25, 1970, the House of Delegates adopted preambles and most of the resolutions proposed by the reference committee. The preambles emphasized "the best interests of the patient," "sound clinical judgment," and "informed patient consent," in contrast to "mere acquiescence to the patient's demand." The resolutions asserted that abortion is a medical procedure that should be performed by a licensed physician in an accredited hospital only after consultation with two other physicians and in conformity with state law, and that no party to the procedure should be required to violate personally held moral principles. Proceedings of the AMA House of Delegates 220 (June 1970). The AMA Judicial Council rendered a complementary opinion.

7. *The position of the American Public Health Association.* In October 1970, the Executive Board of the APHA adopted Standards for Abortion Services. These were five in number:

a. Rapid and simple abortion referral must be readily available through state and local public health departments, medical societies, or other nonprofit organizations.

b. An important function of counseling should be to simplify and expedite the provision of abortion services; it should not delay the obtaining of these services.

c. Psychiatric consultation should not be mandatory. As in the case of other specialized medical services, psychiatric consultation should be sought for definite indications and not on a routine basis.

d. A wide range of individuals from appropriately trained, sympathetic volunteers to highly skilled physicians may qualify as abortion counselors.

e. Contraception and/or sterilization should be discussed with each abortion patient.

Recommended Standards for Abortion Services, 61 Am. J. Pub. Health 396 (1971).

It was said that "a well-equipped hospital" offers more protection "to cope with unforeseen difficulties than an office or clinic without such resources . . . . The factor of gestational age is of overriding importance." Thus, it was recommended that abortions in the second trimester and early abortions in the presence of existing medical complications be performed in hospitals as inpatient procedures. For pregnancies in the first trimester, abortion in the hospital with or without overnight stay "is probably the safest practice." An abortion in an extramural facility, however, is an acceptable alternative "provided arrangements exist in advance to admit patients promptly if unforeseen complications develop." Standards for an abortion facility were listed. It was said that at present abortions should be performed by physicians or osteopaths who are licensed to practice and who have "adequate training." *Id.* at 396.

8. *The position of the American Bar Association.* At its meeting in February 1972 the ABA House of Delegates approved, with 17 opposing votes, the Uniform Abortion Act that had been drafted and approved the preceding August by the Conference of Commissioners of Uniform State Laws. [The Act's text is set forth in a footnote.]

VII

Three reasons have been advanced to explain historically the enactment of criminal abortion laws in the 19th century and to justify their continued existence.

It has been argued occasionally that these laws were the product of a Victorian social concern to discourage illicit sexual conduct. Texas, however, does not advance this justification in the present case, and it appears that no court or commentator has taken the argument seriously. The appellants and *amici* contend, moreover, that this is not a proper state purpose at all and suggest that, if it were, the Texas statutes are overbroad in protecting it since the law fails to distinguish between married and unwed mothers.

A second reason is concerned with abortion as a medical procedure. When most criminal abortion laws were first enacted, the procedure was a hazardous one for the woman. This was particularly true prior to the development of antisepsis. Antiseptic techniques, of course, were based on discoveries by Lister, Pasteur, and others first announced in 1867, but were not generally accepted and employed until about the turn of the century. Abortion mortality was high. Even after 1900, and perhaps until as late as the development of antibiotics in the 1940's, standard modern techniques such as dilation and curettage were not nearly so safe as they are today. Thus, it has been argued that a State's real concern in enacting a criminal abortion law was to protect the pregnant woman, that is, to restrain her from submitting to a procedure that placed her life in serious jeopardy.

Modern medical techniques have altered this situation. Appellants and various *amici* refer to medical data indicating that abortion in early pregnancy, that is, prior to the end of the first trimester, although not without its risk, is now relatively safe. Mortality rates for women undergoing early abortions, where the procedure is legal, appear to be as low as or lower than the rates for normal childbirth. Consequently, any interest of the State in protecting the woman from an inherently hazardous procedure, except when it would be equally dangerous for her to forgo it, has largely disappeared. Of course, important state interests in the areas of health and medical standards do remain. The State has a legitimate interest in seeing to it that abortion, like any other medical procedure, is performed under circumstances that insure maximum safety for the patient. This interest obviously extends at least to the performing physician and his staff, to the facilities involved, to the availability of after-care, and to adequate provision for any complication or emergency that might arise. The prevalence of high mortality rates at illegal "abortion mills" strengthens, rather than weakens, the State's interest in regulating the conditions under which abortions are performed. Moreover, the risk to the woman increases as her pregnancy continues. Thus, the State retains a definite interest in protecting the woman's own health and safety when an abortion is proposed at a late stage of pregnancy.

The third reason is the State's interest — some phrase it in terms of duty — in protecting prenatal life. Some of the argument for this justification rests on the theory that a new human life is present from the moment of conception. The State's interest and general obligation to protect life then extends, it is argued, to prenatal life. Only when the life of the pregnant mother herself is at stake, balanced against the life she carries within her, should the interest of the embryo or fetus not prevail. Logically, of course, a legitimate state interest in this area need not stand or fall on acceptance of the belief that life begins at conception or at some other point prior to live birth. In assessing the State's interest, recognition may be given to the less rigid claim that as long as at least potential life is involved, the State may assert interests beyond the protection of the pregnant woman alone.

Parties challenging state abortion laws have sharply disputed in some courts the contention that a purpose of these laws, when enacted, was to protect prenatal life. Pointing to the absence of legislative history to support the contention, they claim that most state laws were designed solely to protect the woman. Because medical advances have lessened this concern, at least with respect to abortion in early pregnancy, they argue that with respect to such abortions the laws can no longer be justified by any state interest. There is some scholarly support for this view of original purpose. The few state courts called upon to interpret their laws in the late 19th and early 20th centuries did focus on the State's interest in protecting the woman's health rather than in preserving the embryo and fetus. Proponents of this view point out that in many States, including Texas, by statute or judicial interpretation, the pregnant woman herself could not be prosecuted for self-abortion or for cooperating in an abortion performed upon her by another. They claim that adoption of the "quickening" distinction through received common law and state statutes tacitly recognizes the greater health hazards inherent in late abortion and impliedly repudiates the theory that life begins at conception.

It is with these interests, and the weight to be attached to them, that this case is concerned.

VIII

The Constitution does not explicitly mention any right of privacy. In a line of decisions, however, going back perhaps as far as *Union Pacific R. Co. v. Botsford*, 141 U.S. 250, 251 (1891), the Court has recognized that a right of personal privacy, or a guarantee of certain areas or zones of privacy, does exist under the Constitution. In varying contexts, the Court or individual Justices have, indeed, found at least the roots of that right in the First Amendment, *Stanley v. Georgia*, 394 U.S. 557, 564 (1969); in the Fourth and Fifth Amendments, *Terry v. Ohio*, 392 U.S. 1, 8–9 (1968), *Katz v. United States*, 389 U.S. 347, 350 (1967); in the penumbras of the Bill of Rights, *Griswold v. Connecticut*, 381 U.S., at 484–485; in the Ninth Amendment, *id.*, at 486 (Goldberg, J., concurring); or in the concept of liberty guaranteed by the first section of the Fourteenth Amendment, see *Meyer v. Nebraska*, 262 U.S. 390, 399 (1923). These decisions make it clear that only personal rights that can be deemed "fundamental" or "implicit in the concept of ordered liberty," *Palko v. Connecticut*, 302 U.S. 319, 325 (1937), are included in this guarantee of personal privacy. They also make it clear that the right has some extension to activities relating to marriage, *Loving v. Virginia*, 388 U.S. 1, 12 (1967); procreation, *Skinner v. Oklahoma*, 316 U.S. 535, 541–542 (1942); contraception, *Eisenstadt v. Baird*, 405 U.S., at 453–454; *id.*, at 460, 463–465 (White, J., concurring in result); family relationships, *Prince v. Massachusetts*, 321 U.S. 158, 166 (1944); and child rearing and education, *Pierce v. Society of Sisters*, 268 U.S. 510, 535 (1925), *Meyer v. Nebraska, supra.*

This right of privacy, whether it be founded in the Fourteenth Amendment's concept of personal liberty and restrictions upon state action, as we feel it is, or, as the District Court determined, in the Ninth Amendment's reservation of rights to the people, is broad enough to encompass a woman's decision whether or not to terminate her pregnancy. The detriment that the State would impose upon the pregnant woman by denying this choice altogether is apparent. Specific and direct harm medically diagnosable even in early pregnancy may be involved. Maternity, or additional offspring, may force upon the woman a distressful life and future. Psychological harm may be imminent. Mental and physical health may be taxed by child care. There is also the distress, for all concerned, associated with the unwanted child, and there is the problem of bringing a child into a family already unable, psychologically and otherwise, to care for it. In other cases, as in this one, the additional difficulties and continuing stigma of unwed motherhood may be involved. All these are factors the woman and her responsible physician necessarily will consider in consultation.

On the basis of elements such as these, appellant and some *amici* argue that the woman's right is absolute and that she is entitled to terminate her pregnancy at whatever time, in whatever way, and for whatever reason she alone chooses. With this we do not agree. Appellant's arguments that Texas either has no valid interest at all in regulating the abortion decision, or no interest strong enough to support any limitation upon the woman's sole determination, are unpersuasive. The Court's decisions recognizing a right of privacy also acknowledge that some state regulation in areas protected by that right is appropriate. As noted above, a State may properly assert important interests in safeguarding health, in maintaining medical standards, and in protecting potential life. At some point in pregnancy, these respective interests become sufficiently compelling to sustain regulation of the factors that govern the abortion decision. The privacy right involved, therefore, cannot be said to be absolute. In fact, it is not clear to us that the claim asserted by some *amici* that one has an unlimited right to do with one's body as one pleases bears a close relationship to the right of privacy previously articulated in the Court's decisions. The Court has refused to recognize an unlimited right of this kind in the past. *Jacobson v. Massachusetts*, 197 U.S. 11 (1905) (vaccination); *Buck v. Bell*, 274 U.S. 200 (1927) (sterilization).

We, therefore, conclude that the right of personal privacy includes the abortion decision, but that this right is not unqualified and must be considered against important state interests in regulation.

We note that those federal and state courts that have recently considered abortion law challenges have reached the same conclusion. A majority, in addition to the District Court in the present case, have held state laws unconstitutional, at least in part, because of vagueness or because of overbreadth and abridgment of rights. Others have sustained state statutes.

Although the results are divided, most of these courts have agreed that the right of privacy, however based, is broad enough to cover the abortion decision; that the right, nonetheless, is not absolute and is subject to some limitations; and that at some point the state interests as to protection of health, medical standards, and prenatal life, become dominant. We agree with this approach. Where certain "fundamental rights" are involved, the Court has held that regulation limiting these rights may be justified only by a "compelling state interest," and that legislative enactments must be narrowly drawn to express only the legitimate state interests at stake.

. . . .

IX

The District Court held that the appellee failed to meet his burden of demonstrating that the Texas statute's infringement upon Roe's rights was necessary to support a compelling state interest, and that, although the appellee presented "several compelling justifications for state presence in the area of abortions," the statutes outstripped these justifications and swept "far beyond any areas of compelling state interest." Appellant and appellee both contest that holding. Appellant, as has been indicated, claims an absolute right that bars any state imposition of criminal penalties in the area. Appellee argues that the State's determination to recognize and protect prenatal life from and after conception constitutes a compelling state interest. As noted above, we do not agree fully with either formulation.

A. The appellee and certain *amici* argue that the fetus is a "person" within the language and meaning of the Fourteenth Amendment. In support of this, they outline at length and in detail the well-known facts of fetal development. If this suggestion of personhood is established, the appellant's case, of course, collapses, for the fetus' right to life would then be guaranteed specifically by the Amendment. The appellant conceded as much on reargument. On the other hand, the appellee conceded on reargument that no case could be cited that holds that a fetus is a person within the meaning of the Fourteenth Amendment.

The Constitution does not define "person" in so many words. Section 1 of the Fourteenth Amendment contains three references to "person." The first, in defining "citizens," speaks of "persons born or naturalized in the United States." The word also appears both in the Due Process Clause and in the Equal Protection Clause. "Person" is used in other places in the Constitution . . . . But in nearly all these instances, the use of the word is such that it has application only postnatally. None indicates, with any assurance, that it has any possible prenatal application.[1]

---

[1] When Texas urges that a fetus is entitled to Fourteenth Amendment protection as a person, it faces a dilemma. Neither in Texas nor in any other State are all abortions prohibited. Despite broad

All this, together with our observation, *supra*, that throughout the major portion of the 19th century prevailing legal abortion practices were far freer than they are today, persuades us that the word "person," as used in the Fourteenth Amendment, does not include the unborn. . . .

This conclusion, however, does not of itself fully answer the contentions raised by Texas, and we pass on to other considerations.

B. The pregnant woman cannot be isolated in her privacy. She carries an embryo and, later, a fetus, if one accepts the medical definitions of the developing young in the human uterus. The situation therefore is inherently different from marital intimacy, or bedroom possession of obscene material, or marriage, or procreation, or education, with which *Eisenstadt* and *Griswold, Stanley, Loving, Skinner,* and *Pierce* and *Meyer* were respectively concerned. As we have intimated above, it is reasonable and appropriate for a State to decide that at some point in time another interest, that of health of the mother or that of potential human life, becomes significantly involved. The woman's privacy is no longer sole and any right of privacy she possesses must be measured accordingly.

Texas urges that, apart from the Fourteenth Amendment, life begins at conception and is present throughout pregnancy, and that, therefore, the State has a compelling interest in protecting that life from and after conception. We need not resolve the difficult question of when life begins. When those trained in the respective disciplines of medicine, philosophy, and theology are unable to arrive at any consensus, the judiciary, at this point in the development of man's knowledge, is not in a position to speculate as to the answer.

It should be sufficient to note briefly the wide divergence of thinking on this most sensitive and difficult question. There has always been strong support for the view that life does not begin until live birth. This was the belief of the Stoics. It appears to be the predominant, though not the unanimous, attitude of the Jewish faith. It may be taken to represent also the position of a large segment of the Protestant community, insofar as that can be ascertained; organized groups that have taken a formal position on the abortion issue have generally regarded abortion as a matter for the conscience of the individual and her family. As we have noted, the common law found greater significance in quickening. Physicians and their scientific colleagues have regarded that event with less interest and have tended to focus either upon conception, upon live birth, or upon the interim point at which the fetus becomes "viable," that is, potentially able to live outside the mother's womb, albeit with artificial aid. Viability is usually placed at about seven months (28 weeks) but may occur earlier, even at 24 weeks. The Aristotelian theory of "mediate animation," that held sway throughout the Middle Ages and the Renaissance in Europe,

---

proscription, an exception always exists. The exception contained in Art. 1196, for an abortion procured or attempted by medical advice for the purpose of saving the life of the mother, is typical. But if the fetus is a person who is not to be deprived of life without due process of law, and if the mother's condition is the sole determinant, does not the Texas exception appear to be out of line with the Amendment's command?

Further, the penalty for criminal abortion specified by Art. 1195 is significantly less than the maximum penalty for murder prescribed by Art. 1257 of the Texas Penal Code. If the fetus is a person, may the penalties be different?

continued to be official Roman Catholic dogma until the 19th century, despite opposition to this "ensoulment" theory from those in the Church who would recognize the existence of life from the moment of conception. The latter is now, of course, the official belief of the Catholic Church. As one brief *amicus* discloses, this is a view strongly held by many non-Catholics as well, and by many physicians. Substantial problems for precise definition of this view are posed, however, by new embryological data that purport to indicate that conception is a "process" over time, rather than an event, and by new medical techniques such as menstrual extraction, the "morning-after" pill, implantation of embryos, artificial insemination, and even artificial wombs.

In areas other than criminal abortion, the law has been reluctant to endorse any theory that life, as we recognize it, begins before live birth or to accord legal rights to the unborn except in narrowly defined situations and except when the rights are contingent upon live birth. For example, the traditional rule of tort law denied recovery for prenatal injuries even though the child was born alive. That rule has been changed in almost every jurisdiction. In most States, recovery is said to be permitted only if the fetus was viable, or at least quick, when the injuries were sustained, though few courts have squarely so held. In a recent development, generally opposed by the commentators, some States permit the parents of a stillborn child to maintain an action for wrongful death because of prenatal injuries. Such an action, however, would appear to be one to vindicate the parents' interest and is thus consistent with the view that the fetus, at most, represents only the potentiality of life. Similarly, unborn children have been recognized as acquiring rights or interests by way of inheritance or other devolution of property, and have been represented by guardians *ad litem*. Perfection of the interests involved, again, has generally been contingent upon live birth. In short, the unborn have never been recognized in the law as persons in the whole sense.

X

In view of all this, we do not agree that, by adopting one theory of life, Texas may override the rights of the pregnant woman that are at stake. We repeat, however, that the State does have an important and legitimate interest in preserving and protecting the health of the pregnant woman, whether she be a resident of the State or a nonresident who seeks medical consultation and treatment there, and that it has still another important and legitimate interest in protecting the potentiality of human life. These interests are separate and distinct. Each grows in substantiality as the woman approaches term and, at a point during pregnancy, each becomes "compelling."

With respect to the State's important and legitimate interest in the health of the mother, the "compelling" point, in the light of present medical knowledge, is at approximately the end of the first trimester. This is so because of the now-established medical fact that until the end of the first trimester mortality in abortion may be less than mortality in normal childbirth. It follows that, from and after this point, a State may regulate the abortion procedure to the extent that the regulation reasonably relates to the preservation and protection of maternal health. Examples of permissible state regulation in this area are requirements as to the qualifications of the person who is to perform the abortion; as to the licensure of that person; as to the facility in which the procedure is to be performed, that is, whether it must be a hospital or may be a clinic or some other place of less-than-hospital status; as to the licensing of the facility; and the like.

This means, on the other hand, that, for the period of pregnancy prior to this "compelling" point, the attending physician, in consultation with his patient, is free to determine, without regulation by the State, that, in his medical judgment, the patient's pregnancy should be terminated. If that decision is reached, the judgment may be effectuated by an abortion free of interference by the State.

With respect to the State's important and legitimate interest in potential life, the "compelling" point is at viability. This is so because the fetus then presumably has the capability of meaningful life outside the mother's womb. State regulation protective of fetal life after viability thus has both logical and biological justifications. If the State is interested in protecting fetal life after viability, it may go so far as to proscribe abortion during that period, except when it is necessary to preserve the life or health of the mother.

Measured against these standards, the Texas Penal Code, in restricting legal abortions to those "procured or attempted by medical advice for the purpose of saving the life of the mother," sweeps too broadly. The statute makes no distinction between abortions performed early in pregnancy and those performed later, and it limits to a single reason, "saving" the mother's life, the legal justification for the procedure. The statute, therefore, cannot survive the constitutional attack made upon it here.

XI

To summarize and to repeat:

1. A state criminal abortion statute of the current Texas type, that excepts from criminality only a lifesaving procedure on behalf of the mother, without regard to pregnancy stage and without recognition of the other interests involved, is violative of the Due Process Clause of the Fourteenth Amendment.

(a) For the stage prior to approximately the end of the first trimester, the abortion decision and its effectuation must be left to the medical judgment of the pregnant woman's attending physician.

(b) For the stage subsequent to approximately the end of the first trimester, the State, in promoting its interest in the health of the mother, may, if it chooses, regulate the abortion procedure in ways that are reasonably related to maternal health.

(c) For the stage subsequent to viability, the State in promoting its interest in the potentiality of human life may, if it chooses, regulate, and even proscribe, abortion except where it is necessary, in appropriate medical judgment, for the preservation of the life or health of the mother.

2. The State may define the term "physician," as it has been employed in the preceding paragraphs of this Part XI of this opinion, to mean only a physician

currently licensed by the State, and may proscribe any abortion by a person who is not a physician as so defined.

In *Doe v. Bolton*, post, procedural requirements contained in one of the modern abortion statutes are considered. That opinion and this one, of course, are to be read together.

This holding, we feel, is consistent with the relative weights of the respective interests involved, with the lessons and examples of medical and legal history, with the lenity of the common law, and with the demands of the profound problems of the present day. The decision leaves the State free to place increasing restrictions on abortion as the period of pregnancy lengthens, so long as those restrictions are tailored to the recognized state interests. The decision vindicates the right of the physician to administer medical treatment according to his professional judgment up to the points where important state interests provide compelling justifications for intervention. Up to those points, the abortion decision in all its aspects is inherently, and primarily, a medical decision, and basic responsibility for it must rest with the physician . . . .

XI

Our conclusion that Art. 1196 is unconstitutional means, of course, that the Texas abortion statutes, as a unit, must fall . . . .

DOE v. BOLTON
410 U.S 179 (1973)

BLACKMUN, JUSTICE.

[The primary issue in this case is whether the state could require concurrence of a review committee or even of a second physician in the abortion decision.]

IV A.

Roe v. Wade, supra, sets forth our conclusion that a pregnant woman does not have an absolute constitutional right to an abortion on her demand. What is said there is applicable here and need not be repeated . . . .

The appellants recognize that a century ago medical knowledge was not so advanced as it is today, that the techniques of antisepsis were not known, and that any abortion procedure was dangerous for the woman. To restrict the legality of the abortion to the situation where it was deemed necessary, in medical judgment, for the preservation of the woman's life was only a natural conclusion in the exercise of the legislative judgment of that time. A State is not to be reproached, however, for a past judgmental determination made in the light of then-existing medical knowledge. It is perhaps unfair to argue, as the appellants do, that because the early focus was on the preservation of the woman's life, the State's present professed interest in the protection of embryonic and fetal life is to be downgraded.

That argument denies the State the right to readjust its views and emphases in the light of the advanced knowledge and techniques of the day . . . .

We agree with the District Court that the medical judgment may be exercised in the light of all factors — physical, emotional, psychological, familial, and the woman's age — relevant to the well-being of the patient. All these factors may relate to health. This allows the attending physician the room he needs to make his best medical judgment. And it is room that operates for the benefit, not the disadvantage, of the pregnant woman.

This is not to say that Georgia may not or should not, from and after the end of the first trimester, adopt standards for licensing all facilities where abortions may be performed so long as those standards are legitimately related to the objective the State seeks to accomplish. The appellants contend that such a relationship would be lacking even in a lesser requirement that an abortion be performed in a licensed hospital, as opposed to a facility, such as a clinic, that may be required by the State to possess all the staffing and services necessary to perform an abortion safely (including those adequate to handle serious complications or other emergency, or arrangements with a nearby hospital to provide such services). Appellants and various *amici* have presented us with a mass of data purporting to demonstrate that some facilities other than hospitals are entirely adequate to perform abortions if they possess these qualifications. The State, on the other hand, has not presented persuasive data to show that only hospitals meet its acknowledged interest in insuring the quality of the operation and the full protection of the patient. We feel compelled to agree with appellants that the State must show more than it has in order to prove that only the full resources of a licensed hospital, rather than those of some other appropriately licensed institution, satisfy these health interests. We hold that the hospital requirement of the Georgia law, because it fails to exclude the first trimester of pregnancy, see *Roe* v. *Wade, ante,* at 163, is also invalid. In so holding we naturally express no opinion on the medical judgment involved in any particular case, that is, whether the patient's situation is such that an abortion should be performed in a hospital, rather than in some other facility.

2. *Committee approval.* The second aspect of the appellants' procedural attack relates to the hospital abortion committee

Appellants attack the discretion the statute leaves to the committee. The most concrete argument they advance is their suggestion that it is still a badge of infamy "in many minds" to bear an illegitimate child, and that the Georgia system enables the committee members' personal views as to extramarital sex relations, and punishment therefor, to govern their decisions. This approach obviously is one founded on suspicion and one that discloses a lack of confidence in the integrity of physicians. To say that physicians will be guided in their hospital committee decisions by their predilections on extramarital sex unduly narrows the issue to pregnancy outside marriage. (Doe's own situation did not involve extramarital sex and its product.) The appellants' suggestion is necessarily somewhat degrading to the conscientious physician, particularly the obstetrician, whose professional activity is concerned with the physical and mental welfare, the woes, the emotions, and the concern of his female patients. He, perhaps more than anyone else, is knowledgeable in this area of patient care, and he is aware of human frailty, so-called "error," and needs. The good physician — despite the presence of rascals in the medical profession, as in all others, we trust that most physicians are "good" — will have sympathy and understanding for the pregnant patient that probably are not exceeded by those who participate in other areas of professional counseling.

. . . .

Saying all this, however, does not settle the issue of the constitutional propriety of the committee requirement. Viewing the Georgia statute as a whole, we see no constitutionally justifiable pertinence in the structure for the advance approval by the abortion committee. With regard to the protection of potential life, the medical judgment is already completed prior to the committee stage, and review by a committee once removed from diagnosis is basically redundant. We are not cited to any other surgical procedure made subject to committee approval as a matter of state criminal law. The woman's right to receive medical care in accordance with her licensed physician's best judgment and the physician's right to administer it are substantially limited by this statutorily imposed overview . . . .

We conclude that the interposition of the hospital abortion committee is unduly restrictive of the patient's rights and needs that, at this point, have already been medically delineated and substantiated by her personal physician. To ask more serves neither the hospital nor the State.

3. *Two-doctor concurrence* . . . .

. . . the required confirmation by two Georgia-licensed physicians in addition to the recommendation of the pregnant woman's own consultant [remains] (making under the statute, a total of six physicians involved, including the three on the hospital's abortion committee). We conclude that this provision, too, must fall.

The statute's emphasis, as has been repetitively noted, is on the attending physician's "best clinical judgment that an abortion is necessary." That should be sufficient. The reasons for the presence of the confirmation step in the statute are perhaps apparent, but they are insufficient to withstand constitutional challenge. Again, no other voluntary medical or surgical procedure for which Georgia requires confirmation by two other physicians has been cited to us. If a physician is licensed by the State, he is recognized by the State as capable of exercising acceptable clinical judgment. If he fails in this, professional censure and deprivation of his license are available remedies. Required acquiescence by co-practitioners has no rational connection with a patient's needs and unduly infringes on the physician's right to practice. The attending physician will know when a consultation is advisable — the doubtful situation, the need for assurance when the medical decision is a delicate one, and the like. Physicians have followed this routine historically and know its usefulness and benefit for all concerned. It is still true today that "reliance must be placed upon the assurance given by his license, issued by an authority competent to judge in that respect, that he [the physician] possesses the requisite qualifications . . . ."

———————

PLANNED PARENTHOOD OF SOUTHEASTERN
PENNSYLVANIA v. CASEY
505 U.S. 833 (1991)

JUSTICES SOUTER, KENNEDY, and O'CONNER delivered a joint opinion.

Liberty finds no refuge in a jurisprudence of doubt. Yet 19 years after our holding that the Constitution protects a woman's right to terminate her pregnancy in its early stages, *Roe v. Wade*, 410 U.S. 113 (1973), that definition of liberty is still questioned . . . .

After considering the fundamental constitutional questions resolved by *Roe*, principles of institutional integrity, and the rule of *stare decisis*, we are led to conclude this: the essential holding of *Roe v. Wade* should be retained and once again reaffirmed.

It must be stated at the outset and with clarity that *Roe's* essential holding, the holding we reaffirm, has three parts. First is a recognition of the right of the woman to choose to have an abortion before viability and to obtain it without undue interference from the State. Before viability, the State's interests are not strong enough to support a prohibition of abortion or the imposition of a substantial obstacle to the woman's effective right to elect the procedure. Second is a confirmation of the State's power to restrict abortions after fetal viability, if the law contains exceptions for pregnancies which endanger a woman's life or health. And third is the principle that the State has legitimate interests from the outset of the pregnancy in protecting the health of the woman and the life of the fetus that may become a child. These principles do not contradict one another; and we adhere to each.

II

. . . .

The inescapable fact is that adjudication of substantive due process claims may call upon the Court in interpreting the Constitution to exercise that same capacity which by tradition courts always have exercised: reasoned judgment . . . .

Our obligation is to define the liberty of all, not to mandate our own moral code

. . . .

. . . .

Our law affords constitutional protection to personal decisions relating to marriage, procreation, contraception, family relationships, child rearing, and education. Our cases recognize "the right of the individual, married or single, to be free from unwarranted governmental intrusion into matters so fundamentally affecting a person as the decision whether to bear or beget a child." *Eisenstadt v. Baird.* Our precedents "have respected the private realm of family life which the state cannot enter. These matters, involving the most intimate and personal choices a person may make in a lifetime, choices central to personal dignity and autonomy, are central to the liberty protected by the Fourteenth Amendment. At the heart of liberty is the right to define one's own concept of existence, of meaning, of the universe, and of the mystery of human life. Beliefs about these matters could not define the attributes of personhood were they formed under compulsion of the State.

These considerations begin our analysis of the woman's interest in terminating her pregnancy but cannot end it, for this reason: though the abortion decision may originate within the zone of conscience and belief, it is more than a philosophic exercise. Abortion is a unique act. It is an act fraught with consequences for others: for the woman who must live with the implications of her decision; for the persons who perform and assist in the procedure; for the spouse, family, and society which must confront the knowledge that these procedures exist, procedures some deem nothing short of an act of violence against innocent human life; and, depending on one's beliefs, for the life or potential life that is aborted. Though abortion is conduct, it does not follow that the State is entitled to proscribe it in all instances. That is because the liberty of the woman is at stake in a sense unique to the human condition and so unique to the law. The mother who carries a child to full term is subject to anxieties, to physical constraints, to pain that only she must bear . . . . Her suffering is too intimate and personal for the State to insist, without more, upon its own vision of the woman's role, however dominant that vision has been in the course of our history and our culture. The destiny of the woman must be shaped to a large extent on her own conception of her spiritual imperatives and her place in society.

It should be recognized, moreover, that in some critical respects the abortion decision is of the same character as the decision to use contraception, to which *Griswold v. Connecticut, Eisenstadt v. Baird*, and *Carey v. Population Services International*, afford constitutional protection. We have no doubt as to the correctness of those decisions. They support the reasoning in *Roe* relating to the woman's liberty because they involve personal decisions concerning not only the meaning of procreation but also human responsibility and respect for it. The same concerns are present when the woman confronts the reality that, perhaps despite her attempts to avoid it, she has become pregnant.

. . . .

IV

. . . We conclude that the basic decision in *Roe* was based on a constitutional analysis which we cannot now repudiate. The woman's liberty is not so unlimited, however, that from the outset the State cannot show its concern for the life of the unborn, and at a later point in fetal development the State's interest in life has sufficient force so that the right of the woman to terminate the pregnancy can be restricted.

That brings us, of course, to the point where much criticism has been directed at *Roe*, a criticism that always inheres when the Court draws a specific rule from what in the Constitution is but a general standard. We conclude, however, that the urgent claims of the woman to retain the ultimate control over her destiny and her body, claims implicit in the meaning of liberty, require us to perform that function.

Liberty must not be extinguished for want of a line that is clear. And it falls to us to give some real substance to the woman's liberty to determine whether to carry her pregnancy to full term.

We conclude the line should be drawn at viability, so that before that time the woman has a right to choose to terminate her pregnancy. We adhere to this principle for two reasons. First, as we have said, is the doctrine of *stare decisis*. Any judicial act of line-drawing may seem somewhat arbitrary, but *Roe* was a reasoned statement, elaborated with great care. We have twice reaffirmed it in the face of great opposition . . . .

The second reason is that the concept of viability, as we noted in *Roe*, is the time at which there is a realistic possibility of maintaining and nourishing a life outside the womb, so that the independent existence of the second life can in reason and all fairness be the object of state protection that now overrides the rights of the woman . . . .

The woman's right to terminate her pregnancy before viability is the most central principle of *Roe v. Wade*. It is a rule of law and a component of liberty we cannot renounce.

. . . .

Though the woman has a right to choose to terminate or continue her pregnancy before viability . . . . States are free to enact laws to provide a reasonable framework for a woman to make a decision that has such profound and lasting meaning. This, too, we find consistent with *Roe's* central premises, and indeed the inevitable consequence of our holding that the State has an interest in protecting the life of the unborn . . . .

. . . .

. . . Before viability, *Roe* and subsequent cases treat all governmental attempts to influence a woman's decision on behalf of the potential life within her as unwarranted. This treatment is, in our judgment, incompatible with the recognition that there is a substantial state interest in potential life throughout pregnancy.

The very notion that the State has a substantial interest in potential life leads to the conclusion that not all regulations must be deemed unwarranted. Not all burdens on the right to decide whether to terminate a pregnancy will be undue. In our view, the undue burden standard is the appropriate means of reconciling the State's interest with the woman's constitutionally protected liberty.

A finding of an undue burden is shorthand for the conclusion that a state regulation has the purpose or effect of placing a substantial obstacle in the path of a woman seeking an abortion of a nonviable fetus. A statute with this purpose is invalid because the means chosen by the State to further the interest in potential life must be calculated to inform the woman's free choice, not hinder it. And a statute which, while furthering the interest in potential life or some other valid state interest, has the effect of placing a substantial obstacle in the path of a woman's choice cannot be considered a permissible means of serving its legitimate ends . . . . Regulations designed to foster the health of a woman seeking an abortion are valid if they do not constitute an undue burden.

NOTES AND QUESTIONS

5.   Abortion, the Supreme Court, and the right to privacy. Abortion has long been, and remains, the most politicized medical procedure in the United States. It has been the subject of more state and federal legislation than all other medical procedures combined. The U.S. Supreme Court, which almost never hears cases about medical procedures, has regularly heard cases over the past 40 years concerning the constitutionality of various state laws designed to limit abortion. Nonetheless, it is probably not an overstatement to say that *Roe v. Wade* is the most important health-related case of all time. This is not just because it struck down all of the state abortion statutes that existed at the time. It is also because it applied the constitutional "right of privacy" in a way that could potentially protect individual decision-making from state interference in a variety of contexts (such as the right to refuse medical treatment). The Court also adds two new dimensions to "public health" cases: the protection of individual rights, and the protection of the practice of medicine. This means, for example, that state public health rules will have to be consistent not only with the constitutional rights of individuals, they will also have to take into account basic rules of medical practice, including medical ethics and medical licensing. (But see *Gonzales v. Carhart*, below.)

In this regard, *Doe v. Bolton* is an underappreciated case, concentrating as it does on the right of a licensed physician to practice medicine without interference from the state in requiring him or her to present a treatment plan to a committee, or even to another physician, for concurrence. Justice Blackmun, who often said the best years of his life were working as general counsel to the Mayo Clinic, strongly believed that the law should support physicians in their practice of medicine, not hinder it. In his view, expressed in both of these decisions, state licensing of physicians was sufficient for the protection of the public; after that, the doctor-patient relationship should suffice.

6.   Uses of precedent. Note that *Roe* cites both *Jacobson* (Chapter 3, C, *supra*) and *Buck v. Bell, supra*, for the proposition that rights are not absolute. What is the relevance of this citation, especially to the compulsory sterilization case of *Buck*? Can you think of a right that is absolute, in the sense of always taking precedence over state interests? There are many issues that *Roe* and *Doe* left unresolved. For example, could a state require parental consent (in the case of a minor) or spousal consent (in the case of a married woman) to abortion? These and other issues are resolved in later cases, beginning with *Planned Parenthood of Central Missouri v. Danforth*, 428 U.S. 52 (1976), which was the first abortion case decided by the Supreme Court after *Roe. Roe*, although it was decided by a 7 to 2 majority, nonetheless continued to be viewed as the most controversial decision of the Court ever, primarily because of its viability line and its exception for a woman's health that continued even after viability. Thus when the Court had an opportunity to review the entire opinion anew in the case of *Planned Parenthood v. Casey, supra*, many thought the Court would overturn *Roe*. Instead it reinforced it, although it adopted a new test for pre-viability regulations (the so-called "undue burden" test), and reverted to calling the abortion decision an aspect of "liberty" rather than "privacy."

7. **Restrictions v. prohibitions.** The central issue in *Roe, Doe, Danforth* and *Casey* was whether the state has the power to override a woman's right to choose to terminate a pregnancy or make her exercise of that right conditional on approval by others, such as a husband, the father of the fetus, or physicians. After *Casey*, legislation rarely challenged the woman's right itself, but instead imposed conditions on exercising that right. These fall roughly into three categories: (1) prerequisites to obtaining an abortion, such as requiring consent to the procedure to be in writing, a waiting period between the decision and the performance of the procedure, and the provision of state-sanctioned information about abortion; (2) requirements for medical professionals, procedures and facilities, such as prohibitions on specific abortion procedures, building specifications for clinics, requirements to perform a vaginal ultrasound before the abortion procedure, and mandating that physicians who perform abortion obtain privileges from a nearby hospital; and (3) limitations on government funding of abortions. (The Affordable Care Act passed Congress only after the President's assurance of restrictions on federal funding of health insurance coverage of abortions under the Act.) Some of these have been justified as protecting a woman's health and safety, while others have been overturned as unnecessary or violating a woman's right to truthful information. The U.S. Supreme Court has been more sympathetic to legislation conditioning a minor's right to decide to have an abortion.

GONZALES v. CARHART
550 U.S. 124 (2007)

JUSTICE KENNEDY delivered the opinion of the Court.

These cases require us to consider the validity of the Partial-Birth Abortion Ban Act of 2003 (Act), 18 U.S.C. § 1531 (2000 ed., Supp. IV), a federal statute regulating abortion procedures . . . . We conclude the Act should be sustained against the objections lodged by the broad, facial attack brought against it.

. . . .

I

A

. . . .

Abortion methods vary depending to some extent on the preferences of the physician and, of course, on the term of the pregnancy and the resulting stage of the unborn child's development. Between 85 and 90 percent of the approximately 1.3 million abortions performed each year in the United States take place in the first three months of pregnancy, which is to say in the first trimester. The most common first-trimester abortion method is vacuum aspiration (otherwise known as suction curettage) in which the physician vacuums out the embryonic tissue. Early in this trimester an alternative is to use medication, such as mifepristone (commonly known as RU-486), to terminate the pregnancy. The Act does not regulate these procedures.

Of the remaining abortions that take place each year, most occur in the second trimester. The surgical procedure referred to as "dilation and evacuation" or "D&E" is the usual abortion method in this trimester . . . .

A doctor must first dilate the cervix at least to the extent needed to insert surgical instruments into the uterus and to maneuver them to evacuate the fetus. The steps taken to cause dilation differ by physician and gestational age of the fetus . . . .

After sufficient dilation the surgical operation can commence. The woman is placed under general anesthesia or conscious sedation. The doctor, often guided by ultrasound, inserts grasping forceps through the woman's cervix and into the uterus to grab the fetus . . . . The process of evacuating the fetus piece by piece continues until it has been completely removed . . . .

. . . .

The abortion procedure that was the impetus for the numerous bans on "partial-birth abortion, " including the Act, is a variation of this standard D&E The medical community has not reached unanimity on the appropriate name for this D&E variation. It has been referred to as "intact D&E," "dilation and extraction" (D&X), and "intact D&X" For discussion purposes this D&E variation will be referred to as intact D&E The main difference between the two procedures is that in intact D&E a doctor extracts the fetus intact or largely intact with only a few passes. There are no comprehensive statistics indicating what percentage of all D&Es are performed in this manner.

. . . .

In an intact D&E procedure the doctor extracts the fetus in a way conducive to pulling out its entire body, instead of ripping it apart . . . .

. . . .

[The Court describes the procedures in which the skull is collapsed by squeezing or evacuating its contents to enable it to pass through the cervical canal.]

B

. . . In 2003, after this Court's decision in Stenberg [v. Carhart, 530 U.S. 914 (2000) (holding a Nebraska ban on "partial birth abortion procedures" unconstitutional)], Congress passed the Act at issue here. On November 5, 2003, President Bush signed the Act into law . . . .

The Act responded to Stenberg in two ways. First, Congress made factual findings . . . . Congress found, among other things, that "[a] moral, medical, and ethical consensus exists that the practice of performing a partial-birth abortion . . .

is a gruesome and inhumane procedure that is never medically necessary and should be prohibited."

Second, and more relevant here, the Act's language differs from that of the Nebraska statute struck down in Stenberg. The operative provisions of the Act provide in relevant part:

"(a) Any physician who, in or affecting interstate or foreign commerce, knowingly performs a partial-birth abortion and thereby kills a human fetus shall be fined under this title or imprisoned not more than 2 years, or both. This subsection does not apply to a partial-birth abortion that is necessary to save the life of a mother whose life is endangered by a physical disorder, physical illness, or physical injury, including a life-endangering physical condition caused by or arising from the pregnancy itself. This subsection takes effect 1 day after the enactment."

"(b) As used in this section — "

"(1) the term 'partial-birth abortion' means an abortion in which the person performing the abortion — "

"(A) deliberately and intentionally vaginally delivers a living fetus until, in the case of a head-first presentation, the entire fetal head is outside the body of the mother, or, in the case of breech presentation, any part of the fetal trunk past the navel is outside the body of the mother, for the purpose of performing an overt act that the person knows will kill the partially delivered living fetus; and"

"(B) performs the overt act, other than completion of delivery, that kills the partially delivered living fetus; and"

"(2) the term 'physician' means a doctor of medicine or osteopathy legally authorized to practice medicine and surgery by the State in which the doctor performs such activity, or any other individual legally authorized by the State to perform abortions: Provided, however, That any individual who is not a physician or not otherwise legally authorized by the State to perform abortions, but who nevertheless directly performs a partial-birth abortion, shall be subject to the provisions of this section."

. . . .

"(d) (1) A defendant accused of an offense under this section may seek a hearing before the State Medical Board on whether the physician's conduct was necessary to save the life of the mother whose life was endangered by a physical disorder, physical illness, or physical injury, including a life-endangering physical condition caused by or arising from the pregnancy itself."

"(2) The findings on that issue are admissible on that issue at the trial of the defendant. Upon a motion of the defendant, the court shall delay the beginning of the trial for not more than 30 days to permit such a hearing to take place."

"(e) A woman upon whom a partial-birth abortion is performed may not be prosecuted under this section, for a conspiracy to violate this section, or for an offense under section 2, 3, or 4 of this title based on a violation of this section."

. . . .

II

. . . .

We assume the following principles [from the joint opinion in *Planned Parenthood of Southeastern Pa. v. Casey*, 505 U.S. 833 (1992)] for the purposes of this opinion. Before viability, a State "may not prohibit any woman from making the ultimate decision to terminate her pregnancy." It also may not impose upon this right an undue burden, which exists if a regulation's "purpose or effect is to place a substantial obstacle in the path of a woman seeking an abortion before the fetus attains viability." On the other hand, " [r] egulations which do no more than create a structural mechanism by which the State, or the parent or guardian of a minor, may express profound respect for the life of the unborn are permitted, if they are not a substantial obstacle to the woman's exercise of the right to choose." *Casey*, in short, struck a balance. The balance was central to its holding. We now apply its standard to the cases at bar.

III

. . . .

A

The Act punishes "knowingly perform[ing]" a "partial-birth abortion." It defines the unlawful abortion in explicit terms.

First, the person performing the abortion must "vaginally delive[r] a living fetus." The Act does not restrict an abortion procedure involving the delivery of an expired fetus. The Act, furthermore, is inapplicable to abortions that do not involve vaginal delivery (for instance, hysterotomy or hysterectomy). The Act does apply both previability and postviability because, by common understanding and scientific terminology, a fetus is a living organism while within the womb, whether or not it is viable outside the womb. We do not understand this point to be contested by the parties.

Second, the Act's definition of partial-birth abortion requires the fetus to be delivered "until, in the case of a head-first presentation, the entire fetal head is outside the body of the mother, or, in the case of breech presentation, any part of the fetal trunk past the navel is outside the body of the mother." [I]f an abortion procedure does not involve the delivery of a living fetus to one of these "anatomical 'land-marks' " . . . the prohibitions of the Act do not apply.

Third, to fall within the Act, a doctor must perform an "overt act, other than completion of delivery, that kills the partially delivered living fetus." For purposes of criminal liability, the overt act causing the fetus' death must be separate from delivery. And the overt act must occur after the delivery to an anatomical landmark . . . .

Fourth, the Act contains scienter requirements concerning all the actions involved in the prohibited abortion . . . .

B

[The Court finds that the Act satisfies the requirements that a penal statute define the crime with sufficient definiteness and in a manner that does not encourage arbitrary and discriminatory enforcement, in contrast to *Stenberg*.]

C

We next determine whether the Act imposes an undue burden, as a facial matter, because its restrictions on second-trimester abortions are too broad . . . . The Act prohibits intact D&E and . . . it does not prohibit the D&E procedure in which the fetus is removed in parts.

. . . .

Many doctors who testified on behalf of respondents, and who objected to the Act, do not perform an intact D&E by accident. On the contrary, they begin every D&E abortion with the objective of removing the fetus as intact as possible. ("Since Dr. Chasen believes that the intact D&E is safer than the dismemberment D&E, Dr. Chasen's goal is to perform an intact D&E every time"). This does not prove, as respondents suggest, that every D&E might violate the Act and that the Act therefore imposes an undue burden. It demonstrates only that those doctors who intend to perform a D&E that would involve delivery of a living fetus to one of the Act's anatomical landmarks must adjust their conduct to the law by not attempting to deliver the fetus to either of those points. Respondents have not shown that requiring doctors to intend dismemberment before delivery to an anatomical landmark will prohibit the vast majority of D&E abortions. The Act, then, cannot be held invalid on its face on these grounds.

IV

Under the principles accepted as controlling here, the Act, as we have interpreted it, would be unconstitutional "if its purpose or effect is to place a substantial obstacle in the path of a woman seeking an abortion before the fetus attains viability." Casey, 505 U.S., at 878. The abortions affected by the Act's regulations take place both previability and postviability; so the quoted language and the undue burden analysis it relies upon are applicable. The question is whether the Act, measured by its text in this facial attack, imposes a substantial obstacle to late-term, but previability, abortions. The Act does not on its face impose a substantial obstacle, and we reject this further facial challenge to its validity.

A

. . . The Act proscribes a method of abortion in which a fetus is killed just inches before completion of the birth process. Congress stated as follows: "Implicitly approving such a brutal and inhumane procedure by choosing not to prohibit it will further coarsen society to the humanity of not only newborns, but all vulnerable and innocent human life, making it increasingly difficult to protect such life." The Act expresses respect for the dignity of human life.

Congress was concerned, furthermore, with the effects on the medical community and on its reputation caused by the practice of partial-birth abortion. The findings in the Act explain:

> "Partial-birth abortion . . . confuses the medical, legal, and ethical duties of physicians to preserve and promote life, as the physician acts directly against the physical life of a child, whom he or she had just delivered, all but the head, out of the womb, in order to end that life."

There can be no doubt the government "has an interest in protecting the integrity and ethics of the medical profession." Washington v. Glucksberg, 521 U.S. 702, 731 (1997); see also Barsky v. Board of Regents of Univ. of N. Y., 347 U.S. 442, 451 (1954) (indicating the State has "legitimate concern for maintaining high standards of professional conduct" in the practice of medicine). Under our precedents it is clear the State has a significant role to play in regulating the medical profession.

Casey reaffirmed these governmental objectives. The government may use its voice and its regulatory authority to show its profound respect for the life within the woman. A central premise of the opinion was that the Court's precedents after Roe had "undervalue[d] the State's interest in potential life." The plurality opinion indicated "[t]he fact that a law which serves a valid purpose, one not designed to strike at the right itself, has the incidental effect of making it more difficult or more expensive to procure an abortion cannot be enough to invalidate it." This was not an idle assertion. The three premises of Casey must coexist. The third premise, that the State, from the inception of the pregnancy, maintains its own regulatory interest in protecting the life of the fetus that may become a child, cannot be set at naught by interpreting *Casey's* requirement of a health exception so it becomes tantamount to allowing a doctor to choose the abortion method he or she might prefer. Where it has a rational basis to act, and it does not impose an undue burden, the State may use its regulatory power to bar certain procedures and substitute others, all in furtherance of its legitimate interests in regulating the medical profession in order to promote respect for life, including life of the unborn.

The Act's ban on abortions that involve partial delivery of a living fetus furthers the Government's objectives. No one would dispute that, for many, D&E is a procedure itself laden with the power to devalue human life. Congress could nonetheless conclude that the type of abortion proscribed by the Act requires specific regulation because it implicates additional ethical and moral concerns that justify a special prohibition. Congress determined that the abortion methods it proscribed had a "disturbing similarity to the killing of a newborn infant," and thus it was concerned with "draw[ing] a bright line that clearly distinguishes abortion and infanticide". The Court has in the past confirmed the validity of drawing boundaries to prevent certain practices that extinguish life and are close to actions that are condemned. *Glucksberg* found reasonable the State's "fear that permitting assisted suicide will start it down the path to voluntary and perhaps even involuntary euthanasia." 521 U.S., at 732–735.

Respect for human life finds an ultimate expression in the bond of love the mother has for her child. The Act recognizes this reality as well. Whether to have an abortion requires a difficult and painful moral decision. While we find no reliable data to measure the phenomenon, it seems unexceptionable to conclude some women come to regret their choice to abort the infant life they once created and sustained. Severe depression and loss of esteem can follow.

In a decision so fraught with emotional consequence some doctors may prefer not to disclose precise details of the means that will be used, confining themselves to the required statement of risks the procedure entails . . . .

It is, however, precisely this lack of information concerning the way in which the fetus will be killed that is of legitimate concern to the State. The State has an interest in ensuring so grave a choice is well informed . . . .

It is a reasonable inference that a necessary effect of the regulation and the knowledge it conveys will be to encourage some women to carry the infant to full term, thus reducing the absolute number of late-term abortions. The medical profession, furthermore, may find different and less shocking methods to abort the fetus in the second trimester, thereby accommodating legislative demand. The State's interest in respect for life is advanced by the dialogue that better informs the political and legal systems, the medical profession, expectant mothers, and society as a whole of the consequences that follow from a decision to elect a late-term abortion.

It is objected that the standard D&E is in some respects as brutal, if not more, than the intact D&E, so that the legislation accomplishes little . . . . It was reasonable for Congress to think that partial-birth abortion, more than standard D&E, "undermines the public's perception of the appropriate role of a physician during the delivery process, and perverts a process during which life is brought into the world." . . . . In sum, we reject the contention that the congressional purpose of the Act was "to place a substantial obstacle in the path of a woman seeking an abortion."

B

The Act's furtherance of legitimate government interests bears upon, but does not resolve, the next question: whether the Act has the effect of imposing an unconstitutional burden on the abortion right because it does not allow use of the barred procedure where " 'necessary, in appropriate medical judgment, for the preservation of the . . . health of the mother.' " . . . . In *Ayotte* the parties agreed a health exception to the challenged parental-involvement statute was necessary "to avert serious and often irreversible damage to [a pregnant minor's] health." Here, by contrast, whether the Act creates significant health risks for women has been a contested factual question. The evidence presented in the trial courts and before

Congress demonstrates both sides have medical support for their position.

Respondents presented evidence that intact D&E may be the safest method of abortion, for reasons similar to those adduced in *Stenberg*. Abortion doctors testified, for example, that intact D&E decreases the risk of cervical laceration or uterine perforation because it requires fewer passes into the uterus with surgical instruments and does not require the removal of bony fragments of the dismembered fetus, fragments that may be sharp. Respondents also presented evidence that intact D&E was safer both because it reduces the risks that fetal parts will remain in the uterus and because it takes less time to complete. Respondents, in addition, proffered evidence that intact D&E was safer for women with certain medical conditions or women with fetuses that had certain anomalies.

These contentions were contradicted by other doctors who testified in the District Courts and before Congress. They concluded that the alleged health advantages were based on speculation without scientific studies to support them. They considered D&E always to be a safe alternative.

. . . The three District Courts that considered the Act's constitutionality appeared to be in some disagreement on this central factual question. The District Court for the District of Nebraska concluded "the banned procedure is, sometimes, the safest abortion procedure to preserve the health of women." The District Court for the Northern District of California reached a similar conclusion. The District Court for the Southern District of New York was more skeptical of the purported health benefits of intact D&E The court nonetheless invalidated the Act because it determined "a significant body of medical opinion . . . holds that D & E has safety advantages over induction and that [intact D&E] has some safety advantages . . . over D & E for some women in some circumstances."

. . . The Court has given state and federal legislatures wide discretion to pass legislation in areas where there is medical and scientific uncertainty. See Kansas v. Hendricks, 521 U.S. 346, 360, n. 3 (1997); Jacobson v. Massachusetts, 197 U.S. 11, 30–31 (1905); Marshall v. United States, 414 U.S. 417, 427 (1974) ("When Congress undertakes to act in areas fraught with medical and scientific uncertainties, legislative options must be especially broad").

This traditional rule is consistent with *Casey*, which confirms the State's interest in promoting respect for human life at all stages in the pregnancy. Physicians are not entitled to ignore regulations that direct them to use reasonable alternative procedures. The law need not give abortion doctors unfettered choice in the course of their medical practice, nor should it elevate their status above other physicians in the medical community . . . .

Medical uncertainty does not foreclose the exercise of legislative power in the abortion context any more than it does in other contexts. The medical uncertainty over whether the Act's prohibition creates significant health risks provides a sufficient basis to conclude in this facial attack that the Act does not impose an undue burden.

The conclusion that the Act does not impose an undue burden is supported by other considerations. Alternatives are available to the prohibited procedure. As we have noted, the Act does not proscribe D&E . . . . If the intact D&E procedure is truly necessary in some circumstances, it appears likely an injection that kills the fetus is an alternative under the Act that allows the doctor to perform the procedure.

The instant cases, then, are different from Planned Parenthood of Central Mo. v. Danforth, 428 U.S. 52, 77–79 (1976), in which the Court invalidated a ban on saline amniocentesis, the then-dominant second-trimester abortion method. The Court found the ban in *Danforth* to be "an unreasonable or arbitrary regulation designed to inhibit, and having the effect of inhibiting, the vast majority of abortions after the first 12 weeks." Here the Act allows, among other means, a commonly used and generally accepted method, so it does not construct a substantial obstacle to the abortion right.

. . . .

A zero tolerance policy would strike down legitimate abortion regulations, like the present one, if some part of the medical community were disinclined to follow the proscription. This is too exacting a standard to impose on the legislative power, exercised in this instance under the Commerce Clause, to regulate the medical profession. Considerations of marginal safety, including the balance of risks, are within the legislative competence when the regulation is rational and in pursuit of legitimate ends. When standard medical options are available, mere convenience does not suffice to displace them; and if some procedures have different risks than others, it does not follow that the State is altogether barred from imposing reasonable regulations. The Act is not invalid on its face where there is uncertainty over whether the barred procedure is ever necessary to preserve a woman's health, given the availability of other abortion procedures that are considered to be safe alternatives.

V

. . . .

[R]espondents have not demonstrated that the Act would be unconstitutional in a large fraction of relevant cases. We note that the statute here applies to all instances in which the doctor proposes to use the prohibited procedure, not merely those in which the woman suffers from medical complications . . . .

The Act is open to a proper as-applied challenge in a discrete case.

NOTES AND QUESTIONS

8. **The dissent in *Gonzales v. Carhart*.** Justice Ginsburg wrote a lengthy, impassioned dissent in *Gonzales*, 550 U.S. at 168, joined by Justices Stevens, Souter, and Breyer. The excerpts below illustrate her arguments that the majority's decision broke with prior cases and threatened a woman's right to make reproductive decisions:

Today's decision is alarming. It refuses to take *Casey* and *Stenberg* seriously. It tolerates, indeed applauds, federal intervention to ban nationwide a procedure found necessary and proper in certain cases by the American College of Obstetricians and Gynecologists (ACOG). It blurs the line, firmly drawn in *Casey*, between previability and postviability abortions. And, for the first time since *Roe*, the Court blesses a prohibition with no exception safeguarding a woman's health.

. . . .

The Court offers flimsy and transparent justifications for upholding a nationwide ban on intact D&E *sans* any exception to safeguard a woman's health. Today's ruling, the Court declares, advances "a premise central to [*Casey*'s] conclusion" — *i.e.*, the Government's "legitimate and substantial interest in preserving and promoting fetal life." . . . But the Act scarcely furthers that interest: The law saves not a single fetus from destruction, for it targets only a *method* of performing abortion. And surely the statute was not designed to protect the lives or health of pregnant women. In short, the Court upholds a law that, while doing nothing to "preserv[e] . . . fetal life," bars a woman from choosing intact D&E although her doctor "reasonably believes [that procedure] will best protect [her]," *Stenberg*, 530 U.S., at 946 (Stevens, J., concurring).

As another reason for upholding the ban, the Court emphasizes that the Act does not proscribe the nonintact D&E procedure. But why not, one might ask. Nonintact D&E could equally be characterized as "brutal," involving as it does "tear[ing] [a fetus] apart" and "ripp[ing] off" its limbs. "[T]he notion that either of these two equally gruesome procedures . . . is more akin to infanticide than the other, or that the State furthers any legitimate interest by banning one but not the other, is simply irrational." *Stenberg*, 530 U.S., at 946–947 (Stevens, J., concurring).

. . . .

Ultimately, the Court admits that "moral concerns" are at work, concerns that could yield prohibitions on any abortion. Notably, the concerns expressed are untethered to any ground genuinely serving the Government's interest in preserving life. By allowing such concerns to carry the day and case, overriding fundamental rights, the Court dishonors our precedent.

Revealing in this regard, the Court invokes an antiabortion shibboleth for which it concededly has no reliable evidence: Women who have abortions come to regret their choices, and consequently suffer from " [s]evere depression and loss of esteem." Because of women's fragile emotional state and because of the "bond of love the mother has for her child," the Court worries, doctors may withhold information about the nature of the intact D&E procedure. The solution the Court approves, then, is *not* to require doctors to inform women, accurately and adequately, of the different procedures and their attendant risks. Instead, the Court deprives women of the right to make an autonomous choice, even at the expense of their safety.

This way of thinking reflects ancient notions about women's place in the family and under the Constitution — ideas that have long since been discredited. . . .

. . . . In cases on a "woman's liberty to determine whether to [continue] her pregnancy," this Court has identified viability as a critical consideration. . . .

Today, the Court blurs that line [viability], maintaining that "[t]he Act [legitimately] appl[ies] both previability and postviability because . . . a fetus is a living organism while within the womb, whether or not it is viable outside the womb." . . . "One wonders how long a line that saves no fetus from destruction will hold in face of the Court's "moral concerns." . . . . The Court's hostility to the right *Roe* and *Casey* secured is not concealed.

Throughout, the opinion refers to obstetrician-gynecologists and surgeons who perform abortions not by the titles of their medical specialties, but by the pejorative label "abortion doctor." A fetus is described as an "unborn child," and as a "baby," second-trimester, previability abortions are referred to as "late-term," and the reasoned medical judgments of highly trained doctors are dismissed as "preferences" motivated by "mere convenience."

Instead of the heightened scrutiny we have previously applied, the Court determines that a "rational" ground is enough to uphold the Act. And, most troubling, *Casey*'s principles, confirming the continuing vitality of "the essential holding of *Roe*," are merely "assume[d]" for the moment, rather than "retained" or "reaffirmed"

. . . .

The Court further confuses our jurisprudence when it declares that "facial attacks" are not permissible in "these circumstances," *i.e.*, where medical uncertainty exists.

Justice Ginsburg finds "bewildering" the majority's conclusion that Congress can prohibit intact D & E where there is medical uncertainty. She points to language in *Casey* stating that the term "necessary" meant necessary in the medical judgment of the attending physician with respect to an individual patient, not necessary for all. Moreover, a "division in medical opinion 'at most means uncertainty, a factor that signals the presence of risk, not its absence.' " She recounted the evidence of the conditions, in addition to the general risk of uterine perforation and infection, in which intact D&E is safer, including *placenta previa* and *accreta*, uterine scarring, bleeding disorders, heart disease, compromised immune systems, and where fetuses have certain abnormalities, such as severe hydrocephalus. The dissent concludes with the following:

Without attempting to distinguish *Stenberg* and earlier decisions, the majority asserts that the Act survives review because respondents have not shown that the ban on intact D&E would be unconstitutional "in a large fraction of [relevant] cases." . . . It makes no sense to conclude that this facial challenge fails because respondents have not shown that a health exception is necessary for a large fraction of second-trimester abortions, including those for which a health exception is unnecessary: The very purpose of a health *exception* is to protect women in *exceptional* cases.

. . . .

Though today's opinion does not go so far as to discard *Roe* or *Casey*, the Court, differently composed than it was when we last considered a restrictive abortion regulation, is hardly faithful to our earlier invocations of "the rule of law" and the "principles of *stare decisis*." Congress imposed a ban despite our clear prior holdings that the State cannot proscribe an abortion procedure when its use is necessary to protect a woman's health. Although Congress' findings could not withstand the crucible of trial, the Court defers to the legislative override of our Constitution-based rulings. A decision so at odds with our jurisprudence should not have staying power.

In sum, the notion that the Partial-Birth Abortion Ban Act furthers any legitimate governmental interest is, quite simply, irrational. The Court's defense of the statute provides no saving explanation. In candor, the Act, and the Court's defense of it, cannot be understood as anything other than an effort to chip away at a right declared again and again by this Court — and with increasing comprehension of its centrality to women's lives. When "a statute burdens constitutional rights and all that can be said on its behalf is that it is the vehicle that legislators have chosen for expressing their hostility to those rights, the burden is undue." *Stenberg*, 530 U.S., at 952 (Ginsburg, J., concurring).

9. **The reversal of *Stenberg*.** The fact that the Court could simply reverse a decision it had made only seven years prior to *Carhart*, and based exclusively on having Justice O'Connor replaced by Justice Alito, demonstrates that the Court is much more involved in politics than law in the abortion arena. In *Stenberg v. Carhart*, 530 U.S. 914 (2000), the Court struck down a Nebraska statute that was substantially identical to the one it upheld here.

The Nebraska law provided that "no partial birth abortion shall be performed in this state, unless such procedure is necessary to save the life of the mother whose life is endangered by a physical disorder, physical illness, or physical injury, including a life-endangering physical condition caused by or arising from the pregnancy itself." Like the federal acts twice passed by Congress and vetoed by President Bill Clinton, the Nebraska law defined partial-birth abortion as "an abortion in which the person performing the abortion partially delivers vaginally a living unborn child before killing the unborn child and completing the delivery." The law further defined the phrase "partially delivers vaginally a living unborn child before killing the unborn child" to mean "deliberately and intentionally delivering into the vagina a living unborn child, or a substantial portion thereof, for the purpose of performing a procedure that the person performing such procedure knows will kill the unborn child and does kill the unborn child." Violation of the law was a felony that carried a prison term of up to 20 years, a fine of up to $25,000, and automatic revocation of a medical license.

On the basis of information from medical textbooks and the position taken by the American College of Obstetricians and Gynecologists, Justice Breyer, writing for the majority in *Stenberg*, concluded that "intact D&E and D&X [dilation and extraction] are sufficiently similar for us [the Court] to use the terms interchangeably." There are no accurate statistics available on the number of dilation-and-extraction abortions performed in the United States, and Breyer cited estimates ranging from 640 to 5,000 cases per year. He found that such abortions are performed for a variety of reasons, including reducing the danger caused by the passage of sharp bone fragments through the cervix, minimizing the number of surgical instruments used (and thereby decreasing the likelihood of uterine perforation), reducing the likelihood of infection, and helping to ensure the removal of all fetal tissue. Dilation and extraction is also the preferred method for fetuses with hydrocephaly and anomalies incompatible with fetal survival. Regarding the necessity of a health exception, Breyer asked if the ban would in fact adversely affect the health of pregnant women who want to terminate their pregnancies. Breyer concluded that it would, on the basis of the belief of "significant medical authority" that "in some circumstances, D&X would be the safest procedure."

10.   The meaning of *Gonzales v. Carhart*. The major change in the law this opinion brings with it is the new willingness of Congress and the Court to disregard the health of pregnant women and the medical judgment of their physicians. This departure from precedent was made possible by categorizing physicians as "abortion doctors" and infantilizing pregnant women as incapable of making serious decisions about their lives and health. The majority, for example, asserts that giving Congress constitutional authority to regulate medical practice is not new, but identifies no case in which Congress had ever outlawed a medical procedure. Its reliance on the more than 100-year-old case of *Jacobson v. Massachusetts* is especially inapt. *Jacobson* was about mandatory smallpox vaccination during an epidemic. The statute had an exception for "children who present a certificate, signed by a registered physician, that they are unfit subjects for vaccination," and the Court implied that a similar medical exception would be constitutionally required for adults. It is not just abortion regulations that have had a health exception for physicians and their patients — all health regulations have. *See* George J. Annas, *The Supreme Court and Abortion Rights*, 356 NEW ENGL. J. MED. 2201–07 (2007). It is also worth noting that Justice Kennedy went so far as to instruct physicians how to terminate a near term fetus in a way that does not run afoul of Congress's moral disgust with this procedure: "If the D&E procedure is truly necessary in some circumstances, it appears likely an injection that kills the fetus is an alternative under the Act that allows the doctor to perform the [otherwise immoral?] procedure."

C.   PUBLIC HEALTH AND "IMMORAL" BEHAVIOR

Historically, the states' police power has generally been understood as including the (somewhat hazy) authority to regulate "morals." In this area the harms sought to be prevented may often be less concrete and demonstrable, and more speculative or contested, than in the areas described in the preceding materials. The question raised by the cases in this Part is whether the same basic constitutional principles are or should be applied any differently when the powers of the government are justified, either tacitly or explicitly, primarily by moral objections to certain kinds of activities.

LAWRENCE v. TEXAS
539 U.S. 558 (2003)

KENNEDY, JUSTICE.

Liberty protects the person from unwarranted government intrusions into a dwelling or other private places. In our tradition the State is not omnipresent in the home. And there are other spheres of our lives and existence, outside the home, where the State should not be a dominant presence. Freedom extends beyond spatial bounds. Liberty presumes an autonomy of self that includes freedom of thought, belief, expression, and certain intimate conduct. The instant case involves liberty of the person both in its spatial and in its more transcendent dimensions.

. . . .

In Houston, Texas, officers of the Harris County Police Department were dispatched to a private residence in response to a reported weapons disturbance. They entered an apartment where one of the petitioners, John Geddes Lawrence, resided. The right of the police to enter does not seem to have been questioned. The officers observed Lawrence and another man, Tyron Garner, engaging in a sexual act. The two petitioners were arrested, held in custody overnight, and charged and convicted before a Justice of the Peace.

The complaints described their crime as "deviate sexual intercourse, namely anal sex, with a member of the same sex (man)." The applicable state law . . . provides: "A person commits an offense if he engages in deviate sexual inter-course with another individual of the same sex." The statute defines "[d]eviate sexual inter-course" as follows: "(A) any contact between any part of the genitals of one person and the mouth or anus of another person"; or "(B) the penetration of the genitals or the anus of another person with an object."

The petitioners . . . challenged the statute as a violation of the Equal Protection Clause of the Fourteenth Amendment and of a like provision of the Texas Constitution. Those contentions were rejected. The petitioners, having entered a plea of *nolo contendere*, were each fined $200 and assessed court costs of $141.25.

The Court of Appeals for the Texas Fourteenth District considered the petitioners' federal constitutional arguments [to be controlled by *Bowers v. Hardwick*] . . . .

We granted certiorari to consider three questions:

1. Whether petitioners' criminal convictions under the Texas 'Homosexual Conduct' law — which criminalizes sexual intimacy by same-sex couples, but not identical behavior by different-sex couples — violate the Fourteenth Amendment guarantee of equal protection of the laws.

2. Whether petitioners' criminal convictions for adult consensual sexual intimacy

in the home violate their vital interests in liberty and privacy protected by the Due Process Clause of the Fourteenth Amendment.

3. Whether [*Bowers*] should be overruled.

In *Griswold* the Court invalidated a state law prohibiting the use of drugs or devices of contraception and counseling or aiding and abetting the use of contraceptives. The Court described the protected interest as a right to privacy and placed emphasis on the marriage relation and the protected space of the marital bedroom . . . . After *Griswold* it was established that the right to make certain decisions regarding sexual conduct extends beyond the marital relationship. [citing *Eisenstadt v. Baird*]

The opinions in *Griswold and Eisenstadt* were part of the background for the decision in *Roe v. Wade* . . . .

. . . .

The Court began its substantive discussion in *Bowers* as follows: "The issue presented is whether the Federal Constitution confers a fundamental right upon homosexuals to engage in sodomy and hence invalidates the laws of the many States that still make such conduct illegal and have done so for a very long time." That statement, we now conclude, discloses the Court's own failure to appreciate the extent of the liberty at stake. To say that the issue in *Bowers* was simply the right to engage in certain sexual conduct demeans the claim the individual put forward, just as it would demean a married couple were it to be said marriage is simply about the right to have sexual intercourse . . . . The statutes do seek to control a personal relationship that, whether or not entitled to formal recognition in the law, is within the liberty of persons to choose without being punished as criminals.

This, as a general rule, should counsel against attempts by the State, or a court, to define the meaning of the relationship or to set its boundaries absent injury to a person or abuse of an institution the law protects. It suffices for us to acknowledge that adults may choose to enter upon this relationship in the confines of their homes and their own private lives and still retain their dignity as free persons. When sexuality finds overt expression in intimate conduct with another person, the conduct can be but one element in a personal bond that is more enduring. The liberty protected by the Constitution allows homosexual persons the right to make this choice.

[The Court then critiques the summary of prior state and common laws that governed sodomy, as set out in *Bowers*.]

In summary, the historical grounds relied upon in *Bowers* are more complex than the majority opinion and the concurring opinion by Chief Justice Burger indicate. Their historical premises are not without doubt and, at the very least, are overstated.

It must be acknowledged . . . that for centuries there have been powerful voices to condemn homosexual conduct as immoral. The condemnation has been shaped by religious beliefs, conceptions of right and acceptable behavior, and respect for the traditional family. For many persons these are not trivial concerns but profound and deep convictions accepted as ethical and moral principles to which they aspire and which thus determine the course of their lives. These considerations do not answer the question before us, however. The issue is whether the majority may use the power of the State to enforce these views on the whole society through operation of the criminal law. "Our obligation is to define the liberty of all, not to mandate our own moral code."

. . . .

In our own constitutional system the deficiencies in *Bowers* became even more apparent in the years following its announcement. The 25 States with laws prohibiting the relevant conduct referenced in the *Bowers* decision are reduced now to 13, of which 4 enforce their laws only against homosexual conduct. In those States where sodomy is still proscribed, whether for same-sex or heterosexual conduct, there is a pattern of nonenforcement with respect to consenting adults acting in private . . . .

. . . .

As an alternative argument in this case, counsel for the petitioners and some *amici* contend that *Romer* provides the basis for declaring the Texas statute invalid under the Equal Protection Clause. [In *Romer v. Evans*, 517 U.S. 620 (1996), the Court held that a state constitutional amendment attempting to prevent the enactment of any law protecting homosexuals from discrimination was a violation of the federal Constitution because it lacked any legitimate purpose.] That is a tenable argument, but we conclude the instant case requires us to address whether *Bowers* itself has continuing validity. Were we to hold the statute invalid under the Equal Protection Clause some might question whether a prohibition would be valid if drawn differently, say, to prohibit the conduct both between same-sex and different-sex participants.

Equality of treatment and the due process right to demand respect for conduct protected by the substantive guarantee of liberty are linked in important respects, and a decision on the latter point advances both interests. If protected conduct is made criminal and the law which does so remains unexamined for its substantive validity, its stigma might remain even if it were not enforceable as drawn for equal protection reasons. When homosexual conduct is made criminal by the law of the State, that declaration in and of itself is an invitation to subject homosexual persons to discrimination both in the public and in the private spheres . . . .

. . . .

The rationale of *Bowers* does not withstand careful analysis. In his dissenting opinion in *Bowers*, Justice Stevens came to these conclusions:

> Our prior cases make two propositions abundantly clear. First, the fact that the governing majority in a State has traditionally viewed a particular practice as immoral is not a sufficient reason for upholding a law prohibiting the practice; neither history nor tradition could save a law prohibiting miscegenation from constitutional attack. Second, individual decisions by married persons, concerning the intimacies of their physical relationship, even when not intended to produce off-spring, are a form of "liberty" protected by the Due Process Clause of the Fourteenth Amendment.

Moreover this protection extends to intimate choices by unmarried as well as married persons . . . .

Justice Stevens' analysis, in our view, should have been controlling in *Bowers* and should control here.

Bowers was not correct when it was decided, and it is not correct today. It ought not to remain binding precedent. *Bowers v. Hardwick* should be and now is overruled.

  . . . .

The present case does not involve minors. It does not involve persons who might be injured or coerced or who are situated in relationships where consent might not easily be refused. It does not involve public conduct or prostitution. It does not involve whether the government must give formal recognition to any relationship that homosexual persons seek to enter. The case does involve two adults who, with full and mutual consent from each other, engaged in sexual practices common to a homosexual lifestyle. The petitioners are entitled to respect for their private lives. The State cannot demean their existence or control their destiny by making their private sexual conduct a crime. Their right to liberty under the Due Process Clause gives them the full right to engage in their conduct without intervention of the government . . . . The Texas statute furthers no legitimate state interest which can justify its intrusion into the personal and private life of the individual.

Had those who drew and ratified the Due Process Clauses of the Fifth Amendment or the Fourteenth Amendment known the components of liberty in its manifold possibilities, they might have been more specific. They did not presume to have this insight. They knew times can blind us to certain truths and later generations can see that laws once thought necessary and proper in fact serve only to oppress. As the Constitution endures, persons in every generation can invoke its principles in their own search for greater freedom.

The judgment of the Court of Appeals . . . is reversed, and the case is remanded for further proceedings not inconsistent with this opinion.

GOODRIDGE v. DEPARTMENT OF PUBLIC HEALTH
798 N.E.2d 941 (Mass. 2003).

MARSHALL, CHIEF JUSTICE.

Marriage is a vital social institution. The exclusive commitment of two individuals to each other nurtures love and mutual support; it brings stability to our society. For those who choose to marry, and for their children, marriage provides an abundance of legal, financial, and social benefits. In return it imposes weighty legal, financial, and social obligations. The question before us is whether, consistent with the Massachusetts Constitution, the Commonwealth may deny the protections, benefits, and obligations conferred by civil marriage to two individuals of the same sex who wish to marry . . . .

Many people hold deep-seated religious, moral, and ethical convictions that marriage should be limited to the union of one man and one woman, and that homosexual conduct is immoral. Many hold equally strong religious, moral, and ethical convictions that same-sex couples are entitled to be married, and that homosexual persons should be treated no differently than their heterosexual neighbors. Neither view answers the question before us. Our concern is with the Massachusetts Constitution as a charter of governance for every person properly within its reach. "Our obligation is to define the liberty of all, not to mandate our own moral code." [citing *Lawrence*]

Whether the Commonwealth may use its formidable regulatory authority to bar same-sex couples from civil marriage is a question not previously addressed by a Massachusetts appellate court. It is a question the United States Supreme Court left open as a matter of Federal law in *Lawrence*, where it was not an issue . . . . The Massachusetts Constitution is, if anything, more protective of individual liberty and equality than the Federal Constitution; it may demand broader protection for fundamental rights; and it is less tolerant of government intrusion into the protected spheres of private life.

Barred access to the protections, benefits, and obligations of civil marriage, a person who enters into an intimate, exclusive union with another of the same sex is arbitrarily deprived of membership in one of our community's most rewarding and cherished institutions. That exclusion is incompatible with the constitutional principles of respect for individual autonomy and equality under law.

I

. . . .

The Department of Public Health (department) is charged by statute with safeguarding public health. Among its responsibilities, the department oversees the registry of vital records and statistics (registry), which "enforce[s] all laws" relative to the issuance of marriage licenses and the keeping of marriage records, and which promulgates policies and procedures for the issuance of marriage licenses by city and town clerks and registers . . . .

In March and April, 2001, each of the plaintiff couples attempted to obtain a marriage license from a city or town clerk's office . . . . In each case, the clerk either refused to accept the notice of intention to marry or denied a marriage license to the couple on the ground that Massachusetts does not recognize same-sex marriage . . . .

. . . .

II

Although the plaintiffs refer in passing to "the marriage statutes," they focus, quite properly, on G. L. c. 207, the marriage licensing statute, which controls entry into civil marriage . . . . [The Court then determines that the statute does not permit same-sex couples to marry.]

. . . .

III

The larger question is whether, as the department claims, government action that bars same-sex couples from civil marriage constitutes a legitimate exercise of the State's authority to regulate conduct, or whether, as the plaintiffs claim, this categorical marriage exclusion violates the Massachusetts Constitution. We have recognized the long-standing statutory understanding, derived from the common law, that "marriage" means the lawful union of a woman and a man. But that history cannot and does not foreclose the constitutional question.

. . . .

We begin by considering the nature of civil marriage itself. Simply put, the government creates civil marriage. In Massachusetts, civil marriage is, and since pre-Colonial days has been, precisely what its name implies: a wholly secular institution . . . . No religious ceremony has ever been required to validate a Massachusetts marriage.

. . . .

Civil marriage is created and regulated through exercise of the police power . . . . "Police power" (now more commonly termed the State's regulatory authority) is an old-fashioned term for the Commonwealth's lawmaking authority, as bounded by the liberty and equality guarantees of the Massachusetts Constitution . . . . In broad terms, it is the Legislature's power to enact rules to regulate conduct, to the extent that such laws are "necessary to secure the health, safety, good order, comfort, or general welfare of the community."

Without question, civil marriage enhances the "welfare of the community." It is a "social institution of the highest importance." Civil marriage anchors an ordered society by encouraging stable relationships over transient ones. It is central to the way the Commonwealth identifies individuals, provides for the orderly distribution of property, ensures that children and adults are cared for and supported whenever possible from private rather than public funds, and tracks important epidemiological and demographic data.

Marriage also bestows enormous private and social advantages on those who choose to marry. Civil marriage is at once a deeply personal commitment to another human being and a highly public celebration of the ideals of mutuality, companionship, intimacy, fidelity, and family . . . . Because it fulfills yearnings for security, safe haven, and connection that express our common humanity, civil marriage is an esteemed institution, and the decision whether and whom to marry is among life's momentous acts of self-definition.

. . . .

The benefits accessible only by way of a marriage license are enormous, touching nearly every aspect of life and death. The department states that "hundreds of statutes" are related to marriage and to marital benefits . . . .

Exclusive marital benefits that are not directly tied to property rights include the presumptions of legitimacy and parentage of children born to a married couple and evidentiary rights, such as the prohibition against spouses testifying against one another about their private conversations, applicable in both civil and criminal cases. Other statutory benefits of a personal nature available only to married individuals include qualification for bereavement or medical leave to care for individuals related by blood or marriage; an automatic "family member" preference to make medical decisions for an incompetent or disabled spouse who does not have a contrary health care proxy . . . .

Where a married couple has children, their children are also directly or indirectly, but no less auspiciously, the recipients of the special legal and economic protections obtained by civil marriage[,] [n]otwithstanding the Commonwealth's strong public policy to abolish legal distinctions between marital and nonmarital children in providing for the support and care of minors . . . .

. . . The United States Supreme Court has described the right to marry as "of fundamental importance for all individuals" and as "part of the fundamental 'right of privacy' implicit in the Fourteenth Amendment's Due Process Clause." . . .

Without the right to marry — or more properly, the right to choose to marry — one is excluded from the full range of human experience and denied full protection of the laws for one's "avowed commitment to an intimate and lasting human relationship."

Unquestionably, the regulatory power of the Commonwealth over civil marriage is broad, as is the Commonwealth's discretion to award public benefits. Individuals who have the choice to marry each other and nevertheless choose not to may properly be denied the legal benefits of marriage. But that same logic cannot hold for a qualified individual who would marry if she or he only could.

. . . .

The individual liberty and equality safeguards of the Massachusetts Constitution protect both "freedom from" unwarranted government intrusion into protected spheres of life and "freedom to" partake in benefits created by the State for the common good. Both freedoms are involved here. Whether and whom to marry, how to express sexual intimacy, and whether and how to establish a family — these are among the most basic of every individual's liberty and due process rights. And central to personal freedom and security is the assurance that the laws will apply equally to persons in similar situations . . .

The Massachusetts Constitution requires, at a minimum, that the exercise of the State's regulatory authority not be "arbitrary or capricious." Under both the equality and liberty guarantees, regulatory authority must, at very least, serve "a legitimate purpose in a rational way"; a statute must "bear a reasonable relation to a permissible legislative objective." . . .

The plaintiffs challenge the marriage statute on both equal protection and due process grounds. With respect to each such claim, we must first determine the appropriate standard of review. Where a statute implicates a fundamental right or uses a suspect classification, we employ "strict judicial scrutiny." For all other statutes, we employ the " 'rational basis' test." For due process claims, rational basis analysis requires that statutes "bear[] a real and substantial relation to the public health, safety, morals, or some other phase of the general welfare." For equal protection challenges, the rational basis test requires that "an impartial lawmaker could logically believe that the classification would serve a legitimate public purpose that transcends the harm to the members of the disadvantaged class."

For the reasons we explain below, we conclude that the marriage ban does not meet the rational basis test for either due process or equal protection. Because the statute does not survive rational basis review, we do not consider the plaintiffs' arguments that this case merits strict judicial scrutiny.

The department posits three legislative rationales for prohibiting same-sex couples from marrying: (1) providing a "favorable setting for procreation"; (2) ensuring the optimal setting for child rearing, which the department defines as "a two-parent family with one parent of each sex"; and (3) preserving scarce State and private financial resources. We consider each in turn.

The judge in the Superior Court endorsed the first rationale . . . . This is incorrect. Our laws of civil marriage do not privilege procreative heterosexual intercourse between married people above every other form of adult intimacy and every other means of creating a family. General Laws c. 207 contains no requirement that the applicants for a marriage license attest to their ability or intention to conceive children by coitus. Fertility is not a condition of marriage, nor is it grounds for divorce. People who have never consummated their marriage, and never plan to, may be and stay married . . . .

Moreover, the Commonwealth affirmatively facilitates bringing children into a family regardless of whether the intended parent is married or unmarried, whether the child is adopted or born into a family, whether assistive technology was used to conceive the child, and whether the parent or her partner is heterosexual, homosexual, or bisexual. If procreation were a necessary component of civil marriage, our statutes would draw a tighter circle around the permissible bounds of non-marital child bearing and the creation of families by non-coital means . . . .

The "marriage is procreation" argument singles out the one unbridgeable difference between same-sex and opposite-sex couples, and transforms that difference into the essence of legal marriage . . . . In so doing, the State's action confers an official stamp of approval on the destructive stereotype that same-sex relationships are inherently unstable and inferior to opposite-sex relationships and are not worthy of respect.

. . . Protecting the welfare of children is a paramount State policy. Restricting marriage to opposite-sex couples, however, cannot plausibly further this policy. "The demographic changes of the past century make it difficult to speak of an average American family. The composition of families varies greatly from household to household." Moreover, we have repudiated the common-law power of the State to provide varying levels of protection to children based on the circumstances of birth. The "best interests of the child" standard does not turn on a parent's sexual orientation or marital status . . . .

The department has offered no evidence that forbidding marriage to people of the same sex will increase the number of couples choosing to enter into opposite-sex marriages in order to have and raise children. There is thus no rational relationship between the marriage statute and the Commonwealth's proffered goal of protecting the "optimal" child rearing unit. Moreover, the department readily concedes that people in same-sex couples may be "excellent" parents . . . . While the enhanced income provided by marital benefits is an important source of security and stability for married couples and their children, those benefits are denied to families headed by same-sex couples. While the laws of divorce provide clear and reasonably predictable guidelines for child support, child custody, and property division on dissolution of a marriage, same-sex couples who dissolve their relationships find themselves and their children in the highly unpredictable terrain of equity jurisdiction. Given the wide range of public benefits reserved only for married couples, we do not credit the department's contention that the absence of access to civil marriage amounts to little more than an inconvenience to same-sex couples and their children . . . .

. . . .

The third rationale advanced by the department is that limiting marriage to opposite-sex couples furthers the Legislature's interest in conserving scarce State and private financial resources . . . .

An absolute statutory ban on same-sex marriage bears no rational relationship to the goal of economy. First, the department's conclusory generalization — that same-sex couples are less financially dependent on each other than opposite-sex couples — ignores that many same-sex couples, such as many of the plaintiffs in this case, have children and other dependents (here, aged parents) in their care . . . . Second, Massachusetts marriage laws do not condition receipt of public and private financial benefits to married individuals on a demonstration of financial dependence on each other; the benefits are available to married couples regardless of whether they mingle their finances or actually depend on each other for support.

The department [also] argues that broadening civil marriage to include same-sex couples will trivialize or destroy the institution of marriage as it has historically been fashioned . . . .

Here, the plaintiffs seek only to be married, not to undermine the institution of civil marriage. They do not want marriage abolished. They do not attack the binary nature of marriage, the consanguinity provisions, or any of the other gate-keeping provisions of the marriage licensing law. Recognizing the right of an individual to marry a person of the same sex will not diminish the validity or dignity of opposite-sex marriage, any more than recognizing the right of an individual to marry a person of a different race devalues the marriage of a person who marries someone of her own race . . . .

. . . .

The history of constitutional law "is the story of the extension of constitutional rights and protections to people once ignored or excluded." As a public institution and a right of fundamental importance, civil marriage is an evolving paradigm. . . . Alarms about the imminent erosion of the "natural" order of marriage were sounded over the demise of anti-miscegenation laws, the expansion of the rights of married women, and the introduction of "no-fault" divorce. Marriage has survived all of these transformations, and we have no doubt that marriage will continue to be a vibrant and revered institution.

. . . .

The marriage ban works a deep and scarring hardship on a very real segment of the community for no rational reason. The absence of any reasonable relationship between, on the one hand, an absolute disqualification of same-sex couples who wish to enter into civil marriage and, on the other, protection of public health, safety, or general welfare, suggests that the marriage restriction is rooted in persistent prejudices against persons who are (or who are believed to be) homosexual. "The Constitution cannot control such prejudices but neither can it tolerate them. Private biases may be outside the reach of the law, but the law cannot, directly or indirectly, give them effect."

. . . .

We construe civil marriage to mean the voluntary union of two persons as spouses, to the exclusion of all others. This reformulation redresses the plaintiffs' constitutional injury and furthers the aim of marriage to promote stable, exclusive relationships. It advances the two legitimate State interests the department has identified: providing a stable setting for child rearing and conserving State resources. It leaves intact the Legislature's broad discretion to regulate marriage.

. . . We declare that barring an individual from the protections, benefits, and obligations of civil marriage solely because that person would marry a person of the same sex violates the Massachusetts Constitution . . . .

NOTES AND QUESTIONS

1. **Privacy in intimate decisions.** In *Lawrence*, Justices Kennedy, Breyer, Stevens, and Souter, with a separate concurring opinion of Justice O'Connor, did what the Supreme Court has seldom done: It explicitly reconsidered a fairly recent decision, *Bowers v. Hardwick*, 478 U.S. 186 (1986), and held that it was "not correct when it was decided and it is not correct today." *Lawrence* considered a Texas statute (similar to the Georgia statute considered in *Bowers*) making it a crime for two persons of the same sex to engage in intimate sexual conduct. Most importantly, as the excerpt above demonstrates, the majority opinion held that *Bowers* had "demeaned" the constitutional significance of the privacy interest affected by such laws, by characterizing it merely as right to "engage in certain kinds of sexual conduct" rather than as a right to be free of criminally-sanctioned state control of a personal relationship, even if that relationship was not entitled to "formal legal recognition" (by which Kennedy presumably meant some form of civil validation of a same-sex partnership).

The Court compared the private activities of homosexual men to the conduct protected in *Planned Parenthood of Southeastern Pa. v. Casey*, 505 U.S. 833 (1992), and the other abortion cases and — while not using the term "fundamental right" — clearly indicated that their private sexual conduct was entitled to the same degree of judicial protection as that in its previous right to privacy cases:

. . . The case does involve two adults who, with full and mutual consent from each other, engaged in sexual practices common to a homosexual lifestyle. The petitioners are entitled to respect for their private lives. The State cannot demean their existence or control their destiny by making their private sexual conduct a crime. Their right to liberty under the Due Process Clause gives them the full right to engage in their conduct without intervention of the government . . . . The Texas statute furthers no legitimate state interest which can justify its intrusion into the personal and private life of the individual.

539 U.S. at 578.

What standard of review is Justice Kennedy using in the above excerpt? Is it necessary to apply strict scrutiny if the law "furthers no legitimate state interest"? Does this mean that all private sexual conduct is beyond government's reach, regardless of one's sexual preference? Or only that between two (or possibly more) consenting adults?

Significantly, the Court considered whether a state may act to regulate or even prohibit homosexual conduct in order to protect minors, those who might be injured or coerced, or those who have not given their consent, or to prohibit public displays or prostitution, just as the state can regulate contraceptives or abortions where certain compelling or legitimate interests (such as product safety) can properly be served. In such circumstances, the Court seems to contemplate, there may be "injury to a person or abuse of an institution the law protects" that is lacking in the case before it, which by contrast generates no such harm.

2. **Morality and the regulation of intimate relationships.** Since *Lawrence* was decided in 2003, the question is whether, by itself, morality or any particular moral theory remains a legitimate goal of the state sufficient to override personal freedoms, or whether the law must necessarily serve an independent reason of public safety, health, good order, or welfare. Justice Kennedy describes the issue in *Lawrence* as "whether the majority may use the power of the State to enforce these views on the whole society through operation of the criminal law. " His next sentence suggests that the answer is no: " 'Our obligation is to define the liberty of all, not to mandate our own moral code.' " He also concludes that Justice Stevens' analysis, in dissent in *Bowers*, should control the decision in Lawrence, quoting Stevens' statement that "the fact that the governing majority in a State has traditionally viewed a particular practice as immoral is not a sufficient reason for upholding a law prohibiting the practice . . . ." In contrast, Justice Scalia, dissenting, insisted that "the Constitution does not forbid the government to enforce traditional moral and sexual norms." *Lawrence v. Texas*, 539 U.S. at 599 (Scalia, J., dissenting). How broadly should these statements be read?

Justice Kennedy did seem to accept Congress's view of morality as one basis for federal legislation in his opinion upholding the federal prohibition of a medical procedure for abortion in *Gonzales v. Carhart*, Part B, *supra*. There he noted that Congress could express its reverence for life by prohibiting a so-called partial birth abortion method. His opinion asserted, however, that the medical community was divided as to the necessity for this particular procedure — although medical opinions among physicians who actually performed abortion were probably not so divided in reality.

Lawrence concerned a criminal prohibition on individual conduct involving strongly protected constitutional interests. What *Lawrence* did not address, however, is whether a state's interest is sufficient to justify its prevention of other kinds of activities — *e.g.*, gambling or tattooing — that are considered immoral by some members of the public, but do *not* involve the exercise of constitutionally protected interests. Regulation or prohibition of activities of this kind has typically been subject to rationality or some other lower standard of review.

3. **Public morals as a state interest in regulating other matters.** Early definitions of the state's police power included protecting the public's safety, health, welfare, good order, and morals. Laws prohibiting acts considered immoral or disruptive of good order were common in the 18th and 19th centuries, such as laws prohibiting blasphemy, indecent attire and operating a business on the Sabbath, laws prohibiting marriage between races or within certain bounds of consanguinity, or laws prohibiting contraception, abortion, sodomy, and tobacco use. The goal of the federal Comstock Act of 1873, for example, was "the suppression of Trade in and Circulation of obscene Literature and Articles of immoral Use," and imposed criminal penalties for violations. Many such laws provoked controversy. In some cases, advances in scientific knowledge undercut the early rationale for a law, while in others, political or economic objections forced their repeal or limitation. In still others, legal challenges based on constitutional protections of individual liberty succeeded in removing laws prohibiting interracial marriage, contraception, abortion and consensual sodomy, regardless of public opinion. Today, in practice, purely moral justifications are rarely put forth as the sole reason to justify legislation. In the past few decades, for example, Sunday closing laws were upheld as offering a day of rest for workers, rather than a day of worship. Does this mean that morals are no longer a legitimate state interest or a sufficient justification for regulation of activities that are not afforded heightened scrutiny?

Not long after *Lawrence* was decided, a federal court of appeals concluded that morality provided a sufficient basis for a law prohibiting the sale of sex toys. *Williams v. Alabama*, 378 F. 3d 1232 (11th Cir. 2004). The circuit court described Alabama's Anti-Obscenity Enforcement Act as prohibiting, "among other things, the commercial distribution of 'any device designed or marketed as useful primarily for the stimulation of human genital organs for any thing of pecuniary value.' Ala. Code § 13A-12-200.2 (Supp. 2003)." The law did not proscribe any sexual conduct or the possession or use of sexual devices, but prohibited only the purchase and sale of sexual devices. However, the court recognized that a ban on sales burdens one's ability to use the devices, just as a ban on contraceptive sales burdens the right to make reproductive decisions. The district court below had held that the constitution protected a right to sexual privacy, including the right to use sexual devices within private, consensual adult sexual relationships. The circuit court's majority opinion rejected that conclusion, finding no constitutional protection of any right to sexual privacy in general or any right to use sexual devices in particular. Consequently, it held that the Alabama statute targeted activities that merited only rationality review. In the court's view, under a rationality standard, the state could merely find that it had a moral objection to the sale (and, presumably, use) of sex toys: "the promotion and preservation of public morality provided a rational basis" for the criminal proscription. The majority tried to distinguish *Lawrence*, implying that it was incorrectly decided, and concluded that *Lawrence* had not ruled out morality as a basis for legislation. Its reading of *Lawrence* is less than accurate, as the dissent points out. But it does allow the court to address the oft-avoided question: Can the state regulate or prohibit an activity, at least one that is not specially protected by the state or federal constitutions, merely because the state legislature finds it immoral?

Assume for purposes of argument that the *Williams* court was correct about the state's discretion to regulate non-protected activities to achieve moral purposes. What limits would there be on legislative discretion? More to the point for present purposes, what would be the implications for various public health programs? Is it enough, for example, that we find obesity "repulsive" or smoking "stupid"? Is it possible that public health officials should applaud such a broad reading of government power? Can you think of circumstances under which those same officials should fear such a reading of the law?

4.   Same-sex marriage and the US Supreme Court. As of March 2014, the US Supreme Court has not yet decided whether state laws restricting marriage to one man and one woman are constitutional. It determined that it did not have jurisdiction to decide such a challenge in *Hollingsworth v. Perry*, 133 S. Ct. 2652 (2013). The case, brought by two same-sex couples, challenged an amendment to the California constitution that provided, "Only marriage between a man and a woman is valid or recognized in California." The amendment was adopted by ballot initiative (Proposition 8) in response to a decision of the California Supreme Court finding that the earlier statutory limitation of marriage to opposite sex couples violated the equal protection clause of California's Constitution. *In re Marriage Cases*, 183 P. 3d 384 (Cal. 2008).. In *Hollingsworth*, the federal district court found the Proposition 8 amendment unconstitutional and granted the plaintiff couples a permanent injunction against its enforcement. *Perry v. Schwarzenegger*, 704 F. Supp. 2d 921 (ND Cal. 2010). California officials did not appeal. Citizens who were proponents of Proposition 8, however, did appeal to the Ninth Circuit Court of Appeals, which affirmed the district court decision. In *Hollingsworth*, however, the U.S. Supreme Court held that the Proposition 8 proponents had no standing to appeal the district court decision. This left the district court decision intact, but of little precedential value.

Hints of how some U.S. Supreme Court Justices might view laws permitting or forbidding same-sex marriage might be seen in *United States v. Windsor*, Chapter 3, B, *supra*, in which the Court overturned one section of the federal Defense of Marriage Act (DOMA), which defined marriage as exclusively between one man and one woman for purposes of federal law. The *Windsor* majority described the value of marriage in terms similar to those used in *Goodrich, supra*, and even *Lawrence, supra*. Justice Scalia took clear note of the implications in a vigorous dissent. He argued that the majority opinion offered a blueprint to strike down state laws forbidding same-sex marriage. His dissent even included several of the majority opinion's paragraphs, edited in track-changes to demonstrate how the text could also apply to state laws. In his view, "It is enough to say that the Constitution neither requires nor forbids our society to approve of same-sex marriage, much as it neither requires nor forbids us to approve of no-fault divorce, polygamy, or the consumption of alcohol."

In light of the growing number of states that have authorized same-sex marriage, either by statute or court decision, as well as the concurrently growing number that have adopted state constitutional prohibitions against same-sex marriage, the Supreme Court may soon have an opportunity to consider whether the federal constitution protects a right to marry a person of the same sex. If so, it will doubtless confront the arguments considered in state court opinions, like *Goodrich,* *supra.*

5.   ***Goodridge* and the arguments for and against same-sex marriage.** The Massachusetts Supreme Judicial Court, the first to decide a same-sex marriage case, contains most of the arguments for and against a right to marry a person of the same sex. Despite its statements that "whom to marry, how to express sexual intimacy, and whether and how to establish a family — these are among the most basic of every individual's liberty and due process rights, " the Massachusetts court does not rely on *Loving v. Virginia,* 388 U.S. 1 (1967), an obvious precedent. Why not? Are there significant differences between the Virginia law forbidding interracial marriage (which the *Loving* Court held violated the equal protection guarantee of the Fourteenth Amendment) and the Massachusetts law forbidding marriage between persons of the same sex? The Massachusetts court characterizes *Lawrence* as turning on "the core concept of common human dignity." What does that mean? Is it a useful constitutional concept?

The Massachusetts Court also does what some courts do when faced with potentially far-reaching questions of constitutional law: It finds a way to decide the case without deciding some of the more controversial questions that the case had apparently posed. In this case, the court holds that it need not decide whether the Massachusetts marriage laws warrant close judicial scrutiny, because in the court's view, the Massachusetts law does not even satisfy the "rationality" standard. In doing so, the court avoids the need to specify exactly which individual rights are affected by the Massachusetts law or commenting on any other laws that might affect such rights. In a related vein, the court also seems to remain somewhat vague as to whether its analysis and conclusion are based on state-law notions of equal protection, due process, or both. In this respect, its approach is similar to that of *Lawrence.*

Although the court purports to apply "rationality" review, is it really doing so? Note the skepticism with which the court greets several of the bases for the law articulated by the state. Does this track the kind of rationality review we have seen in earlier cases? Under rationality review, a law usually needn't be "perfect" in achieving its goals in order to be upheld. For example, the state's second asserted interest — ensuring the "optimal" setting for child-rearing, and viewing this as fostered by a heterosexual marital couple — is not a "perfect" justification for the law, simply because — even assuming, *arguendo,* that it were generally true — there are surely circumstances in which it will turn out *not* to be true, and in which less traditional families will do better for children's welfare. But why is it, as a constitutional matter, irrational? Under close scrutiny, of course, the imperfect fit may properly be viewed as unnecessarily restrictive. But under deferential scrutiny, such failings don't necessarily transform a law into an "irrational" policy enactment. Further, isn't the court, in substance, requiring the state to prove that the law achieves its interests — in effect, saying to the state, "show me" — rather than simply *presuming* the constitutional sufficiency of the state's interests and their fit with the chosen means, and requiring the *plaintiff* to affirmatively establish why no reasonable person could attach credence thereto? If this is an accurate description of what the court is doing, then it can be seen as an (unarticulated) burden-shifting that, more typically, is done only under "close" scrutiny, and then forthrightly.

Goodridge only briefly touches on the argument that the state may justify its statutory limits on same-sex measures as an effort to protect the morals of the public. Interestingly, in this connection it invokes a definition of the "police power" that includes most of the familiar elements — "the health, safety, good order, comfort, or general welfare of the community" — but omits "morals." In a paragraph not included in the above excerpt, that court rejected the state's argument that the legislature has discretion to prohibit same-sex marriage "in order to assure all citizens of the Commonwealth that . . . the State does not endorse gay and lesbian parenthood as the equivalent of being raised by one's married biological parents." The Court dismisses that argument as inconsistent with the state's many efforts to protect homosexuals from discrimination. Does this make sense? Are anti-discrimination laws grounded in notions of morality? Is it possible — more to the point, is it "rational" — for a state to oppose discrimination against homosexuals but still deny them licenses to marry? If Massachusetts were to repeal its discrimination laws, would it then be constitutionally permissible to disallow same-sex marriage on moral grounds? If notions of morality can be the rational basis for state action such as this, what other activities could be regulated or prohibited? Is there anything that could *not* be?

6. ***Goodridge* and state constitutional provisions.** *Goodridge* is a fascinating case for a number of reasons, not the least of which is the fact that the Massachusetts Supreme Court does in *Goodridge* what all state supreme courts can, but seldom do: It reaches into its own state constitution to build a constitutional foundation for its decision. What reasons do state courts have for taking this approach? One, of course, is clear: Such a decision cannot be overturned by any federal court, even the Supreme Court (except on "supremacy clause" grounds, which would not be available absent a contrary and prohibitive federal rule, either statutory or constitutional). What other reasons might there be? If the Massachusetts (or any other state or federal) court had instead analyzed state-law prohibitions on gay marriage on the basis of federal constitutional doctrine, how might application of *Lawrence* affect that analysis? Many states have adopted amendments to their state constitutions to specify that marriage is permitted only between one man and one woman or that people of the same sex or gender cannot marry. What effect would such state constitutional provisions have if the U.S. Supreme Court were to find that the freedom to marry a person of the same sex is protected by the Fourteenth Amendment's due process or equal protection clause?

7. **Bigamy, polygamy, and other marital combinations.** *State v. Green*, 99 P.3d 820 (Utah 2004), raised some of these same issues, although it does not provide definitive answers. Green, an "avowed polygamist," participated in simultaneous conjugal-type relationships with multiple women. These women all used Green's

surname and bore children who also use the Green surname. Some of the women entered into licensed marriages with Green. The remaining women participated in unlicensed ceremonies, after which they considered themselves married to Green. Green avoided being in more than one licensed marriage at a time by terminating each licensed marriage by divorce prior to obtaining a license for a new marriage. Green then continued his relationships with each of the women he divorced as if no divorce had occurred. Green appeared on various television shows with the women, consistently referring to the women as his wives, and the women likewise acknowledged spousal relationships. In these television appearances, Green acknowledged that his conduct was potentially punishable under Utah criminal statutes.

Utah charged Green with bigamy. A jury found him guilty on four counts. Green appealed claiming that (1) Utah's bigamy statute violated his federal constitutional right to free exercise of religion; (2) Utah's bigamy statute was unconstitutionally vague in light of Green's conduct; and (3) the State's use of Utah's unsolemnized marriage statute to establish a legal marriage to some of his wives was unconstitutional. The state supreme court rejected all of his claims. With respect to his Free Exercise claim, the court reasoned:

> . . . We conclude that Utah's bigamy statute is rationally related to several legitimate government ends. First, this state has an interest in regulating marriage. As stated in *Reynolds* [a 19th Century U.S. Supreme Court case upholding Utah's criminalization of bigamy in its state constitution], marriage may be viewed as a type of "civil contract" : "Upon it society may be said to be built, and out of its fruits spring social relations and social obligations and duties, with which government is necessarily required to deal." . . .

> The State of Utah's interest in regulating marriage has resulted in a network of laws, many of which are premised upon the concept of monogamy . . . .

> Beyond the State's interest in regulating marriage as an important social unit, or in maintaining its network of laws, Utah's bigamy statute serves additional legitimate government ends. Specifically, prohibiting bigamy implicates the State's interest in preventing the perpetration of marriage fraud, as well as its interest in preventing the misuse of government benefits associated with marital status.

> Most importantly, Utah's bigamy statute serves the State's interest in protecting vulnerable individuals from exploitation and abuse. The practice of polygamy, in particular, often coincides with crimes targeting women and children. Crimes not unusually attendant to the practice of polygamy include incest, sexual assault, statutory rape, and failure to pay child support. Moreover, the closed nature of polygamous communities makes obtaining evidence of and prosecuting these crimes challenging. ("Given the highly private nature of sexual abuse and the self-imposed isolation of polygamous communities, prosecution may well prove impossible. This wall of silence may present a compelling justification for criminalizing the act of polygamy, prosecuting offenders, and effectively breaking down the wall

that provides a favorable environment in which crimes of physical and sexual abuse can thrive.")

All of the foregoing interests are legitimate, if not compelling, interests of the State, and Utah's bigamy statute is rationally related to the furthering of those interests. We therefore hold that Utah's bigamy statute does not violate the Free Exercise Clause of the First Amendment of the United States Constitution . . . .

99 P.3d at 829–30.

Note that Green based his primary constitutional claim on his Free Exercise rights. Suppose he had argued that he was exercising his right to privacy, as defined by *Lawrence*. Would this make any difference to either the analysis or the outcome in this case? Should it? Note also that the court goes to considerable length to find some state interest that protects some third party, *e.g.*, exploited women or children, and avoids considering whether the state could object to the practice of polygamy simply because it is regarded as immoral or otherwise inappropriate. If the state had defended the law solely on that ground, which level of review — "close scrutiny" (or its equivalent), or "rationality" — would be properly applicable? Would the state interest be sufficient to survive either level of review? Both levels?

D.   PUBLIC HEALTH AND THE FREE EXERCISE OF RELIGION

"Congress shall make no law respecting an establishment of religion, or prohibiting the free exercise thereof; . . . ."

— First Amendment to the Constitution of the United States

It is no surprise that some public health and safety laws, especially those addressing reproductive health and contagious diseases, may set standards for conduct that some people find morally objectionable. When the objection arises from religious beliefs, it sometimes finds protection under the First Amendment's Free Exercise Clause. Laws that directly disadvantage a particular religion or religious institution are rare (for an example, see *Church of the Lukumi Babalu Aye, infra*). As in the cases concerning the right to privacy, the predominant issue is whether the government's justification for a secular law is sufficiently strong to prevail over an *individual's* religious interest in doing something the law prohibits or constrains. This Part examines examples of laws that have been or could be challenged as interfering with a person's free exercise of religious practices. In a pluralistic society, the goals of protecting public health and accommodating diverse religions can conflict, raising difficult questions of constitutional interpretation.

CURTIS v. SCHOOL COMMITTEE OF FALMOUTH ET AL.
652 N.E.2d 580 (Mass. 1995)

LIACOS, CHIEF JUDGE

. . . This case involves a program of condom availability . . . in the junior and senior high schools of Falmouth.

. . . .

[The court quotes the motion judge's statement of the facts:] "On January 2, 1992, following an authorizing vote of the FSC [Falmouth school committee], the Superintendent of Schools issued a memorandum to the teaching staff of grades 7 through 12, detailing the condom availability program. At Lawrence Junior High School, students could request free condoms from the school nurse. Prior to receiving them, students would be counseled. The nurse was also instructed to give students pamphlets on AIDS/HIV and other sexually transmitted diseases. At Falmouth High School, students could request free condoms from the school nurse, or students could purchase them for $.75 from the condom vending machines located in the lower level boys' and girls' restrooms. Counseling by trained faculty members would be provided to students who requested it, and informational pamphlets were available in the [school] nurses office. The Superintendent's memorandum instructed the staff to reserve their own opinions regarding condom availability in order to respect students' privacy. The memorandum also indicates that the Superintendent's presentation of the condom availability to the student body would stress abstinence as the only certain method for avoiding sexually transmitted diseases. The condom availability program took effect on January 2, 1992."

. . . .

1. *Parental liberty and familial privacy claim.* The plaintiffs [students and parents in the Falmouth schools system] argue that the condom-availability program violates their substantive due process rights, protected by the Fourteenth Amendment, to direct and control the education and upbringing of their children. In the same vein, they argue that the program invades the constitutionally protected "zone of privacy" which surrounds the family. Further, they claim the program intrudes on these rights because it allows their minor children unrestricted access to contraceptives without parental input and within the compulsory setting of the public schools. They claim that in these circumstances parents have the right to intervene and prohibit their children from obtaining the condoms (by an opt-out provision in the program), and that they have a right to parental notification if their child requests and obtains a condom.

We agree that parents possess a fundamental liberty interest, protected by the Fourteenth Amendment, to be free from unnecessary governmental intrusion in the rearing of their children . . . . "The history and culture of Western civilization reflect a strong tradition of parental concern for the nurture and upbringing of their children." *Wisconsin v. Yoder*, 406 U.S. 205, 232 (1972) . . . . Aspects of child rearing protected from unnecessary intrusion by the government include the inculcation of moral standards, religious beliefs, and elements of good citizenship.

. . . .

. . . These cases strongly imply that, in order to constitute a constitutional violation, the State action at issue must be coercive or compulsory in nature. Coercion exists where the governmental action is mandatory and provides no outlet for the parents, such as where refusal to participate in a program results in a sanction or in expulsion.

We discern no coercive burden on plaintiffs' parental liberties in this case. No classroom participation is required of students. Condoms are available to students who request them and, in the high school, may be obtained from vending machines. The students are not required to seek out and accept the condoms, read the literature accompanying them, or participate in counseling regarding their use. In other words, the students are free to decline to participate in the program. No penalty or disciplinary action ensues if a student does not participate in the program. For their part, the plaintiff parents are free to instruct their children not to participate. The program does not supplant the parents' role as advisor in the moral and religious development of their children. Although exposure to condom vending machines may offend the moral and religious sensibilities of the plaintiffs, mere exposure to programs offered at school does not amount to unconstitutional interference with parental liberties without the existence of some compulsory aspect to the program.

The plaintiffs argue that the condom-availability program is coercive because, although participation is voluntary, the program has been implemented in the compulsory setting of the public schools. [T]hey rely on an opinion of a divided lower court (three-to-two decision), *Alfonso v. Fernandez*, 195 A.D.2d 46, 606 N.Y.S.2d 259 (N.Y. 1993), which struck down a similar program in New York public schools as a violation of the parents' right to direct the upbringing of their children. The New York court based its decision, in part, on the fact that State law required the parents to send their children to school in combination with the fact that the program did not include an opt-out provision for parents whereby they could prohibit their children from obtaining condoms. While the case may be read as supporting plaintiff's position, we disagree with its reasoning. Moreover, we point out that the decision was based more directly on a State law which required parental consent for medical treatment. The court concluded, erroneously we think, that the distribution of condoms constituted a medical service for which parental consent was required.

. . . [The court quotes from the dissent in *Alfonso*:] "[T]he mere fact that parents are required to send their children to school does not vest the condom . . . program with the aura of 'compulsion' necessary to make out a viable claim of deprivation of a fundamental constitutional right. Unlike *Meyer v. Nebraska*, [262 U.S. 390 (1923)], where a state attempted to totally prohibit parents from permitting their children to study a foreign language until after completion of the eighth grade, or *Pierce* [*v. Society of Sisters*, 268 U.S. 510 (1944)], where a state attempted to prohibit parents from sending their children to private parochial schools, the element of compulsion is totally absent here."

2. *First Amendment free exercise claim.* Next, the plaintiffs argue that the condom-availability program violates their Federal constitutional rights to the free exercise of religion. . . .

The preliminary inquiry in a free exercise analysis is whether the challenged governmental action creates a burden on the exercise of a plaintiff's religion. Only if a burden is established must the analysis move to the next step: a consideration of the nature of the burden, the significance of the government interest at stake, and the degree to which that interest would be impaired by an accommodation of the religious practice. The degree of interference with free exercise necessary to trigger further analysis of the State's justification . . . must at least rise to the level of a "substantial burden." The Supreme Court has indicated that, just as in the context of a parental liberties claim, a "substantial burden" is one that is coercive or compulsory in nature.

. . . .

The plaintiffs argue that the condom-availability program burdens their right freely to exercise their religion by creating a conflict between the religious teachings of parents as to the issue of premarital sexual intercourse, and the view, allegedly endorsed by the school committee, that sexual activity before marriage is not only permissible but also can be made safe. The plaintiffs contend further . . . that the program is coercive in nature, because it exists in public schools, to which parents are compelled to send their children, and because it lacks an opt-out provision by which parents could choose to prohibit their children from obtaining condoms at school. The plaintiffs also argue that peer pressure may add to the coercive effect of the program.

Although all citizens have a right to freely exercise their religion, the free exercise clause "cannot be understood to require the Government to conduct its own internal affairs in ways that comport with the religious beliefs of particular citizens . . . . The Free Exercise Clause affords an individual protection from certain forms of compulsion . . . . [I]ncidental effects of government programs, which may make it more difficult to practice certain religions but which have no tendency to coerce individuals into acting contrary to their religious beliefs, [do not] require government to bring forward a compelling justification for its otherwise lawful actions." *Lyng v. Northwestern Indian Cemetery Protective Ass'n*, 485 U.S. 439, 448, 450–451 (1988).

. . . .

We conclude that the program in issue which does not violate the plaintiffs' parental liberties or privacy rights also does not violate their rights freely to exercise their religion. There is no requirement that any student participate in the program . . . . The condom-availability program in Falmouth does not penalize students or parents for their religious beliefs or condition the receipt of benefits on a certain belief. Although the program may offend the religious sensibilities of the plaintiffs, mere exposure at public schools to offensive programs does not amount to a violation of free exercise. Parents have no right to tailor public school programs to meet their individual religious or moral preferences.

EMPLOYMENT DIVISION, DEP'T OF HUMAN RESOURCES OF OREGON v. SMITH
494 U.S. 872 (1990)

SCALIA, JUSTICE.

This case requires us to decide whether the Free Exercise Clause of the First   *I*
Amendment permits the State of Oregon to include religiously inspired peyote use
within the reach of its general criminal prohibition on use of that drug, and thus
permits the State to deny unemployment benefits to persons dismissed from their
jobs because of such religiously inspired use.

I

Oregon law prohibits the knowing or intentional possession of a "controlled
substance" unless the substance has been prescribed by a medical practitioner. The
law defines "controlled substance" as a drug classified in Schedules I through V of
the Federal Controlled Substances Act. Persons who violate this provision by
possessing a controlled substance listed on Schedule I are "guilty of a Class B
felony." As compiled by the State Board of Pharmacy under its statutory authority,
see § 475.035, Schedule I contains the drug peyote, a hallucinogen derived from the
plant *Lophophora williamsii Lemaire* . . . .

Respondents Alfred Smith and Galen Black (hereinafter respondents) were fired
from their jobs with a private drug rehabilitation organization because they   *Facts*
ingested peyote for sacramental purposes at a ceremony of the Native American
Church, of which both are members. When respondents applied to petitioner
Employment Division (hereinafter petitioner) for unemployment compensation,
they were determined to be ineligible for benefits because they had been discharged
for work-related "misconduct." The Oregon Court of Appeals reversed that
determination, holding that the denial of benefits violated the respondents' free
exercise rights under the First Amendment. [The Oregon Supreme Court agreed.]

. . . .

II

A.

The Free Exercise Clause of the First Amendment, which has been made
applicable to the States by incorporation into the Fourteenth Amendment . . .
provides that "Congress shall make no law respecting an establishment of religion,
or *prohibiting the free exercise thereof* . . . ." U.S. Const., Amdt. 1 (emphasis
added). The free exercise of religion means, first and foremost, the right to believe
and profess whatever religious doctrine one desires. Thus, the First Amendment
obviously excludes all "governmental regulation of religious *beliefs* as such." The
government may not compel affirmation of religious belief, punish the expression of
religious doctrines it believes to be false, impose special disabilities on the basis of

religious views or religious status, or lend its power to one or the other side in controversies over religious authority or dogma . . . .

But the "exercise of religion" often involves not only belief and profession but the performance of (or abstention from) physical acts: assembling with others for a worship service, participating in sacramental use of bread and wine, proselytizing, abstaining from certain foods or certain modes of transportation. It would be true, we think (though no case of ours has involved the point), that a State would be "prohibiting the free exercise [of religion]" if it sought to ban such acts or abstentions only when they are engaged in them for religious reasons, or only because of the religious belief that they display . . . .

Respondents in the present case, however, seek to carry the meaning of "prohibiting the free exercise [of religion]" one large step further. They contend that their religious motivation for using peyote places them beyond the reach of criminal law that is not specifically directed at their religious practice, and that is concededly constitutional as applied to those who use the drug for other reasons. They assert, in other words, that "prohibiting the free exercise [of religion]" includes requiring any individual to observe a generally applicable law that requires (or forbids) the performance of an act that his religious belief forbids (or requires) . . . .

. . . We have never held that an individual's religious beliefs excuse him from compliance with an otherwise valid law prohibiting conduct that the State is free to regulate . . . . We first had occasion to assert that principle in *Reynolds v. United States*, 98 U.S. 145, 25 L. Ed. 244 (1879), where we rejected the claim that criminal laws against polygamy could not be constitutionally applied to those whose religion commanded the practice. "Laws," we said, "are made for the government of actions, and while they cannot interfere with mere religious belief and opinions, they may with practices . . . ."

Subsequent decisions have consistently held that the right of free exercise does not relieve an individual of the obligation to comply with a "valid and neutral law of general applicability on the ground that the law proscribes (or prescribes) conduct that his religion prescribes (or proscribes)." In *Prince v. Massachusetts*, 321 U.S. 158 (1944), we held that a mother could be prosecuted under the child labor laws for using her children to dispense literature in the streets, her religious motivation notwithstanding. In *Braunfeld v. Brown*, 366 U.S. 599 (1961), we upheld Sunday-closing laws against the claim that they burdened the religious practices of persons whose religions compelled them to refrain from work on other days. In *Gillette v. United States*, 401 U.S. 437, 461 (1971), we sustained the military Selective Service System against the claim that it violated free exercise by conscripting persons who opposed a particular war on religious grounds.

Our most recent decision involving a neutral, generally applicable regulatory law that compelled activity forbidden by an individual's religion was *United States v. Lee*, 455 U.S., at 258–261. There, an Amish employer, on behalf of himself and his employees, sought exemption from collection and payment of Social Security taxes on the ground that the Amish faith prohibited participation in governmental support programs. We rejected the claim that an exemption was constitutionally required. There would be no way to distinguish the Amish believer's objection to

Social Security taxes from the religious objections that others might have to the collection or use of other taxes . . . .

The only decisions in which we have held that the First Amendment bars application of a neutral, generally applicable law to religiously motivated action have involved not the Free Exercise Clause alone, but the Free Exercise Clause in conjunction with other constitutional protections, such as freedom of speech and of the press.

. . . .

The present case does not present such a hybrid situation, but a free exercise claim unconnected with any communicative activity or parental right. Respondents urge us to hold, quite simply, that when otherwise prohibitable conduct is accompanied by religious convictions, not only the convictions but the conduct itself must be free from governmental regulation. We have never held that, and decline to do so now. There being no contention that Oregon's drug law represents an attempt to regulate religious beliefs, the communication of religious beliefs, or the raising of one's children in those beliefs, the rule to which we have adhered ever since *Reynolds* plainly controls . . . .

B.

Respondents argue that even though exemption from generally applicable criminal laws need not automatically be extended to religiously motivated actors, at least the claim for a religious exemption must be evaluated under the balancing test set forth in *Sherbert v. Verner*, 374 U.S. 398 (1963). Under the *Sherbert* test, governmental actions that substantially burden a religious practice must be justified by a compelling governmental interest. Applying that test we have, on three occasions, invalidated state unemployment compensation rules that conditioned the availability of benefits upon an applicant's willingness to work under conditions forbidden by his religion . . . . In recent years we have abstained from applying the *Sherbert* test . . . .

. . . The *Sherbert* test, it must be recalled, was developed in a context that lent itself to individualized governmental assessment of the reasons for the relevant conduct. As a plurality of the Court noted in *Roy*, a distinctive feature of unemployment compensation programs is that their eligibility criteria invite consideration of the particular circumstances behind an applicant's unemployment . . . .

Whether or not the decisions are that limited, they at least have nothing to do with an across-the-board criminal prohibition on a particular form of conduct. Although, as noted earlier, we have sometimes used the *Sherbert* test to analyze free exercise challenges to such laws, we have never applied the test to invalidate one. We conclude today that the sounder approach, and the approach in accord with the vast majority of our precedents, is to hold the test inapplicable to such challenges. The government's ability to enforce generally applicable prohibitions of socially harmful conduct, like its ability to carry out other aspects of public policy, "cannot depend on measuring the effects of a governmental action on a religious objector's spiritual development." . . .

Values that are protected against government interference through enshrinement in the Bill of Rights are not thereby banished from the political process. Just as a society that believes in the negative protection accorded to the press by the First Amendment is likely to enact laws that affirmatively foster the dissemination of the printed word, so also a society that believes in the negative protection accorded to religious belief can be expected to be solicitous of that value in its legislation as well. It is therefore not surprising that a number of States have made an exception to their drug laws for sacramental peyote use. But to say that a nondiscriminatory religious-practice exemption is permitted, or even that it is desirable, is not to say that it is constitutionally required, and that the appropriate occasions for its creation can be discerned by the courts. It may fairly be said that leaving accommodation to the political process will place at a relative disadvantage those religious practices that are not widely engaged in; but that unavoidable consequence of democratic government must be preferred to a system in which each conscience is a law unto itself or in which judges weigh the social importance of all laws against the centrality of all religious beliefs.

Because respondents' ingestion of peyote was prohibited under Oregon law, and because that prohibition is constitutional, Oregon may, consistent with the Free Exercise Clause, deny respondents unemployment compensation when their dismissal results from use of the drug. The decision of the Oregon Supreme Court is accordingly reversed.

RELIGIOUS FREEDOM RESTORATION ACT OF 1993, as amended
42 U.S.C. § 2000bb

§ 2000bb   Congressional findings and declaration of purposes

(a) Findings

The Congress finds that —

(1) the framers of the Constitution, recognizing free exercise of religion as an unalienable right, secured its protection in the First Amendment to the Constitution;

(2) laws "neutral" toward religion may burden religious exercise as surely as laws intended to interfere with religious exercise;

(3) governments should not substantially burden religious exercise without compelling justification;

(4) in Employment Division v. Smith, 494 U.S. 872 (1990) the Supreme Court virtually eliminated the requirement that the government justify burdens on religious exercise imposed by laws neutral toward religion; and

(5) the compelling interest test as set forth in prior Federal court rulings is a workable test for striking sensible balances between religious liberty and competing prior governmental interests.

(b) Purposes

The purposes of this chapter are —

(1) to restore the compelling interest test as set forth in Sherbert v. Verner, 374 U.S. 398 (1963) and Wisconsin v. Yoder, 406 U.S. 205 (1972) and to guarantee its application in all cases where free exercise of religion is substantially burdened; and

(2) to provide a claim or defense to persons whose religious exercise is substantially burdened by government.

§ 2000bb–1.   Free exercise of religion protected

(a) In general

Government shall not substantially burden a person's exercise of religion even if the burden results from a rule of general applicability, except as provided in subsection (b) of this section.

(b) Exception

Government may substantially burden a person's exercise of religion only if it demonstrates that application of the burden to the person —

(1) is in furtherance of a compelling governmental interest; and

(2) is the least restrictive means of furthering that compelling governmental interest.

(c) Judicial relief

A person whose religious exercise has been burdened in violation of this section may assert that violation as a claim or defense in a judicial proceeding and obtain appropriate relief against a government. Standing to assert a claim or defense under this section shall be governed by the general rules of standing under article III of the Constitution.

§ 2000bb–2.   Definitions

As used in this chapter—

(1) the term "government" includes a branch, department, agency, instrumentality, and official (or other person acting under color of law) of the United States, or of a covered entity;

(2) the term "covered entity" means the District of Columbia, the Commonwealth of Puerto Rico, and each territory and possession of the United States;

(3) the term "demonstrates" means meets the burdens of going forward with the evidence and of persuasion; and

(4) the term "exercise of religion" means religious exercise, as defined in section 2000cc–5 of this title.

§ 2000bb–3.   Applicability

(a) In general

This chapter applies to all Federal law, and the implementation of that law, whether statutory or otherwise, and whether adopted before or after November 16, 1993.

(b) Rule of construction

Federal statutory law adopted after November 16, 1993, is subject to this chapter unless such law explicitly excludes such application by reference to this chapter.

(c) Religious belief unaffected

Nothing in this chapter shall be construed to authorize any government to burden any religious belief.

§ 2000bb–4. Establishment clause unaffected

Nothing in this chapter shall be construed to affect, interpret, or in any way address that portion of the First Amendment prohibiting laws respecting the establishment of religion (referred to in this section as the "Establishment Clause"). Granting government funding, benefits, or exemptions, to the extent permissible under the Establishment Clause, shall not constitute a violation of this chapter. As used in this section, the term "granting", used with respect to government funding, benefits, or exemptions, does not include the denial of government funding, benefits, or exemptions.

NOTES AND QUESTIONS

1. **Different perspectives on the role of religion.** Kathleen Sullivan argues that "The constitutional jurisprudence of the Religion Clauses navigates among competing tacit accounts of the role of religious organizations in a democratic society." *The New Religion and the Constitution*, 116 Harv. L. Rev. 1397, 1403 (2003). "The four accounts respectively see religious organizations as, first, dangerous quasi-governments in need of restraint; second, valuable private associations needing autonomy but not public subsidy; third, discrete and insular minorities in need of both equal treatment and affirmative action; or fourth, ordinary interest groups whose gains or losses in the political process may be expected to even out along with others' over time. Each account takes a corresponding view of the appropriate levels of judicial enforcement of the Free Exercise and Establishment Clauses." *Id.* See if you can identify different approaches in the cases in this Part.

2. **Neutral laws of general applicability.** *Smith* holds that a neutral law of general applicability that neither singles out religious activities nor is intended to regulate religious activities does not burden religion — in the constitutional sense. As a consequence, a reviewing court need only find that the law is rationally related to some legitimate state interest; close scrutiny appears to have been abandoned for laws that are characterized this way. The implications of *Smith* are hard to appreciate outside of the context of earlier decisions, especially *Sherbert v. Verner,*

374 U.S. 398 (1963), and *Wisconsin v. Yoder*, 406 U.S. 205 (1972), in which the Supreme Court appeared to strictly scrutinize state laws that had an effect on the practice of religion, even where those laws were laws of "general applicability." In *Smith*, a slim majority of the Court attempted — somewhat unsuccessfully — to distinguish these earlier cases on their facts and claim that *Smith* was a factually different case, one involving a law of general applicability. But the laws in *Sherbert* (denying benefits to people who voluntarily refused employment) and *Yoder* (requiring all people to send their children to school until the age of sixteen) were apparently laws of "general applicability" as well: neither targeted religiously motivated conduct. Nonetheless, the *Smith* majority found these earlier cases distinguishable. Compare the Court's use of precedent in *Smith* and *Gonzales v. Carhart*, Part B, *supra*. Which emphasizes the importance of applying the law uniformly to all and which the necessity for individualizing the inquiry? What might be a reason for the difference?

Curtis offers another example of what could be considered a neutral "law" of general applicability, although at issue was not state legislation, but rather a public school policy. Here, the court emphasized that the policy was not coercive, because it did not force any student or parent to participate in the program of condom availability. Did this allow the court to avoid the question whether the public school's policy burdened the parent's constitutionally protected rights? Note that the parents did not rely exclusively on the First Amendment, but also claimed that their rights to direct the upbringing of the children was protected by the Fourteenth Amendment's Due Process Clause. They also claimed that the program was coercive, because state law required the children to attend school where they could not avoid exposure to the program. Is this the same argument made by those who object to childhood vaccinations as a condition of school attendance?

3. The Religious Freedom Restoration Act. The *Smith* decision upset many religious groups, who preferred to hold courts to the use of strict scrutiny whenever law burdened religious practices. Congress responded by enacting the Religious Freedom Restoration Act (RFRA). Tension between the legislative and judicial branches can be seen in *City of Boerne v. Flores*, 521 U.S. 507 (1997). In that case, the U.S. Supreme Court determined that RFRA exceeded Congress's power by improperly intruding on the power of the judiciary to interpret the Constitution. With respect to RFRA's application to the constitutionality of state laws, Congress necessarily relied on its enforcement power in Section 5 of the Fourteenth Amendment to apply the First Amendment's protection of the free exercise of religion to the States. While Congress has "remedial power" to "enforce" the Fourteenth Amendment's protection of due process and equal protection, the court concluded that Congress has no power to decree what the substance of those protections are. That power is reserved to the judiciary: "The power to interpret the Constitution in a case or controversy remains in the Judiciary." *Id.* at 524.

The Court concluded that RFRA could not be considered to be merely remedial legislation to enforce existing Fourteenth Amendment rights, and thus was unconstitutional as applied to the states:

> It is a reality of the modern regulatory state that numerous state laws, such as the zoning regulations at issue here, impose a substantial burden on

a large class of individuals. When the exercise of religion has been burdened in an incidental way by a law of general application, it does not follow that the persons affected have been burdened any more than other citizens, let alone burdened because of their religious beliefs. In addition, the Act imposes in every case a least restrictive means requirement — a requirement that was not used in the pre-*Smith* jurisprudence RFRA purported to codify — which also indicates that the legislation is broader than is appropriate if the goal is to prevent and remedy constitutional violations.

. . . .

Broad as the power of Congress is under the Enforcement Clause of the Fourteenth Amendment, RFRA contradicts vital principles necessary to maintain separation of powers and the federal balance.

Id. at 535–6.

City of Boerne did not address the effect of the RFRA on federal law. The Court took up that issue in *Gonzales v. O Centro Espírita Beneficente União Do Vegetal* and *Hobby Lobby, infra.*

4. **Religious objections to autopsies.** State law typically authorizes medical examiners to conduct an autopsy where death occurred as a probable result of homicide, suicide or accident or without the attendance of a physician or other medical practitioner. Some religions view autopsies as desecrations of the body, which are prohibited by religious doctrine, or require burial of the dead within a day of death, absent extraordinary circumstances. *See, e.g.*, Jewish Law Case Summaries, http://www.jlaw.com/Summary/autopsy.html (last visited Aug. 14, 2013). Most states have accommodated religious objections to autopsies by allowing the surviving family member to refuse an autopsy, although statutes allowing such refusals often specify exceptions, such as murder and manslaughter investigations, in which autopsies must be performed. Many statutes target autopsies alone, but authorize different procedures for refusing an autopsy. Ohio's statute, for example, allows a friend or family member to petition a court to reverse a coroner's decision to conduct an autopsy, except in cases of homicide; a hearing is to be held within 48 hours. Ohio Rev. Code Ann. § 313.131 (2011). Tennessee allows autopsy objections under its broader Preservation of Religious Freedom Act, which prohibits the state from burdening religious freedom in terms quite similar to the Religious Freedom Restoration Act. Tenn. Code Ann. § 4-1-407 (2011). In *Johnson v. Levy*, 2010 Tenn. App. LEXIS 14 (Jan. 14, 2010), a Tennessee medical examiner sought to perform an autopsy of a man who had been executed by lethal injection, although the man had signed a sworn statement, confirmed by his pastor, objecting to autopsy. The Tennessee court denied the autopsy, finding that its purpose — to benefit medicine and science — was legitimate, but not compelling, as required by the statute. *Johnson* may be an exception to the rule, since most challenges to autopsies have failed, at least prior to the Religious Freedom Restoration Act. *See e.g. Stone v. Allen*, 2007 U.S. Dist. LEXIS 87132 (S.D. Ala. Nov. 27, 2007) (dismissing First Amendment claims); *You Vang Yang v. Sturner*, 750 F. Supp. 558 (Dist. R.I. 1990) (dismissing First and Fourteenth Amendment claims). It is possible, of course, that medical examiners, in consultation with the police, grant the families' wishes in most cases, avoiding disputes.

♦ **5. Conscience clauses.** As we have seen, individuals may not wish to comply with generally applicable law because of their religious beliefs or more general moral convictions. Laws that require the performance of services present a slightly different question than laws that forbid specific practices, such as snake handling. Since *Roe v. Wade*, some health care providers have raised moral or religious objections as reasons for refusing to provide reproductive services, such as contraception, abortion, sterilization, and fertility drugs, as well as end of life care. Many states accommodate at least some of these objections by including religious exemptions from compliance with provider licensure or other requirements. These so-called "conscience clauses" vary considerably with respect to which practitioners and services are covered and in which circumstances. For a review, see Thaddeus Mason Pope, *Legal Briefing: Conscience Clauses and Conscientious Refusal*, 21 J. CLINICAL ETHICS 163 (2010). Conscience clauses are often placed in professional licensure statutes or regulations defining the professional obligations of licensees. Some states prohibit medical schools and hospitals from requiring students to perform services that would otherwise be required of all students in training, if students refuse on the basis of religious, ethical or moral beliefs. For a list of state laws, see The Guttmacher Institute, www.guttmacher.org/ (visited Mar. 2014).

Compare the Idaho and California laws below. Who is covered? What services can be refused? Which better protects patients' access to care? Which better protects religious, ethical or moral beliefs? Which approach do you prefer?

Idaho Code § 18-611.   Freedom of conscience for health care professionals

(1) As used in this section:

(a) "Abortifacient" means any drug that causes an abortion as defined in section 18-604, Idaho Code, emergency contraception or any drug the primary purpose of which is to cause the destruction of an embryo or fetus.

(b) "Conscience" means the religious, moral or ethical principles sincerely held by any person.

(c) "Embryo" means the developing human life from fertilization until the end of the eighth week of gestation.

(d) "Fetus" means the developing human life from the start of the ninth week of gestation until birth.

(e) "Health care professional" means any person licensed, certified or registered by the state of Idaho to deliver health care.

(f) "Health care service" means an abortion, dispensation of an abortifacient drug, human embryonic stem cell research, treatment regimens utilizing human embryonic stem cells, human embryo cloning or end of life treatment and care.

(g) "Provide" means to counsel, advise, perform, dispense, assist in or refer for any health care service.

(h) "Religious, moral or ethical principles," "sincerely held," "reasonably accommodate" and "undue hardship" shall be construed consistently with title VII of the federal civil rights act of 1964, as amended.

(2) No health care professional shall be required to provide any health care service that violates his or her conscience.

(3) Employers of health care professionals shall reasonably accommodate the conscience rights of their employees as provided in this section, upon advanced written notification by the employee. Such notice shall suffice without specification of the reason therefor. It shall be unlawful for any employer to discriminate against any health care professional based upon his or her declining to provide a health care service that violates his or her conscience, unless the employer can demonstrate that such accommodation poses an undue hardship.

(4) No health care professional or employer of the health care professional shall be civilly, criminally or administratively liable for the health care professional declining to provide health care services that violate his or her conscience, except for life-threatening situations as provided for in subsection (6) of this section.

(5) The provisions of this section do not allow a health care professional or employer of the health care professional to refuse to provide health care services because of a patient's race, color, religion, sex, age, disability or national origin.

(6) If a health care professional invokes a conscience right in a life-threatening situation where no other health care professional capable of treating the emergency is available, such health care professional shall provide treatment and care until an alternate health care professional capable of treating the emergency is found.

(7) In cases where a living will or physician's orders for scope of treatment (POST) is operative, as defined by the medical consent and natural death act, and a physician has a conscience objection to the treatment desired by the patient, the physician shall comply with the provisions of section 39-4513(2), Idaho Code, before withdrawing care and treatment to the patient.

(8) Nothing in this section shall affect the rights of conscience provided for in section 18-612, Idaho Code, to the extent that those rights are broader in scope than those provided for in this section.

Cal. Bus. & Prof. Code § 733 (2012).

(a) No licentiate shall obstruct a patient in obtaining a prescription drug or device that has been legally prescribed or ordered for that patient. A violation of this section constitutes unprofessional conduct by the licentiate and shall subject the licentiate to disciplinary or administrative action by his or her licensing agency.

(b) Notwithstanding any other provision of law, a licentiate shall dispense drugs and devices, as described in subdivision (a) of Section 4024, pursuant to a lawful order or prescription unless one of the following circumstances exists:

(1) Based solely on the licentiate's professional training and judgment, dispensing pursuant to the order or the prescription is contrary to law, or the licentiate determines that the prescribed drug or device would cause a harmful drug interaction or would otherwise adversely affect the patient's medical condition.

(2) The prescription drug or device is not in stock. If an order, other than an order described in Section 4019, or prescription cannot be dispensed because the drug or device is not in stock, the licentiate shall take one of the following actions:

(A) Immediately notify the patient and arrange for the drug or device to be delivered to the site or directly to the patient in a timely manner.

(B) Promptly transfer the prescription to another pharmacy known to stock the prescription drug or device that is near enough to the site from which the prescription or order is transferred, to ensure the patient has timely access to the drug or device.

(C) Return the prescription to the patient and refer the patient. The licentiate shall make a reasonable effort to refer the patient to a pharmacy that stocks the prescription drug or device that is near enough to the referring site to ensure that the patient has timely access to the drug or device

(3) The licentiate refuses on ethical, moral, or religious grounds to dispense a drug or device pursuant to an order or prescription. A licentiate may decline to dispense a prescription drug or device on this basis only if the licentiate has previously notified his or her employer, in writing, of the drug or class of drugs to which he or she objects, and the licentiate's employer can, without creating undue hardship, provide a reasonable accommodation of the licentiate's objection. The licentiate's employer shall establish protocols that ensure that the patient has timely access to the prescribed drug or device despite the licentiate's refusal to dispense the prescription or order. For purposes of this section, "reasonable accommodation" and "undue hardship" shall have the same meaning as applied to those terms pursuant to subdivision (l) of Section 12940 of the Government Code.

. . . .

(e) This section imposes no duty on a licentiate to dispense a drug or device pursuant to a prescription or order without payment for the drug or device, including payment directly by the patient or through a third-party payer accepted by the licentiate or payment of any required copayment by the patient.

. . . .

6. Emergency contraception and conscience clauses. Controversy that surrounded the development of emergency contraception (or the morning-after-pill) encouraged the adoption of statutory "conscience clauses" to permit pharmacists to refuse to dispense such drugs. Emergency contraceptives, like Plan B, prevent fertilization of an ovum or implantation of a fertilized ovum, but should be taken within 24 to 72 hours of unprotected intercourse to be effective. Some pharmacists refuse to dispense prescribed emergency contraceptives, because they consider them to be abortifacients. Some states have statutes or regulations that require pharmacies to stock an adequate assortment of drugs to meets its customers' needs or to dispense prescription drugs in a timely fashion. *See, e.g.,* Wash. Admin. Code § 246-869-010; Wash. Admin. Code § 246-869-150. What happens when the only pharmacist in a pharmacy refuses to dispense Plan B to a woman? Does it matter whether or not other pharmacies that do dispense the drugs are nearby? Courts have reached different conclusions on whether the Free Exercise Clause protects a pharmacist's right to refuse to dispense. Compare *Vandersand v. Wal-Mart Stores, Inc.*, 525 F. Supp. 2d 1052 (2007) (pharmacist placed on leave for refusing to dispense Plan B could assert claim for employment discrimination under Illinois Right of Conscience Act); with *Noesen v. Medical Staffing Network*, 2007 U.S. App. LEXIS 10687 (Apr. 25, 2007) (Title VII did not require employer to relieve pharmacist of all telephone and counter duties, as a reasonable accommodation, so that he could avoid dispensing birth control to customers).

The FDA's decision to comply with a court order to approve Plan B for over-the-counter sale may severely limit the use of pharmacist conscience clauses. In April 2013, Judge Edward R. Korman ordered the FDA "to make levonorgestrel-based emergency contraceptives available without a prescription and without point-of-sale or age restrictions within thirty days." *Tummino v. Hamburg*, 936 F. Supp. 2d 162, 197 (E.D.N.Y. 2013). This required the FDA to approve the one-pill version (Plan B One-Step and generic equivalents) for over-the-counter sale to all ages, without a prescription. The court found that the FDA advisory panel had approved the drug as safe and effective, but that the Secretary of Health and Human Services had wrongfully denied approval largely for political reasons. The FDA soon withdrew its appeal of this decision and also agreed to approve the less expensive two-pill version (Plan B) on the same terms. *Tummino v. Hamburg*, 2013 U.S. Dist. LEXIS 82871 (June 12, 2013). In March 2014, after more than a decade of review and litigation, the FDA carried out its agreement. If the pills can be bought off the shelf, like aspirin, do any obstacles remain? What if a pharmacy refuses to stock the pills or a salesperson refuses to let a customer buy the pills?

———

GONZALES v. O CENTRO ESPÍRITA BENEFICENTE UNIÃO DO VEGETAL

UDV wins

546 U.S. 418 (2006)

CHIEF JUSTICE ROBERTS delivered the opinion of the Court.

In *Employment Div., Dept. of Human Resources of Ore. v. Smith*, 494 U. S. 872 (1990), this Court held that the Free Exercise Clause of the First Amendment does not prohibit governments from burdening religious practices through generally applicable laws . . . . In so doing, we rejected the interpretation of the Free Exercise Clause announced in *Sherbert v. Verner*, 374 U. S. 398 (1963), and . . . held that the Constitution does not require judges to engage in a case-by-case assessment of the religious burdens imposed by facially constitutional laws.

Congress responded by enacting the Religious Freedom Restoration Act of 1993 (RFRA), 107 Stat. 1488, as amended, 42 U. S. C. § 2000bb et seq., which adopts a statutory rule comparable to the constitutional rule rejected in *Smith* . . . .

The Controlled Substances Act, 21 U. S. C. § 801 et seq. (2000 ed. and Supp. I), regulates the importation, manufacture, distribution, and use of psychotropic substances. The Act classifies substances into five schedules based on their potential for abuse, the extent to which they have an accepted medical use, and their safety. Substances listed in Schedule I of the Act are subject to the most comprehensive restrictions, including an outright ban on all importation and use, except pursuant to strictly regulated research projects. See §§ 823, 960(a)(1). The Act authorizes the imposition of a criminal sentence for simple possession of Schedule I substances, see § 844(a), and mandates the imposition of a criminal sentence for possession "with intent to manufacture, distribute, or dispense" such substances, see §§ 841(a), (b).

O Centro Espírita Beneficente União do Vegetal (UDV) is a Christian Spiritist sect based in Brazil, with an American branch of approximately 130 individuals. Central to the UDV's faith is receiving communion through *hoasca* (pronounced "wass-ca"), a sacramental tea made from two plants unique to the Amazon region. One of the plants, *psychotria viridis*, contains *dimethyltryptamine* (DMT), a hallucinogen whose effects are enhanced by alkaloids from the other plant, *banisteriopsis caapi*. DMT, as well as "any material, compound, mixture, or preparation, which contains any quantity of [DMT]," is listed in Schedule I of the Controlled Substances Act. § 812(c), Schedule I(c).

In 1999, United States Customs inspectors intercepted a shipment to the American UDV containing three drums of *hoasca*. A subsequent investigation revealed that the UDV had received 14 prior shipments of *hoasca*. The inspectors seized the intercepted shipment and threatened the UDV with prosecution.

[The UDV filed suit against the Attorney General seeking injunctive and declarative relief under the RFRA. The Government conceded that prosecution would substantially burden a sincere exercise of religion.]

The Government argued that this burden did not violate RFRA, because applying the Controlled Substances Act in this case was the least restrictive means of advancing three compelling governmental interests: protecting the health and safety of UDV members, preventing the diversion of *hoasca* from the church to recreational users, and complying with the 1971 United Nations Convention on Psychotropic Substances, a treaty signed by the United States and implemented by the Act.

. . . .

[The Court agreed with the district court that the evidence on the health risks of *hoasca* and the risk of its diversion were about equally balanced between the UDV and the government's positions, and concluded that the government had not carried its burden to establish a compelling interest.]

. . . .

. . . RFRA requires the Government to demonstrate that the compelling interest test is satisfied through application of the challenged law "to the person" — the particular claimant whose sincere exercise of religion is being substantially burdened. RFRA expressly adopted the compelling interest test "as set forth in *Sherbert v. Verner* . . . and *Wisconsin v. Yoder*, 406 U. S. 205 (1972)." In each of those cases, this Court looked beyond broadly formulated interests justifying the general applicability of government mandates and scrutinized the asserted harm of granting specific exemptions to particular religious claimants . . . .

. . . .

Under the more focused inquiry required by RFRA and the compelling interest test, the Government's mere invocation of the general characteristics of Schedule I substances, as set forth in the Controlled Substances Act, cannot carry the day . . . . Congress' determination that DMT should be listed under Schedule I simply does not provide a categorical answer that relieves the Government of the obligation to shoulder its burden under RFRA.

This conclusion is reinforced by the Controlled Substances Act itself. The Act contains a provision authorizing the Attorney General to "waive the requirement for registration of certain manufacturers, distributors, or dispensers if he finds it consistent with the public health and safety." 21 U. S. C. § 822(d) . . . .

. . . .

. . . For the past 35 years, there has been a regulatory exemption for use of peyote — a Schedule I substance — by the Native American Church. See 21 CFR §1307.31 (2005). In 1994, Congress extended that exemption to all members of every recognized Indian Tribe. See 42 U.S.C. § 1996a(b)(1). Everything the Government says about the DMT in *hoasca* — that, as a Schedule I substance, Congress has determined that it "has a high potential for abuse," "has no currently accepted medical use," and has "a lack of accepted safety for use . . . under medical supervision, " — applies in equal measure to the mescaline in peyote, yet both the Executive and Congress itself have decreed an exception from the Controlled Substances Act for Native American religious use of peyote. If such use is permitted in the face of the congressional findings in § 812(b)(1) for hundreds of thousands of Native Americans practicing their faith, it is difficult to see how those same findings alone can preclude any consideration of a similar exception for the 130 or so

American members of the UDV who want to practice theirs . . . .

The Government argues that the existence of a congressional exemption for peyote does not indicate that the Controlled Substances Act is amenable to judicially crafted exceptions. RFRA, however, plainly contemplates that courts would recognize exceptions — that is how the law works.

. . . .

Here, the Government's argument for uniformity . . . rests not so much on the particular statutory program at issue as on slippery-slope concerns that could be invoked in response to any RFRA claim for an exception to a generally applicable law. The Government's argument echoes the classic rejoinder of bureaucrats throughout history: If I make an exception for you, I'll have to make one for everybody, so no exceptions. But RFRA operates by mandating consideration, under the compelling interest test, of exceptions to "rule [s] of general applicability."

. . . .

We do not doubt that there may be instances in which a need for uniformity precludes the recognition of exceptions to generally applicable laws under RFRA. But it would have been surprising to find that this was such a case, given the longstanding exemption from the Controlled Substances Act for religious use of peyote, and the fact that the very reason Congress enacted RFRA was to respond to a decision denying a claimed right to sacramental use of a controlled substance.

. . . .

We have no cause to pretend that the task assigned by Congress to the courts under RFRA is an easy one. Indeed, the very sort of difficulties highlighted by the Government here were cited by this Court in deciding that the approach later mandated by Congress under RFRA was not required as a matter of constitutional law under the Free Exercise Clause. But Congress has determined that courts should strike sensible balances, pursuant to a compelling interest test that requires the Government to address the particular practice at issue. Applying that test, we conclude that the courts below did not err in determining that the Government failed to demonstrate, at the preliminary injunction stage, a compelling interest in barring the UDV's sacramental use of *hoasca*.

[The decision granting UDV a preliminary injunction is affirmed.]

BURWELL v. HOBBY LOBBY STORES, INC.
573 U.S. ____, 2014 U.S. LEXIS 4505 (2014)

JUSTICE ALITO delivered the opinion of the Court

We must decide in these cases whether the Religious Freedom Restoration Act of 1993 (RFRA), 42 U. S. C. § 2000bb et seq., permits the United States Department of Health and Human Services (HHS) to demand that three closely held corporations provide health-insurance coverage for methods of contraception that violate the sincerely held religious beliefs of the companies' owners. We hold that the regulations that impose this obligation violate RFRA, which prohibits the violate Federal Government from taking any action that substantially burdens the exercise of religion unless that action constitutes the least restrictive means of serving a compelling government interest.

. . . .

. . . The owners of the businesses have religious objections to abortion, and according to their religious beliefs the four contraceptive methods at issue are abortifacients. If the owners comply with the HHS mandate, they believe they will be facilitating abortions. . . .

I

B

At issue in these cases are HHS regulations promulgated under the Patient Protection and Affordable Care Act of 2010 (ACA). ACA generally requires employers with 50 or more full-time employees to offer "a group health plan or group health insurance coverage" that provides "minimum essential coverage." 26 U. S. C. § 5000A(f)(2); §§ 4980H(a), (c)(2). . . . [I]f a covered employer provides group health insurance but its plan fails to comply with ACA's group-health-plan requirements, the employer may be required to pay $100 per day for each affected "individual." [26 U.S.C. §§ 4980D] And if the employer decides to stop providing health insurance altogether and at least one full-time employee enrolls in a health plan and qualifies for a subsidy on one of the government-run ACA exchanges, the employer must pay $2,000 per year for each of its fulltime employees.

Unless an exception applies, ACA requires an employer's group health plan or group-health-insurance coverage to furnish "preventive care and screenings" for women without "any cost sharing requirements." 42 U. S. C. § 300gg–13(a)(4). Congress itself, however, did not specify what types of preventive care must be covered. Instead, Congress authorized the Health Resources and Services Administration (HRSA), a component of HHS, to make that important and sensitive decision.

In August 2011, based on the Institute [of Medicine]'s recommendations, the HRSA promulgated the Women's Preventive Services Guidelines. The Guidelines provide that nonexempt employers are generally required to provide "coverage, without cost sharing" for "[a]ll Food and Drug Administration [(FDA)] approved contraceptive methods, sterilization procedures, and patient education and counseling." Although many of the required, FDA-approved methods of contraception work by preventing the fertilization of an egg, four of those methods (those specifically at issue in these cases) may have the effect of preventing an already fertilized egg from developing any further by inhibiting its attachment to the uterus.

HHS also authorized the HRSA to establish exemptions from the contraceptive mandate for "religious employers." 45 CFR § 147.131(a). That category encompasses "churches, their integrated auxiliaries, and conventions or associations of churches," as well as "the exclusively religious activities of any religious order." In its Guidelines, HRSA exempted these organizations from the requirement to cover contraceptive services.

In addition, HHS has effectively exempted certain religious nonprofit organizations, described under HHS regulations as "eligible organizations," from the contraceptive mandate. An "eligible organization" means a nonprofit organization that "holds itself out as a religious organization" and opposes providing coverage for some or all of any contraceptive services required to be covered . . . on account of religious objections." 45 CFR § 147.131(b). To qualify for this accommodation, an employer must certify that it is such an organization. When a group-health-insurance issuer receives notice that one of its clients has invoked this provision, the issuer must then exclude contraceptive coverage from the employer's plan and provide separate payments for contraceptive services for plan participants without imposing any cost-sharing requirements on the eligible organization, its insurance plan, or its employee beneficiaries. § 147.131(c). Although this procedure requires the issuer to bear the cost of these services, HHS has determined that this obligation will not impose any net expense on issuers because its cost will be less than or equal to the cost savings resulting from the services.

In addition to these exemptions for religious organizations, ACA exempts a great many employers from most of its coverage requirements. Employers providing "grandfathered health plans" — those that existed prior to March 23, 2010, and that have not made specified changes after that date — need not comply with many of the Act's requirements, including the contraceptive mandate. And employers with fewer than 50 employees are not required to provide health insurance at all.

All told, the contraceptive mandate "presently does not apply to tens of millions of people." This is attributable, in large part, to grandfathered health plans: Over one-third of the 149 million nonelderly people in America with employer-sponsored health plans were enrolled in grandfathered plans in 2013. The count for employees working for firms that do not have to provide insurance at all because they employ fewer than 50 employees is 34 million workers.

II

Norman and Elizabeth Hahn and their three sons are devout members of the Mennonite Church, a Christian denomination. The Mennonite Church opposes abortion and believes that "[t]he fetus in its earliest stages . . . shares humanity with those who conceived it."

Fifty years ago, Norman Hahn started a wood-working business in his garage, and since then, this company, Conestoga Wood Specialties, has grown and now has 950 employees. Conestoga is organized under Pennsylvania law as a for-profit corporation. The Hahns exercise sole ownership of the closely held business; they control its board of directors and hold all of its voting shares. . . .

. . . .

David and Barbara Green and their three children are Christians who own and operate two family businesses. Forty-five years ago, David Green started an arts and crafts store that has grown into a nationwide chain called Hobby Lobby. There are now 500 Hobby Lobby stores, and the company has more than 13,000 employees. Hobby Lobby is organized as a for-profit corporation under Oklahoma law.

One of David's sons started an affiliated business, Mardel, which operates 35 Christian bookstores and employs close to 400 people. Mardel is also organized as a for-profit corporation under Oklahoma law. . . . David, Barbara, and their children retain exclusive control of both companies.

. . . .

Like the Hahns, the Greens believe that life begins at conception and that it would violate their religion to facilitate access to contraceptive drugs or devices that operate after that point.

. . . .

III

. . . .

According to HHS, the companies cannot sue because they seek to make a profit for their owners, and the owners cannot be heard because the regulations, at least as a formal matter, apply only to the companies and not to the owners as individuals. HHS's argument would have dramatic consequences.

. . . .

As we will show, Congress provided protection for people like the Hahns and Greens by employing a familiar legal fiction: It included corporations within RFRA's definition of "persons." But it is important to keep in mind that the purpose of this fiction is to provide protection for human beings. A corporation is simply a form of organization used by human beings to achieve desired ends. An established body of law specifies the rights and obligations of the people (including shareholders, officers, and employees) who are associated with a corporation in one way or another. When rights, whether constitutional or statutory, are extended to corporations, the purpose is to protect the rights of these people. For example, extending Fourth Amendment protection to corporations protects the privacy interests of employees and others associated with the company. Protecting corporations from government seizure of their property without just compensation protects all those who have a stake in the corporations' financial well-being. And protecting the free-exercise rights of corporations like Hobby Lobby, Conestoga, and Mardel protects the religious liberty of the humans who own and control those companies.

. . . .

. . . Corporations, "separate and apart from" the human beings who own, run, and are employed by them, cannot do anything at all.

B

1

. . . RFRA applies to "a person's" exercise of religion, and RFRA itself does not define the term "person." We therefore look to the Dictionary Act, which we must consult "[i]n determining the meaning of any Act of Congress, unless the context indicates otherwise." 1 U. S. C. § 1.

Under the Dictionary Act, "the wor[d] 'person' . . . include[s] corporations, companies, associations, firms, partnerships, societies, and joint stock companies, as well as individuals.". . .

We see nothing in RFRA that suggests a congressional intent to depart from the Dictionary Act definition. . . . We have entertained RFRA and free-exercise claims brought by nonprofit corporations, see *Gonzales v. O Centro Espírita Beneficiente União do Vegetal*, 546 U. S. 418 (2006) (RFRA); *Hosanna-Tabor Evangelical Lutheran Church and School v. EEOC*, 565 U. S. ___ (2012) (Free Exercise); *Church of the Lukumi Babalu Aye, Inc. v. Hialeah*, 508 U.S. 520 (1993) (Free Exercise), and HHS concedes that a nonprofit corporation can be a "person" within the meaning of RFRA.

. . . No known understanding of the term "person" includes some but not all corporations. The term "person" sometimes encompasses artificial persons (as the Dictionary Act instructs), and it sometimes is limited to natural persons. But no conceivable definition of the term includes natural persons and nonprofit corporations, but not for-profit corporations.

. . . .

4

Finally, HHS contends that Congress could not have wanted RFRA to apply to for-profit corporations because it is difficult as a practical matter to ascertain the sincere "beliefs" of a corporation. HHS goes so far as to raise the specter of "divisive, polarizing proxy battles over the religious identity of large, publicly traded corporations such as IBM or General Electric."

These cases, however, do not involve publicly traded corporations, and it seems unlikely that the sort of corporate giants to which HHS refers will often assert RFRA claims. . . . In any event, we have no occasion in these cases to consider RFRA's applicability to such companies.

HHS has also provided no evidence that the purported problem of determining the sincerity of an asserted religious belief moved Congress to exclude for-profit corporations from RFRA's protection. On the contrary, the scope of RLUIPA [Religious Land Use and Institutionalized Persons Act of 2000] shows that Congress was confident of the ability of the federal courts to weed out insincere claims. RLUIPA applies to "institutionalized persons," a category that consists primarily of prisoners, and by the time of RLUIPA's enactment, the propensity of some prisoners to assert claims of dubious sincerity was well documented. . . . [W]hat reason is there to think that Congress believed that spotting insincere claims would be tougher in cases involving for-profits?

HHS and the principal dissent express concern about the possibility of disputes among the owners of corporations, but that is not a problem that arises because of RFRA or that is unique to this context. . . . State corporate law provides a ready means for resolving any conflicts by, for example, dictating how a corporation can establish its governing structure. Courts will turn to that structure and the underlying state law in resolving disputes.

For all these reasons, we hold that a federal regulation's restriction on the activities of a for-profit closely held corporation must comply with RFRA.

IV

Because RFRA applies in these cases, we must next ask whether the HHS contraceptive mandate "substantially burden[s]" the exercise of religion. We have little trouble concluding that it does.

. . . By requiring the Hahns and Greens and their companies to arrange for [contraceptive] coverage, the HHS mandate demands that they engage in conduct that seriously violates their religious beliefs. . . . If the companies continue to offer group health plans that do not cover the contraceptives at issue, they will be taxed $100 per day for each affected individual. For Hobby Lobby, the bill could amount to $1.3 million per day or about $475 million per year; for Conestoga, the assessment could be $90,000 per day or $33 million per year; and for Mardel, it could be $40,000 per day or about $15 million per year. These sums are surely substantial.

It is true that the plaintiffs could avoid these assessments by dropping insurance coverage altogether and thus forcing their employees to obtain health insurance on one of the exchanges established under ACA. But if at least one of their full-time employees were to qualify for a subsidy on one of the government-run exchanges, . . . [t]he companies could face penalties of $2,000 per employee each year. These penalties would amount to roughly $26 million for Hobby Lobby, $1.8 million for Conestoga, and $800,000 for Mardel.

B

Although these totals are high, amici supporting HHS have suggested that the $2,000 per-employee penalty is actually less than the average cost of providing health insurance, and therefore, they claim, the companies could readily eliminate any substantial burden by forcing their employees to obtain insurance in the government exchanges. [However, the government did not present this argument]. . . .

    . . . .

In sum, we refuse to sustain the challenged regulations on the ground — never maintained by the Government — that dropping insurance coverage eliminates the substantial burden that the HHS mandate imposes. We doubt that the Congress that enacted RFRA — or, for that matter, ACA — would have believed it a tolerable result to put family-run businesses to the choice of violating their sincerely held religious beliefs or making all of their employees lose their existing healthcare plans.

C

. . . HHS's main argument (echoed by the principal dissent) is basically that the connection between what the objecting parties must do (provide health-insurance coverage for four methods of contraception that may operate after the fertilization of an egg) and the end that they find to be morally wrong (destruction of an embryo) is simply too attenuated. HHS and the dissent note that providing the coverage would not itself result in the destruction of an embryo; that would occur only if an employee chose to take advantage of the coverage and to use one of the four methods at issue.

This argument dodges the question that RFRA presents (whether the HHS mandate imposes a substantial burden on the ability of the objecting parties to conduct business in accordance with their religious beliefs) and instead addresses a very different question that the federal courts have no business addressing (whether the religious belief asserted in a RFRA case is reasonable). The Hahns and Greens believe that providing the coverage demanded by the HHS regulations is connected to the destruction of an embryo in a way that is sufficient to make it immoral for them to provide the coverage. This belief implicates a difficult and important question of religion and moral philosophy, namely, the circumstances under which it is wrong for a person to perform an act that is innocent in itself but that has the effect of enabling or facilitating the commission of an immoral act by another. Arrogating the authority to provide a binding national answer to this religious and philosophical question, HHS and the principal dissent in effect tell the plaintiffs that their beliefs are flawed. For good reason, we have repeatedly refused to take such a step.

. . . .

Instead, our "narrow function . . . in this context is to determine" whether the line drawn reflects "an honest conviction," and there is no dispute that it does.

. . . Because the contraceptive mandate forces them to pay an enormous sum of money . . . if they insist on providing insurance coverage in accordance with their religious beliefs, the mandate clearly imposes a substantial burden on those beliefs.

V

. . . .

A

HHS asserts that the contraceptive mandate serves a variety of important interests, but many of these are couched in very broad terms, such as promoting "public health" and "gender equality." RFRA, however, contemplates a "more focused" inquiry: It "requires the Government to demonstrate that the compelling interest test is satisfied through application of the challenged law 'to the person' — the particular claimant whose sincere exercise of religion is being substantially burdened." This requires us to "loo[k] beyond broadly formulated interests" and to "scrutiniz[e] the asserted harm of granting specific exemptions to particular religious claimants". . . . In addition to asserting these very broadly framed interests, HHS maintains that the mandate serves a compelling interest in ensuring that all women have access to all FDA-approved contraceptives without cost sharing. Under our cases, women (and men) have a constitutional right to obtain contraceptives, and HHS tells us that "[s]tudies have demonstrated that even moderate copayments for preventive services can deter patients from receiving those services."

The objecting parties contend that HHS has not shown that the mandate serves a compelling government interest, and it is arguable that there are features of ACA that support that view. As we have noted, many employees — those covered by grandfathered plans and those who work for employers with fewer than 50 employees — may have no contraceptive coverage without cost sharing at all.

HHS responds that many legal requirements have exceptions and the existence of exceptions does not in itself indicate that the principal interest served by a law is not compelling. Even a compelling interest may be outweighed in some circumstances by another even weightier consideration. In these cases, however, the interest served by one of the biggest exceptions, the exception for grandfathered plans, is simply the interest of employers in avoiding the inconvenience of amending an existing plan. Grandfathered plans are required "to comply with a subset of the Affordable Care Act's health reform provisions" that provide what HHS has described as "particularly significant protections." But the contraceptive mandate is expressly excluded from this subset.

We find it unnecessary to adjudicate this issue. We will assume that the interest in guaranteeing cost-free access to the four challenged contraceptive methods is compelling within the meaning of RFRA, and we will proceed to consider the final prong of the RFRA test, i.e., whether HHS has shown that the contraceptive mandate is "the least restrictive means of furthering that compelling governmental interest."

B

The least-restrictive-means standard is exceptionally demanding, and it is not satisfied here. HHS has not shown that it lacks other means of achieving its desired goal without imposing a substantial burden on the exercise of religion by the objecting parties in these cases.

The most straightforward way of doing this would be for the Government to assume the cost of providing the four contraceptives at issue to any women who are unable to obtain them under their health-insurance policies due to their employers' religious objections. This would certainly be less restrictive of the plaintiffs' religious liberty, and HHS has not shown that this is not a viable alternative. HHS has not provided any estimate of the average cost per employee of providing access to these contraceptives, two of which, according to the FDA, are designed primarily for emergency use. Nor has HHS provided any statistics regarding the number of employees who might be affected because they work for corporations like Hobby Lobby, Conestoga, and Mardel. . . . It seems likely, however, that the cost of providing the forms of contraceptives at issue in these cases (if not all FDA-approved contraceptives) would be minor when compared with the overall cost of ACA. . . . If, as HHS tells us, providing all women with cost-free access to all FDA-approved methods of contraception is a Government interest of the highest order, it is hard to understand HHS's argument that it cannot be required under RFRA to pay anything in order to achieve this important goal.

. . . .

In the end, however, we need not rely on the option of a new, government-funded program in order to conclude that the HHS regulations fail the least-restrictive-means test. HHS itself has demonstrated that it has at its disposal an approach that is less restrictive. . . . HHS has already established an accommodation for non-profit organizations with religious objections. Under that accommodation, the organization can self certify that it opposes providing coverage for particular contraceptive services. If the organization makes such a certification, the organization's insurance issuer or third-party administrator must "[e]xpressly exclude contraceptive coverage from the group health insurance coverage provided in connection with the group health plan" and "[p]rovide separate payments for any contraceptive services required to be covered" without imposing "any cost-sharing requirements. . . . on the eligible organization, the group health plan, or plan participants or beneficiaries."

We do not decide today whether an approach of this type complies with RFRA for purposes of all religious claims. At a minimum, however, it does not impinge on the plaintiffs' religious belief that providing insurance coverage for the contraceptives at issue here violates their religion, and it serves HHS's stated interests equally well.

. . . .

HHS and the principal dissent argue that a ruling in favor of the objecting parties in these cases will lead to a flood of religious objections regarding a wide variety of medical procedures and drugs, such as vaccinations and blood transfusions, but HHS has made no effort to substantiate this prediction. . . .

It is HHS's apparent belief that no insurance-coverage mandate would violate RFRA — no matter how significantly it impinges on the religious liberties of employers — that would lead to intolerable consequences. Under HHS's view, RFRA would permit the Government to require all employers to provide coverage for any medical procedure allowed by law in the jurisdiction in question — for instance, third-trimester abortions or assisted suicide. The owners of many closely held corporations could not in good conscience provide such coverage, and thus HHS would effectively exclude these people from full participation in the economic life of the Nation. . . .

. . . Our decision should not be understood to hold that an insurance coverage mandate must necessarily fall if it conflicts with an employer's religious beliefs.

Other coverage requirements, such as immunizations, may be supported by different interests (for example, the need to combat the spread of infectious diseases) and may involve different arguments about the least restrictive means of providing them.

The principal dissent raises the possibility that discrimination in hiring, for example on the basis of race, might be cloaked as religious practice to escape legal sanction. Our decision today provides no such shield. The Government has a compelling interest in providing an equal opportunity to participate in the work-force without regard to race, and prohibitions on racial discrimination are precisely tailored to achieve that critical goal.

HHS also raises for the first time in this Court the argument that applying the contraceptive mandate to for profit employers with sincere religious objections is essential to the comprehensive health-insurance scheme that ACA establishes. HHS analogizes the contraceptive mandate to the requirement to pay Social Security taxes, which we upheld in *Lee* despite the religious objection of an employer, but these cases are quite different. . . . We observed that "[t]he tax system could not function if denominations were allowed to challenge the tax system because tax payments were spent in a manner that violates their religious belief."

Lee was a free-exercise, not a RFRA, case, but if the issue in *Lee* were analyzed under the RFRA framework, the fundamental point would be that there simply is no less restrictive alternative to the categorical requirement to pay taxes. Because of the enormous variety of government expenditures funded by tax dollars, allowing taxpayers to withhold a portion of their tax obligations on religious grounds would lead to chaos. Recognizing exemptions from the contraceptive mandate is very different. ACA does not create a large national pool of tax revenue for use in purchasing healthcare coverage. Rather, individual employers like the plaintiffs purchase insurance for their own employees. And contrary to the principal dissent's characterization, the employers' contributions do not necessarily funnel into "undifferentiated funds." The accommodation established by HHS requires issuers to have a mechanism by which to "segregate premium revenue collected from the eligible organization from the monies used to provide payments for contraceptive services." Recognizing a religious accommodation under RFRA for particular coverage requirements, therefore, does not threaten the viability of ACA's compre-hensive scheme in the way that recognizing religious objections to particular expenditures from general tax revenues would.

The contraceptive mandate, as applied to closely held corporations, violates RFRA.

NOTES AND QUESTIONS

7. **The Religious Freedom Restoration Act and federal laws.** *City of Boerne*, note 3, supra, left open the question whether RFRA could constitutionally apply to the federal government. In *O Centro Espírita*, without expressly answering that question, the U.S. Supreme Court simply applied RFRA to the federal Controlled

Substances Act, in a unanimous decision. There was no substantive discussion of the separation of powers. Of course, the Controlled Substances Act is a federal statute, not a state law. But, one might have expected some mention of the distinct powers of Congress and the judiciary. After *City of Boerne*, federal courts of appeal had not found RFRA applicable in many cases. Perhaps the U.S. Supreme Court no longer worried that RFRA posed a threat to the separation of powers. However, it may encourage challenges to other federal laws, as illustrated in the *Hobby Lobby* case, *supra*, and the Notes below.

The *O Centro Espírita* Court focused on the fact that the RFRA required an individualized analysis of whether the federal law burdened "a person's exercise of religion." Contrast this statutory requirement with the *Smith* Court's conclusion that the First Amendment does not require neutral laws of general applicability to make exceptions. The *O Centro Espírita* Court emphasized that the Controlled Substances Act allowed the Attorney General to make exceptions to the statute's bans and, after *Smith*, Congress amended the Act to exempt the religious use of peyote by all recognized Indian Tribes. Without these provisions, would the Court come to the same conclusion? Could it have mattered that the religion had only about 130 adherents in the United States?

8. **Corporations and religious beliefs**. *Burwell v. Hobby Lobby* held for the first time that for-profit corporations qualify as "persons" who "exercise religion" under RFRA. Justice Alito's decision for the majority — joined by Chief Justice Roberts and Justices, Scalia, Kennedy and Thomas — stated that the ruling was limited to closely held corporations, like Hobby Lobby. Do you agree? What principle did the majority use to define eligible corporations? Should it matter whether a corporation is closely held? Koch Industries, Cargill, and similar companies with multi-billion dollar revenues are closely held. The Walton family owns 84% of the public-traded stock of WalMart. Justice Ginsburg wrote a lengthy dissent, joined by Justices Breyer, Sotomayor and Kagan. However, only Justice Sotomayor joined Ginsburg's argument that for-profit corporations do not exercise religion and were not intended to be covered by RFRA.

According to the majority, who exactly has religious beliefs — the corporation or the owners? For that matter, is having a religious belief that same thing as "exercising religion" for purposes of RFRA? In *Employment Division v. Smith*, the Court said, "the 'exercise of religion' often involves not only belief and profession but the performance of (or abstention from) physical acts: assembling with others for a worship service, . . . proselytizing, abstaining from certain foods or certain modes of transportation." 494 U.S. at 877.

Catholic universities had, in the past, challenged state laws requiring health plans to cover contraception on First Amendment Free Exercise grounds, but these challenged failed under the *Employment Division v. Smith* doctrine. *See, e.g., Catholic Charities of Sacramento, Inc. v. Superior Court*, 10 Cal. Rptr. 3d 283, 315 (2004). Could they challenge state laws under RFRA now? Could Hobby Lobby and Conestoga challenge the HHS contraception regulation under the Free Exercise clause today?

9. **Framing the issue**. Justice Alito's opinion states that the question before the court is whether HHS can demand that the corporations provide health insurance

coverage for contraceptives that violate their sincerely held religious beliefs. The four dissenting Justices view the issue as whether a corporation can deprive its employees of government benefits because of the sincere religious beliefs of its owners. How would you frame the issue? How does the framing affect the analysis?

The majority assumes that the government has a compelling interest in gender equality and access to contraception, but also notes that this assumption could be "arguable." What might be the arguments that these interests are not compelling? What compelling interests might be sufficient to outweigh a religion-based claim of exemption? The dissent argues that the majority's reasoning could give rise to claims that "an employer's sincerely held religious belief is offended by health coverage of vaccines, or paying the minimum wage, ... or according women equal pay for substantially similar work. . . . " Are uniform wage and hour laws sufficiently compelling? What would a less restrictive alternative be? Does the majority opinion answer such questions?

The majority does suggest that uniformity in taxation is a compelling interest, by distinguishing *United States v. Lee*, 455 U.S. 252 (1982), from the RFRA claim. In *Lee*, an Amish taxpayer objected to paying Social Security taxes because the Amish religion obligated believers to take care of their own members. The Court rejected Lee's claim for exemption, noting that "mandatory participation is indispensable to the fiscal vitality of the social security system." *Id*. at 258, 260. How does the goal of uniform taxation differ from uniform benefit coverage?

Alito's opinion notes that, under the government's reasoning, the government could require corporations to pay for abortions and assisted suicide. Do you agree? Does it matter that Congress is almost certain not to do so?

10.   **What is a substantial burden?** What counts as a substantial burden is normally a legal question for the court to decide: how does the HHS regulation burden the exercise of religion? Does the court decide that question? The majority accepts the individual owners' argument that "facilitating" access to the four challenged contraceptives contravenes their religious beliefs, making them complicit in the termination of life. Does this mean that the burden is the act of arranging for or offering a health insurance plan to employees? Is it a "substantial burden"? Chief Judge Briscoe, dissenting in the 10th Circuit's *Hobby Lobby* decision below, argued that the owners' contention "is not one of religious belief, but rather of purported scientific fact, i.e., how the challenged contraceptives operate to prevent pregnancy." 723 F.3d 1114, 1176 (10th Cir. 2013). Should that affect the analysis? The dissent in *Hobby Lobby* argues that the relationship between offering a health plan and the use of specific contraceptives is too attenuated to qualify as a burden. Would Hobby Lobby also object to an employee using her wages to pay for contraceptives directly? After all, any employer's contribution to insurance premiums is part of employee compensation, like wages. If a Hobby Lobby employee died in childbirth paid for by its employee health plan, would Hobby Lobby be complicit in the woman's death?

Alternatively, is the burden at issue the possibility of paying a fee or a tax for offering employee health insurance coverage without full contraceptive coverage? (Note that the $2,000 fee is payable only if an employee obtains a subsidy or tax credit for insurance purchases on a government insurance exchange. The $100 tax, payable by employers that do not comply with federal requirements for employee plans that receive favorable tax treatment under the Internal Revenue Code, pre-dated the ACA.) Is Hobby Lobby required to offer health insurance to its employees or, if it does, to pay any part of the insurance premiums? Compare the Court's rejection of claims that Sunday closing laws burdened the free exercise rights of kosher market customers, *Gallagher v. Crown Kosher Super Market of Mass., Inc.*, 366 U. S. 617 (1961), and Orthodox Jewish merchants, *Braunfeld v. Brown*, 366 U. S. 599 (1961) (noting that the considerable loss of income from closing on both Saturday and Sunday was not a cognizable burden).

11. The least restrictive alternative. Justice Ginsburg opens her dissent with the following:

> In a decision of startling breadth, the Court holds that commercial enterprises, including corporations, along with partnerships and sole proprietorships, can opt out of any law (saving only tax laws) they judge incompatible with their sincerely held religious beliefs. Compelling governmental interests in uniform compliance with the law, and disadvantages that religion-based opt-outs impose on others, hold no sway, the Court decides, at least when there is a "less restrictive alternative." And such an alternative, the Court suggests, there always will be whenever, in lieu of tolling an enterprise claiming a religion-based exemption, the government, i.e., the general public, can pick up the tab.

Justice Ginsburg may be correct that whenever the government must use the least restrictive alternative, the Court can usually conceive of something less restrictive than the government's policy choice. In constitutional doctrine, this requirement has generally been limited to laws impinging on free speech protected by the First Amendment. Although Congress enacted RFRA to restore the strict scrutiny analysis that was applied to First Amendment free exercise claims before*Employment Division v. Smith* , the pre-*Smith* test did not require the least restrictive alternative. Thus, RFRA grants religious claims unusually powerful protection.

Are the less restrictive alternatives suggested by the *Hobby Lobby* majority feasible, either legally or politically? The majority stressed the fact that the HHS rule already offers "accommodation" to religiously-affiliated, non-profit organizations that file a form (with HHS and their health insurers) stating that they have religious objections to covering contraceptives. Just days after the *Hobby Lobby* decision, however, the Court found that a religiously-affiliated college was entitled to an interlocutory injunction against the requirement to file the certification form, pending trial in the lower court. *Wheaton College v. Burwell*, 537 U.S. ___ (2014). Wheaton argued that filing the form makes it com plicit in providing contraceptives by triggering the obligation for someone else to provide the services. Justice Sotomayor, joined by Justices Ginsburg and Kagan, strongly dissented, pointing out that the obligation [on insurers] to cover contraception is already imposed by the ACA, and not the result of filing any form. The dissent also objected that the majority flatly contradicted its statements in *Hobby Lobby* that the accommodation is a less restrictive alternative.

As a practical matter, how are insurers or third-party-administrators of self-insured health plans to know whether or not to provide separate coverage unless told by the employer? Will HHS know who the insurer is? Furthermore, is it safe to assume that private insurers will remain willing to offer separate, cost-free payment for contraception outside the corporation's health plan? If not, what other accommodation could the government offer? Is Congress likely to require the federal government to pay for any health coverage that corporations oppose?

CHURCH OF THE LUKUMI BABALU AYE v. CITY OF HIALEAH
508 U.S. 520 (1993)

JUSTICE KENNEDY delivered the opinion of the Court, except as to Part II-A-2.

I

A

This case involves practices of the Santeria religion, which originated in the 19th century. When hundreds of thousands of members of the Yoruba people were brought as slaves from western Africa to Cuba, their traditional African religion absorbed significant elements of Roman Catholicism. The resulting syncretion, or fusion, is Santeria, "the way of the saints." The Cuban Yoruba express their devotion to spirits, called *orishas*, through the iconography of Catholic saints . . . .

. . . . The basis of the Santeria religion is the nurture of a personal relation with the *orishas*, and one of the principal forms of devotion is an animal sacrifice . . . .

According to Santeria teaching, the *orishas* are powerful but not immortal. They depend for survival on the sacrifice. Sacrifices are performed at birth, marriage, and death rites, for the cure of the sick, for the initiation of new members and priests, and during an annual celebration. Animals sacrificed in Santeria rituals include chickens, pigeons, doves, ducks, guinea pigs, goats, sheep, and turtles. The animals are killed by the cutting of the carotid arteries in the neck. The sacrificed animal is cooked and eaten, except after healing and death rituals . . . .

Santeria adherents faced widespread persecution in Cuba, so the religion and its rituals were practiced in secret. The open practice of Santeria and its rites remains infrequent. . . . The religion was brought to this Nation most often by exiles from the Cuban revolution. The District Court estimated that there are at least 50,000 practitioners in South Florida today.

B

Petitioner Church of the Lukumi Babalu Aye, Inc. (Church), is a not-for-profit corporation organized under Florida law in 1973. The Church and its congregants practice the Santeria religion . . . . In April 1987, the Church leased land in the city of Hialeah, Florida, and announced plans to establish a house of worship as well as a school, cultural center, and museum. Pichardo [the Church president and priest] indicated that the Church's goal was to bring the practice of the Santeria faith, including its ritual of animal sacrifice, into the open . . . .

The prospect of a Santeria church in their midst was distressing to many members of the Hialeah community, and the announcement of the plans to open a Santeria church in Hialeah prompted the city council to hold an emergency public session on June 9, 1987.

. . . First, the city council adopted Resolution 87-66, which noted the "concern" expressed by residents of the city "that certain religions may propose to engage in practices which are inconsistent with public morals, peace or safety," and declared that "the City reiterates its commitment to a prohibition against any and all acts of any and all religious groups which are inconsistent with public morals, peace or safety." Next, the council approved an emergency ordinance, Ordinance 87-40, which incorporated in full, except as to penalty, Florida's animal cruelty laws. Fla. Stat. ch. 828 (1987). Among other things, the incorporated state law subjected to criminal punishment "whoever . . . unnecessarily or cruelly . . . kills any animal." § 828.12.

. . . .

In September 1987, the city council adopted three substantive ordinances addressing the issue of religious animal sacrifice. Ordinance 87-52 defined "sacrifice" as "to unnecessarily kill, torment, torture, or mutilate an animal in a public or private ritual or ceremony not for the primary purpose of food consumption," and prohibited owning or possessing an animal "intending to use such animal for food purposes." It restricted application of this prohibition, however, to any individual or group that "kills, slaughters or sacrifices animals for any type of ritual, regardless of whether or not the flesh or blood of the animal is to be consumed." The ordinance contained an exemption for slaughtering by "licensed establishment [s]" of animals "specifically raised for food purposes." Declaring, moreover, that the city council "has determined that the sacrificing of animals within the city limits is contrary to the public health, safety, welfare and morals of the community," the city council adopted Ordinance 87-71. That ordinance defined "sacrifice" as had Ordinance 87–52, and then provided that "it shall be unlawful for any person, persons, corporations or associations to sacrifice any animal within the corporate limits of the City of Hialeah, Florida." The final Ordinance, 87–72, defined "slaughter" as "the killing of animals for food" and prohibited slaughter outside of areas zoned for slaughterhouse use. The ordinance provided an exemption, however, for the slaughter or processing for sale of "small numbers of hogs and/or cattle per week in accordance with an exemption provided by state law." All ordinances and resolutions passed the city council by unanimous vote. Violations of each of the four ordinances were punishable by fines not exceeding $500 or imprisonment not exceeding 60 days, or both.

. . . .

. . . In addressing the constitutional protection for free exercise of religion, our cases establish the general proposition that a law that is neutral and of general applicability need not be justified by a compelling governmental interest even if the law has the incidental effect of burdening a particular religious practice. *Employment Div., Dept. of Human Resources of Ore.* v. *Smith, supra* . . . . These ordinances fail to satisfy the *Smith* requirements. We begin by discussing neutrality.

. . . .

. . . Although a law targeting religious beliefs as such is never permissible, if the object of a law is to infringe upon or restrict practices because of their religious motivation, the law is not neutral, and it is invalid unless it is justified by a compelling interest and is narrowly tailored to advance that interest . . . . To determine the object of a law, we must begin with its text, for the minimum requirement of neutrality is that a law not discriminate on its face. A law lacks facial neutrality if it refers to a religious practice without a secular meaning discernible from the language or context. Petitioners contend that three of the ordinances fail this test of facial neutrality because they use the words "sacrifice" and "ritual," words with strong religious connotations. We agree that these words are consistent with the claim of facial discrimination, but the argument is not conclusive. The words "sacrifice" and "ritual" have a religious origin, but current use admits also of secular meanings. The ordinances, furthermore, define "sacrifice" in secular terms, without referring to religious practices.

. . . Facial neutrality is not determinative. The Free Exercise Clause, like the Establishment Clause, extends beyond facial discrimination . . . . Official action that targets religious conduct for distinctive treatment cannot be shielded by mere compliance with the requirement of facial neutrality. "The Free Exercise Clause protects against governmental hostility which is masked as well as overt." . . . . The record in this case compels the conclusion that suppression of the central element of the Santeria worship service was the object of the ordinances . . . . Resolution 87-66, adopted June 9, 1987, recited that "residents and citizens of the City of Hialeah have expressed their concern that certain religions may propose to engage in practices which are inconsistent with public morals, peace or safety," and "reiterate[d]" the city's commitment to prohibit "any and all [such] acts of any and all religious groups." No one suggests, and on this record it cannot be maintained, that city officials had in mind a religion other than Santeria.

It becomes evident that these ordinances target Santeria sacrifice when the ordinances' operation is considered . . . . The subject at hand does implicate, of course, multiple concerns unrelated to religious animosity, for example, the suffering or mistreatment visited upon the sacrificed animals and health hazards from improper disposal. But the ordinances when considered together disclose an object remote from these legitimate concerns. The design of these laws accomplishes instead a "religious gerrymander," . . . .

It is a necessary conclusion that almost the only conduct subject to Ordinances 87-40, 87-52, and 87-71 is the religious exercise of Santeria church members. The texts show that they were drafted in tandem to achieve this result. We begin with Ordinance 87-71. It prohibits the sacrifice of animals, but defines sacrifice as "to unnecessarily kill . . . an animal in a public or private ritual or ceremony not for the primary purpose of food consumption." The definition excludes almost all killings of animals except for religious sacrifice, and the primary purpose requirement narrows the proscribed category even further, in particular by exempting kosher slaughter . . . . The net result of the gerrymander is that few if any killings of animals are prohibited other than Santeria sacrifice, which is proscribed because it occurs during a ritual or ceremony and its primary purpose is to make an offering to the *orishas*, not food consumption . . . .

Operating in similar fashion is Ordinance 87-52, which prohibits the "possession, sacrifice, or slaughter" of an animal with the "intent to use such animal for food purposes." This prohibition . . . applies if the animal is killed in "any type of ritual" and there is an intent to use the animal for food, whether or not it is in fact consumed for food. The ordinance exempts, however, "any licensed [food] establishment" with regard to "any animals which are specifically raised for food purposes," if the activity is permitted by zoning and other laws. This exception, too, seems intended to cover kosher slaughter. Again, the burden of the ordinance, in practical terms, falls on Santeria adherents but almost no others: If the killing is — unlike most Santeria sacrifices — unaccompanied by the intent to use the animal for food, then it is not prohibited by Ordinance 87-52; if the killing is specifically for food but does not occur during the course of "any type of ritual," it again falls outside the prohibition; and if the killing is for food and occurs during the course of a ritual, it is still exempted if it occurs in a properly zoned and licensed establishment and involves animals "specifically raised for food purposes." A pattern of exemptions parallels the pattern of narrow prohibitions. Each contributes to the gerrymander.

Ordinance 87-40 incorporates the Florida animal cruelty statute. Its prohibition is broad on its face, punishing "whoever . . . unnecessarily . . . kills any animal." The city claims that this ordinance is the epitome of a neutral prohibition. The problem, however, is the interpretation given to the ordinance by respondent and the Florida attorney general. Killings for religious reasons are deemed unnecessary, whereas most other killings fall outside the prohibition. The city, on what seems to be a *per se* basis, deems hunting, slaughter of animals for food, eradication of insects and pests, and euthanasia as necessary. There is no indication in the record that respondent has concluded that hunting or fishing for sport is unnecessary. Indeed, one of the few reported Florida cases decided under § 828.12 concludes that the use of live rabbits to train greyhounds is not unnecessary. Further, because it requires an evaluation of the particular justification for the killing, this ordinance represents a system of "individualized governmental assessment of the reasons for the relevant conduct." As we noted in *Smith*, in circumstances in which individualized exemptions from a general requirement are available, the government "may not refuse to extend that system to cases of 'religious hardship' without compelling reason." Respondent's application of the ordinance's test of necessity devalues religious reasons for killing by judging them to be of lesser import than nonreligious reasons. Thus, religious practice is being singled out for discriminatory treatment . . . .

The legitimate governmental interests in protecting the public health and preventing cruelty to animals could be addressed by restrictions stopping far short of a flat prohibition of all Santeria sacrificial practice. If improper disposal, not the sacrifice itself, is the harm to be prevented, the city could have imposed a general regulation on the disposal of organic garbage. It did not do so . . . . Thus, these broad ordinances prohibit Santeria sacrifice even when it does not threaten the city's interest in the public health . . . .

. . . With regard to the city's interest in ensuring the adequate care of animals, regulation of conditions and treatment, regardless of why an animal is kept, is the logical response to the city's concern, not a prohibition on possession for the purpose of sacrifice. The same is true for the city's interest in prohibiting cruel methods of killing. Under federal and Florida law and Ordinance 87-40, . . . killing an animal by the "simultaneous and instantaneous severance of the carotid arteries with a sharp instrument" — the method used in kosher slaughter — is approved as humane . . . . If the city has a real concern that other methods are less humane, however, the subject of the regulation should be the method of slaughter itself, not a religious classification that is said to bear some general relation to it.

. . . .

2

. . . .

That the ordinances were enacted " 'because of,' not merely 'in spite of,' " their suppression of Santeria religious practice is revealed by the events preceding their enactment . . . . The public crowd that attended the June 9 meetings interrupted statements by council members critical of Santeria with cheers and the brief comments of Pichardo with taunts. When Councilman Martinez, a supporter of the ordinances, stated that in prerevolution Cuba "people were put in jail for practicing this religion," the audience applauded.

Other statements by members of the city council were in a similar vein. For example, Councilman Martinez, after noting his belief that Santeria was outlawed in Cuba, questioned: "If we could not practice this [religion] in our home-land [Cuba], why bring it to this country?" Councilman Cardoso said that Santeria devotees at the Church "are in violation of everything this country stands for." Councilman Mejides indicated that he was "totally against the sacrificing of animals" and distinguished kosher slaughter because it had a "real purpose." The "Bible says we are allowed to sacrifice an animal for consumption," he continued, "but for any other purposes, I don't believe that the Bible allows that." The president of the city council, Councilman Echevarria, asked: "What can we do to prevent the Church from opening?"

Various Hialeah city officials made comparable comments. The chaplain of the Hialeah Police Department told the city council that Santeria was a sin, "foolishness," "an abomination to the Lord," and the worship of "demons." He advised the city council: "We need to be helping people and sharing with them the truth that is found in Jesus Christ." He concluded: "I would exhort you . . . not to permit this Church to exist." . . . . This history discloses the object of the ordinances to target animal sacrifice by Santeria worshippers because of its religious motivation.

3

In sum, the neutrality inquiry leads to one conclusion: The ordinances had as their object the suppression of religion. The pattern we have recited discloses animosity to Santeria adherents and their religious practices; the ordinances by their own terms target this religious exercise; the texts of the ordinances were gerrymandered with care to proscribe religious killings of animals but to exclude almost all secular killings; and the ordinances suppress much more religious conduct than is necessary in order to achieve the legitimate ends asserted in their defense . . . .

We turn next to a second requirement of the Free Exercise Clause, the rule that laws burdening religious practice must be of general applicability . . . .

The principle that government, in pursuit of legitimate interests, cannot in a selective manner impose burdens only on conduct motivated by religious belief is essential to the protection of the rights guaranteed by the Free Exercise Clause . . . .

Respondent claims that Ordinances 87-40, 87-52, and 87-71 advance two interests: protecting the public health and preventing cruelty to animals. The ordinances are underinclusive for those ends . . . . The underinclusion is substantial, not inconsequential. Despite the city's proffered interest in preventing cruelty to animals, the ordinances are drafted with care to forbid few killings but those occasioned by religious sacrifice. Many types of animal deaths or kills for nonreligious reasons are either not prohibited or approved by express provision. For example, fishing — which occurs in Hialeah — is legal. Extermination of mice and rats within a home is also permitted. Florida law incorporated by Ordinance 87-40 sanctions euthanasia of "stray, neglected, abandoned, or unwanted animals," destruction of animals judicially removed from their owners "for humanitarian reasons" or when the animal "is of no commercial value," the infliction of pain or suffering "in the interest of medical science, " the placing of poison in one's yard or enclosure, and the use of a live animal "to pursue or take wildlife or to participate in any hunting," and "to hunt wild hogs.". . . .

The ordinances are also underinclusive with regard to the city's interest in public health, which is threatened by the disposal of animal carcasses in open public places and the consumption of uninspected meat . . . . The health risks posed by the improper disposal of animal carcasses are the same whether Santeria sacrifice or some nonreligious killing preceded it. The city does not, however, prohibit hunters from bringing their kill to their houses, nor does it regulate disposal after their activity. Despite substantial testimony at trial that the same public health hazards result from improper disposal of garbage by restaurants, restaurants are outside the scope of the ordinances.

. . . .

Ordinance 87-72, which prohibits the slaughter of animals outside of areas zoned for slaughterhouses, is underinclusive on its face. The ordinance includes an exemption for "any person, group, or organization" that "slaughters or processes for sale, small numbers of hogs and/or cattle per week in accordance with an exemption provided by state law." Respondent has not explained why commercial operations that slaughter "small numbers" of hogs and cattle do not implicate its professed desire to prevent cruelty to animals and preserve the public health. Although the city has classified Santeria sacrifice as slaughter, subjecting it to this ordinance, it does not regulate other killings for food in like manner. We conclude, in sum, that each of Hialeah's ordinances pursues the city's governmental interests only against conduct motivated by religious belief . . . .

A law burdening religious practice that is not neutral or not of general application must undergo the most rigorous of scrutiny . . . . A law that targets religious conduct for distinctive treatment or advances legitimate governmental interests only against conduct with a religious motivation will survive strict scrutiny only in rare cases. It follows from what we have already said that these ordinances cannot withstand this scrutiny.

First, even were the governmental interests compelling, the ordinances are not drawn in narrow terms to accomplish those interests. As we have discussed, all four ordinances are overbroad or underinclusive in substantial respects. The proffered objectives are not pursued with respect to analogous nonreligious conduct, and those interests could be achieved by narrower ordinances that burdened religion to a far lesser degree. The absence of narrow tailoring suffices to establish the invalidity of the ordinances.

Respondent has not demonstrated, moreover, that, in the context of these ordinances, its governmental interests are compelling. Where government restricts only conduct protected by the First Amendment and fails to enact feasible measures to restrict other conduct producing substantial harm or alleged harm of the same sort, the interest given in justification of the restriction is not compelling . . . . There can be no serious claim that those interests justify the ordinances.

IV

The Free Exercise Clause commits government itself to religious tolerance, and upon even slight suspicion that proposals for state intervention stem from animosity to religion or distrust of its practices, all officials must pause to remember their own high duty to the Constitution and to the rights it secures. Those in office must be resolute in resisting importunate demands and must ensure that the sole reasons for imposing the burdens of law and regulation are secular. Legislators may not devise mechanisms, overt or disguised, designed to persecute or oppress a religion or its practices. The laws here in question were enacted contrary to these constitutional principles, and they are void.

––––––––––

NOTES AND QUESTIONS

12.   Discrimination against (a) religion. The *Lukumi Babalu Aye* case is a rare example of a law that burdens religion. Such laws have traditionally received heightened scrutiny. The U.S. Supreme Court has struck down a state law that allowed Catholic and Protestant church services, but prohibited Jehovah's Witness preaching, in a public park, *Fowler v. Rhode Island*, 345 U.S. 67 (1953), and a law prohibiting ministers and priests from being elected to the legislature, *McDaniel v. Paty*, 435 U.S. 618 (1978). In *Lukumi*, there was considerable evidence that the city councilors were targeting the Santerians. Its practitioners suffered persecution in Cuba and those who moved to Florida were not welcomed with open arms. City Council meeting participants were surprisingly honest about their intentions, at least by today's standards. This evidence apparently convinced the Court that, despite their neutral language, the ordinances were not neutral and generally applicable laws, but a scheme that targeted a specific religion and thus were subject to strict scrutiny.

Lukumi, decided only a few years after *Smith*, suggests that the Court may be willing, at least in some circumstances, to look behind facially neutral language to determine whether the real purpose of a law of general application is unlawful discrimination against the exercise of a constitutionally protected right or group. What other circumstances would warrant close scrutiny? Is purpose the same as motive? Generally speaking, the judiciary does not consider the legislature's motivation for enacting a neutral and generally applicable law, confining itself to determining whether the law at issue serves a legitimate state interest, especially after *Smith*. Why did the Court conclude that the goals of "protecting the public health and preventing cruelty to animals" were not compelling in *Lukumi*? Certainly such goals sound legitimate, and often compelling. Was the Court simply not persuaded that those were the City Council's actual goals — that they were, instead, pretexts to push the church out of town? Does this mean that courts should always look for the "real" reason for legislation that may burden someone's religious practices?

13. Snake handlers. The United States is home to many religions, some of which hold unconventional beliefs and engage in practices that strike the majority of the population as odd or disturbing. *Swann v. Pack*, 527 S.W.2d 99 (Tenn. 1975), *cert. denied*, 424 U.S. 954 (1976), concerned one such religion, a Holiness Church of God in Jesus Name, whose members, as the court described them, "oppose drinking (to include carbonated beverages, tea and coffee), smoking, dancing, the use of cosmetics, jewelry or other adornment. They regard the use of medicine as a sure sign of lack of faith in God's ability to cure the sick and look upon medical doctors as being for the use of those who do not trust God." What brought them before the court, however, was the practice, during religious services, of handling poisonous snakes. The Church had failed to pay a fine for the violation of the following Tennessee statute:

> *Handling snakes so as to endanger life — Penalty.* — It shall be unlawful for any person, or persons, to display, exhibit, handle or use any poisonous or dangerous snake or reptile in such a manner as to endanger the life or health of any person.

> Any person violating the provisions of this section shall be guilty of a misdemeanor and punished by a fine of not less than fifty dollars ($50.00) nor more than one hundred and fifty dollars ($150), or by confinement in jail not exceeding six (6) months, or by both such fine and imprisonment, in the discretion of the court.

§ 39–2208 T.C.A.

The trial court ordered Church officials to show cause why they should not be jailed for contempt, for failing to pay the fine. The Church then challenged the law as infringing on its religious practices in violation of both the federal and the Tennessee Constitution. The purpose of snake handling was variously described as testing one's faith, demonstrating one's belief or confirming the Word of God. The church's pastor warned, however, that only the "anointed" handle snakes:

> If you've got the Holy Ghost in you, it'll come out and nothing can hurt you. Faith brings contact with God and then you're anointed. It is not tempting God. You can't tempt God by doing what He says do. You can have faith, but if you never feel the anointing, you had better leave the serpent alone.

The Tennessee court concluded that the statute was constitutional, but it struggled — in ways analogous to the helmet and seat belt decisions and not necessarily persuasively — to characterize the legislation as designed exclusively for the protection of third parties:

> At a glance, it is self-evident that it does not forbid snake handling *per se*. It condemns the *manner* and not the *fact* of snake handling. Conversely it permits snake handling if done in a careful and prudent manner or, in the statutory terminology, under any circumstances or in any manner which does not endanger the life or health of any person.
>
> Obviously, it was not intended to prevent zoologists or herpetologists from handling snakes or reptiles as a part of their professional pursuits, nor to preclude handling by those who do so as a hobby, nor those who are engaged in scientific or medical pursuits requiring the handling of snakes.

Consider the statutory language yourself. What does the term "any person" in the first paragraph mean? Perhaps the court, without explanation, was implementing the frequently invoked principle that courts should "strictly" interpret ambiguous criminal statutes, to avoid unfairness and lack of notice to defendants about what conduct is proscribed. Whatever the reason, the court's interpretation of the statute allowed it to avoid a tougher question: whether the state may use the *criminal* law to prohibit a religious practice on the ground that it is hazardous to the practitioner himself. Instead, the Tennessee Supreme Court held "that those who publicly handle snakes in the presence of other persons and those who are present aiding and abetting are guilty of creating and maintaining a public nuisance . . . ." It ordered the trial court to enter a permanent injunction restraining all parties "from handling, displaying or exhibiting dangerous and poisonous snakes." Why would the court avoid *criminal* punishment of persons who engage in religious rituals hazardous to themselves, and at the same time to impose an equally "paternalistic" *civil* injunction against performance of the same rituals? The court stated, "Yes, the state has a right to protect a person from himself and to demand that he protect his own life." Would a court make such a statement today? Recall that later cases at both the state and federal level have made clear that competent adults have the right to refuse to protect their own lives. See the discussion of *Cruzan* in B, Note 2, *supra*.

The Tennessee Supreme Court did find that the Church was "a constitutionally protected religious group." Nonetheless, it found that nothing less than outright prohibition of snake handling could serve the state's goals:

> . . . We gave consideration to limiting the prohibition to handling snakes in the presence of children, but rejected this approach because it conflicts with the parental right and duty to direct the religious training of his children. We considered the adoption of a "consenting adult" standard but, again, this practice is too fraught with danger to permit its pursuit in the frenzied atmosphere of an emotional church service, regardless of age or consent. We considered restricting attendance to members only, but this would destroy the evangelical mission of the church. We considered permitting only the handlers themselves to be present, but this frustrates the purpose of confirming the faith to non-believers and separates the pastor and leaders from the congregation. We could find no rational basis for limiting or restricting the practice, and could conceive of no alternative plan or procedure which would be palatable to the membership or permissible from a standpoint of compelling state interest . . . .

The court upheld the statute's application to the Holiness Church, apparently using strict scrutiny, describing the state's interest as "compelling." *Swann* was decided in 1975, before the U.S. Supreme Court's decision in *Smith, supra*, which found it unnecessary to closely scrutinize neutral statutes of general applicability. Do you think that Tennessee's law was such a statute? How would a court decide *Swann* today? Can you think of any alternative ways, in addition to those mentioned by court in the above excerpt, to permit snake handling that would not endanger others?

14.   Religious objections to medical care. Do parents have the right to use prayer or faith healing in lieu of medical treatment for their children? It is clear that competent adults have the right to refuse medical treatment for themselves for religious reasons or for no reason at all. Well-known examples are competent adult Jehovah's Witnesses' right to refuse blood transfusions for themselves. The state, in its role as *parens patriae*, treats children (minors) — those under 18 — differently. In general, minors are not considered legally competent to make their own medical decisions. There are statutory exceptions to this general rule, such as state laws authorizing minors to obtain treatment for sexually transmitted infections, which are intended to remove any disincentive to obtaining needed treatment that having to obtain parental consent might pose. In addition, state statutes often authorize minors who are married or divorced to make their own medical decisions. (State laws governing consent to abortion are a bit more complicated. These laws do not typically allow minors to consent to medical care beyond that specified in the statutes. The common law in most states allows "mature minors" — those functionally capable of giving informed consent — to make their own medical decisions.

While parents are responsible for a child's upbringing, they (and legal guardians) also have an obligation to provide necessaries for their children, including medical care that is necessary to save the child's life or limb or prevent serious disability. This parental duty is well established in common law; few states have bothered to codify it in legislation. Some religious groups, such as the Church of Christ, Scientist, and the Faith Assembly, eschew medical therapies in favor of faith healing — prayer. The doctrinal foundations may vary, but most include the idea that God alone can heal illness. For parents who belong to such religious groups, their religious beliefs can conflict with their secular responsibilities to their children.

David and Ginger Twitchell were convicted of involuntary manslaughter in 1990 for the death of their two-year-old son from a surgically correctable bowel obstruction. The Twitchells relied on Christian Science prayer sessions, rather than taking the child to a physician. They were sentenced to 10 years' probation. In 2011, news reports found that a 6-month old girl, Alayna Wyland, was discovered with a "baseball-size tumor on her face that pushed her eye out of her socket and could cause blindness." Isolde Raftery, *Changes in Oregon Law Put Faith-Healing Parents on Trial*, New York Times, May 30, 2011, A14. The girl's family had not sought medical care, preferring the "laying on of hands," in accordance with their faith healing religion. *Id.* Children of other church members had died for lack of medical care, prompting Oregon to repeal its law allowing parents to refuse medical care for their children on religious grounds. The parents of teenager Neal Beagley were found criminally responsible for his death from complications of a blocked urinary tract and sentenced to 16 months in prison. The father of 2 year old Ava Worthington was convicted in her death from pneumonia and sentenced to 60 days in prison. *Id.* Are these sentences appropriate punishment? Do they encourage parents to seek medical care for their children?

Church members argue that such prosecutions amount to religious persecution in violation of the Free Exercise Clause. Prosecutors, as well as physicians and child advocates, argue that the parents do not have the right to impose their religious beliefs on their child, when the child could die as a result. Parents who fail to obtain necessary medical care for their children may mistakenly assume that the Free Exercise Clause of the First Amendment protects them. But, as we have seen, there are limits to what that Clause protects. Practices that endanger others are beyond the limit.

In *Prince v. Massachusetts*, 321 U.S. 158 (1944), the U.S. Supreme Court rejected a free exercise defense raised by a woman who claimed she could not constitutionally be prosecuted under child labor laws for having her ward, a child, distribute religious pamphlets. The Court observed: "The [First Amendment] right to practice religion freely does not include liberty *to expose the community or the child to communicable disease or the latter to ill health or death*. . . . Parents may be free to become martyrs themselves. But it does not follow that they are free, in identical circumstances, to make martyrs of their children before they have reached the age of full legal discretion when they can make that choice for themselves." *Id.* at 166–167 (emphasis added). Although *Prince* did not involve any communicable disease or threat to health, this language suggests that the states' interest in children as particular objects of government protection outweighs religiously based objections to compliance. In fact, as we have seen, in *Smith*, Justice Scalia invokes *Prince* as authority for the idea that a "valid and neutral law of general applicability" is not rendered unconstitutional because of its secondary impact on religious freedom.

Parents have more discretion when medical care is not likely to save the child's life or cure a serious disease. Thus, parents are free to refuse treatments with only a small chance of success or treatments that are risky or still experimental. If a parent refuses to consent to necessary care, a court can order treatment without forcing the parent to violate their religious beliefs. This can only happen, however, when the child is brought to the attention of the health care system. It is when a child dies without seeing any physician that criminal prosecution is likely to ensue.

LEPAGE v. STATE
18 P.3d 1177 (Wyoming 2001)

KITE, JUSTICE.

Issues

Appellant Susan LePage presents the following issue: Did the Wyoming Department of Health act arbitrarily and capriciously or otherwise abuse its discretion and legal authority in denying the claimed religious exemption of Appellant? Appellee State of Wyoming, Department of Health phrases the issues as follows: Was the Department of Health's final decision to deny the Appellant's request for a religious exemption in accordance with the law? Was the Department of Health's denial of Appellant's request for a religious exemption constitutional and supported by substantial evidence?

Facts

On March 25, 1999, Mrs. LePage requested a religious exemption from the hepatitis B vaccination pursuant to § 21-4-309(a) on behalf of her daughter. Mrs. LePage outlined her concerns regarding the hepatitis B vaccination in a four-page letter. The State Health Officer for the Department of Health delayed a decision pending receipt of further information to assure that faith served as the basis for the request. In particular, the State Health Officer asked Mrs. LePage to define her beliefs as being religious-based and to explain how she acted upon her faith in a consistent manner. Mrs. LePage responded with a second letter, which restated her concerns. On June 10, 1999, Mrs. LePage's request for exemption was denied, and she was informed that, if her daughter was not immunized, she would be unable to attend school.

Mrs. LePage's initial letter began: "We, the parents . . . are petitioning for religious exemption of the Hepatitis B vaccine. Because of the strong religious beliefs of our family, we do not believe our daughter will engage in behavior that involve[s] exposure to blood or body fluids. We believe that the instituting of mandatory Hepatitis B vaccines is the direct result of our children growing up in a declining moral culture."

Mrs. LePage requested a hearing, and the matter was referred to the Office of Administrative Hearings (OAH). A hearing was held on August 5, 1999, at which time Mrs. LePage stated she had recently concluded that all vaccines were not "[G]od[']s will for our lives." The OAH rendered its decision and determined that Mrs. LePage had failed to provide evidence to justify the religious exemption. The Department of Health issued an amended final decision on September 28, 1999, which specifically found that Mrs. LePage's objection was based on personal, moral, or philosophical beliefs rather than on a principle of religion or a truly held religious conviction. Mrs. LePage appealed from the decision, and the district court certified the case to this court . . . .

[According to the court, the trial evidence shows that LePage did have her children vaccinated against other diseases in the past. It also shows that when LePage initially requested the religious exemption, it was based on her personal belief that the mandatory vaccination condoned immoral behavior which was contrary to how she raised her children. According to the court: "Both of her letters and the attachments provide information which showed that LePage's objection, while religiously based, was in fact philosophical . . . . The first time LePage expressed a truly religious based objection to the hepatitis B vaccine was at the hearing. [The defendants claimed] that the agency does not question that LePage is a devoutly religious individual and that she spent extensive time praying, fasting and reading the Bible. [Nor does it] question the fact that LePage now believes that all vaccinations are contrary to the word of her God and that she believes she sinned when having her children vaccinated in the past."]

Standard of Review

When a case is certified to this court, we examine the administrative agency's decision as if we were the reviewing court of the first instance. The issue presented in this case requires us to interpret [the state's law] . . . . This court affirms an agency's conclusions of law when they are in accordance with the law. When an agency has not invoked and properly applied the correct rule of law, we correct the agency's errors.

Discussion

The United States Supreme Court held in *Jacobson v. Massachusetts* that a state has the authority to enact a mandatory immunization program through the exercise of its police power. Moreover, § 35-4-101 grants the Department of Health the power to prescribe rules and regulations for the management and control of communicable diseases. The question presented in this case requires us to interpret the language of § 21-4-309(a) which provides for mandatory immunization of Wyoming school children. That statute provides in pertinent part: "(a) Any person attending, full or part time, any public or private school, kindergarten through twelfth grade, shall within thirty (30) days after the date of school entry, provide to the appropriate school official written documentary proof of immunization . . . . Waivers shall be authorized by the state or county health officer upon submission of written evidence of religious objection or medical contraindication to the administration of any vaccine."

Mrs. LePage asserts the clear language of the exemption statute confirms that the issuance of a religious exemption is not a discretionary function but is a ministerial duty on the part of the Department of Health. Therefore, the Department of Health exceeded its authority by requiring more than an initial written objection which by statute appears to be sufficient to obtain a waiver. Conversely, the Department of Health argues that Wyoming's immunization waiver allows only for religious objections as opposed to personal or philosophical objections. Therefore, the Department of Health must review the asserted objection and determine whether it is based on sincerely held religious beliefs. The Department of Health determined that Mrs. LePage's religious waiver request was based on concerns regarding the health and safety risks of the vaccination as well as the mode of transmission of the hepatitis B virus. According to the Department of Health, Mrs. LePage failed to establish that the requested waiver was based on sincerely held religious beliefs which would entitle her to a waiver.

In interpreting statutes, we primarily determine the legislature's intent from the words used in the statute . . . . First, we must determine . . . "if the statute is ambiguous by looking at the plain and ordinary meaning of the words contained therein." A "statute is unambiguous if its wording is such that reasonable persons are able to agree as to its meaning with consistency and predictability." "[W]hether an ambiguity exists in a statute is a matter of law to be determined by the court." However, "[s]trict adherence to our Wyoming constitution demands that the judicial branch of government recognize that it is without discretion, nor does it have any latitude, to apply statutes contrary to legislative intent once that intent has been ascertained."

The principal language in the statute which delineates the requirement to obtain a waiver provides: "Waivers shall be authorized." This court has observed that, when the word "shall" is employed, it is usually legally accepted as mandatory. Where a statute uses the mandatory language "shall," a court must obey the statute as a court has no right to make the law contrary to what is prescribed by the legislature.

The choice of the word "shall" intimates an absence of discretion by the Department of Health and is sufficiently definitive of the mandatory rule intended by the legislature. Similarly, the statutory language lacks any mention of an inquiry by the state into the sincerity of religious beliefs. As a result, the Department of Health exceeded its legislative authority when it conducted a further inquiry into the sincerity of Mrs. LePage's religious beliefs.

. . . As a creature of the legislature, an administrative agency has only the powers granted to it by statute, and the justification for the exercise of any authority by the agency must be found within the applicable statute. A statute will be strictly construed when determining the authority granted to an agency . . . . In other words, reasonable doubt of the existence of a power must be resolved against the exercise thereof . . . . The statute provides mandatory language, and the Department of Health may not circumvent the legislature's clear limitation of its powers or expand its power beyond its statutory authority. There is no justification found within the statute for the Department of Health to institute a religious inquiry. As a result, the decision to do so is not in accordance with the law.

Furthermore, construing the statute as the Department of Health suggests raises questions concerning the extent to which the government should be involved in the religious lives of its citizens. Should an individual be forced to present evidence of his/her religious beliefs to be scrutinized by a governmental employee? If parents have not consistently expressed those religious beliefs over time, should they be denied an exemption? Can parents have beliefs that are both philosophical and religious without disqualifying their exemption request? Should the government require a certain level of sincerity as a bench-mark before an exemption can be granted? If the legislature chose to address these types of questions with further legislation, such legislation would call into question the constitutional prohibition against governmental interference with the free exercise of religion under Article 1, section 18 of the Wyoming Constitution. However, those issues need not be addressed in this case because the statute does not provide the authority for such inquiry.

. . . .

We recognize the genuine concern that there could be increased requests for exemption and a potential for improper evasion of immunization. The state certainly has a valid interest in protecting public school children from unwarranted exposure to infectious diseases. However, we have been presented with no evidence that the number of religious exemption waiver requests are excessive and are confident in our presumption that parents act in the best interest of their children's physical, as well as their spiritual, health. Again, if problems regarding the health of Wyoming's school children develop because this self-executing statutory exemption is being abused, it is the legislature's responsibility to act within the constraints of the Wyoming and United States Constitutions.

NOTES AND QUESTIONS

15. Religious exemptions. *LePage* raises nearly the mirror-image problem to that of *Smith*: Can the state constitutionally choose to *exempt* some individuals, on the basis of their religious beliefs, from otherwise-valid public health laws? (Note, at the outset, that the state's general power to require immunization as a condition for attending public school was not at issue, so the court's focus is on the religious basis for exemption.) As *LePage* suggests, the exercise of that legislative largesse toward religious objectors to immunization can itself raise difficult federal and/or state constitutional issues.

The *LePage* court, however, focused on the statutory text, rather than the constitutional issue. It read the statute literally — requiring the state to treat the mere fact of claiming a religious exemption as establishing, *per se*, its legitimacy. The court barred further state inquiry into the basis of the claim. What reasons, both statutory and constitutional, does the *LePage* court give for making this choice? By contrast, many other state courts have insisted (sometimes on the basis of more demanding statutory language) that the claimant prove, for example, that the objector sincerely adheres to a particular religious denomination whose articulated doctrine demonstrably rejects immunization. What arguments might support this more searching form of inquiry? Consider the hazards in both extremes.

Could a state decline to allow religious exemptions to mandatory immunizations? There is case law on point. *See, e.g., Boone v. Boozman*, 217 F. Supp. 2d, 938, 952–55 (E.D. Ark. 2002) (applying *Smith* analysis to conclude that compulsory school immunization law lacking any religious exemption was a law of general applicability that did not merit heightened scrutiny and upholding the law against a free exercise challenge). While most states do allow for exemption on religious grounds, these are properly understood as discretionary policy accommodations, rather than constitutional necessities.

Some states provide exemptions only to "established" religions — presumably in order to limit opportunity for disingenuous invocation of the exemption — "nontraditional" believers may be ineligible. (Similar exemptions are sometimes included in child protection laws, allowing parents to refuse elective medical care in favor of spiritual "treatment" in accordance with the tenets of an established religion.) Such exemptions are vulnerable to claims that the statute favors one religion (or group of religions) over another, in violation of either the establishment clause (*see, e.g., Boone v. Boozman, supra*, 217 F. Supp. at 945–52) or equal protection clause.

In light of such complexities, one might think that avoiding religious exemptions entirely would be the "safest" (and surely the constitutionally simplest) legislative course to follow. The fact that these legislative exemptions are so widely adopted attests to the influence of religion in American political life, and to the felt civic need for its ongoing accommodation.

About 20 states have enacted broader exemptions based on personal philosophy or beliefs about immunization. *See, e.g.,* ARIZ. REV. STAT. § 15-873 (parents authorized to refuse immunization of child based on "personal beliefs," provided parent is informed about risks and benefits of immunization as well as risks of non-immunization) and § 15-873.C. (non-immunized children excluded from school during disease-outbreak periods). Such provisions are broad enough to *include* religiously-based objections, but they largely avoid the complexities of *specifically*-religious exemptions, outlined above. What hazards, if any, do they generate? If you were a legislator, what approach would you favor in this area?

Finally, to complete our review of legislative exemptions, all 50 states recognize exemptions for those who are shown to be medically unfit to receive immunizations. Indeed, *Jacobson* told us in *dictum* that such an exemption is constitutionally necessary, and under proper circumstances the exemption would be implied even were it not included in the law's text.

16.   Vaccine requirements and controversies. The immunization requirements of each state can be found in National Conference of State Legislatures, http://www.ncsl.org/research/health.aspx. Exemptions, with links to statutes, can be found at National Conference of State Legislatures, http://www.ncsl.org/research/health/school-immunization-exemption-state-laws.aspx (visited Aug. 2013). The CDC also publishes reports on state immunization requirements and exemptions, but can be several years out of date. *See* http://www2a.cdc.gov/nip/schoolsurv/schImmRqmt.asp (visited Aug. 2013).

Controversy over mandatory vaccinations continues today. Many parents have religious objections to vaccination against HPV for the same reasons that Mrs. LePage objected to HBV vaccination. Other parents question the efficacy of HPV vaccination. HPV is a sexually transmitted infection, transmitted by close skin-to-skin contact. There is no treatment for HPV. More than 80% of American women will contract HPV by the time they are 50 years old. About 75% of HPV infections clear up by themselves within 30 months; but in some cases, the cells mutate and cause cervical cancer. In the US each year, about 9,700 women are diagnosed with cervical cancer, and about 3,700 die of cervical cancer. Almost all deaths from cervical cancer could be prevented by effective Pap test screening and treatment. In men, HPV appears to cause the majority of the cases of penile cancer (about 1,500 American men per year) and anal cancer (about 1,900 American men per year).

The vaccines protect people from getting the 4 types of HPV that cause 70% of cervical cancers and 90% of genital warts. Immunization is almost 100% effective (against these HPV types) for women who have not already been exposed to HPV before vaccination (mostly those who have not been sexually active). No serious side effects of the vaccine are known. Effective vaccination consists of 3 shots over a 6-month period, and costs about $400 total. Pap tests are still needed even for vaccinated women.

17. Religious exemptions and the Establishment Clause. The Establishment Clause, mentioned first in the First Amendment, raises different issues from those typically found in Free Exercise cases. Nonetheless, the two clauses can compete for supremacy in some circumstances, most notably where laws grant a religious exemption from compliance. Examples include exemptions from mandatory immunizations, as in *LePage*, autopsies, and child protection laws requiring parents to provide necessary medical care to their children. In such cases, there are at least two questions: (1) whether the exemption is necessary to avoid governmental interference with the free exercise of religious practices; and (2) whether the exemption creates a special benefit for a religious group in contravention of the Establishment Clause. A third question may also be pertinent: whether the exemption violates equal protection of the laws by burdening everyone *except* members of religious groups.

Justice Stevens, concurring in *City of Boerne*, raised such concerns:

> In my opinion, the Religious Freedom Restoration Act of 1993 (RFRA) is a "law respecting an establishment of religion" that violates the First Amendment to the Constitution.

> If the historic landmark on the hill in Boerne happened to be a museum or an art gallery owned by an atheist, it would not be eligible for an exemption from the city ordinances that forbid an enlargement of the structure. Because the landmark is owned by the Catholic Church, it is claimed that RFRA gives its owner a federal statutory entitlement to an exemption from a generally applicable, neutral civil law. Whether the Church would actually prevail under the statute or not, the statute has provided the Church with a legal weapon that no atheist or agnostic can obtain. This governmental preference for religion, as opposed to irreligion,

is forbidden by the First Amendment. *Wallace* v. *Jaffree*, 472 U.S. 38, 52–55 (1985).

City of Boerne, 521 U.S. at 536–7.

Chapter 5

CONTAGIOUS DISEASES

A. INTRODUCTION

This chapter examines case studies involving the use of compulsory confinement and other forms of coercion to control the spread of infectious disease. We start with an examination of governmentally-imposed restrictions on liberty in connection with active tuberculosis in Part B. We turn next to HIV/AIDS, in Part C, as an example of responses to newly appearing diseases, and implications for new strains of influenza, like "bird flu."

Three sets of thematic issues are developed in the case studies that follow: (1) the importance of understanding the nature and etiology of the disease in question, particularly the manner and speed with which it is spread and its morbidity and mortality, in evaluating the appropriateness and effectiveness of any use of isolation or quarantine; (2) the availability of therapies, if any, to prevent or cure the disease and their safety, efficacy, and mode of administration, and (3) the implications of applying due process and other constitutional principles in the individually-oriented manner that has characterized judicial application of these constitutional constraints on government action in the past. These themes bracket the range of possible public health responses. On the one hand, modern therapeutic techniques may allow for the control of the spread of disease with minimal supervision of people who are potentially contagious; on the other, some as yet unidentified biological threat may require the type of draconian responses that most Americans have never witnessed in their lifetime. Indeed, there are serious questions as to whether the nation's public health infrastructure, its legal system (as it operated traditionally), and even its basic means for maintaining social order are sufficiently prepared for some of the worst-case scenarios that must at least be considered if not anticipated. The next chapter — Chapter 6 — carries these themes forward to analyze how the states and the federal government can or will react if and when the nation is required to respond to some large-scale emergency, whether it be a rapidly moving disease outbreak, natural disaster, or terrorist attack.

SIDEBAR: A NOTE ON TERMINOLOGY

The terminology used in reference to contagious diseases is sometimes imprecise, but some distinctions can be important. The following summary attempts to clarify commonly used terms.

Infectious, Contagious, and Communicable Diseases. Many diseases are infectious, but not all of these are contagious. An *infectious* disease is any disease that can be transmitted *to* a human being by means of a virus, bacterium or parasite, which infects the person. A *contagious* disease is an infectious disease that can be transmitted *from* one person *to* another. Many statutes use the term "communicable" as a synonym for contagious, to emphasize person-to-person transmissibility and, by implication, to distinguish other kinds of infectious diseases.

Quarantine and Isolation. The terms quarantine and isolation are sometimes used interchangeably in common parlance, and indeed both are aimed at preventing transmission of contagious disease. Statutes and judicial opinions often use quarantine as a generic term for both. Scholars and researchers often distinguish between the two, however.

Generally, isolation means keeping a patient *known* to have a contagious disease separate (isolated) from other people — usually in a room in a hospital or other medical facility — in order to prevent transmission. Isolation is now part of standard medical procedure for anyone with a serious contagious disease in the hospital and is typically accepted voluntarily by patients as part of their treatment. When patients do not accept voluntary isolation, *compulsory* isolation (confinement) may be sought; this requires judicial approval. The circumstances in which it is appropriate are limited, requiring (1) a serious contagious disease that (2) can be spread through casual contact, and (3) the transmission of which cannot readily be prevented voluntarily — either because the patient is unwilling or unable to avoid the risks of infecting others, or because he actually seeks to do so.

Quarantine, a broader intervention, describes steps that restrict the movement or activities of well persons who may have been *exposed* to contagious disease and may thus present the risk of transmitting it further; it may include sealing off ships, houses, or geographic areas thought to harbor such a disease. Quarantine typically keeps a person wherever she may be at the time the restriction is imposed, which will often (but not necessarily) be at home.

Outbreaks, Epidemics, and Pandemics. An *outbreak* of disease is a sudden increase in the number of cases of a disease beyond what is normally expected, ordinarily in a particular locality. An *epidemic* is a broader outbreak in a larger geographic area. However, some epidemiologists treat any outbreak as equivalent to an epidemic. A *pandemic* is an epidemic that spreads to several countries. How many cases of any specific disease can be expected under normal circumstances varies from country to country. In many countries, especially in the developing world, certain diseases (such as malaria) remain constantly in the population and are called *endemic*. MICHAEL GREGG, ed., FIELD EPIDEMIOLOGY (2002). In the United States, diseases like malaria, poliomyelitis, measles, rabies, or plague are normally so rare that any increase in the number of cases warrants an investigation to find and eliminate the cause.

B. TUBERCULOSIS — CONTAGION, CONFINEMENT, AND CLASS

GREENE v. EDWARDS
263 S.E.2d 661 (W. Va. 1980)

PER CURIAM:

William Arthur Greene, the relator in this original habeas corpus proceeding, is involuntarily confined in Pinecrest Hospital under an order of the Circuit Court of McDowell County entered pursuant to the terms of the West Virginia Tuberculosis Act Control Act, W. Va. Code, 265A1, *et seq.* He alleges, among other points, that the Tuberculosis Control Act does not afford procedural due process because: (1) it fails to guarantee the alleged tubercular person the right to counsel; (2) it fails to insure that he may cross-examine, confront and present witnesses; and (3) it fails to require that he be committed only upon clear, cogent and convincing proof. We agree.

A petition alleging that Mr. Greene was suffering from active communicable tuberculosis was filed with the Circuit Court of McDowell County on October 3, 1979. After receiving the petition, the court, in accordance with the terms of . . . [the state law] fixed a hearing in the matter for October 10, 1979. The court also caused a copy of the petition and a notice of the hearing to be served upon Mr. Greene. The papers served did not notify Mr. Greene that he was entitled to be represented by counsel at the hearing.

After commencement of the October 10, 1979 hearing, the court, upon learning that Mr. Greene was not represented, appointed an attorney for him. The court then, without taking a recess so that the relator and his attorney could consult privately, proceeded to take evidence and to order Mr. Greene's commitment.

Section 265A5, the statute under which the commitment proceedings in this case were conducted, provides in part:

> If such practicing physician, public health officer, or chief medical officer having under observation or care any person who is suffering from tuberculosis in a communicable stage is of the opinion that the environmental conditions of such person are not suitable for proper isolation or control by any type of local quarantine as prescribed by the state health department, and that such person is unable or unwilling to conduct himself and to live in such a manner as not to expose members of his family or household or other persons with whom he may be associated to danger of infection, he shall report the facts to the department of health which shall forthwith investigate or have investigated the circumstances alleged. If it shall find that any such person's physical condition is a health menace to others, the department of health shall petition the circuit court of the county in which such person resides, or the judge thereof in vacation, alleging that such person is afflicted with communicable tuberculosis and that such person's physical condition is a health menace to others, and requesting an order of the court committing such person to one of the state

tuberculosis institutions. Upon receiving the petition, the court shall fix a date for hearing thereof and notice of such petition and the time and place for hearing thereof shall be served personally, at least seven days before the hearing, upon the person who is afflicted with tuberculosis and alleged to be dangerous to the health of others. If, upon such hearing, it shall appear that the complaint of the department of health is well founded, that such person is afflicted with communicable tuberculosis, and that such person is a source of danger to others, the court shall commit the individual to an institution maintained for the care and treatment of persons afflicted with tuberculosis . . . .

It is evident from an examination of this statute that its purpose is to prevent a person suffering from active communicable tuberculosis from becoming a danger to others. A like rationale underlies our statute governing the involuntary commitment of a mentally ill person . . . .

In *Hawks v. Lazaro* [202 S.E.2d 109 (1974)], we examined the procedural safeguards which must be extended to persons charged under our statute governing the involuntary hospitalization of the mentally ill. We noted that Article 3, Section 10 of the West Virginia Constitution and the Fifth Amendment to the United States Constitution provide that no person shall be deprived of life, liberty, or property without due process of law; we stated: "This Court recognized in [a 1920 case] that, 'liberty, full and complete liberty, is a right of the very highest nature. It stands next in order to life itself. The Constitution guarantees and safeguards it. An adjudication of insanity is a partial deprivation of it.'"

We concluded that due process required that persons charged under [the state civil commitment law] must be afforded: (1) an adequate written notice detailing the grounds and underlying facts on which commitment is sought; (2) the right to counsel; (3) the right to be present, cross-examine, confront and present witnesses; (4) the standard of proof to warrant commitment to be by clear, cogent and convincing evidence; and (5) the right to a verbatim transcript of the proceeding for purposes of appeal . . . .

Because the Tuberculosis Control Act and the Act for the Involuntary Hospitalization of the Mentally Ill have like rationales, and because involuntary commitment for having communicable tuberculosis impinges upon the right to "liberty, full and complete liberty" no less than involuntary commitment for being mentally ill, we conclude that the procedural safeguards set forth in *Hawks v. Lazaro, supra*, must, and do, extend to persons charged under Section 265A5 . . . .

We noted in [*Hawks*] that where counsel is to be appointed in proceedings for the involuntary hospitalization of the mentally ill, the law contemplates representation of the individual by the appointed guardian in the most zealous, adversary fashion consistent with the Code of Professional Responsibility. Since this decision, we have concluded that appointment of counsel immediately prior to a trial in a criminal case is impermissible since it denies the defendant effective assistance of counsel. It is obvious that timely appointment and reasonable opportunity for adequate preparation are prerequisites for fulfillment of appointed counsel's constitutionally assigned role in representing persons charged with having communicable tuberculosis.

✳ In the case before us, counsel was not appointed for Mr. Greene until after the commencement of the commitment hearing. Under the circumstances, counsel could not have been properly prepared to defend Mr. Greene. For this reason, the relator's writ must be awarded and he must be accorded a new hearing.

. . . .

For the reasons stated above, the writ of habeas corpus is awarded, and the relator is ordered discharged, but such discharge is hereby delayed for a period of thirty days during which time the State may entertain further proceedings to be conducted in accordance with the principles expressed herein.

———

CITY OF NEWARK v. J.S.
652 A.2d 265 (N.J. Super. Ct. 1993)

GOLDMAN, J.

The defendant, J.S., is a 40-year-old African-American male suffering from TB and HIV disease. Hospital authorities requested that Newark intervene when J.S. sought to leave the hospital against medical advice. J.S. was found dressed in street clothes, sitting in the hospital lobby. Once he wandered to the pediatrics ward. He had a prior history of disappearances and of releases against medical advice, only to return via the emergency room when his health deteriorated. Allegedly, J.S. failed to follow proper infection control guidelines or take proper medication when in the hospital and failed to complete treatment regimens following his release. In March of 1993 J.S. had been discharged and deposited in a taxicab, which was given the address of a shelter to which he was to be driven. J.S. was given an appointment at a TB clinic a bus trip away from the shelter. J.S.'s Supplemental Security Income check was being delivered to another hospital, so he had no money. He did not keep his TB clinic appointment and was labeled as "noncompliant."

A sputum sample confirmed that J.S. had *active* TB. TB is a communicable disease caused by a bacteria or bacilli complex, *mycobacterium (M.) tuberculosis*. One of the oldest diseases known to affect humans, it was once known as consumption or the great "white plague" because it killed so many people. Human infection with *M. tuberculosis* was a leading cause of death until anti-tuberculosis drugs were introduced in the 1940s. While it can affect other parts of the body, such as lymph nodes, bones, joints, genital organs, kidneys, and skin, it most often attacks the lungs. It is transmitted by a person with what is called *active* TB by airborne droplets projected by coughing or sneezing. When the organism is inhaled into the lungs of another, TB infection can result. Usually this happens only after close and prolonged contact with a person with *active* TB. Most of those who become infected do not manifest any symptoms because the body mounts an appropriate immune response to bring the infection under control; however, those infected display a positive tuberculin skin test. The infection (sometimes called *latent* TB) can continue for a lifetime, and infected persons remain at risk for developing *active* TB if their immune systems become impaired.

Typical symptoms of *active* TB include fatigue, loss of weight and appetite, weakness, chest pain, night sweats, fever, and persistent cough. Sputum is often streaked with blood; sometimes massive hemorrhages occur if TB destroys enough lung tissue. Fluid may collect in the pleural cavity. Gradual deterioration occurs. If *active* TB is not treated, death is common.

Only persons with *active* TB are contagious. That *active* state is usually easily treated through drugs. Typically a short medication protocol will induce a remission and allow a return to daily activities with safety. A failure to continue with medication may lead to a relapse and the development of MDR-TB (multiple drug resistant TB), a condition in which the TB bacilli do not respond to at least two (isoniazid and rifampin) of the primary treatments, so that the active state is not easily cured and contagiousness continues for longer periods.

Death often results because it takes time to grow cultures and to determine the drugs to which the organism is sensitive. By the time that discovery is made, it may be too late, particularly for a person whose immune system has been compromised by a co-morbidity such as HIV disease. For that reason a wide range of drugs, currently four or five, is tried initially while the cultures are grown and sensitivities detected, particularly if MDR-TB is suspected. Once sensitivities are discovered, medication can be adjusted so that ineffective drugs are eliminated and at least two effective drugs are always used. Medical treatment protocols have been established by the United States Centers for Disease Control and Prevention (CDC) and the American Thoracic Society. These protocols are being used for J.S. as they are for all patients under the supervision of New Jersey's Tuberculosis Control Program.

Active TB of the lungs is considered contagious and requires immediate medical treatment, involving taking several drugs. Usually, after only a few days of treatment, infectiousness is reduced markedly. After two to four weeks of treatment, most people are no longer contagious and cannot transmit TB to others even if they cough or sneeze while living in close quarters. Usually exposure over a prolonged time is required, and less than thirty per cent (30%) of family members living closely with an infected person and unprotected by prophylactic drugs will become infected by the patient with *active* TB.

On the other hand, transmission has been known to occur with as little as a single two-hour exposure to coughing, sneezing, etc., of a person with *active* TB. To cure TB, however, continued therapy for six to twelve months may be required. Failure to complete the entire course of therapy risks a relapse and the development of MDR-TB.

MDR-TB results when only some TB bacilli are destroyed and the surviving bacilli develop a resistance to standard drugs and thus become more difficult to destroy. This resistance may involve several drugs and directly results from a patient's failure to complete therapy. There have been no reports of TDR-TB (totally drug resistant TB) in New Jersey, so J.S. can be cured if effective drugs are found in time.

TB is more serious in persons with impaired immune systems, which can result from poor health, chronic abuse of alcohol or drugs, old age, chemotherapy for cancer, or HIV infection. Such persons are more likely to develop *active* TB if they already harbor the TB bacilli. By way of example, ninety per cent of persons with *latent* TB (these persons are neither sick nor contagious) and with an intact immune system will never develop active TB during their entire lives. On the other hand persons with HIV disease with *latent* TB will develop *active* TB at the rate of eight per cent per year.

. . . .

New Jersey's statutory scheme for dealing with TB dates from 1912 when the predecessor to N.J.S.A. 30:9-57 was first adopted. Only minor amendments have been made since 1917. [That statute now provides:]

> A person with communicable tuberculosis who fails to obey the rules or regulations promulgated . . . by the State Department of Health for the care of tubercular persons and for the prevention of the spread of tuberculosis, or who is an actual menace to the community or to members of his household, may be committed to a hospital or institution, designated by the State Commissioner of Health with the approval of the Commissioner of Human Services for the care and custody of such person or persons by the Superior Court, upon proof of service upon him of the rules and regulations and proof of violation thereafter, or upon proof by the health officer of the municipality in which the person resides, or by the State Commissioner of Health or his authorized representative, that he is suffering from tuberculosis, and is an actual menace to the community, or to members of his household. Two days' notice of the time and place of hearing shall in all cases be served upon the person to be committed. Proof of such service shall be made at the hearing. The court may also make such order for the payment for care and treatment as may be proper. The superintendent or person in charge of said hospital or institution to which such person has been committed shall detain said person until the State Commissioner of Health shall be satisfied that the person has recovered to the extent that he will not be a menace to the community or to members of his household or that the person will so conduct himself that he will not constitute such a menace.

[The foregoing statutory text appears in a footnote in the original opinion.]

This law allows me to enter an order committing a person to a hospital if he or she is "suffering from" TB and "is an actual menace to the community." Notice of the hearing is required and was provided. Neither the statute nor the implementing regulation provides any guidance on the procedures to follow when such applications are made, nor what standards are to be used in issuing such orders. There is no case law in New Jersey providing guidance on these and many other related issues.

The regulatory schemes in other jurisdictions vary widely. There are older schemes like that in New Jersey which provide little or no guidance. There are those that provide detailed procedural details to guarantee due process while still allowing detention, isolation, quarantine, or confinement in the most extreme cases.

. . . .

Newark's attempt to protect the health of its citizenry is an archetypical expression of police power. The claim of "disease" in a domestic setting has the same kind of power as the claim of "national security" in matters relating to foreign policy. Both claims are very powerful arguments for executive action. Both claims are among those least likely to be questioned by any other branch of government and therefore subject to abuse. The potential abuse is of special concern when the other interest involved is the confinement of a human being who has committed no crime except to be sick.

Due Process limits police power. The Fourteenth Amendment requires "that deprivation of life, liberty or property by adjudication be preceded by notice and opportunity for hearing appropriate to the nature of the case." *Mullane v. Central Hanover Trust Co.*, 339 U.S. 306, 317, (1950). The parameters of due process require an analysis of both the individual and governmental interests involved and the consequences and avoidability of the risks of error and abuse. *Mathews v. Eldridge*, 424 U.S. 319, 335 (1976). Here the clash of competing interests is at its peak. Hardly any state interest is higher than protecting its citizenry from disease. Hardly any individual interest is higher than the liberty interest of being free from confinement. The consequences of error and abuse are grave for both the state and the individual.

The United States Supreme Court has recognized that "civil commitment for any purpose constitutes a significant deprivation of liberty that requires due process protection." *Addington v. Texas*, 441 U.S. 418, 425 (1979). A person has the right to notice, counsel, and must be afforded the opportunity to present opposing evidence and argument, and to cross examine witnesses . . . . Illness alone cannot be the basis for confinement. *O'Connor v. Donaldson*, 422 U.S. 563 (1975). To justify confinement it must be shown that the person is likely to pose a danger to self or to others. The proofs must show that there is a "substantial risk of dangerous conduct within the foreseeable future." These proofs must be shown by clear and convincing evidence. The terms of confinement must minimize the infringements on liberty and enhance autonomy. Periodic reviews are required. Lesser forms of restraint must be used when they would suffice to fulfill the government interests.

Covington v. Harris, 419 F.2d 617 (D.C.Cir.1969), held that a court must satisfy itself that there were no less restrictive alternatives available to the "drastic curtailment" of rights inherent in the civil confinement of a person. Quoting *Shelton v. Tucker*, 364 U.S. 479, 488 (1960), the court described the following "axiom of due process" :

> Even though the governmental purpose be legitimate and substantial, that purpose cannot be pursued by means that broadly stifle fundamental personal liberties when the end can be more narrowly achieved. The breadth of legislative abridgement must be viewed in the light of less drastic means for achieving the same basic purpose.

[The court then discusses *Greene*, included *supra* in these materials.]

[The 1987 New Jersey statute governing mental illness] provides a comprehensive set of procedures and standards reflecting modern ideas of mental health treatment and modern concepts of constitutional law.

Some provisions establish procedures to enhance fairness and to reduce the risks of error and abuse. Persons whose confinement is sought must be provided counsel. Such persons are entitled to adequate notice of the hearing and discovery before the hearing. The hearing must be held expeditiously to avoid unnecessary confinement. The hearing must be held *in camera* if requested to protect privacy interests. Prior to the hearing an independent examination paid for by the committing authority must be provided upon request. The person sought to be confined has the right to be present, to cross-examine witnesses and to present testimony. The hearing must be on the record. Evidence must be under oath. Periodic court reviews are mandated. All proofs must be shown by clear and convincing evidence.

There are additional requirements. Illness alone cannot be a basis for involuntary commitment. Persons may not be confined merely because they present a risk of future conduct which is socially undesirable. A court must find that the risk of infliction of serious bodily injury upon another is probable in the reasonably foreseeable future. History, actual conduct, and recent behaviors must be considered. Dangerous conduct is not the same as criminal conduct. Dangerous conduct involves not merely violations of social norms but significant injury to persons or substantial destruction of property. The evaluation of the risk involves considering the likelihood of dangerous conduct, the seriousness of the harm that would ensue if such conduct took place, and its probability within the reasonably foreseeable future. A person's past conduct is important evidence of future conduct. If a person is only dangerous with regard to certain individuals, the likelihood of contact with such individuals must be taken into account.

[M]any commentators have suggested that the most apt analogy for commitments for medical reasons is the model of civil commitments for mental illness. This was the analogy seized upon by the West Virginia Supreme Court in *Greene*. Professor George J. Annas recently similarly referred to the problem of TB:

> The closest legal analogy is provided by court cases that have reviewed the constitutionality of state statutes permitting the involuntary commitment of mental patients on the basis that they have a disease that causes them to be dangerous.

. . . .

> . . . The constitutional concept of due process is designed to prevent irrational discrimination by ensuring a forum that can hear opposing perspectives and by insisting that distinctions are rationally based. "The decisive consideration where personal liberty is involved is that each individual's fate must be adjudged on the facts of his own case, not on the general characteristics of a "class" to which he may be assigned." [Citation omitted.]

. . . .

Thus, it becomes possible to reconcile public health concerns, constitutional requirements, [and] civil liberties . . . simultaneously. Good public health practice considers human rights so there is no conflict. Since coercion is a difficult and expensive means to enforce behaviors, voluntary compliance is the public health goal. Compliance is more likely when authorities demonstrate sensitivity to human rights . . . .

That these interests are reconcilable does not mean that any one case will be easy to reconcile. Any individualized balancing process is a challenge. But it does mean that the principles by which that process is governed can be made clear and without conflict or contradiction. Moreover, to the extent that current laws regarding the commitment of those with TB are so ancient that they fail to meet modern standards of due process . . . it is the responsibility of our courts to ensure that there are procedures to ensure the rights of individuals whose proposed confinement invokes the judicial process. There is no need to declare the New Jersey TB control statute unconstitutional so long as it is interpreted to be consistent with the Constitution . . . . It must be remembered that this statute was first enacted in 1912, yet it had provisions requiring notice and a judicial hearing. The statute required proof that the person be "an actual menace to the community or to members of his household." The Legislature intended to permit the confinement of someone with TB but only under circumstances consistent with due process. Many of the rights we now recognize were unheard of in 1912 . . . . Therefore I construe N.J.S.A. 30:957 so as to include those rights necessitated by contemporary standards of due process . . . .

The first step of the individualized analysis required here is to define precisely what Newark seeks. During the active phase of TB, isolation of J.S., as opposed to confinement or imprisonment, is what is required. If J.S. lived in a college dormitory with other roommates, different quarters would have to be found for him. If J.S. lived in a private home and could be given a private bedroom or others in the household could be given prophylactic antibiotic therapy, confinement to his own home might be appropriate. J.S. is homeless, and a shelter where he would risk infecting others, including those with impaired immune systems, would probably be the worst place for him to stay.

Because *active* TB can be serious and can be potentially contagious by repeated contact, there are few options for the homeless with *active* TB. As Professor Annas said:

> Although these safeguards [constitutional rights] may seem impressive, in fact the only issues likely to concern a judge in a tuberculosis commitment proceeding are two factual ones: Does the person have active tuberculosis, and does the person present a danger of spreading it to others? Since it is unlikely that any case will be brought by public health officials when the diagnosis is in doubt, the primary issues will be the danger the patient presents to others and the existence of less restrictive alternatives to confinement that might protect the public equally well.

I find that the answers to the questions posed by Professor Annas have been provided by Newark and have been established by clear and convincing evidence. There is no question but that J.S. has active TB. There is no question but that he poses a risk to others who may be in contact with him, particularly in close quarters. Because he is homeless, there is no suggestion of any other place he could stay that would be less restrictive than a hospital.

The hearing I conducted was designed to comport to all the requirements of due process and with all the requirements of a commitment hearing under [New Jersey's mental health law] . . . .

I find that J.S. presents a significant risk to others unless isolated. Hospital confinement is the least restrictive mode of isolation proposed to me. The only request at this time is that J.S. be confined until he has shown three negative sputum tests demonstrating that his TB is no longer active. This is narrow, limited, and very reasonable, but because the time period for treatment is indefinite, I will initially set an initial court review to be held in three weeks . . . unless J.S. has earlier been determined to have gone into remission from active TB. In that event J.S. will be released immediately unless Newark seeks confinement for another reason.

. . . Newark will have the burden of proving the need for further confinement . . . . If there is no change, then the current order will likely continue. Obviously J.S. will also have the opportunity to present evidence; however, discovery shall be provided by each side to the other and to me at least one week in advance of the hearing date.

In the interim I will utilize the well-established procedures New Jersey has in place for civil commitments of the mentally ill. Although some procedures may not apply to the confinement of those with contagious diseases like TB, until and unless a more specific law is enacted, the only available and constitutional mechanism is to use these tested mental health statutes, court rules, and the case law thereunder. This is certainly preferable to declaring N.J.S.A. 30: 9–57 unconstitutional and leaving no authority whatsoever to fulfill an essential public police power.

. . . .

Newark also wanted J.S. ordered to provide sputum samples and take his medication as prescribed. The testimony was that a forced sputum sample requires a bronchoscopy, a procedure involving sedation and requiring separate informed consent because of its risks. No facts were shown to justify such a diagnostic procedure where it might cause harm to J.S. As to continued treatment, testimony showed that the medications were quite toxic, dangerous, and some required painful intramuscular administration. J.S. is being asked to take many pills causing numerous side effects, including nausea and pain. The efficacy of the drugs will be unknown until receipt of sensitivity reports.

These facts cannot justify a remedy as broad as Newark seeks. J.S. has the right to refuse treatment even if this is medically unwise . . . . He must remain isolated until he is no longer contagious. Contagiousness cannot be assessed unless he gives sputum samples. While he can refuse to provide sputum samples and refuse bronchoscopy, his release from isolation may be delayed, as he will be unable to satisfy the conditions of release. The same is true with his refusal to take medication. If he refuses, he may not get better. If J.S. continues to suffer from active TB, he will be unable to satisfy the conditions of release.

On the other hand if J.S. cooperates with his caregivers, provides sputum samples, and takes his medication willingly, then upon his improvement, Newark will have a difficult time proving that he needs confinement because he is not cooperative. His in-hospital conduct will go a long way towards demonstrating his ability to follow medical therapy once released and will be considered if after his active TB is cured, J.S.'s confinement is sought because his alleged failure to follow continued therapy will make him a future risk. I would then have to consider an order . . . which would simply require J.S. to take his medication.

NOTES AND QUESTIONS

1. **Tuberculosis — the disease**. Tuberculosis (TB), which is caused by the tubercle bacillus *Mycobacterium tuberculosis*, is the paradigmatic contagious disease because it is transmitted through the air by droplets (most often from coughing or sneezing) without anyone's knowledge. It is a serious disease — often disabling, sometimes fatal, and readily spread (at least to those in close and prolonged contact with a person who has an "active" case, which is the only time it can be transmitted). TB is not easily prevented let alone eradicated. As acknowledged in *J.S.*, TB has been around for a long time and it is likely to be with us for the foreseeable future.

One reason why preventing or treating TB is problematic is its peculiar etiology. Most people who contract the disease don't know they have it. Roughly 10 percent of those who are infected with TB develop "active" cases ("TB disease") and, as a consequence, become contagious. If treated quickly and with the proper regimen of drugs, the infection can essentially always be eliminated. See CDC, Tuberculosis (TB) Treatment, http://www.cdc.gov/tb/topic/treatment/default.htm (visited Aug. 2013). As the *J.S.* decision notes, patients with active TB disease generally are no longer contagious after two weeks of treatment, but can remain infected unless drug therapy is continued for six to nine months, depending on the drug regimen used, to eliminate the infection. After the first few weeks of treatment, patients often feel better (some of the ten approved drugs have unpleasant side effects) and assume that they are cured. People who end their therapy prematurely risk not only relapse, but may develop drug resistant TB (DR-TB, the infection is resistant to one TB drug) or even multidrug resistant TB (MDR-TB, resistance to two or more TB drugs) — which is harder to eliminate, requires considerably lengthier treatment, and, of course, could be transmitted in that form to others. (Incomplete treatment of an individual case, in essence, tends to eliminate the "weaker" germs and to favor replication by those that have developed some resistance to the medications.)

According to the CDC, in 2012, there were 9,951 cases of TB in the United States (a "case rate" of 3.2 cases per 100,000 population), down from nearly 15,000 cases (5.1 per 100,000 population) in 2003, and the twentieth consecutive year of declining rates. All forms of TB accounted for approximately 529 deaths in 2009 (the latest year for which data are available). For current data on TB, see http://www.cdc.gov/tb/ (visited Aug. 2013). About 1 percent of the patients reported with TB in the United States have MDR-TB (98 cases in 2011), more than 80 percent of whom were foreign-born. The prevalence of tuberculosis in the United States is not evenly distributed. While everyone is susceptible — as one authority put it, "we all breathe the same air" — more than half of cases occur in people who are foreign-born. The rates also are higher in Asian, Hispanic, and African-American populations, and among the homeless, people in prisons and other institutions, and in people with weakened immune systems. In 2012, the "TB rate in foreign-born persons in the United States was 11.5 times as high as in U.S.-born persons." Roque Miramontes et al., *Trends in Tuberculosis – 2012*, 61(11) MORBIDITY & MORTALITY REP. 201 (2013), http://www.cdc.gov/mmwr/preview/mmwrhtml/mm6211a2.htm?s_cid=mm6211a2_e (visited Aug. 2013). California, Texas, New York, and Florida reported half of all cases in the country. *Id.*

At the turn of the twentieth century, TB was the leading cause of death in the Western hemisphere countries. In 1950, TB was the leading cause of death in the United States for people between the ages of 15 and 30. Indeed, TB has often been cited as the stereotypical example of a disease that is as much a social problem as it is a medical or even health problem. See, *e.g.*, the classic history of TB by RENE DUBOS & JEAN DUBOS, THE WHITE PLAGUE (1952) (arguing that, even as antibiotics were making headway against the disease, TB was a problem that would persist so long as poor housing, malnutrition, and poverty were widespread). For a good, short history of how public health practitioners identified TB as a contagious disease and used environmental measures to reduce its spread, see GEORGE ROSEN, PREVENTIVE MEDICINE IN THE UNITED STATES 1900–1975, pp. 25–36 (1975). For these reasons, early public health programs were virtually synonymous with TB control and prevention efforts, leading to various public education campaigns, massive screening programs in many communities (chest X-rays to identify "tubercoles," tumors filled with TB bacilli, were considered the preferred diagnostic technique until the 1960s), and, in some parts of the country, rather aggressive efforts to locate and isolate people who were diagnosed with TB. While some of these efforts were voluntary, others were unapologetically not, especially those that focused on low income and homeless populations. For one well-written, illustrative account of this era in TB control and prevention, see BARRON H. LERNER, CONTAGION AND CONFINEMENT: CONTROLLING TUBERCULOSIS ALONG THE SKID ROAD (1998) (describing the programs of forcible detention of people in Seattle, Washington — mostly homeless — in the 1950s and 1960s as the "most aggressive" in the country).

2. **TB around the world**. From a global perspective, TB is a public health problem of much greater magnitude. According to estimates published by the World Health Organization (WHO), in 2011 almost 12 million people worldwide were living with TB, and TB accounted for 1.4 million deaths. World Health Organization, Global Tuberculosis Report 2012, http://www.who.int/tb/publications/global_report/en/index.html (visited Aug. 2013). An estimated 650,000 of these had MDR-TB. About 80 percent of the total number of TB cases worldwide are concentrated in 22 "high burden" countries, primarily in Asia and Sub-Saharan Africa. A bit of good news is that new cases of TB have been declining globally — 2.2 percent from 2010 to 2011. WHO reports that the death rate from TB rate has decreased 41% since 1990, and "the world is on track to achieve the global target of a 50% reduction by 2015." *Id.* Some of the improvements appear to be attributable to intensified efforts by WHO and non-governmental organizations (NGOs) to deliver treatment to those infected. Better diagnostic tests that can diagnose TB and rifampicin resistance in less than two hours have enabled more rapid treatment initiation. Some countries encourage the use of Bacillus Calmette-Guerin (BCG), a vaccine to prevent TB, at least for children in high-risk populations. (The CDC does not recommend the use of BCG in the United States, because of the low risk of TB infection in this country, its variable effectiveness against adult pulmonary TB, and because it can produce a false positive skin reactivity test for TB in vaccine recipients.) Research to develop

better TB drugs and vaccines and methods of delivery are ongoing, but require substantial resources.

Whatever our success in preventing and treating cases of TB in United States, these efforts should not overlook the much larger problem TB represents for the rest of the world. As we have learned, the problem will not be resolved simply by providing better medical care. Public health techniques like sanitation, improved housing, and improved standards of living will have to be employed to combat the social and environmental conditions that allow TB to flourish. TB is likely to remain a problem wherever the conditions that facilitate the spread of diseases like TB persist.

3.   **Substantive due process and civil commitment of persons with contagious diseases.** Both Mr. Greene and J.S. claim that they were confined without due process of law in violation of their rights to liberty under the Fourteenth Amendment. While J.S.'s claim appears to involve both substantive and procedural due process, Mr. Greene's claim is limited to procedural due process. The substantive due process issues raised in J.S. are at the core of modern controversies over proposals to stop disease outbreaks as well as to prepare for possible future epidemics.

A substantive due process claim challenges the state's power to enact and enforce a particular law (its substance) that infringes on an interest in life, liberty or property. The question is whether the government has an adequate reason for infringing on the asserted interest in the particular manner that the law in question allows or requires it to do. Although many judges, including Justices of the U.S. Supreme Court, are reluctant to use the term "substantive due process," they still engage in an analysis of the justification for a law that is claimed to violate rights protected by the Due Process Clause of the Fifth and Fourteenth Amendments.

Since involuntary confinement (or civil detention or commitment, if you prefer) results in committing a person to an institution, it is an obvious infringement of liberty — one that is generally subject to heightened, if not strict, scrutiny. The state's interest in confinement is, of course, preventing the infection of other persons with a harmful, contagious disease. Courts have generally viewed this interest as extremely strong, probably "compelling." These interests are weighed in an individualized analysis of the person whose liberty is at risk.

Thus, the question is whether the individual is likely to expose the public to a dangerous disease. As can be seen, this inquiry really entails two questions. The first is whether the person has a dangerous, contagious disease — one that is transmissible from person to person and can cause serious illness or death. Statutes variously describe the disease as "communicable" or "dangerous" to distinguish committable conditions from other, more benign infections, like the common cold or annual influenza, and from infections that are not casually transmitted by touch or through the air. (Can you imagine confining someone with a cold or a tetanus infection?) The second question is whether the individual is likely to transmit the disease by exposing others to infection. A person who has a dangerous, contagious disease poses no threat to the public if he or she voluntarily avoids contact with other people or takes precautions, such as wearing a mask in public, to prevent exposing others to infection.

Taken together, these two elements — a dangerous, contagious disease and the likelihood of transmitting it to others — create a risk of harm to the public. They also define the constitutional standard for involuntary confinement: the state's justification for limiting an individual's ability (liberty) to expose others to infection. In *City of Newark*, there was no dispute over the fact that J.S. had active (contagious) TB. The New Jersey TB control statute authorized confinement for a person with "communicable tuberculosis who fails to obey the [health department's] rules or regulations" or "who is an actual menace to the community or members of his household . . . ." Does this language satisfy the constitutional standard? How do you interpret the term "actual menace?" Can you identify the passages in the opinion that specify the standard that the court is applying?

Like most courts, the judge in *City of Newark* found the constitutional standard (or requirements) for justifiable civil commitment for mental illness to be an apt analogy for analyzing the New Jersey TB commitment statute. As described in Note 7, *infra*, the state's justification for involuntarily detaining persons with mental illness also rests on the likelihood of danger to the public. In the case of mental illness, however, the danger — possible violence to people or property — results only indirectly from the disease, since mental illness is not contagious. Rather, mental illness may induce the person to engage in violence to others (or to property) or render the person unable to control his or her own violent behavior. In the case of a contagious disease, the disease itself presents a danger only if the person behaves in ways (or lives in circumstances) that expose others to infection. For this reason, courts often focus on the behavior and circumstances of the individual whom the state seeks to confine.

Is confinement of a person with a dangerous, contagious disease simply preventive detention by another name? Why would the courts allow preventive detention of a person with a disease who has committed no crime, when they do not allow preventive detention of a healthy person who is accused of committing a crime or who is not even accused, but merely suspected of planning to commit a crime? (Of course, preventive detention may be ordered for an arrested accused who is suspected of committing violence or fleeing pending trial. Is that a relevant comparison?) Some judges have argued that the reason lies in the fact that civil commitment is, well, civil and not criminal. Is that an answer? What differences do you find between confinement in a TB hospital (or a mental hospital, for that matter) and incarceration in a prison or jail?

4. Substantive due process and involuntary treatment. In addition to confinement, the health department in *City of Newark* also sought an order requiring J.S. "to provide sputum samples and to take his medication as prescribed." One can understand the health department's concern, both for J.S. and the public at large, prompting this request. Nonetheless, the judge summarily rejects it. What principle does the judge rely on for his decision? If J.S. does not take his medication, what is likely to happen?

The problem of incomplete treatment and its relationship to the development of multidrug resistant TB (described in Note 1, *supra*) is one reason why, during the 1990s, some jurisdictions experimented with directly observed therapy (DOT). Under DOT, health care workers actually supervise patients believed more likely to be noncompliant — often targeting homeless persons — in taking and completing their daily dose of medications. This is in fact what happened in the case of J.S., as the judge noted in a final footnote: "At the November 30, 1993 review hearing, Newark presented additional expert testimony and J.S.'s updated medical records showing the situation unchanged. But thereafter, J.S. began to take his medication faithfully and his active TB was arrested. On January 10, 1994, J.S. was released from confinement pursuant to a consent order in which he agreed to DOT and agreed to being committed again if he failed to take his medicine. This consent order was approved in open court in J.S.'s presence as there was no longer any need for isolation once he no longer suffered from active TB." It is of note that the original hearing was conducted by speakerphone — the judge in his chambers, and the patient and his caregivers in his hospital room. A proceeding conducted in this manner can alone convince a judge that the patient is contagious and dangerous.

5. Procedural due process and civil commitment of persons with contagious diseases. Does the West Virginia statute raise substantive due process issues? Does it include the two elements of substantive due process discussed above? Note that the statute requires a hearing before a person is committed to a TB institution. Some state statutes authorize public health officials to detain a person — whom they reasonably believe to be both contagious and likely to spread the infection — for a few days pending the required formal hearing. Is such a procedure compatible with substantive due process requirements? Because he was already confined in a hospital, Mr. Greene brought a *habeas corpus* proceeding to challenge the procedures used in his original confinement hearing. *Habeas corpus* petitions remain a last resort means of challenging wrongful confinement.

The concept of due process of law contemplates, at least, that government must follow fair procedures when it seeks to deprive any person of life, liberty, or property. Procedural due process does not directly question the substance of the law (although there are instances in which procedural choices can affect the substance of the law). Instead, it functions to ensure, insofar as humanly possible, that the law is applied only to those to whom it is intended to apply and not to anyone else. You should recognize, here, a policy assumption that is widespread in the law: that sound *procedures* (which we can endeavor to apply rigorously and conscientiously irrespective of what we think we know about "the facts") will increase the likelihood of accurate *outcomes* (which are often difficult or impossible to know in advance). Appropriate procedural safeguards should increase the likelihood of accurate results — convicting the guilty (and not the innocent), civilly confining those who will expose others to contagion (and not those who won't), and the like.

What "process" is constitutionally due to Mr. Greene? Like the New Jersey court (and most other courts that have addressed the issue), the West Virginia court analogizes civil commitment for a contagious disease to civil commitment for mental illness. The U.S. Supreme Court has not directly pronounced on the procedures due with respect to civil commitment for contagious diseases, but has specified some procedural requirements for civil commitment for the mentally ill. (For a good explanation of the rationale for such procedural requirements, see *Lessard v. Schmidt*, 349 F. Supp. 1078 (E.D. Wisc. 1972).) More generally, the Supreme Court has laid out three somewhat vague factors for courts to evaluate in order to determine what procedures must accompany any governmental deprivation of liberty or property: (1) the private interest that will be affected by the official action (which in the case of civil commitment is physical liberty); (2) the risk of an erroneous deprivation of that interest (liberty) using specific procedures and the probative value, if any, of any additional or different procedural safeguards; and (3) the government's interest, including any fiscal and administrative burdens that additional or different procedures would entail. *Mathews v. Eldridge*, 424 U.S. 319 (1976). While these may be the right questions, the Court has offered incomplete guidance on how they should be weighed or applied in specific settings. For example, how much weight, if any, should the cost to government carry when a person is being involuntarily confined? How much weight should a person's liberty be given when he or she may endanger the public if left free?

The *Greene* court, noting the parallels between the civil commitment of the mentally ill and the involuntary confinement of people with TB, applies its holding in a prior civil commitment decision to read into the West Virginia TB statute the same procedural requirements. Similarly, in *J.S.*, the court reads into the New Jersey statute — enacted (like many) some time ago — considerably more elaborate procedures than its text contained, deeming them constitutionally necessary. What alternatives might the court have? Which approach makes more sense to you? How is civil confinement to prevent contagious disease transmission similar to, and how it is different from, imprisonment for violation of the criminal law? Would you use the same procedures if the government sought instead to require a person to stay at home or to take medication under the personal observation of a physician, nurse or public health practitioner?

6. TB and homelessness. What does it take for a person who is homeless to "comply" with medical treatment recommendations? J.S. was given an appointment to get treatment at a clinic that was "a bus ride away" from a shelter. How likely is it that a person without any income will be able to get to clinic appointments? When people do not show up for their appointments, they may be labeled "noncompliant patients," as J.S. was. What is the cause of noncompliance? Does it matter for purposes of satisfying the dangerousness standard?

In *City of Newark*, Judge Goldman relies heavily on the writings of public health law professors, including Larry Gostin (*Controlling the Resurgent Tuberculosis Epidemic: A 50 State Survey of TB Statutes and Proposals for Reform*, 296 JAMA 255 (1993)), and George J. Annas (*Control of Tuberculosis: The Law and the Public's Health*, 328 NEW ENG. J. MED. 585 (1993)). In that article Annas also writes:

> . . . [T]he burden of involuntary confinement will fall most heavily on the homeless and those who live in crowded, inadequate housing, because they have no place to "confine themselves" during treatment for active tuberculosis. Since the rationale for involuntary commitment is danger to others based on the contagiousness of the patient's disease, under existing state statutes (written before multi-drug-resistant tuberculosis was identified as dangerous to the public) patients have a right to be released when their tuberculosis is no longer communicable and they are therefore no longer a danger to others. The possibility of acquiring and spreading multi-drug-resistant tuberculosis poses a particularly difficult problem. Even though

not currently a danger to others, the patient whose tuberculosis is inactive but not yet cured might be a danger in the future if a treatment regimen that will ultimately cure the patient is not followed and if, instead, the patient takes drugs in such a way as to transform tuberculosis into a multi-drug-resistant variety, which later becomes active and communicable. Because clear and convincing evidence is required to prove dangerousness, the fact that a person might be a risk to others in the future is insufficient reason alone, under current laws, for confinement until cure.

Does the existence of multi-drug-resistant tuberculosis mean that state laws regarding tuberculosis should be changed to permit confinement until cure? The answer depends on the actual danger the patients pose to the public and the relative effectiveness of less restrictive treatment alternatives. In the context of antidiscrimination laws, the Supreme Court has made it clear that more than just the fear of danger is required to exclude a person with tuberculosis from the workplace. In *School Board of Nassau County v. Arline*, 480 U.S. 273 (1987), the Court adopted the position of the American Medical Association as to what factual medical inquiries a court should make in determining the degree of danger posed by a tuberculosis carrier who taught schoolchildren and sought reinstatement in her job after she was fired because she had tuberculosis. Its requirements were that the following be ascertained:

(a) the nature of the risk (how the disease is transmitted), (b) the duration of the risk (how long the carrier is infectious), (c) the severity of the risk (what is the potential harm to third parties) and (d) the probabilities the disease will be transmitted and will cause varying degrees of harm. *Id.*

The Court continued, "In making these findings, courts normally should defer to the reasonable medical judgments of public health officials." *Id.* When the teacher had active tuberculosis, there was no question that she could be excluded from the classroom.

Exclusion from crowded environments is obviously less restrictive than confinement. Nonetheless, if a state legislature concluded after hearing evidence from public health officials that such confinement was required to protect the public's health because there was no effective, less restrictive alternative available, a statute should be passed permitting confinement until cure. The hearings before the legislature could also provide useful education for the public about the epidemic and its control, as well as the opportunity to discuss alternative treatment strategies. Thereafter, if an individual patient were given a timely hearing, legal representation, and other due-process protections and if involuntary confinement were resorted to only when there is clear and convincing evidence that outpatient treatment could not effectively protect the public from that particular patient, confinement until cure would probably be found constitutional. This could be justified, even though confinement of a psychotic patient who did not consistently take medication might not be, because the time of confinement would be limited and relatively short.

Obviously, interventions short of confinement, such as periodic checkups or monitoring, or even the routine administration of therapy under direct observation, are much to be preferred. Moreover, a "technological fix" such as a slow-release implant would eliminate the need for confinement until cure altogether. It is also appropriate to use monetary and other inducements to encourage compliance with outpatient therapy, since the effective treatment of tuberculosis benefits the entire community. In no event, however, should a confined person be physically forced to take medications against his or her will, although confinement might be continued indefinitely as long as the patient continued to be a danger to the public.

Current discussion is properly focusing not on confinement but on less restrictive interventions such as routine and universal use of directly observed therapy. This "methadone maintenance" model of delivery is not now the standard of care, and a survey of state laws found only three states (Maine, Michigan, and Minnesota) that explicitly provide for such monitoring of treatment by state officials. Although the data are incomplete, it appears that from 1976 through 1990, more than 80 percent of all patients with tuberculosis in the United States completed 12 continuous months of drug therapy. The completion rate is much lower for New York, but it still involves a majority. There is an understandable egalitarian desire to try to treat everyone in the same way by subjecting everyone to directly observed therapy. There is, however, insufficient justification for requiring this annoying and inconvenient method of treatment for patients who are virtually certain to take their anti-tuberculosis medications and thus pose no risk to the public health. This is not a case in which there is a conflict between public health and civil rights. It is simply common sense. As Dubos and Dubos rightly observe, measures to prevent the spread of tuberculosis generally do not require legal compulsion, because they "have acquired the compelling strength of common sense."

Requiring all persons to take therapy under direct observation because it is necessary for some is wasteful, inefficient, and gratuitously annoying, and it undercuts the legitimate desire to individualize treatment and to use the least restrictive and intrusive public health interventions. Moreover, in many if not most cases, reasonable discharge planning (including the provision of housing for the homeless) and counseling will greatly improve voluntary compliance. Of course, it can be difficult to predict some patients' degree of compliance accurately, and individualized case-management strategies and monitoring will be necessary.

Directly observed therapy remains clearly preferable to involuntary confinement, however, and diligent and imaginative efforts to deliver therapy on an outpatient basis should be made before involuntary confinement is contemplated. Both these legal interventions, however, concentrate on the victims of social neglect, rather than on the neglect itself. This focus is understandable, since poverty is a much more difficult problem to address than the treatment of tuberculosis, but the history of the disease shows that success in controlling tuberculosis depends much more on the general standard of living than on specific medical or legal interventions.

7.   Civil commitment for mental illness and dangerousness as precedent. As many courts have observed, including those in *Greene* and *City of Newark*, there are obvious parallels between state and local government efforts to involuntarily confine people with tuberculosis or other contagious diseases and the civil commitment of the mentally ill. Thus the extent to which the courts have permitted civil commitment in this related context provides some guidance as to what the state and federal courts should do in cases involving the involuntary commitment of people with contagious diseases.

The Supreme Court has recognized that the due process clauses of the Fifth and Fourteenth Amendments impose substantive limits on the states' discretion to impose civil commitment. Those limits have not been fully articulated, but several cases have developed the two-part illness-plus-dangerousness standard widely used today. In *Jackson v. Indiana*, 406 U.S. 715 (1972), the Court found that there must be a reasonable connection between the state's underlying justification for committing an individual and the nature and length of his commitment. In *O'Connor v. Donaldson*, 422 U.S. 563 (1975), the Court held that a state cannot civilly commit a mentally ill person who is not dangerous or unable to care for himself. In *Jones v. United States*, 463 U.S. 354 (1983), although the Court did not openly retreat from standards it had articulated in earlier holdings, it allowed the states some discretion in the type of evidence that could satisfy the standard for civil commitment. Jones was civilly committed after he was found not guilty by reason of insanity without a separate finding that he was mentally ill and dangerous at the time of his commitment. The Court found that the findings of insanity (at the time of the crime) and dangerousness implicit in his insanity defense were sufficiently probative to allow for his civil commitment without additional post-conviction procedures, although the Court noted that Jones would be entitled to release when he was no longer dangerous or mentally ill. In *Foucha v. Louisiana*, 504 U.S. 71 (1992), the Court consolidated the two-part standard and invalidated the extension of Foucha's original commitment following his successful not guilty by reason of insanity plea. After four years of civil commitment, Foucha's doctors found that he was no longer mentally ill although they still believed he was dangerous and had an antisocial personality. The Court held that without a *current* finding of mental illness, there is no constitutional basis for extending his civil commitment. At the least, the Court held, Foucha was entitled to constitutionally adequate procedures to establish the grounds for his commitment, as discussed in *Jackson*. Most importantly, the Court essentially set out a two-pronged substantive standard for civil commitment: "The State may . . . confine a mentally ill person if it shows by 'clear and convincing evidence that the individual is mentally ill and dangerous.'"

A more difficult question is whether the state may involuntarily confine mentally ill persons who are not dangerous to others but either harm themselves or are not capable of taking care of themselves. Most state civil commitment laws authorize confinement for such conditions, often generally categorized as "dangerous to self." Although the Supreme Court has not addressed the question directly, in *O'Connor*, *supra*, the Court mentions both the state's legitimate interest in helping those in need and its discomfort with a broad principle that would force help on all those who reject it:

> May the State confine the mentally ill merely to ensure them a living standard superior to that they enjoy in the private community? That the State has a proper interest in providing care and assistance to the unfortunate goes without saying. But the mere presence of mental illness does not disqualify a person from preferring his home to the comforts of an institution. Moreover, while the State may arguably confine a person to save him from harm, incarceration is rarely if ever a necessary condition for raising the living standards of those capable of surviving safely in freedom, on their own or with the help of family or friends.

422 U.S. at 575.

In the 1970's, advocates sought recognition of a "right to treatment" for the mentally ill, arguing that involuntary confinement could only be justified if treatment were provided. *See Wyatt v. Aderholt*, 503 F.2d 1305 (5th Cir. 1974). The Supreme Court has never directly addressed the question whether such a right to treatment might exist. In *O'Connor*, the Court largely ignored the state's argument that Donaldson should remain committed to receive treatment, concluding that a person who is not dangerous and can live safely in freedom, with or without the assistance of friends or family, cannot be involuntarily institutionalized. The Court may have discounted the state's claim that Donaldson was receiving "milieu therapy," which the Court described as requiring patients to live in the "milieu" of the institution. *But see also Youngberg v. Romeo*, 457 U.S. 307 (1982) (recognizing a limited "right to habilitation" for the mentally retarded).

8. Civil commitment of sexual predators. Some additional guidance on the scope and limits of civil commitment may be found in a related line of cases involving "sexual predators." In *Kansas v. Hendricks*, 521 U.S. 346 (1997), the Supreme Court upheld a state statute that provides for the civil commitment of "sexual predators" who have been convicted of sexually violent crimes or have been found not guilty of such crimes by reason of insanity. Like civil commitment statutes previously upheld by the Court, the Kansas law requires that the individual be found to be dangerous. The Kansas Sexually Violent Predator Act, like other similar state laws, was enacted largely in the belief that civil commitment laws might not apply to sexual predators, because they do not necessarily have a "mental illness" as that term is understood by the medical profession and used in civil commitment proceedings. The Kansas legislature, therefore, enacted a separate statute that, while almost identical to its civil commitment law, replaced the requirement of "mental illness" with "mental abnormality" or "personality disorder," which it defined as a "volitional capacity which predisposes the person to commit sexually violent offenses in a degree constituting such person a menace to the health and safety of others." This formulation, according to a majority of the Court, satisfied the requirements of substantive due process. Beyond dangerousness, some condition of impaired volition is necessary to justify noncriminal confinement, but the Court did not require "any particular nomenclature" to describe that condition as long as it affected the person's ability to control behavior:

> A finding of dangerousness, standing alone, is ordinarily not a sufficient ground upon which to justify indefinite involuntary commitment. We have sustained civil commitment statutes when they have coupled proof of

dangerousness with the proof of some additional factor, such as "mental illness" or "mental abnormality." These added statutory requirements serve to limit involuntary civil confinement to those who suffer from a volitional impairment rendering them dangerous beyond their control . . . . The precommitment requirement of a "mental abnormality" or "personality disorder" is consistent with the requirements of these other statutes that we have upheld in that it narrows the class of persons eligible for confinement to those who are unable to control their dangerousness.

521 U.S. at 358.

In a subsequent decision, *Kansas v. Crane*, 534 U.S. 407 (2002), the Supreme Court qualified its decision in *Hendricks*. In *Crane*, Kansas applied the same statute at issue in *Hendricks* to involuntarily commit a person who was diagnosed with "exhibitionism and antisocial personality disorder," but for whom there had been no showing that he could not control his dangerous behavior (threats of sexual assault). The state argued that *Hendricks* did not require such a showing in all cases. Justice Breyer, writing for a majority of the Court, responded:

> . . . *Hendricks* set forth no requirement of total or complete lack of control. *Hendricks* referred to the Kansas Act as requiring a "mental abnormality" or "personality disorder" that makes it "difficult, if not impossible [to control the dangerous behavior]." The word "difficult" indicates that the lack of control to which this Court referred was not absolute. Indeed . . . an absolutist approach is unworkable. Moreover, most severely ill people — even those commonly termed "psychopaths" — retain some ability to control their behavior. Insistence upon absolute lack of control would risk barring the civil commitment of highly dangerous persons suffering severe mental abnormalities.

> We do not agree with the State, however, insofar as it seeks to claim that the Constitution permits commitment of the type of dangerous sexual offender considered in *Hendricks* without any lack-of-control determination. *Hendricks* underscored the constitutional importance of distinguishing a dangerous sexual offender subject to civil commitment "from other dangerous persons who are perhaps more properly dealt with exclusively through criminal proceedings." That distinction is necessary lest "civil commitment" become a "mechanism for retribution or general deterrence" — functions properly those of criminal law, not civil commitment . . . .

> In recognizing that fact, we did not give to the phrase "lack of control" a particularly narrow or technical meaning. And we recognize that in cases where lack of control is at issue, "inability to control behavior" will not be demonstrable with mathematical precision. It is enough to say that there must be proof of serious difficulty in controlling behavior. And this, when viewed in light of such features of the case as the nature of the psychiatric diagnosis, and the severity of the mental abnormality itself, must be sufficient to distinguish the dangerous sexual offender whose serious mental illness, abnormality, or disorder subjects him to civil commitment from the dangerous but typical recidivist convicted in an ordinary criminal case . . . .

534 U.S. at 413.

Subsequent to *Crane*, the Supreme Court decided another case from the same jurisdiction, again refining the scope of the state's discretion to confine sexual predators. *McKune v. Lile*, 536 U.S. 24 (2002) (Kansas requirement that sex offender participate in "admission of responsibility" program does not violate his Fifth amendment right to remain silent).

United States v. Comstock, in Chapter 3, Part D, *supra*, illustrates the Court's continued willingness to sanction civil commitment for "sexual predators," although the case was decided on the basis of Congress's power under the Necessary and Proper Clause. Are sexual predators a special class? The Court continues to use the two-pronged test for civil commitment in order to ensure that those whom government seeks to confine have lost at least some control over their dangerous behavior. At the same time, the concept of mental abnormality, as applied in sexual predator cases, poses some conceptual difficulties. A diagnosis of pedophilia, for example, typically is based on the patient's history of sexual offenses against children, which is essentially the same evidence that is used to prove the person's dangerousness to others. This appears to collapse the two-pronged standard into a single prong — dangerousness demonstrated by past offenses. If past offenses are sufficient to justify civil commitment, are sexual predators (or offenders, if you prefer) subject to indefinite confinement? Could they ever be found to no longer have a mental abnormality or no longer be dangerous? Are such offenders more likely than those who commit other crimes to reoffend? There is limited data to answer this last question. *See* U.S. Department of Justice, Bureau of Justice Statistics, *Recidivism of Sex Offenders Released from Prison in 1994* (Nov. 2003) http://www.bjs.gov/index.cfm?ty=pbdetail&iid=1136; http://www.bjs.gov/content/pub/pdf/rsorp94.pdf (visited Aug. 2013)(study of federal prisoners released after 1994 found 43% of sex offenders were rearrested for all types of crimes within 3 years, while 68% of non-sex offenders were rearrested, and 5.3% of sex offenders were rearrested for another sex crime, while 1.3% of non-sex offenders were later arrested for a sex crime).

Could effective treatment render a sexual predator no longer dangerous or "cure" the "mental abnormality?" The psychiatric literature suggests that effective therapy for persons who are predisposed to commit sexual offenses, such as rape, sexual assault or child molestation, remains elusive, perhaps because the etiology of the "abnormality" has not yet been established. Leroy Hendricks, who had a history of molesting children, admitted that he could not control the urge to molest children even though he knew it was wrong; he asserted that "treatment was bull___" and the only certain way he knew to stop was to die. 521 U.S. at 355. In *Hendricks*, the majority of Justices suggested that there is no constitutional bar to the civil commitment of those for whom no treatment is available as long as they pose a danger to others: "A State could hardly be seen as furthering a 'punitive' purpose by involuntarily confining persons afflicted with an untreatable, highly contagious disease." In a dissenting opinion, however, Justice Breyer found that treatment was critical, arguing that "whether the [Due Process] clause requires Kansas to provide treatment that it concedes is potentially available to a person who it concedes is treatable is the basic substantive due process question." The dissent went on to answer the question, arguing that without treatment Hendricks's civil commitment would violate substantive due process requirements (and also would make the commitment punitive and, as a result, an *ex post facto* law). If one were to accept Justice Breyer's argument, what proportion of the targeted population of sexual predators do you imagine could be committed for treatment?

CITY OF MILWAUKEE v. WASHINGTON
735 N.W.2d 111 (Wis. 2007)

Louis B. Butler, Jr., J.

Ruby Washington seeks review of a published decision of the court of appeals affirming a circuit court order confining her to the Milwaukee County Criminal Justice Facility ("CJF") for failure to comply with prior court orders for treatment of tuberculosis. The Milwaukee County Circuit Court . . . found that if Washington continued to refuse treatment she would become contagious and threaten the public health, and issued an order of confinement pursuant to Wis. Stat. § 252.07(9) (2005-06), the long-term confinement provisions of the tuberculosis control statute. Washington asked to be confined to Aurora Sinai Medical Center ("Medical Center"), but the circuit court ordered her confined to the CJF.

. . . .

I

On May 19, 2005, Ruby Washington was evaluated for tuberculosis at the Keenan Health Center Tuberculosis Control Clinic ("TB Clinic"), operated by the City of Milwaukee Health Department ("Department") . . . . On June 17, 2005, Washington was diagnosed with tuberculosis. Washington received tuberculosis medication at the TB Clinic on June 21, 2005. Washington was living in a shelter and had no fixed address at the time. TB Clinic staff provided Washington with bus tickets to ensure that she would return for periodic directly-observed therapy. Washington did not show up for her next two appointments to receive her medication, and could not be located.

The Department issued Washington a directly-observed therapy order ("treatment order") and an isolation order on July 27, 2005, which it intended to serve upon Washington as soon as she could be located. On August 22, 2005, a nurse at the Medical Center informed the Department that Washington had been admitted to the hospital and was giving birth to a baby. The Department served the orders for treatment and isolation on Washington later that day, and requested that Washington stay at the Medical Center.

The next day, after Washington threatened to leave the Medical Center, the City of Milwaukee petitioned the circuit court under Wis. Stat. § 252.07(9) for enforcement of the treatment and isolation orders. The Milwaukee Circuit Court . . . appointed an attorney . . . to represent Washington. Counsel for the parties reached a stipulation whereby Washington would remain confined at the Medical Center [pending a hearing].

At the September 27, 2005, hearing . . ., the City noted that Washington's recovery had progressed to the point where the Department believed that Washington no longer needed to be confined for medical reasons. Counsel for the parties reached a second stipulation under which Washington would be released from confinement at the Medical Center, but would report to the TB Clinic at regular intervals to receive medication by directly-observed therapy, consistent with the July 27 order. Additionally, the stipulation required that Washington follow a nine-month treatment plan and live with her sister, Alwiller Washington, during that time. The stipulation provided that in the event that . . . Washington fails to fully and completely comply with the provisions of this Order [the stipulation], she may be subject to imprisonment, to renewed isolation and inpatient confinement pursuant to Wis. Stat. §§ 252.07(8) and (9) and/or to such other and additional sanctions for contempt of court as this Court may determine.

[handwritten margin note: released but needed to report]

On September 29, 2005, Alwiller Washington called Irmine Reitl, program manager of the TB Clinic, to report that Ruby Washington had left Alwiller's residence shortly after being released from the Medical Center on the 27th, and had yet to return. Alwiller said a friend had spotted (Ruby) Washington near the Jewel/Osco store on North 35th Street in Milwaukee that morning. Reitl and an officer of the Milwaukee Police Department drove to the Jewel/Osco and found Washington in the store parking lot. Reitl caught up with Washington and talked with her on the curb for a few minutes. In an affidavit to the court, Reitl averred that Washington "said many things that [Reitl] was unable to understand" and that Washington "seemed less than coherent in her thoughts."

A Milwaukee Police Department squad car arrived in the parking lot, and Washington left the area and entered a convenience store at the corner of 36th Street and North Avenue. Two additional squad cars arrived, and officers detained Washington. Reitl averred that Ruby was crying and yelling while the police spoke to her. After a few minutes, Ruby was handcuffed and placed in a squad car. While in the police car, she continued to be agitated and was kicking her feet out of the squad car window and kicking the inside roof of the squad car, all the while loudly screaming, yelling and crying.

Washington received an assessment from the Medical Center and was transported to the CJF. The City filed a "Motion of Contempt" with the circuit court seeking Washington's confinement to the CJF for noncompliance with the prior treatment order. Washington was held in the CJF pending a court hearing scheduled for October 3, 2005, on the City's motion.

On October 1, 2005, Washington was mistakenly released from the CJF and went missing . . . . On the morning of October 5, Washington was found at the home of a friend, and was detained by police. She was taken to the Medical Center to be evaluated, and then held at a district police station for a period of hours.

Judge Fiorenza convened a hearing later that afternoon at which Washington contested the City's allegation that she was in violation of the treatment order. The City called Irmine Reitl of the TB Clinic, who explained that Washington was diagnosed with pulmonary tuberculosis, a disease that becomes colonized in the lungs and may be transmitted by coughing, sneezing or otherwise forcing bacteria out of the lungs and into the air. She noted that Washington had one previous bout with tuberculosis, for which she had been successfully treated. She stated that for patients like Washington who have recurrent tuberculosis, a nine-month course of treatment is necessary, which starts with administering a regimen of four medications at regular intervals. Reitl testified that she believed Washington was not presently contagious, but that if she did not resume treatment, she would become contagious, perhaps within a week, and "certainly within a month." Reitl explained that "for [Washington's] own health and everyone's health in the community," Washington "must strictly adhere to the treatment regimen."

. . . .

Washington testified on her own behalf. Washington admitted that she stayed at a friend's house and not with her sister upon her release from the Medical Center on September 27. She also admitted that she had not taken her tuberculosis medication on October 2 as ordered because "[i]t had slipped [her] mind." Based on these statements, which the circuit court determined were admissions of noncompliance, the court found Washington to be in violation of the prior treatment orders. The circuit court concluded that, as a consequence, confinement was appropriate.

The City asked that Washington be confined to the CJF. The City stated that it "d [id] not believe that there [was] any facility . . . other than the [CJF] that would serve the purpose of protecting the public health under these very unusual and extraordinary circumstances. "

Counsel for Washington requested confinement to the Medical Center, arguing that her prior placement there "worked out very well and she was under guard and I would assume she would still be under guard. " Alternatively, counsel asked that the circuit court consider confining Washington to the Milwaukee County Mental Health Complex (Mental Health Complex) . Counsel urged the court to consider "any alternative other than jail . . . . The [Medical Center] situation worked . . . . "

The City opposed Washington's confinement to the Mental Health Complex, arguing that security there was "not assured." The City also opposed placement in the Medical Center, arguing "it would be grossly unfair to the taxpayers of this City to require that [Washington] be placed under police guard on a 24/7 basis, which would be required for a period of nine months. The jail already has security. It would not cost our taxpayers any more. " Counsel for Washington responded that cost to taxpayers was not a permissible factor in a Wis. Stat. § 252.07(9) confinement proceeding.

The circuit court considered the City's request to confine Washington, and determined that it would proceed under Wis. Stat. § 252.07(9), the long-term confinement subsection of the tuberculosis control statute, and not under Wis. Stat. § 785.04(1), the remedial contempt statute. [This court found the contempt statute inapplicable.]

. . . .

The circuit court ordered Washington confined to the CJF for an indeterminate period of time, with a review of her confinement in six months . . . .

. . . .

Washington appealed to the court of appeals, challenging only her placement to the CJF instead of a less restrictive facility, and not whether the court had grounds to order her confinement. [The court of appeals affirmed.]

. . . .

III

The tuberculosis control section of the communicable disease chapter of the Wisconsin statutes, Chapter 252, authorizes the confinement of an individual with tuberculosis under certain circumstances . . . .

Wisconsin Stat. § 252.07(8) [permits confinement of up to 72 hours of a person with "infectious" or "suspect" tuberculosis.]

. . . .

Under Wis. Stat. § 252.07(9)(a), [t]he Wisconsin Department of Health and Family Services [DHFS] or a local health officer may petition any court for a hearing to determine whether an individual with infectious or suspect tuberculosis should be confined for longer than 72 hours in a facility where proper care and treatment will be provided and spread of the disease will be prevented.

The statute further provides that DHFS or a local health officer "shall include in the petition documentation that demonstrates all of the following: " (1) the person has infectious tuberculosis, has noninfectious tuberculosis but is at a high risk of developing infectious tuberculosis or has suspect tuberculosis; (2) the person "has failed to comply with the prescribed treatment regimen . . . or that the disease is resistant to the medication prescribed" to the person; (3) "all other reasonable means of achieving voluntary compliance with treatment have been exhausted and no less restrictive alternative exists; or that no other medication to treat the resistant disease is available"; and (4) the person "poses an imminent and substantial threat to himself or herself or to the public health. " § 252.07(9)(a)1.-4. A person confined under § 252.07(9) "shall remain confined until the department or local health officer . . . determines that treatment is complete or that the individual is no longer a substantial threat to himself or herself or to the public health." § 252.07(9)(c). If the person is to be confined for more than six months, "the court shall review the confinement every [six] months. " Id. . . . .

A

Washington does not challenge the circuit court's basis for ordering her confinement under Wis. Stat. § 252.07(9). She asserts only that the court lacked authority under the statute to order confinement to the CJF. Washington first contends that a jail is not a "facility" as the term is used in § 252.07(9)(a), which authorizes confinement to a "facility where proper care and treatment will be provided and spread of the disease will be prevented. " . . . .

. . . .

While Wis. Stat. § 252.07(9)(a) does not explicitly authorize placement in jail of persons with noninfectious tuberculosis who are noncompliant with a prescribed treatment regimen, the plain language of the statute also does not preclude such a placement. The statute authorizes confinement to a "facility," a word not defined in Chapters 250 (health administration) or 252 (communicable diseases) of the statutes, nor in the tuberculosis subchapter of the administrative code. We therefore turn to a dictionary to ascertain the meaning of the word. Webster's defines "facility" as "something (as a hospital, machinery, plumbing) that is built, constructed, installed or established to perform some particular function or to serve or facilitate some particular end." Under this commonly accepted meaning of the term, "facility" is broad enough to encompass many placement options, including jail.

. . . The tuberculosis control subchapter of the administrative code defines "confinement" as "restriction of a person with tuberculosis to a specified place in order to prevent the transmission of the disease to others, to prevent the development of drug-resistant organisms or to ensure that the person receives a complete course of treatment. " Wis. Admin. Code § HFS 145.08(2) . . . .

. . . .

. . . Webster's defines "confine" as "to keep in narrow quarters," listing "imprison" as a synonym. "Confine" thus connotes not only isolation, but suggests something about the nature of the place to which a person may be isolated or quarantined that is consistent with placement in jail . . . . We conclude that, together, the commonly accepted meanings of "facility" and "confined" indicate that the legislature intended jail to be a permissible placement option under Wis. Stat. § 252.07(9)(a) . . . .

We find support for this interpretation in the legislative history of the statute. Subsections (8) and (9) of Wis. Stat. § 252.07 were created in a 1999 revision of the tuberculosis control statute, authored at the request of the DHFS and included in the biennial budget bill. In a memo addressed to the legislative drafting attorney critiquing an early draft of the proposal, a Department of Administration ("DOA") official suggested that the revised statute include a definition of "facility": "The [DOA] would like to have a definition of 'facility' which could include something other than a health care facility. For example, if the person is incarcerated the facility would be a jail, which would be treating the person for [tuberculosis]." The drafting attorney responded: "[P]lease note that I did not include a definition of 'facility' because I was unsure how the department wanted it defined (other than to make sure it included a penal facility). I do not believe it's a problem to leave it undefined. It would just take a rather broad dictionary definition." As the bill's authors anticipated, we have applied the dictionary definition of "facility" and concluded that the statute authorizes jail as a place of confinement. The above exchange indicates that the authors of the bill intended jail to be a permissible place of confinement and treatment for persons with noninfectious tuberculosis who are noncompliant with a prescribed treatment regimen.

. . . We agree [with Washington] that the purpose of any placement is not to punish the noncompliant person for failing to follow a prescribed treatment regimen, but to provide treatment and to prevent him or her from infecting others. The statutory scheme ensures that jail is not a placement of first resort, but rather is permitted only in cases in which no less restrictive alternate placement is available. Additionally, the particular facility to which a person is to be confined, whether a penal institution or other type of facility, must be a place where proper care and treatment will be provided and spread of the disease will be prevented.

Washington and amicus the American Civil Liberties Union also argue that a penal facility is not "a facility where proper care and treatment will be provided and spread of the disease will be prevented" because the rate of infection is reportedly significantly higher in correctional facilities than among the general population, and the dense congregation of individuals in a jail increases risk of transmission. We take these concerns seriously. Nevertheless, the legislature has provided that confinement is an option, provided all the statutory requirements have been met.

. . . .

B

Washington next argues that if jail is a permissible place of confinement under Wis. Stat. § 252.07(9), confinement to jail is not permitted whenever some less restrictive placement is available, citing "no less restrictive alternative" language in § 252.07(9)(a)3. The court of appeals construed this language to apply only to the fact of confinement and not to the place of confinement. The City asks us to adopt the court of appeals' interpretation. We adopt Washington's interpretation because we conclude it is more reasonable. We interpret Wis. Stat. § 252.07(9)(a)3. to require that "no less restrictive alternative" applies to the place of confinement as well as the fact of confinement.

Wisconsin Stat. § 252.07(9)(a)3. provides that DHFS or the local health official petitioning for confinement of a person with tuberculosis who is noncompliant with a treatment regimen must demonstrate "[t]hat all other reasonable means of achieving voluntary compliance with treatment have been exhausted and no less restrictive alternative exists; or that no other medication to treat the resistant disease is available."

. . . .

. . . Confinement of a person who is noncompliant with a prescribed treatment regimen is not confinement in the abstract, but confinement to a specified place. A person already confined under the short-term tuberculosis confinement statute, Wis. Stat. § 252.07(8), is confined to a specified place selected by DHFS or a local health officer. For the person subject to a petition for long-term confinement who is already confined under § 252.07(8), the court determines whether the existing confinement should be continued.

Portions of Chapter HFS 145 of the administrative code provide additional support for this interpretation. "Confinement" as defined in the tuberculosis control subchapter of HFS 145, means "restriction of a person with tuberculosis to a specified place" to achieve the goals of treatment and prevention of disease transmission. Wis. Admin. Code §HFS 145.08(2) (emphasis added). This language further demonstrates that the tuberculosis control statute contemplates confinement to a particular facility. Likewise, a related subchapter of HFS 145 concerning control of communicable diseases states that the remedy for noncompliance with prescribed treatments should be that which "is the least restrictive on the respondent which would serve to correct the situation and protect the public's health." Wis. Admin. Code §HFS 145.06(5). A remedy that includes confinement would be to a particular place with prevention and treatment as goals, and, taken with Wis. Admin. Code §HFS 145.08(2), these provisions indicate that officials must consider whether no less restrictive alternative exists to the place of confinement.

In light of the legislature's choice to permit confinement to jail of a person with noninfectious tuberculosis who is noncompliant with a prescribed treatment regimen, we conclude that the legislature intended the "no less restrictive alternative" language to apply to the place of confinement as well as the fact of confinement. The legislature did not intend jail to be a placement of first resort for persons with tuberculosis who are noncompliant with a prescribed treatment regimen.

C

Next, Washington argues that the circuit court erred in considering the relative costs to taxpayers of different placements in making its confinement decision. She asserts that cost may not be considered in determining place of confinement because it is not one of the placement criteria set forth in Wis. Stat. § 252.07(9)

. . . .

. . . .

. . . The statute does not explicitly address whether costs may be a factor in determining place of confinement. However, the factors a court must consider in determining the place of confinement under the statute include: The place of confinement must be a facility (a) where proper care and treatment will be provided, (b) where spread of the disease will be prevented, and (c) that is not more restrictive than an alternate place of confinement.

We conclude that a circuit court may take into account cost when determining place of confinement under Wis. Stat. § 252.07(9). A court must first determine that the place of confinement is a facility where proper care and treatment will be provided, spread of the disease will be prevented, and that no less restrictive alternative to the proposed placement exists. Once the court has engaged in this analysis, and two or more placement options remain, a court may consider cost as a factor in making its determination. A party requesting that a court take into account the cost of various placements must offer some proof to support its assertions for the court to consider cost as a factor in placement.

IV

. . . .

Washington contends that the circuit court confined her to jail instead of the Medical Center based solely on its conclusion that the costs to local taxpayers of confinement to the Medical Center were too burdensome. We agree that the court's stated reasons for its placement decision were fiscal in part. However, we conclude the transcript of the circuit court hearing demonstrates that other factors, including the public health of the community and the treatment and care of Washington, were paramount.

. . . .

Additionally, we observe that the circuit court record indicates that in Washington's case, the CJF was a place where proper care and treatment would be provided and spread of the disease would be prevented . . . . Moreover, we note that the court received expert testimony that Washington's tuberculosis was presently noninfectious.

Based on these considerations, we conclude that the order confining Washington to jail was not an erroneous exercise of the circuit court's discretion. Washington was at risk to develop a drug-resistant strain of the disease, had a history of disappearing from sight and was belligerent toward officers. The circuit court reasonably concluded from these factors that medical staff would not have been equipped to handle Washington's outbursts, and that the added security of jail was necessary to ensure that she would continue taking her medication and would not escape confinement. Factoring in taxpayer costs as well was not an erroneous exercise of discretion.

In future cases, courts should follow the guidelines set forth in this opinion when determining place of confinement under Wis. Stat. § 252.07(9). A court proceeding under § 252.07(9) must ascertain whether a proposed place of confinement is a facility where proper care and treatment will be provided, spread of the disease will be prevented and that no less restrictive alternative placement exists. After applying these criteria to potential placement options, if two or more placement options meet the statutory requirements for treatment and disease prevention, and none of these placement options is significantly less restrictive than the others, the court may take into account the relative costs of the different placements. However, a determination based on cost must be supported by more than mere assumptions about the cost of particular placements.

V

[Here the court rejects contempt as a basis for Washington's confinement:] "We therefore disavow the court of appeals' discussion of remedial contempt under Wis. Stat. § 785.04(1) as a separate basis for confinement to jail in this case."

VI

In sum, we conclude that Wis. Stat. § 252.07(9)(a) authorizes confinement to jail for a person with noninfectious tuberculosis who fails to comply with a prescribed treatment regimen, provided that the jail is a place where proper care and treatment will be provided and the spread of disease will be prevented, and that no less restrictive alternative exists to jail confinement. We further conclude that a circuit court may take into account the cost of placement options when determining the place of confinement under § 252.07(9), but only after determining that two or more placement options fulfill the statutory requirements of proper medical treatment and disease prevention, and that none of these options is significantly less restrictive than the other(s).

. . . .

NOTES AND QUESTIONS

9. Civil commitment of noncontagious patients to complete treatment. *City of Milwaukee, supra,* illustrates the practical problems faced by public health professionals, as well as some patients, in contemporary infection control programs. It also raises the difficult question of how to prevent a risk of future illness and possible transmission of TB within the constraints of established constitutional principles governing civil commitment.

After a resurgence of TB in 1988–1992, some states revised their TB control laws to require "non-compliant" patients to take medication, either through directly-observed-therapy or in involuntary confinement. Wisconsin's statute represents this approach to TB control. Note that, unlike the court in *City of Newark, supra,* the *City of Milwaukee* court does not mention any right that Ruby Washington might have to refuse medical treatment. The Supreme Court has not addressed the constitutionality of these new laws; it has not even considered earlier laws that require the presence of a contagious disease. How would you predict the Supreme Court to rule on such a statute, if the Court were to consider it?

As we have seen, the justification for involuntarily confining a person requires that the person is likely to spread a contagious disease to others. The Wisconsin statute authorizing confinement for the purpose taking medication includes the following requirement: the person "poses an imminent and substantial threat to himself or herself or to the public health." A person like Ruby Washington, who is no longer contagious, poses no such threat. The City (through its health department) was concerned about the risk to Ruby Washington of becoming contagious in the future if she did not complete her drug regimen to eliminate the TB infection. The health department and nurse describe this risk as essentially a certainty. Are you convinced? What is a judge likely to do when medical professionals provide such testimony?

A rationale often offered in support of mandatory treatment laws is the risk that incomplete treatment will result in not just contagious TB, but drug resistant TB, or more dramatically (and more often mentioned) MDR-TB. Is this a sensible prevention policy or overreach based on speculation? The handful of courts that have reported decisions on this issue appear to struggle a bit to portray the threat to public health as serious and more than speculative. Such cases often turn on the degree to which the patient has resisted taking medication. *See Levin v. Adalberto M.,* 156 Cal. App. 4th 288 (2007) (holding that "although appellant was no longer contagious, his prior refusal of treatment and attempt to leave isolation demonstrated that he could not be relied upon to complete the treatment without observation. The particular strain of tuberculosis with which appellant is infected was resistant to one of the most common tuberculosis antibiotics. According to Dr. Levin, 'this makes absolute adherence to the remainder of his treatment mandatory.

If [appellant] is not fully compliant he will be at high risk for the development of multi-drug resistant TB which poses a dire threat to the community at large.' ").

Could courts be concerned to avoid authorizing what looks a lot like preventive detention — something they rarely, if ever, allow for persons suspected of violent crimes? But, of course, involuntary confinement of dangerous patients who do have contagious TB could also be seen as preventive detention. Does that affect the analysis?

10.   **The least restrictive alternative and the place of confinement.** In *City of Milwaukee*, the issue before the court was not the constitutionality of the Wisconsin statute (although one might ask why), but whether the statute permitted the City to confine Ms. Washington in jail, rather than in a medical facility. Are you surprised that the Department of Administration urged the legislature to allow confinement in jail, even if only by implication? What reasons would the state or city have to prefer jail to a hospital? The court seems to downplay the cost argument, stating that preventing the spread of disease and Ms. Washington's care and treatment were equally important reasons for the choice of jail. Yet, preventing the spread of disease is more properly seen as the threshold justification for confinement of any kind, not a justification for confinement in jail. Moreover, care and treatment is not typically viewed as a goal of correctional facilities. Whatever you think of the court's parsing of the statute's text, its conclusion begins to blur the boundaries between civil commitment to protect the public health and punitive detention for non-compliant patients.

A California court came to the opposite conclusion in *Souvannarath v. Hadden*, 95 Cal. App. 4th 1115, 1123 (2002), where the governing statute provided that individuals detained for TB control "shall not reside in correctional facilities." In that case, the Fresno County health department argued unsuccessfully first to the legislature and then to the court that it needed to use jails when TB beds were unavailable. The court concluded that it did not have the "power to release [health officials] from their statutory obligations simply because the task given them by the Legislature proves difficult or costly in Fresno County." *Id.* at 1127. [See Note 11, *infra*, for background in this case.] Here again, the court had no occasion to address the question whether the legislature would be justified in permitting the use of jail cells for civil commitment.

A common feature of TB control and similar civil commitment statutes is a requirement that a control order subject the person to "the least restrictive alternative." Whether this is a constitutional requirement for civil commitment remains unaddressed by the U.S. Supreme Court. Of more immediate interest, the concept is open to different interpretations, as seen in *City of Milwaukee*. It could mean that the measures required of the targeted individual must restrict that person's liberty as little as possible consistent with protecting the public's health. This interpretation embeds the concept into the substantive due process analysis in much the same way that the judiciary requires justifiable laws to be narrowly tailored so as to infringe on fundamental rights as little as possible. This is consistent with the principle affirmed by the Supreme Court in *Shelton v. Tucker*, 364 U.S. 479, 488 (1960):

even though the governmental purpose be legitimate and substantial, that purpose cannot be pursued by means that broadly stifle fundamental personal liberties when the end can be more narrowly achieved. The breadth of legislative abridgment must be viewed in the light of less drastic means for achieving the same basic purpose.

If, for example, it were shown that Ruby Washington was capable of isolating herself and taking her medication, the court would probably find confinement in any institution overly restrictive and order some alternative arrangement, such as directly observed therapy. In contrast, some have argued that the least restrictive alternative means only that persons who are confined should not be subjected to additional, unnecessary restrictions. While the latter interpretation should always apply, the former appears to be most consistent with the justification for deprivations of liberty.

11. Public health resource constraints and resort to confinement. The most common subjects of confinement today are TB patients who have other debilitating conditions, particularly homelessness, mental illness, or substance use problems that make it difficult for them to take medications consistently or at all. In this sense, *Greene, City of Newark,* and *City of Milwaukee* are typical of the use of confinement for contagious diseases — although court-ordered confinements remain rare in total.

A more troubling example is that of Hongkham Souvannarath, a tuberculosis patient who was involuntarily jailed in California, allegedly for failing to comply with a TB treatment regimen. Fresno County paid $1.2 million to settle her 1999 federal lawsuit, which claimed violation of her rights under the U.S. Constitution and California state law. She also brought a state action, in which a California appeals court ordered the county to cease using the jail to detain patients with TB. *Souvannarath v. Hadden,* 95 Cal. App. 4th 1115, 116 Cal. Rptr. 2d 7 (5th Dist. Cal. 2002), discussed in Note 10, *supra.* The California Appellate Court noted that fewer than 20 people had been detained in Fresno County for TB since 1995. The federal lawsuit and the events leading to her confinement suggest that confinement may not be necessary (and patients need not become either recalcitrant or dangerous) if appropriate services are made available to patients in need. The relevant facts are not reported in the court decision, but are described in Public Health Institute, TB and the Law Project, *Souvannarath Case Study* (2003), http://changelabsolutions. org/sites/changelabsolutions.org/files/souvannarath.pdf (visited Aug. 2013). *See also* John Roemer, *Reclaiming a Soul,* DAILY JOURNAL (Apr. 30, 2001).

Ms. Souvannarath, a refugee from Laos who came to the United States in 1984, was diagnosed with MDR-TB in California in 1998. She obtained TB treatment from a county clinic for several months, but experienced side effects and understood little of either the disease or its treatment. She spoke very little English and the clinic's translator spoke little Laotian. Ultimately, Souvannarath decided to live with a son in Ohio who could better care for her, but he was delayed in picking her up for the move. The clinic gave Souvannarath a small supply of medications to last until she could enter a prearranged Ohio clinic's program, but she ran out of medications before her son arrived. Feeling fine without taking medications, Souvannarath did not seek more. The clinic discovered she had not arrived in Ohio and had her served with an order in English to appear at the clinic. When she did not appear, the county health officer issued a detention order. She was arrested at gunpoint by two police officers and a communicable disease specialist and confined in the county jail. When she cried that she was afraid of dying, a non-Laotian translator thought she was threatening suicide, so she was confined in a safety cell for 3 days. She remained in jail, where only one guard could attempt translation, for ten months, until she was provided with an attorney and a hearing. The court released her subject to electronic monitoring in May 1999. At a review hearing in July 1999, she was released unconditionally.

Ms. Souvannarath's case suggests several points at which the county clinic might have ensured continued treatment and prevented incarceration. Initially, a translator who could explain the disease, its treatment, length, benefits and side effects might have persuaded Ms. Souvannarath to seek additional medications when she ran out, even though the drugs made her feel worse. If clinic staff had developed a more trusting relationship with Ms. Souvannarath, she might have been more receptive to their requests that she continue taking the medication. Even if all that failed, an order authorizing clinic staff to come to her house and watch her take her medications (directly observed therapy or DOT) would have avoided incarcerating her. The clinic, perhaps the entire TB program, may have had insufficient funds to accomplish these tasks. (The state health department reportedly lobbied against the law prohibiting housing TB patients in jails in order to gain "flexibility in placing TB patients in the event jail beds are the only available beds for the [TB] program." *Souvannarath*, 95 Cal. App. 4th at 1127.) But patients should not be punished simply because their clinic is underfunded. Indeed, it appears that Ms. Souvannarath would never have been considered uncooperative, much less a danger, had the clinic had enough staff and funding to continue the care she willingly accepted originally.

12.   State responses to TB outbreaks. Cases of involuntary confinement for a contagious disease reported since 1980 often involve persons with tuberculosis. Many coincide with a resurgence of tuberculosis in the United States between about 1988 and 1992. Most reported cases cluster around New York City, with a few in other states with large foreign-born populations. *See, e.g., Levin v. Adalberto M.*, 156 Cal. App. 4th 288, 67 Cal. Rptr. 3d 277 (Cal. App. 2d Dist. 2007); *New York v. Antoinette*, 165 Misc. 2d 1014 (N.Y. Sup. Ct. 1995). In addition, most cases target recent immigrants from countries where tuberculosis is prevalent, and people who are homeless or living in shelters, jail or prison, where tuberculosis can easily spread among people living in close quarters. Some suffer from mental illness that impedes their ability to follow treatment regimens, or also have HIV, which increases the likelihood of active TB and complicates treatment. Others speak little English and find the health care system difficult to navigate. Most are poor; almost all are people of color. *See* M. Rose Gasner et al., *The Use of Legal Action in New York City to Ensure Treatment of Tuberculosis*, 340 NEW ENGL. J. MED. 359 (1999) (study of involuntary commitments in New York from 1993–1995 finding that more than 90% of cases involved people of color).

The response to rising rates of tuberculosis varied across the country. Some states tried to rebuild tuberculosis treatment programs that had lost financial support in preceding years. The Institute of Medicine noted that such programs declined when the federal government ended its categorical financing of TB treatment, and concluded that "without question the major reason for the resurgence of tuberculosis was the deterioration of the public health infrastructure essential for the control of tuberculosis. " INSTITUTE OF MEDICINE, ENDING NEGLECT: THE ELIMINATION OF TUBERCULOSIS IN THE UNITED STATES 2 (May 2000). Others argued that the increase in cases was the result of mistaken economic and public health policies in the preceding decade, which reduced services and increased the proportion of the population living in poverty, in prisons or in homeless shelters, all conditions that facilitated the spread of TB. *See, e.g.,* Andrew A. Skolnick, *Some Experts Suggest the Nation's 'War on Drugs' Is Helping Tuberculosis Stage a Deadly Comeback,* 268 JAMA 3177 (1992); FRANK RYAN, THE FORGOTTEN PLAGUE: HOW THE BATTLE AGAINST TUBERCULOSIS WAS WON — AND LOST (1993). New York was particularly hard hit, losing treatment programs and experiencing an especially large rise in TB. Unable to provide enough clinics, New York relied heavily on involuntary confinement and directly observed therapy. (New York abandoned its isolation and quarantine statute in 1959, but adopted a reinvigorated version in response to the rise in tuberculosis in the late 1980s, and expanded it further after the terrorist attack of September 11, 2001.) HIV advocacy groups claimed that New York substituted confinement for treatment. In contrast, Massachusetts, which had preserved its treatment programs, managed to bring tuberculosis under control more rapidly than New York. Massachusetts provided more personal services, including sending public health nurses to take medicines to patients, whether at work or in a shelter, instead of forcing patients to come to a clinic during working hours. The incidence of tuberculosis in the country began to decline again in 1993, with most states claiming that their approach succeeded, even when the approaches were quite different.

13.   **Is a statute specific to TB necessary?** The State of Washington has a statute that delegates broad, general public health power and which reads: "[The State Board of Health] shall have supreme authority in matters of quarantine, and shall provide by rule and regulation procedures for the imposition and use of isolation and quarantine." *See* WASH. REV. CODE ch.70070. State law also gives broad powers over matters relating to public health to local health departments. WASH. REV. CODE §§ 70.05.060 & 70.05.070. The Washington State Constitution grants broad powers to local health officials concerning local public health matters: "Any county, city, town or township may make and enforce within its limits all such local police, sanitary and other regulations as are not in conflict with general laws. " Wash. Const. art. XI, § 11. The Washington Supreme Court has addressed this grant of authority and noted: "This is a direct delegation of the police power as ample within its limits as that possessed by the legislature itself. It requires no legislative sanction for its exercise so long as the subject-matter is local, and the regulation reasonable and consistent with the general laws. " *Spokane County Health Dep't v. Brockett,* 839 P.2d 324, 328 (1992). (Contrast this conclusion with that in *New York Statewide Coalition of Hispanic Chambers of Commerce,* Chapter 3,C, *supra,* finding that the board of health could not properly exercise legislative authority.) Finally, the governor of the state also has both statutory and implied powers (i.e., powers beyond those specified in legislation) to act in response to public health emergencies. *See, e.g., Cougar Business Owners Ass'n v. Washington,* 647 P.2d 481 (Wash. 1982) (discussing the authority of the governor to impose

quarantine on certain areas affected by the Mt. St. Helen's explosion.)

With regard to involuntary confinement, Washington also has a specific statute governing confinement and treatment of people with TB, WASH. REV. CODE § 70.28 *et seq.*; another governing people with sexually transmitted diseases (STDs), WASH. REV. CODE § 70.24.005107; and a statute providing for the civil commitment of the mentally ill. For a detailed discussion of each and their legislative history, see Lisa A. Vincler & Deborah L. Gordon, *Legislative Reform of Washington's Tuberculosis Law: The Tension Between Due Process and Protecting Public Health*, 71 WASH. L. REV. 989 (1996).

Obviously any action by the state or local health departments in Washington State must comply with any applicable statute, and each of these statutes must comply with the dictates of procedural and substantive due process and, for that matter, other requirements of the state and federal constitutions. Just as obviously, there may be a series of preemption and conflict problems (*e.g.*, determining whether a specific state law has overridden the general authority of the local health departments.) This in itself outlines a complicated research problem. But note the unusual breadth of the general power delegated to the state health department and the even broader powers delegated to the local health departments by the state's statutes and its constitution. What are the limits on these truly extraordinary delegations of authority to state and, in some cases, local public health officials? On the one hand, this allows for a maximum of discretion at the agency and local level; on the other, it provides for the greatest risk of abuse. Which is better: To allow the legislature to decide what and how the agencies of the state and local government can act in each particular matter, or to allow state or local officials virtually unlimited discretion in matters relating to public health? Does the separation of powers doctrine suggest that such delegations of authority could go too far?

Note also that to the extent the state legislature has provided specific statutory schemes for dealing with such matters as TB and STIs, the state or local health departments may not be able to exceed the limits of those specific statutes in dealing with TB or STIs, although they have more discretion with regard to other public health problems for which the legislature has not enacted specific legislation. Does this make sense? To what extent is the state poised to deal with future public health problems?

14. The case of Andrew Speaker. The controversy surrounding Andrew Speaker, a lawyer who had traveled in Asia and was diagnosed with MDR-TB in 2007, illustrates the fear that tuberculosis still inspires today. After four months of treatment, Speaker wanted to carry out his plans for marrying his fiancée in Greece before beginning specialized treatment in Denver. Although Georgia county health officials advised against travel, they did not take any action to prevent the trip, apparently because Speaker did not appear to be contagious.

Speaker did have his wedding in Greece, but while he was away, a CDC laboratory concluded (incorrectly, as it turned out) that the infection was extensively-resistant tuberculosis (XDR-TB), a severe form of TB that is resistant to most TB drugs. The CDC then issued a federal order of isolation — the first since 1963. *See United States ex rel. Siegel v. Shinnick*, 219 F. Supp. 789 (E.D.N.Y. 1963) (upholding isolation order for woman who visited Stockholm when cases of smallpox were in Sweden). CDC officials contacted Speaker on his honeymoon in Italy and ordered him to either stay in Italy or hire a private airplane to return to the U.S. (to avoid contact with other people). Unable to pay the cost of a private jet and doubting whether Italy had proper XDR-TB treatment available, Speaker and his wife instead took a commercial airline flight to Canada. They then drove to New York and reported to the health department, where Speaker was placed under the federal quarantine order. He was sent to Denver, as originally planned. Ironically, the Denver specialists determined that Speaker did not have XDR-TB after all, and he responded to treatment at last report.

Public response to Speaker's actions was mostly negative. CDC officials asked the Department of Homeland Security to place Speaker on the "no-fly" list, designed to keep terrorists out of the country. (This did not prevent Speaker and his wife from flying on a regular flight and crossing the Canadian — U.S. border.) Legislators called for tougher laws, although it is not clear what, if any, changes would have altered the outcome. Georgia's TB control law did authorize involuntary confinement for people with contagious TB who are likely to transmit the disease. Health officials apparently did not believe that Speaker was contagious or likely to transmit TB, since he had been entirely cooperative before leaving the country. Despite living with his fiancée/wife, mingling with family and friends (Speaker usually wore a mask), and traveling on a commercial airline, Speaker appears to have infected no one.

The case of Andrew Speaker is unusual in two respects. First, he was an unusual patient, because he was white and middle class. Second, his case raised awareness of TB, albeit in perhaps less than desirable ways. Few patients with TB receive public notoriety, even though thousands are being treated in the country. And few commercial airline passengers worry about the real probability that some of their fellow travelers might have TB without knowing it. While Speaker's actions were not necessarily laudable, they were recognizably human responses to a dangerous disease, the possibility of dying in foreign country, and the absence of resources tailored to his condition.

15. Extensively drug resistant tuberculosis (XDR-TB). This relatively new form of TB is resistant to both the first and second line of TB drugs, including isoniazid, rifampin, ethambutol, streptomycin, kanamycin, and ciprofloxacin. At the Toronto AIDS conference in 2006 an early report from South Africa described a new TB strain that had killed 52 of 53 patients in a rural hospital. Lawrence K. Altman, *Doctors Warn of Powerful and Resistant Tuberculosis Strain*, NEW YORK TIMES, August 18, 2006 at A4. Note that Andrew Speaker was (mistakenly) believed to have XDR-TB in 2007, when concern about its spread may have been especially high. XDR-TB remains a major concern in high risk countries outside the United States. Although it might seem like quarantine would be a reasonable response to the appearance of XDR-TB cases, in fact the individuals with this form of TB typically are so sick they are unable to leave the hospital, and isolation is both reasonable and unlikely to be rejected by the patient.

C. HIV/AIDS — RESPONDING TO NEW DISEASES

CITY OF NEW YORK v. NEW SAINT MARK'S BATHS
130 Misc. 2d 911 (N.Y. Sup. Ct. 1986)

This action by the health authorities of the City of New York is taken against defendant the New St. Mark's Baths (St. Mark's) as a step to limit the spread of the disease known as AIDS (Acquired Immune Deficiency Syndrome). The parties are in agreement with respect to the deadly character of this disease and the dire threat that its spread, now in epidemic proportions, poses to the health and wellbeing of the community . . . [T] here is no disagreement that the rate of incidence of new cases of AIDS in New York State is approaching 200 a month; effective treatment is wholly lacking, and approximately 50% of all persons diagnosed with AIDS have died. The death rate for this disease increases to nearly 85% two years after diagnosis. The same percentage of AIDS patients suffer from special forms of pneumonia or cancer which are untreatable, and about 30% of these patients show symptoms of brain disease or severe damage to the spinal cord.

Immediately relevant to this litigation are the scientific facts with respect to AIDS risk groups. During the five years in which the disease has been identified and studied, 73% of AIDS victims have consisted of sexually active homosexual and bisexual men with multiple partners. AIDS is not easily transmittable through casual body contact or transmission through air, water or food. Direct blood-to-blood or semen-to-blood contact is necessary to transmit the virus. Cases of AIDS among homosexual and bisexual males are associated with promiscuous sexual contact, anal intercourse and other sexual practices which may result in semen-to-blood or blood-to-blood contact.

According to medical evidence submitted by defendants: "The riskiest conduct is thought to be that which allows the introduction of semen into the blood stream. Because anal intercourse may result in a tearing of internal tissues, that activity is considered high-risk for transmission."

Fellatio is also a high risk activity. As stated by the organizer of the AIDS Institute of the New York State Department of Health: "Any direct contact with the semen of an infected person may increase the risk of AIDS transmission. The deposition of semen in areas likely to contain abrasions, open sores, and cuts and concurrent inflammatory processes which could result in the presence of susceptible lymphocytes increase the risk of AIDS transmission. Because the mouth represents such an area (the epithelial tissue in the mouth is more susceptible to injury than the epithelial tissue in the vagina), fellatio presents a high risk for the transmission of AIDS."

PRIOR PROCEEDINGS

On October 25, 1985 the State Public Health Council, with the approval of the intervening New York State Commissioner of Health, adopted an emergency resolution adding a new regulation to the State Sanitary Code. This added regulation, State Sanitary Code (10 NYCRR) § 24.2, specifically authorized local officials, such as the City plaintiffs (City) here, to close any facilities "in which high risk sexual activity takes place." More specifically, in *10 NYCRR 242.2*, the regulation provided: "Prohibited Facilities: No establishment shall make facilities available for the purpose of sexual activities in which high risk sexual activity takes place. Such facilities shall constitute a public nuisance dangerous to the public health. "

In *10 NYCRR 242.1*, the regulation furnished definitions:

   a.   'Establishment' shall mean any place in which entry, membership, goods or services are purchased.

   b.   'High Risk Sexual Activity' shall mean anal intercourse and fellatio.

The Public Health Council based this regulation on the Commissioner's "findings" that: "Establishments including certain bars, clubs and bathhouses which are used as places for engaging in high risk sexual activities contribute to the propagation and spread of such AIDS-associated retroviruses . . . Appropriate public health intervention to discontinue such exposure at such establishments is essential to interrupting the epidemic among the people of the State of New York. "

Thereafter, on or about December 9, 1985, the City commenced this action by order to show cause for an injunction closing St. Mark's as a public nuisance citing the health risks at St. Mark's as defined in the State regulation. On December 19, 1985, following the issuance of a temporary restraining order defendants served papers in opposition to the City's motion for a preliminary injunction and cross-moved to dismiss the complaint for failure to state a cause of action. Defendants challenged the State regulation on the grounds that it was an invasion of defendants' patrons' rights to privacy and freedom of association under the United States Constitution.

Also on December 19, 1985, Paul Corrigan, Charles Dempsey, John Doe and Tom Roe, sought an order to intervene as party defendants. The proposed intervenors-defendants (intervenors) are described as "frequent patrons of the New St. Mark's Baths." The intervenors have also opposed the City's motion for a preliminary injunction. Intervenors also argue that the State regulation violates intervenors' rights to privacy and freedom of association.

On December 20, 1985, the Public Health Council promulgated *10 NYCRR 242.2* as a permanent regulation. The "findings" of the Public Health Council, as they relate to "high risk sexual activity," were similar to the "findings" of the Council in October. The regulation was approved by the Commissioner of Health and became effective on December 23, 1985.

On December 24, 1985, the State Commissioner of Health and the Attorney-General moved to intervene as plaintiffs to defend the validity of the State regulation.

This action is brought pursuant to the Nuisance Abatement Law. Under that law the City is empowered to enjoin public nuisances . . . .

CONSTITUTIONAL CONSIDERATIONS

The City has submitted ample supporting proof that high risk sexual activity has been taking place at St. Mark's on a continuous and regular basis. Following numerous onsite visits by City inspectors, over 14 separate days, these investigators have submitted affidavits describing 49 acts of high risk sexual activity (consisting of 41 acts of fellatio involving 70 persons and 8 acts of anal intercourse involving 16 persons). This evidence of high risk sexual activity, all occurring either in public areas of St. Mark's or in enclosed cubicles left visible to the observer without intrusion therein, demonstrates the inadequacy of self-regulatory procedures by the St. Mark's attendant staff, and the futility of any less intrusive solution to the problem other than closure.

With a demonstrated death rate from AIDS during the first six months of 1985 of 1248 . . . , plaintiffs and the intervening State officers have demonstrated a compelling State interest in acting to preserve the health of the population (*Jacobson v. Massachusetts*, 197 U.S. 11, . . .) Where such a compelling State interest is demonstrated even the constitutional rights of privacy and free association must give way provided, as here, it is also shown that the remedy adopted is the least intrusive reasonably available. Furthermore, it is by no means clear that defendants' rights will, in actuality, be adversely affected in a constitutionally recognized sense by closure of St. Mark's. The privacy protection of sexual activity conducted in a private home does not extend to commercial establishments simply because they provide an opportunity for intimate behavior or sexual release . . . . As stated in *Stratton v. Drumm* (445 F. Supp. 1305, 1309 [D. Conn. 1978]): "privacy and freedom of association . . . rights do not extend to commercial ventures."

No privacy

The private intervenors, of course, are not commercial ventures. However, the closure of this bath house does not extinguish their opportunities for unrestricted association in establishments which avoid creating a serious risk to the public health.

Also, State police power has been upheld over claims of 1st Amendment rights of association where the nature of the assemblage is not for the advancement of beliefs and ideas but predominantly either for entertainment or gratification [citing cases involving a heterosexual "swinging club"; involving a skating rink; "the associational activities of the Elks and Moose are purely social and not political and therefore do not come within the core protection of the right to associate"]. A tangential impact upon association or expression is insufficient to obstruct the exercise of the State's police power to protect public health and safety.

∆ argue bathhouse closing won't reduce aids

To be sure, defendants and the intervening patrons challenge the soundness of the scientific judgments upon which the Health Council regulation is based, citing, *inter alia*, the observation of the City's former Commissioner of Health in a memorandum dated October 22, 1985 that "closure of bathhouses will contribute little if anything to the control of AIDS." . . . Defendants particularly assail the regulation's inclusion of fellatio as a high risk sexual activity and argue that enforced use of prophylactic sheaths would be a more appropriate regulatory response. They go further and argue that facilities such as St. Mark's, which attempts to educate its patrons with written materials, signed pledges, and posted notices as to the advisability of safe sexual practices, provide a positive force in

∆ arg

combating AIDS, and a valuable communication link between public health authorities and the homosexual community. While these arguments and proposals may have varying degrees of merit, they overlook a fundamental principle of applicable law: "It is not for the courts to determine which scientific view is correct in ruling upon whether the police power has been properly exercised. 'The judicial function is exhausted with the discovery that the relation between means and end is not wholly vain and fanciful, an illusory pretense'" . . . . Justification for plaintiffs' application here more than meets that test.

For the foregoing reasons plaintiffs' application for a [sic] preliminary injunctive relief is granted . . . .

Wendy Parmet, *AIDS and Quarantine: The Revival of an Archaic Doctrine*
14 HOFSTRA L. REV. 53, 55–71 (1985)

Quarantine is one of the oldest forms of public health regulation. The word derives from the Italian *quarantenaria* or the Latin *quadraginta*, which means forty days and refers to the forty day detention placed on ships from plague-ridden ports during the late Middle Ages and early Renaissance . . . . The roots of this form of quarantine have been traced as far back as the Book of Leviticus, which prescribes the ostracism of lepers. Following that Biblical precept, lepers were isolated by official edict throughout medieval Europe.

When the plague struck Europe in the fourteenth century, European cities relied on their experience isolating lepers and denied entrance to persons coming from areas afflicted with the plague. Victims of the plague were isolated in their houses for the duration of the illness, as were all who had come into contact with them. Since the plague is usually spread by fleas and rats, the effectiveness of such measures is questionable. However, lacking a scientific understanding of the disease and its transmission, quarantine was one of the few actions that a community could take. Moreover, it set the precedent for a form of public health regulation that was potentially more effective when later applied to other diseases, such as smallpox, that were easily spread by casual contact between individuals.

In England, an early seventeenth century statute required the isolation of plague victims. According to Blackstone, the violation of this statute was a felony, and the matter was of the "highest importance." In colonial America, quarantine was enforced by both local and colonial governments. The earliest reported local quarantine order in America was in 1622 to combat smallpox in East Hampton, Long Island. Historians have found records of maritime quarantines in Boston as far back as 1647. In 1678, individuals with smallpox in Salem, Massachusetts were isolated by local order.

By the time the federal Constitution was drafted in 1787, quarantine had become a well-established form of public health regulation. Although the Constitution does not mention quarantine, article 1, section 10, acknowledges that states may promulgate and enforce inspection laws. This provision has long been thought to give states the power to keep out articles of commerce that are thought to be infectious. In *Gibbons v. Ogden* [22 U.S. (9 Wheat.) 1 (1824)], Chief Justice Marshall noted in *dicta* that a state had the power to quarantine "to provide for the health of its citizens." Quarantine was thus considered a proper exercise of the states' police power.

In 1796, the federal government enacted the first federal quarantine law in response to a yellow fever epidemic. [Act of May 27, 1796, ch. 31, 1 Stat. 474 (repealed 1799)] That law gave the President the power to assist states in enforcing their own quarantine laws. In 1799, the Act was repealed and replaced with one establishing the first federal inspection system for maritime quarantines. [Act of Feb. 25, 1799, ch. 12, 1 Stat. 619] Thereafter, throughout the nineteenth century, the federal government undertook an increasingly prominent role in implementing maritime quarantines.

It was the states, however, usually acting through localities, that enacted and enforced the quarantine regulations that required the isolation of individuals afflicted with, or exposed to, contagious disease. Cases discussing such state and local quarantines thus set the early precedent as to the government's power to deprive individuals of their liberty in order to protect the public health. Modern commentators have relied upon these cases in discussions of the powers of the state to quarantine people with AIDS. Yet, for the most part, these cases do not reflect the dramatic changes that have occurred in public law and science in the last fifty years. As a result, they must be understood in the context of their times, and their principles should not be applied today without modifications made in light of recent changes in law and science . . . .

II. THE LAW OF QUARANTINE

By the mid to late nineteenth century, many states had statutes enabling officials to isolate and detain individuals infected with or exposed to contagious diseases. The Massachusetts public health statute of 1797 was typical. Section 1 stated its purpose: "[T]he better preventing the spread of infection . . . ." [Act of June 22, 1797, ch. 16, GEN. LAWS OF MASS. (1822)] The statute gave the selectmen of a town power to: take care and make effectual provision in the best way they can, for the preservation of the inhabitants, by removing such sick or infected person or persons, and placing him or them in a separate house or houses, and by providing nurses, attendance, and other assistance and necessaries for them. . . .

Despite the broad authority given to state health officials under the nineteenth century quarantine statutes, prior to the second decade of this century there was little discussion about the constitutionality of the state's power to quarantine individuals. Courts and scholars debated the constitutionality of other state actions taken, but they rarely expressed doubts about the validity of quarantine regulations. At that time, the courts presumed that state actions taken within the police power, which was seen as the sovereign power of the state to protect the peace, health and morals of the public, were constitutional. Since quarantine was clearly designed to protect the public from disease, it was easily assumed to be a proper exercise of the police power.

The tacit acceptance of such broad state power over individuals may be understandable when it is remembered that at that time infectious disease was an ever-present threat. It is not surprising that quarantine was seen as emanating from the "higher ground of public welfare" when epidemics were common, and no one was immune from their terror.

The terror of epidemics and the historical roots of quarantine distinguished it as the example of a legitimate use of the police power. The fact that quarantine regulations were universally held to be both constitutional and beneficent, however, does not mean that the courts totally abrogated all review. To the contrary, courts always conducted a limited review. From the middle of the nineteenth century to approximately the time of World War I, the courts were presented with many quarantine cases. Most of these "classic" cases concerned quarantines imposed for acute infectious diseases such as smallpox, yellow fever, and typhus. In such cases, the courts usually upheld the validity of the quarantine statutes or regulations. Nevertheless, they often questioned the actions of particular government officials. Public health officials received their quarantine authority under specific statutes and regulations, and in order for their actions to be valid they had to follow those enactments.

The validity of a detention, however, was rarely contested. Instead, the issue of official authorization usually arose in an action for damages to property caused by a quarantine.

. . . .

Courts sometimes upheld quarantine orders even when the individuals could not be proven contagious, stating that health officials need not wait until a carrier has made someone ill. And yet, some courts set limits, however weak, on the discretion of health officers. These limits appear in the case of *Kirk v. Wyman*. In *Kirk*, the health officers determined that Miss Kirk, a former missionary, had contagious leprosy and ordered her either to leave the city or be quarantined in a pest-house which had previously been used only to incarcerate blacks with smallpox. [83 S.C. 372, 65 S.E. 387 (1909)] The court noted that state quarantine statutes were not violative of constitutional rights because:

> [n]either the right to liberty nor the right of property extends to the use of liberty or property to the injury of others. The maxim *Sic utere tuo ut alienum non laedas* applies to the person as well as to the property of the citizen. The individual has no more right of the freedom of spreading disease by carrying contagion on his person, than he has to produce disease by maintaining his property in a noisome condition.

Nevertheless, in a discussion of the constitutional principles governing state and municipal health regulation, the court stated that health officials cannot be given arbitrary power. According to the court, health officials must ensure that "the means used and the extent of the interference were reasonably necessary for the accomplishment of the purpose to be attained." Reviewing the facts under that standard, the court concluded that the board had acted improperly in ordering that Miss Kirk be sent to a pest-house since she had been safely quarantined in her home and had not made any attempt to violate the quarantine . . . .

Although the court in *Kirk* granted broad deference to the health officials, it interceded, perhaps in part because of its sympathy for Miss Kirk, and ordered the officials to adopt a less restrictive alternative by isolating Miss Kirk in a cottage to be built for her outside the city. As the twentieth century progressed, courts became even more willing to scrutinize the decisions of health officers. Ironically, this heightened form of judicial review came as health officials increasingly used their quarantine power against prostitutes and venereal disease.

*   *   *

Around the time of World War I, health officials began to use quarantine powers against prostitutes on the presumption that they had venereal disease . . . . Until then, quarantine had been used primarily against infectious diseases to which the entire community felt vulnerable . . . [and] was enforced by health officials. But when the power to quarantine was turned against prostitutes, as part of the effort to control venereal disease, a great stigma attached to being quarantined. In addition, it became a complement to police work, a way of holding prostitutes longer than many criminal sentences would allow.

This new association between quarantine and the criminal law led to more petitions for *habeas corpus* and, ultimately, forced courts to recognize that quarantine was not always in the best interest of the individual. The need for judicial review of the facts supporting quarantine, as well as the authority under which it was implemented, became clear. The courts continued to affirm the broad power of health officials to quarantine, but began to demand that health officials base their actions on some reasonable suspicion that the individual was infected.

. . . .

(The application of quarantine to prostitutes illustrates how quarantine can be
used to harass, isolate and exclude socially disfavored groups.)

. . . .

The courts have seldom explicitly addressed the discriminatory potential of quarantine. At the turn of the century, however, at least one federal court did so. In *Wong Wai v. Williamson* [103 F. 1 (C.C.N.D. Cal. 1900)], the court invalidated a quarantine ordinance under the equal protection clause of the fourteenth amendment. The plaintiff was a Chinese resident of San Francisco who challenged a city ordinance that required all Chinese residents of the city to be inoculated against bubonic plague prior to leaving the city. The inoculation, which could cause death, was justified by the city on the grounds that there was plague in the city and Asians as a race were highly susceptible to the disease. The court, however, noted that the regulation discriminated against Asians and could not be justified since the evidence did not support the city's claims. Moreover, the ordinance could not accomplish its stated purpose because the inoculation was only effective if given prior to exposure. The inoculation, in this case, was only administered to Chinese or Asian individuals leaving the city and, therefore, could not possibly stop the spread of disease. The court struck down the regulation, reminding the city that even the police power is subordinate to the Constitution.

. . . .

History of Quarantine

(taken from) A HISTORY OF QUARANTINE
www.pbs.org/wgbh/nova/body/short-history-of-quarantine.html
(visited Mar. 2014)

* * *

583   The Council of Lyons restricts lepers from freely associating with healthy persons.

600s   China detains plague-stricken arrivals in Chinese ports.

1179   Third Lateran Council decrees separation from society.

1200   Europe has some 19,000 leprosaria, or houses for leper patients.

1300s   A number of European and Asian countries begin enforcing quarantines of infected regions by encircling them with armed guards.

1348   Venice establishes the world's first institutionalized system of quarantine, giving a council of three the power to detain ships, cargoes, and individuals in the Venetian lagoon for up to 40 days. The act comes in the midst of the Black Death, a plague epidemic that eventually takes the lives of 14 to 15 million people across Europe.

1403   Venice establishes the world's first known maritime quarantine station on an island in the Venetian lagoon.

1629   Sanitary legislation drawn up in Venice requires health officers to visit houses during plague epidemics and isolate those infected in pest-houses situated away from populated areas.

1663   With plague ravaging parts of continental Europe, the English monarchy issues royal decrees calling for the establishment of permanent quarantines.

1700s   All major towns and cities along the eastern seaboard of the United States have now passed quarantine laws.

1701   A Massachusetts statute stipulates that all individuals suffering from plague, smallpox, and other contagious diseases must be isolated in separate houses.

1712   A plague epidemic around the Baltic Sea leads England to pass the Quarantine Act. During a mandatory 40 day quarantine for arriving ships, goods cannot be removed and serious breaches of the act can result in the death penalty.

1738   With smallpox and yellow fever threatening to strike New York, the City Council sets up a quarantine anchorage off Bedloe's Island (home of the Statue of Liberty today).

1832   After about 30,000 people in Britain alone die in a cholera epidemic in 18311832, New York mandates that no ship can approach within 300 yards of any dock if its captain suspects or knows the ship has cholera aboard

1850   Following horrific epidemics of plague and cholera that spread through

1851	Europe from Egypt and Turkey towards the middle of the 19th century, the first international sanitary conference is held in Paris, with an eye to making quarantine an international cooperative effort. . . .
1863	New York State's new Quarantine Act calls for a quarantine office run by a health officer who has the power to detain any ship entering the port of New York for as long as he deems necessary.
1879	Amid concern about yellow fever, the U.S. Congress establishes the National Board of Health, in part to assume responsibility for quarantine in cases where states' actions had proven ineffective.
1890s	As the era of bacteriology arrives, with major diseases like typhoid and cholera determined to arise from germs, the length and nature of quarantine evolves, now often based on the life cycles of specific microbes.
1892	When an Asiatic cholera epidemic reaches the U.S. in the fall, President Benjamin Harrison has his surgeon general issue an order holding that "no vessel from any foreign port carrying immigrants shall be admitted to enter any port of the United States until such vessel shall have undergone quarantine detention of twenty days. . . ."
1893	The U.S. Congress passes the National Quarantine Act. The act creates a national system of quarantine while still permitting state-run quarantines. . . .
1894	Epidemics of plague in China, Hong Kong, and Taiwan, as well as in India two years later, fly in the face of arguments promulgated by most European scientists of the day that the widespread scourges that ransacked Europe in the middle ages are history.
1900	[A] Chinese [lumberyard] proprietor dies of bubonic plague in the Chinese quarter of San Francisco. Authorities immediately rope off the 15 block neighborhood, quarantining roughly 25,000 Chinese.
1902	The Pan American Sanitary Bureau is established. It is the first of a series of international health organizations formed in the 20th century.
1903	In an attempt to isolate tuberculosis patients, the New York City Department of Health opens a quarantine facility at Riverside Hospital on North Brother Island, an islet in the East River. Mary Mallon, aka "Typhoid Mary," begins what becomes a total of 26 years of quarantine here in 1907.
1916	When an epidemic of polio strikes New York residents, authorities begin forcibly separating children from their parents and placing them in quarantine.
1917 1919	During World War I, American authorities incarcerate more than 30,000 prostitutes in an effort to curb the spread of venereal disease.
1944	The Public Health Service Act is codified, clearly establishing the quarantine authority of the federal government, which has controlled all U.S. quarantine stations since 1921.
1945	Baltimore adopts an ordinance giving health authorities the power to isolate at the city's hospitals those patients with syphilis or gonorrhea who refuse penicillin treatment.
1949	To help stem the spread of tuberculosis, Seattle creates a locked ward for TB sufferers who deny treatment.

1967	The U.S. Department of Health, Education, and Welfare transfers responsibility for quarantine to what is now the Centers for Disease Control and Prevention (CDC).
1986	Treating the first cases of HIV/AIDS in the country as a public health emergency, Cuba begins compulsory, indefinite quarantine for citizens testing positive for HIV.
1990s	To help control multi-drug-resistant tuberculosis, New York City detains more than 200 people who refuse voluntary treatment, confining most of them to the secure ward of a hospital for about six months.
2003	An outbreak of severe acute respiratory syndrome, or SARS, in Asia and Canada occurs in the spring. Officials credit the use of both isolation (for those sick with SARS) and quarantine (for those exposed to the sick) with forestalling an even more severe epidemic. In April, President George W. Bush adds SARS to the list of quarantinable diseases.

NOTES AND QUESTIONS

1. **Public nuisances.** *St. Mark's Baths* is an example of public health regulating business — places rather than people. The state has considerably more leeway to impose rules on organizations, whether for-profit or non-profit, than it does to regulate natural persons. Although the Supreme Court has recognized that organizations have some constitutional rights (*see, e.g., Citizens United v. Federal Election Commission*, 558 U.S. 310 (2010)), organizations like corporations remain legal fictions that do not (yet) enjoy all the constitutional protections afforded to human beings.

The court applies what is today a rarely used state power to stop (abate) public nuisances. The RESTATEMENT (SECOND) OF TORTS, § 821A, cmt. B (1979), describes the common law tort of nuisance as a "human activity or a physical condition that is harmful or annoying to others." Precise definitions, however, are elusive. *See* Warren A. Seavey, *Nuisance, Contributory Negligence and Other Mysteries*, 65 HARV. L. REV. 984, 995 (1952). Classic examples include a rubbish heap and a factory's smoking chimney. As states codified public health and safety standards into legislation regulating commercial endeavors, the need for the tort of nuisance to remedy such harms faded. Nonetheless, some states, like New York, also enacted a statute authorizing the state to enjoin harmful conditions not otherwise expressly regulated as public nuisances. This provides the foundation for the action taken against St. Mark's Bath.

What exactly constitutes the harm that the court finds to be a nuisance? Does the court distinguish between the activities of the business enterprise and the activities of its customers? Recall that this action occurred early in the HIV/AIDS epidemic, before significant therapies were available. If the state sought to close a similar bathhouse today, would the result be the same? If not, what has changed — law, medicine, culture?

2. AIDS and quarantine. Although there were many calls at the beginning of the HIV/AIDS epidemic to respond with mandatory screening followed by quarantine, this strategy was only employed in Cuba. Why wasn't quarantine applied in the U.S. (and in other countries) for HIV/AIDS? Is this an example of so-called "AIDS exceptionalism" or a reflection of the disease process itself?

There are, of course, many reasons for not using quarantine with HIV/AIDS, and you should be able to list them. Nonetheless, the Cuban strategy has its defenders. The U.S. did use quarantine on Guantanamo in 1992 and 1993 to confine Haitian immigrants who were HIV positive. This confinement facility was effectively shut down by Judge Sterling Johnson as being a violation of constitutional, statutory and regulatory rights. *Haitian Centers Council v. Sale*, 817 F. Supp. 336 (1993). *See* George J. Annas, *Detention of HIV Positive Haitians at Guantanamo: Human Rights and Medical Care*, 329 NEW ENG. J. MED. 589 (1993); and Ron Bayer, *Controlling AIDS in Cuba: The Logic of Quarantine*, 320 NEW ENG. J. MED. 1022 (1989). A related early program was an attempt to screen all international travelers, as well as immigrants, for HIV. See Larry Gostin et al., *Screening Immigrants and International Travelers for the Human Immunodeficiency Virus*, 322 NEW ENG. J. MED. 1743 (1990). Current strategies rely as much or more on treatment than prevention, although they work synergistically. *See* Chapter 6.

3. Historical examples of quarantine in the United States. As the Parmet article relates, in *Wong Wai* (1900) a federal court rebuked the city of San Francisco for discriminatory treatment of Chinese people in its efforts to control bubonic plague. Soon thereafter, the city authorized its board of health to adopt quarantines that the board might adjudge "necessary to prevent the spreading of contagious or infectious diseases." Finding that nine deaths from plague had occurred in a particular 12 block area of the city that housed between 10,000 and 15,000 people, the board of health promptly ordered that area quarantined. Jew Ho, a grocer living there, filed another suit in federal court, alleging, *inter alia*, that within the quarantine area the authorities failed to segregate infected persons and households from those unafflicted, thereby increasing risks to the latter; that the area itself was unreasonably large, thereby increasing rather than reducing the likelihood that any disease would spread (both within and beyond the quarantine limits); and that some areas within the quarantine area had actually been plague-free for some time. *Jew Ho v. Williamson*, 103 F. 10 (C.C.N.D. Cal. 1900).

The same federal judge who decided *Wong Wai* determined that the quarantine was in fact drawn and applied as Jew Ho alleged, and ruled that it was unconstitutional on two grounds. First, it was "not a reasonable regulation to accomplish the purposes sought," but rather was "unreasonable, unjust, and oppressive, and therefore contrary to the laws limiting . . . [state and local] police powers . . . ." The court found no fault with either the authorities' "declared purpose" of controlling the spread of bubonic plague (the "ends") or with the proper use of quarantine under state police powers (the "means") in principle. Yet, even under this minimal level of scrutiny, the court found *this* quarantine's enforcement utterly indefensible. Can you determine why? Do you agree?

The second basis for the court's decision to strike down enforcement of the quarantine was that it violated equal protection because it discriminated against the

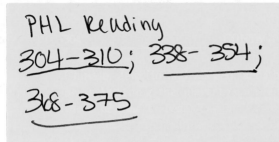

PHL Reading
304-310; 338-354;
368-375

court found, that despite its benign and
orced *only* against Chinese persons and not
serpentined around the area to exclude
appears that San Francisco did not contest
tory application of the quarantine on the
susceptible and "the Chinese may commu-
." (This may roughly translate to: "Plague
Chinatown"). In an understatement of vast
is "is not [a] sufficient" basis for sustaining
w] 'with an evil eye and an unequal hand' "
of equal protection.

the first ground was at all influenced by its
id?

For a good history of the San Francisco plague and the different responses of
different public health officers, see MARILYN CHASE, THE BARBARY PLAGUE: THE BLACK
DEATH IN VICTORIAN SAN FRANCISCO (2003).

4. Quarantine and isolation. Compare the use of the word "quarantine" in
Professor Parmet's article with the definitions presented at the beginning of this
chapter. Like many commentators, Professor Parmet is using the word generically
to include both quarantines of places and "compulsory isolation" of individuals,
because she describes examples of both.

———————

Federal Rules on Interstate Quarantine

In 2005, in connection with federal planning for controlling "bird flu" and other
contagious diseases that fall within federal jurisdiction (explained in Chapter 6,
infra), the CDC proposed revisions to its rules on interstate quarantine. Among
other things, the rules would require airlines to submit detailed passenger lists to
the CDC (rather than to the Federal Aviation Administration) to identify anyone
with a communicable disease.

Two documents follow: first, excerpts of the existing federal regulations on
interstate quarantine; and next, the CDC's proposed revisions to those rules,
announced in November 2005, but not adopted as of April 2014. The new proposal
for "provisional quarantine" offers a useful transition to the next Chapter's
materials on Emergency Preparedness and Bioterrorism.

Interstate Quarantine

42 C.F.R. Part 70 (2014)

§ 70.1 General definitions.

As used in this part, terms shall have the meaning:

Communicable diseases means illnesses due to infectious agents or their
toxic products, which may be transmitted from a reservoir to a susceptible
host either directly as from an infected person or animal or indirectly

through the agency of an intermediate plant or animal host, vector, or the inanimate environment.

Communicable period means the period or periods during which the etiologic agent may be transferred directly or indirectly from the body of the infected person or animal to the body of another.

. . . .

Incubation period means the period between the implanting of disease organisms in a susceptible person and the appearance of clinical manifestation of the disease.

. . . .

§ 70.2   Measures in the event of inadequate local control

Whenever the Director of the Centers for Disease Control and Prevention determines that the measures taken by health authorities of any State or possession (including political subdivisions thereof) are insufficient to prevent the spread of any of the communicable diseases from such State or possession to any other State or possession, he/she may take such measures to prevent such spread of the diseases as he/she deems reasonably necessary, including inspection, fumigation, disinfection, sanitation, pest extermination, and destruction of animals or articles believed to be sources of infection.

. . . .

§ 70.5   Certain communicable diseases; special requirements.

The following provisions are applicable with respect to any person who is in the communicable period of cholera, plague, smallpox, typhus or yellow fever, or who, having been exposed to any such disease, is in the incubation period thereof:

(a) Requirements relating to travelers.

(1) No such person shall travel from one State or possession to another, or on a conveyance engaged in interstate traffic, without a written permit of the Surgeon General or his/her authorized representative.

. . . .

(3) Upon receipt of an application, the Surgeon General or his/her authorized representative shall, taking into consideration the risk of introduction, transmission, or spread of the disease from one State or possession to another, reject it, or issue a permit that may be conditioned upon compliance with such precautionary measures as he/she shall prescribe.

. . . .

§ 70.6   Apprehension and detention of persons with specific diseases.

Regulations prescribed in this part authorize the detention, isolation, quarantine, or conditional release of individuals, for the purpose of preventing the introduction, transmission, and spread of the communicable diseases listed in an Executive Order setting out a list of quarantinable communicable diseases, as provided under section 361(b) of the Public Health Service Act. Executive Order 13295, of April 4, 2003, as amended by Executive Order 13375 of April 1, 2005, contains the current revised list of quarantinable communicable diseases, and may be obtained at http://www.cdc.gov/quarantine and http://www.archives.gov/federal-register. If this Order is amended, HHS will enforce that amended order immediately and update its Website.

Centers for Disease Control, *Proposed Quarantine Regulations, Notice of Proposed Rulemaking* 70 Fed. Reg. 71892 (Nov. 30, 2005)

Sec. 70.1 *Scope and definitions.*

Provisional quarantine means the detention on an involuntary basis of a person or group of persons reasonably believed to be in the qualifying stage of a quarantinable disease until a quarantine order has been issued or until the Director [of the CDC] determines that provisional quarantine is no longer warranted.

Qualifying stage means (i) A communicable stage of the disease; or (ii) A precommunicable stage, if the disease would be likely to cause a public health emergency if transmitted to other persons.

Quarantine means the holding on a voluntary or involuntary basis, including the isolation, of a person or group of persons in such place and for such period of time as the Director deems necessary or desirable to prevent the spread of infection or illness.

Quarantinable diseases means any of the communicable diseases listed in an Executive Order . . . .

. . . .

Sec. 70.13 *Screenings to detect ill persons.*

The Director may, at airports or other locations, conduct screenings of persons or groups of persons to detect the presence of ill persons. Such screenings may be conducted through visual inspection, electronic temperature monitors, or other means determined appropriate by the Director to detect the presence of ill persons.

Sec. 70.14 *Provisional quarantine.*

(a) The Director may provisionally quarantine a person or group of persons who the Director reasonably believes to be in the qualifying stage of a quarantinable disease and: (1) moving or about to move from one state to another state; or (2) a probable source of infection to persons who will be moving from a state to another state.

(b) Provisional quarantine shall commence upon: (1) the service of a written provisional quarantine order; (2) a verbal provisional quarantine order; or (3) actual movement restrictions placed on the person or group of persons.

(c) Provisional quarantine shall end three business days after provisional quarantine commences . . . .

. . . .

(e) A person or group of persons subject to provisional quarantine may be offered medical treatment, prophylaxis or vaccination, as the Director deems necessary to prevent the introduction, transmission or spread of the disease; such persons may refuse such medical treatment, prophylaxis, or vaccination, but remain subject to provisional quarantine.

Sec. 70.16   Quarantine.

(a) The Director may issue a quarantine order whenever the Director reasonably believes that:

> (1) a person or group of persons are in the qualifying stage of a quarantinable disease . . . and either (2) moving or about to move from a state to another state; or (3) a probable source of infection to persons who will be moving from a state to another state.

NOTES AND QUESTIONS

5. Nomenclature. As a matter of nomenclature, note that the CDC's use of the word "quarantine" appears in some places to connote what would be considered involuntary isolation.

6. Responses to the proposed new rules. The CDC's proposed rule-changes have not been promulgated, perhaps because they drew almost unanimous objection. The following comments on the proposed changes were submitted by the New England Coalition for Law and Public Health:

> One of the most notable inventions of the proposed regulations is the institution of a puzzling new procedure called "provisional quarantine," which is actually just involuntary detention — without probable cause or a warrant or a hearing — for up to 3 business days. Proposed 42 C.F.R. §§ 70.15 and 71.18. The purpose of such detention appears to be to allow the CDC time to figure out whether there is probable cause or even reasonable suspicion that a person actually has a contagious disease that will be transmitted to others and could therefore justifiably be subjected to quarantine under the statute or Constitution. Thus, the provisional quarantine provisions appear to be simply a way to avoid meeting any constitutional standards whatsoever prior to involuntarily detaining people.
>
> This conclusion is supported by the text of the legal explanation which states:

A provisional quarantine order is likely to be premised on the need to investigate based on reasonable suspicion of exposure or infection, whereas a quarantine order is more likely to be premised on a medical determination that the individual actually has one of the quarantinable diseases. Thus, during this initial three business day period, there may be very little for a hearing officer to review in terms of factual and scientific evidence of exposure or infection. Three business days may be necessary to collect medical samples, transport such samples to laboratories, and conduct diagnostic testing, all of which would help inform the Director's determination that the individual is infected with a quarantinable disease and that further quarantine is necessary. In addition, because provisional quarantine may last no more than three business days, allowing for a full hearing, with witnesses, almost guarantees that no decision on the provisional quarantine will actually be reached until after the provisional period has ended, thus making such a hearing virtually meaningless in terms of granting release from the provisional quarantine. 70 Fed. Reg. at 71896.

CDC's arguments for failing to provide any oversight for up to *3 business days* is unconvincing and constitutionally troubling. Proposed 42 C.F.R. §§ 70.15(c) and 71.16(c). When there is a weekend or holiday, the provisional quarantine provisions could permit unreviewable detention for up to 6 days. The use of business days is itself puzzling in this context, since it suggests that the CDC does not work on weekends or holidays, even during a threatened epidemic. If a disease is so dangerous that it is arguably necessary to detain someone without evidence that he has the disease, why would public health officials and laboratories be unavailable to work over the weekend? . . .

New England Coalition for Law and Public Health, Comments on Interstate and Foreign Quarantine Regulations Proposed by the Centers for Disease Control and Prevention, 42 C.F.R Parts 70 and 71, Feb. 3, 2006, www.cdc.gov/ncidod/dq/npgm/viewcomments_feb.htm (visited Jan. 2006).

Comments on the proposed revisions submitted by the Center for Biosecurity of the University of Pittsburgh on January 28, 2006, included the following:

The proposed revisions . . . are in many instances inconsistent with available scientific understanding of the nature of person-to-person disease transmission. This is particularly the case with pandemic influenza. The basic premise of the proposed revision, that the identification and quarantine of airline passengers showing symptoms of influenza infection will significantly diminish the spread of pandemic flu, is highly questionable and unsupported by data . . . .

The Center also listed specific issues, including the following:

6) **Monitoring only interstate flights for patients who need to be quarantined does not make sense.** To prevent spread of infection between states, why would the CDC single out air travel? Why do the proposed rules

not apply to interstate train or bus travel? If preventing ill patients from crossing state lines is so fundamentally important to protecting public health, why only apply this principle to air travel? Since this would be impossible, why single out air travel?

. . . .

8) **The rule proposes that arriving persons can be ordered to a medical examination and then placed into provisional quarantine. This element of the proposed rules is highly concerning on a number of levels**. This places unwarranted authority in a single individual ("the quarantine officer") whose medical training is not clearly articulated in the rule. Who will provide medical attention/care and legal resources for these quarantined individuals? Do these individuals have to get their own counsel at their own cost? The details of the administrative hearing which may follow a three day provisional quarantine period are unclear. Who is the "hearing officer"? Is it a judge? A doctor? What are the rights of the detained/quarantined individual?

Jennifer B. Nuzzo, SM, Donald A. Henderson, MD, MPH, Tara O'Toole, MD, MPH, Thomas V. Inglesby, MD, *Comments from the Center for Biosecurity of University of Pittsburgh Medical Center on Proposed Revisions to 42 CFR 70 and 71 (Quarantine Rules)*, www.cdc.gov/ncidod/dq/nprm/viewcomments_jan.htm (visited Jan. 2006).

7. **Implementation in practice**. The CDC's proposal has practical problems as well, especially the limited number and resources of the so-called quarantine stations that actually exist to do the screening at airports and other ports of entry. As the Institute of Medicine reported, "Unlike their namesakes, today's quarantine stations are not stations *per se*, but rather small groups of individuals located at major U.S. airports." INSTITUTE OF MEDICINE, COMMITTEE ON MEASURES TO ENHANCE THE EFFECTIVENESS OF THE CDC QUARANTINE STATION EXPANSION PLAN FOR U.S. PORTS OF ENTRY, QUARANTINE STATIONS AT PORTS OF ENTRY PROTECTING THE PUBLIC'S HEALTH 1 (Sivitz, LB, Stratton K & Benjamin, GC, eds., 2005). The IOM described these stations as follows:

> Unlike physical areas that travelers pass through, the term "station" in this report refers to a group of one to eight individuals located at an airport, land crossing, or seaport who perform activities designed to help mitigate the risk that a microbial and other threats of public health significance may enter the United States or affect travelers in this country. As noted above, all of the established stations (as of May 2005) are located at airports. Although the staff have offices and one or more patient isolation rooms, most interactions between quarantine station staff and travelers or crew take place in public areas of the terminals.

Id. at 20.

When the new regulations were proposed in 2005, there were a total of 8 "stations" in the country. The CDC advocated for increasing the total number to 25, and by November 2005, there were 18 stations. However, it is impossible to believe that the CDC would be able to create a presence at every one of the 474 points of international travel into the United States. As of April 2014, the CDC's website listed total of 20 stations, representing 4.2% of the U.S. ports of entry. http://www.cdc.gov/quarantine/QuarantineStations.html (visited Apr. 2014).

Chapter 6

EMERGENCY PREPAREDNESS AND BIOTERRORISM

A. INTRODUCTION

For many Americans, time is divided by September 11, 2001; there is the world before and the world after. September 11 may not have "changed everything," but it has certainly changed a lot — including major changes in public health funding, laws, and structure. It has caused us to be concerned, even obsessed, with a disease the eradication of which has been seen as public health's greatest triumph: smallpox. It has refocused public health funding, led to new public health laws, and created an entirely new field, "public health preparedness." How should public health and public health lawyers react to the threat of terrorist attacks, including the possible use of a biological agent as a weapon, "bioterrorism"?

The Department of Homeland Security, shortly after 9/11, developed a list of 15 National Planning Scenarios, all of which have public health aspects.

Department of Homeland Security Planning Scenarios

1. Nuclear Detonation — 10-Kiloton Improvised Nuclear
2. Biological Attack — Aerosol Anthrax
3. Biological Disease Outbreak — Pandemic Influenza
4. Biological Attack — Plague
5. Chemical Attack — Blister Agent
6. Chemical Attack — Toxic Industrial Chemicals
7. Chemical Attack — Nerve Agent
8. Chemical Attack — Chlorine Tank Explosion
9. Natural Disaster — Major Earthquake
10. Natural Disaster — Major Hurricane
11. Radiological Attack — Radiological Dispersal Devices
12. Explosive Attack — Bombing Using Improvised Explosive Device
13. Biological Attack — Food Contamination
14. Biological Attack — Foreign Animal Disease (Foot-and-Mouth Disease)
15. Cyber Attack

All of these are based primarily on imagination, and these "worse case scenarios" can cause us and our government to over-react and see these risks as the most important ones the public faces (rather than more everyday risks like smoking, eating processed foods, failure to exercise, etc.). It is worth emphasizing, however, that the rationale for planning to respond to these hypothetical disasters is the same basic rationale for all public health actions: to save lives. This is such a naturally powerful rationale that it even seemed (to Vice President Dick Cheney at least) to justify torture, including waterboarding. Saving lives draws much of its power from its opposite: death. The term that has been developed to describe how Americans cope with the knowledge that we will die is "terror management," which can be done either via religion or secular world views. Ultimately we can either deny death altogether, or imagine end-of-the-world scenarios that are more like fantasy than fact. 9/11 provides examples of both ways of dealing with death. The first is clinging harder to one's ideology; the second is imagining a death-dealing catastrophe so large that a lesser disaster, like the Boston Marathon bombing of 2013, is facilitated.

This chapter on post-9/11 terrorism challenges to public health is designed to encourage students to determine the most effective, efficient and civil-liberties-friendly responses. For example, compulsory measures related to contagious disease epidemics, such as quarantine, are often discussed in the context of preparedness planning. Among the questions that are posed throughout are: Can public health funding really be "dual use" so that we need not sacrifice traditional public health activities for new ones, or will we have to develop new priorities? Does our current "all-hazards" approach to disaster planning make sense given our experience with it in failing to prepare for and respond effectively to Hurricane Katrina? What does "preparedness" mean, and how do we apply public health principles to preventing a bioterrorist attack? Should we expand public health surveillance over medical care in emergency departments and physician offices, and how does this fit into a patient safety program? Should we develop new rules restricting access to bacteria and viruses that can be used as weapons? Should we shift legal power from states and localities to the federal government, or even to multinational or global organizations? How can the trust of the public in public health be maintained and fostered? And, ultimately, are we continuing to overreact to 9/11, and if so, in what areas can or should we return to the pre-9/11 public health?

The materials in this chapter begin with summaries and recommendations from the 9/11 Commission, then moves to Public Health Emergency Preparedness in general, followed by specific case studies of influenza, anthrax, smallpox, and SARS, and concludes with a section on bioterrorism research. As you go through these materials think about the words of physician Kenneth W. Bernard, a former special assistant to the president for biodefense, who has noted that "Public Health and National Security have always been uncomfortable bedfellows," which he describes as two separate tribes, and has encouraged public health professionals to get with the national security agenda "by speaking national security language and eliminating the self-important and sanctimonious lecturing for which global health advocates are known." Kenneth Bernard, *Health and National Security: A*

Contemporary Collision of Cultures, 11 BIOSECURITY & BIOTERRORISM 157, 162 (2013).

B. 9/11

Craig R. Whitney, *Introduction*,
THE 9/11 INVESTIGATIONS
xx–xxi, xxxiii (Steven Strasser ed., 2004)

Until the cold war unraveled after the collapse of the Berlin Wall in 1989, the administrations of presidents Ronald Reagan and George H.W. Bush paid comparatively little attention to terrorism, despite the Hezbollah attack that killed 241 marines in Lebanon in October of 1983 and the Libyan sabotage of Pan American Flight 103 that killed 270 people over Lockerbie, Scotland in 1988. Before the first terrorist attack on the World Trade Center in New York City in 1993 — and the later discovery of a related plot to blow up the city's river tunnels and the United Nations building — terrorism had been considered only a marginal threat to the United States itself. It took time for the implications to sink in.

Not until 1995 did President Bill Clinton establish a working level "Counterterrorism Security Group" inside the White House, chaired by Richard A. Clarke. It was not until 1996, Clarke wrote in a controversial book published on the eve of his public testimony before the 9/11 commission, that the government figured out that it was up against an Islamic terrorist network of global dimensions led by a renegade from a wealthy Saudi Arabian family, Osama bin Laden. And only after terrorist suicide truck bombers destroyed the American embassies in Tanzania and Kenya in August 1998, killing 257 (including 12 Americans) and wounding 5,000 people in Nairobi, did President Clinton order the first direct response against al Qaeda, a cruise missile attack on its training grounds in Afghanistan.

Spending on U.S. defensive actions against terrorism increased in 1999 and 2000, but President Clinton was distracted by the Monica Lewinsky affair. Even after suicide bombers used a boat full of explosives to blow up the U.S.S. *Cole* in Aden on October 12, 2000, killing seventeen sailors and injuring thirty-nine, the Clinton administration did not retaliate against al Qaeda, unsure that it had carried out the attack. Clarke and other officials were left to try to persuade the incoming administration of President George W. Bush that the threat of terrorist strikes on American soil posed an urgent danger. President Bush's first national security briefings, Clarke said, were not about terrorism but about two issues that seemed more important to the president then — Iraq, where his father's administration had left Saddam Hussein in power after Operation Desert Storm, and missile defense.

Then came September 11 . . . September 11 was a warning, but also an opportunity to set in place defenses against new and even more terrible terrorist attacks. With the Arab world in turmoil over the war in Iraq and the Bush administration's unconditional backing of Israel in its showdown with the Palestinian Authority, al Qaeda metastasized rapidly despite losing its sanctuary in Afghanistan. After attacks in Indonesia, Thailand, the Philippines, and then Madrid in the spring of 2004, the threat of terrorism to the United States and its Middle

Eastern and European allies seemed even greater than it had been in 2001. The worst scenario would be an attack using nuclear, biological, or chemical weapons, and al Qaeda and its spawn were known to have tried to acquire them.

NATIONAL COMMISSION ON TERRORIST ATTACKS UPON THE U.S., 9/11 COMMISSION REPORT
361-65, 376, 381-81, 395 (2004)

Three years after 9/11, Americans are still thinking and talking about how to protect our nation in this new era. The national debate continues. Countering terrorism has become, beyond any doubt, the top national security priority for the United States. This shift has occurred with the full support of the Congress, both major political parties, the media, and the American people.

The nation has committed enormous resources to national security and to countering terrorism. Between fiscal year 2001, the last budget adopted before 9/11, and the present fiscal year 2004, total federal spending on defense (including expenditures on both Iraq and Afghanistan), homeland security, and international affairs rose more than 50 percent, from $354 billion to about $547 billion. The United States has not experienced such a rapid surge in national security spending since the Korean War.

This pattern has occurred before in American history. The United States faces a sudden crisis and summons a tremendous exertion of national energy. Then, as that surge transforms the landscape, comes a time for reflection and reevaluation. Some programs and even agencies are discarded; others are invented or redesigned. Private firms and engaged citizens redefine their relationships with government, working through the processes of the American republic. Now is the time for that reflection and reevaluation. The United States should consider *what to do* — the shape and objectives of a strategy. Americans should also consider *how to do it* — organizing their government in a different way.

Defining the Threat

In the post-9/11 world, threats are defined more by the fault lines within societies than by the territorial boundaries between them. From terrorism to global disease or environmental degradation, the challenges have become transnational rather than international. That is the defining quality of world politics in the twenty-first century.

National security used to be considered by studying foreign frontiers, weighing opposing groups of states, and measuring industrial might. To be dangerous, an enemy had to muster large armies. Threats emerged slowly, often visibly, as weapons were forged, armies conscripted, and units trained and moved into place. Because large states were more powerful, they also had more to lose. They could be deterred.

Now threats can emerge quickly. An organization like al Qaeda, headquartered in a country on the other side of the earth, in a region so poor that electricity or telephones were scarce, could nonetheless scheme to wield weapons of unprecedented destructive power in the largest cities of the United States. In this sense, 9/11 has taught us that terrorism against American interests "over there" should be regarded just as we regard terrorism against America "over here." In this same sense, the American homeland is the planet.

But the enemy is not just "terrorism," some generic evil. This vagueness blurs the strategy. The catastrophic threat at this moment in history is more specific. It is the threat posed by Islamist terrorism — especially the al Qaeda network, its affiliates, and its ideology.

. . . .

Our enemy is twofold: al Qaeda, a stateless network of terrorists that struck us on 9/11; and a radical ideological movement in the Islamic world, inspired in part by al Qaeda, which has spawned terrorist groups and violence across the globe. The first enemy is weakened, but continues to pose a grave threat. The second enemy is gathering, and will menace Americans and American interests long after Usama Bin Laden and his cohorts are killed or captured. Thus our strategy must match our means to two ends: dismantling the al Qaeda network and prevailing in the longer term over the ideology that gives rise to *Islamist* terrorism.

Islam is not the enemy. It is not synonymous with terror. Nor does Islam teach terror. American and its friends oppose a perversion of Islam, not the great world faith itself . . . .

The present transnational danger is Islamist terrorism. What is needed is a broad political-military strategy that rests on a firm tripod of policies to:

- Attack terrorists and their organizations;
- Prevent the continued growth of Islamist terrorism; and
- Protect against and prepare for terrorist attacks.

More than a War on Terrorism

Terrorism is a tactic used by individuals and organizations to kill and destroy. Our efforts should be directed at those individuals and organizations. Calling this struggle a war accurately describes the use of American and allied armed forces to find and destroy terrorist groups and their allies in the field, notably in Afghanistan. The language of war also evokes the mobilization for a national effort. Yet the strategy should be balanced.

The first phase of our post-9/11 efforts rightly included military action to topple the Taliban and pursue al Qaeda. This work continues. But long-term success demands the use of all elements of national power: diplomacy, intelligence, covert action, law enforcement, economic policy, foreign aid, public diplomacy, and homeland defense. If we favor one tool while neglecting others, we leave ourselves vulnerable and weaken our national effort.

Certainly the strategy should include offensive operations to counter terrorism. Terrorists should no longer find safe haven where their organizations can grow and flourish. America's strategy should be a coalition strategy that includes Muslim nations as partners in its development and implementation. Our effort should be accompanied by a preventive strategy that is as much, or more, political as it is military. The strategy must focus clearly on the Arab and Muslim world, in all its variety.

Our strategy should also include defenses. America can be attacked in many ways and has many vulnerabilities. No defenses are perfect. But risks must be calculated; hard choices must be made about allocating resources. Responsibilities for America's defense should be clearly defined. Planning does make a difference, identifying where a little money might have a large effect. Defenses also complicate the plans of attackers, increasing their risks of discovery and failure. Finally, the nation must prepare to deal with attacks that are not stopped.

Measuring Success

What should Americans expect from their government in the struggle against Islamist terrorism? The goals seem unlimited: Defeat terrorism anywhere in the world. But Americans have also been told to expect the worst: An attack is probably coming; it may be terrible.

With such benchmarks, the justifications for action and spending seem limitless. Goals are good. Yet effective public policies also need concrete objectives. Agencies need to be able to measure success.

. . . .

We do not believe it is possible to defeat all terrorist attacks against Americans, every time and everywhere. A president should tell the American people:

- No president can promise that a catastrophic attack like that of 9/11 will not happen again. History has shown that even the most vigilant and expert agencies cannot always prevent determined, suicidal attackers from reaching a target.

- But the American people are entitled to expect their government to do its very best. They should expect that officials will have realistic objectives, clear guidance, and effective organization. They are entitled to see some standards for performance so they can judge, with the help of their elected representatives, whether the objectives are being met.

*   *   *

Recommendation: The U.S. government must define what the message is, what it stands for. We should offer an example of moral leadership in the world, committed to treat people humanely, abide by the rule of law, and be generous and caring to our neighbors. America and Muslim friends can agree on respect for human dignity and opportunity. To Muslim parents, terrorists like Bin Laden have nothing to offer their children but visions of violence and death. America and its friends have a crucial advantage — we can offer these parents a vision that might give their children a better future. If we heed the views of thoughtful leaders in the Arab and Muslim world, a moderate consensus can be found.

That vision of the future should stress life over death: individual educational and economic opportunity. This vision includes widespread political participation and contempt for indiscriminate violence. It includes respect for the rule of law, openness in discussing differences, and tolerance for opposing points of view.

* * *

Recommendation: The United States should engage its friends to develop a common coalition approach toward the detention and humane treatment of captured terrorists. New principles might draw upon Article 3 of the Geneva Conventions on the law of armed conflict. That article was specifically designed for those cases in which the usual laws of war did not apply. Its minimum standards are generally accepted throughout the world as customary international law.

* * *

Recommendation: Our report shows that al Qaeda has tried to acquire or make weapons of mass destruction for at least ten years. There is no doubt the United States would be a prime target. Preventing the proliferation of these weapons warrants a maximum effort — by strengthening counter proliferation efforts, expanding the Proliferation Security Initiative, and supporting the Cooperative Threat Reduction program.

* * *

Recommendation: At this time of increased and consolidated government authority, there should be a board within the executive branch to oversee adherence to the guidelines we recommend and the commitment the government makes to defend our civil liberties.

We must find ways of reconciling security with liberty, since the success of one helps protect the other. The choice between security and liberty is a false choice, as nothing is more likely to endanger America's liberties than the success of a terrorist attack at home. Our history has shown us that insecurity threatens liberty. Yet, if our liberties are curtailed, we lose the values that we are struggling to defend.

National Security Preparedness Group, Tenth Anniversary Report Card: The Status of the 9/11 Commission Recommendations
(September 2011)

In 2005, Hurricane Katrina revealed that a catastrophic natural event could produce a chaotic and disorganized response by all levels of government, causing large-scale human suffering. A decade after 9/11, the nation is not yet prepared for a truly catastrophic disaster. Teamwork, collaboration, and cooperation at an incident site are critical to a successful response . . . . We therefore recommend that federal state, and local emergency response agencies nationwide adopt the Incident Command System (ICS); an essential element of this is a unified command with one person in charge of directing the efforts of multiple agencies . . . . While the government has made substantial progress, our recommendation is still a long way from being fully implemented.

The inability of first responders to communicate with each other on demand was a critical failure on 9/11. Incompatible and inadequate communications led to needless loss of life. To remedy this failure, the Commission recommended legislation to provide for the expedited and increased assignment of radio spectrum for public safety purposes. To date, this recommendation continues to languish.

. . . .

An array of security-related policies and programs present significant privacy and civil liberty concerns. . . . the 9/11 Commission recommended creating a Privacy and Civil Liberties Oversight Board to monitor actions across the government. Congress and the president enacted legislation to establish this Board but it has, in fact, been dormant for more than three years.

When we issued our 2004 report, we believed that congressional oversight of homeland security and intelligence functions of government was dysfunctional. It still is . . . . We firmly reinforce what we said in our final report: That it is in our country's security interest that Congress make committee reform a priority.

We are not satisfied with improvement to TSA's explosives screening capability . . . . Explosives detection technology lacks reliability and lags in its capability to automatically identify concealed weapons and explosives.

One area of great progress in securing our borders is the deployment of the biometric entry system known as US-VISIT . . . however, there still is no comprehensive exit system in place.

The delay in compliance with the REAL ID Act [which established standards for the issuance of birth certificates and sources of identification, such as driver's licenses] makes us less safe. No further delay should be authorized; rather, compliance should be accelerated.

Recommendation: "The United States should engage its friends to develop a common coalition approach toward the detention and humane treatment of captured terrorists and [new] principles might draw upon Common Article 3 of the Geneva Conventions on the law of armed conflict."

Within days of his inauguration, President Obama signed a series of executive orders on the treatment of detainees and barring the CIA from using any interrogation methods not already authorized in the U.S. Army Field Manual. This ended the CIA's authority to use harsh interrogation methods, but the administration is still grappling with how to close the Guantanamo prison facilities . . . . Looking forward, however, we are concerned that the issue of prisoner treatment has become highly politicized. This is not good for our country and for our standing in the world. Showing that bipartisan agreement is possible, and intending to reaffirm our values, the five Republicans and five Democrats on the Commission unanimously agreed on this recommendation. Together, we believed that our country's values require adherence to the rule of law and a commitment to human rights and humane treatment. A lingering problem that two presidents have confronted is reconciling the rule of law with indefinitely detaining alleged terrorists. For too long, the President and Congress have delayed resolving this difficult problem.

Today, our country is undoubtedly safer and more secure than it was a decade ago. We have damaged our enemy, but the ideology of violent Islamist extremism is alive and attracting new adherents, including right here in our own country. With important 9/11 Commission recommendations outlined in this report still unfulfilled, we fail to achieve the security we could or should have.

The terrorist threat will be with us far into the future, demanding that we be ever vigilant . . . . Our task is difficult. We must constantly assess our vulnerabilities and anticipate new lines of attack. We have done much, but there is much more to do.

NOTES AND QUESTIONS

1. **The 9/11 Commission** (officially known as "The National Commission on Terrorist Attacks Upon the U.S.") made 41 specific recommendations. Their final report was issued in July 2004 and is available in its entirety on a frozen website that is maintained by the National Archives at www.9-11commission-gov/report/911Report.pdf (last visited Aug. 2014). In December 2005 the Commission issued a report card on its recommendations, giving the government failing grades on many of its most important recommendations, including a "D" on developing critical infrastructure; an "F" on airline passenger pre-screening; a "D" on checked bag and cargo screening; a "D" on international collaboration on borders and document security, a "privacy and civil liberties oversight board, and on developing guidelines for sharing of personal information; and an "F" on "coalition detention standards." Dan Eggen, *U.S. Issued Failing Grades by 9/11 Panel,* WASHINGTON POST, Dec. 6, 2005, at A1.

Perhaps most strikingly, Congress continues to fund preparedness based on congressional districts rather than giving more funds to areas that are the most vulnerable. For the inside story of the Commission by its co-chairs, see THOMAS H. KEAN & LEE H. HAMILTON, WITHOUT PRECEDENT: THE INSIDE STORY OF THE 9/11 COMMISSION (2006). Not everyone was enthusiastic about the Commission's recommendations. Richard Clarke, for example, thought that the quest for bipartisan unanimity led to the commission failing to "admit the obvious: we are less capable of defeating the jihadists because of the Iraq war. Unanimity has its value, but so do debate and dissent in a democracy facing a crisis. " Richard A. Clarke, *Honorable Commission, Toothless Report,* N.Y. TIMES, July 25, 2004, at A11. *See also,* RICHARD A. CLARKE, AGAINST ALL ENEMIES: INSIDE AMERICA'S WAR ON TERROR (2004) .

2. **9/11 Commission findings.** One of the Commission's most striking findings was that the president had received a briefing on bin Laden's plans on August 6, 2001, raising the question of whether warnings and preparations can do much good. The Presidential Daily Brief Memo is reprinted on pages 261–262 of the final report, and contains the following observations about reports that bin Laden has wanted to hijack U.S. aircraft since 1998:

> FBI information since [1998] indicates patterns of suspicious activity in this country consistent with preparation for hijackings or other types of attacks, including recent surveillance of federal buildings in New York. The

FBI is conducting approximately 70 full field investigations throughout the U.S. that it considers bin Laden related. CIA and the FBI are investigating a call to our embassy in the UAE in May saying that a group of bin Laden supporters was in the U.S. planning attacks with explosives.

The Commission concluded that there were no further discussions "before September 11 among the President and his top advisors of the possibility of a threat of an al Qaeda attack on the United States." NAT'L COMM'N ON TERRORIST ATTACKS, *supra*, at 262.

3. **Globalization.** *New York Times* columnist Tom Friedman has argued that dating America from September 11 is a major mistake, and that our country should remain the country of the 4th of July. In his view, globalization should continue to be seen as a positive force for the good of all, rather than as a threat to America. *See, e.g.*, THOMAS FRIEDMAN, THE WORLD IS FLAT: A BRIEF HISTORY OF THE TWENTY-FIRST CENTURY (Updated and expanded ed. 2006).

4. **The Geneva Conventions.** It is striking that the 9/11 Commission highlighted the importance of the Geneva Conventions in our response to 9/11. Only a few months after the attacks, the President signed an executive order declaring that the Geneva Conventions did not apply to the Taliban or to prisoners held at Guantanamo Bay, Cuba. This was the first time in U.S. history that a president has ever claimed an exception for the U.S. from this international treaty that covers the treatment of prisoners and civilians during wartime. In the summer of 2006 the U.S. Supreme Court had its first opportunity to decide if the president could unilaterally declare international law, specifically the Geneva Conventions, null. In what has been described as the most important case the Court has ever decided on the question of executive powers, the Court ruled that the Conventions must be followed as an integral part of international law. *Hamdan v. Rumsfeld*, 548 U.S. 557 (2006). Justice Stevens wrote for the Court:

> [T]here is at least one provision of the Geneva Conventions that applies here even if the relevant conflict is not one between signatories. Article 3, often referred to as Common Article 3 because, like Article 2, it appears in all four Geneva Conventions, provides that in a "conflict not of an international character occurring in the territory of one of the High Contracting Parties, each Party to the conflict shall be bound to apply, as a minimum," certain provisions protecting " [p] ersons taking no active part in the hostilities, including members of armed forces who have laid down their arms and those placed *hors de combat* by . . . detention. " One such provision prohibits "the passing of sentences and the carrying out of executions without previous judgment pronounced by a regularly constituted court affording all the judicial guarantees which are recognized as indispensable by civilized peoples"

> The Court of Appeals thought, and the Government asserts, that Common Article 3 does not apply to Hamdan because the conflict with al Qaeda, being " 'international in scope,' " does not qualify as a " 'conflict not of an international character.' " That reasoning is erroneous. The term "conflict not of an international character" is used here in contradistinction to a conflict between nations. So much is demonstrated by the "fundamental

logic [of] the Convention's provisions on its application." Common Article 2 provides that "the present Convention shall apply to all cases of declared war or of any other armed conflict which may arise between two or more of the High Contracting Parties." High Contracting Parties (signatories) also must abide by all terms of the Conventions vis-à-vis one another even if one party to the conflict is a non-signatory "Power," and must so abide vis-à-vis the non-signatory if "the latter accepts and applies" those terms. Common Article 3, by contrast, affords some minimal protection, falling short of full protection under the Conventions, to individuals associated with neither a signatory nor even a non-signatory "Power" who are involved in a conflict "in the territory of" a signatory. The latter kind of conflict is distinguishable from the conflict described in Common Article 2 chiefly because it does not involve a clash between nations (whether signatories or not). In context, then, the phrase "not of an international character" bears its literal meaning.

Id. at 629–30.

5. Common Article 3 of the Geneva Conventions.

In the case of armed conflict not of an international character occurring in the territory of one of the High Contracting Parties, each Party to the conflict shall be bound to apply, as a minimum, the following provisions:

(1) Persons taking no active part in the hostilities, including members of armed forces who have laid down their arms and those placed *hors de combat* by sickness, wounds, detention, or any other cause, shall in all circumstances be treated humanely, without any adverse distinction founded on race, color, religion or faith, sex, birth or wealth, or any other similar criteria.

To this end, the following acts are and shall remain prohibited at any time and in any place whatsoever with respect to the above mentioned persons:

(a) violence to life and person, in particular murder of all kinds, mutilation, cruel treatment and torture;

(b) taking of hostages;

(c) outrages upon personal dignity, in particular, humiliating and degrading treatment;

(d) the passing of sentences and the carrying out of executions without previous judgment pronounced by a regularly constituted court affording all the judicial guarantees which are recognized as indispensable by civilized peoples.

(2) The wounded and sick shall be collected and cared for. An impartial humanitarian body, such as the International Committee of the Red Cross, may offer its services to the Parties to the conflict.

The Parties to the conflict should further endeavor to bring into force, by means of special agreements, all or part of the other provisions of the present Convention.

The application of the preceding provisions shall not affect the legal status of the Parties to conflict.

6. **Law governing Guantanamo.** The administration's decision to treat the Geneva Conventions as inapplicable helped create a sense that Guantanamo was a legal black hole to which neither U.S. nor international law applied. This attitude in turn helped produce the scandalous abuse and torture of Iraqi prisoners of war at Abu Ghraib prison. The photographs of their humiliating and degrading treatment made it appear that the United States was willing to fight terror with terror. Abu Ghraib negated any American claim of moral superiority in the world and destroyed all human rights rationales for the Iraq war. The "good guys" had become the "evildoers" on prime-time TV for the world to see.

Military physicians performed better when honoring both medical ethics and the human rights provisions of Geneva I, which covers wounded prisoners. After the fiercest battle in Afghanistan (part of Operation Anaconda), for example, the surgeon in command of the U.S. Army field hospital at Bagram Air Base, Lt. Col. Ronald Smith, told reporters who asked him that the Taliban and al Qaeda wounded were being treated side by side with the American wounded at the hospital, noting that "the ethics of combat surgery" require it.

It is also worth noting that the Geneva Conventions themselves affirmatively protect medical ethics. For example, Article 16 of Protocol I (1977) states in relevant part:

> (1) Under no circumstances shall any person be punished for carrying out medical *activities compatible with medical ethics*, regardless of the person benefiting therefrom.

> (2) Persons engaged in medical activities shall not be compelled to perform acts or to carry out work contrary to the *rules of medical ethics* or to other medical rules designed for the benefit of the wounded and sick or to the provisions of the Conventions or this Protocol, or to refrain from performing acts or from carrying out work required by those rules and provisions. (emphasis added)

In short, under international humanitarian law, human rights and medical ethics requirements are symbiotic. *See, e.g.*, George J. Annas, American Bioethics: Crossing Human Rights and Health Law Boundaries 9–10 (2005); Edmund Pellegrino, *Medical Ethics Suborned by Tyranny and War*, 291 JAMA 1505 (2004).

C. PUBLIC HEALTH EMERGENCY PREPAREDNESS

This part explores mass public health emergencies created by contagious disease, whether through an act of bioterror or a widespread, naturally-occurring epidemic. The focus of subpart 1 is on overall public health planning for such emergencies; as such, it concentrates, inevitably, primarily on actions that may be taken by the administrative arms of government at the federal, state and local levels. Subpart 2 focuses more explicitly on "legal planning" — consideration of the adequacy of current legal tools for effectively responding to such events, and exploration of changes in law that may enhance that response. Of course, the distinction between these two subtopics is imperfect, since much of what government can and will do is controlled by the powers and constraints of existing law. Nonetheless, the distinctive focus of subpart 2 on what might be called "public health law reform" seems warranted as we contemplate these unwelcome threats.

1. Planning for Public Health Emergencies: Policy and Administrative Aspects

Thomas V. Inglesby *et al.*, *A Plague on Your City: Observations from TOPOFF*
32 CLINICAL INFECTIOUS DISEASE 436, 437–38 (2001)

*   *   *

The U.S. Congress, in an effort "to assess the nation's crisis and consequence management capacity under extraordinarily stressful conditions," directed the Department of Justice to conduct an exercise that would engage key personnel in the management of mock chemical, biological or cyber-terrorist attacks.

TOPOFF was a $3 million drill that tested the readiness of top government officials to respond to terrorist attacks directed at multiple geographic locations. It was the largest exercise of its kind to date. The exercise, which took place in May 2000 in three cities in the United States, simulated a chemical weapons event in Portsmouth, N.H., a radiological event in the greater Washington, D.C. area, and a bioweapons event in Denver, Colo. The bioterrorism component of the exercise centered on the release of an aerosol of *Yersinia pestis*, the bacteria that causes plague. Denver was selected in part because it had received domestic preparedness training and equipment . . . .

This article seeks to identify the medical and public health observations and lessons discovered in the biological weapons component (*i.e.*, the Denver component) of the TOPOFF exercise . . . .

. . . .

Officials were involved in the event as participants, controllers, or observers. Participants were the actual players of the exercise and, in general, operated within the parameters of their usual roles and authorities. Controllers maintained the structure of the exercise, which helped guide the unfolding scenario. Observers were generally agency heads who had policy responsibilities relevant to the events of the exercise. A number of health agencies (including the county health agency, the state health agency, the Centers for Disease Control and Prevention [CDC], The Office of Emergency Preparedness, and elements of the Public Health Service, as well as three hospitals in the Denver area [Swedish Medical Center, Medical Center of Aurora and Denver Health Medical Center]) participated in the exercise. Many persons from these institutions worked around the clock for days in attempts to cope with the unfolding medical and public health crisis depicted in the exercise.

TOPOFF was intended to be "player driven" which meant that the participants' decisions and the subsequent consequences were to be the primary drivers in the shaping of the exercise . . . .

The scope and complexity of the exercise were such that many of the events that occurred in the exercise could only be "notional" (*i.e.*, they could not be acted out and, thus, occurred on paper only).

. . . .

The exercise began on May 20, 2000, and ended on May 23.

OVERVIEW OF THE EXERCISE

May 17. An aerosol of plague (*Y. pestis*) bacilli is released covertly at the Denver Performing Arts Center.

May 20 (day 1 of exercise). The Colorado Department of Public Health and Environment receives information that increasing numbers of persons began to seek medical attention at Denver area hospitals for cough and fever during the evening of May 19 . . . . By early in the afternoon of May 20, 500 persons with these symptoms have received medical care; 25 of the 500 have died. The Department of Public Health and Environment notifies the CDC of the increased volume of sick patients. Plague is confirmed first by the state laboratory and subsequently, in a patient specimen, by the CDC lab at Ft. Collins, CO . . . .

A public health emergency is declared by the state health officer. The state health officer places an official request for support from the Department of Health and Human Services' Office of Emergency Preparedness. The governor's Emergency Epidemic Response Committee . . . assembles to respond to the unfolding crisis. Thirty-one CDC staff are sent to Denver. The CDC is notified by the Denver police and the Federal Bureau of Investigation (FBI) that a dead man has been found with terrorist literature and paraphernalia in his possession; his cause of death is unknown. Hospitals and clinics in the Denver area, which just a day ago were dealing with what appeared to be an unusual increase in influenza cases, are recalling staffs, implementing emergency plans, and seeking assistance in the determination of treatment protocols and protective measures. By late afternoon, hospital staff are beginning to call in sick, and antibiotics and ventilators are becoming more scarce. Some hospital staff have donned protective respiratory equipment.

The governor issues an executive order that restricts travel (including travel by bus, rail, and air) into or out of 14 Denver metropolitan counties; he also commandeers all antibiotics that can be used to prevent or treat plague. During a VNN press conference, at which a number of agencies are represented, the Denver police is informed that an outbreak of the plague has occurred in the city after a terrorist attack, and it is told of the governor's executive order. The public is also told to seek treatment at a medical facility if they are feeling ill or if they have been in contact with a known or suspected case of plague. Those who are healthy are directed to stay in their homes and to avoid public gatherings. The public is told that the disease can spread from person to person only "if you are within six feet of someone who is infected and coughing," and they are told that dust masks effectively prevent the spread of disease . . . . It is announced that the governor is working with the President of the United States to resolve the crisis and that federal resources are being brought in to support the state agencies. By the end of the day, 783 cases of pneumonic plague have occurred; 123 persons have died.

May 21 (day 2 of exercise). VNN reports that a "national crash effort" is under way that aims to move large quantities of antibiotics to the region as the CDC brings in its "national stockpile," but the quantity of available antibiotics is uncertain. The report explains that early administration of antibiotics is effective in the treatment of plague, but that antibiotic treatment must be started within 24 hours of the development of symptoms. A few hours later, a VNN story reports that hospitals are running out of antibiotics.

A "push-pack" from the National Pharmaceutical Stockpile (NPS) arrives in Denver, but there are great difficulties in moving antibiotics from the stockpile delivery point to the persons who need it for treatment and prophylaxis. Out-of-state cases begin to be reported. The CDC notifies bordering states of the epidemic. Cases are reported in England and Japan. Both Japan and the World Health Organization (WHO) request technical assistance from the CDC.

A number of hospitals in Denver are full to capacity, and by the end of the day, they are unable to see or to admit new patients. Thirteen hundred ventilators from the NPS are to be flown to Colorado. The number of bodies in hospital morgues is reported to have reached critical levels. By 5:00 p.m. mountain time, the CDC has performed an epidemiological investigation on 41 cases. The U.S. Surgeon General flies to Colorado to facilitate communications issues. Many states are now requesting components of the NPS from the CDC. By the end of the day, 1871 plague cases have occurred in persons through-out the United States, London, and Tokyo. Of these, 389 persons have died.

May 22 (day 3 of exercise). Hospitals are understaffed and have insufficient antibiotics, ventilators, and beds to meet demand. They cannot manage the influx of sick patients into the hospitals. Medical care is "beginning to shut down" in Denver. A total of 151 patient charts have been reviewed by state and federal health officials who are pursuing the epidemiological investigation. There are difficulties getting antibiotics from the NPS to the facilities that need them. Details of a distribution plan are still not formalized.

Officials from the Department of Public Health and Environment and the CDC have determined that secondary spread of disease appears to be occurring. The population in Denver is encouraged to wear face masks. The CDC advises that Colorado state borders be cordoned off to limit further spread of plague throughout the United States and other countries. Colorado officials express concern about their ability to get food and supplies into the state. The governor's executive order is extended to prohibit travel into or out of the state of Colorado. By noon, there are reports of 3060 U.S. and international patients with pneumonic plague, 795 of whom have died.

May 23 (day 4 of exercise). There are conflicting reports regarding the number of sick persons and dead persons. Some reports show an estimated 3700 cases of pneumonic plague with 950 deaths. Others are reporting more than 4000 cases and more than 2000 deaths . . . .

. . . .

NOTES AND QUESTIONS

1. **Lessons from TOPOFF.** Inglesby describes a number of what he terms "lessons" from the exercise. Generally he notes that issues of "leadership, the role of authorities, and the processes of decision-making" were all "highly problematic, " and that political considerations often received more attention from "experts" than they might have received from elected officials. He continues:

> Some participants attributed these difficulties to the decision-making processes of public health agencies. One observer commented about how "in public health, more decision-making is through democratic processes and consensus building, but for some decisions, this cannot work." . . . Another observer remarked, "the time frame that public health is accustomed to dealing with is not what is needed for bioterrorism . . . . Some from the CDC, state and local health agencies tried to look at this as a standard epidemiological investigation. In absolutely no way would this [scenario allow] a normal epidemiological investigation." . . .

> The flow of information was another major concern of the participants . . . . It is also unlikely that health departments would have had the resources to acquire and analyze data rapidly enough to know the rate of secondary transmission or to pinpoint the outbreak's origin as quickly as was portrayed in the exercise. Without rapid access to this information and other data, decision-makers would have been even more ill-positioned to make important decisions, such as how and when to distribute antibiotics, make recommendations for containment measures, or communicate public education messages.

> . . . .

> The large numbers of ill persons seeking medical care was one of the most serious challenges identified by the exercise, according to one senior health department official.

Id. at 439–41.

With specific regard to quarantine and isolation of individuals, Inglesby noted:

> Perhaps the issues that provoked the greater concerns and uncertainties with regard to TOPOFF were the series of containment measures that were undertaken to control the spread of the epidemic . . . .

> Early in the crisis, antibiotic prophylaxis and isolation of individual patients in hospitals were the primary epidemic containment measures. Less than one full day into the exercise, the epidemic was rapidly spreading — long before health authorities had sufficient time to characterize the

common source of the outbreak, the rate of secondary transmission, the response to antibiotics, or the results of other containment measures. The unfolding situation precipitated a series of increasingly stringent containment measures . . . . As one observer noted, "They told one million people to stay in their homes. How would we have enforced this?" When asked what would be possible if the situation actually required it, the police and National Guard admitted to the Emergency Epidemic Response Committee that they would be unable to keep people at home. Another participant commented that, by the end of the exercise, "people had been asked to stay in their homes for 72 hours . . . . How were they supposed to get food or medicine?" . . .

. . . .

Comments offered by one senior health participant summarized the implications and lessons of disease containment:

> Many previous bioterrorism exercises dealt with non-contagious diseases. It is just beginning to dawn on us how dramatically different this was as the exercise ended. It terminated arbitrarily and many issues were left unresolved. It is not clear what would have happened if it had gone on . . . . Competition between cities for the NPS has already broken out. It had all of the [characteristics] of an epidemic out of control.

Id. at 441–42.

2.   More lessons from TOPOFF. For additional descriptions of the TOPOFF exercise and the lessons that may have been learned, see Thomas v. Inglesby, *Observations from the TOPOFF Exercise*, 116 PUB. HEALTH REP. 64 (Supp. 2 2001); Richard E. Hoffman & Jane E. Norton, *Lessons Learned From a Full-Scale Bioterrorism Exercise*, 6 EMERGING INFECTIOUS DISEASES 652 (2000).

Since the first TOPOFF, there have been several other simulated exercises, testing the ability of federal, state, and local public health agencies to respond collectively to a disaster — often demonstrating some of the same organizational and management problems encountered in the Colorado exercise. *See, e.g.*, Tara O'Toole, Michael Mair & Thomas V. Inglesby, *Shining Light on "Dark Winter"*, 34 CLINICAL INFECTIOUS DISEASES 972 (2002). The last TOPOFF exercise was conducted in 2007 to simulate an attack with a "dirty bomb." In 2009, the exercises were renamed National Level Exercises and since 2011, they have concentrated primarily on prepping for a cyber attack.

3.   The Role of tabletop exercises. The Department of Homeland Security seems especially fond of running exercises like TOPOFF and involving the public health community in them. The primary rationale for such exercises is to "educate, train, or develop interorganizational and interjurisdictional relationships." As a committee of the Institute of Medicine has put it: " . . . having partnerships is preferable to working in isolation. Furthermore, some level of organization and coordination is essential to help avoid chaos; rehearsing processes may lead to smoother functioning of complex response systems, and in the event of an emergency, for example, a smallpox attack, having personnel that possess certain knowledge and skills (*e.g.*, smallpox diagnosis, vaccination, and search and containment) is better than having personnel that did not receive such education and training."

Nonetheless, the Committee concluded that "The overall effectiveness of exercises as a preparedness strategy has not been well demonstrated, and research is needed to determine, for example, whether exercises could be considered predictors of successful response, what type of exercise would have the greatest positive influence on preparedness, what exercises are most cost-effective, and the best way to assess opportunity costs posed by conducting exercises." COMMITTEE ON SMALLPOX VACCINATION PROGRAM IMPLEMENTATION, INSTITUTE OF MEDICINE, THE SMALLPOX VACCINATION PROGRAM: PUBLIC HEALTH IN AN AGE OF TERRORISM 308–309 (2005). It is, of course, worth noting that the Secretary of Homeland Security failed to respond to the real emergency of Hurricane Katrina and the subsequent flood in New Orleans because while the city was flooding, Secretary Michael Chertoff was in Atlanta at CDC headquarters playing a tabletop game to prepare for a possible bird flu pandemic.

4. **TOPOFF and the "inclination to quarantine."** Shortly after 9/11, and inspired primarily by TOPOFF 2000, Joseph Barbera and colleagues wrote a major article in which they argued that TOPOFF was a "striking example" of the inclination of federal and state officials to resort to quarantine as a tactic to limit the spread of disease. Joseph Barbera *et al.*, *Large-Scale Quarantine Following Biological Terrorism in the United States*, 186 JAMA 2711 (2001). Recall that quarantine applies to healthy people who have been exposed to a disease and may or may not be infected; isolation involves sick people who are infected and who need treatment but who may or may not be contagious. The authors use history to question the effectiveness of quarantine (not used in the US since World War I) and raise a series of questions that should be considered prior to any consideration of quarantine: (1) do public health and medical analyses warrant large-scale quarantine?; (2) is implementation feasible?; and (3) do the potential benefits outweigh the potential adverse consequences (especially loss of public trust)? Most importantly, effective public health intervention requires precise knowledge of the disease and how it is spread, *e.g.* person to person contact, airborne, blood-borne, or some other way. The method of spread may suggest other interventions that could be more effective than quarantine, such as rapid vaccination, isolation and treatment of the sick, hand washing and use of disposable masks, sheltering in place, limiting public events and even closing public schools. Think about what considerations should go into quarantining a population or a geographic area. Is this the same as declaring martial law in this area? What problems should be anticipated if it is decided to invoke a quarantine, and how should the action be explained to the public? (*See* Part G, *infra.*, on the actions of Toronto during the SARS epidemic.) The authors conclude their article by noting, in an understatement, "The development of strategies for communicating with the public throughout a disease outbreak is of paramount importance . . . . Once public credibility is lost, it will be difficult to recover." *Id.*

5. **Reacting to a fast-spreading disease**. The threat of a fast-spreading infectious disease, whether introduced by terrorists or by Mother Nature, presents unique problems that will be measured not only in terms of the immediate impact

— widespread illness and death — but in terms of long-term social and economic consequences. A fast-spreading disease would quickly exhaust local first-aid and medical resources, and, possibly, even the food and water supply. People would stop reporting to work (and some of those people would have first-response and medical responsibilities). The state and the federal governments may act to support local efforts, but even their resources may be at best only able to contain the spread of the disease. Scenarios involving hundreds or even thousands of casualties are reasonably imaginable.

What would happen then? The result might be a loss of confidence in the ability of the government to govern, possibly even a loss of respect for the rule of law. Most Americans have ambivalent feelings about "big government" intervention, but most Americans also have lived their lives in a world in which they could confidently assume that their government, big or otherwise, could maintain order and resolve virtually any widespread problem. For them, an unchecked epidemic disease would be a unique and potentially unsettling experience.

6. **Are we prepared?** Most commentators agree that Americans need to increase their level of preparation for what appears to be the inevitable: either a naturally created, fast-moving outbreak of an infectious disease, or the release by terrorists of some comparable biological threat. Indeed, "preparedness" seems to be the new buzz word of public health policymaking. But what exactly do we have to do to be *prepared*? Part of the answer may simply be to educate ourselves and overcome the "it can't happen here" complacency that many Americans seem to exhibit, or at least exhibited until the fall of 2001. Other suggestions are more concrete:

— more and more coordinated laboratories to identify diseases and biological agents better and quicker;

— more and better trained staff for state and local health departments;

— better (and more sophisticated) communication among local, state, and federal agencies, between government agencies and private health care providers, and between private providers — even those who normally compete for the same health care business and don't like to talk freely to each other;

— better communication between public health agencies and the mass media;

— better education of private health care workers as to what to do (*e.g.*, identify and report signs of contagious diseases) and what *not* to do (*e.g.*, prescribe antibiotics to patients who are worried about future terrorist attacks).

7. **The Stafford Disaster Assistance and Emergency Relief Act** provides for federal assistance to the states in the cases of natural emergencies and disasters, as in the case of floods or hurricanes. *See* 42 U.S.C. § 5121 *et seq.* Note, however, that Stafford Act assistance is not available in the case of biological or disease-related disasters or emergencies.

Apart from the Stafford Act authority, several federal agencies have statutory authority to act in public health and related emergencies, including the Department of Health and Human Services, the Department of Defense and the Department of the Interior, all generally coordinated through the Department of Homeland Security.

8.   **A "model state act."** Shortly after 9/11 the CDC sponsored a "model state act" to, among other things, make compulsory quarantining and treating Americans during a "public health emergency" easier. The proposal drew widespread comment. Of the proposal, Ken Wing wrote:

> [T]he powers outlined in Articles V and VI of the "model act" have drawn the most public attention and controversy . . . .
>
> The provisions of Articles V and VI only outline the powers that the "model act" would allow the state during a declared emergency. In statutory interpretation, as in so many other things in life, the devil may be found in the details as often as in the broad outlines of an enactment. Words like "reasonable and necessary" and "preponderance of the evidence" carry a lot of legal baggage . . . . We would all be better served with a textual description of what is proposed and, most importantly, some justification for creating what, even in its broad outlines, appears to be a public health version of martial law.
>
> . . . .
>
> What is it that we have learned about the public health risks that we face that would counsel creating this elaborate and draconian apparatus? . . . Why do we need all of what is outlined in the "model act"?
>
> . . . .
>
> It is entirely possible that the most basic assumption underlying the "model act" is flawed. If in fact there is a need for some remedial legislation of the type outlined in the "model act," or, for that matter, any other, it may need to be federal legislation, not state legislation . . . .

Kenneth R. Wing, *Policy Choices and Model Acts: Preparing for the Next Public Health Emergency*, 13 HEALTH MATRIX 71 (2003).

Lawrence Gostin has defended the state-based proposal:

> The question faced is not whether the government should have liberty-limiting authority designed to cope with an attack, but what powers the state should have under what circumstances. American society prizes liberty and freedom, openness and tolerance; these values are part of the national identity and seem sometimes to rise to the level of inviolable tenets. These values, important in their own right, need to be balanced against equally valid values of population health and safety. The task for society is to grant government power in a way that clearly separates the warranted from the unwarranted . . . .
>
> . . . .

My refusal to cede to the primacy of individualism is animated by my concern for public safety in a health emergency. It is important that the government has the authority to act quickly should a bioterrorist attack occur . . . .

Lawrence O. Gostin, *When Terrorism Threatens Health: How Far Are Limitations on Personal and Economic Liberties Justified?* 55 FLA. L. REV. 1105, 1159–69 (2003).

9. Federal v. state power. If and when federal agencies respond to a local or state public health problem, there are myriad legal problems involved in sorting out who can do what and under which circumstances. Americans need to be prepared, but American lawyers need to enhance their level of *legal preparedness* as well.

Laws or legal authorities clearly are the beginning point for public health legal preparedness, just as epidemiology is for outbreak investigation. Laws are the authoritative utterances of public bodies and come in many stripes, among them statutes, ordinances, and judicial rulings as well as the policies of such public bodies as school boards, mosquito control districts, transportation commissions, and land use planning bodies . . . .

Laws, however, are neither self-creating nor self-enforcing. Thus the second core element is the competencies of the people who serve as the agents of public health legal preparedness . . . and private citizens . . . . The third core element is information for these agents' use in shaping and applying public health laws . . . . The fourth core element is coordination of legal authorities across the multiple sectors that bear on public health practice and policy and across the vertical dimension of local-state-federal-international jurisdictions. Coordination is critical precisely because the public health system is richly multidisciplinary, multi-sectoral, and cross-jurisdictional.

Anthony Moulton *et al.*, *What is Public Health Legal Preparedness?* 31 J.L. MED. & ETHICS 672, 674 (2003).

10. The interplay of federal and state authority may be particularly problematic. Any use of federal authority will have to be implemented under some specific federal statute (and not just be based on the existence of some connection to interstate commerce), and may only be triggered, in some cases, by specific presidential declaration. Nor does the invitation of a state, by itself, legitimatize federal action. At least at the agency level, all federal action must derive from some federal statutory foundation.

We have already encountered one example of this, in connection with the CDC's statutory authority to prevent diseases from entering the country and to regulate transmission across state lines, including the power to impose quarantine. *See* Chapter 5, Part C, *supra*, discussing 42 U.S.C. § 264 and its implementing regulations (both existing and proposed). Note that 42 C.F.R. § 70.2 provides for federal intervention when a state or local government's efforts to stop the spread of an infectious disease are inadequate; presumably this would provide some basis for federal action, even without the invitation or consent of a state. In addition, 42 U.S.C. § 243 authorizes CDC to act in concert with state or local public health authorities in matters relating to infectious diseases where the CDC is *requested* to do so.

Even where there is statutory authority for the CDC to act in matters relating to bioterrorism or in a naturally-occurring epidemic, there still may be legal problems associated with federal intervention. The legality of the use of military resources is a particularly problematic (and politically volatile) problem that lawyers should be prepared to address — and, as with all other decisions made in these circumstances — address very quickly. The Posse Comitatus Act, 18 U.S.C. § 1385, is a general prohibition on the use of military forces to enforce domestic criminal laws. Among other things, this would prevent the use of the army or other Department of Defense personnel in the enforcement of state or local isolation or quarantine laws, even if other federal personnel, such as those from the CDC, are involved in the implementation of those activities. The President does have the constitutional authority to authorize the use of military force — essentially declaring martial law. The Insurrection Act, 10 U.S.C. §§ 331–334, also allows the President to authorize the use of military personnel in emergencies. There is also limited authority under 10 U.S.C. § 382 for the Secretary of Defense to extend assistance to the Department of Justice in some bioterrorist emergencies. Otherwise, federal military personnel may have to limit their roles to "support" of other federal agencies and avoid engaging in what could be considered a violation of the Posse Comitatus Act. Prior to Hurricane Katrina, the authority to declare a disaster an "incident of national significance" to trigger a federal response was in the hands of the Secretary of Homeland Security.

Establishing the statutory basis for federal action, of course, is only one step in establishing the legal framework within which federal, state, and local public health agencies can act in concert. A myriad of other legal questions will have to be answered. (For just one example, see 42 U.S.C. § 233, limiting liability for health workers who participate in certain specified smallpox counter-measures.) Moreover, as illustrated in the TOPOFF exercise, some of the most difficult legal decisions will have to be made as part of the rapid implementation of the activities that these statutes and regulations authorize. Simply deciding who can decide certain legal questions will be difficult.

---

2. Overreactions and Misusing Public Health to Promote Fear and a Security Agenda

FLORENCE v. BOARD OF CHOSEN FREEHOLDERS OF THE COUNTY OF BURLINGTON
132 S. Ct. 1510 (2012)

JUSTICE KENNEDY

. . . .

In 1998, seven years before the incidents at issue, petitioner Albert Florence was arrested after fleeing from police officers in Essex County, New Jersey. He was charged with obstruction of justice and use of a deadly weapon. Petitioner entered a plea of guilty to two lesser offenses and was sentenced to pay a fine in monthly installments. In 2003, after he fell behind on his payments and failed to appear at an enforcement hearing, a bench warrant was issued for his arrest. He paid the outstanding balance less than a week later; but, for some unexplained reason, the warrant remained in a statewide computer database. Two years later, in Burlington County, New Jersey, petitioner and his wife were stopped in their automobile by a state trooper. Based on the outstanding warrant in the computer system, the officer arrested petitioner and took him to the Burlington County Detention Center. He was held there for six days and then was transferred to the Essex County Correctional Facility. It is the search process at each jail that gives rise to the claims before the Court.

Burlington County jail procedures required every arrestee to shower with a delousing agent. Officers would check arrestees for scars, marks, gang tattoos, and contraband as they disrobed. Petitioner claims he was also instructed to open his mouth, lift his tongue, hold out his arms, turn around, and lift his genitals. Petitioner shared a cell with at least one other person and interacted with other inmates following his admission to the jail. The Essex County Correctional Facility, where petitioner was taken after six days, is the largest county jail in New Jersey. It admits more than 25,000 inmates each year and houses about 1,000 gang members at any given time. When petitioner was transferred there, all arriving detainees passed through a metal detector and waited in a group holding cell for a more thorough search. When they left the holding cell, they were instructed to remove their clothing while an officer looked for body markings, wounds, and contraband. Apparently without touching the detainees, an officer looked at their ears, nose, mouth, hair, scalp, fingers, hands, arms, armpits, and other body openings. This policy applied regardless of the circumstances of the arrest, the suspected offense, or the detainee's behavior, demeanor, or criminal history. Petitioner alleges he was required to lift his genitals, turn around, and cough in a squatting position as part of the process. After a mandatory shower, during which his clothes were inspected, petitioner was admitted to the facility. He was released the next day, when the charges against him were dismissed.

Petitioner sued the governmental entities that operated the jails, one of the wardens, and certain other defendants. . . .

. . . .

The difficulties of operating a detention center must not be underestimated by the courts. Jails (in the stricter sense of the term, excluding prison facilities) admit more than 13 million inmates a year. The largest facilities process hundreds of people every day; smaller jails may be crowded on weekend nights, after a large police operation, or because of detainees arriving from other jurisdictions. Maintaining safety and order at these institutions requires the expertise of correctional officials, who must have substantial discretion to devise reasonable solutions to the problems they face. The Court has confirmed the importance of deference to correctional officials and explained that a regulation impinging on an inmate's constitutional rights must be upheld "if it is reasonably related to legitimate penological interests."

. . . .

[Our] cases establish that correctional officials must be permitted to devise reasonable search policies to detect and deter the possession of contraband in their facilities. The task of determining whether a policy is reasonably related to legitimate security interests is "peculiarly within the province and professional expertise of corrections officials." This Court has repeated the admonition that, " 'in the absence of substantial evidence in the record to indicate that the officials have exaggerated their response to these considerations courts should ordinarily defer to their expert judgment in such matters.' "

. . . .

Correctional officials have a significant interest in conducting a thorough search as a standard part of the intake process. The admission of inmates creates numerous risks for facility staff, for the existing detainee population, and for a new detainee himself or herself. The danger of introducing lice or contagious infections, for example, is well documented. Persons just arrested may have wounds or other injuries requiring immediate medical attention. It may be difficult to identify and treat these problems until detainees remove their clothes for a visual inspection.

Jails and prisons also face grave threats posed by the increasing number of gang members who go through the intake process. . . . These considerations provide a reasonable basis to justify a visual inspection for certain tattoos and other signs of gang affiliation as part of the intake process. The identification and isolation of gang members before they are admitted protects everyone in the facility. Detecting contraband concealed by new detainees, furthermore, is a most serious responsibility. Weapons, drugs, and alcohol all disrupt the safe operation of a jail.

. . . .

People detained for minor offenses can turn out to be the most devious and dangerous criminals. Hours after the Oklahoma City bombing, Timothy McVeigh was stopped by a state trooper who noticed he was driving without a license plate. Johnston, Suspect Won't Answer Any Questions, N.Y. Times, Apr. 25, 1995, p. A1. Police stopped serial killer Joel Rifkin for the same reason. McQuiston, Confession Used to Portray Rifkin as Methodical Killer, N.Y. Times, Apr. 26, 1994, p. B6. One of the terrorists involved in the September 11 attacks was stopped and ticketed for speeding just two days before hijacking Flight 93. The Terrorists: Hijacker Got a Speeding Ticket, N.Y. Times, Jan. 8, 2002, p. A12. Reasonable correctional officials could conclude these uncertainties mean they must conduct the same thorough search of everyone who will be admitted to their facilities . . . .

. . . .

It also may be difficult, as a practical matter, to classify inmates by their current and prior offenses before the intake search. Jails can be even more dangerous than prisons because officials there know so little about the people they admit at the outset.

. . . .

Petitioner's amici raise concerns about instances of officers engaging in intentional humiliation and other abusive practices. There also may be legitimate concerns about the invasiveness of searches that involve the touching of detainees. These issues are not implicated on the facts of this case, however, and it is unnecessary to consider them here.

JUSTICE BREYER, with whom JUSTICE GINSBURG, JUSTICE SOTOMAYOR, and JUSTICE KAGAN join, dissenting.

A strip search that involves a stranger peering without consent at a naked individual, and in particular at the most private portions of that person's body, is a serious invasion of privacy. We have recently said, in respect to a schoolchild (and a less intrusive search), that the "meaning of such a search, and the degradation its subject may reasonably feel, place a search that intrusive in a category of its own demanding its own specific suspicions." The Courts of Appeals have more directly described the privacy interests at stake, writing, for example, that practices similar to those at issue here are "demeaning, dehumanizing, undignified, humiliating, terrifying, unpleasant, embarrassing, [and] repulsive, signifying degradation and submission." (" '[A]ll courts' " have recognized the " 'severe if not gross interference with a person's privacy' " that accompany visual body cavity searches). Even when carried out in a respectful manner, and even absent any physical touching, such searches are inherently harmful, humiliating, and degrading. And the harm to privacy interests would seem particularly acute where the person searched may well have no expectation of being subject to such a search, say, because she had simply received a traffic ticket for failing to buckle a seatbelt, because he had not previously paid a civil fine, or because she had been arrested for a minor trespass.

In *Atwater v. Lago Vista*, 532 U.S. 318, for example, police arrested a mother driving with her two children because their seat belts were not buckled. This Court held that the Constitution did not forbid an arrest for a minor seatbelt offense. But, in doing so, it pointed out that the woman was held for only an hour (before being taken to a magistrate and released on bond) and that the search — she had to remove her shoes, jewelry, and the contents of her pockets — was not " 'unusually harmful to [her] privacy or . . . physical interests.' " Would this Court have upheld the arrest had the magistrate not been immediately available, had the police housed her overnight in the jail, and had they subjected her to a search of the kind at issue here?

. . . .

The lack of justification is fairly obvious with respect to the first two penological interests advanced. The searches already employed at Essex and Burlington include: (a) pat-frisking all inmates; (b) making inmates go through metal detectors (including the Body Orifice Screening System (BOSS) chair used at Essex County Correctional Facility that identifies metal hidden within the body); (c) making inmates shower and use particular delousing agents or bathing supplies; and (d) searching inmates' clothing. In addition, petitioner concedes that detainees could be lawfully subject to being viewed in their undergarments by jail officers or during

Other procedures we employ [handwritten margin note]

showering (for security purposes). No one here has offered any reason, example, or empirical evidence suggesting the inadequacy of such practices for detecting injuries, diseases, or tattoos. In particular, there is no connection between the genital lift and the "squat and cough" that Florence was allegedly subjected to and health or gang concerns.

The lack of justification for such a strip search is less obvious but no less real in respect to the third interest, namely that of detecting contraband. The information demonstrating the lack of justification is of three kinds. First, there are empirically based conclusions reached in specific cases. The New York Federal District Court, to which I have referred, conducted a study of 23,000 persons admitted to the Orange County correctional facility between 1999 and 2003. These 23,000 persons underwent a strip search of the kind described. Of these 23,000 persons, the court wrote, "the County encountered three incidents of drugs recovered from an inmate's anal cavity and two incidents of drugs falling from an inmate's underwear during the course of a strip search." The court added that in four of these five instances there may have been "reasonable suspicion" to search, leaving only one instance in 23,000 in which the strip search policy "arguably" detected additional contraband. The study is imperfect, for search standards changed during the time it was conducted. But the large number of inmates, the small number of "incidents," and the District Court's own conclusions make the study probative though not conclusive.

Similarly, in _Shain v. Ellison_, 273 F.3d 56, 60 (2d Cir. 2001), the court received data produced by the county jail showing that authorities conducted body-cavity strip searches, similar to those at issue here, of 75,000 new inmates over a period of five years. In 16 instances the searches led to the discovery of contraband. The record further showed that 13 of these 16 pieces of contraband would have been detected in a patdown or a search of shoes and outer-clothing. In the three instances in which contraband was found on the detainee's body or in a body cavity, there was a drug or felony history that would have justified a strip search on individualized reasonable suspicion.

Second, there is the plethora of recommendations of professional bodies, such as correctional associations, that have studied and thoughtfully considered the matter. The American Correctional Association (ACA) — an association that informs our view of "what is obtainable and what is acceptable in corrections philosophy," has promulgated a standard that forbids suspicionless strip searches. A standard desk reference for general information about sound correctional practices advises against suspicionless strip searches.

Moreover, many correctional facilities apply a reasonable suspicion standard before strip searching inmates entering the general jail population, including the U.S. Marshals Service, the Immigration and Customs Service, and the Bureau of Indian Affairs. The Federal Bureau of Prisons (BOP) itself forbids suspicionless strip searches for minor offenders, though it houses separately (and does not admit to the general jail population) a person who does not consent to such a search . . . .

Nor do I find the majority's lack of examples surprising. After all, those arrested for minor offenses are often stopped and arrested unexpectedly. And they consequently will have had little opportunity to hide things in their body cavities. Thus, the widespread advocacy by prison experts and the widespread application in many States and federal circuits of "reasonable suspicion" requirements indicates an ability to apply such standards in practice without unduly interfering with the legitimate penal interest in preventing the smuggling of contraband.

NOTES AND QUESTIONS

11. Searches in America. Since 9/11 all Americans who want to board an airplane can be subject to pat downs, virtual strip searches, and with suspicion, real strip searches. These searches all have the same rationale: safety. So on one level, even though not consensual in any way, routine strip searches in jails and prisons may not seem out of the ordinary any longer.

12. Using a public health rationale. Kennedy's first rational is a public health one, the "health of the prisoners," and he lists dangers of bringing in and transmitting lice and infections (including MRSA). Do you find this persuasive or just a pretense? He also accepts a medical rationale: "Persons just arrested may have wounds or other injuries requiring immediate medical attention . . . ."

13. 9/11 and strip searches. Most remarkably, however, Kennedy goes out of his way to discuss two terrorist examples — examples **not** mentioned in any of the briefs, oral argument, or by any of the other Justices: Timothy McVeigh and one of the 9/11 bombers. Both were stopped for traffic violations — McVeigh was arrested because he had a gun; the suicide bomber was given a traffic ticket and sent on his way. Neither had anything to do with strip searches or the reasonableness of a search. They seem to have been included simply to bolster Kennedy's belief that it's a dangerous world out there with dangerous people, and even those who are arrested for a traffic offense could be deadly to prison guards.

14. Physicians as prison guards. It has been argued that the Court's conflation of "strip searches by prison guards with a medical screening examination by a physician or other health care personnel for the health of the person and other prisoners . . . is deeply disturbing in itself, but even more so in that the Court uses it not to promote medicine or public health but rather to endorse the legitimacy of routine strip searches by prison guards." The argument continues by noting that two medical organizations wrote briefs arguing that strip searches "threaten serious and lasting psychological harm and are a fundamental attack on a person's privacy and dignity" and that they are ineffective to detect MRSA. As for the public health rationale, "Routine strip searches will not make jails or prisons safer or healthier. Real public health screening and decent medical care should support, instead of undermine, basic civil and human rights." George J. Annas, *Strip Searches in the Supreme Court — Prisons and Public Health*, 367 NEW ENGL. J. MED. 1653, 1656 (2013).

D. INFLUENZA

In the following excerpt, historian John Barry describes the experience of Paul Lewis, a Navy physician scientist in Philadelphia asked to diagnose sailors taken ill with what turned out to be influenza (often called "Spanish Flu") in September 1918.

JOHN M. BARRY, THE GREAT INFLUENZA: THE EPIC STORY OF THE DEADLIEST PLAGUE IN HISTORY
2–5 (2004)

. . . The blood that covered so many of them did not come from wounds, at least not from steel or explosives that had torn away limbs. Most of the blood had come from nosebleeds. A few sailors had coughed the blood up. Others had bled from their ears. Some coughed so hard that autopsies would later show they had torn apart abdominal muscles and rib cartilage. And many of the men writhed in agony or delirium; nearly all those able to communicate complained of headache, as if someone were hammering a wedge into their skulls just behind the eyes, and body aches so intense they felt like bones breaking. A few were vomiting. Finally the skin of some of the sailors had turned unusual colors; some showed just a tinge of blue around their lips or finger-tips, but a few looked so dark one could not tell easily if they were Caucasian or Negro . . . .

. . . .

[W]hatever was attacking these sailors was not only spreading, it was spreading explosively.

And it was spreading despite a well-planned, concerted effort to contain it. This same disease had erupted ten days earlier at a navy facility in Boston . . . .

. . . .

Philadelphia navy authorities had taken [Milton] Rosenau's warnings seriously, especially since a detachment of sailors had just arrived from Boston, and they had made preparations to isolate any ill sailors should an outbreak occur. They had been confident that isolation would control it.

Yet four days after the Boston detachment arrived, nineteen sailors in Philadelphia were hospitalized with what looked like the same disease. Despite their immediate isolation and that of everyone with whom they had had contract, eighty-seven sailors were hospitalized the next day. They and their contacts were again isolated. But two days later, six hundred men were hospitalized with this strange disease. The hospital ran out of empty beds, and hospital staff began falling ill . . . . Meanwhile, [navy] personnel from Boston, and now Philadelphia, had been and were being sent throughout the country as well.

. . . .

. . . In 1918 an <u>influenza virus</u> emerged — probably in the United States — that would spread around the world . . . . Before that world-wide pandemic faded away in 1920, it would kill more people than any other outbreak of disease in human history. Plague in the 1300's killed a far larger proportion of the population — more than one-quarter of Europe — but in raw numbers influenza killed more than plague then, more than AIDS today.

The lowest estimate of the pandemic's worldwide death toll is twenty-one million, in a world with a population less than one-third today's. That estimate comes from a contemporary study of the disease and newspapers have often cited it since, but it is almost certainly wrong. Epidemiologists today estimate that influenza likely caused at least fifty million deaths worldwide, and possibly as many as one hundred million.

. . . Normally influenza chiefly kills the elderly and infants, but in the 1918 pandemic roughly half of those who died were young men and women in the prime of their life, in their twenties and thirties . . . .

. . . .

. . . Although the influenza pandemic stretched over two years, perhaps two thirds of the deaths occurred in a period of twenty-four weeks, and more than half of those deaths occurred in even less time, from mid-September to early December 1918. Influenza killed more people in a year than the Black Death of the Middle Ages killed in a century; it killed more people in twenty-four weeks than AIDS has killed in twenty-four years.

. . . .

Yet the story of the 1918 influenza virus is not simply one of havoc, death, and desolation, of a society fighting a war against nature superimposed on a war against another human society.

. . . .

For the influenza pandemic that erupted in 1918 was the first great collision between nature and modern science. It was the first great collision between a natural force and a society that included individuals who refused either to submit to that force or to simply call upon divine intervention to save themselves from it, individuals who instead were determined to confront this force directly, with a developing technology and with their minds.

DEPARTMENT OF HEALTH AND HUMAN SERVICES
PANDEMIC INFLUENZA PLAN
17–21, 32 (November 2005)

Emergence of a human influenza virus with pandemic potential presents a formidable response challenge. If such a strain emerged in one or a few isolated communities abroad or within the U.S. and was detected quickly, containment of the outbreak(s), though very difficult, might be feasible, thereby preventing or significantly retarding the spread of disease to other communities. Containment attempts would require stringent infection-control measures such as bans on large public gatherings, isolation of symptomatic individuals, prophylaxis of the entire community with antiviral drugs, and various forms of movement restrictions possibly even including a quarantine.

The resources required for such vigorous containment would almost certainly exceed those available in the affected communities. Thus, if a containment attempt is to have a chance of succeeding, the response must employ the assets of multiple partners in a well-coordinated way. For isolated outbreaks outside the U.S., this means effective multinational cooperation in executing containment protocols designed and exercised well in advance. For isolated outbreaks within the U.S., this would require effective integration of the response assets of local, state, and federal governments and those of the private sector.

The National Response Plan (NRP), based on the principles of incident management, provides an appropriate conceptual and operational framework for a multi-party response to an outbreak of a potential influenza pandemic in one or a few U.S. communities. In particular, the NRP is designed to engage the response assets of multiple public and private partners and bring them to bear in a coordinated way at one or a few incident sites.

If efforts to contain isolated outbreaks within the U.S. were unsuccessful, and influenza spread quickly to affect many more communities either simultaneously or in quick succession — the hallmark of a pandemic — response assets at all levels of government and the private sector would be taxed severely. Communities would need to direct all their influenza response assets to their own needs and would have little to spare for the needs of others. Moreover, as the number of affected communities grows, their collective need would spread the response assets of states and the federal government ever thinner. In the extreme, until a vaccine against the pandemic virus would become available in sufficient quantity to have a significant impact on protecting public health, thousands of communities could be countering influenza simultaneously with little or no assistance from adjacent communities, the state, or the federal government. Preparedness planning for pandemic influenza response must take this prospect into account.

Planning Assumptions

Pandemic preparedness planning is based on assumptions regarding the evolution and impacts of a pandemic. Defining the potential magnitude of a pandemic is difficult because of the large differences in severity for the three 20th century pandemics. While the 1918 pandemic resulted in an estimated 500,000 deaths in the U.S., the 1968 pandemic caused an estimated 34,000 U.S. deaths. This difference is largely related to the severity of infections and the virulence of the influenza viruses that caused the pandemics. The 20th century pandemics have also shared similar characteristics. In each pandemic, about 30% of the U.S. population developed illness, with about half seeking medical care. Children have tended to have the highest rates of illness, though not of severe disease and death. Geographical spread in each pandemic was rapid and virtually all communities experienced outbreaks.

Pandemic planning is based on the following assumptions about pandemic disease:

- Susceptibility to the pandemic influenza subtype will be universal.

• The clinical disease attack rate will be 30% in the overall population. Illness rates will be highest among school-aged children (about 40%) and decline with age. Among working adults, an average of 20% will become ill during a community outbreak.

• Of those who become ill with influenza, 50% will seek outpatient medical care.

• The number of hospitalizations and deaths will depend on the virulence of the pandemic virus. Estimates differ about 10-fold between more and less severe scenarios. Because the virulence of the influenza virus that causes the next pandemic cannot be predicted, two scenarios are presented based on extrapolation of past pandemic experience (Table 1).

• Risk groups for severe and fatal infections cannot be predicted with certainty. During annual fall and winter influenza season, infants and the elderly, persons with chronic illnesses, and pregnant women are usually at higher risk of complications from influenza infections. In contrast, in the 1918 pandemic, most deaths occurred among young, previously healthy adults.

• The typical incubation period (the time between acquiring the infection until becoming ill) for influenza averages two days. We assume this would be the same for a novel strain that is transmitted between people by respiratory secretions.

• Persons who become ill may shed virus and can transmit infection for one-half to one day before the onset of illness. Viral shedding and the risk for transmission will be greatest during the first two days of illness. Children will shed the greatest amount of virus and, therefore, are likely to pose the greatest risk for transmission.

Table 1. Number of Episodes of Illness, Healthcare Utilization, and Deaths Associated with Moderate and Severe Pandemic Influenza Scenarios

Characteristic	Moderate (1957/68-like)	Severe (1918-like)
Illness	90 million (30%)	90 million (30%)
Outpatient Medical care	45 million (50%)	45 million (50%)
Hospitalization	865,000	9,900,000
ICU care	128,750	1,485,000
Mechanical ventilation	64,875	742,500
Deaths	209,000	1,983,000

• On average, about two secondary infections will occur as a result of transmission from someone who is ill. Some estimates from past pandemics have been higher, with up to about three secondary infections per primary case.

• In an affected community, a pandemic outbreak will last about six to eight weeks. At least two pandemic disease waves are likely. Following the pandemic, the new viral subtype is likely to continue circulating and to contribute to seasonal influenza.

• The seasonality of a pandemic cannot be predicted with certainty. The largest waves in the U.S. during 20th century pandemics occurred in the fall and winter. Experience from the 1957 pandemic may be instructive in that the first U.S. cases occurred in June, but no community outbreaks occurred until August, and the first wave of illness peaked in October.

Doctrine for a Pandemic Influenza Response

HHS will be guided by the following principles in initiating and directing its response activities:

1. In advance of an influenza pandemic, HHS will work with federal, state, and local government partners and the private sector to coordinate pandemic influenza preparedness activities and to achieve interoperable response capabilities.

2. In advance of an influenza pandemic, HHS will encourage all Americans to be active partners in preparing their states, local communities, workplaces, and homes for pandemic influenza and will emphasize that a pandemic will require Americans to make difficult choices. An informed and responsive public is essential to minimizing the health effects of a pandemic and the resulting consequences to society.

3. In advance of an influenza pandemic, HHS, in concert with federal partners, will work with the pharmaceutical industry to develop domestic vaccine production capacity sufficient to provide vaccine for the entire U.S. population as soon as possible after the onset of a pandemic and, during the pre-pandemic period, to produce up to 20 million courses of vaccine against each circulating influenza virus with pandemic potential and to expand seasonal influenza domestic vaccine production to cover all Americans for whom vaccine is recommended through normal commercial transactions.

4. In advance of an influenza pandemic, HHS, in concert with federal partners and in collaborations with the States, will procure sufficient quantities of antiviral drugs to treat 25% of the U.S. population and, in so doing, stimulate development of expanded domestic production capacity sufficient to accommodate subsequent needs through normal commercial transactions. HHS will stockpile antiviral medications in the Strategic National Stockpile, and states will create and maintain local stockpiles.

5. Sustained human-to-human transmission anywhere in the world will be the triggering event to initiate a pandemic response by the United States. Because we live in a global community, a human outbreak anywhere means risk everywhere.

6. The U.S. will attempt to prevent an influenza pandemic or delay its emergence by striving to arrest isolated outbreaks of a novel influenza wherever circumstances suggest that such an attempt might be successful, acting in concert with WHO and other nations as appropriate. At the core of this strategy will be basic public health

measures to reduce person-to-person transmission.

7. At the onset of an influenza pandemic, HHS, in concert with federal partners, will work with the pharmaceutical industry to procure vaccine directed against the pandemic strain and to distribute vaccine to state and local public health departments for pre-determined priority groups based on pre-approved state plans.

8. At the onset of an influenza pandemic, HHS, in collaboration with the states, will begin to distribute and deliver antiviral drugs from public stockpiles to healthcare facilities and others with direct patient care responsibility for administration to pre-determined priority groups . . . .

HHS Actions for Pandemic Influenza Preparedness and Response

HHS will follow the WHO published guidance for national pandemic planning, which defines pandemic activities in six phases. WHO Phases 1 and 2 are the Interpandemic Period, which includes phases where no new influenza virus subtypes have been detected in humans.

The Pandemic Alert Period includes a phase when human infection with a novel influenza strain has been identified, but no evidence has been found of transmission between people or, at most, rare instances of spread to a close contact (WHO Phase 3), and includes phases where person-to-person transmission is occurring in clusters with limited human-to-human transmission (WHO Phases 4 and 5). WHO Phase 6 is the Pandemic Period, in which there is increased and sustained transmission in the general population . . . .

Each pandemic phase is associated with a range of preparedness and response activities directed by the Secretary of Health and Human Services, after consultation with international authorities and others, as necessary. Given that an influenza pandemic may not unfold in a completely predictable way, decision-makers must regularly reassess their strategies and actions and make adjustments as necessary . . . .

NOTES AND QUESTIONS

1. **Outbreaks of influenza** can present a major public health problem even if they do not appear as "pandemics." In the United States, cases of "the flu" generally start appearing in late fall and continue through the winter. During a typical year, more than 36,000 Americans will die and over 100,000 will be hospitalized. The risk is particularly high for people over the age of 65, people with chronic heart or lung diseases, people with metabolic diseases, people with impaired immune systems, and children under the age of two. Vaccination is the major public health strategy for limiting the incidence and spread of influenza.

2. **Influenza viruses are grouped into three types:** A, B, and C. Humans can be infected with all three types, but type A is the most common and causes more severe illness. Influenza A viruses are further divided into subtypes or strains on the basis of the number of their protein components, hemagglutinin (H) and neuramini-

dase (N). The 1918 epidemic was caused by influenza A (H1N1). Less severe pandemics occurred in 1957 and 1968 (influenza A (H3N2)). The influenza virus constantly changes the structure of its H and N proteins, because it lacks a "proofreading" mechanism that can repair mutations in replicating its genetic material. This change is called "antigenic drift," and is responsible for annual variations in the influenza that appears in winter seasons around the world. Influenza vaccines must take antigenic drift into account, so vaccine producers try to predict what subtype of influenza is likely to appear each year. Most annual changes are relatively minor, so that vaccines remain relatively effective against any unexpected variation. However, every 10 to 40 years, the virus mutates so dramatically that the human immune system does not recognize it and existing vaccines offer little protection. Such a virus can cause a pandemic — an epidemic that spreads to several countries. This happened with the influenza pandemic in 1918, which claimed more lives than both World Wars, the Korean War, and the Vietnam War combined. Sarah F. Fujimura, *The Purple Death: The Great Flu of 1918*, 8 PERSPECTIVES IN HEALTH MAG., 28, 30 (2003).

We have had one notorious experience with governmental planning for influenza — the so-called "swine flu" epidemic of 1976. Swine flu was expected to be especially serious, and the federal government took the lead in educating the public and attempting (unsuccessfully) to vaccinate the entire population of the country, along with other preventive steps. The flu that year turned out to be nothing particularly hazardous, resulting in a loss of credibility for public health and some presumably-unnecessary morbidity and mortality arising from the widespread vaccination that was in fact achieved (more than 10 million people in 2.5 months). For the authoritative account — which is thorough, fascinating, and illuminating — see RICHARD E. NEUSTADT & HARVEY V. FINEBERG, THE EPIDEMIC THAT NEVER WAS: POLICY-MAKING & THE SWINE FLU AFFAIR (1983).

3. Novel strains of influenza. As described by the material in this Part, the possibility that a new strain of the influenza will emerge creates the threat of a pandemic in the United States, one that could cause many times more deaths, straining both public and private resources, and raising the possibility that more draconian measures might be required to limit the spread of influenza through the population. The "bird" flu (officially identified as H5N1 avian flu virus) represents a prime example, one which has garnered considerable attention over the past couple of years.

In August 2009, the President's Council of Advisors on Science and Technology issued a "Report to the President on U.S. Preparations for 2009-H1N1 Influenza." Perhaps the most important point this report made is that we should not plan based on "worst case scenarios" but based on most likely scenarios. The report made specific reference to what is now known as the 1976 Swine Flu "fiasco" noting that federal response was premised "only on the 'worst case' scenario which ended up being a false alarm." In retrospect the Council noted, "The key policy error in 1976 was to bundle all decisions (*e.g.*, make the vaccine, immunize everyone, make a Presidential announcement) into a single 'go' or 'no-go' decision, with no provision for the monitoring of the situation and continual reconsideration of policy directions based on new evidence." (*Id.* at 9.)

4. Plans and checklists. Mostly we have plans and checklists rather than resources to deal with a potential flu pandemic. But we are nonetheless better off than when President Bush first discussed his reaction to a flu pandemic in the fall of 2005. He suggested that Congress should consider empowering the military to be the "first responders" in any national disaster. Later, the president suggested that the U.S. should confront the risk of a bird flu pandemic by giving him the power to use the U.S. military to quarantine "part[s] of the country" experiencing an "outbreak." Bush said he got the idea by reading John Barry's excellent account of the 1918 Spanish flu pandemic, THE GREAT INFLUENZA, which opened this Part. Although quarantine was only used successfully in that pandemic once, on the island of American Samoa, Barry in his afterword suggests (sensibly) that we need a national plan to deal with a future influenza pandemic. Barry has also said that his other suggestions were only ones that he hoped public health officials and ethicists would consider — but they do read like policy recommendations to some, and apparently including the president. He wrote, for example, "if there is any chance to limit the geographical spread of the disease, officials must have in place the legal power to take extreme quarantine measures." And this recommendation comes shortly after his praise for countries that "moved rapidly and ruthlessly to quarantine and isolate anyone with or exposed to" SARS. In response to the Bush "plan," George Annas wrote an op/ed in the *Boston Globe*:

> Planning makes sense. But planning for "brutal" or "extreme" quarantine of large numbers of people or of areas of the United States makes no sense, and actually creates many more problems than it could possibly solve. First, historically mass quarantines of healthy people who may have been exposed to a pathogen have never worked to control a pandemic, and have almost always done more harm than good because they usually involve vicious discrimination against classes of people who are seen as "diseased" and dangerous. Second, the notion that ruthless quarantine was responsible for preventing a SARS pandemic is a public health myth.
>
> . . . .
>
> Sick people should be treated, but we don't need the military to force treatment. Even in extremes like the anthrax attacks, people seek out and demand treatment. Sending soldiers to quarantine large numbers of people is most likely to create panic, and cause people to flee (and spread disease), as it did in China where a rumor during the SARS epidemic that Beijing would be quarantined led to 250,000 people fleeing the city that night. Not only can't we evacuate Houston [during Hurricane Rita], we cannot realistically quarantine its citizens. The real public health challenge will be shortages of health care personnel, hospital beds, and medicine. Plans to militarize quarantine miss the point in a pandemic. The enemy is not sick or exposed Americans — it is the virus itself. And effective action against any flu virus demands its early identification, and the quick development, manufacture, and distribution of a vaccine and treatment modalities.

George J. Annas, Op/Ed, BOSTON GLOBE, Oct. 8, 2005, at A15.

5. John Warner National Defense Authorization Act. Years after Katrina, and the confusion about authority to call on the U.S. military to respond not only to emergencies such as floods, but also to public health emergencies such as a pandemic flu, the President signed the John Warner National Defense Authorization Act of 2007 on October 17, 2006. Included in the Act is the following amendment to Section 333 of Title 10 (U.S.C.):

(a)   USE OF ARMED FORCES IN MAJOR PUBLIC EMERGENCIES

(1) The President may employ the armed forces, including the National Guard in Federal service, to —

(A) restore public order and enforce the laws of the United States when, as a result of natural disaster, epidemic, or other serious public health emergency, terrorist attack, or incident, or other condition in any State or possession of the United States, the President determines that—

(i) domestic violence has occurred to such an extent that the constituted authorities of the State or possession are incapable of maintaining public order; and

(ii) such violence results in a condition described in paragraph (2); or

(B) suppress, in a State, any insurrection, domestic violence, unlawful combination, or conspiracy results in a condition described in paragraph (2).

(2) A condition described in the paragraph is a condition that—

(A) so hinders the execution of the laws of a State or possession, as applicable, and of the United States within that State or possession, that any part or class of its people is deprived of a right, privilege, immunity, or protection named in the Constitution and secured by law, and the constituted authorities of the State or possession are unable, fail, or refuse to protect that right, privilege, or immunity, or to give that protection; or

(B) opposes or obstructs the execution of the laws of the United States or impedes the course of justice under those laws.

(3) In any situation covered by paragraph (1)(B), the State shall be considered to have denied the equal protection of the laws secured by the Constitution.

This legislation passed Congress with virtually no debate and no public attention or comment. Nonetheless, Senator Edward Kennedy did applaud Senator Warner for the law on the floor of the Senate, saying that the authority of the President to use the military inside the U.S. needed to be clarified: "Late August last year, New Orleans and gulf coast residents saw the devastation nature can sow. We are now in another hurricane season. Communicable disease like SARS and avian flu are still real risks. No one needs reminding that bin Laden and al Qaeda are still are still out there. We need to clarify the applicability of this law to modern problems." Cong. Rec., Sept. 29, 2006, S108060. In 2008, these provisions were repealed in their entirety. Are we better off or worse off without this law? How are terrorism, natural disaster, insurrections, and epidemics alike? How are they different?

PANDEMIC PREPAREDNESS: PROTECTING PUBLIC HEALTH AND CIVIL LIBERTIES
George J. Annas, Wendy K. Mariner & Wendy Parmet
(A report prepared for the American Civil Liberties Union, 2008)

Members of the public are first responders and outbreak managers, too.

Disaster and epidemics are big shocking events that require the judgment, effort, and courage of many people, not just authorities. Research shows that family, friends, coworkers, neighbors, and total strangers often conduct search and rescue activities and provide medical aid before police, fire, and other officials arrive. During epidemics, volunteers have helped run mass vaccination clinics, nurse home-bound patients, support the sick and their families . . . .

Stockpiling in case of an emergency is both too much and too little to ask of Americans . . . realistic planning entails much more than a list of things people should buy to protect themselves. Officials need to work with citizens and community-based organizations before disaster strikes to promote all the ways the public can contribute to preparedness, including taking part in policy decisions, building more robust volunteer networks, and obtaining support for tax or bond measures that help reduce vulnerability and improve health and safety agencies. American ideals about self-sufficiency can inadvertently stymie preparedness by undervaluing the benefits of mutual aid.

In short, plans that promote and rely on a law enforcement/national security model that assumes effective responses are a function of harsh police actions will likely fail to protect the public's health and needlessly trample civil liberties. Plans that democratically engage the community and rely on voluntary actions, including funding research for new drugs and vaccines, are the most likely to succeed.

RECOMMENDATIONS

Both history and current events demonstrate the need for a new, positive paradigm for pandemic preparedness, one that harnesses the talents of all Americans to take effective action to protect the health of all, instead of punishing those who fall ill. This new paradigm should be based on four fundamental principles: Health, Justice, Transparency, and Accountability.

A. GENERAL PRINCIPLES

1. Health. *The goal of preparing for a pandemic is to protect the lives and health of all people in America, not law enforcement or national security.*

A pandemic, no matter how it might be caused, threatens the lives and health of our most valuable asset — our people. Protecting the people's lives and health requires public health measures that effectively limit the spread of disease and provide the resources necessary for survival and health protection. Threats to health will not be limited to a contagious disease, but will include losses of resources necessary for health and survival, such as safe food, water, and shelter, income, communications, as well as medications. In contrast to law enforcement and national security measures, which are designed to punish criminal offenses or acts of war, a public health approach to preparedness rightly focuses on preventing illness, rather than punishing people who are ill. This approach recognizes the need for a robust and well-funded public health system that can keep communities healthy all of the time, not only during a so-called emergency. Moreover, it requires that all individuals have access to affordable health care when they need it. A public health approach treats everyone in the population as deserving of protection, not as the source of disaster.

2. Justice. *Preparation for a potential pandemic (or any disaster) should ensure a fair distribution of the benefits and burdens of precautions and responses and equal respect for the dignity and autonomy of each individual.*

In a democracy based on the rule of law, principles of justice govern the response to disasters, as well as ordinary circumstances. Everyone in the United States should have an equal opportunity for protection against disaster, regardless of existing circumstances. Historically, epidemics and natural disasters have caused substantially more illness and death among people who were already disadvantaged because of social, economic, or medical conditions. Justice requires that people who are unable to protect themselves be provided with the means necessary to do so before disaster strikes. Preparations for emergencies should never be biased against the most vulnerable, but should compensate for resources that are lacking.

3. Transparency. *Pandemic preparedness requires transparent communication of accurate information among all levels of government and the public in order to warrant public trust.*

A healthy democracy depends upon mutual trust between government and the people. Individuals who trust the government to protect their liberties are more likely to trust government to protect their lives and health. Distrust engenders resistance. Similarly, a democratic government should trust its people to respond positively in an emergency. Private individuals are the immediate first responders in an emergency and ordinarily the best judges of their own resources and needs. Civic engagement harnesses the problem-solving talents of individuals, organizations and networks to develop plans for emergencies; and people participate more freely and efficiently in plans they help formulate and implement. The more government officials try to control events, the more they will be blamed for not preventing disasters or for the inevitable mistakes in responding. Transparency is an essential prerequisite for gaining public trust. People are more likely to cooperate with reasonable requests when they are confident that government officials are being honest about the probabilities of risk and outcomes, and are willing to acknowledge uncertainty and admit mistakes.

4. Accountability. *Everyone, including private individuals and organizations and* *government agencies and officials, should be accountable for their actions before, during and after an emergency.*

The rule of law demands protection of rights and duties, even when they are most unpopular. The prospect of accountability is often the only check on temptations to act unjustly during emergencies. The more latitude government officials are granted during emergencies, the more important it is to hold them accountable for significant errors, arbitrary actions and abuses of power.

B. Specific Recommendations

These four general principles are the foundation for the following more specific recommendations concerning measures to prepare for a pandemic.

Protecting Health

1. The government should ensure stockpiling and fair and efficient distribution of vaccines, medications, food, water, and other necessaries in the event of a pandemic.

2. Distribution and rationing decisions for vaccination and treatment should be based on the goal of minimizing the detrimental health effects of the pandemic.

3. Rationing schemes for vaccination and treatment must not be based on race, color, ethnicity, national origin, religion, gender or sexual orientation and can be based on age or disability only if there is good reason to believe particular groups are either at much higher risk of death or have a much higher likelihood of spreading the disease if not vaccinated or treated.

4. Access to vaccination or treatment should not be conditioned on a waiver of one's constitutional rights.

5. The government and the private sector should encourage and support the development of rapid, accurate diagnostic tests for infectious diseases that reduce the possibility for error in identifying individuals who have a dangerous contagious disease.

6. Non-emergency programs to protect the public's health should be supported in order to develop and preserve a healthy population that can optimally survive emergencies.

7. Government plans for responding to a pandemic should be based on the concept of community engagement, rather than individual responsibility.

Protecting Privacy

8. Disease surveillance generally should be conducted using methods, such as syndromic surveillance, that do not require the use of individual names without the individual's consent. Compulsory reports of names and other individually identifiable patient information should be limited to cases in which a person with a contagious disease poses a credible threat of exposing others to infection and an authorized government agency expects to interview the person in order to investigate the outbreak.

9. Mandatory reporting laws should specify procedures for keeping identifiable information strictly confidential and secure (including audit trail) and penalties for failure to maintain confidentiality.

10. Government agencies that legitimately receive identifiable information should not use any identifiable information for purposes other than investigating potential disease outbreaks without the individual's prior authorization.

11. Data collected for purposes of investigating or monitoring the incidence or prevalence of diseases should not be linked with other data that would permit identifying the individual.

12. Federal agencies should not condition funding on the existence of state laws requiring patient names or other PII to be reported to any state or federal agency or private entity.

Protecting Liberty

13. In a pandemic, governments should rely primarily on voluntary social distancing measures, including school closings and voluntary home quarantines, in preference to mandatory quarantines. In order to improve the effectiveness of voluntary social distancing measures, governments should enact laws to protect the jobs and income of people who stay at home, or whose workplaces are closed, under the advice of medical or public health personnel.

14. Governments should ensure that individuals who follow public health advice and stay at home during a pandemic receive food, medicine, and all other necessities.

15. Coercive measures should be imposed only when there is a sound scientific basis for so doing and only when they are the least restrictive alternative and are imposed in the least restrictive manner.

16. Public health measures should not disproportionately burden vulnerable individuals. Coercive measures should never be applied on the basis of race, color, ethnicity, national origin, religion, gender, alienage, sexual orientation, age, or disability.

17. Individuals who are proposed for detention should be provided with counsel and an expeditious judicial hearing to ensure that their detention is in fact legally justified. The government should bear the burden to demonstrate by clear and convincing evidence that the detained individual poses a significant risk of danger to others and that that risk cannot be mitigated by less restrictive measures. Individuals who are detained should be housed in a medical facility, never in a correctional facility,

18. Travel bans should only be imposed when there is a reasonable scientific justification and only to the degree necessary to prevent the spread of disease.

19. Public health-related travel restrictions should never be based on race, color, ethnicity, national origin, religion, gender, alienage, sexual orientation, age or disability.

20. Individuals who are denied the right to travel because they are deemed to be of

high risk should be provided procedural due process, including notice, the right to counsel, and the opportunity to be heard before an independent decision maker.

21. Invasive medical examinations, even at the border, should only be conducted when there is reasonable suspicion of pandemic disease, and only with the individual's informed consent.

Protecting Democracy

22. All public and private entities should remain accountable for their actions in accordance with the law and should not be relieved of liability for gross negligence, recklessness, arbitrary and capricious action, abuse of power, or criminal offenses.

23. Every effort should be made to preserve the operation of the judicial system and to protect the lives and health of judges and personnel needed to ensure the rule of law.

24. Government should provide clear, accurate, and timely information to the public and honestly report uncertainties in the available information.

NOTES AND QUESTIONS

6. **The anthrax attacks.** Less than a month after 9/11, a man was confirmed to be suffering from anthrax. The source was unknown, and a major national attempt was launched to identify it. Within two weeks, additional cases were linked to letters that contained anthrax and were delivered to the U.S. Capitol and New York news workers. In late October, four postal workers at the Brentwood post office (the District of Columbia processing center) were hospitalized with anthrax. A description of the events is in Elin Gursky *et al.*, *Anthrax 2001: Observations on the Medical and Public Health Response*, 1 BIOSECURITY & BIOTERRORISM 97 (2003).

Confusion and contention surrounded both CDC's authority to mandate specific public health actions and state public health officials' responsibility to act on their own best judgments. Noted one state public health official, "We relied on CDC as a consultant. They gave us guidance and knowledge, but we used our own instincts. [We concluded that], if the environment had one spore, you are exposed . . . . A representative of the postal workers noted, "The information [from CDC] changed every day. Nobody knew what was going on."

7. **Anthrax lessons.** Gursky and colleagues drew the following conclusions from the anthrax confusion: (1) Expectations about federal, state, and local public health responsibilities require clarification; (2) Medical preparedness requires better communication among physicians and between medical and public health communities; (3) The public and the medical community must recognize that response to bioterror attacks will evolve based on changing circumstances and new information; (4) Health officials must prepare to handle the media storm; and (5) Public health resources are barely adequate for a small-scale bioterror attack. Gursky *et al.*, *supra*, at 107–09. It is worth noting that this report identified no legal obstacles to public health response and recommended no changes in local, state, or

federal law to enhance public health preparedness. Was this omission a mistake? Could specific legal changes have improved the quality of public health response to the anthrax mailings? If so, what changes would you recommend? Of course, the most critical pieces of information were scientific facts, such as how anthrax is spread. On the other hand, in an emergency there will never be time to obtain all the scientific facts before acting.

The authors conclude:

> It will take considerable vision and leadership — and sustained funding — to build the medical and public health systems needed to appreciably improve the nation's capacity to mitigate the consequences of bioterrorist attacks. *Id.* at 110.

8. **Anthrax vaccine.** A vaccine has been approved for use to prevent cutaneous anthrax and was mandatorily given to the troops in the Gulf War on the basis that it was an approved agent that could be given for an unapproved but closely-related use (inhalation anthrax). This vaccine was developed in 1970. After the Gulf War, DOD signed a sole source contract with a new company, Bioport, to produce anthrax vaccine. In 1998 Secretary of Defense William Cohen ordered that all active duty troops be given the anthrax vaccine, which was to be delivered in a series of six injections over an 18 month period. Some soldiers refused and challenged the orders, arguing that the vaccine was experimental and thus could not be given without informed consent. Many of them were court-martialed. Anthrax vaccination was halted in 2001 when supplies ran out and the sole-source company was shut down by the FDA for failure to maintain proper manufacturing standards. Production and military vaccination resumed in 2002. There is no evidence of any military personnel or installation ever being attacked by anthrax anywhere in the world.

The bioterrorist anthrax attacks in the U.S. were on civilians, none of whom had been vaccinated. The recommended course of treatment for exposure to anthrax is 60 days of antibiotics, and antibiotics were made available to the 10,000 people potentially exposed. The anthrax vaccine was not available to civilians in October or November. In late December 2001, however, DOD agreed to supply sufficient vaccine to vaccinate the 10,000 exposed civilians. Of the 10,000 people eligible for the vaccine, only 152 eventually took it. Since the anthrax vaccine was an investigational drug when used for post-exposure inhalation anthrax, it could only be used in the context of a clinical trial, and then only with the informed consent of the subjects.

The FDA and CDC designed a consent form, together with a counseling process, for use in obtaining the consent of the exposed civilians to participate in the research project. Unlike the case of the military in the Gulf War, or even the peacetime military with the anthrax vaccine, in which the government required soldiers to be vaccinated, the choice was left entirely to individuals. Government officials did not even make a recommendation as to what they thought any individual should do. D.A. Henderson, the chief bioterrorist adviser to the Secretary of Health and Human Services (HHS), justified this failure to recommend for or against taking the anthrax vaccine by saying that there was insufficient information available to make a recommendation. But on what basis could individuals make a decision if those with the most experience with the anthrax vaccine refused even to advise them about what action was medically reasonable?

Although no survey of the exposed civilians has been conducted, it seems likely that the potential subjects mostly decided for themselves that their 60 days (or less) of antibiotics was sufficient protection. It is also unlikely that anyone who actually read and understood the information in the consent forms provided (for adults, adolescents, and children) would have chosen to take the vaccine. Specifically, the consent forms (which are essentially identical) are five-page, single-spaced documents. Designed for a clinical research trial, the forms are nonetheless captioned "Anthrax Vaccine and Drugs Availability Program for Persons Possibly Exposed to Inhaled Spores." Most of the form is in regular typeface, but the following information is in bold:

Before you decide to take part in this program, there are several important things that you should know . . .

> • Anthrax vaccine has not been shown to prevent infection when given to people after exposure to anthrax spores . . .

> • The vaccine that you will receive in this program has not been approved by the Food and Drug Administration (FDA) for this use and is considered investigational . . .

> • FDA has not approved this lot of vaccine (Lot FAV-063) because the company's license to produce the vaccine is under review . . .

> • You should not consider the vaccine as a treatment for anthrax. The vaccine given in this program not been shown to give long term protection against anthrax . . .

> • You may have undesirable side effects from taking this vaccine . . .

> • . . . DHHS is not making any recommendation whether you should or should not take this vaccine. DHHS is making the vaccine available to you to allow you to decide whether or not you wish to use the vaccine.

The FDA does seem to have learned from its experience in the Gulf War, and did seem to understand that there could be no justification for waiving informed consent for competent adults, even in the face of a bioterrorist attack and uncertainty about the usefulness of the anthrax vaccine. Informed consent for research on competent adults is always feasible and is always ethically required. Informed consent is also required for treating competent adult civilians — only military personnel agree to accept reasonable and necessary approved medical procedures without specific consent. That is only one reason why it is dangerous to civilians to argue that after 9/11 "we are all soldiers now." George J. Annas, *Blinded by Bioterrorism: Public Health and Liberty in the 21st Century*, 13 HEALTH MATRIX 33, 38–41 (2003).

See also George J. Annas, *Protecting Soldiers from Friendly Fire: The Consent Requirement for Using Investigational Drugs and Vaccines in Combat*, 24 AM. J.L. & MED. 245 (1996); D.G. McNeil, *Drug Tested in Gulf War is Approved for Troops*, N.Y. TIMES, Feb. 6, 2003, at A19; Michael E. Frisina, *Medical Ethics in Military*

Biomedical Research, in MILITARY MEDICAL ETHICS, Vol. 2, 533–63 (Thomas E. Beam & Linette R. Sparacino eds., 2003).

9. **The first bioterrorist attack.** It is worth noting that the first "bioterrorist" attack in the U.S. is generally credited to a small religious sect in Oregon, which followed Bhagwan Shree Rajneesh, who lived on a ranch approximately a two-hour drive from The Dalles, Oregon. The "attack" took place on September 9, 1984, when members of the sect used agents ordered from the American Type Culture Collection, including *Salmonella typhimurium, Francisella tularensis, Enterobacter cloacae, Neisseria gonorrhoeae,* and *Shigella dysenteriae,* to poison salad bars at various restaurants in The Dalles. The idea was to make people sick in order to prevent them from voting in an election that could have been detrimental to their sect. The attack is described in JUDITH MILLER, STEPHEN ENGELBERG & WILLIAM BROAD, BIOLOGICAL WEAPONS AND AMERICA'S SECRET WAR: GERMS 15–33 (2001).

E. IMPROVISED NUCLEAR DEVICE EXPLOSION

INSTITUTE OF MEDICINE, COMMITTEE ON MEDICAL PREPAREDNESS FOR A
TERRORIST NUCLEAR EVENT,
ASSESSING MEDICAL PREPAREDNESS TO RESPOND TO A TERRORIST
NUCLEAR EVENT: WORKSHOP REPORT
x-xi, 107–110 (2009)

The United States has been struggling for some time to address and plan for the threat of nuclear terrorism and other weapons of mass destruction (WMDs) that terrorists might obtain and use. One of the earliest medical preparedness efforts, the Metropolitan Medical Response System Program, was started in 1995, but it has remained underfunded and its potential has been largely unfulfilled.

There are, of course, a number of public and nonpublic efforts by a variety of federal, state, and local agencies to prevent, mitigate, and respond to the threat of an Improvised Nuclear Device (IND). The latest effort, the Urban Area Security Initiative (UASI), is providing funds to 45 urban areas to improve preparedness for WMDs, including an IND detonation. The Department of Homeland Security, as directed by Congress, asked the Institute of Medicine (IOM) to conduct a workshop to better understand the state of preparedness for an IND detonation in the six UASI cities designated as "Tier 1" (New York/New Jersey; National Capitol Region; Houston; Chicago; Los Angeles; and San Francisco/Bay Area). Public health practitioners are usually asked to figure out how to prevent bad things from happening and to preserve our health. The basic assumption for this workshop, however, was to assume: What if? Specifically, what if the efforts by law enforcement and other security officials failed to prevent the detonation of a 10-kt nuclear device in a central city? The committee's task was basically to ask: Where are we today, and what are the gaps should the unthinkable happen? The committee fulfilled that task.

This report provides a frightening but candid look into our level of preparedness today. It was an informative process; one that did much to confirm that we are not yet prepared for a nuclear event. In fact, in many ways, we are still in the infancy of our planning and response efforts. The workshop identified several key areas in which we might begin to focus our national efforts in a way that will improve the overall level of preparedness.

. . . .

Committee chair Georges Benjamin concluded the workshop by summarizing the main points he had heard during the presentations and discussions. First, the detonation of an IND would be a national catastrophe of unprecedented proportions because of the large number of casualties, reinforced by the social, economic, and psychological impacts. Local and state responses would be overwhelmed immediately, and it would be several days or a week before federal and other resources could be fully mobilized. HHS has developed a playbook outlining how the federal medical response to an IND detonation would evolve and unfold and intends to publish this on the Internet.

Second, it was apparent from the presentations that there are many emergency preparedness efforts going on at multiple levels, and the degree of planning varies among them. Generally, large urban areas and their states have begun to prepare their responses to a radiological event such as a radiological dispersal device (RDD) but are only beginning to think about what they should do to prepare for a possible IND detonation . . . .

Third, many federal agencies are poised to help, but there is a lack of awareness at the local level about what assets would be available and the process. More planning and exercising for an IND detonation contingency is needed at the local level if local and state planners are to understand how these various pieces would fit together in an actual event.

Fourth, in addition to the lack of knowledge of federal plans and resources for responding to an IND event, localities and states generally lack awareness of the number and mix of casualties that would occur in plausible detonation scenarios. There is currently little open-sources information on the conceivable conditions following an IND detonation in a modern U.S. city . . . .

Fifth, there are significant limitations on the effectiveness of a response. Current supplies of specific (e.g., cytokines) and nonspecific (*e.g.*, blood products) medical countermeasures are not matched to the projected requirements of an IND detonation, and the logistical challenges that would have to be overcome in order to administer these countermeasures when they are needed are substantial. There will not be enough vehicles and airplanes to extricate victims and more them to treatment facilities.

Sixth, the nation is not prepared to respond to the medical and public health consequences of an IND detonation, but it is not clear what "prepared" means. Preparedness is a process, not a point in time, and it is not clear what the goal should be. Determining such a goal would help in measuring and evaluating progress toward preparedness.

Seventh, many important strategic decisions have to be made at the national (*i.e.,* combined local, state, and federal) level:

• How to inform and engage the public in the process of deciding what responses would be realistic and appropriate.

• What the triage criteria and process should be, given the mismatch between medical needs and resources: HHS is developing a system, but it is not clear what it will be or how it will be legitimated among providers and the public.

• What the radiation exposure levels for responders should be, and who should apply them: Should each state or locality decide for its people, or should there be a national consensus standards?

• Whether to tell the public to shelter in place or evacuate, and on what criteria to base such a decision: For reasons discussed during the workshop (e.g., the speed of the arrival of fallout and the relatively effective protection that can be provided by buildings versus the probability of gridlock), the default policy probably should be, "Shelter in place until we let you know it is safe enough to evacuate," but no one has stated this officially. Part of the problem is that this or any other blanket policy will not be the best policy for every situation, but the capacity to provide more nuanced advice probably does not exist at this time. No blanket policy is perfect, but the capacity to provide tailored advice during an event is and will continue to be quite limited.

• To what extent plume models should form the basis of decisions to recommend that people should shelter or evacuate: There was evidence presented at the workshop that the footprint of the fallout might well be patchy rather than the sharply defined cigar or fan shape provided by plume models, because the winds at different levels might be going in different directions and shifting at the same time.

• How long-term medical effects should be handled: This was not addressed at the workshop, but steps must be taken soon after the event to identify people exposed to 1 rem (10 mSv) or more, inform them of the long-term risks of cancer, and implement registries to keep track of them. There will also be long-term mental health and behavioral effects that will need to be monitored . . . .

• How to manage public and health care professional concerns and fear: There is no clear strategy for communicating with people and keeping them informed, especially vulnerable populations who have fewer resources to help them make it through a devastating event.

Eighth, there are few medical countermeasures available for victims of radiation exposure, and more are greatly needed . . . . Radiation countermeasures are not going to help people injured by the blast and burn effects if they do not receive trauma care, which poses a great challenge for the reasons mentioned throughout the workshop and described above (e.g., lack of health care facilities, especially for burn patients and other patients needing specialized intensive care; limited assets for moving patients to existing health care facilities, regionally and nationally;

problems with the resupply of health care facilities that have one-day inventories of drugs and other supplies).

Finally, while no preparations could fully mitigate the impacts of a nuclear detonation in the middle of a major U.S. city, the workshop discussions touched on a number of ways that governments at all levels have begun to improve their capacity to respond to such an event, especially by increasing joint information sharing and response planning on a regional basis. Determining how much priority to give such efforts, considering the more likely threats of the occurrence of events such as earthquakes, hurricanes, and other forms of terrorism, was beyond the committee's charge. However, many of these efforts would also help improve the nation's capacity to respond to other types of mass casualty events.

F.   THE SMALLPOX VACCINATION PROGRAM

INSTITUTE OF MEDICINE, COMMITTEE ON SMALLPOX, VACCINATION PROGRAM IMPLEMENTATION, THE SMALLPOX VACCINATION PROGRAM: PUBLIC HEALTH IN AN AGE OF TERRORISM
66–71, 125–26 (2005)

The last case of smallpox in the United States occurred in 1949. General vaccination against smallpox — accomplished with cutaneous administration of a closely related virus, vaccinia virus — ceased in the United States in 1972, when the threat of smallpox disease disappeared due to eradication efforts, which were declared complete by the World Health Organization on May 8, 1980. Only two official stocks of smallpox (variola) virus remained — under the auspices of the governments of the United States and the Soviet Union. It has often been rumored and suggested that some of the virus possessed by the Soviet Union could have been given illegally to people attempting to use the virus as a biological weapon, though factual evidence to support this concern has not been made public. The events of September and October 2001 increased U.S. concerns about all types of possible terrorism, including the potential for biological terrorism. Thus, attention turned to considerations of initiating vaccination against smallpox. CDC has been concurrently developing "post-event" vaccination plans (mass vaccinations after a smallpox release) and — the focus of this committee — "pre-event" plans (precautionary vaccination of smallpox response teams, first responders, and the general public).

On December 13, 2002, President Bush announced his policy on pre-event vaccination against smallpox. Vaccination of select military personnel, including the president in his role as Commander-in-Chief, began immediately thereafter. At the time of this writing, voluntary vaccination of state-based teams of public health disease investigators and of hospital-based teams of health care workers (who would respond to the first case of smallpox, should it ever appear) is scheduled to begin in late January 2003. The president has asked that this round of vaccinations be completed as quickly as possible and that a broader vaccination effort commence thereafter. As currently understood, the subsequent vaccinations will encompass the voluntary vaccination of all health care workers and those commonly defined as first responders, such as firefighters, police, and emergency medical personnel. Vaccination of the general public is specifically not recommended, but the president also announced the intent to provide vaccinations to those members of the public who request the intervention. The IOM's Committee on Smallpox Vaccination Program Implementation met for the first time December 18–20, 2002.

. . . .

The committee realizes that this is an atypical vaccination campaign, and that it is neither a research study nor an ideal public health program. Rather, it is a public health component of bioterrorism preparedness . . . .

For practical reasons, the committee uses the term "phase I" to describe the planned vaccination of 500,000 public health and health care workers who volunteer to be part of smallpox response teams, and "phase II" to refer to the subsequent vaccination of 10 million health care and public health workers and other emergency responders. However, it is unclear what the rounds of vaccination are being called by CDC ("phases" seems most frequently used) and clarification also is needed about the target population for later vaccination efforts.

. . . .

Smallpox Vaccination Program Timeline

Date	Event
June 2001	"Dark Winter," a war game for senior-level officials, is conducted . . . . Exercise included a smallpox outbreak spreading to 25 states and 15 countries . . . .
September 2001	Terrorist attacks in New York, Arlington (Virginia), and Pennsylvania
October 2001	Letters containing anthrax spores delivered through U.S. mail
February 2002	CDC asks ACIP to review its recommendations on smallpox vaccination
June 2002	ACIP meets and drafts supplemental recommendations on smallpox vaccination (vaccinate up to 20,000 health care and public health workers) (ACIP, 2002). Public Health Security and Bioterrorism Preparedness and Response Act of 2002 signed into law . . . .
October 2002	ACIP meets again and updates recommendations on smallpox vaccination. ACIP also recommends offering vaccine to up to 500,000 health care and public health personnel.
November 2002	President signs Homeland Security Act Designated CDC staff members receive smallpox vaccination (epidemiologic investigation teams). Mass media report that Bush administration intelligence review has concluded that four nations (Iraq, North Korea, Russia, and France) may possess covert and illegal stocks of smallpox virus.

Date	Event
December 2002	States submit to CDC smallpox response plans and smallpox pre-event vaccination plans. President announces smallpox vaccination program. HHS telebriefing on smallpox policy; initial goal: vaccinate 500,000 workers in 30 days.
January 2003	Letter to White House issued by minority members of Senate calling for smallpox vaccine injury compensation. CDC begins shipping smallpox vaccine to states. Department of Homeland Security established. DHHS secretary authorizes civilian smallpox vaccinations. Civilian smallpox vaccination begins.
February 2003	Media reports cite lack of a compensation plan as a barrier to smallpox vaccination. DHHS announces contracts to develop safer smallpox vaccines. DoD has vaccinated over 100,000 against smallpox. *Morbidity and Mortality Weekly Report* notifies of one case of angina 4 days after smallpox vaccination. DoD reports first cases of myocarditis among personnel recently immunized with smallpox vaccine.
March 2003	First civilian instances of myo/pericarditis identified, later classified as suspected and probable. DHHS proposes smallpox vaccination compensation plan. Surgeon general, CDC director, and others are vaccinated against smallpox. War with Iraq begins on March 19, 2003. CDC accepts ACIP's exclusion criteria and revises fact sheets, screening materials, and informed consent form.
April 2003	GAO report *Smallpox Vaccination: Implementation of National Program Faces Challenges* finds that 6% of target population has been vaccinated by week 10 of program; data are insufficient to assess safety. On April 30, 2003, president signs into law Smallpox Emergency Personnel Protection Act of 2003, which establishes no-fault Smallpox Vaccine Injury Compensation Program.
May 2003	President declares end of major combat operations in Iraq. Media reports that in April and May, some states have begun offering smallpox vaccine to first responders.
June 2003	ACIP recommends against expansion of smallpox vaccination program beyond "first phase."
December 2003	Federal government issues interim final rule for Smallpox Emergency Personnel Protection Act of 2003 (SEPPA), plan for smallpox vaccine injury compensation.
January 2004	HHS secretary's declaration regarding administration of smallpox countermeasures extended until and including January 23, 2005.

Date	Event
February 2004	DoD reports that 581,183 service members received smallpox shots from December 13, 2002, to February 11, 2004. Seventy-two vaccinees, or about 1 in 8,072, suffered myopericarditis, and there were 30 cases of vaccinia infection in contacts of vaccinees.
June 2004	DoD announces anthrax and smallpox vaccinations for all personnel deployed by Central Command and select units in Pacific Command. Since December 2002, 625,000 troops have been vaccinated against smallpox.
July 2004	The Senate Select Committee on Intelligence issues report which describes evidence on Iraq's possession of smallpox as weak.
October 2004	CIA . . . concludes that, although Iraq had capability to work with smallpox virus, there is "no direct evidence that Iraq either retained or acquired smallpox virus isolates or proceeded with any follow-up smallpox related research."

NOTES AND QUESTIONS

1. **IOM committee report.** In its final report, which also contains complete copies of the above "letter report" and its five subsequent reports, the Committee labels the smallpox vaccination program "a case study at the intersection of public health and national security, two fields brought together by the threat of bioterrorism." It notes that the campaign involved federal agencies that usually do not work together, and problems, such as classified information, that are not encountered in "typical public health programs." Most centrally, it emphasized that "Bioterrorist attacks epitomize 'low-likelihood, high-consequence' events" for which planning is especially problematic and difficult. INSTITUTE OF MEDICINE, *supra*, at 5. Its two recommendations:

> Based on the lessons learned from the smallpox vaccination program, the committee concludes that a policy strategy and a mechanism are needed to balance the need for scientific evidence and public health analysis with the imperatives of national security, ensuring in the process that the authoritative voice of CDC, the nation's public health leader, will be preserved. The committee recommends that, in collaboration with its state and local partners and in the context of broad bioterrorism preparedness, CDC defines smallpox preparedness; set goals that reflect the best available scientific and public health reasoning; conduct regular, comprehensive assessments of preparedness at the national level and by state; and communicate to the public about the status of preparedness efforts.

Id. at 6.

2. **Mandatory v. voluntary vaccination.** The military vaccination program was mandatory. The civilian one, however, was completely voluntary and relied on a combination of public trust and informed consent. In its first report in January

2003, the committee noted specific problems that needed to be addressed, writing that the program was not a "typical public health program" but rather "a matter of national public health preparedness against a national security threat." There was no real way of quantifying the actual threat and the benefit of the vaccine was unknown — the question was how to communicate this. The committee specifically recommended: "all consent documents include a statement that the risks of smallpox vaccine, which are very low, are predictably higher than the risks associated with most other vaccines, but that the benefit is at present unknown — possibly very low (absent exposure to smallpox) or very high (in the event of exposure). The committee further recommends that informed consent forms included explicit notification of the availability, or lack thereof, of compensation for adverse reactions. " *Id.* at 136–38.

3. Failure of the vaccination program. The major reason for the failure of the smallpox vaccination program is that the administration failed to persuade physicians and nurses that the known risks of serious side effects with the vaccine were justified given the fact that there is no evidence that Iraq (or anywhere else) has both smallpox virus and the wish to use it in a terrorist attack. The Director of the CDC, Dr. Julie Gerberding, and the person in charge of the smallpox vaccination program, for example, told a U.S. Senate Appropriations Subcommittee on January 29, 2003, about a month after the smallpox vaccination campaign began,

> I can't discuss all of the details because some of the information is, of course, classified. However, I think our reading of the intelligence that we share with the intelligence community is that there is a real possibility of a smallpox attack either from nations that are likely to be harboring the virus or from individual entities, such as terrorist cells that could have access to the virus. Therefore, we know it is not zero. And, I think that's really what we can say with absolute certainty that there is not a zero risk of a smallpox attack.

This is wonderful doubletalk that proves nothing except that the CDC's director does not seem to know much about the risk of a smallpox attack. Most importantly, however, if the U.S. government knows that an individual, group, or nation has smallpox and is working to make it into a weapon, this information should be made public. It is the terrorists who want to keep their methods and intentions secret; the best defense for a potential target is to make this information public. George J. Annas, *The Statue of Security: Human Rights and Post-9/11 Epidemics*, 38 J. HEALTH L. 319, 330–31 (2005).

Gerberding's approach seems to have been guided by what has become known as the post-9/11 Cheney "One-Percent Doctrine." As described by author Ron Suskind, when asked how to respond to reports that Pakistani scientists may be helping al Qaeda to build a nuclear weapon, Cheney responded, "If there's a one percent chance that Pakistani scientists are helping al Qaeda build or develop a nuclear weapon, we have to treat it as a certainty in terms of response. It's not about our analysis, or finding a preponderance of evidence. It's about our response." In Suskind's words,

> This doctrine — the one percent solution — divided what had largely been indivisible in the conduct of American foreign policy; analysis and action.

> Justified or not, fact-based or not, "our response" is what matters. As to "evidence," the bar was set so low that the word itself almost didn't apply.

RON SUSKIND, THE ONE PERCENT DOCTRINE: DEEP INSIDE AMERICA'S PURSUIT OF ITS ENEMIES SINCE 9/11, 62 (2006). Marc Siegel applies the numbers to try to make sense of post-9/11 alarms regarding public health in his FALSE ALARM: THE TRUTH ABOUT THE EPIDEMIC OF FEAR (2005). D.A. Henderson, who was tasked by the Secretary of HHS to develop a smallpox plan shortly after 9/11, seems to have been able to persuade President Bush that effective containment could be accomplished without widespread prior vaccination. He was, however, unable to persuade the Vice-President, and Cheney ultimately got the limited vaccination program described above. As Henderson put it in 2009, "the program was an abject failure." D.A. HENDERSON, SMALLPOX: THE DEATH OF A DISEASE 296 (2009).

4. Effects of anthrax and smallpox responses on public health. It has reasonably been observed that both the anthrax and smallpox responses were very costly to public health. Hill Cohen and colleagues made this argument in *The Pitfalls of Bioterrorism Preparedness: The Anthrax and Smallpox Experiences*, 94 AM. J. PUB. HEALTH 1667 (2004). They termed the responses "irrational and dysfunctional" arguing that they were not only based on flawed evaluations, but undercut international agreements against biological weapons. They continue: "Even worse, bioterrorism "preparedness" programs now under way include the development of a number of new secret research facilities that will store and handle dangerous materials, thus increasing the risk of accidental release or purposeful diversion." . . . also provides an impetus for a potential global "biodefense race" that would likely spur proliferation of offensive biowarfare capabilities . . . ." They conclude their essay: "Bioterrorism has been a disaster for public health. Instead of leading to more resources for dealing with natural disease as had been promised, there are now fewer such resources. Worse, in response to bioterrorism preparedness, public health institutions and procedures are being reorganized along a military or police model that subverts the relationships between public health providers and the communities they serve."

———

G. SARS

CDC, FACT SHEET: BASIC INFORMATION ABOUT SARS
http://www.cdc.gov/sars/about/fs-SARS.pdf (Jan. 2004)

Severe acute respiratory syndrome (SARS) is a viral respiratory illness caused by a coronavirus, called SARS-associated coronavirus (SARS-CoV). SARS was first reported in Asia in February 2003. Over the next few months, the illness spread to more than two dozen countries in North America, South America, Europe, and Asia before the SARS global outbreak of 2003 was contained.

According to the World Health Organization (WHO), a total of 8098 people worldwide became sick with SARS during the 2003 outbreak. Of these, 774 died. In the United States, only eight people had laboratory evidence of SARS-CoV infection. All of these people had traveled to other parts of the world with SARS.

SARS did not spread more widely in the community in the United States.

In general, SARS begins with a high fever (temperature greater than 100.4°F.) Other symptoms may include headache, an overall feeling of discomfort and body aches. Some people also have mild respiratory symptoms at the outset. About 10 percent to 20 percent of patients have diarrhea. After 2 to 7 days, SARS patients may develop a dry cough. Most patients develop pneumonia.

The main way that SARS seems to spread is by close person-to-person contact. The virus that causes SARS is thought to be transmitted most readily by respiratory droplets (droplet spread) produced when an infected person coughs or sneezes. Droplet spread can happen when droplets from the cough or sneeze of an infected person are propelled a short distance (generally up to 3 feet) through the air and deposited on the mucous membranes of the mouth, nose or eyes of persons who are nearby. The virus also can spread when a person touches a surface or object contaminated with infectious droplets and then touches his or her mouth, nose or eye(s). In addition, it is possible that the SARS virus might spread more broadly through the air (airborne spread) or by other ways that are not now known.

In the context of SARS, close contact means having cared for or lived with someone with SARS or having direct contact with respiratory secretions or body fluids of a patient with SARS. Examples of close contact include kissing or hugging, sharing eating or drinking utensils, talking to someone within three feet, and touching someone directly. Close contact does not include activities like walking by a person or briefly sitting across a waiting room or office.

MARK A. ROTHSTEIN *ET AL.*, QUARANTINE AND ISOLATION: LESSONS LEARNED FROM SARS, A REPORT TO THE CENTERS FOR DISEASE CONTROL AND PREVENTION
23, 24, 26, 44, 54, 55, 58 (2003)
http://biotech.law.lsu.edu/blaw/cdc/SARS_REPORT.pdf

Canada was among the countries hardest hit by SARS. Only the People's Republic of China, Hong Kong, and Taiwan had more probable SARS cases. Toronto was the Canadian city most affected [by] the outbreak. The first (index) SARS case in Toronto was a 78-year-old woman, Mrs. K, who returned home to Toronto on February 23, 2003 from a trip to Hong Kong to visit relatives. Mrs. K, who was never hospitalized, died on March 5 after the onset of an illness later determined to be SARS. Her son, Mr. T, became ill on February 27, was admitted to Scarborough Hospital (Grace Division) on March 7, and died on March 13. Transmission of SARS traceable to Mrs. K is thought to have included 224 other persons in Toronto alone. In all of Canada, there were 438 SARS cases, including 251 probable (1 active) and 187 suspect (0 active) cases. All of the probable cases were reported in two provinces, Ontario, which includes Toronto, and British Columbia. Suspect cases were reported in four other provinces (Alberta, New Brunswick, Prince Edward Island, and Saskatchewan).

. . . Opinions differ about the capability of the Canadian government to respond to SARS or other SARS-like outbreaks [The authors then describe the political and legal structure of Canada.]

On June 12, 2003, SARS was added to the Quarantine Act's schedule of infectious and contagious diseases, together with an established incubation period, thereby bringing SARS cases within the ambit of federal public health authority. [T]he Act provides the Minister of Health with a multitude of powers related to the control of infectious disease. One important means of exercising public health authority in the wake of the SARS outbreak was to develop, coordinate, and provide specific guidance for both public and private entities, including public health workers and health professionals, in identifying and managing SARS cases and related health matters within their jurisdictions. At the federal level, the Department of Health has developed a large number of guidance documents intended to assist both public and private entities to respond to specific SARS-related health matters. These include the following: definition of persons under SARS investigation; definition of a SARS case; interim guidelines for public health authorities in the management of probable and suspect SARS cases; definitions of geo-linked persons for hospital surveillance for SARS; public health protocol for persons meeting the "geo-linked person" definition; recommended laboratory testing for probable SARS cases and SARS contact cases; advisory for laboratory bio-safety; guidelines for health care providers in the identification, diagnosis, and treatment of adults with SARS; guidelines for the use of respirators (masks) among health care workers; and recommendations and guidelines for public health officials for managing probable or suspect SARS cases among air travelers.

. . . .

In contrast to other provincial and local governments — with the exception of British Columbia and to a lesser extent Alberta — only Ontario and the municipality of Toronto have had to invoke their public health authority in a significant and large-scale manner to respond to the SARS outbreak within their jurisdictions

. . . .

On March 25, 2003, in the face of a rising number of SARS cases in the Toronto area, the Ontario government took the critical step of designating SARS as a reportable, communicable, and virulent disease under the province's Health Protection and Promotion Act, which authorized public health authorities to issue orders to detain and isolate persons for purposes of preventing SARS transmission. Eventually, about 30,000 persons in Toronto were quarantined. That number is similar to the number of persons who were quarantined due to the SARS outbreak in Beijing, China, but for the latter the number of probable SARS cases (2500) was ten times larger than Toronto's (about 250).

The fast use of isolation in Toronto occurred early in the SARS outbreak, when the physician treating the index case's son, Mr. T, had Mr. T placed in hospital isolation for suspected tuberculosis (at no time before Mr. T's death was his SARS established) and requested that other family members isolate themselves at home as they, too, might be at risk for tuberculosis infection. Unfortunately, these control measures occurred too late to contain the spread of SARS in Toronto. Mr. T, who had entered Scarborough Hospital through the emergency department, was left in the emergency department for 18-20 hours despite a physician's hospital admission order, and only later admitted to the hospital's Intensive Care Unit (ICU). When he was finally examined by a physician, a tuberculosis isolation order was issued and Toronto Public Health was notified as a routine matter of a possible tuberculosis case. During Mr. T's long wait in the Scarborough Hospital emergency department for admission to the ICU and his short time in the ICU before tuberculosis was suspected, other patients and staff were exposed to SARS. At the time there was no indication that these individuals were at risk of contracting or spreading any communicable disease, let alone SARS.

When tuberculosis was ruled out and public health officials and physicians began to understand the implications of Mr. T's case, steps were taken to remove other members of Mrs. K's family, some of whom were reporting illness, to negative pressure isolation rooms in other area hospitals. These steps undoubtedly limited the spread of SARS. Combining the information from the WHO's international health alert for atypical pneumonia with reports of the Scarborough Hospital cases, both Toronto Public Health and provincial public health authorities activated their emergency response plans. A "Code Orange" (which required all area hospitals to go into emergency mode) was issued, under which area hospitals were required to suspend nonessential services, limit visitors, issue protective equipment for staff, and establish special isolation units for "potential SARS patients." Asymptomatic contacts of SARS patients were not isolated within health facilities, but were asked to adhere to a 10-day home quarantine.

The risk of acquiring SARS was greatest for persons (staff, patients, and visitors) within rather than outside of health care facilities, including doctors' offices; health care workers accounted for over 40% of all SARS patients in Toronto
. . . .

Directives issued by Ontario health authorities instructed hospitals to isolate all patients with fever and respiratory symptoms in the hospital or in the hospital emergency department until SARS had been ruled out. Most hospitals took special precautions for inpatients with respiratory symptoms suggestive of infectious diseases. In Phase I of the Toronto SARS outbreak (March 13–25, 2003), over 20 Toronto area hospitals admitted and cared for SARS patients. No single facility was designated as a "SARS hospital," because both provincial and Toronto area officials feared that such a step would overwhelm the facility so designated. For this reason, capacity for SARS clinical management, including isolation of SARS patients and adequate infection control measures, was built into multiple facilities throughout the Greater Toronto area. Two hospitals (Sunnybrook and Woman's) in the Greater Toronto area appeared to carry the largest volume of SARS patients during Phase I. Unfortunately, many of these two hospitals' physicians with relevant expertise or experience in SARS clinical management were themselves ill or in quarantine . . . . In Phase II of the Toronto SARS outbreak (May 23–June 30, 2003), four hospitals (later termed the SARS Alliance) were designated as SARS facilities. The "Code Orange" described above for Toronto area hospitals was later extended to all Ontario hospitals, meaning they, too, were required to suspend non-essential services, limit visitors, create isolation units for SARS patients, and issue protective equipment (gowns, masks, and goggles) for exposed staff. Some concern was expressed over whether the Code Orange was justified or overly broad.

No persons in transit into or out of Canada were actually quarantined or isolated, although clearly the federal government has the authority to take such measures in appropriate cases . . . . SARS screening for airline passengers took place at Canadian airports, but this screening relied primarily upon information cards that were distributed to and completed by both incoming and outbound passengers. In-person screening questions and secondary assessments were conducted only as needed . . . . As of August 27, 2003, 6.5 million screening transactions had taken place at Canadian airports, with about 9100 passengers referred for further SARS assessment by screening nurses or quarantine officers. None of the passengers who underwent further assessment was found to meet the criteria for a probable or suspect SARS case. The pilot thermal scanner screened 2.4 million passengers, with 832 referred for further assessments, and none met the criteria for a probable or suspect SARS case.

In Toronto, home and workplace quarantines were often imposed for what were definitive "contact" cases, meaning cases in which persons were known to have been in close physical proximity to a probable SARS case with inadequate or no protection from possible exposure. Contact cases included family and household members of SARS patients, hospital visitors and other non-SARS patients within hospitals who may have been exposed to SARS patients, health care staff who provided treatment to SARS patients without adequate protective equipment, and persons at workplaces who may have been exposed to coworkers with SARS. Provided they were timely identified and contacted, these persons were urged to remain at home for a 10-day period, with monitoring, usually by telephone, by a local public health worker . . . .

The federal, provincial, and local governments used a variety of means to convey up-to-date information regarding the SARS outbreak to the public, as well as to health professionals. Features of the public health education and communication measures taken by the government generally and by public health authorities specifically included regular updates to their own websites. Additionally, Toronto Public Health established a SARS Hotline. Hotline staff, primarily public health nurses, provided callers with health information and counseling and case and contact identification, and the recognition and follow-up of emerging issues in SARS-affected institutions and communities. At the height of the outbreak the Hotline had 46 staff on the day shift and 34 staff on the evening shift, including individuals with special language skills. The Hotline received over 300,000 calls between March 15 and June 24, 2003, with a peak of 47,567 calls in a single day.

. . . .

. . . Almost all persons who were asked to submit to quarantine did so voluntarily. In only 27 cases was a written order mandating quarantine issued under Ontario's Health Protection and Promotion Act. Certain actions taken by the federal and provincial governments may have had the effect of increasing public acceptance of SARS-control measures. For example, the federal government has amended its employment insurance regulations under the Employment Insurance Act to remove the waiting period for sickness benefits for certain persons placed under SARS quarantine, as well as to remove the requirement that certain persons under SARS quarantine obtain a medical certificate as a condition of receiving sickness benefits. The federal government also provided special employment insurance coverage for health care workers who were unable to work because of SARS and who were not otherwise eligible for benefits under the government's Employment Insurance Act, as well as tax and mortgage payment relief to persons who were facing difficulties making tax or mortgage payments because of SARS . . . .

The use of quarantine and isolation measures in Toronto cannot be characterized as a uniform, coordinated (and perhaps optimal) response to the SARS outbreak, which is not surprising given the highly decentralized way in which public health functions in Canada are organized. The recently released federal Canadian government report mentioned earlier, *Learning from SARS: Renewal of Public Health Canada*, appears to confirm this, stating, "[t]he SARS experience illustrated that Canada is not adequately prepared to deal with a true pandemic."

. . . .

[In other countries affected by] the SARS outbreak, different types of quarantine and isolation measures were used by public health authorities to control SARS transmission. Isolation was used for persons who posed the greatest risk of transmission, persons who met the criteria used by public health officials for probable SARS cases. Almost all probable SARS cases were isolated in health facilities, generally inpatient acute care hospitals, in which these individuals were actually diagnosed. Often, persons in quarantine, such as persons who met the criteria used by public health officials as suspect SARS cases (*e.g.*, persons who may have been in recent contact with a probable SARS case and are experiencing fever and a cough or breathing difficulty), were subsequently placed in isolation when their symptoms met the criteria for probable SARS cases. Unfortunately, many SARS cases were only diagnosed upon investigation of death or autopsy.

In contrast to isolation, quarantine methods varied greatly, often simply because a particular quarantine method appeared to be the most intuitive and timely response in light of how little was known about the actual risk of transmission. For example, the quarantine of definitive "contact" cases or persons who were known to have been in close physical proximity and who had inadequate or no protection from possible exposure to a probable SARS case or setting, such as household or family members, was perhaps the most intuitive, and in retrospect, rational measure, given what became known about the likely route of transmission (*i.e.*, droplets). This was often referred to as home quarantine or "home isolation," in which the contact cases were urged to remain at home for a 10-day period, with follow-up, usually by telephone, by a local public health worker.

. . . .

While legal authority may have existed or was thought to exist for these quarantine methods, the use of so many different quarantine measures, often without apparent regard to the particularized risk for which control was sought, may have served to undermine public credibility. It is clear that a more considered, careful, and evidence based approach to quarantine and isolation is needed.

Regardless of the wisdom of quarantine and isolation in particular circumstances, these measures are only part of the public health response to an epidemic.

Typically the ordering of quarantine for SARS triggered a whole system of public health measures. Contact tracing was an essential part of the strategy, and this required a staff of trained epidemiologists, public health nurses, and other professionals. Quarantine orders had to be served, and public health officers and law enforcement personnel were used in the countries we studied. Some individuals did not want to stay at home during quarantine because they were afraid of infecting family members. In Singapore, individuals under quarantine had a choice of staying at home or at a designated center (a resort taken over by the government). Taiwan used a public housing center that had not yet opened, military facilities, and a home for the elderly as quarantine facilities. In Hong Kong, "holiday camps" were used for homeless people and those who did not want home confinement. On the other hand, some people did not want to leave their homes because there would be nobody to care for their pets. Every country developed a system for providing meals and other social services.

The vast majority of people under quarantine in all of the countries obeyed requests to stay at home without requiring a court order. Some individuals, however, attempted to escape their confinement, and a variety of means were needed to ensure compliance . . . .

. . . .

A lack of alternatives made the use of quarantine and isolation an important element of controlling SARS in Canada, China, Hong Kong, Singapore, Taiwan, and Vietnam. These jurisdictions had a high rate of compliance with quarantine and isolation. It is not clear whether the United States would have the same compliance rate in a comparable epidemic. Many of the Asian countries are well known for their communitarian culture, and Canada is also known for its commitment to social solidarity as evidenced by its health care system. By contrast, the United States is a heterogeneous society with a strong tradition of individualism and skepticism about government.

George J. Annas, *The Statue of Security: Human Rights and Post-9/11 Epidemics*
38 J. Health L. 331–40 (2005)

The SARS epidemic was our first, and so far only, post-9/11 contagious disease epidemic, but it also returned us to late 19th century Ellis Island days in that its cause and mode of transmission were initially unknown, there is no diagnostic test for it, there is no vaccine, and there is no effective treatment. But SARS also appeared in a society equipped with instant global communication that made management of people through information much more important than management of people through police actions. With the internet information now spreads like a virus, but much faster . . . .

[S]ince the epidemic has ended in all 30 countries in which suspected SARS cases were reported, and only a few countries used quarantine (detained individuals who showed no symptoms), it seems reasonable to conclude that quarantining "contacts" or even "close contacts" was unnecessarily harmful to those affected. It is not only liberty that is at stake in deciding about quarantine, but the effectiveness of public health itself in the 21st century. This is because to be effective in preventing disease spread from either a new epidemic or a bioterrorist attack, public health officials must also prevent the spread of fear and panic. Maintenance of public trust is essential to achieve this.

When any new contagious disease appears, public health officials must answer three related questions: should contacts be quarantined? What test should be used to determine who qualifies as a "contact"?, and should quarantine be voluntary or mandatory? China has been rightly criticized for failing to promptly alert the international community to the existence of a possibly new and contagious virus. Had information about the initial outbreak been properly shared, SARS might never have spread beyond China. Nonetheless when, with the active intervention of the World Health Organization, the epidemic was publicly recognized, China reacted vigorously, even harshly, especially in Beijing and Hong Kong. Mass quarantines were initiated involving two universities, four hospitals, seven construction sites, and other facilities, like apartment complexes. Sixty percent of the approximately 30,000 people quarantined in mainland China were detained at centralized facilities, the remainder were permitted to stay at home. Those quarantined were "close contacts," defined as someone who has shared meals, utensils, place of residence, a hospital room, or a transportation vehicle with a probable SARS patient, or visited a SARS patient or been in contact with the secretions of a SARS patient any time after 14 days before the SARS patient developed symptoms.

Based on the evidence available, it seems reasonable to conclude that these mass quarantines in China had little or no effect on the epidemic. Moreover, the imposition of quarantine led to panic that could have spread the disease if identification of contacts was necessary to contain SARS. When a rumor spread that Beijing itself might be placed under martial law, *China News Service* reported that 245,000 migrant workers from impoverished Henan province fled the city to return home. Even in Hong Kong's Amory Gardens, the site of the initial cluster of SARS cases in Hong Kong, when officials came to relocate residents to a quarantine facility they found no one at home in more than half of the complex's 264 apartments. People were able to evade the police even though the police were working closely with public health officials.

Canada had the only major outbreak of SARS outside of Asia, and it was limited to the Toronto area. Canada had about 440 probable or suspect SARS cases, resulting in 40 deaths, but many more lives were directly affected. Approximately 30,000 people were quarantined, although unlike China, almost all Canadians who were quarantined were confined to their own homes — and staying home, or "sheltering in place" seems to have become the new standard for isolating and protecting individuals in public health emergencies, at least in democracies.

Canadian officials were generally levelheaded in their advice to the public, but seem to have overreacted on two occasions. In mid-April, 2003, before Easter, Ontario health officials published full-page newspaper ads asking anyone who had even one symptom of SARS (severe headache, severe fatigue, muscle aches and pains, fever of 38 Celsius or higher, dry cough and shortness of breath) to stay home for a few days. Ontario's health minister said, "This is a time when the needs of a community outweigh those of a single person." Again, in June, during the second wave of infections in Ontario, the health minister, responding to reports that some people were not completing their 10 day home quarantines, said "I don't know how people will like this, but we can chain them to a bed if that's what it takes." While the request may have arguably been reasonable, the threat was not. At a June 2003 WHO meeting on SARS, Health Canada's senior director general, Paul Gully, noted that intra-hospital transmission was the "most important amplifier of SARS infections" and wondered aloud about the utility of the widespread home quarantines during the Canadian epidemic. His reasoning was that very few of those quarantined wound up exhibiting symptoms of SARS.

There were few cases of SARS in the U.S. and no deaths. The Centers for Disease Control and Prevention (CDC) worked with the World Health Organization and other countries to identify the SARS virus, and issued guidelines and recommendations in press conferences and on its website. Perhaps the most important recommendations involved travel. In this category the CDC issued both travel alerts (which consist of a notification of an outbreak of a specific disease in a geographic area and suggests ways to reduce the risk of infection and what to do if you become ill), and travel advisories (which include the same information, but further recommend against nonessential travel because the risk of disease transmission is considered too high). No attempt was ever made to prohibit Americans from traveling anywhere, although the federal government probably has the authority to do this for international travel (*e.g.*, through passport limitations) should the risk of disease become extreme. Nor do there seem to have been any attempts in the U.S. by public health officials to quarantine asymptomatic contacts of SARS patients.

The CDC also issued reasonable guidance to businesses with employees returning from areas affected with SARS, recommending that while in areas with SARS those "with fever or respiratory symptoms should not travel and should seek medical attention" and upon return asymptomatic travelers "should be vigilant for fever and respiratory symptoms over the 10 days after departure." Most important, the CDC noted that "those persons need not limit their activities and should not be excluded from work, meetings, or other public areas, unless fever or respiratory symptoms develop." In bold letters on its guidelines it underlined the point: "At this time, CDC is not recommending quarantine of persons returning from areas with SARS." The president did, nonetheless, add SARS to the outdated federal list of "quarantinable communicable diseases" on April 4, 2003, and customs and immigration officials were given the authority to detain those entering the U.S. who were suspected of having SARS. This authority was not exercised.

Of course, the public can overreact on its own, and in some cases clearly did — as restaurants in Chinatowns in New York and Boston were virtually empty for a time. The worst offenders were not the uninformed public, however, but academic institutions, some of which forbade their faculty and students to travel to areas that had SARS cases, or required them to spend ten days after they returned in self-imposed quarantine and obtain a physician's certificate that they did not have SARS before returning to campus. Academic institutions with similar policies included both Harvard and Boston University, even though the Boston Public

Health Commission had reasonably advised on April 9, 2003:

> At this point there is no evidence to suggest that a person without symptoms may infect others with SARS. In the absence of fever or respiratory symptoms, anyone who has traveled to high-risk areas or has been exposed to SARS patients may continue normal activities — isolation or quarantine is not recommended. Persons should not be excluded from school or work.

Anita Barry, director of communicable disease control at the Boston Public Health Commission had warned only four days earlier: "The biggest challenge for now with SARS is fear and rumor and panic." As a general matter, local public health officials acted very responsibly, even under extreme pressure. Although there were no quarantines in the U.S., there were cases in which isolation of symptomatic individuals was advised or mandated by local public health departments.

In New York, 27 people were advised by the city health department to stay home for a period of ten days after their SARS fever had returned to normal. In addition, two individuals in New York City and one in Dallas were ordered to be isolated in hospitals because it was suspected they had SARS. The first of these was a young student on a tour around the world. He sought medical care in a New York City hospital and was diagnosed as a suspect case. He would have been quarantined at home, but had none, so he was ordered by the Department to remain in the hospital for ten days after his fever abated, and an unarmed security guard was posted at his door to enforce the order. He was offered an attorney to advise him about fighting the order, but refused. Ten days after the resolution of his fever he left town and has not been heard of since. The second case involved a person who was voluntarily in the hospital, but who became restless and wanted to leave before the ten days was up. He was ordered to stay, and put under guard as well.

The third case, from Dallas, also sought care in a hospital and was diagnosed as a suspect case. He gave a false address. The Dallas County Department of Health and Human Services sought and obtained a court order requiring him to remain in the hospital for ten days. At the hearing all in attendance (including the judge) "were provided with protective gear to wear to avoid any possible exposure to the disease while in the presence of the patient." This alone made it virtually certain that the judge would find the patient a potential danger to the public and order continued isolation, which he did.

In the midst of the SARS epidemic, New York City did, however, change its health code to permit the city's health commissioner to order the quarantine of individuals who "may" endanger the public health because of smallpox, pneumonic plague, or other severe communicable disease. In addition, a contact may also be quarantined: someone who "has been or may have been" in "close, prolonged, or repeated association with a case or carrier." This change in the code from permitting the quarantine of people who actually pose a danger to the public health and who have actually been in close contact with infected individuals, to those who "may" pose a danger and those who "may" have been in close contact with them is breathtaking in its invitation to arbitrariness. Given this, it is disturbing that not one person showed up to testify at the April 28, 2003 public hearing on this change.

In the case of SARS, for example, which the revised rules specifically reference in a section on "post-publication changes," the new regulation would have permitted the department to quarantine New York's entire Chinatown area since all residents there "may" have been in contact with someone who "may" have SARS. No one (thankfully) seems to have even suggested such a rerun of the totally arbitrary San Francisco Chinatown quarantine, allegedly for plague. Nonetheless, it is worth noting that even 19th century U.S. courts, while granting extremely broad powers to public health agencies, condemned the arbitrary use of quarantine, even for smallpox, requiring public health officials to show "facts which warranted isolation."

SARS may return, but the CDC is to be commended for providing the U.S. with a credible and open official (the CDC director, Julie Gerberding, herself) who informed Americans about what they could voluntarily do to avoid contracting or spreading the disease. Nationally, encouragement of sensible voluntary responses became policy, and no state invoked any emergency powers, including quarantine, in response to SARS. As a general rule, sick people seek treatment and accept isolation to obtain it — people do not want to infect others, especially their family members, and will voluntarily follow reasonable public health advice to avoid spreading disease. SARS, like the threat of a bird flu pandemic, emphasizes that effective public health today must rely on actions taken at the national and international level, and that public health should be seen primarily as a global issue. Virtually every country in the world had to take some action to limit the exposure of its people to the disease.

SARS was a major public health challenge; but it is no less a medical challenge. At the beginning of the 21st century, sick people seek medical care. Individuals believed to be infected with the disease were (and continue to be) cared for one-by-one by physicians and nurses in hospitals. In fact, one of the salient aspects of the SARS epidemic is that many (in some countries, most) infections were actually acquired in hospitals, and many of those infected, and some who died, were physicians and nurses who cared for the patients. The dedication of the physicians and nurses who treated SARS patients was exemplary. Neither public health nor medicine alone could have effectively dealt with SARS. The old distinctions between medicine and public health are blurring, and perhaps the most important message is that public health and medicine must work together to be effective.

Of course, SARS is not HIV/AIDS, which is not smallpox, which is not plague or tuberculosis or bioterrorism. Each infectious disease is different, and epidemiology provides the key to any effective public health and medical response to a new disease. The rapid exchange of information, made possible by the internet and an interconnected group of laboratories around the world (set up primarily for influenza identification and tracking), were critical to combating fear with knowledge. Information really does travel faster than even a new virus, and managing information is the most important task of modern public health officials. People around the world, provided with truthful, reasonable information by public health officials who are interested in both their health and human rights will follow their advice.

Isolating sick people seems to have been critical to containing SARS, but better infection-control techniques in hospitals, and adherence to them, are equally necessary. Quarantining contacts, where it was attempted, seems to have been both ineffective (in that many, if not most, contacts eluded quarantine) and useless (in that almost none of those quarantined developed SARS). Mass quarantine is a relic of the past that seems to have outlived its usefulness. Attempts at mass quarantine, as evidenced by the experience in China, are now likely to create more harm than they prevent. They do this both by imposing unnecessary restrictions on liberty on those quarantined, and by encouraging potentially infected people to flee from public health officials.

NOTES AND QUESTIONS

1. **Is SARS unique?** As with tuberculosis, SARS is clearly a serious disease, although, thus far, a major outbreak of SARS has been avoided. But consider some of the characteristics of SARS that make it and diseases like it particularly troubling: Much like TB, people infected with SARS may not know they have it, at least initially. Thus people can be exposed and infected, but asymptomatic for up to 10 days, during which time they can travel and potentially expose many other people. Even when symptoms start, they are indistinguishable from many, more common, and less lethal viral infections such as influenza (although as discussed in the Pandemic Influenza Preparedness and Response Plan, an outbreak of influenza can be a public health problem of epidemic proportions as well). Yet, once these symptoms start, even a casual contact with a person infected with SARS can lead to an infection.

One of the most troubling aspects of the SARS outbreaks in 2003 was the number of health care workers who contracted SARS while caring for hospitalized patients who had not been diagnosed with SARS. To make matters worse, there was no apparent cure or treatment for people with SARS; the disease merely ran its course and was often fatal.

For additional information on SARS, see www.cdc.gov/sars and www.who.int/csr/sars/en/ (visited May 2014).

2. **SARS in the US.** The effects of the SARS epidemic on the United States were limited — more of a warning of what might happen in the future than a first encounter with a full-blown epidemic. Nonetheless, some efforts were made to control the initial and future spread of the disease. As reported by Rothstein:

> The CDC's Global Migration and Quarantine Division has coordinated efforts to prevent and control the spread of infectious diseases with other federal agencies, state and local health departments, the travel industry, and other organizations. The Division has eight permanent quarantine stations at major points of entry staffed by 30 permanent quarantine inspectors. During the SARS outbreak staffing and presence were augmented to 23 quarantine stations (15 new ports of entry) and 150 additional staff in order to provide information to travelers arriving from SARS-affected countries via airplanes, ships or land; distributing health alerts to travelers with information regarding symptoms of SARS and what to do if they should develop SARS-like symptoms; examining travelers aboard

airplanes and ships who have been reported as being ill with SARS-like symptoms; providing updates to other government agencies; and working with the CDC SARS investigation team and local and state health departments. SARS-specific yellow health alert cards were distributed to over 2.7 million arriving passengers disembarking from over 11,000 flights and 62 ships over a three-month period.

3. **Other infectious threats.** Even if there is not another outbreak of SARS, there are many other new and "nasty" infectious diseases that could create a similar pandemic scenario: West Nile virus, Hantavirus, Ebola virus, Nipah virus, Hendra virus, just to name a few that have recently drawn some attention. Are there really more such diseases today and are these contemporary threats any different from those that humans have faced throughout history? In May of 2003, the IOM convened a panel of experts to address that question. Their answers were not comforting and, in general, affirmed the popular impression that there is a surge in new diseases. To explain that apparent trend they pointed to 13 factors that encourage the development of new diseases:

— microbial adaptation

— human susceptibility to infection

— climate and weather changes

— changing ecosystems

— changes in human demographics and behavior

— increased economic development and land use

— international travel and commerce

— spread of technology and industry

— breakdown of public health measures

— poverty and social injustice

— war and famine

— lack of political will

— bioterrorism

Obviously, not all of these factors are references to new phenomena. But the panel made particular reference to the modern trend towards the manipulation of the natural environment, the increasing number of large, crowded urban areas, and the increased level of travel and international commerce. They also noted that many of the new diseases have lived for some time in animals, and have spread to humans more frequently as more people move into habitats that were previously used predominantly by other animals.

For the full report, see IOM, MICROBIAL THREATS TO HEALTH: EMERGENCE, DETECTION, AND RESPONSE (2003).

4. **Federal bioterrorism law.** In June 2002, President Bush signed the Public Health Security and Bioterrorism Preparedness and Response Act of 2002. Among the provisions of that legislation was a clarification of the federal authority to extend isolation and quarantine measures not only to people who are infectious but also to

people who have been exposed to a communicable disease and may potentially become infectious; the legislation also had provisions that clarified procedures for expediting the executive orders under § 264.

Prior to the SARS outbreak, the list of federal diseases subject to federal quarantine authority under § 264 had not been updated since 1983 and was limited to cholera, diphtheria, tuberculosis, plague, small pox, yellow fever, and viral hemorrhagic fevers. Following the outbreak, SARS was added to the list as noted above. This essentially gave CDC and other federal health officials the authority to isolate or quarantine anyone who was considered infectious or who had been exposed to anyone who was considered infectious. This authority was, however, never exercised during the SARS outbreak.

For a broader discussion of the interrelation of federal and state authority in these situations, see James J. Misrahi, Joseph A. Foster, Frederic E. Shaw & Martin S. Cetron, *HHS/CDC Legal Response to SARS Outbreak*, 10(2) EMERGING INFECTIOUS DISEASES 353 (Feb. 2004).

5. SARS myths. While the data and studies done to date confirm that at best, "the effectiveness of quarantine remains in doubt [in the case of SARS]," LAWRENCE GOSTIN, GLOBAL HEALTH LAW 36 (2014), some public health experts continue to believe that it was an important intervention. *See, e.g.*, Harvey V. Fineberg, *Pandemic Preparedness and Response: Lessons from the H1N1 Influenza of 2009*, 370 NEW ENGL. J. MED. 1335 (2014) (asserting that SARS was halted "mainly owing to isolation and quarantine.").

H. BIOTERROR PREPAREDNESS AND RESEARCH

UNITED STATES v. BUTLER
429 F.3d 140 (5th Cir. 2005), *cert. denied*, 574 U.S. 1131 (2006)

BEFORE WIENER, DEMOSS, AND PRADO, CIRCUIT JUDGES.

PER CURIAM

Appellant Dr. Thomas Butler was convicted on 47 of 69 counts of various criminal activity relating to work he performed as a medical researcher at the Texas Tech University Health Sciences Center ("HSC"). Of these 47 counts, Butler was convicted of 44 counts of contract-related crimes, including theft, fraud, embezzle-ment, mail fraud, and wire fraud, (collectively, the "Contract Counts"). Butler was also convicted of three counts relating to the transportation of human plague bacteria ("*Yersinia pestis*" or "YP"), including the illegal exportation of YP to Tanzania, the illegal transportation of hazardous materials, and making a false statement on the waybill accompanying the YP vials shipped to Tanzania, (collec-tively, the "Plague Counts").

Butler was a professor and Chief of Infectious Diseases in HSC's Internal

Medicine Department since 1987. As part of Butler's pay structure, a percentage of his income was provided by the State of Texas while the remainder came from the Medical Practice Income Plan ("MPIP"). Under MPIP, a doctor earned money by seeing patients, receiving research grants, or conducting clinical studies under the auspices of HSC. The monies received from the patients a doctor treated and the funds paid out for the research/studies was remitted to HSC. Part of these monies paid for HSC's overhead costs and other expenses while another part was paid out as the non-state portion of the doctor's income. Any remaining funds from a clinical study was transferred to a developmental account for the researcher's department or division. The money in this account was earmarked for expenses such as professional dues and business travel, none of which was related to any particular project.

When a researcher at HSC was in a position to obtain a research grant or conduct a clinical study, it was required that the accompanying documentation be submitted to the institution for approval. Moreover, any monies paid out as a result of the research grant or clinical study were required to be paid directly to the institution. Consulting contracts, however, received different treatment from research grants or clinical studies. Specifically, a consulting contract was viewed by HSC as a means for a doctor to sell his or her expertise or advice directly to a third party, such as in designing a drug study. The consulting would not involve patient care or patient safety issues, and the consultant would not be using HSC's resources such as labs and personnel. Because of these considerations, consulting contracts were permissible without HSC's financial involvement or approval, unlike contracts covering clinical studies.

Between 1998 and 2001, Butler entered into several clinical study contracts with two different pharmaceutical companies, Pharmacia and Chiron. The first contract entered into with Pharmacia occurred in March 1998. Under this contract, Pharmacia agreed to pay HSC $2,400 for each patient enrolled in the clinical study. Apparently unbeknownst to HSC, however, Pharmacia and Butler entered into another "shadow" or "split" contract that provided Butler with an additional $2,400 per patient enrolled in the same study. A similar contract was entered into between Pharmacia and Butler in the spring of 2000 and again in the fall of 2000.

With respect to the contract in the fall of 2000, there was another HSC researcher, Dr. Casner, who was working on the same study as Butler. Dr. Casner's contract with Pharmacia was not split, and therefore it appeared that he had a budget twice the size of Butler's. A representative with HSC who was aware of Dr. Casner's contract, contacted Butler to inform him that she could get Butler a bigger budget. Butler allegedly refused the offer and informed the HSC representative that he would remain in charge of negotiating his own contracts. Butler had also negotiated two similar contracts with Chiron (another pharmaceutical company), using the contracts with Pharmacia as a template. The contracts with Chiron involved drug studies that were conducted in February 1999 and March 2000. Butler received payments under the contracts with Pharmacia and Chiron until August 2001.

The existence of the shadow contracts first came to the attention of HSC in July 2002, when an HSC representative learned from a Pharmacia representative that

Butler was getting one-half of the money from the Pharmacia studies, while HSC received the other half. HSC initiated a preliminary investigation into the split contracts that continued until January 9, 2003, when HSC informed Butler by letter that an additional investigation by authorities charged with compliance issues was to begin. In the letter, HSC sought a response from Butler by no later than January 21, 2003. For the reasons discussed below, HSC never received the requested response.

In addition to his work at HSC in Texas, Butler conducted plague research in Tanzania in 2001. Then, in April 2002, Butler returned to Tanzania where, for approximately 10 days, he worked on research of plague in human patients at clinics there. Part of his research involved personally culturing and sub-culturing specimens that he planned to bring back to the United States for additional studies.

Having returned to the United States with the *Yersinia pestis* cultures, Butler continued his research. Then, on January 13, 2003, four days after receiving the letter from HSC auditors warning of the impending investigation into the alleged shadow contracts, Butler reported that 30 vials of the *Yersinia pestis* were missing from his HSC laboratory in Lubbock. The FBI was immediately notified and within hours descended upon Lubbock, where Butler was questioned. Eventually, Butler revealed that the *Yersinia pestis* was not actually missing, but that he had destroyed the vials accidentally.

In April 2003, a grand jury returned a 15-count indictment charging Butler with various crimes relating to his transporting of *Yersinia pestis*, the providing of false statements to FBI agents regarding *Yersinia pestis*, and a tax crime. A superseding indictment was returned by the grand jury in August 2003, in which Butler was charged with 54 additional criminal counts, including mail fraud, wire fraud, and embezzlement that arose out of Butler's agreements with the pharmaceutical companies and the Food and Drug Administration (the "FDA"). Butler filed a motion seeking to sever the Contract and Plague Counts, which the district court denied. After a three-week trial in November 2003, the jury returned a mixed-verdict against Butler, finding him guilty on most of the Contract Counts and not guilty on most of the Plague Counts and the tax count. On March 10, 2004, the district court sentenced Butler to 24 months' imprisonment, three years' supervised release, $15,000 in fines, and a $4,700 special assessment. Butler was also ordered to pay HSC restitution in the amount of $38,675. Butler timely filed the instant appeal.

DISCUSSION

I. Whether the district court erred by not severing the Contract Counts and the Plague Counts.

On appeal, Butler argues the Federal Rules of Criminal Procedure and this Circuit's case law prohibit the joinder of unrelated criminal categories charged; here, the Contract Counts and the Plague Counts. Butler contends that trying all the counts together caused him prejudice. Conversely, the Government maintains that joinder was proper because the charges in the superseding indictment were linked as transactions within a common scheme or plan.

The indictment specifically outlines Butler's research into non-plague-related diseases for Pharmacia and Chiron and his plague-related research for the FDA. The indictment's description of Butler's scheme to defraud explained how he failed to disclose material facts to HSC regarding not only the Pharmacia and Chiron contracts, but also the plague-related contracts with the FDA.

The introduction to the superseding indictment details how the FDA offered research opportunities to medical professionals regarding "the development and review of medications for the prevention and treatment of illness that could be caused by terrorists using biological agents." The FDA subsequently purchased Butler's professional service, and specifically, according to the indictment, "for the results of experimental research regarding the postantibiotic effect of drugs on the microorganism *Yersinia pestis*," and later "to provide experimental results from [Butler]'s laboratory about the postantibiotic effect of drugs on various strains of *Yersinia pestis* isolated from plague patients in Tanzania."

Meanwhile, the actual FDA fraud counts charged Butler with attempting to conceal the existence of his FDA contracts from HSC's administrative review and approval process. Butler was alleged to have subsequently obtained payments from the FDA without distributing any monies therefrom to HSC in accordance with HSC's relevant policies for doing so.

The superseding indictment clearly sets forth an alleged common scheme that connects both Butler's plague research and the Pharmacia/Chiron pharmaceutical contracts to the FDA fraud counts. In doing so, the superseding indictment, on its face, creates an overlap that logically intertwines the Contract Counts with the Plague Counts.

* * *

V. Whether the Government presented sufficient evidence as to the Contract and Plague Counts.

. . . Butler maintains there was insufficient evidence to support the jury's finding that he willfully: (1) exported *Yersinia pestis* to Tanzania without a license; (2) described in a misleading manner the *Yersinia pestis* as "laboratory materials" on the FedEx waybill; and (3) violated federal hazardous material regulations when he shipped the *Yersinia pestis* to Tanzania.

As to the first sub-issue, the Government points this panel to evidence introduced at trial that Butler certified on the FedEx waybill that the samples were being "exported . . . in accordance with Export Administration Regulations," when in fact they were not. The Government notes that Butler had in his office a document downloaded from the Center for Disease Control website that clearly indicated a Department of Commerce permit was required to export *Yersinia pestis*. As further evidence of Butler's knowledge of export requirements, the Government observes that Butler previously signed four waybills shipping hazardous materials to Canada and checked the box indicating a Shipper's Export Declaration was not needed (which it is not in those circumstances). Moreover, the Government introduced evidence that during the 1990s, Butler properly shipped infectious substances and other dangerous goods more than 30 times. Based on this evidence, Butler's argument here must fail.

With regard to Butler's conviction for making a false statement by labeling the *Yersinia pestis* as "laboratory materials," he contends that because he did not intend to deceive anyone, he cannot be found to have acted willfully. The Government responds by noting that Butler also certified on that same label that he was not shipping dangerous goods. According to the Government, a reasonable person certainly could conclude that an accomplished researcher, who was the Chief of Infectious Diseases at HSC and had spent considerable time studying plague abroad, would have known that plague was a dangerous good requiring the proper identification thereof. Accordingly, Butler's sufficiency of the evidence argument on this sub-issue is also without merit.

Finally, Butler contends his conviction for violating hazardous material regulations required the Government to prove that his infraction could not have been due to a good faith mistake or misunderstanding of the law. The Government responds with an argument identical to its reason why there was sufficient evidence establishing Butler's unlawful export of *Yersinia pestis* to Tanzania without a license: Butler had successfully and legally shipped hazardous materials at least 30 times before making this particular shipment. Importantly, Butler comes forward with no specific evidence of his own on appeal refuting the Government's evidence, or establishing what about his actions warranted a finding that he made a good faith mistake or misunderstood the law. Without more, a reasonable trier of fact could have found that the evidence established guilt beyond a reasonable doubt.

Having carefully reviewed the entire record of this case, and having fully considered the parties' respective briefing and arguments, we conclude the district court did not commit reversible error by refusing to sever the Contract Counts from the Plague Counts. Moreover, the district court made appropriate discovery and evidentiary rulings. Also, there was sufficient evidence supporting Butler's convictions under the Contract Counts and the Plague Counts . . . . Accordingly, we AFFIRM Butler's conviction and sentence.

NOTES AND QUESTIONS

1. **Butler sentencing.** On January 2, 2006, Butler completed his two-year sentence and was released. A scientific article detailing his plague research in Tanzania, completed while he was in prison, was published shortly thereafter. *See* William Mwengee, Thomas Butler *et al.*, *Treatment of Plague with Gentamicin or Doxycycline in a Randomized Clinical Trial in Tanzania*, 40 CLINICAL INFECTIOUS DISEASE 614 (2006).

2. **Butler's case and science ethics.** The case of physician-researcher Thomas Butler has been the subject of many commentaries — most arguing that his prosecution represents a gross overreaction on the part of federal authorities. Nonetheless, in an article in *Science*, Margaret A. Somerville and Ronald M. Atlas argued that Butler's prosecution "sent a clear signal to the research community,

especially scientists and university researchers, that all ethical and legal require-
·ments must be respected when undertaking research." They continued, "Biosafety
regulations are not merely legal technicalities. They constitute some of the terms of
the pact between science and the public that establishes public trust." *Ethics: A
Weapon to Counter Bioterrorism*, 307 SCIENCE 1881 (2005).

Ethical guidelines for life sciences research that could be related to bioterrorism
do seem critical, and the scientific community should be actively engaged in setting
the standards for such research. As the National Research Council of the National
Academy of Sciences has stated, "biological scientists have an affirmative moral
duty to avoid contributing to the advancement of biowarfare or bioterrorism." It is
reasonable for society to expect that scientists will adopt the equivalent of the
physician's "do no harm" principle. Arguing for such an oath well before September
11, literary scholar Roger Shattuck noted that it could "help scientists scrutinize the
proliferation of research in dubious areas" as well as "renew the confidence of
ordinary citizens" in what is a potentially revolutionary endeavor. FORBIDDEN
KNOWLEDGE 224 (1996).

But can an ethical code be effective? What should it say? Who should write it?
Consider, for example, the National Research Council's seven classes of microbial
experiments that should require special review:

> *The experiments would:*
>
> Demonstrate how to render a vaccine ineffective;
> Confer resistance to therapeutically useful antibiotics or antiviral agents;
> Enhance the virulence of a pathogen or render a non-pathogen virulent;
> Increase transmissibility of a pathogen;
> Alter the host range of a pathogen;
> Enable the evasion of diagnostic and detection methods;
> Enable the weaponization of a biologic agent or toxin.

BIOTECHNOLOGY RESEARCH IN AN AGE OF TERRORISM 5 (2004).

3. **Categorizing biological weapons.** The major approach the administration
has taken toward potential bioterrorism since 9/11 has been to categorize biological
agents according to their risks of being used as a terrorist weapon. The current
scheme has three categories, and the fact that plague is in category A goes a long
way toward explaining why the FBI acted so strongly against Butler.

Category A: Anthrax, botulism, plague, smallpox, tularemia, viral hemorrhagic
fevers.

Category B: Brucellosis, food safety threats, glanders, melioidosis, psittacosis, Q
fever, ricin toxin, staphyloccocococcal enterotoxin B, typhus fever, viral encephalitis,
water safety threats.

Category A, or "high priority agents . . . pose a risk to national security because
they can be easily disseminated or transmitted from person to person; result in high
mortality rates and have the potential for major public health impact; might cause
public panic and social disruption; and, require special action for public health
preparedness."

Category B agents "include those that are moderately easy to disseminate; result in moderate morbidity rates and low mortality rates; and require specific enhancements of CDC's diagnostic capacity and enhanced disease surveillance."

There is also a *Category C* for those agents "that could be engineered for mass dissemination in the future because of availability; ease of production and dissemination; and potential for high morbidity and mortality rates and major health impact." CDC, BIOTERRORISM AGENTS/DISEASES, http://www.bt.cdc.gov/agent/agentlist-category.asp (visited May 2014).

An Institute of Medicine committee suggested that making such lists is not a useful way to counter bioterrorism because they cannot take the future of science into account. They concluded, among other things, that we need a new threat reduction paradigm for the biological sciences. In the Committee's words:

> First, the future is now. Even in the short time since the creation of the committee, we have seen the phenomenon of RNA Interference capture the collective consciousness of the life sciences community, providing entirely new insights into how human genes are normally regulated and how this regulation might be disrupted for malevolent purposes by those intent on doing harm.

> Similarly, "synthetic biology," an approach embraced and discussed by few at the time the Committee was formed, has now been redefined and promoted on the cover of one of the most widely read scientific journals. Neither of these developments could have been foretold even a few years back, pointing to the futility of trying to predict with accuracy what will come in the next few years.

INSTITUTE OF MEDICINE, COMMITTEE ON ADVANCES IN TECHNOLOGY AND THE PREVENTION OF THEIR APPLICATION TO NEXT GENERATION BIOWARFARE THREATS: GLOBALIZATION, BIOSECURITY, AND THE FUTURE OF THE LIFE SCIENCES viii (2006). On the risks to public health from concentrating too much on preparedness, see TERRORISM AND PUBLIC HEALTH: A BALANCED APPROACH TO STRENGTHENING SYSTEMS AND PROTECTING PEOPLE (Barry S. Levy & Victor W. Sidel, eds., 2003).

4. Do thoughts of 9/11 spur overreactions (bioterror and bioart)? There are other examples where an arguably overly-aggressive FBI seems to see bioterrorism where it would not have seen it before 9/11 — including in art — wasting time, effort, and resources that could almost certainly be better spent trying to identify real bioterrorist threats:

> Shortly after Butler's trial, in another part of the country — Buffalo, New York — FBI agents were called in to investigate a suspected act of bioterrorism in the home of Steve Kurtz, a professor and artist at the State University of New York at Buffalo. Kurtz awoke on May 11, 2004, to find his wife dead beside him. Kurtz and his wife previously had cofounded the Critical Art Ensemble, an artists' collective "dedicated to exploring the intersections between art, technology, radical politics and critical theory." Kurtz liked to distinguish what he did from the emerging field of "bioart," which is perhaps best known to the public because of the notoriety of Alba, a rabbit that glowed green because of the insertion of a jellyfish gene. Kurtz

thinks of bioart as consisting of stunts and his own art as an exploration of "the political economy of biotechnology." He had previously argued against the introduction of genetically modified food, and he had encouraged activists to oppose it by means of "fuzzy biological sabotage" — for instance, by releasing genetically mutated and deformed flies at restaurants to stir up paranoia.

The day after his wife's death, the FBI raided his home in full bio-hazard gear. Kurtz had been studying the history of germ warfare for a new project. In connection with this project, he was growing bacterial cultures that he was planning to use to simulate attacks with anthrax and plague. He had obtained the bacteria samples (*Serratia marcescens* and *Bacillus atrophaeus*) from a colleague, Professor Robert Ferrell, a geneticist at the University of Pittsburgh Medical Center, who had ordered them for him from the American Type Culture Collection. Kurtz and Ferrell were suspected almost immediately of being involved in a bioterror ring and were thoroughly investigated. Once the New York Department of Health determined that the bacteria were harmless and that Kurtz's wife had died of natural causes, the bioterrorism investigation was dropped. The Justice Department nonetheless charged both Ferrell and Kurtz with four counts of wire fraud and mail fraud. The allegation was that Ferrell, at Kurtz's request, defrauded the University of Pittsburgh and the American Type Culture Collection by representing that the bacteria samples he ordered would be used in his University of Pittsburgh lab-oratory. [As of January 2007] neither case has yet gone to trial.

Exactly what Kurtz was planning to do with the bacteria is unclear, but serratia, which is known for its ability to form bright red colonies, has been used in biowarfare simulations in the past. Perhaps its most well-known use was a 1950 simulation in which an offshore naval vessel blanketed a 50-square-mile section of San Francisco with an aerosol spray containing serratia to determine what dose could be delivered effectively to the population. Whether using a similar technique as an art exhibit would constitute bioart, biotechnology, or bio-hazard (or even bioterrorism) may be in the eye of the beholder even more than in the eye of the artist or scientist.

Bioart is not bioterrorism, but the two are related politically. As bioart curator and commentator Jens Hauser has said, bioart aims "at the heart of our fears" and is meant to "disturb." He notes, "these artists expose the gulf between the apologetic official discourse about technoscience on the one hand, and paranoia on the other." Like defensive and offensive bioweapons research, bioart and biotechnology may be impossible to distinguish by anything other than the researcher's or creator's intent. Thus, Alba, the bunny with the inserted jellyfish gene, is considered to be and is accepted as a creation of bioart, at least in the contemporary art community; whereas ANDi, the monkey with the inserted jellyfish gene, is considered to be a creation of science, at least in the biotechnology community. Hauser was referring to paranoia in the face of the "rapid acceleration of technical prowess." On the basis of the reaction of federal law enforcement to the actions of Thomas Butler and Steve Kurtz, however, although the advances of biotechnology that have potential applications to bioterrorism and biowarfare are scary, even scarier are the responses — in the name of preventing bioterrorism — of law-enforcement agencies to legitimate scientists and artists whose actions pose no threat to the public.

Butler's arrest came about one year after a simulated bioterrorism event in Lubbock, Texas; this simulation involved the use of aerosolized plague at a civic center. Simulations have been a center-piece of efforts to prepare for acts of bioterrorism. As we should have learned from our obsession with building bomb shelters during the cold war, however, simulations promote fear of worst-case scenarios and make them look much more likely. Bioterrorism simulations such as Dark Winter (smallpox) and Top Officials (TOPOFF) involve more art than science and are likely to provoke a response based more on fear than logic. They should probably be classified as bioart in the sense of performance art, and they should have their most socially useful outlet not in federal law-enforcement agencies or biosafety laboratories but in television dramas like *24*.

George J. Annas, *Bioterror and "Bioart" — A Plague o' Both Your Houses*, 354 NEW ENGL. J. MED. 2715 (2006).

Do you agree? Are law enforcement agencies overreacting or underreacting to the threat of bioterrorism?

Annas concludes:

One reasonable response to the dispute between Butler and the Justice Department and the dispute between Kurtz and the Justice Department could be Mercutio's retort in *Romeo and Juliet*: "A plague o' both your houses." This is because the public is currently more victim and bystander than participant and seems much more likely to be harmed than helped by much of the research. Members of the public recognize this probability, and their skepticism of federal authorities, of the effectiveness of countermeasures, of the existence of weapons of mass destruction in Iraq, and of the entire bioterrorism scare is well illustrated by the few people who took drugs to treat anthrax that were offered after the anthrax attacks. This same skepticism, combined with the lack of evidence of stockpiles of smallpox in Iraq and the certainty of side effects from the drugs, also explains the small number of health professionals who volunteered to take the smallpox vaccine immediately before and shortly after the commencement of the war in Iraq.

Id. at 2719.

5.   Fiction and bioterror. At least some over-reactions can be traced to books highlighting the dangers of a bioterrorist attack. President Bill Clinton, for example, said he first became focused on this risk when he read Richard Preston's novel, THE COBRA EVENT (1997). Preston later wrote a nonfiction book on the dangers of a smallpox attack, THE DEMON IN THE FREEZER: A TRUE STORY (2002). Perhaps more frightening to public health officials were the book by the former Soviet head of bioweapons development, KEN ALIBEK, BIOHAZARD: THE CHILLING

TRUE STORY OF THE LARGEST COVERT BIOLOGICAL WEAPONS PROGRAM IN THE WORLD — TOLD FROM INSIDE BY THE MAN WHO RAN IT (1999), and one by Minnesota epidemiologist MICHAEL OSTERHOLM (WITH JOHN SCHWARTZ), LIVING TERRORS: WHAT AMERICANS NEED TO KNOW TO SURVIVE THE COMING BIOTERRORIST CATASTROPHE (2000). All of these books portray what might be described as worst case scenarios. The value of concentrating on worse cases (instead of likely cases) is debatable. Of course, the nuclear arms race provided the background for over-reaction, complete with its "mutually assured destruction" scenarios, home fallout shelters, and "duck and cover" grade school exercises. *See, e.g.,* HERMAN KAHN, ON THERMONUCLEAR WAR (2d ed. 1961), and SHARON GHAMARI-TABIZI, THE WORLDS OF THERMONUCLEAR WAR (2005).

"Worst case scenarios" are not only popular in emergency preparedness training exercises, but also in more mundane public health problems such as deciding if a particular site for a new post-9/11 research laboratory is safe for the public. Controversy continues, for example, over Boston University's BSL-4 laboratory on the Boston Medical Center campus in the city of Boston.

George J. Annas, *The Statue of Security: Human Rights and Post-9/11 Epidemics*
38 J. HEALTH L. 319-22, 327-28, 330-31, 340-41, 350-51 (2005)

Our enemies are innovative and resourceful, and so are we. They never stop thinking about new ways to harm our country and our people, and neither do we.

President George W. Bush on signing the Defense Appropriations Act, Aug. 5, 2004

Immediately after 9/11 the U.S. government closed the Statue of Liberty to the public. It took almost three years to reopen Liberty Island, just in time for the Republican National Convention. The public can again visit, but little is the same. Those wishing to take the ferry to the island, for example, must submit to airport-like screening, as well as bag checks, including bomb-sniffing dogs, upon arrival. And on the boat trip, the National Park Service has a new recorded "welcome" which asserts that although historically the Statue of Liberty symbol-ized freedom, it is now "a symbol of America's freedom, safety, and security." Similar screening is also required to view the Liberty Bell in Philadelphia. We have not yet renamed the Statue of Liberty, the "Statue of Security"; or the Liberty Bell, the "Safety Bell," but safety and security have been consistently promoted as at least as important as liberty, and often more important, since 9/11.

The next stop after Liberty Island is Ellis Island, the site of screening for more than 2 million immigrants to America in the early 20th century. The most rigorous part of screening immigrants involved federal uniformed public health service physicians whose main duty was to prevent immigrants with contagious diseases from entering the country. Few federal public health officials other than the Surgeon General any longer wear military uniforms, and most public health activities now are done under state or local jurisdiction. But 9/11 has affected public health as well, as public health has been called upon to prepare the nation for a "bioterrorist attack" utilizing lethal disease agents, like smallpox or anthrax. Many public health officials hope that public health can take advantage of the new funding available for terrorism preparedness, and not only do its part in national security, but also make "dual use" of the funding to help it fulfill its core missions of protecting the public's health and preparing for "natural" epidemics.

September 11 was an event, not an epidemic, but the U.S. reacted to it as if it portends an actual epidemic of terrorist attacks against us. In this way, September 11 has been viewed by many in the public health community as a signal of a coming pandemic: akin to the rise of SARS in China, or a novel form of bird flu in Asia. And public health has been asked to prepare for both natural and terrorist-induced epidemics simultaneously. Does 9/11 mean we must make fundamental changes in public health practice regarding epidemic control and revert to 19th century Ellis Island-type quarantine and forced treatment? Must we trade off human rights and civil liberties for increased safety and security? These are important and complex questions. In this article I argue that the answer to both of these questions is no, and that the movement in public health toward the adoption of a modern health and human rights ethical framework begun before 9/11 should continue.

. . . The U.S. is more vulnerable to terrorist attacks than we had believed; and we should strengthen our defenses. But we should not undermine our lives and our values by overreacting to the threat of terrorism. Preserving a human rights framework in the war on terrorists both preserves core American values, and makes it more likely that we will prevail in the long run. Ignoring or marginalizing human and constitutional rights, and treating Americans themselves as suspects or actual enemies is counterproductive and dangerous in itself — a conclusion I will support in this article with specific post-9/11 examples, such as public health preparedness plans for mass smallpox vaccination, the experiences of public health in the SARS epidemic, the enactment of new state public health vaccination and quarantine laws, and the use of torture on terrorist suspects and prisoners of war. Public health professionals are the "good guys" and rightly want to protect the public's health. But the world has changed since the early 19th century, and reliance on coercion rather than education is no longer either legally justifiable or likely to be effective. In this regard, what might be labeled "public health fundamentalism," is as dangerous to the health and safety of Americans as Islamic religious fundamentalism.

The language of human rights also has the great advantage of being universal and thus global. Neither the fight against terrorists, nor the fight against epidemics, can be successfully waged on a local, state, or even national level alone: both can easily cross national boundaries and both can only be effectively confronted by a global, cooperative, strategy. "Safety first" is a good thought, as is the Hippocratic injunction, "first, do no harm"; but neither safety nor inaction are ends in themselves, but only means to promote health and human rights. Sacrificing human rights for safety is almost never necessary and almost always counterproductive in a free society. Benjamin Franklin went further in expressing an American thought from "the land of the free and the home of the brave," saying, "Those who would give up an essential liberty to purchase temporary security deserve neither liberty nor security. "

. . . Bioterrorism continues to be hyped beyond all scientific or historic reality, even in the public health community which should know better. A leading public health lawyer, for example, has asserted that "a single gram of crystalline botulinum toxin, evenly disperse and inhaled, could kill more than 1 million people." But, when looking at actual data, that same lawyer admits that in fact, when Aum Shinrikyo, the Japanese terrorist cult, actually "attempted to disperse aerosolized botulinum toxin both in Tokyo and at several military installations in Japan" the result was not millions dead, or even thousands or hundreds: rather all of these attacks "failed to kill anyone." Likewise, it has been asserted that the release of 100 kilograms of aerosolized anthrax over Washington, D.C. could kill up to three million people. The real anthrax attacks through the U.S. mails were highly effective in sowing terror in the populations, but resulted in only 5 deaths (the number killed in American hospitals by negligence every 30 minutes, or on our nation's highways every hour) . . . .

I wrongly and naively (it turns out) expected the federal government to provide increased funding for public health in the wake of 9/11. There has been some funding for bioterrorism, but mostly public health departments have been struggling with more unfunded federal mandates and suggestions, and have had to actually divert funds from public health programs we know work to save lives and improve health, to bioterrorism preparation which has little or no public health payoff.

My own state of Massachusetts, for example, always a national leader in public health, has made major cuts in tobacco control, domestic violence prevention, and immunizations against pneumonia and hepatitis A and B. Public health dollars have shrunken $30 million in two years, during which time Massachusetts has received $21 million for bioterrorism-related activities, some of which could be categorized as "dual-use. " Public health expert David Ozonoff of the Boston University School of Public Health accurately describes what is happening: "The whole bioterrorism initiative and what it's doing to public health is a cancer, it's hollowing out public health from within . . . . This is a catastrophe for American public health." This was dramatically demonstrated nationally in the fall of 2004 when the U.S. experienced a shortage of flu vaccine and was forced to ration it to Americans most at risk of death and hospitalization from the flu. Cartoonist Matt Davies caught the irony in his cartoon picturing a citizen coming to the door of the "Homeland Security Bio-Terror Readiness Unit" only to be greeted by a note pinned to the door reading, "Out with the Flu."

Other public health experts have put the weakening of public health in even more disturbing terms, noting "Worse, in response to bioterrorism preparedness, public health institutions are being reorganized along a military or police model that subverts the relationships between public health providers and the communities they serve." To the extent that these experts are correct, and I think they are, exaggerated fear of bioterrorism is resulting in overreaction that is already counterproductive in that it is harming both public health's effectiveness and its relationship with the communities' public health serves.

Exaggerated risks produce extreme responses that are based more on fear than facts, so it is not surprising that they have unintended consequences. Public health planning should be based on science not free-floating anxiety and fear. Instead of using the tools of public health, especially epidemiology to gather data and risk-assessment, to identify most likely risks and work on them, our government seems to have adopted the bizarre notion that all threats are equal and that all states and localities should equally prepare for all of them. This philosophy has produced two interrelated epidemics in the U.S. today: an epidemic of fear, and an epidemic of security screening . . . .

In the midst of concern over bioterrorism, but after the SARS epidemic, the New York Academy of Medicine did a survey of the American public asking how they would respond to two types of terrorist attacks: smallpox and a dirty bomb. Published in September 2004, the surveys' results support two lessons that were apparent on 9/11: (1) the primary concern Americans have in a crisis is the safety of their family members; and (2) the most important predictor of whether they will follow the advice of public officials is if they trust them to be telling the truth and to be guided by their welfare. Specifically, the survey found that only 40% of Americans would go to a vaccination site in a smallpox outbreak if told to do so, and only 60% would shelter in place for as long as they were told to in the event of a dirty bomb explosion.

The reasons given for not following advice are instructive. In the smallpox scenario, 60% had worries about the safety of the vaccine itself — twice as many who worried about getting smallpox themselves. The respondents also suggested ways to make them more likely to cooperate. For smallpox, overwhelming majorities (94% and 88%) wanted to speak with someone who knew a lot about smallpox and who they trusted to want what was best for them. A physician not working for the government would fit the bill. In the dirty bomb case, the primary concern respondents had was the safety of their family members. 75% of those who would not shelter in place said they would do so if they could communicate with people they care about or if they knew they were safe. Overall the study concluded that "people are more likely to follow official instructions when they have a lot of trust in what officials tell them to do and are confident that their community is prepared to meet their needs if a terrorist attack occurs."

These survey results are consistent with past bioterrorist exercises as well. As Senator Sam Nunn, who played the part of the president in the smallpox exercise, Dark Winter, in which mass quarantine failed, observed: "There is no force on earth that can make Americans do something that they do not believe is in their own best interests and that of their families." . . .

At the outset of the 21st century bioterrorism, although only one threat to public health, can be the catalyst to effectively federalize and integrate much of what is now uncoordinated and piecemeal state and local public health programs. This should include a renewed effort for national health insurance, national licensure for physicians, nurses, and allied health professionals, and national patient safety standards. Federal public health leadership will also encourage us to look outward, and to recognize that prevention of future bioterrorist attacks and even ordinary epidemics will require international cooperation. As the SARS epidemic illustrates, it is time to not only federalize public health, but to globalize it as well. And universal human rights is the proper foundation for a global public health ethic. . . .

The United States should lead the world in proclaiming a new, global public health, based on transparency, trust, and science, and most importantly, based on respect for human rights. We don't need a new Statue of Security; the Statue of Liberty is just fine.

NOTES AND QUESTIONS

6.   **The national plan** has defined roles for state and local officials as well:

Police, fire, public health and medical, emergency management, public works, environmental response, and other personnel are often the first to arrive and the last to leave an incident site. In some instances, a Federal agency in the local area may act as a first responder, and the local assets of Federal agencies may be used to advise or assist local officials in accordance with agency authorities and procedures. Mutual aid agreements provide mechanisms to mobilize and employ resources from neighboring jurisdictions to support the incident command.

When State resources and capabilities are overwhelmed, Governors may request Federal assistance under a Presidential disaster or emergency declaration. Summarized below are the responsibilities of the Governor, Local Chief Executive Officer, and Tribal Chief Executive Officer.

Governor

As a State's chief executive, the Governor is responsible for the public safety and welfare of the people of that State or territory. The Governor:

- Is responsible for coordinating State resources to address the full spectrum of actions to prevent, prepare for, respond to, and recover from incidents in an all-hazards context to include terrorism, natural disasters, accidents, and other contingencies;

- Under certain emergency conditions, typically has police powers to make, amend, and rescind orders and regulations;

- Provides leadership and plays a key role in communicating to the public and in helping people, businesses, and organizations cope with the consequences of any type of declared emergency within State jurisdiction;

- Encourages participation in mutual aid and implements authorities for the State to enter into mutual agreements with other States, tribes, and territories to facilitate resource-sharing;

- Is the Commander-in-Chief of State military forces . . . ; and

- Requests Federal assistance when it becomes clear that State or tribal capabilities will be insufficient or have been exceeded or exhausted.

Local Chief Executive Officer

A mayor or city or county manager, as a jurisdiction's chief executive, is responsible for the public safety and welfare of the people of that jurisdiction. The Local Chief Executive Officer:

- Is responsible for coordinating local resources to address the full spectrum of actions to prevent, prepare for, respond to, and recover from incidents involving all hazards including terrorism, natural disasters, accidents, and other contingencies;

- Dependent upon State and local law, has extraordinary powers to suspend local laws and ordinances, such as to establish a curfew, direct evacuations, and, in coordination with the local health authority, to order a quarantine;

- Provides leadership and plays a key role in communicating to the public, and in helping people, businesses, and organizations cope with the consequences of any type of domestic incident within the jurisdiction;

- Negotiates and enters into mutual aid agreements with other jurisdictions to facilitate resource-sharing; and

- Requests State and, if necessary, Federal assistance through the Governor of the State when the jurisdiction's capabilities have been exceeded or exhausted.

7. **All-hazards preparedness.** The post-9/11 approach has been an "all-hazards" one. What are the pros and cons to this type of "one-size fits all" planning? Is it true, as President Bush has said, that planning for a pandemic flu will build our capacity to respond to a chemical attack?

8. **Planning.** President Eisenhower, when he was commanding general in Europe, is credited with observing before the D-Day invasion: "It's not the plan, it's the planning." Explain. In March, 1942, Winston Churchill observed, "One cannot always provide against the worst assumptions, and to try to do so prevents the best disposition of limited resources. " What did these leaders mean and are these observations from World War II relevant today?

9. **Hurricane Katrina.** The most notorious example of a complete failure of the national preparedness plan was the response to Hurricane Katrina, despite the fact that only a year earlier the agencies responsible for responding to a hurricane/flood in New Orleans had participated in a simulation of just such a catastrophe, called "Hurricane Pam." Under new rules that existed at the time, the Department of Homeland Security was to be the lead agency, but it did not get involved until days after the flooding. On the day the levees broke, Secretary Chertoff traveled to Atlanta to take part in exercises designed to get the country ready for an avian flu pandemic. Almost a year later Chertoff announced the Department's new plan, which was that:

People should be prepared to sustain themselves for up to 72 hours after a disaster — because first responders might not be able to reach every single person within the first day. That means individuals — especially those in the Gulf states — need to have an emergency plan and an emergency kit with adequate supplied of food, water, and other essentials like a flashlight, first-aid, and medicine.

In the words of Christopher Cooper and Robert Block, who quote this speech from Chertoff to conclude their study of Katrina in DISASTER: HURRICANE KATRINA AND THE FAILURE OF HOMELAND SECURITY (2006): "In the end Chertoff unwittingly defined the most important lesson of all to emerge from Hurricane Katrina: When disaster strikes, we are all on our own." *Id.* at 306. On the actual response of local, state and federal officials during the week after Katrina struck, see DOUGLAS BRINKLEY, THE GREAT DELUGE: HURRICANE KATRINA, NEW ORLEANS, AND THE MISSISSIPPI GULF COAST (2006).

10. Public health as counter-terrorism. Lancet editor Richard Horton noted almost immediately after 9/11 that public health was a "neglected counterterrorist measure." By that he meant,

> [T]he existing narrow range of [counter-terrorism] options could be broadened to find ways of engaging and helping rather than punishing populations at risk . . . .
>
> . . . .
>
> First, foreign-policy goals should incorporate health, development, and human rights as key strategic objectives . . . . Second, the application of sanctions must be judged more wisely . . . . Third, western powers must recommit themselves to international agencies, such as the UN, and to international treaties, such as those on criminal justice and the environment . . . .
>
> The discipline of public health therefore adds fresh perspectives on foreign policy and counterterrorism measures. Principles of harm reduction are more realistic and practicable than false notions of a war on terrorism. Attacking hunger, disease, poverty, and social exclusion might do more good than air marshals, asylum restrictions, and identity cards. Global security will be achieved only by building stable and strong societies. Health is an undervalued measure of our global security.

Richard Horton, *Public Health: A Neglected Counterterrorist Measure*, 358 LANCET 1112 (2001).

11. Public health and bioterrorism. Horton makes a strong case in his editorial. Is he correct about the importance of public health to combat terrorism? Former UN Commissioner for Human Rights, Mary Robinson, has argued that our world is continually becoming less secure because of the increase in global public health problems. She quotes from the 2004 HUMAN DEVELOPMENT REPORT from the United Nations:

> More than 800 million people suffer from undernourishment. Some 100 million children who should be in school are not, 60 million of them girls. More than a billion people survive on less than one dollar a day . . . . And about 900 million people belong to ethnic, religious, racial or linguistic groups that face discrimination . . . . An unprecedented number of coun-

tries saw development slide backwards in the 1990s. In 46 countries people
are poorer today than in 1990. In 25 countries more people go hungry today
than a decade ago.

Id. at 129.

Robinson goes on to note that in the last six years approximately 25,000 people
have died from terrorist attacks. During that same time period, approximately
25,000 people die each day from hunger, malaria, and other preventable diseases.
Mary Robinson, *Connecting Human Rights, Human Development, and Human
Security, in* HUMAN RIGHTS AND THE "WAR ON TERROR" 311 (Richard Ashly Wilson, ed.,
2005).

12.   Development and terrorism. Economist Amartya Sen, cited by Robinson,
has also directly linked health — especially public health — to freedom and
economic development:

> Sometimes the lack of substantive freedoms relates directly to economic
> poverty, which robs people of the freedom to satisfy hunger, or to achieve
> sufficient nutrition, or to obtain remedies for treatable illnesses, or the
> opportunity to be adequately clothed and sheltered, or to enjoy clean water
> or sanitary facilities. In other cases, the unfreedom links closely to the lack
> of public facilities and social care, such as the absence of epidemiological
> programs, or of organized arrangements for health care or educational
> facilities . . . .

AMARTYA SEN, DEVELOPMENT AS FREEDOM 4 (1999). *See also* THE WORLD BANK, WORLD
DEVELOPMENT REPORT 1993: INVESTING IN HEALTH (1993) (relationship between health
and development).

Chapter 7

PRIVACY AND USES OF MEDICAL INFORMATION

A. INTRODUCTION

Sound public health policy depends importantly on accurately identifying health risks and effective methods of decreasing or eliminating those risks. What is causing young men and women in a coastal city to fall ill with vomiting and dizziness — a bacterium in the water, a virus spread by sneezing, a chemical in the workplace, a saboteur, or terrorist plot? How can it be eliminated? Can a viral or chemical agent be removed from the water supply or industrial process? If not, can it be reduced to a tolerable level? What kinds of medical care are effective and are they worth the cost? This chapter examines the programs that gather the information to answer such questions. Throughout the materials, the recurring questions are: What kind of information does government need to protect public health? When can government demand your personal health information without your consent or even your knowledge?

Justice Brandeis called privacy the "right most valued by civilized men," *Olmstead v. United States*, 277 U.S. 438, 478 (1928) (dissenting). Today, it may become the right most challenged by technology, the value of data, and even curiosity. The explosion of information and the technology that makes it easy to use can create tensions between government's legitimate need for good information about health risks and public policy protecting personal privacy. Publicity surrounding the National Security Agency's monitoring of phone, email, and internet information heightened public awareness of how much personal information is being collected and used. Many in the health care and public health communities argue that identifiable information about individuals should be more freely available to government agencies and private researchers without the person's knowledge or consent. Critics of this view do not dispute the value of information, but rather the need for so much individually *identifiable* information. They argue that government agencies, private researchers, and commercial industries always offer a plausibly good reason for obtaining identifiable information without consent, so that such purposes offer no principled protection for privacy.

Part B introduces the array of laws protecting the privacy and confidentiality of personal medical information. Section C examines mandatory reporting laws in light of the relevant U.S. Supreme Court decisions analyzing constitutional protection for information privacy. (These are limited to data collection for civil purposes. This chapter does not cover law enforcement demands for information for purposes of criminal prosecutions. *See* Chapter 10 for related materials on drug testing.)

Part D provides background on the history and evolution of what is today called public health surveillance, focusing on HIV case reporting, which became controversial in part because it highlighted the role of case reporting in identifying people who can be subjected to compulsory isolation (discussed in Chapter 5).

Today, health data is valuable for broader purposes. Part E considers whether and when surveillance programs are conducting research with identifiable data that would require individual consent. It also examines different definitions of Fair Information Practices and how they might mitigate concerns over data collection and use.

Three themes are threaded though the materials in this chapter. First, the value of good information for public health policy sometimes competes for primacy with the values of personal autonomy and privacy. Reasonable people weigh the two differently, often depending upon whether they are the observers or the observed. Second, the way in which courts balance the two depends importantly on the particular law governing each case. For example, different statutes may authorize the ongoing collection of data or require a subpoena for specific documents. Personal health information is subject to a fragmented array of laws governing information privacy, often with ambiguous or unsettled applications and exceptions. The choice of law (or laws) turns not only on what information is collected, but who collects it, from whom, how it is collected, how it is used, whether it is kept secure and confidential, and whether and how it is further disclosed to third parties and for what purpose.

Finally, the explosion of data relevant to public health is challenging traditional conceptions of the types of information that should not be obtained without individual consent and information that should be shared without consent for the good of all, as well as what counts as a public health justification for such data collection. The apex of disease surveillance may have been the decades between 1955 and 1985, when public health officials were most true to Alexander Langmuir's admonition that surveillance should be "information for action" and largely focused on communicable diseases. Courts have generally deferred to public health assessments that personal health information is necessary for "public health purposes" or "disease control." Today, courts and public health practitioners may mean quite different things by those terms. In this age of "Big Data," with public health attention turned to "epidemics" of cancer, diabetes and obesity, the meaning of "disease control" as a justification for surveillance may undergo reexamination. These issues are taken up in Chapter 8, *infra*, concerning surveillance and screening for chronic diseases, including cancer, genetic conditions, and environmental exposures.

B.   ACCESS TO MEDICAL RECORDS

FAA v. COOPER
132 S. Ct. 1441 (2012)

JUSTICE ALITO.

The Privacy Act of 1974, codified in part at 5 U.S.C. § 552a, contains a comprehensive and detailed set of requirements for the management of confidential records held by Executive Branch agencies. If an agency fails to comply with those requirements "in such a way as to have an adverse effect on an individual," the Act authorizes the individual to bring a civil action against the agency. § 552a(g) (1) (D) . For violations found to be "intentional or willful," the United States is liable for "actual damages. " § 552a(g) (4) (A). In this case, we must decide whether the term "actual damages, " as used in the Privacy Act, includes damages for mental or emotional distress. We hold that it does not.

I

The Federal Aviation Administration (FAA) requires pilots to obtain a pilot certificate and medical certificate as a precondition for operating an aircraft. 14 CFR §§ 61.3(a), (c) (2011). Pilots must periodically renew their medical certificates to ensure compliance with FAA medical standards. *See* § 61.23(d). When applying for renewal, pilots must disclose any illnesses, disabilities, or surgeries they have had, and they must identify any medications they are taking. *See* 14 CFR pt. 67.

Respondent Stanmore Cooper has been a private pilot since 1964. In 1985, he was diagnosed with a human immunodeficiency virus (HIV) infection and began taking antiretroviral medication. At that time, the FAA did not issue medical certificates to persons with respondent's condition. Knowing that he would not qualify for renewal of his medical certificate, respondent initially grounded himself and chose not to apply. In 1994, however, he applied for and received a medical certificate, but he did so without disclosing his HIV status or his medication. He renewed his certificate in 1998, 2000, 2002, and 2004, each time intentionally withholding information about his condition.

When respondent's health deteriorated in 1995, he applied for long-term disability benefits under Title II of the Social Security Act, 42 U.S.C. § 401 *et seq.* To substantiate his claim, he disclosed his HIV status to the Social Security Administration (SSA), which awarded him benefits for the year from August 1995 to August 1996.

In 2002, the Department of Transportation (DOT), the FAA's parent agency, launched a joint criminal investigation with the SSA, known as "Operation Safe Pilot," to identify medically unfit individuals who had obtained FAA certifications to fly. The DOT gave the SSA a list of names and other identifying information of 45,000 licensed pilots in northern California. The SSA then compared the list with its own records of benefit recipients and compiled a spreadsheet, which it gave to the DOT.

The spreadsheet revealed that respondent had a current medical certificate but had also received disability benefits. After reviewing respondent's FAA medical file and his SSA disability file, FAA flight surgeons determined in 2005 that the FAA would not have issued a medical certificate to respondent had it known his true medical condition.

When investigators confronted respondent with what had been discovered, he admitted that he had intentionally withheld from the FAA information about his HIV status and other relevant medical information. Because of these fraudulent omissions, the FAA revoked respondent's pilot certificate, and he was indicted on three counts of making false statements to a Government agency, in violation of 18 U.S.C. § 1001. Respondent ultimately pleaded guilty to one count of making and delivering a false official writing, in violation of § 1018. He was sentenced to two years of probation and fined $1,000.

Claiming that the FAA, DOT, and SSA (hereinafter Government) violated the Privacy Act by sharing his records with one another, respondent filed suit in the United States District Court for the Northern District of California. He alleged that the unlawful disclosure to the DOT of his confidential medical information, including his HIV status, had caused him "humiliation, embarrassment, mental anguish, fear of social ostracism, and other severe emotional distress." Notably, he did not allege any pecuniary or economic loss.

[The District Court granted summary judgment against respondent, finding that although the Government had violated the Privacy Act and there was a triable issue of fact as to whether the violation was intentional or willful, the Privacy Act did not authorize the recovery of damages from the Government for nonpecuniary mental or emotional harm. The United States Court of Appeals for the Ninth Circuit reversed and remanded, concluding that the Act permits recovery of nonpecuniary losses.]

II

Because respondent seeks to recover monetary compensation from the Government for mental and emotional harm, we must decide whether the civil remedies provision of the Privacy Act waives the Government's sovereign immunity with respect to such a recovery.

A

. . . .

The question that confronts us here is not whether Congress has consented to be sued for damages under the Privacy Act. That much is clear from the statute, which expressly authorizes recovery from the Government for "actual damages." Rather, the question at issue concerns the scope of that waiver. For the same reason that we refuse to enforce a waiver that is not unambiguously expressed in the statute, we also construe any ambiguities in the scope of a waiver in favor of the sovereign.

. . . .

B

The civil remedies provision of the Privacy Act provides that, for any "intentional or willful" refusal or failure to comply with the Act, the United States shall be liable for "actual damages sustained by the individual as a result of the refusal or failure, but in no case shall a person entitled to recovery receive less than the sum of $1,000."

. . . .

. . . Because Congress declined to authorize "general damages," we think it likely that Congress intended "actual damages" in the Privacy Act to mean special damages for proven pecuniary loss.

. . . .

III

D

We do not claim that the contrary reading of the statute accepted by the Court of Appeals and advanced now by respondent is inconceivable. But because the Privacy Act waives the Federal Government's sovereign immunity, the question we must answer is whether it is plausible to read the statute, as the Government does, to authorize only damages for economic loss. When waiving the Government's sovereign immunity, Congress must speak unequivocally. Here, we conclude that it did not. As a consequence, we adopt an interpretation of "actual damages" limited to proven pecuniary or economic harm. To do otherwise would expand the scope of Congress' sovereign immunity waiver beyond what the statutory text clearly requires.

. . . .

. . . [W]e hold that the Privacy Act does not unequivocally authorize an award of damages for mental or emotional distress. Accordingly, the Act does not waive the Federal Government's sovereign immunity from liability for such harms.

NOTES AND QUESTIONS

1. **Remedies for violations of privacy.** *FAA v. Cooper*, excerpted *supra*, is a relatively rare example of a reported decision concerning invasion of an individual's privacy or a duty of maintaining the confidentiality of person's information. There are relatively few such reported decisions under either state or federal law. Can you think why that might be?

The Privacy Act provides: "No agency shall disclose any record which is contained in a system of records by any means of communication to any person, or to another agency, except pursuant to a written request by, or with the written consent of, the individual to whom the record pertains." 5 U.S.C. § 552a(b). The Act applies only to federal agencies and the personal data they collect and hold. (Other laws, however, authorize record sharing under certain circumstances.)

In *FAA*, there was no dispute that government agencies combined information about Cooper to determine his medical condition without his consent. Neither was there any dispute that the federal Privacy Act allows individuals to bring an action for damages for a government agency's "intentional or willful" violation of its obligations to protect the confidentiality of the personal information it holds. The issue before the Court was whether the federal government could be liable for harm that did not result in financial loss. What harm did Cooper suffer? Whatever you might think of his actions, how, if at all, might his medical condition affect his ability to fly an airplane? Should qualifications for a pilot's license be based on general standards or individualized determinations?

Justice Sotomayor, dissenting, argued that the majority's holding left most individuals without any remedy under the federal Privacy Act:

> Today the Court holds that "actual damages" is limited to pecuniary loss. Consequently, individuals can no longer recover what our precedents and common sense understand to be the primary, and often only, damages sustained as a result of an invasion of privacy, namely mental or emotional distress. That result is at odds with the text, structure, and drafting history of the Act. And it cripples the Act's core purpose of redressing and deterring violations of privacy interests. I respectfully dissent.

132 S. Ct. at 1456.

2. The constitutional right to information privacy. The origin of privacy jurisprudence is often attributed to Warren and Brandeis's now classic exposition of "the right to privacy," the amorphous collection of rights and duties protecting individual control over one's person and reputation. Samuel D. Warren & Louis D. Brandeis, *The Right to Privacy,* 4 HARV. L. REV. 193, 196 (1890) . Their arguments were grounded in common law, but thereafter took on constitutional dimensions. As a Supreme Court Justice, dissenting in *Olmstead v. United States,* 277 U.S. 438 (1928), Brandeis argued that the Fourth Amendment protects a personal "right to be let alone." Since that time, the scope and bounds of individual autonomy to control personal information have been developed and debated, but not fully delineated. In *Katz v. United States,* 389 U.S. 347, 350, n. 5 (1967), the United States Supreme Court agreed with Brandeis's earlier dissent that the Fourth Amendment "protects people, not places." But, the *Katz* court also noted, "Virtually every governmental action interferes with personal privacy to some degree. The question in each case is whether that interference violates a command of the United States Constitution. "

Protections against government intrusions into different personal and private matters can be found in the Fourth Amendment's protection against unreasonable searches and seizures, *Katz, supra*; the First Amendment's protection of freedom of association, *NAACP v. Alabama,* 357 U.S. 449 (1958), and freedom to speak anonymously, *McIntyre v. Ohio Elections Comm'n,* 514 U.S. 334 (1995); and the Fifth Amendment's protection against self-incrimination and the disclosure of some personal information, *Whalen v. Roe,* 429 U.S. 589 (1977). The U.S. Supreme Court has distinguished the line of constitutional cases protecting information privacy or "the individual interest in avoiding disclosure of personal matters" (*see Whalen v. Roe*, Part C, *infra.*), from the cases protecting personal autonomy in personal decision making concerning family, marriage, procreation, and raising children, but the lines blur when sensitive information is at issue. (*See* Part C, *infra.*) Federal courts of appeal have also recognized that the Fourteenth Amendment protects a person's privacy interest in personal information, especially medical information.

Constitutional protection is typically limited to a "reasonable expectation of privacy," based on Justice Harlan's two-prong standard in his concurrence in *Katz*. A person must have an actual expectation of privacy and that expectation must be one that "society is prepared to accept as 'reasonable'." What expectations of privacy are reasonable today? In a 2013 court filing related to National Security Agency revelations, Google reportedly stated that its 425 million email users have no "reasonable expectation" that their email communications will be kept private or confidential. Dominic Rushe, *Google: Don't Expect Privacy When Sending to Gmail*, THE GUARDIAN, Aug. 14, 3013. However, even Google (and Yahoo) reported surprise at the NSA's collection of email and other information that the companies sent or received internationally, and called it "snooping." Charlie Savage, Claire Cain Miller & Nicole Perlroth, *N.S.A. Said to Tap Google and Yahoo Abroad*, NEW YORK TIMES B1, Oct. 31, 2013.

3. Federal legislation. Beyond constitutional protection, federal statutes, and regulations provide some specific protections for personal information that vary with whether the entity seeking the information is public or private, the type of information sought, and how it is to be used. (*See* Box.) Some of these authorize government collection of various types of personal information, with little or no protection. There is no single comprehensive federal (or state) privacy law governing all personal information or even all medical information in all hands, resulting in a patchwork with both gaps and some overlap. The major federal effort at protecting privacy resulted in the Privacy Act of 1974. Congressional hearings on the bill offer a useful history of privacy concerns. *Privacy: The Collection, Use and Computerization of Personal Data (Part 2): Joint Senate Hearings before the Ad Hoc Subcomm. on Privacy and Information Systems of the Comm. on Government Operations and Subcomm. on Constitutional Rights of the Comm. on the Judiciary*, 93rd Cong. 2240, 2246 (1974). The Act created the Privacy Protection Study Commission, whose final 1977 report remained perhaps the most complete analysis of general privacy issues for decades. PRIVACY PROTECTION STUDY COMMISSION, PERSONAL PRIVACY IN AN INFORMATION SOCIETY (1977). Still, most agencies are subject to their own statutory rules. For example, the Public Health Service Act prohibits information obtained by the National Center for Health Statistics from being used for any other purpose without consent and from being published in identifiable form without consent. 42 U.S.C. § 242m. The Department of Health and Human Services issued its HIPAA Privacy Rule, excerpted and discussed *infra*, to provide more consistency in the protection of electronic medical records, but the Rule applies only to specifically covered entities and allows state laws that are more protective of privacy to govern where they apply. Despite publicity surrounding revelations of federal surveillance of domestic telephone calls, emails, and internet use, the substantive law has changed little in the past quarter century. *See The NSA Files*,

The Guardian, www.theguardian.com/world/the-nsa-files (visited Sept. 2013); Joy Pritts *et al.*, *The State of Health Privacy: An Uneven Terrain*, Institute for Health Care Research and Policy, 1999.

Federal Laws Regulating the Privacy of Health Information

- Privacy Act of 1974, 5 U.S.C. § 552a
- Computer Matching and Privacy Protection Act, amending Privacy Act
- Communications Assistance for Law Enforcement Act, Pub. L. 103–414
- Electronic Communications Privacy Act, 18 U.S.C. §§ 2510–2522, 2701–2709

(1986)
- Children's Online Privacy Protection Act, 15 U.S.C. §§ 6501–6506 (1998)
- Driver's Privacy Protection Act of 1994, 18 U.S.C. §§ 2721–2725
- Fair Credit Reporting Act, 15 U.S.C. § 1681 *et seq.*, as amended by the Fair

and Accurate Credit Transactions Act
- Family Educational Rights and Privacy Act, 20 U.S.C. §§ 1221 note, 1232g
- Foreign Intelligence Surveillance Act, 15 U.S.C. §§ 1801–1811
- Freedom of Information Act, 5 U.S.C. § 552(a)
- Food, Drug and Cosmetic Act, 21 U.S.C. § 301 *et seq.*
- Gramm-Leach-Bliley Act of 1999, 15 U.S.C. §§ 6801–6809
- Health Insurance Portability and Accountability Act, Pub. L. 104–191;

Health Information Security and Privacy Regulations, 42 C.F.R. Parts 160 &

164
- Health Information Technology for Economic and Clinical Health

(HITECH) Act, Pub. L. 111–5, 123 Stat. 115 (part of American Recovery and

Reinvestment Act of 2009)
- Health Research Extension Act (1985), Public Health Service Act § 491, and

Federal Policy for the Protection of Human Subjects ("Common Rule"), 42

C.F.R. Part 46.
- Personal Responsibility and Work Opportunity Reconciliation Act of 1996,

Pub. L. 104–193
- Substance Abuse Confidentiality Requirements, Public Health Service Act

§ 543; 42 C.F.R. Part 2, U.S. Safe Harbor Privacy Principles (Developed to

comply with European Union Directive on Data Protection)
- USA-PATRIOT Act of 2001, Pub. L. 107–56

Note: Statutes with Pub. L. numbers are codified in scattered sections of the

United State Code

---

4. State law. Privacy protections can also be found in state constitutional, statutory, and common law. At least 10 states have constitutional provisions protecting privacy. State common law typically recognizes a cause of action for breach of confidentiality against a physician who reveals a patient's medical information without the patient's consent (out of court) . Different causes of action for invasion of privacy are available against those who obtain private information to which they are not otherwise entitled without the person's consent. The reasons for protecting medical information were cogently summarized in *Alberts v. Devine*, 479 N.E.2d 113 (Mass. 1985):

> We continue to recognize a patient's valid interest in preserving the confidentiality of medical facts communicated to a physician or discovered by the physician through examination. "The benefits which inure to the relationship of physician-patient from the denial to a physician of any right to promiscuously disclose such information are self-evident. On the other hand, it is impossible to conceive of any countervailing benefits which would arise by according a physician the right to gossip about a patient's health. " "To foster the best interest of the patient and to insure a climate most favorable to a complete recovery, men of medicine have urged that patients be totally frank in their discussions with their physicians. To encourage the desired candor, men of law have formulated a strong policy of confidentiality to assure patients that only they themselves may unlock the doctor's silence in regard to those private disclosures. The result which these joint efforts of the two professions have produced . . . has been urged or forecast in *una voce* by commentators in the field of medical jurisprudence. " [Internal citations omitted.]

Massachusetts also has a general privacy statute, which states, in its entirety:

> Right of Privacy, Remedy to Enforce. A person shall have a right against unreasonable, substantial or serious interference with his privacy. The superior court shall have jurisdiction in equity to enforce such right and in connection therewith to award damages.

M.G.L. ch. 214, § 1B. How would you interpret this language? How does it compare to the federal Privacy Act and other more specific statutes?

State statutes cover a wide range of specific circumstances, with most targeting financial and business records. Medical licensure laws or regulations may treat breach of confidentiality as unprofessional conduct subject to disciplinary action. Licensure laws governing other health professionals and health care facilities contain comparable requirements for patient confidentiality, medical recordkeeping and data security. Rules of evidence specify certain permitted disclosures and grant (limited) testimonial privileges. The use of genetic information is often the subject of a specific statute. Laws governing research specify privacy protections, while other disease-specific laws strictly limit the disclosure of information about particular diseases, like HIV test results or substance abuse treatment. State public records laws often contain exceptions to public disclosure for medical and other confidential information. Both statutory and common law also specify circumstances in which a person may be compelled to reveal personal medical information, such as in a lawsuit in which the person's medical condition is at issue. *See, e.g.*, *John B. v. Bridget B.*, 137 P.3d 153 (Cal. 2006). Mandatory reporting statutes, discussed in Part C, *infra*, are the best known exceptions to the general rule allowing individuals to decide who can obtain their private health information.

5. **Resources.** Resources on laws affecting privacy are available from the Center for Democracy and Technology at www.cdt.org/issue/health-privacy (visited Sept. 2013) and the Electronic Privacy Information Center, a privacy advocacy organization at www.epic.org (last visited Sept. 2013).

IN THE MATTER OF MIGUEL M.
950 N.E.2d 107 (N.Y. 2011)

Opinion by JUDGE SMITH, CHIEF JUDGE LIPPMAN, and JUDGES CIPARICK, GRAFFEO, READ, PIGOTT, and JONES Concur.

We hold that the Privacy Rule adopted by the federal government pursuant to the Health Insurance Portability and Accountability Act (HIPAA) prohibits the disclosure of a patient's medical records to a State agency that requests them for use in a proceeding to compel the patient to accept mental health treatment, where the patient has neither authorized the disclosure nor received notice of the agency's request for the records.

I

Dr. Charles Barron, as designee of the New York City Department of Health and Mental Hygiene, applied for an order under Mental Hygiene Law § 9.60 requiring "assisted outpatient treatment" (AOT) for Miguel M. The petition alleged that Miguel was suffering from a mental illness; that he was unlikely to survive safely in the community without supervision; that he had a history of failing to comply with treatment; that he was unlikely to participate in necessary treatment voluntarily; and that he needed, and would benefit from, AOT to prevent a relapse or deterioration of his mental status, which would be likely to result in serious harm to Miguel or to others.

. . . Barron offered in evidence records from two hospitals relating to three occasions on which Miguel was hospitalized. A witness called by Barron testified that the hospitals had furnished the records in response to a request — a request made without notice to Miguel. The witness acknowledged that Miguel had not authorized the release of the records, and no court order for their disclosure had been sought or obtained.

The records were received in evidence over Miguel's objection, and Barron's witness described their contents. After the hearing, Supreme Court directed that Miguel "receive and accept assisted outpatient treatment" for a period of six months. The Appellate Division affirmed. We granted leave to appeal, and now reverse.

II

. . . .

Mental Hygiene Law § 9.60, known as "Kendra's Law," was enacted in 1999. It is named for Kendra Webdale, who was killed by a mentally ill man who pushed her off a subway platform. It says that, on a proper showing, a mentally ill person whose lack of compliance with treatment has, twice within the last 36 months, caused him or her to be hospitalized may be the subject of AOT pursuant to a plan stated in a court order. Public officials identified as "directors of community services" are given the duty of enforcing Kendra's Law, and a petition to require AOT may be filed by a director of community services or his or her designee. Mental Hygiene Law § 33.13 (c) (12) permits disclosure of medical records to a director of community services who requests it in the exercise of his or her duties. Thus, the disclosure of a patient's medical records for purposes of an AOT proceeding is permitted by State law, unless the applicable State law is preempted. Miguel argues that it is.

Miguel says that preemption is found in HIPAA (Pub L No 104–191, 110 U.S. Stat 1936, codified in various titles of the United States Code) and the Privacy Rule (45 CFR Titles 160 and 164) promulgated by the United States Department of Health and Human Services under authority granted by HIPAA § 264(c)(1). The Privacy Rule prohibits disclosure of an identifiable patient's health information without the patient's authorization, subject to certain exceptions (45 CFR § 164.508[a][1]). HIPAA § 264(c)(2) and the Privacy Rule (45 CFR § 160.203[b]) say that contrary state laws are preempted unless they offer privacy protections that are "more stringent" than those of the federal law; New York does not offer any more stringent protection that is relevant here. The preemption issue thus comes down to whether the disclosure of Miguel's medical records was permitted by one of the exceptions to the Privacy Rule.

Barron relies on two exceptions, those permitting disclosure for purposes of "public health" and "treatment. ". . . . Considering the apparent purposes of these two exceptions, we conclude that neither fits these facts.

The public health exception permits disclosure of protected information to:

> A public health authority that is authorized by law to collect or receive such information for the purpose of preventing or controlling disease, injury, or disability, including, but not limited to, the reporting of disease, injury, vital events such as birth or death, and the conduct of public health surveillance, public health investigations, and public health interventions.

(45 CFR § 164.512[b][1][i]).

Barron reasons that disclosure of a mentally ill person's hospital records for purposes of requiring that person to accept AOT protects the public health, because mentally ill people might kill or injure other people — like Kendra Webdale — who, of course, are members of the public. Thus Barron, a person designated to enforce Kendra's Law, would be a "public health authority," collecting information for the "purpose of preventing . . . injury, " and his action to require AOT in Miguel's case could be called a public health intervention. We are not convinced, however, that the authors of the Privacy Rule meant "public health" in this literal, but counterintuitive, sense.

The apparent purpose of the public health exception is to facilitate government activities that protect large numbers of people from epidemics, environmental hazards, and the like, or that advance public health by accumulating valuable statistical information. To disclose private information about particular people, for the purpose of preventing those people from harming themselves or others, effects a very substantial invasion of privacy without the sort of generalized public benefit that would come from, for example, tracing the course of an infectious disease. The disclosure to Barron of Miguel's hospital records was not within the scope of the public health exception.

The treatment exception permits disclosure of protected health information "for treatment activities of a health care provider" (45 CFR § 164.506[c][2]). "Treatment" is defined as:

> the provision, coordination, or management of health care and related services by one or more health care providers, including the coordination or management of health care by a health care provider with a third party; consultation between health care providers relating to a patient; or the referral of a patient for health care from one health care provider to another.

(45 CFR § 164.501).

. . . .

Again, Barrons argument is literalistic: AOT — assisted outpatient treatment — is literally "treatment" — "the provision . . . of health care . . . by one or more health care providers." But the thrust of the treatment exception is to facilitate the sharing of information among health care providers working together. We see no indication that the authors of the regulation meant to facilitate "treatment" administered by a volunteer "provider" over the patient's objection. Disclosure for that purpose is a more serious invasion of privacy than, for example, the transmission of medical records from a patient's primary care physician to a specialist — the sort of activity for which the treatment exception seems primarily designed. The treatment exception is inapplicable here.

We find support for our conclusion that the two exceptions Barron relies on are inapposite in the existence of other exceptions that Barron might have invoked but did not. The Privacy Rule authorizes disclosure of health information, subject to certain conditions, "in the course of any judicial or administrative proceeding," in response to either "an order of a court or administrative tribunal" or "a subpoena, discovery request, or other lawful process". Thus, Barron could have pursued Miguel's records either by seeking a court order or by serving a subpoena. To do so in compliance with the Privacy Rule, however, Barron would have had to give notice to Miguel of his request for the records. He could not, absent extraordinary circumstances, have obtained a court order requiring disclosure without giving such notice . . . .

We can see no reason, and Barron has suggested none, why notice should not have been given here. It may well be, in this case as in many others, that no valid ground for withholding the records exists; courts ruling on disclosure issues will surely be conscious, as we are, of the strong public interest in seeing that mentally ill people who might otherwise be dangerous receive necessary treatment. But it seems only fair, and no great burden on the public agencies charged with enforcing Kendra's Law, to give patients a chance to object before the records are delivered.

We emphasize that it is far from our purpose to make the enforcement of Kendra's Law difficult. It may often be possible to avoid all disclosure problems by getting the patient to authorize the disclosure in advance; surely many mentally ill people will, while they are under proper care, recognize that disclosure is very much in their own interest. When . . . they do object, their objections may often be overruled. We hold only that unauthorized disclosure without notice is, under circumstances like those present here, inconsistent with the Privacy Rule.

III

Barron argues in the alternative that, even if the disclosure of the records to him was unlawful — as we have held it was — Supreme Court did not err by admitting the records into evidence at the AOT hearing. HIPAA, as Barron points out, contains its own remedies for violations: civil penalties and, for the knowing and wrongful disclosure of individually identifiable health information, fines and imprisonment. Neither exclusion of the records from evidence nor suppression of evidence obtained by use of the records is among the remedies listed. Barron cites decisions from other states holding that evidence obtained as a result of a HIPAA violation need not be suppressed in a criminal case [citations omitted].

We assume it is correct that, in a criminal case, a HIPAA or Privacy Rule violation does not always require the suppression of evidence. Indeed, we have held that suppression is not required in such a case where evidence was obtained as a result of a violation of New York's physician-patient privilege (*People v Greene*, 9 NY3d 277, 849 N.Y.S.2d 461, 879 N.E.2d 1280 [2007]). But this case is different. It is one thing to allow the use of evidence resulting from an improper disclosure of information in medical records to prove that a patient has committed a crime; it is another to use the records themselves, or their contents, in a proceeding to subject to unwanted medical treatment a patient who is not accused of any wrongdoing. Using the records in that way directly impairs, without adequate justification, the interest protected by HIPAA and the Privacy Rule: the interest in keeping one's own medical condition private. We therefore hold that medical records obtained in violation of HIPAA or the Privacy Rule, and the information contained in those records, are not admissible in a proceeding to compel AOT.

Accordingly, the order of the Appellate Division should be reversed, with costs, and the case remitted to Supreme Court for further proceedings in accordance with this opinion.

HEALTH INSURANCE PORTABILITY AND ACCOUNTABILITY ACT (HIPAA): STANDARDS FOR PRIVACY OF INDIVIDUALLY IDENTIFIABLE HEALTH INFORMATION
45 C.F.R. §§ 164.506, 164.508, 164.512

§ 164.506   Uses and disclosures to carry out treatment, payment or health care operations.

(a) Standard: Permitted uses and disclosures. Except with respect to uses or disclosures that require an authorization under § 164.508(a) (2) through (4) or that are prohibited under § 164.502(a) (5) (i), a covered entity may use or disclose protected health information for treatment, payment, or health care operations as set forth in paragraph (c) of this section, provided that such use or disclosure is consistent with other applicable requirements of this subpart.

. . . .

§ 164.508 Uses and disclosures for which an authorization is required.

(a) Standard: authorizations for uses and disclosures.—(1) Authorization required: General rule. Except as otherwise permitted or required by this subchapter, a covered entity may not use or disclose protected health information without an authorization that is valid under this section. When a covered entity obtains or receives a valid authorization for its use or disclosure of protected health information, such use or disclosure must be consistent with such authorization.

. . . .

§ 164.512 Uses and disclosures for which an authorization or opportunity to agree or object is not required.

A covered entity may use or disclose protected health information without the written authorization of the individual, as described in § 164.508, or the opportunity for the individual to agree or object as described in § 164.510, in the situations covered by this section, subject to the applicable requirements of this section. When the covered entity is required by this section to inform the individual of, or when the individual may agree to, a use or disclosure permitted by this section, the covered entity's information and the individual's agreement may be given orally.

(a) Standard: Uses and disclosures required by law. (1) A covered entity may use or disclose protected health information to the extent that such use or disclosure is required by law and the use or disclosure complies with and is limited to the relevant requirements of such law. (2) A covered entity must meet the requirements described in paragraph (c), (e), or (f) of this section for uses or disclosures required by law.

(b) Standard: uses and disclosures for public health activities.

(1) Permitted disclosures. A covered entity may disclose protected health information for the public health activities and purposes described in this paragraph to:

(i) A public health authority that is authorized by law to collect or receive such information for the purpose of preventing or controlling disease, injury, or disability, including, but not limited to, the reporting of disease, injury, vital events such as birth or death, and the conduct of public health surveillance, public health investigations, and public health interventions; or, at the direction of a public health authority, to an official of a foreign government agency that is acting in collaboration with a public health authority;

(ii) A public health authority or other appropriate government authority authorized by law to receive reports of child abuse or neglect;

(iii) A person subject to the jurisdiction of the Food and Drug Administration (FDA) with respect to an FDA-regulated product or activity for which that person has responsibility, for the purpose of activities related to the quality, safety or effectiveness of such FDA-regulated product or activity. Such purposes include:

(A) To collect or report adverse events (or similar activities with respect to food or dietary supplements), product defects or problems (including problems with the use or labeling of a product), or biological product deviations;

(B) To track FDA-regulated products;

(C) To enable product recalls, repairs, or replacement, or look-back (including locating and notifying individuals who have received products that have been recalled, withdrawn, or are the subject of look-back); or

(D) To conduct post marketing surveillance;

(iv) A person who may have been exposed to a communicable disease or may otherwise be at risk of contracting or spreading a disease or condition, if the covered entity or public health authority is authorized by law to notify such person as necessary in the conduct of a public health intervention or investigation; or

(v) An employer, about an individual who is a member of the workforce of the employer, if:

(A) The covered entity is a covered health care provider who is a member of the workforce of such employer or who provides health care to the individual at the request of the employer:

(1) To conduct an evaluation relating to medical surveillance of the workplace; or

(2) To evaluate whether the individual has a work-related illness or injury;

(B) The protected health information that is disclosed consists of findings concerning a work-related illness or injury or a workplace-related medical surveillance;

(C) The employer needs such findings in order to comply with its obligations, under 29 CFR parts 1904 through 1928, 30 CFR parts 50 through 90, or under state law having a similar purpose, to record such illness or injury or to carry out responsibilities for workplace medical surveillance; and

(D) The covered health care provider provides written notice to the individual that protected health information relating to the medical surveillance of the workplace and work-related illnesses and injuries is disclosed to the employer:

(vi) A school, about an individual who is a student or prospective student of the school, if:

(A) The protected health information that is disclosed is limited to proof of immunization;

(B) The school is required by State or other law to have such proof of immunization prior to admitting the individual; and

(C) The covered entity obtains and documents the agreement to the disclosure from either.

(1) A parent, guardian, or other person acting in loco parentis of the individual, if the individual is an unemancipated minor; or

(2) The individual, if the individual is an adult or emancipated minor.

(2) Permitted uses. If the covered entity also is a public health authority, the covered entity is permitted to use protected health information in all cases in which it is permitted to disclose such information for public health activities under paragraph (b)(1) of this section.

(c) Standard: Disclosures about victims of abuse, neglect or domestic violence.

(1) Permitted disclosures. Except for reports of child abuse or neglect permitted by paragraph (b) (1) (ii) of this section, a covered entity may disclose protected health information about an individual whom the covered entity reasonably believes to be a victim of abuse, neglect, or domestic violence to a government authority, including a social service or protective services agency, authorized by law to receive reports of such abuse, neglect, or domestic violence:

(i) To the extent the disclosure is required by law and the disclosure complies with and is limited to the relevant requirements of such law;

(ii) If the individual agrees to the disclosure; or

(iii) To the extent the disclosure is expressly authorized by statute or regulation and:

(A) The covered entity, in the exercise of professional judgment, believes the disclosure is necessary to prevent serious harm to the individual or other potential victims; or

(B) If the individual is unable to agree because of incapacity, a law enforcement or other public official authorized to receive the report represents that the protected health information for which disclosure is sought is not intended to be used against the individual and that an immediate enforcement activity that depends upon the disclosure would be materially and adversely affected by waiting until the individual is able to agree to the disclosure.

(2) Informing the individual. A covered entity that makes a disclosure permitted by paragraph (c)(1) of this section must promptly inform the individual that such a report has been or will be made, except if:

(i) The covered entity, in the exercise of professional judgment, believes informing the individual would place the individual at risk of serious harm; or

(ii) The covered entity would be informing a personal representative, and the covered entity reasonably believes the personal representative is responsible for the abuse, neglect, or other injury, and that informing such person would not be in the best interests of the individual as determined by the covered entity, in the exercise of professional judgment.

(d) Standard: Uses and disclosures for health oversight activities.

(1) Permitted disclosures. A covered entity may disclose protected health information to a health oversight agency for oversight activities authorized by law, including audits; civil, administrative, or criminal investigations; inspections; licensure or disciplinary actions; civil, administrative, or criminal proceedings or actions; or other activities necessary for appropriate oversight of:

(i) The health care system;

(ii) Government benefit programs for which health information is relevant to beneficiary eligibility;

(iii) Entities subject to government regulatory programs for which health information is necessary for determining compliance with program standards; or

(iv) Entities subject to civil rights laws for which health information is necessary for determining compliance.

(2) Exception to health oversight activities. For the purpose of the disclosures permitted by paragraph (d)(1) of this section, a health oversight activity does not include an investigation or other activity in which the individual is the subject of the investigation or activity and such investigation or other activity does not arise out of and is not directly related to:

(i) The receipt of health care;

(ii) A claim for public benefits related to health; or

(iii) Qualification for, or receipt of, public benefits or services when a patient's health is integral to the claim for public benefits or services.

(3) Joint activities or investigations. [Notwithstanding] paragraph (d)(2) of this section, if a health oversight activity or investigation is conducted in conjunction with an oversight activity or investigation relating to a claim for public benefits not related to health, the joint activity or investigation is considered a health oversight activity for purposes of paragraph (d) of this section.

(4) Permitted uses. If a covered entity also is a health oversight agency, the covered entity may use protected health information for health oversight activities as permitted by paragraph (d) of this section.

(e) Standard: Disclosures for judicial and administrative proceedings.

(1) Permitted disclosures. A covered entity may disclose protected health information in the course of any judicial or administrative proceeding:

(i) In response to an order of a court or administrative tribunal, provided that the covered entity discloses only the protected health information expressly authorized by such order; or

(ii) In response to a subpoena, discovery request, or other lawful process, that is not accompanied by an order of a court or administrative tribunal, if:

(A) The covered entity receives satisfactory assurance, as described in paragraph (e) (1) (iii) of this section, from the party seeking the information that reasonable efforts have been made by such party to ensure that the individual who is the subject of the protected health information that has been requested has been given notice of the request; or

(B) The covered entity receives satisfactory assurance, as described in paragraph (e)(1)(iv) of this section, from the party seeking the information that reasonable efforts have been made by such party to secure a qualified protective order that meets the requirements of paragraph (e)(1)(v) of this section.

(iii) For the purposes of paragraph (e)(1)(ii)(A) of this section, a covered entity receives satisfactory assurances from a party seeking protected health information if the covered entity receives from such party a written statement and accompanying documentation demonstrating that:

(A) The party requesting such information has made a good faith attempt to provide written notice to the individual (or, if the individual's location is unknown, to mail a notice to the individual's last known address);

(B) The notice included sufficient information about the litigation or proceeding in which the protected health information is requested to permit the individual to raise an objection to the court or administrative tribunal; and

(C) The time for the individual to raise objections to the court or administrative tribunal has elapsed, and:

(1) No objections were filed; or

(2) All objections filed by the individual have been resolved by the court or the administrative tribunal and the disclosures being sought are consistent with such resolution.

. . . .

(f) Standard: Disclosure for law enforcement purposes. A covered entity may disclose protected health information for a law enforcement purpose to a law enforcement official if the conditions in paragraphs (f) (1) through (f) (6) of this section are met, as applicable.

(1) Permitted disclosures: Pursuant to process and as otherwise required by law. A covered entity may disclose protected health information:

(i) As required by law including laws that require the reporting of certain types of wounds or other physical injuries, except for laws subject to paragraph (b) (1) (ii) or (c) (1) (i) of this section; or

(ii) In compliance with and as limited by the relevant requirements of:

(A) A court order or court-ordered warrant, or subpoena or summons issued by a judicial officer; or

(B) A grand jury subpoena; or

(C) An administrative request, including an administrative subpoena or summons, a civil or an authorized investigative demand, or similar process authorized under law, provided that:

(1) The information sought is relevant and material to a legitimate law enforcement inquiry;

(2) The request is specific and limited in scope to the extent reasonably practicable in light of the purpose for which the information is sought; and

(3) De-identified information could not reasonably be used.

. . . .

NORTHWESTERN MEMORIAL HOSPITAL v. ASHCROFT
362 F.3d 923 (7th Cir. 2004)

POSNER, JUDGE.

The government appeals from an order by the district court quashing a subpoena commanding Northwestern Memorial Hospital in Chicago to produce the medical records of certain patients on whom Dr. Cassing Hammond had performed late-term abortions at the hospital using the controversial method known variously as "D & X" (dilation and extraction) and "intact D & E" (dilation and evacuation) . . . .

The subpoenaed records, apparently some 45 in number, are sought for use in the forthcoming trial in the Southern District of New York of a suit challenging the constitutionality of the Partial-Birth Abortion Ban Act of 2003. Dr. Hammond is one of the plaintiffs in that suit and will also be testifying as an expert witness. The district court held that the production of the records is barred by regulations issued under the Health Insurance Portability and Accountability Act of 1996 (HIPAA), and let us begin there.

[The court concludes that the HIPAA Privacy Rule, excerpted *supra*, does not bar production of the records, even though it does not supersede state laws that are more protective of privacy and Illinois law prohibits the disclosure of even redacted medical records in judicial proceedings.]

All that [HIPAA] should be understood to do, therefore, is to create a procedure for obtaining authority to use medical records in litigation. Whether the records are actually admissible in evidence will depend among other things on whether they are privileged. And the evidentiary privileges that are applicable to federal question suits are given not by state law but by federal law, *Fed. R. Evid. 501*, which does not recognize a physician-patient (or hospital-patient) privilege. Rule 501 in terms makes federal common law the source of any privileges in federal-question suits unless an Act of Congress provides otherwise. We do not think HIPAA is rightly understood as an Act of Congress that creates a privilege.

The purely procedural character of the HIPAA standard for disclosure of medical information in judicial or administrative proceedings is indicated by the procedure for disclosure in response to a subpoena or other process; the notice to the patient must contain "sufficient information about the litigation or proceeding in which the protected health information is requested to permit the individual to raise an objection to the court." The objection in court would often be based on a privilege — the source of which would be found elsewhere than in the regulations themselves.

. . . .

. . . Northwestern Memorial Hospital concedes that there is no federal common law physician-patient privilege. It is not for us — especially in so summary a proceeding as this litigation to quash the government's subpoena — to create one . . . .

The district court did not reach a further ground urged by Northwestern Memorial Hospital for quashing the government's subpoena, which is simply that the burden of compliance with it would exceed the benefit of production of the material sought by it. *Fed. R. Civ. P. 45(c) (3) (A) (iv)*. However, . . . the judge made findings that are highly germane to — indeed arguably dispositive of — the Rule 45(c) issue. He pointed out that the "government seeks these records on the *possibility* that it may find something therein which would affect the testimony of Dr. Hammond adversely, that is, for its potential value in impeaching his credibility as a witness. What the government ignores in its argument is how little, if any, probative value lies within these patient records." He contrasted the dearth of probative value "with the potential loss of privacy that would ensue were these medical records used in a case in which the patient was not a party" and concluded that "the balance of harms resulting from disclosure severely outweighs the loss to the government through nondisclosure."

These findings were solidly based. The hospital had urged both the lack of probative value of the records and the loss of privacy by the patients. The government had responded in generalities, arguing that redaction would eliminate any privacy concern and that since Dr. Hammond had "made assertions of fact about his experience and his patients that plaintiffs are using to support their claim that, without a health exception, the Act is unconstitutional," the government should be permitted to test those assertions; but the government had not indicated what assertions these were or how the records might bear on them . . . .

At the oral argument we pressed the government's lawyer repeatedly and hard for indications of what he hoped to learn from the hospital records, and drew a blank . . . . The lawyer did suggest that if Hammond testified that patients with leukemia are better off with the D & X procedure than with the conventional D & E procedure but the medical records indicate that not all abortion patients with leukemia undergo D & X abortions, this would both impeach Hammond and suggest that D & X is not the only medically safe abortion procedure available to pregnant women afflicted with leukemia. But such information would be unlikely to be found in *Hammond's* records, given his strongly expressed preference for using the D & X method in the case of patients in fragile health. The information would be much more likely to be found in the records of physicians who perform D & E rather than D & X abortions on such women. Those records, however, the government didn't seek.

[The Court here explains that, the district judge's findings in effect "weighed the competing hardships" of complying with the subpoena. Because of an impending trial of this case, the Court decided remand was not necessary and would weigh the hardships itself.]

Like the district judge, we think the balance weighs in favor of quashing the subpoena. The government does not deny that the hospital is an appropriate representative of the privacy interests of its patients. But it argues that since it is seeking only a limited number of records and they would be produced to it minus the information that would enable the identity of the patient to be determined, there is no hardship to either the hospital or the patients of compliance. The argument is unrealistic and incomplete. What is true is that the *administrative* hardship of compliance would be modest. But it is not the only or the main hardship. The natural sensitivity that people feel about the disclosure of their medical records — the sensitivity that lies behind HIPAA — is amplified when the records are of a procedure that Congress has now declared to be a crime. Even if all the women whose records the government seeks know what "redacted" means, they are bound to be skeptical that redaction will conceal their identity from the world . . . . These women . . . doubtless . . . are also aware that hostility to abortion has at times erupted into violence, including criminal obstruction of entry into abortion clinics, the firebombing of clinics, and the assassination of physicians who perform abortions.

Some of these women will be afraid that when their redacted records are made a part of the trial record in New York, persons of their acquaintance, or skillful "Googlers," sifting the information contained in the medical records concerning each patient's medical and sex history, will put two and two together, "out" the 45 women, and thereby expose them to threats, humiliation, and obloquy. " [W]hether the patients' identities would remain confidential by the exclusion of their names and identifying numbers is questionable at best. The patients' admit and discharge summaries arguably contain histories of the patients' prior and present medical conditions, information that in the cumulative can make the possibility of recognition very high. " . . .

Even if there were no possibility that a patient's identity might be learned from a redacted medical record, there would be an invasion of privacy. Imagine if nude pictures of a woman, uploaded to the Internet without her consent though without identifying her by name, were downloaded in a foreign country by people who will never meet her. She would still feel that her privacy had been invaded. The revelation of the intimate details contained in the record of a late-term abortion may inflict a similar wound.

If Northwestern Memorial Hospital cannot shield its abortion patients' records from disclosure in judicial proceedings, moreover, the hospital will lose the confidence of its patients, and persons with sensitive medical conditions may be inclined to turn elsewhere for medical treatment . . . .

The government has had repeated opportunities to articulate a use for the records that it seeks, and it has failed to do so. What it would like to prove at the trial in New York, to refute Dr. Hammond, is that D & E is always an adequate alternative, from the standpoint of a pregnant woman's health, to the D & X procedure. But the government has failed to explain how the record of a D & X abortion would show this . . . .

None of the records is going to state that Dr. Hammond said that he performed a D & X although he believed that a D & E would be just as good. We thought the government might be hoping to find in the records evidence that Hammond had lied when he said he had performed a D & X on a woman who had leukemia or a woman who had breast cancer, but at argument the government disclaimed any such suggestion. We're still at a loss to understand what it hopes to gain from such discovery. (We begged the government's lawyer to be concrete.) Of course, not having seen the records, the government labors under a disadvantage, although it has surely seen other medical records. And of course, pretrial discovery is a fishing expedition and one can't know what one has caught until one fishes. But *Fed. R. Civ. P. 45(c)* allows the fish to object, and when they do so the fisherman has to come up with more than the government has been able to do in this case despite the excellence of its lawyers.

     . . . .

Were the government sincerely interested in whether D & X abortions are ever medically indicated, one would have expected it to seek from Northwestern Memorial Hospital statistics summarizing the hospital's experience with late-term abortions. Suppose the patients who undergo D & X abortions are identical in all material respects (age, health, number of weeks pregnant, and so on) to those who undergo procedures not forbidden by the Partial-Birth Abortion Ban Act. That would be potent evidence that the D & X procedure does not have a compelling health rationale. No such evidence has been sought . . . . A variant of the suggested approach would be to obtain a random sample of late-term abortion records from various sources and then determine, through good statistical analysis, whether the patient characteristics that lead Dr. Hammond to perform a D & X lead other physicians to perform a conventional D & E instead, and whether there are differences in the health consequences for these two groups of women. If there are no differences, the government might have a good defense of the Act. Gathering records from Hammond's patients alone will not be useful; but if the government has *other* records (say, from VA hospitals) already in its files, then records of Hammond's procedures might enable a useful comparison. The government hasn't suggested doing anything like that either. Its motives in seeking individuals' medical records remain thoroughly obscure.

The fact that quashing the subpoena comports with Illinois' medical-records privilege is a final factor in favor of the district order's action. [C]omity "impels federal courts to recognize state privileges where this can be accomplished at no substantial cost to federal substantive and procedural policy. " Patients, physicians, and hospitals in Illinois rely on Illinois' strong policy of privacy of medical records. They cannot rely completely, for they are not entitled to count on the state privilege's being applied in federal court. But in a case such as this in which, so far as we can determine, applying the privilege would not interfere significantly with federal proceedings, comity has required us not to apply the Illinois privilege, but to consider with special care the arguments for quashing the subpoena on the basis of relative hardship under *Fed. R. Civ. P. 45(c)*.

NOTES AND QUESTIONS

6. The HIPPA Privacy Rule. The Health Insurance Portability and Accountability Act (HIPAA) of 1996, Pub. L. 104–191, 110 Stat. 1936 (1996), authorized the Department of Health and Human Services (DHHS) to issue regulations in the event, as happened, that Congress failed to enact federal legislation to protect the privacy of medical information within three years. HIPAA encouraged health care providers and health insurers to adopt electronic recordkeeping to simplify and expedite insurance administration. (HIPAA's insurance regulation provisions have been modified several times, most dramatically by the Patient Protection and Affordable Care Act of 2010, as itself amended. Major provisions are codified at 42 U.S.C. §§ 300gg *et seq.*, §§ 1320d *et seq.*) Congress recognized that public support for electronic recordkeeping depended importantly on assurance that personal medical information would be kept secure and confidential. The history of HIPAA Privacy Rule can be found in the Introduction to the original rule, Standards for Privacy of Individually Identifiable Health Information, 65 Fed. Reg. 82462 (Dec. 28, 2000), and to the revised rule, Standards for Privacy of Individually Identifiable Health Information, 67 Fed. Reg. 14776 (Mar. 27, 2002). *See also South Carolina Med. Ass'n v. Thompson*, 327 F.3d 346, 348 n.1 (4th Cir. 2003) (explaining effect of HIPAA administrative simplification provisions). The Final Privacy Rule issued by DHSS (excerpted *supra*) took effect April 14, 2003. 45 C.F.R. Parts 160 and 164. In 2009, the Health Information Technology for Economic and Clinical Health (HITECH) Act strengthened civil and criminal enforcement of the HIPAA Rules protecting privacy and security of electronic health information, subjecting business associates (contractors and subcontractors) to the rules, and increasing patient access to their information. At the same, the federal government added financial incentives to providers to increase their adoption and "meaningful use" of electronic medical records. The rules on security have been less controversial than those on privacy, perhaps because there is little dispute over the need for better mechanisms to protect the security of data.

The HIPAA Privacy Rule sets forth general rules for the use or disclosure by "covered entities" of "protected health information" (PHI). Covered entities include health plans, health care clearinghouses, and health care providers who transmit health information in electronic form. 45 C.F.R. § 160.104. The Rule defines "protected health information" as "individually identifiable health information." 45 C.F.R. § 160.103. HIPAA defines "health information" as "any information, whether oral or recorded in any form or medium, that — (A) is created or received by a health care provider, health plan, public health authority, employer, life insurer, school or university, or health care clearinghouse; and (B) relates to the past, present, or future physical or mental health or condition of an individual, the provision of health care to an individual, or the past, present, or future payment for the provision of health care to an individual." 42 U.S.C. § 1320d(4). "Individually identifiable health information" is the subset of health information that "identifies the individual" or "with respect to which there is a reasonable basis to believe that the information can be used to identify the individual. " *Id.* at § 1320d(6). 45 C.F.R. § 164.514 lists 18 data elements that must be removed for data to be considered de-identified (*i.e.*, non-identifiable).

As can be seen from the excerpt above, many sections in 45 C.F.R. Part 164 spell out exceptions to the general principle that PHI cannot be used or disclosed without the individual's authorization. The best understood exception is for patient care. HIPAA does not require that patients provide express consent or authorization for covered entities to use or disclose their health information "for treatment, payment, or health care operations." This is intended to allow physicians and health care facilities to use patient data for regular care, consultations, filing insurance claims for payment, and internal quality assurance reviews. The concept of health care operations remains somewhat unsettled, as increasing pressure to study health care costs and outcomes raises questions about whether certain analyses require individual authorization.

Critics of the HIPAA Privacy Rule argue that it may permit the disclosure of more information without patient authorization than prior law. For example, former Minnesota Attorney General Mike Hatch wrote: "In those few instances where patient authorization is needed, HIPAA permits the health care provider to refuse treatment to a patient who does not sign an authorization form — the "sign or die" provision . . . . HIPAA effectively neutralizes the patient's ability to restrict access to medical information." Mike Hatch, *HIPAA: Commercial Interests Win Round Two*, 86 Minn. L. Rev. 1481, 1485 (2002). *See Citizens for Health v. Leavitt*, 428 F.3d 167 (3d Cir. 2005) (rejecting a challenge to the Rule's promulgation on the ground that whatever violation of constitutionally protected privacy might occur, it would be "at the hands of private entities, " not the government) .

   7.   **The "public health exception. "** In *Matter of Miguel M.*, the public health department official relied on HIPAA's public health exception to get Miguel M's medical records from two hospitals without notifying Miguel M or obtaining his consent. Section 164.512(b) of the HIPAA Privacy Rule, *supra*, permits — but does not require — covered entities, like the hospitals, to disclose PHI for certain public health purposes. How would you construe this public health exception? How is this different from § 164.512(a), which permits covered entities to disclose PHI when "required by law"? The public health purposes stated in the regulation's text are a more limited subset of activities than public health professionals, like Dr. Barron, might wish to include within the meaning of public health. The court — in a unanimous decision — interpreted the language in much the same way that most laypersons and probably most members of Congress would. Similarly, the court interpreted the "treatment" exception to apply to voluntary, personal medical care, rather than care that would be desirable from the public health perspective.

Since the Privacy Rule took effect, there has been some confusion over what kinds of information hospitals and physicians are *permitted* to disclose to public health agencies and what they may be *required* to disclose. Not surprisingly, health care providers can be protective of their patients' information, refusing even public health requests for identifiable data. State laws governing state agencies often contain authorizations to collect information to enable the agencies to receive information relevant to their functions. That type of authorization does not automatically include the power to compel information without consent. Whether any blanket authorization to an agency to obtain information includes the additional power to seize it from the party who holds it entails an analysis of the specific statute at issue. (A federal example is the Cancer Registry Amendments of 2000, discussed in Chapter 8, *infra.*)

The HIPAA statute itself does not alter the authority of any state to enact laws "providing for the reporting of disease or injury, child abuse, birth, or death, public health surveillance, or public health investigation or intervention." 42 U.S.C. § 1320d-7(b). The validity of such laws are determined under the state's own constitution and any federal constitutional limits, as discussed in Part C, *infra.*

A state or local health department ordinarily is not bound by the HIPAA Privacy Rule, because it would not meet the definition of a covered entity. However, divisions within a health department that provide or fund health care for people (as in substance abuse clinics or cholesterol screening programs) or collect mandatory disease reports (discussed in Part C, *infra*) would qualify as covered entities that must comply with the HIPAA Privacy Rule to protect the patient information they hold. The Rule does not protect information handled by parties, such as universities and researchers, who are not covered entities. Covered entities that are authorized to disclose PHI to researchers and other noncovered entities must ensure that recipients of the information preserve its confidentiality. Protection against further disclosure by researchers, therefore, depends upon contractual agreements between the covered entity and the researcher. Can individuals whose information is used or disclosed by third party researchers enforce such a contract?

8. **The HIPAA Privacy Rule and state law.** The HIPAA statute provides that any privacy regulation issued pursuant to its authority shall "not supersede a contrary provision of State law, if the provision of State law imposes requirements, standards, or implementation specifications that are more stringent than the requirements, standards, or implementation specifications imposed under the regulation. " 42 U.S.C. § 1320d(7)(a)(2)(B); HIPAA § 264(c)(2) (1996). Thus, in many states, state law remains the most potent source of privacy protection. New York State, however, had no law that was more protective of private medical information, so HIPAA controlled the decision in Miguel M's case.

Northwestern Memorial Hospital v. Ashcroft, excerpted *supra*, also reviews the relationship of the HIPAA Privacy Rule to other state and federal laws. Unlike New York, Illinois had a law more protective of privacy than the Rule. Are you surprised by the court's conclusion that the HIPAA Rule is merely a procedural device in federal litigation? As the court notes, even if pretrial discovery is a "fishing expedition," the federal rules of evidence (like most state rules) "allow the fish to object. " At issue is the justification for compliance with a subpoena in a civil lawsuit:

"The only issue for us is whether, given that there is a potential psychological cost to the hospital's patients, and a potential cost in lost goodwill to the hospital itself, from the involuntary production of the medical records even as redacted, the cost is offset by the probative value of the records . . . ." 362 F.3d at 930.

9. **Access to abortion records.** As part of the defense of constitutional challenges to the Partial Birth Abortion Ban Act, 18 U.S.C. § 1531, the U.S. Attorney General sought medical records about abortion from hospitals and physicians in several cities, including Chicago, San Francisco, and New York. Resistance to the government's subpoenas met with slightly different court decisions. In *Planned Parenthood Federation of America, Inc. v. Ashcroft*, 2004 U.S. Dist. LEXIS 3383 (N.D. Cal. 2004), Judge Phyllis J. Hamilton did not consider the HIPAA Privacy Rule, but, like the 7th Circuit later in *Northwestern Memorial Hospital*, quashed the subpoena, finding the government's request to be "irrelevant, unduly burdensome" and that the patients' right to privacy outweighed the government's interest in disclosure. In contrast, New York-Presbyterian Hospital was initially ordered to comply with the Justice Department's subpoena on the ground that the records were relevant to the litigation. *National Abortion Federation v. Ashcroft*, 2004 U.S. Dist. LEXIS 4530 (S.D.N.Y. 2004). The Attorney General's Office ultimately abandoned its attempt to obtain medical records, including those in New York, without renouncing future subpoenas. The U.S. Supreme Court upheld the constitutionality of the Act itself in *Gonzales v. Carhart*, 550 U.S. 124 (2007) (excerpted in Chapter 4, B, *supra*), which did not present the issue of information privacy.

The Attorney General used civil litigation and subpoenas to obtain evidence that could support Congress's finding that so-called partial birth abortions are never medically necessary. Why would the Attorney General want only records of D & X abortions? The *Northwestern Memorial Hospital* decision suggests more useful data to determine medical need for specific abortion procedures. Where might such data be found? State laws requiring reports of abortions may not include the type of procedure performed or complications. Should such information also be reported? (For cases discussing what information about patients who have abortions can be reported to the state, see Part C of this chapter.)

10. **What information is identifiable?** *Northwestern Memorial Hospital* presents a more sophisticated analysis of the kinds of information that might identify individuals than had earlier U.S. Supreme Court decisions. Judge Posner is quite sensitive to how medical information might be disseminated and how patients might react, even to data that do not include names. For an analysis and demonstration of ways in which individuals can be identified from as few as three key data elements in apparently "de-identified" data, see Latanya Sweeney, *Maintaining Patient Confidentiality When Sharing Medical Data Requires a Symbiotic Relationship Between Technology and Policy* (MIT Artificial Intelligence Lab. Working Paper No. AIWPWP344b, 1997). *See also* Paul M. Schwartz & Daniel J. Solove, *The PII Problem: Privacy and a New Concept of Personally Identifiable Information*, 86 N.Y.U. L. REV. 1814 (2011).

Judge Manion, dissenting in part in *Northwestern Memorial Hospital*, dismissed the fear of disclosure emphasized by Judge Posner in the following language: "In fact, there is no reason to believe that the women themselves have any idea that their records are among the few sought by the government in this case. But even if they knew, no one else ever would, because all of the information that could reasonably be used to identify them will be redacted, and none of the information — not even the redacted non-identifying information — will ever be made public, much less paraded in court or placed on the Internet . . . . " Judge Manion may be correct that the women would not know that their records were sought or submitted. Is this a reason to permit or prohibit their discovery? In this case, the government obtained a protective order for the records it subpoenaed. Protective orders can be and are granted in cases in which the information meets the requirements for discovery or submission in evidence and also warrants protection against disclosure outside the litigation.

11. **Subpoenas for medical records.** Several different lines of cases consider the power of state agencies to subpoena medical records. *See Schachter v. Whalen*, 581 F.2d 35 (2d Cir. 1978) (finding a state medical licensure board could subpoena patient medical records for purposes of investigating a physician's professional conduct in treating patients with laetrile or MA7); and *U.S. v. Westinghouse*, 638 F.2d 570 (3d Cir. 1980), excerpted in Chapter 8 *infra*. Also distinct is the authority of law enforcement agencies to obtain medical records when the records may provide evidence that the patient or physician committed a crime. For interesting examples, see *Rush Limbaugh v. Florida*, 2004 Fla. App. LEXIS 14653 (Ct. App. Fla. 2004); and *New York City Health & Hosp. Corp. v. Morgenthau (In re Grand Jury Investigation)*, 98 N.Y.2d 525; 779 N.E.2d 173; 749 N.Y.S.2d 462 (2002).

Nicolas P. Terry, *What's Wrong with Health Privacy?*
V J. HEALTH & BIOMEDICAL L. 1, 2–5, 8–9, 12–13, 19, 23–24 (2009)

This essay seeks to identify some of the reasons why "privacy" remains so contentious. Here I suggest several possible answers ranging from "micro" issues such as what we understand by health privacy, to more "macro" and operational issues encountered as we seek to protect health information. First, lawyers have made consistent errors in the terminology applied to the protection of medical privacy; second, both the legal and ethical domains have failed to apply a consistent and robust rationale for health privacy, leaving it prey to consequentialist thought and policy; third, the declining importance of the physician–patient relationship as the touchstone for obligations, particularly confidentiality, has created a "rights" vacuum; fourth, the health information revolution truly is revolutionary in its reach and its concomitant threats to privacy and confidentiality; and, finally, as privacy regulation increasingly lies in the sphere of governmental command-control regulation, it has joined the list of targets in the professionalism-market-regulation conflict over millennial healthcare delivery.

II. Errors in Terminology

. . . .

. . . [U]npacking the legal notion of privacy yields a picture that is both incoherent and incomplete, suggesting not only terminological flaws but also a considerable disconnect between ethical and legal constructs, a disconnect that seems heightened when we examine the protection of health information.

Legal and regulatory systems may potentially utilize three basic models for the protection of personal information: deidentification, collection control, and disclosure control. The first of these models assumes (more or less correctly) that data that is deidentified prior to collection (or, somewhat less successfully, prior to disclosure) reduces or eliminates personal risks associated with its use or processing. The second potential protective model is to place limitations on data collection. Such a model could, for example, prohibit all collection in certain circumstances (*e.g.*, the harvesting of genetic information by life insurers) or limit collection via a proportionality rule (*e.g.*, only information necessary for the purposes of treatment). The third protective model, again primarily focusing on informational privacy, is to place limitations on data disclosure (*e.g.*, hospital records may be disclosed to physicians but not drug companies).

Oddly, our legal systems are only dimly cognizant of the deidentification model. For example, while the federal standards are generally inapplicable to deidentifed health information, they do not require deidentification. Even more surprisingly, the U.S. legal domain recognizes few collection-centric rules. For example, the Restatement's black-letter law of "privacy" provides as follows:

The right of privacy is invaded by

(a) unreasonable intrusion upon the seclusion of another . . . or

(b) appropriation of the other's name or likeness . . . or

(c) unreasonable publicity given to the other's private life . . . or

(d) publicity that unreasonably places the other in a false light before the public.

This "right of privacy" promises far more than it delivers. On its face the Restatement fails to provide any general or comprehensive "right of privacy." It is no more than a listing of modest protections — nominate and discrete tort actions applicable in a narrow range of circumstances rather than fact-sensitive applications of a general principle or theory of privacy . . . .

. . . .

In contrast to deidentification and collection, the third protective model, whereby limitations are placed on data disclosure, is well established in U.S. normative circles . . . . Aside from a few "intrusion upon the seclusion" actions, the modern law of health privacy resides in the far narrower, disclosure-centric model doctrinally captured in cases, statutes, and regulations dealing with breach of confidence. A patient exercises his right of privacy (as recognized by the ethical domain) when he chooses to provide information to his physician (albeit a "right" that is illusory if it is a condition of treatment). Thereafter, dissemination of that information by the physician is limited by ethical and legal standards of confidence, hereinafter referred to as confidentiality. Today, when courts and regulators speak of medical "privacy" they are usually in error, mislabeling what are obligations of "confidentiality."

. . . .

III. An Inadequate "Privacy-Confidence" Rationale

In the ethical domain, the most cogent justification for privacy and confidentiality is the principle of autonomy. For example, Beauchamp and Childress argue that claims to privacy "are justified by rights of autonomous choice that are correlative to the obligations expressed in the principle of respect for autonomy. " As already noted, in the information domain a patient exercises this autonomy-based right of privacy when he or she shares information with his or her physician and thereafter relies on ethical or legal standards of confidentiality to police subsequent disclosure. It is arguable that today's health confidence laws (particularly the federal standards) do not reference any underlying autonomy model. Rather, they are based on more limited and less satisfying instrumental models and, worse, are increasingly justified on utilitarian constructs (specifically, "rule" Utilitarianism) .

. . . .

Instrumental justifications for medical privacy and confidentiality are simply stated. Thus, patients provide information to physicians in the belief that it will further their diagnosis and treatment while physicians respect confidences in order to encourage patients to disclose personal and medical information that will make diagnosis and treatment more effective. This justification may not be an entirely flawed way of looking at the physician-patient discourse. However, it is a notion that stumbles outside of the physician–patient paradigm and becomes unstable when applied in, for example, institutional or industrial models of care. In such models, the notion falls prey to modern utilitarian arguments that see the generation, dispersal, and processing of longitudinal patient health information primarily as a necessity to reduce overall healthcare costs and to minimize medical error. As the context changes, therefore, the simple and probably innocuous instrumental approach becomes increasingly utilitarian.

. . . .

Instrumental fingerprints are all over the federal standards . . . .

The adoption of an almost exclusively instrumental approach is further evidenced by the federal government's choice of enforcement models. The federal standards (in common with the majority of state standards on which they are modeled) do not provide an aggrieved patient with enforcement through a private right of action; rather they provide for a compliance mechanism with regulatory agency oversight and the potential for civil or criminal penalties. The message is that any privacy confidentiality "rights" belong to the healthcare system and not to patients.

. . . .

V. Healthcare Information: Another Domain Unfolds

It is too early to assess the final impact of the ongoing healthcare technology revolution but, inevitably, aspects of the delivery system will be fundamentally changed. Two key sets of technologies are at issue here. The first can be viewed as disruptive — technologies that replace traditional methods of delivery. These include web-based medical content, online consultations, and Internet-prescribing. The second is more integrative — the leveraging of information technologies (IT) by traditional healthcare providers to improve the quality of care and reduce its cost structure. Both sets bring with them difficult privacy issues. Thus, disruptive technologies, in large part because of their novelty, tend to create issues that our ethical and legal constructs have generally failed to address. For example, non-traditional providers, such as those engaged in Internet advice or prescribing generally are not covered by disclosure-centric confidentiality regulation.

. . . .

B. Managing Privacy in the Health Information Domain

In pre-IT times and consistent with an operational paradigm of fragmented record-keeping, the legal protection of patient data was achieved principally through a physician–patient relationship disclosure-centric rule, expressed as breach of confidence and operationalized through implied contract or torts doctrine. Even given the relative weakness of the disclosure-centric confidentiality model or assuming its occasional breach, patient "privacy" was somewhat protected by the sheer inefficiencies of a system built around unstructured, distributed patient data.

This paradigm has now been overwhelmed by the realities of the modern health information domain. The patient data contained in modern longitudinal systems is comprehensive, portable, and manipulatable. The potential for abuse is immense; there are many parties (pharmaceutical companies and government being the obvious examples, inquisitive healthcare employees being the most commonly reported) that crave access to this data. As a result, the privacy and confidentiality costs potentially incurred by patients rise exponentially.

The emerging health information domain has several key properties that extend beyond the confidentiality inherent in the physician–patient relationship. In addition to the confidentiality–privacy–anonymity triumvirate that protects (or should protect) the basic input and output of patient data, the contemporary health information domain has (or should possess) several additional properties (or qualities). These protective rules give rise to "process" controls such as "security" (a confidentiality correlate that restricts access to data to those authorized to receive it) and "integrity" (data "checksum" validation and protection against unauthorized modification). As data is aggregated, additional properties such as "unity," "quality," and "accountability" become paramount because information domains lose their value proposition when they are incomplete or their data is otherwise flawed. "Unity" refers to health information that is "longitudinal," consisting of records from various providers that are consolidated or interlinked to provide a comprehensive view of a patient's healthcare encounters. A longitudinal approach provides the data necessary to interface with other technologies . . . that analyze diagnoses and treatments and support shared care from multiple providers. "Quality" denotes that the data must be current or timely and subject to quality auditing from extrinsic sources such as clinical practice guidelines. Finally, the "accountability" property denotes not only substantive responsibility by providers for the accuracy of the data they enter but also procedural identification of providers responsible for specific data.

The modern health information domain must also take into account and integrate the increasing demands for access to the data it contains. Thus, the "access" property describes the various recognized claims to view and, in some cases, modify patient information. Justice and public health systems make the most persistent claims. However, most mature health information domains also recognize patients' rights of access and correction of their own data. Outcomes assessment and error-reporting mandates will substantially increase demands for access to individual and population-based health records from accreditation bodies and government regulators.

What the discussions of privacy and confidentiality in the context of transaction standards, error reduction, and electronic health records have in common is a heavily instrumental approach to health information. This is because the IT revolution that has brought about the health information domain has less to do with improving or increasing patient access to services and more with business imperatives. Such imperatives include reducing healthcare transaction costs (the expenses associated with medical errors), the inefficiencies associated with multiple providers, and changing roles of physicians in a managed care environment. As a result, individual autonomy tends to be viewed as subordinate to broader goals (*e.g.*, lower costs and a reduction in medical errors) that may or may not directly benefit the individual involved.

NOTES AND QUESTIONS

12. **Approaches to privacy law.** Terry's article, excerpted *supra*, suggests that attitudes toward privacy are imperfectly represented in law, and often only in fragments that fail to cover the territory. He argues that this fragmented approach has failed to develop a coherent principle (or principles) to guide legal policy, especially where both the need for information and the desire to limit its exposure press for acceptance. Note the idea that justifications for laws protecting privacy are often instrumentalist or utilitarian — arguments that privacy should be protected not for its own sake or as an aspect of autonomy, but in order to facilitate an external goal, such as appropriate medical care. Do you agree? Look back at the excerpt from *Alberts v. Devine*, in Note 4, *supra*, explaining the reasons for imposing a duty of confidentiality on physicians. Is this an example of principled or instrumental reasoning? A key reason — undoubtedly instrumental — for adopting the HIPAA Privacy Rule was to facilitate the efficient (and presumably cheaper) electronic exchange of patient information by reassuring patients that their medical information would not be misused or inappropriately disclosed, lest they fail to be completely honest about their conditions. (This assumes that patients are always honest with their physicians, which itself may be questionable.) How do the methods of enforcing HIPAA obligations compare with the enforcement mechanisms in the Privacy Act? What remedies are available to individuals under each of these laws?

European countries have taken a different approach to privacy protection, developing more consistent laws that apply to both the public and private sectors. The European Union's 1995 European Community Directive on Data Protection sets the standards for privacy legislation in EU countries, and new regulations are expected in 2013. A good resource for privacy laws outside the United States is PRIVACY AND HUMAN RIGHTS: AN INTERNATIONAL SURVEY OF PRIVACY LAWS AND DEVELOPMENTS (Marc Rotenberg, Allison Knight & Katitza Rodriguez, eds. 2007).

Marc Rotenberg offers another explanation for the patchwork of laws in the United States:

> . . . [S]omething happened in the 1990s that set the United States on a strange course. At roughly the same point in time that Europe and other governments were developing new legal regimes to protect privacy, the United States was pursuing legal and technical measures to enable surveillance. While Europe faced the challenge of ensuring compliance by all the member states with the requirements of the Data Directive, the U.S. took on the challenge of trying to enforce compliance with the FBI's technical scheme to enable wire surveillance. And when consumers called for privacy safeguards to address the growing problems with the Internet, the United States government turned to the private sector for self-regulatory measures that offered little in the way of actual privacy protection.

> Today industry groups continue to press on with self-regulation . . . that shifts burdens back to consumers and reject the use of public institutions to resolve problems of common concern. Meanwhile, consumer organizations call on their own governments to establish safeguards in law for the emerging digital economy and to extend the approaches that have been established in the past to the technologies of the future.

> One cannot escape the conclusion that privacy policy in the United States today reflects what industry is prepared to do rather than what the public wants done.

Marc Rotenberg, *Fair Information Practices and the Architecture of Privacy (What Larry Doesn't Get)*, 2001 STAN. TECH. L. REV. 1, 117–119. Does Rotenberg's analysis hold true today?

As information technology expands, medical information becomes an increasingly valuable commodity, both for private industry and the development of public policy, including health policy. Amitai Etzioni argues that the public good outweighs individual privacy in matters of public health and safety. AMITAI ETZIONI, THE LIMITS OF PRIVACY (1999). The Affordable Care Act encourages the reporting of data on costs and quality of care, as well as insurance claims, in order to find ways to improve the systems. This often requires analyzing identifiable information. For example, to determine whether appropriate (or costly) care is being provided to patients with a particular medical condition, health departments may wish to review each patient's diagnoses, treatments, and costs in connection with all providers visited, and perhaps also determine whether the patient filled prescriptions and took medication as prescribed. This would require linking all of the patient's records by name (or perhaps a code). Certainly, the goal of improving care (or reducing costs) is valuable. To what extent should the patient's privacy be protected in such circumstances? How should such protection be structured? Do we need entirely new models of privacy of privacy protection in the era of big data? For an analysis of such questions, see Nicolas P. Terry, *Protecting Patient Privacy in the Age of Big Data*, 81 UMKC L. REV. 385 (2012).

13.   Theories of privacy. There is a rich literature on privacy, but delving into it can lead to agreement with Robert Post: "Privacy is a value so complex, so entangled in competing and contradictory dimensions, so engorged with various and distinct meanings, that I sometimes despair whether it can be usefully addressed at all." Robert C. Post, *Three Concepts of Privacy*, 89 GEO. L.J. 2087, 2087 (2001). For thoughtful examinations of the concept of privacy and laws affecting privacy, see DANIEL J. SOLOVE, UNDERSTANDING PRIVACY (2008); JEFFREY ROSEN, THE UNWANTED GAZE: THE DESTRUCTION OF PRIVACY IN AMERICA (2000); ALAN WESTIN, PRIVACY AND FREEDOM (1967). For critical views of the expansion of electronic data mining, see LORI ANDREWS, I KNOW WHO YOU ARE AND I SAW WHAT YOU DID: SOCIAL NETWORKS AND THE DEATH OF PRIVACY (2011); DANIEL J. SOLOVE, NOTHING TO HIDE: THE FALSE TRADEOFF BETWEEN PRIVACY AND SECURITY (2011); and ROBERT O'HARROW, JR., NO PLACE TO HIDE (2005).

14.   Providers and meaningful use of electronic medical records. The federal Centers for Medicare and Medicaid (CMS) offers up to $44,000 to physicians who demonstrate "meaningful use" of electronic medical records. Physicians who fail to qualify will receive reduced Medicare payments after 2015. Health Information Technology for Economic and Clinical Health (HITECH) Act of 2009. The federal Office of the National Coordinator for Health Information Technology helps fund the acquisition of EMR systems. *See* www.healthit.gov/ (visited Apr. 2014). According to one report, an estimated 12.2% of the more than 500,000 eligible physicians in the United States had attested to meaningful use in the Medicare program by May 2012. Adam Wright *et al.*, *Early Results of the Meaningful Use Program for Electronic Health Records*, 368 NEW ENGL. J. MED. 779 (2013). This included 17.8% of primary care physicians and 9.8% of specialists. Providers used 310 different health information technology vendors, but 58.5% of physicians used one of five vendors (Epic, Allscripts, eClinicalWorks, GE Healthcare, and NextGen). Although low in absolute terms, EMR adoption is increasing. Reasons for the slow adoption rates appear to be the initial cost and difficulty of learning the systems, especially among small providers, as well as lack of interoperability among systems and lack of time to implement them.

15.   How medical information is shared. Figure 1 below illustrates how health data about one person (Alice) is shared among providers, insurers, government agencies, researchers and other organizations. A dynamic version of the map is available at the DataMap, http://thedatamap.org/maps.html (visited May 2014). That website allows a comparison of the increased number of organizations that obtain data today with the smaller number that did so in 1997, before the HIPAA Privacy and Security Rule was adopted.

The Data Privacy Lab also analyzes whether and how even de-identified data can be re-identified. In one analysis, the Lab purchased a publicly available database of patients in a Washington state hospital for $50. The database contained hospitalizations, diagnoses, attending physician, procedures, a summary of charges, payment method, and demographic information — but no names. Sweeney identified 43% of the patients by matching information in the database with public records from government and media articles and reports. L. Sweeney, *Matching Known Patients to Health Records in Washington State Data*, Harvard University, Data Privacy Lab. 1089-1 (June 2013), available at http://thedatamap.org/risks.html.

Figure 1

DataMap: A graphic depicting the sharing of a person's health data

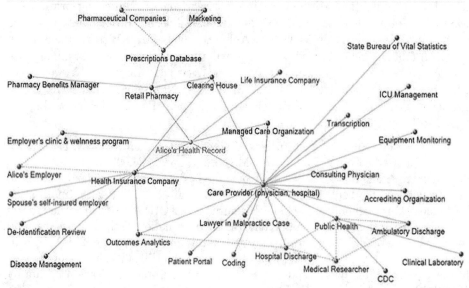

Source: Latanya Sweeney, Data Privacy Lab, Harvard University, 2010.
http://thedatamap.org/maps.html

States often share health data with other state and federal agencies and sell health data to private companies. Jordan Robertson of Bloomberg News surveyed the 20 most populous states to find what entities bought health data. Twelve states responded (AZ, CA, FL, IL, MD, MA, NJ, NY, PA, TN, TX, WA). http://www.bloomberg.com/infographics/2013-06-05/whos-buying-your-medical-records.html. Thirty-four entities were the most frequent buyers of hospital discharge data, including Truven Health Analytic (11 states), Milliman (10 states), WebMD Health (8 states), as well as the CDC and the Federal Trade Commission (3 states each).

16. National health statistics. The National Center for Health Statistics (NCHS) in the Centers for Disease Control and Prevention is a good source of vital statistics concerning births, deaths, disease and injury for the country. *See* www.cdc.gov/nchs (visited Apr. 2014). The NCHS funds several types of state data collection programs and conducts research studies and surveys to describe numbers and rates of disease and disability (morbidity) and death (mortality) in the population as a whole and among subgroups defined by such characteristics as age, sex, race, and residence. Other agencies, such as the Agency for Healthcare Research and Quality, also conduct health-related studies. The Centers for Medicare and Medicaid also allow researchers to use their program claims data to answer many health policy questions. Such data can be essential to determine whether a public health problem exists, its magnitude, whom it most affects, what responses are effective, and how costly they are.

C. COMPULSORY REPORTING OF MEDICAL INFORMATION

WHALEN v. ROE
429 U.S. 589 (1977)

STEVENS, JUSTICE.

The constitutional question presented is whether the State of New York may record, in a centralized computer file, the names and addresses of all persons who have obtained, pursuant to a doctor's prescription, certain drugs for which there is both a lawful and an unlawful market.

The District Court enjoined enforcement of the portions of the New York State Controlled Substances Act of 1972 which require such recording on the ground that they violate appellees' constitutionally protected rights of privacy. We noted probable jurisdiction of the appeal by the Commissioner of Health, and now reverse.

Many drugs have both legitimate and illegitimate uses. In response to a concern that such drugs were being diverted into unlawful channels, in 1970 the New York Legislature created a special commission to evaluate the State's drug control laws. The commission found the existing laws deficient in several respects. There was no effective way to prevent the use of stolen or revised prescriptions, to prevent unscrupulous pharmacists from repeatedly refilling prescriptions, to prevent users from obtaining prescriptions from more than one doctor, or to prevent doctors from overprescribing, either by authorizing an excessive amount in one prescription or by giving one patient multiple prescriptions. In drafting new legislation to correct such defects, the commission consulted with enforcement officials in California and Illinois where central reporting systems were being used effectively.

The new New York statute classified potentially harmful drugs in five schedules. Drugs, such as heroin, which are highly abused and have no recognized medical use, are in Schedule I; they cannot be prescribed. Schedules II through V include drugs which have a progressively lower potential for abuse but also have a recognized medical use. Our concern is limited to Schedule II, which includes the most dangerous of the legitimate drugs.[1]

---

[1] These include opium and opium derivatives, cocaine, methadone, amphetamines, and methaqualone. Pub. Health Law § 3306. These drugs have accepted uses in the amelioration of pain and in the treatment of epilepsy, narcolepsy, hyperkinesia, schizo-affective disorders, and migraine headaches.

With an exception for emergencies, the Act requires that all prescriptions for Schedule II drugs be prepared by the physician in triplicate on an official form. The completed form identifies the prescribing physician; the dispensing pharmacy; the drug and dosage; and the name, address, and age of the patient. One copy of the form is retained by the physician, the second by the pharmacist, and the third is forwarded to the New York State Department of Health in Albany. A prescription made on an official form may not exceed a 30-day supply, and may not be refilled.

The District Court found that about 100,000 Schedule II prescription forms are delivered to a receiving room at the Department of Health in Albany each month. They are sorted, coded, and logged and then taken to another room where the data on the forms is recorded on magnetic tapes for processing by a computer. Thereafter, the forms are returned to the receiving room to be retained in a vault for a five-year period and then destroyed as required by the statute. The receiving room is surrounded by a locked wire fence and protected by an alarm system. The computer tapes containing the prescription data are kept in a locked cabinet. When the tapes are used, the computer is run "offline," which means that no terminal outside of the computer room can read or record any information. Public disclosure of the identity of patients is expressly prohibited by the statute and by a Department of Health regulation. Willful violation of these prohibitions is a crime punishable by up to one year in prison and a $2,000 fine. At the time of trial there were 17 Department of Health employees with access to the files; in addition, there were 24 investigators with authority to investigate cases of over-dispensing which might be identified by the computer. Twenty months after the effective date of the Act, the computerized data had only been used in two investigations involving alleged overuse by specific patients.

A few days before the Act became effective, this litigation was commenced by a group of patients regularly receiving prescriptions for Schedule II drugs, [and] by doctors who prescribe such drugs . . . . Appellees offered evidence tending to prove that persons in need of treatment with Schedule II drugs will from time to time decline such treatment because of their fear that the misuse of the computerized data will cause them to be stigmatized as "drug addicts. "

The District Court held that "the doctor-patient relationship is one of the zones of privacy accorded constitutional protection" and that the patient-identification provisions of the Act invaded this zone with "a needlessly broad sweep, " and enjoined enforcement of the provisions of the Act which deal with the reporting of patients' names and addresses.

I

The District Court found that the State had been unable to demonstrate the necessity for the patient-identification requirement on the basis of its experience during the first 20 months of administration of the new statute. There was a time when that alone would have provided a basis for invalidating the statute. *Lochner v. New York*, 198 U.S. 45 . . . . The holding in *Lochner* has been implicitly rejected many times. State legislation which has some effect on individual liberty or privacy may not be held unconstitutional simply because a court finds it unnecessary, in whole or in part. For we have frequently recognized that individual States have broad latitude in experimenting with possible solutions to problems of vital local concern.

The New York statute challenged in this case represents a considered attempt to deal with such a problem. It is manifestly the product of an orderly and rational legislative decision. It was recommended by a specially appointed commission which held extensive hearings on the proposed legislation, and drew on experience with similar programs in other States. There surely was nothing unreasonable in the assumption that the patient-identification requirement might aid in the enforcement of laws designed to minimize the misuse of dangerous drugs. For the requirement could reasonably be expected to have a deterrent effect on potential violators as well as to aid in the detection or investigation of specific instances of apparent abuse. At the very least, it would seem clear that the State's vital interest in controlling the distribution of dangerous drugs would support a decision to experiment with new techniques for control. For if an experiment fails — if in this case experience teaches that the patient-identification requirement results in the foolish expenditure of funds to acquire a mountain of useless information — the legislative process remains available to terminate the unwise experiment. It follows that the legislature's enactment of the patient-identification requirement was a reasonable exercise of New York's broad police powers. The District Court's finding that the necessity for the requirement had not been proved is not, therefore, a sufficient reason for holding the statutory requirement unconstitutional.

II

Appellees contend that the statute invades a constitutionally protected "zone of privacy." The cases sometimes characterized as protecting "privacy" have in fact involved at least two different kinds of interests. One is the individual interest in avoiding disclosure of personal matters, and another is the interest in independence in making certain kinds of important decisions. Appellees argue that both of these interests are impaired by this statute. The mere existence in readily available form of the information about patients' use of Schedule II drugs creates a genuine concern that the information will become publicly known and that it will adversely affect their reputations. This concern makes some patients reluctant to use, and some doctors reluctant to prescribe, such drugs even when their use is medically indicated. It follows, they argue, that the making of decisions about matters vital to the care of their health is inevitably affected by the statute. Thus, the statute threatens to impair both their interest in the nondisclosure of private information and also their interest in making important decisions independently.

We are persuaded, however, that the New York program does not, on its face, pose a sufficiently grievous threat to either interest to establish a constitutional violation.

Public disclosure of patient information can come about in three ways. Health Department employees may violate the statute by failing, either deliberately or negligently, to maintain proper security. A patient or a doctor may be accused of a violation and the stored data may be offered in evidence in a judicial proceeding. Or, thirdly, a doctor, a pharmacist, or the patient may voluntarily reveal information on a prescription form.

The third possibility existed under the prior law and is entirely unrelated to the existence of the computerized data bank. Neither of the other two possibilities provides a proper ground for attacking the statute as invalid on its face. There is no support in the record, or in the experience of the two States that New York has emulated, for an assumption that the security provisions of the statute will be administered improperly. And the remote possibility that judicial supervision of the evidentiary use of particular items of stored information will provide inadequate protection against unwarranted disclosures is surely not a sufficient reason for invalidating the entire patient-identification program.

Even without public disclosure, it is, of course, true that private information must be disclosed to the authorized employees of the New York Department of Health. Such disclosures, however, are not significantly different from those that were required under the prior law. Nor are they meaningfully distinguishable from a host of other unpleasant invasions of privacy that are associated with many facets of health care. Unquestionably, some individuals' concern for their own privacy may lead them to avoid or to postpone needed medical attention. Nevertheless, disclosures of private medical information to doctors, to hospital personnel, to insurance companies, and to public health agencies are often an essential part of modern medical practice even when the disclosure may reflect unfavorably on the character of the patient. Requiring such disclosures to representatives of the State having responsibility for the health of the community, does not automatically amount to an impermissible invasion of privacy.

Appellees also argue, however, that even if unwarranted disclosures do not actually occur, the knowledge that the information is readily available in a computerized file creates a genuine concern that causes some persons to decline needed medication. The record supports the conclusion that some use of Schedule II drugs has been discouraged by that concern; it also is clear, however, that about 100,000 prescriptions for such drugs were being filled each month prior to the entry of the District Court's injunction. Clearly, therefore, the statute did not deprive the public of access to the drugs.

Nor can it be said that any individual has been deprived of the right to decide independently, with the advice of his physician, to acquire and to use needed medication. Although the State no doubt could prohibit entirely the use of particular Schedule II drugs, it has not done so. This case is therefore unlike those in which the Court held that a total prohibition of certain conduct was an impermissible deprivation of liberty. Nor does the State require access to these drugs to be conditioned on the consent of any state official or other third party. Within dosage limits which appellees do not challenge, the decision to prescribe, or to use, is left entirely to the physician and the patient.

We hold that neither the immediate nor the threatened impact of the patient-identification requirements in the New York State Controlled Substances Act of 1972 on either the reputation or the independence of patients for whom Schedule II drugs are medically indicated is sufficient to constitute an invasion of any right or liberty protected by the Fourteenth Amendment.

. . . .

IV

A final word about issues we have not decided. We are not unaware of the threat to privacy implicit in the accumulation of vast amounts of personal information in computerized data banks or other massive government files. The collection of taxes, the distribution of welfare and social security benefits, the supervision of public health, the direction of our Armed Forces, and the enforcement of the criminal laws all require the orderly preservation of great quantities of information, much of which is personal in character and potentially embarrassing or harmful if disclosed. The right to collect and use such data for public purposes is typically accompanied by a concomitant statutory or regulatory duty to avoid unwarranted disclosures. Recognizing that in some circumstances that duty arguably has its roots in the Constitution, nevertheless New York's statutory scheme, and its implementing administrative procedures, evidence a proper concern with, and protection of, the individual's interest in privacy. We therefore need not, and do not, decide any question which might be presented by the unwarranted disclosure of accumulated private data — whether intentional or unintentional — or by a system that did not contain comparable security provisions. We simply hold that this record does not establish an invasion of any right or liberty protected by the Fourteenth Amendment.

NOTES AND QUESTIONS

1. *Whalen's* holding. *Whalen v. Roe* has been cited most often for the general principle that the due process clause of the constitution protects the "individual['s] interest in avoiding disclosure of personal matters." It has also been cited by commentators for the broad proposition that the state is free to require the reporting of personal medical information without patient consent for almost any reason that might be considered helpful to public health or safety. Does the case support these expansive readings of its holding? The statement that information privacy is protected by the constitution merely describes first principles without suggesting the scope or limits of that protection. Determining what kind of information deserves what kind of protection in what circumstances remains open for development. In contrast, the statement that information may be mandated when it might prove useful to government is more conclusory (always a dangerous approach in interpreting Court decisions) and leaves less room for the nuance necessary in the many different types of cases that involve information disclosure.

The reporting requirement in *Whalen* was initiated and upheld as a means of identifying criminal offenders: patients who attempted to obtain controlled substances and physicians who prescribed them without a medical reason. Can this rationale wholly apply in cases involving the reporting of medical information having no relationship with criminal activity? Might the state have made the prescription or possession of the same drugs for *any* reason a criminal offense? *See Borucki v. Ryan*, 827 F.2d 836, 841 n. 7 (1st Cir. 1987) ("Additional factors apparently underlying the Court's ruling were that the State could have proscribed use of the drugs entirely, and that the decision of whether to use the drugs, within certain prescription limits, was left entirely to the physician and patient."). In *Whalen*, the law at issue was part of the state's Controlled Substances Act, which criminalized the nonmedical prescription or possession of controlled substances, but the data were collected and held by the health department, not law enforcement. How would health agencies become involved in the investigation or prosecution of a criminal offense? (See the discussion in Chapter 5, *supra*, concerning the relationship between public health and law enforcement in detaining and isolating people with communicable diseases.) Compare the Supreme Court's approach to the reporting of drug prescriptions in *Whalen* to its decision on the reporting of pregnant women who used illegal drugs in *Ferguson v. City of Charleston* and to prescription drug monitoring programs (both discussed in Chapter 10, C, *infra*).

2. **Necessary, useful or interesting data**. The *Whalen* Court did not require the state to demonstrate that the reporting law was actually *necessary* to deter or investigate drug crimes, as plaintiffs requested. Instead, the Court appeared confident that the state would repeal the law if it proved to be ineffective or a waste of time or money. Was the Court's confidence well-founded? Not all mandatory reporting laws, or any laws for that matter, are the result of "an orderly and rational legislative decision." Moreover, legislatures rarely bother to repeal unnecessary or even wasteful programs unless there is a major scandal, public outcry or budget crunch. Individuals who object to such programs may find it easier to avoid getting care where they will be reported than to lobby the legislature for repeal. In addition, once the program is in place, a new constituency of groups that benefit from the program is likely to develop. In the case of reporting laws, agencies and private organizations that use the data collected pursuant to reporting laws tend to favor continued reporting, even if their own goals differ from that which justified the program in the first place. For example, substance abuse agencies that have nothing to do with criminal drug diversion may use the data to estimate the number of drug users or trends in the use of specific drugs, or to predict the cost of future treatment programs. Thus, the program may enjoy considerable support in some quarters even if it is not meeting its original goals. There is nothing inherently wrong with retaining a program that no longer serves its original purpose, as long as it now serves a purpose that, by itself, would justify creating the program in the first place. Whether a particular mandatory reporting program meets this test can be a close question.

Compare this type of balancing with that used in *Northwestern Memorial Hospital*, excerpted in Part B, *supra*, where the issue was the relevance of subpoenaed data to a lawsuit. To what degree must the legislature demonstrate the state's need for information to defend the constitutionality of a compulsory reporting law? What difference is there between the information needed to pursue a lawsuit and the information needed to develop public policy?

3. **Collection v. disclosure**. Justice Brennan, concurring in *Whalen*, was concerned with the potential for widespread dissemination of personal information that computers might permit:

> What is more troubling about this scheme, however, is the central computer storage of the data thus collected. Obviously, as the State argues, collection and storage of data by the State that is in itself legitimate is not

rendered unconstitutional simply because new technology makes the State's operations more efficient. However, as the example of the Fourth Amendment shows, the Constitution puts limits not only on the type of information the State may gather, but also on the means it may use to gather it. The central storage and easy accessibility of computerized data vastly increase the potential for abuse of that information, and I am not prepared to say that future developments will not demonstrate the necessity of some curb on such technology . . . . In this case, as the Court's opinion makes clear, the State's carefully designed program includes numerous safeguards intended to forestall the danger of indiscriminate disclosure. Given this serious and, so far as the record shows, successful effort to prevent abuse and limit access to the personal information at issue, I cannot say that the statute's provisions for computer storage, on their face, amount to a deprivation of constitutionally protected privacy interests, any more than the more traditional reporting provisions.

429 U.S. at 606–07.

Should *Whalen* be interpreted to mean that the state may require personally identifiable information to be reported for any plausible reason as long as the information is kept secure? What kinds of information would be susceptible to mandatory reporting using that reasoning? Assurance of enforceable protection of confidentiality appears to be a necessary requirement *in addition* to those of demonstrating that the disclosure is a reasonable means of achieving a legitimate state interest and does not offend reasonable expectations of privacy. The few courts that have addressed the question whether the state violates individual privacy by requiring the reporting of personally identifiable information have emphasized that authorizing legislation contains specific requirements that the personal information be kept confidential, in a secure location, and not be disclosed further, with penalties for any violation of these requirements. *See ACT-UP Triangle v. Comm'n for Health Servs. of North Carolina*, 483 S.E.2d 388 (N.C. 1997) (upholding an AIDS reporting law that enforced the confidentiality of medical records with criminal and civil penalties); *Treants Enters. v. Onslow County*, 350 S.E.2d 365, 374 (N.C. Ct. App. 1986), *aff'd*, 360 S.E.2d 783 (N.C. 1987) (finding that a county licensing ordinance which required companionship services to keep permanent records of their patrons and "grants authority to any law enforcement officer to inspect the records" violated the state and federal constitutions).

In *Whalen*, the Court focused on the possibility of information being disclosed to the public at large. However, that was not the only or even necessarily the primary concern of the plaintiffs. They considered the initial report to the health department itself to be a harmful disclosure. Later cases sometimes conflate these two distinct disclosures. However, more recent cases indicate that the initial disclosure to the health department is the threshold concern; the possibility of disclosure to the public remains part of the "secondary" issue of protecting confidentiality, which appears to mean that a person's identifiable information should not be disclosed to third parties, either deliberately or negligently. *See, e.g., Tucson Woman's Clinic v. Eden*, 371 F3d 1173, 1193 (9th Cir. 2004) ("Even if a law adequately protects against public *disclosure* of a patient's private information, it may still violate informational privacy if an unbounded number of government employees have access to the information.") .

PLANNED PARENTHOOD v. DANFORTH
428 U.S. 52, 80–81 (1976)

[The Court struck down provisions of a Missouri statute requiring pregnant women to obtain their husband's consent to an abortion and requiring minors to obtain parental consent to an abortion. The Court upheld the recordkeeping requirement, as follows:]

BLACKMUN, JUSTICE.

Recordkeeping. Sections 10 and 11 of the Act impose recordkeeping requirements for health facilities and physicians concerned with abortions irrespective of the pregnancy stage. Under § 10, each such facility and physician is to be supplied with forms "the purpose and function of which shall be the preservation of maternal health and life by adding to the sum of medical knowledge through the compilation of relevant maternal health and life data and to monitor all abortions performed to assure that they are done only under and in accordance with the provisions of the law. " The statute states that the information on the forms "shall be confidential and shall be used only for statistical purposes." The "records, however, may be inspected and health data acquired by local, state, or national public health officers. " Under § 11 the records are to be kept for seven years in the permanent files of the health facility where the abortion was performed.

* * *

[T]here are important and perhaps conflicting interests affected by recordkeeping requirements. On the one hand, maintenance of records indeed may be helpful in developing information pertinent to the preservation of maternal health. On the other hand, as we stated in Roe, during the first stage of pregnancy the State may impose no restrictions or regulations governing the medical judgment of the pregnant woman's attending physician with respect to the termination of her pregnancy . . . .

Recordkeeping and reporting requirements that are reasonably directed to the preservation of maternal health and that properly respect a patient's confidentiality and privacy are permissible. As to the first stage [of pregnancy] , one may argue forcefully, as the appellants do, that the State should not be able to impose any recordkeeping requirements that significantly differ from those imposed with respect to other, and comparable, medical or surgical procedures. We conclude, however, that the provisions of §§ 10 and 11, while perhaps approaching impermissible limits, are not constitutionally offensive in themselves. Recordkeeping of this kind, if not abused or overdone, can be useful to the State's interest in protecting the health of its female citizens, and may be a resource that is relevant to decisions involving medical experience and judgment. The added requirements for confidentiality, with the sole exception for public health officers, and for retention for seven years, a period not unreasonable in length, assist and persuade us in our determination of the constitutional limits. As so regarded, we see no legally significant impact or consequence on the abortion decision or on the physician-patient relationship. We naturally assume, furthermore, that these record-keeping and record-maintaining provisions will be interpreted and enforced by Missouri's Division of Health in the light of our decision with respect to the Act's other provisions, and that, of course, they will not be utilized in such a way as to accomplish, through the sheer burden of recordkeeping detail, what we have held to be an otherwise unconstitutional restriction . . . .

THORNBURGH v. AMERICAN COLLEGE OF OBSTETRICIANS AND GYNECOLOGISTS
476 U.S. 747, 765–68 (1986)

[The Court struck down the provisions of a Pennsylvania statute requiring (1) delivering specified information to a woman seeking an abortion; (2) reports on abortions that would be available to the public; (3) a particular standard of care when aborting a viable fetus; and (4) a second physician to be present during an abortion, without an express medical emergency exception. This excerpt from the majority opinion deals with reporting requirements.]

BLACKMUN, JUSTICE.

Section 3214(a) (8), part of the general reporting section, incorporates § 3211(a). Section 3211(a) requires the physician to report the basis for his determination "that a child is not viable." It applies only after the first trimester. The report required by §§ 3214(a) and (h) is detailed and must include, among other things, identification of the performing and referring physicians and of the facility or agency; information as to the woman's political subdivision and State of residence, age, race, marital status, and number of prior pregnancies; the date of her last menstrual period and the probable gestational age; the basis for any judgment that a medical emergency existed; the basis for any determination of nonviability; and the method of payment for the abortion. The report is to be signed by the attending physician.

. . . .

Despite the fact that § 3214(e) (2) provides that such reports "shall not be deemed public records," within the meaning of the Commonwealth's "Right to Know Law," each report "shall be made available for public inspection and copying within 15 days of receipt in a form which will not lead to the disclosure of the identity of any person filing a report." Similarly, the report of complications, required by § 3214(h), "shall be open to public inspection and copying." A willful failure to file a report required under § 3214 is "unprofessional conduct" and the noncomplying physician's license "shall be subject to suspension or revocation."

The scope of the information required and its availability to the public belie any assertions by the Commonwealth that it is advancing any legitimate interest. In

Planned Parenthood of Central Missouri v. Danforth, we recognized that record-keeping and reporting provisions "that are reasonably directed to the preservation of maternal health and that properly respect a patient's confidentiality and privacy are permissible." But the reports required under the Act before us today go well beyond the health-related interests that served to justify the Missouri reports under consideration in *Danforth.* Pennsylvania would require, as Missouri did not, information as to method of payment, as to the woman's personal history, and as to the bases for medical judgments. The Missouri reports were to be used "only for statistical purposes." They were to be maintained in confidence, with the sole exception of public health officers . . . "The decisive factor was that the State met its burden of demonstrating that these regulations furthered important health-related state concerns."

The required Pennsylvania reports, on the other hand, while claimed not to be "public," are available nonetheless to the public for copying. Moreover, there is no limitation on the use to which the Commonwealth or the public copiers may put them. The elements that proved persuasive for the ruling in *Danforth* are absent here. The decision to terminate a pregnancy is an intensely private one that must be protected in a way that assures anonymity. Justice Stevens, in his opinion concurring in the judgment in *Bellotti v. Baird,* 443 U.S. 622, 655 (1979), aptly observed:

> It is inherent in the right to make the abortion decision that the right may be exercised without public scrutiny and in defiance of the contrary opinion of the sovereign or other third parties.

> A woman and her physician will necessarily be more reluctant to choose an abortion if there exists a possibility that her decision and her identity will become known publicly. Although the statute does not specifically require the reporting of the woman's name, the amount of information about her and the circumstances under which she had an abortion are so detailed that identification is likely. Identification is the obvious purpose of these extreme reporting requirements. The "impermissible limits" that *Danforth* mentioned and that Missouri approached have been exceeded here.

We note, as we reach this conclusion, that the Court consistently has refused to allow government to chill the exercise of constitutional rights by requiring disclosure of protected, but sometimes unpopular, activities. Pennsylvania's reporting requirements raise the specter of public exposure and harassment of women who choose to exercise their personal, intensely private, right, with their physician, to end a pregnancy. Thus, they pose an unacceptable danger of deterring the exercise of that right, and must be invalidated.

PLANNED PARENTHOOD v. CASEY
505 U.S. 833, 900–901 (1992)

[The Court upheld provisions of a Pennsylvania statute, including a 24-hour period between consent and performance of abortions, but struck down a requirement that women notify their husbands and, in the following excerpt, upheld part of a reporting requirement.]

O'CONNOR, KENNEDY AND SOUTER, JUSTICES.

Under the recordkeeping and reporting requirements of the statute, every facility which performs abortions is required to file a report stating its name and address as well as the name and address of any related entity, such as a controlling or subsidiary organization. In the case of state funded institutions, the information becomes public.

For each abortion performed, a report must be filed identifying: the physician (and the second physician where required); the facility; the referring physician or agency; the woman's age; the number of prior pregnancies and prior abortions she has had; gestational age; the type of abortion procedure; the date of the abortion; whether there were any preexisting medical conditions which would complicate pregnancy; medical complications with the abortion; where applicable, the basis for the determination that the abortion was medically necessary; the weight of the aborted fetus; and whether the woman was married, and if so, whether notice was provided or the basis for the failure to give notice. Every abortion facility must also file quarterly reports showing the number of abortions performed broken down by trimester. In all events, the identity of each woman who has had an abortion remains confidential.

In *Danforth*, we held that recordkeeping and reporting provisions "that are reasonably directed to the preservation of maternal health and that properly respect a patient's confidentiality and privacy are permissible." . . . The collection of information with respect to actual patients is a vital element of medical research, and so it cannot be said that the requirements serve no purpose other than to make abortions more difficult. Nor do we find that the requirements impose a substantial obstacle to a woman's choice. At most they might increase the cost of some abortions by a slight amount. While at some point increased cost could become a substantial obstacle, there is no such showing on the record before us.

Subsection (12) of the reporting provision requires the reporting of, among other things, a married woman's "reason for failure to provide notice" to her husband. This provision in effect requires women, as a condition of obtaining an abortion, to provide the Commonwealth with the precise information we have already recognized that many women have pressing reasons not to reveal. Like the spousal notice requirement itself, this provision places an undue burden on a woman's choice, and must be invalidated for that reason.

NOTES AND QUESTIONS

4. Sparse case law on mandatory reporting. The *Danforth, Thornburgh*, and *Casey* cases, together with *Whalen*, represent the Supreme Court's body of decisions concerning mandatory reporting laws to date. It is worth pondering why the Supreme Court has only reviewed mandatory reporting laws involving drug crimes and abortion, not contagious diseases, injuries, or other conditions. Drug crimes and abortion appear in a significant number of all cases the Court agreed to decide. They also represent major public health concerns. Might there be other reasons? Perhaps few people are aware of disease reporting laws. Perhaps most people are happy to have their information used. How likely is it that patients who disagree might object to a mandatory reporting law?

5. Heightened scrutiny of information concerning the exercise of constitutional rights. In the cases concerning abortion records, the Court accepted the value of collecting health information, but with the caveat that it was "reasonably directed to the preservation of maternal health." *Danforth*, 428 U.S. at 80. As in *Whalen*, however, it did not analyze whether reporting was necessary for this purpose. (The law offered no benefit to those reported, but permitted the collection of data that might be used in research to identify health risks or better procedures in the future.) Instead, the decisions appear to turn on whether the law "respects a patient's confidentiality and privacy." *Id.* Here, the key concern was whether a woman could be identified from the information reported. In *Thornburgh*, the Court examined the possibility of identification even where the law did not require names to be reported. In *Casey*, it upheld a later Pennsylvania law that did not require reporting the woman's name, even though the information required was somewhat detailed. The Court recognized that state mandatory reporting laws could chill the exercise of constitutionally protected rights when they require the reporting of protected activities, and struck down the requirement to report a woman's reason for not notifying her husband of the abortion. The Court's attention to the types of information at issue and the potential for identification suggest an increasing sophistication with the benefits and risks of data collection.

These decisions suggest that when disclosure of information threatens the exercise of important rights of personal autonomy, more careful scrutiny of the state's purpose may be warranted. Lower courts have used this reasoning to apply heightened scrutiny where sexual or health information is at issue. *See Sheets v. Salt Lake County*, 45 F.3d 1383, 1387 (10th Cir. 1995) (disclosure of sexual or health information may violate a person's right to information privacy unless the disclosure serves a compelling state interest in the least intrusive manner); *Walls v. Petersburg*, 895 F.2d 188, 192 (4th Cir. 1990) ("The more intimate or personal the information, the more justified is the expectation that it will not be subject to public scrutiny."); *Fraternal Order of Police v. City of Philadelphia*, 812 F.2d 105, 110 (3d Cir. 1987) ("Most circuits appear to apply an 'intermediate standard of review' for the majority of confidentiality violations, . . . with a compelling interest analysis reserved for 'severe intrusions' on confidentiality."). *See John B. v. Superior Court*, 137 P.3d 153 (Cal. 2006) (addressing discovery requests for medical records of HIV infection, the court found that where a plaintiff seeks "discovery from a defendant concerning sexual matters protected by the constitutional right of privacy, the intrusion upon sexual privacy may only be done on the basis of practical necessity and the compelled disclosure [must] be narrowly drawn to assure maximum protection of the constitutional interests at stake" (internal quotes omitted)) . There remains some uncertainty about whether more careful scrutiny is required because the type of information itself at issue is especially sensitive or important, or because disclosure of that information would affect the exercise of an important aspect of personal liberty. Further, courts use different levels of scrutiny for somewhat similar types of information, suggesting that there is room for future debate on analytic approaches.

AID FOR WOMEN v. FOULSTON
427 F. Supp. 2d 1093 (D. Kan. 2006)

MARTEN, JUDGE.

Plaintiffs seek to prevent enforcement of Kansas Attorney General Phill Kline's application of the state mandatory reporting statute, through an Attorney General's Opinion [the "Kline Opinion"], to consensual underage sexual activity. [The action was brought pursuant to 42 U.S.C. § 1983 seeking declaratory and injunctive relief by licensed professionals.] Specifically . . . this case turns on whether Kan. Stat. Ann. § 38-1522, commonly referred to as the "Kansas reporting statute," requires reporting of all consensual underage sexual activity as sexual abuse.

. . . [N]either side objects to the reporting of: 1) incest; 2) sexual abuse of a child by an adult; and 3) sexual activities involving a child under the age of twelve. Therefore, the only issue presented is whether consensual underage sexual activity must be reported under the Kansas reporting statute. After extensive review of the record, this court holds that the Kansas reporting statute: 1) does not make all underage sexual activity inherently injurious; and 2) requires that the reporter have reason to suspect both injury and that the injury resulted from illegal sexual activity, as defined by Kansas law, before reporting is required. In addition, to require reporting in accordance with Attorney General Kline's opinion would violate a minor's limited right of informational privacy. Thus, this court permanently enjoins enforcement of Kan. Stat. Ann. § 38-1522 in any manner inconsistent with this decision, which includes the Kline Opinion.

. . . .

As part and parcel of [the state's interest in protecting children], Kansas requires reporting to the state government whenever certain persons have "reason to suspect that a child has been injured as a result of . . . sexual abuse." The mandatory reporting requirement extends to various medical and health care providers, school officials, law enforcement, child care service providers, social workers, counselors, and emergency response personnel . . . "Willful and knowing failure to make a report" is a misdemeanor criminal offense . . . . [S]exual activity of minors younger than sixteen is illegal, regardless of whether the activity is voluntary or the sexual activity involves an age-mate. The only exception to this criminal ban is in the case of consensual sexual contact between a person under sixteen and that person's spouse. Kansas has long allowed twelve-year-old females and fourteen-year-old males to marry with parental or judicial consent, although the Kansas legislature is now considering raising these ages.

. . . .

[The state Department of Social and Rehabilitative Services] has a longstanding policy of screening out consensual underage sexual activity. [Earlier Attorney Generals' opinions required reporters to determine whether sexual activity caused harm.] . . . [O]n June 18, 2003, Kansas Attorney General Phill Kline issued an opinion seeking to significantly change the standard for reporting. His opinion, in part, states:

> Kansas law clearly provides that those who fall under the scope of the reporting requirement must report any reasonable suspicion that a child has been injured as a result of sexual abuse, which would be any time a child under the age of 16 has become pregnant. As a matter of law such child has been the victim of rape or one of the other sexual abuse crimes and such crimes are inherently injurious.

In reaching this conclusion, the Attorney General looked beyond the statute's language and beyond the law of the State of Kansas. His opinion that the minor's pregnancy is "inherently injurious" eliminated the reporter's discretion to determine whether the minor had been "injured." Further, as the Attorney General's opinion acknowledges, such "inherent injury" reaches beyond a minor's pregnancy:

> We are aware that although this opinion is limited to the question posed, the consequences of the conclusion reach further. Other situations that might trigger a mandated reporter's obligation, because sexual activity of a minor becomes known, include a teenage girl or boy who seeks medical attention for a sexually transmitted disease, a teenage girl who seeks medical attention for a pregnancy, or a teenage girl seeking birth control who discloses she has already been sexually active.

Thus, if all illegal sexual activity of a minor is considered sexual abuse and is per se injurious, then pursuant to the Kline Opinion, a mandatory reporter must automatically report any indication that a minor is sexually active.

[The reporting statute] recognizes that a mandatory reporter must identify two things: 1) there is reason to suspect that the child has been injured; and 2) the injury resulted from sexual abuse . . . . [T]he legislature has defined "sexual abuse" in Article 35, Chapter 21 of the Kansas Statutes. However, it has not defined "injury."

. . . .

The legislature included a very specific phrase in the statute: "reason to suspect that a child has been injured as a result of . . . sexual abuse . . . . " This phrase vests a degree of discretion in the reporter not only to determine suspected sexual abuse, but also resulting injury. The legislature acknowledged that not all illegal sexual activity involving a minor necessarily results in "injury;" thus, not all unlawful sexual activity warrants reporting . . . .

Therefore, the court finds that the legislature's inclusion of the phrase "reason to suspect that a child has been injured" requires reporters to determine if there is a reason to suspect injury resulting from sexual abuse. "Injury" and "sexual abuse" are distinct concepts under the statute. Any attempt to conflate the meaning of these terms is contrary to a plain reading of this statute.

. . . .

The narrow constitutional issue before this court is whether minor patients have a right to informational privacy concerning consensual sexual activity with an age-mate where there is no evidence of force, coercion, or power differential. Plaintiffs argue that . . . confidentiality is a cornerstone of treating adolescents and that automatic reporting of all illegal, but non-injurious, sexual activity will deter their minor patients' access to health care. Defendants argue that the state interest in reporting of sexual abuse trumps a minor's privacy interests.

An individual's right to informational privacy may be implicated when the government compels disclosure of that individual's personal sexual or health-related information to the government and/or to other third parties. Compelled disclosure may violate an individual's right to informational privacy unless the disclosure serves a compelling state interest in the least intrusive manner. To determine whether information is of such a personal nature that it demands constitutional protection, the court considers: "1) if the party asserting the right has a legitimate expectation of privacy; 2) if disclosure serves a compelling state interest; and 3) if disclosure can be made in the least intrusive manner. " A "legitimate expectation of privacy, " is based "at least in part, upon the intimate or otherwise personal nature of the material. " . . .

Plaintiffs provided credible evidence of irreparable harm at trial. First, the Kline Opinion places plaintiffs on notice that they may be prosecuted for not reporting illegal sexual activity of minors . . . .

Second, considering the Kline Opinion, plaintiffs do not have fair notice of what is reportable under the statute . . . .

. . . .

Third, based upon the testimony and other evidence, serious questions arise as to whether minors will continue to seek timely medical care and psychological services if all illegal sexual activity is automatically reported . . . .

Since medical and psychological care providers have an obligation to disclose the scope of confidentiality at the onset of treatment, underage minors will be aware of the limits of confidentiality and the potential for state notification of underage sexual activity . . . .

. . . Mandatory reporting of all sexual activity to a state agency can be more frightening given the potential for criminal liability. If minors are told that there may be an investigation, they may be more inhibited in seeking care. Further, minors who otherwise would seek medical care with their parents' involvement may be deterred by the potential to involve their parents in a criminal investigation.

Automatic mandatory reporting of illegal sexual activity involving a minor will change the nature of the relationship between a health care provider and the minor patient to some degree. Based on studies that evaluated the effects of parental notification, there will be a significant decrease in minors seeking care and treatment related to sexual activity. In the context of a reporting statute, the effects may be greater since a state agency will be notified of the alleged "sexual abuse." According to several witnesses, in the long-term, forgoing or delaying medical care leads to risks to minors including the worsening of existing medical conditions and the spreading of undiagnosed diseases. The Wisconsin study indicates that at a minimum, young persons report that they will engage in riskier behavior if confidential care is not available. The cumulative, credible medical evidence presented at trial indicates that minors face irreparable harm in the face of a reporting statute that requires automatic disclosure of all illegal sexual activity.

Finally, . . . SRS Director Sandra Hazlett stated that the Kline Opinion would increase the number of intake reports, increasing the workload without a corresponding increase in funding. Besides overwhelming state agencies, reporting all sexual activity as sexual abuse tends to trivialize actual sexual abuse.

. . . .

The state has a strong interest in protecting minors and promoting public health. But this interest is at its ebb in the present action, where the Attorney General's Opinion goes beyond the scope of the reporting statute, potentially criminalizing the decisions health care providers make in utmost good faith, and solely with the physical and emotional health of their patients in mind. The Attorney General's over-expansive interpretation of the reporting statute not only fails to serve the public interest, it actually serves to undermine it by causing minors to avoid seeking medical services and potentially overburdening SRS.

. . . .

[Permanent injunction granted.]

NOTES AND QUESTIONS

6. **Alternative uses of reporting laws.** *Foulston* presents an unusual use of a state reporting law. Critics claimed that the state attorney general was using the law as a pretext to investigate medical records to identify minors who had abortions. Regardless of the motives for the "Klein opinion," there may be other reasons for the state or a state agency to seek information from surveillance programs in the future. Can you think of some? The opinion notes that sexually transmitted diseases might be evidence of criminal sexual acts. Could data collected pursuant to STI reporting laws be a source of evidence for a criminal investigation? What if the district attorney simply wanted to see who might be engaging in criminal sexual conduct?

The opinion in *Foulston* details considerable expert testimony that the reporting law, enacted in 1982, if applied to all sexual activity in minors, would discourage adolescents from seeking necessary medical care. Are adolescents different from adults in this respect? The court also noted that reporting laws can create a conflict of interest for physicians, because they have an obligation to maintain patient confidentiality and also to violate that confidentiality when required by law. It added, "Because many licensed professionals play a dual role as both mandatory reporters and care providers, the confidentiality between licensed professionals and patients should be breached only sparingly . . . . [C]onfidentiality is the "cornerstone" of the doctor-patient relationship. " Perhaps for this reason, physicians testified at trial that "they personally do not report all cases of underage sexual activity . . . ." The court found that "there is no indication that underreporting is or has been a problem under the Kansas statute," and that the local district attorney had never prosecuted anyone for not reporting abuse in her 17 years in office. Does this failure to report indicate that physicians are using appropriate discretion, adhering to their duty to act in the best interests of their patients, committing a criminal offense, or acting as conscientious objectors?

7. **Public records.** State and federal public records and freedom of information laws give the public access to government agency records. The federal Freedom of Information Act 5 U.S.C. § 552(a), exempts government "personnel and medical files and similar files" from public access, but only the federal agency — not the individual whose information is included — can claim the exemption. Specific statutes have been enacted to permit the agencies to keep some health information confidential, including data collected by some surveillance programs. In the absence of such confidentiality laws, members of the public could claim access to disease reports about individuals that were submitted to the health department. For example, in *Thomas v. Morris*, 36 N.E.2d 141 (N.Y. 1941), the New York Court of Appeals approved the plaintiff's subpoena for health department records indicating whether the defendant was a typhoid carrier in an action for damages for the death of plaintiff's decedent after eating food prepared and served by the defendant at a hotel restaurant:

> We decide . . . that no privilege attaches to these records and that the public policy of the State as expressed in the Public Health Law and the State Sanitary Code confers no privilege. Privilege does not exist unless conferred by statute. Here the statutes point the other way and seem to require that such records, in so far as they refer to known or suspected typhoid carriers, be made available in a case like this. The Sanitary Code . . . requires local health officers to keep the State Department of Health informed of the names, ages and addresses of known or suspected typhoid carriers, . . . to inform the carrier and members of his household of the situation and to exercise certain controls over the activities of the carriers, including a prohibition against any handling by the carrier of food which is to be consumed by persons other than members of his own household. Why should the record of compliance by the County Health Officer with these salutary requirements be kept confidential? Hidden in the files of the health office, it serves no public purpose except a bare statistical one. Made available to those with a legitimate ground for inquiry, it is effective to check the spread of the dread disease . . . .

> The information in the Health Commissioner's files concerning the defendant, if there be any such information there, was not acquired by the Health Commissioner "in attending a patient in a professional capacity" nor was the information "necessary to enable him to act in that capacity. "

Although the information may have come to the commissioner from a physician in private practice, the transmittal from that physician to the public officer was in obedience to the express command of section 25 of the Public Health Law. [That section does not state that the report shall be kept confidential, while other sections concerning reports of TB and two other diseases do provide for confidentiality.] It seems to follow that similar reports as to other communicable diseases are not so privileged.

The court's language may represent an earlier era, but it reflects the basic premise that information collected by public agencies should be available to the public unless expressly exempted by the legislature. It points to the need for statutory requirements for confidentiality if medical information reported to a disease surveillance program should not be made public.

Note the distinction between the confidentiality expected of a physician who receives personal information from a patient and the status of a government agency that receives a report from the physician. The physician may have a common law and in some cases a statutory duty to refrain from revealing the patient's information to others. The health department has no such personal or professional relationship with the patient and no duty to protect the patient's confidentiality absent a statutory mandate. When a health department submits surveillance records to a third party, such as the CDC, to be included in a national data collection system, the third party recipient is even further removed from any duty of confidentiality absent statutory prescriptions. The CDC's obligation to protect the confidentiality of reports it receives from the states is based on the Public Health Service Act and regulations, which do not contain the kind of explicit privilege language that the New York court thought necessary to prevent public disclosure.

D. PUBLIC HEALTH SURVEILLANCE

Ruth L. Berkelman *et al.*, *Public Health Surveillance*, *in* 2 OXFORD TEXTBOOK OF PUBLIC HEALTH
759, 759–60 (Roger Detels *et al.*, eds., 4th ed. 2002)

*   *   *

Public health surveillance is the epidemiological foundation for modern public health.

. . . .

Definition

In 1963, Langmuir defined disease surveillance as "the continued watchfulness over the distribution and trends of incidence through the systematic collection, consolidation, and evaluation of morbidity and mortality reports and other relevant data" together with timely dissemination to those who "need to know". In 1968, the 21st World Health Assembly described surveillance as the systematic collection and use of epidemiological information for the planning, implementation, and assessment of disease control; in short, surveillance implied "information for action."

. . . Thus, health information systems (for example, registration of births and deaths, routine abstraction of hospital records, health surveys in a population) that are general and not linked to specific prevention and control programmes do not, by themselves, constitute surveillance. However, data collected from ongoing health information systems may be useful for surveillance purposes when systematically analysed and applied on a timely basis.

History

. . . Possibly, the first public health action that can be attributed to surveillance occurred in the 1300s when public health authorities in a port near the Republic of Venice prevented passengers from coming ashore during the time of epidemic bubonic plague in Europe. The first Bill of Mortality was issued in London in 1532 as a consequence of fear of a plague epidemic. . . .

William Farr is recognized as the founder of the modern concept of surveillance. As Superintendent of the Statistical Department of the General Registrar's Office in Great Britain from 1839 to 1879, he collected, analysed, and interpreted vital statistics and disseminated the information in weekly, quarterly, and annual reports. . . . [and] took the responsibility of seeing that action was taken on the basis of his analyses.

In the nineteenth century, . . . Edwin Chadwick . . . investigated the relationship between environmental conditions and disease . . . . Louis Rene Villerme . . . analysed the relation between poverty and mortality in Paris. In the United States, Lemuel Shattuck also published data that related deaths, infant and maternal mortality, and infectious diseases to living conditions. He further recommended standardized nomenclature for cause of disease and death, and the collection of health data that included sex, age, locality, and other demographic factors. The first international list of causes of death was developed in 1893.

Increasingly, elements of surveillance were applied to aid in detecting epidemics and in preventing and controlling infectious diseases. In 1899 the United Kingdom began compulsory notification of selected infectious diseases. National morbidity data collection on plague, smallpox, and yellow fever was initiated in 1878 in the United States and by 1925 all states were reporting weekly to the United States Public Health Service on the occurrence of selected diseases. In the public health context, the term surveillance was increasingly applied to programmes of reporting selected infectious diseases in a population, with less emphasis on its application to quarantine of individuals.

Similar reporting activities were occurring in Europe at about the same time . . . . However, many of the morbidity and mortality reporting systems . . . were still largely developed for longterm archival functions.

[Surveillance became important to public health activities in the 1950s.] In 1955 acute poliomyelitis among recipients of the poliomyelitis vaccine in the United States threatened national vaccination programmes that had just begun. [Ed.: This refers to the Cutter incident.] . . . [The CDC and state health departments] developed an intensive national surveillance system [to report polio cases]. The surveillance data assisted epidemiologists in demonstrating that the problem was limited to a single manufacturer of the vaccine and allowed the vaccination programme to continue . . . . During the worldwide malaria control programme, surveillance was used to determine areas of continued transmission and to focus spraying efforts, as well as to document those areas without malaria. With the subsequent decline in malaria control efforts, surveillance data have documented the reemergence of malaria in many areas of the world . . . .

Surveillance was also the foundation for the successful global campaign to eradicate smallpox. When the campaign began in 1967, efforts were focused on achieving a high vaccination level in countries with endemic smallpox; however, it was soon evident that the programme based on surveillance to target vaccination in limited areas would be more efficient. Smallpox reporting sources, usually medical facilities, were contacted on a routine basis . . . .

[Perhaps the greatest surveillance success story was that of HIV/AIDS.] Even before . . . HIV was identified, surveillance data contributed to identifying modes of transmission, population groups at risk for infection, and, equally important, population groups not at risk for infection. These data have been instrumental in directing public health resources to programmes, preventing further spread of HIV, and averting widespread public hysteria.

The need for a strong infrastructure for surveillance systems is currently being reemphasized not only as countries face the emergence and reemergence of infectious diseases but also as a result of the increasing threat of biological terrorism.

The potential usefulness of surveillance as a public health tool to address problems beyond infectious disease was emphasized in 1968 when the 21st World Health Assembly recommended the application of surveillance principles to a wider scope of problems, including cancer, atherosclerosis, and social problems such as drug addiction. Many of the principles of surveillance traditionally applied to acute infectious diseases have also been applied to chronic diseases and conditions, although some differences in surveillance techniques have been observed . . . .

In addition to the increased scope of health problems under surveillance, the methods of surveillance have expanded from general disease notification systems to include survey techniques, sentinel health-provider systems, and other approaches to data collection . . . .

The assimilation of computers into the workplace has made possible more efficient data collection as well as more rapid and sophisticated analyses. In the United States, all state health departments are linked to the CDC by computer for the routine collection and dissemination of selected data on notifiable conditions. . . .

The explosive development of technology will include the development of high-capacity storage devices, expansion of the capabilities of the internet, use of local and wide-area networks for entry of surveillance data at multiple computers simultaneously, and development of new programming tools, video and computer integration, and voice and pen input . . . .

NOTES AND QUESTIONS

1. **Terminology.** The chapter by public health scholars Berkelman, *et al.*, uses the phrase "public health surveillance" in lieu of more traditional terms like "case reporting" or "disease surveillance. " In the middle to late twentieth century, the term "disease surveillance" replaced "case reporting" in order to encompass newer and more sophisticated methods of data collection, including research studies like sample surveys, seroprevalence surveys, and capture-recapture studies. The more recent and even more generic "public health surveillance" expands the definition beyond disease to encompass all matters of interest to public health. A commonly used definition for public health surveillance is "the ongoing, systematic collection, analysis, and use of health-related data to prevent or control disease. " Stephen B. Thacker, *Historical Development*, PRINCIPLES AND PRACTICE OF PUBLIC HEALTH SURVEILLANCE 1 (L. M. Lee *et al.*, eds., 2010). This definition captures the positive, protective role of public health, but still focuses on population-level problems. More recently, public health surveillance has expanded even further into the realm of personal medical treatment. (For examples, see Chapter 8.) Since September 11, 2001, at least one public health scholar has used the term "health intelligence" to describe collecting and linking multiple sources of data about health and health risks.

2. **Case reporting: background.** At the end of the nineteenth century, tuberculosis (TB) was the leading cause of death in the United States. To control the disease, Dr. Hermann M. Biggs wanted information on where the disease was concentrated and made the then controversial recommendation that physicians in New York City report cases of TB to the city health department. *See generally*, C-E.A. WINSLOW, THE LIFE OF HERMANN M. BIGGS: PHYSICIAN AND STATESMAN OF THE PUBLIC HEALTH (1929). Biggs was then Director of the Bacteriological Laboratory of the Department of Health and encouraged public education about how to avoid TB transmission. In 1897, the city adopted a compulsory reporting ordinance, but bills to rescind it were introduced in each of the next two years, in part because of physician opposition to reporting. To encourage voluntary cooperation among resistant physicians, Biggs offered a carrot — free (often overnight) laboratory analysis of sputum specimens to confirm or deny the presence of TB. Physicians gained useful diagnostic information for their patients, and Dr. Biggs got his surveillance data. Patterns of TB cases provided evidence that tuberculosis was a communicable disease, which some physicians had doubted. Physicians began to appreciate the medical value of collecting data on a population of patients and became willing to report their charity patients. *Id.* Nonetheless, physicians objected to reporting their private patients, believing that it would violate physician-patient confidentiality or stigmatize their paid medical practice. In these early years, fewer than half of the cases of active TB were reported to the health department.

Today, physicians generally accept and support case reporting of certain diseases for certain purposes. At the same time, physicians often have little incentive to spend uncompensated time completing reporting forms. Thus, state legislation requires physicians to report cases of "notifiable" diseases to the state or local health department. Reports were first made by sending a post card to the health department; more detailed forms followed. (An example can be seen in Figure 3, *infra.*) Cases requiring urgent intervention are reported by telephone. Electronic reporting is developing, but not yet universal. Many health departments hope to be able, eventually, to "pull" data electronically from provider medical records without relying on providers themselves to actively report. Although the number of notifiable diseases and conditions has grown dramatically, the basic structure of case reporting systems today differs little from the original design.

3. **Mandatory reporting laws.** Statutory requirements for reporting certain diseases were first adopted in European countries in the late 1800s. Rhode Island required tavern owners to report customers with smallpox, yellow fever and cholera to local officials as early as 1741, but Michigan adopted the first American compulsory reporting law in 1893. In the early twentieth century, courts upheld the state's power to require physicians to report cases of communicable disease to the health department. *See* JAMES A. TOBY, PUBLIC HEALTH LAW 110 (3d ed. 1947). Decided before the development of antibiotics and most vaccines, those cases recognized that little could be done to stop the spread of contagious disease besides separating those who were infected from those who were not. The need for immediate intervention made it important to find people with a serious contagious disease as quickly as possible.

All states now have "case reporting" laws requiring physicians (and often hospitals, laboratories and other health entities with relevant knowledge) to report to the state or local health department cases of "notifiable," "communicable," or "dangerous" diseases. (The terminology used depends on when the laws were enacted, with many using terms common in the early twentieth century; yet the terms are basically synonymous.) These notifiable diseases were originally limited to contagious infections that could be easily (and involuntarily) transmitted to others through the air, like tuberculosis, or by touching the same objects, like smallpox, or by drinking the same water, like cholera. Most states also include sexually transmitted infections (STIs; originally called venereal diseases), such as syphilis and gonorrhea, which caused particular concern in the periods surrounding World War I and II. (*See* the discussion of the history of quarantine in Chapter 5, C, *supra.*) Diseases like the common cold and flu are not included, because they typically do not cause severe illness. However, infectious diseases that are new or not yet understood but which appear to be communicable, like SARS, have been added to the list. Some states specify the diseases in the statute, while others authorize the health commissioner to designate diseases for reporting by regulation or rule. An example of a reporting law is shown in Figure 2 *below.*

Beyond diseases, all states require reports of injuries like bullet wounds or injuries from firearms, knives, or other sharp instruments, primarily for the purpose of criminal investigations. Cases of child abuse and, more recently in most states, elder abuse, must be reported to the social services or health department to permit an investigation into whether the person needs protection. In addition, births, deaths, marriages, divorces, and fetal deaths must be reported for compiling vital statistics.

FIGURE 2

Surveillance and Control of Diseases Dangerous to the Public Health and Access to Medical Records, 105 MASS. CODE REGS.. 300.190–.191

300.190: Surveillance and Control of Diseases Dangerous to the Public Health

The Department and local boards of health are authorized to conduct surveillance activities necessary for the investigation, monitoring, control and prevention of diseases dangerous to the public health. Such activities shall include, but need not be limited to:

(A) Systematic collection and evaluation of morbidity and mortality reports.

(B) Investigation into the existence of diseases dangerous to the public health in order to determine the causes and extent of such diseases and to formulate prevention and control measures.

(C) Identification of cases and contacts.

(D) Counseling and interviewing individuals as appropriate to assist in positive identification of exposed individuals and to develop information relating to the source and spread of illness.

(E) Monitoring the medical condition of individuals diagnosed with or exposed to diseases dangerous to the public health.

(F) Collection and/or preparation of data concerning the availability and use of vaccines, immune globulins, insecticides and other substances used in disease prevention and control.

(G) Collection and/or preparation of data regarding immunity levels in segments of the population and other relevant epidemiological data.

(H) Ensuring that diseases dangerous to the public health are subject to the requirements of 105 CMR 300.200 and other proper control measures

300.191: Access to Medical Records and Other Information

The Department or local boards of health are authorized to obtain, upon request, from health care providers and other persons subject to the provisions of 105 CMR 300.000 *et seq.*, medical records and other information that the Department or the local board of health deems necessary to carry out its responsibilities to investigate, monitor, prevent and control diseases dangerous to the public health.

---

4.   Case reporting: expanding reportable conditions. As Table 1 below shows, the diseases recommended for reporting are no longer limited to those that pose an imminent threat of contagion or even person to person transmission. The CDC and the Council of State and Territorial Epidemiologists (CSTE), a professional membership association of epidemiologists employed primarily by state and local departments of health and originally initiated by the CDC, annually recommend diseases for reporting. The CDC manages the National Notifiable Disease Surveillance System (NNDSS), which collects reports of cases of notifiable diseases that are voluntarily submitted to CDC by the states. *See* CDC, National Notifiable Disease Surveillance System, www.cdc.gov/nndss/ (visited Oct. 2013). CSTE/CDC recommendations are highly influential. States, however, have no obligation to accept them and sometimes do not. For example, in 1995 and 1996, CSTE/CDC recommended adding elevated blood lead levels, silicosis, and tobacco use. While some states require the reporting of elevated blood lead levels in children, because lead can cause growth and mental deficits in children less than six years of age, no state has required the reporting of tobacco use — yet. Chapter 8 examines reporting laws targeting non-infectious diseases, cancers, genetic and environmental conditions. For a history affirming the value of disease surveillance, see AMY L. FAIRCHILD, RONALD BAYER & JAMES COLGROVE, SEARCHING EYES: PRIVACY, THE STATE AND DISEASE SURVEILLANCE IN AMERICA (2007).

5. **Justifications for mandatory reporting.** Mandatory reporting laws can be a source of controversy. The rapid increase in data collection of all types and the expansion of public health into areas traditionally reserved to physicians on the one hand and biomedical researchers on the other have begun to test both the state's power to compel the production of information and the law's protection of individual autonomy and control of one's personal information. The threshold legal question in surveillance is whether the state can compel information to be reported without the consent of the person the information is about (*e.g.*, a patient) or the person holding the information (*e.g.*, a physician) . The answer is, of course, it depends. Specifically, it depends upon whether the information is personally identifiable and also upon one or more of the following factors:

- What use will be made of the information, immediately and in the future, and by whom

- Whether subsequent uses will be made with or without consent

- Whether the information will be linked or combined with information from other sources that makes identification possible

- Whether the information will be disclosed to third parties and whether they will subsequently disclose it to fourth and fifth parties

- Whether the information will be kept secure and inaccessible to anyone not authorized to view it, and kept or destroyed after use

- Whether there is an enforceable duty to keep the information secure and confidential on the part of all parties who receive or view it

One approach to answering these questions and creating boundaries for data collection and use lies in adopting Fair Information Practices, described in Part E, *infra*.

Table 1
CDC, RECOMMENDED NATIONAL NOTIFIABLE INFECTIOUS DISEASES   United States 2014   http://wwwn.cdc.gov/NNDSS/script/ConditionList.aspx?Type=0&Yr=2014

• Anthrax	• Malaria
• Arboviral diseases, neuroinvasive and non-neuroinvasive	• Measles
	• Meningococcal disease
• Babesiosis	• Mumps

Table 1

- Botulism
- Brucellosis
- Chancroid
- *Chlamydia trachomatis* infection
- Cholera
- Coccidioidomycosis
- Congenital Syphilis
- Cryptosporidiosis
- Cyclosporiasis
- Dengue virus infections
- Diphtheria
- Ehrlichiosis and Anaplasmosis
- Giardiasis
- Gonorrhea
- *Haemophilus influenzae*, invasive disease
- Hansen's disease
- Hantavirus pulmonary syndrome
- Hemolytic uremic syndrome, post-diarrheal
- Hepatitis A, acute
- Hepatitis B, acute
- Hepatitis B, chronic
- Hepatitis B, perinatal infection
- Hepatitis C, acute
- Hepatitis C, past or present
- HIV Infection (AIDS has been reclassified as HIV Stage III)
- Influenza-associated pediatric mortality
- Invasive Pneumococcal Disease
- Legionellosis
- Leptospirosis
- Listeriosis
- Lyme disease
- Novel influenza A virus infections
- Pertussis
- Plague
- Poliomyelitis, paralytic
- Poliovirus infection, nonparalytic
- Psittacosis
- Q fever
- Rabies, animal
- Rabies, human
- Rubella
- Rubella, congenital syndrome
- Salmonellosis
- Severe Acute Respiratory Syndrome-Associated Coronavirus Disease
- Shiga toxin-producing *Escherichia coli*
- Shigellosis
- Smallpox
- Spotted Fever Rickettsiosis
- Streptococcal toxic-shock syndrome
- Syphilis
- Tetanus
- Toxic shock syndrome (other than Streptococcal)
- Trichinellosis
- Tuberculosis
- Tularemia
- Typhoid fever
- Vancomycin-intermediate *Staphylococcus aureus* and Vancomycin-resistant *Staphylococcus aureus*
- Varicella
- Varicella deaths
- Vibriosis
- Viral Hemorrhagic Fever
- Yellow fever

NEW YORK STATE SOCIETY OF SURGEONS v. AXELROD
572 N.E.2d 605 (N.Y. 1991)

SIMONS, JUDGE.

Petitioners are four medical organizations whose membership consists of New York State physicians. Respondents are the Commissioner of Health and the New York State Public Health Council. In February of 1988, petitioners sent a letter to the Commissioner of Health requesting that infection with the human immunodeficiency virus (HIV infection) be added to the lists of communicable and sexually transmissible diseases pursuant to Public Health Law § 225(5) (h) and § 2311. The Commissioner denied the request on the ground that designation would be contrary to the health of the public because it would discourage cooperation of affected individuals and would lead to the loss of confidentiality for those infected with the disease. Petitioners then commenced this . . . proceeding contending that the statutes imposed a duty on respondents to add HIV infection to the lists or, alternatively, if designation was a matter of discretion, that respondents' refusal to list HIV infection was arbitrary and capricious.

The Commissioner of Health is appointed by the Governor with the consent of the Senate and is charged with the responsibility of taking "cognizance of the interests of health and life of the people of the state, and of all matters pertaining thereto" (Public Health Law § 204[1]; § 206[1][a]) . . . . The Public Health Council . . . appointed by the Governor . . . establishes health and health-related regulations, known as the Sanitary Code of the State of New York, subject to approval by the Commissioner (Public Health Law § 225[4]). The list of communicable diseases is promulgated by the Council with the approval of the Commissioner pursuant to Public Health Law § 225(4) and (5)(h). The list of sexually transmissible diseases is promulgated by the Commissioner pursuant to Public Health Law § 2311. Both are set forth in the Sanitary Code.

HIV infection is a communicable disease. It is transmitted by sexual contact, intravenous drug use or transfusions of infected blood. It can also spread from an infected mother to her infant during pregnancy or at the time of birth. Studies show no evidence that the infection is transmitted by casual contact. Individuals with HIV infection may or may not develop signs of infection and the disease can lead to AIDS. AIDS is a disease which damages the individual's immune system: those who develop it are vulnerable to unusual infections and cancers that do not generally pose a threat to anyone whose immune system is intact. At the present time there is no known cure for AIDS and the percentage of HIV infected individuals who will develop it is not known.

Petitioners contend first that the provisions of section 225(5) (h) and section 2311 require respondents to list HIV infection as a communicable and sexually transmissible disease. We do not construe those sections as imposing a flat, unvarying duty on respondents to designate as such every communicable or sexually transmissible disease in the Sanitary Code.

Section 225(5) (h) of the Public Health Law provides that " [the] sanitary code may . . . designate the communicable diseases which are dangerous to the public health." Petitioners noting that HIV infection is both "communicable" and "dangerous to the public health, " contend that the statute requires respondents to list it. The Legislature's use of the permissive word "may, " however, supports the conclusion that designation is left to the discretion of respondents. Indeed, we find no language in Public Health Law § 225(5) (h) that arguably could be construed as mandating that they list all communicable diseases.

Our construction of the statute is confirmed by the language found in section 225(4) and (5) (a) of the Public Health Law. Section 225(4) authorizes the Council, with the approval of the Commissioner, to "establish, and from time to time, amend and repeal sanitary regulations, to be known as the sanitary code of the state of New York." Subdivision (5) of the same section provides that the Sanitary Code "may," "deal with any matters affecting the security of life or health or the preservation and improvement of public health in the state of New York" . . . [I]n *Chiropractic Assn. v Hilleboe* [we] stated that "the Sanitary Code in general presents a situation where flexibility and the adaptation of the legislative policy to infinitely variable conditions constitute the essence of the program." That observation is pertinent to respondents' powers to amend and adapt the Sanitary Code in order to deal with changing public health concerns regarding HIV infections.

The Commissioner of Health is vested with similar discretion under section 2311 of the Public Health Law. That section provides that the Commissioner shall promulgate a list of sexually transmissible diseases, "such as gonorrhea and syphilis." In determining the diseases to be included in such list, the Commissioner "shall consider those conditions principally transmitted by sexual contact and the impact of particular diseases on individual morbidity and the health of newborns."

Petitioners assert that because HIV infection is principally transmitted by sexual contact and has an impact on individual morbidity and the health of the newborns, respondents must include it on the list of sexually transmissible diseases. However, the statute does not require that every sexually transmitted disease be listed. It identifies the type of diseases to be covered, "such as gonorrhea and syphilis," and directs the Commissioner to "consider" conditions transmitted by sexual contact. Under the terms of the statute, the Commissioner has the discretion to "determin[e] the diseases to be included in such list. " The discretionary nature of the power conferred is confirmed by the legislative history of the statute. As originally proposed, section 2311 could have been read as requiring that all sexually transmitted diseases be listed. Governor Carey vetoed it for that reason . . . .

There are valid reasons for giving the Commissioner discretion in these matters. Placement of any disease on the communicable or sexually transmitted disease lists triggers statutory provisions relating to isolation and quarantine, reporting, mandatory testing, and contact tracing — provisions which, for public health reasons, may not be appropriate in dealing with every type of communicable or sexually transmissible disease. The Commissioner has determined, for example, that no public health purpose is served by placing influenza, a communicable disease, and chlamydia, a sexually transmissible disease, on the lists. Whether HIV infection should be listed or not involves a similar determination by respondents after considering the circumstances attendant to the disease.

Petitioners urge alternatively that if respondents have discretion in these matters, their determination in this case is arbitrary and capricious because they failed to consider the pervasive and serious effect of the disease on the public as a whole and petitioners in particular. They argue that the reporting, mandatory testing and contact tracing requirements contained in the communicable and sexually transmissible disease statutes are crucial in controlling the spread of HIV infection and necessary to allow them to determine whether patients are infected with the disease so that they can take appropriate precautions during treatment.

Our review is limited to whether respondents' determination is rationally based, *i.e.*, whether it is unreasonable, arbitrary or capricious. We cannot substitute our judgment for that of qualified experts in the field of public health unless their judgment is "without justification." We conclude that in this case the evidence in the record provides a rational basis for respondents' determination.

Respondents have declined to add HIV infection to the lists because the provisions triggered by that designation — isolation and quarantine, reporting, mandatory testing and contact tracing — are, in their opinion, ineffective and impractical in dealing with it.

Petitioners acknowledge that isolation and quarantine would not be appropriate for HIV infection because there is no evidence that it is spread by casual contact. Their argument is directed to the provisions of the statute requiring reporting, testing and contact tracing. Under existing requirements, New York State and New York City health officials already have access to reported cases of HIV infection, including most confirmatory test results. Thus, the inquiry narrows to whether respondents' determination to forego contact tracing and mandatory testing of those infected with HIV is rational. In support of their decision, respondents note that, as a practical matter, mandatory testing and contact tracing will not lead to control and prevention because many persons infected with HIV are not tested until their symptoms become apparent and symptoms may not develop for many years. In the interim, between infection and the appearance of symptoms, an individual may have multiple needle sharing, sexual contacts or both. These factors would make contact tracing, without the voluntary cooperation of the infected individuals, an almost impossible task. Moreover, HIV antibodies may take months to develop and infected individuals who have not yet developed antibodies may be capable of carrying and transmitting the disease. Thus, while contact tracing has historically been a useful public health tool in stemming epidemics of readily discoverable communicable diseases which have a short incubation period, that is not the nature of HIV infections.

In addition to these practical limitations, respondents argue that mandatory testing and contact tracing would prevent individuals with HIV infection from cooperating with public health officials. This is so because of the fatal and incurable nature of HIV infection and the segment of the population which has in the past been most affected by that disease. Respondents note that most people affected have strong reasons to avoid disclosing that they have AIDS or HIV infection and confidentiality is critical to them. Intravenous drug users, who make up an ever increasing percentage of new AIDS cases, are engaged in behavior which is illegal and there is little reason to believe they will cooperate with health authorities in identifying their needle sharing contacts. Similar disincentives exist for homosexuals and others at risk of HIV infection because disclosure can result in discrimination in housing, employment and health care. Respondents contend that counseling and active voluntary cooperation are essential to alter private sexual and drug abuse practices which spread HIV infection and they maintain that infected individuals will come forward for counseling and testing only if they are assured that testing will not be coerced and that their test results will remain confidential.

Respondents' approach is in accord with the State policy underlying article 27F of the Public Health Law, a statute enacted to promote voluntary testing for HIV infection. As the Governor emphasized in approving the act, "by enacting this bill, New York rejects coercive measures. As experience in other states has shown, mandatory testing of broad population groups is neither effective nor desirable. "

The relief petitioners seek is inconsistent with that legislation. In article 27F, the Legislature has mandated that written informed consent must be obtained from an individual prior to the performance of any HIV-related test. By contrast, informed consent is not required to test for communicable or sexually transmissible diseases generally. Moreover, article 27F sets strict limits on contact tracing. For example, it permits physicians to warn an identified contact if they believe the contact is in danger, but precludes the physician from revealing the subject's identity. Any individual who does not want a physician to notify contacts can obtain anonymous testing pursuant to section 2781 of the Public Health Law. No such limitations exist on contact tracing once a disease is listed as communicable. Finally, article 27F provides a mechanism for assuring anonymity and confidentiality of test results. No comparable protections are provided to an individual once the disease has been listed as communicable or sexually transmissible.

Finally, respondents' approach to the problem is supported by leading health authorities. The United States Centers for Disease Control has adopted guidelines for dealing with HIV infection which include voluntary testing, counseling and confidentiality of personal information. Similarly, the Institute of Medicine, National Academy of Sciences, has concluded that mandatory testing and contact tracing are inappropriate, at this stage, to deal with the spread of HIV infection. We conclude, therefore, that respondents' determination that designating HIV infection as a communicable or sexually transmissible disease would be detrimental to the public health is rational.

Accordingly, the order of the Appellate Division [holding that designation was discretionary with respondents and that their decision was reasonable] should be affirmed, with costs.

Figure 3

I. STATE/LOCAL USE ONLY

Patient's Name: _____ (Last, First MI.)   Phone No.: (___) _____   Zip _____

Address: _____ City: _____ County: _____ State: _____ Code: _____

RETURN TO STATE/LOCAL HEALTH DEPARTMENT   - Patient identifier information is not transmitted to CDC! -

U.S. DEPARTMENT OF HEALTH & HUMAN SERVICES
Centers for Disease Control and Prevention
TENNESSEE DEPARTMENT OF HEALTH

ADULT HIV/AIDS CONFIDENTIAL CASE REPORT
(Patients ≥13 years of age at time of diagnosis)

CDC — Centers for Disease Control and Prevention

Form Approved OMB number 0920-0009

II. HEALTH DEPARTMENT USE ONLY

DATE FORM COMPLETED — Mo. Day Yr.

REPORT SOURCE: ☐☐

SOUNDEX CODE:

REPORT STATUS:
☐1 New Report
☐2 Update

REPORTING HEALTH DEPARTMENT:
State: _____
City/County: _____

State Patient No.: ☐☐☐☐☐☐☐
City/County Patient No.: ☐☐☐☐☐☐☐

III. DEMOGRAPHIC INFORMATION

DIAGNOSTIC STATUS AT REPORT: (Check one)
☐1 HIV Infection (not AIDS)
☐2 AIDS

AGE AT DIAGNOSIS: ___ Years ___ Years

DATE OF BIRTH: Mo. Day Yr.

CURRENT STATUS:
☐1 Alive ☐2 Dead ☐9 Unk.

DATE OF DEATH: Mo. Day Yr.

STATE/TERRITORY OF DEATH: _____

SEX:
☐1 Male
☐2 Female

RACE/ETHNICITY:
☐1 White (not Hispanic)
☐4 Asian/Pacific Islander
☐2 Black (not Hispanic)
☐5 American Indian/Alaska Native
☐3 Hispanic
☐9 Not specified

COUNTRY OF BIRTH:
☐1 U.S.
☐7 U.S. Dependencies and Possessions (including Puerto Rico) (Specify) _____
☐8 Other (specify) _____
☐9 Unknown

RESIDENCE AT DIAGNOSIS:
City: _____ County: _____ State/Country: _____ Zip Code: ☐☐☐☐☐

IV. FACILITY OF DIAGNOSIS

Facility Name _____

City _____

State/Country _____

FACILITY SETTING (check one)
☐1 Public ☐2 Private ☐3 Federal ☐9 Unknown

FACILITY TYPE (check one)
☐01 Physician, HMO ☐31 Hospital, Inpatient
☐88 Other (specify) _____

This report is authorized by law (Sections 304 and 306 of the Public Health Service Act, 42 USC 242b and 242x). Response in this case is voluntary for federal government purposes, but may be mandatory under state and local statutes. Your cooperation is necessary for the understanding and control of HIV/AIDS. Information in the surveillance system that would permit identification of any individual on whom a record is maintained, is collected with a guarantee that it will be held in confidence, will be used only for the purposes stated in the assurance on file at the local health department, and will not otherwise be disclosed or released without the consent of the individual in accordance with Section 308(d) of the Public Health Service Act (42 USC 242m).

V. PATIENT HISTORY

AFTER 1977 AND PRECEDING THE FIRST POSITIVE HIV ANTIBODY TEST OR AIDS DIAGNOSIS, THIS PATIENT HAD (Respond to ALL Categories):

	Yes	No	Unk.
Sex with male	1	0	9
Sex with female	1	0	9
Injected nonprescription drugs	1	0	9
Received clotting factor for hemophilia/coagulation disorder	1	0	9

Specify disorder: ☐1 Factor VIII (Hemophilia A) ☐2 Factor IX (Hemophilia B) ☐8 Other (Specify) _____

HETEROSEXUAL relations with any of the following:

	Yes	No	Unk.
Intravenous/injection drug user	1	0	9
Bisexual male	1	0	9
Person with hemophilia/coagulation disorder	1	0	9
Transfusion recipient with documented HIV infection	1	0	9
Transplant recipient with documented HIV infection	1	0	9
Person with AIDS or documented HIV infection, risk not specified	1	0	9
Received transfusion of blood/blood components (other than clotting factor)	1	0	9

First: Mo. Yr.   Last: Mo. Yr.

	Yes	No	Unk.
Received transplant of tissue/organs or artificial insemination	1	0	9
Worked in a health-care or clinical laboratory setting	1	0	9

(specify occupation) _____

VI. LABORATORY DATA

1. HIV ANTIBODY TESTS AT DIAGNOSIS: (Indicate first test)

	Pos	Neg	Ind	Not Done	TEST DATE Mo. Yr.
HIV-1 EIA	1	0	–	9	
HIV-1/HIV-2 combination EIA	1	0	–	9	
HIV-1 Western blot/IFA	1	0	8	9	
Other HIV antibody test (specify)	1	0	8	9	

2. POSITIVE HIV DETECTION TEST: (Record earliest test)
☐ culture ☐ antigen ☐ PCR, DNA or RNA probe   Mo. Yr.
Other (specify) _____

3. DETECTABLE VIRAL LOAD TEST: (Record most recent test)
Test type* ☐   COPIES/ML ☐   Mo. Yr.
*Type 11. NASBA (Organon) 12. RT-PCR (Roche) 13. bDNA (Chiron) 18. Other

Date of last documented negative HIV test (specify type) _____   Mo. Yr.

If HIV laboratory tests were not documented, is HIV diagnosis documented by a physician?   Yes 1 No 0 Unk. 9

If yes, provide date of documentation by physician   Mo. Yr.

3. IMMUNOLOGIC LAB TESTS:
AT OR CLOSEST TO CURRENT DIAGNOSTIC STATUS   Mo. Yr.
CD4 Count _____ cells/μL
CD4 Percent _____ %
First <200 μL or <14%   Mo. Yr.
CD4 Count _____ cells/μL
CD4 Percent _____ %

CDC 50.42A REV. 01/2000 (Page 1 of 2)
PH-3273
- ADULT HIV/AIDS CONFIDENTIAL CASE REPORT -
RDA 150

Figure 3 *(continued)*

VI. STATE/LOCAL USE ONLY

Physician's Name: _____ (Last, First, M.I.) Phone No.: ( ) _____ Medical Record No.: _____

Hospital/Facility: _____ Person Completing Form: _____ Phone No.: ( ) _____

- Patient identifier information is not transmitted to CDC! -

VIII. CLINICAL STATUS

CLINICAL RECORD REVIEWED: Yes [1] No [0] ENTER DATE PATIENT WAS DIAGNOSED AS: Asymptomatic (Including acute retroviral syndrome and persistent generalized lymphadenopathy): Mo [ ] Yr [ ] Symptomatic (not AIDS): Mo [ ] Yr [ ]

AIDS INDICATOR DISEASES	INITIAL DIAGNOSIS Def. Pres.	INITIAL DATE Mo Yr	AIDS INDICATOR DISEASES	INITIAL DIAGNOSIS Def. Pres.	INITIAL DATE Mo Yr
Candidiasis, bronchi, trachea, or lungs	[1] NA		Lymphoma, Burkitt's (or equivalent term)	[1] NA	
Candidiasis, esophageal	[1] [2]		Lymphoma, immunoblastic (or equivalent term)	[1] NA	
Carcinoma, invasive cervical	[1] NA		Lymphoma, primary in brain	[1] NA	
Coccidioidomycosis, disseminated or extrapulmonary	[1] NA		*Mycobacterium avium* complex or *M. kansasii*, disseminated or extrapulmonary	[1] [2]	
Cryptococcosis, extrapulmonary	[1] NA		*M. Tuberculosis*, pulmonary*	[1] [2]	
Cryptosporidiosis, chronic intestinal (>1 mo. Duration)	[1] NA		*M. Tuberculosis*, disseminated or extrapulmonary*	[1] [2]	
Cytomegalovirus disease (other than liver, spleen, or nodes)	[1] NA		*Mycobacterium*, of other species or unidentified species, disseminated for extrapulmonary	[1] [2]	
Cytomegalovirus retinitis (with loss of vision)	[1] [2]		*Pneumocystis carinii* pneumonia	[1] [2]	
HIV encephalopathy	[1] NA		Pneumonia, recurrent, in 12 mo. period	[1] [2]	
Herpes simplex chronic ulcer(s) (>1 mo. duration); or bronchitis, pneumonitis or esophagitis	[1] NA		Progressive multifocal leukoencephalopathy	[1] NA	
Histoplasmosis, disseminated or extrapulmonary	[1] NA		Salmonella septicemia, recurrent	[1] NA	
Isosporiasis, chronic intestinal (>1 mo. duration)	[1] NA		Toxoplasmosis of brain	[1] [2]	
Kaposi's sarcoma	[1] [2]		Wasting syndrome due to HIV	[1] NA	

Def. = definitive diagnosis Pres. = presumptive diagnosis * RVCT CASE NO.: [ ][ ][ ][ ][ ][ ][ ]

● If HIV tests were not positive or were not done, does this patient have an immunodeficiency that would disqualify him/her from the AIDS case definition? [1] Yes [0] No [9] Unknown

IX. TREATMENT/SERVICES REFERRALS

Has this patient been informed of his/her HIV infection? [1] Yes [0] No [9] Unk.

This patient's partners will be notified about their HIV exposure and counseled by:
[1] Health department [2] Physician/provider [3] Patient [9] Unknown

This patient received or is receiving:
	Yes	No	Unk.
● Anti-retroviral therapy for HIV treatment	[1]	[0]	[9]
● PCP prophylaxis	[1]	[0]	[9]

This patient has been enrolled at:
Clinical Trial	Clinic
[1] NIH-sponsored	[1] NRSA-sponsored
[2] Other	[2] Other
[3] None	[3] None
[4] Unknown	[4] Unknown

This patient is receiving or has been referred for:
	Yes	No	NA	Unk.
● HIV related medical services	[1]	[0]	–	[9]
● Substance abuse treatment services	[1]	[0]	[8]	[9]

This patient's medical treatment is *primarily* reimbursed by:
[1] Medicaid [2] Private insurance/HMO
[3] No coverage [4] Other Public Funding
[7] Clinical trial/government program [9] Unknown

FOR WOMEN:
● This patient is receiving or has been referred for gynecological or obstetrical services ... [1] Yes [0] No [9] Unknown
● Is this patient currently pregnant? ... [1] Yes [0] No [9] Unknown
● Has this patient delivered live-born infants? ... [1] Yes (if delivered after 1977, provide birth information below for the most recent birth) [0] No [9] Unknown

CHILD'S DATE OF BIRTH: Mo [ ] Day [ ] Yr [ ] Hospital of Birth: _____ City: _____ State: _____ Child's Soundex [ ][ ][ ][ ] Child's State Patient No. [ ][ ][ ][ ][ ][ ][ ]

Would you like the health department to provide (circle Yes or No or A,B,C, and D below)
(A) Post-test counseling: Yes or No (B) Referral for social work/support services: Yes or No
(C) Partner notification: Yes No or (D) Info. about TDH HIV Drug Assistance Program: Yes or No
!!! IMPORTANT NOTICE !!!
IF "YES" TO ANY OF THE ABOVE, PLEASE INFORM YOUR PATIENT THAT HE/SHE WILL BE CONFIDENTIALLY CONTACTED BY A HEALTH DEPARTMENT REPRESENTATIVE

NOTES AND QUESTIONS

6. **The police power and compulsory reporting.** Only a few reported decisions since the 1960s involve disease reporting laws, primarily HIV/AIDS reporting. In

Middlebrooks v. State Board of Health, 710 So. 2d 891 (Ala. 1998), a physician had provided certain statistical data, but refused to provide the names and addresses of his patients with HIV and AIDS as required by Alabama's reporting statute. The court upheld the State Board of Health's power to compel the disclosure in a summary decision without explaining the reasons for its conclusion. The lack of cases on reporting laws and the limited explanations for the decisions that exist could mean that these courts consider reporting laws generally within the state's power to protect public health. Alternatively, it might mean that the courts have not yet been forced to present a clear statement of their reasoning.

7. Official discretion. The *Axelrod* opinion illustrates the discretion typically allowed to state health officials to determine whether cases of disease should be reported to the state by law. The petitioners in *Axelrod* were physicians who wanted to know whether their patients were HIV positive. What might have influenced physicians to advocate for making HIV infection a reportable disease? At the time the *Axelrod* case was decided, many physicians were worried about becoming infected with HIV as a result of treating HIV positive patients. In 1990, Dr. David Acer, a dentist in Florida, was found to be the most likely source of HIV infection in five of his patients, including Kimberly Bergalis, although the precise mechanism of transmission has never been determined. CDC, *Update: Transmission of HIV Infection during an Invasive Dental Procedure — Florida*, MORBIDITY & MORTALITY WKLY. REP., Jan. 18, 1991, at 21. Senator Jesse Helms advocated a $10,000 fine and a 10-year prison sentence for HIV positive physicians who practiced medicine. Some physicians began to advocate for testing physicians for HIV, perhaps in order to justify testing their patients; the risk of transmission from patient to physician was at least verifiable, while the risk of transmission from physician to patient remained unknown and probably infinitesimal. In 1991, the American Medical Association issued a statement that "Physicians who are HIV positive have an ethical obligation not to engage in any professional activity which has an identifiable risk of transmission of that infection to the patient. " AM. MED. ASS'N, STATEMENT ON HIV INFECTED PHYSICIANS (Jan. 17, 1991) . For a description of the controversy, see Leonard H. Glantz, Wendy K. Mariner & George J. Annas, *Risky Business: Setting Public Health Policy for HIV Infected Health Care Professionals*, 70 THE MILBANK Q. 43 (1992) (also arguing that physicians have no duty to disclose their HIV status because it does not affect their ability to practice medicine, but should refrain from engaging in any medical procedure that they cannot perform safely and competently for any reason).

8. Identifying patients for interventions. Judge Simons' opinion in *Axelrod* states that persons with certain reportable diseases could be subjected to mandatory isolation, testing and contact tracing. As discussed in Chapter 5, isolation can be imposed on the basis of clearly defined standards. Is the judge correct that persons can also be tested for a disease without consent?

Today, states that require reporting rarely subject people to compulsory isolation. Instead, health regulations typically recommend approaches tailored to the specific disease, the mode of transmitting any infection, and the availability of medical treatment. See, *e.g.*, Reportable Diseases, 105 MASS. CODE REGS. § 300.200. For example, the recommendations for food handlers with Amebiasis or Giardiasis are restrictions from work until diarrhea has resolved and they have one negative stool sample, while people with cutaneous anthrax are told not to touch other people until their lesions are healed or they are free of anthrax bacilli. People with Hepatitis B are barred from donating blood or organs and counseled on how to avoid transmission to others. There are no restrictions for reported cases of diseases like arbovirus infection, botulism, encephalitis, or Hansen's disease (leprosy). As noted in the *Axelrod* case, interventions can be tailored to the specific risk presented.

9. **Outbreak investigation, contact tracing, and partner notification.** The most immediate use of communicable disease reports still is to investigate the source of an outbreak of contagious disease or environmental toxin and remove the hazard or limit (control) the spread of disease. Indeed, formal case reporting systems may be more valuable in investigating an ongoing outbreak than in discovering it in the first place. *See* Robert A. Weinstein, *Planning for Epidemics — The Lessons of SARS*, 350 NEW ENG. J. MED. 23, 24 (2004) ("The recent highprofile epidemics [*e.g.*, those of SARS, West Nile virus, anthrax, and monkeypox] were all first identified by alert clinicians."). Because outbreaks are now rare, however, outbreak investigations occupy a small proportion of state surveillance program activities.

Where a serious disease is reported, public health investigators often interview the person reported to determine where he or she might have been exposed to a virus, for example. In the case of HIV and STIs, infected persons are interviewed by public health officials to elicit information about their sexual and drug use partners, whom the officials can then confidentially notify of their possible exposure to infection. This process, known as contact tracing, can continue until the source of the problem is found and, ideally, eliminated. If the disease has an environmental source, such as contaminated water for cholera or food for salmonella, investigators may be able to find the source and remove the danger. If the disease is spread by personal contact, like STIs and TB, public health nurses can advise the patient's contacts to seek medical testing and treatment and, if they are not infected, how to avoid infection.

Infected individuals are asked to volunteer information about partners, and a majority does so. Most infected individuals are willing to notify their partners themselves. The more stigma that is attached to the disease being investigated, however, the more reluctant patients may be to reveal their sexual contacts to a public health investigator. Public health officials recognize that contact tracing sometimes poses risks. Some partners may break off the relationship or even abuse the infected person. Partner notification programs have mixed results, depending upon the state and the disease in question. *See* Matthew R. Golden *et al.*, *HIV Partner Notification Programs in the United States: A National Survey of Program Coverage and Results*, 31 SEXUALLY TRANSMITTED DISEASES 709 (2004). New York City's health department reported less success in contacting partners than elsewhere: "Of 4312 persons with newly diagnosed HIV infection in 2003, information on these persons' partners was available for less than a fifth and testing results were confirmed for fewer than 200 partners." Thomas R. Frieden *et al.*, *Applying Public Health Principles to the HIV Epidemic*, 353 NEW. ENG. J. MED. 2397 (2005).

Although the CDC strongly encourages contract tracing and partner notification, it has changed the terms it uses for these activities. In 1998, contact tracing became "contact counseling" and partner notification became "referral services." CDC, 1998 *HIV Partner Counseling and Referral Services Guidance.* In 2008, CDC began to refer to both practices collectively as "partner services," and combined recommendations for how to conduct these activities with its recommendations for STI prevention. CDC, *Recommendations for Partner Services Programs for HIV Infection, Syphilis, Gonorrhea, and Chlamydial Infection,* 57 (RR09) Morbidity & Mortality Weekly Report 1 (Nov. 7, 2008), http://www.cdc.gov/mmwr/preview/mmwrhtml/rr5709a1.htm#How_These_Recommendations_Differ_from_Previous_Partner_Services_Guidelines (visited Sept 2013). These recommendations are directed to state and local health departments. The CDC does not provide direct services to patients.

10. Reporting patients by name. Historically, reports for contagious diseases submitted to state health departments included the patient's name. Reporting systems were originally designed to prevent an epidemic, so health officials often needed to meet the patient. In some cases, it may have been necessary to seek a court order to isolate the person or quarantine a house. Knowledge of personal identity is obviously necessary in such circumstances. When the AIDS epidemic emerged in 1981, states began to require the reporting of symptomatic AIDS cases in the same way sexually transmitted diseases were reported — with the patient's name. Some states simply added AIDS to the list of communicable diseases that were required to be reported. Many, however, adopted separate statutes so that AIDS cases would not automatically be subject to control measures like isolation that applied to other contagious diseases. One reason for this approach was that AIDS was considered incurable, so that isolation could last a lifetime. This seemed unnecessary and unjust to many, especially the growing number of AIDS advocacy groups. In addition, Supreme Court decisions recognizing more explicit constitutional protection of personal autonomy militated against imposing compulsory measures on people with a disease that was spread, not inadvertently through the air, but by particular behaviors, such as unprotected sex and sharing syringes.

After 1985, with the development of reliable diagnostic tests for the HIV virus, antiretroviral therapies and better survival rates for people with HIV infection, some states began to adopt laws requiring the reporting of HIV cases in addition to AIDS cases. HIV/AIDS advocacy organizations objected to including names and other identifiable information. They also believed that names were unnecessary for the purpose of the reports and feared that the identities of individuals would be shared or disclosed to employers, insurers, or others who would discriminate against those reported. (This had not been a major impediment when AIDS reporting laws were first adopted in the early 1980s, probably because most AIDS patients then were too ill to work and insurance coverage was rarely available.) Many people at particular risk for HIV sought testing at centers that did not require their names in order to avoid such problems. There was concern that if names were required, they would not seek testing and might inadvertently infect others if they were in fact HIV positive. Opponents of named HIV reporting pointed to a few cases in which unauthorized people obtained lists of reported names or where old computers were sold to the public with lists of names still on the hard drive. Public health departments, justly proud of their tradition of maintaining confidentiality of individual identities, defended both the need for the information and their ability to keep records confidential. The terminology for reporting systems changed. Reporting systems that require a person's name are now called "confidential reporting," instead of "named" reporting, to indicate that names are collected but kept confidential within the health department. Systems that do not require or collect names are called "anonymous reporting. "

The Institute of Medicine summarized the controversy surrounding the adoption of HIV reporting as follows:

> Public health authorities justified reporting of HIV infection on several grounds. Reporting would alert public health officials to the presence of individuals with a lethal infection; would allow officials to counsel them about what they needed to do to prevent further transmission; would assure the linkage of infected persons with medical and other services [if public health officials referred them to accessible facilities]; and would permit authorities to monitor the incidence and prevalence of infection. In the following years, the CDC continued to press for name-based reporting of HIV cases . . . . Political resistance persisted however, and HIV cases typically became reportable by name only in states that did not have large cosmopolitan communities with effectively organized gay constituencies or high AIDS caseloads. By 1996, although 26 states had adopted HIV case reporting, they represented jurisdictions with only approximately a quarter of total reported AIDS cases.

INSTITUTE OF MEDICINE, MEASURING WHAT MATTERS: ALLOCATION, PLANNING, AND QUALITY ASSESSMENT FOR THE RYAN WHITE CARE ACT 78 (2004) [hereinafter IOM, MEASURING WHAT MATTERS].

ACT-UP Triangle v. Comm'n for Health Servs. of North Carolina, 483 S.E.2d 388 (N.C. 1997), illustrates that resistance. The North Carolina Commission on Health Services adopted a rule to eliminate anonymous HIV testing (which did not record names) at local health departments by September 1994. Advocacy groups and individuals petitioned the Commission to rescind the new rule and to keep offering anonymous testing. Although the court recognized that "arguments can and have been made that the previous program of exempting HIV testing from the reporting requirements is the better policy, " it concluded that confidential testing did not violate petitioners' rights to privacy. The court found that the Commission's decision was based on sufficient evidence in the record and was not arbitrary or capricious.

11. Anonymous reporting. In Massachusetts, California, Maryland, and a few other states with large numbers of people with HIV, physicians recorded a code (numbers or letters) instead of the person's name on the report that went to the health department. In other states, the physician submitted the name, but the health department replaced it with a code. The U.S. National Archives and Records Administration and other organizations use a Soundex code for genealogical and other types of searches and provide instructions on how to construct a Soundex code for names. *See* http://www.archives.gov/research/census/soundex.html; http://searches.rootsweb.ancestry.com/cgi-bin/Genea/soundex.sh (visited Oct. 2013). (The code uses the first letter of a person's surname followed by three numbers assigned to the consonants next appearing in the name. For example, the name Washington is coded W252, and Gutierrez is coded G362. The result gives a phonetic result without the vowels or the consonants H, W and Y. Several websites automatically convert a surname to a soundex code with a click of the mouse. *See, e.g.,* http://resources.rootsweb.ancestry.com/cgi-bin/soundexconverter (visited Oct. 2013). Some states add elements like date of birth to the Soundex code to create a unique identifier.

Physicians, hospitals and laboratories send completed case report forms to the state health department, which sends them on to the CDC's surveillance unit, after removing the physician's name and replacing the patient's name with a Soundex code and adding a 6-digit date of birth and residence at diagnosis. (An example of a report form to the CDC is shown in Figure 3 above.) One pilot study of six states found that a major activity of their surveillance programs was compiling reports for submission to the CDC. The Public Health Service Act authorizes CDC to collect, conduct research, and publish information about diseases. Public Health Service Act § 301(a) , 42 U.S.C. § 241(a).

Is it possible to convert a Soundex code back into a person's name? Would the additional information contained on the form permit identification? Do the concerns about the possibility of identification discussed in *Thornburgh* and *Northwestern Memorial Hospital, supra,* apply here? *See* Notes 10 and 15 in Part B, *supra.*

12. **Name identification as a means of finding duplicate reports.** Providers and health care facilities are typically required to submit a report every time they see a patient with a reportable disease, and laboratories every time they conduct a test for the patient. The same person may be reported several times or by several providers or laboratories (duplicate reports). Like any organization that conducts statistical analyses, the CDC wants to determine which reports refer to the same person so that one person is not counted more than once. Reports with names or the Soundex or similar code enable the CDC to do so. See CDC, SOUNDEX — REFERENCE GUIDE 2 (Dec. 1999) ("By using Soundex in conjunction with other demographic data such as date of birth and sex, CDC programs are able to identify duplicate name reports while adhering to patient confidentiality and privacy laws.") . "De-duplication" is also possible, however, even if different states use different codes that do not permit identification of the patient. The CDC has declined to accept reports from states that use such codes on the ground that it is unable to de-duplicate them. *See* IOM, MEASURING WHAT MATTERS, *supra* (recommending that the CDC accept HIV reports from all states, regardless of whether names or codes are used, and develop better methods of de-duplication). The CDC declined to follow the IOM's recommendation, and conditioned its funding for state surveillance programs on the use of names. By 2008, all states had adopted named reporting of HIV. For a more technical description of how to de-duplicate reports, see CDC, NCIRD, Immunization Information Systems: Patient-Level De-duplication Best Practices (June 25, 2013), www.cdc.gov/vaccines/programs/iis/interop-proj/downloads/de-duplication. pdf.

13. **Secondary and tertiary uses of surveillance data.** The CDC uses the reports it receives from the states for multiple purposes. Perhaps the most common

is to compile monthly and annual summaries of the number of people with a specific disease. Periodic reports are published in the CDC's *Morbidity and Mortality Weekly Review*; summaries are available on the CDC website at www.cdc.gov (visited Oct. 2013). The agency also reviews the reports to see whether a disease is occurring with unusual frequency in particular locations or among specific populations. More detailed analyses may be conducted to determine, for example, whether patients with specific characteristics — like age, race or sex, drug use, or insurance coverage — have a high or low incidence of disease, receive treatment, or survive for given periods of time. The findings can be used to alert both researchers and clinicians to the types of people who might be at risk for a disease.

HIV reporting illustrates a shift in the paradigm for the use of surveillance data — from identifying disease outbreaks to conducting research on risk factors to identifying individuals for treatment. In the case of HIV, this shift may be attributable to the development of antiretroviral treatment for HIV infection, which has proved to be both life-saving and life-prolonging. By 2013, 36 states required HIV case reports to include of CD4 T-lymphocyte (CD4) and HIV viral load (VL) tests by laboratories, which provide data for research on disease stages and treatment options. For a discussion of the advantages of this shift, see Patricia Sweeney, *et al.*, *Shifting the Paradigm: Using HIV Surveillance Data as a Foundation for Improving HIV Care and Preventing HIV Infection*, 91 MILBANK MEM. QRTLY. 558 (2013).

14. Federal financing of state surveillance programs. Many state surveillance systems, including HIV/AIDS and cancer registries (discussed in Chapter 8, C, *infra*), depend significantly on federal funding to operate. A survey conducted for the Institute of Medicine found that " [d]uring 1999-2002, the majority of funds for AIDS and HIV surveillance programs came from the federal government, and in 32 states it was entirely from the federal government." IOM, MEASURING WHAT MATTERS, *supra*, at 241. On average, in the 41 states surveyed, federal funding accounted for more than 95% of state budgets used for HIV and AIDS case reporting. States facing lower revenues may curtail or eliminate surveillance programs.

Funding may also come with strings attached. In the case of HIV case reporting programs, federal funding provided the carrot or stick that persuaded states that used codes instead of names to change their laws to require the reporting of HIV cases with the name of the patient, often against the advice of the health department, AIDS treatment programs, and advocacy organizations. The circumstances surrounding that change demonstrate not only the influence of federal funding on state law, but also the increasing use of surveillance data in formulas for allocating federal funds among the states, and are described in IOM, MEASURING WHAT MATTERS, Note 10 *supra*, at 73–85.

15. Immunization registries. The best defense against infectious disease is an effective vaccine that prevents illness and the ability to transmit the disease. The best known immunizations are those for pediatric diseases. The United States has succeeded in immunizing more than 90% of its children for major childhood diseases: diphtheria, tetanus toxoid and pertussis; poliovirus; *haemophilus influenzae* type b (Hib); measles-mumps-rubella; and hepatitis B. A large majority has also received varicella (chickenpox) vaccine and pneumococcal conjugate vaccine (PCV). To keep track of these immunizations — in addition to national surveys — all states have immunization registries, which collect information from health care providers about the vaccines received by individual children. The CDC administers grants to immunization registries in 50 states. Public Health Service Act § 317b. The data are used to estimate what proportion of the population has been vaccinated against different diseases. Individuals for whom specific vaccinations are not recorded can be contacted and reminded to get immunized. Physicians can use the registry to monitor immunizations and prevent duplicate immunizations. Somewhat more sophisticated registries, called immunization information systems (IIS), also can be used to record adverse events associated with vaccination, maintain a lifetime history of vaccinations, and link with electronic medical records. *See* CDC, Immunization Information Systems, www.cdc.gov/vaccines/programs/iss/about. html (visited Nov. 2013). CDC policy requires participating providers to allow parents to choose whether to participate in an Immunization Information System. *Id.*

The effect of registries on improving immunization rates has been mixed. *Compare* Allison Kempe *et al.*, *The Regional Immunization Registry as a Public Health Tool for Improving Clinical Practice and Guiding Immunization Delivery Policy*, 94 Am. J. Pub. Health 967 (2004) (citing improvement), *with* Arthur J. Davidson *et al.*, *Immunization Registry Accuracy: Improvement with Progressive Clinical Application*, 24 Am. J. Prev. Med. 276, 277–78 (2003) (citing marginal improvement).

Some states require reporting to immunization registries, while others do not. CDC, Survey of State Immunization Information System Legislation, http://www2a.cdc.gov/vaccines/programs/iis/legislation-survey.asp (visited Aug. 2013). Fewer than half of all children voluntarily participate in an immunization registry. Public medical facilities are twice as likely as private providers to submit vaccination information to registries. CDC, *Immunization System Progress, supra*, at 722. Should states require reporting to immunization registries? The CDC favors such laws so that children can be followed and urged to get all their vaccinations. As more providers adopt electronic medical records, they can easily link to immunization registries to report immunization data for their patients. Some CDC funded registries already link information from the registry and medical record systems, such as Medicaid or the special Supplemental Nutrition program of Women, Infants, and Children (WIC).

E. PUBLIC HEALTH SURVEILLANCE AND RESEARCH

Amy L. Fairchild, *Dealing with Humpty Dumpty: Research, Practice, and the Ethics of Public Health Surveillance*
31 J.L. Med. & Ethics 615, 615–20 (2003)

The last third of the twentieth century witnessed the articulation of the ethics governing human subjects research. The federal research legislation and guidelines passed and promulgated in the 1970s built on the Nuremberg Code of 1947 and the 1964 Declaration of Helsinki. All were based on a common set of principles stressing the absolute need to prioritize the rights of the individual over that of society: there could be no exceptions to voluntary participation and informed consent of competent adults in any research protocol. . . . no one could be conscripted into research projects . . . .

In response to the new federal research protections, epidemiologists and ethicists began to discuss whether the principle of informed consent extended to the use of records, and whether the insistence on individual consent would render epidemiological research virtually impossible . . . .

But the discussion . . . did not extend to public health surveillance . . . [which is] based on a principle fundamentally different from that animating biomedical research ethics; individuals may be compelled to do or not do things to protect the common good.

. . . [I]n the 1991 International Guidelines for Ethical Review of Epidemiological Studies, issued by the Council for International Organizations of Medical Sciences (CIOMS) . . . , a relatively narrow definition of public health surveillance was employed to justify exemptions from the requirement of ethical review: "An exception is justified," the guidelines stated, "when epidemiologists must investigate outbreaks of acute communicable diseases. Then they must proceed without delay to identify and control health risks. They cannot be expected to await the formal approval of an ethical review committee." By focusing on the urgency of some surveillance efforts, though, the committee excluded the vast majority of surveillance, which is routine and ongoing . . . .

Blinded HIV Seroprevalence and the Challenge to Surveillance

In 1993, National Institute of Health's (NIH) Office for the Protection from Research Risks (OPRR) received written complaints regarding two CDC studies: a measles vaccine trial intended to compare two different vaccination schedules that the CDC had contracted out to the Kaiser Foundation Research Institute and its own blinded HIV seroprevalence surveillance of childbearing women. [I]t was the serosurvey that raised questions about the bounds between research and practice within the context of federal human research regulations.

The CDC began to explore the feasibility of tracking the HIV epidemic through blinded testing at sentinel hospitals in 1986. When subject to ethical review in the 1980s, experts deemed such screening unproblematic. It involved samples of blood, not identifiable individuals. The privacy of no one could be violated. Informed consent was hence unnecessary. But what made the studies — based on unconsented testing — ethically acceptable also precluded notification of infected individuals. Since there was little that could be done for people with asymptomatic HIV infection in the late 1980s, there was widespread consensus that the blinded surveys were ethically permissible and served a critical public health need.

. . . .

A 12-member OPRR ad hoc advisory group determined that serosurveillance did not fall within the regulatory definition of human subjects research because it met both of two key criteria: first, it "caused no interaction or intervention with living individuals (*i.e.*, the activity resulted in no collection of information or specimens that would not otherwise be obtained)" and, second, it "utilized no information or specimens that could be linked, directly or indirectly, to identifiable living individuals. " . . .

[After investigating, OPRR concluded] that "Discussions with CDC personnel indicated that the distinction between human subjects research and routine, non-research public health practice was poorly understood and inconsistently applied."

. . . But while OPRR raised the prospect of formal IRB review for almost all surveillance activities, they required only that CDC develop a program for educating personnel about the regulatory requirements of human subjects research as well as written guidelines for distinguishing research from practice.

Dixie Snider, the CDC's Associate Director for Science in the Office of the Director, assigned Marjorie Speers, his Deputy Director, the task of addressing the OPRR report. Speers came to the CDC from academia, where all studies are considered research, unaware that surveillance "was such a sacred cow."

Prior to its internal examination of what constituted research, Speers explained, the CDC had traditionally employed a procedure-based approach to determining whether an activity required IRB review: "If they did a blood draw," for example, "they were defining it as research. " Scientists at the CDC were profoundly resistant to labeling an activity research, in part because of a concern that such a designation would invoke a lengthy IRB review and require informed consent.

It was precisely these concerns that had so worried epidemiologists and other social science researchers following passage of the Privacy Act and National Research Act in 1974. Regulations requiring the protection of privacy and informed consent, they feared, would effectively put an end to their research efforts. At the CDC, the concerns of epidemiologists were compounded by the way in which health officials tended to see the relationship between surveillance efforts and the central mission of public health. Speers recalled that on numerous occasions CDC scientists — on hearing that she had determined a protocol to be human subjects research requiring IRB review — would tell her, "You are killing people because you are making me go to the IRB. " . . . In short, the new application of the research regulations "wreaked havoc" on the way things had been done for a century.

. . . .

The 1979 Belmont Report [by the National Commission for the Protection of Human Subjects of Biomedical and Behavioral Research] defined practice as "interventions that are designed solely to enhance the wellbeing of an individual patient or client and that have a reasonable expectation of success." Research, in contrast, "designates an activity designed to test a hypothesis, permit conclusions to be drawn, and thereby to develop or contribute to generalizable knowledge (expressed, for example, in theories, principles, and statements of relationships) . . . . " The NIH subsequently used the Belmont Report as the basis for the definition of research in its 1981 regulations governing human subjects research:

"research is a systematic investigation, including research development, testing and evaluation, designed to contribute to generalizable knowledge. "

. . . .

Although the National Commission formally rejected the notion of intent [as the factor distinguishing practice from research], the first set of CDC guidelines drafted in 1996 made the case that public health surveillance is differentiated from pure research by intent: public health practice is undertaken with "the primary goal . . . to monitor the health of a given population for the purpose of taking public health action." Whereas "The *intent* of research is to contribute to or generate generalizable knowledge; the *intent* of public health practice is to conduct programs to prevent disease and injury and improve the health of communities." [Emphasis added.]

OPRR . . . advanced the notion . . . that all surveillance was research. This alarmed the CDC as well as the Council of State and Territorial Epidemiologists (CSTE) , which protested the position. According to the CDC, "The implications of calling public health surveillance research are broad and far reaching. There are 2088 health departments and over 100 surveillance systems. If all surveillance activities were research, it might mean each local health department would have to form institutional review boards (IRBs) and secure [special CDC assurances that human subjects were being protected] for each system. Whether the surveillance system is mandated by state law is irrelevant. If the research activity is federally funded, it requires assurance of human subjects protection." To the CDC, this was more than a bureaucratic consideration: if surveillance activities were designated research, the CDC feared that "people with TB could prevent their names from being reported to the health department or refuse to provide information about their contacts. "

. . . .

The Effort to Distinguish Research from Practice

. . . .

The CDC, which notably relies on the voluntary reporting of surveillance data by the states, is rarely involved in the use of surveillance for public health interventions like contact tracing. It is thus open to considering many of its activities as directed toward generating "new" knowledge based on the collective experience of the states . . . . [H]owever practical their research might be, it remains research requiring IRB review in the minds of many CDC officials.

States, typically operating under statutes mandating departments of health to collect and act on individual-level disease data for the explicit purpose of controlling disease, tended to view most public health surveillance activities as practice. New York State, for example, described the range of activities it undertook to control a typhoid outbreak in 1989, which included not only case reporting and testing but also one cohort and two case control studies conducted by phone on the sixth day of the outbreak. In the case of the two phone studies, participation was not mandatory, but outbreak investigators were not required to inform individuals about what cooperation was required . . . .

While there was little disagreement between the CDC and the states that activities such as outbreak investigation should not be defined as research, the federal government and the states defined research and practice differently when it came to routine surveillance. These differences were not merely semantic, but carried broad consequences. John Middaugh, Alaska's State Epidemiologist, described an instance in which his state was given legislative authority to conduct birth defects surveillance using federal funds. The funding agency viewed the project as research and demanded a state-level IRB review: "Alaska eventually returned the grant funds because the Attorney General did not want to delegate the decision-making process to an IRB. " . . .

In response to the comments from a meeting with CSTE, the CDC, in its June 1999 draft "Guidelines for Defining Public Health Research and Non-Research" sought to describe more specifically the activities that constituted research. These efforts at clarification provoked more pointed objections on the part of state and local health officials. The guidelines stated that "If the primary intent is to prevent or control disease or injury and no research is intended at the present time, the project is non-research. If the primary intent changes to generating generalizable knowledge, then the project becomes research. " That is, "if subsequent analysis of identifiable private information is undertaken in order to generate or contribute to generalizable knowledge, the analysis constitutes human subjects research that requires IRB review. " Thus, a hallmark of public health practice that was not research was that the "intended benefits of the project are primarily or exclusively for the study participants; data collected are needed to assess and/or improve the health of the participants. "

The New York City Department of Health responded that "the very essence" of its mission was "to prevent or control disease and injury." In doing so, the department argued, "we derive knowledge that may protect the particular 'victims' before us. However, it may also be that it is too late to help the particular victims, but that the activity, or the information derived from it, becomes generalizable so as to protect the general population." CSTE concurred, arguing that "we are rarely able to conduct an investigation that provides any medical benefit to those already infected." For example, in the case of food-borne outbreak investigations, the "major benefit has been to others than those we identified and obtained data and specimens from. "

New York City gave the example of an outbreak investigation of Hepatitis A among young gay men, which was determined to be associated with sexual practices rather than consumption of contaminated food or water: vaccination "was then directed not to the original victims but to the general population of young men who have sex with men. At what stage of this investigation did the Department shift from its 'primary intent' of preventing disease or injury to 'generating generalizable knowledge?' " The department thus adamantly insisted that "Generalizable knowledge can be derived from public health epidemiological investigations, and such investigations can still be deemed not to be human subjects research where there is sufficient statutory authority to conduct the investigation . . . . " And, indeed, New York State Public Health Law specifically noted that "Human research shall not . . . be construed . . . to include epidemiological investigations." For New York City, because surveillance carried the potential for public health impact, broadly construed, this made it practice rather than research, regardless of any research implications it might also carry: "if an inquiry may result in a public health intervention, such as contact notification, Commissioner's Orders or perhaps even rulemaking, then such should be viewed as an epidemiological investigation" that does not constitute research.

Just as surveillance may not always benefit directly the populations from which it was drawn, health officials also drew a distinction between immediate intent and primary intent. CSTE thus explained that it consistently collected data with an eye not only to the present but also the future: "ongoing analysis" of previously collected data sets was "routinely conducted for most, if not all, of the diseases for which data are collected under state law. " By review of previous investigations of trichinosis outbreaks, for example, the state health department in Alaska not only developed an early diagnostic test for the disease but also identified an animal species not previously known to harbor trichinella as well as a new subspecies of the disease-causing organism. "We do not view these activities as research" when conducted by the state, "if conducted by an entity other than the state public health agency, we would define it as research and require an outside research to obtain IRB approval. " Thus it was the provenance of the undertaking that determined whether an activity was research or practice. By definition, then, what public health departments did was not research.

Most alarming to state and local officials was the very narrow conception of when surveillance clearly represented pure practice. The CDC described only disease reporting "conducted to monitor the frequency of occurrence and distribution of disease or a health condition in the population" and surveillance regimes "in which no analytic (etiological) analyses can be conducted" as practice. "[L]ongitudinal data collection systems (*e.g.* follow up surveys and registries)" in which "the scope of the data is broad" and includes "more information than occurrence of a health-related problem," in which "analytic analyses can be conducted," and in which "cases may be identified for subsequent studies" were, according to the CDC guidelines, "likely to be research." The CSTE described this as a contradiction in terms: after all, "by its very nature, mandatory disease reporting is intended to be longitudinal data collection" and "to detect the causal agent to prevent future disease or injury. "

But it also represented a catch 22 for states: New York City and some states found the narrow definition of non-research surveillance "very troubling" because it conflicted with their legal mandate to collect data. For example, the New York State Sanitary Code, in creating the AIDS registry, authorized the health commissioner, after receiving an initial case report, to collect all information "as may be required for the epidemiologic analysis and study of Acquired Immune Deficiency Syndrome. " Thus, for many public health officials, "If an intervention or action is delegated to the health officer by statute or regulation, such intervention is per se ethical and not human subjects research." CSTE broadly concurred that "What distinguishes the activities as non-research at the state level is that the public health authority undertakes them and the data are collected under the authority of explicit state law. "

In the end, the CDC addressed the specific state concerns not by altering its guidelines to meet any of the specific challenges raised by the states, but by holding that "intent is different under the authority of a state/local health department versus a university" and that legal authority or mandate to protect the public health also shaped intent: states acted with such power, the CDC did not. In short, "activities can be viewed differently at federal and state levels. "

Conclusion: Putting Humpty Dumpty Together Again?

It is clear that public health surveillance is simultaneously both research and practice, in some instances more heavily favoring one component than another. Key stakeholders, moreover, can draw the boundary differently at different moments or recognize it not at all. In 1998 and 1999, for instance, the CDC commissioned the drafting of a Model Public Health Privacy Act to help ensure that states keep all surveillance data secure without impeding surveillance efforts. Some AIDS advocates challenged not only the model act but also the very legitimacy of public health surveillance. Advocates did not explicitly frame the debate in terms of whether surveillance should be considered research or practice, but they worried about how easy it was for health officials to conduct research with surveillance data under the model law and thus attempted to require informed consent for all surveillance for all diseases in a way that would have brought even state-mandated data collection under strict human subjects regulation. But not all disease advocates agree that informed consent was desirable. In the context of cancer surveillance, breast cancer advocates led the fight against efforts to make inclusion in state tumor registries voluntary.

It may be that there are few practical consequences for individuals if an activity is defined as practice rather than research, for it may well be the case that health officials protect the rights of citizens as vigilantly as IRBs protect the rights of those same people when they are defined as research subjects. But using the intent of surveillance to determine whether it is research or practice is a slight of hand that in the end is conceptually unsatisfying . . . .

Thus, the time has come to articulate the ethical principles for public health practice that both justify and limit data collection and use and to envision a mechanism for oversight. To be sure, ethical guidelines governing public health practice would not eliminate the thorny problem of determining when surveillance should be governed by the ethics of medical research and when it should be governed by the ethics of public health practice. Nor would such an ethics provide a practical mechanism for challenging legal mandates for states to acquire, use, and disclose surveillance data. But it would provide a systematic means for evaluating legal mandates to conduct surveillance: a practice is not made ethical simply because it is mandatory . . . .

Wendy K. Mariner, *Mission Creep: Public Health Surveillance and Medical Privacy*
87 B.U. L. Rev. 347, 360, 369–375 (2007)

III. FUNCTIONS OF SURVEILLANCE

Mandatory reporting laws are said to be for the purpose of protecting public health or preventing and controlling disease . . . . A closer look at surveillance programs, however, suggests that, in fact, they serve three more specific and immediate functions: outbreak investigation; ensuring essential medical care; and scientific research . . . .

A. Origins and Core Meanings: Outbreak Investigation

. . . Reporting systems were originally conceived and designed to prevent an epidemic of contagious disease. Reports to the health department included the patient's name and address, because of the possible need to contact the person. Timeliness was also a factor. Investigators would need to know that smallpox had been diagnosed within hours or days in order to find the source of infection and investigate whether and where it might have spread to protect other people from imminent infection. Although such outbreaks are rare, this remains a core public health function today.

Outbreak investigations are not limited solely to contagious diseases. They include investigating a source of poisoning, such as pesticides used in the environment, at least where there is no obvious cause. Where a public health agency has the responsibility for investigating the source of an illness that produces a serious injury or disability or death, the source must be identified immediately, and cannot be identified without interviewing the patient, there is ample reason for reporting the patient's identity to the health department. Thus, one useful criterion for characterizing data for outbreak investigation and epidemic control is that the data are needed right away to prevent imminent harm.

. . . If mandatory reporting systems were limited to data needed right away to prevent imminent harm, they would not bother to collect reports about the vast majority of cases, which are handled adequately by attending physicians. Nevertheless, case reporting systems typically insist on reports of every case, just to be sure no case is missed . . . . Yet, the required reports are still rarely submitted or reviewed more often than weekly . . . . Many health departments require physicians to telephone reports of disease cases that need immediate investigation, because ordinary weekly or monthly reports would come too late.

Traditional case reporting systems are not well suited to rapidly detecting epidemics or bioterrorist attacks using biological or chemical agents. New electronic syndromic surveillance systems offer more promise, although perhaps less for early warnings of terrorism and epidemics than for ordinary disease surveillance. Once installed in a location with electronic medical records, like a hospital emergency department, a computer program automatically scans medical records, logs the number of symptoms of interest without picking up personal information, and electronically transmits the totals to the tracking station, typically in a city or state health department. The tracking agency can review the data relatively promptly, often within 24 hours, and contact the hospital to see whether there is a dangerous outbreak.

Advantages of syndromic surveillance include speed and privacy. Most systems do not collect patient names or other identifying information . . . . Systems can be expensive, both to install the computer system and to hire people to monitor them. Because symptoms are common to many diseases, surveillance will produce many false positives and trigger costs to investigate ordinary cases of colds, influenza and other uncomplicated viral illnesses. Like sifting through billions of phone conversations, the task is to sift through billions of health records to find a genuine threat to public health.

. . . .

B. Assuring Essential Medical Care

Newborn genetic screening programs are designed to diagnose newborns with genetic anomalies causing severe developmental disabilities that could be prevented by beginning simple treatments soon after birth. [*See* Section G of this chapter.] Almost all programs are modeled on phenylketonuria (PKU) screening, begun in the 1960's. By the mid 1970's, more than 40 states required PKU testing for newborns. These laws effectively require physicians to provide, and parents to accept, good medical care for an individual child. Indeed, proponents viewed mandatory PKU laws as enforcing both a legal and an ethical duty of parents to their children.

Newborn genetic screening laws, however, do not necessarily ensure treatment for the newborn. By itself, testing serves only a diagnostic function. The disability cannot be prevented without treatment. Screening laws that fail to assure treatment cannot serve the function of protecting children . . . .

. . . Most experts agree that newborns should be tested for a condition that is reasonably serious, can be identified with a reliable test, and can be treated with relatively simple and effective measures. Between six and eight genetic and metabolic conditions meet these criteria.

. . . .

For conditions for which there is no treatment, the blood samples and linked information are used almost exclusively for research, such as testing experimental diagnostic assays to determine their sensitivity, specificity and reliability, estimating the incidence and prevalence of genetic conditions, and searching for risk factors. The screening program effectively creates a DNA bank. As more states expand their mandatory newborn screening laws to include these additional conditions, they may confront the question whether their power to protect children includes the power to create a DNA bank for future research.

. . . .

C. Research

Data collected from surveillance are used for a variety of research studies. Cancer registries are perhaps the most salient example. In the mid-1930's, the Connecticut Medical Society began collecting information about patients with various cancers to see if they could identify cancer treatments that worked . . . . Since then, other organizations have initiated other programs with broader or narrower goals. Cancer registries typically collect detailed personally identifiable information, primarily to permit the registry to contact the patient periodically to update information. The data is ordinarily submitted by hospitals, clinics or physicians, either voluntarily or pursuant to a mandatory reporting law. Most registries receive multiple reports about the same person and de-duplicate the reports by comparing names and dates of birth.

The National Cancer Institute (NCI) established its Surveillance, Epidemiology and End Results (SEER) program in 1973 [in 5 states and 6 cities], with a similar focus on analyzing methods of cancer treatment and outcomes (e.g., survival or death). Consistent with NCI's mission, SEER is primarily oriented toward medical research and uses research techniques. Most sites delegate the actual operation of the registry to a university, where researchers analyze the data and produce reports. They also follow cases annually to find out whether a patient remains alive and calculate survival rates. SEER publishes anonymous statistics on cancer annually, based on data as of about 28 months earlier.

The National Cancer Act was amended in 1992 to authorize the CDC to fund cancer registries in non-SEER states. The Cancer Registries Amendment Act requires, as a condition of eligibility for funding, that the data held by a CDC-funded cancer registry be made available for a wide range of research, both by the registry itself and by unrelated public or private entities. The difference between NCI and CDC registries is typical of the different methods the agencies use to collect data. NCI uses a representative sample of cancer cases to make estimates for the country, based on methods of research used in many other types of NCI studies. CDC prefers to collect data on every case of disease from case reports.

. . . Personal identifiers permit linking cancer registry data to other data bases such as the Behavioral Risk Factor Surveillance Survey, environmental health department records, Medicare and Medicaid health records, health insurance records, the National Death Index, death certificates and other vital statistics, geographic information systems, census data, registries of licensed practitioners (e.g., physicians, nurses, plumbers) and other specific populations (e.g., Vietnam Veterans registry). As information technology advances, the possible linkages are endless.

Several states have gone beyond authorizing the creation of cancer registries and have enacted laws or adopted regulations that either authorize medical providers to voluntarily report cancer cases to a registry or require such reporting without the patient's consent. In some states, advocacy groups lobbied state legislatures or health departments for a centralized source of information about a disease to try to explain unusually high rates of cancer in their communities or in response to fears of exposure to hazards from a local manufacturing plant. The more important factor appears to be the availability of federal grant funds to create or expand a registry. CDC prefers that registries be located in states that require the reporting of cancer cases by law.

. . . .

Arguably, any use of personally identifiable surveillance data — apart from outbreak investigation and newborn treatment — could qualify as research with human subjects. Cancer registries squarely present the question whether the state can demand access to an individual's personally identifiable information for use in research without consent. Since the Nuremberg Code was issued in 1947, research with human subjects has been deemed unethical and unlawful unless the subject voluntarily and knowledgeably consents. The consent requirement is intended to protect the individual's right of self-determination and the dignity of human beings recognized in all international declarations and covenants on human rights . . . . These foundational principles have been embodied in the common law, in regulations governing federally funded research known as the "Common Rule, " and may have constitutional protection. All support the conclusion that the use of personal information without the subject's consent violates the subject's rights. Federal Common Rule regulations expressly specify that research with human subjects includes the use of personally identifiable information.

. . . .

. . . If a project is designed to obtain generalizable knowledge, rather than help an identifiable patient, it is research. In the public health context, this would mean that research includes projects that are designed to identify the incidence and prevalence of diseases, analyze data to see if there is a common risk factor for a disease, compare outcomes to see whether particular preventive or treatment measures work, and similar studies that are disseminated to other researchers or the public.

Summary

Different public health surveillance programs serve very different functions. To complicate matters, the same program can serve a different function at each of the levels of surveillance shown in Surveillance Data Flow Chart [below]. Although some infectious disease programs are designed for outbreak investigation at the first level, they may actually investigate very few outbreaks. And, at the second level, the data reported serves research functions almost exclusively . . . . State public health surveillance programs are third parties who collect data in the first level and then also re-disclose it to fourth parties like CDC in the second level, who may in turn release it to fifth parties. A surveillance program may collect personally identifiable data at the first level for some purposes and uses, but not others, without patient consent. However, even if a surveillance program may collect that information without consent, that does not necessarily answer the question whether it can then further disclose the information to researchers without the person's consent for secondary and tertiary uses.

SURVEILLANCE DATA FLOW CHART

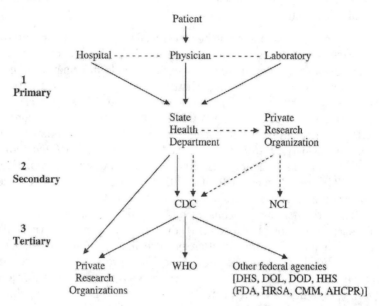

Key: - - - Dashed lines indicate contractual/grant relationship
Arrows show direction of data reporting
Note: In Level 1, provider reports of contagious disease cases sometimes go
their local health department (if immediate response is needed), which
then sends the report on to the state health department.
Also, in Level 1, states sometimes contract with university researchers
to receive data from providers for specific programs like cancer
registries.

NOTES AND QUESTIONS

1.   Research v. practice. The article by Fairchild describes distinctly different
views of what counts as research requiring consent for the use of identifiable data.
Attempts to differentiate public health practice from research appear to be based
on an analogy to the Belmont Report's distinction between medical practice and
medical research. The National Commission distinguished medical practice from
medical research in order to identify which ethical principles apply to various
endeavors by physicians. THE NATIONAL COMMISSION FOR THE PROTECTION OF HUMAN
SUBJECTS OF BIOMEDICAL AND BEHAVIORAL RESEARCH. THE BELMONT REPORT: ETHICAL
PRINCIPLES AND GUIDELINES FOR THE PROTECTION OF HUMAN SUBJECTS OF RESEARCH
(1979) ("For the most part, the term 'practice' refers to interventions that are

designed solely to enhance the wellbeing of an individual patient or client and that have a reasonable expectation of success. The purpose of medical or behavioral practice is to provide diagnosis, preventive treatment or therapy to particular individuals. By contrast, the term 'research' designates an activity designed to test an hypothesis, permit conclusions to be drawn, and thereby to develop or contribute to generalizable knowledge (expressed, for example, in theories, principles, and statements of relationships) . "

As Fairchild describes, some public health officials resist characterizing some (or all) public health surveillance activities as research, perhaps because that might entail obtaining consent from anyone whose identifiable information is collected. *See, e.g.*, LAWRENCE O. GOSTIN, PUBLIC HEALTH LAW: POWER, DUTY, RESTRAINT 309 (2008) ("if routine public health practices were classified as 'research,' health departments would have to submit this activity for review by institutional review boards (IRBs) and obtain informed consent from participants"); James L. Hodge, Jr. & Lawrence O. Gostin, *Public Health Practice v. Research: A Report for Public Health Practitioners* 14 (Atlanta, GA, 2004), www.vdh.virginia.gov/OFHS/policy/documents/2012/irb/pdf/Public%20Health%20Practice%20versus%20Research.pdf (Oct. 2013) (arguing that "[I]dentifiable health data may be collected for public health practice without informed consent and outside of federal and state human subjects research provisions because (1) traditionally, acquisition of these data has been viewed as a quintessential function of government to achieve public health goals; (2) the public has authorized the activity through laws enacted through the political process (*e.g.*, disease reporting requirements pursuant to state or local laws or regulations); (3) administrative protections of individual interests in public health may be built into authorizing laws and regulations; and (4) public health officials are accountable to the public for their activities.").

Mariner argues that the research-practice distinction is misguided and beside the point:

> . . . By itself, the fact that an activity might be considered "practice" does not mean that participation can be compelled. For example, a physician's treatment recommendation to her patient is part of medical practice, but this does not mean that patients must obey it . . . . Similarly, the fact that an activity might be considered research does not always mean that it requires consent.
>
> The real issue is whether the state can compel the reporting of personally identifiable information without first obtaining the person's consent for a specific purpose. The answer to that question depends not on whether an activity is characterized as "research" or "practice, " but on the scope and limits of government's sovereign power and whether compelled disclosure of identifying patient information infringes on constitutionally protected rights.
>
> Furthermore, the idea that there is some special set of endeavors called public health practice may be an illusion. All government agencies can equally call what they do "practice. " Indeed, the programs and activities that public health officials call practice are precisely the same in kind, if not in subject matter, as those of almost every other government agency, from

the Department of Agriculture to the Securities and Exchange Commission. And most of these agencies also conduct research. The fact that public health can be a government function does not exclude surveillance from constitutional constraints. Law enforcement is also a government function, but that does not authorize the police to obtain information about a person in violation of the Fourth Amendment. Similarly, the fact that reporting to a state cancer registry is required by state law does not answer the question of whether the law itself is constitutional.

More far-reaching is the argument that public health surveillance is not research because it *intended* to promote the public good in much the same way that standard medical care is intended to personally benefit a patient. Most medical research is also intended to promote the public good. Similarly, virtually all public health programs are intended to benefit the population as a whole, whether by stopping an epidemic or by collecting data that might be analyzed to identify a risk that might be studied in the future to determine whether it might cause disease. Thus, using intent as a standard would virtually eliminate the rights of research subjects.

Instead, a more objective standard is necessary to identify what counts as a research activity requiring consent. In this vein, the National Commission for the Protection of Human Subjects of Research chose to distinguish research from practice based on how the project is "designed." If a project is designed to obtain generalized knowledge, rather than to help an identifiable patient, it is research. In the public health context, this would mean that research includes projects designed to determine the incidence and prevalence of diseases, to identify common risk factors for diseases by analyzing data, and to evaluate the effectiveness of particular preventive or treatment measures by comparing results, as well as other studies aimed at gleaning similarly generalized knowledge.

Wendy K. Mariner, *Mission Creep: Public Health Surveillance and Medical Privacy*, 87 B.U. L. Rev. 347, 373–75 (2007).

2. Research and the HIPAA Privacy Rule. The HIPAA Privacy Rule does not affect the law governing research with human subjects, including state statutory and common law and the Common Rule governing research funded by or submitted to the Department of Health and Human Services, the Food and Drug Administration, and other federal agencies. *See e.g.*, 45 C.F.R. Part 46 (HHS); 21 C.F.R. Parts 50 and 56 (FDA). Because researchers are not covered entities, HIPAA affects researchers only indirectly — when they seek access to information held by a covered entity. It does not allow researchers to conduct research without subject consent that would not be lawful under laws governing research with human subjects. Nor does it authorize covered entities to give researchers information that would not otherwise be authorized under state or federal law. DHHS considers the creation by a covered entity of a database or repository for research (such as a registry) to be itself a research activity, which must comply with the research requirements. And every time the database is used, the use may be a new research study. Of course, studies may use non-identifiable information without individual consent (and some may obtain a waiver of consent in certain cases), but those that use identifiable information (and do not qualify for a waiver) would require individual consent to the study. For HIPAA rules governing research by covered entities, see 42 C.F.R. § 164.512(i).

As noted in the Fairchild article, *supra*, public health surveillance activities may include creating registries and data repositories and conducting research studies. When might a surveillance program be considered to be collecting data for public health purposes and when might it be considered to be collecting data for research? Even when public health agencies are entitled to obtain data from covered entities, a separate question arises with respect to the later use of that data. Consider the ways in which health departments and federal agencies could use case reports submitted to a surveillance program or registry. The fact that information was lawfully collected by a public health surveillance program does not necessarily imply that it may be disclosed to researchers without the person's consent. Does release to internal health department researchers count as research or as part of surveillance?

Robert Gellman, *Fair Information Practices: A Basic History*
Version 1.92, June 24, 2013
http://bobgellman.com/rg-docs/rg-FIPShistory.pdf

. . . .

[Fair Information Practices] FIPs are a set of internationally recognized practices for addressing the privacy of information about individuals. Information privacy is a subset of privacy. Fair Information Practices are important because they provide the underlying policy for many national laws addressing privacy and data protection matters. The international policy convergence around FIPs as core elements for information privacy has remained in place since the late 1970s. Privacy laws in the United States, which are much less comprehensive in scope than laws in some other countries, often reflect some elements of FIPs but not as consistently as the laws of most other nations.

FIPs began in the 1970s with a document from the Department of Health, Education & Welfare. The Organisation for Economic Cooperation and Development revised the principles in a document that became influential internationally. FIPs have evolved over time, with different formulations coming from different countries and different sources over the decades. There is some evidence that Fair Information Practices may be becoming a generic trademark for privacy principles, whether or not the principles meet any particular standards.

I. Origins of FIPs

In a 1973 report, . . . [t]he [Health, Education and Welfare] Secretary's Advisory Committee on Automated Personal Data Systems issued the report, Records, Computers and the Rights of Citizens . . . .

. . . .

The Privacy Protection Study Commission (PPSC) also may have contributed to the development of FIPs principles in its 1977 report, Protecting Privacy in an Information Society. In chapter 13 on the Privacy Act of 1974, the PPSC credited the work of the Congress in refining the five HEW principles into eight during the drafting of the Privacy Act of 1974 . . . :

1. There shall be no personal-data record-keeping system whose very existence is secret and there shall be a policy of openness about an organization's personal-data record-keeping policies, practices, and systems. (The Openness Principle)

2. An individual about whom information is maintained by a record-keeping organization in individually identifiable form shall have a right to see and copy that information. (The Individual Access Principle)

3. An individual about whom information is maintained by a record-keeping organization shall have a right to correct or amend the substance of that information. (The Individual Participation Principle)

4. There shall be limits on the types of information an organization may collect about an individual, as well as certain requirements with respect to the manner in which it collects such information. (The Collection Limitation Principle)

5. There shall be limits on the internal uses of information about an individual within a record-keeping organization. (The Use Limitation Principle)

6. There shall be limits on the external disclosures of information about an individual a record-keeping organization may make. (The Disclosure Limitation Principle)

7. A record-keeping organization shall bear an affirmative responsibility for establishing reasonable and proper information management policies and practices which assure that its collection, maintenance, use, and dissemination of information about an individual is necessary and lawful and the information itself is current and accurate. (The Information Management Principle)

8. A record-keeping organization shall be accountable for its personal-data record-keeping policies, practices, and systems. (The Accountability Principle)

The structure of the PPSC version closely resembles the later restatement by the Organization for Economic Cooperation and Development. The OECD version of FIPs has some differences from the PPSC version, including renaming of one principle, reorganizing several principles, and some mild substantive revisions.

II. Evolution of FIPs

In the 1970s, European nations began to enact privacy laws applicable to the public and private sectors, beginning with Sweden (1973), the Federal Republic of Germany (1977), and France (1978). These laws were consistent with FIPs . . . .

As privacy laws spread to other countries in Europe, international institutions took up privacy with a focus on the international implications of privacy regulation. In 1980, the Council of Europe adopted a *Convention for the Protection of Individuals with Regard to Automatic Processing of Personal Data* . . . .

. . . .

The Organization for Economic Cooperation and Development (OECD) . . . developed the *OECD Guidelines on the Protection of Privacy and Transborder Flows of Personal Data*. The OECD adopted the recommendation, which became applicable on 23 September 1980.

The eight principles set out by the OECD are:

Collection Limitation Principle

There should be limits to the collection of personal data and any such data should be obtained by lawful and fair means and, where appropriate, with the knowledge or consent of the data subject.

Data Quality Principle

Personal data should be relevant to the purposes for which they are to be used and, to the extent necessary for those purposes, should be accurate, complete, and kept up-to-date.

Purpose Specification Principle

The purposes for which personal data are collected should be specified not later than at the time of data collection and the subsequent use limited to the fulfillment of those purposes or such others as are not incompatible with those purposes and as are specified on each occasion of change of purpose.

Use Limitation Principle

Personal data should not be disclosed, made available or otherwise used for purposes other than those specified in accordance with [the Purpose Specification Principle] except: a) with the consent of the data subject; or b) by the authority of law.

Security Safeguards Principle

Personal data should be protected by reasonable security safeguards against such risks as loss or unauthorized access, destruction, use, modification or disclosure of data.

Openness Principle

There should be a general policy of openness about developments, practices and policies with respect to personal data. Means should be readily available of establishing the existence and nature of personal data, and the main purposes of their use, as well as the identity and usual residence of the data controller.

Individual Participation Principle

An individual should have the right: a) to obtain from a data controller, or otherwise, confirmation of whether or not the data controller has data relating to him; b) to have communicated to him, data relating to him within a reasonable time; at a charge, if any, that is not excessive; in a reasonable manner; and in a form that is readily intelligible to him; c) to be given reasons if a request made under subparagraphs (a) and (b) is denied, and to be able to challenge such denial; and d) to challenge data relating to him and, if the challenge is successful to have the data erased, rectified, completed or amended.

Accountability Principle

A data controller should be accountable for complying with measures, which give effect to the principles stated above.

. . . .

As with other versions of FIPs, the OECD Guidelines generally propose rights and remedies for data subjects while assigning responsibilities to record keepers . . . . Harmonizing national privacy standards was a major purpose of privacy activities by international organizations, along with the protection of individual privacy interests. The goal of harmonization helped to raise interest in privacy among the business community.

III. Statutory and Other Implementations

. . . The Privacy Act of 1974 applies FIPs to federal agencies in the United States. However, it was not until 2002 that the U.S. Congress first formally referenced FIPs in a statute. In establishing a privacy office at the Department of Homeland Security, the Congress assigned the office responsibility for assuring compliance with fair information practices as set out in the Privacy Act of 1974.

. . . .

In 1995, the EU adopted Directive 95/46/EC of the European Parliament and of the Council of 24 October 1995 on the protection of individuals with regard to the processing of personal data and on the free movement of such data. The reliance on FIPs by the European Union in its data protection directive ensured the spread of FIPs throughout Europe.

The Directive restricted the export of personal information to third countries that did not ensure an "adequate level of protection". This encouraged some other countries to conform their laws to the FIPs principles that formed the basis of the directive . . . . [See the EU Data Protection webpage.]

. . . .

IV. More U.S. Versions of FIPs

While there is broad international agreement on the substance of FIPs, different statements of FIPs sometimes look different. Further, statutory implementations of FIPs may vary in different countries, contexts, and sectors. There can be multiple ways to comply with FIPs for different types of records and record keepers.

In the United States, elements of FIPs are occasionally required by law for specific classes of record keepers or categories of records. Otherwise, private sector compliance with FIPs principles, while increasing, is mostly voluntary and sporadic. Also, shortened or incomplete versions of FIPs have sometimes been offered in the United States by federal agencies or trade associations. *Notice and choice* is sometimes presented as an implementation of FIPs, but it clearly falls well short of FIPs standards. Other incomplete versions of FIPs can also be found.

[Here, the author outlines the different versions of FIPS issued by the Federal Trade Commission (2000 and 2012), the Department of Homeland Security (2008), the White House (National Strategies for Trusted Identities in Cyberspace) (2011); National Science and Technology Council report (2011); critical infrastructure cybersecurity (2013); Department of Commerce (2012); Department of Health and Human Services, Office of the National Coordinator for Health Information Technology, Centers for Medicare and Medicaid (2012).]

Overall, the number of versions of FIPs appears to increase with every repetition . . . . However, the variation at the higher level of principle remains curious.

. . . The National Science and Technology Council may have come the closest to the truth when it said, "At present, there is not in place a comprehensive and broadly-accepted application of Fair Information Practice Principles (FIPPs) in the smart grid context." That statement appears to be true in other U.S. contexts. The lack of agreement within the same Administration and even within the same agency [HHS] is noteworthy. The most likely explanation is that FIPs principles expand or contract with each writer and each application. The lack of any central privacy policy apparatus may be a contributing cause.

. . . .

V. Comment and Criticism about FIPs

FIPs are not self-implementing or self-enforcing. Actual implementation of FIPs at the statutory, regulatory, or data controller level can vary widely, depending on the country, the data controller, the type of data, other conflicting goals, and other factors. For example, accountability can be met through many different mechanisms, including criminal or civil penalties; national or provincial supervisory officials; other administrative enforcement; various forms of self-regulation including industry codes and privacy seals; formal privacy policies; compliance audits; employee training; privacy officers at the data controller level; and other methods. Similarly, providing data subjects with access to their own records may have different exceptions, depending on whether the records are employment, educational, credit, or law enforcement records.

Critics of FIPs can be found on both sides. Some in the privacy community believe that FIPs are too weak, allow too many exemptions, do not require a privacy agency, fail to account for the weaknesses of self-regulation, and have not kept pace with information technology. Critics from a business perspective often prefer to limit FIPs to reduced elements of notice, consent, and accountability. They complain that other elements are unworkable, expensive, or inconsistent with openness or free speech principles. Daniel Solove and Chris Hoofnagle offer a different tack, a model regime of privacy protection based on FIPs with more specificity.

In 1999, Mr. Justice Michael Kirby of the High Court of Australia and former chair of the OECD Committee that developed the 1980 Guidelines spoke at an international privacy conference. He noted the many changes brought about by new computer and communication technologies and suggested that it may be time for a review of the guidelines. Among new rights that he mentioned as ripe for review were:

1. A right not to be indexed.

2. A right to encrypt personal information effectively.

3. A right to fair treatment in key public infrastructures so that no person is unfairly excluded in a way that would prejudice that person's ability to protect their privacy.

4. A right to human checking of adverse automated decisions and a right to understand such decisions.

5. A right, going beyond the aspiration of the 'openness principle', of disclosure of the collections to which others will have access and which might affect the projection of the profile of the individual concerned.

No formal attempt to restate FIPs has been undertaken in recent years.

. . . .

On the thirtieth anniversary of the OECD Guidelines, the OECD held a conference on the impact of the Guidelines, sponsored several roundtables, and commissioned papers. Mr. Justice Michael Kirby was one of the participants, and his speech gives new insight on the origins of the original Guidelines and on new challenges, which include new systems of mass surveillance; the need for privacy enhancing technologies; cross-border cooperation in drafting, implementation, and enforcement; end user education; and including developing nations in privacy discussions.

. . . .

NOTES AND QUESTIONS

3. FIPs. Where laws fail to specify — at least clearly or completely — how information must be collected or used or protected, Fair Information Practices sometimes try to fill the gaps. As can be discerned from Gellman's history of FIPs, there is more than one definition of FIPs, and some are clearer than others. He notes the following useful resource: "The Open Identity Exchange published (under a Creative Commons license) a *Fair Information Practice Principles (FIPPs) Comparison Tool.* This document list FIPs principles by subject rather than by source, and it includes principles from more than a dozen sources . . . . http:// openidentityexchange.org/wiki/fair-information-practice-principles-fipps-comparison-tool. "

Can you summarize any consistent principles across the different versions? Which one is most protective of privacy? Which is most supportive of information sharing? What agencies, organizations or groups are likely to prefer which versions? Public agencies and private organizations increasingly consider some version of FIPs when deciding how to use or combine different data collections and whether to seek individual consent for such collection and use. As you consider the various health protection and promotion programs, including the examples in Chapter 8, *infra*, see whether a particular version FIPs should govern such programs or whether existing law serves the needs of individuals or the relevant populations.

For a review of current trends in data processing and privacy risks, see OECD, *The Evolving Privacy Landscape: 30 Years After the OECD Privacy Guidelines* (April 2011), www.oecd-ilibrary.org/content/workingpaper/5kgf09z90c31-en (visited May 2014). For an approach favoring a global framework for FIPS with greater privacy protection, see Public Voice Coalition, Madrid Privacy Declaration (Nov. 2009), http://thepublicvoice.org/madrid-declaration (visited May 2014).

4. **The National Committee on Vital and Health Statistics.** The NCVHS is a public advisory committee to the Secretary of Health and Human Services, which can make recommendations to the Secretary on health information collection, use and disclosure. One focus of the Committee is the collection and use of data that could be studied to find ways to improve the health of communities. Recognizing that such data may come from many sources, including patient care records, public health programs, government agencies, and research studies, the Committee seeks to improve the practices of such data "stewards." The Committee issued a brief letter report to the Secretary outlining a stewardship framework based on the 1973 version of FIPs, described in the Gellman article above. NCVHS, A Stewardship Framework for the Use of Community Health Data (Dec. 5, 2012), http://www.ncvhs.hhs.gov/121205lt.pdf (visited Oct. 2013). The Committee's first principle is "openness, transparency, and choice," emphasizing that there should be no secret data systems. Its endorsement of choice was more qualified:

> The Committee heard testimony that openness and transparency promote trust. For example, a study shows that individuals almost always will consent to research if asked, but they still want to be asked. While we are not suggesting consent is always a proper or feasible step before under-taking a community health initiative, some kind of outreach to subjects — and the communities with which they are associated — can smooth the way for a successful project.

Id. at 4. The Committee also recognized that data collected for one purpose is sometimes used later for a different purpose. Without taking a position on consent for later uses, it encouraged researchers to weigh the pros and cons of seeking consent for a specific purpose only or for open-ended purposes.

> The advantages of narrow specification are that the purposes are easily defined and described, so that communities and individuals may be more likely to trust the data steward and allow the desired uses of their data. This approach, however, may afford less flexibility. A researcher who specifies a more open-ended or unknown purpose gains greater flexibility for future uses but with the risk that individuals or communities may be surprised by future discoveries based on their personal information without separate consent, communication, or other form of outreach.

Id. at 5.

On the subject of accountability, the Committee recommended that someone be identified as responsible for data collection, security, accuracy, protection, and proper use, but left the question of what sanctions or enforcement methods should be adopted. What sanctions would you suggest?

5. **Privacy by design.** Cyber security experts recognize the need to protect the confidentiality of data in large data sets and are developing statistical algorithms intended to omit or alter data elements that would permit re-identification of individuals or groups. Much of this work remains in the academic or investigational stage. The Federal Trade Commission also encourages what it calls privacy by design in its 2012 report, *Protecting Consumer Privacy in an Era of Rapid Change*, available at http://www.ftc.gov/opa/2012/03/privacyframework.shtm. The FTC principle calls for building privacy at every stage of product design.

6. **International privacy protections.** Article 12 of the Universal Declaration of Human Rights, included in Chapter 13, B, *infra*, lists privacy as a human right: "No one shall be subjected to arbitrary interference with his privacy, family, home or correspondence, nor to attacks upon his honor and reputation. Everyone has the right to protection of the law against such interference or attacks." Several international organizations have developed reasonably harmonious rules to protect privacy: the Organisation for Economic Co-operation and Development (OECD); the Council of Europe; the European Court of Human Justice; European Union entities. (OECD Guidelines are described in the Gellman article above.) The United Nations General Assembly adopted Guidelines for the Regulation of Computerized Personal Files in 1990, specifying ten principles, similar to FIPs, which national law should incorporate. Perhaps the most influential law applicable to more than one country is the European Union Data Protection Directive. (Laws protecting privacy outside the United States are generally called data protection laws.) The EU Data Protection Directive can limit the transmission of data to the United States, because, in general, the EU considers U.S. law insufficiently protective of personal data. For a practice-oriented reference, see LOTHAR DETERMANN, DETERMANN'S FIELD GUIDE TO INTERNATIONAL DATA PRIVACY COMPLIANCE (2012).

Chapter 8

CHRONIC DISEASES AND HEALTH PROMOTION

A. INTRODUCTION

In the United States, as in most of the industrialized West, the primary causes of death are chronic diseases, specifically heart disease, stroke, and cancers. As the threat of infectious diseases declined in the twentieth century, largely as a result of successful public health interventions to clean up the country's supplies of water, food, and industrial hazards, chronic diseases gained more prominence. Public health agencies began to consider how to organize programs to reduce mortality and morbidity from chronic diseases, perhaps encouraged by Canada's Lalonde Report, which brought attention to the ways individuals may affect their own health by using illicit drugs like heroin, cocaine or marijuana, drinking alcohol, smoking cigarettes, driving without seatbelts, cycling without a helmet, eating a poor diet, getting little exercise, or engaging in promiscuous unprotected sex. Marc Lalonde, A New Perspective on the Health of Canadians (April 1974), http://www.phac-aspc. gc.ca/ph-sp/pdf/perspect-eng.pdf.) The policy paper, initiated by the Canadian Minister of Health, Marc Lalonde, presented a new direction for health policy in Canada emphasizing prevention and health promotion, rather than curative medical care, and focusing on the environment, human biology, lifestyle, and health care organization. By the end of the twentieth century, however, chronic disease prevention was firmly on the public health agenda, often referred to as "health promotion."

More recent attention to chronic conditions is, in part, a reaction to their treatment costs, often said to account for more than 60% of health care expenditures. However, preventing chronic diseases is even more complicated than preventing infectious diseases, because chronic diseases often result from complex and in many cases still unknown factors, including the environment, one's genetic heritage, personal behavior, and social determinants like wealth, occupation, and education.

To date, the majority of public health promotion policies that seek statutory or judicial changes focus on the risks posed by specific personal behaviors, perhaps because laws addressing other types of risks are more politically controversial or costly. Thus, this chapter considers examples of laws intended primarily to change personal behavior and to improve health in the indefinite future, rather than to prevent imminent death or injury. To be sure, the ultimate goal of most public health legislation is saving lives or at least preventing "premature death," that is, death at an abnormally early age. Still, the adverse effects of many behavioral risks to health lie far in the future. Preventing or reducing the risk may require preventive measures long before anyone could become ill or disabled. The lag between the time for intervention and the materialization of any harm creates some conceptual problems for applying several legal principles. Equally difficult questions arise from the fact that most, though not all, healthful changes in personal behavior benefit the person herself rather than protecting other people from harm.

All public health policy making, but especially that targeted at individual behavior and life style, raises the following questions:

- How does society decide what counts as a public health risk that should be prevented or reduced?
- Which, if any, legal measures should be adopted to prevent such risks?

A wide range of laws might prevent public health risks: criminal prohibitions, financial incentives (taxes, surcharges), tort liability, product standards, environmental controls, or workplace standards by an administrative agency. Although each measure has specific statutory or doctrinal requirements, some of which may be debatable or elusive, those standards may be clearer than the policy or ethical rationale underlying the policy choice. The focus of this chapter is on the policy and doctrinal justifications for measures that reward or penalize individual behavior that affects health.

Section B provides examples of health promotion programs that are gaining popularity. It also examines different justifications for policy measures intended to encourage or compel healthy behavior. The motivation underlying laws that regulate personal behavior, rather than things like products or environmental conditions, may be grounded in health, financial or moral concerns, or a combination of the three. For this reason, this Chapter should be read in light of the materials on perceptions of risk, discussed in Chapter 2, and legislating morality in Chapter 4.

Section C considers measures to identify risk factors for chronic diseases, such as cancer, particularly in the workplace. It also examines screening programs intended to detect diseases, such as cancers, heart disease, and genetic conditions, early enough to prevent serious illness or premature death. Here, the question is not only how, but sometimes whether to take preventive measures, especially where evidence of benefits or risks remains uncertain.

This Chapter lays the foundation for the next two Chapters, which serve as case studies in choosing how to prevent chronic diseases associated with obesity (Chapter 9) and tobacco (Chapter 10).

B. HEALTH PROMOTION PROGRAMS

ANDERSON v. CITY OF TAYLOR
2005 U.S. Dist. LEXIS 44706 (E.D. Mich. Aug. 11, 2005)

The case stems from a wellness program the Taylor Fire Department enacted for its employees, which required a mandatory blood draw. The Federal Emergency Management Agency ("FEMA") created the "Assistance to Firefighters' Grant

Program" to provide funding directly to fire departments for the purpose of protecting the health and safety of the public and firefighting personnel against fire and fire-related hazards.

. . . .

In the late 1990s, the Taylor Fire Service Joint Labor Management Wellness-Fitness Initiative was created. The goal of that initiative was to improve the quality of life of all uniformed personnel. The project sought to maintain fit, healthy and capable firefighters and EMS responders throughout their career.

The FEMA grant application package sets forth the required information for the preparation of the grant proposal. Regarding the wellness and fitness programs, the package states:

> FEMA may make grants for the purpose of establishing and/or equipping wellness and fitness programs for firefighting personnel, including the procurement of medical services to ensure that the firefighting personnel are physically able to carry out their duties . . . .

> . . . .

> . . . Finally, since participation is critical to receiving any benefits from a wellness or fitness program, we will give higher competitive rating to departments whose wellness and fitness programs *mandate* participation as well as programs that provide incentives for participation.

(emphasis added).

The Taylor Fire Department's proposed narrative provided that participation in the program was mandatory along with a fitness incentive for participation in the program. The fitness incentives included a free membership for each employee for the city's recreational facility which contained both cardiovascular and strength training equipment. The proposed incentives also included free rounds of golf at the city owned golf courses and blocks of ice time at the city's arena.

Defendants Fire Chief Kenneth Costella and Deputy Fire Chief Vincent Fedel were notified that the Taylor Fire Department's grant was accepted on August 1, 2001 . . . .

The wellness program instituted by the Taylor Fire Department included health appraisals by the Oakwood Hospital staff. This appraisal included a mandatory blood draw, which forms the basis for this lawsuit. The blood draws were used to obtain a "Lipid Profile test" to find out the Plaintiffs' cholesterol, triglycerides, HDL cholesterol, VLDL cholesterol, and LDL cholesterol.

Plaintiffs [individual firefighters] were required to submit to these blood draws. Plaintiffs contend that these blood draws violated their constitutional rights.

. . . .

ANALYSIS:

. . . .

The Court finds that the mandatory blood draw implicated Plaintiffs' rights under the Fourth Amendment. The Fourth Amendment to the United States Constitution protects "[t]he rights of the people to be secure in their persons, houses, papers, and effects, against unreasonable searches and seizures."

The Court finds that a collection of blood samples constitutes a search under the Fourth Amendment. The Supreme Court in *Skinner v. Railway Labor Executives Ass'n*, 489 U.S. 602 (1989), provided that the act of drawing blood itself, even if the blood is not later tested for the presence of illegal drugs, is a search under the Fourth Amendment. The *Skinner* Court provided:

> In light of our society's concern for the security of one's person, it is obvious that this physical intrusion, penetrating beneath the skin, infringes an expectation of privacy that society is prepared to recognize an reasonable. The ensuing chemical analysis of the sample to obtain physiological data is a further intrusion of the tested employee's privacy interests.

Id. at 616.

Generally, a search or seizure under the Fourth Amendment must be based upon reasonable suspicion of wrongdoing in order to be reasonable, and thus constitutional. The Supreme Court, in evaluating the constitutionality of a search and seizure, generally conducts a balancing test to determine if the intrusion is reasonable.

. . . Defendants argue that under [*National Treasury Employees Union v. Von Raab* 489 U.S. 656 (1989)], the blood draws were reasonable constitutional searches. In *Von Raab*, the Court addressed whether a drug testing program for Customs Service employees was constitutional. The Court noted that the program was not designed to serve the ordinary needs of law enforcement, and used a special needs analysis. The Court found that the government has a compelling interest in ensuring that front line interdiction personnel are physically fit, and have unimpeachable integrity and judgment. Regarding the employees' privacy interests, the Court found that the diminished privacy expectations of those front-line customs were outweighed by the compelling government interest.

The Court finds that the instant blood draws are not constitutional under *Von Raab*; its holding has been limited by the Supreme Court decision in *Chandler v. Miller*, 520 U.S. 305, 313 (1997) . . . . Thus, based upon the fact that the Customs Service employees' job functions required that they were routinely exposed to illegal drugs, the Court found that a special need for the drug testing existed.

In *Chandler v. Miller, supra*, the Supreme Court delineated that before a court balances the public interests at issue regarding a urine drug test, a court must specifically determine whether the program at issue qualifies as a special need.

Stated another way, in certain instances, a search or seizure unsupported by probable cause may be constitutional when special needs, beyond the normal need for law enforcement, make the warrant and probable cause requirements impracticable. . . .

. . . .

. . . Defendants contend that there is no punitive aspect in the blood draw because it is used solely for the benefit of a health screening of Plaintiffs. It is correct that the results of the Plaintiffs' blood draws will not dictate a particular punishment upon the Plaintiffs. However, the Defendants miss the central aspect of the blood draws — they are mandatory. The United States Supreme Court has set forth that a blood draw itself is a search or seizure implicating the Fourth Amendment. *Skinner* at 616. Because the blood draws are mandatory, it follows that Plaintiffs would be subject to some form of punishment for refusing the constitutionally protected intrusion. In fact, Plaintiffs Pochron, Bell, and Lavender set forth in their affidavits that they would have been punished had they not participated in the blood draw. Herein, lies the punitive aspect to the blood draws at issue in this case.

The Court finds that the mandatory blood draws instituted by Defendants, despite the fact that they were intended to benefit Plaintiffs, violates their personal privacy rights protected by the Fourth Amendment. As Justice Brandeis set forth in his landmark dissent in *Olmstead v. United States*, 277 U.S. 438 (1928), albeit addressing a more serious issue, "[e]xperience should teach us to be most on our guard to protect liberty when the Government's purposes are beneficent." *Id.* at 485.

Defendants do not appear to dispute that the *Chandler* special needs test applies instantly. Defendants state that the materials in the FEMA grant process set forth the special need for the blood draws:

> fire fighters and EMS responders respond to emergency incidents that require extreme physical output and often result in adverse physiological and psychological outcomes. These adverse outcomes, over time, can and do affect the overall wellness of the fire fighting and emergency response system. Often, past attempts to address fitness have been piecemeal, such as the recent trends to unilaterally implement timed, task-based performance tests. Such piecemeal approaches have failed to produce universally acceptable and productive results.

The Court finds *Chandler* instructive. In *Chandler,* the state of Georgia passed a law that required potential candidates for state office to pass a urine drug test. The Supreme Court struck the law down as unconstitutional. The Court stated that before it balances the public interests at issue regarding Georgia's law, it must specifically determine whether the program at issue qualifies as a special need. The Court provided:

> Our precedents establish that the proffered special need for drug testing must be substantially important enough to override the individual's acknowledged privacy interest, sufficiently vital to suppress the Fourth Amendment's normal requirement of individualized suspicion.

Id. at 318.

The State of Georgia argued that a special need existed on the grounds that unlawful drug use was incompatible with holding state office because the use of illegal drugs calls into question the official's judgment and integrity; jeopardizes the discharge of public functions; and undermines public confidence. The Court found that State of Georgia's argument notably lacked "any indication of a concrete danger demanding departure from the Fourth Amendment's main rule." *Id.* at 319. The Court found that a demonstrated problem of drug abuse, while not in all cases necessary to the validity of a testing regime, would shore up an assertion of special need for a suspicionless general search program. The *Chandler* Court distinguished its facts from cases where the risk to public safety is substantial and real, such as searches at airports and entrances to courts and other official buildings. The Court went on to state "[b]ut, where, as in this case, public safety is not genuinely in jeopardy, the Fourth Amendment precludes the suspicionless search, no matter how conveniently arranged." *Id.* at 323.

. . . .

The Court finds that the mandatory blood draws at issue are unconstitutional based upon the principles delineated from *Chandler* . . . .

The Court finds that Defendants have failed to establish that there is a special need for the blood draws. . . . [T]here has been no showing by Defendants that there has been a problem with physically unfit fire and emergency response workers . . . .

Defendants have not shown "any indication of a concrete danger [to public safety] demanding departure from the Fourth Amendment's main rule." *Chandler* at 319. The instant blood draws were used to determine employees' cholesterol levels. A cholesterol reading, while an important health barometer, cannot accurately determine the overall physical fitness of an employee as it relates to how that employee is able to respond in an emergency situation. Further, any risk from high cholesterol is likely to take years to manifest. The Court finds that this is not a situation involving a high risk of harm to the public such as an intoxicated employee with a firearm or a drug impaired train conductor. Thus, the Court finds that Defendants have failed to articulate a special need for the blood draws . . . .

. . . .

The Court acknowledges that there is no exact precedent on point. The parties properly analogize the instant blood draws to the long line of Supreme Court precedent relating to drug testing. One possible point of distinction between the drug testing cases and the instant case is that there is no punitive aspect tied to the results of the blood draws. However, the applicable Supreme Court precedent is not based upon the punitive aspect tied to the results of the drug test, but rather the search itself. Further, as noted above, there is a punitive aspect to the blood draws in that the parties are forced to partake in them or be subject to discipline. The Court also notes that *Chandler* has created confusion to the Fourth Amendment doctrine . . . However, for the reasons stated above, the Court finds that the mandatory blood draws violate the Fourth Amendment.

Even if the Court were to find that a special need existed in this case, the Court still finds that the State's interest in maintaining physically fit emergency workers is not advanced by the cholesterol screening, as discussed above. The Court finds that the Plaintiffs' interest to be free from the mandatory search outweighs the public's need for emergency workers with low cholesterol. The Court notes that the special needs test is inextricably tied to this balancing test in that the state's special needs are what is balanced against the individual's privacy interests). . . . Finally, the Court finds it significant that the test results are not provided to the government, but instead, only to the Plaintiffs. This is a significant sign that the government does not need this test for its purposes.

. . . .

Affordable Care Act Wellness Programs
42 U.S.C. § 300gg-4

Prohibiting discrimination against individual participants and beneficiaries based on health status

(a) In general. A group health plan and a health insurance issuer offering group or individual health insurance coverage may not establish rules for eligibility (including continued eligibility) of any individual to enroll under the terms of the plan or coverage based on any of the following health status-related factors in relation to the individual or a dependent of the individual:

(1) Health status.

(2) Medical condition (including both physical and mental illnesses).

(3) Claims experience.

(4) Receipt of health care.

(5) Medical history.

(6) Genetic information.

(7) Evidence of insurability (including conditions arising out of acts of domestic violence).

(8) Disability.

(9) Any other health status-related factor determined by the Secretary.

(b) In premium contributions.

(1)

In general. A group health plan, and a health insurance issuer offering group or individual health insurance coverage, may not require any individual (as a condition of enrollment or continued enrollment under the plan) to pay a premium or contribution which is greater than such premium or contribution for a similarly situated individual enrolled in the plan on the basis of any health status-related factor in relation to the individual or to an individual enrolled under the plan as a dependent of the individual.

(2) Construction. Nothing in paragraph (1) shall be construed—

(A) to restrict the amount that an employer or individual may be charged for coverage under a group health plan except as provided in paragraph (3) or individual health coverage, as the case may be; or

(B) to prevent a group health plan, and a health insurance issuer offering group health insurance coverage, from establishing premium discounts or rebates or modifying otherwise applicable copayments or deductibles in return for adherence to programs of health promotion and disease prevention.

. . . .

(j) Programs of health promotion or disease prevention.

(1) General provisions.

(A) General rule. For purposes of subsection (b)(2)(B), a program of health promotion or disease prevention (referred to in this subsection as a "wellness program") shall be a program offered by an employer that is designed to promote health or prevent disease that meets the applicable requirements of this subsection.

(B) No conditions based on health status factor. If none of the conditions for obtaining a premium discount or rebate or other reward for participation in a wellness program is based on an individual satisfying a standard that is related to a health status factor, such wellness program shall not violate this section if participation in the program is made available to all similarly situated individuals and the requirements of paragraph (2) are complied with.

(C) Conditions based on health status factor. If any of the conditions for obtaining a premium discount or rebate or other reward for participation in a wellness program is based on an individual satisfying a standard that is related to a health status factor, such wellness program shall not violate this section if the requirements of paragraph (3) are complied with.

(2) Wellness programs not subject to requirements. If none of the conditions for obtaining a premium discount or rebate or other reward under a wellness program as described in paragraph (1)(B) are based on an individual satisfying a standard that is related to a health status factor (or if such a wellness program does not provide such a reward), the wellness program shall not violate this section if participation in

the program is made available to all similarly situated individuals. The following programs shall not have to comply with the requirements of paragraph (3) if participation in the program is made available to all similarly situated individuals:

(A) A program that reimburses all or part of the cost for memberships in a fitness center.

(B) A diagnostic testing program that provides a reward for participation and does not base any part of the reward on outcomes.

(C) A program that encourages preventive care related to a health condition through the waiver of the copayment or deductible requirement under group health plan for the costs of certain items or services related to a health condition (such as prenatal care or well-baby visits).

(D) A program that reimburses individuals for the costs of smoking cessation programs without regard to whether the individual quits smoking.

(E) A program that provides a reward to individuals for attending a periodic health education seminar.

(3) Wellness programs subject to requirements. If any of the conditions for obtaining a premium discount, rebate, or reward under a wellness program as described in paragraph (1)(C) is based on an individual satisfying a standard that is related to a health status factor, the wellness program shall not violate this section if the following requirements are complied with:

(A) The reward for the wellness program, together with the reward for other wellness programs with respect to the plan that requires satisfaction of a standard related to a health status factor, shall not exceed 30 percent of the cost of employee-only coverage under the plan. If, in addition to employees or individuals, any class of dependents (such as spouses or spouses and dependent children) may participate fully in the wellness program, such reward shall not exceed 30 percent of the cost of the coverage in which an employee or individual and any dependents are enrolled. For purposes of this paragraph, the cost of coverage shall be determined based on the total amount of employer and employee contributions for the benefit package under which the employee is (or the employee and any dependents are) receiving coverage. A reward may be in the form of a discount or rebate of a premium or contribution, a waiver of all or part of a cost-sharing mechanism (such as deductibles, copayments, or coinsurance), the absence of a surcharge, or the value of a benefit that would otherwise not be provided under the plan. The Secretaries of Labor, Health and Human Services, and the Treasury may increase the reward available under this subparagraph to up to 50 percent of the cost of coverage if the Secretaries determine that such an increase is appropriate.

(B) The wellness program shall be reasonably designed to promote health or prevent disease. A program complies with the preceding sentence if the program has a reasonable chance of improving the health of, or preventing disease in, participating individuals and it is not overly burdensome, is not a subterfuge for discriminating based on a health status factor, and is not highly suspect in the method chosen to promote health or prevent disease.

(C) The plan shall give individuals eligible for the program the opportunity to qualify for the reward under the program at least once each year.

(D) The full reward under the wellness program shall be made available to all similarly situated individuals. For such purpose, among other things:

(i) The reward is not available to all similarly situated individuals for a period unless the wellness program allows—

(I) for a reasonable alternative standard (or waiver of the otherwise applicable standard) for obtaining the reward for any individual for whom, for that period, it is unreasonably difficult due to a medical condition to satisfy the otherwise applicable standard; and

(II) for a reasonable alternative standard (or waiver of the otherwise applicable standard) for obtaining the reward for any individual for whom, for that period, it is medically inadvisable to attempt to satisfy the otherwise applicable standard.

(ii) If reasonable under the circumstances, the plan or issuer may seek verification, such as a statement from an individual's physician, that a health status factor makes it unreasonably difficult or medically inadvisable for the individual to satisfy or attempt to satisfy the otherwise applicable standard.

NOTES AND QUESTIONS

1. **An expanded role for public health.** Thomas Frieden, currently Director of the Centers for Disease Control and Prevention, was an early advocate for expanding the mandate of public health departments into controlling chronic diseases. *See* Thomas Frieden, *Asleep at the Switch: Local Public Health and Chronic Disease*, 94 AM. J. PUB. HEALTH 2059 (2004). He argues that because "noncommunicable diseases, which accounted for less than 20% of US deaths in 1900, now account for about 80% of deaths," public health should apply *traditional* public health measures to chronic diseases. These traditional measure are: surveil-

lance and mandatory reporting; environmental modifications, such as those for water- and mosquito-borne illnesses; regulation; direct delivery of clinical care; outbreak detection, investigation, and control; case management and contact tracing; immunization; and health education." *Id.*

The public health community has taken up Dr. Frieden's challenge, seeking to apply traditional public health activities to chronic diseases in new programs — many explored in this Chapter, others in Chapters 9 and 10. Which of these measures fit chronic diseases?

Look again at the top causes of death in the United States, shown in Chapter 2, *supra* — heart disease, cancer, and stroke. Most Western European countries face the same challenges as the United States to reduce the cost of chronic disease, both physical and financial, although their "solutions" may differ. Chronic diseases are also increasing worldwide, especially as countries become more economically developed.

2. **Programs for public employees.** Policies, including health promotion programs, established by government entities for their employees are, of course, subject to constitutional constraints. *Anderson v. City of Taylor*, excerpted *supra*, raises the most obvious constitutional claim — that of an unreasonable search under the Fourth Amendment. The court here relies on the U.S. Supreme Court's line of cases involving mandatory testing for illicit drugs, which are examined in Chapter 11, *infra*. As the court recognized, this was an unfinished area of Fourth Amendment jurisprudence, and the U.S. Supreme Court has since issued decisions that separately expand and contract protection from searches and seizures for non-criminal purposes.

In *Anderson*, the court granted qualified immunity to the individual city officials, finding "that there is no decision in the Supreme Court or the Sixth Circuit addressing the constitutionality of mandatory warrantless blood tests for health benefit purposes." The court determined that those defendants could not be expected to make a clear legal decision, because "the extension of *Chandler* in this case is close and involves subtle legal distinction." In a follow-up decision, the same court granted summary judgment to the Plaintiffs and against the City of Taylor, rejecting the City's claim that it did not know that the blood draws would be mandatory. The court found that the City's approval of the grant application made it responsible for the policy. *Anderson v. City of Taylor*, 2006 U.S. Dist. LEXIS 38075 (E.D. Mich. June 9 2006).

Constitutional questions aside, what is the purpose of these health promotion programs? How important is the opportunity for federal funding? In *Anderson*, the City provided $45,171.00 to obtain a federal grant of $105,400.00.

3. **The ACA and wellness programs.** The Patient Protection and Affordable Care Act of 2010 (ACA) expanded federal support for incorporating wellness programs into both private and public health plans. The ACA slightly amended a provision of the Health Insurance Portability and Accountability Act (HIPAA) to read as reproduced above. It applies to commercial health insurance plans (referred to as "health insurance issuers in HIPAA) and to private employer self-funded health benefit plans (called "group health plans" in HIPAA), with respect to plan

years beginning on or after January 1, 2014.

The ACA also encourages experimentation with wellness programs in other ways, including authorizing state Medicaid plans to offer such programs to their beneficiaries. 42 U.S.C. § 1396a. Federal grants are available for state Medicaid programs that "provide incentives to Medicaid beneficiaries who 'successfully participate' in wellness programs and 'demonstrate changes in health risk and outcome, including the adoption and maintenance of healthy behaviors by meeting specific targets.'" ACA, Pub. L. 111–148, § 4108(a)(1)(i), (ii), 124 Stat. 119, 561 (2010). The targeted behaviors are stopping tobacco use, weight reduction or control, lowering cholesterol and blood pressure, and avoiding or managing diabetes. *Id.* at § 4108(a)(3)(A)(i)-(v). See the Box below for an example of West Virginia's program that predated the ACA.

As the *Anderson* case suggests, wellness programs are not without controversy. These plans raise many of the questions discussed in the materials in this Section: Are they unjustifiably paternalistic or a fair bargain? Do they offer rewards for staying healthy or penalties for failing to meet health standards? Do they encourage healthy social norms or discriminate against the disadvantaged? And finally, will they work? Will people live longer or better lives? Will health plans and employers save money?

There is widespread support for disease prevention and health promotion programs in general. *See, e.g.*, Howard K. Koh & Kathleen G. Sebelius, *Promoting Prevention Through the Affordable Care Act*, 363 New Eng. J. Med 1296 (2010). Many observers welcome programs that encourage people to take personal responsibility for their own health. On-site gymnasiums, cafeterias with healthy food, and immunization or smoking cessation programs offer benefits without penalties. Others, however, note that most programs target behaviors that are most prevalent among lower income and disadvantaged populations, who may have difficulty meeting targets and can ill afford higher health insurance premiums. *See, e.g.*, Kristin M. Madison *et al.*, *The Law, Policy, and Ethics of Employers' Use of Financial Incentives to Improve Health*, 39 J. L. Med. & Ethics 450 (2011); Wendy K. Mariner, *The Affordable Care Act and Health Promotion: The Role of Insurance in Defining Responsibility for Health Risks and Costs*, 50 Duquesne L. Rev. 271 (2012). Critics worry that voluntary programs can easily be transformed into a condition of employment and that employees who do not participate could be fired or at least priced out of affordable health insurance. The Americans with Disabilities Act (ADA), 42 U.S.C. §§ 12101 *et seq.*, forbids private employers (with 15 or more employees) from discriminating in the terms and conditions of employment on the basis of disability. However, it does not prohibit charging higher insurance fees that are actuarially justified (on the basis of risk). See Chapter 9, Part D, *infra* for a discussion of what counts as a disability for purposes of the ADA.

Refer to the description at the beginning of Chapter 1 of the Pennsylvania State University's imposition of a $100 monthly fee for employees who do not complete a health assessment questionnaire. Faculty members protested the program, and it is on hold as of September 2013. The faculty's action appears to be a rare public protest against such a program. Why might that be? What differences might exist between faculty members and employees of other large corporations or Medicaid beneficiaries?

4. Health promotion and health care costs. In addition to — or perhaps because of — improving health, wellness and other health promotion programs are intended to reduce health care costs. Although the ACA's major goal is to expand health insurance coverage, an implicit objective (left to incentives and possibly later legislation) is to reduce the rate of increase in the nation's $2.6 trillion in health care expenditures (almost 18% of GDP). Before the ACA was finally enacted, reports that Safeway's wellness program had reduced its health insurance costs increased support for the ACA wellness program provision (excerpted above) — so much so that the provision was nicknamed the "Safeway Amendment." Further scrutiny suggests that the program was not necessarily responsible for Safeway's cost savings, after all. John E. McDonough, Inside National Health Reform 192 (2011) (Congressional Budget Office staff concluded that "Safeway is largely a myth). The employer saved money by increasing the employee's share of premiums from 20% to 55%, while less than 9% of its employees enrolled in the wellness program. David S. Hilzenrath, *Misleading Claims about Safeway Wellness Incentives Shape Health-Care Bill*, Wash. Post G01, Jan. 17, 2010.

Disease prevention is widely believed to be an important way to lower costs in the long run by reducing the need for treatment for costly diseases. *See, e.g.*, Trust for America's Health, *A Healthier America 2013: Strategies to Move from Sick Care to Health Care in Four Years* (2013), http://healthyamericans.org/report/104/ (visited Nov. 2013). Childhood immunizations, high blood pressure medication and aspirin to prevent heart disease are good examples of effective preventive measures.

Not everyone agrees that prevention always saves money. There is considerable evidence that most preventive measures increase overall costs, in part because a large population must be treated in order to avoid a smaller number of costly illnesses. *See* Louise B. Russell, *Preventing Chronic Disease: An Important Investment, But Don't Count on Cost Savings*, 28 Health Aff. 42 (Jan/Feb. 2009); Joshua T. Cohen *et al.*, *Does Preventive Care Save Money? Health Economics and the Presidential Candidates*, 358 New Eng. J. Med. 661 (2008). One study recommending greater use of prevention found that health care spending could be reduced, but only by 0.2%, if 90% of the U.S. population used 20 proven preventive services. Michael v.. Maciosek *et al.*, *Greater Use of Preventive Services in U.S. Health Care Could Save Lives at Little or No Cost*, 29 Health Aff. 1646 (2010), http://content.healthaffairs.org/content/29/9/1656.full?sid=6c6c566f-0586-4ddb-96c3-d7c34be0aaa8. How likely is it that 90% of Americans will do so? What might persuade them?

Healthy people tend to live longer. Of course, even healthy people die eventually, and their medical care at the end of life could be reasonable or costly. In the meantime, they may contribute more productive working years to the economy, or they may live their extra years in retirement. These extra years of life may prove expensive, at least to the federal government, which pays for Social Security and Medicare. *See* Table 1 below for a comparison of expenditures for healthy, smoking, and obese cohorts.

So what if good health costs more? Should costs drive prevention policy?

5. How much does the United States spend on prevention? It is commonly reported that the United States spends about 3% of national health expenditures on prevention — give or take a percent or two. Louise Russell reports on an investigation of that number and what it means for the country.

> . . . Researchers at the Altarum Institute have discovered that whatever the estimate, and wherever it appears, the source usually given is a report that appeared in CDC's Morbidity and Mortality Weekly Report in 1992.
>
> It is hard to tell from that brief report, a summary of a larger unpublished study, exactly what the numbers include, but they are based on data for 1988 and are now [more than] 20 years old. So the Altarum group went back to the beginning and developed new estimates. Their estimates show that at least 8 percent to 9 percent of national health spending goes to prevention.
>
> To put even that larger number in perspective, recall that, while treatment takes place only in the medical sector, prevention takes place throughout the economy, as it must to keep people healthy. Examples are everywhere: improvements in highway design, safety features in cars, health inspections for restaurants, water treatment plants, sewage systems, features of buildings required by safety codes, work safety measures, limits on pollutants, and many, many more. An accurate examination of the balance of prevention and treatment needs to look beyond the medical sector.
>
> International comparisons also suggest that spending more of our medical dollars on prevention will not reduce health care costs. In 2004 the Commonwealth Fund surveyed patients in five countries: the U.S., Canada, the United Kingdom, Australia, and New Zealand. With the exception of flu shots for the elderly, where Australia ranked first, the U.K. second, and the U.S. third, the U.S. led on the use of the preventive measures examined: blood pressure checks, screening for cervical cancer, mammography, and advice from a physician on diet and exercise.
>
> The percentages of patients in the U.S. who received these services were higher, sometimes much higher — evidence that the U.S. is already devoting more of its medical spending to prevention than other high-income countries. Yet these other countries all have longer life expectancies and lower health care costs.

Louise B. Russell, *Prevention Will Reduce Medical Costs: A Persistent Myth*, HASTINGS CTR. REP. 1, 2 (June 7, 2009).

WEST VIRGINIA'S MOUNTAIN HEALTH CHOICES

In 2007, the West Virginia Medicaid Program began implementing Mountain Health Choices, a health benefit plan structure to reward personal responsibility and save money. West Virginia Medicaid beneficiaries are enrolled in a "Basic Benefits Plan," which offers fewer benefits than in the past, unless they sign up for an "Enhanced Benefits Plan" by agreeing in writing to the following "member responsibilities," among others, in the West Virginia Medicaid Member Agreement:

— I will do my best to stay healthy. I will go to health improvement programs as directed by my medical home. ["medical home" is defined as "where I go for check-ups or when I am sick and where my health care records will be."]

— I will read the booklets and pamphlets my medical home gives me . . . .

— I will go to my medical home when I am sick.

— I will take the medicines my health care provider prescribes for me.

— I will show up on time when I have my appointments.

— I will bring my children to their appointments on time.

— I will use the hospital emergency room only for emergencies.

West Virginia Medicaid Member Agreement, West Virginia State Plan Amendment, http://www.dhhr.wv.gov/bms/Pages/default.aspx (visited Nov. 2013).

The enhanced benefits (not included in the Basic Benefits package) include diabetes and nutrition education, cardiac and pulmonary rehabilitation, weight management, mental health treatment, and tobacco cessation programs. *Id.* Rewards for patients who meet their health goals were planned, based on expected reports from providers on patient compliance. Michael Hendryx *et al.*, Evaluation of Mountain Health Choices (Aug. 2009), www.rwjf.org/content/dam/farm/reports/evaluations/2009/rwjf45283 (visited Nov. 2013). For a reaction by physicians to monitoring their patients in the plans, *see* Gene Bishop & Amy C. Brodkey, *Personal Responsibility and Physician Responsibility — West Virginia's Medicaid Plan*, 355 New Eng. J. Med. 756 (2006). The program remained in effect, at least temporarily, pursuant to a waiver from the Department of Health and Human Services after the ACA was enacted in 2010.

The program raises the following questions: Do patients who rely on Medicaid for access to health care have a choice about which benefits plan to accept? Are there any limits on the conditions a Medicaid program can impose on its benefits? If patients do not meet their obligations, how will the Basic Benefits plan help them? Will the program reduce state Medicaid costs? West Virginia reported that in 2004, long term care and other services for 122,334 elderly, blind and disabled beneficiaries (1/3 of its Medicaid population) accounted for 65.16% of its expenditures. The Enhanced Benefit Program does not apply to this population.

Table 1
Lifetime Medical Costs
in euros

Outcome Measure	Disease Group	Obese Cohort	"Healthy -Living" Cohort	Smoking Cohort
Remaining life expectancy (years) at age 20	–	59.9	64.4	57.4
Expected remaining lifetime health-care costs (x €1,000) at age 20	–	250	281	220
Expected remaining lifetime health-care costs (x €1,000) per person at age 20 specified by disease group	Coronary heart disease	14	12	14
	Stroke	11	13	12
	Chronic obstructive pulmonary disease	1	1	5
	Diabetes	9	2	2
	Musculoskeletal diseases	15	12	8
	Lung cancer	0	0	3
	Other cancers	5	5	5
	Costs of other diseases	195	236	172

Source: Pieter H. M. van Baal, et al., *Lifetime Medical Costs of Obesity: Prevention No Cure for Increasing Health Expenditure*, 5(2) PLOS MED. e39 (Feb. 5, 2008), http://www.plosmedicine.org/article/info:doi/10.1371/journal.pmed.0050029 (visited Nov. 2013).

Wendy K. Mariner, *Medicine and Public Health: Crossing Legal Boundaries*
10 J. HEALTH CARE L. & POL'Y 121, 121–129 (2007)

On December 14, 2005, the New York City Department of Health and Mental Hygiene adopted a new diabetes surveillance program. The new health code regulation requires medical laboratories to submit to the Health Department the results of every patient's blood sugar tests, together with the patient's name, date of birth, address, medical record number, physician, and other information. [Rules of the City of New York, Title 24: Department of Health and Mental Hygiene, Health Code of the City of New York, Title II, Control of Disease, Article 13, Clinical Laboratories, § 13.04. (24 RCNY Health Code Reg. § 13.04)] The report does not require the patient's consent. The Health Department will review the reports to see which patients are not controlling their blood sugar levels and will contact the physician (or perhaps the patient) to encourage the patient to change his or her behavior, by losing weight, eating better, taking medication and/or seeing a physician more often. Is this an innovative way to improve the health of several hundred thousand New Yorkers, a presumptuous invasion of privacy, or usurpation of the physician's role?

[The City] Commissioner of Health is enthusiastic about the new program, hoping it will reduce the number of people in New York City with uncontrolled . . . Type 2 diabetes.

Critics, on the other hand, worry that the program invades personal privacy. Physicians worry that the city will tell them how to treat their patients. Critics may also be concerned that what begins as a benevolent effort to encourage better medical care may mutate into requiring compliance with a medical regimen as a condition for Medicaid eligibility, private health insurance, public or private employment, or even a general duty to stay healthy. A disproportionate number of diabetics in New York City are Medicaid beneficiaries and/or disadvantaged minorities and the City would benefit financially from any reduction in the cost of their care. If the city or state can monitor a chronic condition like diabetes, why not heart disease, cancers, asthma, hypertension, low back pain, and other chronic conditions?

. . . .

The Health Department's reason for adopting the new program was set forth in its preface to the new ordinance:

> Diabetes, a lifelong disease, has recently become epidemic in New York City (NYC) and is a major public health problem. The prevalence of diabetes in NYC has doubled in the past ten years. The NYC 2003 Community Health Survey (CHS) estimates that 9% (530,000) of adult New Yorkers and 20% of adults over 65 have diagnosed diabetes. People may have diabetes an average of 47 years before being diagnosed, and it is estimated that another 265,000 may have diabetes and not yet know it. Diabetes is now the fourth leading cause of death in New York City, moving up from 6th in 2002. This epidemic condition requires similar or greater urgency in public health response to that traditionally accorded to infectious disease monitoring and control.

. . . .

Beyond the commendable goal of improving health, taking action against diabetes may be financially necessary. The rise in diabetes appears to parallel rising pharmaceutical prices and possible reductions in state Medicaid budgets. The NYC Health Department says that in "New York State, 31% of diabetic patients in commercial managed care and 42% in Medicaid Managed Care have an A1C>9.0%," which is higher than the recommended level of less than 7%. The Health Department further argues that "tight blood sugar control" can reduce "by over 25%" the small blood vessel complications that lead to eye disease, kidney complications and peripheral nerve disorders. Thus, [it] concludes, "Keeping the average blood sugar (A1C) under 7.0% can prevent many diabetes-related complications and deaths."

This goal may prove difficult to achieve, since, as the department acknowledges, the CDC has found that "only 37% of US adults with diabetes have an A1C<7% and 20% have an A1C>9%." Moreover, blood sugar levels are not the only measure of diabetes control . . . .

. . . .

The New York City program was modeled after a genuine experiment currently being conducted in Vermont. Researchers created a research study — a randomized controlled trial funded by a grant from the National Institutes of Health — to test an information system for physicians and their patients . . . [P]atients were invited to become research subjects and only those who did not object were enrolled . . . .

. . . .

What does the NYC health department intend to do with the reports it receives? First, it will enter all the data into a new diabetes registry, the New York City Hemoglobin A1C Registry. It plans to use that data "for public health surveillance and monitoring of trends of blood sugar control in people with diabetes." Specifically, it will "plan programs in the Diabetes Prevention and Control Program" and "measure outcomes of diabetes care". It plans to "report a roster of patients to clinicians, stratified by patient A1C levels, highlighting patients under poor control (*e.g.*, A1C>9%) who may need intensified followup and therapy."

. . . .

There are at least three arguments that New York City does not have the legal authority to adopt or implement its diabetes reporting program. The first is that the health department's regulatory authority over clinical laboratories does not include the power to require the reporting of personally identifiable medical information. The second is that neither the State nor the City of New York has the power to require the reporting of such information in the absence of a credible threat posed by the patients whose information is reported to the health or safety of other people. The third is that, to the extent that the health department uses or discloses this information, it is engaged in research that requires the consent of the patient whose identifiable information is so used.

———

NOTES AND QUESTIONS

6. **Programs for the general public.** An example of applying traditional public health activities to chronic diseases can be seen in the New York City blood sugar (Hemoglobin A1C) registry described above. The registry is part of a program in which a city seeks to improve the health, not just of its employees, but of the city's general population — or at least the population with diabetes Type 2. It also represents a new and highly controversial type of surveillance program that is intended to encourage people to improve their own health. How does this program compare with the surveillance programs discussed in Chapter 7, *supra*? Is this an example of public health stepping up to contemporary problems or intruding into the physician's role? Is it an effective way to find people who need medical care or an unjustifiably paternalistic way to get people to take better care of themselves? (See the article by Wikler on ethical arguments for and against various types of

health promotion policies in this Part B, *infra.*) To analyze the state's power to adopt this type of program, the threshold question is whether it should be tested against the cases and decisions governing traditional disease reporting programs, or those governing informed consent to medical care, or those governing research with human subjects. The Mariner article goes on to examine the three arguments that the program fails to meet legal standards under each of those options. Can you flesh out those arguments and those in rebuttal? Which arguments are most persuasive?

7. **Diabetes.** Diabetes was the seventh leading cause of death in the United States in 2010. It is also a risk factor for heart disease and stroke, which account for the causes of death for about 68% of people with diabetes. About 95% of diabetes cases are Type 2, which typically arises in adulthood from the body's inability to produce or use insulin properly, and is believed to result from poor nutrition. People with Type 2 diabetes sometimes suffer from the stigmatizing view that it is primarily a disease of sedentary, obese people. The majority of research funding goes to Type 1 diabetes, which is a genetic condition that is usually diagnosed in childhood and typically well controlled. A third form of diabetes is gestational diabetes, in which placental hormones block insulin's effect in pregnancy, which affects about 4% of pregnant women, but normally disappears after delivery. The World Health Organization estimates that more than 347 million people worldwide have diabetes, with 80% living in low and middle-income countries. World Health Organization, Diabetes Programme, www.who.int/diabetes/en/ (visited Nov. 2013).

Diabetes affects a growing number of Americans. Researchers at the National Institute of Diabetes and Digestive and Kidney Diseases (NIDDKD, part of NIH) estimated that, in 2010, more than 8% of Americans had diabetes (more than 25 million people), including 7 million who have not been diagnosed. National Institute of Diabetes and Digestive and Kidney Diseases, National Diabetes Information Clearinghouse, www.diabetes.niddk.nih.gov/dm/pubs/overview/ (visited Nov. 2013). NIDDKD also estimated that an additional 79 million Americans have higher than normal blood sugar levels, but not high enough to qualify as diabetes. *Id.*; *see* Catherine C. Cowie *et al.*, *Prevalence of Diabetes and Impaired Fasting Glucose in Adults in the U.S. Population: National Health and Nutrition Examination Survey*, 29 Diabetes Care 1263 (2006). The NIDDKD and CDC now characterize these lower blood sugar levels as "pre-diabetes." Treatment for diabetes Type 2 emphasizes physical activity, proper nutrition, and often weight loss. The cost of treating diabetes, estimated to total $116 billion, is of increased concern to payers of medical care. A disproportionate number of Medicaid beneficiaries have diabetes, especially in New York City. For basic information on diabetes in the U.S., see American Diabetes Association, Diabetes Basics, www.diabetes.org/diabetes-basics/?loc=GlobalNavDB (visited Nov. 2013).

Although diabetes has been increasing as a percentage of the total population, the major health risks associated with diabetes have actually declined in the past two decades. *See* Edward W. Gregg, *et al.*, *Changes in Diabetes-Related Complications in the United States*, 1990-2010, 370 New Engl. J. Med 1514 (2014). Acute myocardial infarction decreased by 67.8%; death from hyperglycemic crisis by 64.4%; stroke by 52.7%; amputations, 51.4%; and end-stage renal disease by 28.3%. *Id.* People with diabetes had larger drops in these diseases than people without diabetes. *Id.* Does this mean that preventive measures may be working? How should you interpret studies that report that the diseases associated with obesity rates decline while obesity among adults does not?

In the Matter of the Proposed Rules of the Department of Health Related to the Collection of Administrative Billing Data
http://mn.gov/oah/multimedia/pdf/090015017.rr.pdf (Dec. 2, 2002)

ALLAN W. KLEIN, ADMINISTRATIVE LAW JUDGE.

This Report is part of a rulemaking proceeding held pursuant to Minn. Stat. §§ 14.131 to 14.20 to hear public comment, determine whether the Department of Health . . . has fulfilled all relevant substantive and procedural requirements of law applicable to the adoption of the rules, and evaluate whether the proposed rules are needed and reasonable . . . .

. . . .

Nature of the Proposed Rules

1. The proposed rules establish requirements for the collection and use of administrative billing data created by health care providers to obtain payment from insurers (or other third-party payors) . . . .

2. . . . Because the capacity exists for these codes to disclose private information about medical care received by individuals, detailed requirements for the handling and use of the data compiled are proposed in these rules. And because of the same privacy concerns, many citizens and groups are opposed to the adoption of these rules.

Statutory Authority

. . . The statute states that [t]he commissioner may adopt rules to implement sections 62J.301 to 62J.452.

. . . Minn. Stat. § 62J.301, subd. 2, [states that the] commissioner of health shall conduct data and research initiatives in order to monitor and improve the efficiency and effectiveness of health care in Minnesota. The Department is obligated to perform a number of duties relating to the collection and use of data [relating to the following functions]:

  (1) collect and maintain data which enable population-based monitoring and trending of the access, utilization, quality, and cost of health care services within Minnesota;

  (2) collect and maintain data for the purpose of estimating total Minnesota health care expenditures and trends;

(3) collect and maintain data for the purposes of setting cost containment goals under section 62J.04, and measuring cost containment goal compliance;

(4) conduct applied research using existing and new data and promote applications based on existing research;

(5) develop and implement data collection procedures to ensure a high level of cooperation from health care providers and health plan companies, as defined in section 62Q.01, subdivision 4;

(6) work closely with health plan companies and health care providers to promote improvements in health care efficiency and effectiveness; and

(7) participate as a partner or sponsor of private sector initiatives that promote publicly disseminated applied research on health care delivery, outcomes, costs, quality, and management.

The proposed rules establish the collection and maintenance of information for a database to be used for research, cost containment, and improvement of health care . . . . Therefore, the Administrative Law Judge finds that the Board has statutory authority to adopt the proposed rules.

Generally speaking, an agency can adopt a rule if the agency shows that the rule is needed and reasonable, and the Legislature has authorized the adoption of the rule in statute. An agency cannot adopt a rule that conflicts with a statute, the Minnesota Constitution, or the United States Constitution.

. . . .

Need for the Proposed Database

The need for the Department to be collecting this data at all was questioned by a large number of commentators. Many considered the existence of such a database of information to have no use other than to serve potential employers, the insurance industry, and others who wanted to obtain otherwise private data about individuals without having to ask for it. Other commentators acknowledged the benefits that could flow from researchers having access to a good database, but they did not believe that this outweighed the harm that would occur if private data were released.

Similar databases are already in existence at the federal level for recipients of Medicaid and Medicare. A collection of databases exists through a voluntary partnership between the federal Agency for Healthcare Research and Quality (AHRQ), thirty states, and the healthcare industry. Such databases are used for research into the effectiveness of treatment, quality of care from particular providers, and the reduction of health care costs. Recently, the findings of research performed with these databases, presented in nonscientific language, have been published to help consumers choose between health plans, medical providers, and long-term care facilities. This research benefits all consumers of healthcare by reducing costs, identifying appropriate and effective treatments, and ensuring the safety of treatments. The University of Minnesota described the database as the "proper tools and information" needed to allow "employers, employees and their families to become better consumers of health care."

. . . .

At the hearing, Dr. Harry Hull, the State Epidemiologist, discussed the need for the database. He stated:

Let me give you a few examples of how I and my staff would use this information:

The Minnesota Department of Health has a newborn screening program. Before a newborn baby leaves the hospital, a couple of drops of blood are taken and put on a piece of filter paper and they are tested for more than 20 genetic diseases. Now, these diseases are rare and the program is expensive, but because treatment of these diseases is so expensive, early identification of these individuals saves huge amounts of money for the state. There is a rare infectious disease called toxoplasmosis. It's a parasite that's passed from cats typically to pregnant women, and they sometimes pass it to their unborn babies. The question is, should we screen additionally for toxoplasmosis? It would be expensive to do so. This database could provide information on the frequency of the disease, the cost of treatment of the disease, and allow us to make a recommendation to the legislature for funding for additional testing.

Another example. It used to be that people on Medicare or citizens over 65 years of age could not be reimbursed for influenza immunizations. Dr. Marshall McBean, who is currently with the University of Minnesota School of Public Health, did a study using Medicare data and found out that the cost to Medicare for hospitalizations related to influenza was between $750,000,000 and a billion dollars per year. The result of that was that Medicare finally decided to reimburse the cost of influenza immunization to help keep our older population out of the hospital as a result of complications of influenza. We need similar data here to look at the total cost of influenza, so that we can evaluate whether or not expanded influenza immunization programs would be desirable.

Another example. The Minnesota legislature, when they revised the immunization law a year and a half ago, at our request (suggestion) stated that we needed to provide data on the cost effectiveness and the incidence of disease related to the vaccinations that we were proposing . . . . Having statewide data on the frequencies of occurrences of this disease and the cost of treating this disease is vital to our providing the information that the people need to know to make a rational recommendation.

. . . .

The Department has shown that there are significant benefits in reducing costs to the public, improving treatment for patients, informing consumer choice in medical care, and preventing inadvertent harm when receiving medical care. Each of these reasons is a sufficient justification for establishing a database populated with billing data created for payment of medical services, so long as patient privacy can be protected.

Consent

. . . .

CCHC [Citizen's Council on Health Care] asserted that obtaining this information without individual consent exceeds the Department's statutory authority . . .

The Department responded that obtaining the encounter data without consent is authorized by Minn. Stat. §§ 62J.321, subd. 1, and 144.335, subd. 3b.[20] Minn. Stat. § 62J.321, subd. 1, states:

> Subdivision 1. Data collection. (a) The commissioner shall collect data from health care providers, health plan companies, and individuals in the most cost-effective manner, which does not unduly burden them. The commissioner may require health care providers and health plan companies to collect and provide patient health records and claim files, and cooperate in other ways with the data collection process. The commissioner may also require health care providers and health plan companies to provide mailing lists of patients. Patient consent shall not be required for the release of data to the commissioner pursuant to sections 62J.301 to 62J.452 by any group purchaser, health plan company, health care provider; or agent, contractor, or association acting on behalf of a group purchaser or health care provider. Any group purchaser, health plan company, health care provider; or agent, contractor, or association acting on behalf of a group purchaser or health care provider, that releases data to the commissioner in good faith pursuant to sections 62J.301 to 62J.42 shall be immune from civil liability and criminal prosecution.

The general standards for access to health records are contained in Minn. Stat. § 144.335. Subdivision 3a generally requires patient consent before health records are to be released. But subdivision 3b of that statute states:

> Subd. 3b. Release of records to commissioner of health or health data institute. Subdivision 3a does not apply to the release of health records to the commissioner of health or the health data institute under chapter 62J, provided that the commissioner encrypts the patient identifier upon receipt of the data.

These statutes unambiguously grant the Department the authority to receive health records without the consent of the individual patient for the purposes of this rule [provided patient identifiers are encrypted. . . .

Fourth Amendment Considerations

A related comment was that the proposed rules violated the Fourth Amendment prohibition against "unreasonable searches and seizures." . . . Similar information to the administrative billing data that is collected under this rule is currently being collected by 44 states. The collection, maintenance, and appropriate handling of such data is governed by federal rule, 45 CFR § 500, *et seq.*, in addition to each individual state's rules . . . . No court has determined such data collection to be constitutionally prohibited . . . .

Constitutional Right to Privacy

. . . .

The leading case on the issue of privacy regarding state-maintained databases containing medical information is *Whalen v. Roe.*

. . . .

As demonstrated by the number of public comments in this proceeding (and as recognized by both the Legislature and the Department), the nature of the information to be provided by this rule is traditionally kept private, and disclosure of the information poses a significant risk of harm to the person and that person's relationship with the medical professionals involved in creating that information . . . . The Department immediately addresses this potential for harm by encrypting the personally identifying data (names and addresses) and storing this information apart from the remaining data that is not personally identified . . . . The proposed rules use this data encryption, as well as physical isolation, designated employee access, use restrictions, and security audits as means of protecting the collected data . . . . The Department has shown the statutory authorization to collect this data and articulated valid public policy reasons for doing so . . . . As with the Fourth Amendment issues discussed in the foregoing Findings, there has been no showing that the proposed rule infringes on a protected privacy right.

. . . .

IT IS HEREBY RECOMMENDED: That the proposed rules be adopted, except where noted above.

* * *

NOTES AND QUESTIONS

8. **Authority to create multiple-use databases.** The Minnesota proposal described in the Administrative Billing Data case excerpted above is an early example of state efforts to collect and analyze data for purposes of making public policy. In Minnesota, legislators and citizens strongly objected to the data collection rule, and the Minnesota Department of Health withdrew the rule in 2003. *See* Department of Health Withdraws Plan to Collect Medical Data (Mar. 21, 2003), http://news.minnesota.publicradio.org/features/2003/03/21_ap_healthdata/ (visited Nov. 2013). Objections were based primarily on concern for personal privacy. The records collected would identify individuals who had any type of medical condition, including stroke, abortion, sexually transmitted disease, and mental disorders, as well as treatment and medicines, such as Prozac, contraception, and high blood pressure medication. Insurance industry representatives also objected to the expense and burdensomeness of collecting the data.

The Minnesota Department of Health relied on MINN. STAT. § 62J.321 (set out in the opinion above) as authority for obtaining patient records without consent. The objections to the proposed rule raise questions about the meaning of that statute. Did the administrative law judge interpret it correctly? Health departments sometimes require access to data held by providers and insurers to investigate violations of licensure and other laws. If legislators were among those opposed to the rule, what might they have believed that the statute authorized? Do you agree with the administrative law judge's conclusion that neither the Fourth Amendment nor the Fourteenth Amendment required consent? How do the department's reasons for collecting the data compare with the reason for the compulsory reporting of contagious diseases? If health departments have the authority to adopt a rule like Minnesota proposed, would they still need other reporting laws for specific diseases?

The Department also rejected the argument that patient consent should be required to obtain the desired data on the ground that not all patients would consent and the resulting data would not represent the entire spectrum of patients in the state. At the same time, the Department's proposed rule in effect limited the data collected to patients with private group health insurance and excluded data from health plans that covered beneficiaries of Medicaid, Medicare, and other government health benefit programs. What effect might that have on the comprehensiveness and utility of the data for the purposes sought by the Department? Would the Department have the authority to require the Centers for Medicare and Medicaid to release their patient records? Would the Department have access to that data from other sources?

9. **State databases of medical records and health insurance claims.** Today, many states and cities seek medical records data to analyze the cost and quality of health care, adding cost control to health policy objectives. To measure patient outcomes, records from one provider may need to be linked with the records of another provider — and perhaps with the patient's employment, social services, and other records as well. Wide-ranging data linkage systems are being developed for policy as well as biomedical research. The U.S. General Accountability Office (GAO) notes that it is less expensive to obtain data by electronic record linkage than by collecting it from scratch, so to speak. GENERAL ACCOUNTING OFFICE, RECORD LINKAGE AND PRIVACY: ISSUES IN CREATING NEW FEDERAL RESEARCH AND STATISTICAL INFORMATION, GAO01126SP (April 2001), *available at* www.gao.gov/products/GAO-01-126SP (visited Nov. 2013). Advances in computer technology permitting large data set transfer and storage, as well as manipulation using sophisticated statistical analyses, simplify and encourage both data mining and data linkage. Linked data creates new information that can be used "to describe or make inferences about a population of individuals, analyze patterns in the data, and evaluate or inform programs or policies." The privacy issues raised by such linkage include "whether consent to linkage was obtained; whether linkages required sharing identifiable data with other organizations; and whether 'deidentified' linked data are subject to re-identification risks when released for research or other purposes." *Id.* Questions may also arise about the authority of specific government agencies to share data with other agencies. For example, if agency A is prohibited from sharing its data, but agency B is not, then agency A cannot give its data to agency B, but agency B

can give its data to agency A. Agency A can then link the data from both agencies.

Data linkage does not necessarily raise new privacy issues, but resolving them may be more complex, because linked data sets create new information, formerly innocuous information may become sensitive, and responsibility for protecting privacy is dispersed over more than one entity. Not surprisingly, researchers, especially those in health fields and government agencies, generally advocate linkage without consent, while consumer groups generally advocate consent to linkage. For a readable accounts of comprehensive data bases, links, monitoring and search systems, *see* ROBERT O'HARROW JR., NO PLACE TO HIDE (2005) (anti-terrorism systems); LORI ANDREWS, I KNOW WHO YOU ARE AND I SAW WHAT YOU DID (2011) (commercial and social media systems).

10.   Federal regulation of state databases. As states collect more and more information to determine how to improve health care quality and efficiency and control costs, an opportunity exists for additional federal regulation — to provide more uniform protection for identifiable information or perhaps to enable more widespread sharing of that information. State agencies that collect and sell personal information could be considered to be engaged in interstate commerce. The U.S. Supreme Court has held that Congress can regulate a state department of motor vehicles' sale of personal information about drivers without violating the Tenth Amendment or principles of federalism. In *Reno v. Condon*, 528 U.S. 141 (2000), South Carolina challenged the federal Driver's Privacy Protection Act of 1994 (DPPA), 18 U.S.C. §§ 2721–2725, which limited the disclosure and sale of drivers' personal information without the driver's consent. In a unanimous opinion by Chief Justice Rehnquist, the Court first concluded that the federal Act was a proper exercise of Congress's Commerce Power, because the driver information it regulates is a " 'thin[g] in interstate commerce,' and . . . the sale or release of that information in interstate commerce is therefore a proper subject of congressional regulation" (quoting *United States v. Lopez*, 514 U.S. 549, 558–559 (1995)). The Court rejected the state's argument that the DPPA "commandeered" state officials. Rather, the DPPA simply regulated all entities — including states — that own databases. It distinguished this permissible regulation of *activities*, from impermissible federal attempts to require the states to regulate their own citizens or to require state officials to enforce federal laws regulating private individuals (as in *New York v. United States*, 505 U.S. 144 (1992), and *Printz v. United States*, 521 U.S. 898 (1997)).

Sections 164.502(a)(5)(ii)(A) and 164.508(a)(4) of the HIPAA Privacy Rule, 45 C.F.R. Part 164 (excerpted *infra*) specifically prohibits the sale of protected health information without patient authorization. However, § 164.502(a)(5)(ii)(B) allows the sale of such information for public health purposes permitted pursuant to §§ 164.512(b) and 164.514(e) [limited data sets]), as well as for research purposes permitted pursuant to §§ 164.512(i) or 164.514(e).

Daniel I. Wikler, *Persuasion and Coercion for Health: Ethical Issues in Government Efforts to Change Life-Styles*
56 Milbank Mem. Fund. Qrtly. 303, 306–12, 314–32 (1978)

What should be the government's role in promoting the kinds of personal behavior that lead to long life and good health? Smoking, overeating, and lack of exercise increase one's chances of suffering illness later in life, as do many other habits . . . . Education, exhortation, and other relatively mild measures may not prove effective in inducing self-destructive people to change their behavior . . . . In this essay, I seek to identify the moral principles underlying a reasoned judgment on whether stronger methods might justifiably be used, and, if so, what limits ought to be observed.

. . . .

Goals of Health Behavior Reform

. . . .

Health as a Goal in Itself: Beneficence and Paternalism

Much of the present concern for the reform of unhealthy life-styles stems from concern over the health of those who live dangerously . . . . There are several steps that might immediately be justified: the government could make the effects of unhealthy living habits known to those who practice them, and sponsor research to discover more of these facts . . . .

Considerably more debate, however, would arise over a decision to use stronger methods. For example, a case in point might be a government "fat tax," which would require citizens to be weighed and taxed if overweight. The surcharges thus derived would be held in trust, to be refunded with interest if and when the taxpayers brought their weight down. This pressure would, under the circumstances, be a bond imposed by the government upon its citizens, and thus can be fairly considered as coercive.

The two signal properties of this policy would be its aim of improving the welfare of obese taxpayers, and its presumed unwelcome imposition on personal freedom. (Certain individual taxpayers, of course, might welcome such an imposition, but this is not the ordinary response to penalties.) The first property might be called "beneficence," and it is generally a virtue. But the second property becomes paternalism; and its status as a virtue is very much in doubt . . . .

What is good about some paternalistic interventions is that people are helped, or saved, from harm. Citizens who have to pay a fat tax, for example, may lose weight, become more attractive, and live longer. In the eyes of many, these possible advantages are more than offset by the chief fault of paternalism, its denying persons the chance to make their own choices concerning matters that affect them. Self-direction, in turn, is valued because people usually believe themselves to be the best judges of what is good for them, and because the choosing is considered a good in itself. These beliefs are codified in our ordinary morality in the form of a moral right to noninterference so long as one does not adversely affect the interests of others . . . .

At the same time, the case for paternalistic intervention on at least some occasions seems compelling. There may be circumstances in which we lose, temporarily or permanently, our capacity for competent self-direction, and thereby inflict harm upon ourselves that serves little purpose. Like Ulysses approaching the Sirens, we may hope that others would then protect us from ourselves. This sort of consideration supports our imposed guardianship of children and of the mentally retarded. Although these persons often resent our paternalistic control, we reason that we are doing what they would want us to do were their autonomy not compromised. Paternalism would be a benefit under the sort of social insurance policy that a reasonable person would opt for if considered in a moment of lucidity and competence.

. . . .

Paternalism: Theoretical Problems. There are a number of reasons to question the general argument for paternalism in the coercive eradication of unhealthful personal practices. First, the analogy between the cases of children and the retarded, where paternalism is most clearly indicated, and of risk-taking adults is misleading. If the autonomy of adults is compromised in one or more of the ways just mentioned, it might be possible to restore that autonomy by attending to the sources of the involuntariness; the same cannot ordinarily be done with the children or the retarded. Thus, adults who are destroying their health because of ignorance may be educated; adults acting under constraint may be freed. If restoration of autonomy is a realistic project, then paternalistic interference is unjustified. The two kinds of interventions are aimed at the same target, *i.e.*, harmful behavior not freely and competently chosen. But they accomplish the result differently. Paternalistic intervention blocks the harm; education and similar measures restore the choice . . . .

It remains true, however, that autonomy sometimes cannot be restored. It may be impossible to reach a given population with the information they need; or, once reached, the persons in question may prove ineducable. Psychological compulsions and social pressures may be even harder to eradicate. In these situations, the case for paternalistic interference is relatively strong, yet even here there is reason for caution. Persons who prove incapable of absorbing the facts about smoking, for example, or who abuse drugs because of compulsion or addiction, may retain a kind of second-order autonomy. They can be told that they appear unable to accept scientific truth, or that they are addicted; and they can then decide to reconsider the facts or to seek a cure . . . .

A second reason for doubting the justifiability of paternalistic interference concerns the subjectivity of the notion of harm. The same experience may be seen as harmful by one person and as beneficial by another . . . . Most of us subscribe to the pluralistic ethic, for better or for worse, which has as a central tenet the proposition that there are multiple distinct, but equally valid, concepts of the good and of the good life. It follows that we must use personal preferences and tastes to determine whether our health-related practices are detrimental.

. . . It is common to feel that one's own preferences reflect values that reasonable people adopt; one can hardly regard oneself as unreasonable. To the extent that government planners employ their own concepts of good in attempting to change health practices for the public's benefit, the social insurance rationale for paternalism is clearly inapplicable.

A third reason for criticism of paternalism is the vagueness of the notion of decision-making disability. The conscientious paternalist intervenes only when the self-destructive individual's autonomy is compromised. It is probably impossible, however, to specify a compromising condition. To be sure, there are cases in which the lack of autonomy is evident, such as that of a child swallowing dangerous pills in the belief that they are candy. But the sorts of practices that would be the targets of coercive campaigns to reform health-related behavior are less dramatic and their involuntary quality much less certain . . . .

. . . .

The difficulty for the paternalist at this point is plain. The desire to interfere only with involuntary risk-taking leads to designating individuals for intervention whose behavior proceeds from externally-instilled values. Pluralism commits the paternalist to use the persons' own values in determining whether a health-related practice is harmful. What is needed is some way of determining individuals' "true" personal values; but if these cannot be read off from their behavior, how can they be known?

In certain individual cases, a person's characteristic preferences can be determined from wishes expressed before losing autonomy, as was Ulysses' desire to be tied to the mast. But this sort of data is hardly likely to be available to government health planners. The problem would be at least partially solved if we could identify a set of goods that is basic and appealing, and that nearly all rational persons value. Such universal valuation would justify a presumption of involuntariness should an individual's behavior put these goods in jeopardy . . . .

The crucial question for health planners is whether health is one of these primary goods. Considered alone, it certainly is: it is valued for its own sake; and it is a means to almost all ends. Indeed, it is a necessary good. No matter how eccentric a person's values and tastes are, no matter what kinds of activities are pleasurable, it is impossible to engage in them unless alive . . . .

But the significance of health as a primary good should not be overestimated. The health planner may attempt to argue for coercive reform of health-destructive behavior with a line of reasoning that recalls Pascal's wager. Since death, which precludes all good experience, must receive an enormously negative valuation, contemplated action that involves risk of death will also receive a substantial negative value after the good and bad consequences have been considered. And this will hold true even if the risk is small, since even low probability multiplied by a very large quantity yields a large quantity. Hence anyone who risks death by living dangerously must, on this view, be acting irrationally . . . .

This argument, or something like it, may lie behind the willingness of some to endorse paternalistic regulation of the life-styles of apparently competent adults. It is, however, invalid. Its premises may sometimes be true, and so too may its conclusion, but the one does not follow from the other. Any number of considerations can suffice to show this. For example, time factors are ignored. An act performed at age 25 that risks death at age 50 does not threaten every valued activity. It simply threatens the continuation of those activities past the age of 50. The argument also overlooks an interplay between the possible courses of action: if every action that carries some risk of death or crippling illness is avoided, the enjoyment of life decreases . . . .

. . . .

The trouble for a government policy of life-style reform is that a given intervention is more likely to be tailored to practices and habits than to people. Although we may someday have a fat tax to combat obesity, it would be surprising indeed to find one that imposed charges only on those whose obesity was due to involuntary factors. It would be difficult to reach agreement on what constituted diminished voluntariness; harder still to measure it; and perhaps administratively impractical to make the necessary exceptions and adjustments . . . . Perhaps the firmest conclusion one may draw from all this is that a thoroughly reasoned moral rationale for a given kind of intervention can be very difficult to carry out.

Paternalism: Problems in Practice. Even if we accept the social insurance rationale for paternalism in the abstract, then, there are theoretical reasons to question its applicability to the problem of living habits that are injurious to health . . . .

First, there is the distinct possibility that the government takes over decision-making power from partially-incompetent individuals may prove even less adept at securing their interests that they would have been if left alone. Paucity of scientific data may lead to misidentification of risk factors. The primitive state of the art in health promotion and mass-scale behavior modification may render interventions ineffective or even counterproductive. And the usual run of political and administrative tempests that affect all public policy may result in the misapplication of such knowledge as is available in these fields . . . .

. . . .

Second, there is some possibility that what would be advertised as concern for the individual's welfare (as that person defines it) would turn out to be simple legal moralism, i.e., an attempt to impose the society's or authorities' moral prescriptions upon those not following them. In Knowles' call for life-style reform (1976) the language is suggestive:

> The next major advances in the health of the American people will result from the assumption of individual responsibility for one's own health. This will require a change in lifestyle for the majority of Americans. The cost of sloth, gluttony, alcoholic overuse, reckless driving, sexual intemperance, and smoking is now a national, not an individual responsibility.

All save the last of these practices are explicitly *vices*; indeed, the first two — sloth and gluttony — use their traditional names . . . . Skiing and football produce injuries as surely as sloth produces heart disease; and the decision to postpone childbearing until the thirties increases susceptibility to certain cancers in women.

If it is the unhealthiness of "sinful" living habits that motivates the paternalist toward reform, then ought not other acts also be targeted on occasions when persons exhibit lack of self-direction? . . . If enthusiasm for paternalistic intervention slackens in these latter cases, it may be a signal for reexamination of the motives.

A third problem is the involuntariness of some self-destructive behavior may make paternalistic reform efforts ineffective. To the extent that the unhealthy behavior is not under the control of the individual, we cannot expect the kind of financial threat involved in a "fat tax" to exert much influence. Paradoxically, the very conditions under which paternalistic intervention seems most justified are those in which many of the methods available are least likely to succeed . . . .

. . . .

[The author then examines two other possible goals of health behavior reform:]

Fair Distribution of Burdens

[Some people argue that the healthy should not have to pay for costs incurred by risk-takers.] In the view of these persons, those who indulge in self-destructive practices and present their medical bills to the public are free riders in an economy kept going by the willingness of others to stay fit and sober . . . .

. . . .

This sort of argument presupposes a certain theory of justice . . . . A number of considerations lead to the conclusion that the fairness argument as a justification of coercive intervention, despite initial appearances, is anything but straightforward. Underlying this argument is an empirical premise that may well prove untrue of at least some unhealthy habits: that those who take chances with their health do place a significant financial burden upon society. It is not enough to point to the costs of medical care for lung cancer and other diseases brought on by individual behavior. [O]ne must also determine what the individual would have died of had he not engaged in the harmful practice, and subtract the cost of the care which that condition requires. There is no obvious reason to suppose that the diseases brought on by self-destructive behavior are costlier to treat than those that arise from "natural causes."

. . . It may turn out, for all we know prior to investigation, that smoking tends to cause few problems during a person's productive years and then to kill the individual before the need to provide years of social security and pension payments

. . . .

A second doubt concerning the claim that the burdens of unhealthy behavior are unfairly distributed also involves an unstated premise. The risk taker, according to the fairness argument, should have to suffer not only the illness that may result from the behavior but also the loss of freedom attendant to the coercive measures used in the attempt to change the behavior. What, exactly, is the cause cited by those complaining of the financial burdens placed upon society by the self-destructive? It is not simply the burden of caring and paying for care of these persons when they become sick. Many classes of persons impose such costs on the

public besides the self-destructive. For example, diabetics, and others with hereditary dispositions to contract diseases, incur unusual and heavy expenses, and these
are routinely paid by others. Why are these costs not resisted as well?

One answer is that there is resistance to these other costs . . . . But even those
willing to pay for the costs of caring for diabetics, or the medical expenses of the
poor, may still bridle when faced by the needs of those who have compromised their
own health . . . . One possible reason to distinguish the costs of the person with a
genetic disease from those of the person with a life-style-induced disease is simply
that one can be prevented and the other cannot . . . .

But this is not the argument we seek. The medical costs incurred by diseases
caused by unhealthy life-styles may be preventable, if our behavior-modifying
methods are effective; but . . . [i]f costs must be reduced, perhaps they should be
reduced some other way (*e.g.*, by lessening the quality of care provided for all); or
perhaps costs should not be lowered and those feeling burdened should be made to
tolerate the expense. The fact that money could be saved by intruding into the
choice of life-styles of the *self-destructive* does not itself show that it would be
particularly fair to do so.

If intrusion is to be justified on the grounds that unhealthy lifestyles impose
unfair financial burdens on others, then, something must be added to the argument.
That extra element, it seems, is *fault* . . . .

      . . . .

The argument thus depends crucially on the premise that the person who
engages in an unhealthy life-style is responsible for the costs of caring for the illness
that it produces . . . . [R]esponsibility . . . seems to involve the actions of choice
and voluntariness. If the chronic diseases resulting from life-style were not the
result of voluntary choices, then there could be no assignment of responsibility in
the sense in which the term is being used . . . . Since much self-destructive
behavior is the result of suggestion, constraint, compulsion, and other factors, the
applicability of the fairness argument is limited.

Even if the behavior leading to the illness is wholly voluntary, there is not
necessarily any justification for intervention *by the state*. The only parties with
rights to reform life-styles on these grounds are those who are actually being
burdened by the costs involved. A wealthy man who retained his own medical
facilities would not justifiably be a target of any of these interventions, and a
member of a prepaid health plan would be liable to intervention primarily from
others in his payment pool. He would then, of course, have the option of resigning
and continuing his self-destructive ways; or he might seek out an insurance scheme
designed for those who wish to take chances but who also want to limit their losses
 . . . . Measures undertaken by the government and applied indiscriminately to all
who indulge in a given habit may thus be unfair to some (unless other justification
is provided) . . . .

This objection may lose force should there be a national health insurance
program in which membership would be mandatory . . . . But this only establishes
another ground for disputing the responsibility of the self-destructive individual for
the costs of his medical care. To state this objection, two classes of acts must be

distinguished: the acts constituting the life-style that causes the disease and creates the need for care; and the acts of imposing financial shackles upon an unwilling public. Unless the acts in the first group are voluntary, the argument for imposing behavior change does not get off the ground. Even if voluntary, those acts in the second class might not be . . . . If the financial arrangement is mandatory, then the individual may not have *chosen* that his acts should have these effects on others. The situation will have been this: an individual is compelled by law to enter into financial relationships with certain others as a part of an insurance scheme; the arrangement causes the individual's acts to have effects on others that the others object to; and so they claim the right to coerce the individual into desisting from those acts. It seems difficult to assign to this individual responsibility for the distribution of financial burdens . . . .

. . . .

There is, however, a response that would seem to have more chance of success: allowing those with unhealthy habits to pay their own way. Users of cigarettes and alcohol, for example, could be made to pay an excise tax, the proceeds of which would cover the costs of treatment for lung cancer and other resulting illnesses. Unfortunately, these costs would also be paid by users who are not abusers: those who drink only socially would be forced to pay for the excesses of alcoholics. Alternatively, only those contracting the illnesses involved could be charged; but it would be difficult to distinguish illnesses resulting from an immoderate life-style from those due to genetic or environmental causes . . . .

This kind of policy has its good and bad points. Chief among the favorable ones is that it allows a maximum retention of liberty in a situation in which liberty carries a price. Under such a policy, those who wished to continue their self-destructive ways without pressure could continue to do so, provided that they absorbed the true costs of their practices themselves. Should they not wish to shoulder these costs, they could submit to the efforts of the government to induce changes in their behavior . . . .

The negative side of this proposal stems from the fact that under its terms the only way to retain one's liberty is to pay for it. This, of course, offers very different opportunities to rich and poor . . . . Only the poor would be forced to submit to loss of privacy, loss of freedom from pressure, and regulation aimed at behavior change. Such liberties are what make up full citizenship, and one might hold that they ought not to be made contingent on one's ability to purchase them.

. . . .

. . . The central difficulty for the fairness argument, mentioned above, is that much of the self-destructive behavior that burdens the public is not really the fault of the individual; various forces, internal and external, may conspire to produce such a behavior independently of the person's will. Conversely, a problem for the paternalist is that much of the harm from which the individual would be "protected" may be the result of free, voluntary choices, and hence beyond the paternalist's purview. The best reason to be skeptical of the first rationale, then, is doubt over the *presence* of voluntariness; the best reason to doubt the second concerns the *absence* of voluntariness. Whatever weighs against the one will count for the other.

. . . .

Public Welfare

Aside from protecting the public from unfair burdens imposed by those with poor health habits, there may be social benefits to be realized by inducing immoderates to change their behavior. Health behavior change may be the most efficient way to reduce the costs of health care in this country . . . . A healthier work force means a stronger economy, for example, and the availability of healthy soldiers enhances national security . . . .

. . . .

Means of Health Behavior Reform

Two questions arise in considering the ethics of government attempts to bring about healthier ways of living. The first question is: Should coercion, intrusion, and deprivation be used as methods for inducing change? The other question is: How do we decide whether a given health promotion is coercive, intrusive, or inflicts deprivations? These questions are independent of each other . . . .

. . . .

. . . What is the difference between persuasion and manipulation? Can offers and incentives be coercive, or is coerciveness a property only of threats? . . .

Health Education

Health education seems harmless. Education generally provides information and this generally increases our power, since it enhances the likelihood that our decisions will accomplish our ends . . . .

. . . .

The main threat of coerciveness in health education programs, in my opinion, lies in the possibility that such programs may turn from providing information to manipulating attitude and motivation. Education, in the sense of providing information, is a means of inducing belief and knowledge. A review of the literature indicates, however, that when health education programs are evaluated, they are not judged successful or unsuccessful in proportion to their success in *inducing belief*. Rather, evaluators look at *behavior change*, the actions which, they hope, would stem from those beliefs. If education programs are to be evaluated favorably, health educators may be led to take a wider view of their role. This would include attempts to motivate the public to adopt healthy habits, and this might have to be supplied by covert appeals to other interests ("smokers are unpopular," and so on). Suggestion and manipulation may replace information as the tools used by the health educators to accomplish their purpose. Indeed, health education may call for actual and deliberate misinformation: directives may imply or even state that the scientific evidence in favor of a given health practice is unequivocal even when it is not.

A fine line has been crossed in these endeavors. Manipulation and suggestion go well beyond providing information to enhance rational decision making. These measures bypass rational decision-making faculties and thereby inflict a loss of personal control. Thus, health education, except when restricted to information, requires some justification . . . .

Incentives, Subsidies, and Taxes

. . . .

Generally speaking, justification is required only for coercive measures, not for incentives. However, the distinction is not as clear as it first appears. Suppose, for example, that the government wants to induce the obese to lose weight, and that a mandatory national health insurance plan is about to go into effect. The government's plan threatens the obese with higher premiums unless they lose their excess weight. Before the plan is instituted, however, someone objects that the extra charges planned for eager eaters make the program coercive. No adequate justification is found. Instead of calling off the program, however, some subtle changes are made. The insurance scheme is announced with higher premiums than had been originally planned. No extra charges are imposed on anyone; instead, discounts are offered to all those who avoid overweight. Instead of coercion, the plan now uses positive incentives; and this does not require the kind of justification needed for the former plan. Hence the new program is allowed to go into effect.

The effect of the rate structure in the two plans is, of course, identical: The obese would pay the higher rate, the slender the lower one. It seems that the distinction between coercion and incentive is merely semantic. But this is the wrong conclusion . . . . Ultimately, I believe, the judgment required for the obesity measure would require us to decide what a fair rate would have been for the insurance; any charges above that fair rate would be coercive, and any below, incentive . . . . [T]his shows that one cannot judge the coerciveness of a few structure merely by checking it for surcharges . . . .

. . . .

Regulative Measures

. . . A different way of effecting a reform is to deprive self-destructive individuals of the means needed to engage in their unhealthy habits. Prohibition of the sale of cigarettes would discourage smoking at least as effectively as exhortations not to smoke or insurance surcharges for habitual tobacco use. Yet, these regulative measures are surely as coercive, although they do not involve direct interaction with the individuals affected. They are merely one more way of intervening in an individual's decision to engage in habits that may cause illness. As such, they are clearly in need of the same or stronger justification as those involving threats, despite the argument that these measures are taken only to combat an unhealthy environment, and thus cannot be counted as coercing the persons who have unhealthy ways of living . . . . What distinguishes these "environmental" causes of illness from, say, carcinogens in the water supply, is the active connivance of the victims. "Shielding" the "victims" from these external forces must involve making them behave in a way they do not choose. This puts regulative measures in the same category as those applied directly to the self-destructive individuals.

Conclusions

. . . It is apparent that more is needed than a simple desire on the part of government to promote health and/or reduce costs. When the measures taken are intrusive, coercive, manipulative, and/or inflict deprivations — in short, when they are of the sort many might be expected to dislike — the moral justification required may be quite complex. The principles that would be used in making a case for these interventions may have limited scope and require numerous exceptions and qualifications; it is unlikely that they can be expressed as simple slogans such as "individuals must be responsible for their own health" or "society can no longer afford self-destructiveness."

. . . .

Inherent in the subject matter is a danger that reform efforts, however rationalized and advertised, may become "moralistic," in being an imposition of the particular preferences and values of one (powerful) group upon another. . . .

Leonard H. Glantz, *Control of Personal Behavior and the Informed Consent Model*
(2006)

Control of Personal Behavior

. . . [T]he greatest achievements in public health and those that have best protected the population produced clean water, safe milk, clean air, effective sanitation, habitable living conditions and safer work-places. All of these interventions have one thing in common — they protect the health of the population without individuals being required to take action to protect themselves.

In recent years, in addition to these environmental interventions, there has been much more focus on changing the personal behaviors of large numbers of individuals. In 1993, an influential article was published in the Journal of the American Medical Association entitled "Actual Causes of Death in the United States," 270 JAMA 2207 (1993). The authors note that death certificates list the cause of death as the immediate medical condition that resulted in death: heart disease, cancer, cerebrovascular disease, pneumonia, influenza, diabetes, and the like. The authors claim, however, that while these are the conditions from which people die, they do not account for the underlying causes of those medical conditions. The authors propose that the actual causes of death are tobacco use, diet/activity patterns, alcohol use, firearms, sexual behavior, motor vehicles, and illicit drug use. (Ask yourself if the authors are correct in their approach. In law, the term "causation" has a pretty distinct definition and usually refers to proximate causation. This is because there is almost no limit to how far back in time one can go to ascribe causation to a multiple of factors. For example, while describing tobacco use as the cause of death, one could ask whether the classmate in the playground who provided the first cigarette is the cause of death, or whether the tobacco farmer is the cause of death, or whether it is the economic conditions that the led the farmer to grow tobacco instead of some other crop. Ascription of causation can have a substantial political component to it.)

The "actual" causes of death are seemingly all within the control of individuals. Rather than being victims of the environment people become victims of their own activity or inactivity. As this perspective became accepted one would go about preventing death and disability by getting people to cease engaging in behaviors that caused such conditions or to engage in activities that would prolong their lives and well-being. Unlike the traditional public health interventions which would make people healthier by changing their environment, these interventions are based on the notion that if each individual acts in way that makes him or her healthier, the population on the whole will be healthier — the ultimate goal of public health.

The goal of changing people's behavior, however, is not new. The seven deadly sins, which include sloth and gluttony, were seen as moral failings, not public health matters. Prohibitionists in the United States and elsewhere were opposed to the drinking of alcoholic beverages because this indulgence was perceived as unhealthy for the soul, as well as or perhaps even more than unhealthful for the body. Historically, those concerned with the moral fiber of society have tried to keep people from drinking, smoking, taking drugs, and having sex outside of marriage — all issues that are also addressed by the public health community. Is there a difference between moralistic interventions and public-health interventions? An example of the cumulative effect of public health and moralistic concerns on social policy is found in an early United States Supreme Court case that upheld the Kansas prohibition against the manufacture of intoxicating liquors, *Mugler v. Kansas*, 123 U.S. 623 (1887). The petitioner argued that the state had no business regulating the manufacturer of liquor for his own use. The Court upheld the statute, saying that it could not ignore the fact that "Public health, public morals, and the public safety may be endangered by the general use of intoxicating drinks; nor the fact established by statistics accessible to every one, that the idleness, disorder, pauperism, and crime existing in the country are, in some degree at least, traceable to this evil." 123 U.S. at 662.

While activities that are discouraged for either moralistic or public health reasons may be similar, the methods and goals should be different. Furthermore, public health interventions should be based on scientific knowledge about the nature of risky activities and the effectiveness of interventions designed to reduce or eliminate the risk. In the absence of a scientific and rational foundation for inducing individual behavior change, the change is being proposed for moral or aesthetic reasons rather than its implications for health.

Does the Informed Consent Model Have a Place in Public Health Interventions?

The doctrine of informed consent for medical treatment was adopted by courts and ethicists in the late 1960s and early 1970s. Prior to its adoption, the general sense was that patients should listen to "doctor's orders." Physicians and even some family members often proposed that a patient not even be told his or her diagnosis, especially gloomy ones like cancer, so that the patient would not be come upset or "lose hope." It was not uncommon that medically proven treatments were not disclosed by physicians to their patients if those treatments were different from those the physician preferred. A stark example of this involves the treatment of breast cancer. For many years breast cancer was treated by performing a radical mastectomy, which removed all of the breast and all underlying muscle and tissue. As less radical and deforming treatments were developed, such as the removal of the cancerous tissue while saving the breast (lumpectomy), physicians who continued to believe that radical mastectomy was more likely to save lives did not discuss the availability of the less radical surgical or medical treatments. Ultimately, under pressure from organizations of women, some states adopted specific legislation requiring disclosure of alternative breast cancer therapies.

Physicians often withheld information because they feared that patients would not understand it or would act "irrationally," by which they typically meant that the patient would not choose what the physician believed to be the best chance for survival. In the breast cancer scenario, physicians who withheld information about lumpectomy often were concerned that "mere vanity" would keep women from choosing radical mastectomy. Many believed that longevity was so desirable a goal that other considerations should not be relevant.

The doctrine of informed consent to medical care created by courts in the early 1970s enables individuals to make important decisions about their health care based on their own perception of their needs, desires and fears. As the California Supreme Court noted in *Cobbs v. Grant*, 8 Cal. 3d 229, 502 P.2d 1 (1972), physicians are experts in knowing what the likely risks and benefits are of a recommended treatment, but, "the weighing of these risks against the individual subjective fears and hopes of the patient is not an expert skill. Such evaluation and decision is a nonmedical judgment reserved for the patient alone." 8 Cal. 3d at 243. This type of analysis, adopted by courts in other states, caused a reconsideration of the goals of medicine.

The goal of doctrine of informed consent is to create patients who are armed with the information they need to decide *whether or not* to accept medical care recommended by their physician. It is the fact that patients were to be well enough informed to knowledgeably *reject* a physician's recommendation that made the doctrine "radical" to physicians. It also means that a good outcome of the physician-patient interaction is not an obedient or "compliant" patient but an informed patient. Patient knowledge and autonomy became more important values than their health or longevity.

In time the medical profession came to adopt the doctrine of informed consent as a fundamental ethical underpinning of the practice of medicine:

> It is a fundamental ethical requirement that a physician should at all times deal honestly and openly with patients . . . . Only through full disclosure is a patient able to make informed decisions regarding future medical care.

AMA Opinion E-8.12 Patient Information (1994)

> The patient's right of self-decision can be effectively exercised only if the patient possesses enough information to enable an intelligent choice. The patient should make his or her own determination on treatment. The

physician's obligation is to present the medical facts accurately to the patient . . . . and to make recommendations for management in accordance with good medical practice.

AMA E-8.08 Informed Consent (1981)

It is notable that the AMA acknowledged patient "self-decision" as a "right." The AMA has further acknowledged that physicians must provide a patient with accurate facts but it is the patient's right to make "his or her own determination on treatment."

The question this raises is whether the philosophy behind the doctrine of informed consent plays any role in the practice of public health. Leaders in the public health profession recently adopted what is referred to as "Principles of the Ethical Practice of Public Health." Nowhere in these principles is the doctrine of informed consent mentioned. The closest to informed consent these principles come is paragraph 6:

6. Public health institutions should provide communities with the information they have that is needed for decisions on policies or programs and should obtain the community's consent for their implementation.

92 AM. J. PUB. HEALTH 1058 (July 2002).

It is far from clear what it means to provide communities with information and to obtain "the community's consent." Indeed the code does not require anything of a public health practitioner, unlike the AMA code of ethics that requires individual physicians to act in certain ways. Rather "public health institutions" are assigned to provide information to communities.

In the "old public health" paradigm this approach makes a certain amount of sense. If the public health goal is to create a safer water supply for a community by replacing lead water pipes, no consent of every individual who might drink that water could sensibly be required. Indeed, no particular individual in the community could "reject" the recommended water improvement project. Furthermore, community leaders such as mayors, city councilors or other elected representatives would make the decision about the water supply and should be informed about the risks and benefits of alternative approaches before making such decisions. But this is a long way from individual informed consent. It is simply a description of how policymakers arrive at decisions.

With the new public health paradigm that focuses on behavior change, there is no "community" that needs information, nor any "community" that gives consent. Behavior change is squarely focused on individuals, not communities. What might the goals of public health be in this context? Is it to have a citizenry that behaves the way public health agencies think people ought to behave or a citizenry that has enough information to make knowledgeable choices? For example, should the goal of public health be to ensure that nobody smokes cigarettes, or should the goal be to ensure that everybody knows the risks of cigarette smoking so they can make their own decision whether or not to smoke?

This raises the question of how truthful public health education campaigns need to be. If the goal is to ensure that people behave in a certain way, truth-telling could be counterproductive. For example, Viscusi argues that people in the United States tend to think that smoking is even more risky than it actually is. W. Kip Viscusi, Smoking: Making The Risky Decision (1992). If the goal is to prevent people from smoking or to get smokers to stop smoking, such misinformation will help further that goal. If the goal is to have an informed populace, this goal is not met. Do public health professionals have an obligation to present accurate information even if that runs counter to their behavioral goals? If there is no obligation to tell the truth, is there some obligation not to mislead the public about risks and benefits of behavior change? If there is such an obligation, what is its source?

Behavior Change Methods

There are many ways to change people's behavior. One way is to provide them with knowledge. This is very close to the informed consent model in which one tells the truth about risks and benefits of particular activities and leaves it up to the individual to decide whether or not to engage in those activities. For example, there can be educational advertising campaigns or even laws mandating signs in cars to inform people that they are less likely to die in an accident if they wear their seatbelts. It is well-known that education will affect some people's behaviors. Still, there will be people who will ignore or reject the information and continue to drive without seatbelts. We can try to persuade these people to use seatbelts with more appealing or effective notices or by adding a strong emotional component. For example, an advertisement might show a young family in a cemetery grieving for a family member who would be alive if only he had worn his seatbelt. This emotional manipulation will create an additional number of seatbelt users, but there will certainly still be people who do not use seatbelts. To reach this last group, the legislature might pass a law making it a crime to drive while not wearing a seatbelt. It is this last approach, state action that criminalizes otherwise innocent behaviors, that raise both legal and ethical issues.

The use of coercive measures to force people to conform their behavior in ways we think best for raises the problem of paternalism. Paternalism assumes we know what is in a person's interests better than that person does. For young children or incompetent adults, this is the case, and both law and ethics permit making decisions on their behalf. For competent adults, however, paternalism deprives them of the ability to make decisions for themselves based on what they conclude is best for themselves. As described above, in the pre-informed consent era physicians were endowed with paternalistic power. The movement towards in-formed consent was a rejection of this paternalistic way of making medical decisions. In a free and pluralistic society, Americans tend to resist paternalistic actions by the state. Indeed, one of the underpinnings of being a free adult is the ability to make poor decisions for ourselves. Because state paternalism is such a suspect doctrine in a free society, states often deny their paternalistic motives for passing legislation.

———

NOTES AND QUESTIONS

11. Ends and means. Wikler's article was published almost four decades ago, but the questions he posed remain quite contemporary. The general goals of health policies and laws — health itself; fair distribution of (financial) burdens; and public welfare — are widely accepted. It is the measures used to achieve those goals that generate controversy, particularly measures that compel individuals to change their personal behavior. The article examines individual policy goals in isolation, but also acknowledges that "in actuality most government programs would probably be expected to serve several purposes at once." (Wikler, *supra*, at 305.) Does the fact that a measure serves more than one goal improve its chances of justification as a matter of law, as a matter of moral theory, as a matter of political acceptability?

For arguments for and against paternalism, see Gerald Dworkin, *Paternalism*, 56 The Monist 64 (Jan. 1972); John Kleinig, Paternalism (1984); Joel Feinberg, Harm To Self: The Moral Limits of the Criminal Law (1986); Gregory Mitchell, *Libertarian Paternalism Is an Oxymoron*, 99 Nw. U. L. Rev. 1245 (2005); Cass R. Sunstein & Richard H. Thaler, *Libertarian Paternalism Is Not an Oxymoron*, 70 U. Chi. L. Rev. 1159 (2003); Thaddeus Mason Pope, *Counting the Dragon's Teeth and Claws: The Definition of Hard Paternalism*, 20 Ga. State U. L. Rev. 659 (2004); Jeffrey J. Rachlinski, *Cognitive Errors, Individual Differences, and Paternalism*, 73 U. Chi. L. Rev. 207 (2006); Sarah Conly, Against Autonomy: Justifying Coercive Paternalism (2013); Riccardo Rebonato, Taking Liberties: A Critical Examination Of Libertarian Paternalism (2012); Cass R. Sunstein, *Behavioral Economics and Paternalism*, 122 Yale. L. J. 1826 (2013).

Does public health policy treat similar risks to health consistently? Are skiing, playing football, or other recreational sports less risky than using marijuana? Risk is the result of multiplying two factors: the probability of a specific harm occurring, and the magnitude of that harm. As we saw in Chapter 2, one's perception of risk may differ, depending upon whether one focuses on the magnitude of the harm or on the probability that it may occur. (And the values of each factor may themselves be uncertain.) The probability of catching the common cold may be high during winter, but few people consider it a serious risk, because the harm it causes, while annoying, is not dreadful (unless you are immunocompromised). Moreover, as noted in Chapter 2, people may assign very different values to the same harm and to what they lose by preventing the harm. This suggests that policies may or may not be accepted depending upon whose ox is being gored. How should society decide which risks are socially acceptable and which are not? Is a simple majority vote of the legislature enough, as long as the measure serves a legitimate state purpose? Wikler's article challenges policy makers to think carefully about the accuracy of assumptions about how different measures serve legitimate public health goals. In particular, his discussion of paternalism emphasizes that measures intended to improve an individual's health for his or her own sake, rather than to prevent harm to others (as was the primary focus of Chapter 5), are both conceptually and empirically difficult to justify in a principled manner. Wikler presents an ethical analysis, not a legal one, although the arguments are relevant to legal analysis. Are the various legal doctrines applicable to criminal laws, tax laws, administrative regulation, and general civil rights and obligations sufficient to distinguish acceptable from unacceptable public health policies?

Note that Wikler mentions diabetes as an example of a disease that is beyond an individual's control. Contrast that view with current public health campaigns to reduce the incidence of diabetes by encouraging people to lose weight and take their medications consistently, as seen in other materials in this Chapter and in Chapter 9, *infra*. Is the change in how the condition is viewed the result of better scientific and epidemiological information? Are there other explanations?

12. Regulating things instead of people. A criticism of the emphasis on personal behavioral risk factors, one recognized by Wikler in his article (*supra*, at 305), is that it may distract attention from more important sources of risk, such as environmental, economic, and occupational factors. Contemporary study of the social determinants of health may have been inspired by WHY ARE SOME PEOPLE HEALTHY AND OTHERS ARE NOT? THE DETERMINANTS OF HEALTH OF POPULATIONS (Robert G. Evans, *et al.*, eds. 2004). Some, perhaps most, environmental interventions can be less costly and more effective than laws intended to change personal behavior, primarily because they do not depend upon individual willingness to take specific actions. Moreover, they largely avoid arguments that the law violates some aspect of personal liberty. For example, building roads with safe curves, graded banking, and lighting may reduce the risk of motor vehicle crashes as much or more than enforcing speed limits. Some of these contributors to risk may be more difficult and expensive to remove. Think about what might be more appealing to you as a legislator: a bill requiring all people in motor vehicles to wear seat belts or a bill requiring the automobile industry to install air bags in all vehicles sold in the state. What constituencies might support and oppose each bill? What might each bill cost the state itself?

State laws requiring motor vehicle drivers (and more recently passengers) to wear seatbelts were encouraged as an alternative to regulatory requirements that automobile manufacturers install airbags or passive restraints in cars, which the industry had opposed since 1969. The Department of Transportation issued final standards requiring passive restraints for all cars by 1984, but reopened the rulemaking process in 1981 and ultimately rescinded the standard, when it appeared that auto makers were going to install passive seat belts instead of airbags in 99% of new cars. Some of the history of the regulatory battle between the automobile industry and the Department of Transportation is found in *Motor Vehicle Manufacturers Association of the United States v. State Farm Mutual Automobile Insurance Co.*, 463 U.S. 29 (1983). In that case, the U.S. Supreme Court overturned the agency's rescission of the standard because it was not "the product of reasoned decisionmaking." Although substantial evidence supported issuing the standard, the agency rescinded it primarily because of industry practice, which the Court found arbitrary and capricious: "If, under the statute, the agency should not defer to the industry's failure to develop safer cars, which it surely should not do, *a fortiori* it may not revoke a safety standard which can be satisfied by current technology simply because the industry has opted for an ineffective seatbelt design." 463 U.S. at 49. A presidential election resulted in a new Secretary of Transportation, however, who reached agreement with the industry that the airbag standard would not be issued as a final rule if two-thirds of the states enacted legislation requiring people to wear seatbelts. The effort to pass such laws was successful, although it prompted occasionally heated debates over whether such laws were unjustifiably paternalistic or a safety-conscious condition on the privilege of driving. Largely ignored in the arguments was the reason for having the debate in the first place — rejection of effective safety standards for motor vehicles.

13. Informed consent. Glantz pushes several themes raised by Wikler, most importantly in asking whether public health policies can or do accommodate the informed consent model of the physician-patient relationship. As Glantz notes, the medical profession's acceptance of patient decision making, autonomy, and the doctrine of informed consent was substantially nudged by ethical and judicial opinions. Jay Katz chronicled physicians' earlier paternalistic attitude toward patients in THE SILENT WORLD OF DOCTOR AND PATIENT (1984), in which he describes a conversation on breast cancer treatment he had with a surgeon-friend:

> We first discussed at some length all the uncertainties that plague the treatment of breast cancer. We readily agreed on what was known, unknown, or conjectural about the varieties of therapeutic modalities offered to patients, such as surgery, radiation, and chemotherapy. I then asked how he would speak with a patient. . . . . [H]e related to me this recent experience.
>
> At the beginning of their encounter, he had briefly mentioned a number of available treatment alternatives. He added that he had done so without indicating that any of the alternatives to radical surgery deserved serious consideration. Instead, he had quickly impressed on his patient the need for submitting to this operation [complete mastectomy]. I commented that he had given short shrift to other treatment approaches even though a few minutes earlier he had agreed with me that we still are so ignorant about which treatment is best. He seemed startled by my comment but responded with little hesitation that ours had been a theoretical discussion, of little relevance to practice.

KATZ, THE SILENT WORLD OF DOCTOR AND PATIENT at 166–67.

Dr. Katz was struck by the surgeon's confidence that patients "could neither comprehend nor tolerate an exploration of the certainties and uncertainties inherent in the treatment of breast cancer." *Id.* at 168.

Public health traditionally considered population-wide problems, not the personal health concerns of individuals. Health promotion programs, paradoxically perhaps, are intended to achieve population-wide results by having individuals stop risky behaviors for their own personal benefit. The informed consent model Glantz describes could be applied in population-based educational programs that allow individuals to make informed choices about behavioral health risks. Allowing choice respects autonomy, but it also means some people may not make the healthy choice. If the success of a public health program were judged by the extent to which population rates of mortality or morbidity decrease, then the informed consent model would be judged a failure. At the same time, more coercive measures to ensure compliance confront the problem of justifying paternalism.

14. Who behaves badly? Many recent public health policies have wide support among people who are relatively affluent and educated. Smoking, excessive alcohol consumption, illicit drug use, and obesity, for example, are more likely to be found among people in lower socioeconomic groups than the better off and well educated classes. James Morone concludes that since the colonial days in America, the most coercive measures were directed most often at lower socioeconomic classes, especially people of color and immigrants, but also the working poor. *See* James Morone, HELLFIRE NATION: THE POLITICS OF SIN IN AMERICAN HISTORY (2003). Can you think of public health measures that forbid behaviors that are most prevalent among the affluent?

Great Britain engaged in a public debate over the so-called "nanny state." One report argued for the careful use of paternalistic measures. Karen Jochelson, Nanny or Steward: *The Role of the State in Public Health* (Kings Fund, Oct. 2005). Public surveys have reported class differences in attitudes toward different public health measures, "with poorer socio-economic groups . . . more likely to feel that health is beyond an individual's control and that tackling poverty is the most effective way for a government to prevent illness." *Id.* at 7. Other surveys indicate that more educated, affluent groups support laws regulating personal behavior, while lower socioeconomic groups fear they would bear the primary burdens and instead prefer programs that improve the environment, such as bicycle paths and public parks for those who could not afford health clubs or cars.

C.   HEALTH PROTECTION: SCREENING AND EARLY DETECTION OF DISEASE

UNITED STATES v. WESTINGHOUSE ELECTRIC CORP.
638 F.2d 570 (3d Cir. 1980)

SLOVITER, JUDGE.

In this case, we attempt to reconcile the privacy interests of employees in their medical records with the significant public interest in research designed to improve occupational safety and health.

The National Institute for Occupational Safety and Health (NIOSH) was established by the Occupational Safety and Health Act of 1970, 29 U.S.C. §§ 651 *et seq.* (1976). NIOSH has the authority to "develop and establish recommended occupational safety and health standards," and to conduct research concerning occupational safety and health. In particular, it has the authority to conduct a health hazard evaluation, which entails an investigation to determine following a written request by any employer or authorized representative of employees, specifying with reasonable particularity the grounds on which the request is made, whether any substance normally found in the place of employment has potentially toxic effects in such concentrations as used or found.

On February 22, 1978, NIOSH received a written request for a health hazard evaluation from an officer of the International Union of Electrical Workers, Local 601, an authorized representative of the employees at Westinghouse Electric Corporation's plant in Trafford, Pennsylvania. The Trafford plant manufactures, inter alia, electric insulators by means of an epoxy mold process. The complaint concerned two areas in the Trafford plant, the "bushings aisle" or TC72, and the "epoxy aisle" or TC74, and alleged that workers were suffering allergic reactions as a result of exposure to methyl ethyl ketone. The Director of NIOSH initiated an investigation pursuant to his authority under 29 U.S.C. § 669(a) (6).

On April 21, 1978, an industrial hygienist and two physicians employed by NIOSH performed a walkthrough inspection. They determined that the conditions which led to the complaint concerning TC72 had been remedied and no further evaluation of that area was required. However, although methyl ethyl ketone was found not to be a potential health hazard, hexahydrophthalic anhydride, or HHPA, was used in significant quantities in TC74, and the physicians suspected that it might be causing allergic reactions in some workers. The physicians therefore recommended that environmental and medical testing be done regarding the presence and effect of HHPA in the TC74 area.

Dr. Thomas Wilcox, a Medical Project Officer in . . . NIOSH, and G. Edward Burroughs, an industrial hygienist, visited the site and requested access to the company's medical records of potentially affected employees in the TC74 area. A Westinghouse official replied that access would be difficult because the records were considered confidential. [A footnote describes the records at issue as including "the employee's reported medical history," and "reports of physical examinations given to employees at the time they are hired," which "generally includes a chest xray, a pulmonary function test, hearing and visual tests, a blood count, an examination by a medical doctor."]

. . . .

Thereafter, the Director of NIOSH issued a subpoena duces tecum to Westinghouse's custodian of records at the Trafford plant, requiring the production of "(medical) records of all employees presently employed in the TC74 area and the medical records of all employees who formerly worked in the TC74 area and who now work elsewhere in the plant." Westinghouse refused to honor the subpoena.

. . . .

NIOSH then filed this action in the district court seeking an order to enforce its subpoena. Following a hearing, the district court granted NIOSH's petition and ordered full enforcement of the subpoena . . . . Westinghouse filed this appeal . . . .

[The court finds that Westinghouse had standing to assert its employee's privacy interests in this case and that the documents requested by NIOSH were relevant to an investigation within its statutory authority.]

IV

. . . .

Proliferation in the collection, recording and dissemination of individualized information has made the public, Congress and the judiciary increasingly alert to the threat such activity can pose to one of the most fundamental and cherished rights of American citizenship, falling within the right characterized by Justice Brandeis as "the right to be let alone." . . . Much of the concern has been with governmental accumulation of data and the ability of government officials to put information technology to uses detrimental to individual privacy, which have been facilitated by the spread of data banks and by the increasing storage in computers of sensitive information relating to the personal lives and activities of private citizens . . . .

. . . .

Although the full measure of the constitutional protection of the right to privacy has not yet been delineated, we know that it extends to two types of privacy interests: "One is the individual interest in avoiding disclosure of personal matters, and another is the interest in independence in making certain kinds of important decisions." (citation to *Whalen*) The latter decisions have encompassed "matters relating to marriage, procreation, contraception, family relationships, and child rearing and education." The privacy interest asserted in this case falls within the first category referred to in *Whalen v. Roe*, the right not to have an individual's private affairs made public by the government.

There can be no question that an employee's medical records, which may contain intimate facts of a personal nature, are well within the ambit of materials entitled to privacy protection. Information about one's body and state of health is matter which the individual is ordinarily entitled to retain within the "private enclave where he may lead a private life." It has been recognized in various contexts that medical records and information stand on a different plane than other relevant material. For example, the Federal Rules of Civil Procedure impose a higher burden for discovery of reports of the physical and mental condition of a party or other person than for discovery generally. Medical files are the subject of a specific exemption under the Freedom of Information Act. 5 U.S.C. § 552(b) (6) (1976). This difference in treatment reflects a recognition that information concerning one's body has a special character. The medical information requested in this case is more extensive than the mere fact of prescription drug usage by identified patients considered in *Whalen v. Roe* and may be more revealing of intimate details. Therefore, we hold that it falls within one of the zones of privacy entitled to protection.

Westinghouse concedes that even material which is subject to protection must be produced or disclosed upon a showing of proper governmental interest . . . . In recognition that the right of an individual to control access to her or his medical history is not absolute, courts and legislatures have determined that public health or other public concerns may support access to facts an individual might otherwise choose to withhold. On this basis, disclosures regarding past medical history, present illness, or the fact of treatment have been required . . . . Generally, the reporting requirements which have been upheld have been those in which the government has advanced a need to acquire the information to develop treatment programs or control threats to public health.

. . . .

In the cases in which a court has allowed some intrusion into the zone of privacy surrounding medical records, it has usually done so only after finding that the societal interest in disclosure outweighs the privacy interest on the specific facts of the case. In *Detroit Edison Co. v. NLRB*, 440 U.S. 301, 31317 (1979), the interests of the NLRB and the labor union in giving the union access to employees' scores in psychological aptitude tests to assist the union in processing a grievance were weighed against the strong interest of the Company and its employees in maintaining confidentiality. The Court held the NLRB had improperly compelled disclosure because "(t)he Board has cited no principle of national labor policy to warrant a remedy that would unnecessarily disserve (the Company's interest in test secrecy) and we are unable to identify one."

Thus, as in most other areas of the law, we must engage in the delicate task of weighing competing interests. The factors which should be considered in deciding whether an intrusion into an individual's privacy is justified are the type of record requested, the information it does or might contain, the potential for harm in any subsequent nonconsensual disclosure, the injury from disclosure to the relationship in which the record was generated, the adequacy of safeguards to prevent unauthorized disclosure, the degree of need for access, and whether there is an express statutory mandate, articulated public policy, or other recognizable public interest militating toward access.

Applying those factors in this case, we consider first that NIOSH was established as part of the comprehensive statutory scheme dealing with occupational health and safety embodied in the Occupational Safety and Health Act of 1970. In enacting that statute, Congress noted the " 'grim current scene'. . . (i)n the field of occupational health," and sought, by passage of the statute, "to reduce the number and severity of work-related injuries and illnesses which, despite current efforts of employers and government, are resulting in ever-increasing human misery and economic loss." It was hoped and expected that NIOSH would "provide occupational health and safety research with the visibility and status it merits . . . ." Among the special "research, experiments, and demonstrations" which it is statutorily mandated to conduct are those "necessary to produce criteria . . . identifying toxic substances,"; those necessary to development of criteria "which will describe exposure levels that are safe for various periods of employment;" and those necessary "to explore new problems, including those created by new technology in occupational safety and health, which may require ameliorative action" beyond that provided for in the Act. The research activity in this case, a health hazard evaluation, requires that the Secretary determine "whether any substance normally found in the place of employment has potentially toxic effects in such concentrations as used or found . . . ."

Thus, the interest in occupational safety and health to the employees in the particular plant, employees in other plants, future employees and the public at large is substantial. It ranks with the other public interests which have been found to justify intrusion into records and information normally considered private.

Turning next to the degree of need for access, we have found in section III that NIOSH has shown a reasonable need for the entire medical file of the employees as requested. It seeks those records in order to be able to compare its findings of high levels of antibodies to HHPA and reduced pulmonary function with the comparable findings in the employees before they were exposed to the substances in the TC74 area, and during the course of such exposure. Its need for all of the medical files requested in their complete form has also been satisfactorily demonstrated.

Westinghouse has not produced any evidence to show that the information which the medical records contain is of such a high degree of sensitivity that the intrusion could be considered severe or that the employees are likely to suffer any adverse effects from disclosure to NIOSH personnel. Most, if not all, of the information in the files will be results of routine testing, such as X-rays, blood tests, pulmonary function tests, hearing, and visual tests. This material, although private, is not generally regarded as sensitive. Furthermore, since Westinghouse's testing and NIOSH's examination of the records are both conducted for the purpose of protecting the individual employee from potential hazards, it is not likely that the disclosures are likely to inhibit the employee from undergoing subsequent periodic examinations required of Westinghouse employees.

Finally, we must consider whether there are effective provisions for security of the information against subsequent unauthorized disclosure. Westinghouse argues that the security of the information in this case is inadequate. It stresses that the statute authorizes use of outside contractors for data processing and analysis, and contains neither means to police compliance with nondisclosure nor adequate sanctions for unwarranted disclosure. It also argues that removal by NIOSH of individual identifiers before disclosure to those parties is made will be inadequate, since only obvious identifiers, such as names and addresses, are deleted, but that identification may still be possible because more idiosyncratic identifiers will be included in the disclosed materials. For these reasons, Westinghouse conditioned its compliance with NIOSH's request for the records in issue on the provision by the government of written assurance that the contents of the employees' medical records will not be disclosed to third parties, a condition the government has refused to accept.

The district court . . . concluded that the "evidence indicates that NIOSH's procedures of safekeeping the records and of removing the names and addresses of the individuals in its compilation of published data represents sufficiently adequate assurance of nondisclosure by [NIOSH]." We see no reason to disturb this conclusion.

The applicable regulation expressly provides that unless otherwise specifically provided, "no disclosure will be made of information of a personal and private nature, such as information in personnel and medical files, . . . and any other information of a private and personal nature." Only aggregate data is included in the forms of the study distributed to employees and others. The excerpted data which is retained by NIOSH is maintained in locked cabinets, inside the Medical Section of the agency, in rooms locked during non-office hours. Material from small studies is not placed on computers; data from large studies is removed from the computer after six months. NIOSH has represented that no outside contractors are used for small studies, such as the one in issue here, and that when such contractors are used, they are bound to nondisclosure by their contract with NIOSH, as required by 5 U.S.C. § 552a(m). In the absence of any contrary evidence produced by Westinghouse, we cannot conclude that there are inadequate safeguards against disclosure.

Accordingly, we believe that the strong public interest in facilitating the research and investigations of NIOSH justify this minimal intrusion into the privacy which surrounds the employees' medical records, and that Westinghouse is not justified in its blanket refusal to give NIOSH access to them or to condition their disclosure on compliance with its unilaterally imposed terms.

V

. . . We recognize, however, that there may be information in a particular file which an employee may consider highly sensitive. Westinghouse has represented that the files are not limited to employment-related concerns but include records of the employees' personal consultations with the company physician and the physician's ministrations on a broad spectrum of health matters. Employees absent from work for medical reasons must clear through the medical department on their return. The medical records also contain reference to payments made under Westinghouse's comprehensive medical insurance program. Since the employees had no prior notice that their medical records might be subject to subsequent examination, they may have raised with the company physician medical matters unrelated to their employment which they consider highly confidential. We cannot assume that an employee's claim of privacy as to particular sensitive data in that employee's file will always be outweighed by NIOSH's need for such material.

Although Westinghouse has been permitted to assert the general claim of privacy on behalf of all of the employees, and has done so vigorously on the employees' behalf, each employee is entitled to make an individual judgment as to whether s/he regards the information so sensitive that it outweighs that employee's interest in assisting NIOSH in a health hazard investigation that may benefit the employee. We do not think it appropriate to permit Westinghouse to assert the claims of individual employees to privacy in particular documents. Each employee is uniquely capable of evaluating the degree of confidentiality which s/he attaches to discrete items of information in his or her file.

Westinghouse has suggested that the employees' privacy rights will not be adequately preserved unless their written consents are obtained. One district court has already conditioned the disclosure of personal identifiers on conducting a due process hearing. We believe that the requirement of securing written consent may impose too great an impediment to NIOSH's ability to carry out its statutory mandate. Although the number of employees involved in this particular investigation is not unwieldy, totalling no more than 100 employees, there may be other instances where the number of employees involved makes securing written consent difficult. Furthermore, there is the possibility that some employees will withhold consent either arbitrarily or because they do not understand the full nature of the investigation. Finally, some employees may withhold consent because they believe that is the course desired by their employer.

Under the circumstances, we believe the most appropriate procedure is to require NIOSH to give prior notice to the employees whose medical records it seeks to examine and to permit the employees to raise a personal claim of privacy, if they desire. The form of notice may vary in each case . . . . The touchstone should be provision for reasonable notice to as many affected individuals as can reasonably be reached; an opportunity for them to raise their objections, if any, expeditiously and inexpensively; preservation of confidentiality as to the objections and the material itself from unwarranted disclosure; and prompt disposition so that NIOSH's evaluation is not hampered. We are confident that the district court will be able to oversee this procedure which should, in the main, be self-executing by the parties.

. . . .

NOTES AND QUESTIONS

1. **Investigation, research or surveillance?** *Westinghouse* illustrates one way that an administrative agency can obtain data to investigate health risks to a particular person or group of people. How would you characterize NIOSH's actions? The court introduces its opinion by saying that it is asked "to reconcile the privacy interests of employees in their medical records with the significant public interest in research designed to improve occupational safety and health." Is NIOSH conducting research? NIOSH issued a subpoena asking the company to produce employee medical records to determine whether those employees had experienced adverse health effects from HHPA in the workplace. And it did so at employees' request. The "research" activity in this case appears to be an investigation directly for the benefit of existing Westinghouse employees (which might also provide information for former employees). If NIOSH later uses the results of its investigation to develop standards that limit (or permit) exposure to HHPA in the workplace, is it then conducting research?

NIOSH's request was a one-off demand for specific records, not for the continuing or perpetual submission of information, as in a surveillance program. Westinghouse could and did contest the subpoena, leaving it to a court to determine the legitimacy of NIOSH's demand. While the governing statute included NIOSH's authority to conduct certain investigations and research activities, NIOSH did not assume that it could automatically obtain medical records without a subpoena, which would be subject to objection by the recipient or the workers whose information would be disclosed. Does this statutory structure authorize NIOSH to demand employee medical records without a subpoena? An agency's scope of authority to conduct research is specified by its own governing statute, so that it is unwise to generalize from one statute to another.

The NIOSH request in *Westinghouse* was prompted by the employees at risk; it was not spontaneously generated by the agency. How might this affect the court's view of the need for the information? Can NIOSH represent the employees? Companies may have little incentive to encourage investigations into workplace hazards. Is there greater justification for obtaining access to employee records than patient records? Do patients have more bargaining power than employees? Are there any limits on when a company is entitled to assert the privacy interests of its employees?

2. **A balancing test.** The *Westinghouse* court suggests six factors to weigh the government's interest in obtaining medical information and the individual's interest in preventing disclosure to the government: "The factors which should be consid-

ered in deciding whether an intrusion into an individual's privacy is justified are the type of record requested, the information it does or might contain, the potential for harm in any subsequent nonconsensual disclosure, the injury from disclosure to the relationship in which the record was generated, the adequacy of safeguards to prevent unauthorized disclosure, the degree of need for access, and whether there is an express statutory mandate, articulated public policy, or other recognizable public interest militating toward access." Although the U.S. Supreme Court has not had occasion to consider this six-factor balancing test, some of its elements can be discerned from the high court's earlier decisions. It remains unclear whether all of these factors should be considered and how much each should weigh.

Westinghouse has also been cited as endorsing a public health exception to privacy, sometimes in *dictum. See, e.g., Sterling v. Borough of Minersville*, 232 F.3d 190, 195 (3d Cir. 2000) ("Public health or like public concerns may justify access to information an individual may desire to remain confidential"); *Fraternal Order of Police v. City of Philadelphia*, 812 F.2d 105, 110 (3d Cir. 1987) ("Disclosure may be required if the government interest in disclosure outweighs the individual's privacy interest"). Consider what is meant by public health in each of these cases. How would you interpret such references?

   3. **Environmental disease surveillance.** There is growing interest in identifying sources in the environment that might cause disease. To study the possible relationships between exposure to such hazards and disease, many states have created surveillance systems, which collect data on exposures and diseases — primarily chronic diseases — that are suspected to be caused by environmental sources. Environmental hazards include chemical, biological, and physical agents in the indoor or outdoor environment at home or at work, such as pesticides, dioxins, tobacco smoke, and radiation. Some environmental specialists also include social concerns like biomechanical stressors, such as repetitive motion, and psychological stress, as from sexual harassment in the workplace. Of particular concern are environmental hazards that potentially or actually cause illness in humans. Chronic diseases or genetic conditions that may be caused or aggravated by exposure to something in the environment can be considered environmental diseases. Thus, environmental diseases can include any illness or condition that is not an infectious disease caused by a virus, bacterium, or parasite.

   Environmental surveillance, or tracking as it often called, can mean obtaining information about one or more of the following: the source of an environmental hazard; human exposure to a hazard; or human health outcomes from exposure to the hazard. In order to determine whether a particular chemical, for example, causes disease in human beings, it would be necessary to find out whether the people who are exposed to that chemical ultimately get a particular disease (that is not attributable to some other source). This may require linking exposure to the chemical to specific health outcomes. More sophisticated studies of environmental diseases seek to determine what is produced, when and where it is released, who is exposed to it, and what happens to them later. Such studies could use anonymous data to correlate exposures with disease in populations with specific characteristics, such as workplace, age or sex. Alternatively, identifiable data can be used to link particular individuals with specific environmental exposures. That data could be obtained from medical records, cancer registries or government agencies like the

Social Security Administration, Medicare, or worker compensation systems. The type of data that could be obtained from other sources includes a person's name or unique identifier such as social security number, gender, date of birth, diagnostic code (ICD9) for disease, date of diagnosis, race/ethnicity, address or latitude/longitude of residence, occupational history, school, and smoking history. An efficient environmental health surveillance system would be linked with some or all of these other registries or records.

    4.   **Environmental tracking or mandatory reporting?** Recall the discussion in Chapter 7, *supra*, on surveillance programs that rely on mandatory reporting. Do chronic disease surveillance programs meet the criteria for mandatory reporting? The Massachusetts Department of Public Health considered just this question and adopted the following regulation as part of its disease surveillance regulations:

> Surveillance of Diseases Possibly Linked to Environmental Exposures, 105 MASS CODE REGS. 300.192

>   The Department is authorized to collect from health care providers and other persons subject to 105 CMR 300.000 *et seq.*, and/or prepare data, as detailed in 105 CMR 300.190 and 105 CMR 300.191, on individuals evaluated for or diagnosed with the following diseases possibly linked to environmental exposures:

> > Amyotrophic Lateral Sclerosis (ALS)
> > Aplastic Anemia
> > Asthma
> > Autism Spectrum Disorder (ASD)
> > Multiple Sclerosis (MS)
> > Myelodysplastic Syndrome (MDS)
> > Scleroderma
> > Systemic Lupus Erythematosus

    Does the above regulation authorize the Department to demand the information without patient consent? The Department concluded that the text gave the Department the authority to *receive* the data, but did not require the Department to demand the information without patient consent. Other states have adopted statutes or regulations that do authorize or permit compulsory reporting without individual consent. Their goal is to ensure that the data collected include all (or, realistically, almost all) cases of disease in order to accurately analyze any relationship to environment sources. Which approach do you favor?

NATIONAL PROGRAM OF CANCER REGISTRIES
42 U.S.C. § 280e

(a) In general.

    (1) Statewide cancer registries. The Secretary, acting through the Director of the Centers for Disease Control [and Prevention], may make grants to States, or may make grants or enter into contracts with

academic or nonprofit organizations designated by the State to operate the State's cancer registry in lieu of making a grant directly to the State, to support the operation of population-based, statewide registries to collect, for each condition specified in paragraph (2) (A), data concerning—

(A) demographic information about each case of cancer;

(B) information on the industrial or occupational history of the individuals with the cancers, to the extent such information is available from the same record;

(C) administrative information, including date of diagnosis and source of information;

(D) pathological data characterizing the cancer, including the cancer site, stage of disease (pursuant to Staging Guide), incidence, and type of treatment; and

(E) other elements determined appropriate by the Secretary.

. . . .

(c) Eligibility for grants.

(1) In general. No grant shall be made by the Secretary under subsection (a) unless an application has been submitted to, and approved by, the Secretary. Such application shall be in such form, submitted in such a manner, and be accompanied by such information, as the Secretary may specify. No such application may be approved unless it contains assurances that the applicant will use the funds provided only for the purposes specified in the approved application and in accordance with the requirements of this section, that the application will establish such fiscal control and fund accounting procedures as may be necessary to assure proper disbursement and accounting of Federal funds paid to the applicant under subsection (a) of this section, and that the applicant will comply with the peer review requirements under sections 491 and 492 [42 USC § 289 and § 289a].

(2) Assurances. Each applicant, prior to receiving Federal funds under subsection (a), shall provide assurances satisfactory to the Secretary that the applicant will —

(A) provide for the establishment of a registry in accordance with subsection (a);

(B) comply with appropriate standards of completeness, timeliness, and quality of population-based cancer registry data;

(C) provide for the annual publication of reports of cancer data under subsection (a); and

(D) provide for the authorization under State law of the statewide cancer registry, including promulgation of regulations providing —

(i) a means to assure complete reporting of cancer cases (as described in subsection (a)) to the statewide cancer registry by hospitals or other facilities providing screening, diagnostic or therapeutic services to patients with respect to cancer;

(ii) a means to assure the complete reporting of cancer cases (as defined in subsection (a)) to the statewide cancer registry by physicians, surgeons, and all other health care practitioners diagnosing or providing treatment for cancer patients, except for cases directly referred to or previously admitted to a hospital or other facility providing screening, diagnostic or therapeutic services to patients in that State and reported by those facilities;

(iii) a means for the statewide cancer registry to access all records of physicians and surgeons, hospitals, outpatient clinics, nursing homes, and all other facilities, individuals, or agencies providing such services to patients which would identify cases of cancer or would establish characteristics of the cancer, treatment of the cancer, or medical status of any identified patient;

(iv) for the reporting of cancer case data to the statewide cancer registry in such a format, with such data elements, and in accordance with such standards of quality timeliness and completeness, as may be established by the Secretary;

(v) for the protection of the confidentiality of all cancer case data reported to the statewide cancer registry, including a prohibition on disclosure to any person of information reported to the statewide cancer registry that identifies, or could lead to the identification of, an individual cancer patient, except for disclosure to other State cancer registries and local and State health officers;

(vi) for a means by which confidential case data may in accordance with State law be disclosed to cancer researchers for the purposes of cancer prevention, control and research;

(vii) for the authorization or the conduct, by the statewide cancer registry or other persons and organizations, of studies utilizing statewide cancer registry data, including studies of the sources and causes of cancer, evaluations of the cost, quality, efficacy, and appropriateness of diagnostic, therapeutic, rehabilitative, and preventative services and programs relating to cancer, and any other clinical, epidemiological, or other cancer research; and

(viii) for protection for individuals complying with the law, including provisions specifying that no person shall be held liable in any civil action with respect to a cancer case report provided to the statewide cancer registry, or with respect to access to cancer case information provided to the statewide cancer registry.

SOUTHERN ILLINOISAN v. ILLINOIS DEP'T OF PUBLIC HEALTH
844 N.E. 2d 1 (Ill. 2006)

McMORROW, JUDGE.

Plaintiff, the Southern Illinoisan newspaper, requested the Illinois Department of Public Health (Department) to release from the Illinois Health and Hazardous Substances Registry (Cancer Registry) certain data about incidents of neuroblastoma, a rare form of childhood cancer. The Department denied plaintiff's request. Thereafter, plaintiff filed a complaint in the circuit court of Jackson County pursuant to the Freedom of Information Act (FOIA) (5 ILCS 140/1 *et seq.* (West 1998)), requesting judicial review of the Department's denial. The circuit court . . . ordered the Department to release the requested data. [The appellate court affirmed.]

. . . Plaintiff, the Southern Illinoisan, is a daily newspaper published in Carbondale, Illinois . . . . [Plaintiff requested copies of documents including type of cancer, zip code and date of diagnosis — but not names — relating to the incidence of neuroblastoma in Illinois from 1985 to 1997.]

. . . .

. . . [The Department argued that] although the [Illinois] FOIA provides that "each public body shall make available to any person for inspection or copying all public records", there are certain exceptions to disclosure, including "information specifically prohibited from disclosure by . . . State law." The Department argued that the information requested by plaintiff was prohibited from disclosure under this provision because the Registry Act precludes disclosure of information which reveals "the identity, or any group of facts which tends to lead to the identity, of any person whose condition or treatment is submitted to the Illinois Health and Hazardous Substances Registry."

In support of its position, the Department attached the affidavit of Dr. Latanya Sweeney, Ph.D., a professor of computer science and public policy at Carnegie Mellon University. In her affidavit, Dr. Sweeney attested that, at the behest of the Department, she conducted an experiment to determine if persons listed in the Cancer Registry could be identified from only the three information fields requested by plaintiff: the type of cancer, the date of diagnosis, and the patient's ZIP code. According to Dr. Sweeney, she compared the data in these three information fields to other data sets that are available to the general public, such as patient names, addresses, phone numbers, financial information, and other medical information. Even though the data in the Cancer Registry did not have identifiers such as names, addresses and telephone numbers, Dr. Sweeney attested that through her experiment she could "show how persons can be re-identified from the Illinois Cancer Registry when the combination of data elements that includes only type of cancer, date of diagnosis, and zip code is provided." According to Dr. Sweeney, her experiment "established that a significant number of individuals in the general public with access to a personal computer, using traditional database software, who purchase or acquire public data sets will be able to reidentify individuals in the

Illinois Cancer Registry," as this "seemingly anonymous information can be re-identified by linking the information to databases that are made available to the public."

. . . .

This appeal presents the sole question of whether the information requested from the Department by plaintiff pursuant to the [Illinois] FOIA "tends to lead to the identity" of patients listed in the Cancer Registry, thereby violating section 4(d) of the Registry Act (410 ILCS 525/4(d) (West 1998)). If so, then the information requested by plaintiff is exempt from disclosure under section 7(1)(a) of the FOIA.

. . . .

. . . Plaintiff contends that the FOIA is to be interpreted in favor of disclosure and that the exemptions from disclosure are to be read narrowly. In addition, plaintiff asserts, the public policy concerns which underpin the Registry Act — most specifically that the Registry information be used to alert citizens about risks, early detection and treatment of cancers known to be elevated in their communities — favor disclosure of the information requested by plaintiff. Although plaintiff acknowledges that the Registry Act has an "inherent tension" between patient privacy and a community's right to know about elevated levels of cancer in its geographic area, plaintiff argues that the balance is tipped by the fact that the FOIA is to be given a liberal interpretation and that the exceptions to disclosure are narrow.

. . . .

. . . In sections 2(b) and (c), the legislature enumerated the purposes of the Registry Act:

"(b) It is the purpose of this Act to establish a unified Statewide project to collect, compile and correlate information on public health and hazardous substances. Such information is to be used to assist in the determination of public policy and to provide a source of information for the public, except when public disclosure of the information would violate the provisions of subsection (d) of Section 4 concerning confidentiality.

(c) In particular, the purpose of the collection of cancer incidence information is to:

(1) monitor incidence trends of cancer to detect potential public health problems, predict risks and assist in investigating cancer clusters;

(2) more accurately target intervention resources for communities and patients and their families;

(3) inform health professionals and citizens about risks, early detection and treatment of cancers known to be elevated in their communities; and

(4) promote high quality research to provide better information for cancer control and to address public concerns and questions about cancer."

. . . . [S]ection 4(d) of the Registry Act provided in pertinent part:

"The identity, or any group of facts that tends to lead to the identity, of any person whose condition or treatment is submitted to the Illinois Health and Hazardous Substances Registry is confidential and shall not be open to public inspection or dissemination."

. . . .

. . . We must determine the meaning of the phrase "tends to lead to the identity" as it is used in section 4(d) of the Registry Act. Because this is an issue of statutory interpretation, our review is *de novo*.

. . . .

. . . [W]e find that it is not entirely clear from section 4(d) of the Registry Act whether the legislature intended that disclosure of the Registry information is prohibited upon a showing by the Department that the challenged information "tends to lead to the identity" of Registry patients based upon experiments conducted by *experts*, such as Dr. Sweeney, or if disclosure is prohibited upon a showing that the *general public at large* is capable of making such identifications . . . . Given this uncertainty in interpretation, we are especially mindful of the public policy which underpins both the Registry Act and the FOIA: to ensure public disclosure of government information that is not otherwise protected. We also note, as stated above, that under the FOIA, public records are presumed to be open and accessible, with exceptions to disclosure to be read narrowly. Accordingly, in light of these public policies, we conclude that information "tends to lead to the identity" of Registry patients only if that information can be used by the general public to make those identifications.

. . . .

In sum, we conclude, as did the lower courts in this matter, that the Department failed to demonstrate that the release of the Cancer Registry information requested by plaintiff tends to lead to the identity of the specific persons described in that data. [I]t was the Department's burden under the FOIA to establish that its refusal to release the requested material to plaintiff fell within the exemption set forth in section 7(1)(a) of the FOIA, by establishing that the information was prohibited from disclosure pursuant to section 4(d) of the Registration Act. In the absence of more definitive proof that individuals of the general public would have the ability to duplicate Dr. Sweeney's multistep experiment, our decision is guided by the public policy of this state, which "encourages a free flow and disclosure of information between government and the people." [W]e we conclude that the lower courts properly instructed the Department to disclose to plaintiff the information contained in its FOIA request.

As a final matter, we note that in granting plaintiff access to the requested information from the Cancer Registry, the circuit court ordered plaintiff not to identify those on the Cancer Registry list. We believe that the court's order expressly forbidding plaintiff to use the information in an improper manner will ensure its confidentiality.

NOTES AND QUESTIONS

5. Cancer registries. The National Cancer Registries Amendments were enacted with the goal of building a national database of cancer cases. States are encouraged to create state registries by the offer of federal funding. The text of the statute included above states that applicants for funding must provide an assurance that, among other things, the applicant will "provide for the authorization under State law of the statewide cancer registry, including promulgation of regulations providing . . . a means to assure complete reporting of cancer cases . . . to the [registry] by hospitals or other facilities providing screening, diagnostic or therapeutic services to patients with respect to cancer . . . by physicians, surgeons, and all other health practitioners diagnosing or providing treatment for cancer patients . . . " How might those goals be accomplished? Must the information provided be personally identifiable? Section 208e(a) (1) (A) seeks data on "demographic information," which the CDC interprets to include a person's name, street address, city, county, state, zip code, census tract, race, sex, birth date, social security number, and industrial or occupational history. It would be difficult to study causes of specific cancers without being able to link individual cases to past exposures to cancer risks or to investigate whether particular treatments are effective without knowing how each patient fared. Cancer researchers generally assume that, to be useful for research, registries must contain identifiable information about each patient.

Does "authorization under State law" require that the data be collected or reported without the patient's knowledge or consent? Can Congress require the states to enact a mandatory reporting law as a condition of federal funding? *See* the discussion of conditions on federal spending in Chapter 3, Part E, and federal funding of surveillance programs in Chapter 7, Part D, Note 14, *supra*. Many states have adopted mandatory cancer reporting laws as the most efficient or desirable means of collecting the data. Would states that do not adopt a mandatory reporting law qualify for federal funding? If not, could the state claim that the condition was beyond the power of Congress to impose in order to obtain funding nonetheless? *See United States v. Am. Library Ass'n*, 539 U.S. 194 (2003); *New York v. United States*, 505 U.S. 144 (1992); *South Dakota v. Dole*, 483 U.S. 203 (1987). As a practical matter, it might be difficult to convince the CDC that a registry's data are "complete" in the absence of a law requiring that all cases be reported without patient consent. Could patients or physicians challenge the state's power to require reporting without consent? Would the law meet the *Westinghouse* balancing test? Does that test even apply to the ongoing collection of data?

6. Public access to registry information. The Illinois cancer registry at issue in Southern Illinoisan, excerpted above, required data to be submitted without patient consent by 400 different mandated reporters, including all Illinois hospitals, ambulatory surgical centers and radiation treatment centers, as well as voluntary reporting by some physicians and laboratories. The state also obtained data on patients who moved out of state through agreements with systems in 13 other states. *Southern Illinoisan*, 218 Ill.2d at 400. The data includes demographic information that identifies the patient (including address, county of residence, race and gender, and whether the patient used alcohol and/or tobacco) and medical information (including type of cancer, how it was diagnosed, date of diagnosis, how much it has spread, and treatment and survival information). *Id.* Public data sets with limited aggregate information are available from the Department. The newspaper wanted individual level data to report on possible links between local hazards and cancer, but did not seek the individuals' identities. Is this a legitimate goal of the media? The Registry? The Department first tried to protect the data's release by stating that it was data "collected in a medical study." *Id.* at 395. It argued that data should not be released except for purposes of investigations. Do you see any problems with this argument? Certainly the data were used for research of various sorts.

7. **Using registries to identify environmental hazards.** Cancer registries provide some data to study whether particular environmental hazards can cause specific cancers. Environmental and occupational health specialists and epidemiologists are especially supportive of such registries for that reason. In principle, information about industrial hazards could be obtained from industry. In practice, legislation compelling industry reporting has faced political opposition. Cancer registries may be the fallback option. However, cancer registries do not typically collect relevant data about a patient's occupational or geographic exposures, which would be needed for linking exposures to illness. Occupations are often listed by category rather than employer and location. By the time they are diagnosed, many cancer patients are listed simply as retired. To investigate the relationship between health and environmental hazards, a different approach may be needed.

The CDC's National Environmental Public Health Tracking Program provides grants to 23 states (and one city) to create their own tracking systems that could be linked to the CDC's National Tracking Network. CDC, National Environmental Public Health Tracking Program, www.cdc.gov/nceh/tracking/ (visited Nov. 2013). California received a CDC grant in 2002 to develop its program. A working group, created to develop the system, recommended collecting data on the use and distribution of chemical, physical, and biological hazards, rather than relying on patient medical records alone. *See* STRATEGIES FOR ESTABLISHING AN ENVIRONMENTAL HEALTH SURVEILLANCE SYSTEM IN CALIFORNIA: REPORT OF THE SB 702 WORKING GROUP XV (California Policy Research Center, 2004. The group also favored research studies on hazards and health outcomes, rather than physician reporting, to collect data, noting that "Physician case reporting has not generally proven to be fruitful or reliable outside the framework of infectious disease because of widespread underreporting and inconsistency of diagnostic criteria." *Id.* at 32.

The results of such studies may help researchers learn more about the causes of disease, especially cancer, asthma, and lead poisoning, and where certain diseases are concentrated. Studies may also discover that certain racial, ethnic, or age groups are more or less susceptible to chronic diseases. Policy makers could use the results for future policy decisions with respect to water purity and pollution, safe methods for handling toxic substances, or recommendations to physicians to offer tests for certain chemicals to patients who work in industries using those chemicals. Cities and states could use the information to change standards for construction, land use, zoning, and licensing certain businesses. It may also create baseline information about the kinds of risks that people who live or work in particular places may be subject to, which may interest their employers and insurers. Policymakers might be able to determine whether, for example, a large chemical spill is likely to add a small or large risk of cancer to people in that neighborhood. The cost of a large environmental tracking system may be quite high, however. A statewide California registry for Parkinson's and Alzheimer's diseases alone was estimated to require at least $8.3 million to create and more than $1 million a year to operate. If a federal agency did not fund such programs, where might a state obtain the necessary resources to pay for them?

8. **Student educational records.** For an interesting case involving claims that a survey of student behaviors and exposures to health risks violated the Family Educational Records Privacy Act, the Protection of Pupil Rights Amendment, and the United States Constitution, *see C. N. v. Ridgewood Board of Education*, 430 F.3d 159 (3d Cir. 2005).

H. GILBERT WELCH, OVERDIAGNOSED — MAKING PEOPLE SICK IN THE PURSUIT OF HEALTH,
11–13, 15–16, 23, 24, 32, 37–38, 173–178, 190 (2011)

Genesis

A couple of winters ago, Mr. Bailey's name appeared on a list given to me by clinic administrators identifying which of my patients had blood pressures that the VA [Department of Veterans Affairs] considered somehow suboptimal. His diastolic blood pressure had been fine, in the 70 to 90 range. But his systolic blood pressure had been high at his last two visits — both measurements in the 160s . . . .

. . . No doctor wants to be identified as being out of step with practice norms . . . .

So I started Mr. Bailey on one twenty-five milligram tablet of hydrochlorothiazide every morning. Hydrochlorothiazide is a diuretic: it makes a person urinate more, which lowers the amount of fluid in the body (part of the reason it lowers blood pressure) . . . . His blood pressure was down and was normal throughout the spring. Then we had a spell of hot, humid weather. That sort of thing doesn't stop Mr. Bailey. One day he was outside rebuilding a stone wall, lifting heavy rocks and dripping with sweat. And since he's not the kind of guy to tote a water bottle around with him, he got dehydrated. He blood pressure got too low and he collapsed.

When he woke up, he called me . . . . I told him to stop the medicine, drink more water, and see me in clinic.

. . . .

While the treatment of diastolic hypertension dates back to the 1960s, the treatment of systolic hypertension is much more recent. The study that changed our practice was a randomized trial published in 1991 . . . . The study was big — almost five thousand patients. And the follow-up was long — almost five years . . . . If a huge effect exists, it will be found using a small number of people in a short amount of time. If a study is really large and has a long follow-up, that's a clue that the effect the researchers are looking for is small.

In the study of isolated systolic hypertension, the researchers were looking for

. . . death and problems stemming from damage to the blood vessels supplying the heart and brain . . . . [I]n the No Treatment group — 18 percent had bad events over five years. The Treatment group did somewhat better — 13 percent had bad events over five years. [Mr. Bailey decided against treatment.]

* * *

The management of hypertension represented a true paradigm shift in medicine: from treating patients experiencing health problems now to treating people who may develop problems in the future. It marked the beginning of treatment for people without symptoms — people who felt well but who were more likely than the average person to develop disease.

While treatment does save lives, it doesn't save everyone's life. It doesn't prevent every heart attack and stroke. And some people with hypertension aren't destined to experience these problems even without treatment. They face a different problem: overdiagnosis.

We Change the Rules

How Numbers Get Changed to Give You Diabetes, High Cholesterol, and Osteoporosis

[H]ypertension is defined by a numerical rule. If your blood pressure is above a certain number, you have hypertension. If it isn't above that number, you don't. There are many conditions that you can be labeled with simply because you are on the wrong side of a number, not because you have any symptoms. Diabetes is defined by a number for blood sugar; hyperlipidemia is defined by a number for cholesterol; and osteoporosis is defined by a number for bone density. [I]n each of these conditions doctors are trying to get ahead of symptoms — we are trying to make diagnoses early in order to prevent bad events such as leg amputation and blindness from diabetes, heart attacks and strokes from high cholesterol, and wrist and hip fractures from osteoporosis. But whenever we make diagnoses ahead of symptoms, overdiagnosis becomes a problem. Some people diagnosed with diabetes, high cholesterol, and osteoporosis will never develop symptoms or die from the conditions. And this is most likely for those in whom the condition is mild.

. . . These numbers — called cutoffs or thresholds — determine who has a condition and who doesn't. They determine who gets treatment and who doesn't. And they determine how much overdiagnosis occurs.

Cutoffs are set by expert panels of physicians. I wish I could say that their determinations result from purely scientific processes. But they are more haphazard than that: they involve value judgments, and even financial interests. The experts who select the cutoffs have particular sets of beliefs about what is important. Because these doctors care greatly about the conditions they specialize in, I believe they sometimes lose a broader perspective. Their focus is to do everything they can to avoid the bad events associated with the conditions; their main concern is not missing anyone who could possibly benefit from diagnosis and treatment. So they tend to set cutoffs that are expansive, leading many to be labeled abnormal. They tend to either ignore or downplay the major pitfall of this strategy: treating those who will not benefit.

. . . .

You can see [in the Table below] how changing cutoffs dramatically increased the number of people labeled with the conditions (and who were then said to need treatment). Whether or not that was a good thing for the affected individuals is a tough question. But there's no question about whether or not it was a good thing for business. . . .

Effect of Lower Diagnostic Thresholds on the Number of "Diseased" Americans				
Condition		**Disease Prevalence**		
Change in Threshold	Old Definition	New Definition	New Cases	Increase
Diabetes				
Fasting sugar 140 ≤ 126	11,697,000	13,378,000	1,681,000	14%
Hypertension				
Systolic BP 160 ≤ 140	38,690,000	52,180,000	13,490,000	35%
Diastolic BP 100 ≤ 90				
Hyperlipidemia				
Total cholesterol 240 ≤ 200	49,480,000	92,127,000	42,647,000	86%
Osteoporosis in women				
T score −2.5 ≤ −2.0	8,010,000	14,791,000	6,781,000	85%

We Are Able to See More

. . . .

Imaging technologies [X-rays, ultrasounds, CT scans, MOR scans, PET scans] are very helpful in finding the abnormalities that are making patients sick. But they are also increasingly able to find abnormalities in people who are well . . . . While some may be helped, others are overdiagnosed — a patient is told he has an abnormality, but the abnormality is not destined to progress to cause symptoms or death.

. . . .

. . . A few years ago there was considerable enthusiasm for doing total-body CT scans. . . . One radiologist who had scanned more than ten thousand individuals noted, "The realities are, with this level of information, I have yet to see a normal patient." . . . . In a recent study of over a thousand people who elected to undergo total-body CT screening — people with no symptoms — 86 percent had at least one abnormality detected . . . . [T]he researchers calculated that the average individual had 2.8 abnormalities!

By revealing more and more abnormalities, imaging technologies shift the diagnostic spectrum of abnormalities by including increasingly subtle forms of abnormality. Thus, they decrease the importance of the typical abnormal finding. In other words, because we can see more, the typical abnormality means less. Abnormalities that are detectable only by the new imaging technologies generally include less severe variants, those are less likely to cause symptoms or death. The basic problem was well illustrated by an expert in fractal geometry who posed the deceptively simple question "How many islands surround Britain's coast?" There is no single correct answer; it depends on how many you can see. The number of island will increase with the resolution of the map used to identify them . . . .

. . . .

Get the Big Picture

. . .The rationale behind making more diagnoses works something like this: First, medical science identifies that some intervention improves an important health outcome in a high-risk group. Then someone makes the following supposition: what's good for a group on the severe side of the spectrum of abnormality (the high-risk group) is probably good for a group on the mild side of the spectrum of abnormality (the low risk group). This is a problem of excessive extrapolation.

The issue with extrapolating from severe to mild abnormalities is that, practically speaking, it is often not known whether the same important benefits of treatment will appear in people with mild abnormalities. By *important benefits* I mean avoiding death or major complications of disease (such as a hip fracture or an advanced cancer). These events are so rare in those with mild abnormalities that it would require enormous studies to learn if treatment actually has an important benefit for this group. The studies required may need to be larger than any we could reasonably expect to conduct. So investigators focus on less important but more measurable outcomes — such as bone density or PSA level — as surrogates . . . .

Once someone decides that what is good for a high-risk group must be good for a low-risk group, the stage is set for more diagnosis . . . .

. . . [I]t's a positive feedback loop . . . . Here's how it works. Someone somewhere makes an excessive extrapolation and suggests something that leads to more diagnosis: perhaps that something is more screening, or an expanded definition of abnormal, or more testing in general. Immediately, doctors notice that there are more abnormalities out there than they had previously thought, which in itself promotes more diagnosis. Then population-based statistics, which reflect how many people have the disease (prevalence) or how many are newly diagnosed (incidence), appear to rise. Now the population appears sicker than previously thought. Someone uses the word *epidemic*. To make sure no cases are missed, more diagnosis is recommended. At the same time, the spectrum of detected abnormalities shifts toward milder forms. . . .that in itself is seen as an accomplishment — an effect of better medical care — thereby promoting more diagnosis. Then diseased-based health statistics (such as measurement of five-year survival) appear to improve. Someone uses the phrase *save lives*. To "save" lives, more diagnosis is recommended.

More diagnosis, the resulting "epidemics," and claims that testing can save lives make the public want to seek more diagnosis as well . . . . It's a second self-reinforcing cycle . . . .

. . . [I]magine that you have no symptoms and decide to undergo screening . . . . But now that your results have come back normal and [the possibility of cancer, for example] is off the table, you feel good . . . .

But what has really happened? Basically, the system that promotes early diagnosis induced a measure of anxiety and then took it away. Some have pointed out that the reassurance is largely an illusion — a single normal screening exam has little effect on your overall chance of dying from cancer . . . . Once your anxiety has been raised about a disease, you want to be sure you don't forgo the chance to avoid it in the future. In fact, if you don't get screened and you get sick, you think it will be your own fault. This "anticipated regret" also promotes more testing.

. . . .

. . . What if you learn you really have the disease . . . ? So you go for surgery. If you do well, you assume that you owe your life to early detection. So does everyone else. That is the most powerful positive feedback for more testing. Of course, it is assumed that the tumor was destined to kill you. But the truth is that no one knows whether it was a deadly cancer or whether you were overdiagnosed.

. . . .

Pursuing Health with Less Diagnosis

One reason it is so hard to think more critically about early diagnosis is that it has become synonymous with preventive medicine. Preventive medicine is widely viewed as an unambiguous good — thus, early detection must be an unambiguous good. And it's hard to think critically about things that are assumed to be unambiguously good. So it's important to recognize that early detection is only one aspect of preventive medical care. In fact, some would argue that early detection has nothing to do with prevention, since its whole purpose is to find disease, not prevent it. Of course, the idea is to find abnormalities early in their course and then prevent their consequences. But as you know, many of us harbor abnormalities that are not destined to produce consequences. . . .

Luckily, preventive medicine also involves health promotion. Think of health promotion as what your grandmother might have told you when you were young: don't smoke, eat your fruits and vegetables, and go play outside . . . . Her idea was simple: lead a healthy life.

NOTES AND QUESTIONS

9. When is screening beneficial? Successfully identifying and treating high blood pressure with drugs helped to encourage screening for other conditions. Dr. Welch notes that, according to the CDC, the prevalence of high blood pressure among Americans in 2000 was half of what it was in 1960. Yet his book offers cautionary tales of screening for prostate cancer, breast cancer, thyroid cancer, melanoma and other conditions, when the results cause anxiety, surgery, and side-effects without necessarily preventing premature death. As Welch observes, "The problem with overdiagnosis is overtreatment." WELCH, OVERDIAGNOSIS, at 88.

This concern has been one reason for traditionally limiting screening to populations that are at higher risk of a particular disease than the general population. When low-risk populations are screened, the results are more likely to yield false positives that subject people to further testing and treatment, without preventing disease. Limiting the target population for screening also avoids expense. Therefore, the threshold indicators for screening often become a delicate balancing act.

Overdiagnosis and overtreatment are receiving increased attention. Gilbert Welch, M.D., M.P.H., Professor Medicine at Dartmouth Medical School, after all, is hardly a rebel in medicine, and he is not alone. However, pressures on physicians to detect problems before they become serious — and perhaps seriously costly — and pressures on patients to stay healthy, combined with an emphasis on prevention in general, may make it difficult to resist unnecessary treatment.

Angelina Jolie became the face of prevention when she announced her double mastectomy. Jeffrey Kluger & Alice Park, *The Angelina Effect*, 181(20) TIME 28 (May 27, 2013). In her case, genetic testing — not mammography — found that she carried a BRCAI gene, which, although found among less than 0.24% of women, dramatically increases the risk of breast cancer and is linked with about 10% of breast cancer cases.

10. Breast cancer screening. Breast cancer screening is a politically volatile subject. The National Cancer Institute created controversy in 1997 by concluding that there was little evidence that the benefits of mammography outweighed its risks in women age 40 to 50. The panel's recommendation provoked outrage and was widely ignored. The process repeated itself in 2009, when the U.S. Preventive Services Task Force recommended that women under 50 years of age did not need to get mammograms unless they had specific risk factors, such as a family history of breast cancer. After reviewing the evidence, the panel concluded that screening women under 50 produced too many false positives, which led to unnecessary biopsies and anxiety. Even with false positives, early detection had not decreased breast cancer deaths in that age group. As before, this recommendation provoked an outcry from women who believed that they were being deprived of life-saving care. Judith Graham & Thomas H. Maugh II, *Mammogram Guidelines Spark Heated Debate*, L.A. TIMES, Nov. 17, 2009. After all, some women could benefit. The problem is, our tools are rarely precise enough to identify who could benefit and who could be harmed.

For an informative description of the uncertainties surrounding breast cancer screening, *see* Peggy Orenstein, *The Problem with Pink: The Public Relations War on Breast Cancer Has Been Won. So Why Aren't More Lives Being Saved?*, NEW YORK TIMES MAGAZINE 36, Apr. 28, 2013. Orenstein examines the campaign to encourage women to get mammograms, the somewhat disappointing accuracy of mammograms themselves, and the difficulty of distinguishing benign lumps from those that would develop into symptomatic cancer. The author wonders whether her self-image as a cancer survivor is a delusion. She quotes Gilbert Welch's estimates that mammography benefits about 3 to 13% of women with mammography diagnoses of possible cancer. This translates to between 4,000 and 18,000 women out of the estimated 138,000 women whose screening resulted in a diagnosis of breast cancer. *See also* Steven Woloshin *et al.*, *Cancer Screening Campaigns — Getting Past Uninformative Persuasion*, 367 NEW ENGL. J. MED. 1677, 1678 (2012) (arguing that too many cancer screening campaigns fail to provide the accurate information needed to make responsible decisions).

11.   Screening, testing, treatment, and prevention. In 2006, the CDC recommended universal HIV testing. Is universal testing any different from universal screening? The recommendation to test everyone, regardless of risk factors, has not been widely adopted. The CDC's stated goal is to encourage people who are HIV positive to get treatment, since there is good evidence that antiretroviral drugs substantially reduce morbidity and mortality from HIV, effectively converting HIV into a less threatening chronic disease for most patients. It also cited studies finding that people who get tested are more likely to take precautions to prevent infecting others. However, testing does not necessarily get everyone into treatment. The CDC, of course, does not provide treatment. Note that since HIV is a notifiable disease, more testing would increase the reporting of HIV cases — largely by name. *See* Chapter 7, Part D. Reporting helps achieve a different goal — obtaining more accurate, comprehensive data on the incidence and prevalence of HIV infection. More recently, the CDC recommended using HIV surveillance data to conduct outreach to individuals to get them into medical care. Improving access to care is a priority for both the medical and public health professions. Should health departments use surveillance data to find individuals with positive tests and encourage them to obtain medical care?

George J. Annas, Leonard H. Glantz, & Patricia A. Roche,
Drafting the Genetic Privacy Act:
Science, Policy, and Practical Considerations
23 J. L. MED. & ETHICS 360–66 (1995)

. . . A central question presented by genetic screening and testing is whether the genetic information so obtained is different in kind from other medical information (such as family history and cholesterol levels), and, if so, whether this means that it should receive special legal protection. Genetic information can be considered uniquely private or personal information, for at least three reasons: it can predict an individual's likely medical future for a variety of conditions; it divulges personal information about one's parents, siblings, and children; and it has historically been used to stigmatize and victimize individuals.

The highly personal nature of the information contained in one's DNA can be illustrated by thinking of DNA as containing an individual's coded "future diary." A diary is perhaps the most personal and private document an individual can create. It contains a person's innermost thoughts and perceptions, and is usually hidden and locked to assure its secrecy. Diaries describe the past. The information in one's genetic code can be thought of as a coded probabilistic future diary because it describes an important part of a person's unique future and, as such, can affect and undermine an individual's view of his/her life's possibilities. Unlike ordinary diaries that are created by the writer, the information contained in one's DNA, which is stable and can be stored for long periods of time, is in code and is largely unknown to the person. Most of the code cannot now be broken, but parts are being deciphered almost daily. As decoding techniques get better, and if one's DNA is deciphered without permission, another person could learn intimate details of the individual's likely health future that even the individual does not know. Thus even if one concludes that genetic information that can currently be derived from DNA analysis is like other sensitive medical information, the DNA sample itself, with its ability to yield far more information in the future, remains unique.

Deciphering an individual's genetic code also provides the reader of that code with probabilistic health information about that individual's family, especially close relatives like parents, siblings, and children. Finally, genetic information and misinformation has been used by governments (in U.S. immigration and sterilization policies and in Nazi racial hygiene policies, for example) to discriminate viciously against those perceived as genetically unfit and to restrict their reproductive decisions.

We began our own work by trying to develop rules for gene banks. We soon concluded, however, that although regulating gene banks is necessary to protect genetic privacy, it is not sufficient. We believe that we need federal legislation to protect individual privacy by protecting not only stored DNA samples (which will be mostly in the form of blood samples), but also the genetic information obtained from analyzing DNA samples. To be effective, such legislation must govern activities at least at four points: collection of DNA, analysis of DNA, storage of DNA and information derived from it, and distribution of DNA samples and information derived from DNA samples. We believe that, as a general rule, no collection or analysis of an individual's DNA should be permitted without an informed and voluntary authorization by the individual or the individual's legal representative. Research on nonidentifiable DNA samples need not be inhibited; but research on DNA from identifiable individuals should proceed only with informed consent.

We drafted the Genetic Privacy Act of 1995 (GPA) to codify these rules and to make them uniform throughout the United States. The core of the GPA prohibits individuals from analyzing DNA samples unless they have verified that written authorization for the analysis has been given by the individual or the individual's representative. The individual has the right to do the following:

- determine who may collect and analyze DNA;
- determine the purposes for which a DNA sample can be analyzed;

- know what information can reasonably be expected from the genetic analysis;

- order the destruction of DNA samples;

- delegate authority to another party to order the destruction of the DNA sample after death;

- refuse to permit the use of the DNA sample for research or commercial activities; and

- inspect and obtain copies of records containing information derived from genetic analysis of the DNA sample.

Under the GPA, a written summary of these principles must be supplied to the individual by the person who collects the DNA sample. The GPA requires that the person who holds private genetic information in the ordinary course of business keep such information confidential, and it prohibits the disclosure of private genetic information unless the individual has authorized the disclosure in writing or unless the disclosure is limited to specified researchers for compiling data. Although the GPA itself does not prohibit the use of genetic information by employers and insurance companies (because this is a separate problem from privacy), we believe it would be reasonable public policy to prohibit both employers and health insurance companies from using genetic information in making employment and coverage decisions. Congress should act to protect genetic privacy. While we await congressional action, states can act, and private companies and health care practitioners can voluntarily adopt these privacy rules. The remainder of this summary describes how we made some of the choices that shaped the GPA. The full text of the GPA and Commentary available at: http://web.ornl.gov/sci/techresources/Human_Genome/resource/privacyact.pdf

The most difficult task for anyone wanting to protect genetic privacy is defining what genetic information to protect, as the variety of definitions that have been used in other legislative proposals and enactments indicates. Creating laws for control of genetic information is pointless if there is no real distinction between genetic information and any other medical information . . . .

We began with this definition: The term *private genetic information* means any information about an identifiable individual that has been obtained:

(1) from an analysis of the individual's DNA;

(2) from an analysis of the DNA of a person to whom the individual is genetically related; or

(3) from knowing the status of the individual in a pedigree or family history that has been developed or analyzed for a particular hereditary condition; and that

(4) confirms the diagnosis of a disease;

(5) determines the presence of a gene or genes, or a specific gene marker or gene markers;

(6) indicates that the individual is at increased or decreased risk of developing a disease as a result of having inherited a gene; or

(7) establishes that the individual is a carrier of a gene.

One advantage of this definition is its comprehensiveness; but this is also a problem. Strict adherence to the information practices that the GPA applies to private genetic information would require changes in all medical records and record-keeping practices if such records contain family histories. When doctors ask patients about family histories of heart disease or cancer, they do so because such information may help them assess risk factors about the patient. In a real sense, they are asking for genetic information.

But to regulate this type of genetic information, we believe, is impractical. We were thus presented with this choice: either create a definition for genetic information that is consistent from the viewpoint of theory and principle, but not of much practical value, or design provisions that are capable of practical application that would have the effect of protecting the most private and potentially stigmatizing genetic information. Our final definition thus covers DNA analysis exclusively.

The term *private genetic information* means any information about an identifiable individual that is derived from the presence, absence, alteration, or mutation of a gene or genes, or the presence or absence of a specific DNA marker or markers, and that has been obtained: (1) from an analysis of the individual's DNA; or (2) from an analysis of the DNA of a person to whom the individual is related . . . .

The rules contained in the first sections of the GPA apply to collecting, storing, and analyzing *identifiable* samples, meaning samples that are linkable to an identifiable individual. These rules:

- require particular verbal disclosures before the collection of an identifiable DNA sample for analysis;
- prohibit DNA analysis without prior written authorization;
- prescribe the content of written authorizations;
- acknowledge that a DNA sample is the property of the person who is the source of the DNA;
- provide for routine destruction of DNA samples; and
- require that a notice of rights and assurances be provided to individuals before the collection of a sample.

These provisions require that prior to any DNA analysis, for example, the person be informed about the information that can reasonably be expected to be derived from the analysis, and about the utility, if any, that such information might have to that individual . . . . Given the potential dangers and uncertain benefits of genetic information, genetic counseling is often useful for individuals faced with making the decision to have DNA analyzed. The GPA requires that the person be informed that such counseling exists. It does not require that such counseling be provided to or by anyone; if and how such counseling is obtained is a matter of individual interests and resources.

After verbal disclosures are made, and before any analysis of an identifiable DNA sample can legally be performed, the GPA requires that written authorization be obtained either from the sample source or that person's legal representative. The prescribed contents of a valid authorization are similar to authorizations for other medical diagnostic tests, but contain a few novel items, mostly related to the storage of DNA samples for possible future tests. . . . Under the GPA, the sample source has the right to order the destruction of an identifiable sample at anytime, and has the right to inspect records containing in formation derived from analysis of the sample . . . . The GPA presumes destruction of DNA samples after the authorized analysis has been completed, unless otherwise directed by the sample source . . . . Not all individuals will have the same desire to protect or care about the storage of DNA samples that could be analyzed in the future. To protect autonomy, however, legislation must accommodate a range of individual needs and intentions. By establishing an individually identifiable sample as the property of the sample source, the GPA not only serves the interests of those who would want to maintain exclusive control over their DNA, but also enables those who desire to share or transfer such control to do so . . . Owning one's DNA sample allows transfer of control of the sample in accordance with property law principles.

The GPA limits some of the discretion parents have to consent to genetic testing by prohibiting the analysis of the DNA of children under the age of sixteen for any condition that will not be manifested until after the child reaches adulthood, unless some effective measure can be taken before that time to prevent or ameliorate the condition. This prohibition is consistent with the position of many experts on the effects of genetic testing who strongly caution against childhood testing unless an effective therapy exists that must be instituted during minority.

This is a departure from the American tradition of granting broad discretion to parents in the areas of decision making and access to information about their children. One reader asked after examining an early draft of the GPA, "You mean I can consent to surgery for my kid, but I can't consent to a painless, harmless genetic test?" The GPA's answer is yes, if that test is to determine that she has a gene associated with an untreatable, unpreventable condition that will not in reasonable medical judgment manifest itself until after the child reaches adulthood. The problem with comparing surgery and drawing a blood or tissue sample to test DNA is in the characterization of the genetic test as "harmless." Although creating no physical risk or harm, it is the risk to the child's privacy interests, in circumstances that present no countervailing benefit for the child, that are protected by prohibiting such predictive testing. The prohibition is similar to that against parental consent for research on children when a risk of harm but no benefit to the child exists. The goal is to protect the genetic information that is really private information about the adult the child will become, unless a compelling reason can be made not to protect that person's genetic information . . . .

The GPA makes no exception that permits health care professionals to warn genetic relatives who may be at risk for developing a genetic condition. The reasons for this are detailed in an appendix to the GPA. They are both ethical and practical. For example, it would be difficult, if not impossible, to set logical boundaries on such an exception. This "no exception rule" also maximizes the privacy between individuals who receive services that result in private genetic information and their health care providers. It also places the responsibility for informing relatives of their potential genetic risks on the family member who has such knowledge, which is where we believe it morally belongs.

Further, we think it is reasonable to assume that with proper counseling and guidance from supportive and informed practitioners, family members will act in a protective manner toward other family members.

Unlike some existing state laws and proposed federal legislation governing medical information, the GPA does not carve out any emergency exceptions from the requirement that an individual's written authorization be obtained for disclosures of private genetic information. We were unable to identify any emergency situation that would warrant breaches of confidentiality of genetic information in order to protect another individual. The GPA does, however, contain exceptions from the requirement of prior authorization for identification of dead bodies, identification for law enforcement purposes, and in relation to court ordered genetic analysis. Paternity actions and any genetic information resulting from tests conducted for such actions would be covered by the latter provisions. Therefore, no specific section was devoted specifically to paternity actions. The GPA relies on civil remedies, civil penalties, and the possibility of injunctive relief for violations. We did not think criminal sanctions were appropriate for violations of genetic privacy. Criminal penalties could, however, be added were it determined that they would better deter violations.

The gene has become more than a piece of information; it has become "a cultural icon, a symbol, almost a magical force." To the extent that we accord special status to our genes and what they reveal, genetic information is uniquely powerful and uniquely personal, and thus merits unique privacy protection . . . .

. . . .

George J. Annas, Patricia A. Roche, & Robert C. Green, *GINA, Genism, and Civil Rights*
22 BIOETHICS ii (2008)

Culminating its 13-year legislative gestation, The Genetic Information Nondiscrimination Act (GINA), was signed by President George W. Bush on May 21, 2008 . . . . The centerpiece of GINA lies in its broad definitions of genetic information and genetic test. *Genetic information* includes information about an individual or a family member's genetic tests, information about manifestation of a disease in a family member, information about receipt of genetic services and information about participation in clinical research that involves genetic services. Family members include an individual's dependents and first, second, third or fourth degree relatives. Group health plans and health insurers are prohibited from collecting genetic information for underwriting purposes, such as determining eligibility for benefits or setting premiums or employee contribution levels. They are also prohibited from requesting or requiring that an individual or a family member undergo a genetic test.

A *genetic test* refers to any analysis that detects genotypes, genetic mutations or chromosomal changes. It does not include an analysis of proteins or metabolites that is directly related to a manifested disease. Consequently, it does not change the rules on how group health plans and insurers acquire or use information about an enrollee's history of genetic or any other type of illness. Nor does it prevent the insurance company from increasing an employer's premium based on the manifestation of a disease of an employee already enrolled in the plan. As an example, GINA protects a woman who has had a genetic test that reveals that she has a BRAC1 or a BRAC2 mutation, as long as she does not have breast cancer. Once she has breast cancer, she is no longer protected by the act, whether or not her disease was genetically caused. The Act also does not cover other types of insurance, such as long-term care insurance and disability insurance. The long-term care industry has, so far successfully, argued that permitting individuals to get predictive genetic testing, like APOE testing, and then letting them use that information to decide whether to purchase long-term care insurance without disclosing the results, could put the insurers out of business. The Act places restrictions on the collection and uses of genetic information in employment by generally prohibiting employers from requesting or requiring genetic information of an employee or a family member.

Senator Judd Gregg has termed GINA 'the first civil rights bill of the 21st Century,' a phrase often quoted by the Senate's main sponsor of the bill, Senator Olympia Snow and others, and endorsed by the American Civil Liberties Union as well. There are some similarities between racism and what one of us (GJA) has termed 'genism.' It has been suggested, for example, that concentration on the small portion of the genome that makes individuals different from others could encourage racism to be 'replaced or supplemented by genism'. GINA, however, provides narrower protections than existing civil rights laws that prohibit discrimination on the basis of race, or even laws that prohibit discrimination on the basis of sex because it applies only to health insurance and employment discrimination. In this respect it is more like the federal Emergency Medical Treatment and Active Labor Act (EMTALA), which prohibits discrimination in hospital emergency departments based on inability to pay . . . .

Discrimination based on genetics by health insurers and employers is important. But because of the mystique of genetics, the personal reactions to genetic information by individuals themselves, family members, and friends may be even more important. This is because genetic information can radically alter an individual's perception of themselves and their life's prospects, as well as alter how they are perceived by their family members and friends. This helps us see that the broader policy issue in the new genetics is privacy, an issue tangential to GINA . . . .

An act designed to protect genetic privacy would focus on the major actions needed before genetic discrimination is even possible: the collection of DNA samples, the testing of DNA samples, the storage of DNA samples, and the rules regarding the sharing of results of DNA testing. As we suggested in a 1995 ELSI report, a genetic privacy act would forbid the taking of a DNA sample for the purpose of doing a genetic test without the individual's informed consent, would require that consent for genetic testing and the sharing of any test results be specific, and would prohibit the storage of identifiable DNA samples without authorization . . . .

NOTES AND QUESTIONS

12. Federal protection of genetic information. The federal Genetic Information Nondiscrimination Act of 2008 (GINA) combined with the provisions in the ACA prohibiting denial of insurance on the basis of pre-existing conditions, effectively prohibit the use of genetic information to deny health insurance coverage. Long-term care insurance, disability insurance, and other types of insurance are not affected. Whether or not GINA should be expanded remains a controversial issue. *See, e.g.*, Kira Peikoff, *Fearing Punishment for Bad Genes*, NEW YORK TIMES D1, April 8, 2014. Do you think it should cover life insurance and/or disability insurance?

Genetic testing conducted by governmental agents for entirely different purposes has also been challenged on constitutional grounds. In 1995, employees in a federally funded research laboratory brought a lawsuit against their employers claiming that they had been subjected to nonconsensual testing for several conditions including sickle cell trait and that the testing violated their rights to privacy as guaranteed by the constitutions of California and the United States (as well as some statutes). The trial court dismissed the plaintiffs' claims, but in *Norman Bloodsaw v. Lawrence Berkeley Laboratory*, 135 F.3d 1260 (9th Cir. 1998), the circuit court reinstated the constitutional claims, recognizing that few subject areas are more personal and more likely to implicate privacy interests than one's health or genetic makeup. As a result the case went back to the trial court. Neither the California Supreme Court nor the U.S. Supreme Court has subsequently addressed or ruled on the privacy issues raised in *Bloodsaw*. Therefore, the relationship between constitutionally protected rights to privacy and secret or nonconsensual genetic testing of governmental employees has yet to be authoritatively defined by any court.

13. Newborn genetic testing. About 4 million babies are born each year in the United States. Almost all are tested for a variety of genetic conditions. In the 1960s, Dr. Robert Guthrie developed a bacterial assay for phenylketonuria (PKU), which became the model for all newborn screening in the country. A few drops of blood are taken from a newborn (usually from the heel) and placed on what became known as a Guthrie card. PKU is caused by a defective enzyme for metabolizing phenylalanine, a common amino acid in protein rich food, and results in severe neurological damage. In the 1950s, Horst Bickel, a German pediatrician, found that a special diet low in phenylalanine could reduce or prevent the development of mental retardation. Guthrie's test made it easy to identify newborns with PKU in time to start them on the diet that could prevent lifelong damage. This success encouraged a search for other conditions that might be prevented by early intervention. PKU remains the paradigm condition for testing in a newborn because of the relative simplicity and accuracy of the diagnostic test, the need for immediate intervention to prevent severe illness or disability, and the availability of a relatively accessible intervention (the diet) that can prevent the condition. Even the test for PKU, however, produced false positives in the early years, and the special diet given to newborns mistakenly diagnosed with PKU caused neurological damage in those children. Norman Fost, *Genetic Diagnosis and Treatment: Ethical Considerations*, 147 AM. J. DISEASES CHILD. 1190 (1993). Adhering to the diet presents its own challenges, especially for adolescents. It can be more expensive than an ordinary diet. Is such a diet medical treatment? Do health insurance plans pay for such foods as a covered benefit? Who is responsible for providing this "treatment"?

14. Mandatory newborn screening. PKU screening began as a voluntary test, but by the mid 1970's more than 40 states had laws requiring PKU testing for all newborns, some with religious exceptions. In addition to PKU, all states require testing for congenital hypothyroidism and classical galactosemia. Almost all states require testing for hemoglobinopathies (sickle cell), and most states require it for congenital adrenal hyperplasia, biotinidase deficiency, maple syrup urine disease, and homocystinuria. Most expert groups agree that at least the first six of these disorders should be identified by screening, because some form of treatment is available to prevent or ameliorate the condition when given or begun in infancy. For the specific screening requirements in each state, see About Newborn Screening/ Conditions Screened by State, www.babysfirsttest.org/newborn-screening/states (visited Nov. 2013).

Currently, about 38 states require parents to be notified that screening tests will be done, but do not afford the parents the right to refuse. Another 10 states do not require notification or consent. Two states require parental consent. Several states, including Massachusetts, require consent only for pilot studies about conditions for which there is as yet either no satisfactory test or no effective treatment. For an excellent study of how newborn screening works in practice, see STEFAN TIMMERMANS & MARA BUCHBINDER, SAVING BABIES: THE CONSEQUENCES OF NEWBORN GENETIC SCREENING (2013).

What is the justification for mandatory newborn screening laws? Parents have a common law obligation to provide lifesaving and medically necessary medical care for their children. They also have an obligation to act in the best interest of their children. The state also has the *parens patriae* power to protect children in need of necessary medical care. Faden and others argue that parents have a moral obligation to determine whether their newborns have a genetic condition that can be treated, and that such testing should be required by law because there is no reasonable issue of judgment on the prospect of benefit to the child. Ruth R. Faden, *Parental Rights, Child Welfare, and Public Health: The Case of PKU Screening*, 72 AM. J. PUB. HEALTH 1396 (1982). Others argue that because newborn screening is simply another diagnostic test for the newborn's own benefit, it is not justified without parental consent unless effective treatment must begin in the newborn period to prevent significant disability. *See* Sheila Wildeman & Jocelyn Downie, *Genetic and Metabolic Screening of Newborns: Must Health Care Providers Seek Explicit Parental Consent?*, 9 HEALTH L.J. 61 (2001). Since almost all parents want to find out whether their children have a medical problem that can be prevented or treated and there may be some risks associated with false positive tests or the absence of effective treatment, Annas concludes that it is difficult to justify mandatory screening. George J. Annas, *Mandatory PKU Screening: The Other Side of the Looking Glass*, 72 AM. J. PUBLIC HEALTH 1401 (1982). Some parents may object to newborn screening for religious reasons. *See e.g., Douglas County Nebraska v. Anaya*, 269 Neb. 552 (2005). Are there any circumstances in which such objections would permit refusing a test? See the discussion in Chapter 4, *supra*.

A state survey of screening programs found that only 22 states followed up to ensure that parents of newborns are notified of test results, advised about how to care for a child with a positive test, and confirm that treatment has begun. Kenneth D. Mandl *et al.*, *Newborn Screening Program Practices in the United States: Notification, Research and Consent*, 109 PEDIATRICS 269 (2002). How might this affect the justification for mandatory screening programs? How might it affect estimates of costs and benefits?

Is newborn screening a "public health activity"? How does the reason for newborn screening compare with the reason for laws requiring communicable diseases to be reported? What is done to the patient in each case? Are there laws requiring adults to be tested for any genetic or medical condition? How does it compare with the New York City diabetes blood sugar test reporting law, discussed above?

With the "$1,000 genome" approaching at least some physicians have begun advocating whole genome screening for newborns. Is this a good idea? Why or why not? Do newborns have any privacy interests in not having their genomes routinely screened? Do parents have a right to refuse (or to demand) such screening? Where should the records of any such screening be stored, and who should have access to them? Should the genome screen simply be made part of the newborn's medical record? *See, e.g.*, Jocelyn Kaiser, *Researchers to Explore Promise, Risks of Sequencing Newborns' DNA*, 341 SCIENCE 1163 (2013).

15. What conditions should be identified? Several groups have offered criteria for selecting conditions that should be identified in the neonatal period. *See* JeanLouis Dhondt & JeanPierre Farriaux, *Impact of French Legislation on Neonatal Screening, in* HUMAN DNA: LAW AND POLICY 285, 286 (Bartha Maria Knoppers, ed. 1997). The essential elements common to all can be summarized as follows:

1 — the disease will result in severe morbidity (mental and physical) and/or mortality if not diagnosed in the neonatal period;

2 — clinical screening by simple physical examination is not totally effective to identify the disease;

3 — an effective treatment is available;

4 — there is a significant improved prognosis with early treatment;

5 — there is a simple rapid, reliable, inexpensive screening test.

Are these criteria for physicians to use in determining whether to recommend testing or are they criteria for assessing the validity of statutory requirements for tests?

Tandem mass spectronomy and DNA analysis make it possible to screen a single blood sample for many genetic and metabolic conditions. The technology is less expensive than conducting independent analyses for each condition to be identified. To what extent might technology or cost drive decisions about the conditions for which screening is used?

16. Testing or treatment? Genetic testing simply identifies a genetic condition or anomaly; it does not prevent or cure it. Unfortunately, more genetic conditions can be identified than can be prevented or treated. As technology advances, a recurring question is whether to require or even offer tests for conditions that cannot be treated or genetic variations about which little is known. The Institute of Medicine recommended against screening for conditions for which there is no beneficial treatment: "Newborn screening is not a trivial intervention and may raise important health and social issues. For example, detection of an affected child can disrupt the relationship between the parents and the newborn. Parents often experience guilt at having passed on a genetic disorder to their child. In addition, there may be social stigma, and such stigma may be increased if a reliable carrier screening test was available *before* pregnancy or birth." INSTITUTE OF MEDICINE, ASSESSING GENETIC RISKS: IMPLICATIONS FOR HEALTH AND SOCIAL POLICY (Lori Andrews *et al.*, eds. 1994). Does routine screening for genetic conditions foster the idea that genetic variations are so abnormal that they should be prevented or fixed or that parents should not have children with genetic abnormalities? Would it encourage prospective parents to seek genetic enhancements for their future children? For an analysis of the prospects for and implications of genetic enhancement, see MAXWELL J. MEHLMAN, WONDERGENES: GENETIC ENHANCEMENT AND THE FUTURE OF SOCIETY (2003).

In 2005, the American College of Medical Genetics recommended that all newborns be screened for 29 diseases. *Newborn Screening: Toward a Uniform Screening Panel and System — Report for Public Comment*, 70 Fed. Reg. (March 8, 2005), *available at* www.mchb.hrsa.gov/screening (last visited Aug. 2006). States have generally adopted this recommendation, even though not all conditions recommended for screening can yet be prevented or treated.

17. **Genetic research.** Parents of children with a genetic or metabolic condition may have a special interest in encouraging newborn testing. Parents of children with Canavan's disease encouraged a research scientist to develop a genetic test for the disease, collecting tissue samples and medical histories from other families. Although a test was developed, disputes over patent rights divided the families, the investigator, his university, and its assignees. The parents, who had intended for the test to be widely used, affordable or free, objected to the university's royalty demands and brought an unsuccessful suit alleging unjust enrichment, conversion, lack of informed consent, fraudulent concealment, breach of fiduciary duty, and misappropriation of trade secrets. After a federal district court found that the families did not retain any property interest in their genetic information or tissue samples, *Greenberg v. Miami Children's Hospital, Inc.*, 264 F. Supp. 2d 1064 (S.D. Fla. 2003), the families reached a settlement with the university allowing certain universities to use the test royalty-free. Another group did retain control over their samples and information. One family created a foundation to collect tissue samples and genetic information about children with PXE (pseudoxanathoma elasticum) and provided the data to a researcher, who developed a genetic test for the disease. The founder participated in the research sufficiently to be named as a co-inventor on the resulting patent, which allowed the foundation to maintain some control over the use of the test. *See* Eliot Marshall, *Patient Advocate Named Co-Inventor on Patent for PXE Disease Gene*, 305 SCIENCE 1226 (2004), www.sciencemag.org/cgi/content/full/305/5688/1226a (visited Apr. 2014).

18. **Other research with newborn testing samples.** States often keep newborn blood spot samples for research. *See* INSTITUTE OF MEDICINE, CHALLENGES AND OPPORTUNITIES IN USING RESIDUAL NEWBORN SCREENING SAMPLES FOR TRANSLATIONAL

RESEARCH 51–54 (S. Olson & A.C. Berger, Rapporteurs, 2010). In some states, including Texas and Minnesota, parents who discovered this practice objected that they had not been asked for their consent to use the samples for research. *See Bearder v. State of Minn.*, 806 N.W.2d 766 (Minn. 2011); *Beleno v. Tex. Dep't of State Health Servs.* No. 5:09-cv-00188-FB (W.D.Tex., San Antonio Division, filed Mar. 12, 2009). A Texas court ordered the state to destroy its samples.

Are blood samples property? Who owns the blood samples retained by newborn screening programs? *See generally* ROBERT F. WEIR & R. S. OLICK, THE STORED TISSUE ISSUE: BIOMEDICAL RESEARCH, ETHICS AND LAW IN THE ERA OF GENOMIC MEDICINE (2004); Gary E. Marchant, *Property Rights and Benefit-Sharing for DNA Donors?*, 45 JURIMETRICS 153 (2005). Should researchers obtain the parents' consent to allow their children's blood samples to be used in a research study? In *Ande v. Rock*, 647 N.W.2d 265 (Wis. Ct. App. 2002), *reh'g denied*, 650 N.W.2d 840 (Wis. 2002), *cert. denied sub nom. Ande v. Fost*, 537 U.S. 1107 (2003), parents brought a medical malpractice action against researchers for failing to obtain their informed consent to a test for cystic fibrosis in their children and failing to notify them of the results. Their malpractice claim was dismissed because the researchers had no physician-patient relationship with the Andes or their children. The Wisconsin court did not address the substance of any claim that the Andes should have been asked to donate their child's blood sample for the research, because they claimed no injury from the initial collection of blood. Might they have? *See* Ellen Wright Clayton *et al.*, *Informed Consent for Genetic Research on Stored Tissue Samples*, 274 JAMA 1786 (1995) (discussing informed consent to donating tissue samples for genetic research and whether consent should be required for a later different research study using such samples). Might the Andes have brought a successful negligence claim against the researchers for failure to tell them the results of their child's test? The research protocol specified that parents would not be told, and the researchers apparently did not see the results of individual tests for the control group. Who would ordinarily be responsible for advising the parents of the results of a child's diagnostic test? It depends on whether the test was conducted as part of the child's medical care or solely for purposes of research.

19. Genomic research. A real world example of a dispute over the uses of genetic samples arose in Arizona. The Havasupai tribe had given blood samples to Arizona State University researchers to see if there was a genetic reason for the high rate of diabetes Type 2 among tribal members and possibly a cure. The researchers received grants from the university and the National Alliance for Research on Schizophrenia and Depression to study genes believed related schizophrenia, metabolic disorders, and alcoholism, as well as diabetes. No gene linked to diabetes was found among the Havasupai, but the tribe said it was not told of the results. Tribe members later learned, by accident, that doctoral students used the stored DNA to analyze tribe members' DNA for genetic determinants of schizophrenia and to determine whether the tribe descended from ancestors who crossed the Bering Strait, rather than being created in the Grand Canyon as their religious and cultural traditions held. When discovered, the researchers argued that they had permission to use the samples for many types of research, a claim fiercely disputed by the tribe. *See* Katherine Drabiak-Syed, *Lessons from Havasupai Tribe v. Arizona State University Board of Regents: Recognizing Group, Cultural, and*

Dignitary Harms as Legitimate Risks Warranting Integration into Research Practice, 6 J. HEALTH & BIOMED. L. 175 (2010). The tribe sued the university with pro bono legal counsel and finally agreed to a settlement of $700,000, as well as scholarships and assistance in getting funding for a health clinic. Amy Harmon, *Indian Tribe Wins Fight to Limit Research of Its DNA*, THE NEW YORK TIMES, Apr. 21, 2010. *See Tilousi v. Ariz. State Bd. of Regents, Havasupai Tribe v. Ariz. State Univ. Bd. of Regents*, 204 P.3d 1063 (Ariz. 2008), *review granted, review denied by Havasupai Tribe v. Ariz. State Univ. Bd. of Regents*, 2009 Ariz. Lexis 82 (Apr. 20, 2009).

Chapter 9

WEIGHT AND HEALTH

A. INTRODUCTION

Americans have long had an obsession with weight. Ideal body shapes wax and wane — often quite literally. Views on the health effects of too much or too little weight may also vary in light of scientific research and cultural values. This chapter considers whether and how weight or obesity becomes a public health problem. It begins with a description (in Part B) of how different perspectives on weight might define or "frame" size or fat as a problem and how each such definition suggests a different set of responses. The remaining Parts sample materials that support and sometimes refute the different approaches. Part C provides background on weight as a risk factor for chronic diseases. Part D examines weight as a target of discrimination. Part E considers environmental and social measures that affect weight gain. Finally, Part F examines litigation as a way to alter the food supply.

Together, these materials offer a case study of ways to prevent chronic diseases associated with obesity. As you read the materials, consider how you define the problem of weight and what legal options are responsive to that definition.

B. DEFINING THE PROBLEM

Abigail C. Saguy, What's Wrong With Fat?
10–11, 13, 28–30 (2013)

Framing Matters

. . . .

. . . [D]ifferent ways of framing blame and responsibility for obesity imply different courses of action. Believing that weight is under personal control may give some individuals a sense of agency and facilitate positive lifestyle changes. However, people who fail to lose weight despite their best efforts may end up feeling guilt and shame. The belief that body size is under personal control would also justify policies that make people personally accountable, by, say, charging people more for health insurance if they fall into the obese category or obligating them to buy two seats on an airplane if they are too big to fit in a single seat. In contrast, if being fat is seen as due to factors beyond personal control, one can reason that fat people deserve public accommodations, like the disabled enjoy. If being fat as a child is a serious

565

health risk that is due to poor parenting or parental neglect, it may be seen as desirable that social services try to educate the families of fat children or, in extreme cases, even remove fat children from their parents' custody.

If, however, one attributes high rates of obesity among the poor to food insecurity, defined as lacking the money to buy food at some point in the past 12 months, then different policy solutions are likely to be on the table. For instance, one might argue that the food stamp program needs to be more generous so that people do not experience food acquisition cycles, in which food-spending peaks in the first three days after benefits are received and sharply drops at the end of the month when food stamps run out. This perspective relies on research suggesting that this cycle leads to binging on high-calorie foods when the new month's supply of food stamps arrives.

If blame is heaped on the food industry for encouraging unhealthy eating, this implies a need for greater regulation of this industry. If obesity, particularly among the underprivileged, is economically driven by the high cost of fruits and vegetables and the low cost of high-calorie processed foods, this would suggest a need to increase access (*e.g.*, via subsidies) to fruits and vegetables or decrease access (*e.g.*, via taxes) to "bad" foods and drinks. If people are fat because they do not have a safe place to exercise, this may point to a need to improve neighborhood safety and provide public gymnasiums and recreational spaces. If the working poor's weight stems from the fact that they cannot look after their health due to the pressures of working two or three minimum-wage jobs, one could argue that the minimum wage needs to be raised so that people working in these jobs have more time to eat well and exercise. Alternatively, if a penchant for cooking and eating fried food or an aesthetic preference for curvy women is to blame for higher body mass among certain ethnic groups or social classes, some sort of educational intervention may be justified. If obesity is genetically or biologically determined, it may be desirable to invest more in biological interventions. As these examples illustrate, different ways of framing blame and responsibility imply different solutions.

While advocates for these various positions disagree about the causes of and best solutions for the "obesity epidemic," they agree that obesity is a health crisis that urgently needs to be addressed. Indeed, the shared framing of higher body weight as obesity, that is, as medically pathological, allows a wide range of social actors to gloss over different views regarding the causes of fatness and appropriate public health responses to it. Diverse commentators may disagree about why people are getting fatter or how to stop or reverse trends in "obesity," while concurring that higher body weights represent a pressing medical and public health problem. This is an advantage for anti-obesity advocates, as concern over a given issue if more likely to spread when there are multiple causal frames available, and when it is possible to gloss over disagreements regarding these frames, so long as the issue itself is generally acknowledged to be a problem.

. . . .

Framing fatness as a matter of health raises the stakes. No longer merely a question of appearance, fatness becomes a matter of life and death. At the same time, the reframing of fatness as a health problem, rather than, say, as a feminist issue, obscures the ways in which women are judged more harshly based on their appearance than men and are more likely to go on weight-loss diets, take weight-loss drugs, and undergo weight-loss surgery.

Women's concerns about weight are as much or more about class as about health. Achieving and maintaining thinness is an important way in which the contemporary elite in rich nations, and especially elite women, signal their status . . . . The pursuit of (female) thinness is an integral part of elite and middle-class (but not working class) habitus, or a largely unconscious, taken-for-granted, and embodied worldview. The reframing of fatness as unhealthy lends medical authority to this century-old dislike for fatness among the elite and white middle classes. At the same time, it casts as irresponsible cultural preferences for heft among the working classes and, in the American context, some ethnic minorities. The idea that "obesity kills" thus can and is used as a justification for imposing elite white preferences of thinness onto working classes and people of color . . . . At the same time, the framing of obesity as illness brought on by bad personal choices can and is used to blame the poor, rather than poverty or inequality, for negative health outcomes.

. . . .

Problem Frames

Obesity is a disease. Obesity is an epidemic. Obesity is a public health crisis. Obesity is a frame.

Obesity, that is, an understanding of fatness as a medical problem, is the dominant way of understanding fatness in the contemporary United States and Europe. And yet this has not always been the case and is not true everywhere . . . . And it was not until quite recently in the United States, in the middle of the twentieth century, that fatness came to be viewed as a medical problem and even later — at the end of the twentieth century — as a public health crisis. Today, in the United States, a small but vocal group of activists, clinicians, and researchers is attempting to reframe fat as healthy, beautiful, and/or as a basis for group identity and rights . . . .

. . . Problem frames are the different ways in which fat is framed as a problem or as *not* a problem. In addition to the medical frame, these include an *immorality frame*, in which fatness is seen as a moral problem, and a *public health crisis frame*, in which corpulence is viewed as a public health crisis affecting the nation and justifying government intervention. I also identify three problem frames that refute the notion of fatness as a problem, including the Health At Every Size® frame, according to which corpulence is potentially compatible with health; the beauty frame, in which fatness is seen as beautiful; and a fat rights frame, according to which weight-based discrimination, not fatness itself, is the problem.

Table [1] provides an overview of the six problem frames . . . , showing what each frame implies about: what (if anything) is wrong with fatness, what should be done, associated analogies, key supporters, the gender of proponents, and the master frame on which the particular problem frame draws.

TABLE 1

	Immorality	Medical	Public Health Crisis	Health at Every Size	Beauty	Fat Rights
What's wrong with fat?	Fat is evidence of sloth and gluttony, a *moral* problem.	Excess weight/fat is a *medical* problem	Increasing population weights is a *public health* crisis.	The focus on weight loss and dieting are *health* problems.	Tendency to equate thinness with beauty is an *aesthetic* problem.	Weight-based discrimination is a *social justice* problem
What should be done?	People need to exercise moral restraint.	We need to find medical means to help individuals lose weight.	We need to reduce BMI at the population level.	Fat should be seen as beautiful.	Fat should be seen as beautiful.	We need to combat fat bias and weight-based discrimination in employment, public spaces, health care, and elsewhere.
Master frame	Sin	Health	Health, Economic	Health	Aesthetics	Equal Rights
Analogies	Sexual immorality	Cancer, smoking	Epidemic, smoking	Yellow teeth, baldness	Clear complexion	Race, gender, sexual orientation, disability

	Immorality	Medical	Public Health Crisis	Health at Every Size	Beauty	Fat Rights
Proponents	Religious authorities	Bariatric doctors, medical journals	CDC, WHO, IASO, NAASO, IOTE, Hoffman-La Roche, commercial weight-loss companies	ASDAH, NAAFA	NAAFA, fat admirers	Fat rights movement and organizations
Gender of proponents	Male dominated	Male dominated	Male dominated	Female dominated	Male dominated	Female dominated

NOTES AND QUESTIONS

1. **Framing the problem.** Abigail Saguy examines different opinions of weight or size or fat from a sociological perspective. Her work recalls Daniel Kahneman's emphasis on the significance of framing (in Chapter 2, *supra*): how one frames an issue largely determines the permissible array of responses. Is Saguy's Table above a useful tool for differentiating among views of fatness? As you read the articles and cases in the rest of this Chapter, try to identify what each one means by "obesity" and whether that definition circumscribes, expands or dictates appropriate responses.

2. **Obesity as a medical or public health problem.** What does it mean to characterize obesity as a medical problem? What responses would be appropriate? If something is a medical problem, is it a private matter that should be addressed solely within the personal physician-patient relationship? If so, what should physicians do? When does something cross over from a medical problem to a public health crisis? Is it a matter of numbers or money or something else? Saguy notes that, "by current standards, more than 50% of the U.S. population were overweight in the 1970's. Yet it took more than twenty years and concerted advocacy before widespread public concern erupted over an 'obesity epidemic.'" SAGUY, WHAT'S WRONG WITH FAT? at 15. The idea of an obesity epidemic may have found support in research indicating that people tend to associate with others within similar weight categories. *See* Nicholas A. Christakis & James H. Fowler, *The Spread of Obesity in a Large Social Network over 32 Years*, 357 NEW ENGL. J. MED. 370 (2007). Saguy argues that characterizing obesity as a public health crisis converts it into a matter of public policy that justifies government intervention. Do you agree? If government interventions are called for, which interventions are justified?

3. **Cultural frames.** Non-medical frames of fat are rare in medical and public health materials on obesity. For examinations of social views of fat, *see, e.g.,* DEBORAH L. RHODE, THE BEAUTY BIAS: THE INJUSTICE OF APPEARANCE IN LIFE AND LAW (2010); ESTER D. ROTHBLUM & SONDRA SOLOVAY, THE FAT STUDIES READER (2009); KELLY D. BROWNELL *ET AL.*, WEIGHT BIAS: NATURE, CONSEQUENCES, AND REMEDIES (2005); KATHLEEN LEBESCO, REVOLTING BODIES: THE STRUGGLE TO REDEFINE FAT IDENTITY (2004); CHARLOTTE COOPER, FAT AND PROUD: THE POLITICS OF SIZE (1998). The prevalence of anorexia and bulimia has appeared to increase over time alongside obesity. For an examination of the culture encouraging girls to be supermodel thin, see. SHARLENE HESS-BIBER, AM I THIN ENOUGH YET? THE CULT OF THINNESS AND THE COMMERCIALIZATION OF IDENTITY (1996). For works suggesting that fat is often seen as a moral issue, see LYNNE GERBER, SEEKING THE STRAIGHT AND NARROW (2011); AGAINST HEALTH: HOW HEALTH BECAME THE NEW MORALITY (Jonathan M. Metzl & Anna Kirkland, eds., 2010); DEBORAH LUPTON, THE IMPERATIVE OF HEALTH: PUBLIC HEALTH AND THE REGULATED BODY (1995).

4. **Financial frames.** Some critics of the focus on obesity as a health problem point to the money to be made from obesity prevention by makers of diet drugs and weight-loss programs, as well as increased funding for obesity researchers and government agencies responsible for prevention. *See, e.g.,* J. ERIC OLIVER, FAT

POLITICS: THE REAL STORY BEHIND AMERICA'S OBESITY EPIDEMIC (2005). The movie "Super Size Me" gave audiences a glimpse of how much weight could be gained by an exclusive diet of fast food. The food and beverage industries may promote a consumer/personal responsibility frame in order to avoid being blamed for marketing and profiting from unhealthy or fattening products. *See* KELLY D. BROWNELL & KATHERINE BATTLE HORGEN, FOOD FIGHT: THE INSIDE STORY OF THE FOOD INDUSTRY, AMERICA'S OBESITY CRISIS, AND WHAT WE CAN DO ABOUT IT (2004); MARIAN NESTLE, FOOD POLITICS: HOW THE FOOD INDUSTRY INFLUENCES NUTRITION AND HEALTH (2002).

C. HEALTH IMPLICATIONS OF WEIGHT

SURGEON GENERAL, A CALL TO ACTION TO PREVENT & DECREASE OVERWEIGHT & OBESITY
1–2,4,6,8,10–14 (2001)

This *Surgeon General's Call To Action* seeks to engage leaders from diverse groups in addressing a public health issue that is among the most burdensome faced by the Nation: the health consequences of overweight and obesity. This burden manifests itself in premature death and disability, in health care costs, in lost productivity, and in social stigmatization. The burden is not trivial. Studies show that the risk of death rises with increasing weight. Even moderate weight excess (10 to 20 pounds for a person of average height) increases the risk of death, particularly among adults aged 30 to 64 years.

Overweight and obesity are caused by many factors. For each individual, body weight is determined by a combination of genetic, metabolic, behavioral, environmental, cultural, and socioeconomic influences. Behavioral and environmental factors are large contributors to overweight and obesity and provide the greatest opportunity for actions and interventions designed for prevention and treatment.

For the vast majority of individuals, overweight and obesity result from excess calorie consumption and/or inadequate physical activity. Unhealthy dietary habits and sedentary behavior together account for approximately 300,000 deaths every year. Thus, a healthy diet and regular physical activity, consistent with the *Dietary Guidelines for Americans*, should be promoted as the cornerstone of any prevention or treatment effort . . . . Much work needs to be done to ensure the nutrient adequacy of our diets while at the same time avoiding excess calories. Dietary adequacy and moderation in energy consumption are both important for maintaining or achieving a healthy weight and for overall health.

. . . Many experts also believe that physical *inactivity* is an important part of the energy imbalance responsible for the increasing prevalence of overweight and obesity. Our society has become very sedentary; for example, in 1999, 43 percent of students in grades 9 through 12 viewed television more than 2 hours per day.

. . . .

MEASURING OVERWEIGHT AND OBESITY

The first challenge in addressing overweight and obesity lies in adopting a common public health measure of these conditions. An expert panel, convened by the National Institutes of Health (NIH) in 1998, has utilized Body Mass Index (BMI) for defining overweight and obesity. BMI is a practical measure that requires only two things: accurate measures of an individual's weight and height. BMI is a measure of weight in relation to height. BMI is calculated as weight in pounds divided by the square of the height in inches, multiplied by 703 [to adjust for comparisons to weights based on the metric system]. Alternatively, BMI can be calculated as weight in kilograms divided by the square of the height in meters.

Studies have shown that BMI is significantly correlated with total body fat content for the majority of individuals. BMI has some limitations, in that it can overestimate body fat in persons who are very muscular, and it can underestimate body fat in persons who have lost muscle mass, such as many elderly. . . . These definitions are based on evidence that suggests health risks are greater at or above a BMI of 25 kg/m2 compared to those at a BMI below that level. The risk of death, although modest until a BMI of 30 kg/m2 is reached, increases with an increasing Body Mass Index.

. . . .

In children and adolescents, overweight has been defined as a sex and age-specific BMI at or above the 95th percentile, based on revised Centers for Disease Control and Prevention (CDC) growth charts. Neither a separate definition for obesity nor a definition for overweight based on health outcomes or risk factors is defined for children and adolescents.

. . . .

HEALTH RISKS

. . . .

Morbidity from obesity may be as great as from poverty, smoking, or problem drinking. Overweight and obesity are associated with an increased risk for coronary heart disease; type 2 diabetes; endometrial, colon, postmenopausal breast, and other cancers; and certain musculoskeletal disorders, such as knee osteoarthritis. Both modest and large weight gains are associated with significantly increased risk of disease. For example, a weight gain of 11 to 18 pounds increases a person's risk of developing type 2 diabetes to twice that of individuals who have not gained weight, while those who gain 44 pounds or more have four times the risk of type 2 diabetes.

A gain of approximately 10 to 20 pounds results in an increased risk of coronary heart disease (nonfatal myocardial infarction and death) of 1.25 times in women and 1.6 times in men. Higher levels of body weight gain of 22 pounds in men and 44 pounds in women result in an increased coronary heart disease risk of 1.75 and 2.65, respectively. In women with a BMI of 34 or greater, the risk of developing endometrial cancer is increased by more than six times. Overweight and obesity are also known to exacerbate many chronic conditions such as hypertension and elevated cholesterol. Overweight and obese individuals also may suffer from social stigmatization, discrimination, and poor body image.

Although obesity-associated morbidities occur most frequently in adults, important consequences of excess weight, as well as antecedents of adult disease, occur in overweight children and adolescents. Overweight children and adolescents are more likely to become overweight or obese adults; this concern is greatest among adolescents. Type 2 diabetes, high blood lipids, and hypertension, as well as early maturation and orthopedic problems also occur with increased frequency in overweight youth. A common consequence of childhood overweight is psychosocial — specifically discrimination.

. . . .

EPIDEMIOLOGY

The United States is experiencing substantial increases in overweight and obesity (as defined by a BMI ≥ 25 for adults) that cut across all ages, racial and ethnic groups, and both genders. According to self-reported measures of height and weight, obesity (BMI ≥ 30) has been increasing in every state in the nation. Based on clinical height and weight measurements in the 2000 National Health and Nutrition Examination Survey (NHANES), 34 percent of U.S. adults aged 20 to 74 years are overweight (BMI 25 to 29.9), and an additional 27 percent are obese (BMI ≥ 30). This contrasts with the late 1970s, when an estimated 32 percent of adults aged 20 to 74 years were overweight, and 15 percent were obese.

. . . .

The most recent data (1999) estimate that 13 percent of children aged 6 to 11 years and 14 percent of adolescents aged 12 to 19 years are overweight. During the past two decades, the percentage of children who are overweight has nearly doubled (from 7 to 13 percent), and the percentage of adolescents who are overweight has almost tripled (from 5 to 14 percent).

. . . .

DISPARITIES IN PREVALENCE

. . . Disparities in overweight and obesity prevalence exist in many segments of the population based on race and ethnicity, gender, age, and socioeconomic status. For example, overweight and obesity are particularly common among minority groups and those with a lower family income.

. . . .

In general, the prevalence of overweight and obesity is higher in women who are members of racial and ethnic minority populations than in non-Hispanic white women. Among men, Mexican/Americans have a higher prevalence of overweight and obesity than non-Hispanic whites or non-Hispanic blacks. For non-Hispanic men, the prevalence of overweight and obesity among whites is slightly greater than among blacks.

. . . .

In addition to racial and ethnic and gender disparities, the prevalence of overweight and obesity also varies by age. Among both men and women, the prevalence of overweight and obesity increases with advancing age until the sixth decade, after which it starts to decline.

. . . .

Disparities in the prevalence of overweight and obesity also exist based on socioeconomic status. For all racial and ethnic groups combined, women of lower socioeconomic status (income ≤ 130 percent of poverty threshold) are approximately 50 percent more likely to be obese than those with higher socioeconomic status (income > 130 percent of poverty threshold). Men are about equally likely to be obese whether they are in a low or high socioeconomic group.

⤷ interesting!

HEALTH BENEFITS OF WEIGHT LOSS

The recommendations to treat overweight and obesity are based on two rationales. First, overweight and obesity are associated with an increased risk of disease and death, as previously discussed. Second, randomized controlled trials have shown that weight loss (as modest as 5 to 15 percent of excess total body weight) reduces the risk factors for at least some diseases, particularly cardiovascular disease, in the short term. Weight loss results in lower blood pressure, lower blood sugar, and improved lipid levels. While few published studies have examined the link between weight loss and reduced disease or death in the long-term, current data, as well as scientific plausibility suggest this link.

Studies have shown that reducing risk factors for heart disease, such as blood pressure and blood cholesterol levels, lowers death rates from heart disease and stroke. Therefore, it is highly probable that weight loss that reduces these risk factors will reduce the number of deaths from heart disease and stroke . . . .

. . . .

UNITED NATIONS FOOD & AGRICULTURE ORGANIZATION/WORLD HEALTH ORGANIZATION, JOINT REPORT ON DIET, NUTRITION, AND THE PREVENTION OF CHRONIC DISEASES
61–68, 70 (2003)

Almost all countries (high-income and low-income alike) are experiencing an obesity epidemic, although with great variation between and within countries. In low-income countries, obesity is more common in middle-aged women, people of higher socioeconomic status and those living in urban communities. In more affluent countries, obesity is not only common in the middle-aged, but is becoming increasingly prevalent among younger adults and children. Furthermore, it tends to be associated with lower socioeconomic status, especially in women, and the urban-rural differences are diminished or even reversed.

It has been estimated that the direct costs of obesity accounted for 6.8 percent of total health care costs . . . in the United States in 1995. Although direct costs in other industrialized countries are slightly lower, they still consume a sizeable proportion of national health budgets. Indirect costs, which are far greater than direct costs, include work days lost, physician visits, disability pensions and premature mortality. Intangible costs such as impaired quality of life are also enormous. Because the risks of diabetes, cardiovascular disease and hypertension rise continuously with increasing weight, there is much overlap between the prevention of obesity and the prevention of a variety of chronic diseases, especially type 2 diabetes . . . .

The increasing industrialization, urbanization, and mechanization occurring in most countries around the world is associated with changes in diet and behavior; in particular, diets are becoming richer in high-fat, high energy foods and lifestyles more sedentary. In many developing countries undergoing economic transition, rising levels of obesity often co-exist in the same population (or even the same household) with chronic undernutrition. Increases in obesity over the past 30 years have been paralleled by a dramatic rise in the prevalence of diabetes.

. . . .

Physical activity is an important determinant of body weight. In addition, physical activity and physical fitness (which relates to the ability to perform physical activity) are important modifiers of mortality and morbidity related to overweight and obesity. There is firm evidence that moderate to high fitness levels provide a substantially reduced risk of cardiovascular disease and all-cause mortality and that these benefits apply to all BMI levels. Furthermore, high fitness protects against mortality at all BMI levels in men with diabetes. Low cardiovascular fitness is a serious and common comorbidity of obesity, and a sizeable proportion of deaths in overweight and obese populations are probably a result of low levels of cardio-respiratory fitness rather than obesity per se. Fitness is, in turn, influenced strongly by physical activity in addition to genetic factors. These relationships emphasize the role of physical activity in the prevention of overweight and obesity, independently of the effects of physical activity on body weight.

. . . .

The effectiveness over the long term of most dietary strategies for weight loss, including low-fat diets, remains uncertain unless accompanied by changes in behaviour affecting physical activity and food habits. These latter changes at a public health level require an environment supportive of healthy food choices and an active life . . . . A variety of popular weight-loss diets that restrict food choices may result in reduced energy intake and short term weight loss in individuals but most do not have trial evidence of long-term effectiveness and nutritional adequacy and therefore cannot be recommended for populations.

. . . .

Part of the consistent, strong relationships between television viewing and obesity in children may relate to the food advertising to which they are exposed. Fast food restaurants and foods and beverages that are usually classified under the "eat least" category in dietary guidelines are among the most heavily marketed products, especially on television. Young children are often the target group for the advertising of these products because they have a significant influence on the foods bought by parents. The huge expenditure on marketing fast-foods and other "eat least" choices was considered to be a key factor in the increased consumption of food prepared outside the home in general and of energy-dense, micronutrient-poor foods in particular. Young children are unable to distinguish programme content from the persuasive intent of advertisements. The evidence that the heavy marketing of these foods and beverages to young children causes obesity is not unequivocal . . . . [T]here is sufficient indirect evidence to warrant this practice being placed in the "probable" category and thus becoming a potential target for interventions.

Diets that are proportionally low in fat will be proportionally higher in carbohydrate (including a variable amount of sugars) . . . . The physiological effects of energy intake on satiation and satiety appear to be quite different for energy in solid foods as opposed to energy in fluids. Possibly because of reduced gastric distension and faster transit times, the energy contained in fluids is less well "detected" by the body and subsequent food intake is poorly adjusted to account for the energy taken in through beverages . . . . The high and increasing consumption of sugars-sweetened drinks by children in many countries is of serious concern. It has been estimated that each additional can or glass of sugars-sweetened drink that they consume every day increases the risk of becoming obese by 60 percent. Most of the evidence relates to soda drinks but many fruit drinks and cordials are equally energy-dense and may promote weight gain if drunk in large quantities. Overall, the evidence implicating a high intake of sugars-sweetened drinks in promoting weight gain was considered moderately strong.

. . . The mechanisms by which socioeconomic status influences food and activity patterns are probably multiple and need elucidation. However, people living in circumstances of low socioeconomic status may be more at the mercy of the obesogenic environment because their eating and activity behaviours are more likely to be the "default choices" on offer. The evidence for an effect of low socioeconomic status on predisposing people to obesity is consistent (in higher income countries) across a number of cross-sectional and longitudinal studies, and was thus rated as a "probable" cause of increased risk of obesity.

. . . .

. . . In many countries, there has been a steady increase in the proportion of food eaten that is prepared outside the home. In the United States, the energy, total fat, saturated fat, cholesterol and sodium content of foods prepared outside the home is significantly higher than that of home prepared food. People in the United States who tend to eat in restaurants have a higher BMI than those who tend to eat at home.

. . . .

. . . Studies have not shown consistent associations between alcohol intake and obesity despite the high energy density of the nutrient . . . .

. . . .

Low-income groups globally and populations in countries in economic transition often replace traditional micronutrient-rich foods by heavily marketed, sugars-sweetened beverages (*i.e.*, soft drinks) and energy-dense, fatty, salty, and sugary foods. These trends, coupled with reduced physical activity, are associated with the rising prevalence of obesity. Strategies are needed to improve the quality of diets by increasing consumption of fruits and vegetables, in addition to increasing physical activity, in order to stem the epidemic of obesity and associated diseases.

. . . .

NOTES AND QUESTIONS

1. **An epidemic of obesity.** Public health is concerned with weight because obesity is associated with hypertension, high LDL cholesterol, low HDL cholesterol, high triglyceride levels, and type 2 diabetes — all of which are associated with coronary heart disease and stroke — as well as gall bladder disease, osteoarthritis, sleep apnea, and some cancers (breast, endometrial, and colon). It is also concerned because of numbers; the more people with a health condition, the more the public health community views it as a matter of *public* health. Some experts even projected that the rising rates of obesity in the United States will eventually result in a reduction in average life expectancy in the United States. S. Jay Olshansky *et al.*, *A Potential Decline in Life Expectancy in the United States*, 352 NEW ENG. J. MED. 1138 (2005). For general information on obesity, see CDC, Overweight and Obesity, www.cdc.gov/obesity/data/index.html (visited Nov. 2013).

According to the Surgeon General's report summarized in this Part — and a host of other public health experts — obesity is a problem of epidemic proportions in the United States. Indeed, the CDC has labeled obesity an epidemic. The CDC estimates that 35.7% of adults and 16.9% of children (under age 20) were obese in 2009 — 2010. For current data, see the annual reports — *Health, United States* — by the National Center for Health Statistics, available at www.cdc.gov/nchs/hus (visited Nov. 2013).

The percentage of obese adults grew after 1976 and leveled off somewhat after 2010. Cynthia L. Ogden *et al.*, *Prevalence of Obesity Adults: United States, 2011–2012*, NCHS Data Brief, No. 131 (Oct. 2013), www.cdc.gov/nchs/data/databriefs/db131.htm (visited Nov. 2013). For children, the percentages have not increased since 2000. See Figures 1 and 2 below. Has the epidemic paused — or even peaked? For a review confirming that we don't know yet, see B. Rokholm, J.L. Baker & T.I. Sørensen, *The Levelling Off of the Obesity Epidemic Since the Year 1999 — A Review of the Evidence and Perspectives*, 11 OBESITY REVIEW 835 (2010).

Figure 1

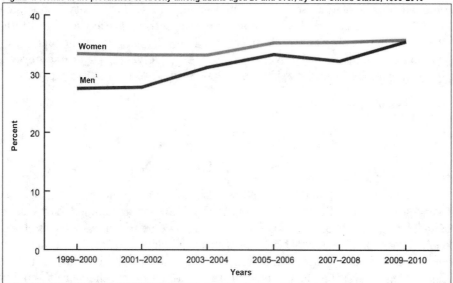

Figure 4. Trends in the prevalence of obesity among adults aged 20 and over, by sex: United States, 1999-2010

[1]Significant increasing linear trend 1999-2000 to 2009-2010 (p < 0.0001).
NOTE: Estimates were age adjusted by the direct method to the 2000 U.S. Census population using the age groups 20-39, 40-59, and 60 and over.
SOURCE: CDC/NCHS, National Health and Nutrition Examination Survey, 2009-2010.

Figure 2

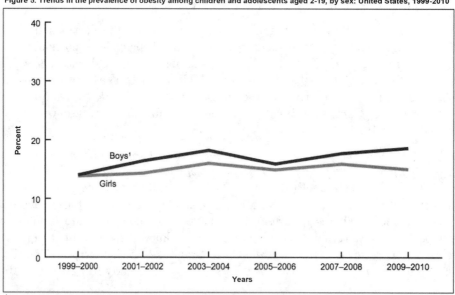

Figure 5. Trends in the prevalence of obesity among children and adolescents aged 2-19, by sex: United States, 1999-2010

[1]Significant increasing linear trend 1999-2000 to 2009-2010 (p < 0.05).
SOURCE: CDC/NCHS, National Health and Nutrition Examination Survey, 2009-2010.

Note that some reports use the term "obesity" somewhat generically to describe people who are classified as *either* "overweight" or "obese," according to Body Mass

Index (BMI). In some calculations, the distinction makes an important difference. For example, CDC estimates that about 34% of the US adult population is overweight and 35.7% is obese are sometimes mistakenly understood as meaning that more than two-thirds of Americans are obese.

2. **Body Mass Index (BMI).** In humans, the most common statistical measurement of obesity is the body mass index (BMI). *See* CDC, About BMI for Adults, www.cdc.gov/healthyweight/assessing/bmi/adult_bmi/index.html (visited Nov. 2013). As the Surgeon General's report summarized above explains, BMI is a logarithmic calculation of weight in kilograms divided by height in meters squared (kg/m2). Current categories for adults are:

Underweight	<18.5
Normal	18.5–<25.0
Overweight	25.0–<30.0
Obese	≥30.0
Grade 1	30.0–<35.0
Grade 2	35.0–<40.0
Grade 3 (morbid)	≥40.0

The Belgian statistician Adolphe Quetelet created the BMI in the nineteenth century. The cut-off points between categories are occasionally redefined and have differed from country to country. In June 1998, the National Institutes of Health brought official US category definitions into line with those used by the World Health Organization, moving the American "overweight" threshold from BMI 27 to BMI 25. About 30,000,000 Americans moved from "normal" or "ideal" weight to being 1-10 pounds "overweight" as a result.

BMI is intended to measure body fat, but it has acknowledged limitations. For example, athletes in excellent "shape" may have a BMI in the overweight range because of well-developed — and heavier — muscles. The above adult BMI categories are not recommended for use with children. Instead, a sex-specific body mass index-age-percentile compares a child with the population of children of the same sex in the same age range, with 5%–85% considered "healthy weight" (normal), 85%–≥95% overweight, and ≥95% obese. www.cdc.gov/healthyweight/ assessing/bmi/childrens_bmi/about_childrens_bmi.html#What%20is%20BMI% 20percentile (visited Nov. 2013). According to the National Center for Health Statistics:

> The percentage of children aged 2–5 who were obese rose from 7% in 1988–1994 to 10% in 1999–2000 and has not increased significantly since that time. The prevalence of obesity among 6 to 11 year olds increased from 11% in 1988–1994 to 15% in 1999–2000 and has not increased significantly since then. Among adolescents aged 12 to 19, the prevalence of obesity rose from 11% in 1988–1994 to 15% in 1999–2000 and has not increased significantly since that time.

CDC, NCHS, *Health, United States*, 2012, http://www.cdc.gov/nchs/data/hus/hus12. pdf#063.

CDC defines children to include anyone younger than age 20, which can complicate comparing CDC data with other sources of data about children that use the more typical age of 18 as the cut-off age.

3. **Obesity and mortality.** Proving precisely how increased weight leads to bad outcomes is difficult and has produced some conflicting results. In less than a year, U.S. government agencies reported that obesity caused 414,000 deaths, 280,000 deaths, and 112,000 deaths. *See* David H. Mark, *Deaths Attributable to Obesity*, 293 JAMA 1918 (2005); Edward W. Gregg *et al.*, *Secular Trends in Cardiovascular Disease Risk Factors According to Body Mass Index in US Adults*, 293 JAMA 1868 (July 14, 2005). Underweight is also associated with a higher risk of death. Katherine M. Flegal *et al.*, *Excess Deaths Associated With Underweight, Over-weight, and Obesity*, 293 JAMA 1861 (2005). Why might that be?

More recent mortality estimates confirmed higher risk for people with a BMI ≥35.0, but also found a slight advantage for people in the overweight category. Katherine M. Flegal *et al.*, *Association of All-Cause Mortality with Overweight and Obesity Using Standard Body Mass Index Categories: A Systematic Review and Meta-analysis*, 309 JAMA 71 (2013). CDC researchers in the National Center for Health Statistics analyzed studies of mortality associated with BMI categories and reported hazard ratios, shown below. *Id.* The hazard ratio is the ratio of the risk of death (from all causes) for the overweight and obese categories to the risk of death (from all causes) for normal weight people, in which the normal weight risk equals one (1). A ratio of less than 1.0 means that the risk of death is lower than for normal weight people; a ratio greater than 1.0 means that the risk of death is higher than for normal weight people.

Category	BMI	Hazard Ratio
Overweight	25.0–<30.0	0.94
All Obese	≥30.0	1.18
Grade 1	30.0–<35.0	0.95 (not statistically significant)
Grades 2 & 3	≥35.0	1.29

Some of the improved mortality for overweight people may come from better medical care. While high blood pressure and high cholesterol are risk factors for heart disease, the incidence of high blood pressure and high cholesterol among people who are obese has been declining since 1960. BMI is also an imperfect predictor of risk. Some nutrition researchers find it hard to believe that overweight people — and especially Grade 1 obese people — could have a lower risk of death than people of normal weight. Are there advantages or disadvantages to different groups from finding larger numbers of deaths or a higher rate of mortality from obesity?

4. **Obesity and costs.** Health conditions often become a public health problem — or at least a matter of public interest — when the cost of treating them rises. Obesity is associated with many chronic diseases that account for a major share of national health expenditures in the U.S. Since Medicare and Medicaid pay for almost half the costs of medical care, it should surprise no one that obesity is one

target of cost control efforts. Yet, because obesity is associated with so many different adverse health problems, the actual costs attributable to obesity alone are hard to quantify. The annual medical costs for obesity in 2006 were estimated to be $86 billion or almost 10% of total national medical costs, while more recent estimates suggest more than twice that amount. Overall costs follow a U-shaped curve, with higher costs in the underweight category, lowest costs in the normal and overweight categories, and highest costs in the more severely obese grades. For some good efforts to summarize and assess the costs of obesity, see John Cawley & Chad Meyerhoefer, *The Medical Care Costs of Obesity: An Instrumental Variables Approach*, 31 J. HEALTH ECON. 219 (2012); Eric A. Finkelstein *et al.*, *Annual Medical Spending Attributable to Obesity: Payer- and Service-Specific Estimates*, 28(5) HEALTH AFF. w822 (2009).

Paul Campos, Abigail Saguy, Paul Ernsberger, Eric Oliver & Glenn Gaesser, *The Epidemiology of Overweight and Obesity: Public Health Crisis or Moral Panic?*
35 INTERNATIONAL J. EPIDEMIOLOGY 55, 55–59 (2006)

. . . This article evaluates four central claims made by those who are calling for intensifying the war on fat: that obesity is an epidemic; that overweight and obesity are major contributors to mortality; that higher than average adiposity is pathological and a primary direct cause of disease; and that significant long-term weight loss is both medically beneficial and a practical goal. Given the limited scientific evidence for any of these claims, we suggest that the current rhetoric about an obesity-driven health crisis is being driven more by cultural and political factors than by any threat increasing body weight may pose to public health.

> "Claim #1: 'Almost all countries (high-income and low-income alike) are experiencing an obesity epidemic . . .' WHO, 2003 (p. 61)."

The claim that we are seeing an 'epidemic' of overweight and obesity implies an exponential pattern of growth typical of epidemics. The available data do not support this claim. Instead, what we have seen, in the US, is a relatively modest rightward skewing of average weight on the distribution curve, with people of lower weights gaining little or no weight, and the majority of people weighing ~3–5 kg more than they did a generation ago. The average American's weight gain can be explained by 10 extra calories a day, or the equivalent of a Big Mac once every 2 months . . . .

While there has been significant weight gain among the heaviest individuals the vast majority of people in the 'overweight' and 'obese' categories are now at weight levels that are only slightly higher than those they or their predecessors were maintaining a generation ago. In other words we are seeing subtle shifts, rather than an alarming epidemic. Biologist Jeffery Friedman offers this analogy: 'Imagine that the average IQ was 100 and that five percent of the population had an IQ of 140 and were considered to be geniuses. Now let's say that education improves and the average IQ increases to 107 and 10% of the population has an IQ of >140.

You could present the data in two ways. You could say that average IQ is up seven points or you could say that because of improved education the number of geniuses has doubled. The whole obesity debate is equivalent to drawing conclusions about national education programmes by saying that the number of geniuses has doubled.'

In the US, . . . the so-called 'obesity epidemic' is almost wholly a product of tens of millions of people with BMIs formerly in the 23–25 range gaining a modest amount of weight and thus now being classified as 'overweight', and, similarly, tens of millions of people with BMIs formerly in the high 20s now having BMIs just >30. This movement of population cohorts from just below to just above the formal definitions of overweight and obesity is what public health officials are referring to when they point out that rates of obesity have exploded over the course of the last generation . . . .

. . . .

> "Claim #2: 'Mortality rates increase with increasing degrees of overweight, as measured by BMI.' — WHO, 2003 (p. 61)"

This claim, central to arguments that higher than average body mass amount to a major public health problem, is at best weakly supported by the epidemiological literature. Except at true statistical extremes, high body mass is a very weak predictor of mortality, and may even be protective in older populations. In particular, the claim that 'overweight' (BMI 25–29.9) increases mortality risk in any meaningful way is impossible to reconcile with numerous large-scale studies that have found no increase in relative risk among the so-called 'overweight', or have found a lower relative risk for premature mortality among this cohort than among persons of so-called 'normal' or 'ideal' [sic] weight. Among the obese, little or no increase in relative risk for premature mortality is observed until one reaches BMIs in the upper 30s or higher. In other words, the vast majority of people labelled 'overweight' and 'obese' according to current definitions do not in fact face any meaningful increased risk for early death. Indeed the most recent comprehensive analysis of this question within the context of the US population found more premature deaths associated with a BMI of <25 than with a BMI above it. This was largely owing to the finding that lowest death rates fell within the BMI range of 25–29.9 — some 86 000 fewer 'excess' deaths than was observed in the referent group, the so-called 'normal weight' BMI range of 18.5–24.9. Additional analyses that controlled for potential confounders such as length of follow-up, weight stability, weight loss caused by illness, or smoking status did not change the results. For this nationally representative cohort of US adults — National Health and Nutrition Examination Surveys I, II, and III — the 'ideal' weight for longevity was 'overweight'.

. . . .

These findings from representative US cohorts are consistent with global observations. In a quantitative analysis of a number of previously published studies, involving >600 000 men and women, Troiano et al., observed a similar U-shaped relationship between BMI and mortality, with the lowest mortality rates between BMIs of 23 and 29. Most of the range considered 'overweight' was not associated with higher risk. On the other hand, low BMI was. For example, mortality rates for men with BMIs between 19 and 21 were the same as those for men with BMIs between 29 and 31 . . . .

     . . . .

But the greatest problem with the statistical linkages between body mass and mortality is that other confounding factors are not considered, leaving little basis for drawing causal inferences. Most epidemiological studies estimating the relationship between body weight and mortality do not control for fitness, exercise, diet quality, weight cycling, diet drug use, economic status, or family history. Furthermore, in studies that control for some of these factors, the data are usually self-reported and thus of extremely questionable reliability. (See, for example, the five-point exercise scale used in the Nurses' Health Study.) By contrast, when one or more confounders are controlled for in a rigorous fashion, the already weak association between higher body mass and greater mortality tends to be greatly attenuated or disappear altogether. For example, all of the excess mortality associated with obesity in the Framingham study can be accounted for by the impact of weight cycling. Obese Framingham residents with stable body weights were not at increased risk. The same result has been obtained in NHANES.

Fitness is closely intertwined with obesity, and has powerful influences on health and mortality. Data from the Aerobics Center Longitudinal Study show that low cardiovascular fitness accounted for all of the excess all-cause mortality among obese men. Similar data by these researchers have been reported for women. In short, it seems probable that body weight, like height or baldness, is for the most part a proxy for many unmeasured variables. From a public health perspective, the most significant aspect of such a conclusion is that most of these unmeasured variables, especially the lifestyle factors, are more readily modifiable than body mass.

Many common weight loss treatments generate particularly problematic confounders. For example, over-the-counter diet pills used by millions, including phenylpropanoloamine and herbal ephedra, have been linked to heart attack and strokes and recently banned. The adjusted odds ratio for stroke in women taking phenylpropanolamine for weight loss was 16.6, many times higher than the relative risk for stroke associated with a BMI > 30, which in one typical study was 1.29 (not significant). And the higher a person's BMI, the more likely they are to use these and other hazardous weight loss methods, including surgery. One study found that 22% of weight loss clinic clients surveyed used phenylpropanoloamine for weight loss. If only one in 13 obese persons were exposed to over-the-counter diet pills containing phenylpropanolamine, then all of the excess risk of obesity could be accounted for by increased diet pills use. No epidemiological study to date has assessed mortality risks after taking the known hazards of stimulant diet pills into account.

     . . . We actually know little about why the very thin and the very heavy are more likely to die than those in the 'normal,' 'overweight', and 'Type I obese' (BMI = 30–34.9) categories, and it is likely that there are multiple causal pathways across the weight spectrum . . . .

"Claim #3: 'The data linking overweight and obesity to adverse health outcomes are well established and incontrovertible.' "

. . . [I]t is sometimes asserted that BMI is an inexact measure of adiposity and that high levels of body fat, rather than high body mass per se, represent the real health risk. Yet when epidemiological studies have compared BMI with percentage of body fat as a marker for disease risk, BMI is consistently superior to percentage of body fat. This suggests that body build rather than fatness may be the source of risks associated with high BMI. Despite much speculation, very little evidence has been produced regarding the question of exactly how adiposity is supposed to cause disease. With the exception of osteoarthritis, where increased body mass contributes to wear on joints, and a few cancers where oestrogen originating in adipose tissue may contribute, causal links between body fat and disease remain hypothetical. It is quite possible, and even likely, that higher than average body fat is merely an expression of underlying metabolic processes that themselves may be the sources of the pathologies in question. For example, much evidence suggests that insulin resistance is a product of an underlying metabolic syndrome that also predisposes persons to higher adiposity because compensatory insulin secretion promotes fat storage. Modern molecular genetics confirms the thrifty gene hypothesis that mutations favouring fat storage and survival of famine also confer risk of diabetes. Thus, obesity may be an early symptom of diabetes rather than its underlying cause.

. . . .

Indeed, disentangling the presumed cause-effect link between body fat and 'weight-related' health problems is fairly straightforward. Exercise and nutrition can effectively reduce blood pressure — an effect that is independent of changes in body weight. In the DASH trial the reductions in blood pressure among participants with hypertension were comparable with those achieved with pharmacotherapy. Blood lipids can also be improved with changes in exercise and diet, largely independent of changes in body weight or body fat.

. . . .

. . . This illustrates a more general point: discussions about obesity and overweight as a health risk tend to treat weight as a health behaviour, akin to smoking. Thus overweight and obesity are commonly referred to as 'preventable causes of illness'. Yet the relationship between behaviour and weight is complex, and intertwined with immutable factors such as genetics, and body build and shape. The average individual's control over his or her weight is limited at best. This brings us to Claim #4.

"Claim #4: Significant long-term weight loss is a practical goal, and will improve health."

. . . It is a remarkable fact that the central premise of the current war on fat — that turning obese and overweight people into so-called 'normal weight' individuals will improve their health — remains an untested hypothesis. One main reason the hypothesis remains untested is because there is no method available to produce the result that would have to be produced — significant long-term weight loss, in statistically significant cohorts — in order to test the claim. It is particularly striking that studies that have found health benefits associated with various levels of weight loss generally record no dose response: in other words, people who lose a small amount of weight, or even gain weight, get as much health benefit from the intervention as those who lose larger amounts.

Data from the National Health Interview Survey (follow-up from 1989 through 1997) illustrate the point. Among overweight and obese men and women, with and without type 2 diabetes, those who reported trying to lose weight (but without success) experienced a reduction in mortality rate that was the same as, or greater than, those who reported that they were successful at weight loss. In other words weight loss itself did not appear to be beneficial. Indeed, in this same study, weight loss was associated with a mortality hazard ratio of 3.36 and weight cycling with a hazard ratio of 1.83. By contrast, obese people with stable body weight had no increase in mortality.

On the whole, body weight seems like a poor target for public health remediation, particularly in the absence of any safe or effective tools for weight loss. Furthermore, many of the tools that are currently employed towards that end (diet drugs, weight loss surgery, eating disordered behaviour, fad diets, and the chronic weight cycling they induce) have serious side effects, up to and including death. Thus public health interventions designed to lessen rates of obesity and overweight are striving to achieve a presently unachievable goal of unknown medical efficacy. In contrast, as noted above, many studies have found striking health benefits associated with lifestyle changes that produce little or no long-term weight loss. Furthermore, dozens of double blind randomized controlled clinical trials have shown that obese patients are protected from death and heart disease by lipid lowering and antihypertensive medications, without losing any weight whatsoever. One class of drugs, the thiazolidinediones, improves multiple risk factors in obese diabetics while causing significant increases in body fat. Under such circumstances, for public health agencies to focus on trying to make people thinner, at the potential expense of initiatives that will improve lifestyle but are unlikely to produce significant long term weight loss, seems grossly inefficient.

Social and political contributors to the obesity panic

. . . [B]etween 1980 and 2004, media attention to obesity increased exponentially, from 62 articles published in the Lexis-Nexis US News Sources with 'obesity' in the headings, lead paragraphs, or key terms in 1980, to over 6500 in 2004. If such heightened concern does not reflect scientific reality, what is driving it?

Part of the answer may lie with overlapping (and often conflicting) sets of economic interests among various public health constituencies. For example, many of the leading obesity researchers who have created the official standards for what constitutes 'overweight' and 'obese' have also received sizable funding from the pharmaceutical and weight-loss industries. These obesity researchers also manage weight loss clinics and have an economic interest in defining unhealthy weight as broadly as possible, by overstating the hazards of obesity, and thus providing justifications for regulatory approvals, as well as for government and insurance industry subsidization of their products. In particular, organizations like the International Obesity Task Force (which has authored many of the WHO reports on obesity) and the American Obesity Association (which has actively campaigned to have obesity officially designated as a 'disease') have been largely funded by pharmaceutical and weight-loss companies. Notably, although expert panels on obesity are largely devoted to evaluating epidemiological evidence and claims, qualified epidemiologists are almost never included as members. In addition, government health agencies, like the Centers for Disease Control and Prevention in the United States, have promoted the urgency of the 'obesity epidemic' while lobbying for greater programme funding and policy setting authority.

Targeting obesity has support across the political spectrum. In the US, discussions of the supposed obesity epidemic usually take place within the context of a larger discussion, which assumes that the increasing weight of the population is a sign of increasing moral laxity and that overweight and obesity are playing a significant role in driving up health care costs. This linkage is attractive for those who are ideologically committed to a focus on 'individual responsibility', rather than on structural factors that continue to drive health care costs ever upward . . . . Anxieties about increasing weight resonate with those on the left of the political spectrum as well, who tend to interpret the 'obesity epidemic' as both a by-product and a symbol of rampant consumer overconsumption and greedy corporations.

The exponential increase in mass media attention to obesity in the US and abroad seems to have many of the elements of what social scientists call a 'moral panic'. Moral panics are typical during times of rapid social change and involve an exaggeration or fabrication of risks, the use of disaster analogies, and the projection of societal anxieties onto a stigmatized group . . . .

Public opinion studies also show that negative attitudes towards the obese are highly correlated with negative attitudes towards minorities and the poor, such as the belief that all these groups are lazy and lack self-control and will power. This suggests that anxieties about racial integration and immigration may be an underlying cause of some of the concern over obesity . . . .

. . . .

Yet despite all of the moral connotations ascribed to weight gain, we have little idea exactly why people weigh somewhat more now than they did a generation ago. Not surprisingly, some works suggest that increasing caloric intake and decreasing activity levels, in some combination, are sufficient explanations for this trend. However, other works suggest that some portion of the population's weight gain can be attributed to smoking cessation, which runs counter to the assumption that the country's weight gain is evidence of both moral laxity and a harbinger of declining overall health.

So what if the so-called 'obesity epidemic' is largely an illusion? What if higher than average weight turns out to have neither much medical nor moral significance? The answer to these questions, all of which we believe are strongly suggested by the epidemiological literature, go far beyond the issues of body mass and health. The current scientific evidence should prompt health professionals and policy makers to consider whether it makes sense to treat body weight as a barometer of public health. It should also make us pause to consider how propagating the idea of an 'obesity epidemic' furthers the political and economic interests of certain groups, while doing immense damage to those whom it blames and stigmatizes.

———

NOTES AND QUESTIONS

5. **Reframing the problem.** Paul Campos and colleagues offer another point of view — one that does not view weight itself as the problem. They argue that public policy should focus on health rather than weight. They also favor reducing the stigma of obesity and making a healthy lifestyle possible for everyone. These are not necessarily controversial points. However, they touch a nerve among obesity researchers by suggesting that the rise in population weight has not been all that dramatic and by highlighting the gaps in our knowledge about the relationship between weight and health.

In his earlier book, THE OBESITY MYTH: WHY AMERICA'S OBSESSION WITH WEIGHT IS HAZARDOUS TO YOUR HEALTH (2004), Campos argues that the health hazards of obesity have been overstated or, at least, not convincingly proven. For example:

> . . . [H]ere are some figures from what — at the time it was compiled — was the world's largest epidemiological study to date. This study, conducted in Norway in the mid-1980s, followed 1.8 million people for ten years. Consider the following data in light of the government's and the medical establishment's claims that a BMI of 18.5 to 24.9 is optimal and that people with BMI figures of 25 and above are running major health risks. The highest life expectancy (79.7 years) was found among people with BMI figures between 26 and 28 . . . . The lowest life expectancy (74.2 years) was found among those with BMI figures below 18 (A woman of average height who is 5 pounds below what the government claims to be her "optimal" BMI will fall into that category). Those with BMI figures between 18 and 20 . . . had a lower life expectancy than those with BMI figures between 34 and 36 . . . .

CAMPOS at 10.

Campos, a law professor, may not be a member of the medical community, but he is not alone. A growing number of books have appeared critiquing the weight-loss focus of controlling the obesity epidemic. *See* MICHAEL GARD & JAN WRIGHT, THE OBESITY EPIDEMIC: SCIENCE, MORALITY AND IDEOLOGY (2005); J. ERIC OLIVER, OBESITY: THE MAKING OF AN AMERICAN EPIDEMIC (2005). Some point to potential conflicts of interest among investigators funded by the weight-loss industry. The National Institutes of Health have increased grant opportunities for obesity research, making it an attractive subject for academic researchers. Weight loss programs and drugs continue to proliferate, but success is hard to achieve. Programs may be considered effective if they result in a loss of 5% of one's body weight. And what works for one person may not work for another. *See* GINA KOLATA, RETHINKING THIN: THE NEW SCIENCE OF WEIGHT LOSS — AND THE MYTH AND REALITIES ABOUT DIETING (2007). Keeping weight lost off can be even harder. *See* J. W. Anderson *et al.*, *Long-Term Weight Loss Maintenance: A Meta-Analysis of US Studies*, 74 AM. J. CLINICAL NUTRITION 579 (2001)(finding that the majority of obese dieters did not maintain their reduced weight); WILLIAM BENNETT & JOEL GURIN, THE DIETER'S

DILEMMA: EATING LESS AND WEIGHING MORE (1982) (introducing set point theory). Bariatric surgery has grown significantly; its success rate in weight reduction appears to be considerably better than exhortations to diet and exercise.

6. **What about genetics or biology?** Is obesity "a predictable consequence of modern life," as Kelly Brownell and Katherine Battle Horgan say in FOOD FIGHT 5 (2004)? Researchers are investigating whether certain viruses or bacteria play a role in regulating weight, while others are studying genetic and hormonal influences, including a possible hormonal resistance to weight loss. *See, e.g.,* Chin Jou, *The Biology and Genetics of Obesity — A Century of Inquiries,* 370 NEW ENGL. J. MED 1874 (2014); Barbara E. Corkey, *Diabetes: Have We Got It All Wrong? Insulin Hypersecretion and Food Additives: Cause of Obesity and Diabetes?,* 35 DIABETES CARE 2432 (2012); Priya Suminthra *et al., Long Term Persistence of Hormonal Adaptations to Weight Loss,* 365 NEW ENGL. J. MED 1597 (2011).

Brownell and Horgan explain what we are up against when ancient biology confronts the modern world:

> The lives of your ancestors, dating back many thousands of years, reside in your genes. Unpredictable food supplies and looming starvation were their everyday realities. Those who adapted ate voraciously when food appeared, stored energy (as body fat) with extreme efficiency, survived later scarcity, and contributed to the gene pool from which you draw your DNA.
>
> Married to this food biology are genes related to physical activity. Extreme exertion was once required to hunt and gather food. The body functioned optimally with bouts of heavy activity punctuated by periods of rest needed to conserve energy. Modern culture has removed strenuous exercise.
>
> You are an exquisitely efficient calorie conservation machine. Your genes match nicely with a scarce food supply, but not with modern living conditions . . . .

BROWNELL & HORGAN, FOOD FIGHT at 5–6. The result, they conclude, is that our bodies are not prepared to cope with what they call a "toxic environment." *Id.* at 7.

7. **Sugar or fat?** For decades, physicians, dieticians, and even self-help manuals have repeated the orthodoxy that reducing the amount of fat consumed would improve health, avoid illness, and control weight gain. This is reflected in the Dietary Guidelines for Americans issued by the US Departments of Agriculture and Health and Human Services every five years — the source of the "food pyramid" of your youth. U.S. DEP'T OF AGRICULTURE & U.S. DEP'T OF HEALTH & HUMAN SERVICES, DIETARY GUIDELINES FOR AMERICANS, 2010 (Dec. 2010), www.dietaryguidelines.gov (visited Nov. 2013). It is also a key element of alternative food pyramids or plates. *See* WALTER C. WILLETT, EAT, DRINK AND BE HEALTHY (2005).

A growing body of research casts doubt on the assumption that fat is a meaningful risk factor for heart disease, suggesting that added sugars may be the culprit. A meta-analysis of more than 70 studies including over half a million subjects found no support for guidelines that recommend low consumption of saturated fats in favor of polyunsaturated fatty acids. Rajiv Chowdhury *et al.*, *Association of Dietary, Circulating, and Supplement Fatty Acids With Coronary Risk: A Systematic Review and Meta-analysis*, 160 ANNALS INTERNAL MED. 398 (2014). A separate study found higher risks of death from cardiovascular diseases among those who consumed more than 25% of their calories in the form of added sugar (hazard ratio of 2.75, confidence interval: 1.40–5.42, P= .004) compared with those who consumed less than 10% of their calories in added sugar. Quanhe Yang, *et al.*, *Added Sugar Intake and Cardiovascular Diseases Mortality Among US Adults*, JAMA INTERNAL MED. (Feb. 3, 2014), http://archinte.jamanetwork.com/article.aspx?articleid=1819573 (visited Mar. 2014). A Mediterranean diet with olive oil, nuts, fish, beans, fruits, vegetables, and even wine with dinner was found to prevent heart attacks and stroke, even though it did not result in weight loss. Ramón Estruch *et al.*, *Primary Prevention of Cardiovascular Disease with a Mediterranean Diet*, 368 NEW ENGL. J. MED. 1279 (2013).

Robert Lustig, a pediatrician, offers evidence that too much sugar is a major contributor to obesity as well as a health hazard. His book, FAT CHANCE: BEATING THE ODDS AGAINST SUGAR, PROCESSED FOOD, OBESITY, AND DISEASE (2013), explains the effects of sugar on metabolism, insulin response and resistance, and the role of insulin in storing energy in fat cells. He notes that the processed food industry responded to public health advice to reduce fat in the American diet by adding sugar — primarily in the form of high-fructose corn syrup — to compensate for the loss of flavor caused by removing tasty fat.

According to Mark Bittman, author of FOOD MATTERS (2008), cookbooks, and food critic for the New York Times, "The most efficient summary might be to say 'eat real food' and 'avoid anything that didn't exist 100 years ago.'" Mark Bittman, *Butter Is Back*, NEW YORK TIMES, Mar. 25, 2014, www.nytimes.com/2014/03/26/opinion/bittman-butter-is-back.html?ref=dining&_r=0. So, perhaps grandma was right. Her family probably ate limited quantities of red meat, probably from grass-fed cattle, whereas today's corn-fed beef has many times the fat content of grass fed beef. Her family also probably cooked most of the food they ate, without additives or preservatives, and had cakes, pies and ice cream only occasionally.

8. Evaluating the research. How do we know what the studies mean? A large, carefully controlled study of the effects of a low-fat diet completed in 2005 illustrates how studies may be interpreted differently. As set out in the introductory summaries to three articles in the JOURNAL OF THE AMERICAN MEDICAL ASSOCIATION, the study found:

> Among postmenopausal women, a low-fat dietary pattern did not result in a statistically significant reduction in invasive breast cancer risk over an 8.1 year average follow-up period . . . Ross L. Prentiss *et al.*, *Low Fat Dietary Pattern and Risk of Invasive Breast Cancer*, 295 JAMA 629 (2005).

> . . . [A] dietary intervention that reduced total fat and increased intakes of vegetables, fruits, and grains did not significantly reduce the risk of [coronary heart disease or] stroke in postmenopausal women . . . *Barbara v. Howard, Low-Fat Dietary Pattern and Risk of Cardiovascular Disease*, 295 JAMA 655 (2005).

. . . [A] low-fat dietary pattern intervention did not reduce the risk of colorectal cancer in postmenopausal women during 8.1 years of follow-up. Shirley A.A. Beresford *et al.*, *Low-Fat Dietary Pattern and Risk of Colorectal Cancer*, 295 JAMA 643 (2005).

Like the 2014 studies mentioned in the preceding note, these results perplexed, perhaps even embarrassed, a number of public health experts who had long endorsed the belief that low-fat diets were better and healthier. Little could be said about the quality of the study: The researchers had followed nearly 50,000 women over the course of eight years, carefully dividing them between a group that maintained the prescribed diet and a control group that had no measurable change in their pre-study eating habits. There were some ways to qualify the results. The study only included women between the ages of 50 and 79 years. Only their diets were changed and monitored; activity levels, for examples, were not measured or controlled.

The authors of the study identified several possible sub-groupings within their study populations that appeared to have better results than the low-fat group taken as a whole, *e.g.*, women who had a higher BMI to begin with seemed to benefit more from the low-fat diets than those with lower BMI to begin with (although not in statistically measurable ways).

The surprising results were quickly picked up by the mass media, usually under headlines of the type "Fat Not As Bad As Believed" or "Low-Fat Over-rated!" There also was some criticism of the presentation of the results in JAMA as the authors of the study seemed eager — almost to the point of losing their scientific objectivity — to put a positive (and pro low-fat) spin on their results. The whole point, after all, of such a carefully controlled testing of a scientific hypothesis is to produce quantifiable results that speak for themselves. In theory, a hypothesis that is not proven is as useful as one that is confirmed, even if that is not what the authors or anyone else had hoped the data would show.

This is only one example of a larger problem: interpreting data — whether positive or negative or equivocal — in terms that the public can understand and put to use but not exaggerate. Just what a study proves or disproves involves understanding what a study is: an attempt to isolate one variable that may or may not have a causal connection to some outcome. Even a study with 50,000 people is just a sample. Whether it can be generalized or not depends on how representative the sample is, whether it is large enough to have statistical power, and the statistical methods used to calculate results. Even if it can be generalized, it might prove far less than most Americans and the media they rely on would like to believe. And even the best designed and controlled study can only attempt to isolate other influences well enough to assess the influence of one factor. No single study can account for all the complex influences on human biology and behavior.

The best advice is the one most Americans are not in a position to take: If you want to know what a study says or does not say, you should read the study in full text, apply some basic principles of statistical design, analysis, and logic, and evaluate conclusions in light of other relevant studies, just as you should do with a judicial opinion.

9. Open questions. Whether any of the above assessments is correct, it is clear that we know far less about the health effects of obesity than we do about most disease-related health problems. There is a growing body of empirical research finding an association between obesity and a number of medical conditions, but determining whether there is a direct causal relationship between obesity and illness — or vice versa — is a more complicated epidemiological problem. *See, e.g.,* Krista Casazza *et al., Myths, Presumptions, and Facts About Obesity,* 386 N. ENGL. J. MED. 446, 451, Table 3 (2013). We also don't know very much about some important practical questions, questions that need answers in order to shape effective, remedial solutions. In this regard, consider the following:

a. The data concerning morbidity and mortality are most convincing for people who are "very obese". So far, the data show no higher risk of death for overweight people. Contrast smoking: There seems to be a direct, dose-response type of correlation between increased exposure to tobacco smoke and increased risk of death or illness. Perhaps obesity is only a health risk beyond some threshold BMI. Is there some sort of species-specific, natural limit to population weight? Even so, don't people feel better at normal weights, regardless of their risk of death?

b. Smokers who quit can improve their health and lower their risk of illness and death. Is the same true for obesity? Is a formerly obese person healthier than a current one — but less healthy than someone who has avoided the problem throughout their lifetime? What about people who gain and lose weight cyclically? Again, are the answers different for "overweight," "slightly obese" or "very obese" people?

c. More recent research suggests that factors besides food and exercise — such as your genetic or metabolic make-up, gut bacteria, insulin production, how much sleep you get, where you live, or who your friends are — may affect weight gain and loss. How do we isolate genetic or biological factors from nutrition and physical activity? How important a role does culture or social norms play?

Note how the answers to these questions may bear on the questions of whether and how to regulate food production and sales, food products, drugs, weight loss programs, health benefit plans, advertising, public parks and transportation, workplaces, schools, and potential liability for so-called "obesogenic" products.

D. WEIGHT AND DISCRIMINATION

FRANK v. LAWRENCE UNION FREE SCHOOL DISTRICT
688 F. Supp. 2d 160 (E.D.N.Y. 2010)

JOANNA SEYBERT, UNITED STATES DISTRICT JUDGE.

In 2003 and 2004, the Lawrence Union Free School District denied Plaintiff Michael D. Frank tenure, then fired him. Mr. Frank responded by commencing suit asserting discrimination . . . claims under the Americans with Disabilities Act of 1990 ("ADA"), the Rehabilitation Act, and the New York State Human Rights Law ("NYSHRL"). Currently before the Court is Defendants' summary judgment motion . . . .

BACKGROUND

In 2000, Lawrence hired Mr. Frank as a junior high school mathematics teacher, on a probationary basis. Mr. Frank never needed any assistance to perform his teaching duties . . . .

. . . .

. . . Mr. Frank received a very positive annual appraisal for the 2000–2001 school year. This appraisal reported that Mr. Frank "demonstrates knowledge of his subject matter, establishes and achieves lesson and unit objectives and provides for active student participation." . . . . The appraisal also commended Mr. Frank for the "meticulous care" he takes in performing aspects of his job, his "excellent" attendance record, his openness to "supervisor suggestions," and his consistent "professional manner and appearance." . . .

[Individual reports of classroom lesson observations (typically 4 times a year) for the next academic year were similarly positive, but also recommended that Mr. Frank improve his lesson timing, because he sometimes ran out of time to complete class exercises.]

. . . .

Mr. Frank was eligible for tenure during the 2002–2003 school year. During this school year, Dr. [Mark] Kavarsky supervised him . . . .

During this time, Michelle Lineal was Lawrence's Assistant Superintendent of Curriculum and Instruction. In January or February of 2003, Ms. Lineal observed Mr. Frank's teaching, to determine whether to recommend him for tenure. After observing his lesson, Ms. Lineal informally spoke with Mr. Frank to provide her comments. Sometime later, she and Dr. Kavarsky conducted a formal conference with Mr. Frank. At this conference, Mr. Frank recalls that Ms. Lineal told him he was "so big and sloppy."

Dr. Kavarsky does not recall Ms. Lineal using that phrase. But Dr. Kavarsky does recall Ms. Lineal making remarks about Mr. Frank's "attire," indicating that she said something like "for a big man, that bowling shirt doesn't look good." Dr. Kavarsky remarked that this statement "somewhat caught my breath." He understood her statement to mean that "holistically she did not like the way he appeared in the classroom." Dr. Kavarsky also recalled that Ms. Lineal asked him to "work with [Mr. Frank] to get him better dressed." Dr. Kavarsky had no problems with Mr. Frank's attire, no one besides Ms. Lineal brought any such problems to his attention, and he never spoke with Mr. Frank concerning Ms. Lineal's remarks.

In the spring of 2003, Ms. Lineal met with Superintendent Dr. Mark Rosenbaum and Dr. Kavarsky to discuss, among other things, Mr. Frank's tenure application. Dr. Kavarsky believed that Mr. Frank satisfied his objectives and goals for all three years he had taught, and strongly supported awarding him tenure. Ms. Lineal disagreed. She indicated that she would not approve Mr. Frank's tenure because "he had not met the standards." Dr. Kavarsky then asked Ms. Lineal to "share with me any documentation" she had prepared to support her view. But "[t]here was nothing forthcoming," as Ms. Lineal "did not choose to share any notes." Ms. Lineal then demanded Mr. Frank's "immediate dismissal." Dr. Kavarsky responded by "attempting to strike a compromise," and asked Dr. Rosenbaum if "he would consider a fourth year for Mr. Frank." Dr. Rosenbaum agreed, and they decided to offer Mr. Frank a fourth [probationary] year . . . .

Despite not receiving tenure, Mr. Frank['s annual appraisal for the 2002–2003 school year] indicated that Mr. Frank "worked hard" to meet his yearly goals, "developed creative and innovative ideas to make his classroom a place where students enjoy learning," and had "very good" "knowledge of the curriculum."

. . . But, at the beginning of Mr. Frank's fourth year [2003–2004], Mr. Akst replaced [Dr. Kavarsky as Frank's immediate supervisor]. Dr. Kavarsky did not believe there was "any professional rationale in terms of appraisal or staff development" for replacing him as Mr. Frank's supervisor, especially because Mr. Akst was "not a math licensed supervisor" and had never supervised math teachers before. Dr. Kavarsky commented that one might "conjecture" that Mr. Akst replaced him because "he was up for tenure that year and so could be vulnerable to [Ms. Lineal's] persuasion."

[In 2003, Mr. Akst, Dr. Kavarsky, and Karen Lazare observed Mr. Frank's class. Their reports were substantively the same as earlier reports, praising his performance except for time management.]

. . . .

. . . Then, after a meeting with Ms. Lineal, Mr. Akst "emphatically" told Dr. Kavarsky that "Ms. Lineal put the kibosh on [Mr. Frank's] tenure and he would not be receiving any tenure." Dr. Kavarsky "was shocked and appalled" when he learned this, especially because "Ms. Lineal was not part of any observation process that year nor part of any conversations regarding Mr. Frank."

. . . .

In the Spring of 2004, . . . Dr. Fitzsimons met with Dr. Kavarsky, Mr. Akst, and Ms. Lineal to discuss Mr. Frank's prospective tenure. Dr. Kavarsky believed that Mr. Frank satisfied his objectives and goals for his fourth year of teaching. Ms. Lineal and Mr. Akst opposed granting Mr. Frank tenure . . . . Dr. Kavarsky believes that Mr. Frank's "size and appearance" was a "factor" in Ms. Lineal recommending against tenure. Prior to Mr. Frank's case, no superintendent or assistant superintendent had ever vetoed one of Dr. Kavarsky's tenure recommendations. Indeed, the District had a "general practice [ ] to defer to either the principal or the immediate supervisors" in making tenure decisions.

. . . Dr. Fitzsimons decided against . . . tenure because Mr. Frank: (1) used ineffective teaching techniques; (2) had poor execution of lesson planning; and (3) did not reach "the level of expectations of Lawrence Public Schools." Dr. Kavarsky does not believe Mr. Frank had "ineffective teaching techniques" and has "no clue as to what that means." Likewise, Dr. Kavarsky also does not believe that Mr. Frank had "poor execution of lesson planning," and does believe that Mr. Frank met Lawrence's expectations for public school teachers.

[O]n May 19, 2004, Lawrence Board of Education members . . . voted to terminate Mr. Frank's employment . . . .

On December 13, 2004, Mr. Frank filed a charge with the Equal Employment Opportunity Commission.

. . . .

DISCUSSION

. . . .

A. Discrimination Under the ADA and the NYHRL

To establish a prima facie case of disability discrimination under the ADA or the NYSHRL, a plaintiff must show that: (1) the employer is subject to the relevant statute; (2) the plaintiff is disabled within the statute's meaning; (3) the plaintiff was otherwise qualified to perform the essential functions of his job, with or without reasonable accommodation; and (4) "he suffered adverse employment action because of his disability." *Heyman v. Queens Village Committee for Mental Health*, 198 F.3d 68, 72 (2d Cir. 1999); *Attis v. Solow Realty Development Co.*, 522 F. Supp. 2d 623, 627 (S.D.N.Y. 2007) (standards for a prima facie case the same under NYSHRL).

Here, there is no dispute that Lawrence is subject to both the ADA and the NYSHRL, or that Mr. Frank is otherwise qualified to serve as a mathematics teacher. Thus, the only disputed questions concern: (1) whether Mr. Frank was disabled, or regarded as disabled, under the ADA, Rehabilitation Act and NY-SHRL; and (2) whether Defendants discriminated against him based on that disability or perceived disability.

B. Is Obesity a Disability?

Defendants correctly argue, and Mr. Frank does not dispute, that obesity is not a disability under the ADA. *See Francis v. City of Meriden*, 129 F.3d 281, 286 (2d Cir. 1997). Similarly, because there is no evidence that Mr. Frank's obesity "constitute[d] or result[ed] in a substantial impediment to employment," Mr. Frank was also not disabled for Rehabilitation Act purposes. Thus, Defendants are entitled to summary judgment on Mr. Frank's ADA and Rehabilitation Act claims predicated on Mr. Frank's alleged disability.

The law is less clear with respect to Mr. Frank's NYSHRL claim. In *State Div. of Human Rights on Complaint of McDermott v. Xerox Corp.*, 65 N.Y.2d 213, 219, 491 N.Y.S.2d 106, 480 N.E.2d 695 (1985), the New York Court of Appeals held that "clinically diagnosed" obesity constituted a disability under the NYSHRL. But then, in *Delta Air Lines v. New York State Div. of Human Rights*, 91 N.Y.2d 65, 72–73, 666 N.Y.S.2d 1004, 689 N.E.2d 898 (N.Y. 1997), the Court of Appeals limited

Xerox. There, the Court of Appeals rejected disability discrimination claims brought by plaintiffs who challenged Delta's weight requirements for flight attendants. Distinguishing *Xerox*, the Court held that the plaintiffs had failed to show that they were "medically incapable of meeting Delta's weight requirements due to some cognizable medical condition." The Court stated that the presence of such a "condition" was "crucial in *Xerox* and is utterly absent here." With the plaintiffs lacking such a condition, the Court found that their claims failed because "weight, in and of itself, does not constitute a disability" under the NYSHRL.

There is little law interpreting *Delta*. In perhaps the only case discussing *Delta's* limits on *Xerox*, *Spiegel v. Schulmann*, 03-CV-5088, 2006 U.S. Dist. LEXIS 86531, *43–45 (E.D.N.Y. Nov. 30, 2006), the Court interpreted *Delta* as requiring plaintiffs asserting "weight" disability claims to show that their weight problems resulted from another medical condition.

This Court disagrees with *Spiegal's* interpretation. *Delta* stopped short of overturning *Xerox*. And, in *Xerox*, the plaintiff's obesity did not result "from any other disorder causally related" to her weight. Rather, the plaintiff's obesity "was probably due to bad dietary habits." Accordingly, this Court understands *Delta* to have distinguished *Xerox* on the grounds that, in *Xerox*, the plaintiff had "clinically diagnosed" obesity, and thus, a "cognizable medical condition," while the *Delta* plaintiffs did not. Indeed, there is no indication that the *Delta* plaintiffs were even overweight. Rather, the issue concerned whether the plaintiffs satisfied *Delta* Airlines' weight requirements for flight attendants. Thus, construing *Xerox* and *Delta* together, the Court understands New York's Court of Appeals to recognize NYSHRL disability claims predicated on "clinically diagnosed" conditions — such as obesity — but not claims based on weight alone.

C. Was Mr. Frank Obese?

Because clinically diagnosed obesity is an NYSHRL disability, the question then turns to whether Mr. Frank was clinically obese during the applicable time period. The Court finds that Mr. Frank has satisfied his *McDonnell-Douglas* burden for this prong. Specifically, Mr. Frank has produced affidavits from himself and his former treating physician, Dr. Paul Orbon, along with copies of Dr. Orbon's medical reports. These medical reports establish that Mr. Frank weighed between 343 and 348 pounds in 2000 and 2001. Dr. Orbon's affidavit sets forth that Mr. Frank's weight during this period constituted "morbid obesity," a "medically diagnosable condition." Likewise, Mr. Frank's affidavit establishes that "[a]t all times in my employment, I was 6 feet, 5 inches tall and weighed approximately 340 pounds." . . . Thus, Mr. Frank has set forth a triable issue of fact concerning whether he was clinically obese when Defendants denied him tenure and then fired him.

D. Did Defendants "Regard" Mr. Frank as Disabled?

Mr. Frank also contends that Defendants "regarded" him as disabled. Specifically, in his affidavit, Mr. Frank sets forth that Ms. Lineal told him that his "size and weight were not conducive to learning" and "were preventing me from fulfilling the job functions of a teacher."

. . . [T]he Court finds that it suffices to show that Ms. Lineal regarded him as disabled.

Mr. Frank also asserts "regarded as" claims under the ADA and the Rehabilitation Act. For the same reasons that Mr. Frank's "regarded as" claim survives summary judgment under the NYSHRL, it also survives under the ADA and the Rehabilitation Act.

E. Did Mr. Frank Suffer an Adverse Employment Action due to his Obesity?

The final element of Mr. Frank's prima facie case concerns whether he suffered an adverse employment action due to his obesity, or due to Defendants regarding him as disabled. Here, Mr. Franks has submitted ample amounts of direct and circumstantial evidence to establish Defendants' discriminatory animus. Viewing the evidence in the light most favorable to Mr. Frank, Mr. Frank has shown — among other things — that: (1) both Mr. Frank and Dr. Kavarsky testified that Ms. Lineal made inappropriate comments about Mr. Frank's weight and appearance, although they differed on certain details (i.e., whether she called Mr. Frank "big and sloppy" or a "big man"); (2) Ms. Lineal put the "kibosh" on Mr. Frank's tenure, but failed to support or justify her reasoning; (3) Mr. Akst inexplicably replaced Dr. Kavarsky as Mr. Frank's supervisor, even though he had no experience supervising math teachers, possibly because Ms. Lineal could exert improper influence over him; (4) after meeting with Ms. Lineal, Mr. Akst reversed his position on granting Mr. Frank tenure; (5) Dr. Kavarsky strongly supported Mr. Frank, and his tenure recommendations had never been overruled before; and (6) after learning about Mr. Frank's discrimination complaint, Defendants purposefully destroyed Ms. Lineal's file on Mr. Frank, which included "[a]nectodal notes" she took while observing his classroom performance.

In addition, even if Defendants arguably set forth legitimate non-discriminatory reasons for denying Mr. Frank tenure and firing him, Mr. Frank has more than shown — for summary judgment purposes — that these reasons were a pretext. Among other things, Mr. Frank has set forth that: (1) issues serious enough to deny tenure are typically mentioned in a teacher's annual appraisals; (2) Mr. Frank's annual appraisals did not list any of these purported problems with his performance and, in fact, praised his work; (3) Mr. Frank's own principal, Dr. Kavarsky, has "no clue" what Mr. Frank's supposed "ineffective teaching techniques" were, and likewise rejects Defendants' claim that Mr. Frank had "poor execution of lesson planning" and did not meet Lawrence's expectations; and (4) Defendants granted tenure to several non-obese teachers with similar purported performance issues.

Accordingly, the Court finds that: (1) Mr. Frank's ADA and Rehabilitation Act claims survive on a "regarded as" disabled theory; and (2) Mr. Frank's NYSHRL claim survives on both a disability discrimination theory and a "regarded as" theory.

———

LOWE v. AMERICAN EUROCOPTER, LLC
2010 U.S. Dist. LEXIS 133343 (N.D. Miss. Dec. 16, 2010)

Plaintiff, who is an allegedly disabled forty-eight year old African American female, was employed as a receptionist from July 17, 2007, until May 22, 2009, when she was terminated. Plaintiff claims that she was replaced by a younger non-disabled Caucasian female, and that she was terminated, harassed, and forced to perform more work due to her disability. . . . Plaintiff — who is proceeding pro se — filed this Complaint alleging [*inter alia*] disability discrimination and disability-based hostile work environment under the Americans with Disabilities Act (ADA), 42 U.S.C.A. § 12101 *et seq.* . . . Defendant filed a Motion to Dismiss . . . .

. . . .

Plaintiff claims that her termination was a result of her disability in violation of the ADA. Under the ADA, as amended, a disability is "(A) a physical or mental impairment that substantially limits one or more major life activities of such individual; (B) a record of such an impairment; or (C) being regarded as having such an impairment." 42 U.S.C. § 12102(1). A "qualified individual with a disability" is "an individual with a disability who, with or without reasonable accommodation, can perform the essential functions of the employment position that such individual holds or desires." 42 U.S.C. § 12111(8).

Plaintiff claims that she is disabled due to her weight. In response, Defendant contends that obesity is not a disabling impairment under the ADA. Despite Defendant's blanket contention, the Court is unable to say that obesity can never be a disability under the ADA, especially given that on September 25, 2008, the ADA was amended by the Americans with Disabilities Act Amendments Act of 2008 ("ADAAA"). See Americans with Disabilities Act Amendments Act of 2008, Pub.L. No. 110-325, 112 Stat. 3553, 110th Cong., 2d Sess. (Sept. 25, 2008) (effective Jan. 1, 2009).

Prior to the ADAAA, the Interpretive Guidance created by the EEOC on Title I of the ADA provided that except in "rare circumstances," obesity is not considered a disabling impairment. See *Melson v. Chetofield*, 2009 U.S. Dist. LEXIS 19025, at *3 (E.D. La. Mar. 4, 2009). Furthermore, many courts presented with the issue of obesity as a disability have held that such an impairment is not recognized under the ADA. *See, e.g., Merker v. Miami-Dade County Fla.*, 485 F. Supp. 2d 1349, 1353 (S.D. Fla. 2007) (citing *EEOC v. Watkins Motor Lines, Inc.*, 463 F.3d 436, 440–443 (6th Cir. 2007)("we hold that to constitute an ADA impairment, a person's obesity, even morbid obesity, must be the result of a physiological condition.")); *Francis v. City of Meriden*, 129 F.3d 281, 286 (2d Cir. 1997) ("obesity, except in special cases where the obesity relates to a physiological disorder, is not 'physical impairment' within the meaning of the [ADA] statutes."); *Marsh v. Sunoco, Inc.*, 2006 U.S. Dist. LEXIS 88887, at *4 (E.D. Pa. Dec. 6, 2006) (same); *Coleman v. Georgia Power Co.*, 81 F. Supp. 2d 1365, 1369 (N.D. Ga. 2000) (same); *Fredregill v. Nationwide Agribusiness Ins. Co.*, 992 F. Supp. 1082, 1088–89 (S.D. Iowa 1997) (collecting cases)). However, these cases were all before the ADAAA took effect. This is especially important due to the expansion of what "substantially limits" and "major life activities" mean under the ADAAA. The ADAAA appears to have legislatively pre-empted the Supreme Court's past definitions of "substantially limits," stating that the Court's standard was "too high," and that "substantially limits" should be more broadly interpreted. 122 Stat. 3552, sec. 2, § a(8); 42 U.S.C.A. § 12101. The ADAAA details a nonexhaustive list of what constitutes a major life activity, stating that in general such activities are, but not limited to "caring for oneself, performing manual tasks, seeing, hearing, eating, sleeping, walking, standing, lifting, bending, speaking, breathing, learning, reading, concentrating, thinking, communicating, and working." 42 U.S.C.A. § 12102(2)(A). Further, under the ADAAA, bodily function limitations are now considered a major life activity. 42 U.S.C.A. § 12102(2)(B). Here, Plaintiff asserts that her weight affects the major life activity of walking.

Also affected by the ADAAA is the "regarded as having" a disability prong of the ADA. In this case, Plaintiff states that her "[e]mployer was informed of this situation [referring to her obesity and her inability to walk from the regular parking lot]." The Court reads this as Plaintiff's attempt to show that her employer regarded her as having such a disability. Under the ADAAA, an individual is now not required to demonstrate that the disability she is regarded as having is an actual qualified disability under the ADA or that it substantially limits a major life activity. See 42 U.S.C.A. §§ 12102(1)(C), (3). The ADAAA requires a plaintiff to only show "that he or she has been subjected to an action prohibited under this chapter because of an actual or perceived physical or mental impairment whether or not the impairment limits or is perceived to limit a major life activity." Thus, a plaintiff now might be considered disabled due to obesity under the ADA if her employer perceived her weight as an impairment.

Based on the substantial expansion of the ADA by the ADAAA, Defendant's assertion that Plaintiff's weight cannot be considered a disability is misplaced. See *Melson v. Chetofield*, 2009 U.S. Dist. LEXIS 19025, at *3 (E.D. La. Mar. 4, 2009) (finding that plaintiff pled sufficient facts showing that her obesity was a disabling impairment to overcome a motion to dismiss); but see *Frank v. Lawrence Union Free Sch. Dist.*, 688 F. Supp. 2d 160, 169 (E.D.N.Y. 2010) (citing case law prior to the ADAAA and holding that obesity is not a disability under the ADA). Whether or not Plaintiff can in fact prove that her weight rises to the level of a disability under the ADA is not at issue here, as a motion to dismiss is not the proper method for evaluating the merits of Plaintiff's specific assertions. Swierkiewicz, 534 U.S. at 514, 122 S. Ct. 992 ("claims lacking merit may be dealt with through summary judgment under Rule 56."). As such, Plaintiff has pled enough facts, taken as true, to allege she qualifies as "disabled" within the meaning of the ADA.

Upon finding that Plaintiff has plausibly alleged that she is disabled, Plaintiff must also show that "[s]he is 'qualified' for the job . . . and [that] an adverse employment decision was made [ ] because of [her] disability" in order to establish an ADA discrimination claim. Here, Plaintiff sufficiently pleads that she was qualified for her job, that her employer knew of her impairment, that she was terminated due to this impairment, and that she was not reasonably accommodated . . . . Accordingly, Plaintiff's claim is plausible on its face, and Defendant's Rule 12(b)(6) motion to dismiss Plaintiff's disability discrimination claim is denied.

———

NOTES AND QUESTIONS

1. **Is obesity a disease or disability?** The *Frank* and *Lowe* cases illustrate the significance of classifying obesity as a disease or disability for purposes of determining whether a person falls within a class protected by the Americans with Disabilities Act and state anti-discrimination laws. Courts have attempted to distinguish between weight problems that themselves can be characterized as a disease (or perhaps the product of a disease) from those that are — for lack of a better description — the person's own choice. Is this a useful or even accurate distinction?

Ms. Lowe did not succeed in her claim. (After she filed for bankruptcy without disclosing the lawsuit to the bankruptcy court, the court granted summary judgment to her employer, and the Fifth Circuit Court of Appeals affirmed that judgment. *Lowe v. Am. Eurocopter, LLC*, 2012 U.S. App. LEXIS 4708 (5th Cir. Mar. 7, 2012).) But, the question of whether "weight rises to the level of a disability" remains an issue of law, as well as a problem for policy.

2. **AMA recognizes obesity as a disease.** In 2013, the American Medical Association recognized obesity as a disease. American Medical Ass'n, Recognition of Obesity as a Disease (June 2013) ("Resolved: That our American Medical Association recognizes obesity as a disease state with multiple pathophysiological aspects requiring a range of interventions to advance obesity treatment and prevention. (Res. 420, A-13)"), http://www.ama-assn.org/assets/meeting/2013a/a13-resolutions. pdf. (visited Oct. 2013). What advantages or disadvantages could result from classifying obesity as a disease? Would the American Medical Association's resolution persuade a court that Mr. Frank or Ms. Lowe had a disability within the meaning of the ADA? What effect might defining obesity as a disease have on health insurance or life insurance coverage? How might it affect how obesity is perceived by the public?

3. **ADA claims.** Title I of the Americans with Disabilities Act, 42 U.S.C. §§ 12101 et seq., prohibits discrimination in employment on the basis of disability by employers with at least 15 employees. (It does not apply to the federal government, the Indian Tribes, or tax-exempt private membership organizations.) In the Act, "The term 'disability" means, with respect to an individual: (A) a physical or mental impairment that substantially limits one or more major life activities of such individual; (B) a record of such an impairment; or (C) being regarded as having such an impairment." 42 U.S.C. § 12102(1). Major life activities are defined "to include, but are not limited to, caring for oneself, performing manual tasks, seeing, hearing, eating, sleeping, walking, standing, lifting, bending, speaking, breathing, learning, reading, concentrating, thinking, communicating, and working." *Id.* at § 12102(2). The definitions also specify that "a major life activity also includes the operation of a major bodily function, including but not limited to, functions of the immune system, normal cell growth, digestive, bowel, bladder, neurological, brain, respiratory, circulatory, endocrine, and reproductive functions." *Id.*

Discrimination in employment is broadly defined to include discrimination with respect to hiring, firing, training, promotion, compensation, benefits, and any other condition of employment. The ADA makes discrimination unlawful only against a qualified employee — one who is qualified for the job at issue — and only if the discriminatory action is *on the basis of* (because of) a real or perceived disability. *Id.* at § 12112. An employer remains free to take adverse action against an employee on grounds unrelated to disability, such as poor performance, as long as those grounds are not merely a pretext for discrimination on the basis of disability. The employee has the burden of proving pretext. *See McDonnell-Douglas Corp. v. Green*, 411 U.S. 792 (1973).

IN RE: BRITTANY T.
Family Court, Chemung County, New York (Feb. 7, 2007)

This court is called upon once again ultimately to determine whether it is in the best interest of a morbidly obese child, who also suffers from numerous co-morbidities, to be removed from parents who have consistently failed to address her severe medical concerns and who have also failed to ensure her proper school attendance . . . .

[Brittany was 13 years old with a BMI of 50 at the time of hearing. William J. Cochran, the pediatric gastroenterologist and nutritionist concluded that Brittany's weight was due to excessive caloric intake and a sedentary lifestyle and not genetic or psychiatric disease. The court had earlier ordered the child to be placed in a nutrition program, including behavior modification, dietary assistance, exercise therapy, and lifestyle changes, and required the parents to ensure that the child attend school, go to the gym at least twice a week, and sign releases to permit the department of social services to monitor progress. The parents' earlier failures to comply fully had resulted in an order granting legal custody to the department, but the child was later returned to her parents.]

. . . Cochran expressed his concern that after two and a half years, the attempts to deal with Brittany and the parents regarding her obesity has, overall, been "unsuccessful." Very much concerning to Cochran was that in the Fall of 2005 (when the child left his program and was returned to the respondents), she weighed 238; by February of 2005 (when she was ordered to reenter it), she weighed in at 261, a gain of approximately five pounds per month. This all occurred while a weight loss of one to two pounds per month had been achieved and was a realistic expectation for the future . . . .

. . . Typical of his concerns was an incident he described in November of 2004. He testified that he had just spent a long session with Brittany and Mrs. T. regarding Brittany's health. Right after the appointment, he went to an eating establishment across from the hospital. There he saw Brittany eating french fries and a "hamburger or something of that nature." . . . More recently, he noted, food logs continue to reflect regular ingestion by the child of foods he would certainly not recommend, including "lots of chicken nuggets, lots of pop tarts, hot dogs and pizza."

. . . .

. . . [A clinical dietician] explained that Brittany suffers from a significant amount of emotional distress related to her excessive weight [which] has a detrimental effect on her physical and emotional well-being . . . . She opined that she knew of no children removed from their homes due to weight and that she felt that being with any parent was better than being with no parent at all.

. . . [Brittany's father] is confined to a wheelchair and, he testified, suffers from cardiomyopathy, muscular dystrophy, arthritis and scoliosis . . . . Much of Brittany's tardiness, he said, was because he thought school started at 8:15, not 8:00 . . . .

. . . Mrs. T herself is very obese . . . . She offered that there were numerous difficulties during the period of supervision including such things as weather and transportation troubles and a hospital stay for herself for gallstones. She was aware that Brittany often had snacks after school and after dinner in the evening and that the child was known to "sneak food" at home. She also attributed some of the compliance difficulties to Brittany getting "frustrated" at "all she needs to do" and that the child "hates all of what the court has ordered the parents to do." On a positive note, the mother indicated that Brittany was now enjoying and doing better in school, to which she or her husband regularly drive her the half mile.

Distilled to its essence, the parents disagreed with particular dates and times, but did not refute that there have been missed appointments, missed school days and numerous tardies . . . . [T]hey indicated they had tried their best. Essentially, however, they each offered numerous excuses for their noncompliance and argued that the child has not been negatively impacted by their noncompliance. The court frankly finds the respondents' explanations regarding their inability to comply with the terms to be spurious, unpersuasive and largely lacking in credibility.

. . . .

The long history of this unfortunate case demonstrates that the respondents have unequivocally evinced an unwillingness to follow doctors' and others' advice, so as to justify a finding that they willfully violated the terms of the order of disposition . . . . The court recognizes the physical limitations of the respondents but finds that this neither excuses nor prohibits them from executing their parental and court-ordered responsibilities.

. . . .

It is clear in New York that a child is neglected when his or her "physical, mental or emotional condition has been impaired as a result of the failure of his or her parent to exercise a minimum degree of care in supplying the child with adequate education or medical care though financially able to do so." Family Ct. Act § 1012(f). The respondents, due to their continued failures with respect to Brittany's educational and medical needs, have not provided that minimum degree of care, which is measured against the behavior of reasonable and prudent parents faced with the same circumstances.

This court is cognizant of potential concerns regarding the power of the state to drastically intervene in the regulation of family affairs with respect to morbid obesity. It is also very aware of the emotional impact that disruptions in the parent-child relationship may have. This court also agrees and holds that state intervention would generally "not be justified simply because a child was overweight, or did not simply engage in a healthy and fit lifestyle." [citation omitted]

Capsule

However, where, as here, there are clear medical standards and convincing evidence that there exist severe, life-threatening dangers due to parental lifestyle and persistent neglect, removal is justified. This is no less a cause for determining neglect and ordering removal than is a matter where a child is at risk of life-limiting consequences due to malnourishment, inadequate supervision or other heretofore well-established bases for removal. Indeed, "the obesity must be of a severe nature reaching the life-threatening or morbid state, which has also manifested itself in physical problems, such as those present here, or mental problems." *In re* D.K., [58 Pa. D. & C. 4th 353], 358 (Pa. Com. Pl. 2002).

Holding

. . . The court finds that Brittany's continued residency in the home is contrary to her health, welfare and safety and that the best interest of the child warrants her removal from the care and custody of the parents and placement once again with the Department.

NOTES AND QUESTIONS

4. Denormalization or shaming. A few scholars have encouraged shaming as a way to encourage reductions in obesity. Gregg Bloche, for example, argues that public health strategies to discourage "sedentary living and risky eating" could be modeled after anti-smoking campaigns to change cultural attitudes from acceptance to disapproval. This approach, he adds, "should not shy away from judicious use of shame: portraying obesity as a burden to others (medically and financially) and a sign of self-indulgence can lend force to calls for self-restraint." Gregg Bloche, *Obesity and the Struggle Within Ourselves*, 93 Geo. L. J. 1335, 1354 (2005). *See also* Daniel Callahan, *Obesity: Chasing an Elusive Epidemic*, 43 Hasting Ctr. Report 34, 34 (2013) (advocating "strong social pressure" to persuade people that "excessive weight and outright obesity are not socially acceptable any longer.").

Others counter that the general public has long disapproved of excess weight. Evidence of discrimination against those who are not slim or at least of normal weight is not hard to find. Persons who are overweight are subject to intentional as well as unrecognized prejudice, which results in reduced employment opportunities and lower average income. *See* Amy Erdman Farrell, Fat Shame: Stigma and the Fat Body in American Culture (2011); John Cawley, *The Impact of Obesity on Wages*, 39(2) J. Human Resources 451 (2004). There is even evidence that some physicians and other health care providers exhibit bias against overweight patients. *See, e.g.,* Abigail C. Saguy, What's Wrong with Fat? 141–144 (2013); Geraldine M. Budd *et al.*, *Health Care Professionals' Attitudes about Obesity: An Integrative Review*, 24 Applied Nursing Research 127 (2011). A Texas hospital made news after adopting a policy refusing to hire anyone with a BMI over 35. Emily Ramshaw, *Victoria Hospital Won't Hire Very Obese Workers*, The Texas Tribune, March 26, 2012, www.texastribune.org/2012/03/26/victoria-hospital-wont-hire-very-obese-workers/. The hospital defended its policy as projecting the proper image of health care professionals, adding that its "patients have expectations that cannot be ignored in terms of personal appearance." *Id.* In contrast, the "fat rights" movement seeks to turn the paradigm around to protect body size as an aspect of liberty. *See* Yofi Tirosh, *The Right to Be Fat*, 12 Yale J. Health Pol'y, L. & Ethics 264 (2012).

5. Parental and state responsibilities. All states hold parents responsible for providing necessaries — food, shelter, clothing, and life-saving medical care — to their children. The case of Brittany T. is unusual in that the state sought to remove custody from her parents almost entirely on the basis of Brittany's weight. How much responsibility should parents' have for their children's size? How much control do parents actually have over their children's diet and physical activity? Does the child's age make a difference? *See* Lindsey Murtagh, David S. Ludwig, *State Intervention in Life-Threatening Childhood Obesity*, 306 JAMA 206 (2011) (arguing that obesity is sufficiently harmful to children that it can justify custody removal). How confident should the courts be of the correlations among parental control, diet, physical activity, size, and disease? Even in the case of clear evidence, what action should be taken? For example, should parents face criminal penalties for neglect in such cases? *See* Lauren Cox, *Courts Charge Mother of 555-pound Boy: A Mother Facing Felony Charges for Her Son's Obesity*, ABCNews.com, June 29, 2009, http://abcnews.go.com/Health/WellnessNews/story?id=7941609 (visited Nov. 2013).

6. Normal BMI as a prerequisite for care. Recall the Medicaid programs that encourage recipients to lose weight and improve their health, discussed in Chapter 8, *supra*. Should a normal weight be a precondition for receiving health care — or any other public benefit, for that matter? The Scottish newspaper Express reported that, after October 1, 2012, the National Health Service would no longer pay for in vitro fertilization for a woman with a BMI of 30 or above or for couples where both parents smoke. David Scott, *Fat Smokers Banned from Trying for Test Tube Babies*, Scottish Express, Sept. 22, 2012, www.express.co.uk/news/uk/347527/Fat-smokers-banned-from-trying-for-test-tube-babies (visited Nov. 2013). The Health Service, facing budget cuts, sought to save taxpayer funds, but NHS patients are taxpayers, too. Is infertility treatment a "luxury" that can be limited? The NHS Fife was reported to say "Treatment criteria have been revised to improve the success of the treatment and the outcomes for mothers and babies." *Id.* The Scots may be unusually severe when it comes to obesity. *See* Lauren Cox, *Scottish Courts Briefly Take Obese Mother's Newborn Child*, ABCNews.com, Oct. 27, 2009, http://abcnews. go.com/Health/Diet/courts-obese-familys-newborn-neglect/story?id=8921808 (visited Nov 2013).

E. THE ENVIRONMENT FOR FOOD AND PHYSICAL ACTIVITY

Eric A. Finkelstein & Kiersten L. Strombotne, *The Economics of Obesity*
91(Suppl) Am. J. Clin. Nutr. 1520s, 1520s–1522s (2010)

Economics is at the heart of the obesity epidemic. Economic forces have made it easier and cheaper to consume high-energy, tasty, affordable foods and have allowed us to be increasingly sedentary at work, at home, and in between. Moreover, medical advances have lowered the health costs (*i.e.*, consequences), if not the financial costs, that result from excess weight, and have perhaps decreased the motivation to diet and exercise. In other words, the rise in obesity rates is a direct result of changes in relative prices (or costs) that promote excess food consumption and inactivity and that decrease the motivation to engage in health-seeking behaviors.

Food consumption

One of the basic tenets of economics is the inverse relation between price and quantity demanded. As prices decrease, quantity demand is expected to increase. Demand for food is no exception. During the past several decades, food prices have been steadily dropping. Since 1978, food prices have dropped 38% relative to the prices of other goods and services.

Even more relevant, high-calorie foods have become much cheaper than more healthful alternatives. US data show that since 1983 the price of fresh fruit and vegetables has increased by 190%, all fruit and vegetables by 144%, fish by 100%, and dairy products by 82%, whereas the price of fats and oils, sugars and sweets, and carbonated beverages, for example, increased at much lower rates (70%, 66%, and 32%, respectively), which suggests that the relative prices of associated foods have decreased. Much of the decrease in relative prices is a result of advances in food technology that disproportionately affect processed foods (*e.g.*, freeze drying, vacuum packaging, and the discovery and mass production of high-fructose corn syrup). Generous subsidies for corn and soy-based products, the primary ingredients of many energy-dense foods, have also contributed to the decrease. Regardless of the cause, as these calorie-dense foods become cheaper than more healthful alternatives, people shift their consumption toward more affordable, more fattening options.

In addition to falling monetary costs, technology has decreased the amount of time and energy it takes to prepare food. Decreasing nonmonetary costs are also expected to increase consumption. For example, the widespread availability and convenience of the microwave oven have made it even easier for prepackaged food, which tends to be higher in calories than food cooked from scratch, to play a more prominent role in the home. Today, 95% of US homes have a microwave oven, compared with 8% in 1978. Decreases in the acquisition cost of food is also supported by the sheer volume of restaurants, cafeterias, snack bars, vending machines, and other locations where prepackaged foods can be purchased at low prices and with minimal preparation time. These options were not available a few decades ago.

So has food consumption increased consistently with falling food costs, both monetary and nonmonetary? In the United States, between the late 1970s and today, men increased their daily food intake by ≈80 calories, and women increased their daily food intake by ≈360 calories. On the assumption of no change in energy expenditure, these increases are more than enough to generate the rise in adult obesity rates and, consistent with these findings, women have experienced greater weight gain than men. Children have also increased their caloric intake. Adolescent boys now average ≈2800 calories/d, an increase of 250 calories from the mid-1970s. Similarly, adolescent girls now average ≈1900 calories, an increase of 120 calories.

Much of the increase in calorie consumption has occurred between meals, when the time costs were historically too high to prepare a high-calorie snack. As a consequence of innovations in technology and falling prices, the prevalence of snacking and the number of calories per snack have both increased. Jahns et al showed that the prevalence of snackers among children of all ages increased from 77% to 91% from 1977 to 1996. Piernas and Popkin showed that sugar-sweetened beverages and desserts were among the highest contributors to snacking caloric intake in youth.

Energy expenditure

Although the cost of calorie consumption has decreased, the cost of expending those calories has increased significantly. Consider energy expenditure in the workplace. As a result of advances in workplace technology, even the most blue-collar occupations have been automated to the point where employees burn very few calories in the workplace. This technology has allowed employees to be increasingly productive and to earn a higher wage as a result, but partly at the expense of their growing waistlines. One study suggests that after 18 y, an average male worker would weigh 25 pounds more if he worked in the lowest fitness-demanding jobs than if he had worked in the highest fitness-demanding jobs. Yet not only are jobs that burn large numbers of calories increasingly hard to find, they also pay low wages, and few people would be willing to take a substantial pay-cut in exchange for a few extra pounds of weight loss.

One strategy to offset the increase in calories consumed and the decrease in calories expended in the workplace is to increase leisure-time physical activity. However, that too requires significant costs when one considers what needs to be given up to engage in that activity (what economists term opportunity costs). Over the past few decades, a host of sedentary new technologies, which include computers, the Internet, video games, cable television, and others, have been introduced that compete for our free time. It is estimated that children aged 8–18 y spend >3 h per day on average watching TV, DVDs, and movies and playing video games. To engage in physical activity requires taking a break from these and other technologies, which many people are not willing to do. As a result, leisure-time physical activity levels remain low. In the United States, only 4 out of 10 adults meet physical activity guidelines. The US Surgeon General reports that ≈25% of US youth (aged 12–21 y) report no vigorous physical activity and ≈14% of young people report no vigorous or light-to-moderate physical activity. Children also spend less time being physically active in school. In 2003, 28% of adolescents participated in physical education courses, compared with 42% in 1991.

Motivation to engage in health-seeking behaviors

There is at least one more potential cause behind the rise in obesity rates, or at least behind the lack of efforts among the obese to lose weight. And this, too, is based on economics. As a result of advances in medical technology, the health consequences of being obese have decreased. Over the past few decades, there has been a tremendous increase in medical, pharmacologic, and surgical treatments for the risk factors and diseases that obesity promotes, which suggests that the health consequences, one form of the cost of obesity, are not as great as they once were. For example, many drugs and surgical procedures have been introduced over the past 40 years that effectively treat cholesterol, blood pressure, and other risk factors that obesity promotes. Partly as a result of these new technologies, obese adults in the United States have better blood pressure and cholesterol concentrations than normal-weight individuals did a few decades ago. They are also likely to take newly developed medications to keep their diabetes under control. As a result of these and other medical advancements, they may be less concerned about their weight and therefore less likely to make an effort to decrease it.

. . . .

Classical economic theory suggests that, given all possible choices, individuals will choose the options that make them best off (in economic terms, they make the choices that maximize their utility) given their preferences and constraints. These choices concern where they work, how much they eat and exercise, and whether they engage in activities to control excess weight, among others. The underlying assumption is not that individuals have perfect information about these choices, but that they make the decisions that are best for them given the information they do have. Moreover, the decision to acquire additional information, such as how many calories are in a meal, is also a choice that individuals can make if they perceive the benefits as worth the costs.

It is possible that food addictions, manipulation by marketers, short-sightedness, or other factors make it difficult for individuals to make optimal choices when it comes to their weight. However, it is also possible, and quite likely, that many rational, utility-maximizing individuals will engage in behaviors that are obesity promoting simply because — in today's obesity-promoting environment — it is just too costly (in economic terms) to weigh less.

. . . .

Given our contention that obesity results from market forces and technologic advances that lower the costs of behaviors that promote obesity, successful efforts to prevent obesity will need to do just the opposite: make it easier and cheaper to engage in a healthy diet and regular physical activity. This will require policy and environmental changes that extend beyond that which can be achieved through changes in health care financing and delivery. It will not be an easy feat, but anything short of that is unlikely to have a significant effect on the worldwide obesity epidemic.

Jennifer L. Harris *et al.*,
Fast Food FACTS 2013: Measuring Progress in Nutrition and Marketing to Children and Teens,
Executive Summary vi–vii
Yale Rudd Center for Nutrition Policy and Obesity (2013)
www.fastfoodmarketing.org/media/FastFoodFACTS_Report.pdf

Nutrition results

Kids' meal options have improved since 2010. Most [fast food] restaurants offer more healthy sides and beverages and some also offer healthy main dishes for their kids' meals. Restaurants also added a few new healthy options to their regular menus. However, nearly all items on fast food menus — including kids' meal items — exceed recommended levels of calories, saturated fat, sodium, and/or sugar for children and teens.

From 2010 to 2013, the nutritional quality of individual items offered with kids' meals improved at some restaurants. All restaurants except Taco Bell offered at least one healthy side option for their kids' meals; three-quarters of restaurants with kids' meals increased healthy beverage options; and McDonald's introduced half-portions of french fries and apples as the default sides in Happy Meals. There was also a 54% increase in the number of different kids' meals available, consisting of a kids' main dish, side, and beverage. In total, the 12 restaurants examined in 2013 with special kids' menus offered 5,427 possible kids' meal combinations.

However, there was no change in the percent of kids' meal combinations that qualified as healthy meals for children. As in 2010, less than 1% of all kids' meal combinations met recommended nutrition standards . . . . Only five restaurants (Subway, Burger King, Taco Bell, Arby's, and Jack in the Box) offered even one kids' meal main dish option that was not too high in saturated fat and/or sodium . . . .

On regular menus, there was also a dramatic increase in the number of menu items offered by fast food restaurants, but the proportion of healthy versus unhealthy menu items remained the same. From 2010 to 2013, McDonald's, Subway, Burger King, and Taco Bell averaged 71 additional menu items per restaurant (+35%), and the number of snack and dessert items offered increased 88%. McDonald's continued to have the highest proportion of menu items that met nutrition criteria for teens (24%). At Burger King, Subway, and Wendy's, no more than 20% of items qualified as nutritious. McDonald's, Subway, Taco Bell, and Sonic did advertise healthy menus consisting of items they designated as healthier or lower-calorie. However, less than half of healthy menu items at McDonald's, Subway, and Sonic met all nutrition criteria. Healthy menus from Subway and Sonic were less likely to meet nutrition criteria in 2013 than in 2010. In addition, all restaurants continued to offer large or extra-large soft drinks with 350 to 850 calories per serving and burger restaurants offered large french fries with 470 to 610 calories.

Marketing results

In 2012, fast food restaurants spent $4.6 billion in total on all advertising, an 8% increase over 2009. For context, the biggest advertiser, McDonald's, spent 2.7 times as much to advertise its products ($972 million) as all fruit, vegetable, bottled water, and milk advertisers combined ($367 million).

On average, U.S. preschoolers viewed 2.8 fast food ads on TV every day in 2012, children (6 to 11 years) viewed 3.2 ads per day, and teens viewed 4.8 ads per day. Six companies were responsible for more than 70% of all TV ads viewed by children and teens: McDonald's, Subway, Burger King, Domino's, Yum! Brands (Taco Bell, Pizza Hut, KFC), and Wendy's.

Marketing to children

There were a few positive developments in fast food marketing to children. From 2009 to 2012, total fast food TV advertising seen by children ages 6 to 11 declined by 10%. McDonald's and Burger King (the two biggest advertisers in 2009) reduced their advertising to children by 13% and 50%, respectively. Marketing to children on the internet also declined. Three popular child-targeted websites (Dairy Queen's DeeQs.com, McDonald's LineRider.com, and Burger King's ClubBK.com) were discontinued, as was McDonald's site for preschoolers (Ronald.com). Just one site (HappyMeal.com) had more than 100,000 monthly unique child visitors in 2012, compared with four sites in 2009.

However, there are many reasons for continued concern. Despite the decline in TV advertising to 6 to 11-year-olds, advertising to very young children (ages 2 to 5) did not change from 2009 to 2012, and the majority of fast food restaurants stepped up their TV advertising to children. Among the top-25 advertisers, 19 increased advertising to preschoolers, and 14 increased ads to older children. Of note, Domino's and Wendy's increased advertising to children by 44% and 13%, respectively, which were approximately six times their rates of increase in advertising to teens. Further, McDonald's continued to advertise more to children than to teens or adults on TV — the only restaurant to do so. On the internet, McDonald's also placed 34 million display ads for Happy Meals per month — up 63% from 2009. Three-quarters of Happy Meal ads appeared on kids' websites, such as Nick.com, Roblox.com, and CartoonNetwork.com. In addition, child-targeted advergames (i.e., branded games) have gone mobile with McDonald's "McPlay" and Wendy's "Pet Play Games" mobile apps.

A few restaurants did advertise their healthier kids' meals, but kids' meals represented only one-quarter of fast food ads viewed by children on TV. McDonald's Happy Meals were the most frequently advertised products to children, followed by Domino's pizza, Subway sandwiches, Wendy's lunch/ dinner items, and Pizza Hut pizza. Burger King and Subway kids' meals ranked 16 and 19, respectively. In apparent contradiction of Children's Advertising Review Unit (CARU) guidelines that advertising to children must focus primarily on the product being sold (i.e., food), Subway placed ads with a primary focus on the brand (not the food) on children's networks, and Burger King placed ads that focused primarily on child-targeted promotions. In addition, Wendy's and Subway advertised regular menu items — including Frostys, Baconator burgers, and Footlong sandwiches — directly to children on children's networks, including Nickelodeon and Cartoon Network. McDonald's advertised its Filet-o-fish sandwich and other regular menu items on kids' websites, including Nick.com and CartoonNetwork.com.

Marketing to teens

There were fewer positive trends in fast food marketing to teens. The overall nutritional quality of fast food products advertised to teens on TV did improve. Although the average number of fast food TV ads viewed by teens did not change from 2009 to 2012, average calories in TV ads viewed declined 16%, and the proportion of calories from sugar and saturated fat improved from 37% in 2010 to 28% in 2013. In addition, the number of display ads placed by fast food restaurants on youth websites declined by more than half, from 470 million ad views per month in 2009 to 210 million in 2012.

However, several restaurants continued to target teens directly with marketing for unhealthy products. Although teens watch 30% less TV than do adults, they saw as many or more TV advertisements for Taco Bell, Sonic, and Starbucks compared with adults. Thus these restaurants likely purchased advertising in media viewed by relatively more adolescents than adults. Burger King Smoothies were the only nutritious regular menu item among those advertised most frequently to teens. In addition, three restaurants substantially increased their display advertising on youth websites: KFC (+138%), Subway (+450%), and Starbucks (+330%). In contrast to the decline in child visits to restaurant websites, the number of teen visitors increased for more than half of the websites analyzed both in 2010 and 2013, including Subway.com (+102%), Starbucks.com (+92%), and McDonald's.com (+75%). Three fast food websites (PizzaHut.com, McDonalds.com, and Dominos.com) averaged 270,000 or more unique teen visitors per month.

Further, fast food marketing via mobile devices and social media — media that are popular with teens — grew exponentially in the three years examined. Fast food restaurants placed six billion display ads on Facebook in 2012, 19% of all their online display advertising. Dunkin' Donuts and Wendy's placed more than one-half of their online ads on Facebook. Starbucks was most popular on social media, with 35 million Facebook likes and 4.2 million Twitter followers, followed by McDonald's and Subway, which each had 23+ million Facebook likes and 1.4+ million Twitter followers. From 2010 to 2013, increases in the number of Facebook likes and Twitter followers ranged from 200% to 6400%. Six fast food restaurants had more than 10 million likes on Facebook in 2013. Taco Bell's YouTube videos were viewed nearly 14 million times. In addition, ten restaurants offered branded smartphone apps with interactive features, including order functions and special offers. Papa John's and Pizza Hut mobile apps averaged 700,000+ unique visitors per month.

Targeted marketing to racial and ethnic minority youth

Fast food restaurants also continued to target black and Hispanic youth, populations at high risk for obesity and related diseases. Increased advertising on Spanish-language TV raises special concerns. Combined advertising spending on Spanish-language TV by all fast food restaurants increased 8% from 2009 to 2012. KFC and Burger King increased their spending by 35% to 41% while reducing English- language advertising, and Domino's and Subway increased Spanish-language advertising by more than 15%. Hispanic preschoolers' exposure to fast food ads on Spanish-language TV increased by 16% reaching almost one ad viewed per day. They also saw 100 more of these ads than older Hispanic children or teens saw. However, just 5% of Spanish-language ads viewed by Hispanic children promoted kids' meals.

As in 2009, black children and teens saw approximately 60% more fast food ads than white youth, due largely to greater TV viewing. However, advertising for Starbucks, Popeyes, Papa John's, and some Burger King products appeared during programming watched relatively more often by black youth. Black and Hispanic youth were more likely than their white and non-Hispanic peers to visit one-third or more of all fast food websites. For instance, Hispanic youth were 30% more likely to visit HappyMeal.com, and black youth were 44% more likely to visit the site.

Kelly Brownell *et al.*, *Personal Responsibility and Obesity: A Constructive Approach to a Controversial Issue*
29 HEALTH AFF. 379, 380, 382–86 (2010)
http://content.healthaffairs.org/content/29/3/379.full

* * *

The notion that obesity is caused by the irresponsibility of individuals, and hence not corporate behavior or weak or counterproductive government policies, is the centerpiece of food industry arguments against government action. Its conceptual cousin is that government intervention unfairly demonizes industry, promotes a "nanny" state, and intrudes on personal freedoms. This libertarian call for freedom was the tobacco industry's first line of defense against regulation. It is frequently sounded today by the food industry and its allies, often in terms of vice and virtue that are deeply rooted in American history and that cast problems like obesity, smoking, heavy drinking, and poverty as personal failures.

. . . .

Industry had some early success with these arguments. Public policy reforms such as restricting junk food in schools and menu labeling were successfully blocked for years in various U.S. jurisdictions, as critics invoked personal responsibility claims at every turn. A recent example occurred in the early Senate and House discussion of health care reform that included the possibility of a tax on sugared beverages. Discussion ceased after a $24 million lobbying and advertising campaign in 2009 mounted by the beverage industry and funneled partly through an industry front group called Americans Against Food Taxes. And the personal responsibility frame was most clearly deployed in the Personal Responsibility in Food Consumption Act, created to ban lawsuits against the fast-food industry. The legislation passed in the U.S. House but failed in the Senate. Versions of it have been adopted in twenty-three states.

. . . .

If irresponsibility is the cause of obesity, one might expect evidence that people are becoming less responsible overall. But studies suggest the opposite. [A graph shows declining rates of alcohol use, riding with an impaired driver, not using seatbelts, and intercourse without a condom, in US adolescents and adults.] . . . . What might make behaviors related to diet and activity such an exception?

. . . .

Humans gain weight when their environment promotes highly palatable food. Consider the Pima Indians. Native to northern Mexico, the Mexican Pimas are physically active as subsistence farmers, eat indigenous food, and rarely suffer from obesity and diabetes. Among a related group of Pimas living in southern Arizona, researchers have found much higher average weights and the world's highest rate of diabetes. Research has shown consistently that people moving from less to more obese countries gain weight, and those moving to less obese countries lose weight.

Some conditions common to the modern food environment undermine or damage the body's delicate balance of hunger, satiety, and body weight. Rising portion sizes and increasing amounts of sugar in food are examples of such conditions . . . .

. . . .

A relatively new but compelling area of research examines whether some food can trigger an addictive process. Bartley Hoebel and colleagues have shown that animals taken on and off high-sugar diets show behavioral and neurological effects similar to those characterizing classic substances of abuse such as morphine. Other work has shown similarities in reward pathways for drugs and food.

. . . .

Until recently, American approaches to diet, physical activity, and obesity have largely focused on the individual. Predominant approaches have been to educate individuals and implore them to alter their behavior. This view, emphasized in the surgeon general's 1979 Healthy People report and reaffirmed in various government reports since, is consistent with the American focus on individualism in culture and politics.

Studies demonstrate repeatedly that judgments about obesity are linked to values of individualism, self-determination, political conservatism, and secular morality. The resulting "just world" belief is that people get what they deserve, that they are responsible for their life situation, and that to behave in ways contrary to expectations is immoral. These attributions echo Max Weber's Protestant work ethic, reflecting beliefs that hard work, determination, and self-discipline create success (for example, weight loss); that failure reflects personal weakness; and that obese people are lazy, gluttonous, and undisciplined. Numerous weight-based stereotypes have emerged from personal responsibility attributions, making obese people frequent targets of bias, stigma, and discrimination.

. . . .

Changes in disease prevalence are often brought about most rapidly and effectively through structural interventions that change the environment. Elimination of adverse agents at an early and common source is almost always more effective and efficient than depending on individuals to identify and avoid exposure or to treat the consequences. A safe water system prevents waterborne illness such as cholera and is far more effective than asking each person to purify water . . . The "upstream" approach is effective for several reasons: specific individuals can be employed to prevent or control exposure as their primary responsibility; and systems can be devised that include redundancy, monitoring, and feedback loops to optimize control.

The right to health is a fundamental and widely recognized aspect of human rights. Around the world, poor diet and obesity threaten this right. For people to be healthy, personal behavior, safe conditions, and an environment that supports healthy choices must combine in complementary ways.

The use of collective action to support personal responsibility is central to public health. It has been discussed in a variety of political and economic contexts using language such as "asymmetric paternalism," "optimal defaults" and "libertarian paternalism," and "choice architecture." The underlying notion is that choices must be made, but the environment affects the content of choice. Children in a school cafeteria will select food, but which choice they make is affected by the availability of some foods and not others . . . .

. . . .

The public holds nuanced views of the obesity problem that encompass personal and collective responsibility. In a nationally representative poll of 1,326 U.S. adults, Colleen Barry and colleagues asked about reasons for the high prevalence of obesity. The lowest-rated cause was personal behavior related to sloth and gluttony, while the highest was the food environment. Rated above personal behavior were "time crunch" issues, pressures such as food marketing, and addiction to certain food. In addition, the public perceived multiple causes: 66 percent of the sample chose three or more explanatory factors. There was support for a number of government actions including improving school nutrition (69 percent support) and even an outright ban on junk-food advertising (51 percent).

. . . .

The challenge is to combine personal and collective responsibility approaches in ways that best serve the public good. This begins with viewing these approaches as complementary, if not synergistic, and recognizing that conditions can be changed to create more optimal defaults that support informed and responsible decisions and hence enhance personal freedoms. Conditions that subvert responsible behavior have been identified. Attention can now turn to creating conditions that enhance responsible choices.

. . . .

Legislative and regulatory actions become more probable if there are identifiable victims who are unavoidably harmed without their consent. Children have traditionally been seen as just such victims. Food companies formulate and market food in ways that have powerful psychological and biological effects on children, thus undermining parents' ability to provide their children with a safe nutritional environment and making it difficult for children to develop responsible behavior.

Some of the first policy victories have been in schools. The federal government has stopped short of requiring changes in school food, but through reauthorization of the Special Supplemental Nutrition Program for Women, Infants, and Children (WIC) in 2004 it required all school districts to have wellness policies. In addition, dozens of school districts and several states (such as Connecticut and California) have taken action to change food in schools. There is great hope that the reauthorization of the Child Nutrition Act in 2010 will help change the nutrition landscape in schools by promoting healthier food in breakfast and lunch programs and by eliminating unhealthy foods that compete with the nation's nutrition guidelines . . . .

Regulations that promote the disclosure of information promote personal choice and responsibility by ameliorating information asymmetries in the marketplace. If consumers are to make better food choices, they must be armed with accurate, truthful information about what they purchase. This philosophy was the basis for the Nutrition Labeling and Education Act of 1990, which requires nutrition labels on packaged food. Menu labeling legislation is the more recent variant designed so that consumers see, at the very least, calorie information on restaurant menus and posted food options at fast-food outlets.

. . . .

Consumers must also be protected from inaccurate, misleading, or deceptive information, thus making enforcement of federal and state consumer protection laws a public health priority. A case in point is the "Smart Choices" program in which the food industry set its own nutrition standards and applied a Smart Choices label to products it considered healthy. Products such as mayonnaise and cereals such as Lucky Charms and Froot Loops received this designation, but the industry withdrew the program after criticism by the FDA and, perhaps most important, legal action announced by Connecticut's attorney general.

Food marketing has a negative impact on the nation's diet and hence health, particularly affecting children. Marketing is relentless, is overwhelming in amount, is carried out in many new forms referred to by industry as "stealth" approaches (for example, when built into online video games), often occurs outside the awareness of parents, and hence erodes the nation's goal of fostering healthier eating . . . . The vast majority of marketed products have poor nutritional quality. For example, a 2009 report on the marketing of breakfast cereals found almost perfect overlap between the cereals with the worst nutrition ratings and those marketed most aggressively to children.

A number of federal agencies have authority to affect food marketing, including the FTC, the FDA (labeling), and the U.S. Department of Agriculture (USDA; marketing of food in schools). Congress has the authority to set tighter standards for what can be marketed; states, particularly through the attorneys general, may be in a position to take action.

Two industry actions must be anticipated if government acts to curtail food marketing. Any change is virtually certain to be challenged in the courts using First Amendment protection of commercial speech as the basis. Second, as public scrutiny of industry intensifies, companies will continue issuing self-regulatory promises to act in the public good. The tobacco industry voluntarily withdrew its television advertising in the 1970s in exchange for the right to market in all other media. What seemed at the time to be a public health victory turned out otherwise, as industry used other more cost-effective means of marketing. Similar traps must be avoided with food and obesity, and there is every reason to be cautious when industry promises self-regulation.

. . . [G]overnment can set specific standards for food products . . . through legislation or administrative regulation . . . .

An example is the ban on trans fats in restaurants . . . . Although not particularly relevant to obesity (fats that replace trans fats have equivalent calories), the precedent could be very important. Salt is the next most likely ingredient to be the target of regulatory authority, but fat and sugar might be possibilities at some point.

. . . .

Perhaps the most controversial public policy proposal, and the one to evoke greatest outcry from industry about government intrusion, is to tax food, particularly sugar-sweetened beverages as a starting point . . . .

Changing food prices is a means of creating better defaults. Industry arguments that this would create hardship or remove one of life's simple pleasures are difficult to swallow, considering that, although a tax of a penny per ounce would reduce population consumption of sugared beverages, it would still leave the average American consuming 38.5 gallons of sugary beverages per year. Arguments that the tax is regressive are countered by knowledge that obesity and diabetes are regressive diseases that affect the poor in greater numbers. Moreover, revenues from the tax could be used for programs that would specifically help the poor.

Creating conditions that foster and support personal responsibility is central to public health. Default conditions now contribute to obesity, a reality that no amount of education or imploring of individuals can reverse. Government has a wide variety of options at its command to address the obesity problem. Judicious use of this authority can increase responsibility, help individuals meet personal goals, and reduce the nation's health care costs.

INSTITUTE OF MEDICINE, ACCELERATING PROGRESS IN OBESITY
PREVENTION: SOLVING THE WEIGHT OF THE NATION
2, 7, 10–16 (2012)

The Critical Importance of Obesity Prevention

Although the obesity epidemic in the United States has been instrumental in bringing worldwide attention to the problem, obesity also has become a problem worldwide. In the United States alone, one-third of adults are now obese, and the prevalence of obesity among children has risen from 5 to 17 percent in the past 30 years. Equally disturbing, these percentages generally are higher for ethnic minorities, for those who are low-income or less educated, and for rural populations. With obesity at these levels and with current trajectories suggesting the possibility of further increases, future health, social, and economic costs are likely to be devastating. Obesity is associated with major causes of death and disability, and its effect on predisposing individuals to the development of type 2 diabetes is so strong that the onset of this disease now is occurring in childhood.

In economic terms, the estimated annual cost of obesity-related illness based on data from the Medical Expenditure Panel Survey for 2000–2005 is $190.2 billion (in 2005 dollars), or nearly 21 percent of annual medical spending in the United States. Childhood obesity alone is responsible for $14.1 billion in direct medical costs. Many of these health-related obesity costs are absorbed by Medicare and Medicaid, important programs already under attack because of their national price tag. Moreover, obesity-related medical costs in general are expected to rise significantly, especially because today's obese children are likely to become tomorrow's obese adults. In fact, U.S. military leaders report that obesity has reduced their pool of potential recruits to the armed forces. As the U.S. economy struggles to stabilize and grow, obesity projections reveal that beyond the impact of growing medical costs attributable to obesity, the nation will incur higher costs for disability and unemployment benefits, and businesses will face the additional costs associated with obesity-related job absenteeism and lost productivity.

. . . .

Engagement and Equity

It is essential to recognize that accelerating progress toward obesity prevention will need to occur at every level, from individual, to family, to community, to society as a whole. Acceleration will require engagement among all levels and all sectors in order to build capacity and achieve impact so that individuals and families can successfully manage and support healthy changes in lifestyle.

. . . .

It is important to recognize as well that not all individuals, families, and communities are similarly situated. In many parts of the United States, low-income individuals and families live, learn, work, and play in neighborhoods that lack sufficient health-protective resources such as parks and open space, grocery stores, walkable streets, and high-quality schools . . . . To change this situation, robust and long-term community engagement and civic participation among these disadvantaged populations become essential.

. . . .

Recommendations and Strategies

The committee offers five recommendations, along with strategies for their implementation, under five respective overarching goals. Specific actions associated with each strategy, a detailed systems map illustrating the interactions among the recommendations and strategies, and indicators that can serve as measures of progress are presented in the body of the report . . . .

Goal 1: Make physical activity an integral and routine part of life.

Recommendation 1: Communities, transportation officials, community planners, health professionals, and governments should make promotion of physi-

cal activity a priority by substantially increasing access to places and opportunities for such activity.

Strategy 1-1: Enhance the physical and built environment. Communities, organizations, community planners, and public health professionals should encourage physical activity by enhancing the physical and built environment, rethinking community design, and ensuring access to places for such activity.

Strategy 1-2: Provide and support community programs designed to increase physical activity. Communities and organizations should encourage physical activity by providing and supporting programs designed to increase such activity.

Strategy 1-3: Adopt physical activity requirements for licensed child care providers. State and local child care and early childhood education regulators should establish requirements for each program to improve its current physical activity standards.

Strategy 1-4: Provide support for the science and practice of physical activity. Federal, state, and local government agencies should make physical activity a national health priority through support for the translation of scientific evidence into best-practice applications.

Goal 2: Create food and beverage environments that ensure that healthy food and beverage options are the routine, easy choice.

Recommendation 2: Governments and decision makers in the business community/private sector should make a concerted effort to reduce unhealthy food and beverage options and substantially increase healthier food and beverage options at affordable, competitive prices.

Strategy 2-1: Adopt policies and implement practices to reduce overconsumption of sugar-sweetened beverages. Decision makers in the business community/private sector, in nongovernmental organizations, and at all levels of government should adopt comprehensive strategies to reduce overconsumption of sugar-sweetened beverages.

Strategy 2-2: Increase the availability of lower-calorie and healthier food and beverage options for children in restaurants. Chain and quick-service restaurants should substantially reduce the number of calories served to children and substantially expand the number of affordable and competitively priced healthier options available for parents to choose from in their facilities.

Strategy 2-3: Utilize strong nutritional standards for all foods and beverages sold or provided through the government, and ensure that these healthy options are available in all places frequented by the public. Government agencies (federal, state, local, and school district) should ensure that all foods and beverages sold or provided through the government are aligned with the age-specific recommendations in the current Dietary Guidelines for Americans. The business community and the private sector operating venues frequented by the public should ensure that a variety of foods and beverages, including those recommended by the Dietary Guidelines for Americans, are sold or served at all times.

Strategy 2-4: Introduce, modify, and utilize health-promoting food and beverage retailing and distribution policies. States and localities should utilize financial incentives such as flexible financing or tax credits, streamlined permitting processes, and zoning strategies, as well as cross-sectoral collaborations (*e.g.*, among industry, philanthropic organizations, government, and the community) to enhance the quality of local food environments, particularly in low-income communities. These efforts should include encouraging or attracting retailers and distributors of healthy food (*e.g.*, supermarkets) to locate in underserved areas and limiting the concentration of unhealthy food venues (*e.g.*, fast-food restaurants, convenience stores). Incentives should be linked to public health goals in ways that give priority to stores that also commit to health-promoting retail strategies (*e.g.*, through placement, promotion, and pricing).

Strategy 2-5: Broaden the examination and development of U.S. agriculture policy and research to include implications for the American diet. Congress, the Administration, and federal agencies should examine the implications of U.S. agriculture policy for obesity, and should ensure that such policy includes understanding and implementing, as appropriate, an optimal mix of crops and farming methods for meeting the Dietary Guidelines for Americans.

Goal 3: Transform messages about physical activity and nutrition.

Recommendation 3: Industry, educators, and governments should act quickly, aggressively, and in a sustained manner on many levels to transform the environment that surrounds Americans with messages about physical activity, food, and nutrition.

Strategy 3-1: Develop and support a sustained, targeted physical activity and nutrition social marketing program. Congress, the Administration, other federal policy makers, and foundations should dedicate substantial funding and support to the development and implementation of a robust and sustained social marketing program on physical activity and nutrition. This program should encompass carefully targeted, culturally appropriate messages aimed at specific audiences (*e.g.*, tweens, new parents, mothers); clear behavior-change goals (*e.g.*, take a daily walk, reduce consumption of sugar-sweetened beverages among adolescents, introduce infants to vegetables, make use of the new front-of-package nutrition labels); and related environmental change goals (*e.g.*, improve physical environments, offer better food choices in public places, increase the availability of healthy food retailing).

Strategy 3-2: Implement common standards for marketing foods and beverages to children and adolescents. The food, beverage, restaurant, and media industries should take broad, common, and urgent voluntary action to make substantial improvements in their marketing aimed directly at children and adolescents aged 2–17. All foods and beverages marketed to this age group should support a diet that accords with the Dietary Guidelines for Americans in order to prevent obesity and risk factors associated with chronic disease risk . . . .

Strategy 3-3: Ensure consistent nutrition labeling for the front of packages, retail store shelves, and menus and menu boards that encourages healthier food choices. The Food and Drug Administration (FDA) and the U.S. Department of Agriculture should implement a standard system of nutrition labeling for the front of packages and retail store shelves that is harmonious with the Nutrition Facts panel, and restaurants should provide calorie labeling on all menus and menu boards.

Strategy 3-4: Adopt consistent nutrition education policies for federal programs with nutrition education components. USDA should update the policies for Supplemental Nutrition Assistance Program Education and the policies for other federal programs with nutrition education components to explicitly encourage the provision of advice about types of foods to reduce in the diet, consistent with the Dietary Guidelines for Americans.

Goal 4: Expand the role of health care providers, insurers, and employers in obesity prevention.

Recommendation 4: Health care and health service providers, employers, and insurers should increase the support structure for achieving better population health and obesity prevention.

Strategy 4-1: Provide standardized care and advocate for healthy community environments. All health care providers should adopt standards of practice (evidence-based or consensus guidelines) for prevention, screening, diagnosis, and treatment of overweight and obesity to help children, adolescents, and adults achieve and maintain a healthy weight, avoid obesity-related complications, and reduce the psychosocial consequences of obesity. Health care providers also should advocate, on behalf of their patients, for improved physical activity and diet opportunities in their patients' communities.

Strategy 4-2: Ensure coverage of, access to, and incentives for routine obesity prevention, screening, diagnosis, and treatment. Insurers (both public and private) should ensure that health insurance coverage and access provisions address obesity prevention, screening, diagnosis, and treatment.

Strategy 4-3: Encourage active living and healthy eating at work. Worksites should create, or expand, healthy environments by establishing, implementing, and monitoring policy initiatives that support wellness.

Strategy 4-4: Encourage healthy weight gain during pregnancy and breastfeeding, and promote breastfeeding-friendly environments. Health service providers and employers should adopt, implement, and monitor policies that support healthy weight gain during pregnancy and the initiation and continuation of breastfeeding. Population disparities in breastfeeding should be specifically addressed at the federal, state, and local levels to remove barriers and promote targeted increases in breast-feeding initiation and continuation.

Goal 5: Make schools a national focal point for obesity prevention.

Recommendation 5: Federal, state, and local government and education authorities, with support from parents, teachers, and the business community and the private sector, should make schools a focal point for obesity prevention.

Strategy 5-1: Require quality physical education and opportunities for physical activity in schools. Through support from federal and state governments, state and local education agencies and local school districts should ensure that all students in grades K-12 have adequate opportunities to engage in 60 minutes of physical activity per school day. This 60-minute goal includes access to and participation in quality physical education.

Strategy 5-2: Ensure strong nutritional standards for all foods and beverages sold or provided through schools . . . . Federal, state, and local decision makers are responsible for ensuring that nutrition standards based on the Dietary Guidelines are adopted by schools; these decision makers, in partnership with regulatory agencies, parents, teachers, and food manufacturers, also are responsible for ensuring that these standards are implemented fully and that adherence is monitored so as to protect the health of the nation's children and adolescents.

Strategy 5-3: Ensure food literacy, including skill development, in schools. Through leadership and guidance from federal and state governments, state and local education agencies should ensure the implementation and monitoring of sequential food literacy and nutrition science education, spanning grades K-12, based on the food and nutrition recommendations in the Dietary Guidelines for Americans.

NOTES AND QUESTIONS

1. **A grand coalition to devise remedies.** By now, Americans should be aware that many factors contribute to weight gain in complicated ways, so that weight reduction may require complex interventions. For the past decade, however, public health recommendations focused on changing individual behaviors — encouraging physical activity and eating healthier foods. The IOM Report above recognizes — even emphasizes — environmental factors that encourage weight gain and is sensitive to the problems faced by disadvantaged populations. Are its recommendations equally sensitive? How many recommendations target individual behavior? How many require business or government to take action?

The IOM recommendations also follow a pattern adopted in the earlier Surgeon General's report and, to a lesser extent, the WHO/FAO report, excerpted in Part C *supra*: They envision a grand, cooperative partnership of everyone involved — government, business, food producers, schools, etc. — that would work together to solve the problem of obesity. There is little discussion of the role that some of these actors play in producing the problem in the first place. Nor is there any realistic game plan for what should happen if this fanciful coalition does not join hands in cooperation. Is advocacy of a "grand cooperative effort" to fight obesity aspirational? Naïve? Politically disingenuous? Even if a grand coalition does not materialize, are specific recommendations worth pursuing?

2. **Economic factors influencing weight.** As Brownell and colleagues argue, Americans don't just eat too much and exercise too little because many of them are stupid. They do so, in part, because of the social and economic environment in which they live. And at least part of that environment has been structured by the entities that directly profit from Americans' bad eating habits. Moreover, since these entities profit from that environment, they resist changes in that environment, whatever the merits of the public health-based justifications for doing so.

For other interesting works with similar political messages, see ERIC SCHLOSSER, FAST FOOD NATION (2002); DAVID G. HOGAN, SELLING 'EM BY THE SACK (1998) (the history of White Castle hamburgers and their pioneering of various means for increasing consumption of fast food); and references in Part B, Note 4, *supra*. For an early examination of how economic and political interests favor characterizing health concerns as matters of personal choice and responsibility and often oppose regulation of commercial or economic interests or provision of government benefits, see SYLVIA TESH NOBLE, HIDDEN ARGUMENTS: POLITICAL IDEOLOGY AND DISEASE PREVENTION POLICY (1988).

Finkelstein and Strombotne point to food prices and a more sedentary workforce as plausible explanations for weight gain. They note the "generous subsidies for corn and soy that lower prices below market levels for products with these ingredients." Finkelstein and Strombotne at 1523s. The documentary film "King Korn," which illustrates how corn and high-fructose corn syrup pervaded the food supply after a reversal of federal agricultural policy in the early 1970's, supports this view. *See also* David Wallinga, *Agricultural Policy and Childhood Obesity: A Food Systems and Public Health Commentary*, 29 HEALTH AFF. 405 (2010); MICHAEL POLLAN, THE OMNIVORE'S DILEMMA (2006). For a contrary view, see Bradley J. Rickard, Abigail M. Okrent & Julian M. Alston, *How Have Agricultural Policies Influenced Caloric Consumption in the United States?*, 22 HEALTH ECON. 316 (2013). From the perspective of classical economics, the market forces that gave us cheap and fast food have allocated resources efficiently, if not to the benefit of our physique, "by producing affordable and convenient foods and labor-saving goods and services that are increasingly demanded by consumers." Finkelstein and Strombotne at 1522s. Finkelstein and Strombotne argue that government regulation is not necessary — except perhaps to protect children — because true market failures do not appear to have arisen. With respect to a possible lack of places to exercise, they have this to say: "Are too few public goods causing rising rates of obesity? Not likely. For example, the US government provides >84 million acres of public parks and recreation facilities, which is more than twice as many as there were in the late 1970s, when obesity rates were markedly lower." *Id.*

3. **McDonald's advice.** McDonald's, the fast-food company, offered financial planning advice to its employees make the most of their low income. A typical McDonald's cashier reportedly earns $7.72 per hour, which, after taxes, would be

about $1,105 per month. McDonald's sample monthly budget assumed a net income of $2,060, which included 2 jobs (one earning $1,105; the other $955). Monthly expenses totaled $1,260, which included $600 in rent — a seemingly low sum unless the employee is sharing a home — car payments of $150, car/home insurance of $100, health insurance of $20, savings of $100, electric, cable and phone payments of $190, but zero for heat. This left $27 per day for food, clothing, gas, and other expenses. Perhaps the company assumed that programs like Medicaid and food stamps would supplement employee wages. For the sample budget, see Jordan Weissman, *McDonald's Can't Figure Out How Its Workers Survive on Minimum Wage*, THE ATLANTIC, July 16, 2013, http://www.theatlantic.com/business/archive/2013/07/mcdonalds-cant-figure-out-how-its-workers-survive-on-minimum-wage/277845/ (visited May 2014).

4. **Policy options.** The emphasis on personal responsibility in much of public health policy might wane in response to researchers and scholars who advocate changing commercial or government policies and practices instead. *See, e.g.*, Cheryl L. Hayne, Patricia A. Moran & Mary M. Ford, *Regulating Environments to Reduce Obesity*, 25 J. PUB. HEALTH POL'Y 391 (2005). There is growing research on how weight and/or health may be affected by the built environment (buildings, sidewalks, parks, roads, and public transportation), financing (taxes and subsidies), product standards (ingredient bans or requirements), and food and physical activities that take place (or don't) in schools and workplaces. Who would be responsible for each of these alternatives? Who pays? How do these factors affect its political and economic support?

5. **Healthy choices.** Brownell and colleagues advocate changing the products available in the environment so that healthy choices are the default option. They rely on theories of default rules, choice architecture, and libertarian paternalism in psychology and behavioral economics, finding that people are most likely to accept what is offered first, rather than take affirmative action to find an alternative or "opt-out." Does steering people's choices with healthy default rules preserve their freedom of choice, as Sunstein and Thaler argue? *See* CASS SUNSTEIN & RICHARD THALER, NUDGE (2008). How much does it demand of commercial enterprises or government agencies?

6. **Consumer disclosure requirements.** One way to let people know how fattening food is or its nutritional content is to require restaurants and perhaps other retail operations to post nutrition and calorie information about their meals. Just which restaurants — and other establishments — should do so and for which foods, however, can get complicated. The Nutrition Labeling and Nutrition Act of 1990 amended the Food, Drug and Cosmetic Act to require labeling of packaged food products sold for human consumption, 21 U.S.C. § 343(q), but excluded restaurants. Packaged foods are considered to be misbranded unless their labels contain information about calories, calories from fat (unless the product contains less than 0.5 g of fat), total fat, saturated fat, trans fat, cholesterol, sodium, total carbohydrate, dietary fiber, sugars, protein, vitamins, and minerals. The Affordable Care Act amended the FDCA to require labeling by restaurants and retail food establishments that are part of a chain with at least 20 locations doing business under the same name and offering essentially the same menu items. ACA § 4205, 21 U.S.C. § 343(q)(5)(H). Such establishments are to provide calorie information for

standard menu items; nutrition information must be provided on consumer request. Although these requirements took effect on March 23, 2010, actual implementation depends on more detailed FDA regulations. *See* FDA, Menu and Vending Machines Labeling Requirements, www.fda.gov/Food/IngredientsPackagingLabeling/LabelingNutrition/ucm217762.htm (visited Nov. 2013). While consumers generally appreciate this type of labeling, it is not clear that it translates into reduced rates of obesity.

7. **Banning foods, drinks or ingredients.** The Food and Drug Administration has proposed eliminating trans fats from the processed food supply. FDA, FDA Opens 60-day Comment Period on Measure to Further Reduce Trans Fat in Processed Foods (Nov. 7, 2013), www.fda.gov/Food/NewsEvents/ConstituentUpdates/ucm373925.htm (visited Nov. 2013). The FDA's preliminary determination that trans fats are not Generally Recognized as Safe (GRAS) — if finally adopted — means that food producers could not use trans fats without FDA approval. Trans fats include partially hydrogenated oils that food producers add during processing to improve the texture and shelf life of food, such as Crisco (now available without trans fats), some crackers and microwave popcorn. There is evidence that trans fats raise low density lipoprotein (LDL or "bad") cholesterol, which increases the risk of heart disease and may have other adverse health effects. Whether the FDA's action suggests greater willingness to regulate industry is unclear. It may be an easy case. Even if their risks are not dramatic, trans fats have little benefit beyond industrial utility, and there are satisfactory, affordable substitutes.

For a description of trans fats, see FDA, Talking About Trans Fats: What You Need to Know, www.fda.gov/Food/ResourcesForYou/Consumers/ucm079609.htm (visited Nov. 2013).

More limited "bans," including portion size restrictions like the one at issue in *New York Statewide Coalition of Hispanic Chambers of Commerce, et al. v. New York City Dep't of Health and Mental Hygiene*, excerpted in Chapter 3, Part C, *supra*, also regulate commercial businesses, rather than individuals. To be sure, this sort of default rule may restrict the ease with which a person obtains a large quantity of food or drink, but it does not eliminate choice entirely. Is there an analogy here to municipal ordinances requiring fluoridation of the public water supply? (*See* Chapter 3, Part C, Note 17, *supra*.) Is there a difference between mandating fluoride in water and mandating portion sizes? How do each of these compare to product standards, such as safety features in automobiles and children's toys, that are imposed by regulatory agencies? Are the latter product standards more like a ban on trans fats or portion size limits?

Compare the standard of judicial review for state laws regulating commercial products with that for restricting important personal freedoms. Which is easier to satisfy? If the legal threshold for the former is relatively easy to cross, why are there so few similar regulations?

8. **"Fat taxes."** A few local communities and states have experimented with "fat taxes," taxes on soft drinks, fast foods, or other less-than-healthy food. Apparently such taxes can be a good source of revenue and, as "sin taxes," are somewhat less controversial than other forms of taxation. Whether they can have any effect on the

consumption of these foods is harder to assess, although they have been credited with reducing cigarette purchases, at least among adolescents. In theory, sin taxes are supposed to internalize the extra costs of the "sin," so the tax should approximate those costs. How easily can these costs be determined? What if they prove to be less than costs for the average population? For an extended review of "fat taxes," their effects, and related matters, see Jeff Strnad, *Conceptualizing the "Fat Tax": The Role of Food Taxes in Developed Economies*, 78 S. CAL. L. REV. 1221 (2005).

Recall Wikler's discussion of "sin taxes" in Chapter 8, Part B, *supra*. Is eating fattening food — or a lot of it — a sin? Do such junk food taxes interfere with individual choice any more than taxes on alcohol or cigarettes? Admittedly, such taxes are regressive, burdening lower income people more than middle and high-income groups. And distinguishing sugary foods and drinks that should be taxed from hand-crafted baked goods, orange juice and martinis may prove a thorny problem. Yet, those are primarily policy issues. When examined as a matter of state power, how hard would it be to justify imposing such taxes?

9. Advertising restrictions. Does food advertising induce demand or provide misinformation about the products advertised? Any effort to regulate food advertising, of course, would have to overcome First Amendment protection of advertising. See the discussion of advertising and the First Amendment in Chapter 10, Part D, *infra*.

Alternatively, should the government engage in more counter-advertising and consumer education? Some obesity prevention advertising can be fairly dramatic. *See, e.g.*, David Kiefaber, *This "Toxic Fat" PSA Is Super Gross, but Effective*, ADWEEK, June 27, 2012; The Fatsmack campaign, http://fatsmack.org/; Bob Curley, *Georgia Anti-Obesity Campaign Wins Attention, Critics*, WELL-BEING WIRE, May 4, 2011, http://wellbeingwire.meyouhealth.com/physical-health/georgia-anti-obesity-campaign-wins-attention-critics/ (visited Nov. 2013).

10. Saving the children. Policies aimed at improving the lot of children seem to be more enthusiastically accepted than policies directed at adults. After all, who can oppose saving children's lives? Moreover, the state can exercise it *parens patriae* power to protect the health and welfare of children. And there are more opportunities to intervene on behalf of children than adults. One is in school. Children spend a lot of time in school, where adults control physical activities, school lunches, and, for some students, breakfasts. So, how much influence does a school have on the weight of its students?

One source of seemingly unnecessary calories lies in sodas — or "sugary drinks" as they are often called. Many schools depend on revenues from vending machines that sell such sugary drinks, along with other non-nutritious snacks. Nonetheless, an increasing number of schools have eliminated sugary drinks from the machines. The Clinton Foundation is credited with influencing the beverage industry to reduce the size and calorie count of drinks sold in many more schools. Other voluntary efforts, such as First Lady Michelle Obama's Let's Move initiative, encourage everyone — but especially children — to drink water instead of soda and engage in more physical activity. *See* www.letsmove.gov/ (visited Nov. 2013).

Some school districts advocate a consumer education approach by weighing their students and sending "BMI report cards" (sometimes called "fat letters") home to their parents. Recommended by the Institute of Medicine, the report cards are intended to alert parents to their children's weight. What should parents do with this information? The practice is not without controversy, and some jurisdictions have stopped it. Can you think why?

11. State v. federal regulation. Many of the regulatory actions noted above were first initiated by cities and towns, but they are slowly moving to the national level where Congress has constitutional authority — and sometimes the political will — to legislate or where federal agencies have statutory jurisdiction to regulate. Menu labeling and a ban on trans fat are only two examples. Federal programs like the Supplemental Nutrition Assistance Program (SNAP) — known as food stamps — may add limits to the food and drink that SNAP pays for in order to encourage healthy diets. *See* U.S. Dep't of Agriculture, Food and Nutrition Service, www.fns. usda.gov/snap/supplemental-nutrition-assistance-program-snap (visited Nov. 2013). (At this writing, however, many in Congress seek to reduce SNAP benefits.) The Healthy, Hunger-Free Kids Act of 2010, P.L. 111–296, is intended to improve nutrition in several federal programs, including the National School Lunch Program, the School Breakfast Program, and the Special Supplemental Nutrition Program for Women, Infants and Children (WIC), all administered by the U.S. Department of Agriculture. Are Congress and executive branch agencies following the lead of state and local governments or has public support for such programs pushed federal action or both?

As regulatory reforms were being considered — or threatened — the food and beverage industries began changing their own policies. The Yale Rudd Center monitors fast food companies' products and advertising intended for children and adolescents. Jennifer Harris and colleagues at the Center report that industry has improved its nutritional offerings somewhat, but not enough to be counted as a source of good nutrition.

Perhaps consumers are demanding healthier choices, such as fresh produce from local farms, but demand has not yet risen enough to make fruits and vegetables cheaper than fast food.

F. LITIGATING RESPONSIBILITY FOR OBESITY

Richard A. Daynard, P. Tim Howard & Cara L. Wilking, *Private Enforcement: Litigation as a Tool to Prevent Obesity*
25 J. Pub. Health Pol'y 408–14 (2004)

Unlike tobacco, which is harmful when consumed in any quantity, food is necessary for life. But successful tobacco litigation was based not on the dangers of the products but on the misdeeds of the manufacturers. Similarly, cases against food manufacturers are likely to be based on evidence that manufacturers misrepresented nutritional properties of products, took advantage of the credulity of children to sell them high calorie density products that helped launch them on a career of unhealthy eating, marketed addictive high calorie sodas to teenagers in their own school buildings, or otherwise violated consumer protection laws that prohibit "unfair or deceptive acts or practices in commerce.

. . . .

One of litigation's first benefits is access to industry documents through the discovery process. Evidence essential to proving cases of unfair trade practices, negligence, or product liability, will undoubtedly flow from discovery requests made of food manufacturers and retailers, and information obtained through depositions and interrogatories answered under oath . . . .

An increase in industry self-policing is another benefit of litigation. Some food manufacturers and retailers already are responding to public concerns about obesity and their own concerns about litigation, and have chosen to modify certain business practices . . . . This self-regulation is not merely an incidental effect of litigation: consumer protection laws and product liability principles, like almost all law, are primarily designed to discourage the proscribed conduct, with the application of legal sanctions and compensatory damage awards reserved for the occasional instance where the legal standard was violated nonetheless.

APPLICABLE LEGAL PRINCIPLES

Unfair and Deceptive Trade Practices

State and federal consumer protection laws prohibit manufacturers and retailers of food and other products from inducing consumers to purchase products through unfair, deceptive, and misleading trade practices. The Federal Trade Commission Act (FTCA) proscribes unfair and deceptive trade practices, but it can only be invoked by the Federal Trade Commission.

State consumer protection laws are largely modeled after the FTCA but, with the exception of one state, provide consumers with a private right of legal action. State consumer protection statutes are broadly drafted and deem unlawful such unfair and deceptive trade practices as direct misrepresentation and failure to disclose material information. State consumer protection jurisprudence, however, reflects disparities in the willingness of state courts to enforce consumer protection laws. State statutes, moreover, vary considerably with respect to the requirement that a plaintiff prove intent to deceive and/or induce reliance by consumers on false or misleading statements made . . . .

An early example of use of consumer protection laws to counter practices that encourage childhood obesity is the 1983 California Supreme Court decision Committee on *Children's Television v. General Food.* The plaintiff NGO alleged that advertisements on children's television programs for high-sugar breakfast cereals made by General Foods and other manufacturers were unfair and deceptive because they were designed to make children believe these products would help make them strong and healthy, whereas they were minimally nutritious and tended to cause tooth decay . . . .

The strength of claims brought under *unfair and deceptive acts* and *practices statutes* is that while plaintiffs must show that the representations and/or omissions made by the defendant in the marketing of the food product was unfair and deceptive, they do not have to show that the consumption of the product caused obesity and its medical consequences. However, finding private counsel willing to take on a consumer protection case may be difficult. The financial losses to each consumer, measured by the money spent on unfairly or deceptively marketed products, are likely small. While consumer protection laws generally allow successful plaintiffs to recover their attorneys' fees, courts are not always sufficiently generous in awarding such fees to provide economic incentives commensurate with the enormous resources necessary to successfully litigate such a claim. Class action claims, which could combine the small financial losses suffered by each of tens or hundreds of thousands of consumers, may prove to be the most effective vehicle to make a case "large" enough to justify a large award in the minds of most judges.

Personal Injury Claims

Personal injury claims may also provide relief to consumers harmed by food products and can be brought either on the theory that there was something wrong with the product or the manufacturer improperly marketed the product. In general, for a *product liability* action to be successful, a plaintiff must prove that: (1) the danger from the food was not apparent to the average consumer; (2) the food was unreasonably dangerous for its intended use; and (3) the harm would not have occurred had an adequate warning about the food been given.

Defining the "average consumer" depends on the age and sophistication of the consumer. Courts may be more receptive to claims brought on behalf of children because they lack the ability to analyze critically advertising claims and promotions directly targeted at them . . . .

The *improper marketing theory*, which can be based either on consumer protection laws or on traditional common law negligence or fraud, requires that the seller deceived the consumer in a material way about the health effects of eating the food, and that this deception caused the consumer to consume the food. If a seller explicitly or implicitly represented, for example, that one could eat a typical McDonald's meal every day without putting on weight, and a customer reasonably relied on this representation, such a case could be brought. The consumer, however, would have to prove that his reliance on these misrepresentations continued to be reasonable even as he put on weight and his waistline expanded.

Under either a product liability or improper marketing theory, the plaintiff must prove that his obesity and its sequelae were caused by consuming the food in question. This requires the plaintiff to show, at a minimum, that the defendant's food was a "substantial factor" in causing the obesity, and that the obesity was a "substantial factor" in causing the subsequent medical condition. The latter link can frequently be proven through ordinary etiological evidence — studies in the public health or medical literature. Establishing a causal link between a particular food product and an individual's weight gain, while more difficult, may not be impossible . . . .

. . . .

Personal Responsibility of the Plaintiff

Resistance to obesity-related litigation is consistently couched in personal responsibility terms — responsibility for the injury should lie entirely on the afflicted consumer. This argument was frequently used to discredit attempts to hold the tobacco industry responsible for harms to consumers, and, while an initially attractive argument, does not withstand analysis. Various factors mitigate consumers' blameworthiness. Predictable over-consumption on the part of a consumer does not excuse decisions by food marketers to exploit this consumer behavior for their own benefit and to the detriment of consumers' health.

Attributing primary causal responsibility to the individual consumer denies the power of the new food environment — ubiquitous and inexpensive food with little nutritional value . . . .

DIRECT RESPONSES TO THE THREAT OF LITIGATION: PROPOSED IMMUNITY FOR THE FOOD INDUSTRY

In the United States, widespread media attention to the threat of obesity-related litigation has inspired federal and state *tort reform* legislation that would grant the food industry blanket immunity from obesity-related lawsuits . . . . Dubbed "cheeseburger bills" by the popular media, state-level legislation would bar lawsuits by consumers alleging harm in the form of obesity and obesity-related illness . . . .

CONCLUSION

Food producers and restaurants argue that obesity-related litigation is inherently frivolous, and that they will be bankrupted from the legal costs of defending against such litigation. Defendants, they certainly know, can quickly get genuinely frivolous litigation dismissed, and may even obtain their attorneys' fees from the plaintiffs if the lawsuit is found to be frivolous . . . . There has not been, and there will not be, a flood of frivolous obesity-related lawsuits. The industry's real fear, rather, is of well-founded lawsuits, amply supported by compromising memos, obtained in discovery from company files that would demonstrate how many food companies engage in unfair or deceptive acts and practices that substantially contribute to the obesity epidemic.

PELMAN *et al.*, v. McDONALD'S CORP.
272 F.R.D. 82 (S.D.N.Y. 2010)

Donald C. Pogue, Judge.

Plaintiffs in this action are New York State consumers claiming, pursuant to Section 349 of New York's General Business Law ("GBL § 349"), exposure to and injury from Defendant McDonald's Corporation's allegedly deceptive marketing scheme. Plaintiffs claim that the effect of Defendant's affirmative representations and material omissions throughout this marketing scheme — from 1985 until the filing of this case in 2002 — was to mislead consumers into falsely believing that Defendant's food products may be consumed on a daily basis without incurring any adverse health effects, and that, as a result of this marketing scheme, Plaintiffs and putative class members suffered injury in the form of, inter alia, the development of certain adverse medical conditions . . . .

Before the court is Plaintiffs' motion for class certification pursuant to Federal Rule of Civil Procedure 23(b)(3) or, in the alternative, for class certification solely with respect to the litigation of issues common to all putative class members, pursuant to Rule 23(c)(4). As explained below, because establishment of the causation and injury elements of Plaintiffs"claims will necessitate extensive individualized inquiries, the court finds that the questions of law and fact which would be common to putative class members would not predominate over questions affecting only individual members. Accordingly, certification of this action for class litigation under Rule 23(b)(3) is not appropriate. See Fed. R. Civ. P. 23(b)(3).

. . . .

BACKGROUND

A. Procedural History

Plaintiffs originally commenced this suit in the State Supreme Court of New York, Bronx County, on August 22, 2002. Plaintiffs claimed that Defendants McDonald's Corporation, McDonald's Restaurants of New York, Inc., McDonald's 1865 Bruckner Boulevard Bronx, New York, and McDonald's 2630 Jerome Avenue, Bronx, New York (collectively "McDonald's") engaged in deceptive business practices in making and selling their products, and that "this deception has caused the minors who have consumed McDonald[']s' products to injure their health by becoming obese." *Pelman v. McDonald's Corp.*, 237 F. Supp. 2d 512, 516 (S.D.N.Y. 2003) ("Pelman I").

. . . .

Plaintiffs filed their first amended complaint ("FAC") on February 19, 2003. On September 3, 2003, the court again granted Defendant's renewed Rule 12(b)(6) motion, dismissing Plaintiffs' complaint in its entirety, without leave to amend. *Pelman v. McDonald's Corp.*, No. 02 Civ. 7821 (RWS), 2003 U.S. Dist. LEXIS 15202, at *14 (S.D.N.Y. Sept. 3, 2003) ("Pelman II"). [The court noted that, in Pelman I, "[t]he plaintiffs ha[d] been warned that they must make specific allegations about particular advertisements that could have caused plaintiffs' injuries, and to provide detail on the alleged connection between those injuries and the consumption of McDonald's foods." Pelman II, 2003 U.S. Dist. LEXIS 15202, at *14. Plaintiffs failed to do so.]

Plaintiffs appealed solely the district court's dismissal of counts I, II and III — each brought under GBL § 349 — of their FAC. *Pelman v. McDonald's Corp.*, 396 F.3d 508, 509–11 (2d Cir. 2005) ("Pelman III").[4] The United States Court of Appeals

---

[4] GBL § 349 makes unlawful "[d]eceptive acts or practices in the conduct of any business, trade or

for the Second Circuit ("Second Circuit") vacated the district court's dismissal of these claims, holding that, "because a private action under [GBL] § 349 does not require proof of the same essential elements (such as reliance) as common-law fraud, an action under [GBL] § 349 is not subject to the pleading-with-particularity requirements of Rule 9(b), Fed. R. Civ. P., but need only meet the bare-bones notice-pleading requirements of Rule 8(a), Fed. R. Civ. P.," and that "[s]o far as the [GBL] § 349 claims are concerned, the [FAC] more than meets the requirements of Rule 8(a)."

Following a remand to this Court for further proceedings consistent with the Second Circuit's opinion in Pelman III, the court granted in part Defendant's Rule 12(e) motion for a more definite statement, requiring Plaintiffs to "identify the advertisements that collectively amount to the alleged deceptive nutritional scheme." *Pelman v. McDonald's Corp.*, 396 F. Supp. 2d 439, 445 (S.D.N.Y. 2005) ("Pelman IV"). In addition, the court required Plaintiffs to provide "a brief explanation of why the advertisements are materially deceptive to an objective consumer." In addition, "in accordance with GBL § 349's requirement that [P]laintiffs' injuries be 'by reason of' [D]efendant's conduct, the court directed Plaintiffs [to] provide a brief explanation of how [P]laintiffs were aware of the nutritional scheme[] they allege to have been deceptive." The court also required Plaintiffs to "outline the injuries that were suffered by each plaintiff 'by reason of' defendant's alleged deceptive nutritional scheme."

Plaintiffs filed their second amended complaint ("SAC") on December 12, 2005. By opinion of September 16, 2006, the court denied Defendant's motion to strike and dismiss the SAC for failure to comport with the court's orders in *Pelman v. McDonald's Corp.*, 452 F. Supp. 2d 320, 328 (S.D.N.Y. 2006) ("Pelman V"). The court noted that:

> the SAC identifies a number of advertisements being claimed as part of the Defendant's deceptive practices[;] . . . outlines why the advertisements are objectively deceptive[;] . . . alleges that Plaintiffs were aware of McDonald's deceptive practices through their exposure to the advertisements and statements annexed to their pleading and that such statements were disseminated in the specified fora of[] television, radio, internet, magazine, periodical, in-store poster advertisements, and press releases issued in New York State from 1985 and continuing through filing in 2002[;] . . . [and] alleges that each named Plaintiff was injured as a result of Defendant's practices, in the following respects: obesity, elevated levels of

commerce or in the furnishing of any service" in the State of New York, N.Y. Gen. Bus. L. § 349(a), and provides a private right of action to any person "injured by reason of" such acts or practices to seek an injunction, actual damages, or both. Count I of Plaintiffs' FAC alleged that the combined effect of Defendant's advertising scheme during the years from 1987 until 2002 "was to create the false impression that [Defendant's] food products were nutritionally beneficial and part of a healthy lifestyle if consumed daily." Pelman III, 396 F.3d at 510. Count II alleged that Defendant's food products were substantially less healthy than represented by Defendant, in light of Defendant's manner of food processing and use of certain additives. *Id.* And Count III alleged that Defendant "deceptively represented that it would provide nutritional information to its New York customers when in reality such information was not readily available at a significant number of McDonald's outlets in New York visited by the plaintiffs and others." *Id.* (footnote omitted).

Low-Density Lipoprotein, or LDL, more commonly known as 'bad' choles-terol ["LDL"], significant or substantial increased factors in the develop-ment of coronary heart disease, pediatric diabetes, high blood pressure, and/or other detrimental and adverse health effects and/or diseases as medically determined to have been causally connected to the prolonged use of Defendant's products[].

The court then held that, because "Plaintiffs need not have seen or heard each advertisement, but rather only to have been exposed to them in some manner," the SAC sufficiently described how Plaintiffs were aware of the marketing scheme alleged to be deceptive, and that, "[c]ontrary to McDonald's contentions, . . . the SAC outlines the injuries sustained by each Plaintiff in a manner sufficient for McDonald's to answer."

B. The Claims of the Second Amended Complaint ("SAC")

Count I of Plaintiffs' SAC alleges that Defendant, "its respective agents, servants, and[/]or employees, engaged in unfair and deceptive acts and practices, in violation of [GBL § 349], by allegedly representing, subjecting, exposing, and/or attempting to mislead the Plaintiffs, putative class members, New York State users and consumers, from 1985 and continuing thereafter to 2002, that its certain foods, including but not limited to[] Chicken McNuggets, Filet-O-Fish, Chicken Sandwich, French Fries and/or Hamburgers were substantially healthier-than-in-fact, in contradiction to medically and nutritionally established acceptable guidelines."

Specifically, Plaintiffs allege that Defendant subjected, exposed and/or at-tempted to mislead Plaintiffs and putative class members, from 1985 until 2002, "with misleading nutritional claims, in widespread advertising campaigns, promo-tions, brochures, press releases, 'consumer-oriented' statements, in various media and print outlets, that its certain foods were healthy, nutritious, of a beneficial nutritional nature, and/or were easily part of anyone's healthy daily diet, each and/or all claims being in contradiction to medically and nutritionally established acceptable guidelines." Plaintiffs claim that, "as a direct, foreseeable and proximate result of the Defendant's deceptive practice to misrepresent the nutritional attributes of its foods," Plaintiffs and putative Class Members suffered injury in the form of the financial costs of Defendant's products; "false beliefs and understand-ings as to the nutritional contents and effects of Defendant's food products"; and "obesity, elevated levels of [LDL], significant or substantial increased factors in the development of coronary heart disease, pediatric diabetes, high blood pressure and/or other detrimental and adverse health effects and/or diseases as medically determined to have been causally connected to the prolonged use of Defendant's products . . . ."

Count II of Plaintiffs' SAC alleges that Defendant, "its respective agents, servants, and[/] or employees, engaged in unfair and deceptive acts and practices, in violation of [GBL § 349], by engaging in an ingredient disclosure scheme, from 1985 and continuing thereafter to 2002, whereby the Defendant is alleged to have failed to adequately disclose its use of certain additives and that the manner of its food processing rendered certain of its foods, specifically French Fries, hash browns, chicken McNuggets, fish and/or chicken products, substantially less healthy than were represented to Plaintiffs, putative Class Members, New York State residents and consumers, in widespread advertising campaigns, 'consumer-oriented' statements, promotions, brochures, press releases, corporate nutritionist statements, and Internet disseminations, store-posters, and other means of media communications." Plaintiffs allege that, "as a direct, foreseeable and proximate result of the Defendant's deceptive ingredient disclosure scheme," Plaintiffs and putative Class Members suffered injuries identical to those claimed in Count I.

Count III of Plaintiffs' SAC alleges that Defendant, "its respective agents, servants, and[/]or employees, engaged in unfair and deceptive acts and practices, in violation of [GBL § 349], by representing, warranting and issuing promissory statements, that it provide[d], and w[ould] continue to provide, nutritional brochures including disclosures regarding the ingredients, and amount of calories, protein, carbohydrates, fat, cholesterol and sodium, on all of its products, at all its store/franchise and drive-through locations in conspicuous locations for study by consumers prior to purchase", when in fact "the nutritional information which the Defendant represent[ed] and warrant[ed] was not adequately available to the Plaintiff consumers and putative Class members at a significant number of the Defendant's New York stores for inspection upon request." Plaintiffs allege that, "by reason of the Defendant's deceptive practices, the Infant-Plaintiffs [and putative Infant Class Members] have been caused to believe said nutritional material]s were present, when in fact said data was not available[,] resulting [in] preventing the Infant-Plaintiff[s] and purchaser[s] from making informed decisions about the consumption of Defendant's certain foods."

Because Counts I, II, and III of Plaintiffs' SAC each claim identical injuries as a result of the same allegedly deceptive marketing scheme — alleged in each count to be materially deceptive as a result of affirmative misrepresentations (Count I) and/or material omissions or non-disclosures (Counts II and III) — the court concludes that Plaintiffs' SAC presents a single cause of action under GBL § 349.

C. Plaintiffs' Request for Class Certification

Plaintiffs' putative Class Members consist of New York State residents, infants, and consumers, who were exposed to Defendant's deceptive business practices, and as a result thereof, purchased and consumed the Defendant['s] products in New York State stores/franchises, directly causing economic losses in the form of the financial costs of the Defendant's goods, causing significant or substantial factors in the development of diabetes, coronary heart disease, high blood pressure, obesity, elevated levels of [LDL], and/or other detrimental and adverse health effects and/or diseases as medically determined to have been causally connected to the prolonged use of Defendant's certain products." [Plaintiffs define Class members who consumed these products at least once a week as "Heavy-Users" and those who consumed the products at least 4 times per week as "Super Heavy-Users."] Plaintiffs concede that "[t]he exact number of putative class members . . . [is] not known", arguing that "[t]he number and identities of the class members can only be ascertained through appropriate investigation and discovery", but estimating a class size numbering in the thousands.

. . . .

STANDARD OF ANALYSIS

FRCP23

Federal Rule of Civil Procedure 23 governs the certification of federal class actions. "Rule 23(a) requires that a class action possess four familiar features: (1) numerosity; (2) commonality; (3) typicality; and (4) adequacy of representation. If those criteria are met, the district court must next determine whether the class can be maintained under any one of the three subdivisions of Rule 23(b)." *McLaughlin v. Am. Tobacco Co.*, 522 F.3d 215, 222 (2d Cir. 2008). . . . . Plaintiffs argue that their proposed class or issue class can be maintained under 23(b)(3), which requires the court to find that "the questions of law or fact common to class members predominate over any questions affecting only individual members, and that a class action is superior to other available methods for fairly and efficiently adjudicating the controversy."

π's arg

. . . .

DISCUSSION

. . . .

"The Rule 23(b)(3) predominance inquiry tests whether proposed classes are sufficiently cohesive to warrant adjudication by representation." *Amchem Prods, Inc. v. Windsor*, 521 U.S. 591, 623 (1997) (citation and footnote omitted). . . . . Plaintiffs must establish that "the issues in the class action that are subject to generalized proof, and thus applicable to the class as a whole, predominate over those issues that are subject only to individualized proof."

What π must show

. . . .

To prevail on the elements of their cause of action under GBL § 349, Plaintiffs must prove that Defendant "[1] made misrepresentations or omissions that were likely to mislead a reasonable consumer in the plaintiff's circumstances, [2] that the plaintiff was deceived by those misrepresentations or omissions and [3] that as a result the plaintiff suffered injury." *Solomon v. Bell Atl. Corp.*, 9 A.D.3d 49, 777 N.Y.S.2d 50, 55 (N.Y. App. Div. 2004) (citation omitted). As explained below, the court concludes that individualized inquiries are necessary to determine whether each plaintiff suffered injury as a result of being deceived by Defendant's allegedly misleading representations. Accordingly, the court decides that the cause of action fails to satisfy the predominance requirement of Rule 23(b)(3). Further, although the cause of action does present discrete issues which otherwise satisfy the criteria for Issue Class certification pursuant to Rule 23(c)(4), the court concludes that, because Plaintiffs have failed to present specific evidence of a sufficiently numerous class of individuals who were both exposed to Defendant's allegedly deceptive marketing scheme and have subsequently suffered from the same adverse medical conditions as those alleged by Plaintiffs to have been the result of their exposure, Plaintiffs have also not met their burden for Issue Class certifiability at this time

holding

. . . .

A. The Cause of Action Fails to Meet Rule 23(b)(3)'s Predominance Requirement.

. . . .

Plaintiffs claim to have suffered three types of harm or injuries "by reason of" Defendant's allegedly deceptive nutritional marketing scheme — the financial costs of Defendant's products; "false beliefs and understandings as to the nutritional contents and effects of Defendant's food products"; and "obesity, elevated levels of [LDL], significant or substantial increased factors in the development of coronary heart disease, pediatric diabetes, high blood pressure and/or other detrimental and adverse health effects and/or diseases as medically determined to have been causally connected to the prolonged use of Defendant's products." However, allegations of "false beliefs and understandings" do not state a claim for "actual injury" under GBL § 349, *Small v. Lorillard Tobacco Co.*, 252 A.D.2d 1, 679 N.Y.S.2d 593, 599 (N.Y. App. Div. 1998) ("Neither the case law nor the statutory language [of GBL § 349] supports [the] argument that the deception is the injury." (emphasis in original)), *aff'd*, 94 N.Y.2d 43, 698 N.Y.S.2d 615, 720 N.E.2d 892 (N.Y. 1999); and neither do allegations of pecuniary loss for the purchase of Defendant's products. *Small*, 720 N.E.2d at 898 ("[Plaintiffs] posit that consumers who buy a product that they would not have purchased, absent a manufacturer's deceptive commercial practices, have suffered an injury under [GBL] § 349. We disagree."). Accordingly, the only alleged injuries for which Plaintiffs and putative Class members may claim damages under GBL § 349 are those related to the development of certain medical conditions.

All proposed experts who have given their opinion in this case regarding the possibility of a causal link between the consumption of Defendant's products and the development of these medical conditions essentially agree that the presence of such causal connection, if any, depends heavily on a range of factors unique to each individual. As Dr. Raman, Defendant's proposed nutritional expert, concludes, "[b]ecause there are so many factors that contribute to obesity and to obesity related illnesses, it is improper to generalize and make assumptions as to causation in any individual." *See, e.g., In re* Rezulin, 210 F.R.D. at 66 ("[T]he issue of whether [ingestion of Defendant's product due to Defendant's failure to warn of risks] caused physical injury to a specific class member will depend on his or her unique characteristics[,] such as[,] [inter alia,] family and medical background, preexisting medical conditions, age, gender, life style, drug or alcohol use, quantity of [product] ingested, [etc.].") . . . .

Plaintiffs' own proposed nutritional expert, Dr. Barnard, attests to the lack of certainty with regard to a generalized causal connection between consumption of Defendant's products and the medical injuries Plaintiffs identify . . . Dr. Barnard asserts that a general causal link between consumption of Defendant's products and the development of certain medical conditions can be determined because Defendant's products are high in fat, salt, and cholesterol, low in fiber and certain vitamins, and contain beef and cheese. However, because many foods are high in fat, salt, and cholesterol, low in fiber and certain vitamins, and contain beef and cheese, and because there is no evidence to suggest that all who consume such foods develop the kinds of medical conditions which are at issue in this case, the central proposition upon which Dr. Barnard's argument is based necessarily admits the conclusion that, in the absence of individualized inquiries regarding various other factors, no necessary generalizable causal connection is manifest* between the consumption of Defendant's products and the development of certain medical conditions.

Dr. Frieden, whose declaration in a prior action is also submitted in support of Plaintiffs' motion for class certification, similarly presents no evidence establishing a direct and necessary causal connection, obviating the need for individualized inquiries, between the consumption of Defendant"s products and the development of the sort of medical conditions allegedly suffered by Plaintiffs . . . . Because, as Dr. Frieden points out, "increasing weight results from an imbalance between calories consumed (nutrition) and energy expended (physical activity)", individualized inquiries predominate in this case regarding the extent of each plaintiff's consumption and energy expenditure.

The court therefore concludes that, because factual questions with regard to, at the very least, the nutritional composition of food products consumed by each plaintiff from sources other than Defendant's facilities, as well as the level of regular physical activity engaged in by each plaintiff, predominate in the inquiry with respect to an essential element of Plaintiffs' cause of action, this case is not appropriate for adjudication on a class-wide basis.

Moreover, Defendant is correct that whether or not Plaintiffs' claims — that they ate McDonald's food because they believed it to be healthier than it was in fact — are true for any particular person is an inquiry which also requires individualized proof.

As Defendant points out, "[a] person's choice to eat at McDonald's and what foods (and how much) he eats may depend on taste, past experience, habit, convenience, location, peer choices, other non-nutritional advertising, and cost", and although "[b]eliefs about nutrition may influence a person's decision in some cases, [it will] not always [be the case]."

[I]ndividualized inquiries will also predominate regarding the causal connection between each plaintiff's exposure to the allegedly misleading aspects of Defendant's advertising scheme and each Plaintiff's subsequent consumption of Defendant's allegedly injurious products.

Accordingly, the court concludes that, "[w]hile some common questions concerning [Defendant's nutritional marketing scheme] exist, individual questions about causation would overwhelm them[,] [and therefore] Plaintiff[s'] Section 349 claim is not appropriate for class certification." *In re* Currency Conversion, 230 F.R.D. at 311.

B. Class Certification for the Litigation of Certain Issues Pursuant to Rule 23(c)(4) Is Also Not Appropriate.

[T]the court will now consider Plaintiffs' request to certify an Issue Class "for a determination of Defendant's liability for its deceptive conduct on consumers under [GBL] § 349."

"When appropriate, an action may be brought or maintained as a class action with respect to particular issues." Fed. R. Civ. P. 23(c)(4) . . . .

"Issue certification is especially appropriate . . . where Defendants' liability can *Rule*
be determined once, on a class-wide basis, through common evidence." . . . .

. . . .

As mentioned, there are three elements to Plaintiffs' cause of action under GBL § 349: "first, that the challenged act or practice was consumer-oriented; second, that it was misleading in a material way; and third, that the plaintiff suffered injury as a result of the deceptive act." . . . .

While the court has concluded that proof of the element of injury as a result of the allegedly deceptive acts would require a level of individualized inquiry that precludes the class-wide litigation of the action as a whole, questions of the consumer-orientation and material deceptiveness of Defendant's acts and omissions are evaluated on the basis of objective standards, and are therefore subject to proof based on evidence common to the class of individual plaintiffs who claim or may claim exposure to and injury from these acts and omissions.

. . . Plaintiffs list a number of specific advertisements which they allege to comprise the nutritional scheme that is the subject of this litigation.[35] . . .

The 1) existence; 2) consumer-orientation; and 3) materially misleading nature of the marketing scheme alleged by Plaintiffs as the basis of their cause of action against Defendant are each questions which can be settled upon a showing of objective evidence and legal argument. Such evidence and argumentation are commonly applicable to the entire class of existing and potential plaintiffs who claim to have been exposed to and injured by this marketing scheme.

Because these issues "are precisely the common questions of law and fact," and because "when a Court chooses to limit class certification only to certain common issues . . . , those issues necessarily predominate [in the resulting class action]," the commonality and typicality requirements of Rule 23(a), . . . are met, with respect to these issues, for the set of individuals in Plaintiffs' position. Persons who are in Plaintiffs' position are those persons who had not yet reached the age of twenty-one as of August 2002, who were exposed to McDonald's nutritional marketing scheme in New York during the years from 1985 until 2002, who ate regularly at McDonald's, and who subsequently developed the same medical conditions as Plaintiffs.

---

[35] Specifically, Plaintiffs list the following distinct representations allegedly made by Defendant: 1) that "only delicious chunks of juicy breast and thigh meat go into Chicken McNuggets"; 2) that Defendant's Chicken McNuggets were made with "100 percent chicken"; 3) that include 22 percent of a person's recommended daily allowance for protein, 32 percent of the allowance for calcium, and 26 percent of the allowance for riboflavin; 13) that Defendant's products are made with "beef that's leaner than the kind of beef most people buy in the supermarket"; 14) that Defendant does not add additives, fillers, or extenders to its beef products, and that its beef products are comprised of "[s]elected cuts including sirloin, chuck and round steak"; 15) that Defendant's French Fries are cooked in 100 percent vegetable oil; 16) that Defendant's McLean Deluxe was 91 percent fat-free; 17) that daily consumption of meat products "can make it easier to do things like climb higher and ride [a] bike farther"; 18) that Defendant's Fish Filet was made with "'100% cod' [and] with only a pinch of salt added to taste after cooking".

With respect to the numerosity requirement of Rule 23(a), however, although Plaintiffs argue that "[New York State] product sales records, frequency and customer-product-use surveys can reveal hundreds of thousands [of] consumers within the ambit of the class", Plaintiffs have not presented the court with any specific evidence that there are any other persons who had not yet reached the age of twenty-one as of August 2002, were exposed to McDonald's nutritional marketing scheme in New York during the years from 1985 until 2002, ate regularly at McDonald's, and subsequently developed the same medical conditions as Plaintiffs.

. . . .

Because Plaintiffs have not yet established that there are any other persons within the relevant age group who were exposed to the nutritional marketing at issue, then regularly ate at McDonald's, and subsequently developed the same medical injuries as those allegedly suffered by Plaintiffs, and because Plaintiffs have not submitted sufficient evidence from which these facts may be reasonably inferred, the court cannot conclude that the putative class of persons with claims identical to those of Plaintiffs' in this case "is so numerous that joinder of all members is impracticable." Fed. R. Civ. P. 23(a). Accordingly, Plaintiffs have failed to meet their burden of proving that the putative Issue Class satisfies all requirements of Rule 23, and the motion for certification of an Issue Class in this case must therefore also be denied.

CONCLUSION

For all of the foregoing reasons, Plaintiffs' motion for class certification and, in the alternative, for issue class certification, is DENIED in its entirety.

NOTES AND QUESTIONS

1. **Litigation as a public health policy strategy.** Some commentators argue that bringing lawsuits against the food or restaurant industry has the potential to change public policy. Kersh and Morone, for example, expect an increase in lawsuits "to remake health policy" in the face of legislative stalemate. Rogan Kersh & James A. Morone, *Obesity, Courts, & the New Politics of Public Health*, 30 J. HEALTH POL., POL'Y & L. 839 (2005). They may be correct that the judiciary is familiar with deciding individual (and class action) claims for unfair or deceptive trade practices and products liability. How, if at all, does the *Pelman* litigation, excerpted above, fit this model? Daynard and colleagues correctly predicted that few lawsuits would be brought. Is this the result of restraint on the part of potential litigants or the difficulty of proving individual causation or something else?

There is a larger question here: whether public health policy should be made by the legislature — state or federal — or whether it should be made by the judiciary as part of resolving lawsuits initiated by individuals or other representatives of the public. Plaintiffs brought litigation against the tobacco industry and the food industry after failing to persuade the legislature to take action. Are litigants more representative of the public than the legislature? If legislators are so secure in their seats that they do not need to respond to voters' concerns, is there any alternative? Advocates of litigation may view lawsuits as more influential than they really are, but courts can at least respond to specific controversies.

As with tobacco, public acceptance of social policies to address obesity increased dramatically when obesity was characterized as a serious health problem, rather than an aesthetic concern. Whether or not litigation is a realistic tool, both the public and policy makers are increasingly considering legislation and liability rules to improve public health.

2. Population-based and individualized risk. Note the difference between the general population-based data used by public health experts and the individualized evidence required to carry the plaintiff's burden of proof in *Pelman*. The court describes and rejects two expert affidavits for failing to provide evidence beyond increased risk at the population level. Regarding the first affidavit, by Dr. Frieden (now Director of the CDC), the court highlighted the following statement as population-based rather than individualized: "People who are overweight are at *increased risk* for diabetes, heart disease, stroke, high blood pressure, arthritis, and cancer." (Emphasis added by the court.)

How easy or difficult would it be for plaintiffs to satisfy the requirements for class certification? How different is this burden from the requirements to satisfy an individual claim?

3. What, if any, legal claims should be pursued? Are lawsuits such as *Pelman* viable? If they are, will they help reduce obesity or improve health? The answer to the first question is yet to be determined. *Pelman VI* left the plaintiff with a viable cause of action, at least sufficient to survive summary judgment, but the plaintiffs face substantial problems of proof if they take their case to trial — especially that of tracing advertising (or food) to individual harm. Moreover, the courts seem to have rejected most of the causes of action except for those under the New York trade laws; there may not be analogous legislation in other jurisdictions. On the other hand, both the trial judge and the appellate judges imply that they had some sympathy for the plaintiffs and some animus for the behavior of the defendants.

4. Anti-litigation legislation. The barriers faced by future plaintiffs may be even greater than those faced by the *Pelman* plaintiffs. At least 26 states have enacted laws — often called Common Sense Consumption Acts — to immunize the fast food industry from these sorts of lawsuits. For a review of pending lawsuits, legislation intended to immunize potential defendants, and references to other sources, see Public Health Advocacy Institute, Study of State Cheeseburger Bills Finds They Go Well Beyond "Tort Reform" (Aug. 26, 2013) http://www.phaionline.org/tag/obesity-litigation/ (visited Nov. 2013).

The public reaction to these lawsuits often parallels the apparent view of these state legislatures. Many people think it is silly to claim that fast food purveyors have caused, in the legal sense of the term, people to become obese. But are these lawsuits as specious as they may appear at first glance? Are there parallels to the tobacco litigation discussed in Chapter 10, *infra* — which many people thought were silly until all of the facts came out? Can you imagine some set of facts that may be discovered, comparable to the revelations about the fraudulent practices of the tobacco companies that might make these lawsuits more factually plausible or legally viable?

Assume for the moment that "cheeseburger lawsuits" are not completely mooted by immunizing legislation or rejected outright by the courts. What *should be* the standard for liability, even if causation and other related issues can be satisfied? Consider the following options:

a.   sellers or manufacturers of food should be liable if they fail to disclose a substantial health risk of which the average consumer would otherwise be unaware (a negligence standard)

b.   sellers or manufacturers of food should be liable if it is found that any product they sell is unreasonably dangerous (a strict liability standard)

c.   sellers or manufacturers of food should be liable if it is found that they have affirmatively concealed a substantial health risk associated with their product (a requirement of intentional malfeasance).

Chapter 10

TOBACCO AND HEALTH

A. INTRODUCTION

This Chapter examines the health problems associated with smoking tobacco products and the various ways in which the local, state, and federal governments have attempted to reduce the impact of tobacco on the public's health. It offers another opportunity to explore the legal tools available to reduce the risks of chronic diseases. In one sense, the decline of smoking in the United States is a public health success story. The percentage of the population that smokes cigarettes dropped more than 60% — from about 46% in 1960 to 18% in 2012. *See* Table 1 below. At the same time, a large number of Americans, both former and current smokers, remain at higher risk of lung cancer, heart disease, respiratory illnesses, and a shorter lifespan than non-smokers. Thus, while the public health goal of raising a generation of tobacco-free youth now seems possible, eradicating smoking among the remaining population of users may prove difficult.

The Chapter begins in Part B with the Surgeon General's report on contemporary evidence of the health risks of tobacco use and the Framework Convention on Tobacco Control, together with a reading suggesting some of the reasons for the persistence of smoking, notwithstanding widespread knowledge of its hazards. Part C explores the scope and limits of federal, state, and local powers to regulate tobacco sales and use, including issues of preemption that arise when state laws conflict with federal legislation and local ordinances conflict with state laws. It also examines the Food and Drug Administration's authority to regulate tobacco products before and after the federal Family Smoking Prevention and Tobacco Control Act of 2009.

The justifications for tobacco regulation, both constitutional and political, have evolved from protecting individuals from a dangerous product — by banning its sale or use — to the more classic public health rationale of protecting the broader public from harmful effects of second hand and even third hand smoke. Where governments shift away from outright prohibitions to less draconian forms of regulation, however, they sometimes confront more difficult constitutional barriers. Part D examines efforts to regulate tobacco advertising and promotion. The cases addressing tobacco advertising examine First Amendment principles that also apply to government programs that restrict the marketing of other potentially dangerous products or behaviors.

Part E explores the role of the private sector in reducing smoking by employees, with potential implications for other disfavored conduct. Such actions raise questions about the boundary between public and private activities in light of a growing perception of smoking as a *non*-private activity. Finally, Part F reviews causes of action in private lawsuits that have been brought by consumers of tobacco products against sellers and manufacturers of tobacco, as a vehicle for considering the role of private litigation in influencing public health policy. Here, too, preemption affects the available causes of action. Finally, the material discusses the "Master Settlement Agreement," designed to end the litigation that states brought against tobacco companies to recover public funds spent on medical care for conditions attributed to tobacco use.

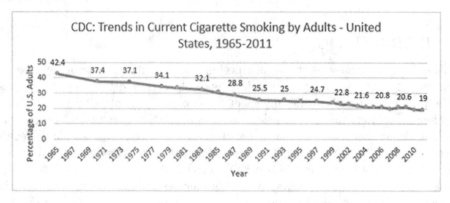

B.   THE HEALTH CONSEQUENCES OF SMOKING TOBACCO

THE HEALTH CONSEQUENCES OF SMOKING — 50 YEARS OF PROGRESS, A REPORT OF THE SURGEON GENERAL, U.S. DEPARTMENT OF HEALTH AND HUMAN SERVICES, EXECUTIVE SUMMARY 1–17 (2014)
http://www.surgeongeneral.gov/library/reports/50-years-of-progress/

For the United States, the epidemic of smoking-caused disease in the twentieth century ranks among the greatest public health catastrophes of the century, while the decline of smoking consequent to tobacco control is surely one of public health's greatest successes. However, the current rate of progress in tobacco control is not fast enough, and much more needs to be done to end the tobacco epidemic. . . . If smoking persists at the current rate among young adults in this country, 5.6 million of today's Americans younger than 18 years of age are projected to die prematurely from a smoking-related illness. More than 20 million Americans have died as a result of smoking since the first Surgeon General's report on smoking and health was released in 1964. Most were adults with a history of smoking, but nearly 2.5 million were nonsmokers who died from heart disease or lung cancer caused by exposure to secondhand smoke . . . .

. . . .

More than 10 times as many U.S. citizens have died prematurely from cigarette smoking than have died in all the wars fought by the United States during its history. Study after study has confirmed the magnitude of the harm caused to the human body by exposure to toxicants and carcinogens found in tobacco smoke. Since 1964, the 31 previous Surgeon General's reports have chronicled a still growing but already conclusive body of evidence about the adverse impact of tobacco use on human cells and organs and on overall health. . . .

Previous Surgeon General's reports have tracked the evolution of cigarettes into the current highly engineered, addictive, and deadly products containing thousands of chemicals that are harmful in themselves, but the burning of tobacco produces the complex chemical mixture of more than 7,000 compounds that cause a wide range of diseases and premature deaths as a result. . . .

. . . .

The 2006 report concluded that the scientific evidence indicates that there is no risk-free level of exposure to secondhand smoke . . . . Fifty years after the first report in 1964, it is striking that the scientific evidence in this report expands the list of diseases and other adverse health effects caused by smoking and exposure of nonsmokers to tobacco smoke . . . . These new findings include:

- Liver cancer and colorectal cancer are added to the long list of cancers caused by smoking;

- Exposure to secondhand smoke is a cause of stroke;

- Smoking increases the risk of dying from cancer and other diseases in cancer patients and survivors;

- Smoking is a cause of diabetes mellitus; and

- Smoking causes general adverse effects on the body including inflammation and it impairs immune function. Smoking is a cause of rheumatoid arthritis.

Progress has been made in tobacco control. During the 50 years since the 1964 report, approaches have moved from single measures, such as small text-only pack warnings, to implementing comprehensive control programs, including indoor smoking bans, support for cessation, restrictions on advertising and promotion, media campaigns, and tax hikes to raise prices. Smoking rates have declined, as have mortality rates for some diseases caused by smoking, such as heart disease and lung cancer for which smoking is the major cause.

Nonetheless, between 2005–2009, smoking was responsible for more than 480,000 premature deaths annually among Americans 35 years of age and older. More than 87% of lung cancer deaths, 61% of all pulmonary disease deaths, and 32% of all deaths from coronary heart disease were attributable to smoking and exposure to secondhand smoke. . . .

. . . .

Section 1. Historical Perspective, Overview, and Conclusions

When Dr. Luther L. Terry released the first Surgeon General's report on smoking and health in January 1964, few could have anticipated the long-term impact it would have on this nation's health. . . .

. . . In 1964, more than one-half of men and nearly one-third of women were regular smokers; it took approximately 15 years for rates of smoking among men to drop by one-quarter or more. The scientific evidence helped to launch public health campaigns about the dangers of smoking. The tobacco industry attempted to counter these campaigns through aggressive advertising. . . .

During the decades that followed, however, a number of local, state, and federal laws and policies addressed tobacco product marketing and advertising, labeling and packaging, youth access, and exposure to secondhand smoke. Social norms that had made smoking acceptable everywhere began to change as a grassroots movement aimed at protecting nonsmokers emerged. Surgeon General's reports on the impact of tobacco use on specific populations, the changing cigarette, nicotine addiction, specific smoking-related diseases, and secondhand smoke gave impetus to a steady movement away from smoking as an acceptable social norm . . . . A 2011 Gallup poll reported that for the first time, a majority of Americans supported a ban on smoking in all public places.

. . . .

Section 2. The Health Consequences of Active and Passive Smoking: The Evidence in 2014.

Since 1964, the evidence on smoking and health has expanded greatly; the list of adverse consequences of tobacco smoking has lengthened progressively; and since the 1970s, scientific research has linked the inhalation of secondhand smoke by nonsmokers to specific diseases and other adverse effects. . . .

. . . .

Cancer: Lung cancer, the first of many deadly diseases to be identified in a Surgeon General's report as being caused by smoking, is now the nation's most common cancer killer among men and women. Two studies carried out by the American Cancer Society have been key sources of information on the risks of lung cancer in smokers. These two studies each followed more than 1 million U.S. men and women, starting in 1959 for the first study and then again in 1982 for the second. Results from these studies have now been compared with data combined from several large populations followed from 2000–2010. Although the risk of lung cancer for never smokers in all three studies stayed about the same, the risk to smokers increased steadily . . . . In the 1959 study, women smokers were 2.7 times more likely than women never smokers to develop lung cancer; by 2000–2010 that additional risk for women smokers had jumped nearly tenfold, to 25.7. For men who smoked, the risk more than doubled, from 12.2 to 25.0 between the first and last studies. These relative risks increased over the same period as the prevalence of smoking and the average number of cigarettes consumed per smoker decreased. Although the incidence of squamous cell carcinoma of the lung — the type of lung cancer most often diagnosed among smokers at the start of the lung cancer epidemic — declined as smoking rates dropped, the incidence of adenocarcinoma of the lung increased dramatically. Evidence suggests that changes in the composition and design of the cigarette itself may have had some impact on the relative risk of lung cancer, as well as on the shift in the types of lung cancer occurring in the contemporary cohorts of smokers.

This latest Surgeon General's report also evaluated the evidence on other cancers, and concluded that smoking is a cause of liver cancer and of colorectal cancer, the fourth most diagnosed cancer in the United States and the cancer responsible for the second largest number of cancer deaths annually. The report found that the evidence is suggestive but insufficient to conclude that smoking and exposure to secondhand smoke cause breast cancer, and that smoking is not a cause for prostate cancer. . . .

Respiratory diseases: In the 1964 Surgeon General's report, smoking was found to be a cause of "chronic bronchitis," a term used then for the disease now generally referred to as chronic obstructive pulmonary disease (COPD). Because smoke is inhaled into the lung and its components are deposited and absorbed in the lungs, it has long been linked to adverse effects on the respiratory system, causing malignant and nonmalignant diseases, exacerbating chronic lung diseases, and increasing the risk for respiratory infections. The scientific literature showing associations with multiple diseases of the respiratory tract is extensive as is the evidence supporting the biologic plausibility of smoking as a cause of these associations. This report has reviewed the updated evidence on COPD. Mortality from COPD continues to rise, and smoking remains responsible for the vast majority of cases. As for lung cancer, comparison of the findings of the two American Cancer Society studies with the more recent studies spanning 2000–2010 showed rising risks for COPD, particularly in women. . . .

For asthma, another obstructive lung disease, the evidence was found to be sufficient to infer that smoking worsens asthma in adults who smoke . . . .

Cardiovascular diseases: Although lung cancer is often assumed to be the largest smoking-attributable cause of death in the United States, cardiovascular disease actually claims more lives of smokers 35 years of age and older every year compared with lung cancer. Exposure to secondhand smoke causes significantly more deaths due to cardiovascular disease than due to lung cancer, and this new report finds that exposure to second-hand smoke is also a cause of stroke. Exposure to second-hand smoke increases the risk for stroke by an estimated 20–30%. Even so, the evidence is clear that reductions in smoking and exposure to secondhand smoke have contributed to the decline in death rates from cardiovascular diseases since the late 1960s. Smokefree laws and policies have been proven to reduce the incidence of heart attacks and other coronary events among people younger than 65 years of age, and evidence suggests that there could be a relationship between such laws and policies and a reduction in cerebrovascular events.

Diabetes: Previous Surgeon General's reports have found that smoking complicates the treatment of diabetes and that smokers who have been diagnosed with diabetes are at a higher risk for kidney disease, blindness, and circulatory complications leading to amputations. This report concludes that smoking is a cause of type 2 diabetes mellitus, and that the risk of developing diabetes is 30–40% higher for active smokers than nonsmokers. Furthermore, the risk of developing diabetes increases as the number of cigarettes smoked grows.

Immune and autoimmune disorders: This report finds that smoking is a cause of general adverse effects on the body, including systemic inflammation and impaired immune function. One result of this altered immunity is increased risk for pulmonary infections among smokers. For example, risks for Mycobacterium tuberculosis and for death from tuberculosis disease are higher for smokers than nonsmokers. Additionally, smoking is known to compromise the equilibrium of the immune system, increasing the risk for several immune and autoimmune disorders. This report finds that smoking is a cause of rheumatoid arthritis, and that smoking interferes with the effectiveness of certain treatments for rheumatoid arthritis.

Reproductive effects: Several additional adverse reproductive effects are now found to be attributable to smoking. One is ectopic pregnancy, in which the embryo implants in the Fallopian tube or elsewhere outside the uterus. Ectopic pregnancy is very rarely a survivable condition for the fetus and is a potentially fatal condition for the mother. This report finds that maternal smoking during early pregnancy is causal for orofacial clefts in infants, and evidence suggests that smoking could be associated with certain other birth defects. This report also finds that the evidence is now sufficient to conclude that there is a causal relationship between smoking and erectile dysfunction in men.

Eye disease: The retina is a delicate, light-sensitive tissue that lines the inside of the eye. The macula is the most sensitive part of the retina and is the part of the eye that supplies sharp vision. Age-related macular degeneration (AMD) gradually destroys the macula and can ultimately lead to loss of vision in the center of the eye. This report finds that smoking is a cause of AMD. Evidence in the report also suggests that quitting smoking may reduce the risk for AMD, but the reduced risk may not appear for 20 or more years after smoking cessation.

General health: Smokers have long been known to suffer from poorer general health than nonsmokers, beginning at an early age and extending throughout adult life. Although emphasis has been given to smoking as a cause of specific and avoidable diseases, it is a powerful cause of ill-health generally. These health deficits not only reduce the quality of life of smokers but also affect their participation in the workplace and increase their costs to the health care system.

All-cause mortality: The evidence in this report reaffirms that smoking is a major cause of premature death. During the past 50 years, as generations of men and women who began smoking in adolescence and continued to smoke into middle and older ages have been stricken with the health consequences of lifetime smoking, the relative risk for all-cause mortality associated with current cigarette smoking has increased. The age-standardized relative risk, comparing the all-cause death rate in current smokers to that of never smokers, has more than doubled in men and more than tripled in women during the years since the release of the first Surgeon General's report on smoking and health. The lives of smokers are cut short by the development of the many diseases caused by smoking and by their greater risk of dying from common health events, such as complications of routine surgeries and pneumonia. Smoking shortens life far more than most other risk factors for early mortality; smokers are estimated to lose more than a decade of life. Smoking cessation by 40 years of age reduces that loss approximately 90%. Even stopping by about 60 years of age reduces that loss approximately 40%. However, reducing the number of cigarettes smoked per day is much less effective than quitting entirely for avoiding the risks of premature death from all smoking-related causes of death.

. . . .

Section 3: Tracking and Ending the Epidemic

. . . .

. . . The annual costs attributed to smoking in the United States are between $289 billion and $333 billion, including at least $130 billion for direct medical care of adults, over $150 billion for lost productivity due to premature death, and more than $5 billion for lost productivity from premature death due to exposure to secondhand smoke.

Despite decades of warnings on the dangers of smoking, nearly 42 million adults and more than 3.5 million middle and high school students continue to smoke cigarettes. Significant disparities in tobacco use persist among certain racial/ethnic populations, and among groups defined by educational level, socioeconomic status, geographic region, sexual minorities (including individuals who are gay, lesbian, bisexual, and transgender, and individuals with same-sex relationships or attraction), and severe mental illness. The majority (88%) started smoking before 18 years of age, and nearly all first use of cigarettes occurs before 26 years of age. The fraction of smoking initiation occurring after 18 years of age has been increasing over the past decade.

Tobacco industry advertising and promotional activities cause youth and young adults to start smoking, and nicotine addiction keeps people smoking past those ages. Each year, for every adult who dies prematurely from a smoking-related cause, more than two youth or young adults become replacement smokers. Although the prevalence of current smoking among high school-aged youth has declined, the total number of youth and young adults who started smoking increased from 1.9 million in 2002 to 2.3 million in 2012. However, progress has been made in reducing initiation among youth younger than 18 years of age, with the total number of youth who initiated smoking before age 18 declining from 1.5 million in 2009 down to 1.2 million in 2012.

While attention has focused primarily on cigarette smoking, this and recent Surgeon General's reports review health risks and emphasize the need to monitor patterns of use of all combusted tobacco products, particularly the use of cigarette-like cigars and roll-your-own cigarettes using pipe tobacco. Most commonly, these products are used along with cigarettes. According to recent trends, the percentage of adults, 18 years of age and older — who smoke either cigarettes, cigars, or roll-your-own cigarettes made with pipe tobacco — has remained relatively steady (25–26%) since 2009 and has declined only a small amount since 2002.

. . . Today, in the United States there are more former smokers than current smokers, and success rates for quitting have been increasing among recent birth cohorts. Interest in quitting is high across all segments of society. Patterns of tobacco use are also changing, with more people smoking intermittently and smoking fewer cigarettes; however, there is an increase in the use of tobacco products other than cigarettes, often concurrent with cigarettes.

The burden of smoking-attributable disease and pre-mature death and its high costs to the nation will continue for decades unless smoking prevalence is reduced more rapidly than the current trajectory. The evidence in this report shows that the nation may fail to achieve the Healthy People 2020 objective of reducing the prevalence of smoking among adults to 12%. Model estimates suggest that if the status quo in tobacco control in 2008 were maintained, the projected prevalence of smoking among adults in 2050 could still be as high as 15% . . . .

. . . .

Therefore, this report addresses the question: what steps are needed to end the tobacco epidemic? There are different ways to achieve this vision. Should the emphasis be on ending cigarette use?; ending the use of the most harmful tobacco products while reducing the harm of remaining products?; or ending the use of all tobacco products?

. . . .

. . . This and previous reports outline effective programs and policies: raising the retail price of cigarettes and other tobacco products, smokefree indoor air policies, high-impact media campaigns, full access to cessation treatments, and funding of comprehensive statewide tobacco control programs. . . .

However, these five actions are not all that needs to be done . . . . For example, selected state experience suggests that all levels of government can enhance revenue collection and minimize tax avoidance and evasion through several promising policy approaches, such as implementing a high-tech cigarette tax stamp, improving tobacco licensure management, and making the stamps harder to counterfeit. These state practices could also be expanded to the national level with a track and trace system. A track and trace system, in the tobacco control context, is a system that can track goods from manufacture to distribution to sale, identifying points in the supply chain where taxes should be paid and confirm payment. Implementing such systems would also simultaneously retain the positive public health effects of taxation and protect product regulation in the market.

. . . [O]ther factors in society can significantly affect social norms. Portrayals of tobacco use in U.S. films appear to have rebounded upward in the past 2 years. In 2012, youth were exposed to an estimated 14.9 billion in-theater tobacco-use impressions in youth-rated films. Youth who are exposed to images of smoking in movies are more likely to smoke; those who get the most exposure to onscreen smoking are about twice as likely to begin smoking as those who get the least exposure. Actions that would eliminate the depiction of tobacco use in movies, which are produced and rated as appropriate for children and adolescents, could have a significant effect on preventing youth from becoming tobacco users.

Faced with the challenge of achieving a vision of a society free of tobacco-related death and disease, a discussion has begun within the field of tobacco control about what has come to be called the tobacco "end game" in the published literature. This literature considers strategies that could be used . . . to accelerate declines in the use of cigarettes and other combusted tobacco products and end the epidemic of disease and premature death caused by tobacco.

. . . .

Examples of end game options . . . include but are not limited to:

1. Reducing the nicotine content to make cigarettes less addictive; and

2. Greater restrictions on sales, particularly at the local level, including bans on entire categories of tobacco products.

End game strategies might be aided by future approaches and devices for nicotine delivery that better substitute for the cigarette. [V]arious new products are increasingly being introduced into the market. In 2012 Lorillard acquired Blu Electronic Cigarettes, in 2013 R.J. Reynolds Tobacco Company introduced VUSE electronic cigarettes in limited markets, and Altria announced that it will introduce an electronic cigarette in 2014. Additionally, other electronic nicotine delivery systems have been developed and marketed by companies with little or no experience in developing and marketing traditional tobacco products. As these new products are entering the marketplace rapidly, significant questions remain about (1) how to assess the potential toxicity and health effects of the more than 250 electronic cigarette brands; (2) the magnitude of reduced risk from electronic cigarettes versus continuing use of conventional cigarettes for individual smokers; (3) the need to weigh the potential individual benefits versus population risks; (4) how the advertising and marketing of these new products should be regulated; and (5) even assuming that electronic cigarettes could be sufficiently safe to the users and offer net public health benefits, there are significant questions about the manner in which they should be regulated. Further research and attention to the consequences as well as regulatory measures will be necessary to fully address these questions. However, the promotion of electronic cigarettes and other innovative tobacco products is much more likely to be beneficial in an environment where the appeal, accessibility, promotion, and use of cigarettes are being rapidly reduced.

. . . . .

RICHARD KLUGER, ASHES TO ASHES
xiii, xv, xvii, xix (1996)

The proverbial visitor from a distant planet would likely find no earthling custom more pointless or puzzling than the swallowing of tobacco smoke followed by its billowy emission and accompanying odor. Told that the act neither warms nor cleanses the human interior, that it neither repels enemies nor attracts lovers, our off-planet visitor would be still more baffled. The utility of the exercise, he would be informed, is traceable to the changing pace, scale, and nature of daily living in this century. Lives used to be simpler and shorter, given over largely to the struggle for survival. But the technological marvels of our age have provoked attendant stresses from congested living and our often grating interdependence; from the irksome nature of our duties and lack of time to accomplish them; from a welter of conflicting values and emotions born of unattainable expectations and unmanageable frustrations; and from the often careening velocity of life. Many of us have lacked the inner resources to get through the battle and gain a little repose without help wherever and however we could find it, and no device, product, or pastime has been more readily seized upon for this pur-pose than the cigarette. It has been the preferred and infamous pacifier of the twentieth century, even as — or if — it has been our worst killer. Its users have found it their all-purpose psychological crutch, their universal coping device, and the truest, cheapest, most accessible opiate of the masses.

Let us consider, then, this protean usefulness of the cigarette, which, practically speaking, is the tobacco business in the United States, accounting for some 95 percent of the industry's revenues. The unique value of the cigarette to its users has resided in its perceived dual (and contradictory) role as both stimulant and sedative. Clinically, smoking has been found to speed up a number of bodily functions, most notably the flow of adrenaline, with its quickening effect on the beat of the heart, but the smoker when questioned will most often characterize the cigarette as a relaxant. This seeming paradox is the essence of the product's appeal, for in fact, the smoker uses it to meet both needs.

The smoker smokes when feeling up or in the dumps, when too harassed and overburdened or too unchallenged and idle, when threatened by the crowd at a party or when lonely in a strange place. A smoke is a reward for a job well done or consolation for a job botched. It can fuel the smoker for the intensity of life's daily confrontations yet seem to insulate him from the consuming effects of any given encounter. It defines and punctuates the periods of the smoker's day, and nothing helps as much in dealing on the telephone with trying people or unpleasant matters. The cigarette, in short, has been the peerless regulator of its user's moods, the merciful stabilizing force against the human tendency to over-respond to the infinite stimuli that inescapably impinge upon us.

. . . .

That smoking is equally a boon to the soul as to the body, few partakers would claim, but most believe it helps them think. Samuel Johnson, among the eighteenth century's more celebrated pipe-puffers, modestly praised the practice as "a thing which requires so little exertion and yet preserves the mind from total vacuity." Freud went a good deal further. "I owe to the cigar a great intensification of my capacity to work." This was written in his seventy-second year after thirty agonizing operations for cancer of the jaw, by which time the connection between the two was not likely lost on him . . . .

Is there clinical support for smoking as brain food? Some experimenters have found, though the evidence is equivocal at best, that nicotine, tobacco's psycho-activating ingredient, excites the brain waves, can increase vigilance in the performance of repetitive (one might say mindless) tasks, and may improve the processing of sensory stimuli — provided, that is, one keeps on smoking. Does any of this amount to a boost in productive mental energy? Some scientists have theorized that smoking creates an apparent heightening effect by neutralizing (one might say numbing) the edges of one's consciousness and thereby reducing distractions. Translation: Smoking may help you concentrate by emptying the mind of all but the subject of the moment.

. . . .

Nor to be minimized, either, has been the usefulness of smoking as coded defiance of authority, of the hand fate has dealt you, of sweet reason itself. It is most favored, in the first instance, by juvenile smokers as an initiator into the mysteries and empowerment of the adult world; the accompanying displeasures of nausea and dizziness assaulting the novice inhaler are tolerated as rites of passage and the price to be paid for partaking of forbidden fruit . . . .

For those millions enslaved by nicotine, the weightier charge that the addiction can ultimately prove lethal inspires a lot of fast talking and whistling by the graveyard. The catechism of the hopelessly habituated runs something like this: (1) Even if those busybody biostatisticians are right, only one of four smokers will die due, more or less, to smoking, so the odds are on my side. (2) Besides, you've got to die of something, so why not from a source of pleasure? (3) Anyway, it takes decades for the diseases linked to smoking to develop, and those years I might lose aren't exactly quality time, coming late in life when many human faculties and the yen for living are diminished. (4) Life is full of dangers — to live is to take risks of all sorts every day; I may get hit by a truck tomorrow. I'm here and want to enjoy myself to the fullest extent possible, and cigarettes help me do that. And (5), let's face it, I might have gone cuckoo a long while back without smoking or stressed out terminally, as they say. So, (6) if you don't mind — or even if you do — please get out of my face and tend to your own garden P.S. (7) When your number's up, it's up; you can't mess with your karma.

Why, given the enormity of the crimes against humanity with which it has been charged, the cigarette has not been outlawed or its ingredients and design modified by government command is thus explainable in the first place by the immense and continuing consumption of the product for all the above uses and excuses. It must then be added at once, without excessive moralizing, that the tobacco industry, understandably devoted to its own survival ahead of all others', has labored prodigiously to reassure its customers, disarm its foes, purchase allies in high places, and minimize government intrusion into its gravely suspect business. But the success of that industry cannot be facilely dismissed as greedy capitalism at its most predatory, for in many nations, capitalist and socialist alike, the manufacture and sale of tobacco products have been reserved as an operation of the state, carried out in the name of the public interest if not the public health . . . .

Around the world, moreover, the pro-smoking cause is championed by millions dependent on the tobacco industry for their livelihood. Most numerous among these are the growers of what the industry claims is the most widely cultivated non-food plant on earth. In the United States, tobacco remains the most profitable cash crop on a per-acre basis, and in many places throughout Latin America, Africa, and Asia, where subsistence farming is the obligatory way of life for the masses, pending the creation of viable domestic industry, tobacco has been considered a godsend . . . .

. . . .

Governments, furthermore, have themselves become addicted to the cigarette because of the taxes it harvests for them. Cigarettes are the most heavily taxed consumer product in the world . . . . In China, they have been the largest source of capital formation for broadening the country's industrial base. Few politicians have been willing to forgo such revenues, as well as the votes and support of smokers and all those battening on the habit. . . .

. . . .

The question, then, is whether cigarette merchants are businessmen basically like any other, selling a product judged to be highly hazardous long after its usefulness to millions was well established, and are now sorely abused by "health fascists" and moralizing busybodies, or are they moral lepers preying on the ignorant, the miserable, the emotionally vulnerable, and the genetically susceptible?

NOTES AND QUESTIONS

1.   **American tobacco history.** Tobacco has been used in one form or another for centuries. However, the vast majority of such use was in chewing tobacco, snuff, cigars, and pipes of various sorts. This changed with several new technologies that made it possible to inhale cigarette smoke and produce cigarettes in large quantities. Tobacco grew wild and was cultivated in the American colonies, but typically produced harsh smoke. Milder tobaccos were imported, but by 1620, an even milder smoke was produced by changing the method for curing the leaves from piling them on the ground to hanging the leaves in a barn. This method turned the leaves a bright yellow — hence the name "bright" tobacco. This even milder bright tobacco generated more demand and a prosperous industry. An even more important technological change came in the early 1800's. Flue-cured tobacco altered the *ph* of the smoke, making inhalation both possible and necessary. This, in turn, fostered an addiction to nicotine not found in pipe, cigar and snuff use, and demand soared. (*See* Box below.) After 1880, James Bonsack's cigarette manufacturing device made mass production possible. James Buchanan Duke cemented his family's fortune in cigarette sales, using Bonsack's machine to increase production to meet demand. Duke formed the giant American Tobacco Company in 1890, which was broken into the American, Liggett and Myers, Lorillard, and Reynolds companies in the trust-busting actions of 1911.

The excerpt above from Richard Kluger's book, ASHES TO ASHES: AMERICA'S HUNDRED-YEAR CIGARETTE WAR, THE PUBLIC HEALTH, AND THE UNABASHED TRIUMPH OF PHILIP MORRIS, indicates the potency of nicotine not only in the rise of the industry, but also in attitudes toward smoking. His book provides a detailed social history of the tobacco industry. For the definitive early history of the tobacco industry, see NANNIE MAE TILLEY, THE BRIGHT TOBACCO INDUSTRY: 1860–1929 (1948). For a history of cigarettes in the twentieth century, see ALLAN BRANDT, THE CIGARETTE CENTURY (2007).

The Rise of Flue-Cured Tobacco, Inhalable Nicotine, and Addiction

In 1980, William Ira Bennett, MD, first described how a new method of flue-curing tobacco, introduced around 1810, changed the *ph* of bright tobacco leaves from alkaline (as in the harsher tobacco in pipes and cigars), to acid, making it both possible and necessary to inhale — and thereby induce addiction:

[In the early seventeenth century] demand for the so-called bright leaf was substantial, but it increased relatively little until early in the nineteenth century, when European tastes, influenced by exposure to mild Turkish tobaccos, began to favor it.

. . . .

Once again innovations in curing were needed, both to reduce the cost of production and to improve the quality of the leaf. Curing had been controlled mostly through the use of tight barns with open fires in them. A shift from wood to charcoal curing made the tobacco even more pleasant to smoke than before — though it still could not be comfortably inhaled. The crucial innovation, developed as early as 1810, was to heat the barns with flues running through them, so that the tobacco was not directly exposed to wood or charcoal smoke.

. . . .

The reason why flue-curing made such a difference was that it produced a mildly acid, instead of alkaline, smoke. Nicotine is efficiently absorbed only from an alkaline medium. Fire-cured tobaccos — those used for snuff, plug, and pipe tobaccos, and even for cigarettes, by and large, before the 1870's — are alkaline and thus permit nicotine to be absorbed through the lining of the mouth or nose. Chewing, snuffing, and pipe or cigar smoking are all conducive to a gradual intake of nicotine without inhaling. The alkalinity of smoke from this sort of tobacco also makes it unpleasant for all but the hardiest smokers to inhale, even when it originates from the bright leaf.

The smoke of modern cigarettes, by contrast, comes from flue-cured tobacco and is slightly acid. Not only can it be inhaled, it *must* be for any significant amount of nicotine to be absorbed, because only in the lungs is the smoke converted from acid to alkaline. The nicotine is, moreover, absorbed in a series of very concentrated doses, each of which reaches the brain about seven seconds after it enters the lungs (that is, about twice as fast as heroin traveling from the forearm).

. . . .

In general, the non-inhaling smoker of pipes and cigars obtains a low-to-moderate blood level of nicotine through a process of gradual absorption. Although nicotine is an essential component of the pleasure, the dose is administered along with a host of cozy associations and little bits of comforting business. Provided some nicotine is absorbed, the routine is thoroughly habit-forming, but not often intensely addictive.

The inhaler of tobacco smoke . . . has a different experience. He or she draws smoke onto the enormous absorbing surface of the lung, which neutralizes the acidity sufficiently to permit absorption to occur. In this process, an entire cross-section of the bloodstream is loaded with nicotine. It travels to the heart and then to the brain without dilution. (By contrast, a drug shot into a vein in the forearm is mixed with blood returning from other veins as it approaches the heart, and so is diluted before it reaches the brain.)

> . . . . it appears to be these periodic jolts of nicotine that the cigarette smoker is after. Each puff is followed by a transitory, but very high, level of nicotine in the blood. . . .
>
> The basis of addiction, then, is a requirement for intermittent, tiny "highs." But because nicotine begins to have unpleasant side effects as it builds up in the blood, the smoker must also guard against overdose. A given individual's pattern of smoking is a compromise between the frequency of rewards that he or she can achieve and the need to keep the average level of nicotine in the blood below a tolerable maximum. . . .
>
> William Bennett, *The Nicotine Fix*, 82(6) HARVARD MAGAZINE 10, 12–13 (July/ Aug. 1980).

2. **Reports of the Surgeon General.** The Surgeon General's Report excerpted above marks the 50th anniversary of Dr. Luther L. Terry's landmark first Surgeon General's report on smoking and health linking smoking and lung cancer. Subsequent reports have cataloged the evidence for smoking as a cause of other cancers, heart disease, stroke, respiratory diseases, and potentially damage to virtually every organ of the body. These reports encouraged wide dissemination of information about the dangers of smoking cigarettes, such that today no one would claim that cigarettes are harmless. Consider the change in public opinion about smoking in the last century. During World War II, when almost half the population smoked, cigarettes were considered as essential a ration for combat troops as food. Cigarettes provided actors with a prop to express various emotions on the movie screen. Women smoked cigarettes to demonstrate their independence.

While the proportion of the population using cigarettes declined in the last half-century, Surgeon General reports described an increasing number of deaths attributable to smoking cigarettes. Can you discern why? How many diseases were found to be caused by smoking in 1964 compared with 2014? The 2014 report, excerpted above, also states, "today's cigarette smokers — both men and women — have a much higher risk for lung cancer and chronic obstructive pulmonary disease (COPD) than smokers in 1964, despite smoking fewer cigarettes." How can that be? Note that the reports attribute deaths of non-smokers to exposure to secondhand smoke.

For current information about the number of people in the U.S. who use tobacco, as well as summary data on tobacco and health, see www.cdc.gov/tobacco/ (visited Feb. 2014).

3. **Secondhand smoke or environmental tobacco smoke.** The risks posed by secondhand smoke are the reason for most, if not all, legislation and ordinances adopted to reduce tobacco use in the United States, including those discussed in this Chapter. Modern regulatory measures are intended to protect the non-smoking public from exposure to the risks of secondhand smoke — not to protect the smokers themselves. As seen in earlier Chapters, it is relatively easy to justify protecting people from external sources of harm. (A complete ban on smoking or selling tobacco might be justified to protect the smoker from serious danger.) Thus, the evidence of harm from secondhand smoke is critical to public health laws to reduce tobacco use.

The various effects on non-smokers who are exposed to tobacco smoke were first mentioned in a Surgeon General's 1986 report. By 2006, the Surgeon General's Report was unequivocal in its conclusion that "secondhand smoke" is a major health hazard and still another reason to reduce smoking. These and subsequent reports collect the evidence that exposure to secondhand smoke increases a person's risk of heart disease, cancers, and other diseases. In 2006, the CDC reported that secondhand smoke contained 4,000 chemicals, including 50 carcinogens. By 2014, its website reported that secondhand smoke contains 7,000 chemicals, of which 70 can cause cancer. According to CDC estimates, for example, exposure to secondhand smoke causes 46,000 premature deaths from heart disease and 3,400 deaths from lung cancer among non-smokers each year. CDC, Smoking and Tobacco Use, Health Effects of Secondhand Smoke, www.cdc.gov/tobacco/data_statistics/fact_sheets/secondhand_smoke/health_effects/index.htm (visited Feb. 2014).

The evidence regarding the health consequences of smoking provides an interesting demonstration of the inherent problems facing epidemiologists and other experts when they attempt to assess the causal linkage between morbidity and mortality and various potential risks such as smoking. The Surgeon General's Reports classify causation into four levels: "proven to cause the disease;" "may cause the disease;" "there is not enough proof that smoking does or does not cause the disease;" and "probably does not cause the disease." Typically, a panel of experts reviews the available literature and makes a determination (by majority or consensus), considering questions like the following:

— Do multiple high-quality studies show a consistent association between smoking and disease?

— Are the measured effects large enough and statistically strong?

— Does the evidence show that smoking occurs before the disease occurs (*i.e.*, a temporal association)?

— Is the relationship between smoking and disease coherent or plausible in terms of known scientific principles, biologic mechanisms, and observed patterns of disease?

Note that all of these questions call for a mix of good scientific research, expert opinion about that research, data analysis, and — particularly when the state of knowledge becomes relevant to policymaking — value-laden judgments. In some cases, lung cancer for example, the evidence is overwhelming: There is no doubt that smoking tobacco is a direct and primary cause of lung cancer in smokers. In other cases, any assessment of a causal link must be made with some qualification. Research may be limited and the results may be hard to interpret. Direct measures of effect may be difficult to obtain, especially if there are many causes for a disease or if exposure to a potential cause may result in the disease in some but not all of those who are exposed. For that matter, it may be both scientifically and ethically impossible to engage in the kind of controlled clinical trial that might provide the most probative evidence. (Recall the court's rejection of EPA's report in the *Flue-Cured Tobacco Cooperative* case in Chapter 2, B, Note 2, *supra*. The Surgeon General included the EPA's evidence in his own report, perhaps for lack of alternative studies.) Studying the health effects of "secondhand" smoke is particularly problematic, even more so than studying the effects of smoking on smokers.

Yet more difficult may be research concerning third-hand smoke, that is, the residue left from smoking on walls, furniture and clothing.

WHO FRAMEWORK CONVENTION ON TOBACCO CONTROL (2003)

PART II: OBJECTIVE, GUIDING PRINCIPLES AND GENERAL OBLIGATIONS

Article 3

Objective

The objective of this Convention and its protocols is to protect present and future generations from the devastating health, social, environmental and economic consequences of tobacco consumption and exposure to tobacco smoke by providing a framework for tobacco control measures to be implemented by the Parties at the national, regional and international levels in order to reduce continually and substantially the prevalence of tobacco use and exposure to tobacco smoke.

. . . .

PART III: MEASURES RELATING TO THE REDUCTION OF DEMAND FOR TOBACCO

Article 6

Price and tax measures to reduce the demand for tobacco

1. The Parties recognize that price and tax measures are an effective and important means of reducing tobacco consumption by various segments of the population, in particular young persons.

2. Without prejudice to the sovereign right of the Parties to determine and establish their taxation policies, each Party should take account of its national health objectives concerning tobacco control and adopt or maintain, as appropriate, measures which may include:

(a) implementing tax policies and, where appropriate, price policies, on tobacco products so as to contribute to the health objectives aimed at reducing tobacco consumption; and

. . . .

Article 8

Protection from exposure to tobacco smoke

. . . .

2. Each Party shall adopt and implement in areas of existing national jurisdiction as determined by national law and actively promote at other jurisdictional levels the

adoption and implementation of effective legislative, executive, administrative and/or other measures, providing for protection from exposure to tobacco smoke in indoor workplaces, public transport, indoor public places and, as appropriate, other public places.

. . . .

Article 11

Packaging and labelling of tobacco products

1. Each Party shall, within a period of three years after entry into force of this Convention for that Party, adopt and implement, in accordance with its national law, effective measures to ensure that:

(a) tobacco product packaging and labelling do not promote a tobacco product by any means that are false, misleading, deceptive or likely to create an erroneous impression about its characteristics, health effects, hazards or emissions, including any term, descriptor, trademark, figurative or any other sign that directly or indirectly creates the false impression that a particular tobacco product is less harmful than other tobacco products. These may include terms such as "low tar", "light", "ultra-light", or "mild"; and

(b) each unit packet and package of tobacco products and any outside packaging and labelling of such products also carry health warnings describing the harmful effects of tobacco use, and may include other appropriate messages. These warnings and messages:

   (i)   shall be approved by the competent national authority,

   (ii) shall be rotating,

   (iii) shall be large, clear, visible and legible,

   (iv) should be 50% or more of the principal display areas but shall be no less than 30% of the principal display areas,

   (v)   may be in the form of or include pictures or pictograms.

2. Each unit packet and package of tobacco products and any outside packaging and labelling of such products shall, in addition to the warnings specified in paragraph 1(b) of this Article, contain information on relevant constituents and emissions of tobacco products as defined by national authorities.

. . . .

Article 13

Tobacco advertising, promotion and sponsorship

1. Parties recognize that a comprehensive ban on advertising, promotion and sponsorship would reduce the consumption of tobacco products.

2. Each Party shall, in accordance with its constitution or constitutional principles, undertake a comprehensive ban of all tobacco advertising, promotion and sponsorship. . . . ;

3. A Party that is not in a position to undertake a comprehensive ban due to its constitution or constitutional principles shall apply restrictions on all tobacco advertising, promotion and sponsorship. . . . ;

4. As a minimum, and in accordance with its constitution or constitutional principles, each Party shall:

(a) prohibit all forms of tobacco advertising, promotion and sponsorship that promote a tobacco product by any means that are false, misleading or deceptive or likely to create an erroneous impression about its characteristics, health effects, hazards or emissions;

(b) require that health or other appropriate warnings or messages accompany all tobacco advertising and, as appropriate, promotion and sponsorship;

(c) restrict the use of direct or indirect incentives that encourage the purchase of tobacco products by the public;

(d) require, if it does not have a comprehensive ban, the disclosure to relevant governmental authorities of expenditures by the tobacco industry on advertising, promotion and sponsorship not yet prohibited. . . . ;

(e) undertake a comprehensive ban or, in the case of a Party that is not in a position to undertake a comprehensive ban due to its constitution or constitutional principles, restrict tobacco advertising, promotion and sponsorship on radio, television, print media and, as appropriate, other media, such as the internet, within a period of five years; and

(f) prohibit, or in the case of a Party that is not in a position to prohibit due to its constitution or constitutional principles restrict, tobacco sponsorship of international events, activities and/or participants therein.

. . . .

PART IV: MEASURES RELATING TO THE REDUCTION OF THE SUPPLY OF TOBACCO

. . . .

Article 16

Sales to and by minors

1. Each Party shall adopt and implement effective legislative, executive, administrative or other measures at the appropriate government level to prohibit the sales of tobacco products to persons under the age set by domestic law, national law or eighteen. These measures may include:

(a) requiring that all sellers of tobacco products place a clear and prominent indicator inside their point of sale about the prohibition of tobacco sales to minors and, in case of doubt, request that each tobacco purchaser provide appropriate evidence of having reached full legal age;

(b) banning the sale of tobacco products in any manner by which they are directly accessible, such as store shelves;

(c) prohibiting the manufacture and sale of sweets, snacks, toys or any other objects in the form of tobacco products which appeal to minors; and

(d) ensuring that tobacco vending machines under its jurisdiction are not accessible to minors and do not promote the sale of tobacco products to minors.

2. Each Party shall prohibit or promote the prohibition of the distribution of free tobacco products to the public and especially minors.

3. Each Party shall endeavour to prohibit the sale of cigarettes individually or in small packets which increase the affordability of such products to minors.

. . . .

Article 19

Liability

1. For the purpose of tobacco control, the Parties shall consider taking legislative action or promoting their existing laws, where necessary, to deal with criminal and civil liability, including compensation where appropriate.

. . . .

NOTES AND QUESTIONS

4. The Framework Convention on Tobacco Control. The WHO Framework Convention on Tobacco Control (FCTC) was adopted in 2003 by the World Health Assembly, WHO's governing body composed of representatives of member nations. This first (and so far only) convention negotiated by WHO came into force on February 27, 2005. As of September 2013, 177 countries were Parties to the FCTC. The excerpts above indicate the FCTC's broad scope. It includes general statements of principle as well as recommendations for measures to reduce tobacco sales and its harmful effects on health. For background and the complete text of the FCTC, *see* WHO FCTC, www.who.int/fctc/about/en/index.html (visited May 2014).

Note that the FCTC focuses its most prescriptive statements on the supply side of the tobacco industry. Article 14 encourages reduction in the demand for tobacco, but does not include a ban on smoking or the use of tobacco (although Article 16 does include a ban on *sales* to minors). Instead, it charges the Parties with taking "effective measures to promote cessation of tobacco use and adequate treatment for tobacco dependence." Why might this be?

The United States signed but has not ratified the convention. Can you think why? Treaties and conventions often allow the parties to decline to be bound by specific provisions, unless such provisions are deemed to be "non-derogable." The convention's Article 30, however, states, "No reservations may be made to this Convention." Nonetheless, the federal government has taken steps to implement some FCTC provisions, including regulating the advertising of cigarettes, as discussed in Sections C and D, *infra*.

Article 5 of the FCTC states that each Party, "shall, in accordance with its capabilities . . . adopt and implement effective legislative, executive, administrative and other measures . . . for preventing and reducing tobacco consumption, nicotine addiction and exposure to tobacco smoke." Similar language can be found in most of the articles. How much leeway does that give the Parties in deciding what, if any, binding laws to enact? How might the convention be enforced? The convention provides for periodic progress reports. Does WHO or the United Nations or any Party to the FCTC have enforcement authority?

5. **Smoking cessation measures.** The excerpt above from Kluger suggests how and why some people find smoking appealing, despite knowledge of its harm and addictive quality. Still, most people who continue to smoke say they want to stop. The FCTC and the Surgeon General's Report recommend the adoption and implementation of "effective" measures to reduce the number of people who smoke or otherwise use tobacco products. But which anti-tobacco programs are actually effective? And, what does "effective" mean in this context?

If by "effective," one means quitting smoking forever, the evidence can seem disappointing. Most smoking cessation studies report that 5% to 15% of participants stop smoking at the end of the program, but more intensive interventions may have better results. Studies do not always follow participants for more than 6 to 12 months, and many former smokers relapse. Most experts consider quitting to be a process, with multiple attempts before finally quitting for good. Some reports conclude that the majority of smokers who stop permanently go "cold turkey," without entering a cessation program or using nicotine replacements, but studies of this "method" are rare. For an overview, see Karen Messer *et al.*, *Smoking Cessation Rates in the United States: A Comparison of Young Adults and Older Smokers*, 98 Am. J. Pub. Health 317 (2008).

For a description of smoking cessation treatments, see the National Institute on Drug Abuse, The Science of Drug Addiction and Treatment, http://www.drugabuse.gov/publications/topics-in-brief/tobacco-addiction (visited Feb. 2014).

6. **Comprehensive tobacco control programs.** Smoking cessation programs are only one element of what tobacco control experts describe as "comprehensive tobacco control programs." These include laws restricting locations that permit smoking, enforcing prohibitions on tobacco sales to minors, taxing tobacco sales, integrating smoking cessation into clinical medical care, insurance coverage of smoking cessation products and programs, surveillance of smoking incidence and prevalence, public education campaigns, and increased funding for tobacco control programs. *See* CDC, Best Practices for Comprehensive Tobacco Control Programs — 2014, www.cdc.gov/tobacco/stateandcommunity/best_practices/index.htm (visited Feb. 2014).

Tobacco control programs can be evaluated in terms of whether they save money, such as the costs of hospitalization for smoking-related diseases like heart disease, cancer, and emphysema. Comprehensive programs have been deemed successful for reducing the prevalence of smoking by between 0.4% and 1% per year in states like California and Massachusetts. However, they may depend heavily on public funding and suffer during economic recessions.

California was an early initiator of smoking control programs. In 2012, the city of San Rafael earned the distinction of adopting the country's strictest smoking ban. It prohibited smoking in multifamily residential units, as well as indoor and outdoor common areas. It also prohibited smoking on sidewalks in the downtown area except when the smoker is "actively passing on the way to another destination." Lori Preuitt, *San Fafael Passes Country's Toughest Smoking Ban*, NBC, Oct. 16, 2013, www.nbcbayarea.com/news/local/San-Rafael-Passes-Countrys-Toughest-Smoking-Ban-174418071.html (visited Feb. 2014).

For an interactive map showing the types of tobacco control laws in the states, see Robert Wood Johnson Foundation, Interactive Tobacco Map, www.rwjf.org/en/research-publications/find-rwjf-research/2010/03/interactive-tobacco-map-provides-latest-data-on-state-smoking-la.html (visited Feb. 2014).

C. CONSTITUTIONAL AND STATUTORY AUTHORITY TO REGULATE TOBACCO

AUSTIN v. TENNESSEE
179 U.S. 343 (1900)

BROWN, JUSTICE.

It is charged that the act in question [a state law criminalizing the sale or importation into Tennessee of cigarettes for sale or distribution] is an infringement upon the exclusive power of Congress to regulate commerce between the states. This is the sole question presented for our determination.

We are not disposed to question the general principle that the states cannot, under the guise of inspection or revenue laws, forbid or impede the introduction of products, and more particularly of food products, universally recognized as harmless or otherwise burden foreign or interstate commerce by regulations adopted under the assumed police power of the state, but obviously for the purpose of taxing such commerce or creating discriminations in favor of home producers or manufacturers . . . . "If, therefore, a statute purporting to have been enacted to protect the public health, the public morals, or the public safety has no real or substantial relation to those objects, or is a palpable invasion of rights secured by the fundamental law, it is the duty of the courts to so adjudge, and thereby give effect to the Constitution."

[The Tennessee Supreme Court had upheld Austin's conviction, ruling that the law's enforcement against him did not violate the commerce clause for two reasons: cigarettes were not "legitimate articles of commerce," and Austin's sale of cigarettes was "not the sale of an original package." The Court rejected the first in the following terms:]

. . . Whatever product has from time immemorial been recognized by custom or law as a fit subject for barter or sale, particularly if its manufacture has been made the subject of Federal regulation and taxation, must, we think, be recognized as a legitimate article of commerce although it may to a certain extent be within the police power of the states. Of this class of cases is tobacco. From the first settlement of the colony of Virginia to the present day tobacco has been one of the most profitable and important products of agriculture and commerce, and while its effects may be injurious to some, its extensive use over practically the entire globe is a remarkable tribute to its popularity and value. We are clearly of opinion that it cannot be classed with diseased cattle or meats, decayed fruit, or other articles, the use of which is a menace to the health of the entire community. Congress, too, has recognized tobacco in its various forms as a legitimate article of commerce by requiring licenses to be taken for its manufacture and sale, imposing a revenue tax upon each package of cigarettes put upon the market, and by making express regulations for their manufacture and sale, their exportation and importation. Cigarettes are but one of the numerous manufactures of tobacco, and we cannot take judicial notice of the fact that it is more noxious in this form than in any other. Whatever might be our individual views as to its deleterious tendencies, we cannot hold that any article which Congress recognizes in so many ways is not a legitimate article of commerce. . . .

[The Court then analogized tobacco to intoxicating liquors and reviewed its cases approving the states' authority to regulate the latter, up to and including the prohibition of intrastate sales. The Court said of those cases:]

These cases recognize the fact that intoxicating liquors belong to a class of commodities which, in the opinion of a great many estimable people, are deleterious in their effects, demoralizing in their tendencies, and often fatal in their excessive indulgence; and that, while their employment as a medicine may sometimes be beneficial, their habitual and constant use as a beverage, whatever it may be to individuals, is injurious to the community. It may be that their evil effects have been exaggerated, and that, though their use is usually attended with more or less danger, it is by no means open to universal condemnation. It is, however, within the power of each state to investigate the subject and to determine its policy in that particular. If the legislative body comes deliberately to the conclusion that a due regard for the public safety and morals requires a suppression of the liquor traffic, there is nothing in the commercial clause of the Constitution, or in the 14th Amendment to that instrument, to forbid its doing so. While, perhaps, it may not wholly prohibit the use or sale of them for medicinal purposes, it may hedge about their use as a general beverage such restrictions as it pleases. Nor can we deny to the legislature the power to impose restrictions upon the sale of noxious or poisonous drugs, such as opium and other similar articles, extremely valuable as medicines, but equally baneful to the habitual user.

Cigarettes do not seem until recently to have attracted the attention of the public as more injurious than other forms of tobacco; nor are we now prepared to take judicial notice of any special injury resulting from their use or to indorse the opinion of the supreme court of Tennessee that "they are inherently bad and bad only." At the same time we should be shutting our eyes to what is constantly passing before them were we to affect an ignorance of the fact that a belief in their deleterious effects, particularly upon young people, has become very general, and that communications are con-stantly finding their way into the public press denouncing their use as fraught with great danger to the youth of both sexes. Without undertaking to affirm or deny their evil effects, we think it within the province of the legislature to say how far they may be sold, or to prohibit their sale entirely, after they have been taken from the original packages or have left the hands of the importer, provided no discrimination be used as against such as are imported from other states, and there be no reason to doubt that the act in question is designed for the protection of the public health.

We have had repeated occasion to hold, where state legislation has been attacked as violative either of the power of Congress over interstate commerce, or of the 14th Amendment to the Constitution, that, if the action of the state legislature were as a *bona fide* exercise of its police power, and dictated by a genuine regard for the preservation of the public health or safety, such legislation would be respected, though it might interfere indirectly with interstate commerce.

. . . .

We are therefore of opinion that although the state of Tennessee may not wholly interdict commerce in cigarettes it is not, in the language of Chief Justice Taney in *The License Cases*, "bound to furnish a market for [them], nor to abstain from the passage of any law which it may deem necessary or advisable to guard the health or morals of its citizens, although such law may discourage importation, or diminish the profits of the importer, or lessen the revenue of the general [federal] government."

. . . .

There is doubtless fair ground for dispute as to whether the use of cigarettes is not hurtful to the community, and therefore it would be competent for a state, with reference to is own people, to declare, under penalties, that cigarettes should not be manufactured within its limits . . . . [We reject the view that] . . . the reserved power of the state to protect the health of its people, by reasonable regulations, has application only in respect of articles manufactured within its own limits, and that an open door exists for the introduction into the State, against its will, of all kinds of property which may be fairly regarded as injurious in their use to health. . . .

D.A.B.E., Inc. v. CITY OF TOLEDO
393 F.3d 692 (6th Cir. 2005)

Martin, Judge.

The City of Toledo has regulated smoking in public places since 1987, when it enacted the original Clean Indoor Air Ordinance. In early 2003, the City Council formed a task force to consider strengthening the ordinance in order to protect employees and non-smoking patrons from the harmful effects of secondhand smoke. After holding numerous meetings and public hearings, the City Council unanimously repealed the 1987 Clean Indoor Air Ordinance and enacted a new Clean Indoor Air Ordinance, No. 509-03.

Ordinance No. 509-03 regulates the ability to smoke in public places, such as retail stores, theaters, courtrooms, libraries, museums, health care facilities, and — most relevant to the instant case — restaurants and bars. [Proprietors of restaurants and bars were the plaintiffs-appellants in this case.] In enclosed public places, smoking is generally prohibited except in a "separate smoking lounge" that is designated for the exclusive purpose of smoking and that satisfies the following criteria:

(1) it cannot constitute more than thirty percent of the total square footage of space to which the public is invited;

(2) it must be completely enclosed on all sides by floor-to-ceiling walls;

(3) it must have a separate ventilation system not used by the non-smoking potion of the establishment;

(4) it must not incorporate the sole path to or from the restrooms, to or from the non-smoking portion of the establishment, or into or out of the building or waiting areas; and

(5) it cannot be located in an area where employees are required to work.

. . . .

A. Regulatory Taking Claim

The Takings Clause of the Fifth Amendment, made applicable to the States through the Fourteenth Amendment, provides that private property shall not "be taken for public use, without just compensation." The Supreme Court has recognized two categories of takings: regulatory and physical. Appellants allege the former. Furthermore, their attack on the ordinance is limited to a facial challenge, which requires them to prove that the "mere enactment" of the ordinance constitutes a taking of their property. According to the Supreme Court, the test to be applied in considering facial challenges such as this one is "fairly straightforward." Under that test, "[a] statute regulating the uses that can be made of property effects a taking if it denies an owner economically viable use of his [property]."

The evidence presented in this case fails to establish that, on its face, the Clean Indoor Air Ordinance denies appellants "economically viable use" of their respective properties. Appellants have submitted affidavits alleging that they have lost — or fear they will lose — customers as a result of the ordinance, because smoking is an activity in which many customers wish to engage while patronizing their establishments. Even if true, however, those allegations are simply not enough to satisfy appellants' burden of proof.

. . . First, there is nothing on the face of the Clean Indoor Air Ordinance that prevents the "beneficial use" of appellants' property. To the contrary, the ordinance has absolutely no effect on any aspect of appellants' businesses other than to restrict the areas in which appellants' patrons may smoke. Second, the ordinance does not "categorically prohibit" smoking inside appellants' establishments; it "merely regulates the conditions under which" smoking is permitted. We recognize that the construction of separate smoking lounges in most cases will require some financial investment, but an ordinance does not effect a taking merely because compliance with it "requires the expenditure of money." Finally, for obvious reasons, the ordinance does not "purport to regulate alternative uses" of appellants' respective properties. Therefore, . . . , it is clear that appellants have failed to establish that the Clean Indoor Air Ordinance, on its face, effects a regulatory taking of their property.

B. Preemption Claim

Appellants' second argument is that the Clean Indoor Air Ordinance conflicts with — and, therefore, is preempted by — Section 3791.031(A) of the Ohio Revised Code.

A state statute takes precedence over a local ordinance when (1) the ordinance is in conflict with the statute, (2) the ordinance is an exercise of police power, rather than of local self-government, and (3) the statute is a general law.

. . . .

"In determining whether an ordinance is in 'conflict' with general laws, the test is whether the ordinance permits or licenses that which the statute forbids or prohibits, and vice versa." To the extent that the statute does not address or apply to an item or issue, however, an ordinance regulating the excluded item or issue does not conflict with the statute, even if it deals with the same general subject matter . . . . "The law in Ohio on 'conflict' is stringent. Preemption is not easily demonstrated. "

In this case, Section 3791.031 regulates indoor smoking throughout the State of Ohio within "places of public assembly. " It explicitly provides, however, that "[r]estaurants, food service establishments, dining rooms, cafes, cafeterias, or other rooms used primarily for the service of food, as well as bowling alleys and places licensed by the division of liquor control to sell intoxicating beverages for consumption on the premises, are not places of public assembly. " As discussed, the City of Toledo's Clean Indoor Air Ordinance prohibits smoking in all public places, including restaurants and bars, except in separate smoking lounges.

Appellants argue that because smoking is allowed in their establishments under state law but not under the ordinance, there is a conflict that renders the ordinance preempted by state law. The City argues, by contrast, that the statute "simply does not regulate the establishments" that are subject to the ordinance and, therefore, municipalities within the State of Ohio are free to regulate smoking within these establishments in the exercise of their "home rule" authority. *See* Ohio Const. art. XVIII, § 3 ("Municipalities shall have authority to exercise all powers of local self-government and to adopt and enforce within their limits such local policy, sanitary and other similar regulations, as are not in conflict with general laws.")

. . . [B]y stating that certain types of establishments — such as restaurants, bars, bowling alleys, etc. — "are not places of public assembly," the legislature indicated not that these establishments were immune to smoking-related regulation, but that they simply did not fall within the ambit of the statute.

Our independent research reveals that other courts that have considered whether smoking-related ordinances are preempted by state law have reached similar conclusions. . . .

In an attempt to overcome this persuasive authority supporting the City's position, appellants point to the case . . . in which a New Jersey trial court held that a local ordinance prohibiting smoking in "restaurants, bars, cabarets, and taverns" in an attempt to protect the public from the deleterious effects of smoking was preempted by a state law that did not prohibit smoking in restaurants, but merely "encourage[d] restaurants to establish non-smoking areas." That case, however, is significantly distinguishable from the present one. The statute . . . [therein] provided that any guidelines suggested by political subdivisions such as municipalities would "in no case . . . be mandatory." The court also found it significant that the statute explicitly stated that its provisions "shall supersede" any municipal ordinance concerning smoking in restaurants except ordinances that are enacted "for purposes of protecting life and property from fire." . . . Because none of the factors that compelled . . . [that] court's decision is present here, that case fails to undermine our conclusion that Section 3791.031 does not preempt the City of Toledo's Clean Indoor Air Ordinance.

NOTES AND QUESTIONS

1. **State power to regulate tobacco sale and use.** *Austin v. Tennessee* recognizes the power of the states to regulate or, should they choose to do so, prohibit the sale, possession, or use of tobacco products within the state. Tennessee made it misdemeanor "for any person, firm or corporation to·sell, offer to sell, or to bring into the State for the purpose of selling, giving away, or otherwise disposing of, any cigarettes, cigarette paper, or substitute for the same." Austin appealed his conviction under that law on the ground, *inter alia*, that only the federal government could regulate the sale of cigarettes.

Here, the Court is concerned with defining the line between the congressional authority to regulate interstate commerce and the states' authority to regulate items of commerce once they have entered the state. At the time of *Austin*, the Supreme Court had a somewhat limited view of the congressional authority to regulate interstate commerce: Congress could only regulate commercial activities that were, in the most literal sense, interstate in nature, and all commercial activities were defined as either intrastate or interstate. If an activity were an intrastate activity, the state could regulate it; if it were an interstate activity, only the Congress could regulate it. Each activity was either one or the other. Within this framework, the Court regards the state's decision to regulate tobacco (at least in the manner that Tennessee did) as constitutional.

Today, state and federal power are no longer so separate and exclusive. If there is a rational basis for concluding that an intrastate activity has an effect on interstate commerce, Congress can choose to regulate that activity. *See* Chapter 3,

D, *supra*. In any event, as the cases discussed *infra* illustrate, there has been little debate over the extent of the federal government's constitutional authority to tax, regulate, or prohibit tobacco products; the economic effects on interstate commerce of the sale of cigarettes and other tobacco products would be easy to document. The major limitation on constitutional exercises of federal authority today are those that implicate the First Amendment, *i.e.*, efforts to limit advertising as discussed in Section D, *infra*.

2. State preemption of municipal ordinances. As demonstrated by *D.A.B.E.*, there have been many challenges to local laws that attempt to regulate or prohibit smoking. These cases are usually a matter of statutory (and sometimes state constitutional) interpretation and differ from jurisdiction to jurisdiction. The most successful challenges have been those that argue that the local government is exercising powers that are reserved for the general (meaning state) government or that the local law has been preempted by the state legislature.

None of the above questions the state's power to prohibit the sale of cigarettes. A lesser step might be seen in more recent proposals to increase the age at which one can lawfully purchase tobacco products from 18 to 21. *See* Jonathan P. Winickoff, Mark Gottlieb & Michelle M. Mello, *Tobacco 21 — An Idea Whose Time Has Come*, 370 NEW ENGL. J. MED. 295 (2014).

FDA v. BROWN & WILLIAMSON TOBACCO CORP.
529 U.S. 120 (2000)

O'CONNOR, JUSTICE.

. . . In 1996, the Food and Drug Administration (FDA), after having expressly disavowed any such authority since its inception, asserted jurisdiction to regulate tobacco products. The FDA concluded that nicotine is a "drug" within the meaning of the Food, Drug, and Cosmetic Act (FDCA or Act), and that cigarettes and smokeless tobacco are "combination products" that deliver nicotine to the body. Pursuant to this authority, it promulgated regulations intended to reduce tobacco consumption among children and adolescents. The agency believed that, because most tobacco consumers begin their use before reaching the age of 18, curbing tobacco use by minors could substantially reduce the prevalence of addiction in future generations and thus the incidence of tobacco-related death and disease.

Regardless of how serious the problem an administrative agency seeks to address, however, it may not exceed its authority "in a manner that is inconsistent with the administrative structure that Congress enacted into law." And although agencies are generally entitled to deference in the interpretation of statutes that they administer, a reviewing "court, as well as the agency, must give effect to the unambiguously expressed intent of Congress." [citing *Chevron U.S.A., Inc.*]. In this case, we believe that Congress has clearly precluded the FDA from asserting jurisdiction to regulate tobacco products. Such authority is inconsistent with the intent that Congress has expressed in the FDCA's overall regulatory scheme and in the tobacco-specific legislation that it has enacted subsequent to the FDCA. In light of this clear intent, the FDA's assertion of jurisdiction is impermissible.

The FDCA grants the FDA, as the designee of the Secretary of Health and Human Services (HHS), the authority to regulate, among other items, "drugs" and "devices." The Act defines "drug" to include "articles (other than food) intended to affect the structure or any function of the body." It defines "device," in part, as "an instrument, apparatus, implement, machine, contrivance, . . . or other similar or related article, including any component, part, or accessory, which is . . . intended to affect the structure or any function of the body." The Act also grants the FDA the authority to regulate so-called "combination products," which "constitute a combination of a drug, device, or biological product." The FDA has construed this provision as giving it the discretion to regulate combination products as drugs, as devices, or as both.

. . . .

On August 28, 1996, the FDA issued a final rule [and] determined that nicotine is a "drug" and that cigarettes and smokeless tobacco are "drug delivery devices," and therefore it had jurisdiction under the FDCA to regulate tobacco products as customarily marketed — that is, without manufacturer claims of therapeutic benefit. First, the FDA found that tobacco products "affect the structure or any function of the body" because nicotine "has significant pharmacological effects." Specifically, nicotine "exerts psychoactive, or mood-altering, effects on the brain" that cause and sustain addiction, have both tranquilizing and stimulating effects, and control weight. Second, the FDA determined that these effects were "intended" under the FDCA because they "are so widely known and foreseeable that [they] may be deemed to have been intended by the manufacturers," [and because] consumers use tobacco products "predominantly or nearly exclusively" to obtain these effects, and the statements, research, and actions of manufacturers revealed that they "have designed cigarettes to provide pharmacologically active doses of nicotine to consumers." Finally, the agency concluded that cigarettes and smokeless tobacco are "combination products" because, in addition to containing nicotine, they include device components that deliver a controlled amount of nicotine to the body."

Having resolved the jurisdictional question, the FDA next explained the policy justifications for its regulations, detailing the deleterious health effects associated with tobacco use . . . . The agency also determined that the only way to reduce the amount of tobacco-related illness and mortality was to reduce the level of addiction, a goal that could be accomplished only by preventing children and adolescents from starting to use tobacco. . . .

Based on these findings, the FDA promulgated regulations concerning tobacco products' promotion, labeling, and accessibility to children and adolescents. The access regulations prohibit the sale of cigarettes or smokeless tobacco to persons younger than 18; require retailers to verify through photo identification the age of all purchasers younger than 27; prohibit the sale of cigarettes in quantities smaller than 20; prohibit the distribution of free samples; and prohibit sales through self-service displays and vending machines except in adult-only locations. The promotion regulations require that any print advertising appear in a black-and-white, text-only format unless the publication in which it appears is read almost exclusively by adults; prohibit outdoor advertising within 1,000 feet of any public playground or school; prohibit the distribution of any promotional items, such as T-shirts or hats, bearing the manufacturer's brand name; and prohibit a manufacturer from sponsoring any athletic, musical, artistic, or other social or cultural event using its brand name. The labeling regulation requires that the statement, "A Nicotine-Delivery Device for Persons 18 or Older," appear on all tobacco product packages.

The FDA promulgated these regulations pursuant to its authority to regulate "restricted devices." The FDA construed § 353(g) [of the FDCA] as giving it the discretion to regulate "combination products" using the Act's drug authorities, device authorities, or both, depending on "how the public health goals of the act can be best accomplished." Given the greater flexibility in the FDCA for the regulation of devices, the FDA determined that "the device authorities provide the most appropriate basis for regulating cigarettes and smokeless tobacco." Under § 360j(e) the agency may "require that a device be restricted to sale, distribution, or use . . . upon such other conditions as [the FDA] may prescribe in such regulation, if, because of its potentiality for harmful effect or the collateral measures necessary to its use, [the FDA] determines that there cannot otherwise be reasonable assurance of its safety and effectiveness." The FDA reasoned that its regulations fell within [its authority] because they related to the sale or distribution of tobacco products and were necessary for providing a reasonable assurance of safety.

Respondents, a group of tobacco manufacturers, retailers, and advertisers, filed suit . . . challenging the regulations. . . .

. . . .

II

. . . .

Because this case involves an administrative agency's construction of a statute that it administers, our analysis is governed by *Chevron U.S.A., Inc.* Under *Chevron*, a reviewing court must first ask "whether Congress has directly spoken to the precise question at issue. " If Congress has done so, the inquiry is at an end; the court "must give effect to the unambiguously expressed intent of Congress . ." But if Congress has not specifically addressed the question, a reviewing court must respect the agency's construction of the statute so long as it is permissible.

. . . .

[W]e find that Congress has directly spoken to the issue here and precluded the FDA's jurisdiction to regulate tobacco products.

A

Viewing the FDCA as a whole, it is evident that one of the Act's core objectives is to ensure that any product regulated by the FDA is "safe" and "effective" [terms defined in the Act] for its intended use. This essential purpose pervades the FDCA . . . . Thus, the Act generally requires the FDA to prevent the marketing of any drug or device where the "potential for inflicting death or physical injury is not offset by the possibility of therapeutic benefit. "

In its rulemaking proceeding, the FDA quite exhaustively documented that "tobacco products are unsafe," "dangerous," and "cause great pain and suffering from illness." It found that the consumption of tobacco products presents "extraordinary health risks" and that "tobacco use is the single leading cause of preventable death in the United States." . . .

These findings logically imply that, if tobacco products were "devices" under the FDCA [as the FDA found in its rulemaking proceeding], the FDA would be required to remove them from the market. Consider, first, the FDCA's provisions concerning the misbranding of drugs or devices. The Act prohibits "[t]he introduction or delivery for introduction into interstate commerce of any food, drug, device, or cosmetic that is adulterated or misbranded." In light of the FDA's findings, two distinct FDCA provisions would render cigarettes and smokeless tobacco misbranded devices . . . . Given the FDA's conclusions concerning the health consequences of tobacco use, there are no directions that could adequately protect consumers . . . . Thus, were tobacco products within the FDA's jurisdiction, the Act would deem them misbranded devices that could not be introduced into interstate commerce . . . .

Second, the FDCA requires the FDA to place all devices that it regulates into one of three classifications. The agency relies on a device's classification in determining the degree of control and regulation necessary to ensure that there is "a reasonable assurance of safety and effectiveness." The FDA has yet to classify tobacco products. Instead, the regulations at issue here represent so-called "general controls," which the Act entitles the agency to impose in advance of classification . . . . Given the FDA's findings regarding the health consequences of tobacco use, the agency would have to place cigarettes and smokeless tobacco in Class III because, even after the application of the Act's available controls, they would "presen[t] a potential unreasonable risk of illness or injury." As Class III devices, tobacco products would be subject to the FDCA's premarket approval process. Under these provisions, the FDA would be prohibited from approving an application for premarket approval without "a showing of reasonable assurance that such device is safe under the conditions of use prescribed, recommended, or suggested in the proposed labeling thereof." In view of the FDA's conclusions regarding the health effects of tobacco use, the agency would have no basis for finding any such reasonable assurance of safety. Thus, once the FDA fulfilled its statutory obligation to classify tobacco products, it could not allow them to be marketed.

The FDCA's misbranding and device classification provisions therefore make evident that were the FDA to regulate cigarettes and smokeless tobacco, the Act would require the agency to ban them. In fact, based on these provisions, the FDA itself has previously taken the position that if tobacco products were within its jurisdiction, "they would have to be removed from the market because it would be impossible to prove they were safe for their intended us[e]." . . .

Congress, however, has foreclosed the removal of tobacco products from the market. A provision of the United States Code currently in force states that "[t]he marketing of tobacco constitutes one of the greatest basic industries of the United

[handwritten margin note: Congress knows the dangers of tabacco but has still not banned it.]

States with ramifying activities which directly affect interstate and foreign commerce at every point, and stable conditions therein are necessary to the general welfare." 7 U.S.C. § 1311(a). More importantly, Congress has directly addressed the problem of tobacco and health through legislation on six occasions since 1965. [A list of statutes is omitted.] When Congress enacted these statutes, the adverse health consequences of tobacco use were well known, as were nicotine's pharmacological effects. Nonetheless, Congress stopped well short of ordering a ban. Instead, it has generally regulated the labeling and advertisement of tobacco products, expressly providing that it is the policy of Congress that "commerce and the national economy may be . . . protected to the maximum extent consistent with" consumers "be[ing] adequately informed about any adverse health effects." . . . [T]he collective premise of these [specifically tobacco-related] statutes [enacted subsequently to and independently of the FDCA,] is that cigarettes and smokeless tobacco will continue to be sold in the United States. A ban of tobacco products by the FDA would therefore plainly contradict congressional policy.

[handwritten margin note: ✗ FDA ration for reg. but NOT banning — to determine Safeness & contradicts expressed goals of FDCA]

The FDA apparently recognized this dilemma and concluded, somewhat ironically, that tobacco products are actually "safe" within the meaning of the FDCA. In promulgating its regulations, the agency conceded that "tobacco products are unsafe, as that term is conventionally understood." Nonetheless, the FDA reasoned that, in determining whether a device is safe under the Act, it must consider "not only the risks presented by a product but also any of the countervailing effects of use of that product, including the consequences of not permitting the product to be marketed." Applying this standard, the FDA found that, because of the high level of addiction among tobacco users, a ban would likely be "dangerous." In particular, current tobacco users could suffer from extreme withdrawal, the health care system and available pharmaceuticals might not be able to meet the treatment demands of those suffering from withdrawal, and a black market offering cigarettes even more dangerous than those currently sold legally would likely develop. The FDA therefore concluded that, "while taking cigarettes and smokeless tobacco off the market could prevent some people from becoming addicted and reduce death and disease for others, the record does not establish that such a ban is the appropriate public health response under the act."

It may well be, as the FDA asserts, that "these factors must be considered when developing a regulatory scheme that achieves the best public health result for these products." But the FDA's judgment that leaving tobacco products on the market "is more effective in achieving public health goals than a ban," is no substitute for the specific safety determinations required by the FDCA's various operative provisions. Several provisions in the Act require the FDA to determine that the product itself is safe as used by consumers. That is, the product's probable therapeutic benefits must outweigh its risk of harm. In contrast, the FDA's conception of safety would allow the agency, with respect to each provision of the FDCA that requires the agency to determine a product's "safety" or "dangerousness," to compare the aggregate health effects of alternative administrative actions. This is a qualitatively different inquiry. Thus, although the FDA has concluded that a ban would be "dangerous, " it has not concluded that tobacco products are "safe" as that term is used throughout the Act.

. . . .

A straightforward reading of [the FDCA] dictates that the FDA must weigh the probable therapeutic benefits of the device to the consumer against the probable risk of injury. Applied to tobacco products, the inquiry is whether their purported benefits — satisfying addiction, stimulation and sedation, and weight control — outweigh the risks to health from their use. To accommodate the FDA's conception of safety, however, one must read "any probable benefit to health" to include the benefit to public health stemming from adult consumers' continued use of tobacco products, even though the reduction of tobacco use is the raison d'etre of the regulations. In other words, the FDA is forced to contend that the very evil it seeks to combat is a "benefit to health." This is implausible.

The FDA's conception of safety is also incompatible with the FDCA's misbranding provision . . . .

. . . .

The dissent contends that our conclusion means that "the FDCA requires the FDA to ban outright 'dangerous' drugs or devices," and that this is a "perverse" reading of the statute. This misunderstands our holding. The FDA, consistent with the FDCA, may clearly regulate many "dangerous" products without banning them. Indeed, virtually every drug or device poses dangers under certain conditions. What the FDA may not do is conclude that a drug or device cannot be used safely for any therapeutic purpose and yet, at the same time, allow that product to remain on the market. Such regulation is incompatible with the FDCA's core objective of ensuring that every drug or device is safe and effective.

 Considering the FDCA as a whole, it is clear that Congress intended to exclude tobacco products from the FDA's jurisdiction. A fundamental precept of the FDCA is that any product regulated by the FDA — but not banned — must be safe for its intended use. Various provisions of the Act make clear that this refers to the safety of using the product to obtain its intended effects, not the public health ramifications of alternative administrative actions by the FDA. That is, the FDA must determine that there is a reasonable assurance that the product's therapeutic benefits outweigh the risk of harm to the consumer. According to this standard, the FDA has concluded that, although tobacco products might be effective in delivering certain pharmacological effects, they are "unsafe" and "dangerous" when used for these purposes. Consequently, if tobacco products were within the FDA's jurisdiction, the Act would require the FDA to remove them from the market entirely. But a ban would contradict Congress' clear intent as expressed in its more recent, tobacco-specific legislation. The inescapable conclusion is that there is no room for tobacco products within the FDCA's regulatory scheme. If they cannot be used safely for any therapeutic purpose, and yet they cannot be banned, they simply do not fit.

B

In determining whether Congress has spoken directly to the FDA's authority to regulate tobacco, we must also consider in greater detail the tobacco-specific legislation that Congress has enacted over the past 35 years. . . .

[The opinion then reviews the Federal Cigarette Labeling and Advertising Act and a number of other federal laws that require that health warnings appear on all packaging and in all print and outdoor advertisements, prohibit the advertisement of tobacco products in the electronic media, require the Secretary of HHS to report every three years to Congress on research findings concerning "the addictive property of tobacco," and make States' receipt of certain federal block grants contingent on their making it unlawful "for any manufacturer, retailer, or distributor of tobacco products to sell or distribute any such product to any individual under the age of 18."]

In adopting each statute, Congress has acted against the backdrop of the FDA's consistent and repeated statements that it lacked authority under the FDCA to regulate tobacco absent claims of therapeutic benefit by the manufacturer. In fact, on several occasions over this period, and after the health consequences of tobacco use and nicotine's pharmacological effects had become well known, Congress considered and rejected bills that would have granted the FDA such jurisdiction. Under these circumstances, it is evident that Congress' tobacco-specific statutes have effectively ratified the FDA's long-held position that it lacks jurisdiction under the FDCA to regulate tobacco products. . . .

. . . .

By no means do we question the seriousness of the problem that the FDA has sought to address. The agency has amply demonstrated that tobacco use, particularly among children and adolescents, poses perhaps the single most significant threat to public health in the United States. Nonetheless, no matter how "important, conspicuous, and controversial" the issue, and regardless of how likely the public is to hold the Executive Branch politically accountable, an administrative agency's power to regulate in the public interest must always be grounded in a valid grant of authority from Congress. . . . Reading the FCDA as a whole, as well as in conjunction with Congress' subsequent tobacco-specific legislation, it is plain that Congress has not given the FDA the authority that it seeks to exercise here. . . .

FAMILY SMOKING PREVENTION AND TOBACCO CONTROL ACT
P.L. 111–31, 123 Stat. 1782 (enacted June 22, 2009)
21 U.S.C. §§ 387 *et seq.*

§ 901 [21 U.S.C. § 387a].   FDA authority over tobacco products

(a) In general. Tobacco products, including modified risk tobacco products for which an order has been issued in accordance with section 911 [21 USCS § 387k], shall be regulated by the Secretary under this chapter [21 USCS §§ 387 *et seq.*] and shall not be subject to the provisions of chapter V [21 USCS §§ 351 *et seq.*].

(b) Applicability. This chapter [21 USCS §§ 387 *et seq.*] shall apply to all cigarettes, cigarette tobacco, roll-your-own tobacco, and smokeless tobacco and to any other tobacco products that the Secretary by regulation deems to be subject to this chapter.

. . . .

§ 903 [21 U.S.C. § 387c].   Misbranded tobacco products

(a) In general. A tobacco product shall be deemed to be misbranded—

(1) if its labeling is false or misleading in any particular;

(2) if in package form unless it bears a label containing—

(A) the name and place of business of the tobacco product manufacturer, packer, or distributor;

(B) an accurate statement of the quantity of the contents in terms of weight, measure, or numerical count;

(C) an accurate statement of the percentage of the tobacco used in the product that is domestically grown tobacco and the percentage that is foreign grown tobacco; and

(D) the statement required under section 920(a) [21 USCS § 387t(a)], except that under subparagraph (B) reasonable variations shall be permitted, and exemptions as to small packages shall be established, by regulations prescribed by the Secretary;

(3) if any word, statement, or other information required by or under authority of this chapter [21 USCS §§ 387 *et seq.*] to appear on the label or labeling is not prominently placed thereon with such conspicuousness (as compared with other words, statements, or designs in the labeling) and in such terms as to render it likely to be read and understood by the ordinary individual under customary conditions of purchase and use;

(4) if it has an established name, unless its label bears, to the exclusion of any other nonproprietary name, its established name prominently printed in type as required by the Secretary by regulation;

(5) if the Secretary has issued regulations requiring that its labeling bear adequate directions for use, or adequate warnings against use by children, that are necessary for the protection of users unless its labeling conforms in all respects to such regulations;. . . .

(9) if it is a tobacco product subject to a tobacco product standard established under section 907 [21 USCS § 387g], unless it bears such labeling as may be prescribed in such tobacco product standard; or

. . . .

(b) Prior approval of label statements. The Secretary may, by regulation, require prior approval of statements made on the label of a tobacco product to ensure that such statements do not violate the misbranding provisions of subsection (a) and that such statements comply with other provisions of [this] Act (including the amendments made by such Act). No regulation issued under this subsection may require prior approval by the Secretary of the content of any advertisement, except for modified risk tobacco products as provided in section 911. No advertisement of a tobacco product published after the date of enactment of [this Family Smoking Prevention and Tobacco Control Act [enacted June 22, 2009] shall, with respect to the language of label statements as prescribed under section 4 of the Federal Cigarette Labeling and Advertising Act and section 3 of the Comprehensive Smokeless Tobacco Health Education Act of 1986 or the regulations issued under such sections, be subject to the provisions of sections 12 through 15 of the Federal Trade Commission Act.

. . . .

§ 906 [21 U.S.C. § 387f]. General provisions respecting control of tobacco products

. . . .

(d) Restrictions.

(1) In general. The Secretary may by regulation require restrictions on the sale and distribution of a tobacco product, including restrictions on the access to, and the advertising and promotion of, the tobacco product, if the Secretary determines that such regulation would be appropriate for the protection of the public health. The Secretary may by regulation impose restrictions on the advertising and promotion of a tobacco product consistent with and to full extent permitted by the first amendment to the Constitution. The finding as to whether such regulation would be appropriate for the protection of the public health shall be determined with respect to the risks and benefits to the population as a whole, including users and nonusers of the tobacco product, and taking into account—

(A) the increased or decreased likelihood that existing users of tobacco products will stop using such products; and

(B) the increased or decreased likelihood that those who do not use tobacco products will start using such products.

No such regulation may require that the sale or distribution of a tobacco product be limited to the written or oral authorization of a practitioner licensed by law to prescribe medical products.

(2) Label statements. The label of a tobacco product shall bear such appropriate statements of the restrictions required by a regulation under subsection (a) as the Secretary may in such regulation prescribe.

(3) Limitations.

(A) In general. No restrictions under paragraph (1) may —

(i) prohibit the sale of any tobacco product in face-to-face transactions by a specific category of retail outlets; or

(ii) establish a minimum age of sale of tobacco products to any person older than 18 years of age.

. . . .

(f) Research and development. The Secretary may enter into contracts for research, testing, and demonstrations respecting tobacco products and may obtain tobacco products for research, testing, and demonstration purposes.

. . . .

§ 907 [21 U.S.C. § 387g].   Tobacco product standards

(a) In general.

(1) Special rules.

(A) Special rule for cigarettes. [A] cigarette or any of its component parts (including the tobacco, filter, or paper) shall not contain, as a constituent (including a smoke constituent) or additive, an artificial or natural flavor (other than tobacco or menthol) or an herb or spice, including strawberry, grape, orange, clove, cinnamon, pineapple, vanilla, coconut, licorice, cocoa, chocolate, cherry, or coffee, that is a characterizing flavor of the tobacco product or tobacco smoke. Nothing in this subparagraph shall be construed to limit the Secretary's authority to take action under this section or other sections of this Act [21 USCS §§ 301 *et seq.*] applicable to menthol or any artificial or natural flavor, herb, or spice not specified in this subparagraph.

. . . .

(d) Promulgation

. . . .

(3) Limitation on power granted to the Food and Drug Administration. Because of the importance of a decision of the Secretary to issue a regulation—

(A) banning all cigarettes, all smokeless tobacco products, all little cigars, all cigars other than little cigars, all pipe tobacco, or all roll-your-own tobacco products; or

(B) requiring the reduction of nicotine yields of a tobacco product to zero, the Secretary is prohibited from taking such actions under this Act [21 USCS §§ 301 *et seq.*].

. . . .

§ 910 [21 U.S.C. § 387j].   Application for review of certain tobacco products

(a) In general.

(1) New tobacco product defined. For purposes of this section the term "new tobacco product" means—

(A) any tobacco product (including those products in test markets) that was not commercially marketed in the United States as of February 15, 2007; or

(B) any modification (including a change in design, any component, any part, or any constituent, including a smoke constituent, or in the content, delivery or form of nicotine, or any other additive or ingredient) of a tobacco product where the modified product was commercially marketed in the United States after February 15, 2007.

(2) Premarket review required.

(A) New products. An order under subsection (c)(1)(A)(i) for a new tobacco product is required unless—

(i) the manufacturer has submitted a report under section 905(j) [21 USCS § 387e(j)]; and the Secretary has issued an order that the tobacco product—

(I) is substantially equivalent to a tobacco product commercially marketed (other than for test marketing) in the United States as of February 15, 2007; and

(II) is in compliance with the requirements of this Act [21 USCS §§ 301 *et seq.*]; or

(ii) the tobacco product is exempt from the requirements of section 905(j) [21 USCS § 387e(j)] pursuant to a regulation issued under section 905(j)(3) [21 USCS § 387(j)(3)].

. . . .

§ 911 [21 U.S.C. § 387k].   Modified risk tobacco products

(a) In general. No person may introduce or deliver for introduction into interstate commerce any modified risk tobacco product unless an order issued pursuant to subsection (g) is effective with respect to such product.

(b) Definitions. In this section:

(1) Modified risk tobacco product. The term "modified risk tobacco product" means any tobacco product that is sold or distributed for use to reduce harm or the risk of tobacco-related disease associated with commercially marketed tobacco products.

(2) Sold or distributed.

(A) In general. With respect to a tobacco product, the term "sold or distributed for use to reduce harm or the risk of tobacco-related disease associated with commercially marketed tobacco products" means a tobacco product—

(i) the label, labeling, or advertising of which represents explicitly or implicitly that—

(I) the tobacco product presents a lower risk of tobacco-related disease or is less harmful than one or more other commercially marketed tobacco products;

(II) the tobacco product or its smoke contains a reduced level of a substance or presents a reduced exposure to a substance; or

(III) the tobacco product or its smoke does not contain or is free of a substance;

(ii) the label, labeling, or advertising of which uses the descriptors "light", "mild", or "low" or similar descriptors; or

(iii) the tobacco product manufacturer of which has taken any action directed to consumers through the media or otherwise, other than by means of the tobacco product's label, labeling, or advertising, after the date of enactment of [this Act, enacted June 22, 2009], respecting the product that would be reasonably expected to result in consumers believing that the tobacco product or its smoke may present a lower risk of disease or is less harmful than one or more commercially marketed tobacco products, or presents a reduced exposure to, or does not contain or is free of, a substance or substances.

(B) Limitation. No tobacco product shall be considered to be "sold or distributed for use to reduce harm or the risk of tobacco-related disease associated with commercially marketed tobacco products", except as described in subparagraph (A).

(C) Smokeless tobacco product. No smokeless tobacco product shall be considered to be "sold or distributed for use to reduce harm or the risk of tobacco-related disease associated with commercially marketed tobacco products" solely because its label, labeling, or advertising uses the following phrases to describe such product and its use: "smokeless tobacco", "smokeless tobacco product", "not consumed by smoking", "does not produce smoke", "smokefree", "smoke-free", "without smoke", "no smoke", or "not smoke".

. . . .

(c) Tobacco dependence products. A product that is intended to be used for the treatment of tobacco dependence, including smoking cessation, is not a modified risk tobacco product under this section if it has been approved as a drug or device by the Food and Drug Administration and is subject to the requirements of chapter V [21 USCS §§ 351 *et seq.*].

. . . .

§ 914 [21 U.S.C. § 387n]. Jurisdiction of and coordination with the Federal Trade Commission

(a) Jurisdiction.

(1) In general. Except where expressly provided in this chapter [21 USCS §§ 387 *et seq.*], nothing in this chapter shall be construed as limiting or diminishing the authority of the Federal Trade Commission to enforce the laws under its jurisdiction with respect to the advertising, sale, or distribution of tobacco products.

. . . .

§ 916 [21 U.S.C. § 387p].   Preservation of State and local authority

(a) In general.

(1) Preservation. Except as provided in paragraph (2)(A), nothing in this chapter, or rules promulgated under this chapter , shall be construed to limit the authority of a Federal agency (including the Armed Forces), a State or political subdivision of a State, or the government of an Indian tribe to enact, adopt, promulgate, and enforce any law, rule, regulation, or other measure with respect to tobacco products that is in addition to, or more stringent than, requirements established under this chapter, including a law, rule, regulation, or other measure relating to or prohibiting the sale, distribution, possession, exposure to, access to, advertising and promotion of, or use of tobacco products by individuals of any age, information reporting to the State, or measures relating to fire safety standards for tobacco products. No provision of this chapter shall limit or otherwise affect any State, tribal, or local taxation of tobacco products.

(2) Preemption of certain State and local requirements.

(A) In general. No State or political subdivision of a State may establish or continue in effect with respect to a tobacco product any requirement which is different from, or in addition to, any requirement under the provisions of this chapter relating to tobacco product standards, premarket review, adulteration, misbranding, labeling, registration, good manufacturing standards, or modified risk tobacco products.

(B) Exception. Subparagraph (A) does not apply to requirements relating to the sale, distribution, possession, information reporting to the State, exposure to, access to, the advertising and promotion of, or use of, tobacco products by individuals of any age, or relating to fire safety standards for tobacco products. Information disclosed to a State under subparagraph (A) that is exempt from disclosure under section 552(b)(4) of title 5, United States Code, shall be treated as a trade secret and confidential information by the State.

(b) Rule of construction regarding product liability. No provision of this chapter [21 USCS §§ 387 *et seq.*] relating to a tobacco product shall be construed to modify or otherwise affect any action or the liability of any person under the product liability law of any State.

. . . .

NOTES AND QUESTIONS

3.   **Federal regulation of tobacco.** The *FDA v. Brown & Williamson* analyzes the jurisdictional limits on FDA authority to regulate tobacco products arising from its governing statute, the Food, Drug and Cosmetic Act (FDCA), and the Federal Cigarette Labeling and Advertising Act of 1965 (FCLAA) and other federal laws. Speaking for a closely (5-4) divided Court, Justice O'Connor found that the FDA's proposed regulations were beyond its authority. The FDCA legislation gives the agency the authority to approve new drugs or devices only if they are safe their intended use. Because there is essentially no medicinal benefit from the use of tobacco that outweighs its inherently dangerous effects, the statute would require the FDA to ban tobacco products. The FDA made a somewhat strained argument that regulation was preferable to prohibition, because of the immediate effects of a total prohibition on the existing nicotine-addicted population. The Court rejected the logic of this position.

The Court found additional support for its conclusion in other Congressional actions — particularly the FCLAA and its subsequent amendments. These suggested that Congress assumed that cigarettes and other products would be available to adults, even if subject to various forms of state and federal regulation of their advertising or promotion, and of the terms and conditions of their sale (*e.g.*, package warnings and size limits). Because of these laws, O'Connor found that Congress could not have intended to give the FDA the authority to prohibit cigarettes or other tobacco products, even if the FDA legislation, read alone, might allow that authority. (For an argument that the text of the FDA could be so read, see Justice Breyer's dissenting opinion.)

4.   **The Tobacco Control Act.** The *Brown & Williamson* opinion, of course, addressed only the authority granted to the FDA by the Food, Drug and Cosmetic Act as of 2000, not Congress's authority itself to regulate tobacco. After considerable debate, Congress enacted the Family Smoking Prevention and Tobacco Control Act of 2009 (FSPTCA), excerpted above, which amended the FDCA to grant the FDA the regulatory authority it sought in its proposed regulations. Note that this authority includes much of what is required of countries that ratify the Framework Convention on Tobacco Control. One point of minor contention was whether the FDA was the appropriate agency to regulate tobacco. Since the FDA's primary mission is to prevent the distribution of risky drugs and devices that do not offer compensating benefit to users, its regulation of tobacco products is something of an anomaly, to say the least. Why might Congress lodge this authority in the FDA, instead of another agency, such as the Consumer Products Safety Commission or the Federal Trade Commission, or an entirely new agency?

The tobacco industry was not wholly opposed to the Tobacco Control Act. Why not? Note that the Act prohibits the FDA from banning all cigarettes and other tobacco products and from requiring that the products contain no nicotine. § 907. It also prohibits regulations that would ban sales of tobacco products to persons older than 18 years of age. § 906. Could states ban the sale of cigarettes to older persons? For that matter, could states ban the sale of cigarettes in the state entirely?

The Tobacco Control Act amended the FDCA to prohibit any tobacco manufacturer from making any express or implied representation that "conveys, or misleads or would mislead consumers into believing, that (1) the product is approved by the Food and Drug Administration; (2) the Food and Drug Administration deems the product to be safe for use by consumers; (3) the product is endorsed by the Food and Drug Administration for use by consumers; or (4) the product is safe or less harmful by virtue of — (A) its regulation or inspection by the Food and Drug Administration; or (B) its compliance with regulatory requirements set by the Food and Drug Administration." 21 U.S.C. § 331(tt). Would this prohibit a package statement that the product is approved by the FDA or labeled in accordance with FDA rules? Does FDA regulation of labeling imply approval? Section 906 of the Tobacco Control Act allows the FDA "to impose restrictions on the advertising and promotion of a tobacco product consistent with and to full extent permitted by the first amendment to the Constitution." Could the tobacco industry argue that this labeling restriction is not permitted by the first amendment?

5. **Flavored cigarettes.** Note that FSPTCA section 907 prohibits adding certain flavors to cigarettes. (The U.S. tobacco industry generally does not produce cigarettes with flavors, except for menthol cigarettes.) Indonesia (the largest producer of clove cigarettes) challenged the Act's ban on clove cigarettes before the World Trade Organization. A WTO panel found the ban discriminatory, because it accorded less favorable treatment to cigarettes with clove flavoring than cigarettes with menthol flavoring and was inconsistent with the Technical Barriers to Trade Agreement. The status of the dispute is available at World Trade Organization, United States — Measures Affecting the Production and Sale of Menthol Cigarettes, Dispute DS406, http://www.wto.org/english/tratop_e/dispu_e/cases_e/ds406_e.htm (visited May 2014). Although menthol is not included among the flavors banned in the FSPTC, the provision does not preclude FDA from "tak[ing] action" on menthol. Why might this be? In 2013, the FDA sought public comments on whether it should propose a tobacco product standard for allowable menthol in cigarettes or restrict or ban sales of menthol cigarettes. FDA, Menthol in Cigarettes; Request for Comments, https://federalregister.gov/a/2013-17805 (visited Feb. 2014). The Federal Register notice includes a link to a report by FDA's Tobacco Products Scientific Advisory Committee on evidence concerning the effects of menthol in cigarettes. Tobacco companies have challenged the composition of that Committee and its report, in litigation pending as of this writing. *Lorillard, Inc. v. FDA*, 2012 U.S. Dist. LEXIS 120163, (D.D.C. Aug. 1, 2012).

6. **Electronic cigarettes.** E-cigarettes are electronic devices that typically look like plastic cigarettes (so far), but contain no tobacco. The device uses an atomizer to heat clear, odorless liquid into vapor that users inhale, and then exhale. This gives the sensation of smoking without inhaling the ingredients in tobacco (like tar) that can harm the smoker or exhaling second-hand smoke. The liquid is usually a harmless solution of propylene glycol, vegetable glycerin, and/or polyethylene glycol 400 mixed with flavors. Most, but not all, versions include nicotine. Definitive evidence on what, if any, health risks these products may pose is not yet available.

E-cigarettes offer a potential replacement market for the $80 billion tobacco industry, which sees the U.S. market for regular cigarettes declining. (At least one e-cigarette maker does not make tobacco products.) Controversy exists over how e-cigarettes will be used. On one hand, they may help people stop smoking tobacco. On the other hand, they may initiate nicotine addiction among youth who might then begin smoking tobacco products. Sabrina Tavernise, *Hot Debate Over E-Cigarettes As Path to Tobacco, or From It*, NEW YORK TIMES A1, 18, Feb. 23, 2014 (visited Feb. 2014). E-cigarettes with fruit flavors may prove appealing to youth. There is particular concern over internet sales of e-cigarettes, since age is not verifiable. (All states prohibit the sale of nicotine-replacement therapies, like gum and patches, to people less than 18 years of age, but do not necessarily include e-cigarettes in their definitions of nicotine-replacement therapies.)

The FDA could regulate e-cigarettes that are intended for therapeutic purposes, as it regulates nicotine replacement therapies, through its Center for Drug Evaluation and Research. In late 2013, the FDA proposed to extend the authority of its Center for Tobacco Products to e-cigarettes. *See* www.fda.gov/newsevents/publichealthfocus/ucm172906.htm (visited Feb. 2014). Does the FDA have authority to deem e-cigarettes to be tobacco products under the Tobacco Control Act? Are they nicotine delivery devices that can or should be regulated under FDA's authority over drugs or devices? What about e-cigarettes that do not contain any nicotine? The head of the FDA Center for Tobacco Products was reported as saying that while nicotine is not benign, tobacco is much worse, because "people smoke for the nicotine and die from the tar." Toni Clarke, *E-cig Industry on Tenterhooks Ahead of U.S. Regulation*, REUTERS, Feb. 20, 2014, www.reuters.com/article/2014/02/20/us-usa-health-ecigarettes-idUSBREA1J1JJ20140220 (visited Feb. 2014).

D. ADVERTISING AND THE FIRST AMENDMENT

LORILLARD TOBACCO v. REILLY
533 U.S. 525 (2001)

O'CONNOR, JUSTICE.

In January 1999, pursuant to his authority to prevent unfair or deceptive practices in trade, the Massachusetts Attorney General (Attorney General) promulgated regulations governing the sale and advertisement of cigarettes, smokeless tobacco, and cigars. The purpose of the cigarette and smokeless tobacco regulations is "to eliminate deception and unfairness in the way cigarettes and smokeless tobacco products are marketed, sold and distributed in Massachusetts in order to address the incidence of cigarette smoking and smokeless tobacco use by children under legal age . . . [and] in order to prevent access to such products by underage consumers." [The cigar regulations have similar purposes.] . . .

The cigarette and smokeless tobacco regulations being challenged before this Court provide: . . . "Except as otherwise provided . . . it shall be an unfair or deceptive act or practice for any person who sells or distributes cigarettes or smokeless tobacco products through a retail outlet located within Massachusetts to engage in any of the following retail outlet sales practices: . . . (c) Using self-service displays of cigarettes or smokeless tobacco products; (d) Failing to place cigarettes and smokeless tobacco products out of the reach of all consumers, and in a location accessible only to outlet personnel." . . . (5) [I]t shall be an unfair or deceptive act or practice for any manufacturer, distributor or retailer to engage in any of the following practices: (a) Outdoor advertising, including advertising in enclosed stadiums and advertising from within a retail establishment that is directed toward or visible from the outside of the establishment, in any location that is within a 1000 foot radius of any public playground, playground area in a public park, elementary school, or secondary school; (b) Point-of-sale advertising of cigarettes or smokeless tobacco products any portion of which is placed lower than five feet from the floor of any retail establishment which is located within a one thousand foot radius of any public playground, playground area in a public park, elementary school or secondary school, and which is not an adult-only retail establishment."

[The Court then sets out the regulations concerning cigar sales and the definition of advertising.]

. . . .

II

Before reaching the First Amendment issues, we must decide to what extent federal law pre-empts the Attorney General's regulations. . . .

A

[The Court notes that that the supremacy clause (Art. VI, cl. 2) is the constitutional basis of federal pre-emption; that its "relatively clear and simple mandate has generated considerable discussion" by the Court, which is surely an understatement; and that pre-emption may arise in several different ways: from (1) "express" Congressional language pre-empting state and local activity in a given area; (2) by implication, where the "depth and breadth" of a congressional scheme "occupies the legislative field"; or (3) by implication "because of a conflict with a congressional enactment."]

In the FCLAA [Federal Cigarette Labeling and Advertising Act], Congress has crafted a comprehensive federal scheme governing the advertising and promotion of cigarettes. The FCLAA's pre-emption provision [21 U.S.C. § 1334] provides:

(a) Additional statements. No statement relating to smoking and health, other than the statement required by section 1333 of this title, shall be required on any cigarette package.

(b) State regulations. No requirement or prohibition based on smoking and health shall be imposed under State law with respect to the advertising or promotion of any cigarettes the packages of which are labeled in conformity with the provisions of this chapter.

The FCLAA's preemption provision does not cover smokeless tobacco or cigars.

. . . .

. . . In the pre-emption provision, Congress unequivocally precludes the requirement of any additional statements on cigarette packages beyond those provided in § 1333. Congress further precludes States or localities from imposing any requirement or prohibition based on smoking and health with respect to the advertising and promotion of cigarettes. Without question, the second clause is more expansive than the first; it employs far more sweeping language to describe the state action that is pre-empted. We must give meaning to each element of the pre-emption provision. We are aided in our interpretation by considering the predecessor pre-emption provision and the circumstances in which the current language was adopted.

In 1964, the ground-breaking Report of the Surgeon General's Advisory Committee on Smoking and Health concluded that "[c]igarette smoking is a health hazard of sufficient importance in the United States to warrant appropriate remedial action." In 1965, Congress enacted the FCLAA as a proactive measure in the face of impending regulation by federal agencies and the States. The purpose of the FCLAA was twofold: to inform the public adequately about the hazards of cigarette smoking, and to protect the national economy from interference due to diverse, non-uniform, and confusing cigarette labeling and advertising regulations with respect to the relationship between smoking and health. The FCLAA prescribed a label for cigarette packages: "Caution: Cigarette Smoking May Be Hazardous to Your Health.". . .

Section 5 of the FCLAA included a pre-emption provision . . . which . . . prohibited any requirement of additional statements on cigarette packaging . . . . As we have previously explained, "on their face, [the pre-emption] provisions merely prohibited state and federal rule making bodies from mandating particular cautionary statements on cigarette labels . . . or advertisements. . . ."

. . . [Between 1965 and 1969], Congress received reports and recommendations from the HEW Secretary [of Health, Education, and Welfare] and the FTC [Federal Trade Commission]. . . .

. . . The . . . Public Health Cigarette Smoking Act of 1969 . . . made three significant changes to the FCLAA. First, Congress drafted a new label that read: "Warning: The Surgeon General Has Determined That Cigarette Smoking Is Dangerous to Your Health." Second, Congress declared it unlawful to advertise cigarettes on any medium of electronic communication subject to the jurisdiction of the FCC [Federal Communications Commission]. Finally, Congress enacted the current pre-emption provision, which proscribes any "requirement or prohibition based on smoking and health . . . imposed under State law with respect to the advertising or promotion" of cigarettes. The new [provision] did not pre-empt regulation by federal agencies, freeing the FTC to impose warning requirements in cigarette advertising. The new pre-emption provision, like its predecessor, only applied to cigarettes, and not other tobacco products.

In 1984, Congress again amended the FCLAA in the Comprehensive Smoking Education Act . . . . The Act established a series of warnings to appear on a rotating basis on cigarette packages and in cigarette advertising, and directed the Health and Human Services Secretary to create and implement an educational program about the health effects of cigarette smoking.

. . . .

The scope and meaning of the current pre-emption provision become clearer once we consider the original pre-emption language and the amendments to the FCLAA. Without question, "the plain language of the pre-emption provision in the 1969 Act is much broader." Rather than preventing only "statements," the amended provision reaches all "requirement[s] or prohibition[s] . . . imposed under State law." And, although the former statute reached only statements "in the advertising," the current provision governs "with respect to the advertising or promotion" of cigarettes. Congress expanded the pre-emption provision with respect to the States, and at the same time, it allowed the FTC to regulate cigarette advertising. Congress also prohibited cigarette advertising in electronic media altogether. Viewed in light of the context in which the current pre-emption provision was adopted, we must determine whether the FCLAA pre-empts Massachusetts' regulations governing outdoor and point-of-sale advertising of cigarettes.

B

. . . .

Turning first to the language in the pre-emption provision . . . , we reject the notion that the Attorney General's cigarette advertising regulations are not "with respect to" advertising and promotion . . . . [T]here is no question about an indirect relationship between the regulations and cigarette advertising because the regulations expressly target cigarette advertising.

. . . The Attorney General argues that the cigarette advertising regulations are not "based on smoking and health," because they do not involve health-related content in cigarette advertising but instead target youth exposure to cigarette advertising. [W]e cannot agree with the Attorney General's narrow construction of the phrase.

. . . In the 1969 amendments, Congress not only enhanced its scheme to warn the public about the hazards of cigarette smoking, but also sought to protect the public, including youth, from being inundated with images of cigarette smoking in advertising. In pursuit of the latter goal, Congress banned electronic media advertising of cigarettes. And to the extent that Congress contemplated additional targeted regulation of cigarette advertising, it vested that authority in the FTC.

The context in which Congress crafted the current pre-emption provision leads us to conclude that Congress prohibited state cigarette advertising regulations motivated by concerns about smoking and health. Massachusetts has attempted to address the incidence of underage cigarette smoking by regulating advertising much like Congress' ban on cigarette advertising in electronic media. At bottom, the concern about youth exposure to cigarette advertising is intertwined with the concern about cigarette smoking and health. Thus the Attorney General's attempt to distinguish one concern from the other must be rejected.

The Attorney General next claims that the State's outdoor and point-of-sale advertising regulations for cigarettes are not pre-empted because they govern the location, and not the content, of advertising . . . . But the content/location distinction cannot be squared with the language of the pre-emption provision, which reaches all "requirements" and "prohibitions" "imposed under State law." A distinction between the content of advertising and the location of advertising in the FCLAA also cannot be reconciled with Congress' own location-based restriction, which bans advertising in electronic media, but not elsewhere. We are not at liberty to pick and choose which provisions in the legislative scheme we will consider . . . .

Moreover, any distinction between the content and location of cigarette advertising collapses once the implications of that approach are fully considered . . . . We believe that Congress wished to ensure that "a State could not do through negative mandate (*e.g.*, banning all cigarette advertising) that which it already was forbidden to do through positive mandate (*e.g.*, mandating particular cautionary statements)." . . .

. . . .

In sum, we fail to see how the FCLAA and its pre-emption provision permit a distinction between the specific concern about minors and cigarette advertising and the more general concern about smoking and health in cigarette advertising, especially in light of the fact that Congress crafted a legislative solution for those very concerns. We also conclude that a distinction between state regulation of the location as opposed to the content of cigarette advertising has no foundation in the text of the pre-emption provision. Congress pre-empted state cigarette advertising regulations like the Attorney General's because they would upset federal legislative choices to require specific warnings and to impose the ban on cigarette advertising in electronic media in order to address concerns about smoking and health. Accordingly, we hold that the Attorney General's outdoor and point-of-sale advertising regulations targeting cigarettes are pre-empted by the FCLAA.

C

[The FCLAA's] language still leaves significant power in the hands of States to impose generally applicable zoning regulations and to regulate conduct . . . . For instance, the FCLAA does not restrict a State or locality's ability to enact generally applicable zoning restrictions. We have recognized that state interests in traffic safety and esthetics may justify zoning regulations for advertising. . . .

The FCLAA also does not foreclose all state regulation of conduct as it relates to the sale or use of cigarettes. The FCLAA's pre-emption provision explicitly governs state regulations of "advertising or promotion." Accordingly, the FCLAA does not pre-empt state laws prohibiting cigarette sales to minors. To the contrary, there is an established congressional policy that supports such laws; Congress has required States to prohibit tobacco sales to minors as a condition of receiving federal block grant funding for substance abuse treatment activities.

In Massachusetts, it is illegal to sell or distribute tobacco products to persons under the age of 18. Having prohibited the sale and distribution of tobacco products to minors, the State may prohibit common inchoate offenses that attach to criminal conduct, such as solicitation, conspiracy, and attempt. States and localities also have at their disposal other means of regulating conduct to ensure that minors do not obtain cigarettes.

. . . .

III

By its terms, the FCLAA's pre-emption provision only applies to cigarettes. Accordingly, we must evaluate the smokeless tobacco and cigar petitioners' First Amendment challenges to the State's outdoor and point-of-sale advertising regulations. The cigarette petitioners did not raise a pre-emption challenge to the sales practices regulations. Thus, we must analyze the cigarette as well as the smokeless tobacco and cigar petitioners' claim that certain sales practices regulations for tobacco products violate the First Amendment. *[handwritten: for smokeless & cigars]*

A

For over 25 years, the Court has recognized that commercial speech does not fall outside the purview of the First Amendment. Instead, the Court has afforded commercial speech a measure of First Amendment protection "commensurate" with its position in relation to other constitutionally guaranteed expression. In recognition of the "distinction between speech proposing a commercial transaction, which occurs in an area traditionally subject to government regulation, and other varieties of speech," we developed a framework for analyzing regulations of commercial speech that is "substantially similar" to the test for time, place, and manner restrictions. The analysis contains four elements:

> At the outset, we must determine whether the expression is protected by the First Amendment. For commercial speech to come within that provision, it at least must concern lawful activity and not be misleading. Next, we ask whether the asserted governmental interest is substantial. If both inquiries yield positive answers, we must determine whether the regulation directly advances the governmental interest asserted, and whether it is not more extensive than is necessary to serve that interest. *Central Hudson Gas & Electric Corp. v. Public Serv. Comm'n*, 447 U.S. 557 (1980).

[handwritten margin note: Central Hudson commercial speech elements]

Petitioners urge us to reject this analysis and apply strict scrutiny. They are not the first litigants to do so. Admittedly, several Members of the Court have expressed doubts about the *Central Hudson* analysis and whether it should apply in particular cases. But here we see no need to break new ground. *Central Hudson* provides an adequate basis for decision.

Only the last two steps of the four-part analysis are at issue here. The Attorney General has assumed for purposes of summary judgment that petitioners' speech is entitled to First Amendment protection. With respect to the second step, none of the petitioners contests the importance of the State's interest in preventing the use of tobacco products by minors.

The third step concerns the relationship between the harm that underlies the State's interest and the means identified by the State to advance that interest. It requires that[:]

> the speech restriction directly and materially advanc[e] the asserted governmental interest. This burden is not satisfied by mere speculation or

conjecture; rather, a governmental body seeking to sustain a restriction on commercial speech must demonstrate that the harms it recites are real and that its restriction will in fact alleviate them to a material degree.

We do not, however, require that "empirical data come . . . accompanied by a surfeit of background information. . . . [W]e have permitted litigants to justify speech restrictions by reference to studies and anecdotes pertaining to different locales altogether, or even, in a case applying strict scrutiny, to justify restrictions based solely on history, consensus, and simple common sense."

The last step of the analysis "complements" the third step, "asking whether the speech restriction is not more extensive than necessary to serve the interests that support it." We have made it clear that "the least restrictive means" is not the standard; instead, the case law requires a reasonable "fit between the legislature's ends and the means chosen to accomplish those ends . . . [and] a means narrowly tailored to achieve the desired objective." Focusing on the third and fourth steps, we first address the outdoor advertising and point-of-sale advertising regulations for smokeless tobacco and cigars. We then address the sales practices regulations for all tobacco products.

B

The outdoor advertising regulations prohibit smokeless tobacco or cigar advertising within a 1000-foot radius of a school or playground. The District Court and Court of Appeals concluded that the Attorney General had identified a real problem with underage use of tobacco products, that limiting youth exposure to advertising would combat that problem, and that the regulations burdened no more speech than necessary to accomplish the State's goal. The smokeless tobacco and cigar petitioners take issue with all of these conclusions.

1

The smokeless tobacco and cigar petitioners . . . maintain that although the Attorney General may have identified a problem with underage cigarette smoking, he has not identified an equally severe problem with respect to underage use of smokeless tobacco or cigars. The smokeless tobacco petitioner emphasizes the "lack of parity" between cigarettes and smokeless tobacco. The cigar petitioners catalog a list of differences between cigars and other tobacco products, including the characteristics of the products and marketing strategies. The petitioners finally contend that the Attorney General cannot prove that advertising has a causal link to tobacco use such that limiting advertising will materially alleviate any problem of underage use of their products.

In previous cases, we have acknowledged the theory that product advertising stimulates demand for products, while suppressed advertising may have the opposite effect . . . . The FDA promulgated the advertising regulations after finding that the period prior to adulthood is when an overwhelming majority of Americans first decide to use tobacco products, and that advertising plays a crucial role in that decision. (We later held that the FDA lacks statutory authority to regulate tobacco products. [See *FDA v. Brown & Williamson, supra*]) Nevertheless, the Attorney General relies on the FDA's proceedings and other studies to support his decision that advertising affects demand for tobacco products.

. . . .

The FDA also made specific findings with respect to smokeless tobacco. The FDA concluded that "[t]he recent and very large increase in the use of smokeless tobacco products by young people and the addictive nature of these products has persuaded the agency that these products must be included in any regulatory approach that is designed to help prevent future generations of young people from becoming addicted to nicotine-containing tobacco products." . . .

. . . .

. . . There was no data on underage cigar use prior to 1996 because the behavior was considered "uncommon enough not to be worthy of examination." In 1995, the FDA decided not to include cigars in its attempted regulation of tobacco product advertising, explaining that "the agency does not currently have sufficient evidence that these products are drug delivery devices . . . ."

Cigars

More recently, however, data on youth cigar use has emerged. The National Cancer Institute concluded in its 1998 Monograph that the rate of cigar use by minors is increasing and that, in some States, the cigar use rates are higher than the smokeless tobacco use rates for minors. . . .

Studies have also demonstrated a link between advertising and demand for cigars. After Congress recognized the power of images in advertising and banned cigarette advertising in electronic media, television advertising of small cigars "increased dramatically in 1972 and 1973," "filled the void left by cigarette advertisers," and "sales . . . soared." In 1973, Congress extended the electronic media advertising ban for cigarettes to little cigars. In the 1990's, cigar advertising campaigns triggered a boost in sales.

Ct in favor of Atty G.

Our review of the record reveals that the Attorney General has provided ample documentation of the problem with underage use of smokeless tobacco and cigars. In addition, we disagree with petitioners' claim that there is no evidence that preventing targeted campaigns and limiting youth exposure to advertising will decrease underage use of smokeless tobacco and cigars. On this record and in the posture of summary judgment, we are unable to conclude that the Attorney General's decision to regulate advertising of smokeless tobacco and cigars in an effort to combat the use of tobacco products by minors was based on mere "speculation [and] conjecture."

step 3

2

Whatever the strength of the Attorney General's evidence to justify the outdoor advertising regulations, however, we conclude that the regulations do not satisfy the fourth step of the Central Hudson analysis. The final step, the "critical inquiry in this case," requires a reasonable fit between the means and ends of the regulatory scheme. The Attorney General's regulations do not meet this standard. The broad sweep of the regulations indicates that the Attorney General did not "carefully calculat[e] the costs and benefits associated with the burden on speech imposed" by the regulations.

The outdoor advertising regulations prohibit any smokeless tobacco or cigar advertising within 1000 feet of schools or playgrounds. In the District Court, petitioners maintained that this prohibition would prevent advertising in 87% to 91% of Boston, Worcester, and Springfield, Massachusetts. The 87% to 91% figure appears to include not only the effect of the regulations, but also the limitations imposed by other generally applicable zoning restrictions. The Attorney General disputed petitioners' figures but "concede[d] that the reach of the regulations is substantial." Thus, the Court of Appeals concluded that the regulations prohibit advertising in a substantial portion of the major metropolitan areas of Massachusetts.

The substantial geographical reach of the Attorney General's outdoor advertising regulations is compounded by other factors. "Outdoor" advertising includes not only advertising located outside an establishment, but also advertising inside a store if that advertising is visible from outside the store. The regulations restrict advertisements of any size and the term advertisement also includes oral statements.

In some geographical areas, these regulations would constitute nearly a complete ban on the communication of truthful information about smokeless tobacco and cigars to adult consumers. The breadth and scope of the regulations, and the process by which the Attorney General adopted the regulations, do not demonstrate a careful calculation of the speech interests involved.

First, the Attorney General did not seem to consider the impact of the 1000-foot restriction on commercial speech in major metropolitan areas. The Attorney General apparently selected the 1000-foot distance based on the FDA's decision to impose an identical 1000-foot restriction when it attempted to regulate cigarette and smokeless tobacco advertising. But the FDA's 1,000-foot regulation was not an adequate basis for the Attorney General to tailor the Massachusetts regulations. The degree to which speech is suppressed — or alternative avenues for speech remain available — under a particular regulatory scheme tends to be case specific. And a case specific analysis makes sense, for although a State or locality may have common interests and concerns about underage smoking and the effects of tobacco advertisements, the impact of a restriction on speech will undoubtedly vary from place to place. The FDA's regulations would have had widely disparate effects nationwide. Even in Massachusetts, the effect of the Attorney General's speech regulations will vary based on whether a locale is rural, suburban, or urban. The uniformly broad sweep of the geographical limitation demonstrates a lack of tailoring.

In addition, the range of communications restricted seems unduly broad. For instance, it is not clear from the regulatory scheme why a ban on oral communications is necessary to further the State's interest. Apparently that restriction means that a retailer is unable to answer inquiries about its tobacco products if that communication occurs outdoors. Similarly, a ban on all signs of any size seems ill suited to target the problem of highly visible billboards, as opposed to smaller signs. To the extent that studies have identified particular advertising and promotion practices that appeal to youth, tailoring would involve targeting those practices while permitting others. As crafted, the regulations make no distinction among practices on this basis.

. . . .

The State's interest in preventing underage tobacco use is substantial, and even compelling, but it is no less true that the sale and use of tobacco products by adults is a legal activity. We must consider that tobacco retailers and manufacturers have an interest in conveying truthful information about their products to adults, and adults have a corresponding interest in receiving truthful information about tobacco products . . . . As the State protects children from tobacco advertisements, tobacco manufacturers and retailers and their adult consumers still have a protected interest in communication. . . .

In some instances, Massachusetts' outdoor advertising regulations would impose particularly onerous burdens on speech. For example, we disagree with the Court of Appeals' conclusion that because cigar manufacturers and retailers conduct a limited amount of advertising in comparison to other tobacco products, "the relative lack of cigar advertising also means that the burden imposed on cigar advertisers is correspondingly small." If some retailers have relatively small advertising budgets, and use few avenues of communication, then the Attorney General's outdoor advertising regulations potentially place a greater, not lesser, burden on those retailers' speech. Furthermore, to the extent that cigar products and cigar advertising differ from that of other tobacco products, that difference should inform the inquiry into what speech restrictions are necessary.

In addition, a retailer in Massachusetts may have no means of communicating to passersby on the street that it sells tobacco products because alternative forms of advertisement, like newspapers, do not allow that retailer to propose an instant transaction in the way that onsite advertising does. The ban on any indoor advertising that is visible from the outside also presents problems in establishments like convenience stores, which have unique security concerns that counsel in favor of full visibility of the store from the outside. It is these sorts of considerations that the Attorney General failed to incorporate into the regulatory scheme.

We conclude that the Attorney General has failed to show that the outdoor advertising regulations for smokeless tobacco and cigars are not more extensive than necessary to advance the State's substantial interest in preventing underage tobacco use. . . .

A careful calculation of the costs of a speech regulation does not mean that a State must demonstrate that there is no incursion on legitimate speech interests, but a speech regulation cannot unduly impinge on the speaker's ability to propose a commercial transaction and the adult listener's opportunity to obtain information about products. After reviewing the outdoor advertising regulations, we find the calculation in these cases insufficient for purposes of the First Amendment.

C

Massachusetts has also restricted indoor, point-of-sale advertising for smokeless tobacco and cigars. Advertising cannot be "placed lower than five feet from the floor of any retail establishment which is located within a one thousand foot radius of" any school or playground. . . .

We conclude that the point-of-sale advertising regulations fail both the third and fourth steps of the Central Hudson analysis. . . . [T]he State's goal is to prevent minors from using tobacco products and to curb demand for that activity by limiting youth exposure to advertising. The 5-foot rule does not seem to advance that goal. Not all children are less than 5 feet tall, and those who are certainly have the ability to look up and take in their surroundings.

. . . .

Massachusetts may wish to target tobacco advertisements and displays that entice children, much like floor-level candy displays in a convenience store, but the blanket height restriction does not constitute a reasonable fit with that goal. The Court of Appeals recognized that the efficacy of the regulation was questionable, but decided that "in any event, the burden on speech imposed by the provision is very limited." There is no *de minimis* exception for a speech restriction that lacks sufficient tailoring or justification. We conclude that the restriction on the height of indoor advertising is invalid under *Central Hudson*'s third and fourth prongs.

D

The Attorney General also promulgated a number of regulations that restrict sales practices by cigarette, smokeless tobacco, and cigar manufacturers and retailers. Among other restrictions, the regulations bar the use of self-service displays and require that tobacco products be placed out of the reach of all consumers in a location accessible only to salespersons . . . . Two of the cigarette petitioners . . . and the cigar petitioners challenge the sales practices regulations on First Amendment grounds. . . .

. . . .

. . . As we read the regulations, they basically require tobacco retailers to place tobacco products behind counters and require customers to have contact with a salesperson before they are able to handle a tobacco product.

. . . .

Massachusetts' sales practices provisions regulate conduct that may have a communicative component, but Massachusetts seeks to regulate the placement of tobacco products for reasons unrelated to the communication of ideas . . . . We conclude that the State has demonstrated a substantial interest in preventing access to tobacco products by minors and has adopted an appropriately narrow means of advancing that interest. *United States v. O'Brien*, 391 U.S. 367 (1968).

Unattended displays of tobacco products present an opportunity for access without the proper age verification required by law. Thus, the State prohibits self-service and other displays that would allow an individual to obtain tobacco products without direct contact with a salesperson. It is clear that the regulations leave open ample channels of communication. The regulations do not significantly impede adult access to tobacco products. Moreover, retailers have other means of exercising any cognizable speech interest in the presentation of their products. We presume that vendors may place empty tobacco packaging on open display, and display actual tobacco products so long as that display is only accessible to sales personnel. As for cigars, there is no indication in the regulations that a customer is unable to examine a cigar prior to purchase, so long as that examination takes place through a salesperson.

We conclude that the sales practices regulations withstand First Amendment scrutiny. The means chosen by the State are narrowly tailored to prevent access to tobacco products by minors, are unrelated to expression, and leave open alternative avenues for vendors to convey information about products and for would-be customers to inspect products before purchase.

. . . .

IV

We have observed that "tobacco use, particularly among children and adolescents, poses perhaps the single most significant threat to public health in the United States." From a policy perspective, it is understandable for the States to attempt to prevent minors from using tobacco products before they reach an age where they are capable of weighing for themselves the risks and potential benefits of tobacco use, and other adult activities. Federal law, however, places limits on policy choices available to the States.

In these cases, Congress enacted a comprehensive scheme to address cigarette smoking and health in advertising and pre-empted state regulation of cigarette advertising that attempts to address that same concern, even with respect to youth. The First Amendment also constrains state efforts to limit advertising of tobacco products, because so long as the sale and use of tobacco is lawful for adults, the tobacco industry has a protected interest in communicating information about its products and adult customers have an interest in receiving that information.

To the extent that federal law and the First Amendment do not prohibit state action, States and localities remain free to combat the problem of underage tobacco use by appropriate means . . . .

NOTES AND QUESTIONS

1. Preemption. In *Lorillard Tobacco v. Reilly*, the Supreme Court had to determine the extent to which the federal FCLAA legislation enacted in the 1960s (and amended several times thereafter) preempted state anti-tobacco laws — at least the advertising and sales practice laws that the Massachusetts attorney general attempted to implement in 2001. (Note that the attorney general undertook the tobacco initiative, and determined its content, under the state's consumer-protection statute prohibiting unfair and deceptive trade practices. That is, there was no tobacco-specific legislative mandate to do so; the campaign arose administratively). The FCLAA required the now-familiar warning labels on cigarettes and other tobacco advertising and limited advertisement of cigarettes and most other forms of tobacco (but not cigars and smokeless products) on electronic media.

The FCLAA preemption provision targeted state laws arising out of public health concerns — the health effects of smoking: "No requirement or prohibition *based on smoking and health* shall be imposed under State law with respect to the advertising or promotion of any cigarettes the packages of which are labeled in conformity with the provisions of this chapter." 15 U.S.C. § 1334(b) (emphasis added.) The Massachusetts regulations were clearly inspired by — and designed to reduce — smoking and its health risks. Thus, the Court had little difficulty finding them to be preempted insofar as they applied to the advertising and promotion of cigarettes.

The preemption provision, however, did not extend to cigars or smokeless tobacco products. Nor did it address laws that did not involve advertising or promotion, such as prohibitions on sales, whether or not based on "smoking or health." *See Cipollone v. Liggett Group*, 505 U.S. 504 (1992). Could Massachusetts have prohibited the sale of cigarettes to adults, as well as minors? Is there an argument that the FCLAA preempts this type of legislation? Could the tobacco industry argue that the federal legislation requires labels on cigarettes and prohibits some forms of advertising — restrictions that anticipate that, within these restrictions, tobacco products and their use would be permitted? Is that enough to infer preemption?

2. The First Amendment and advertising restrictions. Since the FCLAA preemption applied only to cigarettes, and because Massachusetts was attempting to regulate cigars and smokeless tobacco products as well, the *Lorillard* decision also addressed the First Amendment problem that arises when government attempts to impose restrictions on the advertising or promotion of otherwise legal commercial goods.

In this and other commercial speech cases, the Court makes a critical, threshold distinction between viewpoint-based and viewpoint-neutral regulation. Viewpoint (or content) neutral regulation imposes the same restrictions on the advertising of all products, such as limitations on where billboards of any kind can be placed, times of day in which loudspeakers can be used, and the like. Such regulations of "time, place or manner" are typically subject to minimum scrutiny; government needs only a rational basis for believing that such restrictions will serve a legitimate state interest, such as peace and quiet. Similarly, regulation intended to protect consumers from "commercial harms," such as false advertising, receives minimum scrutiny.

Where government seeks to regulate advertising because it disfavors (or favors) the product or service being advertised, however, the law is not viewpoint neutral. It imposes restrictions only a specific product — such as tobacco, alcoholic beverages or contraceptives — for the purpose of discouraging consumption of the product. Such regulations do not seek to protect consumers from "commercial harms." The majority of Justices on the U.S. Supreme Court have raised the standard of judicial review of such measures. For early decisions concerning advertising regulations, see *Bigelow v. Virginia*, 421 U.S. 809 (1975) (state law banning advertisements of abortion services violated First Amendment; although the law was not purely commercial, commercial speech "enjoys a degree of constitutional protection"); *Virginia Bd. of Pharmacy v. Virginia Citizens Consumer Council, Inc.*, 425 U.S. 748 (1976) (blanket state ban on advertising the price of prescription drugs violated the First Amendment).

The Court uses the standard of review for regulations affecting "commercial speech" laid out in *Central Hudson Gas & Electric Corp. v. Public Serv. Comm'n*, 447 U.S. 557 (1980). The Court first decides whether the commercial speech is not misleading or fraudulent and whether it concerns a lawful activity, in order to determine whether it warrants heightened scrutiny. (Note that with noncommercial speech, neither of these elements would disqualify the speech from First Amendment protection.) If commercial speech is not misleading and concerns lawful activities, the Court requires the government to demonstrate that its purpose is "substantial," that the regulation at issue (the means) "directly advances" that purpose, and that the restriction on speech is no more extensive than necessary to achieve its purpose.

In *Lorillard*, as in prior cases, Massachusetts had little difficulty satisfying the first prong, since the state certainly has a substantial interest in protecting children from the risks of tobacco use. It found studies linking advertising with cigar use to meet the demanding third prong, which requires more than mere "speculation or conjecture." Evidence directly linking advertising with increased consumption is often unavailable, despite the fact that common sense supports causation. In *44 Liquormart, Inc. v. Rhode Island*, 517 U.S. 484, 493 (1996), the Court found that Rhode Island offered no evidence that its ban on advertising alcoholic beverage prices would reduce alcohol consumption or promote temperance, noting that states without bans had lower consumptions rates.

The fourth prong often presents an insurmountable obstacle to regulation, because banning, taxing or restricting sales of a product are less intrusive on First Amendment rights and probably more effective. *See e.g., Rubin v. Coors Brewing Company*, 514 U.S. 476 (1995). *Lorillard* fits this pattern.

The Court has so far declined to find that governments have broader discretion to restrict the advertising of "vices." Several Justices remain hostile to what they perceive to be paternalistic advertising restrictions, such as regulations limiting nonmisleading advertising. *See, e.g., 44 Liquormart*, 517 U.S. at 503. ("The First Amendment directs us to be especially skeptical of regulations that seek to keep people in the dark for what the government perceives to be their own good.") A few Justices have questioned whether government can ban commercial speech at all, at least if it is truthful about a lawful product. *See e.g., Central Hudson*, 447 U.S. at 579 (Justices Blackmun and Brennan, concurring) ("[We] seriously doubt whether suppression of information concerning the availability and price of a legally offered product is ever a permissible way for the State to dampen demand for or use of the product."). Note, however, that these stances are applied most strictly to adults. The Court appears to apply a more "paternalistic" standard to restrictions designed to protect children from exposure to advertisements of products whose sales are limited to adults.

The result in *Lorillard* is not without irony. Had Massachusetts decided to ban the sale, use, or possession of tobacco in more draconian ways, the Court probably would have applied a more deferential "rationality" standard to the state's ban. Having chosen to limit only the advertising of tobacco products, Massachusetts must meet a more demanding constitutional burden.

Massachusetts — indeed all states — have additional options. Counter-advertising or public service advertisements that highlight the unattractiveness of smoking and its adverse effects have had some success in reducing smoking. In perhaps another irony, smoking rates increased slightly after the FCC banned cigarettes advertising in electronic media, perhaps because the anti-smoking ads that had accompanied such advertising were believed to be unnecessary and also ended.

3. Expressive conduct. The *Lorillard* opinion makes reference to *United States v. O'Brien*, 391 U.S. 367 (1968). The O'Brien "expressive conduct" doctrine allows the government to regulate conduct that also involves some elements of speech or expression, again under a form of heightened scrutiny. Essentially, as long as the court finds that the government's purpose is to regulate the conduct and not the speech and the impact on the speech is "incidental," the *O'Brien* test will be satisfied. In *Lorillard,* the Court used this analysis to uphold some of the Massachusetts laws that limited the manner in which tobacco products can be displayed and other related sales practices. *O'Brien* may be applied in other cases where the regulated activity has elements of both conduct and expression and the courts are unwilling to make a determination that the activity is exclusively one or the other.

R.J. REYNOLDS TOBACCO COMPANY. v. FOOD & DRUG ADMINISTRATION
696 F. 3d 1205 (D.C. Cir. 2012)

BROWN, CIRCUIT JUDGE:

The Family Smoking Prevention and Tobacco Control Act of 2009 ("the Act") . . . directed the Secretary of the U.S. Department of Health and Human Services to issue regulations requiring all cigarette packages manufactured or sold in the United States to bear one of nine new textual warnings, as well as "color graphics depicting the negative health consequences of smoking." . . . Pursuant to this authority, the Food and Drug Administration ("FDA") initiated a rulemaking proceeding through which it selected the nine images that would accompany the statutorily-prescribed warnings. Five tobacco companies ("the Companies") challenged the rule, alleging that FDA's proposed graphic warnings violated the First Amendment . . . . The district court granted the Companies' motion for summary judgment on February 29, 2012. FDA appeals, and we affirm.

. . . .

I. Background

The Act gives FDA the authority to regulate the manufacture and sale of tobacco products, including cigarettes. In addition to requiring cigarette packages and advertisements to bear one of nine new warning statements, the Act mandates that the new warning labels comprise the top 50 percent of the front and rear panels of cigarette packages and 20 percent of the area of each cigarette advertisement. . . .

Pursuant to the statutory directive, FDA issued a Proposed Rule seeking comment on thirty-six potential images for the new graphic warning labels . . . . In accordance with the requirements of the Act, FDA proposed a dramatic expansion of the existing health warnings, which it justified based on scientific literature and a "strong worldwide consensus" regarding the relative effectiveness of graphic warnings compared to the text-only warnings the United States currently requires . . . . The agency explained that by "clearly and effectively convey[ing] the negative health consequences of smoking," the new warnings would discourage nonsmokers, particularly minors, from "initiating cigarette use," and encourage current smokers to quit. . . .

FDA promulgated the final set of nine images — one for each warning statement — by regulations issued on June 22, 2011 . . . . FDA also required each graphic image to bear the phone number of the National Cancer Institute's "Network of Tobacco Cessation Quitlines," which uses the telephone portal "1-800-QUIT-NOW." . . .

FDA based its selection of the final images on an 18,000-person internet-based consumer study it commissioned. The study divided respondents into two groups: a control group that was shown the new text in the format of the current warnings (located on the side of cigarette packages), and a separate treatment group that was shown the proposed graphic warnings . . . . Each group then answered questions designed to assess, among other things, whether the graphic warnings, relative to the text-only control, (1) increased viewers' intention to quit or refrain from smoking; (2) increased viewers' knowledge of the health risks of smoking or second-hand smoke; and (3) were "salient," which FDA defined in part as causing viewers to feel "depressed, " "discouraged, " or "afraid. " . . .

In selecting these nine images, FDA reviewed and responded to over a thousand public comments, including joint comments submitted by plaintiffs-appellees RJ Reynolds, Lorillard, and Commonwealth Brands . . . . Several comments — including comments from cancer researchers, nonprofits, and academics — criticized the single exposure study design, noting it prevented the government from assessing the long-term or actual effects of the proposed warnings. . . . FDA conceded the study did not permit it to reach "firm" conclusions about the "long-term, real-world effects" of the proposed warnings, but claimed the existing scientific literature "provides a substantial basis for our conclusion that the required warnings will effectively communicate the health risks of smoking, thereby encouraging smoking cessation and discouraging smoking initiation." . . . Still other comments asserted that FDA's research study failed to provide evidence that the proposed warnings would actually affect smoking rates, significantly affect consumers knowledge of the risks of smoking, or bring about actual behavior change . . . . But FDA disagreed, again relying on the "substantial research" showing the effectiveness of similar graphic health warnings in other countries. . . .

Some comments also criticized the lack of statistical evidence supporting FDA's belief that requiring cigarette packages to bear the graphic warnings would reduce smoking rates. For example, the Companies noted that the Canadian data revealed no statistically significant decline in smoking rates for adolescents and adults after the introduction of similar graphic warnings, which implied that the warnings were ineffective and that FDA's warnings would be ineffective as well. FDA summarily disagreed, stating that the images it selected would satisfy its "primary goal, which is to effectively convey the negative health consequences of smoking on cigarette packages and in advertisements," which can help "both to discourage nonsmokers . . . from initiating cigarette use and to encourage current smokers to consider cessation." . . . FDA also explained that the data from Canada did not indicate that the warnings had been ineffective, because other studies showed that the warnings had been "effective at providing . . . smokers with health information, making consumers think about the health effects of smoking, and increasing smokers' motivations to quit smoking." . . .

After FDA finalized the Rule, the Companies filed suit in the district court, claiming the cigarette warnings required under the Act and FDA's implementing regulations violated the First Amendment. . . .

II. Level of Scrutiny

. . . The only question before us is whether FDA's promulgation of the graphic warning labels — which incorporate the textual warnings, a corresponding graphic image, and the "1-800-QUIT-NOW" cessation hotline number — violates the First Amendment. We begin our analysis by determining the applicable level of scrutiny.

Both the right to speak and the right to refrain from speaking are "complementary components of the broader concept of individual freedom of mind" protected by the First Amendment . . . . Any attempt by the government either to compel individuals to express certain views . . . or to subsidize speech to which they object . . . is subject to strict scrutiny. . . .

This case contains elements of compulsion and forced subsidization. The Companies contend that, to the extent the graphic warnings go beyond the textual warnings to shame and repulse smokers and denigrate smoking as an antisocial act, the message is ideological and not informational. "[B]y effectively shouting well-understood information to consumers," they explain, "FDA is communicating an ideological message, a point of view on how people should live their lives: that the risks from smoking outweigh the pleasure that smokers derive from it, and that smokers make bad personal decisions, and should stop smoking." . . . No one doubts the government can promote smoking cessation programs; can use shock, shame, and moral opprobrium to discourage people from becoming smokers; and can use its taxing and regulatory authority to make smoking economically prohibitive and socially onerous. And the government can certainly require that consumers be fully informed about the dangers of hazardous products. But this case raises novel questions about the scope of the government's authority to force the manufacturer of a product to go beyond making purely factual and accurate commercial disclosures and undermine its own economic interest — in this case, by making "every single pack of cigarettes in the country [a] mini billboard" for the government's anti-smoking message.

. . . .

Even assuming the Companies' marketing efforts (packaging, branding, and other advertisements) can be properly classified as commercial speech, and thus subject to less robust First Amendment protections, a thorny question remains: how much leeway should this Court grant the government when it seeks to compel a product's manufacturer to convey the state's subjective — and perhaps even ideological — view that consumers should reject this otherwise legal, but disfavored, product? . . .

Courts have recognized a handful of "narrow and well-understood exceptions" to the general rule that content-based speech regulations — including compelled speech — are subject to strict scrutiny. . . . There are two primary exceptions in the commercial speech context. First, "purely factual and uncontroversial" disclosures are permissible if they are "reasonably related to the State's interest in preventing deception of consumers," provided the requirements are not "unjustified or unduly burdensome." *Zauderer [v. Office of Disciplinary Counsel of Supreme Court*, 471 U.S. 626, 651 (1985)]. Second, restrictions on commercial speech are subject to less stringent review than restrictions on other types of speech. For a statute burdening commercial speech to survive, the government must affirmatively prove that (1) its asserted interest is substantial, (2) the restriction directly and materially advances that interest, and (3) the restriction is narrowly tailored. *See Cent. Hudson Gas & Elec. Corp., v. Pub. Serv. Comm'n*, 447 U.S. 557, 566 (1980). While this test is not quite as demanding as strict scrutiny, it is significantly more stringent than *Zauderer's* standard, which is akin to rational-basis review.

. . . .

a. Applicability of the *Zauderer* Standard

In *Zauderer*, the Court applied a lower level of scrutiny to regulations requiring attorneys to fully disclose information about the actual cost and consequences of services . . . . Noting that the First Amendment's protection of commercial speech is premised on its informational value to consumers, the Court reasoned that an advertiser's constitutional interest in not providing additional factual information was "minimal." . . . Although the Court acknowledged that "unjustified or unduly burdensome disclosure requirements might offend the First Amendment by chilling protected commercial speech," it "h[e]ld that an advertiser's rights are adequately protected as long as disclosure requirements are reasonably related to the State's interest in preventing deception of consumers." *Id.* . . .

The Supreme Court has never applied *Zauderer* to disclosure requirements not designed to correct misleading commercial speech. FDA argues that *Zauderer's* lenient standard of scrutiny applies to regulations that serve a different governmental interest: disclosure of the health and safety risks associated with commercial products. . . .

But by its own terms, *Zauderer's* holding is limited to cases in which disclosure requirements are "reasonably related to the State's interest in preventing deception of consumers." . . . And as the Court explained in *Pacific Gas*, "[n]othing in *Zauderer* suggests . . . that the State is equally free to require [entities] to carry the messages of third parties, where the messages themselves are biased against or are expressly contrary to the [entity's] views." . . .

          . . . .

In fact, the Court's only recent application of the *Zauderer* standard involved a disclosure requirement that "share[d] the essential features of the rule at issue in *Zauderer*." . . . In *Milavetz*, a law firm challenged a provision of the Bankruptcy Abuse Prevention and Consumer Protection Act of 2005 ("BAPCPA") that required professionals qualifying as debt relief agencies to "clearly and conspicuously disclose in any advertisement of bankruptcy assistance services . . . that the services or benefits are with respect to bankruptcy relief under this title." . . . The Court upheld the statute's disclosure requirement because, as in *Zauderer*, the law firm's advertisements were "inherently misleading" — in this case, because they "promis[ed] . . . debt relief without any reference to the possibility of filing for bankruptcy, which has inherent costs." . . .

 Zauderer, Ibanez, and Milavetz thus establish that a disclosure requirement is only appropriate if the government shows that, absent a warning, there is a self-evident — or at least "potentially real" — danger that an advertisement will mislead consumers . . . . In this case, the . . . Act bans any labeling or advertising representing that any tobacco product "presents a lower risk of tobacco-related disease or is less harmful than one or more other commercially marketed tobacco products," "contains a reduced level of a substance or presents a reduced exposure to a substance," or "does not contain or is free of a substance." . . . The Act also bans advertising or labeling using the descriptors "light," "mild," "low," or similar descriptors . . . . In light of these restrictions, and in the absence of any congressional findings on the misleading nature of cigarette packaging itself, there is no justification under *Zauderer* for the graphic warnings.

          . . . .

The *amicus* States suggest that the graphic warnings be evaluated in the context of the years of deception that preceded them. . . . [T]hey claim this Court has found that even advertisements that do not appear deceptive in isolation can constitute "part of a continuing deception of the public" absent highly visible warnings . . . . But the States' argument overlooks the broader context of that decision. *Warner-Lambert* involved a petition for review of an FTC order requiring the Warner-Lambert company to cease and desist from advertising that its product, Listerine mouthwash, prevents, cures, or alleviates the common cold . . . . As a remedial measure, the Commission required Warner-Lambert to include the following disclosure in every future advertisement for Listerine for a defined period: "Contrary to prior advertising, Listerine will not help prevent colds or sore throats or lessen their severity." . . . In other words, the disclosure statement was required as part of a corrective order which the Commission found necessary to "dissipate the effects of respondent's deceptive representations." . . .

. . . .

By contrast, FDA does not frame this rule as a remedial measure designed to counteract specific deceptive claims made by the Companies, nor did it offer a remedial justification for the graphic warnings during the rulemaking proceeding . . . . Nor did it show that absent disclosure, consumers would likely be deceived by the Companies' packaging in the future. Rather, FDA framed the warnings as general disclosures about the negative health effects of smoking. The warnings thus represent an ongoing effort to discourage consumers from buying the Companies' products, rather than, as in *Warner-Lambert*, a measure designed to combat specific deceptive *claims*.

. . . .

Moreover, the graphic warnings do not constitute the type of "purely factual and uncontroversial" information . . . to which the *Zauderer* standard may be applied. The disclosures approved in *Zauderer* and *Milavetz* were clear statements that were both indisputably accurate and not subject to misinterpretation by consumers.. . .

The FDA's images are a much different animal. FDA concedes that the images are not meant to be interpreted literally, but rather to symbolize the textual warning statements, which provide "additional context for what is shown." . . . But many of the images chosen by FDA could be misinterpreted by consumers. For example, the image of a man smoking through a tracheotomy hole might be misinterpreted as suggesting that such a procedure is a common consequence of smoking — a more logical interpretation than FDA's contention that it symbolizes "the addictive nature of cigarettes," which requires significant extrapolation on the part of the consumers . . . . Moreover, the graphic warnings are not "purely" factual because — as FDA tacitly admits — they are primarily intended to evoke an emotional response, or, at most, shock the viewer into retaining the information in the text warning. . . .

In fact, many of the images do not convey any warning information at all, much less make an "accurate statement" about cigarettes. For example, the images of a woman crying, a small child, and the man wearing a T-shirt emblazoned with the words "I QUIT" do not offer any information about the health effects of smoking. And the "1-800-QUIT-NOW" number, when presented without any explanation about the services provided on the hotline, hardly sounds like an unbiased source of information. These inflammatory images and the provocatively-named hot-line cannot rationally be viewed as pure attempts to convey information to consumers. They are unabashed attempts to evoke emotion (and perhaps embarrassment) and browbeat consumers into quitting . . . . While none of these images are patently false, they certainly do not impart purely factual, accurate, or uncontroversial information to consumers. Consequently, the images fall outside the ambit of *Zauderer*.

b. Applicability of *Central Hudson*

Because this case does not fall within the narrow enclave carved out by *Zauderer*, we must next determine which level of scrutiny — strict or intermediate — is appropriate . . . . The government argues that we should view the graphic warnings as restrictions on commercial speech, which are analyzed under the less rigorous standard established by *Central Hudson*. Despite the contrary views of other circuits, our governing precedent makes clear that *Central Hudson* is the appropriate standard.

. . . .

III. Evaluating the Graphic Warnings Under Intermediate Scrutiny

Under *Central Hudson*, the government must first show that its asserted interest is "substantial." . . . If so, the Court must determine "whether the regulation directly advances the governmental interest asserted, and whether it is not more extensive than is necessary to serve that interest." . . . The party seeking to uphold a restriction on commercial speech bears the burden of justifying it . . . . Because this case involves a challenge to final agency action, the Administrative Procedure Act governs our review of the record . . . . The APA requires us to "hold unlawful and set aside agency action, findings, and conclusions found to be . . . unsupported by substantial evidence." . . .

Unlike rational-basis review, the *Central Hudson* standard does not permit this Court to "supplant the precise interests put forward by [FDA] with other suppositions." . . . We thus begin by identifying FDA's asserted interests.

A review of the statute and the administrative record makes clear that the graphic warnings are intended to encourage current smokers to quit and dissuade other consumers from ever buying cigarettes. One of the Act's many stated purposes is "promot[ing] cessation to reduce disease risk and the social costs associated with tobacco-related diseases." . . . The only explicitly asserted interest in either the Proposed or Final Rule is an interest in reducing smoking rates. . . . Although counsel attempted to disclaim this interest at oral argument, the administrative record shows otherwise: the primary objective of the Rule was "both to discourage nonsmokers from initiating cigarette use and to encourage current smokers to consider quitting." . . .

Assuming FDA's interest in reducing smoking rates is substantial, we next evaluate whether FDA has offered substantial evidence showing that the graphic warning requirements "directly advance[] the governmental interest asserted," . . . A restriction that "provides only ineffective or remote support for the government's purposes," . . . is not sufficient, and the government cannot satisfy its burden "by mere speculation or conjecture." . . . .

FDA has not provided a shred of evidence — much less the "substantial evidence" required by the APA — showing that the graphic warnings will "directly advance" its interest in reducing the number of Americans who smoke. FDA makes much of the "international consensus" surrounding the effectiveness of large graphic warnings, but offers no evidence showing that such warnings have directly caused a material decrease in smoking rates in any of the countries that now require them. While studies of Canadian and Australian youth smokers showed that the warnings on cigarette packs caused a substantial number of survey participants to think — or think more — about quitting smoking . . . . . it is mere speculation to suggest that respondents who report increased thoughts about quitting smoking will actually follow through on their intentions. And at no point did these studies attempt to evaluate whether the increased thoughts about smoking cessation led participants to actually quit. Another Australian study reported increased quit attempts by survey participants after that country enacted large graphic warnings, but found "no association with short-term quit success." . . . Some Canadian and Australian studies indicated that large graphic warnings might induce individual smokers to reduce consumption, or to help persons who have already quit smoking remain abstinent . . . . But again, the study did not purport to show that the implementation of large graphic warnings has actually led to a reduction in smoking rates.

FDA's reliance on this questionable social science is unsurprising when we consider the raw data regarding smoking rates in countries that have enacted graphic warnings. FDA claims that Canadian national survey data suggest that graphic warnings may reduce smoking rates. But the strength of the evidence is underwhelming, making FDA's claim somewhat misleading. In the year prior to the introduction of graphic warnings, the Canadian national survey showed that 24 percent of Canadians aged 15 or older smoked cigarettes. In 2001, the year the warnings were introduced, the national smoking rate dropped to 22 percent, and it further dropped to 21 percent in 2002 . . . . FDA concedes it cannot directly attribute any decrease in the Canadian smoking rate to the graphic warnings because the Canadian government implemented other smoking control initiatives, including an increase in the cigarette tax and new restrictions on public smoking, during the same period . . . . Although FDA maintains the data "are suggestive" that large graphic warnings "may" reduce smoking consumption . . . it cannot satisfy its First Amendment burden with "mere speculation and conjecture." . . .

FDA's Regulatory Impact Analysis ("RIA") essentially concedes the agency lacks any evidence showing that the graphic warnings are likely to reduce smoking rates. One way in which the RIA analyzed the expected benefits of the Rule was by comparing the impact of similar warnings introduced in Canada in 2000 . . . . It (1) analyzed the change in smoking trends in Canada before and after 2000; (2) assumed any difference in the post-2000 change between Canada and the United States was solely attributable to the introduction of graphic warnings; and (3) assumed similar warnings would have an identical impact on U.S. smoking rates. . . .

    . . . .

Logic dictates that these procedural shortcuts would, if anything, lead to an overly optimistic prediction of the efficacy of the proposed graphic warnings. Not so. The RIA estimated the new warnings would reduce U.S. smoking rates by a mere 0.088% . . . a number the FDA concedes is "in general not statistically distinguishable from zero." . . .

FDA has thus presented us with only two studies that directly evaluate the impact of graphic warnings on actual smoking rates, and neither set of data shows that the graphic warnings will "directly" advance its interest in reducing smoking rates "to a material degree." . . . And one of the principal researchers on whom FDA relies recently surveyed the relevant literature and conceded that "[t]here is no way to attribute . . . declines [in smoking] to the new health warnings." . . . In light of the number of foreign jurisdictions that have enacted large graphic warning labels, the dearth of data reflecting decreased smoking rates in these countries is somewhat surprising, and strongly implies that such warnings are not very effective at promoting cessation and discouraging initiation. . . .

FDA attempts to downplay the significance of the RIA . . . by noting the analysis made only the "unremarkable point" that it is "difficult [to] determine with statistical precision the relative causal impact of the relevant contributing factors," particularly given the very small data sets to which FDA had access . . . . But FDA cannot get around the First Amendment by pleading incompetence or futility . . . .

. . . .

Alternatively, FDA asserts an interest in "effectively communicating health information" regarding the negative effects of cigarettes . . . . But as FDA concedes, this purported "interest" describes only the means by which FDA is attempting to reduce smoking rates: "[t]he goal of effectively communicating the risks of cigarette smoking is, of course, related to the viewer's decision to quit, or never to start, smoking." . . . . The government's attempt to reformulate its interest as purely informational is unconvincing, as an interest in "effective" communication is too vague to stand on its own. Indeed, the government's chosen buzzwords, which it reiterates through the rulemaking, prompt an obvious question: "effective" in what sense? Allowing FDA to define "effectiveness" however it sees fit would not only render *Central Hudson's* "substantial interest" requirement a complete nullity, but it would also eviscerate the requirement that any restriction "directly advance" that interest . . . . In this case, both the statute and the Rule offer a barometer for assessing the effectiveness of the graphic warnings — the degree to which they encourage current smokers to quit and dissuade would-be smokers from taking up the habit . . . . As such, FDA's interest in "effectively communicating" the health risks of smoking is merely a description of the means by which it plans to accomplish its goal of reducing smoking rates, and not an independent interest capable of sustaining the Rule.

. . . .

IV. Conclusion

In the Proposed Rule, FDA lamented that their previous efforts to combat the tobacco companies' advertising campaigns have been like bringing a butter knife to a gun fight. According to the FTC, tobacco companies spent approximately $12.49 billion on advertising and promotion in 2006 alone, employing marketing and advertising experts to incorporate current trends and target their messages toward certain demographics . . . . The graphic warnings represent FDA's attempt to level the playing field, not only by limiting the Companies' ability to advertise, but also by forcing the Companies to bear the cost of disseminating an anti-smoking message. But as the Supreme Court recently reminded us, "[t]hat the [government] finds expression too persuasive does not permit it to quiet the speech or to burden its messengers." . . . The First Amendment requires the government not only to state a substantial interest justifying a regulation on commercial speech, but also to show

that its regulation directly advances that goal. FDA failed to present any data —
much less the substantial evidence required under the APA — showing that
enacting their proposed graphic warnings will accomplish the agency's stated
objective of reducing smoking rates. The Rule thus cannot pass muster under
Central Hudson. . . . We therefore vacate the graphic warning requirements and
remand to the agency. . . .

NOTES AND QUESTIONS

4. FDA regulation of tobacco and graphic images. The Family Smoking
Prevention and Tobacco Control Act amended the FDCA to give the FDA authority
to regulate tobacco and also amended the FCLAA to require new text and
formatting of warnings on cigarette packages and advertising. (Package warnings
must cover the top 50% of each package front and back.) The new § 4(d) of the
FCLAA requires the Secretary to "issue regulations that require color graphics
depicting the negative health consequences of smoking to accompany the label
statements." *R.J. Reynolds Tobacco Company* is a challenge to the FDA's proposed
regulations governing specific graphic images, which can be seen at www.fda.gov/
TobaccoProducts/Labeling/ucm259214.htm (visited May 2014). Several countries
adopted similar graphic warnings — a popular measure — perhaps to implement
the Framework Convention on Tobacco Control. The decision of the Court of
Appeals for the District of Columbia, however, demonstrates how the First
Amendment circumscribes the FDA's options. The FDA did not appeal the Circuit
Court's decision, presumably because it concluded that the U. S. Supreme Court
would uphold the ruling, despite a lengthy dissent by Judge Rogers. The FDA
retains the authority to propose new and different graphic images. What type of
image would meet First Amendment standards?

Note that the court does not accept the FDA's conclusions that graphic warnings
will help reduce smoking. In analyzing the regulation under the third prong of
Central Hudson, the court dismissed the FDA's evidence, because it did not satisfy
the requirement for evidence that the regulation would "directly advance" the goal
of reducing smoking. Were you surprised that the estimated effect of the graphic
warnings was only a 0.088% reduction in smoking rates? Surely the FDA would
present the best evidence available to support its conclusions. How do you think
smokers or prospective smokers would react to the images? Does it matter that
people would have to ask for a package of cigarettes (often behind the counter) in
order to see the images?

The court does not reach the fourth *Central Hudson* prong — whether the
regulations are more extensive than necessary to achieve the FDA's goal. The FDA
argued that its regulations should not be reviewed under *Central Hudson*, but with
minimum scrutiny under *Zauderer*. The court found that the type of regulations
subject to a *Zauderer* minimum scrutiny standard of review require only factual
information to be presented to consumers — information needed to prevent
consumer deception. The court viewed the graphic images — and especially the
1-800-QUIT-NOW message — as presenting the government's point of view. Would
the same images be acceptable without the addition of the 1-800-QUIT-NOW

message? What other images might be permissible? Are there other ways in which the government might educate the public about the risk of smoking? Is there anything preventing the federal or state governments from initiating their own public education campaigns?

5. **Justice Oliver Wendell Holmes and freedom of speech.** Justice Oliver Wendell Holmes was, until late 1919, a believer in a powerful government with almost no constitutional protection of freedom of speech. In 1915, he wrote the opinion for a unanimous U.S. Supreme Court upholding the conviction of a journalist who wrote an editorial supporting a private nudist camp in an isolated area and encouraging continuing a boycott of the "prudes" who reported them for prosecution under laws forbidding indecent exposure. *Fox v. Washington*, 236 U.S. 273 (1915) (Washington state law forbade any printed matter having a tendency to encourage, incite or advocate disrespect for the law.) Privately, Holmes reportedly told Learned Hand that the state's power to imprison those who might spread "dangerous" ideas was analogous to the state's power to vaccinate those who might spread dangerous diseases. *See* THOMAS HEALY, THE GREAT DISSENT: HOW OLIVER WENDELL HOMES CHANGED HIS MIND — AND CHANGED THE HISTORY OF FREE SPEECH IN AMERICA (2013). (What do you think of Holmes' apparent reference to *Jacobson v. Massachusetts* as precedent for the power to criminalize controversial opinions?)

Justice Holmes' opinion for a unanimous Court in *Schenck v. United States*, 249 U.S. 47 (1919), upheld the criminal conviction of three Socialist Party members for conspiracy to obstruct the World War I draft in violation the Espionage Act of June 15, 1917. The defendants' crime was distributing leaflets saying that conscription was "a monstrous wrong against humanity in the interest of Wall Street's chosen few" and arguing for repeal of the Act. *Id.* at 51.

Yet later that same year, Holmes changed his view of the First Amendment's protection of speech, apparently after considerable debate with judges and academics like Learned Hand, Zechariah Chafee, Harold Laski, and Felix Frankfurter. *See* HEALY, THE GREAT DISSENT, *supra*. The change appeared in *Abrams v. United States*, 250 U.S. 616 (1919), which upheld the defendants' conviction under the Sedition Act of 1918 for distributing leaflets denouncing the sending of troops to Russia and advocating the cessation of weapons production for the war in Russia. (That decision also announced the "clear and present danger" test.) Holmes, joined by Justice Brandeis, dissented, arguing that "the defendants were deprived of their rights under the Constitution." *Id.* at 631. His "great dissent" would become the core of modern free speech doctrine:

> But as against dangers peculiar to war, as against others, the principle of the right to free speech is always the same. It is only the present danger of immediate evil or an intent to bring it about that warrants Congress in setting a limit to the expression of opinion where private rights are not concerned. Congress certainly cannot forbid all effort to change the mind of the country. Now nobody can suppose that the surreptitious publishing of a silly leaflet by an unknown man, without more, would present any immediate danger that its opinions would hinder the success of the government arms or have any appreciable tendency to do so . . . .

. . . .

[T]he ultimate good desired is better reached by free trade in ideas — that the best test of truth is the power of the thought to get itself accepted in the competition of the market, and that truth is the only ground upon which their wishes safely can be carried out. That at any rate is the theory of our Constitution. . . . I think that we should be eternally vigilant against attempts to check the expression of opinions that we loathe and believe to be fraught with death, unless they so imminently threaten immediate interference with the lawful and pressing purposes of the law that an immediate check is required to save the country.

Id. at 630.

For a thoughtful exploration of the First Amendment's protection of freedom of speech, see ANTHONY LEWIS, FREEDOM FOR THE THOUGHT WE HATE: A BIOGRAPHY OF THE FIRST AMENDMENT (2007).

6. Alternative theories of freedom of speech. In the wake of Supreme Court decisions striking down restrictions on advertising alcohol and cigarettes, some public health scholars are developing alternative theories of First Amendment protections that would permit restricting the advertising of dangerous products. Wendy Parmet, for example, argues that freedom of speech is not an absolute, individual right:

[T]o be meaningful, individual autonomy requires the recognition of positive liberty. More generally, individual liberty requires an environment in which individuals face reduced risks so that they can make authentic and meaningful choices about how to live their lives. After all, without population health protection, individuals cannot "develop their faculties," nor are they presented with choices that are meaningful to them . . . .

This idea that freedom of speech must coexist with protection for population health is at times evident in the Supreme Court's own commercial speech cases. Indeed, in the earliest commercial speech cases, such as *Bigelow* and *Virginia Board of Pharmacy*, the state's restriction of speech was likely detrimental to, rather than protective of, population health. In those cases, the Court expanded its protection of commercial speech partially in an effort to assist public health, or at least access to health care . . . .

A population-based approach, however, would alter the way that the Court actually applies the Central Hudson test in two critical ways. First, it would focus the analysis on the impact of speech on populations, rather than on individuals. Courts would thus look more closely at the impact of the regulated speech on different affected populations, rather than solely or even primarily on the speaker. Second, a population approach would take empirical evidence seriously.

WENDY PARMET, POPULATIONS, PUBLIC HEALTH, AND THE LAW 182–183 (2009) (footnotes omitted).

How would you apply "population-level analysis" to cigarette advertising? Parmet offers an example involving advertising high-calorie, low-nutrition food during children's television programming. She argues that the population approach would require the court to "consider the impact of the speech and the regulation on the multiple populations at special risk for the health problem at issue." *Id.* at 183. It would also require recognition that food advertising operates at a population level, altering the environment in ways that individuals cannot control. Although any one individual parent can turn off the television, or even throw it away, short of removing a child from the environment (perhaps the planet), a parent cannot shield him or her from the environmental impact and culture-altering effect of advertising. A typical child, after all, will want to eat what all of his or her peers want to eat even if the child has never seen the commercials that helped to influence the peers. Moreover, the weight of a child's peers may alter the child's sense of what weight is normal. *Id.* at 183–184.

How, if at all, would the result differ from *Central Hudson* analysis? *Central Hudson's* third prong requires the restriction to "directly advance" the government's substantial interest. This ordinarily requires empirical evidence. The *R.J. Reynolds Tobacco Company* decision found that the FDA produced no significant evidence that its regulations would reduce smoking. Empirical evidence that sorts out the specific contribution of advertising fatty foods to childhood weight gain, as opposed to other possible contributing factors, is also difficult to obtain. In the absence of such evidence, Parmet suggests that courts should consider the role that advertising plays in shaping the environment in which children live and recognize that individuals may not be able to make the choices they would prefer in such an environment. *Id.* at 184. Courts have been sympathetic to restrictions on advertising that is directed at children, but rather hostile to restrictions on advertising for adults.

7. **Controversial "public service" advertising.** *AIDS Action Committee of Massachusetts, Inc. v. Massachusetts Bay Transportation Authority*, 42 F.3d 1 (1st Cir. 1994), presented a First Amendment challenge similar to that presented in *Christ's Bride Ministries*, excerpted in Chapter 2, B, *supra*. The MBTA placed seven public service advertisements from AIDS Action Committee on Boston subways and trolleys. The ads showed a color picture of a packaged condom and stated that latex condoms are an effective means of preventing HIV transmission. The ad campaign provoked complaints, one-third of which included "explicit homophobic statements," 42 F.3d at 3, perhaps because the ads included text using double entendres and sexual innuendo. Shortly thereafter, the MBTA issued a new policy that required advertising to meet guidelines "with respect to good taste, decency and community standards as determined by the Authority." The policy described these standards as follows:

> [T]he average person applying contemporary community standards must find that the advertisement, as a whole, does not appeal to a prurient interest. The advertisement must not describe, in a patently offensive way, sexual conduct specifically defined by the applicable state law . . . . Advertising containing messages or graphic representations pertaining to sexual conduct will not be accepted.

Quoted in 42 F.3d at 3-4.

The following year, the MBTA rejected six AIDS Action ~~~~~ violated the new policy. All the ads included text saying~~~~~ Barring abstinence, it's the best way to prevent AIDS. For ~~~~~ HIV and AIDS, call the AIDS Action Committee Hotl~~~ ~~ ~ ~~~-~~~-~~~~." Introducing this text were different headlines: "Haven't you got enough to worry about in bed?"; "Simply having one on hand won't do any good."; "You've got to be putting me on."; "Tell him you don't know how it will ever fit."; "One of these will make you 1/1000th of an inch larger."

The Court of Appeals found that the MBTA's rejection of the ads was content-based, in violation of the First Amendment. The Court said that the policy was not content-neutral because it did not permit sexually explicit words. Although "the MBTA has not opposed expression of the view that the use of condoms is effective in the fight against AIDS," *id.* at 10, the MBTA did discriminate against the AIDS Action ads on the basis of viewpoint. The MBTA had accepted more overtly sexual advertisements for the 1993 movie "Fatal Instinct," which also used sexual innuendo and double entendres and which the court found to be "at least as sexually explicit and/or patently offensive as the AAC ads." *Id.* at 10. It added, "One might easily infer that ads tend to be screened not because they threaten to violate the Policy but because they appear likely to generate controversy or, even more surely, where controversy actually results." *Id.* at 11–12. The Court did not reach the question whether the interiors of subway cars were designated public fora. Whether or not the MBTA could lawfully refuse to accept sexually explicit ads, it could not pick and choose among those it did accept.

Risk behaviors involving sex and drug use are often also behaviors that spark controversy. Public education directed at preventing or avoiding such risks may need to be explicit — and therefore controversial — to reach the target audience. Whether the public education materials present political content or commercial advertising, an analysis of the relevant First Amendment standards is a necessary element of deciding how to communicate. Does that analysis distinguish between advertising that states a risk and advertising that presents a way to prevent the same risk?

———— *Reg is constitutional*

E. EMPLOYMENT AND SHIFTING NORMS ON THE CONCEPT OF "PRIVATE" CONDUCT

CITY OF NORTH MIAMI, FLORIDA v. KURTZ
653 So. 2d 1025 (Fla. 1995), *cert denied*, Kurtz v. City of N. Miami, 516 U.S. 1043 (1996)

OVERTON, JUDGE.

. . . [T]he district court . . . certified . . . the following question as one of great public importance:

DOES ARTICLE I, SECTION 23 OF THE FLORIDA CONSTITUTION PRO-

HIBIT A MUNICIPALITY FROM REQUIRING JOB APPLICANTS TO RE-
FRAIN FROM USING TOBACCO OR TOBACCO PRODUCTS FOR ONE YEAR
BEFORE APPLYING FOR, AND AS A CONDITION FOR BEING CONSID-
ERED FOR EMPLOYMENT, EVEN WHERE THE USE OF TOBACCO IS
NOT RELATED TO JOB FUNCTION IN THE POSITION SOUGHT BY THE
APPLICANT?

. . . .

The record establishes the following unrefuted facts. To reduce costs and to
increase productivity, the City of North Miami adopted an employment policy
designed to reduce the number of employees who smoke tobacco. In accordance
with that policy decision, the City issued Administrative Regulation 1-46, which
requires all job applicants to sign an affidavit stating that they have not used
tobacco or tobacco products for at least one year immediately preceding their
application for employment. The intent of the regulation is to gradually reduce the
number of smokers in the City's work force by means of natural attrition.
Consequently, the regulation only applies to job applicants and does not affect
current employees. Once an applicant has been hired, the applicant is free to start
or resume smoking at any time. Evidence in the record, however, reflects that a high
percentage of smokers who have adhered to the one year cessation requirement are
unlikely to resume smoking.

Additional evidence submitted by the City indicates that each smoking employee
costs the City as much as $4611 per year in 1981 dollars over what it incurs for
non-smoking employees. The City is a self-insurer and its taxpayers pay for 100%
of its employees' medical expenses. In enacting the regulation, the City made a
policy decision to reduce costs and increase productivity by eventually eliminating
a substantial number of smokers from its work force. Evidence presented to the
trial court indicated that the regulation would accomplish these goals.

The respondent in this case, Arlene Kurtz, applied for a clerk-typist position with
the City. When she was interviewed for the position, she was informed of Regulation
1-46. She told the interviewer that she was a smoker and could not truthfully sign
an affidavit to comply with the regulation. The interviewer then informed Kurtz that
she would not be considered for employment until she was smoke-free for one year.
Thereafter, Kurtz filed this action seeking to enjoin enforcement of the regulation
and asking for a declaratory judgment finding the regulation to be unconstitutional.

. . . [T]he trial judge recognized that Kurtz has a fundamental right of privacy
under [the state constitution]. The trial judge noted that Kurtz had presented the
issue in the narrow context of whether she has a right to smoke in her own home.
While he agreed that such a right existed, he concluded that the true issue to be
decided was whether the City, as a governmental entity, could regulate smoking
through employment. Because he found that there is no expectation of privacy in
employment and that the regulation did not violate any provision of either the
Florida or the federal constitutions, summary judgment was granted in favor of the
City.

The Third District Court of Appeal reversed. . . .

Florida's constitutional privacy provision provides as follows:

District Court

> Right of privacy: Every natural person has the right to be let alone and free from governmental intrusion into his private life except as otherwise provided herein. This section shall not be construed to limit the public's right of access to public records and meetings as provided by law.

This right to privacy protects Florida's citizens from the government's uninvited observation of or interference in those areas that fall within the ambit of the zone of privacy afforded under this provision. Unlike the implicit privacy right of the federal constitution, Florida's privacy provision is, in and of itself, a fundamental one that, once implicated, demands evaluation under a compelling state interest standard. The federal privacy provision, on the other hand, extends only to such fundamental interests as marriage, procreation, contraception, family relationships, and the rearing and educating of children.

→ strict scrutiny?

Although Florida's privacy right provides greater protection than the federal constitution, it was not intended to be a guarantee against all intrusion into the life of an individual. First, the privacy provision applies only to government action, and the right provided under that provision is circumscribed and limited by the circumstances in which it is asserted. Further, "[d]etermining 'whether an *individual* has a legitimate expectation of privacy in any given case must be made by considering all the circumstances, especially objective manifestations of that expectation.' " Thus, to determine whether Kurtz, as a job applicant, is entitled to protection . . . we must first determine whether a governmental entity is intruding into an aspect of Kurtz's life in which she has a "legitimate expectation of privacy." If we find in the affirmative, we must then look to whether a compelling interest exists to justify that intrusion and, if so, whether the least intrusive means is being used to accomplish the goal.

Analysis pt. 1

pt. 2

In this case, we find that the City's action does not intrude into an aspect of Kurtz' life in which she has a legitimate expectation of privacy. In today's society, smokers are constantly required to reveal whether they smoke. When individuals are seated in a restaurant, they are asked whether they want a table in a smoking or non-smoking section. When individuals rent hotel or motel rooms, they are asked if they smoke so that management may ensure that certain rooms remain free from the smell of smoke odors. Likewise, when individuals rent cars, they are asked if they smoke so that rental agencies can make proper accommodations to maintain vehicles for non-smokers. Further, employers generally provide smoke-free areas for non-smokers, and employees are often prohibited from smoking in certain areas. Given that individuals must reveal whether they smoke in almost every aspect of life in today's society, we conclude that individuals have no reasonable expectation of privacy in the disclosure of that information when applying for a government job and, consequently, that Florida's right of privacy is not implicated under these unique circumstances.

Is privacy illegal?

In reaching the conclusion that the right to privacy is not implicated in this case, however, we emphasize that our holding is limited to the narrow issue presented. Notably, we are not addressing the issue of whether an applicant, once hired, could be compelled by a government agency to stop smoking. Equally as important, neither are we holding today that a governmental entity can ask any type of information it chooses of prospective job applicants.

↳ holding is very specific to this situation

Having determined that Kurtz has no legitimate expectation of privacy in revealing that she is a smoker under the Florida constitution, we turn now to her claim that the regulation violates her rights under the federal constitution. As noted, the federal constitution's implicit privacy provision extends only to such fundamental interests as marriage, procreation, contraception, family relationships, and the rearing and educating of children. Clearly, the "right to smoke" is not included within the penumbra of fundamental rights protected under that provision . . . . On these facts, the City's policy cannot be deemed so irrational that it may be branded arbitrary. In fact, under the special circumstances supported by the record in this case, we would find that the City has established a compelling interest to support implementation of the regulation. As previously indicated, the record reflects that each smoking employee costs the City as much as $4611 per year in 1981 dollars over what it incurs for non-smoking employees; that, of smokers who have adhered to the one year cessation requirement, a high percentage are unlikely to resume smoking; and that the City is a self-insurer who pays 100% of its employees' medical expenses. We find that the elimination of these costs, when considered in combination with the other special circumstances of this case, validates a compelling interest in the City's policy of gradually eliminating smokers from its work force. We also find that the City is using the least intrusive means in accomplishing this compelling interest because the regulation does not prevent current employees from smoking, it does not affect the present health care benefits of employees, and it gradually reduces the number of smokers through attrition. Thus, we find the regulation to be constitutional under both the federal and Florida constitutions.

For the reasons expressed, we answer the question in the negative, finding that Florida's constitutional privacy provision does not afford the applicant, Arlene Kurtz, protection because she has no reasonable expectation of privacy under the circumstances of this case. Accordingly, we quash the district court's decision, and we remand this case with directions that the district court of appeal affirm the trial court judgment.

. . . .

KOGAN, JUDGE, dissenting.

As the majority itself notes, job applicants are free to return to tobacco use once hired. I believe this concession reveals the anti-smoking policy to be rather more of a speculative pretense than a rational governmental policy. Therefore I would find it unconstitutional under the right of due process.

The privacy issue is more troublesome, to my mind. There is a "slippery-slope" problem here because, if governmental employers can inquire too extensively into off-job-site behavior, a point eventually will be reached at which the right of privacy clearly will be breached. An obvious example would be an inquiry into the lawful sexual behavior of job applicants in an effort to identify those with the "most desirable" lifestyles. Such an effort easily could become the pretext for a constitutional violation. The time has not yet fully passed, for example, when women job applicants have been questioned about their plans for procreation in an effort to eliminate those who may be absent on family leave. I cannot conceive that such an act is anything other than a violation of the right of privacy when done by a governmental unit.

Health-based concerns like those expressed by the City also present a definite slippery slope to the courts. The time is fast approaching, for example, when human beings can be genetically tested so thoroughly that susceptibility to particular diseases can be identified years in advance. To my mind, any governmental effort to identify those who might eventually suffer from cancer or heart disease, for instance, itself is a violation of bodily integrity guaranteed by [the state constitution]. Moreover, I cannot help but note that any such effort comes perilously close to the discredited practice of eugenics.

The use of tobacco products is more troubling, however. While legal, tobacco use nevertheless is an activity increasingly regulated by the law. If the federal government, for instance, chose to regulate tobacco as a controlled substance, I have no trouble saying that this act alone does not undermine anyone's privacy right. However, regulation is not the issue here because tobacco use today remains legal. The sole question is whether the government may inquire into off-job-site behavior that is legal, however unhealthy it might be. In light of the inherently poor fit between the governmental objective and the ends actually achieved, I am more inclined to agree with the district court that the right of privacy has been violated here. I might reach a different result if the objective were better served by the means chosen.

NOTES AND QUESTIONS

1. **Privacy claims.** *Miami v. Kurtz* raises a series of interesting questions and answers only one relatively narrow one: Are there constitutional infirmities in a governmental policy that requires job applicants to refrain from smoking for one year prior to their application? As a matter of federal constitutional law, the answer is clearly no; there is no fundamental or otherwise constitutionally protected interest affected by such a policy and the policy is clearly within the bounds of the "rationality" standard typically applied in such cases. Nor is there, according to the *Miami* court, a violation of Florida state constitutional limits on government action. Nor is this a violation of any federal prohibition on discrimination (*e.g.*, this is not discrimination based on disability).

The court's federal constitutional analysis seems forthrightly to engage the question whether personal *use* of tobacco off the job can be disqualifying for employment. Its treatment of the *state* constitutional claim, however, is somewhat more limited, and seems incomplete. The court treats the state-constitutional "privacy" violation as arising only from the forced *disclosure* of personal tobacco use (Ms. Kurtz is required to "reveal" her usage-status by signing a statement). But is this the question certified for resolution by the district court? (Hint: No). Assume Ms. Kurtz (or another claimant) raised no objection to the disclosure itself, or was "seen" smoking before her job interview, rendering the disclosure unimportant. Couldn't she still argue — wasn't she *in fact* arguing — that the rule, if enforced, violates her state constitutional "privacy" because of its impact on her non-working life, irrespective of the disclosure issue? The state constitutional analysis, unlike the federal one, sheds no light on this question.

Ironically, the Florida cities in *Kurtz* rescinded their hiring policies after they reduced the number of job applicants and failed to lower health insurance premiums. Linda Florea, *St. Cloud Ends Smoke-Free Hiring: The City Found Its No-Tobacco Rule Limited Its Ability to Hire Employees*, SENTINEL (May 24, 2006).

The Scotts Company, a private corporation that provides landscaping services, adopted a policy in 2006 not to hire tobacco users. Scott Rodrigues submitted the required urine sample and was fired when test results were returned positive for nicotine. The court dismissed his state common law claim for wrongful termination, because he was an employee at will, as well as a claim for violation of the Massachusetts Civil Rights Act, without questioning the employer's prerogative to adopt its no-smoker policy. It later dismissed his claim for violation of the state's privacy statute, concluding, "Rodrigues does not have a protected privacy interest in the fact that he is a smoker because he has never attempted to keep that fact private." *Rodrigues v. EG Sys.*, 639 F. Supp. 2d 131, 134 (D. Mass. 2009).

2. From smoke-free to smoker-free workplaces. Banning smoking from workplaces is justified as protecting coworkers and customers from exposure to secondhand smoke. As the number of smoke-free workplaces proliferated and smoking became denormalized, however, employers began to shift from simply banning smoking in the workplace to banning smokers themselves from employment, even when they do not smoke at the workplace. Such workers do not expose coworkers to secondhand smoke. So, what is the reason for not hiring them?

Some entities, like the Department of Defense, local fire departments and athletic teams that need employees to be physically fit, forbid smoking as a legitimate condition of participating in military combat or job performance. Most employers, however, like the Florida cities in *Kurtz*, offer different reasons: they want to encourage good health on the part of their employees; non-smokers are more productive than smokers; and smokers increase health insurance costs because of higher rates of illness. Cost appears to be the most salient motivator. If costs savings do not materialize, will employers drop such policies, as did North Miami? Health care organizations, like the Cleveland Clinic (Ohio's second largest employer) and the World Health Organization, adopted no-smoker hiring policies for more symbolic reasons: smoking is inconsistent with their health-related mission.

Private employers have considerable discretion in their hiring policies. The vast majority of workers in the United States are employees at will, who can be fired for any reason or no reason. (Some states require the employer to show good cause, but usually only in quite limited circumstances.) Collective bargaining units are able to bargain in good faith with employers, but cover a small percentage of employees in the country. National Labor Relations Act, 29 U.S.C. §§ 151 *et seq.*

3. Weighing the pros and cons of no-smoker policies. Houle and Siegel provide a model for research to analyze the advantages and disadvantages of not hiring workers who smoke outside employment. Brian Houle & Michael Siegel, *Smoker-free Workplace Policies: Developing a Model of Public Health Conse-*

quences of Workplace Policies Barring Employment to Smokers, 18 Tobacco Control 64 (2009). On the positive side, workers may stop smoking, improve their health, and retain their jobs and employer-sponsored health insurance. They may also become more productive, although the evidence on productivity is limited so far. On the other hand, employees who are unable or unwilling to quit may or may not find other employment. Those who do not find a new job may suffer the adverse health outcomes, social and economic stresses, and stigma that are associated with lower income and marginalized populations. *Id.* Employers may — or may not — find equally or more qualified employees who do not smoke and may — or may not — reduce their health insurance premiums. *Id.*

Can the model be applied to other kinds of conduct? What other sorts of actions should be considered within the bounds of legal behavior? In what other ways can individuals or groups choose to discriminate, in the broader sense of the term, *i.e.*, distinguish or treat differently smokers and non-smokers? Obviously the government has to stay within constitutional limits, but as outlined in this chapter, those limits allow for a great deal of discretion. Can an employer refuse to hire a non-smoker whose spouse smokes, as Weyco Inc. did? Can a private club exclude smokers? Can I refuse to sell my home to a smoker? Can public or nonprofit agencies provide discretionary services only to nonsmokers? Can universities deny enrollment or financial aid to smokers? The list goes on and on. What is at stake here? How do you measure the benefits of such actions? What are the costs?

4. Discrimination in employment. Employer policies that exclude people who smoke provoke controversy less for their health implications than because of the more general principle they reflect — that employers can prescribe behavior in their employees' private lives. Is there an analogy with employer objections to paying for health insurance coverage of contraception for their employees? *See* Chapter 4, C, *supra*. Where the policy is motivated by cost, it suggests that an employer is entitled to refuse employment to anyone who might increase costs for any reason. Several anti-discrimination laws, including those banning discrimination based on race, color, national origin, religion, sex, age, and disability, are intended to preclude the argument, among others, that employers can make hiring decisions on the basis of employee costs. *See, e.g.*, Civil Rights Act of 1964, 42 U.S.C. §§ 2000e; Americans with Disabilities Act, 42 U.S.C. §§ 12101 *et seq.*; Genetic Information Nondiscrimination Act, P. L. 110-233, 29 U.S.C. § 1182. Of course, such laws do not prohibit discrimination against smokers as a class. But neither would they protect employees who engage in risky activities like NASCAR. The Affordable Care Act requires health insurance coverage regardless of health status or pre-existing conditions, so that premiums cannot be individually rated on the basis of a person's costly medical conditions, such as heart disease, diabetes, and cancers. At the same time, the ACA does permit increased premiums for smokers and older persons, and those who do not participate in employer wellness programs. *See* Chapter 8, B, Note 1. (Massachusetts decided not to permit increased premiums for smokers, in order to encourage them to obtain insurance coverage and use its benefits for smoking cessation programs.)

The following editorial responded to the World Health Organization's announcement that it would no longer hire smokers:

. . . .

With the hanging of the "No Smokers Need Apply" sign on its door, WHO has joined a long line of bigots who would not hire people of color, members of religious minorities, or disabled or gay people because of who they are or what they lawfully do.

To outlaw discriminatory hiring practices, both state and federal governments have passed a series of anti-discrimination laws that all share an underlying basis: The only legitimate job requirements are those that are related to the applicant's ability to do the work, as long as they do not endanger others.

. . . .

Thus, it is one thing to ban smoking in the workplace but quite another to ban employees who smoke away from the workplace. What WHO's new policy says is that it will not hire any member of a group that [smokes] — no matter how well qualified, dedicated and caring they are — because of activities away from the workplace that have no impact on their job performance.

Under WHO's policy, if Franklin Roosevelt, Winston Churchill, Albert Einstein and Adolf Hitler applied for a job, only Hitler, the sole nonsmoker in the group (and someone who would not allow anyone to smoke near him), would be eligible for consideration.

The organization's "principled" stand could, and logically should, be applied to other unhealthful activities. While WHO would be the first to note that smoking is the leading cause of premature deaths, there is no reason this policy should not be applied to the second- and third-leading causes and to various other unhealthful activities in which so many engage. And, of course, if WHO succeeds in eliminating smoking, some other activity will take its place as the number-one cause of premature death. WHO's logical next step in amending its application form is to ask for the height and weight of applicants so it can discard the applications of obese people.

In adopting this policy, WHO is not acting in its capacity as a health care organization but rather as an employer. And the principle that it argues for is that employers can impose job requirements based on what its employees do off the job. One can only imagine WHO's reaction to a tobacco company that requires all its employees to smoke or a gun company that requires them all to keep a gun and ammunition in their homes. The position that WHO has adopted would neatly support such ludicrous employment requirements.

. . . .

Other than the very rich, people must work, and WHO's position is that smokers should not be allowed to work.

. . . .

Leonard Glantz, *Smoke Got In Their Eyes*, Boston Globe B7, December 18, 2005.

Professor Glantz observed that once smokers can be eliminated from employment, employers may then attempt to exclude obese people or people with chronic diseases? Was he alarmist or prescient? *See* Chapter 9, D, *supra*.

Controversy over hiring practices prompted at least 29 states to enact statutes forbidding discrimination in employment on the basis of an employee's lawful activity away from the workplace. Some laws are specific to tobacco use, while others include any lawful activity. *See, e.g.*, Discrimination on Basis of Using Tobacco Products Prohibited, New Hampshire Revised Statutes, Title XXIII, § 275.37a ("No employer shall require as a condition of employment that any employee or applicant for employment abstain from using tobacco products outside the course of employment, as long as the employee complies with any workplace policy"); State Policy Against Discrimination, North Dakota Century Code, title 14, ch. 14-02.4-01 ("lawful activity off the employer's premises during nonworking hours which is not in direct conflict with the essential business-related interests of the employer").

5. Smoking and medical care. Not very many decades ago, a significant number of physicians smoked cigarettes. Today medical school graduates might find it difficult to be accepted into a medical residency if they use tobacco. Concerns about the health risks of tobacco have also influenced medical criteria for certain therapies for patients. A news story out of England, for example, reported that the National Health Service declined to treat a man's broken ankle as long as he smoked cigarettes, citing tobacco's effects of delaying wound healing. Chris Brooke, *Doctors Refuse to Fix Builder's Broken Ankle Unless He Stops Smoking*, The Daily Mail, Sept. 13, 2007. In Scotland, the NHS reportedly decided to deny NHS-funded in vitro fertilization (IVF) services to any family in which both spouses smoke. David Scott, *Fat Smokers Banned from Trying for Test Tube Babies*, Scottish Express, Sept. 12, 2012, http://www.express.co.uk/news/uk/347527/Fat-smokers-banned-from-trying-for-test-tube-babies (visited Feb. 2014). (Women with a BMI of 30 or above are also excluded.) Smokers' rights organizations objected, arguing that they have already paid taxes into the system for the right to treatment. *Id.* Is this an example of reserving services to those who are most likely to benefit, reducing program costs, or discrimination against persons who smoke (or are obese)?

F. LITIGATION AND PUBLIC POLICY CONCERNING SMOKING AND TOBACCO USE

EVANS v. LORILLARD TOBACCO CO.
990 N.E.2d 997 (Mass. 2013)

Gants, J.

Marie R. Evans (Marie) died in 2002, at the age of fifty-four, from small cell lung cancer caused by smoking cigarettes. A jury found that the defendant, Lorillard

Tobacco Company (Lorillard), the designer and manufacturer of Newport brand cigarettes, caused her wrongful death based on various theories of liability: breach of the implied warranty of merchantability because of design defect and inadequate warning of Newport cigarettes' health hazards and addictive properties; negligence in the design, marketing, or distribution of Newport cigarettes; negligent distribution by giving free samples of Newport cigarettes to minors; and negligent performance of a duty Lorillard voluntarily undertook in 1954 to research the health hazards of smoking and disclose accurate information regarding the results of that research to the smoking public. As to the negligence claims, the jury found Marie also to be negligent, and apportioned thirty per cent of the comparative negligence to her. The jury awarded $21 million to her son, Willie Evans (plaintiff), for the loss of his mother's companionship, comfort, and counsel; and $50 million to Marie's estate for her conscious pain and suffering. The jury also found that Lorillard was grossly negligent and acted in a manner that was malicious, wilful, wanton, or reckless, and awarded punitive damages in the amount of $81 million. The judge found that Lorillard had violated G. L. c. 93A, § 2 [the state consumer fraud statute], but did not award any additional compensatory or punitive damages for its violation, finding that any further award of damages would be "duplicative" of the jury's award.

Following trial . . . [t]he judge [allowed Lorillard's motion remittitur in part], reducing the amount of compensatory damages to the plaintiff to $10 million, and to Marie's estate to $25 million, but denying any remittitur as to punitive damages. The plaintiff accepted the remittitur, Lorillard appealed from the judgment, and we granted the plaintiff's application for direct appellate review.

. . . .

Background. Because Lorillard contends that the evidence is insufficient as a matter of law to sustain the jury's verdict, we summarize the evidence at trial in the light most favorable to the plaintiff . . . .

1. Marie's smoking history. In 1960, when Marie was thirteen years old, she began smoking Newport cigarettes. She started smoking cigarettes because she saw other people smoking "and they looked attractive doing it," and because "[i]t made you grown up, made you feel like an adult." She testified that, when she was a child, "there would be campaigns going on for Newport"; they had "free giveaways" of cigarettes after school in a playground in the Orchard Park neighborhood of the Roxbury section of Boston, where she grew up. "So I would stand out there and get free cigarettes. That's how I started smoking." The "free giveaways" occurred "quite a bit; maybe about fifty times." She smoked Newport cigarettes because she "had free access to them," "[t]hey were pretty packaged," and "[t]hey were always available." Marie testified that, at least in the early years of her smoking, she felt that she received certain benefits from cigarette smoking: she enjoyed the taste and aroma of the cigarette, smoking helped her relieve stress and anxiety, smoking helped keep her alert, smoking helped her keep her weight under control, and smoking helped her fit in socially with her friends.

When she was a child and teenager, she heard people refer to cigarette smoking as an addiction. She remembered the 1964 United States Surgeon General's report describing cigarette smoking as habit forming and as a cause of lung cancer.

manufacturer, or even considered for commercial use, at the time of sale." Third Restatement, § 2 comment d.

A broad range of factors may be considered in determining whether an alternative design is reasonable *and* whether its omission renders a product not reasonably safe. The factors include, among others, the magnitude and probability of the foreseeable risks of harm[;] the instructions and warnings accompanying the product[;] the nature and strength of consumer expectations regarding the product, including expectations arising from product portrayal and marketing[;] [t]he relative advantages and disadvantages of the product as designed and as it alternatively could have been designed[;] the likely effects of the alternative design on production costs; the effects of the alternative design on product longevity, maintenance, repair, and esthetics; and the range of consumer choice among products . . . .

Third Restatement, § 2 comment f.

While consumer expectations may be considered in the risk-utility balancing, the Third Restatement makes it clear that, in sharp contrast with the Second Restatement, "consumer expectations do not play a determinative role in determining defectiveness." Third Restatement, § 2 comment g. "The mere fact that a risk presented by a product design is open and obvious, or generally known, and that the product thus satisfies expectations, does not prevent a finding that the design is defective." *Id.* Thus, the Third Restatement recognizes the possibility that a product may be made significantly safer through a reasonable alternative design even when consumers, unaware of the alternative design, expect the product to be no safer than it is.

[handwritten margin note: Just b/c you know it's danger ≠ not defective]

[handwritten margin note: Holding]

The vast majority of States have adopted the risk-utility balancing test of the Third Restatement rather than the consumer expectations test of the Second Restatement. . . .

. . . Since 1978, we have . . . recognized that the determination whether a product is unreasonably dangerous depends on many factors, including "the gravity of the danger posed by the challenged design, the likelihood that such danger would occur, the mechanical feasibility of a safer alternative design, the financial cost of an improved design, and the adverse consequences to the product and to the consumer that would result from an alternative design." And since 1978 we have recognized that a product may be found unreasonably dangerous even where all the products in the industry were designed with the alleged defect and where the product conformed to all safety standards in the industry. In short, in determining whether a product's design is unreasonably dangerous, we have been applying a risk-utility balancing standard, where consumer expectations are a factor but not necessarily the determinative factor, since well before the Third Restatement articulated this liability standard.

. . . .

Therefore, the judge did not err in instructing the jury that they "may," rather than that they "must," consider whether Newport cigarettes met consumers' reasonable expectations as to safety. And because reasonable consumer expectations are simply one of many factors that may be considered and not necessarily the determinative factor, the plaintiff was not obligated to prove that Newport cigarettes were more dangerous than consumers reasonably expected.

b. Reasonable alternative design of a cigarette. "To establish a prima facie case of defect, the plaintiff must prove the availability of a technologically feasible and practical alternative design that would have reduced or prevented the plaintiff's harm." Third Restatement, § 2 comment f.

The plaintiff presented evidence at trial that cigarettes are a highly engineered product, that the defendant manipulated its product to give the smoker a particular dose of tar and nicotine, that an addictive level of nicotine was approximately 0.4 to 0.5 milligrams of nicotine per cigarette, and that Lorillard never sold a cigarette with nicotine levels at or below 0.4 milligrams per cigarette. Dr. Farone testified that there are "some [fifty-seven] or [fifty-eight] different things that one takes into account in designing a cigarette to deliver a certain amount of tar and a certain amount of nicotine." The plaintiff proposed as a reasonable alternative a cigarette without menthol where the carcinogens in the tar are at a level that was relatively safe and where the level of nicotine is nonaddictive. Dr. Farone testified that this could be accomplished by using a "filter that has a very, very high efficiency" and perforating the filter with holes "such that when you suck on it or draw on it, very little smoke comes out," or by using "expanded tobacco," which is tobacco which has had the nicotine removed and which has become very light "so when you burn it, you have very little tar." To avoid the complete loss of flavor, Dr. Farone testified that a cigarette manufacturer such as Lorillard could put a flavor on the filter, "so when the air draws back in you get that flavor." He noted that, to design a cigarette with a nonaddictive level of nicotine, "you have to get virtually all of it out" to avoid the risk that smokers will become addicted to the remaining nicotine, and maintain or increase their risk of cancer by puffing harder or smoking more cigarettes.

There was abundant evidence that this alternative was technologically feasible. . . .

There was also evidence that a safer alternative cigarette was feasible as to cost. According to a 1977 Lorillard memorandum, the manufacturing costs for a hypothesized Lorillard cigarette with "ultra-low tar" and 0.35 milligrams of nicotine per cigarette would be higher than usual, but "these costs [would] be more than offset by the reduction in the amount of tobacco used."

Lorillard, however, contends that, even if a low tar, low nicotine cigarette were a technologically feasible alternative design that could be produced at comparable cost, it was not a reasonable alternative design because "carcinogenic levels of tar and addictive levels of nicotine . . . are inherent in all ordinary cigarettes," and the "inherent risks of smoking . . . cannot be removed without fundamentally altering the nature of the product." The jury rejected this argument through their verdict . . . .

Having failed to persuade the jury, Lorillard contends on appeal that the evidence at trial was insufficient as a matter of law to support a finding of a reasonable alternative design. It essentially makes two arguments. First, it contends that the alternative design proffered at trial was not truly a cigarette, and that the jury essentially found that all cigarettes were defective, thereby imposing categorical product liability on all cigarettes. We agree with Lorillard that, in a case where the allegedly defective product is a cigarette, the reasonable alternative design must also be a cigarette, and that a jury may not impose categorical liability on all cigarettes. But the evidence was more than sufficient to permit a reasonable jury to conclude that the alternative design proffered by the plaintiff was a cigarette, especially where the plaintiff's experts identified brands of cigarettes that implement the alternative design that have long been sold commercially as cigarettes. . . .

Second, Lorillard contends that, even if the alternative design proffered by the plaintiff were a cigarette, the reduced tar and nicotine in that alternative cigarette so fundamentally alters the nature of the product that no reasonable jury could find that it was a reasonable alternative to Newport cigarettes . . . . Here, Lorillard's claim that all "ordinary cigarettes" have the same design flaws alleged by the plaintiff does not protect Lorillard from liability, and the judge did not err in refusing to instruct the jury that the plaintiff had to prove that a defect was present in Lorillard's cigarettes that was not present in other cigarettes on the market.

The essential question is not whether the safer alternative design is an "ordinary cigarette" but whether adoption of the safer alternative design would result in undue interference with the cost or performance of the product, thereby making the alternative unreasonable. Whether any interference with the cost or performance of the product is "undue" is generally a question for the jury, because many safer alternatives may increase the cost of a product or interfere to some degree with its performance, such as where the addition of a safety shield to a machine tool makes it both more expensive and harder and slower to operate. But the question becomes one of law where, viewing the evidence in the light most favorable to the plaintiff, the interference with the cost or performance of the product is so substantial that no reasonable jury could conclude that it offers a reasonable alternative to consumers of the product. For example, an automobile is not a reasonable alternative to a motorcycle, even if it were proven safer, solely because it has four wheels rather than two. To add two wheels to a motorcycle would create a fundamentally different product and destroy the product's distinct utility in the eyes of any potential consumer.

Lorillard contends that the safer alternative cigarette proffered by the plaintiff is not a reasonable alternative as a matter of law because, as the plaintiff's experts conceded at trial, "ordinary smokers" — meaning smokers who are addicted to the nicotine in tobacco — will not smoke cigarettes that will not provide them with the nicotine they crave to satiate their addiction, which is why the alternative cigarettes that are commercially sold have a small share of the market. Before we address this argument, we look first to the expert testimony offered at trial regarding what motivates people to smoke. Drs. Benowitz and Cummings testified that those who start smoking do so for social reasons, not for nicotine. Dr. Cummings noted that, at first, "[m]ost people get a little light-headed, they may even get nauseous, and you overcome that usually because your friends are" smoking. He added that when people start to smoke, they are freely making a choice to smoke, and the choice, especially for teenagers, is usually for "psychosocial reasons." However, once one goes beyond the experimentation phase and "you get into the daily use pattern, your choice to smoke becomes diminished by the physiological effects of nicotine on your brain . . . . It's the daily use pattern . . . that distinguishes somebody . . . smoking for nicotine from somebody who is not smoking for nicotine." Dr. Benowitz testified that, with continued exposure to nicotine, "smoking changes from social smoking to drug-reinforced smoking or to pharmacologic smoking." Once people become regular, daily smokers, what keeps them smoking is nicotine addiction. The evidence at trial was that Lorillard manipulated the level of nicotine in its cigarettes to ensure that those who smoked would continue to be addicted to nicotine. The evidence at trial also showed that the addiction produced by "ordinary" levels of nicotine in cigarettes is so powerful that, in a given year, approximately seventy per cent of cigarette smokers want to stop smoking, but only approximately one-half of those who wish to quit will attempt to quit and, of those who attempt to quit, only approximately three per cent will succeed.

Therefore, the evidence at trial would adequately support a finding that a cigarette with low tar and nicotine was a reasonable alternative to an individual who retained the unimpaired ability to make a rational, informed choice whether to smoke, such as an individual who was considering whether to start smoking or an individual who smoked infrequently or in small quantities. However, the plaintiff's proposed alternative cigarette was not a reasonable alternative to one who already was addicted to nicotine, whose freedom of choice was physiologically impaired by the effects of the nicotine. In short, the evidence in this case is sufficient to support a finding that low tar, low nicotine cigarettes are a safer, reasonable alternative design to the design used by Lorillard in their Newport cigarettes for the subclass of cigarette consumers who are not yet addicted but is not sufficient to support a finding that such cigarettes are a reasonable alternative for the subclass of consumers who are already addicted.

The question, then, is which subclass of consumers should be considered in evaluating the reasonableness of the alternative design? Lorillard's argument, stripped to its essence, is that the chemical in a product that causes consumers to be powerfully addicted to the product can never be found to constitute an unreasonably dangerous defect because no alternative design that did not contain addictive levels of the chemical will satisfy addicts' craving for the chemical and therefore be purchased by those addicted. If this argument were to prevail, addictive chemicals would be the only substance whose presence in a product could not, as a matter of law, be found to constitute a defect in the product's design, because there could be no reasonable alternative design that did not include them. And the more powerfully addictive the chemical, the more it would be protected from product liability.

We decline to place addictive chemicals outside the reach of product liability and give them special protection akin to immunity based solely on the strength of their addictive qualities. To do so would eliminate any incentive for cigarette manufacturers to make safer perhaps the most dangerous product lawfully sold in the market through reasonable alternative designs. Rather, we conclude that, in determining as a matter of law whether the evidence presented at trial was sufficient for a reasonable jury to conclude that the plaintiff's proposed design was a reasonable alternative to the defendant's product, we must determine whether the design alternative unduly interfered with the performance of the product from the perspective of a rational, informed consumer, whose freedom of choice is not substantially impaired by addiction. Applying that standard to the evidence in this case, we conclude that a reasonable jury could find from the evidence presented that a low tar, low nicotine cigarette constituted a safer reasonable alternative to Lorillard's Newport cigarettes.

Few courts appear to have addressed this question, perhaps because the only legally sold product so addictive as to raise the question is nicotine, and the courts that have done so provide little relevant guidance. The United States Court of Appeals for the Seventh Circuit, in evaluating whether "the average consumer at the time in question" fully appreciated the health risks of smoking, recognized that it needed to "define this imaginary 'average consumer.'" *Insolia v. Philip Morris Inc.*, 216 F.3d 596, 599 (7th Cir. 2000). Recognizing "[n]icotine's addictive grip," the court concluded that "the state of knowledge of the average consumer must be measured before the average person is hooked and is no longer capable of making a rational choice."

. . . .

Because cigarettes are unique among lawfully sold products in being so powerfully addictive, it is doubtful that our ruling requiring a reasonable alternative design to be evaluated through the eyes of a rational, informed consumer, whose freedom of choice is not substantially impaired by addiction, will have any significant consequence on liability actions involving any other product. In *Haglund* [*v. Philip Morris Inc.*, 446 Mass. 741 (2006)], we recognized that cigarettes are unusual in that any reasonable use of the product is foreclosed by the dual risks of serious disease and addiction, and we therefore barred cigarette manufacturers in most circumstances from offering as a defense in a product liability action the plaintiff's unreasonable use of cigarettes, the so-called *Correia* defense. *See Correia v. Firestone Tire & Rubber Co.*, 388 Mass. 342, 446 N.E.2d 1033 (1983). Just as we needed in *Haglund* to adapt our product liability jurisprudence to the inherent danger of smoking, so too do we need here to adapt our product liability jurisprudence to the inherent addictive potency of certain cigarettes. And just as the defendants in that case argued that we had eviscerated the *Correia* defense, so too does the defendant here contend that we will be paving the way for product liability claims that nonalcoholic whiskey and beer are reasonable alternatives to whiskey and beer. Such fears are wholly unwarranted. In contrast with cigarette smokers, the vast majority of whiskey and beer drinkers are not addicted to alcohol, so limiting the risk-utility evaluation of a reasonable alternative design to the perspective of rational, informed consumers of these products would have no bearing on the risk of product liability for these beverages.

Finally, even though the evidence was essentially undisputed that the tar and nicotine in Newport brand cigarettes caused Marie's lung cancer, Lorillard argues that no reasonable jury could have found that any design defect in Newport cigarettes caused her death because the evidence at trial was that she tried and rejected a brand of cigarettes with lower tar and nicotine. In making this argument, Lorillard misunderstands the meaning of causation in products liability. Where a plaintiff proves that a product is defective, she may establish causation by proving that the defect caused her injury; the plaintiff need not prove that she would have used a reasonable alternative design had one been available.

Here, the plaintiff submitted sufficient evidence for a reasonable jury to conclude that the combined effect of the nicotine and tar consumed by smokers of Lorillard's Newport cigarettes was a substantial factor in bringing about Marie's addiction, lung cancer, and wrongful death, and that her injury would have been reduced or avoided had she smoked cigarettes with a reasonable alternative design that would have resulted in a nonaddictive level of nicotine and a reasonably safe level of carcinogenic tar being consumed by the smoker. Lorillard does not escape liability for its defective product simply because an addicted smoker continued to use a product that sated her addiction rather than switch to a safer product that would not do so.

c. Warning defect for the period before 1970. As noted earlier, the jury found that Lorillard violated the implied warranty of merchantability not only because of a design defect, but also because of a warning defect arising from its failure to provide Marie an adequate warning of the health hazards or addictive properties of Newport cigarettes before 1970. Lorillard contends that the evidence was insufficient as a matter of law to support this finding because the risks of smoking were widely reported before Marie started smoking in 1960 and there is no common-law duty to warn of a known or an obvious risk.

"Even if a product is properly designed, it is unreasonably dangerous and, therefore, it is not fit for the purposes for which such goods are used, if foreseeable users are not adequately warned of dangers associated with its use." *Hayes v. Ariens Co.*, 391 Mass. 407, 413, 462 N.E.2d 273 (1984). "However, we have recognized that, 'where the danger presented by a given product is obvious, no duty to warn [exists] because a warning will not reduce the likelihood of injury.'" *Bavuso v. Caterpillar Indus., Inc.*, 408 Mass. 694, 699, 563 N.E.2d 198 (1990). This is consistent with the Third Restatement, which provides, in § 2 comment j: "In general, a product seller is not subject to liability for failing to warn or instruct regarding risks and risk-avoidance measures that should be obvious to, or generally known by, foreseeable product users."

Marie began to smoke in 1960. In 1965, the United States Congress enacted the Federal Cigarette Labeling and Advertising Act (Labeling Act), which required all cigarette packages to bear the warning, "Caution: Cigarette Smoking May Be Hazardous to Your Health." Before this requirement took effect in 1966, there were no warnings on retail packages of Newport cigarettes, on free sample packages of Newport cigarettes, or in any advertising materials for Newport cigarettes. Marie testified that she remembered seeing the warning when it first appeared on cigarette packages.

In 1967, the Federal Trade Commission (FTC) issued a report stating that the warning label on cigarette packages had "not succeeded in overcoming the prevalent attitude toward cigarette smoking created and maintained by the cigarette companies through their advertisements, particularly the barrage of commercials on television, which portray smoking as a harmless and enjoyable social activity that is not habit forming and involves no hazards to health." The report concluded that "[c]igarette commercials continue to appeal to youth and continue to blot out any consciousness of the health hazards." In 1970, Congress amended the mandated warning label on cigarette packages to state: "Warning: The Surgeon General Has Determined That Cigarette Smoking Is Dangerous To Your Health," with the warning becoming effective on November 1, 1970. Public Health Cigarette Smoking Act of 1969. The 1969 Act also declared that, apart from this warning, "[n]o requirement or prohibition based on smoking and health shall be imposed under State law with respect to the advertising or promotion of any cigarettes." Because the 1969 Act preempts any State law claim imposing liability based on a showing that a cigarette manufacturer's "post-1969 advertising or promotions should have included additional, or more clearly stated, warnings," *Cipollone v. Liggett Group, Inc.*, 505 U.S. 504, 524 (1992), the plaintiff limited the failure to warn claims to the period ending in 1969.

Viewing the evidence in the light most favorable to the plaintiff, we conclude that a reasonable jury could find that the risks of cigarette smoking were certainly not obvious before 1966, when the warning on cigarette packages ordered by Congress provided only that "cigarette smoking *may* be hazardous to your health", and were still not obvious before 1970, when the warning was stiffened to declare that "the Surgeon General has determined that cigarette smoking *is* dangerous to your health" (emphases added). As the United States Court of Appeals for the Sixth Circuit declared in *Tompkin v. American Brands*, 219 F.3d 566, 572 (6th Cir. 2000):

> "The pertinent issue here is not whether the public knew that smoking was hazardous to health at some undifferentiated level, but whether it knew of the specific linkages between smoking and lung cancer. Public awareness of a broad-based and ambiguous risk that smoking might be tenuously connected to lung cancer does not suggest 'common knowledge' of the known scientific fact that cigarette smoking is a strong precipitant of lung cancer . . . . It is one thing to be aware generally that a product might have an attenuated and theoretical connection with a deadly disease like lung cancer; it is another altogether to comprehend that it is the cause of an overwhelming majority of lung cancer cases . . . .

While the general public may have understood before 1970 that cigarettes posed a general risk to health, the plaintiff presented considerable evidence that Lorillard, along with other cigarette manufacturers, engaged in a calculated effort through advertising and public statements to raise doubts whether the causative link between cigarettes and cancer was scientifically proven, and that the FTC in 1967 acknowledged the success of these efforts. In fact, Lorillard has a bit of chutzpah to claim that it was obvious to the general public by 1960 that cigarettes were addictive and caused cancer when, in 1994, during sworn testimony before a congressional subcommittee, Andrew H. Tisch, Lorillard's chairman and chief executive officer, declared that he did not believe that cigarette smoking was addictive or caused cancer.

. . . Viewing the evidence in the light most favorable to the plaintiff, a reasonable jury could conclude that Marie was not aware of the health risks of smoking when she started to smoke in 1960 at the age of thirteen and that, in 1964 when she became aware of the publicity surrounding the Surgeon General's report, she did not appreciate the danger of smoking Lorillard's Newport cigarettes to the same extent as a warning would have provided. . . .

Finally, Lorillard argues that there was no evidence that its failure to warn of the foreseeable dangers arising from the use of Newport cigarettes caused Marie's injury because she did not heed the warnings placed on Lorillard's cigarette packages since 1966. We are not persuaded by this argument. In Massachusetts, "[t]he law permits an inference that a warning, once given, would have been followed." Once a plaintiff establishes that a warning should have been given, the burden is on "the defendants to come forward with evidence tending to rebut such an inference." There was substantial evidence that, by 1966, Marie was addicted to cigarettes. Evidence that an addicted smoker failed to heed a warning that was given to her after she was already addicted is insufficient to rebut the presumption that, had she received adequate warning before she started smoking, she would have heeded the warning and avoided the addiction.

In conclusion, the jury were appropriately instructed as to both a design defect and a warning defect and, although we do not know whether the jury found causation as to one or both defects, the evidence was sufficient to support the jury's finding on either theory.

2. Negligence. The jury found that Lorillard was "negligent in the design, marketing and/or distribution of Newport cigarettes," that Lorillard was "negligent in failing to warn Marie Evans of the health hazards and/or addictive properties of Newport cigarettes at any time prior to 1970," and that Lorillard "negligently distribute[d] Newport cigarettes by giving samples of such cigarettes to minors, including Marie Evans." However, as with breach of the implied warranty, the jury were not asked to find causation as to each theory of negligence but instead were asked whether "any negligence" of Lorillard was "a substantial factor in causing Marie Evans's lung cancer." Therefore, because we cannot know on which theory or theories the jury found causation, the jury's finding of liability for negligence may stand only if the jury were correctly and adequately instructed on each theory of negligence.

As to negligent design, the judge instructed the jury that they "may" but were "not required to consider whether there was a safer alternative design available." This instruction was timely objected to by the defendant at trial and constituted prejudicial error. In claims alleging negligence in the design of a product, as with claims of a design defect . . . , the plaintiff must show "an available design modification which would reduce the risk without undue cost or interference with the performance of the [product]," and the jury must consider whether a safer alternative design was available in deciding whether the defendant was negligent for failing to adopt that design. Therefore, we conclude that the jury were incorrectly instructed on the law regarding the plaintiff's claim of negligent design.

As to negligent marketing, the judge provided the jury with no guidance as to the duty a cigarette manufacturer would owe in the marketing of its products, which, if breached, could give rise to a cognizable claim of negligence. Presumably, the plaintiff's theory of negligent marketing was that Lorillard had marketed cigarettes to minors when Marie was a minor, because the plaintiff offered evidence to support this claim. But the plaintiff also offered substantial evidence that Lorillard marketed its Newport cigarettes to African-American adults. Some of this evidence may have been relevant to show that Lorillard marketed its products to African-

American children at a time when Marie, who was African-American, was a child, but the jury were not limited in the use of this evidence. Lorillard timely objected to the imprecise marketing instruction and asked that it be limited to the "give-aways" of cigarettes when Marie was a minor, but the jury were not instructed as to any limitation.

We conclude that the absence of guidance as to the meaning of negligent marketing and of any limitation as to its scope was prejudicial because we cannot know what marketing duty the jury found Lorillard to have breached. Specifically, we cannot know whether the jury found that Lorillard engaged in negligent marketing by targeting African-American adults, which would not constitute a breach of any legal duty.

Where we cannot ascertain on which theory the jury relied in finding causation, the jury's finding of liability as to negligence cannot stand. Therefore, we must vacate the jury's finding of liability for wrongful death based on the theory of negligence because we conclude that the jury were incorrectly instructed as to negligent design and inadequately instructed as to negligent marketing.

. . . .

4. Punitive damages. Because we have vacated the finding of negligence liability . . . , we must also vacate the jury's findings that Lorillard was grossly negligent and that Lorillard acted in a manner that was malicious, willful, wanton, or reckless. We cannot be confident that the jury's findings on these issues were untainted by the aforementioned errors. Consequently, we must also vacate the jury's award of punitive damages for wrongful death under G. L. c. 229, § 2.

. . . .

7. Compensatory damages. The defendant contends that the award of compensatory damages, even after being reduced by the remittitur, was excessive.

The judge granted Lorillard's motion for remittitur in part, finding that, "[g]iven the extent of [Marie's] pain, suffering and death," a compensatory award of $25 million for Marie's conscious pain and suffering would be "appropriate, reasonable and just," and that "the largest reasonable compensatory award for [the plaintiff's] significant loss is $10 million." "[A]n award of damages must stand unless to make it or to permit it to stand was an abuse of discretion on the part of the court below, amounting to an error of law." We find no abuse of discretion; the judge's remittitur award was not disproportionate to the injuries suffered and did not represent a miscarriage of justice.

. . . .

Conclusion. We affirm the jury's finding of liability on the claim of wrongful death caused by breach of the implied warranty of merchantability, and affirm the award of compensatory damages, as reduced by the remittitur. . . . We vacate the jury's findings as to the claim of wrongful death on the theory of negligence and their findings that Lorillard was grossly negligent and acted in a manner that was malicious, wilful, wanton, or reckless, and therefore vacate the jury's award of punitive damages. We remand the case for a new trial on the issue whether Lorillard is liable for any conduct that would give rise to punitive damages under G. L. c. 229,

§ 2, and if so, the amount of punitive damages that should be awarded. We vacate the judge's finding of liability on plaintiff's claim that Lorillard violated G. L. c. 93A and remand the case to the judge for further action consistent with this opinion.

[Note: In October 2013, the parties in *Evans* settled the suit for $79 million, representing $35 million in compensatory damages plus interest.]

NOTES AND QUESTIONS

1. **Preemption and early litigation on behalf of smokers.** Private lawsuits by smokers claiming that they have been injured by smoking tobacco products have been based on a variety of theories. Prior to the 1990s, virtually all such efforts were unsuccessful, either because of a failure to prove causation or due to some variation on the argument that "everybody knows smoking is unhealthy and anyone who smokes is choosing to accept the consequent risks."

In *Cipollone v. Liggett Group*, 505 U.S. 504 (1992), a plurality of the Supreme Court addressed the preemptive impact of the FCLAA and other federal laws on smokers' state-law-based claims against tobacco companies. The Court found that the 1964 federal legislation preempted state legislation and regulations imposing additional or different "warnings" from those required by the federal law, but did not preempt private litigation based on state common law theories. The FCLAA was amended by the Public Health Cigarette Smoking Act of 1969, which, in addition to strengthening the federal warnings, preempted many private common law claims as well: "No requirement or prohibition based on smoking and health shall be imposed under State law with respect to the advertising or promotion of any cigarettes the packages of which are labeled in conformity with the provisions of this [Act]." 15 U.S.C. § 1334(b). A plurality of the *Cipollone* court found that the 1969 Act preempts state common law causes of action, such as failure to warn, that claim that the manufacturers should have provided additional or different warnings to the public or the claimant or minimized the health risks of smoking. 505 U.S. at 524. This prevented smokers and their estates from pursuing state claims that warnings issued after 1969 (when the Act became effective) were inadequate.

Cipollone did not preclude all state claims, however. The plurality opinion indicated that claims based on express warranties, fraudulent misrepresentation or concealment, unfair and deceptive trade practices, and product defects are not preempted where they are unrelated to advertising and promotion. The Supreme Court confirmed this interpretation in *Altria Group, Inc. v. Good*, 555 U.S. 70 (2008), allowing a claim that the cigarette company violated Maine's Unfair Trade Practices Act by fraudulent advertising indicating that its "light" cigarettes deliver less tar and nicotine than regular brands. This state statutory claim was not preempted, because it was based on a manufacturer's duty not to deceive, and not on any duty "based on smoking and health."

After *Cipollone*, private litigants began to meet with occasional success, at least where they were seeking damages for injuries prior to 1969. *See, e.g., Burton v. R.J. Reynolds Tobacco Co.*, 397 F.3d 906 (10th Cir. 2005). Also pivotal were the revelations in the 1990s that smoking was, in fact, far more dangerous than had been previously believed and that the nicotine levels in cigarettes were being adjusted by the tobacco manufacturers, despite claims to the contrary. In 1994, Lorillard's chairman and CEO, Andrew H. Tisch, testified before a congressional hearing that he did not believe that cigarettes were addictive or caused cancer. The discovery process in the *Cipollone* litigation revealed that the industry had known some of the harms from smoking for many years. Public and political attention was particularly galvanized when a Congressman released documents that a former employee of Brown & Williamson, a British-American tobacco company, had stolen from his employer, revealing that the tobacco companies' knowledge of the enhanced risks of smoking and of the addictive properties of nicotine was far more extensive than they had claimed — even in their courtroom statements. The results were devastating to the tobacco companies' public and judicial standing.

The "Brown & Williamson documents" have been used in subsequent lawsuits. To view the documents and related papers, see www.library.ucsf.edu/tobacco (visited Feb. 2014). For information on tobacco litigation before 2011, see www.nolo.com/legal-encyclopedia/tobacco-litigation-history-and-development-32202.html (visited Feb. 2014). For litigation involving exposure to second hand smoke, see http://smokelitigation.org/ (visited Feb. 2014).

2. Products liability and negligence. *Evans* presents a more far-reaching view of the causes of action available to smokers today — one that could threaten the cigarette industry itself. The decision offers a nice overview of the different requirements for claims in negligence and products liability. (A quirk of Massachusetts law subsumes products liability claims under the concept of warranty of merchantability, more commonly viewed as a contractual undertaking, but nonetheless explains the elements consistently with most jurisdictions — with a few added twists, discussed below.)

Products liability causes of action allow persons who are injured by a defective product to seek compensation in the form of damages. Claims can address three categories of product defects: manufacturing defects; design defects; and defects in warnings or instructions. Manufacturing defects are defects in the product arising out of the manufacturing process; the product that emerges is not what the manufacturer intended in every respect. Such defects are relatively rare and have not been at issue in tobacco litigation. Products with inherent risks can be considered defective if not accompanied by adequate warnings or instructions for use. However, risks that are obvious or common knowledge do not require express warnings. (Hence the tobacco industry's arguments that the health risks of cigarettes were common knowledge.) Claims of defective warnings — or failure to warn — have been preempted for post-1969 labeling and advertising, at least where the claimant argues that a company should have warned of a health risk from smoking.

Design defect claims challenge products that are properly manufactured, just as the manufacturer intended, but "unreasonably dangerous" in ways that cannot be overcome by proper warnings. Here, the challenge to the claimant is to establish that an alternative design — product specifications — would pose fewer risks without undermining the product's function. Like the *Evans* court, most states refer to the Restatements in discussions of products liability law. Section 402(a) of the

RESTATEMENT (SECOND) OF TORTS provided a basis for relatively consistent doctrine concerning inherently dangerous products for many years. Its successor, section 2 of the RESTATEMENT (THIRD) OF TORTS: PRODUCTS LIABILITY, describes a somewhat more demanding burden for claimants to shoulder — the risk-utility balancing test. Consider how the *Evans* court uses aspects of both Restatements to determine whether cigarettes are unreasonably dangerous.

In theory, products liability differs from negligence in that it focuses on the characteristics of the product (whether it is defective), rather than on the duty or conduct of the manufacturer. Products liability eliminated the requirement of privity, enabling consumers to sue the manufacturer of a product directly. In practice, however, the distinction between products liability and negligence is not so clear, especially in cases based on design defects. This is because a claimant must demonstrate that a manufacturer could have used a different, safer design — a claim that entails examining the manufacturer's conduct. For a discussion of the similarities and differences, see Alani Golanski, *Paradigm Shifts in Products Liability and Negligence*, 71 U. PITT. L. REV. 673 (2010). In negligence actions, the claimant may have to prove that the manufacturer actually knew that a safer design could be produced. In many states, the products liability concept of design defect eases the claimant's burden somewhat by holding the manufacturer to the knowledge of an expert in the field and requiring only that a safer design was available, regardless of the manufacturer's actual knowledge.

3. **Cigarettes as defective products.** The *Evans* court arrived at two potentially far-reaching conclusions. The first, and potentially most significant, is its holding, "We decline to place addictive chemicals outside the reach of product liability . . . ." The court's considers a cigarette with very low (or no?) tar and nicotine to be a reasonable alternative design for Lorillard's cigarettes, rejecting the company's objection that such a product is not really a cigarette. It described two classes of smokers — those who are addicted to smoking and those who are not — and concludes that what counts as a reasonable alternative design should be determined from the perspective of a rational person who has not become addicted to nicotine. What does this mean for the future marketing of "regular" cigarettes, the mainstay of the industry? Could a cigarette with any amount of nicotine or tar, no matter how small, be found to be a defective product? For that matter, what could it mean for other products, like alcoholic beverages? The court rejects the analogy with alcohol, reasoning that most drinkers are not addicted to alcohol. Do you agree? Are cigarettes truly unique for purposes of products liability?

The court's second conclusion limits a manufacturer's defense to causation — that a smoker failed to stop smoking after being warned or discovering a disease caused by smoking. Comment j to § 402A of the RESTATEMENT (SECOND) states: "Where warning is given the seller may reasonably assume that it will be read and heeded; and a product bearing such a warning, which is safe for use if it is followed, is not in defective condition, nor is it unreasonably dangerous." The Third Restatement omits this language, casting doubt on the presumption that a person would have heeded a warning (had it existed) and thereby avoided injury. The court, however, arguably expanded the presumption in favor of claimants. Even if an *addicted* smoker would not have heeded a warning, she can be presumed to have heeded a warning given before she became addicted. How would a tobacco company rebut such a presumption? In the absence of rebuttal, the presumption can cement causation.

Massachusetts might prove to be an outlier. In an earlier case, *Haglund v. Philip Morris Inc.*, 847 N.E.2d 315 (Mass. 2006), the same court allowed the plaintiff to overcome what is often the most difficult barrier to lawsuits brought by smokers against tobacco manufacturers: the plaintiff-smoker's knowledge of the risks of smoking. As described in the opinion, typically a defendant in a suit based on product liability or a related cause of action can claim that the plaintiff(s) knew of the defect or "unreasonable risk," but used the product anyway. The court found that this "unreasonable risk" defense is not available where there is no "*non*unreasonable" (the court's word) use of the product; that is, the product is inherently dangerous even if used as intended by the manufacturer.

Consider the application of the Massachusetts approach in similar actions brought against manufacturers of high-fat foods, firearms, alcoholic beverages, or other potential risks to the public's health. Are such cases essentially the same as the tobacco cases, or are there legally significant differences? Phrased otherwise, if you find *Evans* well reasoned, is that because you favor its standard for determining reasonable alternative designs or its rejection of the "unreasonable risk" defense generally, or because you think tobacco is particularly dangerous and should be regarded differently from other public health risks? (*See* related discussions of private litigation against food producers in Chapter 9 and against gun manufacturers in Chapter 12.)

None of these privately initiated lawsuits fits neatly into the usual concept of "public health." Their significance in the present context lies in their potential impact on the tobacco (or food or firearms) industry. Any large-scale award would affect the profitability and, possibly, the financial stability of the complex of industries that produce and sell such products. While this seems unlikely, if the award of damages were great enough — the amount paid by the companies would have to be measured in tens of billions of dollars to really affect their stability — the net result could have a more widespread effect on the availability of tobacco (or certain foods or firearms) in the United States than any of the governmental "public health" measures that have been undertaken thus far. To what extent should litigation be a public policy tool?

4. **Punitive damages.** The *Evans* court avoided addressing the amount of punitive damages by vacating the jury's findings on the underlying causes of action. In *Philip Morris, USA. v. Williams*, 549 U.S. 346 (2007), however, the U. S. Supreme Court limited the rationale for awarding punitive damages:

> "In our view, the Constitution's Due Process Clause forbids a State to use a punitive damages award to punish a defendant for injury that it inflicts upon nonparties or those whom they directly represent, i.e., injury that it inflicts upon those who are, essentially, strangers to the litigation. For one thing, the Due Process Clause prohibits a State from punishing an individual without first providing that individual with 'an opportunity to present every available defense.' Yet a defendant threatened with punishment for injuring a nonparty victim has no opportunity to defend against the charge, by showing, for example in a case such as this, that the other

victim was not entitled to damages because he or she knew that smoking was dangerous or did not rely upon the defendant's statements to the contrary."

. . . .

"Evidence of actual harm to nonparties can help to show that the conduct that harmed the plaintiff also posed a substantial risk of harm to the general public, and so was particularly reprehensible — although counsel may argue in a particular case that conduct resulting in no harm to others nonetheless posed a grave risk to the public, or the converse. Yet for the reasons given above, a jury may not go further than this and use a punitive damages verdict to punish a defendant directly on account of harms it is alleged to have visited on non-parties."

. . . .

"We did not previously hold explicitly that a jury may not punish for the harm caused others. But we do so hold now."

549 U.S. at 353–356.

At issue in *Williams* was a jury award of $79.5 million in punitive damages to a smoker's estate for negligence and deceit by a tobacco company. The Court remanded the case to allow the Oregon court to apply the newly announced standard. Justices Scalia, Thomas, and Ginsburg dissented, with Justice Thomas also writing separately "to reiterate [his] view that 'the Constitution does not constrain the size of punitive damages awards.'" *Id.* at 362.

A BRIEF SUMMARY OF THE 1998 MASTER SETTLEMENT AGREEMENT BETWEEN THE STATES AND TOBACCO MANUFACTURERS

As evidence mounted in the 1990s that the manufacturers of tobacco products knew much more about the dangers of smoking and the addictive properties of nicotine than they had previously claimed, a number of individual states initiated lawsuits against the tobacco companies, essentially asking for the recovery of the states' Medicaid funds spent for smoking-related health care. Some of the states' lawsuits were based on common law equity theories, others on claims of fraud or antitrust violations. Many of these claims did not survive even initial judicial examination. One obstacle was linking the manufacturers' actions (causing disease in smokers) to losses that the state incurred for medical care for smokers' illnesses. In 1996, faced with both privately initiated lawsuits and the remaining state claims, and the FDA's pursuit of jurisdiction over tobacco products, some of the larger tobacco companies began negotiating with several of the states to strike some sort of settlement.

The negotiations culminated in the Master Settlement Agreement of 1998, authored by the attorneys general of Washington State and several other key states, and the "Big Four" companies — Philip Morris, RJR Nabisco, Brown & Williamson, and Lorillard. Four states (Florida, Minnesota, Mississippi, and Texas) concluded separate, multi-billion dollar settlements with the larger tobacco companies. Eventually all of the states that had not previously settled individual lawsuits, signed on to the agreement, as did most other domestic (and some foreign) tobacco companies.

The key terms of the agreement are described below:

Financial payments to the states

The tobacco companies agreed to make annual payments to the states in perpetuity, estimated to total over $206 billion at least through the year 2025 (and to continue as long as the companies exist). These payments were intended to compensate states for the Medicaid-related costs of the states' smokers. In addition, they agreed to pay $1.5 billion in attorney fees to private lawyers who had represented the states.

The tobacco companies make annual payments into a fund based on their sales. The initial amounts of payments are adjusted each year by 3 percent or the Consumer Price Index, whichever is greater, and further adjusted to account for changes in the volume of sales; *i.e.*, the payments of each tobacco company rise or fall as their sales increase or decrease. Payments can also be adjusted to reflect federal legislation affecting these obligations. The states receive their payments from a master fund. Each state's share is based on a formula reflecting its efforts in resolving the initial lawsuits and reaching the settlement.

Limits on advertising and promotion

The tobacco companies agreed to various advertising limits, including a ban on outdoor advertising and in public transit, bans on advertising at sporting events, and prohibitions on product placement in movies and videos and on merchandise bearing cigarette brand logos. The companies also agreed to stop using Joe Camel and other cartoons in advertising and promotion, packaging, or labeling.

The companies agreed not to oppose proposed state or local laws intended to limit youth access or consumption of tobacco products or to oppose legislation banning the manufacture or sale of cigarettes in packages containing fewer than twenty cigarettes.

They agreed to release their secret documents concerning the health effects of tobacco products and to shut down the research institute that had produced tobacco-friendly research.

The companies agreed to provide $250 million ($25 million a year for the first ten years) for a foundation [American Legacy Foundation] dedicated to reducing youth smoking and $1.5 billion for national anti-smoking advertising campaigns.

Settlement of past and future lawsuits

Under the terms of the settlement, the states and local governments are precluded from pursuing lawsuits for past or future actions by the tobacco companies or anyone else involved in the production, marketing, or sale of tobacco products, except for criminal violations and except for civil actions brought to enforce the provisions of the settlement.

The text of the Master Settlement Agreement and related information can be found at: www.naag.org/backpages/naag/tobacco/msa/ (visited Feb. 2014).

NOTES AND QUESTIONS

5. Reasons for the Master Settlement Agreement. Why would the tobacco companies agree to these restrictions and, in particular, to make payments, in perpetuity, to the states, especially payments that may total hundreds of billions of dollars? What do they gain from doing so?

The answer is *not* that they feared losing the state-initiated lawsuits. The answer has more to do with the indirect and direct effects of the settlement on the future of the tobacco companies and their business. The states now have a very good reason not to unduly hinder tobacco sales, through taxes that might ultimately reduce demand or through other measures. The more tobacco products that are sold, the more money each state will get. If a state decides to reduce the sale or use of tobacco, the obligations of the companies are reduced accordingly. For that matter, if the sales of a particular company changes, the payments by that company are changed accordingly. Each state must be aware of the implications for its own treasury.

As long as the companies can raise their prices to cover their obligations to pay the states, they don't really lose money; rather they maintain their rather profitable status and that status is secured into the future. Moreover, one major category of litigant — the states — has settled all past and future lawsuits. Not a bad deal, is it?

6. Where does the money go? From the states' perspective, a key goal of the Master Settlement Agreement was to reduce smoking, especially among young people. Most public health experts assumed that the states would spend their tobacco settlement payments on smoking abatement, anti-smoking education, or, at least, covering smoking-related health care costs. But there is nothing in the settlement that requires the funds to be spent for any particular program or to be spent at all. In fact, as the years distanced the annual revenue received from its origins, many states realized that the income from the settlement agreement is revenue that can be spent for anything. Thus, many states use that revenue to pay for other pressing expenses, especially in difficult economic times, and have come to depend on it to meet budget obligations. In 2014, states are estimated to spend 1.9% of their $25 billion settlement dollars on tobacco control programs. *See* Campaign for Tobacco Free Kids, Broken Promises to Our Children: The 1998 Tobacco Settlement 15 Years Later, www.tobaccofreekids.org/what_we_do/state_local/tobacco_settlement (visited Feb. 2014).

A key advantage of the settlement funds for states is that the payments provide revenue that does not require imposing taxes on the general population. People who buy tobacco are paying more for their cigarettes and other tobacco products, but that is part of what they pay the seller, not a tax they pay the state — a fine point of economics, but an important point of politics. (Of course, states also impose taxes on cigarette sales.) How might this affect a state legislature's view of enforcing the settlement agreement or proposals to reduce tobacco sales? What if public health officials or the attorneys general think that the tobacco industry has transgressed some of the settlement's prohibitions, but state budget officials prefer to accept the settlement payments and ignore the possible violation of the settlement?

7. **The Settlement and the FDA.** The Family Smoking Prevention and Tobacco Control Act (Part C, *supra*) includes provisions that overlap with those of the Master Settlement Agreement, particularly with respect to advertising and marketing. These raise questions of which agency — the FDA, the FTC, or a state attorney general — has jurisdiction to enforce specific obligations on the part of a tobacco company. The FDA's Center for Tobacco Control is not necessarily in the habit of seeking the advice of attorneys general or the National Association of Attorneys General, which monitors the Master Settlement Agreement. What is the function of the Master Settlement Agreement today, beyond settling old claims and providing revenue to the states? How much freedom do states have to regulate marketing?

8. **RICO claims.** The Master Settlement does not preclude criminal prosecutions. In 1999, the U.S. Attorney General filed suit against cigarette manufacturers and related organizations claiming that they had engaged in a fraudulent pattern of covering up the dangers of tobacco use and had disguised their efforts to market cigarettes to minors. In large part, these allegations were based on the "tobacco papers" that had been discovered during the privately initiated lawsuits discussed above. The government argued that under the federal Racketeer Influenced and Corrupt Organizations Act (RICO), 18 U.S.C. §§ 1961–68, the courts could order both injunctive relief and disgorgement of all profits from the allegedly unlawful activities — essentially asking for hundreds of billions of dollars in damages. In 2000, the district court dismissed most of the other claims, but allowed the government to proceed on the RICO claim. In 2005, the D.C. Circuit issued an opinion holding that disgorgement of profits is not available under the RICO legislation, and that the government could seek only injunctive relief, severely undercutting the government's case. *United States v. Philip Morris USA, Inc.*, 396 F.3d 1190 (D.C. Cir. 2005), *cert. denied*, 546 U.S. 960 (2005).

The companies were ultimately found liable for conducting "a joint enterprise through a pattern of wire and mail fraud in a scheme to deceive American consumers" about the health effects and addictiveness of cigarettes. *United States v. Philip Morris USA, Inc.*, 566 F.3d 1095 (D.C. Cir. 2009). The circuit court's opinion offers a good summary of this lengthy and complex litigation. The evidence showed that the major companies agreed not to take competitive advantage of each other by suggesting that their products were less risky than another's products. The district court rejected the companies' argument that Master Settlement Agreement made an injunction against similar future actions unnecessary. The district court imposed broad injunctions on seven companies, prohibiting them "from committing any act of racketeering, as defined in 18 U.S.C. § 1961(1), relating in any way to the manufacturing, marketing, promotion, health consequences or sale of cigarettes in the United States." *Id.* at 1137. (No injunction was imposed on Liggett, because it had withdrawn from the conspiracy by admitting that smoking is addictive and causes cancer.) The circuit court affirmed the district court's decisions on liability and remedies, and the U.S. Supreme Court denied certiorari in multiple petitions. *See, e.g.*, 130 S. Ct. 3501 (2010).

What effect, if any, does the Family Smoking Prevention and Tobacco Control Act of 2009 have on the remedies imposed in RICO case? Are they duplicative or additive? For that matter, what bearing might the findings in that case — that the tobacco companies knew of the addictiveness and health risks of tobacco — have on individual claims that a tobacco company should be liable for personal injuries under products liability, negligence or fraud claims? Several claimants have sought to apply offensive collateral estoppel against tobacco companies, to preclude the companies from contesting the findings of fact in the RICO case that they acted fraudulently. So far, courts have declined to grant collateral estoppel. *See Aspinall v. Philip Morris Cos.*, 2012 Mass. Super. LEXIS 218 (Supr. Ct. Mass. Mar. 14, 2012); *Curtis v. Altria Group*, 792 N.W.2d 836 (Minn. 2010); *Schwab v. Philip Morris USA, Inc.*, 449 F. Supp. 2d 992, 1079 (E.D.N.Y. 2006), *rev'd on other groundssub. nom. McLaughlin v. American Tobacco Co.*, 522 F.3d 215 (2d Cir. 2008).

Chapter 11

DRUGS AND ALCOHOL

A. INTRODUCTION

According to the National Institute of Drug Abuse, illicit drugs cost the country $193 billion in crime, lost productivity, and health care each year. www.drugabuse.gov/related-topics/trends-statistics (visited Mar. 2014). Crime accounted for most expenses, with health care estimated to cost $11 billion. This Chapter focuses on health concerns, not criminal law, but public health regulations can subject violators to criminal sanctions, such as incarceration and monetary fines. In particular, it examines prevention and treatment programs that sometimes become intertwined with criminal law enforcement. Part B begins with attempts to distinguish between drug or alcohol use, on one hand, and addiction, on the other, in order to examine what counts as criminal responsibility and what counts as a medical concern. Part C examines instances in which medical care facilities cooperate with police to get people — mostly women — into treatment or at least to stop using controlled substances. It then compares drug screening programs used by employers, schools, and funding agencies as a condition of employment or receiving benefits. In many of these examples, government agencies face Fourth Amendment challenges to their drug screening or testing policies. Part D considers the responsibility of private actors for harm caused by intoxicated persons. Alcoholic beverages raise many of the same issues as narcotics or opioids, despite their lawful use by adults today. In turn, the history of regulating alcoholic beverages in the United States often influences public policy concerning other risks.

B. DEFINING CRIMINAL RESPONSIBILITY FOR INTOXICATION

ROBINSON v. CALIFORNIA
370 U.S. 660 (1962), *reh. den.*, 371 U.S. 905 (1962)

Mr. Justice Stewart delivered the opinion of the Court.

A California statute makes it a criminal offense for a person to "be addicted to the use of narcotics."[3] This appeal draws into question the constitutionality of that

---

[3] The statute is § 11721 of the California Health and Safety Code. It provides: "No person shall use, or be under the influence of, or be addicted to the use of narcotics, excepting when administered by or

provision of the state law, as construed by the California courts in the present case.

The appellant was convicted after a jury trial in the Municipal Court of Los Angeles. The evidence against him was given by two Los Angeles police officers. Officer Brown testified that he had had occasion to examine the appellant's arms one evening on a street in Los Angeles some four months before the trial. The officer testified that at that time he had observed "scar tissue and discoloration on the inside" of the appellant's right arm, and "what appeared to be numerous needle marks and a scab which was approximately three inches below the crook of the elbow" on the appellant's left arm. The officer also testified that the appellant under questioning had admitted to the occasional use of narcotics.

Officer Lindquist testified that he had examined the appellant the following morning in the Central Jail in Los Angeles. The officer stated that at that time he had observed discolorations and scabs on the appellant's arms, and he identified photographs which had been taken of the appellant's arms shortly after his arrest the night before. Based upon more than ten years of experience as a member of the Narcotic Division of the Los Angeles Police Department, the witness gave his opinion that "these marks and the discoloration were the result of the injection of hypodermic needles into the tissue into the vein that was not sterile." He stated that the scabs were several days old at the time of his examination, and that the appellant was neither under the influence of narcotics nor suffering withdrawal symptoms at the time he saw him. This witness also testified that the appellant had admitted using narcotics in the past.

The appellant testified in his own behalf, denying the alleged conversations with the police officers and denying that he had ever used narcotics or been addicted to their use. He explained the marks on his arms as resulting from an allergic condition contracted during his military service. His testimony was corroborated by two witnesses.

The trial judge instructed the jury that the statute made it a misdemeanor for a person "either to use narcotics, or to be addicted to the use of narcotics . . . . That portion of the statute referring to the 'use' of narcotics is based upon the 'act' of using. That portion of the statute referring to 'addicted to the use' of narcotics is based upon a condition or status. They are not identical . . . . To be addicted to the use of narcotics is said to be a status or condition and not an act. It is a continuing offense and differs from most other offenses in the fact that [it] is chronic rather than acute; that it continues after it is complete and subjects the offender to arrest at any time before he reforms. The existence of such a chronic condition may be ascertained from a single examination, if the characteristic reactions of that condition be found present."

The judge further instructed the jury that the appellant could be convicted under a general verdict if the jury agreed either that he was of the "status" or had committed the "act" denounced by the statute. "All that the People must show is either that the defendant did use a narcotic in Los Angeles County, or that while in

---

under the direction of a person licensed by the State to prescribe and administer narcotics. . . . Any person convicted of violating any provision of this section is guilty of a misdemeanor and shall be sentenced to serve a term of not less than 90 days nor more than one year in the county jail . . . ."

the City of Los Angeles he was addicted to the use of narcotics . . . ."

Under these instructions the jury returned a verdict finding the appellant "guilty of the offense charged." An appeal was taken . . . . Although expressing some doubt as to the constitutionality of "the crime of being a narcotic addict," the reviewing court in an unreported opinion affirmed the judgment of conviction . . . . We noted probable jurisdiction of this appeal because it squarely presents the issue whether the statute as construed by the California courts in this case is repugnant to the Fourteenth Amendment of the Constitution.

The broad power of a State to regulate the narcotic drugs traffic within its borders is not here in issue. More than forty years ago, in *Whipple v. Martinson, 256 U.S. 41,* this Court explicitly recognized the validity of that power: "There can be no question of the authority of the State in the exercise of its police power to regulate the administration, sale, prescription and use of dangerous and habit-forming drugs . . . . The right to exercise this power is so manifest in the interest of the public health and welfare, that it is unnecessary to enter upon a discussion of it beyond saying that it is too firmly established to be successfully called in question." 256 U.S. at 45. Such regulation, it can be assumed, could take a variety of valid forms. A State might impose criminal sanctions, for example, against the unauthorized manufacture, prescription, sale, purchase, or possession of narcotics within its borders. In the interest of discouraging the violation of such laws, or in the interest of the general health or welfare of its inhabitants, a State might establish a program of compulsory treatment for those addicted to narcotics. Such a program of treatment might require periods of involuntary confinement. And penal sanctions might be imposed for failure to comply with established compulsory treatment procedures. *Cf. Jacobson v. Massachusetts, 197 U.S. 11.* Or a State might choose to attack the evils of narcotics traffic on broader fronts also — through public health education, for example, or by efforts to ameliorate the economic and social conditions under which those evils might be thought to flourish. In short, the range of valid choice which a State might make in this area is undoubtedly a wide one, and the wisdom of any particular choice within the allowable spectrum is not for us to decide. Upon that premise we turn to the California law in issue here.

It would be possible to construe the statute under which the appellant was convicted as one which is operative only upon proof of the actual use of narcotics within the State's jurisdiction. But the California courts have not so construed this law. Although there was evidence in the present case that the appellant had used narcotics in Los Angeles, the jury were instructed that they could convict him even if they disbelieved that evidence. The appellant could be convicted, they were told, if they found simply that the appellant's "status" or "chronic condition" was that of being "addicted to the use of narcotics." And it is impossible to know from the jury's verdict that the defendant was not convicted upon precisely such a finding.

. . . .

This statute, therefore, is not one which punishes a person for the use of narcotics, for their purchase, sale or possession, or for antisocial or disorderly behavior resulting from their administration. It is not a law which even purports to provide or require medical treatment. Rather, we deal with a statute which makes the "status" of narcotic addiction a criminal offense, for which the offender may be prosecuted "at any time before he reforms." California has said that a person can be continuously guilty of this offense, whether or not he has ever used or possessed any narcotics within the State, and whether or not he has been guilty of any antisocial behavior there.

It is unlikely that any State at this moment in history would attempt to make it a criminal offense for a person to be mentally ill, or a leper, or to be afflicted with a venereal disease. A State might determine that the general health and welfare require that the victims of these and other human afflictions be dealt with by compulsory treatment, involving quarantine, confinement, or sequestration. But, in the light of contemporary human knowledge, a law which made a criminal offense of such a disease would doubtless be universally thought to be an infliction of cruel and unusual punishment in violation of the Eighth and Fourteenth Amendments.

We cannot but consider the statute before us as of the same category. In this Court counsel for the State recognized that narcotic addiction is an illness. Indeed, it is apparently an illness which may be contracted innocently or involuntarily. We hold that a state law which imprisons a person thus afflicted as a criminal, even though he has never touched any narcotic drug within the State or been guilty of any irregular behavior there, inflicts a cruel and unusual punishment in violation of the Fourteenth Amendment. To be sure, imprisonment for ninety days is not, in the abstract, a punishment which is either cruel or unusual. But the question cannot be considered in the abstract. Even one day in prison would be a cruel and unusual punishment for the "crime" of having a common cold.

We are not unmindful that the vicious evils of the narcotics traffic have occasioned the grave concern of government. There are, as we have said, countless fronts on which those evils may be legitimately attacked. We deal in this case only with an individual provision of a particularized local law as it has so far been interpreted by the California courts.

Reversed.

POWELL v. TEXAS
392 U.S. 514 (1968)

Mr. Justice Marshall announced the judgment of the Court and delivered an opinion in which the Chief Justice, Mr. Justice Black, and Mr. Justice Harlan join.

In late December 1966, appellant was arrested and charged with being found in a state of intoxication in a public place, in violation of Texas Penal Code, Art. 477 (1952), which reads as follows:

"Whoever shall get drunk or be found in a state of intoxication in any public place, or at any private house except his own, shall be fined not exceeding one hundred dollars."

Appellant was tried in the Corporation Court of Austin, Texas, found guilty, and fined $20. He appealed to the County Court at Law No. 1 of Travis County, Texas, where a trial de novo was held. His counsel urged that appellant was "afflicted with the disease of chronic alcoholism," that "his appearance in public [while drunk was] . . . not of his own volition," and therefore that to punish him criminally for that conduct would be cruel and unusual, in violation of the Eighth and Fourteenth Amendments to the United States Constitution. The trial judge in the county court, sitting without a jury, ruled as a matter of law that chronic alcoholism was not a defense to the charge. He found appellant guilty, and fined him $50.

. . . .

III

. . . .

Appellant . . . seeks to come within the application of the Cruel and Unusual Punishment Clause announced in *Robinson v. California* [*supra*], which involved a state statute making it a crime to "be addicted to the use of narcotics." . . .

On its face the present case does not fall within that holding, since appellant was convicted, not for being a chronic alcoholic, but for being in public while drunk on a particular occasion. The State of Texas thus has not sought to punish a mere status, as California did in *Robinson*; nor has it attempted to regulate appellant's behavior in the privacy of his own home. Rather, it has imposed upon appellant a criminal sanction for public behavior which may create substantial health and safety hazards, both for appellant and for members of the general public, and which offends the moral and esthetic sensibilities of a large segment of the community. This seems a far cry from convicting one for being an addict, being a chronic alcoholic, being "mentally ill, or a leper . . . ."

. . . .

It is suggested in dissent that *Robinson* stands for the "simple" but "subtle" principle that "[criminal] penalties may not be inflicted upon a person for being in a condition he is powerless to change." In that view, appellant's "condition" of public intoxication was "occasioned by a compulsion symptomatic of the disease" of chronic alcoholism, and thus, apparently, his behavior lacked the critical element of *mens rea*. Whatever may be the merits of such a doctrine of criminal responsibility, it surely cannot be said to follow from *Robinson*. The entire thrust of *Robinson*'s interpretation of the Cruel and Unusual Punishment Clause is that criminal penalties may be inflicted only if the accused has committed some act, has engaged in some behavior, which society has an interest in preventing, or perhaps in historical common law terms, has committed some *actus reus*. It thus does not deal with the question of whether certain conduct cannot constitutionally be punished because it is, in some sense, "involuntary" or "occasioned by a compulsion."

Likewise, as the dissent acknowledges, there is a substantial definitional distinction between a "status," as in *Robinson*, and a "condition," which is said to be involved in this case. Whatever may be the merits of an attempt to distinguish between behavior and a condition, it is perfectly clear that the crucial element in this case, so far as the dissent is concerned, is whether or not appellant can legally be held responsible for his appearance in public in a state of intoxication. The only relevance of *Robinson* to this issue is that because the Court interpreted the statute there involved as making a "status" criminal, it was able to suggest that the statute would cover even a situation in which addiction had been acquired involuntarily. That this factor was not determinative in the case is shown by the fact that there was no indication of how *Robinson* himself had become an addict.

Ultimately, then, the most troubling aspects of this case, were *Robinson* to be extended to meet it, would be the scope and content of what could only be a constitutional doctrine of criminal responsibility. In dissent it is urged that the decision could be limited to conduct which is "a characteristic and involuntary part of the pattern of the disease as it afflicts" the particular individual, and that "[it] is not foreseeable" that it would be applied "in the case of offenses such as driving a car while intoxicated, assault, theft, or robbery." That is limitation by fiat. In the first place, nothing in the logic of the dissent would limit its application to chronic alcoholics. If Leroy Powell cannot be convicted of public intoxication, it is difficult to see how a State can convict an individual for murder, if that individual, while exhibiting normal behavior in all other respects, suffers from a "compulsion" to kill, which is an "exceedingly strong influence," but "not completely overpowering." Even if we limit our consideration to chronic alcoholics, it would seem impossible to confine the principle within the arbitrary bounds which the dissent seems to envision.

. . . .

Traditional common-law concepts of personal accountability and essential considerations of federalism lead us to disagree with appellant. We are unable to conclude, on the state of this record or on the current state of medical knowledge, that chronic alcoholics in general, and Leroy Powell in particular, suffer from such an irresistible compulsion to drink and to get drunk in public that they are utterly unable to control their performance of either or both of these acts and thus cannot be deterred at all from public intoxication. And in any event this Court has never articulated a general constitutional doctrine of *mens rea*.

We cannot cast aside the centuries-long evolution of the collection of interlocking and overlapping concepts which the common law has utilized to assess the moral accountability of an individual for his antisocial deeds. The doctrines of *actus reus*, *mens rea*, insanity, mistake, justification, and duress have historically provided the tools for a constantly shifting adjustment of the tension between the evolving aims of the criminal law and changing religious, moral, philosophical, and medical views of the nature of man. This process of adjustment has always been thought to be the province of the States.

. . . .

Affirmed.

Mr. Justice White, concurring in the result. If it cannot be a crime to have an irresistible compulsion to use narcotics, *Robinson v. California*, I do not see how it can constitutionally be a crime to yield to such a compulsion. Punishing an addict for using drugs convicts for addiction under a different name. Distinguishing between the two crimes is like forbidding criminal conviction for being sick with flu or epilepsy but permitting punishment for running a fever or having a convulsion.

Unless *Robinson* is to be abandoned, the use of narcotics by an addict must be beyond the reach of the criminal law. Similarly, the chronic alcoholic with an irresistible urge to consume alcohol should not be punishable for drinking or for being drunk.

Powell's conviction was for the different crime of being drunk in a public place. Thus even if Powell was compelled to drink, and so could not constitutionally be convicted for drinking, his conviction in this case can be invalidated only if there is a constitutional basis for saying that he may not be punished for being in public while drunk. The statute involved here, which aims at keeping drunks off the street for their own welfare and that of others, is not challenged on the ground that it interferes unconstitutionally with the right to frequent public places. No question is raised about applying this statute to the nonchronic drunk, who has no compulsion to drink, who need not drink to excess, and who could have arranged to do his drinking in private or, if he began drinking in public, could have removed himself at an appropriate point on the path toward complete inebriation.

. . . .

The sober chronic alcoholic has no compulsion to be on the public streets; many chronic alcoholics drink at home and are never seen drunk in public. Before and after taking the first drink, and until he becomes so drunk that he loses the power to know where he is or to direct his movements, the chronic alcoholic with a home or financial resources is as capable as the nonchronic drinker of doing his drinking in private, of removing himself from public places and, since he knows or ought to know that he will become intoxicated, of making plans to avoid his being found drunk in public. For these reasons, I cannot say that the chronic alcoholic who proves his disease and a compulsion to drink is shielded from conviction when he has knowingly failed to take feasible precautions against committing a criminal act, here the act of going to or remaining in a public place. On such facts the alcoholic is like a person with smallpox, who could be convicted for being on the street but not for being ill, or, like the epileptic, who could be punished for driving a car but not for his disease.

The fact remains that some chronic alcoholics must drink and hence must drink somewhere. Although many chronics have homes, many others do not. For all practical purposes the public streets may be home for these unfortunates, not because their disease compels them to be there, but because, drunk or sober, they have no place else to go and no place else to be when they are drinking. This is more a function of economic station than of disease, although the disease may lead to destitution and perpetuate that condition. For some of these alcoholics I would think a showing could be made that resisting drunkenness is impossible and that avoiding public places when intoxicated is also impossible. As applied to them this statute is in effect a law which bans a single act for which they may not be convicted under the Eighth Amendment — the act of getting drunk.

It is also possible that the chronic alcoholic who begins drinking in private at some point becomes so drunk that he loses the power to control his movements and for that reason appears in public. The Eighth Amendment might also forbid conviction in such circumstances, but only on a record satisfactorily showing that it was not feasible for him to have made arrangements to prevent his being in public when drunk and that his extreme drunkenness sufficiently deprived him of his faculties on the occasion in issue.

These prerequisites to the possible invocation of the Eighth Amendment are not satisfied on the record before us. Whether or not Powell established that he could not have resisted becoming drunk on December 19, 1966, nothing in the record indicates that he could not have done his drinking in private or that he was so inebriated at the time that he had lost control of his movements and wandered into the public street. Indeed, the evidence in the record strongly suggests that Powell could have drunk at home and made plans while sober to prevent ending up in a public place. Powell had a home and wife, and if there were reasons why he had to drink in public or be drunk there, they do not appear in the record.

. . . .

NOTES AND QUESTIONS

1.   **Criminal acts, personal status, and conditions.** The *Robinson* court does not question the state's power to enact criminal prohibitions against the sale or use of narcotics. Is the rationale for such laws protecting the public from violence associated with drug abusers who need money to buy drugs, protecting the public from the sight of dissolute addicts, protecting the population from the harmful effects of drugs, some combination of factors, or something else?

Robinson makes clear that, by itself, one's status or medical condition cannot be a criminal offense. In particular, it accepted the concept of addiction as an illness, as California had recognized, without actually explaining what it meant by that term. The majority nonetheless concludes that being ill cannot be a crime. The court proceeds from the assumption that the Fourteenth Amendment places substantive limits the state's power to define crimes. It then concludes that punishment for illness would violate the Eighth Amendment's prohibition on cruel and unusual punishment, made applicable to the states through the Fourteenth Amendment, without highlighting this first incorporation of Eighth Amendment limits into the Fourteenth Amendment's protections.

In 1977, the Court found that the Eighth Amendment's cruel and unusual punishment clause limits the state's power in three ways: "First, it limits the kinds of punishment that can be imposed on those convicted of crimes; second, it proscribes punishment grossly disproportionate to the severity of the crime; and third, it imposes substantive limits on what can be made criminal and punished as such." *Ingraham v. Wright*, 430 U.S. 651, 667 (1977).

2.   **Implications for criminal responsibility.** *Powell* effectively limited the reach of *Robinson*. Leroy Powell was employed as a shoeshine man, but he was also a chronic alcoholic who had been arrested dozens of times for being drunk in public. He was typically found asleep on a sidewalk. His case challenged the legitimacy of very old laws against public drunkenness at a time when the Supreme Court was recognizing new procedural protections for criminal defendants in state courts, such as prohibiting involuntary confessions, excluding evidence obtained in unreasonable

searches under the Fourth Amendment, and requiring the state to provide indigent defendants with counsel.

The Justices split 4-4 in *Powell*, with Justice White, who had dissented in *Robinson*, writing a separate concurrence to give Justice Marshall a majority. The major disagreement among the Justices was whether addiction or loss of control over one's actions could excuse otherwise criminal behavior. Stated this way, it is easy to see how barring the state from prosecuting alcoholics for public drunkenness could be interpreted as establishing a more far-reaching precedent — one that could excuse dangerous behavior by persons addicted to drugs or alcohol or impaired by a mental disorder. Four dissenting Justices in *Powell* argued that *Robinson* stood for the following principle: "Criminal penalties may not be inflicted upon a person for being in a condition he is powerless to change." 392 U.S. at 567. They did not challenge laws prohibiting public intoxication, but argued that Powell's conviction was improper, because his addiction rendered him powerless to avoid being in a public place.

Justice Marshall's plurality opinion worries about the question of criminal responsibility. The law generally presumes that people will act in accordance with the law. Defenses to criminal charges based on insanity recognize that a person with certain mental disorders cannot act rationally; the law cannot deter crime by a person who is incapable of recognizing the law's requirements. If the court were to extend *Robinson* to cover cases like *Powell*, any defendant could escape conviction by claiming that his condition deprived him of control over his actions, such that he or she could not have the *mens rea* necessary to intend the harm caused. Thus, Justice Marshall rejects the dissent's view that the class of people who would escape prosecution on the ground of addiction would be insignificant, calling it "limitation by fiat."

Justice White's concurrence raises questions about the differences between chronic alcoholics and those who drink without becoming intoxicated, between those who can and cannot get drunk in the privacy of their own homes, and between the decision to take the first drink and the compulsion to continue. Assuming that such distinctions are factually correct, how might they affect criminal responsibility?

3. **Two lawful acts can be a crime.** The majority in *Powell* found that the act of appearing in public (while drunk) satisfied the requirement that the defendant commit an act that constitutes an offense — even though neither appearing in public nor being intoxicated is itself a crime. What exactly is the risk that the law seeks to prevent? To be sure, people who are intoxicated can commit violent acts against others (unlike Leroy Powell), but those acts are themselves crimes that can be punished regardless of intoxication. Can a statute be drafted that prevents only drunks prone to violence from harming others? Preventing harm to others has been the goal of other laws that criminalize the combination of two otherwise lawful activities. An obvious example is a law that prohibits driving while intoxicated. It is not a crime to drive, to drink alcoholic beverages (if you are an adult), or even to be intoxicated. Yet an adult who engages in two of these lawful activities at the same time commits a crime. What about laws prohibiting persons with uncontrolled epilepsy from driving? Or driving and texting? To what extent does the probability of harm justify such laws? How much is that probability determined by the

individual and how much by the person's condition? If science finds genetic predispositions to some addictions, should that knowledge affect the definition of criminal responsibility?

4. **Criminal punishment v. civil commitment.** The *Powell* majority declined to carve out a defense — loss of control — to constitutionally permissible grounds for criminal punishment. Compare the Court's later discussion of loss of control as a permissible substitute for mental illness for purposes of civil commitment of "sexual predators" in *Kansas v. Crane*, described in Chapter 5, B, *supra*. How do the purposes of the concept differ in the criminal and civil contexts?

The civil rights movements in the 1960s included private organizations that advocated not only for the rights of criminal defendants, but also for more therapeutic approaches to those afflicted with alcohol or drug addiction, one that could keep them out of jail and provide a path to sobriety. (This is also an objective of the Colorado constitutional amendment concerning marijuana reproduced below.) Advocates were concerned about the revolving door between the streets and jail, especially for disadvantaged populations. Would civil commitment of addicts be fairer than criminal prosecution? (*See* Chapter 5, B, *supra*.) When would the addict no longer be under the influence of addiction? Most states have adopted special statutes authorizing the civil commitment of persons addicted to narcotics or alcohol, primarily because the target population does not readily meet the standards for civil commitment of the mentally ill and dangerous. Treatment for addiction is not always successful. Substance abuse commitment statutes therefore often impose time limits, although the period of involuntary detention can be weeks or months. Criminal convictions for public intoxication typically carry minimal sentences: a day or two in jail until the person sobers up.

In recent decades, the policy trends have favored providing education to prevent substance abuse, including alcohol abuse, and increased access to treatment programs, both voluntary and involuntary alternatives to criminal detention. For information on the prevalence of drug and alcohol use and treatment programs, see the Substance Abuse and Mental Health Services Administration, Data, Outcomes, and Quality, http://samhsa.gov/data/ (visited Mar. 2014).

5. **Vagrancy.** States and cities have used other laws to remove intoxicated persons from public places, such as prohibitions on public urination, disorderly conduct, panhandling, camping and sleeping in public parks and streets, and vagrancy. Such laws are defended as necessary to protect public health and safety. Laws against camping in public areas or vagrancy attract controversy, because they can effectively forbid homeless people from living in a particular municipality, at least where there are not enough shelter beds to accommodate all in need – which is common. Courts have reached different conclusions as to the constitutionality of such ordinances. In *Jones v. City of Los Angeles*, 444 F.3d 1118, 1132 (9th Cir. 2006), *vacated and remanded after settlement*, 505 F.3d 1006 (9th Cir. 2007), the ninth circuit court of appeals found, "Because there is substantial and undisputed evidence that the number of homeless persons in Los Angeles far exceeds the number of available shelter beds at all times, including on the nights of their arrest or citation, Los Angeles has encroached upon Appellants' Eighth Amendment protections by criminalizing the unavoidable act of sitting, lying, or sleeping at night

while being involuntarily homeless." The eleventh circuit court of appeals, however, found no Eighth Amendment violation, where a homeless shelter had space, also noting that that the city had authority to regulate the places where people were entitled to camp. *Joel v. City of Orlando*, 232 F.3d 1353, 1362 (11th Cir. 2000).

6.   Impediments to prosecution for drug crimes. Most criminal laws concerning controlled substances ban possession, manufacture, sale, and distribution. (*See* the Colorado statute below.) Fewer proscribe the *use* of narcotics. Why might that be? How easy is it for law enforcement officers — or anyone else for that matter — to observe a person in the act of using illegal drugs? Anyone who might have been present may be reluctant or downright opposed to providing evidence to the police. Thus, even in jurisdictions where use is prohibited, minor offenders with small quantities of a drug are more likely to be prosecuted for possession, while those with large quantities are more likely to be charged with possession with intent to distribute, which carries more severe penalties.

Justice White, dissenting in *Robinson*, took the view that the conviction should be deemed to be for the use of narcotics, not the status of addiction, because proof of addiction would entail proof of frequent use of narcotics. He pointed out that the "State's only purpose in allowing prosecutions for addiction was to supersede its own venue requirements applicable to prosecutions for the use of narcotics and in effect to allow convictions for use where there is no precise evidence of the county where the use took place." 370 U.S. at 686–7. Might the state have other alternatives? Could the legislature authorize prosecutions in any county in which the defendant is found?

7.   The War on Drugs. For a critical analysis of the history of imprisonment in the United States, including the role of the "war on drugs," see Eric Blumenson, *Two Moral Mistakes in the American Criminal Justice System*, in THE TRAGEDY OF LIBERTY (Andras Sajo & Renata Uitz, eds., 2013).

Constitution of the State of Colorado
Article XVIII, Miscellaneous

Section 16.

(a) In the interest of the efficient use of law enforcement resources, enhancing revenue for public purposes, and individual freedom, the people of the state of Colorado find and declare that the use of marijuana should be legal for persons twenty-one years of age or older and taxed in a manner similar to alcohol.

(b) In the interest of the health and public safety of our citizenry, the people of the state of Colorado further find and declare that marijuana should be regulated in a manner similar to alcohol so that:

(I) Individuals will have to show proof of age before purchasing marijuana;

(II) Selling, distributing, or transferring marijuana to minors and other individuals under the age of twenty-one shall remain illegal;

(III) Driving under the influence of marijuana shall remain illegal;

(IV) Legitimate, taxpaying business people, and not criminal actors, will conduct sales of marijuana; and

(V) Marijuana sold in this state will be labeled and subject to additional regulations to ensure that consumers are informed and protected.

(c) In the interest of enacting rational policies for the treatment of all variations of the cannabis plant, the people of Colorado further find and declare that industrial hemp should be regulated separately from strains of cannabis with higher delta-9 tetrahydrocannabinol (THC) concentrations.

(d) The people of the state of Colorado further find and declare that it is necessary to ensure consistency and fairness in the applications of this section throughout the state and that, therefore, the matters addressed by this section are, except as specified herein, matters of statewide concern.

―――――

The Colorado Uniform Controlled Substances Act
Article 18
Co. Rev. Stat. Ann. § 18-18-406 (2013)

§ 18-18-406. Offenses relating to marijuana and marijuana concentrate.

(1)

(a) The sale, transfer, or dispensing of more than two and one half pounds of marijuana or more than one pound of marijuana concentrate to a minor if the person is an adult and two years older than the minor is a Level 1 Drug Felony subject to the mandatory sentencing provision in Section 18-1.3-401.5(7).

(b) The sale, transfer, or dispensing of more than six ounces, but not more than two and one-half pounds of marijuana or more than three ounces, but not more than one pound of marijuana concentrate to a minor if the person is an adult and two years older than the minor is a Level 2 Drug Felony.

(c) The sale, transfer, or dispensing of more than one ounce, but not more than six ounces of marijuana or more than one-half ounce, but not more than three ounces of marijuana concentrate to a minor if the person is an adult and two years older than the minor is a Level 3 Drug Felony.

. . . . .

(d) The sale, transfer, or dispensing of not more than one ounce of marijuana or not more than one-half ounce of marijuana concentrate to a minor if the person is an adult and two years older than the minor is a Level 4 Drug Felony.

(2)

(a)

(I) It is unlawful for a person to knowingly process or manufacture any marijuana or marijuana concentrate or knowingly allow to be processed or manufactured on land owned, occupied, or controlled by him or her any marijuana or marijuana concentrate except as authorized pursuant to Part 1 of Article 42.5 of Title 12, C.R.S., or Part 2 of Article 80 of Title 27, C.R.S.

(II) A person who violated the provisions of subparagraph (I) of this paragraph (a) commits a Level 3 Drug Felony.

(b)

(I) Except as otherwise provided in Subsection (7) of this Section and except as authorized by Part 1 of Article 42.5 of Title 12, C.R.S., Part 2 of Article 80 of Title 27, C.R.S., or Part 2 or 3 of this Article, it is unlawful for a person to knowingly dispense, sell, distribute, or possess with intent to manufacture, dispense, sell or distribute marijuana or marijuana concentrate; or attempt, induce, attempt to induce, or conspire with one or more other persons, to dispense, sell, distribute, or possess with intent to manufacture, dispense, sell or distribute marijuana or marijuana concentrate.

. . . .

(III) A person who violates any of the provisions of Subparagraph (I) of this Paragraph (b) commits:

(A) A Level 1 Drug Felony and is subject to the mandatory sentencing provision in Section 18-1.3.401.5(7) if the amount of marijuana is more than fifty pounds or the amount of marijuana concentrate is more than twenty-five pounds;

(B) A Level 2 Drug Felony if the amount of marijuana is more than five pounds but not more than fifty pounds or the amount of marijuana concentrate is more than two and one-half pounds but not more than twenty-five pounds;

(C) A Level 3 Drug Felony if the amount is more than twelve ounces but not more than five pounds of marijuana or more than six ounces but not more than two and one-half pounds of marijuana concentrate;

. . . .

(D) A Level 4 Drug Felony if the amount is more than four ounces, but not more than twelve ounces of marijuana or more than two ounces but not more than six ounces of marijuana concentrate; or

(E) A Level 1 Drug Misdemeanor if the amount is not more than four ounces of marijuana or not more than two ounces of marijuana concentrate.

(3) It is unlawful for a person to knowingly cultivate, grow, or produce a marijuana plant or knowingly allow a marijuana plant to be cultivated, grown, or produced on land that the person owns, occupies, or controls. A person who violates the provisions of this Subsection (3) commits:

(a) A Level 3 Drug Felony if the offense involves more than thirty plants;

(b) A Level 4 Drug Felony if the offense involves more than six but not more than thirty plants; or

(c) A Level 1 Drug Misdemeanor if the offense involves not more than six plants.

(4)

(a) A person who possesses more than twelve ounces of marijuana or more than three ounces of marijuana concentrate commits a Level 4 Drug Felony.

(b) A person who possesses more than six ounces of marijuana but not more than twelve ounces of marijuana or not more than three ounces of marijuana concentrate commits a Level 1 Drug Misdemeanor.

(c)

A person who possesses more than two ounces of marijuana but not more than six ounces of marijuana commits a Level 2 Drug Misdemeanor.

(5)

(a)

(I) Except as described in Section 18-1-711, a person who possesses not more than two ounces of marijuana commits a drug petty offense and, upon conviction thereof, shall be punished by a fine of not more than one hundred dollars.

. . . .

(b)

(I) Except as described in Section 18-1-711, a person who openly and publicly displays, consumes, or uses two ounces or less of marijuana commits a drug petty offense and, upon conviction thereof, shall be punished by a fine of up to one hundred dollars and up to twenty-four hours of community service.

(II) Open and public display, consumption, or use of more than two ounces of marijuana or any amount of marijuana concentrate is deemed possession thereof, and violations shall be punished as provided for in Subsection (4) of this Section.

(III) Except as otherwise provided for in Subparagraph (I) of this Paragraph (b), consumption or use of marijuana or marijuana concentrate is deemed possession thereof, and violations must be punished as provided for in Paragraph (a) of the Subsection (5) and Subsection (4) of this Section.

(c) Transferring or dispensing not more than two ounces of marijuana from one person to another for no consideration is a drug petty offense and is not deemed dispensing or sale thereof.

(6) The provisions of this Section do not apply to any person who possesses, uses, prescribes, dispenses, or administers any drug classified under Group C Guidelines of the National Cancer Institute, as amended, approved by the federal Food and Drug Administration.

(7) The provisions of this Section do not apply to any person who possesses, uses, prescribes, dispenses, or administers dronabinol (synthetic) in sesame oil and encapsulated in a soft gelatin capsule in a federal Food and Drug Administration approved drug product, pursuant to Part 1 of Article 42.5 of Title 12, C.R.S., or Part 2 of Article 80 of Title 27, C.R.S.

. . . .

18-18-433. Constitutional provisions. The provisions of this Part 4 do not apply to a person twenty-one years of age or older acting in conformance with Section 16 of Article XVIII of the State Constitution [reproduced above] and do not apply to a person acting in conformance with Section 14 of Article XVIII of the State Constitution [authorizing the "medical use of marijuana for persons suffering from debilitating medical conditions" under detailed conditions].

NOTES AND QUESTIONS

8. **Federal v. state regulation.** Notwithstanding the constraints imposed by state or federal constitutional limitations, both the state and the federal governments have considerable discretion to regulate or prohibit the use or even the possession of narcotic or other potentially dangerous drugs. *Gonzales v. Raich*, 545 U.S. 1 (2005), excerpted in Chapter 3, D, *supra*, summarizes the federal government's long history of regulating illicit drugs, including marijuana. Early federal legislation, as the court notes, relied on financial incentives rather than prohibitions. The Harrison Narcotics Act of 1914, 38 Stat. 785 (repealed 1970), imposed taxes on producers of opiates and cocaine, while the Marihuana Tax Act, 50 Stat. 551 (repealed 1970), taxed marijuana; the sale of marijuana without a stamp indicating payment was a criminal offense. These approaches were overhauled and replaced in 1970 by the Controlled Substances Act (Title II of the Comprehensive Drug Abuse Prevention and Control Act, 21 U.S.C. §§ 801 *et seq.*), which contains both criminal prohibitions and regulates uses of narcotics, according to a statutory schedule of drugs ranked according to Congress's view of each drug's dangerous and palliative properties — hence the term "controlled substances." Marijuana possession is a federal misdemeanor that carries a sentence of up to one year in prison and a minimum fine of $1,000. Cultivation, sale, and distribution are felonies that carry more severe penalties — up to five years in prison and a fine of up to $250,000.

The Obama administration advised federal prosecutors that they "should not focus federal resources . . . on individuals whose actions are in clear and unambiguous compliance with existing state laws providing for the medical use of marijuana." Memorandum for U.S. Attorneys from James M. Cole, Deputy Attorney General, *Guidance Regarding the Ogden Memo in Jurisdictions Seeking to Authorize Marijuana for Medical Use* (Oct. 19, 2009). This exercise of prosecutorial discretion, however, does not necessarily extend to large-scale cultivation or dispensing operations. Moreover, its continuance depends upon the particular view of drugs espoused by whichever administration is in power.

Recall that *Employment Division v. Smith*, excerpted in Chapter 4, D, *supra*, considered a denial of unemployment benefits to state employees who had been fired for the ceremonial use of peyote in their Native American religious rituals. Congress responded by exempting Native American ritual use of peyote from the Controlled Substances Act's prohibition. The interplay of federal and state authority in matters relating to drug use and possession can also be seen in *State v. Mooney*, 98 P. 3d 420 (Utah 2004), where the federal exemption was incorporated into state law criminalizing the use of peyote.

Congress has not taken similar action with respect to medical marijuana. At the end of the majority opinion in *Raich*, Justice Stevens hinted that Congress might be persuaded to change marijuana's classification to permit its medical use if supporters brought credible evidence to that body. One obstacle may be the difficulty of conducting clinical trials to evaluate marijuana's safety and efficacy in treating particular medical conditions. Advocates of the use of marijuana for medical purposes complain that the FDA controls access to cannabis for use in medical research and that what is available is unsuitable for sound studies.

9. **Contemporary state initiatives decriminalizing marijuana use.** The *Raich* decision did not end state efforts to permit the use of marijuana for medical purposes. By 2014, 21 states and the District of Columbia had decriminalized the medical use of marijuana, with varying restrictions. For a state-by-state summary of laws, see http://healthcare.findlaw.com/patient-rights/medical-marijuana-laws-by-state.html (visited Mar. 2014).

Decriminalization has gone further — to encompass the recreational use of marijuana — in Colorado and Washington, so far. The amendment to the Colorado constitution reproduced above, adopted by the voters in November 2012, states that the goal of adding Section 16 to Article XVIII of the constitution is to regulate marijuana like alcohol. (In 2000, Colorado voters had amended the state's constitution — Article XVIII, Section 14 — to permit the medical use of marijuana.) What would be necessary to regulate marijuana like alcohol? Decriminalizing marijuana is only the first step in a process of making marijuana available — for medical or other purposes. There are questions about whether to license and limit cultivation and dispensaries and, if so, on what terms, whether to impose excise taxes on sales (the real question is probably how much tax and whether to tax marijuana sold for medical use at a different rate), whether to limit sales to adults only, and whether laws governing driving while intoxicated cover marijuana intoxication. Even where protective state regulations are in place, marijuana dispensaries face practical challenges stemming from federal law, which prohibits banks from receiving funds derived from sales that are unlawful under the Controlled Substances Act. Dispensaries that are refused bank accounts must operate a cash business, which is vulnerable to theft. Although the Department of Justice announced in early 2014 that it favors allowing banks to hold funds for dispensaries, in the absence of changing the federal law, this remains a matter of administrative (and prosecutorial) discretion.

In May 2013, Colorado Governor John Hickenlooper signed lengthy regulations intended to carry out the state's constitutional decriminalization of marijuana under Article XCIII, Section 16. These include limiting marijuana possession to people over age 21 and sales of marijuana to no more than ounce in a single transaction to a Colorado resident (not more than one-quarter ounce to a non-resident). Adults can buy marijuana in person in a licensed retail store upon proof of being over age 21. Adults may also grow up to six plants. Sales are limited to licensed retail stores, which are prohibited from selling over the internet and from giving away free products. Excise and sales taxes are expected to cover some of the expenses of inspecting premises, reviewing required reports, and enforcing the regulations. Retail establishments must meet detailed requirements comparable to those governing clinical laboratories; these include advertising restrictions and security and video surveillance of cultivation and retail sales to track plants from "seed to sale." For licensure requirements, see Dept. of Revenue, Marijuana Enforcement Division, Retail Marijuana Code, 1 Colorado Code of Regulations 212-2 (2013). The first licensed retailers opened their doors January 1, 2014.

Colorado's Uniform Controlled Substances Act, also excerpted above, is a somewhat more typical statute defining drug crimes, although it includes more modern provisions encouraging diversion of offenders to parole and treatment. Note that the Act's last section, 18-18-433, makes clear that it does not apply to anyone acting in accordance with the Constitution's decriminalization of marijuana. Where would you expect this Act to apply? The Colorado legislature amended its Controlled Substances Act, effective October 2013, after its Commission on Criminal and Juvenile Justice recommended changes to the criminal law. The recommended changes were intended to increase collaboration with primary health care, behavioral health, criminal justice and social services, encourage therapeutic services, reduce incarceration, and use the savings to encourage therapeutic services to treat substance abuse. Note that this Act does not eliminate all crimes related to marijuana. Instead, it ranks drug offenses according to the *amount* of marijuana at issue, not the *purpose* for which is sold or used (other than a special exception for marijuana used in connection with NIH guidelines). It also specifies increasing penalties for those who are convicted of other, especially violent, crimes. Possession or consumption of less than 2 ounces of marijuana carries a penalty of not more than $100 upon conviction. Moreover, offenders can petition to seal their records one year after conviction of a petty drug offense. As a practical matter, it may not be worth law enforcement's time or energy to pursue arrests for this "petty drug offense." Who would these provisions apply to?

The District of Columbia was poised to follow suit in February 2014. A city council panel in the District of Columbia approved a measure in January 2014 that would reduce the penalty for possessing less than an ounce of marijuana to a $25 fine, akin to a parking ticket. Congress's reaction may illustrate where trends are going. As of February 2014, Congress had not offered an opinion on the measure, in contrast to vocal opposition from Representatives during a 1998 DC city council debate over a similar law. Ryan J. Reilly, *Feds Mum as D.C. Prepares to*

Decriminalize Pot Possession, HUFFINGTON POST, Feb. 4, 2014, www.huffingtonpost. com/2014/02/04/dc-marijuana-decriminalization_n_4724232.html (visited Mar. 2014).

Proponents of decriminalization measures argue that marijuana is not a primary cause of death, that incarcerating drug users consumes vast resources that could be used for more important objectives, and that tax revenues from the lawful sale of marijuana could augment ailing state budgets. Opponents argue that marijuana use remains a serious risk to health, could lead teenagers to smoke tobacco or take more dangerous drugs, and could reduce workforce productivity. How do the health risks of marijuana compare with those of other controlled substances — or, for that matter, tobacco, alcohol, and other risks to health and safety?

10. Prescribing for suicide. The Controlled Substances Act (CSA) was also at issue in *Gonzales v. Oregon*, 546 U.S. 243 (2006), which held that the United States Attorney General did not have the statutory authority to override Oregon's physician-assisted suicide legislation. Oregon's law permitted physicians to prescribe drugs for patients who wished to use them to commit suicide, provided that they followed a detailed procedure to ensure that the patient was terminally ill, competent, and making a fully informed decision. Then Attorney General John Ashcroft issued an Interpretative Rule finding that "assisting suicide is not a 'legitimate medical practice' within the meaning" of CSA regulations. None of the Justices in *Oregon* challenged the conclusion that Congress had the power, if it chose, to prohibit physician-assisted suicide. The majority, however, found that Congress had not done so and had not granted the Attorney General the power to decide that prescribing medications for a patient's use to commit suicide was not legitimate medical practice.

The results in *Raich* and *Oregon* can seem paradoxical, since California could not authorize patients to use marijuana to alleviate pain or even survive, while Oregon could permit physicians to prescribe drugs that patients could use to end their own lives. Of course, *Raich* concerned Congress's power under the Commerce Clause to use the CSA to regulate intrastate marijuana use, while the issue in *Oregon* was what the CSA itself said. Nonetheless, the case raises policy questions about the proper locus of regulation for the practice of medicine and public health. As George Annas notes:

> Congress historically has been loath to legislate medical practice, preferring to see the areas in which it legislated — such as drug trafficking, recreational drug use, female genital mutilation, and even so-called partial birth abortion — not as the practice of medicine at all, but something outside it.

George J. Annas, *Congress, Controlled Substances, and Physician-Assisted Suicide — Elephants in Mouseholes,* 354 NEW ENG. J. MED. 1079, 1083–84 (2006).

Although Annas says that national medical standards have merit, he concludes: "It is one thing to decide that national standards will be set by the relevant specialty boards or other national medical organizations on the basis of evidence that supports the relevance of such standards to the health and welfare of patients; it is quite another to say that standards will be set by Congress or the attorney general on the basis of the political winds of the day." *Id.* at 1084.

C. TESTING AND SCREENING: CRIMINAL AND CIVIL USES

REGINA KILMON v. MARYLAND
KELLY LYNN CRUZ v. MARYLAND
905 A.2d 306 (Md. 2006)

WILNER, J.

Maryland Code, § 3-204(a)(1) of the Criminal Law Article (CL) makes it a misdemeanor for a person recklessly to engage in conduct that creates a substantial risk of death or serious physical injury to another person. The question before us is whether the intentional ingestion of cocaine by a pregnant woman can form the basis for a conviction under that statute of the reckless endangerment of the later-born child. The answer is "no."

BACKGROUND

We deal here with two prosecutions in the Circuit Court for Talbot County. In August, 2004, the State's Attorney filed a criminal information charging Regina Kilmon with second degree child abuse, contributing to conditions that render a child delinquent, reckless endangerment, and possession of a controlled dangerous substance . . . . The reckless endangerment count charged that Ms. Kilmon, "on or about the 3rd day of June through the 4th day of June, 2004, in Talbot County, Maryland, did recklessly engage in conduct, to wit: using cocaine while pregnant with Andrew Kilmon that created a substantial risk of death and serious physical harm to Andrew Kilmon."

In January, 2005, Ms. Kilmon entered a plea of guilty on the reckless endangerment count in exchange for the State's commitment to *nol pros* the other charges. [T]he State's Attorney offered . . . the following statement of facts in support of the guilty plea:

> "On June the 3rd, 2004, the Defendant . . . gave birth at the Easton Memorial Hospital to a baby boy subsequently named Andrew W. Kilmon. At the time of the birth the baby weighed 5.5 pounds. The baby was tested through a drug screen which at the hospital which showed the presence of cocaine at the level of 675 nanograms per milliliter . . . [T]he minimum sensitivity level for cocaine is 300 nanograms per milliliter. The State would have produced expert testimony that the result of using cocaine by a pregnant woman . . . is as follows: that they are more likely to experience premature separation of the placenta, spontaneous abortion and premature delivery. That cocaine may cause blood clots to develop in the brain of the fetus. May also interfere with the development of the fetus. And that low

birth weight in bab[ies] born with cocaine in their system may lead to many health problems versus normal size babies. There would be further testimony that the only source of cocaine in the baby's system would have been that as derived from the blood stream of the mother prior to birth . . . ."

[T]he court accepted the plea, found Ms. Kilmon guilty of reckless endangerment, and sentenced her to four years in prison. Ms. Kilmon [appealed but the Court of Appeals granted *certiorari* before the appeal proceeded].

[In the companion case, Kelly Lynn Cruz was charged with the same crimes for using cocaine while pregnant with her child, who was born at 3 pounds 2 ounces on January 13, 2005. Cruz entered a *nol pros* to three charges, but pled not guilty to the reckless endangerment charge. The court] found her guilty and imposed a sentence of five years in prison, with two-and-a-half years suspended in favor of five years of supervised probation and drug treatment commencing on release from prison . . . .

DISCUSSION

We pointed out in *Holbrook v. State*, 364 Md. 354, 365, 772 A.2d 1240, 1246 (2001), that "[r]eckless endangerment is purely a statutory crime" in Maryland. It exists and is defined solely by CL § 3-204. Because the issue is therefore entirely one of statutory construction, it is necessary to determine whether, in enacting § 3-204(a) (1) and its relevant antecedents, the General Assembly intended that the statute include the conduct charged . . . .

The relevant part of CL § 3-204, subsection (a) (1), makes it a misdemeanor for a person recklessly to "engage in conduct that creates a substantial risk of death or serious physical injury to another." By "another," it obviously meant another person. Aware of the Constitutional issues that may arise from regarding a fetus or embryo as a person, the State, in its briefs, makes clear its position that, for purposes of the convictions under § 3-204(a) (1), the "person" allegedly endangered by each appellant's conduct was not the fetus, but the child, after the child's live birth. The offense, in this context, according to the State, is that the prenatal ingestion of cocaine recklessly endangers the child immediately upon and after his or her live birth.

The reckless endangerment statute was first enacted in Maryland in 1989 as Art. 27, § 120. [I]t was modeled after § 211.2 of the Model Penal Code, first proposed by the American Law Institute in 1962. The later-published Commentary to § 211.2 notes that specific kinds of reckless conduct had previously been made criminal in various States — everything from reckless driving to shooting at an airplane to placing an obstruction on railway tracks — and that § 211.2 was intended to "replace the haphazard coverage of prior law with one comprehensive provision" that "reaches any kind of conduct that 'places or may place another person in danger of death or serious bodily injury.'" MODEL PENAL CODE AND COMMENTARIES, PART II (1980) at 195–96.

We have tended to construe the Maryland statute in that manner as well. In *Minor v. State*, 326 Md. 436, 443, 605 A.2d 138, 141 (1992), we held that guilt under the statute does not depend on whether the defendant actually intended that his reckless conduct create a substantial risk of death or serious injury, but whether his conduct, viewed objectively, "was so reckless as to constitute a gross departure from the standard of conduct that a law-abiding person would observe, and thereby create the substantial risk that the statute was designed to punish." In *State v. Pagotto*, 361 Md. 528, 549, 762 A.2d 97, 108 (2000), we confirmed the further point made in *Minor* that the statute was "aimed at deterring the commission of potentially harmful conduct before an injury or death occurs."

Unquestionably, the proscription against recklessly endangering conduct is, and was intended to be, a broad one. Whether it was intended to include conduct of a pregnant woman that might endanger in some way the child she is carrying is not so clear, however, as that brings into play some important policy-laden considerations not relevant with respect to acts committed by third persons.

In support of its argument that the statute should be read as including that conduct, the State observes that an injury committed while a child is still *in utero* can produce criminal liability if the child is later born alive . . . .

     . . . .

The appellants respond that acceptance of the "born alive" rule with respect to the common law relating to homicides that arise from acts committed by others does not inform whether the Legislature intended CL §3-204(a) (1) to criminalize conduct committed by a pregnant woman that might endanger the child she is carrying. The statute itself, though certainly broad in its language, does not specifically address that question. In the absence of any direct evidence of legislative intent in this regard, either clear or implicit from the language of the statute, we look for other relevant indications, and there are some very cogent ones.

Notwithstanding occasional flights of fancy that may test the proposition, the law necessarily and correctly presumes that Legislatures act reasonably, knowingly, and in pursuit of sensible public policy. When there is a legitimate issue of interpretation, therefore, courts are required, to the extent possible, to avoid construing a statute in a manner that would produce farfetched, absurd, or illogical results which would not likely have been intended by the enacting body. . . .

Keeping in mind that recklessness, not intention to injure, is the key element of the offense, if, as the State urges, the statute is read to apply to the effect of a pregnant woman's conduct on the child she is carrying, it could well be construed to include not just the ingestion of unlawful controlled substances but a whole host of intentional and conceivably reckless activity that could not possibly have been within the contemplation of the Legislature — everything from becoming (or remaining) pregnant with knowledge that the child likely will have a genetic disorder that may cause serious disability or death, to the continued use of legal drugs that are contraindicated during pregnancy, to consuming alcoholic beverages to excess, to smoking, to not maintaining a proper and sufficient diet, to avoiding proper and available pre-natal medical care, to failing to wear a seat belt while driving, to violating other traffic laws in ways that create a substantial risk of producing or exacerbating personal injury to her child, to exercising too much or too little, indeed to engaging in virtually any injury-prone activity that, should an injury occur, might reasonably be expected to endanger the life or safety of the child. Such ordinary things as skiing or horseback riding could produce criminal liability. If the State's position were to prevail, there would seem to be no clear basis for categorically excluding any of those activities from the ambit of the statute; criminal liability would depend almost entirely on how aggressive, inventive, and persuasive any particular prosecutor might be.

Confirming the strong inference that the General Assembly did not intend CL § 3-204(a) (1) to include any of this kind of self-induced activity, including the ingestion of controlled substances, is the manner in which they actually dealt with that kind of activity when they chose to deal with it.

In the same 1989 session that produced the initial enactment of the reckless endangerment law, House Bill 809 was introduced. That bill would have expanded the definition of "abuse" to include the physical dependency of a newborn infant on any controlled dangerous substance for the purposes of the Family Law Article provisions requiring reporting and investigation of suspected child abuse. The bill was opposed by the Secretary of Human Resources, the American Civil Liberties Union (ACLU), and the Foster Care Review Board, and it died in the House Judiciary Committee.

In 1990, a number of bills were introduced on the subject, taking differing approaches. . . .

All of those bills died in the House Judiciary Committee. . . . [T]he Department of Human Services [opposed the bills and] observed (1) that it was often difficult to establish a cause-and-effect relationship between a woman's drug use and injuries to the fetus, (2) in most cases, a woman's use of drugs during pregnancy is the result of her inability to control her addiction, the absence of adequate treatment programs, or her lack of awareness of the possible effects of her drug use on the fetus, and (3) in those States where criminal sanctions exist for drug use by pregnant women, the data did not indicate any decrease in the number of drug-using pregnant women. It is noteworthy that the opposition to those bills that would have established criminal liability, from both State agencies and private groups that dealt with the problem of drug-addicted pregnant women and babies, was not that the bills were unnecessary because criminal liability already existed under the reckless endangerment law, but that the approach they embraced was not good public policy.

. . . .

. . . In 1997, by 1997 Md. Laws, ch. 367 and 368, the Legislature opted to address the problem in a tripartite civil context. It first attached to the definition of a "child in need of assistance" a presumption that a child is not receiving ordinary and proper care and attention if the child was born addicted to or dependent on cocaine, heroin, or a derivative of either, or was born with a significant presence of those drugs in his or her blood. That circumstance could be taken into account by a Juvenile Court in deciding whether the child is in need of assistance. Second, the bills amended the law pertaining to the termination of parental rights to add that circumstance, plus the parent's refusal to participate in a drug treatment program, as a consideration in determining whether termination is in the child's best interest.

Finally, the Legislature required the Departments of Human Resources and Health and Mental Hygiene to develop and implement pilot drug intervention programs for the mothers of children who were born drug-exposed. As part of that intervention program, the Department of Human Resources was required to file a child in need of assistance petition on behalf of a child who was born drug-exposed if the mother failed to complete drug treatment and she and the father were unable to provide adequate care for the child. See Maryland Code, § 3-818 of the Cts. & Jud. Proc. Article and §§ 5-323(d) (3) (ii) and 5-706.3 of the Family Law Article.

In the 2004 session, Senate Bill 349 and House Bill 802, both captioned as the Unborn Victims of Violence Act, were introduced. Among other provisions dealing with murder, manslaughter, and assault, they would have defined the term "another," as used in CL § 3-204(a) (1), to include an unborn child, thereby making it a criminal offense recklessly to create a substantial risk of death or serious physical injury to an unborn child. There was no exemption for the conduct of the child's mother, other than in the context of a legal abortion. Neither bill passed. . . .

In 2005, the Legislature, in a more limited version of the 2004 bills, extended the law of murder and manslaughter to permit a prosecution for the murder or manslaughter of a viable fetus. *See* 2005 Md. Laws, Ch. 546, enacting CL § 2-103. The statute provides that such a prosecution is warranted only if the defendant intended to cause the death of or serious physical injury to the viable fetus or wantonly or recklessly disregarded the likelihood that the defendant's action would cause death or serious physical injury to the fetus. There are at least two important differences between the 2005 enactment and the failed 2004 bills. First, the 2005 Act did not encompass the reckless endangerment statute but dealt only with unlawful homicides. At least equally significant, and perhaps more so, the Legislature was careful, in § 2-103(f), to make clear that "[n]othing in this section applies to an act or failure to act of a pregnant woman with regard to her own fetus."

That provision was added to the bill specifically to allay concerns expressed by the Secretary of Health and Mental Hygiene, the ACLU, and the National Organization for Women that, absent such a provision, women might be subject to prosecution for not accessing available prenatal care or causing the death of a fetus by reason of reckless behavior during pregnancy, including a drug overdose . . . .

This sixteen-year history, from 1989 to 2005, shows rather clearly that, although a pregnant woman, like anyone else, may be prosecuted for her own possession of controlled dangerous substances, the General Assembly, despite being importuned on numerous occasions to do so, has chosen not to impose additional criminal penalties for the effect that her *ingestion* of those substances might have on the child, either before or after birth. It has consistently rejected proposals that would have allowed such conduct to constitute murder, manslaughter, child abuse, or reckless endangerment. In doing so, the Legislature obviously gave credence to the evidence presented to it that criminalizing the ingestion of controlled substances — in effect criminalizing drug addiction for this one segment of the population, pregnant women — was not the proper approach to the problem and had, in fact, proved ineffective in other States in deterring either that conduct or addiction generally on the part of pregnant women. It deliberately opted, instead, to deal with the problem by providing drug treatment programs for pregnant women and using the child in need of assistance and termination of parental rights remedies if the women failed to take advantage of the treatment programs and, as a result, were unable to provide proper care for the child.

Given the exemption added to the 2005 legislation, it would be an anomaly, indeed, if the law were such that a pregnant woman who, by ingesting drugs, recklessly caused the death of a viable fetus would suffer no criminal liability for manslaughter but, if the child was born alive and did not die, could be imprisoned for five years for reckless endangerment. A *non-fatal* injury resulting from reckless conduct would be culpable; a *fatal injury* resulting from the same reckless conduct would not be.

Maryland is not the only State to address this issue. These kinds of cases — prosecutions for reckless endangerment, child abuse, or distribution of controlled substances based on a pregnant woman's ingestion of a controlled dangerous substance, or, in some cases, excessive amounts of alcohol — have arisen in other States, and the overwhelming majority of courts that have considered the issue have concluded that those crimes do not encompass that kind of activity. Indeed, only one State — South Carolina — has so far held to the contrary.

In conformance with this nearly universal view, but most particularly in light of the way in which the Maryland General Assembly has chosen to deal with the problem, we hold that it was not the legislative intent that CL § 3-204(a) (1) apply to prenatal drug ingestion by a pregnant woman. We therefore reverse the judgments entered by the Circuit Court.

NOTES AND QUESTIONS

1.   **Drug use by pregnant women.** *Kilmon v. Maryland* illustrates the issues and arguments presented in most cases concerning drug use by pregnant women, regardless of the criminal statute at issue. It collects the cases in the following footnote:

> For specific holdings, *see Johnson v. State*, 602 So. 2d 1288 (Fla. 1992) (statute prohibiting delivery of controlled substance to person under 18 not applicable to ingestion of controlled substance prior to giving birth) and *cf. State v. Ashley*, 701 So. 2d 338 (Fla. 1997) (confirming *Johnson*); *State v. Gray*, 62 Ohio St. 3d 514, 584 N.E.2d 710 (Ohio 1992) (statute prohibiting creation of substantial risk to health or safety of child not applicable to abuse of drugs during pregnancy); *State v. Aiwohi*, 109 Haw. 115, 123 P.3d 1210, 1214 (Hawaii 2005) (manslaughter statute not applicable; court recognizes that "overwhelming majority of jurisdictions confronted with the prosecution of a mother for her own prenatal conduct, causing harm to the subsequently born child, refuse to permit such prosecutions"); *Com. v. Welch*, 864 S.W.2d 280 (Ky. 1993) (legislature did not intend child abuse statute to apply to prenatal self-abuse that caused drugs to be transmitted through umbilical cord to child); *Sheriff v. Encoe*, 110 Nev. 1317, 885 P.2d 596 (Nev. 1994) (child endangerment statute does not apply to transmission of illegal substances from mother to newborn through umbilical cord);

Reinesto v. Superior Court, 182 Ariz. 190, 894 P.2d 733 (Ariz. App. 1995) (child abuse statute not applicable); *Reyes v. Superior Court*, 75 Cal. App. 3d 214, 141 Cal. Rptr. 912 (Cal. App. 1977) (child endangerment statute not applicable); *People v. Hardy*, 188 Mich. App. 305, 469 N.W.2d 50 (Mich. App. 1991) (statute prohibiting delivery of cocaine did not apply to transmission of cocaine through umbilical cord from mother to child); *People v. Morabito*, 151 Misc. 2d 259, 580 N.Y.S.2d 843 (City Ct. 1992) (child endangerment statute not applicable to that circumstance); *Collins v. State*, 890 S.W.2d 893 (Tex. App. 1994) (reckless injury statute not applicable); *State v. Deborah J.Z.*, 228 Wis. 2d 468, 596 N.W.2d 490 (Wis. App. 1999) (reckless injury statute not applicable to ingestion of excessive amount of alcohol during pregnancy causing injury to child). Compare *Whitner v. State*, 328 S.C. 1, 492 S.E.2d 777 (S.C. 1997), *cert. denied*, 523 U.S. 1145, 118 S. Ct. 1857, 140 L. Ed. 2d 1104 (1998) (holding that woman could be prosecuted for endangering fetus by prenatal substance abuse).

Like *Kilmon*, most of these cases were decided largely on public policy grounds — interpreting the statute in light of its probable effects, often bolstered by a legislative history of rejecting proposed bills that would have criminalized drug use in pregnancy in one way or another. There is little or no discussion of the woman's right to liberty or the state's power to protect the fetus or delivered child. Many state legislatures have engaged in a policy debate similar to Maryland's and described in the opinion. Would the state have the power to enact a criminal prohibition, even if it were not good policy? If so, would it have the power to impose other standards of behavior on women during pregnancy or whenever they might be or become pregnant? Many of the most serious risks to a fetus, particularly from cocaine, occur during the first trimester of pregnancy, perhaps even before a woman realizes she is pregnant.

2. The South Carolina exception. Only one state — South Carolina — has interpreted its criminal statutes to include drug use during pregnancy. *Whitner v. State*, 492 S.E.2d 777 (S.C. 1997), *cert. denied*, 523 U.S. 1145 (1998). In 1992, Cornelia Whitner was sentenced to eight years in prison after pleading guilty to criminal child neglect for taking crack cocaine during her third trimester of pregnancy. Her baby was born with cocaine metabolites in its system, but otherwise healthy. Her attorney did not advise her that the child neglect law might not apply to prenatal drug use. Whitner later petitioned for post conviction relief, claiming ineffective assistance of counsel and lack of subject matter jurisdiction. Her petition was granted on both grounds, but reversed by the state Supreme Court.

The child neglect statute at issue, S.C. CODE ANN. § 20-7-50 (1985), provided:

> Any person having the legal custody of any child or helpless person, who shall, without lawful excuse, refuse or neglect to provide, as defined in § 20-7-490, the proper care and attention for such child or helpless person, so that the life, health or comfort of such child or helpless person is endangered or is likely to be endangered, shall be guilty of a misdemeanor and shall be punished within the discretion of the circuit court.

In addition, under the Children's Code, "child" means a "person under the age of eighteen." S.C. CODE ANN. § 20-7-30(1) (1985).

The Supreme Court of South Carolina held that a viable fetus was a "person" for purposes of the Children's Code. The State argued that any maternal act that endangered or was likely to endanger "the life, comfort, or health of a viable fetus" qualified as child neglect, and the Court agreed. The Court rejected Whitner's arguments, similar to those accepted in *Kilmon* and the decisions in other states, that including viable fetuses within the definition of "child" would lead to absurd results and that the legislature had rejected bills using that approach. Instead, the Court found that the "plain meaning" of child included a viable fetus. It supported this conclusion with a discussion of developments in tort and criminal law to permit actions against a third party who injures a pregnant woman and her fetus:

. . . .

In 1960, this Court decided *Hall v. Murphy*, 236 S.C. 257, 113 S.E.2d 790 (1960). That case concerned the application of South Carolina's wrongful death statute to an infant who died four hours after her birth as a result of injuries sustained prenatally during viability. The Appellants argued that a viable fetus was not a person within the purview of the wrongful death statute, because, inter alia, a fetus is thought to have no separate being apart from the mother.

We found such a reason for exclusion from recovery "unsound, illogical and unjust," and concluded there was "no medical or other basis" for the "assumed identity" of mother and viable unborn child. In light of that conclusion, this Court unanimously held: "We have no difficulty in concluding that a fetus having reached that period of prenatal maturity where it is capable of independent life apart from its mother is a person."

. . . .

Since a viable child is a person before separation from the body of its mother and since prenatal injuries tortuously inflicted on such a child are actionable, it is apparent that the complaint alleges such an "act, neglect or default" by the defendant, to the injury of the child . . . . Once the concept of the unborn, viable child as a person is accepted, we have no difficulty in holding that a cause of action for tortious injury to such a child arises immediately upon the infliction of the injury.

. . . .

Similarly, we do not see any rational basis for finding a viable fetus is not a "person" in the present [criminal] context. Indeed, it would be absurd to recognize the viable fetus as a person for purposes of homicide laws and wrongful death statutes but not for purposes of statutes proscribing child abuse . . . .

328 S.C. at 6–7.

Are there differences between allowing parents a cause of action in tort for the loss of a child at the hands of a third party and holding the mother criminally responsible for injuring her own child before birth?

Whitner argued that the statute burdened her right to privacy, specifically her right to carry her pregnancy to term. But the Court rejected the very idea of any such right:

> [W]e do not think any fundamental right of Whitner's — or any right at all, for that matter — is implicated under the present scenario. It strains belief for Whitner to argue that using crack cocaine during pregnancy is encompassed within the constitutionally recognized right of privacy. Use of crack cocaine is illegal, period. No one here argues that laws criminalizing the use of crack cocaine are themselves unconstitutional.

328 S.C. at 18.

Ultimately, it found that the law did not affect Whitner's right to privacy, because she remained free to carry the pregnancy to term. And, pregnant or not, she never had any right to use cocaine. (This conclusion might be disputed where criminal laws prohibit only the possession, sale or distribution, and not the *use*, of a controlled substance.) Finally, the court found that the state had not only a legitimate, but a compelling interest in the potential life of the fetus, citing *Planned Parenthood of Southeastern Pennsylvania v. Casey*. Thus, the Court construed the statute's use of the term child — in South Carolina's child neglect and endangerment statute — to include a viable fetus, and the ingestion of cocaine as endangering a child.

But the court's treatment of the constitutional issue goes beyond the statute at issue. It concludes, "If the State wishes to impose additional criminal penalties on pregnant women who engage in this already illegal conduct because of the effect the conduct has on the viable fetus, it may do so. We do not see how the fact of pregnancy elevates the use of crack cocaine to the lofty status of a fundamental right." 328 S.C. at 18. But, can the state impose a harsher sentence for cocaine use on pregnant women than on everyone else? Here, the constitutional argument should focus on the status that triggers the enhanced penalty and the relationship between the mother and child. Both would appear to be the type of interest that has been regarded as "fundamental" under traditional federal constitutional analysis. Should not the state have to show a compelling interest and that the statute achieves that interest in the narrowest possible way? Can the state do so? Is protecting the health of the future child a compelling interest? The Attorney General of South Carolina argued publicly that the purpose of prosecuting pregnant women was to prevent harm to children, not to put women in prison. (An example of how hospitals cooperated in that endeavor is found *Ferguson v. City of Charlestown*, below.) In April 2014, Tennessee enacted a new law ostensibly for the same purpose. Tenn. Code. Anno. § 39-13-107(c)(1) (2014). A pregnant woman who uses an illegal narcotic while pregnant can be charged with assault if her child is born addicted to or harmed by the drug, unless the woman entered a drug treatment program before delivery and completed the program. The law is to sunset in 2016, but could be enacted anew if an evaluation finds it gets pregnant women into drug treatment or reduces illegal drug use.

3.   The effects of drug use in pregnancy. Illicit drugs are risky for both adults and babies. Several can cause premature birth. Heroin and other opiates, as well as dextroamphetamine and methamphetamine, can induce withdrawal symptoms in newborns, such as jitteriness and trouble sleeping and feeding. Heroin withdrawal symptoms can last several months. Longer lasting risks can include growth deficits, hyperactivity, and learning problems. *See* the National Institute of Drug Abuse, above; Robert Wood Johnson University Hospital, Illegal Drug Use and Pregnancy, www.rwjuh.edu/health_information/adult_pregnant_drug.html (visited Mar. 2014).

As is the case with many risks, it is often difficult to determine whether any newborn will suffer drug-related harm and, if so, which harm. The South Carolina court takes the view that a fetus exposed to drugs like cocaine will almost certainly suffer serious damage: "the consequences of abuse or neglect which takes place after birth often pale in comparison to those resulting from abuse suffered by the viable fetus before birth." 328 S.C. at 8. Child protection professionals in state child welfare and social service agencies might dispute this claim, since they deal with often horrifying cases of physical abuse, neglect and death of children at many ages. Nonetheless, serious injury from drug exposure in utero was feared when crack cocaine became widely available in the late 1980s and early 1990s. By the end of the 1990s, however, scientific evidence showed far less long term damage than originally suspected. Researchers found that even children who appeared to have some developmental delays could improve with appropriate education. A key problem is the difficulty of isolating the effect of one drug on the child of a woman who has multiple problems of her own. Pregnant women who used cocaine often used other drugs, including alcohol and tobacco, had poor nutrition, unstable housing, sometimes with abusive partners, no pre-natal care, and were often poor, all of which are factors that can jeopardize the physical or mental development of their children. Of course, parents who abuse or neglect their children after they are born are subject to having the children removed from their custody and even prosecution under ordinary child abuse statutes. In the absence of conditions that threaten the child, however, state child welfare agencies typically attempt to provide services to families in order to enable them to properly care for their children.

Most substance abuse treatment professionals, the American Public Health Association, and other health organizations recommend providing drug treatment services to pregnant women. The Maryland court in *Kilmon* notes that Maryland proposed offering treatment programs, but it was not followed up because of cost. The cost of providing drug treatment services, however, is typically less that the cost of confining someone in prison. Experts in the field argue that pregnant women who use drugs need treatment programs tailored specifically to pregnant women and that such programs almost always have long waiting lists, so that the pregnancy is likely to end before space becomes available.

4. References. For background information and data on controlled substances, such as cocaine, marijuana, heroin, and other drugs, see The National Institute for Drug Abuse, www.drugabuse.gov/ (visited Mar. 2014), and the Substance Abuse and Mental Health Services Administration, http://samhsa.gov/ (visited Mar. 2014). More references can be found at the site of the NIH National Library of Medicine, www.nlm.nih.gov/medlineplus/drugabuse.html (visited Mar. 2014). There is also a separate national institute, the National Institute for Alcohol Abuse and Alcoholism, dedicated to alcohol. *See* www.niaaa.nih.gov/.

FERGUSON v. CITY OF CHARLESTON
532 U.S. 67 (2001)

Stevens, J.

In this case, we must decide whether a state hospital's performance of a diagnostic test to obtain evidence of a patient's criminal conduct for law enforcement purposes is an unreasonable search if the patient has not consented to the procedure. More narrowly, the question is whether the interest in using the threat of criminal sanctions to deter pregnant women from using cocaine can justify a departure from the general rule that an official nonconsensual search is unconstitutional if not authorized by a valid warrant.

I

In the fall of 1988, staff members at the public hospital operated in the city of Charleston by the Medical University of South Carolina (MUSC) became concerned about an apparent increase in the use of cocaine by patients who were receiving prenatal treatment. In response to this perceived increase, as of April 1989, MUSC began to order drug screens to be performed on urine samples from maternity patients who were suspected of using cocaine. If a patient tested positive, she was then referred by MUSC staff to the county substance abuse commission for counseling and treatment. However, despite the referrals, the incidence of cocaine use among the patients at MUSC did not appear to change.

Some four months later, Nurse Shirley Brown, the case manager for the MUSC obstetrics department, heard a news broadcast reporting that the police in Greenville, South Carolina, were arresting pregnant users of cocaine on the theory that such use harmed the fetus and was therefore child abuse. Nurse Brown discussed the story with MUSC's general counsel, Joseph C. Good, Jr., who then contacted Charleston Solicitor Charles Condon in order to offer MUSC's cooperation in prosecuting mothers whose children tested positive for drugs at birth.

After receiving Good's letter, Solicitor Condon took the first steps in developing the policy at issue in this case. He organized the initial meetings, decided who would participate, and issued the invitations, in which he described his plan to prosecute women who tested positive for cocaine while pregnant. The task force that Condon formed included representatives of MUSC, the police, the County Substance Abuse Commission and the Department of Social Services. Their deliberations led to MUSC's adoption of a 12-page document entitled "POLICY M-7," dealing with the subject of "Management of Drug Abuse During Pregnancy."

The first three pages of Policy M-7 set forth the procedure to be followed by the hospital staff to "identify/assist pregnant patients suspected of drug abuse." The first section, entitled the "Identification of Drug Abusers," provided that a patient should be tested for cocaine through a urine drug screen if she met one or more of nine criteria.[3] It also stated that a chain of custody should be followed when

---

[3] Those criteria were as follows:

obtaining and testing urine samples, presumably to make sure that the results could be used in subsequent criminal proceedings. The policy also provided for education and referral to a substance abuse clinic for patients who tested positive. Most important, it added the threat of law enforcement intervention that "provided the necessary 'leverage' to make the [p]olicy effective." That threat was, as respondents candidly acknowledge, essential to the program's success in getting women into treatment and keeping them there.

The threat of law enforcement involvement was set forth in two protocols, the first dealing with the identification of drug use during pregnancy, and the second with identification of drug use after labor. Under the latter protocol, the police were to be notified without delay and the patient promptly arrested. Under the former, after the initial positive drug test, the police were to be notified (and the patient arrested) only if the patient tested positive for cocaine a second time or if she missed an appointment with a substance abuse counselor. In 1990, however, the policy was modified at the behest of the solicitor's office to give the patient who tested positive during labor, like the patient who tested positive during a prenatal care visit, an opportunity to avoid arrest by consenting to substance abuse treatment.

The last six pages of the policy contained forms for the patients to sign, as well as procedures for the police to follow when a patient was arrested. The policy also prescribed in detail the precise offenses with which a woman could be charged, depending on the stage of her pregnancy. If the pregnancy was 27 weeks or less, the patient was to be charged with simple possession. If it was 28 weeks or more, she was to be charged with possession and distribution to a person under the age of 18 — in this case, the fetus. If she delivered "while testing positive for illegal drugs," she was also to be charged with unlawful neglect of a child. Under the policy, the police were instructed to interrogate the arrestee in order "to ascertain the identity of the subject who provided illegal drugs to the suspect." Other than the provisions describing the substance abuse treatment to be offered to women who tested positive, the policy made no mention of any change in the prenatal care of such patients, nor did it prescribe any special treatment for the newborns.

II

Petitioners are 10 women who received obstetrical care at MUSC and who were arrested after testing positive for cocaine. Four of them were arrested during the

---

"1. No prenatal care

"2. Late prenatal care after 24 weeks gestation

"3. Incomplete prenatal care

"4. Abruptio placentae

"5. Intrauterine fetal death

"6. Preterm labor 'of no obvious cause'

"7. IUGR [intrauterine growth retardation] 'of no obvious cause'

"8. Previously known drug or alcohol abuse

"9. Unexplained congenital anomalies."

initial implementation of the policy; they were not offered the opportunity to receive drug treatment as an alternative to arrest. The others were arrested after the policy was modified in 1990; they either failed to comply with the terms of the drug treatment program or tested positive for a second time. Respondents include the City of Charleston, law enforcement officials who helped develop and enforce the policy, and representatives of MUSC.

Petitioners' complaint challenged the validity of the policy under various theories, including the claim that warrantless and nonconsensual drug tests conducted for criminal investigatory purposes were unconstitutional searches. Respondents advanced two principal defenses to the constitutional claim: (1) that, as a matter of fact, petitioners had consented to the searches; and (2) that, as a matter of law, the searches were reasonable, even absent consent, because they were justified by special non-law-enforcement purposes. . . . [The jury found for the respondents.]

. . . . The Court of Appeals for the Fourth Circuit affirmed, but without reaching the question of consent. . . .

III

Because MUSC is a state hospital, the members of its staff are government actors, subject to the strictures of the Fourth Amendment. Moreover, the urine tests conducted by those staff members were indisputably searches within the meaning of the Fourth Amendment. Neither the District Court nor the Court of Appeals concluded that any of the nine criteria used to identify the women to be searched provided either probable cause to believe that they were using cocaine, or even the basis for a reasonable suspicion of such use. Rather, the District Court and the Court of Appeals viewed the case as one involving MUSC's right to conduct searches without warrants or probable cause. Furthermore, given the posture in which the case comes to us, we must assume for purposes of our decision that the tests were performed without the informed consent of the patients.

Because the hospital seeks to justify its authority to conduct drug tests and to turn the results over to law enforcement agents without the knowledge or consent of the patients, this case differs from the four previous cases in which we have considered whether comparable drug tests "fit within the closely guarded category of constitutionally permissible suspicionless searches." In three of those cases, we sustained drug tests for railway employees involved in train accidents, for United States Customs Service employees seeking promotion to certain sensitive positions, and for high school students participating in interscholastic sports. [*See Earles, infra.*] In the fourth case, we struck down such testing for candidates for designated state offices as unreasonable.

In each of those cases, we employed a balancing test that weighed the intrusion on the individual's interest in privacy against the "special needs" that supported the program. As an initial matter, we note that the invasion of privacy in this case is far more substantial than in those cases. In the previous four cases, there was no misunderstanding about the purpose of the test or the potential use of the test results, and there were protections against the dissemination of the results to third parties. The use of an adverse test result to disqualify one from eligibility for a particular benefit, such as a promotion or an opportunity to participate in an extracurricular activity, involves a less serious intrusion on privacy than the unauthorized dissemination of such results to third parties. The reasonable expectation of privacy enjoyed by the typical patient undergoing diagnostic tests in a hospital is that the results of those tests will not be shared with non-medical personnel without her consent. In none of our prior cases was there any intrusion upon that kind of expectation.

The critical difference between those four drug-testing cases and this one, however, lies in the nature of the "special need" asserted as justification for the warrantless searches. In each of those earlier cases, the "special need" that was advanced as a justification for the absence of a warrant or individualized suspicion was one divorced from the State's general interest in law enforcement . . . . In this case, however, the central and indispensable feature of the policy from its inception was the use of law enforcement to coerce the patients into substance abuse treatment. This fact distinguishes this case from circumstances in which physicians or psychologists, in the course of ordinary medical procedures aimed at helping the patient herself, come across information that under rules of law or ethics is subject to reporting requirements, which no one has challenged here.

Respondents argue in essence that their ultimate purpose — namely, protecting the health of both mother and child — is a beneficent one . . . . In this case, a review of the M-7 policy plainly reveals that the purpose actually served by the MUSC searches "is ultimately indistinguishable from the general interest in crime control."

. . . In this case, as Judge Blake put it in her dissent below, "it . . . is clear from the record that an initial and continuing focus of the policy was on the arrest and prosecution of drug-abusing mothers . . . ." Tellingly, the document codifying the policy incorporates the police's operational guidelines. It devotes its attention to the chain of custody, the range of possible criminal charges, and the logistics of police notification and arrests. Nowhere, however, does the document discuss different courses of medical treatment for either mother or infant, aside from treatment for the mother's addiction.

Moreover, throughout the development and application of the policy, the Charleston prosecutors and police were extensively involved in the day-to-day administration of the policy. Police and prosecutors decided who would receive the reports of positive drug screens and what information would be included with those reports. Law enforcement officials also helped determine the procedures to be followed when performing the screens. In the course of the policy's administration, they had access to Nurse Brown's medical files on the women who tested positive, routinely attended the substance abuse team's meetings, and regularly received copies of team documents discussing the women's progress. Police took pains to coordinate the timing and circumstances of the arrests with MUSC staff, and, in particular, Nurse Brown.

While the ultimate goal of the program may well have been to get the women in question into substance abuse treatment and off of drugs, the immediate objective of the searches was to generate evidence *for law enforcement purposes* in order to reach that goal. The threat of law enforcement may ultimately have been intended as a means to an end, but the direct and primary purpose of MUSC's policy was to ensure the use of those means. In our opinion, this distinction is critical. Because law enforcement involvement always serves some broader social purpose or objective, under respondents' view, virtually any nonconsensual suspicionless search could be immunized under the special needs doctrine by defining the search solely in terms of its ultimate, rather than immediate, purpose. Such an approach is inconsistent with the Fourth Amendment. Given the primary purpose of the Charleston program, which was to use the threat of arrest and prosecution in order to force women into treatment, and given the extensive involvement of law enforcement officials at every stage of the policy, this case simply does not fit within the closely guarded category of "special needs."

The fact that positive test results were turned over to the police does not merely provide a basis for distinguishing our prior cases applying the "special needs" balancing approach to the determination of drug use. It also provides an affirmative reason for enforcing the strictures of the Fourth Amendment. While state hospital employees, like other citizens, may have a duty to provide the police with evidence of criminal conduct that they inadvertently acquire in the course of routine treatment, when they undertake to obtain such evidence from their patients *for the specific purpose of incriminating those patients*, they have a special obligation to make sure that the patients are fully informed about their constitutional rights, as standards of knowing waiver require.

. . . While respondents are correct that drug abuse both was and is a serious problem, "the gravity of the threat alone cannot be dispositive of questions concerning what means law enforcement officers may employ to pursue a given purpose."

Accordingly, the judgment of the Court of Appeals is reversed, ...

. . . .

JUSTICE SCALIA, with JUSTICES REHNQUIST and THOMAS, dissenting.

. . . .

I

. . . What petitioners [and] the Court, . . . really object to is not the urine testing, but the hospital's reporting of positive drug-test results to police. But the latter is obviously not a search. At most it may be a "derivative use of the product of a past unlawful search," which, of course, "work[s] no new Fourth Amendment wrong" and "presents a question, not of rights, but of remedies." There is only one act that could conceivably be regarded as a search of petitioners in the present case: the taking of the urine sample. I suppose the *testing* of that urine for traces of unlawful drugs could be considered a search of sorts, but the Fourth Amendment protects only against searches of citizens' "persons, houses, papers, and effects"; and it is entirely unrealistic to regard urine as one of the "effects" (i.e., part of the property) of the person who has passed and abandoned it.

It is rudimentary Fourth Amendment law that a search which has been consented to is not unreasonable. There is no contention in the present case that the urine samples were extracted forcibly. The only conceivable bases for saying that they were obtained without consent are the contentions (1) that the consent was coerced by the patients' need for medical treatment, (2) that the consent was uninformed because the patients were not told that the tests would include testing for drugs, and (3) that the consent was uninformed because the patients were not told that the results of the tests would be provided to the police.

. . . .

Until today, we have *never* held — or even suggested — that material which a person voluntarily entrusts to someone else cannot be given by that person to the police, and used for whatever evidence it may contain . . . . I would adhere to our established law, which says that information obtained through violation of a relationship of trust is obtained consensually, and is hence not a search.

There remains to be considered the first possible basis for invalidating this search, which is that the patients were coerced to produce their urine samples by their necessitous circumstances, to wit, their need for medical treatment of their pregnancy. If that was coercion, it was not coercion applied by the government — and if such nongovernmental coercion sufficed, the police would never be permitted to use the ballistic evidence obtained from treatment of a patient with a bullet wound. And the Fourth Amendment would invalidate those many state laws that require physicians to report gunshot wounds, evidence of spousal abuse, and like the South Carolina law relevant here, evidence of child abuse.

BOARD OF EDUCATION OF INDEPENDENT SCHOOL DISTRICT NO. 92 OF POTTAWATOMIE COUNTY v. EARLS
536 U.S. 822 (2002)

THOMAS, JUSTICE.

The city of Tecumseh, Oklahoma, is a rural community located approximately 40 miles southeast of Oklahoma City. The School District administers all Tecumseh public schools. In the fall of 1998, the School District adopted the Student Activities Drug Testing Policy (Policy), which requires all middle and high school students to consent to drug testing in order to participate in any extracurricular activity. In practice, the Policy has been applied only to competitive extracurricular activities sanctioned by the Oklahoma Secondary Schools Activities Association, such as the Academic Team, Future Farmers of America, Future Homemakers of America, band, choir, pom pom, cheerleading, and athletics. Under the Policy, students are required to take a drug test before participating in an extracurricular activity, must submit to random drug testing while participating in that activity, and must agree to be tested at any time upon reasonable suspicion. The urinalysis tests are designed to detect only the use of illegal drugs, including amphetamines, marijuana, cocaine, opiates, and barbiturates, not medical conditions or the presence of authorized prescription medications.

At the time of their suit, both respondents attended Tecumseh High School. Respondent Lindsay Earls was a member of the show choir, the marching band, the Academic Team, and the National Honor Society. Respondent Daniel James sought to participate in the Academic Team. Together with their parents, Earls and James brought a 42 U.S.C. § 1983 action against the School District, challenging the Policy both on its face and as applied to their participation in extracurricular activities. They alleged that the Policy violates the Fourth Amendment . . . . They also argued that the School District failed to identify a special need for testing students who participate in extracurricular activities, and that the "Drug Testing Policy neither addresses a proven problem nor promises to bring any benefit to students or the school."

Applying the principles articulated in *Vernonia School Dist. 47J v. Acton*, 515 U.S. 646 (1995), in which we upheld the suspicionless drug testing of school athletes, the United States District Court for the Western District of Oklahoma rejected respondents' claim that the Policy was unconstitutional . . . .

The United States Court of Appeals for the Tenth Circuit reversed, holding that the Policy violated the Fourth Amendment. . . .

II

The Fourth Amendment to the United States Constitution protects "the right of the people to be secure in their persons, houses, papers, and effects, against unreasonable searches and seizures." . . .

In the criminal context, reasonableness usually requires a showing of probable cause. The probable-cause standard, however, "is peculiarly related to criminal investigations" and may be unsuited to determining the reasonableness of administrative searches where the "Government seeks to prevent the development of hazardous conditions." *Treasury Employees v. Von Raab* . . . . The Court [in Vernonia] also held that a warrant and finding of probable cause are unnecessary in the public school context because such requirements "'would unduly interfere with the maintenance of the swift and informal disciplinary procedures [that are] needed.'"

Given that the School District's Policy is not in any way related to the conduct of criminal investigations, respondents do not contend that the School District requires probable cause before testing students for drug use. Respondents instead argue that drug testing must be based at least on some level of individualized suspicion. It is true that we generally determine the reasonableness of a search by balancing the nature of the intrusion on the individual's privacy against the promotion of legitimate governmental interests. But we have long held that "the Fourth Amendment imposes no irreducible requirement of [individualized] suspicion." "In certain limited circumstances, the Government's need to discover such latent or hidden conditions, or to prevent their development, is sufficiently compelling to justify the intrusion on privacy entailed by conducting such searches without any measure of individualized suspicion." *Von Raab* . . . . Therefore, in the context of safety and administrative regulations, a search unsupported by probable cause may be reasonable "when 'special needs, beyond the normal need for law enforcement, make the warrant and probable-cause requirement impracticable.' "

Significantly, this Court has previously held that "special needs" inhere in the public school context. While school children do not shed their constitutional rights when they enter the schoolhouse, "Fourth Amendment rights . . . are different in public schools than elsewhere; the 'reasonableness' inquiry cannot disregard the schools' custodial and tutelary responsibility for children." In particular, a finding of individualized suspicion may not be necessary when a school conducts drug testing.

In *Vernonia*, this Court held that the suspicionless drug testing of athletes was constitutional. The Court, however, did not simply authorize all school drug testing, but rather conducted a fact-specific balancing of the intrusion on the children's Fourth Amendment rights against the promotion of legitimate governmental interests. . . .

A

We first consider the nature of the privacy interest allegedly compromised by the drug testing. . . .

A student's privacy interest is limited in a public school environment where the State is responsible for maintaining discipline, health, and safety. School children are routinely required to submit to physical examinations and vaccinations against disease. Securing order in the school environment sometimes requires that students be subjected to greater controls than those appropriate for adults. Without first establishing discipline and maintaining order, teachers cannot begin to educate their students. And apart from education, the school has the obligation to protect pupils from mistreatment by other children, and also to protect teachers themselves from violence by the few students whose conduct in recent years has prompted national concern.

Respondents argue that because children participating in non-athletic extracurricular activities are not subject to regular physicals and communal undress, they have a stronger expectation of privacy than the athletes tested in *Vernonia*. This distinction, however, was not essential to our decision in *Vernonia*, which depended primarily upon the school's custodial responsibility and authority.

In any event, students who participate in competitive extracurricular activities voluntarily subject themselves to many of the same intrusions on their privacy as do athletes. Some of these clubs and activities require occasional off-campus travel and communal undress. All of them have their own rules and requirements for participating students that do not apply to the student body as a whole. For example, each of the competitive extracurricular activities governed by the Policy must abide by the rules of the Oklahoma Secondary Schools Activities Association, and a faculty sponsor monitors the students for compliance with the various rules dictated by the clubs and activities. This regulation of extracurricular activities further diminishes the expectation of privacy among school children.

B

Next, we consider the character of the intrusion imposed by the Policy. Urination is "an excretory function traditionally shielded by great privacy." But the "degree of intrusion" on one's privacy caused by collecting a urine sample "depends upon the manner in which production of the urine sample is monitored."

Under the Policy, a faculty monitor waits outside the closed restroom stall for the student to produce a sample and must "listen for the normal sounds of urination in order to guard against tampered specimens and to insure an accurate chain of custody." The monitor then pours the sample into two bottles that are sealed and placed into a mailing pouch along with a consent form signed by the student. This procedure is virtually identical to that reviewed in *Vernonia*, except that it additionally protects privacy by allowing male students to produce their samples behind a closed stall. Given that we considered the method of collection in *Vernonia* a "negligible" intrusion, the method here is even less problematic.

In addition, the Policy clearly requires that the test results be kept in confidential files separate from a student's other educational records and released to school personnel only on a "need to know" basis. Respondents nonetheless contend that the intrusion on students' privacy is significant because the Policy fails to protect effectively against the disclosure of confidential information and, specifically, that the school "has been careless in protecting that information: for example, the Choir teacher looked at students' prescription drug lists and left them where other students could see them." But the choir teacher is someone with a "need to know," because during off-campus trips she needs to know what medications are taken by her students. . . . This one example of alleged carelessness hardly increases the character of the intrusion.

Moreover, the test results are not turned over to any law enforcement authority. Nor do the test results here lead to the imposition of discipline or have any academic consequences. Rather, the only consequence of a failed drug test is to limit the student's privilege of participating in extracurricular activities. Indeed, a student may test positive for drugs twice and still be allowed to participate in extracurricular activities. After the first positive test, the school contacts the student's parent or guardian for a meeting. The student may continue to participate in the activity if within five days of the meeting the student shows proof of receiving drug counseling and submits to a second drug test in two weeks. For the second positive test, the student is suspended from participation in all extracurricular activities for 14 days, must complete four hours of substance abuse counseling, and must submit to monthly drug tests. Only after a third positive test will the student be suspended from participating in any extracurricular activity for the remainder of the school year, or 88 school days, whichever is longer.

Given the minimally intrusive nature of the sample collection and the limited uses to which the test results are put, we conclude that the invasion of students' privacy is not significant.

C

Finally, this Court must consider the nature and immediacy of the government's concerns and the efficacy of the Policy in meeting them. This Court has already articulated in detail the importance of the governmental concern in preventing drug use by school children. The drug abuse problem among our Nation's youth has hardly abated since *Vernonia* was decided in 1995. In fact, evidence suggests that it has only grown worse. As in *Vernonia*, "the necessity for the State to act is magnified by the fact that this evil is being visited not just upon individuals at large, but upon children for whom it has undertaken a special responsibility of care and direction." The health and safety risks identified in *Vernonia* apply with equal force to Tecumseh's children. Indeed, the nationwide drug epidemic makes the war against drugs a pressing concern in every school.

Additionally, the School District in this case has presented specific evidence of drug use at Tecumseh schools. Teachers testified that they had seen students who appeared to be under the influence of drugs and that they had heard students speaking openly about using drugs. A drug dog found marijuana cigarettes near the school parking lot. Police officers once found drugs or drug paraphernalia in a car driven by a Future Farmers of America member. And the school board president reported that people in the community were calling the board to discuss the "drug situation." We decline to second-guess the finding of the District Court that "viewing the evidence as a whole, it cannot be reasonably disputed that the [School District] was faced with a 'drug problem' when it adopted the Policy."

Respondents consider the proffered evidence insufficient and argue that there is no "real and immediate interest" to justify a policy of drug testing non-athletes. We have recognized, however, that "[a] demonstrated problem of drug abuse . . . [is] not in all cases necessary to the validity of a testing regime," but that some showing does "shore up an assertion of special need for a suspicionless general search program." The School District has provided sufficient evidence to shore up the need for its drug testing program.

Furthermore, this Court has not required a particularized or pervasive drug problem before allowing the government to conduct suspicionless drug testing. For instance, in *Von Raab* the Court upheld the drug testing of customs officials on a purely preventive basis, without any documented history of drug use by such officials. In response to the lack of evidence relating to drug use, the Court noted generally that "drug abuse is one of the most serious problems confronting our society today," and that programs to prevent and detect drug use among customs officials could not be deemed unreasonable. Likewise, the need to prevent and deter the substantial harm of childhood drug use provides the necessary immediacy for a school testing policy. Indeed, it would make little sense to require a school district to wait for a substantial portion of its students to begin using drugs before it was allowed to institute a drug testing program designed to deter drug use.

Given the nationwide epidemic of drug use, and the evidence of increased drug use in Tecumseh schools, it was entirely reasonable for the School District to enact this particular drug testing policy. We reject the Court of Appeals' novel test that "any district seeking to impose a random suspicionless drug testing policy as a condition to participation in a school activity must demonstrate that there is some identifiable drug abuse problem among a sufficient number of those subject to the testing, such that testing that group of students will actually redress its drug problem." Among other problems, it would be difficult to administer such a test. As we cannot articulate a threshold level of drug use that would suffice to justify a drug testing program for schoolchildren, we refuse to fashion what would in effect be a constitutional quantum of drug use necessary to show a "drug problem."

Respondents also argue that the testing of non-athletes does not implicate any safety concerns, and that safety is a "crucial factor" in applying the special needs framework. They contend that there must be "surpassing safety interests," or "extraordinary safety and national security hazards," in order to override the usual protections of the Fourth Amendment. Respondents are correct that safety factors into the special needs analysis, but the safety interest furthered by drug testing is undoubtedly substantial for all children, athletes and non-athletes alike. We know all too well that drug use carries a variety of health risks for children, including death from overdose.

We also reject respondents' argument that drug testing must presumptively be based upon an individualized reasonable suspicion of wrongdoing because such a testing regime would be less intrusive. In this context, the Fourth Amendment does not require a finding of individualized suspicion, and we decline to impose such a requirement on schools attempting to prevent and detect drug use by students. Moreover, we question whether testing based on individualized suspicion in fact would be less intrusive. Such a regime would place an additional burden on public school teachers who are already tasked with the difficult job of maintaining order and discipline. A program of individualized suspicion might unfairly target members of unpopular groups. The fear of lawsuits resulting from such targeted searches may chill enforcement of the program, rendering it ineffective in combating drug use. In any case, this Court has repeatedly stated that reasonableness under the Fourth Amendment does not require employing the least intrusive means, because "the logic of such elaborate less-restrictive-alternative arguments could raise insuperable barriers to the exercise of virtually all search-and-seizure powers."

Finally, we find that testing students who participate in extracurricular activities is a reasonably effective means of addressing the School District's legitimate concerns in preventing, deterring, and detecting drug use. While in *Vernonia* there might have been a closer fit between the testing of athletes and the trial court's finding that the drug problem was "fueled by the 'role model' effect of athletes' drug use," such a finding was not essential to the holding. *Vernonia* did not require the school to test the group of students most likely to use drugs, but rather considered the constitutionality of the program in the context of the public school's custodial responsibilities. Evaluating the Policy in this context, we conclude that the drug testing of Tecumseh students who participate in extracurricular activities effectively serves the School District's interest in protecting the safety and health of its students.

III

Within the limits of the Fourth Amendment, local school boards must assess the desirability of drug testing school children. In upholding the constitutionality of the

Policy, we express no opinion as to its wisdom. Rather, we hold only that Tecumseh's Policy is a reasonable means of furthering the School District's important interest in preventing and deterring drug use among its schoolchildren. . . .

. . . .

Justice Ginsberg with Stevens, O'Connor, and Souter, dissenting.

Seven years ago, in *Vernonia School Dist. 47J v. Acton*, 515 U.S. 646 (1995), this Court determined that a school district's policy of randomly testing the urine of its student athletes for illicit drugs did not violate the Fourth Amendment. In so ruling, the Court emphasized that drug use "increased the risk of sports-related injury" and that Vernonia's athletes were the "leaders" of an aggressive local "drug culture" that had reached "'epidemic proportions.'" Today, the Court relies upon *Vernonia* to permit a school district with a drug problem its superintendent repeatedly described as "not . . . major," to test the urine of an academic team member solely by reason of her participation in a non-athletic, competitive extracurricular activity — participation associated with neither special dangers from, nor particular predilections for, drug use.

. . . The particular testing program upheld today is not reasonable, it is capricious, even perverse: Petitioners' policy targets for testing a student population least likely to be at risk from illicit drugs and their damaging effects. I therefore dissent.

. . . .

This case presents circumstances dispositively different from those of *Vernonia*. True, as the Court stresses, Tecumseh students participating in competitive extracurricular activities other than athletics share two relevant characteristics with the athletes of *Vernonia*. First, both groups attend public schools. . . . Concern for student health and safety is basic to the school's care-taking, and it is undeniable that "drug use carries a variety of health risks for children . . . ."

Those risks, however, are present for all schoolchildren. *Vernonia* cannot be read to endorse invasive and suspicionless drug testing of all students upon any evidence of drug use, solely because drugs jeopardize the life and health of those who use them. Many children, like many adults, engage in dangerous activities on their own time; that the children are enrolled in school scarcely allows government to monitor all such activities. If a student has a reasonable subjective expectation of privacy in the personal items she brings to school, surely she has a similar expectation regarding the chemical composition of her urine. Had the *Vernonia* Court agreed that public school attendance, in and of itself, permitted the State to test each student's blood or urine for drugs, the opinion in *Vernonia* could have saved many words. . . .

The second commonality to which the Court points is the voluntary character of both interscholastic athletics and other competitive extracurricular activities. "By choosing to 'go out for the team,' [school athletes] voluntarily subject themselves to a degree of regulation even higher than that imposed on students generally." Comparably, the Court today observes, "students who participate in competitive extracurricular activities voluntarily subject themselves to" additional rules not applicable to other students.

The comparison is enlightening. While extracurricular activities are "voluntary" in the sense that they are not required for graduation, they are part of the school's educational program; for that reason, the petitioner (hereinafter School District) is justified in expending public resources to make them available. Participation in such activities is a key component of school life, essential in reality for students applying to college, and, for all participants, a significant contributor to the breadth and quality of the educational experience. Students "volunteer" for extracurricular pursuits in the same way they might volunteer for honors classes: They subject themselves to additional requirements, but they do so in order to take full advantage of the education offered them. ·

Voluntary participation in athletics has a distinctly different dimension: Schools regulate student athletes discretely because competitive school sports by their nature require communal undress and, more important, expose students to physical risks that schools have a duty to mitigate. For the very reason that schools cannot offer a program of competitive athletics without intimately affecting the privacy of students, *Vernonia* reasonably analogized school athletes to "adults who choose to participate in a closely regulated industry." Industries fall within the closely regulated category when the nature of their activities requires substantial government oversight. Interscholastic athletics similarly require close safety and health regulation; a school's choir, band, and academic team do not.

In short, *Vernonia* applied, it did not repudiate, the principle that "the legality of a search of a student should depend simply on the reasonableness, *under all the circumstances*, of the search." Enrollment in a public school, and election to participate in school activities beyond the bare minimum that the curriculum requires, are indeed factors relevant to reasonableness, but they do not on their own justify intrusive, suspicionless searches. *Vernonia*, accordingly, did not rest upon these factors; instead, the Court performed what today's majority aptly describes as a "fact-specific balancing." Balancing of that order, applied to the facts now before the Court, should yield a result other than the one the Court announces today.

Vernonia initially considered "the nature of the privacy interest upon which the search [there] at issue intruded." The Court emphasized that student athletes' expectations of privacy are necessarily attenuated:

. . . .

Competitive extracurricular activities other than athletics, however, serve students of all manner: the modest and shy along with the bold and uninhibited. Activities of the kind plaintiff-respondent Lindsay Earls pursued — choir, show choir, marching band, and academic team — afford opportunities to gain self-assurance, to "come to know faculty members in a less formal setting than the typical classroom," and to acquire "positive social supports and networks [that] play a critical role in periods of heightened stress."

On "occasional out-of-town trips," students like Lindsay Earls "must sleep together in communal settings and use communal bathrooms." But those situations are hardly equivalent to the routine communal undress associated with athletics;

the School District itself admits that when such trips occur, "public-like restroom facilities," which presumably include enclosed stalls, are ordinarily available for changing, and that "more modest students" find other ways to maintain their privacy.

After describing school athletes' reduced expectation of privacy, the *Vernonia* Court turned to "the character of the intrusion . . . complained of." Observing that students produce urine samples in a bathroom stall with a coach or teacher outside, *Vernonia* typed the privacy interests compromised by the process of obtaining samples "negligible." As to the required pretest disclosure of prescription medications taken, the Court assumed that "the School District would have permitted [a student] to provide the requested information in a confidential manner — for example, in a sealed envelope delivered to the testing lab." On that assumption, the Court concluded that Vernonia's athletes faced no significant invasion of privacy.

In this case, however, Lindsay Earls and her parents allege that the School District handled personal information collected under the policy carelessly, with little regard for its confidentiality. Information about students' prescription drug use, they assert, was routinely viewed by Lindsay's choir teacher, who left files containing the information unlocked and unsealed, where others, including students, could see them; and test results were given out to all activity sponsors whether or not they had a clear "need to know."

. . . .

Finally, the "nature and immediacy of the governmental concern," faced by the Vernonia School District dwarfed that confronting Tecumseh administrators. Vernonia initiated its drug testing policy in response to an alarming situation. . . . Tecumseh, by contrast, repeatedly reported to the Federal Government during the period leading up to the adoption of the policy that "types of drugs [other than alcohol and tobacco] including controlled dangerous substances, are present [in the schools] but have not identified themselves as major problems at this time." As the Tenth Circuit observed, "without a demonstrated drug abuse problem among the group being tested, the efficacy of the District's solution to its perceived problem is . . . greatly diminished."

The School District cites *Treasury Employees v. Von Raab*, 489 U.S. 656 (1989), in which this Court permitted random drug testing of customs agents absent "any perceived drug problem among Customs employees," given that "drug abuse is one of the most serious problems confronting our society today." The tests in *Von Raab* and *Railway Labor Executives*, however, were installed to avoid enormous risks to the lives and limbs of others, not dominantly in response to the health risks to users invariably present in any case of drug use.

Urging that "the safety interest furthered by drug testing is undoubtedly substantial for all children, athletes and non-athletes alike," the Court cuts out an element essential to the *Vernonia* judgment. Citing medical literature on the effects of combining illicit drug use with physical exertion, the *Vernonia* Court emphasized that "the particular drugs screened by [Vernonia's] Policy have been demonstrated to pose substantial physical risks to athletes." We have since confirmed that these special risks were necessary to our decision in *Vernonia*.

At the margins, of course, no policy of *random* drug testing is perfectly tailored to the harms it seeks to address. The School District cites the dangers faced by members of the band, who must "perform extremely precise routines with heavy equipment and instruments in close proximity to other students," and by Future Farmers of America, who "are required to individually control and restrain animals as large as 1500 pounds." For its part, the United States acknowledges that "the linebacker faces a greater risk of serious injury if he takes the field under the influence of drugs than the drummer in the halftime band," but parries that "the risk of injury to a student who is under the influence of drugs while playing golf, cross country, or volleyball (sports covered by the policy in *Vernonia*) is scarcely any greater than the risk of injury to a student . . . handling a 1500-pound steer (as [Future Farmers of America] members do) or working with cutlery or other sharp instruments (as [Future Homemakers of America] members do)." Notwithstanding nightmarish images of out-of-control flatware, livestock run amok, and colliding tubas disturbing the peace and quiet of Tecumseh, the great majority of students the School District seeks to test in truth are engaged in activities that are not safety sensitive to an unusual degree. There is a difference between imperfect tailoring and no tailoring at all.

The Vernonia district, in sum, had two good reasons for testing athletes: Sports team members faced special health risks and they "were the leaders of the drug culture." No similar reason, and no other tenable justification, explains Tecumseh's decision to target for testing all participants in every competitive extracurricular activity.

Nationwide, students who participate in extracurricular activities are significantly less likely to develop substance abuse problems than are their less-involved peers. Even if students might be deterred from drug use in order to preserve their extracurricular eligibility, it is at least as likely that other students might forgo their extracurricular involvement in order to avoid detection of their drug use. Tecumseh's policy thus falls short doubly if deterrence is its aim: It invades the privacy of students who need deterrence least, and risks steering students at greatest risk for substance abuse away from extracurricular involvement that potentially may palliate drug problems.

NOTES AND QUESTIONS

5. Fourth Amendment basics. As set out in the *Ferguson* decision, the Fourth Amendment generally prohibits "unreasonable searches and seizures." In most ordinary criminal investigations, this requires that a warrant be issued on the showing of probable cause; exceptions are allowed for consensual searches, searches incident to an arrest, and a few other circumstances where there is some immediate and individualized showing of probable cause. But the Supreme Court also has on a few occasions acknowledged an additional exception for certain "permissible suspicionless searches." In each of those cases, the Court has employed a balancing test that weighed the intrusion on the individual's interest in privacy against the "special needs" that supported the search. In *Skinner v. Railway Labor Executives' Ass'n*, 489 U.S. 602 (1989), the Court upheld warrantless drug testing of railway employees; in *Treasury Employees v. Von Raab*, 489 U.S. 656 (1989), the Court allowed similar testing of customs officials who were applying for promotion; in *Vernonia School Dist. 47J v. Acton*, 515 U.S. 646 (1995), the Court allowed warrantless, random drug testing of athletes participating in sports at public schools (discussed extensively in *Earls*). However, in *Chandler v. Miller*, 520 U.S. 305 (1997) the Court refused to allow for warrantless testing of candidates for political office.

These exceptional "suspicionless" search cases all derive their reasoning from a more general principle essentially distinguishing between governmental efforts to identify individual criminal conduct and government's "special need" to preemptively protect the public safety. As articulated by the *Earls* majority: "[T]he Government's need to discover such latent or hidden conditions, or to prevent their development, is sufficiently compelling to justify the intrusion on privacy entailed by conducting such searches without any measure of individualized suspicion." The Supreme Court developed this "special needs" analysis in cases involving "administrative searches" or inspections of premises, not people, in regulated industries. Examples included health and safety inspections of coal mines and warehouses, either without a warrant or with reasonable suspicion, a standard lower than probable cause. *See*, e.g., *Marshall v. Barlow's*, 436 U.S. 307 (1978). Other cases required that a warrant be issued prior to an administrative search (*e.g.*, a search that is part of a citywide inspection of rental property), but that the warrant could be issued based on legislative or administratively determined criteria. *See Camara v. Municipal Court of City & County of San Francisco*, 387 U.S. 523 (1967).

The administrative search exception was initially justified primarily on the ground that a premises search was not personal. Later decisions, however, emphasized both the government's goal in conducting the search (the "special need") and the fact that regulated industries — and ultimately their employees — should have a limited expectation of privacy. In the "special needs" cases noted above, the Court has sometimes strained to find reasons why those who are subjected to drug testing are engaged in safety-sensitive jobs and how drug use would result in harm to others, such as passengers on trains. Dissenting Justices often question both the likelihood of harm and the coherence of the "special needs" exception. For example, in *Skinner*, Justice Marshall wrote, "There is no drug exception to the Constitution, any more than there is a Communism exception or an exception for any other real or imagined sources of domestic unrest." The *Chandler* court insisted, "Our precedents establish that the proffered special need for drug testing must be substantial," adding that the special needs categories are "closely guarded" and limited to the state's concerns for public safety and its role as guardian of school children. *Chandler*, 520 U.S. at 318. Nevertheless, as illustrated by the *Earls case*, the Court continues to apply the special needs exception to a widening range of drug testing policies.

6. *Ferguson*: **special needs v. law enforcement.** In *Ferguson*, the Court rejected the government's claim that a special needs exception comparable to that in *Skinner, Von Raab*, and *Vernonia*, justified the hospital's policy. The Court found that the invasion of privacy in this case "is far more substantial than in those cases" and that, in any event, the government's "special need" was little different than it was in any other criminal prosecution. Do you agree? The Court distinguished the special needs line of cases from the general rule that searches used for law enforcement (including investigations) require a warrant or consent and found that the hospital's policy fell within the general rule. In particular, it insisted that the determining factor was the specific — and immediate — purpose of the drug testing, not its ultimate or long-term goal. Although both the hospital and law enforcement personnel may have intended to protect mothers and children, the policy itself was limited to law enforcement — threatened or actual arrest and criminal prosecution for drug crimes. The Court cautioned that "Because law enforcement always serves some broader social purpose or objective, virtually any nonconsensual suspicionless search could be immunized under the special needs doctrine by defining the search solely in terms of its ultimate, rather than immediate, goal."

The Court has maintained the conceptual distinction between searches whose immediate purpose is law enforcement and those intended to address internal organizational safety policies. A critical factor in these cases, including *Ferguson*, is how drug test results are used. (Another factor, of rather less conceptual weight, is how privately and sensitively the drug test itself is conducted, as a component of its reasonableness.) The Court has approved policies that require the results of drug testing to be kept confidential within the agency and used solely for (civil) personnel decisions, such as hiring and firing or identifying and treating employees whose drug use may pose safety risks to others, as in *Skinner*; but has struck down policies that give test results to police for purposes of criminal investigations.

7. **Is reporting medical information a search or seizure?** As the dissent points out in *Ferguson*, this sort of drug testing is not the usual sort of search or seizure. How would you respond to the Justice Scalia's claims that there may not be a search, consensual or otherwise, that is subject to the Fourth Amendment limitations at all — or, alternatively, that the only search is the taking of the urine sample, a procedure to which the patients may have consented? Compare his view of patient expectations of privacy in medical care with that expressed in the majority opinion.

Justice Scalia also argues that the special needs exception presumably upholds the validity of laws requiring physicians and other providers to report gunshot wounds, evidence of child abuse, and other data. Do you agree? If so, is this because patients have no privacy interest in controlling the use of medical information (like test results or diagnoses) that is acquired by providers as part of ordinary medical treatment? Might this view mean that any government agency programs could have unfettered access to anything in patients' medical records? (*See* Chapter 7.) Alternatively, might the dissent base his presumption on the idea that such reporting laws demonstrate a special need unrelated to law enforcement? The information provided by physicians under most reporting laws goes to public health or social welfare agencies, not law enforcement. The reference to the compulsory reporting of gunshot wounds, which might be sent to the police for criminal investigations, however, undermines this interpretation. Is the dissent in *Ferguson* suggesting that the state can require generalized reporting of any information for purposes of criminal investigation or prosecution without a warrant or probable cause? See the discussion of prescription drug monitoring programs in Notes 16–17 *infra*.

8. ***Earls* and the expansion of special needs.** *Earls* represents a significant expansion of the special needs exception. The drug policy met some of the requirements for a special needs exception, however. The test results were kept confidential within the school (despite some possible laxity in keeping them secure from prying eyes) and were not delivered to law enforcement officials or used for criminal investigations. The more difficult question was whether the school had a special need for precluding participation in extracurricular programs by students who used drugs. The several opinions in *Earls* illustrate the Justices' different views of what counts as a special need.

The majority opinion emphasizes the *parens patriae* role of the state — and by extension the school — as protector of children. Who is the school protecting by its policy — the students tested or other students with whom they have contact? Is this the same approach used in the cases in which a government agency's special need is to ensure the safety of its customers and passengers? The Court is obviously concerned with what it calls "the nationwide epidemic of drug use." What other risks might threaten school children? As a practical matter, how effective is the school's policy in deterring drug use among students? What other measures might a school take to protect its students from harm?

Justice Ginsberg's dissent lays out the factual differences between the students affected in *Vernonia* and those in *Earls*. Not surprisingly, the majority minimize or ignore factual differences between the circumstances in *Earls* and *Vernonia* that are emphasized by the dissent. Do you agree with the majority that "students who participate in competitive extracurricular activities voluntarily subject themselves to many of the same intrusions in their privacy as do athletes"? Was *Vernonia* itself correctly decided? The dissent argues that the risks to students in the extracurricular programs are no different from the risks for all students and that the majority's reasoning would permit drug testing for all students. Do you agree?

9. **Drug testing proliferates.** As *Earls* demonstrates, the special needs exception has encouraged the adoption of drug testing policies by many government agencies, including police departments, fire departments, and schools. *See, e.g., Knox County Educ. Ass'n v. Knox County Bd. of Educ.*, 158 F.3d 361 (6th Cir. 1998) (applicants for all safety-sensitive positions in a school district); *Tanks v. Greater Cleveland Regional Transit Auth.*, 930 F.2d 475 (6th Cir. 1991) (municipal bus drivers); *Penny v. Kennedy*, 915 F.2d 1065 (6th Cir. 1990) (police); *Shoemaker v. Handel*, 795 F.2d 1136 (3rd Cir. 1986) (jockeys after horse race). How effective have such policies been? Not all such programs have been upheld. *See, e.g., Petersen v. City of Mesa*, 207 Ariz. 35, *cert. denied*, 543 U.S. 814 (2004) (random, suspicionless drug testing of firefighters); *Capua v. City of Plainfield*, 643 F.Supp 1507 (D.N.J. 1986) (firefighters); *Horsemen's Benevolent Association v. State Racing Commission*, 532 N.E. 2d 644 (Mass. 1989) (jockeys). Nonetheless, the trend has been to uphold drug testing of public school students and public employees in anything that can be considered safety sensitive jobs.

Private organizations, of course, are not subject to any Fourth Amendment constraints on requiring drug testing for their employees. What, if any, differences are there between an employer's policy forbidding its employees to use unlawful controlled substances and a policy forbidding employees to smoke? Private universities and research organizations that receive federal grants and other federal funds must comply with federal policies requiring certification that staff in the funded program do not use controlled substances. Universities might also consider drug testing for enrolled students. How might a state university justify such testing?

10.   Drug testing recipients of government benefits. Federal and state agencies have proposed or implemented programs to require drug testing of all or some categories of persons receiving public assistance. For example, the federal Temporary Assistance for Needy Families (TANF) authorizes states to require drug testing of aid recipients. 21 U.S.C. § 862(b). In 2012, the Social Security Act was amended in a similar fashion, allowing states to deny unemployment compensation for persons who do not pass drug tests. Federal laws that simply allow states to impose drug testing do not directly impose drug testing, but state laws acting on that authority may. What special need would such a requirement serve?

In *Marchwinski v. Howard*, 113 F. Supp. 2d 1134 (E.D. Mich. 2000), *aff'd*, 2003 U.S. App. LEXIS 6893 (6th Cir. Apr. 7 2003) (by an equally divided en banc panel), a federal district court enjoined a Michigan statute that authorized the suspicionless drug testing of welfare recipients. The state argued that drug use impairs one's ability to be a responsible parent, contributes to child abuse and neglect, impedes becoming economically self-sufficient, and that the state has a special need to insure that the money it gives recipients is not spent on drugs. The district court disagreed, finding that public safety was not in jeopardy from welfare recipients. Relying on several of the Supreme Court's Fourth Amendment decisions noted above (except *Earls*, decided later), the district court concluded that the Michigan law violated the Fourth Amendment.

On appeal, the court of appeals reversed, and accepting the state's arguments, found that special needs could include more than just public safety. 309 F. 3d 330 (6th Cir. 2002), *vacated*, 60 Fed. Appx. 601, 2003 U.S. App. LEXIS 6893 (6th Cir. Apr. 7, 2003). Alternatively, it found that the law could be interpreted as imposing a condition prohibiting drug use by welfare recipients, with the testing simply a means of enforcing that condition. However, the sixth circuit held a rehearing en banc, in which the judges were equally divided (6 for reversal; 6 for affirmance), so the first appellate decision was vacated, and the district court's decision finding that the challengers were likely to succeed on the merits of their Fourth Amendment claim was affirmed. The case was then settled, with the state agreeing to require drug testing only for aid recipients who are reasonably suspected of using drugs. *Settlement reached in Lawsuit Over Mandatory Drug Testing of Welfare Recipients*, Am. Civil Liberties Union Press Release, Dec. 18, 2003, www.aclumich.org/issues/search-and-seizure/2003-12/1044 (visited Mar. 2014).

A similar Florida statute was challenged by a TANF recipient. *See Lebron v. Sec'y, Fla. Dep't of Children and Families* 710 F. 3d 1202 (11th Cir. 2013). The district granted a preliminary injunction against the drug testing. The eleventh circuit court affirmed, finding that the district court did not abuse its discretion in concluding that the plaintiff was likely to succeed on the merits:

> Instead, the only pertinent inquiry is whether there is a substantial special need for mandatory, suspicionless drug testing of TANF recipients when there is no immediate or direct threat to public safety, when those

being searched are not directly involved in the frontlines of drug interdiction, when there is no public school setting where the government has a responsibility for the care and tutelage of its young students, or when there are no dire consequences or grave risk of imminent physical harm as a result of waiting to obtain a warrant if a TANF recipient, or anyone else for that matter, is suspected of violating the law. We conclude that, on this record, the answer to that question of whether there is a substantial special need for mandatory suspicionless drug testing is "no."

Id. at 16 (slip op.)

The district court then granted plaintiff's motion for summary judgment, holding the drug testing program in violation of the Fourth Amendment, because no special need justified dispensing with individualized suspicion. *Lebron v. Wilkins*, 2013 U.S. Dist. LEXIS 182492 (M.D. Fla. Dec. 31, 2013). The case is subject to appeal as of February 2014.

11.   **Highway checkpoints.** A slightly different line of cases concerns random stops of the public at highway roadblocks or checkpoints. Such stops constitute a seizure within the meaning of the Fourth Amendment. The Supreme Court has upheld brief, suspicionless seizures at highway checkpoints to keep intoxicated drivers off the road, *Michigan Department of State Police v. Sitz*, 496 U.S. 444 (1990), and to ask drivers if they had witnessed a hit-and-run accident, *Illinois v. Lidster*, 540 U.S. 419 (2004). In City of *Indianapolis v. Edmond*, 531 U.S. 32 (2000), however, the Supreme Court held that a police roadblock set up to find drugs without individualized suspicion violated the Fourth Amendment. The police stopped all vehicles at six locations, checked the driver's license and registration, looked in and around the car from the outside, and walked a narcotics-detection dog around the car. About nine percent of drivers were arrested, 55% on charges of drug-related crimes. As in *Ferguson*, the Court found that "what principally distinguishes these checkpoints from those we have previously approved is their primary purpose . . . interdicting illegal narcotics." It added, "We have never approved a checkpoint program whose primary purpose was to detect evidence of ordinary criminal wrongdoing." *Id.* at 40–41. The safety risk posed by drivers who are impaired by drugs or alcohol may be more apparent than that presented by a customs officer, although there is little evidence that highway checkpoints have identified a significant number of impaired drivers. Are there alternative ways to keep intoxicated drivers off the road?

12.   **Searches for criminal offenses involving drugs.** The foregoing examples of special needs suspicionless searches must be distinguished from law enforcement investigations of criminal activity. The U.S. Supreme Court has approved searches of individuals suspected of having controlled substances in several circumstances, including *United States v. Montoya*, 473 U.S. 531 (1985) (approving holding a woman suspected of being a drug mule for 72 hours at the border), as well as upholding a full strip and body cavity search of a person arrested by mistake in a routine "health" check for jail inmates in *Florence v. Board of Chosen Freeholders of City of Burlington*, 132 S. Ct. 1510 (2012) (excerpted in Chapter 6, C, 3, *supra.*)

Kristin M. Finklea, Erin Bagalman, & Lisa N. Sacco,
Prescription Drug Monitoring Programs
Congressional Research Service Report for Congress R42593, pp. 1–5, 11–12, 20 (Jan. 3, 2013),
http://fas.org/sgp/crs/misc/R42593.pdf

In the midst of national concern over illicit drug use and abuse, prescription drug abuse has been described by the Centers for Disease Control as an epidemic in the United States. Seven million individuals aged 12 or older (2.7% of this population) were current nonmedical users of prescription — or psychotherapeutic — drugs in 2010. Over 1 million emergency department visits involved nonmedical use of pharmaceuticals in 2010.

. . . .

Prescription drug overdoses caused 20,044 deaths in the United States in 2008; of these, 74% (14,800) involved opioid pain relievers. Of those individuals who used prescription painkillers non-medically in 2010, nearly three-quarters received the drugs from a friend or relative — either for free, through a purchase, or via stealing the drugs. Aside from prescription painkillers such as oxycodone, other commonly abused medications include benzodiazepines and amphetamine-like drugs.

. . . .

Nearly all prescription drugs involved in overdoses are originally prescribed by a physician (rather than, for example, being stolen from pharmacies). Thus, attention has been directed toward preventing the diversion of prescription drugs after the prescriptions are dispensed. Prescription drug monitoring programs (PDMPs) maintain statewide electronic databases of prescriptions dispensed for controlled substances. PDMP information can aid those in law enforcement and/or health care in identifying patterns of prescribing, dispensing, or receiving controlled substances that may indicate abuse.

Information collected by PDMPs may be used to support access to and legitimate medical use of controlled substances; identify or prevent drug abuse and diversion; facilitate the identification of prescription drug-addicted individuals and enable intervention and treatment; outline drug use and abuse trends to inform public health initiatives; or educate individuals about prescription drug use, abuse, and diversion as well as about PDMPs.

For over a decade, Congress has provided financial support for state-level PDMPs using electronic databases. In 2002, Congress established the Harold Rogers PDMP grant, administered by the Department of Justice (DOJ), to help law enforcement, regulatory entities, and public health officials analyze data on prescriptions for controlled substances. Three years later, Congress passed the National All Schedules Prescription Electronic Reporting Act of 2005 (NASPER) requiring the Secretary of Health and Human Services (HHS) to award grants to states to establish or improve PDMPs.

Congress has demonstrated a particular interest in facilitating interoperability among state-level PDMPs, as well as in establishing national programs. Policymakers have focused on enhancing state-level databases and interstate information sharing, and some have suggested establishing a national system. A related issue that policymakers may consider is whether PDMPs and their interstate information sharing platforms adequately protect personally identifiable and related health information and whether they can ensure that patients with legitimate medical needs have access to prescriptions. . . .

. . . .

PDMPs maintain statewide electronic databases of designated information on specified prescription drugs dispensed within the states. Data are made available to individuals or organizations as authorized under state law; these may include prescribers, law enforcement officials, licensing boards, or others. Possible uses of PDMPs include

- supporting patient access to controlled substances for legitimate medical use;

- identifying or preventing drug abuse and diversion;

- facilitating the identification of prescription drug-addicted individuals and appropriate intervention and treatment;

- outlining use and abuse trends to inform public health initiatives; and

- educating individuals about prescription drug use, abuse, and diversion.

In addition to uses of PDMPs aimed at drug abuse and diversion, an explicit goal of PDMPs is supporting access to controlled substances for legitimate medical use. This may best be understood by viewing PDMPs in comparison to earlier, paper-based programs called multiple copy prescription programs. For example, in 1914 a New York state law required physicians to use state-issued, serialized, duplicate prescription forms for certain drugs. Similarly, California began a multiple-copy prescription program using triplicate forms for specified narcotics in 1939; it expanded to monitor all schedule II narcotics in 1972 and schedule II non-narcotics in 1981. Studies of multiple-copy prescription programs found that many prescribers did not order the required prescription forms, rendering them unable to prescribe specified controlled substances even when medically appropriate. In addition, the ability to check a patient's prescription history using an electronic PDMP might give prescribers more confidence when considering the use of drugs with high risk of abuse.

. . . .

The entity responsible for administering the PDMP varies by state and may be pharmacy boards, departments of health, professional licensing agencies, law enforcement agencies, substance abuse agencies, or consumer protection agencies. Of the 49 authorized PDMPs, two-thirds are administered by either state pharmacy boards (18) or health departments (15).

. . . .

Access to information contained in the PDMP database is determined by state law and varies by state. The majority of states allow pharmacists and practitioners to access information related to their patients, and some also allow other entities — law enforcement, licensing and regulatory boards, state Medicaid Programs, state medical examiners, and research organization — to access the information under certain circumstances. State laws outline the procedures by which information from the PDMP may be accessed.

With respect to how the states identify and investigate cases of potential prescription drug diversion or abuse, PDMPs may be classified as *reactive* or *proactive*. In essence, "[s]tates with [r]eactive PDMPs . . . generate solicited reports only in response to a specific inquiry made by a prescriber, dispenser, or other party with appropriate authority" while "[s]tates with [p]roactive PDMPs . . . identify and investigate cases, generating unsolicited reports whenever suspicious behavior is detected."

. . . .

PDMPs may have unintended consequences beyond reducing prescription drug diversion and abuse. Prescribers may hesitate to prescribe medications monitored by the PDMP — even for appropriate medical use — if they are concerned about potentially coming under scrutiny from law enforcement or licensing authorities . . . . Their concerns may lead prescribers to replace medications that are monitored by the PDMP with medications that are not monitored by the PDMP, even if the unmonitored medications are inferior in terms of effectiveness or side effects. Studies showed that after benzodiazepines were added to New York's paper-based program in 1989, a decrease in benzodiazepine prescriptions was accompanied by an increase in prescriptions for other sedatives. . . .

Like prescribers, patients may fear coming under scrutiny from law enforcement if they use medications monitored by the PDMP, even if they have a legitimate medical need for the medications. Patients may worry about changes in prescribing behavior, which may limit their access to needed medications. Patients may worry about the additional cost of more frequent office visits if prescribers become more cautious about writing prescriptions with refills. Patients may also have concerns about the privacy and security of their prescription information if it is submitted to a PDMP.

. . . .

A PDMP may also have positive unintended consequences. For example, when accessing information from a PDMP, a prescriber or dispenser may identify a patient who is receiving legitimate prescriptions for multiple controlled substances and who is therefore at risk of harmful drug interactions. PDMPs may also enable prescribers to monitor their own DEA number to determine whether someone else is using it to forge prescriptions.

. . . .

While establishment and enhancement of PDMPs (such as interstate data sharing and real-time data access) enjoy broad support, some stakeholders express concerns about (1) health care versus law enforcement uses of PDMP data, particularly with regard to protection of personally identifiable health information, and (2) maintaining access to medication for patients with legitimate medical needs.

Research has demonstrated that PDMPs save law enforcement officials time in investigations, *if law enforcement officials have access to PDMP information.*

Concerns about potential law enforcement uses of PDMP data are expressed by stakeholder organizations representing prescribers. The American Medical Association (AMA), . . . supports the use of PDMPs and recommends that PDMPs be housed in health-related agencies (rather than law enforcement agencies). AMA further recommends that information from PDMPs "be used first for education of the specific physicians involved prior to any civil action against these physicians." The American Society of Addiction Medicine (ASAM), . . . likewise expresses concern about the use of PDMP data for purposes other than health care: "[L]aw enforcement, the judiciary, corrections professionals, employers, and others outside of the health care system should not be granted access to PDMP data except via the means available to them to secure access to other personally identifiable health information."

NOTES AND QUESTIONS

13.   **Prescription drugs.** Illegal drugs are not the only concern. Prescription drug overdoses (primarily from opioid pain relievers) are responsible for more deaths today than heroin and cocaine together. *See* Substance Abuse and Mental Health Services Administration, Results from the 2011 National Survey on Drug Use and Health: Summary of National Findings (2011); www.samhsa.gov/data/NSDUH/2k11Results/NSDUHresults2011.pdf (visited Oct. 2013). As sales of prescription drugs increased, so did deaths from overdoses of those drugs — from 3 per 100,000 population in 1991 to 11.8 per 100,000 in 2007. CDC, *CDC Grand Rounds: Prescription Drug Overdoses — A U.S. Epidemic*, 61 MORB. MORTAL. WKLY. REP. 10 (2012). The increase in prescribing may be attributable to professional recommendations encouraging physicians to recognize and better treat pain. *See* the Joint Commission on Health Care Organizations; Institute of Medicine, Relieving Pain in America: A Blueprint for Transforming Prevention, Care, Education, and Research (2011). However, more recent evidence suggests that the expense of prescription pain medication has encouraged patients to seek out cheaper relief — heroin.

14.   **FDA rules for opioids.** The Food and Drug Administration can play a role in preventing the misuse of controlled substances used by prescription. In 2013, the FDA issued new rules requiring more specific warnings in the labels of all extended-release and long-acting (ER/LA) opioid analgesics. The labeling is to state that ER/LA opioid should be reserved for patients whose pain cannot be adequately controlled by alternative medication, because of the risk of addiction. It also requires a boxed warning that chronic use during pregnancy can result in symptoms of withdrawal in newborns, which can be life-threatening. Of course, the FDA does not regulate physician prescribing practices. Rather, it has required opioid makers to provide physicians with educational material on safe prescription practices as part of its ER/LA Opioid Analgesics Risk Evaluation and Mitigation Strategy. The new rules also amend the requirements for postmarketing studies. *See* FDA News Release, Sept. 10, 2013, http://www.fda.gov/NewsEvents/Newsroom/PressAnnouncements/ucm367726.htm?source=govdelivery&utm_medium=email&utm_source=govdelivery; and FDA Letter to ER/LA opioid ap-

plication holders, http://www.fda.gov/downloads/Drugs/DrugSafety/InformationbyDrugClass/UCM367697.pdf (visited Mar. 2014). Should physician licensure boards place prescribing restrictions on physicians, in addition to those imposed under the federal Controlled Substances Act?

Restricting pain relief medication is not without controversy. Critics argue, for example, that limitations on refills require unnecessary visits to a physician, a special hardship for frail elderly in nursing homes, and undermine efforts to encourage physicians to prescribe adequate pain relief for terminally ill patients. Others warned, perhaps presciently, that limits could "produce a whack-a-mole effect, pushing up abuse of other drugs, like heroin . . . ." Sabrina Tavernise, *FDA Likely to Add Limits on Painkillers*, NEW YORK TIMES A-1, A-13, Jan. 26, 2013.

15. Variation in state PDMPs. The Congressional Research Service Report excerpted above describes considerable state to state variation among PDMPs: "Each state determines which agency houses the PDMP; which controlled substances must be reported; which types of dispensers are required to submit data (e.g., pharmacies); how often data are collected; who may access information in the PDMP database (e.g., prescribers, dispensers, or law enforcement); the circumstances under which the information may (or must) be accessed; and what enforcement mechanisms are in place for noncompliance." Finklea *et al., Prescription Drug Monitoring Programs*, at i. Program start-up costs have ranged from $450,000 to more than $1.5 million. *Id.* at 8. The federal government has helped with some funding from the Harold Rogers PDMP grand program, administered by the Department of Justice, and the National All Schedules Prescription Electronic Reporting Act of 2005, administered by the Department of Health and Human Services. *Id.* at 2.

All but one state has authorized a prescription drug monitoring program (PDMP). (Not all are operational at this writing.) They have been credited with reducing narcotic prescribing as well as hospital admissions for overdoses. Nathaniel Katz et al., *Usefulness of Prescription Monitoring Programs for Surveillance — Analysis of Schedule II Opioid Prescription Data in Massachusetts*, 1996–2006, 19 PHARMACOEPIDEMIOL. DRUG SAF. 115 (2010). They have also been criticized for missing data and not linking to a patient's medical record. Far less is known about whether PDMPs improve the accuracy of prescribing decisions. A recent study compared the prescribing decisions of emergency physicians treating adult emergency patients under 65 years of age whose chief complaint was headache, back pain or dental pain – before and after consulting the state's PDMP for information on past drug prescriptions for each patient. Before consulting the PDMP, the physicians believed that 35.6% of patients were drug-seeking (i.e., asking for opioids for recreational use or for addiction). The PDMP criteria defined 23.2% of patients as drug-seeking, suggesting that physicians mistakenly attributed drug-seeking behavior to a third of the patients in pain. After reviewing the PDMP, the physicians decided to prescribe opioids only for an additional 6.5% of patients and also not to prescribe them for 3.0% of patients first thought to have real pain. It is unclear why consulting the PDMP had such a small effect on prescribing. Scott G. Weiner et al., *Clinician Impression Versus Prescription Drug Monitoring Program Criteria in the Assessment of Drug-Seeking Behavior in the Emergency Department*, 62 ANNALS EMERG. MED. 281 (2013).

16. PDMP data collection and the Fourth Amendment. In *Ferguson* and *Earles*, the Court made clear that drug testing is a search within the meaning of the Fourth Amendment. The growing number of PDMPs, as well as registries of other medical data, raises the question whether reporting a person's prescription drug information is a search or seizure. The CRS Report suggests that PDMPs are modern successors to earlier paper prescription drug reporting programs, like the one at issue in *Whalen v. Roe* (excerpted in Chapter 7, C, *supra*), which upheld the compulsory reporting of prescriptions for controlled substances to the health department. The primary purpose of reporting was to detect or investigate unlawful conduct — stolen prescriptions, improper prescribing practices, dispensing unauthorized refills, and drug diversion — some of which could be crimes. Neither the majority nor the dissent in *Ferguson* mentions the court's 1977 *Whalen* decision. The *Whalen* court addressed only information privacy claims, not Fourth Amendment claims. Moreover, the *Whalen* decision focused on the collection and storage of prescriptions, not their later use or disclosure; it did not consider the possibility that the health department could turn over information to law enforcement. Would that make a difference?

The majority of Justices in *Ferguson, supra,* found that the South Carolina suspicionless drug-testing program violated the Fourth Amendment, because "the immediate objective of the searches was to generate evidence *for law enforcement purposes.*" 532 U.S. at 83 (emphasis in original). How immediate must the objective be? Are PDMPs permissible as long as they collect information for medical purposes? In other words, if PDMP data are not used *exclusively* for criminal investigations, could they be considered to be collected for a "special need unrelated to law enforcement"? In *Earles, supra,* the Court found that the school district demonstrated a special need, in part because student test results were not turned over to law enforcement. Can you reconcile *Ferguson, Earles* and *Whalen*?

17. Law enforcement access to PDMP data and the Fourth Amendment. The federal government encourages the adoption of prescription drug monitoring programs, to assist both physicians who prescribe controlled substances to their patients and civil and criminal law enforcement agencies to investigate a variety of prescription-drug related problems. Does a state law authorizing law enforcement to have access to PDMP data implicate the Fourth Amendment's prohibition on unreasonable searches or seizures? A federal district court in Oregon answered yes to that question, finding that law enforcement requests to use the data could be an unreasonable search and seizure in violation of the Fourth Amendment. *Oregon Prescription Drug Monitoring Program v. U.S. Drug Enforcement Agency,* 2014 U.S. Dist. LEXIS 17047 (Dist. Ore. 2014). While a single district court decision is not a final answer, its decision illustrates several factors that are likely to be considered in future cases.

Oregon law requires pharmacies to report prescriptions of drugs listed in Schedules II–IV of the Controlled Substances Act (CSA) to the state's PDMP, which is operated by the Oregon Health Authority. The CSA gives the federal Drug Enforcement Agency (DEA) broad authority to issue administrative subpoenas to investigate drug crimes. 21 U.S.C. § 876. The Oregon PDMP sought declaratory judgment on the question whether § 876 preempted Oregon's PDMP law, which limits disclosure of PDMP data. The Oregon PDMP takes the position that it has no authority to comply with any DEA administrative subpoena unless a court orders its enforcement.

The Oregon federal district court "conclude[d] that the DEA's use of administrative subpoenas to obtain prescription records from the PDMP violates the Fourth Amendment." 2014 U.S. Dist. LEXIS 17047 at *27. Having no exact precedent on this issue, the court reviewed the broad principles of earlier cases. It found that patients have an objectively reasonable expectation of privacy in their prescription information, within the meaning of *Katz v. United States*, 389 U.S. 347 (1967). It cited *Ferguson* to distinguish law enforcement purposes from "special needs." Both cases supported access by medical and pharmacist personnel for the purpose of patient care, but not necessarily "unfettered access" by law enforcement. This reasoning led the court to find inapplicable the business records (or third party) doctrine, which holds that people have no reasonable expectation of privacy in business records held by third parties. *See United States v. Miller*, 425 U.S. 435 (1976) (depositor had no reasonable expectation of privacy in his bank records); *Smith v. Maryland*, 442 U.S. 735 (1979) (dialed phone numbers or "pen registers"). Moreover, the court noted that *Whalen v. Roe* (*supra*, Chapter 7, C) did not even address the Fourth Amendment issue, "because the case did not 'involve affirmative, unannounced, narrowly focused intrusions into individual privacy during the course of criminal investigations.' 429 U.S. at 604 n. 32." 2014 U.S. Dist. LEXIS 17047 at *18.

The court found that two provisions of Oregon's PDMP authorizing statute almost compelled its decision. The first deems the prescription information submitted to the PDMP to be "protected health information" that is not subject to disclosure except as specified in the statute. The statute permits physicians and pharmacists to obtain PDMP prescription information if they certify that the request "is for the purpose of evaluating the need for or providing medical or pharmaceutical treatment for a patient to whom the practitioner or pharmacist anticipates providing, is providing or has provided care." ORS 431.966(2)(a)(A). It also permits disclosure pursuant "to a valid court order based on probable cause and issued at the request of a federal, state or local law enforcement agency engaged in an authorized drug-related investigation involving a person to whom the requested information pertains." ORS 431.966(2)(a)(C).

This decision does not necessarily preclude the DEA (or any other law enforcement agency) from obtaining a court order to enforce a subpoena if the agency can demonstrate probable cause with respect to a particular individual suspected of criminal actions. Even if other courts accept the Oregon district court's reasoning, would they come to the same conclusion in the absence of the specific Oregon PDMP statutory provisions protecting PDMP data?

18. Reconsidering reasonable expectations of privacy under the Fourth Amendment. Assumptions about what individuals can reasonably expect to be kept private may be challenged in the age of big data. *See, e.g.*, JARON LANIER, WHO OWNS THE FUTURE? (2013). The Supreme Court, in *United States v. Miller*, 425 U.S. 435, 443 (1976), held that a bank depositor "takes the risk, in revealing his affairs to another, that the information will be conveyed by that person to the Government." This so-called business records doctrine has been viewed as precluding a Fourth

Amendment challenge to government demands for personal information held by third parties. Is this view unassailable? In *United States v. Jones*, 132 S. Ct. 945 (2012), the Supreme Court found that the FBI and the District of Columbia Metropolitan Police violated the Fourth Amendment by attaching a GPS device to a criminal suspect's car and monitoring its whereabouts for 28 days. The decision is notable for Justice Scalia's 5:4 opinion relying on theories of trespass. A separate concurrence by Justice Sotomayor, however, argues that government intrusions on privacy include, but are not limited to, physical interventions. "More fundamentally," she continues, "it may be necessary to reconsider the premise that an individual has no reasonable expectation of privacy in information voluntarily disclosed to third parties," citing *Miller*, 425 U.S. 435. She concludes by saying, "I would not assume that all information voluntarily disclosed to some member of the public for a limited purpose is, for that reason alone, disentitled to Fourth Amendment protection." *Id.*

Riley v. California, 134 S. Ct. 2473 (2014), further suggests that the Supreme Court Justices may be reexamining the scope of Fourth Amendment privacy protection in light of contemporary technology. In *Riley*, the Court held that the police may not, "without a warrant, search digital information on a cell phone seized from an individual who has been arrested." (A warrantless search incident to an arrest has been seemed reasonable in order to remove weapons that could threaten police or prevent the destruction of evidence.) The Court found that even arrestees have significant privacy interests in their cell phone data, because that data includes vast amounts of personal information "from the mundane to the intimate," such as prescriptions, bank statements, and Internet browsing history. Such a search could obtain acess to files stored in the cloud, and even the government conceded that a "search incident to arrest could not be stretched to cover a search of the files accessed remotely [i.e., in the cloud]." Although the Court's Fourth Amendment jurisprudence is largely limited to criminal cases, its reasoning could inform the analysis of demands for information for civil purposes. What might a reconsideration of reasonable expectations of privacy mean for government access to social media records or medical, pharmacy or health insurance records for purposes of monitoring health care quality, cost and outcomes or disease prevalence and risk factors or even research?

D. CIVIL LIABILITY

"After one year from the ratification of this article the manufacture, sale, or transportation of intoxicating liquors within, the importation thereof into, or the exportation thereof from the United States and all territory subject to the jurisdiction thereof for beverage purposes is hereby prohibited."

U.S. Constitution, Amendment XVIII (1919)

"The eighteenth article of amendment to the Constitution of the United States is hereby repealed."

U.S. Constitution, Amendment XXI (1933)

People have consumed alcoholic beverages for centuries, with varying consequences. For most, they enhance a meal without adverse effects. For others, alcohol initiates an addiction that can be as personally debilitating and financially destructive as addiction to narcotics. And for still others, alcohol can unleash terrible violence against others. These different effects complicate policy-making to prevent the risks that drinking alcoholic beverages can pose. The Eighteenth Amendment to the Constitution was one – ultimately unsuccessful – effort to end alcohol's adverse effects. For excellent examinations of the origins and aftermath of the Eighteenth Amendment, see the Ken Burns and Lynn Novick documentary film, *Prohibition*, available from the Public Broadcasting Service, http://www.pbs.org/kenburns/prohibition/ (visited Mar. 2014), and DANIEL OKRENT, LAST CALL: THE RISE AND FALL OF PROHIBITION (2010).

DELFINO v. GRIFFO
257 P.3d 917 (N.M. 2011)

SERNA, J.

. . . .

On April 29, 2005, Plaintiff was in an automobile accident caused by Ms. Gonzales, who was speeding and had a blood alcohol content level of more than twice the legal limit. Plaintiff's minor son was killed, and Plaintiff and her passengers suffered grave injuries.

Ms. Gonzales had spent the hours prior to the accident with the individual pharmaceutical representatives: Griffo and Gonzales, employees of Schering; Donahue, an employee of Abbot; and Paz, an employee of Merck. The pharmaceutical representatives hosted an out-of-office business luncheon for Ms. Gonzales and her colleagues from Dr. David Leech's office. The employers of the pharmaceutical representatives had policies that authorized the entertainment of physicians and their staff, through the purchase of food and alcohol, to further the business interests of the companies. . . .

The luncheon began at Chili's Restaurant. After consuming multiple alcoholic beverages over the course of several hours, Ms. Gonzales drove to Uptown Bar & Grill with Griffo as her passenger. At Uptown, Ms. Gonzales, Griffo, and Donahue consumed more alcohol, and then Ms. Gonzales drove to Doc & Eddy's, again with Griffo in her car. After one and one half hours of drinking at Doc & Eddy's, Ms. Gonzales, obviously intoxicated, departed in her vehicle. The fatal accident occurred approximately 14 minutes later. Griffo purchased alcoholic beverages for Ms. Gonzales at all three bars; Gonzales, Donahue, and Paz purchased alcohol for Ms. Gonzales in at least one bar.

Plaintiff filed a wrongful death suit against Pharmaceutical Defendants and the owners and operators of the various bars and restaurants where Ms. Gonzales had consumed alcohol that evening (collectively, Bar Defendants). Plaintiff's complaint included 21 counts against the various Defendants. The counts at issue in this appeal are those alleging common-law negligence against the individual pharmaceutical representatives for purchasing alcohol for Ms. Gonzales and permitting her to drive, recklessness for the same actions under the Liquor Liability Act, and against their employers under respondeat superior (Counts 7-9); negligent hiring, retention and training against the pharmaceutical companies (Counts 13-15); and prima facie tort, negligent infliction of emotional distress, intentional infliction of emotional distress, and loss of consortium against all Defendants (Counts 16-18). The theories underlying the claims asserting liability against Pharmaceutical Defendants are that they owed a common-law duty to prevent Ms. Gonzales from driving while intoxicated; that Pharmaceutical Defendants were aiding and abetting Ms. Gonzales in committing a tortious action under Restatement (Second) of Torts Section 876(B) (1977); and that Pharmaceutical Defendants are social hosts who acted recklessly and thus liable under the Liquor Liability Act.

. . . . The district court concluded that Pharmaceutical Defendants were not social hosts under the Liquor Liability Act; that the Liquor Liability Act precludes any common-law cause of action that may have existed against Pharmaceutical Defendants; and that the complaint states no cause of action under the Restatement. . . .

II.

. . . .

B. The Liquor Liability Act Imposes a Duty on All Social Hosts.

The Liquor Liability Act provides for the tort liability of liquor licensees and social hosts who sell, serve, or provide alcohol. The Act was passed in 1983, in response to *Lopez v. Maez*, in which this Court recognized a common-law cause of action against a tavern that had furnished alcoholic beverages to an intoxicated individual who later caused injury to a third party. 98 N.M. 625, 632, 651 P.2d 1269, 1276 (1982) ("In light of the use of automobiles and the increasing frequency of accidents involving drunk drivers, we hold that the consequences of serving liquor to an intoxicated person whom the server knows or could have known is driving a car is reasonably foreseeable." (footnote omitted)). . . . The Liquor Liability Act imposes liability based on varying relationships between plaintiffs and defendants. For a suit by an injured third party against a licensee, the plaintiff must show that the licensee was negligent — that it was "reasonably apparent" that the person being served was intoxicated. Section 41-11-1(A)(2). For a suit against a licensee by a patron, the plaintiff must show "gross negligence and reckless disregard for the safety of the person who purchased or was served the alcoholic beverages." Section 41-11-1(B). For a suit against a gratuitous provider, or social host, the plaintiff must show that the host provided alcoholic beverages "recklessly in disregard of the rights of others, including the social guest." Section 41-11-1(E).

With the social host provision of Liquor Liability Act, "the legislature intended to limit the rights of third parties to recover against social hosts who provided alcoholic beverages to intoxicated guests who negligently injure a third party." *Walker v. Key*, 101 N.M. 631, 636, 686 P.2d 973, 978 (Ct. App. 1984). The social host provision of the Liquor Liability Act states:

> No person who has gratuitously provided alcoholic beverages to a guest in a social setting may be held liable in damages to any person for bodily injury, death or property damage arising from the intoxication of the social guest unless the alcoholic beverages were provided recklessly in disregard of the rights of others, including the social guest.

. . . .

1. The Liquor Liability Act does not limit social host liability to private settings.

. . . .

. . . The plain language of the statute does not indicate a legislative intent to limit social host liability to *private* settings; rather, a social host is one who provides his or her guest with gratuitous alcohol in a *social* setting. The Liquor Liability Act is silent on whether the duty imposed on social hosts is limited to *only* those who are entertaining in their homes, or whether it is extended to individuals who host events, and otherwise provide alcohol, in public spaces, including when the actual service of alcoholic beverages is performed by licensed servers. As such, we turn to other tools of statutory construction. . . .

. . . .

Turning to the structure of the Liquor Liability Act, we do not find evidence that the Legislature intended to limit social host liability to instances in which no licensed alcohol server was involved in providing the alcohol. Most subsections of the Act describe the duty on licensees based on different relationships; Subsection (E), discussed above, sets forth the duty on social hosts. The only subsection of the Act that discusses both licensees and social hosts is Subsection (H), the exclusivity provision, which states that the Act is the exclusive remedy for injuries proximately caused by the sale or service of alcohol, *not* that a suit against one class of liquor providers is exclusive of a suit against another. The absence of any language expressly precluding social host liability when alcohol is consumed in a licensed establishment indicates the intent of the Legislature to permit concurrent social host and licensee liability.

. . . .

We conclude that the Liquor Liability Act permits a cause of action against a social host who recklessly provides alcohol to a guest when the alcohol is consumed in a licensed establishment.

. . . .

[W]e turn to the question of who may be considered a social host. Social host liability under the Liquor Liability Act,. . . requires "some degree of control over the service or consumption of alcohol." [C]ontrol is implicit in the statutory language, applicable to a social host "who has gratuitously provided" alcohol. This Legislative choice of language is reflected in case law from other jurisdictions, where courts have imposed social host liability only when the social host had performed some sort of affirmative act in the service or provision of alcohol.

[Here, the court summarizes cases from other states.]

We perceive the following common themes in these well-reasoned cases that are instructive in determining what our Legislature envisioned when it statutorily enacted social host liability. Social hosting need not occur in a home; one may host in a bar or restaurant where the actual delivery of alcoholic beverages to the guests is performed by a licensed server. Factors that are key to determining whether one is a social host in a public establishment are whether the alleged social host exercised control over the alcohol consumed by the guests; whether the alleged social host convened the gathering for a specific purpose or benefit to the alleged social host, such as promoting business good will; and whether the alleged host intended to act as a "host" of the event, meaning arrange for the service of and full payment for all food and beverages served to the guests.

None of these factors is determinative, and this Opinion will not attempt to capture the myriad host/guest relationships that may exist. The presence of a business incentive, as corroborated by a corporate policy of encouraging entertainment to foster a business relationship, is evidence which could persuade a jury that a guest/host relationship exists. However, it is equally apparent that this kind of business atmosphere is not essential, and factors indicating whether one is acting as a social host, and thereby assuming some responsibility for the service of alcohol to guests, may be present in a purely social setting.

In our view, the guest/host relationship implies a certain degree of control by the host over the guest and the provision of alcohol. The host creates the environment and has the power to change it. It is the degree of control and responsibility envisioned by the Legislature in its careful choice of wording that distinguishes the present case, and others like it, from the more casual social arrangement in which each individual is responsible for herself or himself. Unless the social arrangement fits within the guest/host paradigm, the Legislature has not imposed a duty of care. Friends sharing drinks, regardless of who pays, normally would not rise to a guest/host relationship. When one is put in a position of being another's guest, it is implied that the host will be in the position of some responsibility, albeit only a responsibility not to be reckless in providing gratuitous alcohol.

3. The recklessness standard limits social host liability.

Our construction of social host to include individuals and companies who host in licensed establishments does not . . . create a slippery slope leading to the creation of a duty to the whole world or, at least, to the whole bar . . . . [I]n this case the Liquor Liability Act imposes a duty on social hosts not to act recklessly in the service of alcohol beverages to their guest, Section 41-11-1(E). Recklessness, as defined by the Uniform Jury Instructions for liquor liability, is "the intentional doing of an act with utter indifference to or conscious disregard for a person's [rights or safety]." A plaintiff, therefore, has two sizeable hurdles to be successful in a suit under a social host liability theory: to establish facts from which a well-instructed jury could identify a guest/host relationship, and to prove reckless misconduct resulting from that relationship.

. . . .

. . . The mere presence of an individual in a bar is not enough to impose a duty on her or him; nor is merely purchasing a round for friends, or even a stranger.

. . . .

4. Pharmaceutical Defendants were social hosts.

Plaintiff's complaint properly characterized Pharmaceutical Defendants as social hosts, and pleaded facts that raise the question of recklessness, thus stating a cause of action against them under the Liquor Liability Act. The individual pharmaceutical representatives invited Ms. Gonzales and her co-workers to a business luncheon, organized for business purposes under corporate policies of "wining and dining" medical office personnel in order to develop business goodwill and eventually increase sales to that office. The representatives arranged the business luncheon, paid for all of Ms. Gonzales' many alcoholic beverages at multiple licensed establishments, accompanied her at and between the multiple establishments, and escorted her to her car at the end of the evening . . . . We reverse the district court's order granting the motion to dismiss for failure to state a claim, and hold that Plaintiff stated a claim against Pharmaceutical Defendants as social hosts under the Liquor Liability Act.

We need not reach Plaintiff's argument that Pharmaceutical Defendants owed her a common-law tort duty or that a duty was stated under the Restatement, because the Liquor Liability Act is the exclusive remedy for injuries caused by social hosts.

NOTES AND QUESTIONS

1.   **Dram shop liability**. State laws prohibiting bars, restaurants, and liquor stores from selling alcoholic beverages to intoxicated persons became widespread after the end of Prohibition. Such so-called dram shop laws sometimes impose criminal penalties for violations. *See Gregory H. Adamian v. Three Sons, Inc.*, 233 N.E.2d 18 (Mass. 1968). Dram shop statutes were initially limited to prohibiting sales to intoxicated persons, without addressing the establishment's responsibility for harms caused by its customers to third parties. However, increasing attention to the risks of driving while intoxicated encouraged tort claims against bars and restaurants that continued to serve patrons who then injured or killed third parties when they drove home while drunk. Among the first cases were *Waynick v. Chicago's Last Dept. Store*, 269 F. 2d 322 (7th Cir. 1959), and *Rappaport v. Nichols*, 31 N.J. 188 (1959). Although the driver remains responsible, some cases involve individuals without sufficient assets to pay compensatory damages, perhaps inspiring plaintiffs to find a more financially secure defendant. As with many tort duties, the dram shop's responsibility to third parties has been codified in statutes like New Mexico's Liquor Liability Act at issue in *Delfino v. Griffo*.

2.   **Social host liability**. Bars and restaurants are no longer the only parties who may be responsible for serving too much alcohol. Social hosts may be liable for the harmful actions of their guests if the hosts continue to provide the guests with alcohol after the hosts knew — or should have known — that the guests were intoxicated. *Delfino v. Griffo* mentions several possible causes of action in tort, in

addition to statutory liability. Perhaps the most troubling case is one in which parents serve liquor to young people under the legal drinking age (21). However, courts may be reluctant to impose liability in the absence of evidence that the parents should have known that person was intoxicated, continued to serve alcohol, and let the person drive, resulting in injury or death to a passenger or person outside the driver's care. *See, e.g., Commonwealth v. McGeoghegan*, 449 N.E.2d 349 (Mass. 1983). Furthermore, social hosts are not responsible for an intentional crime, such as rape or robbery, committed by the intoxicated person, because such actions are not foreseeable consequences of intoxication.

3. **Driving while intoxicated.** The percentage of miles driven with a blood alcohol level of more than 0.05 is only 0.9% of all miles driven, but drunk driving is estimated to cost the country $125 billion a year. Christopher A. Kahn, *Locked Out or Locked Up: Are Ignition Interlocks the Answer?*, 63 ANN. EMERG. MED. 475 (2014). According to the National Highway Safety Transportation Administration (NHSTA), 10,228 people were killed in "alcohol-impaired-driving crashes" in 2010, representing 31% of all motor vehicle deaths in the US. The NHSTA considers drivers to be alcohol-impaired "when their blood alcohol concentration (BAC) is 0.08 grams per deciliter (g/dL) or higher." U.S. Dept. of Transportation, National Highway Traffic Safety Administration, Alcohol-Impaired Driving, DOT HS 811 606, http://www-nrd.nhtsa.dot.gov/Pubs/811606.pdf (last visited Mar. 2014). The number of deaths includes drivers (65%), passengers (28%), and others outside the vehicle (7%). *Id.* The NHTSA notes "The term 'alcohol-impaired' does not indicate that a crash or a fatality was caused by alcohol impairment." *Id.* Of the 9,694 alcohol-impaired drivers involved in fatal crashes, 6,652 or 68% had BAL of 0.15 or higher. *Id.* The number of alcohol-impaired driving fatalities has declined by 29% since 2001, from 0.48 per 100 million miles traveled in 2001 to 0.34 per 100 million miles traveled in 2010. Not surprisingly, fatal crashes are more frequent at night and on weekends than during the day or on weekdays. Younger drivers are more likely to be killed than drivers over 35 years of age. *Id.*

Alcohol is not the only source of driving error by any means. The NHSTA also has information on "distracted driving," including information about the risks of texting while driving. *See* http://www.distraction.gov/ (visited Mar. 2014). Consider also whether criminal statutes prohibiting driving while intoxicated require amendment to include marijuana intoxication,, and if so, how to measure punishable levels of marijuana.

4. **Alternative preventive measures.** Criminal and civil responsibilities are not, of course, the only policy options to reduce harm or death caused by persons who are intoxicated. All states have programs to require or allow courts to order the installation of ignition interlocks in the cars of people convicted of driving while intoxicated — to prevent the car from starting if the driver is impaired. Because the specific requirements vary by state, the National Highway Traffic Safety Administration issued guidelines for best practices. *See* National Highway Traffic Safety Administration, *Model Guideline for State Ignition Interlock Programs*, Report No. DOT HS 811 859 (2013), http://www.nhtsa.gov/Impaired (visited Mar. 2014).

Penalties such as revoking a driver's license, however, have not proved uniformly effective, perhaps because the sanction is imposed only after serious harm occurs or because enforcement is difficult and spotty. Engineering improvements, including airbags and passive restraints, in vehicles lessen injuries when accidents do occur.

As with the decline in tobacco use, increased public awareness of the dangers of driving after drinking alcoholic beverages has undoubtedly contributed to decreasing number deaths from motor vehicle crashes each year. All fatalities from motor vehicle crashes (related to alcohol or not) declined from 43,005 in 2002 to 32,367 in 2011. U.S. Dept. of Transportation, *Fatality Analysis Reporting System, General Estimates System, 2011 Data Summary*, at 5 (April 2013). http://www-nrd.nhtsa.dot.gov/Pubs/811755DS.pdf (visited Mar. 2014). Public education campaigns may also have increased the use of designated drivers. The private group, Mothers Against Drunk Driving, was influential in raising public awareness and tightening penalties for driving while intoxicated. *See* http://www.madd.org/. Government can also regulate advertising by makers of alcoholic beverages within the parameters of First Amendment protections. See the materials on advertising and the First Amendment in Chapter 10, D, including the discussion of *44 Liquormart, Inc. v. Rhode Island*, 517 U.S. 484 (1996) (striking down state ban on advertising liquor prices).

Chapter 12

INJURY PREVENTION

A. INTRODUCTION

We often think of injuries as accidental, but many "accidents" can be prevented. Federal and state consumer protection laws require certain products to be designed in ways that reduce harm. Examples include safety guards for cutting blades in machines like lawnmowers and industrial saws, maximum spaces between slates in baby cribs, fire retardant fabrics in clothing and upholstery, and minimum strengths for building materials in construction. Laws requiring smoke detectors have substantially decreased the number of fires in the country. Indeed, laws requiring such environmental measures are among the greatest success stories of public health. Good lighting and banked curves on highways helped reduce car accidents. Deaths from car crashes have declined about 25% since 2005 and dropped out of the top 10 causes of death in 2009, according to data from the National Highway Traffic Administration, www.nhtsa.gov (last visited January 2013). For more examples of successes in injury prevention, see DAVID HEMENWAY, WHILE WE WERE SLEEPING: SUCCESS STORIES IN VIOLENCE AND INJURY PREVENTION (2009).

Notably, laws requiring safety measures to be installed in products and in the environment are typically more effective in preventing injuries than laws that require people to protect themselves. Inanimate objects can't forget to take precautions. Moreover, and especially important for the purpose of identifying laws that promote public health and safety, things do not have legal rights, but people do. As long as there is a plausible basis for believing that a product standard will protect public health or safety, state legislatures have considerable authority under the police power to require manufacturers, construction companies, and other organizations to install safety measures in their products and workplaces. The federal government can also require similar measures for products and companies in interstate and foreign commerce.

Requiring people to take protective measures is less reliable, both legally and in practice. As earlier chapters should have demonstrated, there are some limits to what government can require people to do or not do. Perhaps more important, even valid laws may not overcome human forgetfulness or resistance. For example, drivers routinely ignore speed limits (none reading this chapter, of course), despite the demonstrated success of lower limits in reducing automobile accidents. Enforcement requires substantial resources and is unlikely to be completely effective, because obeying the law depends on human will. In reading the materials in this chapter, consider who controls the source of injury and whether regulation should target products or people.

Part B examines the case of medical injuries, which, while not always thought of as a public health issue, account for more deaths than motor vehicle crashes, breast cancer, or firearms. The materials illustrate the factors to consider when deciding whether to focus on systems or incentives to guide human behavior. Part C examines injuries and deaths caused by firearms — or the people who use them. More importantly, viewing these examples in the same manner as other public health topics allows us to shift away from identifying individual "culprits" and affixing individual blame for death and harm — or at least from doing so exclusively — and towards the identification of causation in the broader sense of the term: What are the causal factors that lead to harm in various populations? How can those causal links be altered to reduce the frequency of death and injury? What is the most cost-effective way to produce the maximum beneficial impact — given the range of interventions public health analysis invites us to consider?

B. PATIENT SAFETY IN MEDICAL CARE

INSTITUTE OF MEDICINE, TO ERR IS HUMAN: BUILDING A SAFER HEALTH SYSTEM
1–4 (2000)

The knowledgeable health reporter for the Boston Globe, Betsy Lehman, died from an overdose during chemotherapy. Willie King had the wrong leg amputated. Ben Kolb was eight years old when he died during "minor" surgery due to a drug mix-up.

These horrific cases that make the headlines are just the tip of the iceberg. Two large studies, one conducted in Colorado and Utah and the other in New York, found that adverse events occurred in 2.9 and 3.7 percent of hospitalizations, respectively. In Colorado and Utah hospitals, 6.6 percent of adverse events led to death, as compared with 13.6 percent in New York hospitals. In both of these studies, over half of these adverse events resulted from medical errors and could have been prevented.

When extrapolated to the over 33.6 million admissions to U.S. hospitals in 1997, the results of the study in Colorado and Utah imply that at least 44,000 Americans die each year as a result of medical errors. The results of the New York Study suggest the number may be as high as 98,000. Even when using the lower estimate, deaths due to medical errors exceed the number attributable to the 8th-leading cause of death. More people die in a given year as a result of medical errors than from motor vehicle accidents (43,458), breast cancer (42,297), or AIDS (16,516).

Total national costs (lost income, lost household production, disability and health care costs) of preventable adverse events (medical errors resulting in injury) are estimated to be between $17 billion and $29 billion, of which health care costs represent over one-half.

In terms of lives lost, patient safety is as important an issue as worker safety. Every year, over 6,000 Americans die from workplace injuries. Medication errors alone, occurring either in or out of the hospital, are estimated to account for over 7,000 deaths annually.

Medication-related errors occur frequently in hospitals and although not all result in actual harm, those that do, are costly. One recent study conducted at two prestigious teaching hospitals, found that about two out of every 100 admissions experienced a preventable adverse drug event, resulting in average increased hospital costs of $4,700 per admission or about $2.8 million annually for a 700-bed teaching hospital. If these findings are generalizable, the increased hospital costs alone of preventable adverse drug events affecting inpatients are about $2 billion for the nation as a whole.

These figures offer only a very modest estimate of the magnitude of the problem since hospital patients represent only a small proportion of the total population at risk, and direct hospital costs are only a fraction of total costs . . . .

. . . .

Yet silence surrounds this issue. For the most part, consumers believe they are protected. Media coverage has been limited to reporting of anecdotal cases. Licensure and accreditation confer, in the eyes of the public, a "Good Housekeeping Seal of Approval." Yet, licensing and accreditation processes have focused only limited attention on the issue, and even these minimal efforts have confronted some resistance from health care organizations and providers. Providers also perceive the medical liability system as a serious impediment to systematic efforts to uncover and learn from errors.

The decentralized and fragmented nature of the health care delivery system (some would say "nonsystem") also contributes to unsafe conditions for patients, and serves as an impediment to efforts to improve safety. Even within hospitals and large medical groups, there are rigidly-defined areas of specialization and influence. For example, when patients see multiple providers in different settings, none of whom have access to complete information, it is easier for something to go wrong than when care is better coordinated. At the same time, the provision of care to patients by a collection of loosely affiliated organizations and providers makes it difficult to implement improved clinical information systems capable of providing timely access to complete patient information. Unsafe care is one of the prices we pay for not having organized systems of care with clear lines of accountability.

Lastly, the context in which health care is purchased further exacerbates these problems. Group purchasers have made few demands for improvements in safety. Most third party payment systems provide little incentive for a health care organization to improve safety, nor do they recognize and reward safety or quality.

The goal of this report is to break this cycle of inaction. The status quo is not acceptable and cannot be tolerated any longer. Despite the cost pressures, liability constraints, resistance to change and other seemingly insurmountable barriers, it is simply not acceptable for patients to be harmed by the same health care system that is supposed to offer healing and comfort. "First do no harm" is an often quoted term from Hippocrates. Everyone working in health care is familiar with the term. At a very minimum, the health system needs to offer that assurance and security to the public.

. . . .

In this report, safety is defined as freedom from accidental injury. This definition recognizes that this is the primary safety goal from the patient's perspective. Error is defined as the failure of a planned action to be completed as intended or the use of a wrong plan to achieve an aim. According to noted expert James Reason, errors depend on two kinds of failures: either the correct action does not proceed as intended (an error of execution) or the original intended action is not correct (an error of planning). Errors can happen in all stages in the process of care, from diagnosis, to treatment, to preventive care.

Not all errors result in harm. Errors that do result in injury are sometimes called preventable adverse events. An adverse event is an injury resulting from a medical intervention, or in other words, it is not due to the underlying condition of the patient. While all adverse events result from medical management, not all are preventable (i.e., not all are attributable to errors). For example, if a patient has surgery and dies from pneumonia he or she got postoperatively, it is an adverse event. If analysis of the case reveals that the patient got pneumonia because of poor hand washing or instrument cleaning techniques by staff, the adverse event was preventable (attributable to an error of execution). But the analysis may conclude that no error occurred and the patient would be presumed to have had a difficult surgery and recovery (not a preventable adverse event).

Much can be learned from the analysis of errors. All adverse events resulting in serious injury or death should be evaluated to assess whether improvements in the delivery system can be made to reduce the likelihood of similar events occurring in the future. Errors that do not result in harm also represent an important opportunity to identify system improvements having the potential to prevent adverse events.

Preventing errors means designing the health care system at all levels to make it safer. Building safety into processes of care is a more effective way to reduce errors than blaming individuals (some experts, such as Deming, believe improving processes is the only way to improve quality). The focus must shift from blaming individuals for past errors to a focus on preventing future errors by designing safety into the system. This does not mean that individuals can be careless. People must still be vigilant and held responsible for their actions. But when an error occurs, blaming an individual does little to make the system safer and prevent someone else from committing the same error.

. . . .

To err is human, but errors can be prevented. Safety is a critical first step in improving quality of care. The Harvard Medical Practice Study, a seminal research study on this issue, was published almost ten years ago; other studies have corroborated its findings. Yet few tangible actions to improve patient safety can be found. Must we wait another decade to be safe in our health system?

CLARK v. ST. DOMINIC-JACKSON MEMORIAL HOSPITAL
660 So. 2d 970 (Miss. 1995)

HAWKINS, CHIEF JUSTICE, for the court:

Dollie H. Clark filed a wrongful death action on August 1, 1990, against St. Dominic-Jackson Memorial Hospital and Dr. James Hays for the death of her husband, Arthur Clark, in the circuit court of the First Judicial District of Hinds County. After discovery St. Dominic moved for summary judgment, which was granted. Mrs. Clark has appealed.

On Saturday July 30, 1988, Arthur Clark, a circuit court judge, at his home in Indianola, began experiencing discomfort in his chest, and having a difficult time catching his breath. The next Monday Judge Clark and his wife went to a local doctor who recommended that he go to Jackson for an examination by a cardiologist, Dr. James Crosthwait. Judge Clark and his wife arrived in Jackson the following Thursday for an appointment with Dr. Crosthwait. After conducting a physical, Dr. Crosthwait recommended that Judge Clark undergo a treadmill test for purposes of evaluating his cardiac functioning. Judge Clark did not perform well on the test, and Dr. Crosthwait then suggested that Judge Clark have a cardiac catheterization — a procedure by which the condition of coronary arteries can be determined. Judge Clark agreed.

Late Thursday afternoon Judge Clark was admitted to St. Dominic-Jackson Memorial Hospital. The catheterization was scheduled for the next morning, August 5. Prior to the procedure Judge Clark was asked to sign a consent form, which stated in part, "I also understand that the cardiac catheterization laboratory is equipped and personnel assisting the doctor are trained to handle emergencies that may arise in order to make the test as safe as possible." Mrs. Clark returned to Indianola.

The next morning, August 5, Judge Clark was taken to the catheterization lab. Dr. James Hays was the attending physician. During the procedure Dr. Hays found a serious lesion on Judge Clark's left coronary artery. Shortly after the catheterization was completed, Judge Clark began to experience chest pains, and ultimately went into cardiac arrest. Because both operating rooms were in use, bypass surgery could not be performed at St. Dominic. Dr. Hays was unaware that the operating rooms were in use when he began the catheterization. Thereafter, inquiries were made to determine whether other local hospitals had operating rooms available. Although numerous other measures were taken to try and save his life — including the use of an intra-aortic balloon pump — Judge Clark's condition worsened. He died in the catheterization lab at approximately 11:00 a.m.

At the time Judge Clark was admitted, it was not St. Dominic's policy to reserve operating rooms for patients undergoing routine cardiac catheterization. The guidelines for the American College of Cardiology recommend that catheterizations only be performed at hospitals that have cardiac surgery capability. According to a number of hospital employees, several patients died while undergoing catheterizations before Judge Clark.

In her complaint, Mrs. Clark alleged that (1) St. Dominic had failed to provide the necessary emergency support facilities, and (2) St. Dominic had failed to fully disclose the nature of the catheterization procedure to Judge Clark before obtaining his consent. The hospital denied both charges.

During discovery Mrs. Clark designated three experts as potential witnesses. In his deposition, Dr. Nathaniel Reich, a specialist in internal medicine, stated that the facilities at St. Dominic were insufficient to provide minimally competent care, although he did not find that any hospital employee had acted negligently. According to Dr. Reich, Dr. Hays should have identified Judge Clark as a high risk patient and instructed the hospital to have an operating room available. Dr. Reich did admit that for routine diagnostic catheterization it was not necessary to have an operating room on standby. Dr. Reich stated that after Judge Clark's condition became serious he should have been transported to a hospital that had an operating room available.

Dr. Yadin David, a biomedical engineer, was also deposed by the defense. Dr. David stated that he had examined the service records of the hospital's intra-aortic balloon pumps, [such pumps are designed to reduce cardiac overload during cardiac arrest] and found that they indicated some malfunction had occurred at approximately the same time Judge Clark was being treated. He also concluded that the consent form which Judge Clark executed was misleading in that it stated that the hospital was prepared to handle emergencies, and it failed to mention the risk of death.

Finally, Dr. Alan Kravitz, a board certified cardiologist, was deposed. Dr. Kravitz testified that in his experience catheterization patients were rated as being either high or low risk, and that for high risk patients an operating room was kept on standby. According to Dr. Kravitz, the attending physician should rate the patients, and then inform the hospital of their status. After reviewing Judge Clark's records, Dr. Kravitz found that he was a high risk patient. Although he stated that the hospital would not normally be liable if the attending physician failed to inform it of a patient's condition, Dr. Kravitz contended that the hospital should have required physicians to inform it of the condition of every patient prior to beginning a catheterization.

STANDARD OF CARE

It is important to note that this case does not concern physician malpractice. Absent special circumstances, a hospital may not be held liable for a physician's malpractice. However, it may be liable for its own negligence and the negligence of its employees. As is true of all negligence actions, a hospital must exercise reasonable care in preventing foreseeable injuries to foreseeable plaintiffs.

Mrs. Clark's first claim against St. Dominic focused on the hospital's failure to provide adequate facilities and support staff. Prior to Judge Clark's death, a number of patients had experienced difficulty while undergoing catheterizations at St. Dominic.[1] In some of those cases, the patients were taken to an operating room

---

[1] The American College of Cardiology recommends that catheterizations be done at hospitals that

for bypass surgery, while in others the patients were treated in the catheterization lab because an operating room was unavailable. An undetermined number of patients had died at St. Dominic during the catheterization procedure. Accordingly, the hospital was on notice that people might die as a result of the procedure.

St. Dominic counters by contending its conduct was appropriate under the applicable standard of care. In particular, it notes that operating rooms are not normally reserved for patients undergoing routine cardiac catheterizations.[2] St. Dominic contends that only when a patient is classified as high risk should an operating room be kept on standby during a catheterization. Furthermore, the hospital argues — and plaintiff's experts seem to agree — that unless the attending physician notifies the hospital that a patient is high risk, there is no duty to reserve an operating room, and that because it followed the customary practice of hospitals throughout the nation, it cannot be found liable. However, in *George B. Gilmore Co. v. Garrett*, we noted:

> Indeed in most cases reasonable prudence is in fact common prudence; but strictly it is never its measure; a whole calling may have unduly lagged in the adoption of new and available devices. It never may set its own tests, however persuasive be its usages. Courts must in the end say what is required; there are precautions so imperative that even their universal disregard will not excuse their omission. *582 So. 2d 387, 394 (Miss. 1991)* (quoting *The T.J. Hooper, 60 F.2d 737, 740 (2d Cir. 1932)*).

In the field of medicine, the Court has held:

> Conformity with established medical custom practiced by minimally competent [hospitals] . . . while evidence of performance of the duty of care, may never be conclusive of such compliance. The content of the duty of care must be objectively determined by reference to the availability of medical and practical knowledge which would be brought to bear in the treatment of like or similar patients under like or similar circumstances . . . given the facilities, resources and options available. The content of the duty of care may be informed by . . . medical custom but never subsumed by it. *Hall v. Hilbun, 466 So. 2d 856, 872 (Miss. 1985)*.

The same is true of the instant case. Testimony from several employees indicated that the hospital was aware that catheterizations could be life threatening before the Judge Clark episode. Several patients had in fact died during catheterizations before. Despite this, the hospital continued to operate under its previous policy. Given that notice, it would not be unreasonable to conclude that the hospital failed to exercise reasonable care.

In assessing reasonable conduct, there is a vast difference between taking a chance when unavoidable and when avoidable. Taking a 1% chance when necessary

---

have cardiac surgery capability. Mrs. Clark contends that because both of its operating rooms were occupied when Judge Clark entered cardiac arrest, St. Dominic actually had no capability for all practical purposes.

[2] At the time Judge Clark underwent the catheterization, Drs. Crosthwait and Hays termed the procedure routine. Plaintiff's experts, Drs. Reich and Kravitz, however, would have classified the judge as high-risk.

might be exemplary, but taking the same chance when unnecessary might be negligence.

The hospital was on notice that (1) upon occasion the operating room would be needed because of an emergency arising during a catheterization procedure, and (2) when such a need did arise, it would be critically important to the life of the patient. Why else would the American College of Cardiology have recommended that such procedures only be performed at hospitals that have cardiac surgery capability?

Under such circumstances the hospital was under a duty to show, at least more than is shown in this record, why no operating room was kept available as a matter of course during catheterization procedures. If patients are undergoing procedures in one part of a hospital that can be life threatening, and there are known methods by which physicians can meet such emergencies which are available in another part of the hospital, the question naturally arises, why should hospital regulations permit any life threatening procedure without also having safeguards in place? St. Dominic favors us with no such explanation.

Giving Mrs. Clark the benefit of all reasonable inferences, genuine issues of material fact did exist. The summary judgment entered in favor of St. Dominic is, therefore, reversed.

REVERSED AND REMANDED

George J. Annas, *The Patient's Right to Safety — Improving the Quality of Care Through Litigation Against Hospitals*
354 NEW ENGL. J. MED. 2063–66 (2006)

It is the consensus of experts in the patient-safety field that little has changed to improve the safety of hospital care since the Institute of Medicine's 1999 report, To Err Is Human. The report noted that in order to be successful, "safety must be an explicit organizational goal that is demonstrated by clear organizational leadership . . . . This process begins when boards of directors demonstrate their commitment to this objective by regular, close oversight of the safety of the institutions they shepherd." Leape and Berwick agree, noting that safety cannot become an institutional priority "without more sustained and powerful pressure on hospital boards and leaders — pressure that must come from outside the health industry." In hospital care, the challenge is to reform corporate governance to make hospital boards take their responsibility for patient safety at least as seriously as they take the hospital's financial condition.

Most patient-safety experts continue to believe that the threat of liability is the primary barrier to the development of effective and comprehensive patient safety programs in hospitals. I suggest, on the contrary (and no doubt controversially among physicians), that judicial recognition of an explicit "right to safety" for hospital patients, with a correlative duty of hospitals to implement patient-safety measures, can become the primary motivator for the development of systems to improve patient safety. Hospitals that do not take specific actions to improve safety should be viewed as negligent and be subject to malpractice lawsuits when a violation of the right to safety results in injury.

HOSPITALS AND CORPORATE RESPONSIBILITY

Patients have rights, even when they are in the hospital. Such rights, most centrally, include the right to information (often termed informed consent or informed choice), the right to refuse any treatment, the right to privacy and confidentiality, the right to emergency treatment, and the right to be treated with dignity. A patient's right to safety could be derived from the fiduciary nature of the doctor-patient relationship. But physicians do not control all possible risks of injury in the hospital setting. Therefore, it is more appropriate to focus on the hospital and to define the scope of the right to safety as a reflection of corporate responsibility: the obligation of a hospital to maintain a safe environment for patients and for their health care providers.

Hospitals are corporations (artificial persons created by law), and their obligations are imposed on them by law, their own bylaws, their mission statements, their internal rules, licensing regulations, and accreditation standards. Hospitals are responsible for their own negligence under the doctrine of corporate responsibility, which courts have applied directly to hospitals. Although the law usually permits industries and professions to set their own practice standards, courts have also ruled that entire industries and professions can be negligent by failing to adopt new technologies, especially those that are inexpensive and effective, and that judges and juries must ultimately determine what is reasonable.

The famous 1932 *T.J. Hooper* case, for example, involved the question of whether it was negligent for a tugboat not to have a wireless radio on board to get weather reports. The tugboat sank with the plaintiff's cargo during a predicted storm that the tugboat could easily have avoided had the captain listened to weather forecasts. The practice in the tugboat industry was not to carry wireless radios, but the court rejected this "nobody does it" defense:

> A whole calling may have unduly lagged in the adoption of new and available devices.

> It never may set its own tests, however persuasive be its usages. Courts must in the end say what is required; there are precautions so imperative that even their universal disregard will not excuse their omission.

Specifically with respect to health care, other courts have held that "conformity with established medical custom practiced by minimally competent physicians, . . . while evidence of performance of the duty of care, may never be conclusive of such compliance."

The major safety-related reasons for which hospitals have been successfully sued are inadequate nursing staff and inadequate facilities. Since providing a safe environment for patient care is a corporate responsibility, understaffing is corporate negligence. The best known of such suits is the 1965 case of Darling v. Charlestown Community Memorial Hospital, in which the Supreme Court of Illinois determined that a jury could find that a hospital was negligent for not having a sufficient number of qualified nurses to monitor a patient, whose leg had to be amputated because his cast had been put on too tight — a fact that was not discovered by the nursing staff in time to prevent injury.

In another case, the Supreme Court of Mississippi held that it was for the jury to decide if a hospital was negligent for failing to keep an operating room available in case a high-risk patient undergoing cardiac catheterization required emergency surgery to survive. The patient died because all of the hospital's operating rooms were in use when he needed emergency surgery as a result of the cardiac catheterization. Even though other hospitals followed the same practice, the court ruled: "In assessing reasonable conduct there is a vast difference between taking a chance when unavoidable and when avoidable. Taking a 1 percent chance when necessary might be exemplary, but taking the same chance when unnecessary might be negligence."

Although courts have not explicitly adopted a specific right to safety, they have discussed the protection of the patient's safety as an aspect of corporate responsibility. Hospitals are more than hotels that rent out bedrooms. In 1991, for example, the Pennsylvania Supreme Court stated simply, "Corporate negligence is a doctrine under which the hospital is liable if it fails to uphold the proper standard of care owed the patient, which is to ensure the patient's safety and wellbeing while at the hospital." The court also listed four specific examples that previous courts had identified as hospital safety obligations: the maintenance of safe and adequate facilities and equipment, the selection and retention of competent physicians, the oversight of medical practice within the hospital, and the adoption and enforcement of adequate rules and policies to ensure the quality of care for patients.

Specific hospital obligations would flow from the recognition of a patient's right to safety. For example, courts could determine that a hospital's failure to adopt a new technology to prevent the injury of patients — such as a computerized drug ordering system — could subject the hospital to liability for injury in cases in which it could be demonstrated that adoption of the technology would not have been prohibitively expensive and would probably have prevented the injury. Nosocomial infections resulting from a hospital's failure to adopt or enforce hand-washing policies would be even easier to demonstrate as a breach of a hospital's duty to keep patients safe. The 100,000 Lives Campaign of the Institute for Healthcare Improvement is promoting six evidence based safety interventions: deployment of rapid response teams, reliable care for acute myocardial infarction, medication reconciliation, and prevention of central-line infections, surgical-site infections, and ventilator-associated pneumonia. More than half of all U.S. hospitals have already joined the campaign, which helps make these six safety interventions the "standard of care" for all hospitals.

Potential liability for not adopting these safety measures should give the remaining hospitals an added incentive either to adopt them or to explain why particular interventions will not improve patient safety in their institutions.

ENFORCING THE RIGHT TO SAFETY

In the absence of a comprehensive social insurance system, the patient's right to safety can be enforced only by a legal claim against the hospital. The hospital, not the physician, satisfies or breaches the duty to ensure patient safety. And more liability suits against hospitals may be necessary to motivate hospital boards to take patient safety more seriously. The question of whether to take the additional step of moving to enterprise liability — in which all medical liability suits (including those alleging negligence by physicians) are brought against hospitals — deserves more serious consideration than it has had to date. It should be emphasized that the goal is not to encourage more litigation for its own sake. The goal is the prevention of injury, and focusing on litigation provides a strong incentive for hospitals to make their environments safer.

Patient-safety experts almost uniformly insist that hospitals need to establish a system of reporting errors and near misses, both for quality control and to make sure patients are told when their injuries were caused by errors. Most experts believe that reporting by physicians cannot be achieved without drastically limiting or eliminating legal liability. The view that physicians fail to report errors (both to patients and to hospitals) because they are afraid of being sued is plausible and has intuitive appeal. But as Hyman and Silver recently reported, no empirical study has shown a negative correlation between "the intensity of malpractice risk and the frequency of error reporting, or has shown that liability correlates inversely with health care quality." A 2005 survey of patients found that only one quarter of U.S. physicians disclosed errors to their patients; but the result was not that much different in New Zealand, a country that has had no-fault malpractice insurance for more than three decades and where 61 percent of physicians still fail to report errors to their patients.

Thus, adoption of the confidentiality-immunity model may produce little or no change in the reporting practices of physicians. Nor should this be surprising. There are many reasons why physicians do not report errors, including a general reluctance to communicate with patients and a fear of disciplinary action or a loss of position or privileges. Nonetheless, even Congress seems to have accepted the prevailing medical view on liability, as evidenced by the July 2005 passage of the Patient Safety and Quality Improvement Act, which establishes federal confidentiality protections for a new system of reporting medical errors. If my analysis is correct, this law will have little or no effect on reporting patterns and even less on patient safety.

Like most defendants in tort litigation, physicians have always despised malpractice suits. Even those who consider litigation appropriate in cases of serious injury to a patient still think of the system as fundamentally flawed and corrupt. But modifying the traditional tort system in ways that will benefit both physicians and patients is much more difficult than is usually recognized by the medical profession and requires sustained and constructive dialogue with the legal profession. With respect to the issue of patient safety, at least, lawyers and physicians should see themselves as natural allies, rather than as predator and prey. The patient-safety problem is complicated, and no single change in the tort system (including a recognition of a right to safety) will solve it, any more than the elimination of legal liability for vaccine manufacturers will solve our chronic vaccine shortages.

MAKING A PATIENT SAFETY A REALITY

A right to safety will have to be implemented by hospital systems, but physicians will be central to its success. The most appropriate model for physicians is the success of the patient-safety programs for anesthesiologists, which were motivated by liability suits and high rates of medical malpractice insurance. Because of the successful 25-year program to make anesthesia safer for patients, the risk of death from anesthesia dropped from 1 in 5000 to about 1 in 250,000. As a consequence, the malpractice insurance rate for anesthesiologists, once the highest in medicine, is now among the lowest.

The anesthesiologists provide an instructive example for patient safety; the Joint Commission on Accreditation of Healthcare Organizations has recently provided a less constructive one. One of the commission's most recent patient-safety initiatives is to encourage physicians to wear a button that reads, "Ask me if I have washed my hands." This is an example of putting the responsibility for patient safety on patients themselves. The fact that the commission sees patient self-defense actions as an important safety strategy is a symptom of the problem, not a solution. Patients should, of course, be encouraged to participate actively in their care, but they cannot and should not be responsible for their own safety in an environment over which they have no control.

Hospitals can decide on their own to take the patient's right to safety seriously. But few have done so, and the jury is still out on how seriously hospitals will take their commitments to the 100,000 Lives Campaign. Effective pressure for a change in safety culture seems most likely to come from an increased risk of liability, which is signaled by an increase in patient-safety lawsuits, one incentive to which hospitals (at least those not still covered by charitable immunity) seem to respond. Legal actions that are focused on patient-safety systems in hospitals, rather than on the actions of individual physicians, could help encourage more serious consideration of other reforms as well.

Physicians cannot change a hospital's safety culture by themselves. But by working with patients (and their lawyers) to establish a patient's right to safety, and by proposing and supporting patient-safety initiatives, physicians can help pressure hospitals to change their operating systems to provide a safer environment for the benefit of all patients.

NOTES AND QUESTIONS

1. **Patient safety improvements.** Although patient safety has been widely recognized as a critical issue in improving the quality and outcomes of medical care in hospitals, progress on changing the culture of hospitals to prioritize patient safety has been depressingly slow. 15 years after the IOM report, some progress has been made, but even "never events" (such as operating on the wrong patient or removing the wrong limb) still occur, and universal physician hand-washing

between patients cannot yet be assured. On the other hand, there is increasing awareness that simple steps, such as adopting operating room checklists similar to those used by airplane pilots, can cut down on patient injuries. *See, e.g.* ATUL GAWANDE, THE CHECKLIST MANIFESTO (2010), and Alex B. Haynes *et al.*, *A Surgical Safety Checklist to Reduce Morbidity and Mortality in a Global Population*, 360 NEW. ENGL. J. MED. 491–499 (2009).

There are some steps, such as tagging all surgical instruments and sponges with a radio frequency tag, that could cut down and perhaps eliminate the problem of retained surgical instruments and sponges. Hospitals are, nonetheless, reluctant to adopt such patient safety advances. *See* Anahad O'Connor, *No Sponge Left Behind*, NEW YORK TIMES D5, September 25, 2012. When should hospitals be held legally liable for failure to adopt patient safety measures such as this one?

For an examination of how the Affordable Care Act might — or might not — encourage improvements in patient safety, see Barry R. Furrow, *Regulating Patient Safety: The Patient Protection and Affordable Care Act*, 159 U. PA. L. REV. 101 (2011).

2. Medical malpractice. There is, of course, some tension between traditional medical malpractice litigation which seeks to identify individual physicians and nurses who have injured patients by behaving in a negligent manner, and attempting to treat patient injuries as "systems problems" for which individuals are not responsible. Of course, these two views are not incompatible. On the other hand, many physicians continue to argue that they will not report dangerous actions, near-misses, or personal involvement in patient injury until they are guaranteed legal immunity. The challenge is to hold negligent physicians accountable for their actions, while making sure patients are promptly informed about them and immediate steps are taken to care for injured patients, and to provide them with fair compensation for their injuries. How do you think this can be done? What role does the trend toward immediate physician apology have? For a historical perspective, see George J. Annas, *Doctors, Patients, and Lawyers: Two Centuries of Health Law*, 367 NEW ENGL. J. MED. 445 (2012).

3. Judging physician quality. A 2013 article in the New England Journal of Medicine reported that of 20 bariatric (obesity) surgeons, those judged by their peers to be in the bottom quartile (as compared with those in the upper quartile) had longer surgeries with higher complication rates (14% vs. 5%), and higher death rates (.25% vs. .05%). John D. Birkmeyer *et al*, *Surgical Skill and Complication Rates after Bariatric Surgery*, 369 NEW ENGL. J. MED. 1434 (2013). What implications do numbers like this have for patient safety? Do patients have a right to know which quartile their surgeon is in? Is this information relevant in a medical malpractice suit?

C. FIREARMS

At first encounter, any suggestion that firearms and gun control should be considered public health issues may seem somewhat overreaching. After all, as gun enthusiasts are fond of saying, guns don't kill people; people kill people. If there is a public health problem, it is the individual who misbehaves, not the instrument used by the individual. Moreover, to the extent that guns and the people who use them should be controlled, much of gun-related death and injury arises out of activities that are already governed by the criminal law, as the materials in Part C.1 below illustrate. What value is there in viewing guns and their use through the same lens that we used to examine such things as unhealthy behavior, exposure to disease, and other traditional public health matters?

To begin with, guns are not really that qualitatively different than many of the other matters already discussed in these materials. Tobacco, as we have seen, appears to provide pleasure notwithstanding its well-established dangers to its users; junk food is not all that bad for your health unless and until it is ingested excessively; cars without seat belts and airbags (and motorcyclists without helmets) are not unsafe to their occupants until there is an accident. Yet in these cases, government policymakers may regulate the products themselves, not just the individuals who use (or abuse) them. Indeed, countless products must meet health and safety requirements in order to be sold at all. For that matter, civil and/or criminal law enforcement and public health remedies are not mutually exclusive, either as a matter of efficiency or political choice.

Most critically, at least from a legal perspective, the options for gun control must be considered in light of the limits on government action created by the Second Amendment to the federal Constitution as well as by the comparable language included in most state constitutions, examined in Part C.2. At the same time that gun control and regulatory measures are being debated in legislative bodies and the courts, a second judicial debate has concerned the extent to which private parties and, in some cases, state and local governments can bring lawsuits against gun owners, distributors, and manufacturers seeking injunctive relief or damages for the harm caused by their guns. These are examined in Part C.3. below.

---

1. The Fatal Appeal of Firearms

Walter Kirn, *I've Owned Six Guns; I've Drawn Them on Bad Guys; I Want to BeUnderstood*
The New Republic 31, 33, 35 (Feb. 11, 2013)

They push back when they're fired. That's the elemental fact involved, the deep Newtonian heart of the whole business. They kick at your will in the instant they also project it, reminding you that force is always two-sided. It's a shock the first time, an insult to the senses, but once you've learned to expect it, absorb it, ride it, recoil becomes a source of pleasure . . . . You want to do it again, again — again! — and the urge becomes part of your body, your nervous system. It feels as though it was always there, this appetite, this desire for a small, acute struggle that you can win. Win consistently. Repeatedly.

Semi-automatically.

When I shoot at the range, I don't feel personally powerful but like the custodian of something powerful. I feel like a successful disciplinarian of something radically alien and potent. Analyze this sensation all you want; you still can't make it go away. But that's the primitive, underlying fear, of course, which the likes of LaPierre [Wayne LaPierre, President of the National Rifle Association] exploit: the fear that it will be curtailed, suppressed, prohibited — perhaps not any time soon, but ultimately.

We're not talking rights here; we're talking instincts. It's not the gun that the so-called "clingers" cling to and don't like the thought of anybody screwing with. It's not even the power of the gun. It's the power *over* the power of the gun.

. . . .

Will there be fewer murders with tighter gun laws — the modest laws that might actually materialize rather than the grand ones that probably won't but will surely rev up the rhetoric and the hoarding — or only fewer or smaller massacres? Can we expect less violence altogether or merely less outrageous acts of violence? And if the answer is fewer catastrophes, fewer Auroras and Sandy Hooks, would that be a worthwhile accomplishment in itself? I think so. Horror and panic themselves are a form of violence, and diminishing them, restricting their dimensions, is itself a civilizing act.

To civilize, I think, is the key verb. It's a crossover word, with a cultural legacy and a practical, specific meaning — to order; to, yes, regulate — that the gun-owning mind responds to and respects. In westerns, the gun . . . is a tool of civilization, not a totem. It tames, the gun, but only if it's first tamed. Those who won't tame it, or can't — because they're unable to tame themselves — must face being disarmed. Especially hard-to-tame types of guns, moreover, must be closely, vigilantly, watched.

. . . .

. . . [W]hat will be lost by giving [assault rifles] up? Nothing but their destabilizing allure for the grandiose, image-obsessed mass killers who favor them — and whose crimes represent a far greater risk to gun rights than does the perceived hostility of certain politicians. By assenting to such a ban, the gun-owning community can demonstrate precisely the sort of reasonable public-mindedness of which some believe it incapable. Otherwise, the showdown will go on and we will have only ourselves to blame if our self-destructive intransigence leaves us despised and cornered, with no way out.

———————

Matthew Miller, Deborah Azrael, & David Hemenway, *Firearms and Violent Death in the United States,* REDUCING GUN VIOLENCE IN AMERICA
3–13, 15 (D.W. Webster, J.S. Vernick, eds. 2013)

Firearm-Related Deaths in the United States

In 2010, there were more than 31,000 firearm deaths in the United States: 62% were suicides, 36% were homicides, and 2% were unintentional. Almost as many Americans die from gunfire as die from motor vehicle crashes (almost 34,000 in 2010). Americans under age 40 are more likely to die from gunfire than from any specific disease.

Homicide

The United States is not a more violent country than other high-income nations. Our rates of car theft, burglary, robbery, sexual assault, and aggravated assault are similar to those of other high-income countries; our adolescent fighting rates are also similar. However, when Americans are violent, the injuries that result are more likely to prove fatal. For example, the U.S. rate of firearm homicide for children 5 to 14 years of age is thirteen times higher than the firearms homicide rate of other developed nations, and the rate of homicide overall is more than three times higher (Table 1.1).

U.S. homicide rates vary cyclically over time. Current rates are at a 30-year low, but as recently as 1991 rates were nearly twice as high. Changes in homicide rates over the past several decades are largely attributable to changes in firearm homicide rates, mostly driven by changes in firearm homicide rates among adolescent and young men in large cities.

The U.S. homicide rate is much higher in urban than in rural areas, as are rates of all violent crime. Nine out of ten homicide offenders are male, and 75% of victims are male. African Americans are disproportionately represented among both perpetrators and victims.

Suicide

Compared with other high-income countries, the U.S. adult suicide rate falls roughly in the middle. Among younger persons, however, our suicide mortality is relatively high: for children under 15 years of age, the overall suicide rate in the United States is 1.6 times that of the average of other high-income countries, largely accounted for by a firearm suicide rate eight times that of the average of these countries.

Over the past several decades, suicide rates have been more stable than have rates of homicide. Nevertheless, after declining from a peak of 12.9/100,000 in 1986 to 10.4 in 2000, driven largely by a decline in the rate of firearm suicide, the suicide rate has increased over the past decade to 12.4/100,000 in 2010, mostly due to an increase in suicide by hanging.

Age, sex, race, and other demographic characteristics — including marital status, income, educational attainment, and employment status — all influence suicide mortality. Suicide rates are higher, for example, for white and Native Americans than for black, Hispanic, and Asian Americans. A consistent finding across numerous studies is that the strongest individual-level risk factor for a fatal suicidal act is having previously attempted suicide; other strong risk factors include psychiatric and substance abuse disorders.

In contrast to homicide rates, suicide rates are higher in rural than in urban areas almost entirely due to higher rates of firearm suicide in rural areas.

Table 1.1 Homicide, suicide, and unintentional gun deaths among 5-14 year olds: The United States versus 25 other high-income populous countries (yearly 2003)	
Mortality	**Rate ratio**
Homicides	
Gun homicides	13.2
Non-gun homicides	1.7
Total	3.4
Suicides	
Gun suicides	7.8
Non-gun suicides	1.3
Total	1.7
Unintentional firearm deaths	10.3
Source: Richardson and Hemenway, 2011	

Unintentional Firearm Deaths

Approximately 675 Americans per year were killed unintentionally with firearms between 2001 and 2010. Data from the National Violent Death Reporting System show that two-thirds of the accidental shooting deaths occurred in someone's home, about half of the victims were younger than 25 years, and half of all deaths were other-inflicted. In other-inflicted shootings, the victim was typically shot accidentally by a friend or family member — often an older brother.

Firearm Ownership in the United States

The United States has more private guns per capita (particularly more handguns) and higher levels of household gun ownership than other developed countries.

Most of what we know about gun ownership levels in the United States over the past several decades comes from the General Social Survey (GSS 2010), a relatively small biannual survey of U.S. adults. Data from the GSS show that the percentage of households with firearms has fallen from approximately 50% in the late 1970s to 33% today. Changing household demographics are believed to explain the decline in the household ownership of guns chiefly due to a fall in the number of households with an adult male. Notably, however, the percentage of individuals owning firearms has remained relatively constant over the past several decades.

The GSS does not speak to the number of guns in civilian hands or the distribution of guns within households. For this information, researchers have turned to data from two medium-sized national surveys conducted a decade apart. These surveys suggest that the number of guns in civilian hands grew from approximately 200 million in 1994 to 300 million in 2004 — and that the average gun owner now owns more guns than previously.

Compared with other Americans, gun owners are disproportionately male, married, older than 40, and more likely to live in nonurban areas. Their long guns (rifles, shotguns) are owned mainly for sport (hunting and target shooting). People who own only handguns typically own the guns for protection against crime.

In 2001, 2002, and 2004, but not before or since, information on household gun ownership from the General Social Survey was supplemented by information from the National Behavioral Risk Factor Surveillance System. The BRFSS is of sufficient size (more than 200,000 respondents annually) that household gun ownership could, for the first time, be determined at the state level for all 50 states and for some Metropolitan Statistical Areas.

Prior to these three iterations of the BRFSS, researchers generally used proxies to measure firearm ownership rates at the state and sub-state level. A validation study by Azrael, Philip, and Miller (2004) found that from among all proxies, the fraction of suicides that are committed with firearms (FS/S) correlates most strongly and consistently with cross-sectional survey-based measures of household firearm ownership at the county, state, and regional levels.

Household firearm ownership is probably a good measure of the accessibility of guns used in suicides, since most suicides involving firearms occur in the home and involve a firearm owned by a member of the household. Household gun ownership levels seem also to be the key exposure variable for firearm homicides that take place in the home, where women, children and older adults are particularly likely to be killed. The most common perpetrator in such instances is a family member. By contrast, older adolescent and young adult males are more often killed outside the home by guns owned by a nonfamily member.

In this essay, we focus on studies that assess the relationship between gun prevalence and violent death. As such, the essay does not examine studies of gun carrying nor any literature on illegal gun markets. It also does not address research that investigates the relationship between firearm regulations and violent death. Note, however, that firearm prevalence and firearm regulation are highly collinear. Strong regulations may limit firearm ownership, and low levels of firearm ownership make it easier to pass stronger regulations.

This essay is also not an exhaustive review of the literature examining the association of firearm availability and violent death. Rather, it briefly summarizes (a) international ecologic studies comparing the United States to other countries, (b) ecologic studies of U.S. regions, states, and metropolitan areas, and (c) individual case-control and cohort studies.

Studies included in this brief review met a minimal threshold of attempting to control for important confounders: studies had to compare likes to likes. For case-control studies of homicide, that means — at a minimum — controlling for age, gender, and neighborhood; in suicide studies, for age, sex, and psychiatric risk factors for suicidal behavior. For international studies of homicide, it means comparing high-income countries to high-income countries. International comparisons of adult suicide rates are confounded by large differences in religion, culture and recording practices (i.e., the social meaning and cultural acceptance of adult suicide), as evidenced by tenfold differences in suicide rates across high-income nations. Thus, the only international studies of suicide included focus on the suicides of children — which all countries hold to be tragedies. For ecologic studies in the United States, making "like to like" comparisons means comparing states to states with similar levels of urbanization (or, for homicide, similar crime rates), cities to cities, and rural areas to rural areas.

Firearms and Homicide

Ecologic Studies

Killias (1993) evaluated rates of violence in 14 developed countries: 11 in Europe, along with the United States, Canada, and Australia. He used data from the 1989 International Crime Survey, a telephone survey of 14 countries and 28,000 respondents, to measure firearm prevalence. Respondents were asked whether there were any firearms in their household and, if so, whether any were a handgun or a long gun. Military firearms were excluded. In this study, which did not include control variables, rates of firearm ownership and homicide were positively correlated, while rates of firearm ownership and non-firearm homicide were not.

A study by Hemenway and Miller (2000) included 26 high-income nations with populations greater than one million. To measure gun availability, the authors used two proxies, including FS/S. No control variables were included in the analysis. Firearm availability was strongly and significantly associated with homicide across the 26 countries.

A follow-up study (Hemenway, Shinoda-Tagawa, and Miller 2002) examined homicide rates among women across high-income countries. The validated proxy (FS/S, or the percentage of suicides committed with a firearm) was used to estimate firearm ownership in each country. Urbanization and income inequality were included as control variables. The United States accounted for 70% of all female homicide victims in the study and had the highest firearm ownership rates. The U.S. homicide rate for women was five times higher than that of all of the other countries combined; its female firearm homicide rate was eleven times higher.

U.S. Studies

Cook (1979) conducted a cross-sectional analysis of 50 large cities in the United States to explore the relationship between gun availability and robbery, including robbery-murder. Using data on the number of robberies in 1975, Cook examined how firearm availability (as proxied by Cook's index) was related to robbery and robbery-murder rates, controlling for measures of the effectiveness of the criminal justice system, population density, and other regional and state differences. Increased gun availability was not associated with overall robbery rates, but it was positively associated with the proportion of robberies that involved a gun — and with the per capita robbery-murder rate, through an increased rate of gun robbery.

Miller et al. (2002) evaluated the relationship between levels of firearm ownership at the state and regional level and the incidence of homicide from 1988 to 1997 for 50 states and 9 regions. At the state level, they used the percentage of suicides with a firearm as a proxy for ownership and they measured gun availability at the regional level with data from the GSS. Five potential confounders were included: poverty, urbanization, unemployment, alcohol consumption, and (non-homicide) violent crime rates. In the multivariate analyses, a positive and significant association between gun ownership and homicide rates was found for the entire population and for every age group (except ages 0–4), primarily due to higher firearm homicide rates.

A similar study (Miller et al. 2007) used survey estimates of household gun ownership for each state from the Behavioral Risk Factor Surveillance System. It examined data from 2001 to 2003 and controlled for state-level rates of aggravated assault, robbery, unemployment, urbanization, alcohol consumption, poverty, income inequality, the percentage of the population that was black, and the percentage of families headed by a single female parent. Again, states with higher rates of household firearm ownership had significantly higher homicide victimization rates for men, for women, and for children. The association was driven by gun-related homicide victimization rates; non-gun-related victimization rates were not significantly associated with rates of firearm ownership.

Individual Level Studies

Ecologic studies provide evidence about whether more guns in the community are associated with more homicides in the community. Case-control and cohort studies provide data more germane to the question of whether a gun in the home increases or reduces the risk of homicide victimization for members of the household.

Kellermann et al. examined approximately 400 homicide victims from three metropolitan areas who were killed in their homes (Kellermann et al. 1993). All died from gunshot wounds. In 83% of the homicides, the perpetrator was identified; among these cases, 95% of the time, the perpetrator was not a stranger. In only 14% of all the cases was there evidence of forced entry. After controlling for illicit drug use, fights, arrests, living alone, and whether the home was rented, the presence of a gun in the home remained strongly associated with an increased risk for homicide in the home. Gun ownership was most strongly associated with an increased risk of homicide by a family member or intimate acquaintance.

Whereas most men are murdered away from home, most children, older adults, and women are murdered at home (Table 1.2). A gun in the home is a particularly strong risk factor for female homicide victimization — with the greatest danger for women coming from their intimate partners.

. . . .

Other case-control studies have also found that a gun in the home is a risk for homicide in the home, with especially heightened risk for women. Results from perpetrator based case-control homicide studies also find that gun ownership is a risk for homicide perpetration. For example, a study of women murdered by intimate partners found that compared with a control group of living battered women, a gun in the house was present for 65% of perpetrators of murder versus 24% of perpetrators of nonfatal abuse. Access to a firearm by the battered woman had no protective effect.

. . . .

Firearm Prevalence and Suicide

Firearm suicide rates and overall suicide rates in the United States are higher where guns are more prevalent. By contrast, rates of suicide by methods other than firearms are not significantly correlated with rates of household firearm ownership. This pattern has been reported in ecologic studies that have adjusted for several potential confounders, including measures of psychological distress, alcohol and illicit drug use and abuse, poverty, education, and unemployment.

Household firearm ownership has also been consistently found to be a strong predictor of suicide risk in studies that examined individual-level data. U.S. case-control studies find that the presence of a gun in the home or purchase from a licensed dealer is a risk factor for suicide The relative risk is large (two-to-tenfold), depending on the age group and, for younger persons, how firearms in the home are stored.

The only large U.S. cohort study to examine the firearm-suicide connection found that suicide rates among California residents who purchased handguns from licensed dealers were more than twice as likely to die by suicide as were age/sex matched members of the general population, not only immediately after the purchase but throughout the six-year study period. Here, too, the increase in suicide risk was attributable entirely to an excess risk of suicide with a firearm.

Drawing causal inferences about the relation between firearm availability and the risk of suicide from existing case-control and ecologic studies has been questioned on the grounds that these studies may not adequately control for the possibility that members of households with firearms are inherently more suicidal than members of households without firearms (NRC 2005). Additional cited limitations include the possibility of differential recall (by cases compared with controls) of firearm ownership and comorbid conditions, and reverse causation (whereby suicidal persons purchase firearms with the idea of committing suicide).

It is very unlikely, however, that the strong association between firearms and suicide reported consistently in U.S. studies is either spurious or substantially overstated. First, individual-level studies have often controlled for measures of psychopathology.

Second, directly answering the reverse causation critique, the risk of suicide associated with a household firearm pertains not only to gun owners but to all household members; the relative risk is larger for adolescents than for the gun owner; and for the gun owner the risk persists for years after firearms are purchased.

Third, studies that have examined whether people who live in homes with guns have higher rates of psychiatric illness, substance abuse, or other known suicide risk factors generally fail to find any indication of heightened risk. For example, four case-control studies found comparable rates of psychiatric illness and psychosocial distress among households with versus without firearms.

Fourth, there appears to be a hierarchy of suicide risk among children and young adults, depending on how securely household firearms are stored, suggesting a dose-response relationship.

Finally, the consistency in magnitude, direction, and specificity of method related risk observed in both the many individual-level and ecologic studies (the latter not being subject to recall bias or the reverse causation criticism) leads to only one conclusion: a gun in the home increases the likelihood that a family member will die from suicide.

Unintentional Firearm Deaths

Not surprisingly, ecologic and case-control studies find that where there are more guns and more guns poorly stored, there are more unintentional firearm deaths. U.S. children aged 5 to 14 have eleven times the likelihood of being killed accidentally with a gun compared with similarly aged children in other developed countries (Richardson and Hemenway 2011).

Conclusion

The United States, with its many guns and highly permissive gun laws, faces a far more serious problem of lethal firearms violence than other high-income nations. The relative magnitude of our problem is illustrated in Table 1.1. This table, which compares U.S. children aged 5-14 with children of other developed countries, illustrates the stark fact that U.S. children are *thirteen* times more likely to die from a firearm homicide and *eight* times more likely to a die of a firearm suicide than children in comparable developed nations. There is no evidence that U.S. children are more careless, suicidal, or violent than children in other high-income nations. Rather, what distinguishes children in the United States from children in the rest of the developed world is the simple, devastating fact that they die — mostly by firearms — at far higher rates.

Within the United States itself, the evidence is similarly compelling: where there are more guns, there are more violent deaths — indeed, many more. The magnitude of this relationship is illustrated in Table 1.3, which compares the number of lives lost between 2001 and 2007 to homicide, suicide, and unintentional firearm accidents by sex and age groups in states with the highest compared with the lowest gun ownership rates. The consistency of findings across different populations, using different study designs, and by different researchers is striking. No credible evidence suggests otherwise.

Firearm policy is often focused on guns used in crime. What is notable about the studies reviewed here, however, is the consistency of the story they tell about *all* firearms — not just those used in crime. In the United States, there are more firearm suicides than firearm homicides, and women, children, and older adults are more likely to die by gunfire from a household gun (typically, legally acquired and possessed) than from illegal guns.

The first step in ameliorating a public health problem is to identify what the problem is. For the purposes of this essay, the problem is that, year after year, many more Americans are dying by gunfire than people in any other high-income nation. Good firearm policy has the potential to reduce the toll of lethal firearm violence in the United States. Efforts to reduce this uniquely American problem will, however, be less effective than they could be if good policy is not accompanied by a shift in the kind of discussions politicians, academicians, and citizens engage in about firearms. Science can provide the content — and better science based on better data, better content. The best chance for durable and large-scale reductions in lethal violence in the United States is for all of us to commit to keeping the conversation about the costs and benefits of guns in American society civil, ongoing, and factually grounded.

NOTES AND QUESTIONS

1. Firearm prevalence.   How many guns are there (in private hands) in the United States? No one really knows; there is no national reporting system for sale or ownership. Most estimates of private gun ownership are just that — estimates. The NRA estimates that there are nearly 300 million firearms in the US, including perhaps 100 million handguns. Another organization of gun owners, Gun Owners of America, which sometimes criticizes the NRA, claims 300,000 members. The Bureau of Alcohol, Tobacco, Firearms, and Explosives (ATF) estimated that 192 million guns were privately owned in the United States in 1999, 65 million of which were handguns. More recent estimates of firearms owned by civilians range from 270,000 to 310,000. William J. Krouse, *How Many Guns Are in the United States? — Gun Control Legislation*, pp. 8–9. (United States Congressional Research Service, Nov. 14, 2012). These include an estimated 110,000 rifles, 86,000 shotguns, and 114,000 handguns. *Id.* This translates to about 101 firearms for every 100 persons. *Id.*

The U.S. military is estimated to have 2,700,00 firearms, while police departments have 1,150,000 firearms. Aaron Karp, *Armed Actors — Data Sources and the Estimation of Military-Owned Small Arms*. Table 4 (Geneva: Small Arms Survey, the Graduate Institute of International and Development Studies, Sept. 1, 2013); Aaron Karp, Small Arms Survey 2006: Unfinished Business (2006).

For international comparisons, see www.gunpolicy.org/firearms/region/united-states (visited Mar. 2014). For an attempt to assess the accuracy of data and interesting comparisons between gun ownership in Canada and the United States, see Philip J. Cook & Jens Ludwig, *Principles for Effective Gun Policy*, 73 Fordham L. Rev. 589, 590–92 (2004).

2. Firearm deaths and injuries.   Data about how much harm these guns cause is also surprisingly sparse. All sources seem to agree that there is some good news: Gun-related injuries declined in the 1990s. Deaths rose slightly after 2001 and the death rate has remained at just over 10 per 100,000 population since 1999. Nonetheless, firearms are the second leading cause of *injury* mortality in the United States. National Center for Health Statistics data for 2010 show more than 35,000 people died from gun injuries. This is comparable to the numbers of deaths that year from motor vehicle accidents (33,687) and from breast cancer (41,435). More than half of firearm fatalities — 19,392 — were suicides; homicides accounted for 16,259 deaths that year. Sherry Murphy *et al., Deaths: Final Data for 2010*, 61 NAT'L VITAL STAT. REP. No. 4 (2013), www.cdc.gov/nchs/data/nvsr/nvsr61/nvsr61_04.pdf (visited Mar. 2014). Firearms were used in about half of the 38,364 suicides in 2010. *Id. See also* United Nations Office on Drugs and Crime, *Global Study on Homicide 2011: Trends, Context, Data* (June 26, 2013).

Firearms are estimated to have caused about twice as many injuries as deaths in 2010. INSTITUTE OF MEDICINE & NATIONAL RESEARCH COUNCIL, PRIORITIES FOR RESEARCH TO REDUCE THE THREAT OF FIREARMS INJURIES (June 2013), http://www.iom.edu/Reports/2013/Priorities-for-Research-to-Reduce-the-Threat-of-Firearm-Related-Violence.aspx. The CDC has almost no current data on firearms deaths or injuries. Its Injury Center now focuses on motor vehicle related injuries, violence against children and youth, prescription painkiller overdoses, and traumatic brain injury. *See* www.cdc.gov/injury/overview/index.html (visited Apr. 2014). But, in 2013, President Obama ordered the CDC to resume research on violence related to firearms.

There are, of course, no reliable sources of quantifiable data on the many other "costs" associated with gun ownership and use, *e.g.*, the number of people intimidated or harassed with guns, the loss of property values in neighborhoods associated with gun use, the increased insecurity or loss of "peace of mind" of people who live near gun use areas, and so on.

3. **Mass shootings.** The United States experienced 67 mass shootings (killing 4 or more people) between 1984 and April 2014. For a timeline and analysis of these events, see Mark Follman, Gavin Aronsen & Deanna Pan, *A Guide to Mass Shootings in America*, MOTHER JONES (2012, updated April 2014), http://www.motherjones.com/politics/2012/07/mass-shootings-map?page=1 (visited Apr. 2014). Among the more recent, on April 2, 2014, Ivan Lopez, an army soldier, killed three people and himself at Fort Hood, Texas, which had seen another soldier, Nidal Malik Hasan, kill 13 people in 2009; Adam Lanza killed 20 children and seven adults, including his mother, in Newtown, Connecticut, before killing himself on December 14, 2012; Wade Michael Page killed seven people at a Sikh temple in Oak Creek, Wisconsin, August 5, 2012; and James Holmes opened fire in a movie theater in Aurora, Colorado, killing or injuring 70 people on July 20, 2012. The authors analyzed all cases and found that 44 of the killers were white males and that more than 3/4 of the guns used in these killings were obtained legally. *Id.* Of the 143 weapons used, 71 were semiautomatic handguns, most with high capacity magazines. They also suggest that many of the killers had displayed signs of mental illness before taking violent action. *Id.* Mass shootings receive far more publicity than do individual gun fatalities, but they still remain relatively rare

events, and thus, difficult to predict or prevent. Mass shootings killed about 35 people each year from 2009 and 2013, compared with about 9,000 killed annually by guns in other homicides. *See* Jeffrey W. Swanson, *Explaining Rare Acts of Violence: The Limits of Population Research Evidence*, 62 PSYCHIATRIC SERVICES 1369–1371 (2010).

4. **Mental illness, suicide, and firearms.** A common reaction to the tragedy of a mass shooting is that the killer must be insane, since it is hard to imagine that anyone "in his right mind" would want to kill a large group of people, often strangers. Is this reaction correct? As a group, people with mental illnesses are no more likely to commit violence than the general population. Nonetheless, there is concern that the perpetrators of mass shooting may have experienced some form of mental illness, whether or not it was recognized or treated. Several perpetrators have been described as isolated and withdrawn, which may encourage antisocial reactions, with or without mental illness. *See* John T. Walkup & David H. Rubin, *Social Withdrawal and Violence — Newtown, Connecticut*, 368 NEW ENGL. J. MED. 399 (2013). For a parent's personal perspective, see Andrew Solomon, *The Reckoning — The Father of the Sandy Hook Killer Searches for Answers*, THE NEW YORKER 36, Mar. 17, 2014.

It is difficult to estimate the prevalence of mental illness in the United States. First, the term mental illness means different things to different people and may or may not include substance abuse disorders. Second, research methods vary from collecting data on diagnosed illness to surveys requesting self-reported symptoms, without clinical psychiatric evaluations. Third, research may or may not distinguish "serious disorders" from any form of mental illness. Psychiatrists diagnose specific illnesses guided by the American Psychiatric Association's DIAGNOSTIC AND STATISTICAL MANUAL OF MENTAL DISORDERS, 5TH EDITION (2013) (DSM-5). Thus, estimates vary considerably. *See* Erin Bagalman & Angela Napili, *Prevalence of Mental Illness in the United States: Data Sources and Estimates*, CONGRESSIONAL RESEARCH SERVICE (Feb. 28, 2014). According to the review conducted by Bagalman & Napili, two major national surveys have estimated that between 26.2% and 32.4% of adults had a mental illness (including substance abuse; 18.6% excluding substance abuse) in 2001–2003. *Id.* at 4. The prevalence was 40.3% among adolescents, although serious mental illness was estimated to be 8.0%. *Id.* at 8. However, the more recent National Survey on Drug Use and Health, which focuses primarily on the use of illegal drugs, alcohol, and tobacco among non-institutionalized civilians over 11 years of age, estimated that the prevalence of any mental illness excluding substance abuse disorders among adults (aged 18 or older) was 18.6% in 2012 and 4.1% for serious mental illness. *Id.* at 7–8.

As Miller *et al.* describe above, the majority of firearms deaths are suicides. Suicide and attempted suicide are often thought to result from clinical depression or another mental illness. What does this suggest about how to define the problem? How does it affect the range of solutions?

5. **Public opinion.** Days after the December 2012 Newtown, CT, shooting, a USA/Gallup Poll survey reported that 47% of respondents supported new, stricter gun control laws, while 6% said laws should be less strict. Lydia Saad, *Americans Want Stricter Gun Control, Still Oppose Bans*, GALLUP POLITICS (Dec. 27, 2012),

www.gallup.com/poll/159569/americans-stricter-gun-laws-oppose-bans.aspx (visited Apr. 2014). Nevertheless, in the year following the Newtown, CT, shooting, 30 laws were enacted restricting access to guns, while 70 laws loosened restrictions on guns. Karen Yourish et al., *State Gun Laws Enacted in the Year Since Newtown*, NEW YORK TIMES, Dec. 10, 2013, www.nytimes.com/interactive/2013/12/10/us/state-gun-laws-enacted-in-the-year-since-newtown.html (visited Apr. 2014). A January 2014 Gallup Poll found that those wanting less strict laws had increased from 5% in 2013 to 16% in 2014, while those favoring stricter gun control decreased from 38% in 2013 to 31% in 2014. Rebecca Rifkin, *Americans' Dissatisfaction with Gun Laws Highest Since 2001*, GALLUP POLITICS, Jan. 30, 2014, www.gallup.com/poll/167135/americans-dissatisfaction-gun-laws-highest-2001.aspx (visited Apr. 2014).

6. Policy options. What does the above data — or lack thereof — tell us about how to prevent or reduce deaths and injuries from firearms? Some argue that more and more restrictive measures limiting the availability of firearms are necessary. Others argue that selective access to firearms should keep guns out of the hands of dangerous persons. For many people, fewer guns mean lower rates of morbidity and mortality from gunshots. Alternatively, making guns safer — with technological advances that disable firing by non-owners, for example, may reduce accidental injuries or the use of stolen guns by criminals. These all seem like plausible policy options. Experience, however, does not necessarily conform to the dictates of common sense. Both the District of Columbia and the city of Chicago have among the strictest gun regulations in the country, yet both have high rates of gun injuries and death.

Some argue that increased gun ownership — at least among those without criminal records or significant mental illness — is the best way to prevent gun injuries. John R. Lott, Jr., makes the case for this approach in his book, MORE GUNS, LESS CRIME: UNDERSTANDING CRIME AND GUN CONTROL LAWS (2d ed. 2000). Focusing on the United States, Lott argues that nondiscretionary (i.e., mandatory) concealed handgun laws are the most cost-effective means of reducing crime. According to Lott, states that adopt "shall issue" concealed weapons laws may reduce their rates of murder and other violent crimes, presumably because criminals are afraid that their potential victims could be carrying concealed weapons. He emphasizes that guns give physically weak potential victims a way to equalize the threat of a confrontation. He also suggests that outlawing guns by law-abiding citizens may leave most guns in the hands of criminals. Lott backs up his claims with empirical evidence. Nonetheless, not everyone accepted either the reliability or validity of the data he amassed or the conclusions that he drew from that data. Indeed, his critics have challenged the sources of his data, some of the ways in which he has analyzed it, and even his motives. None, however, have been completely successful in discounting his work. For one example, see Ian Ayres & John J. Donohue III, *Shooting Down the 'More Guns, Less Crime' Hypothesis*, 55 STAN. L. REV. 1193 (2003). For another work that attempts to develop a thesis similar to that of Lott with regard to gun ownership and crime rates in Great Britain, see JOYCE LEE MALCOM, GUNS AND VIOLENCE: THE ENGLISH EXPERIENCE (2002) (comparing the experience with and without gun control laws in England and the United States, making the case that gun control laws do not reduce gun-related violence).

For other works attempting to assess the effectiveness of various gun control measures, see REDUCING GUN VIOLENCE IN AMERICA (D.W. Webster, J.S. Vernick, eds. 2013); DAVID HEMENWAY, PRIVATE GUNS, PUBLIC HEALTH (2006); NATIONAL RESEARCH COUNCIL, NATIONAL ACADEMIES, FIREARMS AND VIOLENCE: A CRITICAL REVIEW (2004); PHILLIP COOK & JENS LUDWIG, EVALUATING GUN POLICY (2003); Arthur L. Kellerman *et al., Gun Ownership as a Risk Factor for Homicide in the Home*, 329 NEW ENG. J. MED. 1084 (2005); Steven D. Levitt, *Understanding Why Crime Fell in the 1990s: Four Factors that Explain the Decline and Six That Do Not*, 18 J. ECON. PERSPECTIVES 163 (2004).

7. The Affordable Care Act and gun ownership. Opponents of gun control scrutinize all kinds of proposed legislation for measures that could be perceived as gun control. Opposition to anything resembling a registry that lists gun owners is especially fierce. The NRA succeeded in including a provision in the Affordable Care Act, entitled "Protection of Second Amendment Gun Rights," stating that no authority given to the Secretary of Health and Human Services by the ACA "shall be construed to authorize or may be used for the collection of any information relating to— (A) the lawful ownership or possession of a firearm or ammunition; (B) the lawful use of a firearm or ammunition; or (C) the lawful storage of a firearm or ammunition. . . . [or] to maintain records of individual ownership or possession of a firearm or ammunition." 42 U.S.C. § 300gg–17(c)(2),(3). The same provision also prohibits wellness programs, otherwise encouraged in the ACA (discussed in Chapter 8, *supra*), from requiring the collection of any information relating to the lawful use, possession, or storage of a firearm or ammunition by an individual and prohibits health insurance plans from denying insurance to lawful gun owners or charging them higher premiums or cost sharing rates. 42 U.S.C. § 300gg–17(c)(1),(4).

The NRA also opposed President Obama's nominee for U.S. Surgeon General, Vivek Hallegere Murthy, MD, because Dr. Murthy thinks guns are a public health problem. Jeremy W. Peters, *Senate Balks at Obama Pick for Surgeon General*, NEW YORK TIMES, Mar. 14, 2014, www.nytimes.com/2014/03/15/us/senate-balks-at-obama-pick-for-surgeon-general.html (visited Apr. 2014).

* * *

2. The Second Amendment and Constitutional Authority to Regulate Firearms

"A well-regulated Militia being necessary to the security of a free State, the right of the people to keep and bear Arms, shall not be infringed."

— U.S. Constitution, Amendment II (1791)

The Second Amendment is an anomaly in the Bill of Rights, because it includes a prefatory clause. The United States Supreme Court did not address the nature of the right protected under the Amendment until its 2008 decision in *District of Columbia v. Heller* (excerpted below). In *Silveira v. Lockyer*, 312 F.3d 1052 (9th Cir. 2002), the Ninth Circuit described the debate over the meaning of the Amendment in the years preceding the *Heller* decision: "A robust constitutional debate is currently taking place in this nation regarding the scope of the Second Amendment, a debate that has gained intensity over the last several years . . . . There are three principal schools of thought that form the basis for the debate. The first, which we will refer to as the "traditional individual rights" model, holds that the Second Amendment guarantees to individual private citizens a fundamental right to possess and use firearms for any purpose at all, subject only to limited government regulation. This view, urged by the NRA and other firearms enthusiasts, as well as by a prolific cadre of fervent supporters in the legal academy, had never been adopted by any court until the recent Fifth Circuit decision in *United States v. Emerson*, 270 F.3d 203 (5th Cir. 2001). The second view, a variant of the first, we will refer to as the "limited individual rights" model. Under that view, individuals maintain a constitutional right to possess firearms insofar as such possession bears a reasonable relationship to militia service. The third, a wholly contrary view, commonly called the "collective rights" model, asserts that the Second Amendment right to "bear arms" guarantees the right of the people to maintain effective state militias, but does not provide any type of individual right to own or possess weapons. Under this theory of the amendment, the federal and state governments have the full authority to enact prohibitions and restrictions on the use and possession of firearms, subject only to generally applicable constitutional constraints, such as due process, equal protection, and the like . . . ."

DISTRICT OF COLUMBIA v. DICK ANTHONY HELLER
554 U.S. 570 (2008)

SCALIA, J., delivered the opinion of the Court, in which ROBERTS, C. J., and KENNEDY, THOMAS, and ALITO, JJ., joined. STEVENS, J., filed a dissenting opinion, in which SOUTER, GINSBURG, and BREYER, JJ., joined. BREYER, J., filed a dissenting opinion, in which STEVENS, SOUTER, and GINSBURG, JJ., joined.

We consider whether a District of Columbia prohibition on the possession of usable handguns in the home violates the Second Amendment to the Constitution.

I

The District of Columbia generally prohibits the possession of handguns. It is a crime to carry an unregistered firearm, and the registration of handguns is prohibited . . . . Wholly apart from that prohibition, no person may carry a handgun without a license, . . . District of Columbia law also requires residents to keep their lawfully owned firearms, such as registered long guns, "unloaded and dissembled or bound by a trigger lock or similar device" unless they are located in a place of business or are being used for lawful recreational activities. . . .

Respondent Dick Heller is a D. C. special police officer authorized to carry a handgun while on duty at the Federal Judicial Center. He applied for a registration certificate for a handgun that he wished to keep at home, but the District refused. He thereafter filed a lawsuit in the Federal District Court for the District of Columbia seeking, on Second Amendment grounds, to enjoin the city from enforcing the bar on the registration of handguns, the licensing requirement insofar as it prohibits the carrying of a firearm in the home without a license, and the trigger-lock requirement insofar as it prohibits the use of "functional firearms within the home."

II

. . . .

A

The Second Amendment provides: "A well regulated Militia, being necessary to the security of a free State, the right of the people to keep and bear Arms, shall not be infringed." In interpreting this text, we are guided by the principle that "[t]he Constitution was written to be understood by the voters; its words and phrases were used in their normal and ordinary as distinguished from technical meaning." . . .

. . . Petitioners and today's dissenting Justices believe that it protects only the right to possess and carry a firearm in connection with militia service. Respondent argues that it protects an individual right to possess a firearm unconnected with service in a militia, and to use that arm for traditionally lawful purposes, such as self-defense within the home.

. . . The Amendment could be rephrased, "Because a well regulated Militia is necessary to the security of a free State, the right of the people to keep and bear Arms shall not be infringed. Although this structure of the Second Amendment is unique in our Constitution, other legal documents of the founding era, particularly individual-rights provisions of state constitutions, commonly included a prefatory statement of purpose.

Logic demands that there be a link between the stated purpose and the command. . . .

1. Operative Clause.

a. "Right of the People." The first salient feature of the operative clause is that it codifies a "right of the people." The unamended Constitution and the Bill of Rights use the phrase "right of the people" two other times, in the First Amendment's Assembly-and-Petition Clause and in the Fourth Amendment's Search-and-Seizure Clause . . . . All three of these instances unambiguously refer to individual rights, not "collective" rights, or rights that may be exercised only through participation in some corporate body.

Three provisions of the Constitution refer to "the people" in a context other than "rights" — the famous preamble ("We the people"), § 2 of Article I (providing that "the people" will choose members of the House), and the Tenth Amendment (providing that those powers not given the Federal Government remain with "the States" or "the people"). Those provisions arguably refer to "the people" acting collectively — but they deal with the exercise or reservation of powers, not rights.

Nowhere else in the Constitution does a "right" attributed to "the people" refer to anything other than an individual right.

. . . .

We start therefore with a strong presumption that the Second Amendment right is exercised individually and belongs to all Americans.

b. "Keep and Bear Arms." . . .

Before addressing the verbs "keep" and "bear," we interpret their object: "Arms." The 18th-century meaning is no different from the meaning today. . . .

The term was applied, then as now, to weapons that were not specifically designed for military use and were not employed in a military capacity.

Some have made the argument, bordering on the frivolous, that only those arms in existence in the 18th century are protected by the Second Amendment. We do not interpret constitutional rights that way. Just as the First Amendment protects modern forms of communications, and the Fourth Amendment applies to modern forms of search, the Second Amendment extends, prima facie, to all instruments that constitute bearable arms, even those that were not in existence at the time of the founding.

We turn to the phrases "keep arms" and "bear arms." Johnson defined "keep" as, most relevantly, "[t]o retain; not to lose," and "[t]o have in custody." Thus, the most natural reading of "keep Arms" in the Second Amendment is to "have weapons."

The phrase "keep arms" was not prevalent in the written documents of the founding period that we have found, but there are a few examples, all of which favor viewing the right to "keep Arms" as an individual right unconnected with militia service. William Blackstone, for example, wrote that Catholics convicted of not attending service in the Church of England suffered certain penalties, one of which was that they were not permitted to "keep arms in their houses." Petitioners point to militia laws of the founding period that required militia members to "keep" arms in connection with militia service, and they conclude from this that the phrase "keep Arms" has a militia-related connotation. This is rather like saying that, since there are many statutes that authorize aggrieved employees to "file complaints" with federal agencies, the phrase "file complaints" has an employment-related connotation. "Keep arms" was simply a common way of referring to possessing arms, for militiamen *and everyone else.*

At the time of the founding, as now, to "bear" meant to "carry." When used with "arms," however, the term has a meaning that refers to carrying for a particular purpose — confrontation. Although the phrase implies that the carrying of the weapon is for the purpose of "offensive or defensive action," it in no way connotes participation in a structured military organization.

In numerous instances, "bear arms" was unambiguously used to refer to the carrying of weapons outside of an organized militia . . . . Nine state constitutional provisions written in the 18th century or the first two decades of the 19th, . . . enshrined a right of citizens to "bear arms in defense of themselves and the state" or "bear arms in defense of himself and the state." . . . Justice James Wilson interpreted the Pennsylvania Constitution's arms-bearing right, for example, as a recognition of the natural right of defense "of one's person or house" — what he called the law of "self-preservation." . . .

. . . .

In any event, the meaning of "bear arms" that petitioners and Justice Stevens propose is *not even* the (sometimes) idiomatic meaning. Rather, they manufacture a hybrid definition, whereby "bear arms" connotes the actual carrying of arms . . . but only in the service of an organized militia. No dictionary has ever adopted that definition, and we have been apprised of no source that indicates that it carried that meaning at the time of the founding. But it is easy to see why petitioners and the dissent are driven to the hybrid definition. Giving "bear Arms" its idiomatic meaning would cause the protected right to consist of the right to be a soldier or to wage war — an absurdity that no commentator has ever endorsed. . . .

. . . .

c. **Meaning of the Operative Clause.** Putting all of these textual elements together, we find that they guarantee the individual right to possess and carry weapons in case of confrontation. This meaning is strongly confirmed by the historical background of the Second Amendment. We look to this because it has always been widely understood that the Second Amendment, like the First and Fourth Amendments, codified a *pre-existing* right. The very text of the Second Amendment implicitly recognizes the pre-existence of the right and declares only that it "shall not be infringed." . . .

Between the Restoration and the Glorious Revolution, the Stuart Kings Charles II and James II succeeded in using select militias loyal to them to suppress political dissidents, in part by disarming their opponents. Under the auspices of the 1671 Game Act, for example, the Catholic Charles II had ordered general disarmaments of regions home to his Protestant enemies. These experiences caused Englishmen to be extremely wary of concentrated military forces run by the state and to be jealous of their arms. They accordingly obtained an assurance from William and Mary, in the Declaration of Right (which was codified as the English Bill of Rights), that Protestants would never be disarmed: "That the subjects which are Protestants may have arms for their defence suitable to their Conditions, and as allowed by Law." This right has long been understood to be the predecessor to our Second Amendment. It was clearly an individual right, having nothing whatever to do with service in a militia . . . .

By the time of the founding, the right to have arms had become fundamental for English subjects. Blackstone, whose works, we have said, "constituted the preeminent authority on English law for the founding generation," cited the arms provision of the Bill of Rights as one of the fundamental rights of Englishmen . . . . It was, he said, "the natural right of resistance and self-preservation," and "the right of having and using arms for self-preservation and defence". Other contemporary authorities concurred. . . .

And, of course, what the Stuarts had tried to do to their political enemies, George III had tried to do to the colonists. In the tumultuous decades of the 1760's and 1770's, the Crown began to disarm the inhabitants of the most rebellious areas. That provoked polemical reactions by Americans invoking their rights as Englishmen to keep arms. They understood the right to enable individuals to defend themselves. . . .

There seems to us no doubt, on the basis of both text and history, that the Second Amendment conferred an individual right to keep and bear arms. Of course the right was not unlimited, just as the First Amendment's right of free speech was not. Thus, we do not read the Second Amendment to protect the right of citizens to carry arms for *any sort* of confrontation, just as we do not read the First Amendment to protect the right of citizens to speak for *any purpose*. Before turning to limitations upon the individual right, however, we must determine whether the prefatory clause of the Second Amendment comports with our interpretation of the operative clause.

2. Prefatory Clause. . . .

a. **"Well-Regulated Militia."** In *United States* v. *Miller*, 307 U.S. 174 (1939), we explained that "the Militia comprised all males physically capable of acting in concert for the common defense." That definition comports with founding-era sources. See, *e.g.*, Webster ("The militia of a country are the able bodied men organized into companies, regiments and brigades . . . and required by law to attend military exercises on certain days only, but at other times left to pursue their usual occupations") . . . .

Petitioners take a seemingly narrower view of the militia, stating that "[m]ilitias are the state- and congressionally-regulated military forces described in the Militia Clauses (art. I, § 8, cls. 15–16)." . . . [W]e believe that petitioners identify the wrong thing, namely, the organized militia. Unlike armies and navies, which Congress is given the power to create, the militia is assumed by Article I already to be *in existence*. Congress is given the power to "provide for calling forth the Militia," § 8, cl. 15; and the power not to create, but to "organiz[e]" it — and not to organize "a" militia, which is what one would expect if the militia were to be a federal creation, but to organize "the" militia, connoting a body already in existence. This is fully consistent with the ordinary definition of the militia as all able-bodied men. From that pool, Congress has plenary power to organize the units that will make up an effective fighting force. That is what Congress did in the first militia Act, which specified that "each and every free able-bodied white male citizen of the respective states, resident therein, who is or shall be of the age of eighteen years, and under the age of forty-five years (except as is herein after excepted) shall severally and respectively be enrolled in the militia." Act of May 8, 1792. . . . . Although the militia consists of all able-bodied men, the federally organized militia may consist of a subset of them.

Finally, the adjective "well-regulated" implies nothing more than the imposition of proper discipline and training.

b. **"Security of a Free State."** The phrase "security of a free State" meant "security of a free polity," not security of each of the several States . . . .

There are many reasons why the militia was thought to be "necessary to the security of a free State." First, of course, it is useful in repelling invasions and suppressing insurrections. Second, it renders large standing armies unnecessary —

an argument that Alexander Hamilton made in favor of federal control over the militia. Third, when the able-bodied men of a nation are trained in arms and organized, they are better able to resist tyranny.

3. Relationship Between Prefatory Clause and Operative Clause.

We reach the question, then: Does the preface fit with an operative clause that creates an individual right to keep and bear arms? It fits perfectly, once one knows the history that the founding generation knew and that we have described above . . . .

. . . .

It is therefore entirely sensible that the Second Amendment's prefatory clause announces the purpose for which the right was codified: to prevent elimination of the militia. The prefatory clause does not suggest that preserving the militia was the only reason Americans valued the ancient right; most undoubtedly thought it even more important for self-defense and hunting. But the threat that the new Federal Government would destroy the citizens' militia by taking away their arms was the reason that right — unlike some other English rights — was codified in a written Constitution. Justice Breyer's assertion that individual self-defense is merely a "subsidiary interest" of the right to keep and bear arms is profoundly mistaken. He bases that assertion solely upon the prologue — but that can only show that self-defense had little to do with the right's *codification*; it was the *central component* of the right itself.

. . . .

D

We now address how the Second Amendment was interpreted from immediately after its ratification through the end of the 19th century. . . .

1. Postratification Commentary.

Three important founding-era legal scholars interpreted the Second Amendment in published writings. All three understood it to protect an individual right unconnected with militia service.

St. George Tucker's version of Blackstone's Commentaries . . . conceived of the Blackstonian arms right as necessary for self-defense. He equated that right . . . with the Second Amendment . . . . : "This may be considered as the true palladium of liberty . . . . The right to self defence is the first law of nature: in most governments it has been the study of rulers to confine the right within the narrowest limits possible. Wherever standing armies are kept up, and the right of the people to keep and bear arms is, under any colour or pretext whatsoever, prohibited, liberty, if not already annihilated, is on the brink of destruction." . . .

In 1825, William Rawle, a prominent lawyer who had been a member of the Pennsylvania Assembly that ratified the Bill of Rights, published an influential treatise, which analyzed the Second Amendment as follows:

"The first [principle] is a declaration that a well regulated militia is necessary to the security of a free state; a proposition from which few will dissent . . . .

"The corollary, from the first position is, that the right of the people to keep and bear arms shall not be infringed.

"The prohibition is general. No clause in the constitution could by any rule of construction be conceived to give to congress a power to disarm the people. Such a flagitious attempt could only be made under some general pretence by a state legislature. But if in any blind pursuit of inordinate power, either should attempt it, this amendment may be appealed to as a restraint on both."

. . . Rawle clearly differentiated between the people's right to bear arms and their service in a militia: "In a people permitted and accustomed to bear arms, we have the rudiments of a militia, which properly consists of armed citizens, divided into military bands, and instructed at least in part, in the use of arms for the purposes of war." Rawle further said that the Second Amendment right ought not "be abused to the disturbance of the public peace," such as by assembling with other armed individuals "for an unlawful purpose" — statements that make no sense if the right does not extend to *any* individual purpose.

Joseph Story published his famous Commentaries on the Constitution of the United States in 1833. . . . Story [compared] the [right included in the] English Bill of Rights . . . with the Second Amendment: "§ 1891. A similar provision [to the Second Amendment] in favour of protestants (for to them it is confined) is to be found in the bill of rights of 1688, it being declared, 'that the subjects, which are protestants, may have arms for their defence suitable to their condition, and as allowed by law.' . . . " (Footnotes omitted.)

This comparison to the Declaration of Right would not make sense if the Second Amendment right was the right to use a gun in a militia, which was plainly not what the English right protected . . . .

Antislavery advocates routinely invoked the right to bear arms for self-defense. Joel Tiffany, for example, citing Blackstone's description of the right, wrote that "the right to keep and bear arms, also implies the right to use them if necessary in self defence; without this right to use the guaranty would have hardly been worth the paper it consumed." In his famous Senate speech about the 1856 "Bleeding Kansas" conflict, Charles Sumner proclaimed:

> The rifle has ever been the companion of the pioneer and, under God, his tutelary protector against the red man and the beast of the forest. Never was this efficient weapon more needed in just self-defense, than now in Kansas, and at least one article in our National Constitution must be blotted out, before the complete right to it can in any way be impeached
> . . . .

We have found only one early-19th century commentator who clearly conditioned the right to keep and bear arms upon service in the militia — and he recognized that the prevailing view was to the contrary. "The provision of the constitution, declaring the right of the people to keep and bear arms, &c. was probably intended to apply to the right of the people to bear arms for such [militia-related] purposes only, and not to prevent congress or the legislatures of the different states from enacting laws to prevent the citizens from always going armed. A different construction however has been given to it."

2. Pre-Civil War Case Law.

The 19th-century cases that interpreted the Second Amendment universally support an individual right unconnected to militia service . . . . In the famous fugitive-slave case of _Johnson_ v. _Tompkins_, 13 F. Cas. 840, 850 (CC Pa. 1833), Baldwin, sitting as a Circuit Judge, cited both the Second Amendment and the Pennsylvania analogue for his conclusion that a citizen has "a right to carry arms in defence of his property or person, and to use them, if either were assailed with such force, numbers or violence as made it necessary for the protection or safety of either."

Many early-19th century state cases indicated that the Second Amendment right to bear arms was an individual right unconnected to militia service, though subject to certain restrictions. A Virginia case in 1824 holding that the Constitution did not extend to free blacks explained: "[n]umerous restrictions imposed on [blacks] in our Statute Book, many of which are inconsistent with the letter and spirit of the Constitution, both of this State and of the United States as respects the free whites, demonstrate, that, here, those instruments have not been considered to extend equally to both classes of our population . . . ." . . . An 1829 decision by the Supreme Court of Michigan said: "The constitution of the United States also grants to the citizen the right to keep and bear arms. But the grant of this privilege cannot be construed into the right in him who keeps a gun to destroy his neighbor. No rights are intended to be granted by the constitution for an unlawful or unjustifiable purpose." _United States_ v. _Sheldon_, in 5 Transactions of the Supreme Court of the Territory of Michigan 337, 346 (W. Blume ed. 1940). It is not possible to read this as discussing anything other than an individual right unconnected to militia service. . . .

      . . . .

Those who believe that the Second Amendment preserves only a militia-centered right place great reliance on the Tennessee Supreme Court's 1840 decision in _Aymette_ v. _State,_ 21 Tenn. 154. The case does not stand for that broad proposition . . . . _Aymette_ held that the state constitutional guarantee of the right to "bear" arms did not prohibit the banning of concealed weapons. The opinion first recognized that both the state right and the federal right were descendents of the 1689 English right, but (erroneously, and contrary to virtually all other authorities) read that right to refer only to "protect[ion of] the public liberty" and "keep[ing] in awe those who are in power". The court then adopted a sort of middle position, whereby citizens were permitted to carry arms openly, unconnected with any service in a formal militia, but were given the right to use them only for the military purpose of banding together to oppose tyranny. This odd reading of the right is, to be sure, not the one we adopt — but it is not petitioners' reading either. More importantly, seven years earlier the Tennessee Supreme Court had treated the state constitutional provision as conferring a right "to all the free citizens of the State to keep and bear arms for their defence"; and 21 years later the court held that the "keep" portion of the state constitutional right included the right to personal self-defense: "[T]he right to keep arms involves, necessarily, the right to use such arms for all the ordinary purposes, and in all the ordinary modes usual in the country, and to which arms are adapted, limited by the duties of a good citizen in times of peace."

3. Post-Civil War Legislation.

In the aftermath of the Civil War, there was an outpouring of discussion of the Second Amendment in Congress and in public discourse, as people debated whether and how to secure constitutional rights for newly free slaves. Since those discussions took place 75 years after the ratification of the Second Amendment, they do not provide as much insight into its original meaning as earlier sources. Yet those born and educated in the early 19th century faced a widespread effort to limit arms ownership by a large number of citizens; their understanding of the origins and continuing significance of the Amendment is instructive.

Blacks were routinely disarmed by Southern States after the Civil War. Those who opposed these injustices frequently stated that they infringed blacks' constitutional right to keep and bear arms. Needless to say, the claim was not that blacks were being prohibited from carrying arms in an organized state militia . . . .

. . . .

Congress enacted the Freedmen's Bureau Act on July 16, 1866. Section 14 stated:

> "[T]he right . . . to have full and equal benefit of all laws and proceedings concerning personal liberty, personal security, and the acquisition, enjoyment, and disposition of estate, real and personal, including the constitutional right to bear arms, shall be secured to and enjoyed by all the citizens . . . without respect to race or color, or previous condition of slavery . . . ."
> 14 Stat. 176–177.

The understanding that the Second Amendment gave freed blacks the right to keep and bear arms was reflected in congressional discussion of the bill, with even an opponent of it saying that the founding generation "were for every man bearing his arms about him and keeping them in his house, his castle, for his own defense."

Similar discussion attended the passage of the Civil Rights Act of 1871 and the Fourteenth Amendment. For example, Representative Butler said of the Act: "Section eight is intended to enforce the well-known constitutional provision guaranteeing the right of the citizen to 'keep and bear arms,' and provides that whoever shall take away, by force or violence, or by threats and intimidation, the arms and weapons which any person may have for his defense, shall be deemed guilty of larceny of the same." With respect to the proposed Amendment, Senator Pomeroy described as one of the three "indispensable" "safeguards of liberty . . . under the Constitution" a man's "right to bear arms for the defense of himself and family and his homestead." Representative Nye thought the Fourteenth Amendment unnecessary because "[a]s citizens of the United States [blacks] have equal right to protection, and to keep and bear arms for self-defense."

It was plainly the understanding in the post-Civil War Congress that the Second Amendment protected an individual right to use arms for self-defense.

4. Post-Civil War Commentators.

Every late-19th century legal scholar that we have read interpreted the Second Amendment to secure an individual right unconnected with militia service. The most famous was the judge and professor Thomas Cooley, . . . :

> "Among the other defences to personal liberty should be mentioned the right of the people to keep and bear arms . . . . The alternative to a standing army is 'a well-regulated militia,' but this cannot exist unless the people are trained to bearing arms. How far it is in the power of the legislature to regulate this right, we shall not undertake to say, as happily there has been very little occasion to discuss that subject by the courts."

That Cooley understood the right not as connected to militia service, but as securing the militia by ensuring a populace familiar with arms, is made even clearer in his 1880 work, General Principles of Constitutional Law . . . . :

> "It might be supposed from the phraseology of this provision that the right to keep and bear arms was only guaranteed to the militia; but this would be an interpretation not warranted by the intent. The militia, as has been elsewhere explained, consists of those persons who, under the law, are liable to the performance of military duty, and are officered and enrolled for service when called upon. But the law may make provision for the enrolment of all who are fit to perform military duty, or of a small number only, or it may wholly omit to make any provision at all; . . . . The meaning of the provision undoubtedly is, that the people, from whom the militia must be taken, shall have the right to keep and bear arms; and they need no permission or regulation of law for the purpose . . . ."

All other post-Civil War 19th-century sources we have found concurred with Cooley. [The Court gives one example from each decade.]

E

We now ask whether any of our precedents forecloses the conclusions we have reached about the meaning of the Second Amendment.

United States v. Cruikshank [1876], in the course of vacating the convictions of members of a white mob for depriving blacks of their right to keep and bear arms, held that the Second Amendment does not by its own force apply to anyone other than the Federal Government. The opinion explained that the right "is not a right granted by the Constitution [or] in any manner dependent upon that instrument for its existence. The second amendment . . . means no more than that it shall not be infringed by Congress." States, we said, were free to restrict or protect the right under their police powers. The limited discussion of the Second Amendment in

Cruikshank supports, if anything, the individual-rights interpretation. There was no claim in *Cruikshank* that the victims had been deprived of their right to carry arms in a militia; indeed, the Governor had disbanded the local militia unit the year before the mob's attack. We described the right protected by the Second Amendment as " 'bearing arms for a lawful purpose' " and said that "the people [must] look for their protection against any violation by their fellow-citizens of the rights it recognizes" to the States' police power. That discussion makes little sense if it is only a right to bear arms in a state militia.

Presser v. *Illinois*, 116 U.S. 252 (1886), held that the right to keep and bear arms was not violated by a law that forbade "bodies of men to associate together as military organizations, or to drill or parade with arms in cities and towns unless authorized by law." This does not refute the individual-rights interpretation of the Amendment; . . . .

Justice Stevens places overwhelming reliance upon this Court's decision in *Miller.* "[H]undreds of judges," we are told, "have relied on the view of the Amendment we endorsed there," and "[e]ven if the textual and historical arguments on both sides of the issue were evenly balanced, respect for the well-settled views of all of our predecessors on this Court, and for the rule of law itself . . . would prevent most jurists from endorsing such a dramatic upheaval in the law." And what is, according to Justice Stevens, the holding of *Miller* that demands such obeisance? That the Second Amendment "protects the right to keep and bear arms for certain military purposes, but that it does not curtail the Legislature's power to regulate the nonmilitary use and ownership of weapons."

. . . *Miller* did not hold that and cannot possibly be read to have held that. The judgment in the case upheld against a Second Amendment challenge two men's federal indictment for transporting an unregistered short-barreled shotgun in interstate commerce, in violation of the National Firearms Act. It is entirely clear that the Court's basis for saying that the Second Amendment did not apply was *not* that the defendants were "bear[ing] arms" not "for . . . military purposes" but for "nonmilitary use". Rather, it was that the *type of weapon at issue* was not eligible for Second Amendment protection: "In the absence of any evidence tending to show that the possession or use of a [short-barreled shotgun] at this time has some reasonable relationship to the preservation or efficiency of a well regulated militia, we cannot say that the Second Amendment guarantees the right to keep and bear *such an instrument*." (emphasis added). "Certainly," the Court continued, "it is not within judicial notice that this weapon is any part of the ordinary military equipment or that its use could contribute to the common defense." Beyond that, the opinion provided no explanation of the content of the right.

This holding is not only consistent with, but positively suggests, that the Second Amendment confers an individual right to keep and bear arms (though only arms that "have some reasonable relationship to the preservation or efficiency of a well regulated militia"). Had the Court believed that the Second Amendment protects only those serving in the militia, it would have been odd to examine the character of the weapon rather than simply note that the two crooks were not militiamen. . . . *Miller* stands only for the proposition that the Second Amendment right, whatever its nature, extends only to certain types of weapons.

. . . .

We may as well consider at this point (for we will have to consider eventually) *what* types of weapons *Miller* permits. Read in isolation, *Miller*'s phrase "part of ordinary military equipment" could mean that only those weapons useful in warfare are protected. That would be a startling reading of the opinion, since it would mean that the National Firearms Act's restrictions on machineguns (not challenged in *Miller*) might be unconstitutional, machineguns being useful in warfare in 1939. We think that *Miller*'s "ordinary military equipment" language must be read in tandem with what comes after: "[O]rdinarily when called for [militia] service [able-bodied] men were expected to appear bearing arms supplied by themselves and of the kind in common use at the time." . . . "In the colonial and revolutionary war era, [small-arms] weapons used by militiamen and weapons used in defense of person and home were one and the same." Indeed, that is precisely the way in which the Second Amendment's operative clause furthers the purpose announced in its preface. We therefore read *Miller* to say only that the Second Amendment does not protect those weapons not typically possessed by law-abiding citizens for lawful purposes, such as short-barreled shotguns. That accords with the historical understanding of the scope of the right.

We conclude that nothing in our precedents forecloses our adoption of the original understanding of the Second Amendment. It should be unsurprising that such a significant matter has been for so long judicially unresolved. For most of our history, the Bill of Rights was not thought applicable to the States, and the Federal Government did not significantly regulate the possession of firearms by law-abiding citizens. Other provisions of the Bill of Rights have similarly remained unilluminated for lengthy periods . . . . It is demonstrably not true that, as Justice Stevens claims, "for most of our history, the invalidity of Second-Amendment-based objections to firearms regulations has been well settled and uncontroversial." For most of our history the question did not present itself.

III

Like most rights, the right secured by the Second Amendment is not unlimited. From Blackstone through the 19th-century cases, commentators and courts routinely explained that the right was not a right to keep and carry any weapon whatsoever in any manner whatsoever and for whatever purpose. For example, the majority of the 19th-century courts to consider the question held that prohibitions on carrying concealed weapons were lawful under the Second Amendment or state analogues. [N]othing in our opinion should be taken to cast doubt on longstanding prohibitions on the possession of firearms by felons and the mentally ill, or laws forbidding the carrying of firearms in sensitive places such as schools and government buildings, or laws imposing conditions and qualifications on the commercial sale of arms.

We also recognize another important limitation on the right to keep and carry arms. *Miller* said, as we have explained, that the sorts of weapons protected were those "in common use at the time." We think that limitation is fairly supported by the historical tradition of prohibiting the carrying of "dangerous and unusual weapons."

It may be objected that if weapons that are most useful in military service — M-16 rifles and the like — may be banned, then the Second Amendment right is completely detached from the prefatory clause. But as we have said, the conception of the militia at the time of the Second Amendment's ratification was the body of all citizens capable of military service, who would bring the sorts of lawful weapons that they possessed at home to militia duty. It may well be true today that a militia, to be as effective as militias in the 18th century, would require sophisticated arms that are highly unusual in society at large . . . . But the fact that modern developments have limited the degree of fit between the prefatory clause and the protected right cannot change our interpretation of the right.

IV

Issue Here

We turn finally to the law at issue here. As we have said, the law totally bans handgun possession in the home. It also requires that any lawful firearm in the home be disassembled or bound by a trigger lock at all times, rendering it inoperable.

As the quotations earlier in this opinion demonstrate, the inherent right of self-defense has been central to the Second Amendment right. The handgun ban amounts to a prohibition of an entire class of "arms" that is overwhelmingly chosen by American society for that lawful purpose. The prohibition extends, moreover, to the home, where the need for defense of self, family, and property is most acute. Under any of the standards of scrutiny that we have applied to enumerated constitutional rights, banning from the home "the most preferred firearm in the nation to 'keep' and use for protection of one's home and family," would fail constitutional muster.

Few laws in the history of our Nation have come close to the severe restriction of the District's handgun ban. And some of those few have been struck down. In *Nunn* v. *State*, the Georgia Supreme Court struck down a prohibition on carrying pistols openly (even though it upheld a prohibition on carrying concealed weapons). In *Andrews* v. *State*, the Tennessee Supreme Court likewise held that a statute that forbade openly carrying a pistol "publicly or privately, without regard to time or place, or circumstances," violated the state constitutional provision (which the court equated with the Second Amendment). That was so even though the statute did not restrict the carrying of long guns.

Rationale

It is no answer to say, as petitioners do, that it is permissible to ban the possession of handguns so long as the possession of other firearms (*i.e.*, long guns) is allowed. It is enough to note, as we have observed, that the American people have considered the handgun to be the quintessential self-defense weapon. There are many reasons that a citizen may prefer a handgun for home defense: . . . Whatever the reason, handguns are the most popular weapon chosen by Americans for self-defense in the home, and a complete prohibition of their use is invalid.

We must also address the District's requirement (as applied to respondent's handgun) that firearms in the home be rendered and kept inoperable at all times. This makes it impossible for citizens to use them for the core lawful purpose of self-defense and is hence unconstitutional. The District argues that we should interpret this element of the statute to contain an exception for self-defense. But we think that is precluded by the unequivocal text, and by the presence of certain other enumerated exceptions: . . . The nonexistence of a self-defense exception is also suggested by the D. C. Court of Appeals' statement that the statute forbids residents to use firearms to stop intruders.

Apart from his challenge to the handgun ban and the trigger-lock requirement respondent asked the District Court to enjoin petitioners from enforcing the separate licensing requirement "in such a manner as to forbid the carrying of a firearm within one's home or possessed land without a license." The Court of Appeals did not invalidate the licensing requirement, but held only that the District "may not prevent [a handgun] from being moved throughout one's house." [The Court then briefly discusses the licensing requirement.] We therefore assume that petitioners' issuance of a license will satisfy respondent's prayer for relief and do not address the licensing requirement.

Justice Breyer has devoted most of his separate dissent to the handgun ban. He says that, even assuming the Second Amendment is a personal guarantee of the right to bear arms, the District's prohibition is valid. He first tries to establish this by founding-era historical precedent, pointing to various restrictive laws in the colonial period. These demonstrate, in his view, that the District's law "imposes a burden upon gun owners that seems proportionately no greater than restrictions in existence at the time the Second Amendment was adopted." Of the laws he cites, only one offers even marginal support for his assertion. A 1783 Massachusetts law forbade the residents of Boston to "take into" or "receive into" "any Dwelling-House, Stable, Barn, Out-house, Ware-house, Store, Shop or other Building" loaded firearms, and permitted the seizure of any loaded firearms that "shall be found" there. That statute's text and its prologue, which makes clear that the purpose of the prohibition was to eliminate the danger to firefighters posed by the "depositing of loaded Arms" in buildings, give reason to doubt that colonial Boston authorities would have enforced that general prohibition against someone who temporarily loaded a firearm to confront an intruder (despite the law's application in that case). In any case, we would not stake our interpretation of the Second Amendment upon a single law, in effect in a single city, that contradicts the overwhelming weight of other evidence regarding the right to keep and bear arms for defense of the home . . . . Nothing about those fire-safety laws undermines our analysis; they do not remotely burden the right of self-defense as much as an absolute ban on handguns. Nor, correspondingly, does our analysis suggest the invalidity of laws regulating the storage of firearms to prevent accidents.

Justice Breyer points to other founding-era laws that he says "restricted the firing of guns within the city limits to at least some degree" in Boston, Philadelphia, and New York. Those laws provide no support for the severe restriction in the present case. The New York law levied a fine of 20 shillings on anyone who fired a gun in certain places (including houses) on New Year's Eve and the first two days of January, and was aimed at preventing the "great Damages . . . frequently done on [those days] by persons going House to House, with Guns and other Fire Arms and being often intoxicated with Liquor." It is inconceivable that this law would have been enforced against a person exercising his right to self-defense on New Year's Day against such drunken hooligans. The Pennsylvania law to which Justice Breyer refers levied a fine of five shillings on one who fired a gun or set off fireworks in Philadelphia without first obtaining a license from the Governor. Given Justice Wilson's explanation that the right to self-defense with arms was protected by the Pennsylvania Constitution, it is unlikely that this law (which in any event amounted to at most a licensing regime) would have been enforced against a person who used firearms for self-defense. [The Court next refers to similar laws cited by Justice Breyer that were promulgated in Rhode Island and Massachusetts.]

A broader point about the laws that Justice Breyer cites: All of them punished the discharge (or loading) of guns with a small fine and forfeiture of the weapon (or in a few cases a very brief stay in the local jail), not with significant criminal penalties. They are akin to modern penalties for minor public-safety infractions like speeding or jaywalking. And although such public-safety laws may not contain exceptions for self-defense, it is inconceivable that the threat of a jaywalking ticket would deter someone from disregarding a "Do Not Walk" sign in order to flee an attacker, or that the government would enforce those laws under such circumstances. Likewise, we do not think that a law imposing a 5-shilling fine and forfeiture of the gun would have prevented a person in the founding era from using a gun to protect himself or his family from violence, or that if he did so the law would be enforced against him. The District law, by contrast, far from imposing a minor fine, threatens citizens with a year in prison (five years for a second violation) for even obtaining a gun in the first place.

Justice Breyer moves on to make a broad jurisprudential point: He criticizes us for declining to establish a level of scrutiny for evaluating Second Amendment restrictions. He proposes, explicitly at least, none of the traditionally expressed levels (strict scrutiny, intermediate scrutiny, rational basis), but rather a judge-empowering "interest-balancing inquiry" that "asks whether the statute burdens a protected interest in a way or to an extent that is out of proportion to the statute's salutary effects upon other important governmental interests." After an exhaustive discussion of the arguments for and against gun control, Justice Breyer arrives at his interest-balanced answer: Because handgun violence is a problem, because the law is limited to an urban area, and because there were somewhat similar restrictions in the founding period (a false proposition that we have already discussed), the interest-balancing inquiry results in the constitutionality of the handgun ban. QED.

We know of no other enumerated constitutional right whose core protection has been subjected to a freestanding "interest-balancing" approach. The very enumeration of the right takes out of the hands of government — even the Third Branch of Government — the power to decide on a case-by-case basis whether the right is *really worth* insisting upon. A constitutional guarantee subject to future judges' assessments of its usefulness is no constitutional guarantee at all. Constitutional rights are enshrined with the scope they were understood to have when the people adopted them, whether or not future legislatures or (yes) even future judges think that scope too broad . . . . The First Amendment contains the freedom-of-speech guarantee that the people ratified, which included exceptions for obscenity, libel, and disclosure of state secrets, but not for the expression of extremely unpopular and wrong-headed views. The Second Amendment is no different. Like the First, it is the very *product* of an interest balancing by the people — which Justice Breyer would now conduct for them anew. And whatever else it leaves to future evaluation, it surely elevates above all other interests the right of law-abiding, responsible citizens to use arms in defense of hearth and home.

Justice Breyer chides us for leaving so many applications of the right to keep and bear arms in doubt, and for not providing extensive historical justification for those regulations of the right that we describe as permissible. But since this case represents this Court's first in-depth examination of the Second Amendment, one should not expect it to clarify the entire field . . . . And there will be time enough to expound upon the historical justifications for the exceptions we have mentioned if and when those exceptions come before us.

In sum, we hold that the District's ban on handgun possession in the home violates the Second Amendment, as does its prohibition against rendering any lawful firearm in the home operable for the purpose of immediate self-defense. Assuming that Heller is not disqualified from the exercise of Second Amendment rights, the District must permit him to register his handgun and must issue him a license to carry it in the home.

* * *

We are aware of the problem of handgun violence in this country, and we take seriously the concerns raised by the many *amici* who believe that prohibition of handgun ownership is a solution. The Constitution leaves the District of Columbia a variety of tools for combating that problem, including some measures regulating handguns. But the enshrinement of constitutional rights necessarily takes certain policy choices off the table. These include the absolute prohibition of handguns held and used for self-defense in the home. Undoubtedly some think that the Second Amendment is outmoded in a society where our standing army is the pride of our Nation, where well-trained police forces provide personal security, and where gun violence is a serious problem. That is perhaps debatable, but what is not debatable is that it is not the role of this Court to pronounce the Second Amendment extinct.

MOORE v. MADIGAN, ATTORNEY GENERAL OF ILLINOIS
702 F.3d 933 (7th Cir. 2012)

POSNER, CIRCUIT JUDGE.

These two appeals, consolidated for oral argument, challenge denials of declaratory and injunctive relief sought in materially identical suits under the *Second Amendment*. An Illinois law forbids a person, with exceptions mainly for police and other security personnel, hunters, and members of target shooting clubs, *720 ILCS 5/24-2*, to carry a gun ready to use (loaded, immediately accessible — that is, easy to reach — and uncased). There are exceptions for a person on his own property (owned or rented), or in his home (but if it's an apartment, only there and not in the apartment building's common areas), or in his fixed place of business, or on the property of someone who has permitted him to be there with a ready-to-use gun . . . . Even carrying an unloaded gun in public, if it's uncased and immediately

Illinois law

accessible, is prohibited, other than to police and other excepted persons, unless carried openly outside a vehicle in an unincorporated area and ammunition for the gun is not immediately accessible . . . .

The appellants contend that the Illinois law violates the *Second Amendment* as interpreted in *District of Columbia v. Heller, 554 U.S. 570 (2008)*, and held applicable to the states in *McDonald v. City of Chicago, 130 S. Ct. 3020 (2010)*. *Heller* held that the *Second Amendment* protects "the right of law-abiding, responsible citizens to use arms in defense of hearth and home." But the Supreme Court has not yet addressed the question whether the *Second Amendment* creates a right of self-defense outside the home. The district courts ruled that it does not, and so dismissed the two suits for failure to state a claim.

The parties and the amici curiae have treated us to hundreds of pages of argument, in nine briefs. The main focus of these submissions is history. The supporters of the Illinois law present historical evidence that there was no generally recognized private right to carry arms in public in 1791, the year the *Second Amendment* was ratified — the critical year for determining the amendment's historical meaning, according to *McDonald v. City of Chicago*. Similar evidence against the existence of an eighteenth-century right to have weapons in the home for purposes of self-defense rather than just militia duty had of course been presented to the Supreme Court in the *Heller* case. . . . The District of Columbia had argued that "the original understanding of the Second Amendment was neither an individual right of self-defense nor a collective right of the states, but rather a civic right that guaranteed that citizens would be able to keep and bear those arms needed to meet their legal obligation to participate in a well-regulated militia." . . . .

The Supreme Court rejected the argument. The appellees ask us to repudiate the Court's historical analysis. That we can't do. Nor can we ignore the implication of the analysis that the constitutional right of armed self-defense is broader than the right to have a gun in one's home. The first sentence of the *McDonald* opinion states that "two years ago, in *District of Columbia v. Heller*, we held that the *Second Amendment* protects the right to keep and bear arms for the purpose of self-defense,". . . and later in the opinion we read that "*Heller* explored the right's origins, noting that the 1689 English *Bill of Rights* explicitly protected a right to keep arms for self-defense, and that by 1765, Blackstone was able to assert that the right to keep and bear arms was 'one of the fundamental rights of Englishmen,' " . . . . And immediately the Court adds that "Blackstone's assessment was shared by the American colonists."

Both *Heller* and *McDonald* do say that "the need for defense of self, family, and property is *most* acute" in the home (emphasis added); but that doesn't mean it is not acute outside the home. *Heller* repeatedly invokes a broader *Second Amendment* right than the right to have a gun in one's home, as when it says that the amendment "guarantee[s] the individual right to possess and carry weapons in case of confrontation." Confrontations are not limited to the home.

The *Second Amendment* states in its entirety that "a well regulated Militia, being necessary to the security of a free State, the right of the people to keep *and bear* Arms, shall not be infringed" (emphasis added). The right to "bear" as distinct from the right to "keep" arms is unlikely to refer to the home. To speak of "bearing" arms within one's home would at all times have been an awkward usage. A right to bear arms thus implies a right to carry a loaded gun outside the home.

And one doesn't have to be a historian to realize that a right to keep and bear arms for personal self-defense in the eighteenth century could not rationally have been limited to the home. Suppose one lived in what was then the wild west — the Ohio Valley for example (for until the Louisiana Purchase the Mississippi River was the western boundary of the United States), where there were hostile Indians. One would need from time to time to leave one's home to obtain supplies from the nearest trading post, and en route one would be as much (probably more) at risk if unarmed as one would be in one's home unarmed.

The situation in England was different — there was no wilderness and there were no hostile Indians and the right to hunt was largely limited to landowners, who were few. Defenders of the Illinois law reach back to the fourteenth-century Statute of Northampton, which provided that unless on King's business no man could "go nor ride armed by night nor by day, in Fairs, markets, nor in the presence of the Justices or other Ministers, nor in no part elsewhere." 2 Edw. III, c. 3 (1328). Chief Justice Coke interpreted the statute to allow a person to possess weapons inside the home but not to "assemble force, though he be extremely threatened, to go with him to church, or market, or any other place." Edward Coke, *Institutes of the Laws of England* 162 (1797). But the statute enumerated the locations at which going armed was thought dangerous to public safety (such as in fairs or in the presence of judges), and Coke's reference to "assemble force" suggests that the statutory limitation of the right of self-defense was based on a concern with armed gangs, thieves, and assassins rather than with indoors versus outdoors as such.

. . . .

Blackstone described the right of armed self-preservation as a fundamental natural right of Englishmen, on a par with seeking redress in the courts or petitioning the government. The Court in *Heller* inferred from this that eighteenth-century English law recognized a right to possess guns for resistance, self-preservation, self-defense, and protection against both public and private violence. The Court said that American law was the same. And in contrast to the situation in England, in less peaceable America a distinction between keeping arms for self-defense in the home and carrying them outside the home would, as we said, have been irrational. All this is debatable of course, but we are bound by the Supreme Court's historical analysis because it was central to the Court's holding in *Heller*.

Twenty-first century Illinois has no hostile Indians. But a Chicagoan is a good deal more likely to be attacked on a sidewalk in a rough neighborhood than in his apartment on the 35th floor of the Park Tower. A woman who is being stalked or has obtained a protective order against a violent ex-husband is more vulnerable to being attacked while walking to or from her home than when inside. She has a stronger self-defense claim to be allowed to carry a gun in public than the resident of a fancy apartment building (complete with doorman) has a claim to sleep with a loaded gun under her mattress. But Illinois wants to deny the former claim, while compelled by *McDonald* to honor the latter. That creates an arbitrary difference. To confine the right to be armed to the home is to divorce the *Second Amendment* from the right of self-defense described in *Heller* and *McDonald*. It is not a property right — a right to kill a houseguest who in a fit of aesthetic fury tries to slash your copy of Norman Rockwell's painting *Santa with Elves*. That is not self-defense, and this case like *Heller* and *McDonald* is just about self-defense.

A gun is a potential danger to more people if carried in public than just kept in the home. But the other side of this coin is that knowing that many law-abiding citizens are walking the streets armed may make criminals timid. Given that in Chicago, at least, most murders occur outside the home, . . . the net effect on crime rates in general and murder rates in particular of allowing the carriage of guns in public is uncertain both as a matter of theory and empirically. "Based on findings from national law assessments, cross-national comparisons, and index studies, evidence is insufficient to determine whether the degree or intensity of firearms regulation is associated with decreased (or increased) violence." Robert A. Hahn et al., "Firearms Laws and the Reduction of Violence: A Systematic Review," 28 *Am. J. Preventive Med.* 40, 59 (2005); cf. John J. Donohue, "The Impact of Concealed-Carry Laws," in *Evaluating Gun Policy Effects on Crime and Violence* 287, 314–21 (2003). "Whether the net effect of relaxing concealed-carry laws is to increase or reduce the burden of crime, there is good reason to believe that the net is not large . . . . [T]he change in gun carrying appears to be concentrated in rural and suburban areas where crime rates are already relatively low, among people who are at relatively low risk of victimization — white, middle-aged, middle-class males. The available data about permit holders also imply that they are at fairly low risk of misusing guns, consistent with the relatively low arrest rates observed to date for permit holders. Based on available empirical data, therefore, we expect relatively little public safety impact if courts invalidate laws that prohibit gun carrying outside the home, assuming that some sort of permit system for public carry is allowed to stand." Philip J. Cook, Jens Ludwig & Adam M. Samaha, "Gun Control After Heller: Threats and Sideshows from a Social Welfare Perspective," *56 UCLA L. Rev. 1041, 1082 (2009)*; . . . . But we note with disapproval that the opening brief for the plaintiffs in appeal no. 12-1788, in quoting the last sentence above from the article by Cook and his colleagues, deleted without ellipses the last clause — "assuming that some sort of permit system for public carry is allowed to stand."

If guns cannot be carried outside the home, an officer who has reasonable suspicion to stop and frisk a person and finds a concealed gun on him can arrest him, . . . and thus take the gun off the street before a shooting occurs; and this is argued to support the ban on carrying guns outside the home. But it is a weak argument. Often the officer will have no suspicion (the gun is concealed, after all). And a state may be able to require "open carry" — that is, require persons who carry a gun in public to carry it in plain view rather than concealed . . . . Many criminals would continue to conceal the guns they carried, in order to preserve the element of surprise and avoid the price of a gun permit; so the police would have the same opportunities (limited as they are, if the concealment is effective and the concealer does not behave suspiciously) that they do today to take concealed guns off the street.

Some studies have found that an increase in gun *ownership* causes an increase in homicide rates . . . . But the issue in this case isn't ownership; it's carrying guns in public. Duggan's study finds that even the concealed carrying of guns, which many states allow, doesn't lead to an increase in gun ownership . . . . Moreover, violent crime in the United States has been falling for many years and so has gun ownership, . . . — in the same period in which gun laws have become more permissive.

A few studies find that states that allow concealed carriage of guns outside the home and impose minimal restrictions on obtaining a gun permit have experienced increases in assault rates, though not in homicide rates . . . . But it has not been shown that those increases persist. Of another, similar paper by Ayres and Donohue, "Shooting Down the 'More Guns, Less Crime' Hypothesis," *55 Stan. L. Rev. 1193, 1270–85 (2003)*, it has been said that if they "had extended their analysis by one more year, they would have concluded that these laws [laws allowing concealed handguns to be carried in public] reduce crime." . . . Ayres and Donohue disagree that such laws reduce crime, but they admit that data and modeling problems prevent a strong claim that they *increase crime* . . . .

Concealed carriage of guns might increase the death rate from assaults rather than increase the number of assaults. But the studies don't find that laws that allow concealed carriage increase the death rate from shootings, and this in turn casts doubt on the finding of an increased crime rate when concealed carriage is allowed; for if there were more confrontations with an armed criminal, one would expect more shootings. Moreover, there is no reason to expect Illinois to impose *minimal* permit restrictions on carriage of guns outside the home, for obviously this is not a state that has a strong pro-gun culture, unlike the states that began allowing concealed carriage before *Heller* and *MacDonald* enlarged the scope of *Second Amendment* rights.

Charles C. Branas et al., "Investigating the Link Between Gun Possession and Gun Assault," 99 *Am. J. of Pub. Health* 2034, 2037 (2009), finds that assault victims are more likely to be armed than the rest of the population is, which might be thought evidence that going armed is not effective self-defense. But that finding does not illuminate the deterrent effect of knowing that potential victims may be armed. David Hemenway & Deborah Azrael, "The Relative Frequency of Offensive and Defensive Gun Uses: Results from a National Survey," 15 *Violence & Victims* 257, 271 (2000), finds that a person carrying a gun is more likely to use it to commit a crime than to defend himself from criminals. But that is like saying that soldiers are more likely to be armed than civilians. And because fewer than 3 percent of gun-related deaths are from accidents . . . and because Illinois allows the use of guns in hunting and target shooting, the law cannot plausibly be defended on the ground that it reduces the accidental death rate, unless it could be shown that allowing guns to be carried in public causes gun ownership to increase, and we have seen that there is no evidence of that.

In sum, the empirical literature on the effects of allowing the carriage of guns in public fails to establish a pragmatic defense of the Illinois law . . . . Anyway the Supreme Court made clear in *Heller* that it wasn't going to make the right to bear arms depend on casualty counts . . . . If the mere possibility that allowing guns to be carried in public would increase the crime or death rates sufficed to justify a ban, *Heller* would have been decided the other way, for that possibility was as great in the District of Columbia as it is in Illinois.

And a ban as broad as Illinois's can't be upheld merely on the ground that it's not irrational . . . . Otherwise this court wouldn't have needed . . . to marshal extensive empirical evidence to justify the less restrictive federal law that forbids a person "who has been convicted in any court of a misdemeanor crime of domestic violence" to possess a firearm in or affecting interstate commerce. *18 U.S.C. § 922(g)(9)*. In *Skoien* we said that the government had to make a "strong showing" that a gun ban was vital to public safety — it was not enough that the ban was "rational." . . . Illinois has not made that strong showing — and it would have to make a stronger showing in this case than the government did in *Skoien*, because the curtailment of gun rights was much narrower: there the gun rights of persons convicted of domestic violence, here the gun rights of the entire law-abiding adult population of Illinois.

A blanket prohibition on carrying gun in public prevents a person from defending himself anywhere except inside his home; and so substantial a curtailment of the right of armed self-defense requires a greater showing of justification than merely that the public *might* benefit on balance from such a curtailment, though there is no proof it would. In contrast, when a state bans guns merely in particular places, such as public schools, a person can preserve an undiminished right of self-defense by not entering those places; since that's a lesser burden, the state doesn't need to prove so strong a need. Similarly, the state can prevail with less evidence when, as in *Skoien*, guns are forbidden to a class of persons who present a higher than average risk of misusing a gun . . . . And empirical evidence of a public safety concern can be dispensed with altogether when the ban is limited to obviously dangerous persons such as felons and the mentally ill. Illinois has lots of options for protecting its people from being shot without having to eliminate all possibility of armed self-defense in public.

Remarkably, Illinois is the *only* state that maintains a flat ban on carrying ready-to-use guns outside the home, though many states used to ban carrying concealed guns outside the home, . . . — a more limited prohibition than Illinois's, however. Not even Massachusetts has so flat a ban as Illinois, though the District of Columbia does, . . . and a few states did during the nineteenth century, . . . — but no longer.

It is not that all states but Illinois are indifferent to the dangers that widespread public carrying of guns may pose. Some may be. But others have decided that a proper balance between the interest in self-defense and the dangers created by carrying guns in public is to limit the right to carry a gun to responsible persons rather than to ban public carriage altogether, as Illinois with its meager exceptions comes close to doing. Even jurisdictions like New York State, where officials have broad discretion to deny applications for gun permits, recognize that the interest in self-defense extends outside the home. There is no suggestion that some unique characteristic of criminal activity in Illinois justifies the state's taking a different approach from the other 49 states. If the Illinois approach were demonstrably superior, one would expect at least one or two other states to have emulated it.

Apart from the usual prohibitions of gun ownership by children, felons, illegal aliens, lunatics, and in sensitive places such as public schools, the propriety of which was not questioned in *Heller* . . . , some states sensibly require that an applicant for a handgun permit establish his competence in handling firearms. A person who carries a gun in public but is not well trained in the use of firearms is a menace to himself and others. . . . States also permit private businesses and other private institutions (such as churches) to ban guns from their premises. If enough private institutions decided to do that, the right to carry a gun in public would have much less value and might rarely be exercised — in which event the invalidation of the Illinois law might have little effect, which opponents of gun rights would welcome.

Recently the Second Circuit upheld a New York state law that requires an applicant for a permit to carry a concealed handgun in public to demonstrate "proper cause" to obtain a license. *Kachalsky v. County of Westchester,* . . . This is the inverse of laws that forbid dangerous persons to have handguns; . . .

The New York gun law upheld in *Kachalsky,* although one of the nation's most restrictive such laws (under the law's "proper cause" standard, an applicant for a gun permit must demonstrate a need for self-defense greater than that of the general public, such as being the target of personal threats) is less restrictive than Illinois's law. Our principal reservation about the Second Circuit 's analysis is . . . its suggestion that the *Second Amendment* should have much greater scope inside the home than outside simply because other provisions of the Constitution have been held to make that distinction. For example, the opinion states that "in *Lawrence v. Texas*, the [Supreme] Court emphasized that the state's efforts to regulate private sexual conduct between consenting adults is especially suspect when it intrudes into the home." . . . Well of course — the interest in having sex inside one's home is much greater than the interest in having sex on the sidewalk in front of one's home. But the interest in self-protection is as great outside as inside the home . . . .

      . . . .

We are disinclined to engage in another round of historical analysis to determine whether eighteenth-century America understood the *Second Amendment* to include a right to bear guns outside the home. The Supreme Court has decided that the amendment confers a right to bear arms for self-defense, which is as important outside the home as inside. The theoretical and empirical evidence (which overall is inconclusive) is consistent with concluding that a right to carry firearms in public may promote self-defense. Illinois had to provide us with more than merely a rational basis for believing that its uniquely sweeping ban is justified by an increase in public safety. It has failed to meet this burden. The Supreme Court's interpretation of the *Second Amendment* therefore compels us to reverse the decisions in the two cases before us and remand them to their respective district courts for the entry of declarations of unconstitutionality and permanent injunctions. Nevertheless we order our mandate stayed for 180 days to allow the Illinois legislature to craft a new gun law that will impose reasonable limitations, consistent with the public safety and the *Second Amendment* as interpreted in this opinion, on the carrying of guns in public.

———————

NOTES AND QUESTIONS

1. The role of history in interpreting the Second Amendment. To an extraordinary extent, the majority and dissenting Justices in *Heller* rely on historical sources to support their very different views of what the Framers intended the Second Amendment to protect. The search for the historical meaning is understandable in light of the unique structure and ambiguity of the text. Yet the historical literature is itself somewhat ambiguous. In such circumstances, what role should history play in interpreting constitutional text? How much confidence do you have in the Justice's historical research? How do their analyses compare with those of historians? In an article in THE NEW REPUBLIC, Judge Richard A. Posner, called this "law office history":

> The judge sends his law clerks scurrying to the library and to the Web for bits and pieces of historical documentation. When the clerks are the numerous and able clerks of Supreme Court justices, enjoying the assistance of the capable staffs of the Supreme Court Library and the Library of Congress, and when dozens and sometimes hundreds of amicus curiae briefs have been filed, many bulked out with the fruits of their authors' own law-office historiography, it is a simple matter, especially for a skillful rhetorician such as Scalia, to write a plausible historical defense of his position.

Richard A. Posner, *In Defense of Looseness*, THE NEW REPUBLIC, Aug. 27, 2008, www.tnr.com.

In the same article, Judge Posner argued that the *Heller* decision was "questionable in method and result, and it is evidence that the Supreme Court, in deciding constitutional cases, exercises a freewheeling discretion strongly flavored with ideology." Strong words from a conservative federal judge on the 7th Circuit Court of Appeals. Posner was most critical of Justice Scalia's interpretive method, which, according to Posner, "denies the flexible interpretation designed to adapt the Constitution (so far as the text permits) to current conditions." *Id.* Posner argued that the original motivation for the Second Amendment was the fear that the federal government could call up "the Militia" under its Article I power and disarm its members. If the purpose of the Second Amendment was to preserve the ability of state militias to resist a tyrannical federal government, then individuals need not keep arms in their homes either for personal self-defense or hunting. In Posner's view, the *Heller* majority "cut[] loose the Second Amendment from any concern with state militias", because "modern military weapons are not appropriate for home defense." He also argued that true originalism — the way in which the Framers understood legislative interpretation — took into account *"the spirit and reason of the law."* (Emphasis in original.) Thus, he concluded, the decision was not originalist, but a loose construction that allowed the majority to achieve their preferred result, in much the same way that more liberal justices had done with earlier civil rights cases. For Posner, decisions that forbid Congress from interfering with particular rights, such as *Roe v. Wade* (in Chapter 4) and *Kennedy v. Louisiana* (holding that capital punishment for a child rapist is cruel and unusual punishment prohibited by the Eighth Amendment), impose constitutional restraints that tie the federal government's hands, often in improper or inefficient ways.

2. An individual right to own firearms. The *Heller* case answered one question that had remained open for decades — whether the Second Amendment protected the right of individuals to own a firearm independent of any connection to the militia — at least against federal prohibition. Since Congress establishes the law governing the District of Columbia, the decision addressed only the Second Amendment's effect on federal power. In 2010, the Supreme Court held that the Second Amendment also applied to the states. *McDonald v. Moore*, 561 U.S. 742 (2010). In *McDonald*, the Supreme Court summarized *Heller* as holding that "the Second Amendment protects the right to keep and bear arms for the purpose of self-defense." Note how, in *Moore v. Madigan, supra*, Judge Posner emphasizes this self-defense rationale as the reason for finding that the Amendment protects a right to carry firearms outside the home: "The theoretical and empirical evidence (which overall is inconclusive) is consistent with concluding that a right to carry firearms in public may promote self-defense." Since Judge Posner disagreed with *Heller's* conclusion, is his decision a necessary application of *Heller* or a way to show the Supreme Court how *Heller* opened a Pandora's Box?

After *Moore v. Madigan*, Illinois enacted a new law, generally consistent with the Seventh Circuit's decision, authorizing licenses for carrying concealed firearms. In follow-up litigation, the Seventh Circuit described that law's key provisions as follows: "to be entitled to a license, the applicant must have 16 hours of approved firearms training; be at least 21 years old; have a currently valid Firearm Owner's Identification Card . . . ; and not have been convicted of assault, drunk driving, or certain other offenses or be in pending proceedings that could lead to disqualification for a gun license, and not have been treated recently for alcoholism or drug addiction. 430 I.L.C.S. 66/25." *Shepard v. Madigan*, 734 F.3d 748, 749 (7th Cir. 2013).

3. Standard of review for firearms regulations. In *Heller*, the Supreme Court did not decide the applicable level of judicial review of laws implicating the Second Amendment. Recognition of an individual right to bear arms does not answer the question whether a particular regulatory method is constitutional, as can be seen with laws restricting the constitutionally protected rights of privacy, religion, and speech. Thus, courts are faced with deciding the level of scrutiny that should apply to restrictions on the right to bear arms. In *Moore v. Madigan*, the Seventh Circuit requires the state to demonstrate "more than merely a rational basis for believing that its uniquely sweeping ban is justified by an increase in public safety." Is the court requiring heightened or even strict scrutiny? What governmental purposes might be sufficiently important to justify regulation or denial of "the right to bear arms"? How necessary or effective or "tailored" does that legislation have to be?

Note that the court put the burden on the state to demonstrate not only a legitimate (substantial or perhaps compelling) purpose, but also that the law would increase public safety — although to what degree remains unclear. Who should bear the burden of proof in these cases? Is this like freedom of speech, for which it is presumed that all Americans are free to say what they like unless government can produce a very good reason to limit expression? Or should individuals be required to produce a very good reason to own or carry firearms?

Is a general objection to some types of guns, *e.g.*, assault rifles, enough of a justification for a categorical ban? If misuse of a gun is a crime, is a prohibition on the possession of guns to avoid that misuse an overbroad effort to prevent the crime? Perhaps most important from a public health perspective, will the courts require advocates of gun control to show empirical support for their claims that one or another gun control law is constitutionally justified? *See* Mark V. Tushnet, Out of Range: Why the Constitution Can't End the Battle over Guns (2007).

4. State constitutional provisions. Some state constitutions protect a "right to bear arms," although not always using the same terminology as the Second Amendment. These state constitutional provisions would not enable state or local governments to adopt regulatory schemes that violate the Second Amendment, but they may provide a wholly separate basis for opposing a state or local gun control law.

For example, Article 1, § 24 of the State of Washington Constitution provides:

> The right of the individual citizen to bear arms in defense of himself, or the state, shall not be impaired, but nothing in this section shall be construed as authorizing individuals or corporations to organize, maintain, or employ an armed body of men.

How might this provision affect the employment of security personnel to protect corporate facilities or the private engagement of a bodyguard?

5. Gun control references. For a good source of gun control laws on a state-by-state basis, see www.bradycampaign.org/stategunlaws/ (visited Apr. 2014). For an additional source with a somewhat different orientation, *see* www. keepandbeararms.com (visited Apr. 2014).

---

3. Firearms Legislation

Summary of Key Provisions of the
Gun Control Act of 1968, as amended
18 U.S.C. § 921 *et seq.*

The Gun Control Act of 1968 was one of several major federal statutes enacted during the era of civil rights legislation. The Act limits the sale of firearms and ammunition to manufacturers, importers and vendors who obtain a federal license (often called a federal firearms license or FFL). It also prohibits certain individuals from buying, possessing or transporting firearms in foreign or interstate commerce. The major provisions are summarized below.

Federal firearms licensees. Section 922(a) prohibits anyone except a licensed manufacturer, licensed importer or licensed dealer to engage in the business of importing, manufacturing or dealing in firearms or ammunition in interstate or foreign commerce. They are prohibited from shipping or receiving firearms to or from anyone other than another licensed entity. Licensees must sell to retail customers in face-to-face transactions. Licensed entities must provide anyone who received a handgun with a secure gun storage or safety device. § 922(z)(1). Licenses are issued by the Attorney General of the United States. § 923.

Section 922(b) prohibits a licensee from selling or delivering a firearm or ammunition to anyone whom the licensee knows or has reasonable cause to believe is prohibited from obtaining it under the Act. The prohibitions apply to sales to anyone under age 21 (age 18 for shotguns and rifles), anyone who is not a resident of the state where the sale takes place, and to any sale that would violate state law. Sales or deliveries of machine guns, short-barreled shotguns, and short-barreled rifles and "destructive devices" are entirely prohibited, except upon authorization of the U.S. Attorney General "consistent with public safety and necessity." Other persons prohibited from buying a firearm are listed below.

Persons prohibited from obtaining firearms. Section 922(g) lists the persons who are prohibited from shipping, transporting or receiving any firearm or ammunition that has been shipped or transported in interstate commerce:

- A person convicted of (or under indictment for) a crime carrying a sentence of more than one year

- A fugitive from justice

- An unlawful user of, or addicted to, a controlled substance

- A person who has been adjudicated as a "mental defective" or has been committed to any mental institution

(Regulations issued by the Attorney General include in this category persons who have been found incompetent to stand trial or not guilty of a crime by reason of insanity.)

- An alien unlawfully present in the United States

- A person discharged from the U.S. armed forces "under dishonorable conditions"

- A person who has renounced United States citizenship

- A person who has been convicted of a crime of domestic violence or is under a restraining order for domestic violence

The Act states that such "prohibited persons" are forbidden "to ship or transport in interstate or foreign commerce, or possess in or affecting commerce, any firearm or ammunition; or to receive any firearm or ammunition which has been shipped or transported in interstate or foreign commerce." Individuals are also prohibited from transferring a firearm to anyone who is not a resident of the same state.

Background checks. The Brady Handgun Violence Act of 1993, P.L. 103-159, added the provisions that require background checks. § 922(t). Interim requirements were found unconstitutional. *See* note 2 *infra*.) The permanent provisions became operative in 1998, when the Federal Bureau of Investigation (FBI) implemented its National Instant Criminal Background Check System (NICS). (This system does not require any state or local official to carry out the federal law.) Licensed entities are to request background checks for sales of handguns and long guns to customers (except other licensed entities). The licensee is to submit (directly or through a state agency voluntarily created by the state) the customer's name, sex, race, date of birth and state of residence to the NICS, which checks several databases to determine whether the customer is a prohibited person. The NCIS does not inform the licensed entity of the reason why a person is prohibited. If the NICS finds information suggesting, but not confirming, a prohibited status, it can delay the purchase for 3 business days to get more information; it then has 90 days to finalize a decision. If the gun has been sold to someone found to be a prohibited person during that period, the FBI can start a process to retrieve the gun. People who are mistakenly identified as prohibited can appeal the decision to the FBI.

Purchasers are required to attest that they are the actual buyers, and not buying for someone else. But straw purchases ("lying and buying for the other guy") can be difficult to detect in practice. Checking for disqualification for mental illness factors may not be wholly reliable. Some states decline to report adjudications of civil commitment or incompetence to the FBI, and some state laws restrict the disclosure of mental health records.

Individuals are not required to conduct background checks. However, the Act prohibits anyone who is not a licensed entity under the Act to transport or receive a firearm in the state where he resides if the firearm was obtained in another state, § 922(a)(3), or to deliver a firearm to an unlicensed person in another state, § 922(a)(5). Violations are punishable by a fine and/or up to 5 years in prison.

No background check record maintenance. The Brady Act prohibits creating any electronic registry of firearms, owners, or approved transactions. A 1999 amendment to the Gun Control Act prohibited charging fees for NCIS background checks. Another amendment required that background check records be destroyed within 24 hours was enacted in 2004 and made permanent in 2012.

Immunity from liability. Section 992(z)(3) grants qualified immunity from civil liability in certain circumstances. The text provides in part:

(A) In general. Notwithstanding any other provision of law, a person who has lawful possession and control of a handgun, and who uses a secure gun storage or safety device with the handgun, shall be entitled to immunity from a qualified civil liability action.

(B) Prospective actions. A qualified civil liability action may not be brought in any Federal or State court.

(C) Defined term. As used in this paragraph, the term "qualified civil liability action"—

(i) means a civil action brought by any person against a person described in subparagraph (A) for damages resulting from the criminal or unlawful misuse of the handgun by a third party, if—

(I) the handgun was accessed by another person who did not have the permission or authorization of the person having lawful possession and control of the handgun to have access to it; and

(II) at the time access was gained by the person not so authorized, the handgun had been made inoperable by use of a secure gun storage or safety device; and

(ii) shall not include an action brought against the person having lawful possession and control of the handgun for negligent entrustment or negligence per se.

Preemption: Some states require individuals to obtain a license to purchase, own, or carry various types of firearms, with or without a waiting period. The Act does not preempt state laws unless they are in direct and positive conflict with the Act. § 927.

Florida "Stand Your Ground Law"

Florida Statutes § 766.013 (effective October 1, 2005)

§ 776.013. Home protection; use of deadly force; presumption of fear of death or great bodily harm

(1) A person is presumed to have held a reasonable fear of imminent peril of death or great bodily harm to himself or herself or another when using defensive force that is intended or likely to cause death or great bodily harm to another if:

(a) The person against whom the defensive force was used was in the process of unlawfully and forcefully entering, or had unlawfully and forcibly entered, a dwelling, residence, or occupied vehicle, or if that person had removed or was attempting to remove another against that person's will from the dwelling, residence, or occupied vehicle; and

(b) The person who uses defensive force knew or had reason to believe that an unlawful and forcible entry or unlawful and forcible act was occurring or had occurred.

(2) The presumption set forth in subsection (1) does not apply if:

(a) The person against whom the defensive force is used has the right to be in or is a lawful resident of the dwelling, residence, or vehicle, such as an owner, lessee, or titleholder, and there is not an injunction for protection from domestic violence or a written pretrial supervision order of no contact against that person; or

(b) The person or persons sought to be removed is a child or grandchild, or is otherwise in the lawful custody or under the lawful guardianship of, the person against whom the defensive force is used; or

(c) The person who uses defensive force is engaged in an unlawful activity or is using the dwelling, residence, or occupied vehicle to further an unlawful activity; or

(d) The person against whom the defensive force is used is a law enforcement officer, as defined in s. 943.10(14), who enters or attempts to enter a dwelling, residence, or vehicle in the performance of his or her official duties and the officer identified himself or herself in accordance with any applicable law or the person using force knew or reasonably should have known that the person entering or attempting to enter was a law enforcement officer.

(3) A person who is not engaged in an unlawful activity and who is attacked in any other place where he or she has a right to be has no duty to retreat and has the right to stand his or her ground and meet force with force, including deadly force if he or she reasonably believes it is necessary to do so to prevent death or great bodily harm to himself or herself or another or to prevent the commission of a forcible felony.

(4) A person who unlawfully and by force enters or attempts to enter a person's dwelling, residence, or occupied vehicle is presumed to be doing so with the intent to commit an unlawful act involving force or violence.

NOTES AND QUESTIONS

1. **Gun Control Act.** The federal Gun Control Act created a system of federal licensure for manufacturers, importers, and dealers in firearms, and prohibits the sale or transfer of firearms to several categories of individuals believed to pose a risk of violence. The *Heller* decision (Part C. 2., *supra*) appears to assume that at least some individuals can be constitutionally barred from obtaining at least some kinds of firearms. Prohibiting persons who are "mentally defective" (an unfortunate term) may be the most contentious of these categories. How would you define persons who should not be allowed to obtain guns but who have not been convicted of any crime? *See* Garen J. Wintemute, Anthony A Braga, & David M Kennedy, *Private-Party Gun Sales, Regulation, and Public Safety*. 363 NEW ENGL. J. MED. 508 (2010).

Since most persons who commit suicide have not been adjudicated as mentally ill or convicted of a crime, they are not prohibited from purchasing a gun under the federal Gun Control Act. Public health education programs may help to educate federal licensees on how to identify a person who may be seeking a gun to commit suicide. Should people who are voluntarily getting mental health treatment services be on the prohibited list? What effect would that have on willingness to seek treatment? *See* Paul S. Appelbaum & Jeffrey W. Swanson, *Gun Laws and Mental Illness: How Sensible Are the Current Restrictions?*, 61 PSYCHIATRIC SERVICES 652–654 (2010).

Firearms are defined at some length in the Act, 18 U.S.C. § 921, but not all firearms are governed by the Act. The National Firearms Act of 1934 required that machine guns — which continue to fire automatically when the trigger is pressed — must be registered with the federal government. The *Heller* decision did not face the issue of whether civilians could be forbidden from owning particular types of firearms under the Second Amendment. But its discussion of *Miller* did suggest that not all weapons need to be permitted. What should count as "arms" under the Second Amendment? Do arms include tanks or nuclear weapons? Semi-automatic assault weapons and large capacity ammunition feeding devices were banned from 1994 to 2004 (except those lawfully owned or available when the provision took effect). Semi-automatic weapons fire one shot with each pull of the trigger without reloading. 18 U.S.C. § 921(a)(30). Some observers thought that the mass shootings in 2011 and 2012 would prompt renewal of that or a similar ban, but Congress has failed to do so as of April 2014. For a more detailed analysis of the Act, see William J. Krouse, *Gun Control Legislation*, CONGRESSIONAL RESEARCH SERVICE (Nov. 14, 2013).

2. The Brady Act. A different constitutional debate was sparked by the enactment of the Brady Handgun Violence Act of 1993, amending the Gun Control Act to require dealers to conduct background checks to determine whether purchasers of handguns were eligible under state and federal law to own handguns. The 1993 amendments included an interim requirement that federally licensed gun dealers submit information to state and local law enforcement agencies who were required to make "reasonable efforts" to verify the accuracy of the information obtained by the dealers. The legislation anticipated that eventually the National Instant Criminal Background Check System would be developed, as it later was.

In *Printz v. United States*, 521 U.S. 898 (1997), the U.S. Supreme Court held that the requirements imposed on state and local law enforcement by the Brady Act were unconstitutional. According to the Court, Tenth Amendment principles of federalism prohibit Congress from imposing mandatory obligations on state officials (and their local counterparts). The Court did not invalidate the entire Brady Act. If found only that Congress cannot commandeer state or local officials to carry out federal statutory requirements.

The Brady Act has not necessarily lived up to its expectations. *See* Philip J. Cook & Jens Ludwig, *The Effects of the Brady Act on Gun Violence*, GUNS, CRIME, AND PUNISHMENT IN AMERICA (Bernard E. Harcourt, ed., 2003). However, there is some evidence that preventing gun purchases by those under a restraining order for domestic violence has some effect. E.R. Vigdor & J.A. Mercy, *Do Laws Restricting Access to Firearms by Domestic Violence Offenders Prevent Intimate Partner Homicide?*, 30 EVALUATION REVIEW 266 (2006); Garen J. Wintemute *et al.*, *Firearms and Domestic Violence Education and Intervention Project: Final Report of Process and Outcome Evaluations*, Violence Prevention Research Program, University of California, Davis (2012). The Act prohibits anyone convicted of "a misdemeanor crime of domestic violence" from possessing firearms. In *United States v. Castleman*, 134 S. Ct. 1405 (2014), the U.S. Supreme Court interpreted the definition somewhat broadly, finding that domestic violence does not require physical force beyond what qualifies for a common law battery conviction — offensive touching.

3. Florida's "Stand Your Ground" law. Laws governing lawful ownership of firearms, of course, do not preclude other (primarily state) laws prohibiting the use of firearms to commit crimes. Florida's statute gained notoriety when George Zimmerman was acquitted of second degree murder and manslaughter for fatally shooting Trayvon Martin in February 2012 in Sanford, Florida. The law abolished the common law duty to retreat and expanded the right of self-defense to prevent imminent great bodily harm or death, effectively creating an affirmative defense to using deadly force. *Dorsey v. State*, 74 So.3d 521 (Fla. Dist. Ct. App. 2011); *Little v. State*, 111 So.3d 214 (Fla. Dist. Ct. App. 2013). An objective standard — whether a reasonable and prudent person in the same circumstances would have used deadly force — may be required. *Mobley v. State*, 2014 Fla. App. LEXIS 8425 (May 29, 2014). Note that most sections of the statute pertain to defending one's home against unlawful intruders, while subsection (3) applies in public settings. By July 2013, when Zimmerman was acquitted, more than 20 states had enacted similar laws. For a summary of the case, see Lizette Alvarez & Cara Buckley, *Zimmerman Is Acquitted in Trayvon Martin Killing*, NEW YORK TIMES, July 13, 2013, www.nytimes.com/2013/07/14/us/george-zimmerman-verdict-trayvon-martin.html?pagewanted=all&_r=1& (visited Apr. 2014).

4. **Alternative regulatory approaches.** In the wake of mass shooting and renewed controversy over firearms, cities, and states have enacted a remarkable range of different laws. While some adopted more restrictive laws governing licensure to possess firearms and ammunition, others expanded the freedom to possess and carry. Both the Gun Control Act and some state laws protect people from liability for the unauthorized use of their gun by a third party who uses it to commit a crime or other unlawful act.

An interesting example arose in Iowa, whose law prohibits sheriffs to deny permits to carry a firearm on the basis of disability. This placed some sheriffs in a quandary when blind citizens applied for firearms permits. *See* Jason Clayworth, *Iowa Grants Permits for Blind Residents to Carry Guns in Public*, DesMoinesRegister.com, Sept. 8, 2013, www.desmoinesregister.com/article/20130908/NEWS/309080061/Iowa-grants-permits-blind-residents-carry-guns-public?nclick_check=1 (visited Apr. 2014). The Gun Control Act does not mention blindness as a prohibited status, although some states do. There are online firearms training programs, but not all states (including Iowa) require an in-person shooting test.

As long as universal prohibitions on gun ownership or possession implicate the Second Amendment, states continue to seek different approaches to reduce firearm death and injury. These include:

- A minimum age for gun purchases
- Limits on the number of guns or bullets a person is allowed to buy at one time or within a period of time
- Product standards, such as non-removable identification numbers, safety or trigger locks, and load indicators
- Requirements for safe storage of guns
- Gun buy-back programs

These policies have mixed results. There is little correlation between the prevalence of gun deaths and strict gun control laws. Age limits face pushback from families who farm or hunt and want their children to know how to use a gun for protection or hunting. Gun buy-back programs do not necessarily collect many guns used in crimes. *See* Joe Nocera, *Notes from a Gun Buyback*, NEW YORK TIMES, Feb. 15, 2013, www.nytimes.com/2013/02/16/opinion/nocera-notes-from-a-gun-buyback.html (visited Apr. 2014). Law enforcement personnel sometimes object to firearms designed to be fired only by the owner, for fear that they may need use a fellow officer's weapon in an emergency. By far the greatest resistance by gun owners — and the NRA in particular — is to any government registry of gun purchases or owners. A registry could help trace guns used in crimes, but opposition has made registries politically impossible so far.

Approaches that have yet to gain much traction are substantially increased sales or excise taxes on firearms or ammunition and a form of strict liability for the owner of any gun that is used to threaten, injure, or kill another person.

5. When may I shoot a student? For a tongue-in-cheek reaction to the flurry of gun access laws, see Greg Hampikian, *When May I Shoot a Student?*, NEW YORK TIMES, Feb. 27, 2014, www.nytimes.com/2014/02/28/opinion/when-may-i-shoot-a-student.html?emc=eta1&_r=0 (visited, Apr. 2014). Hampikian, a biology professor, wrote in response to an Idaho bill permitting guns on the state's university campuses. He asks, "If I am working out a long equation on the board and several students try to correct me using their laser sights, am I allowed to fire a warning shot?" His answer to the concern that drunken frat boys will fire guns is: "The problem . . . is that they are drunken frat boys. Arming them is clearly not the issue. They would cause damage with or without guns." He adds that he hopes the Legislature will consider providing faculty with bullet proof windows and body armor in the school colors.

6. Resources. Resources on gun control policies include: Brady Campaign to Prevent Gun Violence, www.bradycampaign.org/; U.S. Dept. of Justice, Bureau of Alcohol, Tobacco, Firearms and Explosives, www.atf.gov/; National Institute of Justice, www.nij.gov/; Johns Hopkins Center for Gun Policy and Research, www.jhsph.edu/research/centers-and-institutes/johns-hopkins-center-for-gun-policy-and-research/. Sources supporting gun rights include the National Rifle Association, http://home.nra.org/, and Gun Owners of America, www.gunowners.org/.

---

4. The Role of Litigation in Determining Public Policy on Gun Use and Ownership

PROTECTION OF LAWFUL COMMERCE IN ARMS ACT
Pub. L. No. 109-92, 15 U.S.C. §§ 7901–7903 (2005)

§ 7902. Prohibition on bringing of qualified civil liability actions in federal or state court.

(a) In general. A qualified civil liability action may not be brought in any Federal or State court.

(b) Dismissal of pending actions. A qualified civil liability action that is pending on the date of enactment of this Act shall be immediately dismissed by the court in which the action was brought or is currently pending.

§ 7903.   Definitions. In this Act:

(1) Engaged in the business. The term "engaged in the business" . . . as applied to a seller of ammunition, means a person who devotes time, attention, and labor to the sale of ammunition as a regular course of trade or business with the principal objective of livelihood and profit through the sale or distribution of ammunition.

(2) Manufacturer. The term "manufacturer" means, with respect to a qualified product, a person who is engaged in the business of manufacturing the product in interstate or foreign commerce and who is licensed to engage in business as such a manufacturer . . . .

(3) Person. The term "person" means any individual, corporation, company, association, firm, partnership, society, joint stock company, or any other entity, including any governmental entity.

(4) Qualified product. The term "qualified product" means a firearm . . . , including any antique firearm . . . , or ammunition (as defined in section 921(a) (17) (A) of such title), or a component part of a firearm or ammunition, that has been shipped or transported in interstate or foreign commerce.

(5) Qualified civil liability action.

(A) In general. The term "qualified civil liability action" means a civil action or proceeding or an administrative proceeding brought by any person against a manufacturer or seller of a qualified product, or a trade association, for damages, punitive damages, injunctive or declaratory relief, abatement, restitution, fines, or penalties, or other relief, resulting from the criminal or unlawful misuse of a qualified product by the person or a third party, but shall not include—

(i) an action brought against a transferor convicted under [the Gun Control Act], or a comparable or identical State felony law, by a party directly harmed by the conduct of which the transferee is so convicted;

(ii) an action brought against a seller for negligent entrustment or negligence per se;

(iii) an action in which a manufacturer or seller of a qualified product knowingly violated a State or Federal statute applicable to the sale or marketing of the product, and the violation was a proximate cause of the harm for which relief is sought, including — . . .

(I) any case in which the manufacturer or seller knowingly made any false entry in, or failed to make appropriate entry in, any record required to be kept under Federal or State law with respect to the qualified product, or aided, abetted, or conspired with any person in making any false or fictitious oral or written statement with respect to any fact material to the lawfulness of the sale or other disposition of a qualified product; or

(II) any case in which the manufacturer or seller aided, abetted, or conspired with any other person to sell or otherwise dispose of a qualified product, knowing, or having reasonable cause to believe, that the actual buyer of the qualified product was prohibited from possessing or receiving a firearm or ammunition under [the Gun Control Act] § 922(g) or (n).

(iv) an action for breach of contract or warranty in connection with the purchase of the product;

(v) an action for death, physical injuries or property damage resulting directly from a defect in design or manufacture of the product, when used as intended or in a reasonably foreseeable manner, except that where the discharge of the product was caused by a volitional act that constituted a criminal offense, then such act shall be considered the sole proximate cause of any resulting death, personal injuries or property damage; or

(vi) an action or proceeding commenced by the Attorney General to enforce [the Gun Control Act] or 26 U.S.C. § 5801 *et seq.*

(B) Negligent entrustment. As used in subparagraph (A) (ii), the term "negligent entrustment" means the supplying of a qualified product by a seller for use by another person when the seller knows, or reasonably should know, the person to whom the product is supplied is likely to, and does, use the product in a manner involving unreasonable risk of physical injury to the person or others.

(C) Rule of construction. The exceptions enumerated under clauses (i) through (v) of subparagraph (A) shall be construed so as not to be in conflict, and no provision of this Act shall be construed to create a public or private cause of action or remedy.

(D) Minor child exception. Nothing in this Act shall be construed to limit the right of a person under 17 years of age to recover damages authorized under Federal or State law in a civil action that meets one of the requirements under clauses (i) through (v) of subparagraph (A).

. . . .

(9) Unlawful misuse.— The term "unlawful misuse" means conduct that violates a statute, ordinance, or regulation as it relates to the use of a qualified product.

CITY OF NEW YORK v. BERETTA U.S.A. CORP.
524 F.3d 384 (2d Cir. 2008), *cert. denied*, 556 U.S. 1104 (2009)

Miner, Circuit Judge:

Defendants-appellants-cross-appellees, manufacturers and wholesale sellers of firearms ("Firearms Suppliers"), appeal from so much of an order entered in the United States District Court for the Eastern District of New York as denies their motion, grounded on the claim restriction provisions of the Protection of Lawful Commerce in Arms Act, for dismissal of the complaint. In the complaint, plaintiff-appellee-cross-appellant, the City of New York, seeks injunctive relief to inhibit the diversion of firearms into illegal markets. The District Court determined that the Act did not violate the United States Constitution, and that the Act's statutory exception for claims based on the violation of a state statute applicable to the sale or marketing of firearms is met by New York's criminal nuisance statute. The City cross appeals from so much of the above-described order as rejects, in accordance with the position taken by intervenor United States of America, various constitutional challenges to the Act raised by the City. Because we conclude that the PLCAA (1) bars the instant action and (2) represents a permissible exercise of Congress's power under the Commerce Clause, we affirm the order of the District Court in part and reverse in part.

BACKGROUND

I. Introduction

The action giving rise to this appeal was commenced on June 20, 2000, when the City filed a complaint against the Firearms Suppliers seeking injunctive relief and abatement of the alleged public nuisance caused by the Firearms Suppliers' distribution practices. The City claimed that the Firearms Suppliers market guns to legitimate buyers with the knowledge that those guns will be diverted through various mechanisms into illegal markets. . . .

. . . .

On the day the PLCAA [Protection of Lawful Commerce in Arms Act, October 2005] was enacted, the Firearms Suppliers moved to dismiss the Amended Complaint pursuant to section 7902(b) [providing for dismissal of pending actions]. In its opposition to the Firearms Suppliers' motion to dismiss, the City argued that the Act did not bar its causes of action because this case fell within an exception to the forbidden qualified civil liability actions. [A] suit may proceed when a plaintiff adequately alleges that a "manufacturer or seller of [firearms transported in interstate or foreign commerce] knowingly violated a State or Federal statute applicable to the sale or marketing of [firearms], and the violation was the proximate cause of the harm for which relief is sought." This provision has been called the "predicate exception," which appellation we adopt. For purposes of this opinion, a statute upon which a case is brought under the predicate exception is referred to as a "predicate statute." The predicate statute at issue in this case is

New York Penal Law § 240.45, Criminal Nuisance in the Second Degree. The Firearms Suppliers claimed that New York Penal Law § 240.45 may not serve as a predicate statute because the predicate exception is meant to apply to statutes that are expressly and specifically applicable to the sale and marketing of firearms, and not to statutes of general applicability, such as § 240.45. The City also challenged the constitutionality of the Act on various grounds. The United States intervened to defend the constitutionality of the PLCAA, taking no position on the PLCAA's effect, if any, on the litigation.

. . . .

For the reasons that follow, we conclude that the City's claim . . . does not fall within an exception to the claim restricting provisions of the Act . . . We also hold that the PLCAA is a valid exercise of the powers granted to Congress pursuant to the Commerce Clause and that the PLCAA does not violate the doctrine of separation of powers or otherwise offend the Constitution in any manner alleged by the City.

II. The City's Allegations

. . . The City seeks "injunctive relief and abatement of the public nuisance that defendants cause, contribute to and maintain by their marketing and distribution practices." The City alleges that the Firearms Suppliers know that firearms distributed to legitimate retailers are diverted into illegal markets and that the Firearms Suppliers "could, but do not, monitor, supervise or regulate the sale and distribution of their guns by their downstream distributors or dealer-customers"; "could, but do not, monitor, supervise or train distributors or dealers to avoid sales that feed the illegal secondary market"; and "make no effort to determine those distributors and dealers whose sales disproportionately supply the illegal secondary market." In spite of New York City's strict controls on gun possession, "thousands of guns manufactured or distributed by defendants were used to commit crimes in the City of New York. This number includes only guns that were recovered in the course of a crime. The actual number of defendants' 'crime guns' used in New York City over the last five years is vastly higher." Amended Complaint P 62.

According to the City, among the mechanisms that serve to facilitate the movement of legally distributed handguns into illegal markets are: (i) gun shows, at which non-licensed persons can sell to other private citizens; (ii) private sales from "non-stocking" or "kitchen table" sellers, who are not required to conduct background checks or to maintain records that Federal Firearms Licensees ("FFL") are required to maintain; (iii) "straw purchases," in which persons qualified to purchase handguns make purchases on behalf of those who are not so qualified; (iv) "multiple sales," in which a purchaser buys more than one gun at the same time or during a limited period of time for the purpose of transferring the guns to unqualified purchasers; (v) intentional illegal trafficking by corrupt FFLs; (vi) thefts from FFLs with poor security, as well as false reports of theft by corrupt FFLs; and (v) oversupplying of markets where gun regulations are lax. The City seeks injunctive relief requiring the Firearms Suppliers to take assorted measures that would effectively inhibit the flow of firearms into illegal markets.

DISCUSSION

. . . .

III. Constitutionality of the PLCAA

The City advances four arguments on cross-appeal with respect to the constitutionality of the PLCAA: (i) the PLCAA is not a permissible exercise of Congress's power to regulate interstate commerce; (ii) the PLCAA violates basic principles of separation of powers by dictating the outcome of pending cases; (iii) the PLCAA, by recognizing predicate exceptions defined by statute, i.e. by a state's legislative branch, but not by common law as interpreted by state courts, violates the Tenth Amendment by dictating which branch of states' governments may authoritatively pronounce state law; and (iv) the PLCAA violates the First Amendment's guarantee of the right to petition the government to redress grievances through access to the courts. For the reasons that follow, we agree with the District Court that "[t]here is no violation of the United States Constitution".

A. Commerce Clause Regulatory Power

. . . .

The City claims that the activity that the PLCAA concerns itself with — civil litigation against members of the gun industry for unlawful acts committed by third parties — is not commercial in nature and therefore is outside of Congress's regulatory power. In support of its argument that Congress has exceeded its power by regulating litigation, the City relies on *Lopez* and *United States v. Morrison*, 529 U.S. 598 (2000) . . . .

. . . .

[W]e agree with the District Court that "the connection between the regulated activity and interstate commerce under the Act is far more direct than that in *Morrison* [and *Lopez*]." In enacting the PLCAA, Congress explicitly found that the third-party suits that the Act bars are a direct threat to the firearms industry, whose interstate character is not questioned. Furthermore, the PLCAA only reaches suits that "have an explicit connection with or effect on interstate commerce." The claim-preclusion provisions of § 7902 apply to actions "brought . . . against a manufacturer or seller of a qualified product" for relief from injuries "resulting from the criminal or unlawful misuse of a qualified product,"; where "qualified product means a firearm . . . or a component part of a firearm or ammunition, *that has been shipped or transported in interstate or foreign commerce*" (emphasis added). Accordingly, unlike the Gun-Free School Zones Act and Violence Against Women Act, the PLCAA raises no concerns about Congressional intrusion into "truly local" matters. The City itself, in the Amended Complaint, stressed the interstate character of the firearms industry. A foundation of the City's claim is that New York City's strict limitations on gun possession are undermined by the uncontrolled seepage into New York of guns sold in other states.

We agree that the firearms industry is interstate — indeed, international — in nature . . . . We find that Congress has not exceeded its authority in this case, where there can be no question of the interstate character of the industry in question and where Congress rationally perceived a substantial effect on the industry of the litigation that the Act seeks to curtail.

B. Principles of Separation of Powers

The doctrine of separation of powers is "one of the organizing principles of our system of government."

Here, the City claims that the Act's mandate of dismissal of pending actions against firearms manufacturers violates *United States v. Klein*, [80 U.S. 128, 146 (1871)] by legislatively directing the outcome of specific cases without changing the applicable law. The government, however, argues that *Klein* does not prohibit Congress from enacting statutes that set forth new rules of law applicable to pending cases, provided the new rule of law is also made applicable prospectively to cases commenced after enactment. We agree with the government that the Act permissibly sets forth a new rule of law that is applicable both to pending actions and to future actions.

. . . .

C. The Tenth Amendment and Fundamental Principles of Federalism

. . . The City claims that the PLCAA impermissibly dictates to the states which branch of their government may authoritatively articulate state law — to wit, that the Act prohibits courts from giving effect to the states' exercise of their lawmaking power through the judicial branch. According to the City, the Act recognizes the authority of states' legislatures to create a predicate exception to qualified civil liability actions by enacting a statute expressly applicable to the sale of firearms, whereas if a state court interprets a general statute as applicable to the sale of firearms, such an interpretation would not create a predicate exception under the Act.

According to the City, the Act "impermissibly oversteps [] fundamental limits when it determines which branch of state government will be recognized by the Federal Government as the authoritative expositor of any state's pertinent laws." . . .

In any event, the critical inquiry with respect to the Tenth Amendment is whether the PLCAA commandeers the states. As the City concedes, the PLCAA does not. We have explained that "[[f]ederal statutes validly enacted under one of Congress's enumerated powers . . . cannot violate the Tenth Amendment unless they commandeer the states' executive officials."] [citations omitted]. The PLCAA "does not commandeer any branch of state government because it imposes no affirmative duty of any kind on any of them." The PLCAA therefore does not violate the Tenth Amendment.

D. First Amendment Right of Access to the Courts

. . . .

By its terms, the Act bars plaintiffs from courts for the adjudication of qualified civil liability actions, allowing access for only those actions that fall within the Act's exceptions. We conclude that these restrictions do not violate plaintiffs' right of access to the courts. "The constitutional right of access [to the courts] is violated where government officials obstruct legitimate efforts to seek judicial redress." The right to petition exists in the presence of an underlying cause of action and is not violated by a statute that provides a complete defense to a cause of action or curtails a category of causes of action.

The PLCAA immunizes a specific type of defendant from a specific type of suit. It does not impede, let alone entirely foreclose, general use of the courts by would-be plaintiffs such as the City. For these reasons, the PLCAA cannot be said to deprive the City of its First Amendment right of access to the courts.

IV. Does the PLCAA Require Dismissal of the City's Action?

A. Predicate Exception to Qualified Civil Liability Actions

The Firearms Suppliers maintain that the PLCAA requires immediate dismissal of this suit, which is a qualified civil liability action under the statute. . . .

The Act also sets forth certain exceptions to the definition of qualified civil liability action, allowing suits to proceed that meet any of the following criteria [excerpted above in this Chapter].

The City has predicated its claims in this case on the Firearms Suppliers' alleged violation of New York Penal Law § 240.45 Criminal Nuisance in the Second Degree, which provides:

> A person is guilty of criminal nuisance in the second degree when:
>
> 1. By conduct either unlawful in itself or unreasonable under all the circumstances, he knowingly or recklessly creates or maintains a condition which endangers the safety or health of a considerable number of persons; or
>
> 2. He knowingly conducts or maintains any premises, place or resort where persons gather for purposes of engaging in unlawful conduct.

The City claims that its suit falls within the [third] exception set forth in § 7903(5)(A)(iii), because § 240.45 is a statute "applicable to the sale or marketing of [firearms]." The Firearms Suppliers disagree, arguing that the predicate exception was intended to include statutes that specifically and expressly regulate the firearms industry. The District Court agreed with the City, finding that, "[b]y its plain meaning, New York [Penal Law . . . satisfies the language of the predicate exception requiring a 'statute applicable to the sale or marketing of [a firearm].' " It is not disputed that New York Penal Law § 240.45 is a statute of general applicability that has never been applied to firearms suppliers for conduct like that complained of by the City.

B. Is New York Penal Law § 240.45 "Applicable" to the Sale of Firearms?

Central to the issue under examination is what Congress meant by the phrase "applicable to the sale or marketing [firearms]." . . .

We conclude, for the reasons set forth in subsection "1" below, that the meaning of the term "applicable" must be determined in the context of the statute. We find nothing in the statute that requires any express language regarding firearms to be included in a statute in order for that statute to fall within the predicate exception. We decline to foreclose the possibility that, under certain circumstances, state courts may apply a statute of general applicability to the type of conduct that the City complains of, in which case such a statute might qualify as a predicate statute. Accordingly, while the mere absence in § 240.45 of any express reference to firearms does not, in and of itself, preclude that statute's eligibility to serve as a predicate statute under the PLCAA, § 240.45 is a statute of general applicability that does not encompass the conduct of firearms manufacturers of which the City complains. It therefore does not fall within the predicate exception to the claim restricting provisions of the PLCAA.

1. "Applicable" In Context

The City relies on the dictionary definition of "applicable," which is, simply, "capable of being applied."

On the other hand, the Firearms Suppliers contend that the phrase "statute applicable to the sale or marketing of [a firearm]" in the context of the language in the entire statute limits the predicate exception to statutes specifically and expressly regulating the manner in which a firearm is sold or marketed — statutes specifying when, where, how, and to whom a firearm may be sold or marketed. We agree that the examples of state and federal statutory violations in the predicate exception itself refer to state and federal laws that specifically and expressly govern firearms. We also agree with the District Court's rejection of the Firearms Suppliers' argument that the predicate exception is necessarily limited to statutes that expressly regulate the firearms industry. However, for the reasons set forth below, we disagree with the District Court's adoption of the out-of-context "plain meaning" of the term "applicable" and its conclusion that the dictionary definition of the term "applicable" accurately reflects the intent of Congress.

The meaning of the term "applicable" must be determined here by reading that term in the context of the surrounding language and of the statute as a whole. . . .

. . . The PLCAA provides that predicate statutes are those that are "applicable to the sale or marketing of [firearms]." The universe of predicate statutes is further defined as "including" the examples set forth in subsections (I) and (II). . . .

2. Canons of Statutory Construction

. . . .

[The] meaning of doubtful terms or phrases may be determined by reference to their relationship with other associated words or phrases (*noscitur a sociis*). [In addition, "where general words" are accompanied by "a specific enumeration of persons or things, the general words should be limited to persons or things similar to those specifically enumerated (*ejusdem generis*)."]

. . . .

The general language contained in section 7903(5)(A)(iii) (providing that predicate statutes are those "applicable to" the sale or marketing of firearms) is followed by the more specific language referring to statutes imposing record-keeping requirements on the firearms industry, § 7903(5)(A)(iii)(I), and statutes prohibiting firearms suppliers from conspiring with or aiding and abetting others in selling firearms directly to prohibited purchasers, § 7903(5)(A)(iii)(II). Statutes applicable to the sale and marketing of firearms are said to include statutes regulating record-keeping and those prohibiting participation in direct illegal sales. Thus, the general term — "applicable to" — is to be "construed to embrace only objects similar to those enumerated by" sections 7903(5)(A)(iii)(I) and (II). We accordingly conclude that construing the term "applicable to" to mean statutes that clearly can be said to regulate the firearms industry more accurately reflects the intent of Congress.

. . . .

We think Congress clearly intended to protect from vicarious liability members of the firearms industry who engage in the "lawful design, manufacture, marketing, distribution, importation, or sale" of firearms. [In the PLCAA] Congress stated that it had found that "[t]he manufacture, importation, possession, sale, and use of firearms and ammunition in the United States are heavily regulated by Federal, State, and local laws. Such Federal laws include the Gun Control Act of 1968, the National Firearms Act, and the Arms Export Control Act." We think the juxtaposition of these two subsections demonstrates that Congress meant that "lawful design, manufacture, marketing, distribution, importation, or sale" of firearms means such activities having been done in compliance with statutes like those. . . .

This conclusion is supported by the "interpretive principle that statutory exceptions are to be construed 'narrowly in order to preserve the primary operation of the [general rule].' " [R]esort to the dictionary definition of "applicable" — i.e. capable of being applied — leads to a far too-broad reading of the predicate exception. Such a result would allow the predicate exception to swallow the statute, which was intended to shield the firearms industry from vicarious liability for harm caused by firearms that were lawfully distributed into primary markets.

3. Legislative History

. . . .

. . . [W]e think that the [statements made by the legislators] support the view that the predicate exception was meant to apply only to statutes that actually regulate the firearms industry . . . . In sum, we hold that the exception created by 15 U.S.C. § 7903(5)(A)(iii): (1) does not encompass New York Penal Law § 240.45; (2) does encompass statutes (a) that expressly regulate firearms, or (b) that courts have applied to the sale and marketing of firearms; and (3) does encompass statutes that do not expressly regulate firearms but that clearly can be said to implicate the purchase and sale of firearms.

CONCLUSION

For the foregoing reasons, the judgment of the District Court denying the Firearms Suppliers' motion to dismiss based on the claim restricting provisions of the PLCAA is REVERSED. The judgment of the District Court with respect to the constitutionality of the PLCAA is AFFIRMED. The case is remanded to the District Court with instructions to enter judgment dismissing the case as barred by the PLCAA.

ADAMES v. SHEAHAN

909 N.E.2d 742 (Ill. 2009), *cert. denied*, 558 U.S. 1100 (2009)

Opinion by THOMAS:

On May 5, 2001, William (Billy) Swan accidentally shot and killed his friend Joshua (Josh) Adames while playing with his father's service weapon. At the time, Billy's father, David Swan, was employed by the Cook County sheriff's department as a correctional officer. Plaintiffs, Hector Adames, Jr., and Rosalia Diaz, as co-special administrators of the estate of Josh Adames, filed suit against numerous defendants. At issue in this case are plaintiffs' claims against defendant Michael F. Sheahan (Sheahan), in his official capacity as Cook County sheriff, and defendant Beretta U.S.A. Corporation (Beretta).

. . . .

BACKGROUND

. . . .

Billy Swan's Testimony

On the morning of May 5, 2001, Billy Swan, who then was 13 years old, was home alone. Billy's mother was at work and his father, David, had taken Billy's brother to a movie. Billy called his friend Josh Adames and invited him over to play. Billy then went to his parents' bedroom to watch for Josh through the bedroom window. Billy knew that both going into his parents' bedroom and inviting friends over when no one else was home were against house rules.

While in his parents' bedroom, Billy . . . saw a box on the top shelf of the closet, so he took the box down to see what was inside. Billy opened the box, which he said was unlocked, and saw three guns. One of the guns was a Beretta 92FS handgun, the gun at issue in this case. Billy had never seen his father carry a gun or clean a gun in the house, although he thought that his father might have a gun. Billy had never handled a gun before.

Billy picked up each gun and examined it. Billy said that the magazine or clip was in the Beretta. When Billy picked up the Beretta, he pushed a button that released the magazine. Billy could see the bullets in the magazine. Billy then put the magazine back in the Beretta. Billy moved the slide at the top of the gun and a bullet popped out. Billy again removed the magazine and put the bullet back in the magazine. Billy repeatedly removed and replaced the bullets and magazine from the gun. Billy knew that the Beretta was loaded when the magazine was in the gun, but thought it was unloaded when the magazine was taken out. He thought that the bullet came out of the top of the magazine when the handgun was fired, and did not know that a bullet remained in the chamber. Billy did not read the instruction manual for the Beretta.

After playing with the guns for several minutes, Billy saw his friend Michael riding his bike outside. Billy put the three guns in his pockets and went downstairs and opened the front door. Billy invited Michael in and showed him the guns. Billy jokingly told Michael that he was feeling "trigger happy" and that he was going to shoot Josh. Billy left the guns on the couch while he and Michael went in another room to play on the computer. Approximately 10 minutes later, Josh came over. Billy showed Josh the guns and the boys began playing around. While Billy was holding the Beretta, Josh tried to reach for it to take it out of Billy's hand. Billy pushed the button on the Beretta, took the magazine out and put it in his pocket. At this point, Josh was by the front door. Billy pretended that he was firing the gun, then pulled the trigger, discharging the gun. The gunshot was loud, causing Billy's ears to ring. Billy was afraid he would be in trouble if the neighbors heard the noise, so he ran upstairs and put the guns away.

When Billy came back downstairs, he saw Josh sitting against the door holding his stomach. Josh told Billy that he had been shot. Billy first thought that Josh was kidding, but when he moved Josh's hand, he saw a hole. Billy called 911 and told the dispatcher that he had found a gun and accidentally shot his friend while playing. Billy testified that he knew he was handling a real firearm and real ammunition when he shot Josh. Michael left as soon as the shooting happened.

Billy was found delinquent in juvenile court proceedings for the shooting and was placed on probation. The delinquency determination was based on a finding that Billy committed involuntary manslaughter, and reckless discharge of a firearm . . . .

David Swan's Testimony

. . . .

At the time of the shooting, David owned three firearms, the .38 Special, a .25 semiautomatic and the Beretta 92FS. The .25 semiautomatic was David's personal weapon and was never carried on the job. Although David no longer carried a gun once he was promoted to lieutenant, David kept his guns for his own protection and in case he was transferred to a different unit of the Cook County sheriff's office where he would again need a firearm. . . .

On May 5, 2001, David took his younger son to the movies while his wife was at work. Billy did not want to go to the movie. David told Billy that no one was allowed in the house. Billy said that he was going to the park to play. David testified that prior to May 5, 2001, the last time he had seen his guns was in the summer of 2000, when he completed his annual certification at the Cook County sheriff's gun range. After qualifying with the weapons, David cleaned them and locked them in his lock box. David placed the lockbox with the guns in it on the top shelf of his bedroom closet. There were two keys to the lockbox. David kept one key on his key ring and one key in his top dresser drawer. David disagreed with Billy's testimony that the lockbox was not locked; however, for purposes of summary judgment, it was presumed that the lockbox was unlocked.

David understood that the sheriff's department required deputies to secure and store their weapons in either a locking box, like the one David used, or with a trigger lock. David testified that he stored the ammunition separately from the handgun, and stored the handgun without a bullet in its chamber, in accordance with department requirements. David was not aware that the Beretta would fire a bullet if the magazine was removed.

Following the shooting, Sheahan filed a complaint against David before the Cook County sheriff's merit board. The complaint alleged that each officer has a duty to safely store his weapon, that David did not do that, and that this failure allowed David's son to gain access to the weapon, which in turn resulted in Josh's death. The complaint noted that Sheahan's general order required the safe storage of weapons to avoid accidents. David's guns were taken from him by the police in the investigation and were never returned to him, although David was able to continue to work for the Cook County sheriff's office as a correctional officer after serving a suspension.

David also was charged pursuant to the [Illinois] Criminal Code of 1961, which prohibits improper storage of a firearm in a premise in which a minor under the age of 14 is likely to gain access to the firearm. David was found not guilty of the criminal charges.

. . . .

The Beretta 92FS

The Beretta 92FS is a semiautomatic nine-millimeter pistol. The instruction manual for the Beretta states that "[t]he Beretta 92FS semiautomatic pistol is primarily designed as a personal defense firearm for military and police use," and that "[i] has become the choice of military and police forces throughout the world." The manual lists the Beretta's safety features, including: an ambidextrous safety-decocking lever; a firing pin unit; a hammer drop catch; an automatic firing pin catch; a chamber-loaded indicator, and a slide overtravel stop. The manual repeatedly cautions users to keep fingers off the trigger until ready to fire and to make sure the muzzle is pointing in a safe direction. The manual also warns that to prevent accidents due to wrongful unloading practice, the user should remember to remove the magazine and clear the chamber.

Expert Testimony

Plaintiffs presented experts in their case against Beretta to testify that the Beretta 92FS was unreasonably dangerous. Stanton Berg, a firearms consultant, testified that a magazine disconnect device would have prevented the shooting in this case. The magazine disconnect was invented in 1910 and disables a semiautomatic pistol from firing when the magazine is removed. Berg testified that Beretta produced and sold Beretta 92 Series handguns with a magazine disconnect for use by police departments such as the Royal Canadian Mounted Police, the United States Veterans Administration and the correctional department of New York City. Berg noted more than 300 other models of handguns that incorporate a magazine disconnect safety, and testified that, in his opinion, any handgun without a magazine disconnect is defective. In addition, Berg testified that, in the absence of a magazine disconnect, the Beretta required a good chamber-loaded indicator. Berg said that the chamber-loaded indicator on the Beretta 92FS was not sufficient to warn a user that the chamber had a bullet in it because the user could hardly see the indicator. Berg also believed that the Beretta required a warning on the weapon stating that it was capable of being fired with the magazine removed.

Wallace Collins, a firearms and ammunition design and safety expert, also testified on behalf of plaintiffs that the Beretta was unnecessarily dangerous. Collins stated that the Beretta required a magazine disconnect safety; a warning that the gun would fire when the magazine was removed; a marking to make plain what the chamber-loaded indicator means; a chamber-loaded indicator in an optimum position; and a key lock. Collins testified that the chamber-loaded indicator on the Beretta was not well designed. Collins said that the safety features required were readily available, inexpensive, and commercially feasible.

Professor Stephen Teret testified on behalf of plaintiffs as an expert in injury epidemiology. Teret was a professor of epidemiology for the School of Public Health at Johns Hopkins University. Teret testified concerning a survey designed by the Johns Hopkins Center for Gun Policy and Research, reported in the Journal of Public Health Policy. The survey asked respondents whether they thought that a pistol can be shot when the magazine is removed. Out of 1,200 respondents, 65% said that the pistol could be fired if the magazine was removed, 20.3% thought that a pistol could not be discharged after the magazine was removed, 14.5% did not know, and 0.2% refused to answer. Of those that answered either that the pistol could not be discharged after the magazine was removed or that they did not know, 28% lived in a gun-owning household. Teret testified that the absence of a magazine disconnect caused Josh's shooting. Teret further testified that the chamber-loaded warning on the Beretta was not effective. Teret's opinion was that the chamber-loaded warning did not convey that the handgun was loaded.

Beretta's witnesses testified that Beretta has manufactured handguns with magazine disconnects, which adds at most $10 to the $500 price of the gun. Beretta's witnesses agreed that the shooting in this case would not have happened if a magazine disconnect safety had been installed on the gun. Beretta did not include a magazine disconnect safety feature on the Beretta 92FS because there was no market demand for that feature. Beretta's witnesses also testified that for the past 20 years, the vast majority of law enforcement agencies have consistently expressed a preference for no magazine disconnect safety or internal locking device. Law enforcement officers and agencies do not want weapons that may become inoperable by an inadvertent release of the magazine, which could possibly jeopardize the safety of officers and the public.

The Complaint and Summary Judgment

With regard to Sheahan, plaintiffs' third amended complaint contained a wrongful-death claim and a survival claim. Plaintiffs alleged that Sheahan assumed and exercised control over David Swan as Sheehan's employee and servant with regard to the safe and secure handling and storage of David's duty firearm and ammunition. . . .

. . . Plaintiffs asserted that Sheahan was vicariously liable for David's negligent acts and/or omissions in the scope of his employment as an officer of the Cook County sheriff's office, both at common law and pursuant to statute.

. . . .

With regard to Beretta, plaintiffs' third amended complaint contained claims for product liability design defect, negligent design, failure to warn, and breach of the implied warranty of merchantability. Specifically, plaintiffs alleged that the Beretta was inherently dangerous and defective because it did not incorporate safety features, including: a magazine disconnect safety that would prevent the gun from being fired if the magazine is removed; an effective chamber-loaded indicator to make users aware of when a bullet is loaded into the gun's chamber; and other safety devices such as a built-in lock, a child-resistant manual safety, a grip safety, and personalized gun technology that would have prevented unauthorized users, such as children, from firing the gun.

Plaintiffs also alleged that the gun was defective because it did not include adequate warnings concerning the foreseeable use of the gun by unauthorized persons, including children. Plaintiffs asserted that the defects included a failure to warn that: the gun may be loaded and can be fired even if the magazine is empty or disconnected from the gun; that the gun is loaded when there is red showing on the extractor; that the gun is loaded when the extractor is protruding; that the gun can be fired by children and other unauthorized users; that the gun automatically loads bullet cartridges into the gun's chamber after being fired or after the gun is released from a lockback position; and that the gun should not be used or stored without additional safety devices.

In its summary judgment motion, Beretta argued that its product was not unreasonably dangerous, and that the Beretta 92F S performed as safely as ordinary consumers of firearms would expect. Beretta also argued that it had no duty to warn because the dangers of pointing a firearm at another human being and pulling the trigger are open and obvious. Finally, Beretta contended that Billy's actions were an intervening and superseding cause.

The trial court granted Beretta's motion in its entirety . . . .

. . . .

ANALYSIS

This case comes before us on the grant of summary judgment in favor of defendants. . . .

Sheahan's Appeal

. . . .

. . . Pursuant to the theory of *respondeat superior*, an employer can be liable for the torts of his employee when those torts are committed within the scope of the employment. Under *respondeat superior*, an employer's vicarious liability extends to the negligent, willful, malicious or even criminal acts of its employees, when those acts are committed within the scope of employment.

. . . .

. . . David's negligent storage of his guns was not the kind of conduct David was employed to perform, nor was it incidental to his employment . . . .

. . . .

For the same reasons, David's negligent storage of the gun was not within the authorized time and space limits of his employment. . . .

Similarly, there is no evidence that David was motivated, at least in part, by a desire to serve his employer when he negligently stored his gun. . . .

. . . Here, no reasonable person could conclude from the evidence that David was acting within the scope of his employment when he negligently stored his weapon. Consequently, Sheahan was entitled to summary judgment in his favor on the issue of *respondeat superior*. The appellate court erred in finding that David was acting within the scope of employment and that Sheahan was thereby liable for David's allegedly tortious acts.

. . . .

Beretta's Appeal

Plaintiffs' claim against Beretta contained counts alleging design defect, failure to warn, and breach of the implied warranty of merchantability. As noted, the trial court granted summary judgment in favor of Beretta on all of plaintiffs' claims. Plaintiffs appealed the dismissal of their design defect and failure to warn claims, arguing that the trial court erred in holding that the handgun was not unreasonably dangerous for failing to include a magazine disconnect, or a sufficient chamber-loaded indicator, and in finding that Beretta had no duty to warn. Plaintiffs also asserted that the trial court erred in finding that Billy's conduct was an independent intervening cause superseding Beretta's legal responsibility.

. . . .

The appellate court affirmed the trial court's finding that the Beretta was not unreasonably dangerous or defectively designed. However, the appellate court did find that plaintiffs' failure to warn claim presented a question of fact, so that summary judgment was improperly entered in favor of Beretta on that claim.

. . . .

The appellate court found that there was a question of fact concerning whether plaintiffs' failure to warn claim fit within the section 7903(5)(A)(v) exception [of the PLCAA]. That exception allows for claims alleging a defect in design or manufacturing absent a volitional criminal act. . . .

In this court, Beretta argues that the appellate court erred in finding that Beretta had a duty to warn. Beretta contends that the danger of pointing a gun at another person and pulling the trigger is open and obvious, even if the person pointing the gun mistakenly believes that the gun is not loaded. In addition, the appellate court ignored the fact that Beretta did provide numerous warnings, any one of which would have prevented Josh's shooting if read and heeded. Beretta also argues that the appellate court erred in holding that plaintiffs' failure to warn claim fit within the exception for manufacturing and design defect claims set forth in the PLCAA.

We first address Beretta's claim that the PLCAA bars plaintiffs' sole remaining claim against Beretta. Whether plaintiffs' failure to warn claim is barred by the PLCAA presents a question of statutory interpretation, which is a question of law. Accordingly, our review is *de novo*.

. . . .

In this court, plaintiffs deny that their lawsuit is a qualified civil liability action [which is barred by the PLCAA]. Plaintiffs do not dispute that their lawsuit is a civil action or proceeding against a manufacturer of a qualified product and that the Beretta is a qualified product. However, plaintiffs deny that their civil action results from the criminal or unlawful misuse of a qualified product.

The PLCAA defines unlawful misuse as "conduct that violates a statute, ordinance, or regulation as it relates to the use of a qualified product." The PLCAA does not define "criminal" misuse. As Beretta notes, however, the word "criminal" in this portion of the statute is used as an adjective to modify the term "misuse." Black's Law Dictionary defines "criminal" in its adjective form as, "1. Having the character of a crime; in the nature of a crime (criminal mischief). 2. Connected with the administration of penal justice (the criminal courts)."

In this case, Billy was adjudicated delinquent based upon the finding of the court in the juvenile proceeding that Billy committed involuntary manslaughter and reckless discharge of a firearm when he shot Josh with his father's Beretta. This finding was affirmed on appeal. Billy's use of the Beretta, therefore, certainly violated the Criminal Code, a statute, when he was adjudicated delinquent for involuntary manslaughter and reckless discharge of a firearm, satisfying the definition of "unlawful misuse."

In addition, involuntary manslaughter and reckless discharge of a firearm are criminal offenses [in Illinois]. It follows, then, that Billy's misuse of the Beretta in this case also had the character of a crime and was in the nature of a crime" and, therefore, was a criminal misuse.

Plaintiffs, however, argue that this court may not look to Billy's juvenile adjudication in determining whether there was a criminal or unlawful misuse because that adjudication was described in an unpublished order pursuant to Illinois Supreme Court Rule 23. Plaintiffs also argue that Billy's conduct could not be criminal or unlawful because Billy was adjudicated delinquent, and thus was not "convicted" of anything. Moreover, Billy had no criminal intent, so that his conduct could not be criminal. Finally, plaintiffs contend that Billy was not "using" the handgun, so there could be no unlawful "misuse" of the handgun, as required under the statute.

. . . .

[T]he definition of qualified civil liability action . . . does not contain a requirement that there be criminal intent or a criminal conviction. The statute only requires "the criminal or unlawful misuse of a qualified product by the person or a third party." With regard to intent, the PLCAA does not limit criminal misuse to specific intent crimes.

Likewise, the PLCAA does not require a criminal conviction. As Beretta observes, Congress did require a conviction in order for another exception to the PLCAA to apply. See 15 U.S.C. § 7903(5)(A)(i) (2006) ("an action brought against a transferor *convicted* under section 924(h) of Title 18, or a comparable or identical State felony law, by a party directly harmed by the conduct of which the transferee is so *convicted*" (emphases added)). When Congress includes particular language in one section of a statute but omits it in another section of the same act, courts presume that Congress has acted intentionally and purposely in the inclusion or exclusion. Therefore, because Congress specifically included language requiring a conviction in § 7903(5)(A)(i), but did not include such language in § 7903(5)(A), we presume that Congress did not intend criminal misuse to require proof of a criminal conviction.

Finally, there is no merit to plaintiffs' claim that Billy was not "using" the Beretta, so he could not have "misused" the weapon as set forth in the definition of a qualified civil liability action. Plaintiffs assert that the PLCAA implies the weapon is being used proactively for the purpose of firing or threatening to fire a projectile, and was not designed to apply, for example, where someone "using" a weapon by holding it drops the weapon, causing it to discharge. Plaintiffs claim that Billy was not using the Beretta as a weapon because he did not intend to fire it, so that Billy was not using the firearm as that word is used in the PLCAA.

We again note that the definition of a qualified civil liability action contains no intent requirement, so it does not matter whether Billy intended to fire the Beretta. The relevant inquiry is whether the misuse of the Beretta was criminal or unlawful. Moreover, this is not a case where Billy dropped the Beretta, causing it to accidentally discharge. Rather, Billy took his father's Beretta from his parents' bedroom closet, pointed the Beretta at Josh, and pulled the trigger. Billy therefore "used" the Beretta, and that "use" constituted a criminal or unlawful misuse of the Beretta for purposes of the PLCAA. Accordingly, we find that plaintiffs' lawsuit is a qualified civil liability action as defined in the PLCAA.

Because we find that plaintiffs' lawsuit was a qualified civil liability action, we next address whether the exceptions to the PLCAA apply in this case. The appellate court held that the only exception that applied in this case was the exception set forth in § 7903(5)(A)(v) . . . . Section 7903(5)(A)(v) provides that a qualified civil liability action shall not include:

> "an action for death, physical injuries or property damage resulting directly from a defect in design or manufacture of the product, when used as intended or in a reasonably foreseeable manner, except that where the discharge of the product was caused by a volitional act that constituted a criminal offense, then such act shall be considered the sole proximate cause of any resulting death, personal injuries or property damage."

. . . .

We initially note that, like the definition of qualified civil liability action in § 7903(5)(A), the exception in § 7903(5)(A)(v) does not require a criminal conviction. The statute requires only that the volitional act constitute a criminal offense. As discussed, *supra*, Billy's act of shooting Josh constituted a criminal offense.

. . . Although this court in *Taylor* held that a juvenile adjudication was not tantamount to a criminal conviction, we also noted that the Juvenile Court Act was radically altered in 1999 "to provide more accountability for the *criminal acts* of juveniles." (Emphasis added.) Moreover, the purpose and policy section of article V of the Juvenile Court Act declares that it is the intent of the General Assembly "to promote a juvenile justice system capable of dealing with the problem of juvenile delinquency" and, to effectuate that intent, declares among the important purposes of the Act "[t]o protect citizens from *juvenile crime*." (Emphasis added.) Consequently, the fact that Billy was adjudicated delinquent does not mean that his actions were not criminal for purposes of § 7903(5)(A)(v).

We also find that Billy's act was a volitional act. Black's Law Dictionary defines volition as: " "1. The ability to make a choice or determine something. 2. The act of making a choice or determining something. 3. The choice or determination that someone makes." "

. . . .

Plaintiffs and the appellate court read volitional to require a finding that Billy intended to shoot Josh or understood the ramifications of his conduct. We disagree. As Beretta argues, even if Billy did not intend to shoot Josh, Billy did choose and determine to point the Beretta at Josh and did choose and determine to pull the trigger. Although Billy did not intend the consequences of his act, his act nonetheless was a volitional act. Accordingly, pursuant to the PLCAA, the discharge of the Beretta in this case was caused by a volitional act that constituted a criminal offense, which the PLCAA provides "shall be considered the sole proximate cause of any resulting death, personal injuries or property damage." The exception for qualified civil liability actions, therefore, does not apply, and plaintiffs' failure to warn claims are barred by the PLCAA.

Plaintiffs also argue that section 7903(5)(A)(v) does not apply because Billy's act was not the sole cause of Josh's injury. Plaintiffs, however, have misread the PLCAA. The PLCAA does not require a finding that the volitional act that constituted a criminal offense be the sole proximate cause of any resulting death. Rather, the PLCAA provides that "where the discharge of the product was caused by a volitional act that constituted a criminal offense, *then such act shall be considered the sole proximate cause of any resulting death* ***." (Emphasis added.)

. . . .

As stated, we find that the PLCAA requires dismissal of plaintiffs' failure to warn claim against Beretta. We therefore reverse the appellate court's finding that there was an issue of fact concerning whether the PLCAA barred plaintiffs' failure to warn claim.

Plaintiffs' Cross-Appeal

Finally, we note that plaintiffs have filed a cross-appeal challenging the appellate court's finding that the trial court properly dismissed plaintiffs' design defect claims because the Beretta was not unreasonably dangerous as a matter of law. Plaintiffs claim that the Beretta is unreasonably dangerous under both the consumer expectation test and the risk-utility test.

Upon review, we find that we need not consider whether the appellate court erred in finding that the Beretta was not unreasonably dangerous under the consumer expectation test and the risk-utility test . . . . As noted, the exception to the PLCAA set forth in section 7903(5)(A)(v) applies to "an action for death, physical injuries or property damage resulting directly from *a defect in design or manufacture of the product*, when used as intended or in a reasonably foreseeable manner." (Emphasis added.) We have held that the exception set forth in section 7903(5)(A)(v) does not apply in this case because the discharge of the Beretta was caused by a volitional act that constituted a criminal offense, which act shall be considered the sole proximate cause of any resulting death. Accordingly, plaintiffs' design defect claims, as well as their failure to warn claims, are barred by the PLCAA. For that reason, we affirm the dismissal of those claims.

CONCLUSION

For all the foregoing reasons, the judgment of the appellate court is affirmed in part and reversed in part and the judgment of the circuit court is affirmed.

NOTES AND QUESTIONS

1. Litigation by state and local governments. By 2005, cities facing high crime rates increasingly sought to achieve some of the same objectives of gun control legislation through litigation claiming, among other things, that gun manufacturers and distributors were negligent in allowing the distribution of potentially dangerous products or liable for the inherent dangers of their products, or that gun manufacturers and distributors were creating a public nuisance. None of these government-sponsored lawsuits were fully successful and most were rejected or withdrawn. *See, e.g., In Re Firearms*, 126 Cal. App. 4th 959 (2005); *City of Chicago v. Beretta U.S.A. Corp.*, 821 N.E.2d 1099 (Ill. 2004); *City of Gary v. Smith & Wesson Corp.*, 801 N.E.2d 1222 (Ind. 2003); *City of Philadelphia v. Beretta U.S.A. Corp.*, 277 F.3d 415 (3d Cir. 2002). *City of Cincinnati v. Beretta U.S.A. Corp.*, 768 N.E.2d 1136 (Ohio 2002) is atypical, because the Ohio Supreme Court allowed the city to proceed to trial. During the discovery process, however, political support for the lawsuit waned and the Cincinnati city council voted to drop the lawsuit. The decision is of historical interest, because it describes most of the claims and arguments that were typical of these cases. The city argued that this particular gun manufacturer had declined to incorporate safety devices into its guns, misled the public about the advantages of having a gun in the home, and engaged in distributional practices that fostered a large, illegitimate "secondary" market for guns.

From a public health policy point of view, does it make sense for cities and other local governments to pursue gun control through this type of litigation? Are these efforts to sidestep the political process? Would it make a difference if the plaintiff-governmental body were precluded from seeking regulatory gun control legislation by state preemption legislation? For that matter, what do you think the plaintiffs are trying to achieve: recovery of actual damages? limits on the distribution of guns? Would you feel differently if, in fact, these lawsuits were being orchestrated by a larger, nationwide "antigun conspiracy" and intended to force gun manufacturers or distributors out of business or into bankruptcy?

2. The Protection of Lawful Commerce in Arms Act (PCLAA). Congress's response to the increasing number of lawsuits by cities was the Protection of Lawful Commerce in Arms Act (PCLAA) — to protect manufacturers and dealers in firearms from liability for death and injury resulting from the "criminal or unlawful misuse" of guns (the "qualified civil liability actions"). It begins with a section of Congressional findings, which include a statement that litigation against a lawful industry constitutes "an abuse of the legal system." § 7901(a)(6).

Several cities challenged the constitutionality of the PCLAA, but the courts have rejected such challenges, largely for the reasons expressed in *City of New York v. Beretta*, above. When Congress precludes civil liability claims, it often creates an alternative compensation system, such as workers' compensation. Is that constitutionally required? How might such a (hypothetical) system operate to replace the liability claims precluded by the PCLAA?

The PCLAA includes 6 exceptions to immunity from civil suit, although the few cases that have interpreted them so far have found them to be somewhat circumscribed in their application. *City of New York v. Beretta* focuses on the third exception, known as the "predicate exception," because the plaintiff must prove that a manufacturer or seller knowingly violated a state or federal law (the "predicate statute"). The Second Circuit rejected the City's argument that New

York's criminal nuisance law could be considered a predicate statute, because it was not "applicable to the sale or marketing of [firearms]. Do you agree with the Second Circuit's interpretation? In *Beretta*, the Second Circuit suggested that other statutes might be deemed "applicable" under other circumstances. Can you identify those circumstances? What kind of laws might qualify?

The Ninth Circuit also found that state negligence and nuisance laws could not be predicate statutes for claims for saturating the market and creating an illegal secondary market for guns. *Ileto v. Glock, Inc.*, 565 F.3d 1126 (9th Cir. 2009). Like *Beretta*, the Ninth Circuit concluded that the predicate statute exception to preemption must be a statute that regulates firearms, not a generally applicable statute. However, it allowed a cause of action against defendant China North, because it was not a federally licensed entity — the PLCAA does not protect non-licensed entities. (China North has been banned from importing into the U.S. because of its earlier arms deals with Iran and could not get a federal license.) *See also, Dist. of Columbia v. Beretta U.S.A. Corp.*, 940 A.2d 163 (D.C. 2008) (rejecting District of Columbia's law imposing strict liability on assault weapons manufacturers as a predicate statute).

There are a few examples of the successful use of the exception permitting civil actions against dealer practices that violate the Gun Control Act. *See City of New York v. Bob Moates' Sport Shop, Inc.*, 253 F.R.D. 237 (E.D.N.Y. 2008); *Smith & Wesson Corp. v. City of Cary, Indiana*, 875 N.E.2d 422 (Ind. Ct. App. 2007). In both cases, the cities claimed that licensed retailers created a public nuisance by allowing straw purchases in violation of the Gun Control Act — clearly a predicate statute. However, in contrast to the Second Circuit in *Beretta*, the Indiana court also interpreted "applicable" as meaning "capable of being applied," which could include nuisance laws and other statutes that do not directly target gun manufacturers or dealers. That interpretation may not have affected the case, and remains of limited precedential value.

3. Private claims of products liability and negligence. Individuals also sought to hold the gun industry responsible for failing to produce safety mechanisms to prevent accidental shootings or at least for failing to provide warnings that unseen ammunition could be fired. The *Adames* case suggests that the PLCAA makes it almost impossible for plaintiffs to pursue a negligence or products liability claim against a gun manufacturer when a child (or anyone, for that matter) pulls the trigger on a gun, even without realizing that the gun was loaded and without any intent to actually shoot or hurt anyone else. The PLCAA foreclosed most avenues for imposing liability on a gun manufacturer, including some that had begun to achieve success.

For example, *Smith v. Bryco Arms*, 33 P.3d 638 (N.M. 2001), a case with similar facts to those in *Adames*, found that New Mexico would permit a claim in products liability for design defect against the manufacturer of a .22 caliber handgun, referred to as the J22, for failing to have a safety mechanism preventing the gun from firing a bullet when the ammunition magazine was removed or a chamber indicator showing that the weapon was loaded with a bullet even when the magazine was removed. The *Smith* court noted that "In response to Defendants' contentions that the J-22 had sufficient safety devices and warnings as designed,

Plaintiffs provided evidence that patents for magazine-out safeties have been filed in 1912, 1914, 1916, 1921, 1922, 1927, 1945, 1949, 1951, 1977, 1980, 1981, 1984, and 1986. These patent applications specifically articulate the known danger that people will remove the gun magazine and think they have unloaded the gun and then fire it, unintentionally injuring someone. The United States Patent Office granted the first patent for a magazine-out safety device on April 30, 1912." The court found that plaintiffs' claims fit within New Mexico's products liability law and that there were sufficient material issues of fact to allow those claims to proceed to trial.

For a description of poor handgun manufacturer practices in the 1990's, *see* VIOLENCE PREVENTION RESEARCH PROGRAM, UNIV. OF CALIFORNIA, DAVIS, RING OF FIRE: THE HANDGUN MAKERS OF SOUTHERN CALIFORNIA (1994), www.ucdmc.ucdavis.edu/ vprp/pdf/RingofFire1994.pdf (visited Apr. 2014).

4. What causes of action are left? What types of lawsuits against which defendants are still viable? The PCLAA does not preempt lawsuits against entities that are not federally licensed. Nevertheless, it limits many "upstream" lawsuits — *i.e.*, licensed importers, manufacturers, dealers, and even sellers have been immunized from most lawsuits resulting from harm caused by gun owners or possessors long after they have passed through the stream of commerce, with rather limited and rather specific exceptions. Does this make sense (a) as a matter of law or (b) as a matter of public policy? Are lawsuits attempting to impose a liability limitation on commerce in guns? Or are they attempts to insure that guns only fall into the hands of lawful consumers? Are we concerned that guns will be used, either illegally or accidentally, in a way that we want to avoid, or that guns are inherently dangerous even in the hands of lawful purchasers? Importers, manufacturers, dealers, and sellers are clearly links in the chain of events that lead to various bad outcomes, ranging from homicides to accidental injuries. Are they in the best position to break that chain of causation? Or are they being blamed for something that is really caused — in the legal sense of the term — by other actors?

Viewing the federal law somewhat more broadly, does the extension of immunity incorporated into this law reflect policy judgments about the appropriate locus for liability, or was it a more crassly political decision? In this regard, the extensive statements of purposes and findings at the beginning of the statute are instructive. Congress has made some clear policy judgments about the importance of commerce in guns, the legitimacy of judicial determinations of liability, and even the proper interpretation of the Second Amendment.

Chapter 13

GLOBAL HEALTH

A. INTRODUCTION

The final chapter of this textbook is devoted to "global health." In legal and human rights terms the chapter could also be entitled "Health and Human Rights," with the emphasis on public health, as in public health and human rights. The core of the health and human rights movement is to encourage relevant national and international actors to live up to the World Health Organization's founding principle to maximize the health of the world's population, the right to the "highest attainable standard of health." Although we cover this subject in a legal textbook, it is worth underlining at the beginning that most of the relevant legal instruments do not bind countries to act in specific ways, and when they do, enforcement is not readily available. We are mostly talking about "soft law," including the formation of international norms for behavior on the part of governments, especially those related to social justice and health equity. The field, however, also contains many private entities, including private foundations and nongovernmental organizations (NGOs), and multinational corporations. The professions of law and medicine, both transnational in their own norms, are also becoming increasingly important.

We begin with an overview of "Global Governance and Public Health", including the global state of public health and the use of human rights instruments (including the Universal Declaration of Human Rights) to attempt to improve it and to promote the right to health. Part C then addresses the use of litigation to promote the right to health. Part D concludes the chapter with the most developed area of global health rights, rules governing research on human beings.

B. GLOBAL GOVERNANCE AND PUBLIC HEALTH

Richard Horton, Robert Beaglehole, Ruth Bonita et al., *From Public to Planetary Health: A Manifesto*
383 THE LANCET 847 (2014)

This manifesto for transforming public health calls for a social movement to support collective public health action at all levels of society — personal, community, national, regional, global, and planetary. Our aim is to respond to the threats we face: threats to human health and wellbeing, threats to the sustainability of our civilisation, and threats to the natural and human-made systems that support us. Our vision is for a planet that nourishes and sustains the diversity of life with which we coexist and on which we depend. Our goal is to create a movement for planetary health.

Our audience includes health professionals and public health practitioners, politicians and policy makers, international civil servants working across the UN and in development agencies, and academics working on behalf of communities. Above all, our audience includes every person who has an interest in their own health, in the health of their fellow human beings, and in the health of future generations.

The discipline of public health is critical to this vision because of its values of social justice and fairness for all, and its focus on the collective actions of interdependent and empowered peoples and their communities. Our objectives are to protect and promote health and wellbeing, to prevent disease and disability, to eliminate conditions that harm health and wellbeing, and to foster resilience and adaptation. In achieving these objectives, our actions must respond to the fragility of our planet and our obligation to safeguard the physical and human environments within which we exist.

Planetary health is an attitude towards life and a philosophy for living. It emphasises people, not diseases, and equity, not the creation of unjust societies. We seek to minimise differences in health according to wealth, education, gender, and place. We support knowledge as one source of social transformation, and the right to realise, progressively, the highest attainable levels of health and wellbeing.

Our patterns of overconsumption are unsustainable and will ultimately cause the collapse of our civilisation. The harms we continue to inflict on our planetary systems are a threat to our very existence as a species. The gains made in health and wellbeing over recent centuries, including through public health actions, are not irreversible; they can easily be lost, a lesson we have failed to learn from previous civilisations. We have created an unjust global economic system that favours a small, wealthy elite over the many who have so little.

The idea of unconstrained progress is a dangerous human illusion: success brings new and potentially even more dangerous threats. Our tolerance of neoliberalism and transnational forces dedicated to ends far removed from the needs of the vast majority of people, and especially the most deprived and vulnerable, is only deepening the crisis we face. We live in a world where the trust between us, our institutions, and our leaders, is falling to levels incompatible with peaceful and just societies, thus contributing to widespread disillusionment with democracy and the political process.

An urgent transformation is required in our values and our practices based on recognition of our interdependence and the interconnectedness of the risks we face. We need a new vision of cooperative and democratic action at all levels of society and a new principle of planetism and wellbeing for every person on this Earth — a principle that asserts that we must conserve, sustain, and make resilient the planetary and human systems on which health depends by giving priority to the wellbeing of all. All too often governments make commitments but fail to act on them; independent accountability is essential to ensure the monitoring and review of these commitments, together with the appropriate remedial action.

The voice of public health and medicine as the independent conscience of planetary health has a special part to play in achieving this vision. Together with empowered communities, we can confront entrenched interests and forces that jeopardise our future. A powerful social movement based on collective action at every level of society will deliver planetary health and, at the same time, support sustainable human development.

———————

University of Oslo Commission on Global Governance for Health, Ole Petter Ottersen, Jashodhara Dasgupta, Chantal Blouin, *et al., The Political Origins of Health Inequity: Prospects for Change*
383 THE LANCET 631–37, 641–42, 651, 657–58, 660–61 (2014)

"We are challenged to develop a public health approach that responds to the globalised world. The present global health crisis is not primarily one of disease, but of governance . . . ." *Ilona Kickbusch*

The Commission on Global Governance for Health is motivated by a shared conviction that the present system of global governance fails to adequately protect public health. This failure strikes unevenly and is especially disastrous for the world's most vulnerable, marginalised, and poorest populations. Health inequalities have multiple causes, some of which are rooted in how the world is organised (Table 1).

Table 1: Global health inequities

- About 842 million people worldwide are chronically hungry, one in six children in developing countries is underweight, and more than a third of deaths among children younger than 5 years are attributable to malnutrition. Unequal access to sufficient, safe, and nutritious food persists even though global food production is enough to cover 120% of global dietary needs.

- 1.5 billion people face threats to their physical integrity, their health being undermined not only by direct bodily harm, but also by extreme psychological stress due to fear, loss, and disintegration of the social fabric in areas of chronic insecurity, occupation, and war.

- Life expectancy differs by 21 years between the highest-ranking and lowest-ranking countries on the human development index. Even in 18 of the 26 countries with the largest reductions in child deaths during the past decade, the difference in mortality is increasing between the least and most deprived quintiles of children.

- More than 80% of the world's population are not covered by adequate social protection arrangements. At the same time, the number of unemployed workers is soaring. In 2012, global unemployment rose to 197.3 million, 28.4 million higher than in in 2007. Of those who work, 27% (854 million people) attempt to survive on less than US$2 per day. More than 60% of workers in southeast Asia and sub-Saharan Africa earn less than $2 per day.

- Many of the 300 million Indigenous people face discrimination, which hinders them from meeting their daily needs and voicing their claims. Girls and women face barriers to access education and secure employment compared with boys and men, and women worldwide still face inequalities with respect to reproductive and sexual health rights. These barriers diminish their control over their own life circumstances.

Although the poorest population groups in the poorest countries are left with the heaviest burden of health risks and disease, the fact that people's life chances differ so widely is not simply a problem of poverty, but one of socioeconomic inequality. The differences in health manifest themselves as gradients across societies, with physical and mental ills steeply increasing for each step down the social ladder, along with other health-related outcomes such as violence, drug misuse, depression, obesity, and child wellbeing. It is now well established that the more unequal the society, the worse the outcomes for all — including those at the top.

The WHO Commission on Social Determinants of Health recognised that societal inequalities skew the distribution of health. It concluded that "social norms, policies, and practices that tolerate or actually promote unfair distribution of, and access to, power, wealth, and other necessary social resources" create systematic inequalities in daily living conditions. In a groundbreaking analysis, the report showed how daily living conditions make a major difference to people's life chances. These conditions include safe housing and cohesive communities, access to healthy food and basic health care, decent work, and safe working conditions. They also include underlying factors: political empowerment, non-discriminatory inclusion in social and political interactions, and the opportunity to voice claims.

In our view, the report rightly characterised vast health gaps between groups of people as unfair, labelling them health inequities rather than inequalities. According to Margaret Whitehead, health equity implies that: "ideally everyone should have a fair opportunity to attain their full health potential and, more pragmatically, that no one should be disadvantaged from achieving this potential, if it can be avoided. The aim of policy for equity and health is not to eliminate all health differences so that everyone has the same level and quality of health, but rather to reduce or eliminate those that result from factors considered to be both avoidable and unfair."

Nation states are responsible for respecting, protecting, and fulfilling their populations' right to health, but with globalisation many important determinants of health lie beyond any single government's control, and are now inherently global. Besides local and national action, combating health inequity increasingly requires improvement of global governance . . . .

. . . .

. . . We assert that health inequity requires a moral judgment — it must be considered unfair and avoidable by reasonable means . . . .

. . . .

. . . We follow Weiss and Thakur's definition of global governance as: "The complex of formal and informal institutions, mechanisms, relationships, and pro-cesses between and among states, markets, citizens, and organisations, both intergovernmental and non-governmental, through which collective interests on the global plane are articulated, rights and obligations are established, and differences are mediated."

. . . Global governance for health is distinct from the concept of global health governance, which is defined as: "The use of formal and informal institutions, rules, and processes by states, intergovernmental institutions, and non-state actors to deal with challenges to health that require cross-border collective action to address effectively."

. . . .

The present system of international political organisation is rooted in the post-World War II era when the victors established the UN, the Bretton Woods institutions (the International Monetary Fund [IMF] and the World Bank), and the General Agreement on Tariffs and Trade (precursor to the World Trade Organiza-tion [WTO]), to secure post-war order and prosperity. Each organisation was built on the principle of sovereign states coming together at will to address transnational issues.

The nation state has been the fundamental building block of the global polity since the 1648 Treaty of Westphalia, which established a set of sovereign European nation states. Nation states have proliferated, particularly over the past half century, largely due to decolonisation and the division of existing states into new, independent political entities. 51 member states joined the UN charter in 1945, increasing to 193 at present. However, the roles of nation states have changed as the importance of international organisations and groups of actors has grown. Market actors have entered the global governance arena, and private foundations, civil society organisations, and individuals have obtained more influence in global decision-making processes . . . .

. . . The Commission on Social Determinants of Health argued convincingly that the basic, root causes of health inequity lie in the unequal distribution of power, money, and resources. Power disparities and dynamics suffuse all aspects of life: relations between men and women, or old and young people, as well as between countries, firms, and organisations . . . .

In principle, states are political equals in the global system. In reality, power disparities remain vast, especially between the most advanced and the least developed countries. The skewed distribution of wealth between countries reflects their economic power: high-income countries account for only 16% of the global population, but two-thirds of global gross domestic product (GDP). The military spending of the USA exceeds that of any other country, and constitutes nearly half of total military spending worldwide. Although the "one-state, one-vote" decision-making rules of many UN bodies reflect the legal notion that sovereign states are equals in the international system, the choice of five permanent members of the UN Security Council and the weighting of IMF and World Bank votes by financial contribution reflect the greater influence of states with the greatest military and economic capacity.

. . . .

Private firms have an influential role in contemporary global governance. Large transnational companies wield tremendous economic power, which they can deploy to further their interests in global governance processes and global markets. The combined market capitalisation of the five largest tobacco corporations is more than US$400 billion. For the five largest beverage firms the total is more than $600 billion, and for the five largest pharmaceutical firms more than $800 billion. These industries dwarf most national economies. Of 184 economies for which the World Bank reported GDP data in 2011, 124 had a GDP of less than $100 billion. Although governments have the authority to regulate any private actor operating on their soil, in practice states face difficulties governing transnational corporations, not only because of their formidable economic power, but also because firms can change jurisdictions with relative ease to avoid or deter regulation — in other words, they seem to be beyond any one state's control. Although transnational corporations can yield enormous benefits by creating jobs, raising incomes, and driving technological advances, they can also harm health through dangerous working conditions, inadequate pay, environmental pollution, or by producing goods that are a threat to health (e.g., tobacco).

Other non-state actors such as foundations also wield substantial economic power. The Bill & Melinda Gates Foundation has become one of the most influential players in global health. Its enormous contributions to global health initiatives have not only improved health for many, but also inspired financial contributions from other wealthy actors. In 2013, the Foundation had an estimated endowment of more than US$36 billion. With its vast economic power, the Foundation has the power to set global agendas and to direct efforts and action via its grant-making priorities.

In addition to economic and military power, normative power — the ability to shape beliefs about what is ethical, appropriate, or socially acceptable — has proven influential, even without huge material resources. International non-governmental organisations (NGOs), such as Oxfam and Médecins Sans Frontières, can wield considerable influence through their global networks, access to media, and public reputations. The media too can exert power to outrage the public and inspire political mobilisation, and through their editorial decisions they can drive issues up or down the global agenda. Scientific or expert bodies such as the Intergovernmental Panel on Climate Change can provide authoritative scientific evidence that puts pressure on governments to act.

. . . .

Recent years have witnessed a heavy emphasis on biomedical approaches to tackling global health challenges. The biomedical model is oriented towards the individual in illness and health. It focuses on the immediate biological, and sometimes behavioural, causes of illness and disease . . . .

. . . .

. . . The biomedical approach cures disease, but it alone cannot address the root causes of health inequity. Biomedical interventions should be accompanied by a broader understanding of health-depriving forces found in the global political economy. The deep causes of health inequity cannot be diagnosed and remedied with technical solutions, or by the health sector alone, because the causes of health inequity are tied to fairness in the distribution of power and resources rather than to biological variance . . . .

HUMAN RIGHTS NORMS

For more than 60 years, a unified normative global framework relevant for health has been encapsulated in the 1948 Universal Declaration of Human Rights. The Declaration articulates not only the right to life and to health, but also rights related to the major social and political determinants of health, including the right to an adequate standard of living and the right to participate in political life. These rights extend to all human beings irrespective of race, colour, sex, language, religion, political or other opinion, national or social origin, property, birth, or other status. Articulated further in the 1966 International Covenant on Economic, Social and Cultural Rights, and in the International Covenant on Civil and Political Rights, and their respective optional protocols, these norms have the status of international law. The duty to realise these rights sits primarily with states, acting individually and cooperatively.

However, the internalisation stage of human right norms, including the right to health, remains weak and woefully incomplete. Although an international system is in place to monitor treaty compliance, both formal (e.g., the UN Human Rights Council and other mechanisms such as the independent UN Special Rapporteurs) and informal (e.g., reports from civil society and the media), in practice there is little that other states can or will do to compel an unwilling state to adhere to their human rights obligations. Additionally, few mechanisms are in place to effectively monitor and protect human rights across sectors and issue areas . . . .

These challenges in ensuring compliance with international human rights law across sectors and actors have attracted renewed attention through the post-2015 UN development agenda. The UN General Secretary has reminded the world about the need to base a vision of the future in human rights and the universally accepted values and principles (such as accountability and transparency) encapsulated in the Charter, Universal Declaration on Human Rights, and the Millennium Declaration, to achieve sustainable development. The vision must be agreed upon within strengthened partnerships for development, representing both state and non-state actors from all sectors of society.

. . . .

The purpose of this Commission is to draw attention to the global political determinants of health. We maintain that it is the responsibility of nation states to respect, protect, and fulfil the right to health of their populations. However, when health is compromised by transnational forces, the response must be in the realm of global governance.

The tremendous health inequities that exist are morally unacceptable and "not in any sense a 'natural' phenomenon, but the results of a toxic combination of poor social policies and programs, unfair economic arrangements, and bad politics" . . . .

. . . .

We perceive this upwelling of collective efforts as an expression of a shared vision, an emerging global social norm: that the global economic system should serve a global population of healthy people in sustainable societies, within the boundaries of nature. The main ambition of this Commission is to add our voice and weight to push this norm towards its tipping point, by urging policy makers across all sectors, as well as international organisations and civil society, to recognise how global political determinants affect health inequities, and to launch a global public debate about how they can be addressed.

. . . .

One of the main sets of global rules that govern health-related knowledge production and access is the WTO Agreement on Trade-Related Aspects of Intellectual Property Rights (TRIPS). A central policy objective of protecting intellectual property is to incentivise the creation and disclosure of information and knowledge . . . .

TRIPS requires countries to ensure a harmonised minimum level of intellectual property protection, based on the standards in industrialised countries, including: minimum 20-year patents in all areas of technology, including drugs; restrictions on the policy space for states to exclude specific technologies from patentability; and limits on permissible public interest safeguards in patent laws, such as compulsory licences.

Before TRIPS, many countries — including those in Western Europe — had made special exceptions for food, drugs, agricultural technologies, and education in their national patent and copyright laws. But the introduction of patents on drugs, in many countries for the first time, enabled monopoly pricing for these products, raising concerns about affordability, particularly for poor populations. Although the right to health includes access to essential drugs, the adverse effect of patent monopolies on prices and availability of drugs has made it difficult for many countries to comply with their obligations to respect, protect, and fulfil the right to health. Additionally, patents alone do not drive sufficient investment to counter diseases that predominantly affect poor people, because they do not offer a sufficiently profitable market; as a result, some diseases — or rather, some populations — are neglected. This problem was characterised by the Global Forum for Health Research in the 1990s as the 10/90 gap, on the basis of estimates that only 10% of research funding was spent on the major health needs of 90% of the world's population. TRIPS shows clearly how economic power can shape global rule making, with far-reaching consequences for health. Globalisation of patent rules creates a net transfer of resources from poor countries to rich countries in the form of royalties, while simultaneously restricting access to the knowledge and technologies that could improve health and spur economic development.

. . . .

Although concerns about the health effects of TRIPS have been widely voiced by civil society and many developing countries, the agreement has become increasingly important with the continuing growth of the knowledge economy. TRIPS is nearly impossible to amend because WTO rules require all members to agree on any changes — an unlikely outcome since the more advanced industrialised countries benefit handsomely from these rules. Thus, TRIPS shows how major power disparities shaped the initial rules of the game, and continue to perpetuate such disparity.

. . . .

PATTERNS OF ARMED VIOLENCE AND EFFECTS ON HEALTH

Throughout the world in the past 15–20 years, patterns of armed violence have been changing and expanding beyond the traditional features of organised armed conflict. Compared with the vast interstate wars of the 20th century, armed conflicts between large nation states are now relatively rare. Civil wars — those between a standing government and a rebel force — have fallen in number since a peak in the 1990s, although they often persist for many years and contribute to protracted refugee and internal displacement crises, and long-lasting border insecurities.

. . . .

Armed conflicts lead to civilian death, injury, disability, illness, and mental anguish. Although data are woefully incomplete, estimates show that between 191 million and 231 million people died as a direct or indirect result of conflict during the 20th century. Civilian deaths have come to far outnumber combatant deaths, and this heavy preponderance arises from deliberate war strategies: direct targeting of civilians; gross inattention to principles of distinction, protection, and proportionality; and wanton destruction of health systems, basic societal functions, and infrastructure necessary to support civilian life and function.

. . . .

[M]ajor internal and international wars of the new century, such as those in Syria, Iraq, and Afghanistan, have claimed civilian lives estimated in the hundreds of thousands. In one of few systematic efforts to collect data for civilian deaths, the Oxford Research Group reported that the war in Syria killed 11 420 children younger than 17 years over a period of only 30 months. The deliberate targeting of health-care infrastructure and health professionals has been a recurring feature in Iraq and Syria, and the same tactic has been reported in the Democratic Republic of the Congo. Hospitals in Iraq have been called killing fields; in Syria, most hospitals in conflict zones have been severely damaged or abandoned, and many physicians, viewed as war targets, have been forced to flee the country.

An inevitable result of the deliberate targeting of civilians is forced migration. When armed groups or armies attack specific neighbourhoods or communal groups, residents flee en masse and, dependent on geographical and security constraints, become either internally displaced or refugees in neighbouring countries. UNHCR estimates that by the end of 2011 there were 42.5 million refugees and internally displaced people worldwide, the highest cumulative total since 1994. The average length of protracted refugee situations is approaching 20 years (an increase from 9 years in 1993).

. . . .

TACKLING POLITICAL DETERMINANTS OF HEALTH

. . . .

Transformational change is needed in the way in which policies and global decisions that affect health are made, and in the norms that inform them. A new, interconnected global agenda for sustainable development will require a more democratic distribution of political and economic power and a transformed global governance architecture . . . .

. . . .

The Commission offers two proposals to fill existing gaps in the institutional framework of global governance for health, which could be within reach as an agenda for change and should be further explored: a UN Multistakeholder Platform on Global Governance for Health and an Independent Scientific Monitoring Panel on Global Social and Political Determinants of Health. These proposals could also be extended to include mandatory health equity impact assessments for all global institutions and strengthened sanctions against non-state actors for rights violations. As an immediate action, governments and the UN Human Rights Council could strengthen the roles of existing human rights instruments for health. These proposals should be viewed within the broader context of, and as a contribution to, global discussions about how to strengthen global governance for sustainable development . . . .

. . . .

We . . . also propose some immediate actions that are intended, not to root out the very causes of persistent health inequities, but to remedy the effects of the inequitable distribution of health through improved sanctions and security.

STRENGTHEN THE USE OF HUMAN RIGHTS INSTRUMENTS FOR HEALTH

The report of the UN Secretary General, *A life of dignity for all*, highlights the growing emphasis on a rights-based agenda for sustainable development, noting that "people across the world are demanding more responsive governments and better governance based on rights". The Commission underlines the importance of building on this momentum.

Although the human rights system has important mechanisms in place to drive an agenda of this type, the application of human rights instruments for health, including access to drugs, sexual and reproductive rights, and violence against women, has been controversial and therefore underused. The opportunity should now be taken to seek improved recognition of health as a human right, integrated with other social, economic, political, and civil rights in the agenda of global governance. Calling attention to violations of agreed human rights standards by state and non-state actors is crucial.

The mandate, reports, and recommendations of the Special Rapporteur on the Right to Health can be better used to inform policies and strategies that affect health, including by having the Special Rapporteur report to the World Health

Assembly. Governments and other actors should work to strengthen links between the existing international human rights system to make better use of existing surveillance capacities, with reports and guidance taken into account in multilateral arenas such as the IMF, the UN Security Council, WHO, the World Intellectual Property Organization, WTO, and the World Bank. Governments on the UN Human Rights Council should expand the mandates for the Special Rapporteurs to include human rights audit of the decision-making processes of international organisations. . . .

To strengthen weak accountability at the transnational level, stronger mechanisms for sanctions are needed. Sanctions can lead to punishment of those actors who violate agreed-upon standards, or to remedy for harms committed, whether in the form of an apology, commitment not to repeat, policy changes, or reparations.

Although national courts can play an important part in sanctioning violations, when they are unable or unwilling to try specific cases, international courts might be needed. In view of the many global power imbalances that can limit the effectiveness of national courts, the international judicial system is an important backstop to national systems and could offer a useful mechanism for strengthened transnational accountability. The state-based international judicial system should, however, be strengthened to encompass a broader range of non-state actors and to enforce sanctions against a broader range of violations.

The existing patchwork of international courts has wide gaps, especially for cases in which non-state actors are potential plaintiffs or defendants. For example, the ICC does not accept cases brought by non-state actors such as minority groups or civil society organisations, and transnational corporations cannot be brought before the ICC, since its mandate is restricted to prosecuting human beings . . . . Recognising the many challenges involved in broadening the formal mandate of the ICC, we suggest as a first step the creation of a regularly scheduled forum at which civil society organisations could present reports on alleged violations requiring greater attention from the court.

Global governance for health must be rooted in commitments to global solidarity and shared responsibility, building on national and international commitments to work together to ensure fulfilment of the right to health. . . .

    . . . .

Strengthened and transformed mechanisms for global solidarity and shared responsibility based in financing models beyond traditional development assistance are highly relevant and need priority attention. Examples include health research that meets the needs of poor people and mechanisms for global social protection transfers.

Proposals have been tabled by many actors, including the WHO Consultative Expert Working Group on Research and Development, to ensure sufficient investment in health-related research and development in areas for which market incentives are insufficient. One of the options is a treaty under which countries would commit to finance research and development in accordance with their ability to pay, while the research would be oriented towards the most important global public health needs. This proposal would have the effect of mandatory financial transfers — albeit indirect — from wealthy countries to poorer countries (which would benefit most from the research). If a binding treaty is not politically feasible, an alternative model could be the non-binding assessed contribution scheme used for the replenishments of the International Development Association (the arm of the World Bank that provides grants and soft loans to low-income countries), contributions to which are roughly proportional to a country's share of the global economy.

Universal health coverage is about "solidarity between the healthy and the sick and between population groups in all income classes". Just as social health insurance schemes and risk pooling for medical expenditure are central to universal health coverage, social protection is key to the whole social dimension of sustainable development. Good reasons might exist for applying these principles beyond state borders. Global social protection would entail appropriate distribution of national and international responsibilities, with mechanisms to collect and redistribute transfers that are both duty-based and rights-based. Whether a single global social health protection fund would be better than the present patchwork of thousands of bilateral and multilateral global social protection transfers remains a controversial issue, but these are important questions that need to be further explored and debated.

. . . .

Health is a precondition, outcome, and indicator of a sustainable society, and should be adopted as a universal value and a shared social and political objective for all.

Daniel Tarantola & Sofia Gruskin, *Human Rights Approach to Public Health Policy*, in HEALTH AND HUMAN RIGHTS IN A CHANGING WORLD
43–56 (Grodin, Tarantola, Annas & Gruskin, eds., 2013)

Health and human rights are not distinct but intertwined aspirations. Viewed as a universal aspiration, the notion of health as the attainment of physical, mental, and social well-being implies its dependency on and contribution to the realization of all human rights. From the same perspective, the enjoyment by everyone of the highest attainable standard of physical and mental health is in itself a recognized human right. From a global normative perspective, health and human rights are closely intertwined in many international treaties and declarations supported by mechanisms of monitoring and accountability (even as their effectiveness can be questioned) that draw from both fields . . . . Health and human rights individually occupy privileged places in the public discourse, political debates, public policy, and the media, and both are at the top of human aspirations. There is hardly a proposed political agenda that does not refer to health in its own right, as well as justice, security, housing, education, and employment opportunities — all with relevance to health. These aspirations are often not framed as human rights but the fact that they are contained in human rights treaties and often translated into national constitutions and legislations provides legal support for efforts in these areas.

Incorporating human rights in public health policy therefore responds to the demands of people, policy makers, and political leaders for outcomes that meet public aspirations. It also creates opportunities for helping decipher how all human rights and other determinants of well-being and social progress interact. It allows progress toward these goals to be measured and shapes policy directions and agendas for action.

This article highlights the evolution that has brought human rights and health together in mutually reinforcing ways. It draws from the experience gained in the global response to HIV/AIDS, summarizes key dimensions of public health and of human rights and suggests a manner in which these dimensions intersect that may be used as a framework for health policy analysis, development, and evaluation.

Human rights constitute a set of normative principles and standards which, as a philosophical concept can be traced back to antiquity, with mounting interest among intellectuals and political leaders since the seventeenth century. The atrocities perpetrated during World War II gave rise, in 1948, to the Universal Declaration of Human Rights (United Nations, 1948) and later to a series of treaties and conventions that extended the aspirational nature of the UDHR into instruments that would be binding on states under international human rights law. Among these are the International Covenant on Civil and Political Rights (ICCPR) and the International Covenant on Economic, Social, and Cultural Rights (ICESCR), both of which came into force in 1976.

Human rights are legal claims that persons have on governments simply on the basis of their being human. They are "what governments can do to you, cannot do to you and should do for you." Even though people hold their human rights throughout their lives, they are nonetheless often constrained in their ability to fully realize them. Those who are most vulnerable to violations or neglect of their rights are also often those who lack sufficient power to claim the impact of the lack of enjoyment of their rights on their well-being, including their state of personal health. Human rights are intended to be inalienable (individuals cannot lose these rights any more than they can cease being human beings); they are indivisible (individuals cannot be denied a right because it is deemed less important or nonessential); they are interdependent (all human rights are part of a complementary framework, one right impacting on and being impacted by all others). They bring into focus the relationship between the State — the first-line provider and protector of human rights — and individuals who hold their human rights simply for being human. In this regard, governments have three sets of obligations toward their people:

- They have the obligation to respect human rights, which requires governments to refrain from interfering directly or indirectly with the enjoyment of human rights. In practice, no health policy, practice, program, or legal measure should violate human rights. Policies should ensure the provision of health services to all population groups on the basis of equality and freedom from discrimination, paying particular attention to vulnerable and marginalized groups.

- They have the obligation to protect human rights, which requires governments to take measures that prevent non-state actors from interfering with human rights, and to provide legal means of redress that people know about and can access. This relates to such important non-state actors as private health-care providers, pharmaceutical companies, health insurance companies and, more generally, the health-related industry, but also national and multinational enterprises whose actions can impact significantly on lifestyle, labor, and the environment such as oil and other energy-producing companies, car manufacturers, agriculture, food industry, and labor-intensive garment factories.

■ They have the obligation to fulfill human rights, which requires States to adopt appropriate legislative, administrative, budgetary, judicial, promotional, and other measures toward the full realization of human rights, including putting into place appropriate health and health-related policies that ensure human rights promotion and protection. In practice, governments should be supported in their efforts to develop and apply these measures and monitor their impact, with an immediate focus on vulnerable and marginalized groups.

Government responsibility for health exists in several ways. The right to the highest attainable standard of health appears in one form or another in most international and regional human rights documents, and equally importantly, nearly every article of every document can be understood to have clear implications for health.

THE RIGHT TO HEALTH

The right to the highest attainable standard of health builds on, but is by no means limited to, Article 12 of the International Covenant on Economic, Social, and Cultural Rights (ICESCR). Rights relating to autonomy, information, education, food and nutrition, association, equality, participation, and nondiscrimination are integral and indivisible parts of the achievement of the highest attainable standard of health, just as the enjoyment of the right to health is inseparable from all other rights, whether they are categorized as civil and political, economic, social, or cultural. This recognition is based on empirical observation and on a growing body of evidence that establishes the impact that lack of fulfillment of any and all of these rights has on people's health status: Education, nondiscrimination, food and nutrition epitomizing this relationship. Conversely, ill-health constrains the fulfillment of all rights as the capacity of individuals to claim and enjoy all their human rights depends on their physical, mental, and social well-being.

The right to health does not mean the right to be healthy as such, but the obligation on the part of the government to create the conditions necessary for individuals to achieve their optimal health status. . . . In 2000, the United Nations Committee on Economic, Social, and Cultural Rights adopted a General Comment further clarifying the substance of government obligations relating to the right to health. In addition to clarifying governmental responsibility for policies, programs and practices impacting the underlying conditions necessary for health, it sets out requirements related to the delivery of health services including their availability, acceptability, accessibility, and quality. It lays out directions for the practical application of Article 12 and proposes a monitoring framework. Reflecting the mounting interest in determining international policy focused on the right to health, the UN Commission on Human Rights appointed in 2002 a Special Rapporteur whose mandate concerns the right of everyone to the enjoyment of the highest attainable standard of physical and mental health . . . . All international human rights treaties and conventions contain provisions relevant to health as defined in the preamble of the Constitution of the World Health Organization (WHO), repeated in many subsequent documents and currently adopted by the 191 WHO Member States: Health is a "state of complete physical, mental, and social well-being, and not merely the absence of disease or infirmity." . . .

The focus of public health from its inception in the eighteenth century through the mid-1970s remained on combating disease and some of its most blatant social, environmental, and occupational causes. The state acted as a benevolent provider of services and the source of policies, laws, regulations, and practices generally based on the disease prevention and control model emphasizing risk — and impact-reduction strategies through immunization, case finding, treatment, and changes in domestic, environmental, and occupational hygiene.

In 1978, the Alma Ata conference solidified a new international health agenda. The aim of achieving Health for All by the Year 2000 was put forward, and this was to be achieved through a Primary Health Care (PHC) approach. Invoking the human right to the highest attainable standard of health, the Declaration of Alma Ata called on nations to ensure the availability of the essentials of primary health care, including education concerning health conditions and the methods for preventing and controlling them; promotion of food supply and proper nutrition; an adequate supply of safe water and basic sanitation; maternal and child health care, including family planning; immunization against major infectious diseases; prevention and control of locally endemic diseases; appropriate treatment of common disease and injuries; and provision of essential drugs.

The 1980s also witnessed the recognition that health was not merely determined by social and economic status but was dependent on dynamic social and economic determinants that could be acted upon through policy and structural changes . . . . The late 1980s and the 1990s saw growing attention being directed in the policy discourse to human rights and to their particular implications for health, and this resulted from several factors. First, the ICCPR and IESCR entered into force in 1976, and in the 1980s the UN Committees responsible for the monitoring of their implementation had begun to decipher their actual meaning and core contents, making the obligations of governments explicit and measurable. Second, the decay of the world geopolitical block ideologies of the late 1980s and the advent of economic neoliberalism created a space for alternate paradigms to help shape public policy and international relations. Human rights entered the scene of geopolitical reconstruction and became common parley after the Glasnost and the fall of the Berlin Wall, in 1989, regardless of whether in reality they were used or abused by new political leaders. Third, the connection between human rights and health was increasingly being shaped around focal causes in various social and political movements. This resulted in the creation of NGOs, some of which engaged in human rights work (responding to torture in particular), others in advocacy around reproductive health and rights issues, while others provided health assistance in armed conflicts and natural disasters, all with the intent of positively impacting on policy and practice. Fourth, and particularly important for the ways this contributed to the integration of human rights concepts into health policy, the emergence of AIDS in 1981, and the recognition of HIV as a global pandemic, resulted in a variety of human rights violations by those seeking to address this mounting public health problem. As traditional disease control policies that had marked the earlier history of public health were put in place by state authorities, with a few exceptions, community-based and advocacy organizations, supported by academic groups, voiced the necessity for policies that afforded greater protections for the rights of people living with or vulnerable to HIV.

Until this time, the focus of public health had generally been to promote the collective physical, mental, and social well-being of people, even if in order to achieve public health goals, policies had to be implemented that sacrificed individual choice, behavior, and action for the common good. This was, and continues to be, exemplified by the principles and practices that guide the control of such communicable diseases as tuberculosis, typhoid, or sexually transmitted infections, where quarantine or other restrictions of rights are imposed on affected individuals. In a number of instances, in particular where health policy addressed communicable diseases and mental illness, restrictions of such rights as privacy, free movement, autonomy, or bodily integrity have been imposed by public health authorities with the commendable intention to protect public health even without valid evidence of their intended public health benefit. The current resurgence of this issue in the context of systematic testing for HIV in health facilities or within entire populations, advocated by some in order to enhance the early access to care and treatment by people found infected, illustrates that disease control methods blind to human rights have by no means vanished. Insufficient attention has been devoted to assessing and monitoring the impact of such policies on the life of people whose rights were being restricted or denied, and to the negative consequences such impositions can have on their willingness to participate supportively in public health efforts that concern them. Public health abuses have also been exemplified by policies which result in the excessive institutionalization of people with physical or mental impairments where alternate care and support approaches have not been adequately considered. In the fields of disability and in mental health, in a number of countries national policies have been found to be discriminatory and, in the case of mental health, at times when carried out in practice to amount to inhuman and degrading treatment. And far from uncommon was — and remains — something often invisible to policy but invidious if not adequately addressed, discrimination in the health-care setting on the basis of health status, gender, race, color, language, religion, or social origin, or any other attribute that can influence the quality of services provided to individuals by or on behalf of the State.

Cognizant of the need to engage HIV-affected communities in the response to the fast-spreading epidemics in order to achieve their public health goals, human rights were understood as valuable by policy makers not for their moral or legal value but to open access to prevention and care for those who needed these services most, away from fear, discrimination and other forms of human rights violations, and as a way to ensure communities that needed to be reached did not go underground. The deprivation of such entitlements as access to health and social services, employment, or housing imposed on people living with HIV was understood to constrain their capacity to become active subjects rather than the objects of HIV programs, and this was recognized as unsound from a public health perspective . . . . Stemming from an instrumental approach rather than moral or legal principles, the response to HIV had exposed the congruence between sound public health policy and the upholding of human rights norms and standards . . . .

International activism and a series of international political conferences that took place in this period facilitated similar changes in the approach taken to a wide range of diseases and health conditions, in particular with respect to reproductive and sexual health issues. The 1994 Cairo International Conference on Population and Development was a watershed in recognizing the responsibility of governments worldwide to translate their international-level commitments into national laws, policies, programs, and practices that promote and do not hinder sexual and reproductive health among their populations. National laws and policies were thus open to scrutiny to determine both the positive and negative influences they could have on sexual and reproductive health programming, information, services, and choices. Human rights concerns, including legal, policy, and practice barriers that impact on the delivery and use of sexual and reproductive health services thereafter became a valid target for international attention.

As, from a theoretical perspective, the interaction between health and human rights was drawing increased attention from policy makers in an expanding array of health-related domains, two issues were and continue to be cited as creating obstacles to the translation of theory into practice. The first is that the realization of the right to health cannot be made real in view of the structures, services, and resources it requires. The second, often cited by those concerned with communicable disease control, is that the protection of human rights should not be the prime concern of policy makers when and where such public health threats as emerging epidemics call for the restriction of certain individual rights. As these two obstacles are often used and misused to question the validity of the health and human rights framework, they are discussed briefly below.

PROGRESSIVE REALIZATION OF HEALTH-RELATED HUMAN RIGHTS

In all countries, resource and other constraints can make it impossible for a government to fulfill all rights immediately and completely. The principle of progressive realization is fundamental to the achievement of human rights as they apply to health. And applies equally to resource-poor countries as to wealthier countries whose responsibilities extend not only to what they do within their own borders, but also their engagement in international assistance and cooperation.

Given that progress in health necessitates infrastructure and human and financial resources that may not match existing or future needs in any country, the principle of progressive realization takes into account the inability of governments to meet their obligations overnight. Yet, it creates an obligation on governments to set their own benchmarks, within the maximum of the resources available to them, and to show how and to what extent, through their policies and practices, they are achieving progress toward the health goals they have agreed to in international forums such as the World Health Assembly, as well as those they have set for themselves. In theory, States account for progress in health (or lack thereof) through a variety of mechanisms that include global monitoring mechanisms, as well as national State of the Health of the Nation reports or similar forms of domestic public reporting.

HUMAN RIGHTS LIMITATIONS IN THE INTEREST OF PUBLIC HEALTH

There remains a deeply rooted concern of many in the health community that application of a health and human rights approach to health policy will deprive the State from applying such measures as isolation or quarantine or travel restrictions when public health is at stake. Public health and care practitioners alike, acting on behalf of the State, are used to applying restrictions to individual freedom in cases where the enjoyment of these rights creates a real or perceived threat to the population at large. The SARS and Avian flu epidemics have demonstrated that such restrictions can also be applied globally under the revised International Health Regulations (IHR), the only binding agreement thus far under the auspices of WHO. They stipulate that WHO can make recommendations on an ad hoc, time-limited, risk-specific basis, as a result of a public health emergency of international concern, and that implementation of these Regulations "shall be with full respect for the dignity, human rights and fundamental freedoms of persons." The human rights framework recognizes that these are situations where there can be legitimate and valid restriction of rights, and this under several circumstances relevant to the creation of health policies: Public emergencies and public health imperatives. Public emergencies stipulate that in time of a public emergency that threatens the life of the nation and the existence of which is officially proclaimed, the States Parties to the present Covenant may take measures derogating from their obligations under the present Covenant to the extent strictly required by the exigencies of the situation, provided that such measures are not inconsistent with their other obligations under international law and do not involve discrimination solely on the ground of race, color, sex, language, religion, or social origin. Public health imperatives give governments the right to take the steps they deem necessary for the prevention, treatment, and control of epidemic, endemic, occupational, and other diseases.

Public health may therefore justify the limitation of certain rights under certain circumstances. Policies that interfere with freedom of movement when instituting quarantine or isolation for a serious communicable disease — for example, Ebola fever, syphilis, typhoid, or untreated tuberculosis, more recently SARS and pandemic influenza — are examples of limitation of rights that may be necessary for the public good and therefore may be considered legitimate under international human rights law. Yet arbitrary restrictive measures taken or planned by public health authorities that fail to consider other valid alternatives may be found to be both abusive of human rights principles and in contradiction with public health best practice. The limitation of most rights in the interest of public health remains an option under both international human rights law and public health laws, but the decision to impose such limitations must be achieved through a structured and accountable process. Increasingly, such consultative processes are put in place by national authorities to debate over the approach taken to public health issues as they arise, such as in the case of immunization, disability, mental health, HIV, smoking, and more recently pandemic influenza preparedness.

Limitations on rights are considered a serious issue under international human rights law — as noted in specific provisions within international human treaties — regardless of the apparent importance of the public good involved. When a government limits the exercise or enjoyment of a right, this action must be taken only as a last resort and will only be considered legitimate if the following criteria are met: [Saracusa Principles]

1. The restriction is provided for and carried out in accordance with the law.

2. The restriction is in the interest of a legitimate objective of general interest.

3. The restriction is strictly necessary in a democratic society to achieve the objective.

4. There are no less intrusive and restrictive means available to reach the same goal.

5. The restriction is not imposed arbitrarily, *i.e.*, in an unreasonable or otherwise discriminatory manner.

The restriction of rights, if legitimate, is therefore consistent with human rights principles. Both principles of progressive realization and legitimate limitations of rights are directly relevant to public health policy as they can inform decisions on how to achieve the optimal balance between protecting the rights of the individual and the best interest of the community. Examples of the impact of human rights violations and protection on public health are set out below. Discrimination — a frequent, severe, and persistent issue confronted both in society and in the health-care setting — has been chosen to illustrate how public health can be hampered by the neglect of human rights and enhanced by their incorporation in public health policy.

DISCRIMINATION

Discrimination can impact directly on the ways that morbidity, mortality, and disability — the burden of disease — are both measured and acted upon. In fact, the burden of disease itself discriminates: Disease, disability, and death are not distributed randomly or equally within populations, nor are their devastating effects within communities. Tuberculosis, for example, is exploding in disenfranchised communities, in particular among prison inmates and people already affected by HIV and subjected to dual discrimination both in their communities and in the health-care setting.

Far from uncommon, discrimination in health systems, including health centers, hospitals, or mental institutions, may further contribute to exacerbating disparities in health. A few examples of myriads that could be cited are named here. Undocumented migrant workers receive poor or no treatment for fear of having to justify their civil status. Documented migrant workers, refugees, and asylum seekers and their families may not avail themselves of services that have not been designed to suit their culture and respond to their specific needs. People with hemophilia have been given unsafe blood products on the premise that this adds only a marginal risk to their lives. People with physical or mental disabilities receive substandard care; they are unable to complain or if they do, they fare poorly in legal action. . . . Discrimination can also be at the root of unsound human development policies and programs that may impact directly or indirectly on health. For example, an infrastructure development project may require the displacement of entire populations and fail to pay sufficient attention to the new environment to which these populations will have to adjust. In the developing world, when the health impact of large-scale development programs at the local level is considered, it is often from the perspective of the possible further spread of such infectious diseases as malaria and other waterborne diseases . . . .

The ongoing international movement toward poverty alleviation has emphasized the critical importance of health in the fight against poverty. The eight Millennium Development Goals (MDGs) — which set targets for 2015 to halve extreme poverty, halt the spread of HIV/AIDS, and improve health and education — have been agreed to by all the world's countries and all the world's leading development institutions. Arguably, all MDGs have a linkage to health either by their direct bearing on health outcomes and the needed services (e.g., through efforts to reduce child and maternal mortality, HIV, malaria, and other diseases) or by underscoring principles central to public health policy (e.g., gender equality) or else by calling for the creation of policies addressing the underlying conditions for progress in health (e.g., education, environmental sustainability, and global partnerships).

PUBLIC HEALTH POLICY AND THE VALUE OF HEALTH AND HUMAN RIGHTS

A distinction exists between public policy affecting health (most of them do) and public health policy (often emerging from public health governmental authorities or on their initiative). Policies affecting health — for example, those related to gender, trade, intellectual property, the environment, migration, education, housing, or labor — are contingent upon national laws and international treaties or agreements which often overlook — by omission or commission — their potential health consequences. As the Health Impact Assessment of development and social policies gained credence in the 1990s, the development of a human rights assessment for the formulation and evaluation of public health policies emerged. Health Impact Assessment (HIA), applying different methods, has become more frequently practiced to guide policy options both nationally and internationally . . . .

Public health policy should seek the optimal synergy between health and human rights, building on the premise that the optimal quality of a public health policy is attained when the highest possible health outcome and the fullest realization of human rights are both attained. This requires a close interaction between public health professionals, human rights practitioners and representatives of affected communities. The response to HIV has been shaped by such an interaction with significant positive impact — at least in the short term — in such countries as Australia, Sweden, Thailand, Brazil, or Uganda. Where misconceptions about either sound public health or human rights have distorted HIV policies and programs, the epidemic has continued to strive, as illustrated by the situation in South Africa or China.

Both public health policy and human rights emphasize the importance of outcome and impact, crudely measured in public health terms by the reduction of mortality, morbidity and disability, and the improvement of quality of life, along with economic measurement enabling an assessment of the value for money of particular policies or programs that can guide priority setting. The extent to which outcome includes the fulfillment of human rights is seldom factored in. For example, one would like to see the value of policies that promote sex education in school measured not only in terms of reduction of teenage pregnancy or the incidence of sexually transmitted diseases, but how the right of the child to information is fulfilled in this way and how it impacts on further demands for other health-related, life-saving information. Likewise, when assessing the outcome and impact of policies that prioritize childhood immunization programs, one would want to know not only how immunization makes people healthier, both early and later in their childhood, but also how such public health policies will advance the right of the child to growth and development and her right to education by improving her attendance to and performance at school . . . .

Health and human rights, together and independently from each other, have achieved today a degree of prominence in the political and public discourse never witnessed before. The fields of health and rights are illuminated today by their commonalties, no longer by their differences. Both are obligations of governments toward their people; and each supports and requires the fulfillment of the other.

Overall, health and human rights provide a framework for all aspects of policy and program development. In practice, human rights considerations are often built into public health policy through the application of what are today called rights-based approaches . . . .

UNIVERSAL DECLARATION OF HUMAN RIGHTS
United Nations (1948)

Whereas recognition of the inherent dignity and of the equal and inalienable rights of all members of the human family is the foundation of freedom, justice and peace in the world,

Whereas disregard and contempt for human rights have resulted in barbarous acts which have outraged the conscience of mankind, and the advent of a world in which human beings shall enjoy freedom of speech and belief and freedom from fear and want has been proclaimed as the highest aspiration of the common people,

Whereas it is essential, if man is not to be compelled to have recourse, as a last resort, to rebellion against tyranny and oppression, that human rights should be protected by the rule of law,

Whereas it is essential to promote the development of friendly relations between nations,

Whereas the peoples of the United Nations have in the Charter reaffirmed their faith in fundamental human rights, in the dignity and worth of the human person and in the equal rights of men and women and have determined to promote social progress and better standards of life in larger freedom,

Whereas Member States have pledged themselves to achieve, in co-operation with the United Nations, the promotion of universal respect for and observance of human rights and fundamental freedoms,

Whereas a common understanding of these rights and freedoms is of the greatest importance for the full realization of this pledge,

Now, Therefore THE GENERAL ASSEMBLY proclaims THIS UNIVERSAL DECLARATION OF HUMAN RIGHTS as a common standard of achievement for all peoples and all nations, to the end that every individual and every organ of society, keeping this Declaration constantly in mind, shall strive by teaching and education to promote respect for these rights and freedoms and by progressive measures, national and international, to secure their universal and effective recognition and observance, both among the peoples of Member States themselves and among the peoples of territories under their jurisdiction.

Article 1.

All human beings are born free and equal in dignity and rights. They are endowed with reason and conscience and should act towards one another in a spirit of brotherhood.

Article 2.

Everyone is entitled to all the rights and freedoms set forth in this Declaration, without distinction of any kind, such as race, colour, sex, language, religion, political or other opinion, national or social origin, property, birth or other status. Furthermore, no distinction shall be made on the basis of the political, jurisdictional or international status of the country or territory to which a person belongs, whether it be independent, trust, non-self-governing or under any other limitation of sovereignty.

Article 3.

Everyone has the right to life, liberty and security of person.

Article 4.

No one shall be held in slavery or servitude; slavery and the slave trade shall be prohibited in all their forms.

Article 5.

No one shall be subjected to torture or to cruel, inhuman or degrading treatment or punishment.

Article 6.

Everyone has the right to recognition everywhere as a person before the law.

Article 7.

All are equal before the law and are entitled without any discrimination to equal protection of the law. All are entitled to equal protection against any discrimination in violation of this Declaration and against any incitement to such discrimination.

Article 8.

Everyone has the right to an effective remedy by the competent national tribunals for acts violating the fundamental rights granted him by the constitution or by law.

Article 9.

No one shall be subjected to arbitrary arrest, detention or exile. Article 10.

Article 10.

Everyone is entitled in full equality to a fair and public hearing by an independent and impartial tribunal, in the determination of his rights and obligations and of any criminal charge against him.

Article 11.

(1) Everyone charged with a penal offence has the right to be presumed innocent until proved guilty according to law in a public trial at which he has had all the guarantees necessary for his defense.

(2) No one shall be held guilty of any penal offence on account of any act or omission which did not constitute a penal offence, under national or international law, at the time when it was committed. Nor shall a heavier penalty be imposed than the one that was applicable at the time the penal offence was committed.

Article 12.

No one shall be subjected to arbitrary interference with his privacy, family, home or correspondence, nor to attacks upon his honour and reputation. Everyone has the right to the protection of the law against such interference or attacks.

Article 13.

(1) Everyone has the right to freedom of movement and residence within the borders of each state.

(2) Everyone has the right to leave any country, including his own, and to return to his country.

Article 14.

(1) Everyone has the right to seek and to enjoy in other countries asylum from persecution.

(2) This right may not be invoked in the case of prosecutions genuinely arising from non-political crimes or from acts contrary to the purposes and principles of the United Nations.

Article 15.

(1) Everyone has the right to a nationality.

(2) No one shall be arbitrarily deprived of his nationality nor denied the right to change his nationality.

Article 16.

(1) Men and women of full age, without any limitation due to race, nationality or religion, have the right to marry and to found a family. They are entitled to equal rights as to marriage, during marriage and at its dissolution.

(2) Marriage shall be entered into only with the free and full consent of the intending spouses.

(3) The family is the natural and fundamental group unit of society and is entitled to protection by society and the State.

Article 17.

(1) Everyone has the right to own property alone as well as in association with others.

(2) No one shall be arbitrarily deprived of his property.

Article 18.

Everyone has the right to freedom of thought, conscience and religion; this right includes freedom to change his religion or belief, and freedom, either alone or in community with others and in public or private, to manifest his religion or belief in teaching, practice, worship and observance.

Article 19.

Everyone has the right to freedom of opinion and expression; this right includes freedom to hold opinions without interference and to seek, receive and impart information and ideas through any media and regardless of frontiers.

Article 20.

(1) Everyone has the right to freedom of peaceful assembly and association.

(2) No one may be compelled to belong to an association.

Article 21.

(1) Everyone has the right to take part in the government of his country, directly or through freely chosen representatives.

(2) Everyone has the right of equal access to public service in his country.

(3) The will of the people shall be the basis of the authority of government; this will shall be expressed in periodic and genuine elections which shall be by universal and equal suffrage and shall be held by secret vote or by equivalent free voting procedures.

Article 22.

Everyone, as a member of society, has the right to social security and is entitled to realization, through national effort and international co-operation and in accordance with the organization and resources of each State, of the economic, social and cultural rights indispensable for his dignity and the free development of his personality.

Article 23.

(1) Everyone has the right to work, to free choice of employment, to just and favorable conditions of work and to protection against unemployment.

(2) Everyone, without any discrimination, has the right to equal pay for equal work.

(3) Everyone who works has the right to just and favorable remuneration ensuring for himself and his family an existence worthy of human dignity, and supplemented, if necessary, by other means of social protection.

(4) Everyone has the right to form and to join trade unions for the protection of his interests.

Article 24.

Everyone has the right to rest and leisure, including reasonable limitation of working hours and periodic holidays with pay.

Article 25.

(1) Everyone has the right to a standard of living adequate for the health and well-being of himself and of his family, including food, clothing, housing and medical care and necessary social services, and the right to security in the event of unemployment, sickness, disability, widowhood, old age or other lack of livelihood in circumstances beyond his control.

(2) Motherhood and childhood are entitled to special care and assistance. All children, whether born in or out of wedlock, shall enjoy the same social protection.

Article 26.

(1) Everyone has the right to education. Education shall be free, at least in the elementary and fundamental stages. Elementary education shall be compulsory. Technical and professional education shall be made generally avail-able and higher education shall be equally accessible to all on the basis of merit.

(2) Education shall be directed to the full development of the human personality and to the strengthening of respect for human rights and fundamental freedoms. It shall promote understanding, tolerance and friendship among all nations, racial or religious groups, and shall further the activities of the United Nations for the maintenance of peace.

(3) Parents have a prior right to choose the kind of education that shall be given to their children.

Article 27.

(1) Everyone has the right freely to participate in the cultural life of the community, to enjoy the arts and to share in scientific advancement and its benefits.

(2) Everyone has the right to the protection of the moral and material interests resulting from any scientific, literary or artistic production of which he is the author.

Article 28.

Everyone is entitled to a social and international order in which the rights and freedoms set forth in this Declaration can be fully realized.

Article 29.

(1) Everyone has duties to the community in which alone the free and full development of his personality is possible.

(2) In the exercise of his rights and freedoms, everyone shall be subject only to such limitations as are determined by law solely for the purpose of securing due recognition and respect for the rights and freedoms of others and of meeting the just requirements of morality, public order and the general welfare in a democratic society.

(3) These rights and freedoms may in no case be exercised contrary to the purposes and principles of the United Nations.

Article 30.

Nothing in this Declaration may be interpreted as implying for any State, group or person any right to engage in any activity or to perform any act aimed at the destruction of any of the rights and freedoms set forth herein.

INTERNATIONAL COVENANT ON CIVIL AND POLITICAL RIGHTS

United Nations (1966)

Article 1.

All peoples have the right of self-determination . . . .

. . . .

Article 4.

1. In time of public emergency which threatens the life of the nation and the existence of which is officially proclaimed, the States Parties to the present Covenant may take measures derogating from their obligations under the present Covenant to the extent strictly required by the exigencies of the situation, provided that such measures are not inconsistent with their other obligations under international law and do not involve discrimination solely on the ground of race, colour, sex, language, religion or social origin.

2. No derogation from articles 6, 7, 8 (paragraphs 1 and 2), 11, 15, 16 and 18 may be made under this provision.

3. Any State Party to the present Covenant availing itself of the right of derogation shall immediately inform the other States Parties to the present Covenant, through the intermediary of the Secretary-General of the United Nations, of the provisions from which it has derogated and of the reasons by which it was actuated . . . .

. . . .

Article 6.

1. Every human being has the inherent right to life. This right shall be protected by law. No one shall be arbitrarily deprived of his life . . . .

Article 7.

No one shall be subjected to torture or to cruel, inhuman or degrading treatment or punishment. In particular, no one shall be subjected without his free consent to medical or scientific experimentation.

Article 8.

1. No one shall be held in slavery; slavery and the slave-trade in all their forms shall be prohibited.

2. No one shall be held in servitude . . .

. . . .

Article 11.

No one shall be imprisoned merely on the ground of inability to fulfill a contractual obligation.

. . . .

Article 15.

No one shall be held guilty of any criminal offence on account of any act or omission which did not constitute a criminal offence, under national or international law, at the time when it was committed . . .

Article 16.

Everyone shall have the right to recognition everywhere as a person before the law.

. . . .

Article 18.

Everyone shall have the right to freedom of thought, conscience, and religion . . .

INTERNATIONAL COVENANT ON ECONOMIC, SOCIAL, AND CULTURAL RIGHTS
United Nations (1966)

Article 2.

1. Each State Party to the present Covenant undertakes to take steps, individually and through international assistance and co-operation, especially economic and technical, to the maximum of its available resources, with a view to achieving progressively the full realization of the rights recognized in the present Covenant by all appropriate means, including particularly the adoption of legislative measures . . . .

. . . .

Article 11.

1. The States Parties to the present Covenant recognize the right of everyone to an adequate standard of living for himself and his family, including adequate food, clothing and housing, and to the continuous improvement of living conditions . . . .

Article 12.

1. The States Parties to the present Covenant recognize the right of everyone

to the enjoyment of the highest attainable standard of physical and mental health.

2. The steps to be taken by the States Parties to the present Covenant to achieve the full realization of this right shall include those necessary for:

(a) The provision for the reduction of the stillbirth-rate and of infant mortality and for the healthy development of the child;

(b) The improvement of all aspects of environmental and industrial hygiene;

(c) The prevention, treatment and control of epidemic, endemic, occupational and other diseases;

(d) The creation of conditions which would assure to all medical service and medical attention in the event of sickness.

Article 13.

1. The States Parties to the present Covenant recognize the right of everyone to education . . . .

NOTES AND QUESTIONS

1. **The United Nations** was formed at the end of World War II as a permanent peace-keeping organization. The charter of the United Nations, signed by the 50 original member nations in San Francisco on June 26, 1945, spells out the organization's goals. The first two goals are "to save succeeding generations from the scourge of war. . . . and to reaffirm faith in fundamental human rights, in the dignity and worth of the human person, in the equal rights of men and women and of nations large and small." After the charter was signed, the adoption of an international bill of rights with legal authority proceeded in three steps: a declaration, treaty-based covenants, and implementation measures.

2. **The Universal Declaration of Human Rights** was adopted by the United Nations General Assembly in 1948, with 48 member states voting in favor of adoption and 8 (Saudi Arabia, South Africa, and the Soviet Union together with 5 other countries whose votes it controlled) abstaining. The declaration was adopted as a "common standard for all people and nations." As Henry Steiner notes, "No other document has so caught the historical moment, achieved the same moral and rhetorical force, or exerted so much influence on the human rights movement as a whole." The rights enumerated in the declaration "stem from the cardinal axiom that all human beings are born free and equal, in dignity and rights, and are endowed with reason and conscience. All the rights and freedoms belong to everybody." These points are spelled out in Articles 1 and 2. Nondiscrimination is the overarching principle. Article 7, for example, is explicit: "All are equal before the law and are entitled without any discrimination to equal protection of the law." Other articles prohibit slavery, torture, and arbitrary detention and protect freedom of expression, assembly, and religion, the right to own property, and the right to work and receive an education. Of special importance to health care professionals is Article 25, which states, in part, "Everyone has the right to a standard of living adequate for the health and well-being of himself and his family,

including food, clothing, housing, and medical care and necessary social services."

Human rights are primarily rights individuals have in relation to governments. Human rights require governments to refrain from doing certain things, such as torturing persons or limiting freedom of religion, and also require that they take actions to make people's lives better, such as providing education and nutrition programs. The United Nations adopted the Universal Declaration of Human Rights as a statement of aspirations. The legal obligations of governments were to derive from formal treaties that member nations would individually sign and incorporate into domestic law. On the development of the UDHR, *see* MARY ANN GLENDON, A WORLD MADE NEW: ELEANOR ROOSEVELT AND THE UNIVERSAL DECLARATION OF HUMAN RIGHTS (2002).

3. **International covenants.** Because of the cold war, with its conflicting ideologies, it took almost 20 years to reach an agreement on the texts of the two human-rights treaties. On December 16, 1966, both the **International Covenant on Civil and Political Rights** and the **International Covenant on Economic, Social, and Cultural Rights** were adopted by the General Assembly and offered for signature and ratification by the member nations. The United States ratified the International Covenant on Civil and Political Rights in 1992, but not surprisingly, given our capitalist economic system with its emphasis on private property, we have yet to act on the International Covenant on Economic, Social, and Cultural Rights. The division of human rights into two separate treaties illustrates the tension between liberal states founded on civil and political rights and socialist and communist welfare states founded on solidarity and the government's obligation to meet basic economic and social needs.

The rights spelled out in the International Covenant on Civil and Political Rights include equality, the right to liberty and security of person, and freedom of movement, religion, expression, and association. The International Covenant on Economic, Social, and Cultural Rights focuses on well-being, including the right to work, the right to receive fair wages, the right to make a decent living, the right to work under safe and healthy conditions, the right to be free from hunger, the right to education, and "the right of everyone to the enjoyment of the highest attainable standard of physical and mental health."

Given the horrors of poverty, disease, and civil wars over the past 50 years, it is easy to dismiss the rights enunciated in these documents as empty gestures. Indeed, Amnesty International, in marking the 50th anniversary of the Universal Declaration of Human Rights, labeled the rights it articulates "little more than a paper promise" for most people in the world. It is certainly true that unadulterated celebration is not in order, but as Kunz noted almost 60 years ago in writing about the birth of the declaration, "In the field of human rights as in other actual problems of international law it is necessary to avoid the Scylla of a pessimistic cynicism and the Charybdis of mere wishful thinking and superficial optimism." Joseph L. Kunz, *The United Nations Declaration of Human Rights*, 43 AM. J. INT'L L. 316, 321 (1949).

4. **The right to health** has been given more precise definition in a report of the Committee on Economic, Social, and Cultural Rights, the treaty entity formed to help implement the International Covenant on Economic, Social, and Cultural

Rights. The document is known as General Comment No. 14 and was issued in 2000. Among its most important provisions are the following:

Health is a fundamental human right indispensable for the exercise of other human rights . . .

4. . . . the right to health embraces a wide range of socio-economic factors that promote conditions in which people can lead a healthy life, and extends to the underlying determinants of health, such as food and nutrition, housing, access to safe and potable water and adequate sanitation, safe and healthy working conditions, and a healthy environment.

8. The right to health is not to be understood as a right to be healthy. The right to health contains both freedoms and entitlements. The freedoms include the right to control one's health and body, including sexual and reproductive freedom, and the right to be free from interference, such as the right to be free from torture, non-consensual medical treatment and experimentation. By contrast, the entitlements include the right to a system of health protection which provides equality of opportunity for people to enjoy the highest attainable level of health.

11. . . . . the right to health . . . [is] an inclusive right extending not only to timely and appropriate health care but also to the underlying determinants of health, such as access to safe and potable water and adequate sanitation, an adequate supply of safe food, nutrition and housing, healthy occupational and environmental conditions, and access to health-related education and information, including on sexual and reproductive health . . .

12. The right to health in all its forms and at all levels contains the following interrelated and essential elements, the precise application of which will depend on the conditions prevailing in a particular State party:

(a) *Availability.* Functioning public health and health-care facilities, goods and services, as well as programs, have to be available . . . .

(b) *Accessibility.* Health facilities, goods and services have to be accessible to everyone without discrimination . . . physical accessibility . . . economic accessibility (affordability) . . . information accessibility . . . .

(c) *Acceptability* . . . All health facilities, goods and services must be respectful of medical ethics and culturally appropriate . . . .

(d) *Quality.* . . . must also be scientifically and medically appropriate and of good quality. This requires, *inter alia*, skilled medical personnel, scientifically approved and unexpired drugs and hospital equipment, safe and potable water, and adequate sanitation. . . .

17. The right to health facilities . . . [includes] the provision of . . . equal and timely access to basic preventive, curative, rehabilitative health services and health education; regular screening programs; appropriate treatment of prevalent diseases, illnesses, injuries and disabilities, prefer-

ably at community level; the provision of essential drugs; and appropriate mental health treatment and care . . . .

. . . .

33. The right to health, like all human rights, imposes three types or levels of obligations on States parties: the obligations to *respect, protect,* and *fulfill.*

34. States are under the obligation to *respect* the right to health by, *inter alia*, refraining from denying or limiting equal access for all persons, including prisoners or detainees, minorities, asylum seekers and illegal immigrants, to preventive, curative and palliative health services; abstaining from enforcing discriminatory practices as a State policy; and abstaining from imposing discriminatory practices relating to women's health status and needs . . . .

35. Obligations to *protect* include, *inter alia*, the duties of States to adopt legislation or to take other measures ensuring equal access to health care and health-related services provided by third parties; to ensure that privatization of the health sector does not constitute a threat to the availability, accessibility, acceptability and quality of health facilities, goods and services; to control the marketing of medical equipment and medicines by third parties; and to ensure that medical practitioners and other health professionals meet appropriate standards of education, skill and ethical codes of conduct . . . .

36. The obligation to *fulfill* requires States parties, *inter alia*, to give sufficient recognition to the right to health in the national political and legal systems, preferably by way of legislative implementation, and to adopt a national health policy with a detailed plan for realizing the right to health. States must ensure provision of health care, including immunization programs against the major infectious diseases, and ensure equal access for all to the underlying determinants of health, such as nutritiously safe food and potable drinking water, basic sanitation and adequate housing and living conditions. Public health infrastructures should provide for sexual and reproductive health services, including safe motherhood, particularly in rural areas . . . .

. . . .

43. . . . . core obligations [minimum essential level of the right] include at least the following obligations:

    (a) To ensure the right of access to health facilities, goods and services on a nondiscriminatory basis, especially for vulnerable or marginalized groups;

    (b) To ensure access to the minimum essential food which is nutritionally adequate and safe, to ensure freedom from hunger to everyone;

(c) To ensure access to basic shelter, housing, and sanitation, and an adequate supply of safe and potable water;

(d) To provide essential drugs, as from time to time defined under the WHO Action Program on Essential Drugs;

(e) To ensure equitable distribution of all health facilities, goods and services;

(f) To adopt and implement a national public health strategy and plan of action, on the basis of epidemiological evidence, addressing the health concerns of the whole population; the strategy and plan of action shall be devised, and periodically reviewed, on the basis of a participatory and transparent process; they shall include methods, such as right to health indicators and benchmarks, by which progress can be closely monitored; the process by which the strategy and plan of action are devised, as well as their content, shall give particular attention to all vulnerable or marginalized groups.

. . . .

47. . . . a State party cannot, under any circumstances whatsoever, justify its noncompliance with the core obligations set out in paragraph 43, which are non-derogable.

5. **Global public health and human rights.** World War II, arguably the first truly global war, led many nations to acknowledge the universality of human rights and the responsibility of governments to promote them. Jonathan Mann perceptively noted that the AIDS epidemic can be viewed as the first global epidemic, because it is taking place at a time when all countries are linked both electronically and by easy transportation. Like World War II, this tragedy requires us to think in new ways and to develop effective methods to prevent and treat disease on a global level. Globalization is a mercantile and ecologic fact; it is also a reality in health care. The challenge facing medicine and health care is to develop a global language and strategy to improve the health of all the world's citizens.

Clinical medicine is practiced one patient at a time. The language of medical ethics is the language of self-determination and beneficence: Doing what is in the best interests of the patient with the patient's informed consent. This language is powerful, but often has little application in countries where physicians are scarce and medical resources very limited.

Public health deals with populations and prevention of disease — the necessary frame of reference in the global context. In the context of clinical practice, the treatment of human immunodeficiency virus infection with a combination of antiretroviral medicines makes sense. In the context of worldwide public health, however, such treatment was initially available to less than 5% of people with AIDS. To control AIDS, it was necessary to deal directly with discrimination, immigration status, and access to health care. Population-based prevention is required to address all global epidemics effectively. Nonetheless, the field of public health itself has had an extraordinarily difficult time developing ethical language. This problem of language has two basic causes: the incredibly large array of factors that influence health at the population level, and the emphasis by contemporary public health professionals on individualism and market forces rather than on the collective responsibility for social welfare.

On the 50th anniversary of the Universal Declaration of Human Rights, George Annas, following the lead of Jonathan Mann, the father of the "health and human rights" field, suggested that the declaration itself sets forth the ethics of public health, since its goal is to provide the conditions under which people can flourish. This is also the goal of public health. The unification of public health and human-rights efforts throughout the world could be a powerful force to improve the lives of every person. George J. Annas, *The Universal Declaration of Human Rights at 50*, 339 NEW ENG. J. MED 1778 (1998).

6. The "Siracusa Principles" describe the conditions under which emergency powers can be used by the state to limit human rights. U.N., ECONOMIC AND SOCIAL COUNCIL, SUB-COMMISSION ON PREVENTION OF DISCRIMINATION AND PROTECTION OF MINORITIES, SIRACUSA PRINCIPLES ON THE LIMITATION AND DEROGATION OF PROVISIONS IN THE INTERNATIONAL COVENANT ON CIVIL AND POLITICAL RIGHTS, U.N. Doc. E/CN4/ 1984/4, Annex (1984):

LIMITATION CLAUSES

A.   General Interpretative Principles Relating to the Justification of Limitations

1.   No limitations or grounds for applying them to rights guaranteed by the Covenant are permitted other than those contained in the terms of the Covenant itself.

2.   The scope of a limitation referred to in the Covenant shall not be interpreted so as to jeopardize the essence of the right concerned.

3.   All limitation clauses shall be interpreted strictly and in favor of the rights at issue.

4.   All limitations shall be interpreted in the light and context of the particular right concerned.

. . . .

9.   No limitation on a right recognized by the Covenant shall discriminate contrary to Article 2, paragraph 1.

10.   Whenever a limitation is required in the terms of the Covenant to be "necessary," this term implies that the limitation:

> (a) is based on one of the grounds justifying limitations recognized by the relevant article of the Covenant,

> (b) responds to a pressing public or social need,

> (c) pursues a legitimate aim, and

> (d) is proportionate to that aim.

Any assessment as to the necessity of a limitation shall be made on objective considerations.

11.   In applying a limitation, a state shall use no more restrictive means than are required for the achievement of the purpose of the limitation.

12.   The burden of justifying a limitation upon a right guaranteed under the Covenant lies with the state.

B.   Interpretative Principles Relating to Specific Limitation Clauses

. . . .

iv.   "public health"

25.   Public health may be invoked as a ground for limiting certain rights in order to allow a state to take measures dealing with a serious threat to the health of the population or individual members of the population. These measures must be specifically aimed at preventing disease or injury or providing care for the sick and injured.

26.   Due regard shall be had to the international health regulations of the World Health Organization.

7.   **International health regulations**, promulgated by the WHO, have always been problematic because the WHO itself is founded on the theory that each state party retains its complete sovereignty. WHO is the premier health organization of the United Nations. (Up to date information on its ongoing activities is available on its website: www.who.int.) Since WHO is a UN organization, each member state has a vote in policy-making, and individual states must voluntarily agree to take actions (such as monitoring and reporting infectious diseases). As noted in the discussion on SARS in Chapter 6, state sovereignty can obstruct health regulation goals if a country wants to prevent an investigation of an outbreak by WHO because it is worried about discouraging trade and tourism.

After the SARS epidemic, the International Health Regulations were amended in 2005. The new regulations are designed, among other things, to encourage the development of more effective public health surveillance methods and to encourage information sharing, especially for "potential public health emergencies of international concern" defined as "an extraordinary event which is determined, as provided in these regulations, (i) to constitute a public health threat to other States through the international spread of disease, and (ii) to potentially require a coordinated response." Other provisions include:

Article 5, Surveillance

Each State Party shall develop, strengthen and maintain, as soon as possible but not later than five years from the entry into force of these Regulations for that State Party, the capacity to detect, assess, notify and report events in accordance with these Regulations, as specified in Annex 1 [of the regulations].

Article 6, Notification

1. Each State Party shall assess events occurring within its territory by using the decision instrument in Annex 2. Each State Party shall notify WHO, by the most efficient means of communication available, by way of the National IHR Focal Point, and within 24 hours of assessment of public health information, of all events which may constitute a public health emergency of international concern, within its territory in accordance with the decision instrument, as well as any health measure implemented in response to those events . . . .

2. Following a notification, a State Party shall continue to communicate to WHO timely, accurate and sufficiently detailed public health information available to it on the notified event, where possible including case definitions, laboratory results, source and type of the risk, number of cases and deaths, conditions affecting the spread of the disease and the health measures employed; and report, when necessary, the difficulties faced and support needed in responding to the potential public health emergency of international concern.

8. **Biological Conventions.** There are also treaties that apply directly to bioterrorism and biowarfare, the most important of which is the 1972 Biological and Toxin Weapons Convention. Article I sets forth its basic operative language:

Each State Party to this Convention undertakes never in any circumstance to develop, produce, stockpile or otherwise acquire or retain:

(1) Microbial or other biological agents, or toxins whatever their origin or method of production, of types and in quantities that have no justification for prophylactic, protective or other peaceful purposes;

(2) Weapons, equipment or means of delivery designed to use such agents or toxins for hostile purposes or in armed conflict.

C.   LITIGATING THE RIGHT TO HEALTH

MINISTER OF HEALTH v. TREATMENT ACTION CAMPAIGN
South Africa Constitutional Court, 2002(10) BCLR 1033(CC)

The HIV/AIDS pandemic in South Africa has been described as "an incomprehensible calamity" and "the most important challenge facing South Africa since the birth of our new democracy" and government's fight against "this scourge" as "a top priority". It "has claimed millions of lives, inflicting pain and grief, causing fear and uncertainty, and threatening the economy." These are not the words of alarmists but are taken from a Department of Health publication in 2000 and a ministerial foreword to an earlier departmental publication.

This appeal is directed at reversing orders made in a High Court against government because of perceived shortcomings in its response to an aspect of the

HIV/AIDS challenge. The court found that government had not reasonably addressed the need to reduce the risk of HIV-positive mothers transmitting the disease to their babies at birth. More specifically the finding was that government had acted unreasonably in (a) refusing to make an antiretroviral drug called Nevirapine available in the public health sector where the attending doctor considered it medically indicated, and (b) not setting out a time-frame for a national program to prevent mother-to-child transmission of HIV.

The case started as an application in the High Court in Pretoria on 21 August 2001. The applicants were a number of associations and members of civil society concerned with the treatment of people with HIV/AIDS and with the prevention of new infections. In this judgment they are referred to collectively as "the applicants." The principal actor among them was the Treatment Action Campaign (TAC). The respondents were the national Minister of Health and the respective members of the executive councils (MECs) responsible for health in all provinces save the Western Cape. They are referred to collectively as "the government" or "government."

Government, as part of a formidable array of responses to the pandemic, devised a program to deal with mother-to-child transmission of HIV at birth and identified Nevirapine as its drug of choice for this purpose. The program imposes restrictions on the availability of Nevirapine in the public health sector. This is where the first of two main issues in the case arose. The applicants contended that these restrictions are unreasonable when measured against the Constitution, which commands the State and all its organs to give effect to the rights guaranteed by the Bill of Rights. This duty is put thus by sections 7(2) and 8(1) of the Constitution respectively:

> 7(2) The State must respect, protect, promote and fulfill the rights in the Bill of Rights.
>
> . . . .
>
> 8(1) The Bill of Rights applies to all law, and binds the legislature, the executive, the judiciary and all organs of State.

At issue here is the right given to everyone to have access to public health care services and the right of children to be afforded special protection. These rights are expressed in the following terms in the Bill of Rights:

27(1) Everyone has the right to have access to—

(a) health care services, including reproductive health care; . . .

(2) The State must take reasonable legislative and other measures, within its available resources, to achieve the progressive realization of each of these rights . . . .

28(1) Every child has the right . . . .

(c) to basic nutrition, shelter, basic health care services and social services.

The second main issue also arises out of the provisions of sections 27 and 28 of the Constitution. It is whether government is constitutionally obliged and had to be ordered forthwith to plan and implement an effective, comprehensive and progressive program for the prevention of mother-to-child transmission of HIV throughout the country.

. . . .

The State is obliged to take reasonable measures progressively to eliminate or reduce the large areas of severe deprivation that afflict our society. The courts will guarantee that the democratic processes are protected so as to ensure accountability, responsiveness and openness, as the Constitution requires in section 1. As the Bill of Rights indicates, their function in respect of socio-economic rights is directed towards ensuring that legislative and other measures taken by the State are reasonable. As this Court said in *Grootboom*, "[i]t is necessary to recognize that a wide range of possible measures could be adopted by the State to meet its obligations . . . ." As was said in *Soobramoney*: "The State has to manage its limited resources in order to address all these claims. There will be times when this requires it to adopt a holistic approach to the larger needs of society rather than to focus on the specific needs of particular individuals within society."

Courts are ill-suited to adjudicate upon issues where court orders could have multiple social and economic consequences for the community. The Constitution contemplates rather a restrained and focused role for the courts, namely, to require the State to take measures to meet its constitutional obligations and to subject the reasonableness of these measures to evaluation. Such determinations of reasonableness may in fact have budgetary implications, but are not in themselves directed at rearranging budgets. In this way the judicial, legislative and executive functions achieve appropriate constitutional balance

We therefore conclude that section 27(1) of the Constitution does not give rise to a self-standing and independent positive right enforceable irrespective of the considerations mentioned in section 27(2). Sections 27(1) and 27(2) must be read together as defining the scope of the positive rights that everyone has and the corresponding obligations on the State to "respect, protect, promote and fulfill" such rights. The rights conferred by sections 26(1) and 27(1) are to have "access" to the services that the State is obliged to provide in terms of sections 26(2) and 27(2)

. . . .

It is the applicants' case that the measures adopted by government to provide access to health care services to HIV-positive pregnant women were deficient in two material respects: first, because they prohibited the administration of Nevirapine at public hospitals and clinics outside the research and training sites; and second, because they failed to implement a comprehensive program for the prevention of mother-to-child transmission of HIV . . . . The applicants' contentions raise two questions, namely, is the policy of confining the supply of Nevirapine reasonable in the circumstances; and does government have a comprehensive policy for the prevention of mother-to-child transmission of HIV.

In deciding on the policy to confine Nevirapine to the research and training sites, the cost of the drug itself was not a factor . . . . In substance four reasons were advanced in the affidavits for confining the administration of Nevirapine to the research and training sites. First, concern was expressed about the efficacy of

Nevirapine where the "comprehensive package" is not available . . . . Secondly, there was a concern that the administration of Nevirapine to the mother and her child might lead to the development of resistance to the efficacy of Nevirapine and related antiretrovirals in later years. Thirdly, there was a perceived safety issue. Nevirapine is a potent drug and it is not known what hazards may attach to its use. Finally, there was the question whether the public health system has the capacity to provide the package. It was contended on behalf of government that Nevirapine should be administered only with the "full package" and that it was not reasonably possible to do this on a comprehensive basis because of the lack of trained counselors and counseling facilities and also budgetary constraints which precluded such a comprehensive scheme being implemented.

We deal with each of these issues in turn. First, the concern about efficacy. It is clear from the evidence that the provision of Nevirapine will save the lives of a significant number of infants even if it is administered without the full package and support services that are available at the research and training sites. Mother-to-child transmission of HIV can take place during pregnancy, at birth and as a result of breastfeeding . . . . The wealth of scientific material produced by both sides makes plain that seroconversion of HIV takes place in some, but not all, cases and that Nevirapine thus remains to some extent efficacious in combating mother-to-child transmission even if the mother breast-feeds her baby. As far as resistance is concerned, the only relevance is the possible need to treat the mother and/or the child at some time in the future. Although resistant strains of HIV might exist after a single dose of Nevirapine, this mutation is likely to be transient. At most there is a possibility of such resistance persisting, and although this possibility cannot be excluded, its weight is small in comparison with the potential benefit of providing a single tablet of Nevirapine to the mother and a few drops to her baby at the time of birth. The prospects of the child surviving if infected are so slim and the nature of the suffering so grave that the risk of some resistance manifesting at some time in the future is well worth running.

The evidence shows that safety is no more than a hypothetical issue. The only evidence of potential harm concerns risks attaching to the administration of Nevirapine as a chronic medication on an ongoing basis for the treatment of HIV-positive persons. There is, however, no evidence to suggest that a dose of Nevirapine to both mother and child at the time of birth will result in any harm to either of them . . . . The policy of confining Nevirapine to research and training sites fails to address the needs of mothers and their newborn children who do not have access to these sites. It fails to distinguish between the evaluation of programs for reducing mother-to-child transmission and the need to provide access to health care services required by those who do not have access to the sites.

In *Grootboom* (supra) this Court held that: "[t]o be reasonable, measures cannot leave out of account the degree and extent of the denial of the right they endeavor to realize. Those whose needs are the most urgent and whose ability to enjoy all rights therefore is most in peril, must not be ignored by the measures aimed at achieving realization of the right . . . . "

In evaluating government's policy, regard must be had to the fact that this case is concerned with newborn babies whose lives might be saved by the administration of Nevirapine to mother and child at the time of birth. . . . the provision of a single dose of Nevirapine to mother and child where medically indicated is a simple, cheap and potentially lifesaving medical intervention.

CHILDREN'S RIGHTS

There is another consideration that is material. This case is concerned with newborn children. Sections 28(1) (b) and (c) of the Constitution provide that

[e]very child has the right—

    (b)   to family care or parental care, or to appropriate alternative care when removed from the family environment;

    (c)   to basic nutrition, shelter, basic health care services and social services.

The provision of a single dose of Nevirapine to mother and child for the purpose of protecting the child against the transmission of HIV is, as far as the children are concerned, essential. Their needs are "most urgent" and their inability to have access to Nevirapine profoundly affects their ability to enjoy all rights to which they are entitled. Their rights are "most in peril" as a result of the policy that has been adopted and are most affected by a rigid and inflexible policy that excludes them from having access to Nevirapine.

The State is obliged to ensure that children are accorded the protection contemplated by section 28 that arises when the implementation of the right to parental or family care is lacking. Here we are concerned with children born in public hospitals and clinics to mothers who are for the most part indigent and unable to gain access to private medical treatment which is beyond their means. They and their children are in the main dependent upon the State to make health care services available to them . . . .

We are also conscious of the daunting problems confronting government as a result of the pandemic. And besides the pandemic, the State faces huge demands in relation to access to education, land, housing, health care, food, water and social security. These are the socio-economic rights entrenched in the Constitution, and the State is obliged to take reasonable legislative and other measures within its available resources to achieve the progressive realization of each of them. In the light of our history this is an extraordinarily difficult task. Nonetheless it is an obligation imposed on the State by the Constitution . . . .

South African courts have a wide range of powers at their disposal to ensure that the Constitution is upheld. These include mandatory and structural interdicts. How they should exercise those powers depends on the circumstances of each particular case. Here due regard must be paid to the roles of the legislature and the executive in a democracy. What must be made clear, however, is that when it is appropriate to do so, courts may — and if need be must — use their wide powers to make orders that affect policy as well as legislation.* * * In the present case we have identified aspects of government policy that are inconsistent with the Constitution. The decision not to make Nevirapine available at hospitals and clinics other than the research and training sites is central to the entire policy. Once that restriction is removed, government will be able to devise and implement a more comprehensive policy that will give access to health care services to HIV-positive mothers and their newborn children, and will include the administration of Nevirapine where that is appropriate. The policy as reformulated must meet the constitutional requirement of providing reasonable measures within available resources for the progressive realization of the rights of such women and new-born children. This may also require, where that is necessary, that counselors at places other than at the research and training sites be trained in counseling for the use of Nevirapine. We will formulate a declaration to address these issues . . . .

It is essential that there be a concerted national effort to combat the HIV/AIDS pandemic. The government has committed itself to such an effort. We have held that its policy fails to meet constitutional standards because it excludes those who could reasonably be included where such treatment is medically indicated to combat mother-to-child transmission of HIV. . . . We consider it important that all sectors of the community, in particular civil society, should co-operate in the steps taken to achieve this goal. In our view that will be facilitated by spelling out the steps necessary to comply with the Constitution. We will do this on the basis of the policy that government has adopted as the best means of combating mother-to-child transmission of HIV, which is to make use of Nevirapine for this purpose. Government must retain the right to adapt the policy, consistent with its constitutional obligations, should it consider it appropriate to do so. The order that we make has regard to this . . . . We accordingly make the following orders:

1. The orders made by the High Court are set aside and the following orders are substituted.

2. It is declared that:

    (a) Sections 27(1) and (2) of the Constitution require the government to devise and implement within its available resources a comprehensive and coordinated program to realize progressively the rights of pregnant women and their newborn children to have access to health services to combat mother-to-child transmission of HIV.

    (b) The program to be realized progressively within available resources must include reasonable measures for counseling and testing pregnant women for HIV, counseling HIV-positive pregnant women on the options open to them to reduce the risk of mother-to-child transmission of HIV, and making appropriate treatment available to them for such purposes.

    (c) The policy for reducing the risk of mother-to-child transmission of HIV as formulated and implemented by government fell short of compliance with the requirements in subparagraphs (a) and (b) in that:

        (i) Doctors at public hospitals and clinics other than the research and training sites were not enabled to prescribe Nevirapine to reduce the risk of mother-to-child transmission of HIV even where it was medically indicated and adequate facilities existed for the testing and counseling of the pregnant women concerned.

        (ii) The policy failed to make provision for counselors at hospitals and clinics other than at research and training sites to be trained in counseling for the use of Nevirapine as a means of reducing the risk of mother-to-child transmission of HIV.

3. Government is ordered without delay to:

    (a) Remove the restrictions that prevent Nevirapine from being made available for the purpose of reducing the risk of mother-to-child transmission of HIV at public hospitals and clinics that are not research and training sites.

    (b) Permit and facilitate the use of Nevirapine for the purpose of reducing the risk of mother-to-child transmission of HIV and to make it available for this purpose at hospitals and clinics when in the judgment of the attending medical practitioner acting in consultation with the medical superintendent of the facility concerned this is medically indicated, which shall if necessary include that the mother concerned has been appropriately tested and counseled.

    (c) Make provision if necessary for counselors based at public hospitals and clinics other than the research and training sites to be trained for the counseling necessary for the use of Nevirapine to reduce the risk of mother-to-child transmission of HIV.

    (d) Take reasonable measures to extend the testing and counseling facilities at hospitals and clinics throughout the public health sector to facilitate and expedite the use of Nevirapine for the purpose of reducing the risk of mother-to-child transmission of HIV.

4. The orders made in paragraph 3 do not preclude government from adapting its policy in a manner consistent with the Constitution if equally appropriate or better methods become available to it for the prevention of mother-to-child transmission of HIV . . . .

NOTES AND QUESTIONS

1. The South African constitution. The provisions in the South African constitution discussed in this case are modeled on those in the International Covenant on Economic, Social and Cultural Rights — and placing the provisions of this international treaty in legislation and constitutional provisions of individual states is an especially effective way of making international law integral to national law. Note that Article 12 of the Covenant includes not only appropriate health care, but also the underlying determinants of health, including clean water, sanitation, safe food, housing, and health-related education. In addition, South Africa's constitution adopts specific provisions in the Convention on the Rights of the Child, which, of course, have special application in this case.

2. Access to drugs and litigation. The decision in the Nevirapine case illustrates both the strength and the weakness of relying on courts to determine specific applications of the right to health. The strength is that the right to health is a legal right, and since there can be no legal right without a remedy, courts will provide a remedy for violations of the right to health. In this regard, it is worth noting not only that the right to health and access to health care articulated in the Universal Declaration of Human Rights has been given more specific meaning in the International Covenant on Economic, Social, and Cultural Rights and other internationally binding documents on human rights, but also that these rights have been written into the constitutions of many countries, including South Africa. The widespread failure of governments to take the right to health seriously, however, means that we are still a long way from the realization of this right. Nonetheless, the activism of many nongovernmental organizations, such as the Treatment Action Campaign, in the area of health rights, provides some ground for optimism that government inaction will not go unchallenged.

The weakness of relying on courts is that the subject matter of the right to health in a courtroom struggle is likely to be narrow, involving interventions such as kidney dialysis or Nevirapine therapy. The HIV epidemic demands a comprehensive strategy of treatment, care and prevention, including education, adequate nutrition, clean water, and nondiscrimination.

3. **Social rights and resource allocation.** The Nevirapine case was the third case in which the Constitutional Court had been asked to enforce a socioeconomic right under the South African constitution. The first, *Soobramoney v. Minister of Health*, 1997 (12) BCLR 1696 (CC), was also a right-to-health case. It involved a 41-year-old man with chronic renal failure and a history of stroke, heart disease and diabetes, who was not eligible for a kidney transplant and therefore required lifelong dialysis to survive. The renal-dialysis unit in the region where he lived, which had 20 dialysis machines — not nearly enough to provide dialysis for everyone who required it — had a policy of accepting only patients with acute renal failure. The health department argued that this policy met the government's duty to provide emergency care under the constitution. Patients with chronic renal failure, like the petitioner, did not automatically qualify.

In considering whether the constitution required the health department to provide a sufficient number of machines to offer dialysis to everyone whose life could be saved by it, the court observed that under the constitution, the state's obligation to provide health care services was qualified by its "available resources." The court noted that offering extremely expensive medical treatments to everyone would make "substantial inroads into the health budget . . . to the prejudice of the other needs which the state has to meet." The Constitutional Court ultimately decided that the administrators of provincial health services, not the courts, should set budgetary priorities and that the courts should not interfere with decisions that are rational and made "in good faith by those political organs and medical authorities whose responsibility it is to deal with such matters."

Likewise, in *South Africa v. Grootboom*, 2000 (11) BCLR 1169 (CC), a case involving the right to housing, the Constitutional Court determined that although the state is obligated to act positively to ameliorate the conditions of the homeless, it "is not obligated to go beyond available resources or to realize these rights immediately." The constitutional requirement is that the right to housing be "progressively realized." Nonetheless, the court noted, there is "at the very least, a negative obligation placed upon the state and all other entities and persons to desist from preventing or impairing the right of access to adequate housing."

Applying the rulings in these two cases to the Nevirapine case, the Constitutional Court reasonably concluded that the right to health care services "does not give rise to a self-standing and independent fulfillment right" that is enforceable irrespective of available resources. Nonetheless, the government's obligation to respect rights, as articulated in the housing case, applies equally to the right to health care services. *See* George J. Annas, *The Right to Health and the Nevirapine Case in South Africa*, 348 NEW ENG. J. MED. 750 (2003). For a discussion of a similar case from Venezuela, see Mary Ann Torres, *The Human Right to Health, National Courts, and Access to HIV/AIDS Treatment: A Case Study from Venezuela*, 3 CHICAGO J. INT'L L. 1 (2002). For a discussion of ways governments might address budget constraints, see the World Bank report by Ajay Tandon and Cheryl Cashin, ASSESSING PUBLIC EXPENDITURE ON HEALTH FROM A FISCAL SPACE PERSPECTIVE (2010).

4. **Jonathan Mann and Paul Farmer.** Jonathan Mann was the first to observe that "health and human rights are inextricably linked." Jonathan M. Mann, *Human Rights and AIDS: The Future of the Pandemic*, in HEALTH AND HUMAN RIGHTS: A READER 216–26 (Jonathan M. Mann et al. eds., 1999). Paul Farmer has argued that "the most important question facing modern medicine involves human rights." Farmer noted that many poor people have no access to modern medicine and concluded, "The more effective the treatment, the greater the injustice meted out to those who do not have access to care." Paul Farmer, *The Major Infectious Diseases in the World — To Treat or Not to Treat?* 345 N. ENG. J MED. 208 (2001). *See also* PAUL FARMER, INFECTIONS AND INEQUALITIES: THE MODERN PLAGUES (Updated Ed. 1999); AMARTYA SEN, DEVELOPMENT AS FREEDOM (1999); LAURIE WERMUTH, GLOBAL INEQUALITY AND HUMAN NEEDS: HEALTH AND ILLNESS IN AN INCREASINGLY UNEQUAL WORLD (2003).

5. **The war on terror and human rights.** A major concern, of course, is that the entire human rights movement could fall victim to the "war on terror." As Richard Falk has expressed it:

> By highlighting "terrorism" there is an almost unavoidable tendency to perceive issues through the lens of the September 11 attacks, and to downplay such other issues as are associated with the inequities arising from the operation of the world economy or with the practices that produce environmental decay. In these respects from the perspective of human rights' priorities, the highlighting of the security agenda inevitably leads to a downplaying of economic and social rights, the right of self-determination, health issues, and rights associated with environmental protection. It is to be expected that academic discussions of security would take different forms in other parts of the world, that the American context of discussion is in this respect rather the exception than the rule.

Richard Falk, *Human Rights: A Descending Spiral*, in HUMAN RIGHTS IN THE "WAR ON TERROR" 229 (Richard Ashby Wilson ed., 2005).

6. **HIV/AIDS and poverty.** Many commentators approach the HIV/AIDS pandemic from the perspective they would describe as "social justice." How does this perspective differ from a "health and human rights" perspective? Jonathan Mann, the founder of the health and human rights field, has observed that most of the problems of health are problems of poverty — nonetheless, he also noted that

framing them as poverty problems makes them seem insurmountable and intractable. Better, he thought, to focus on the basic human rights which most people support and whose recognition can dramatically improve health status. *See* MADISON POWERS & RUTH FADEN, SOCIAL JUSTICE (2006); Emi Suzuki et al., POVERTY AND HEALTH MONITORING REPORT (World Bank, 2012).

7. **HIV/AIDS and priority setting.** Consider how treatment and prevention go hand in hand. Assuming that not everyone can get access to treatment immediately, how should public health officials prioritize who should get access first? Do we need an explicit rationing scheme that puts parents, workers, children, or some other group at the top of the priority list? How should such a list be constructed and who should construct it? Would it be an inherent violation of the nondiscrimination basis of the human rights movement?

Of course, these same issues will be faced in the event of an epidemic or bioterrorist attack — who should be treated first with available drugs and vaccines? In this regard, the CDC has suggested priorities for flu vaccinations, both in the yearly flu (when supplies are short) and in the event of an avian pandemic, when vaccine will not be immediately available to anyone. Who should be at the top of the distribution list and why? *See, e.g.,* Alfred I. Tauber, *Medicine, Public Health, and the Ethics of Rationing,* 45 PERSPECTIVES IN BIOLOGY & MED. 16 (2002); Ezekiel Emanuel & Alan Wertheimer, *Who Should Get Influenza Vaccine When Not All Can?,* 312 SCIENCE 854 (2006); George J. Annas, *The Prostitute, the Playboy, and the Poet: Rationing Schemes for Organ Transplantation,* 75 AM. J. PUB. HEALTH 187 (1985).

8. **Universal access to treatment.** The editor of *The Lancet,* Richard Horton, was far less impressed by the August 2006 International AIDS meeting in Toronto than others. The meeting, for example, committed to a goal of "universal access to comprehensive prevention programs, treatment, care and support by 2010." Unfortunately, as Horton notes,

> . . . the opportunity to produce a roadmap to reach the 2010 target of universal access was squandered. Rarely has there been a meeting that felt so disengaged from a global predicament of such historic proportions. The agenda in Toronto was unfocused, giving prime air time to celebrities, such as Bill Gates and Bill Clinton, while largely ignoring Africa [even though] Africa bears the greatest burden of AIDS today — 24.5 million of 38.6 million people with HIV.

Richard Horton, *A Prescription for AIDS 2006–10,* 368 THE LANCET 726–28 (2006). Horton's essay echoes the more generalized arguments of LAURIE GARRETT, BETRAYAL OF TRUST: THE COLLAPSE OF GLOBAL PUBLIC HEALTH (2000), a critical pre-9/11 look at global public health dedicated to Jonathan Mann. The President's Emergency Plan for AIDS Relief (PEPFAR), initiated in 2003, has made some progress. *See* Wafaa M. El-Sadr et al., *Scale-Up of HIV Treatment through PEPFAR: A Historic Public Health Achievement,* 60 (Supp. 3) J. ACQUIR. IMMUNE DEFIC. SYNDR. S96 (2012). A criticism of PEPFAR is that its focus on HIV/AIDS deflects attention and resources from other health problems.

9.   **The role of private foundations.** The stars of the 2006 AIDS meeting were Bill Gates and Bill Clinton, based largely on their work in donating and raising private funds for AIDS research and treatment. Their activities and status raise some fundamental questions for public health advocates. Why do governments fail to adequately fund public health programs? And what is the role of the private sector in public health? Are public-private partnerships the future of public health? *See* Public Health, Ethics, and Equity (Sudhir Anand et al., eds, 2004).

Bill Gates has decided that his foundation will put most of its resources into global health initiatives, especially HIV/AIDS, because he believes that this is the area in which you can get the most return on your investment in terms of lives saved. Warren Buffet, the second richest man in the US after Gates, has announced that he will leave most of his fortune to the Gates Foundation, because he believes they have the right approach and his own foundation could not do it better. Private charity is to be admired and foundation funding is almost always welcome. But what does this say about public health to note that the Gates Foundation annually provides more funding for public health initiatives than the entire budget of the World Health Organization? Gates has said that he got most of his philanthropic investment ideas from reading a report by the World Bank, which is still well worth reading. World Bank, World Development Report 1993: Investing in Health (1993).

The Bill and Melinda Gates Foundation was interested in developing an AIDS vaccine, but has branched out. In 2000, Foundation financing launched the Global Alliance for Vaccines and Immunisation (GAVI), a public-private partnership that also includes WHO, UNICEF, and the World Bank. Vaccines are, of course, the most basic of successful public health interventions, in that they can prevent disease in populations. Nonetheless, even the limited quest to provide already existing and effective vaccines to the world's children has been often overwhelmed by politics. *See, e.g.,* William Muraskin, The Politics of International Health: The Children's Vaccine Initiative and the Struggle to Develop Vaccines for the Third World (1998).

10.   **Pharmaceutical patenting.** One of the major legal issues involving world health of the past decade has been the debate around pharmaceutical patenting and profits. Although almost everyone now realizes that by itself providing drugs, without a public health infrastructure to deliver them and care for patients, is not practical, nonetheless the cost of drugs remains a critical issue to providing decent care, especially for HIV/AIDS, in many countries. An excellent introduction to this subject is contained in Symposium, *Globalization of Pharmaceuticals: International Regulatory Issues*, 32 Am. J. L. & Med. 153 (2006). *See also* Ellen 't Hoen, *TRIPS, Pharmaceuticals Patents, and Access to Essential Medicines: A Long Way from Seattle to Doha*, 3 Chi. J. Int'l L. 27 (2002); Kevin Outterson, *Pharmaceutical Arbitrage: Balancing Access and Innovation in International Prescription Drug Markets*, 5 Yale J. Health Pol'y L. & Ethics 193 (2005).

11.   **Social justice.** Norman Daniels has argued persuasively that bioethics should broaden its agenda from the doctor-patient relationship to include public health and population problems and should do so based on a social justice rather

than a human rights perspective. The last three items he urges bioethicists to add
to their agenda are to:

10)   assess the implications of the obligation not to harm for reducing health
inequalities internationally;

11)   develop an account of justice for the evolving international institutions and
rule-making bodies that have an impact on international health inequalities; and

12)   examine Promethean challenges from the perspective of their impact on
international health inequalities and obligations of justice regarding them.

Norman Daniels, *Equity and Population Health: Toward a Broader Bioethics
Agenda*, 36(4) HASTINGS CENTER REP. 22, 33 (2006).

12.   Bioethics. Other commentators prefer to keep bioethics at some distance
from public health. Jonathan Mann, for example, has written that he believes
bioethics is the correct language for medicine, but that human rights is the proper
language for public health. *See, e.g.*, Jonathan Mann, *Medicine and Public Health,
Ethics and Human Rights*, 27(3) HASTINGS CENTER REP. 6 (1997). Ron Bayer and
Amy Fairchild would go much further, arguing that modern bioethics has no place
in public health ethics. In their words, "Bioethics cannot serve as a basis for
thinking about the balances required in the defense of the public's health. As we
commence the process of shaping an ethics of public health, it is clear that bioethics
is the wrong place to start." Ronald Bayer & Amy L. Fairchild, *The Genesis of
Public Health Ethics*, 18 BIOETHICS 473, 492 (2004).

Of course, the real answer may be that when medicine and public health work
together (usually the case), public health must take account of bioethics (sometimes
called simply "medical ethics"), and that in real life there are no sharp borders
between health law, bioethics, and human rights in public health practice. *See, e.g.*,
GEORGE J. ANNAS, AMERICAN BIOETHICS: CROSSING HUMAN RIGHTS AND HEALTH LAW
BOUNDARIES (2005); BRITISH MEDICAL ASSOCIATION, THE MEDICAL PROFESSION AND
HUMAN RIGHTS: HANDBOOK FOR A CHANGING AGENDA (2001); DAVID J. ROTHMAN & SHEILA
M. ROTHMAN, TRUST IS NOT ENOUGH: BRINGING HUMAN RIGHTS TO MEDICINE (2006).

D.   HUMAN RIGHTS IN RESEARCH

THE NUREMBERG DOCTORS' TRIAL, OPENING STATEMENT OF THE PROSECUTION
(Dec. 9, 1946)

Trials of War Criminals Before the Nuremberg Military Tribunal Under Control Council Law 10, Vol. 1 (Washington, D.C.: Superintendent of Documents, U.S. Government Printing Office, 1950); Military Tribunal, Case 1, *United States v. Karl Brandt* **et al., pp 27–74.**

Teleford Taylor

The defendants in this case are charged with murders, tortures, and other atrocities committed in the name of medical science. The victims of these crimes are numbered in the hundreds of thousands. A handful only are still alive; a few of the survivors will appear in this courtroom. But most of these miserable victims were slaughtered outright or died in the course of the tortures to which they were subjected.

For the most part they are nameless dead. To their murderers, these wretched people were not individuals at all. They came in wholesale lots and were treated worse than animals. They were 200 Jews in good physical condition, 50 gypsies, 500 tubercular Poles, or 1,000 Russians. The victims of these crimes are numbered among the anonymous millions who met death at the hands of the Nazis and whose fate is a hideous blot on the page of modern history.

The charges against these defendants are brought in the name of the United States of America. They are being tried by a court of American judges. The responsibilities thus imposed upon the representatives of the United States, prosecutors and judges alike, are grave and unusual. It is owed, not only to the victims and to the parents and children of the victims, that just punishment be imposed on the guilty, but also to the defendants that they be accorded a fair hearing and decision. Such responsibilities are the ordinary burden of any tribunal. Far wider are the duties which we must fulfill here.

These larger obligations run to the peoples and races on whom the scourge of these crimes was laid. The mere punishment of the defendants, or even of thousands of others equally guilty, can never redress the terrible injuries which the Nazis visited on these unfortunate peoples. For them it is far more important that these incredible events be established by clear and public proof, so that no one can ever doubt that they were fact and not fable; and that this Court, as the agent of the United States and as the voice of humanity, stamp these acts, and the ideas which engendered them, as barbarous and criminal.

We have still other responsibilities here. The defendants in the dock are charged with murder, but this is no mere murder trial. We cannot rest content when we have shown that crimes were committed and that certain persons committed them. To kill, to maim, and to torture is criminal under all modern systems of law. These defendants did not kill in hot blood, nor for personal enrichment. Some of them may be sadists who killed and tortured for sport, but they are not all perverts. They are not ignorant men. Most of them are trained physicians and some of them are distinguished scientists. Yet these defendants, all of whom were fully able to comprehend the nature of their acts, and most of whom were exceptionally qualified to form a moral and professional judgment in this respect, are responsible for wholesale murder and unspeakably cruel tortures. It is our deep obligation to all peoples of the world to show why and how these things happened. It is incumbent upon us to set forth with conspicuous clarity the ideas and motives which moved these defendants to treat their fellow men as less than beasts. The perverse thoughts and distorted concepts which brought about these savageries are not dead. They cannot be killed by force of arms. They must not become a spreading cancer in the breast of humanity. They must be cut out and exposed for the reason so well stated by Mr. Justice Jackson in this courtroom a year ago — "The wrongs which we seek to condemn and punish have been so calculated, so malignant, and so devastating, that civilization cannot tolerate their being ignored because it cannot survive their being repeated."

To the German people we owe a special responsibility in these proceedings. Under the leadership of the Nazis and their war lords, the German nation spread death and devastation throughout Europe. This the Germans now know. So, too, do they know the consequences to Germany: defeat, ruin, prostration, and utter demoralization. Most German children will never, as long as they live, see an undamaged German city.

To what cause will these children ascribe the defeat of the German nation and the devastation that surrounds them? Will they attribute it to the overwhelming weight of numbers and resources that was eventually leagued against them? Will they point to the ingenuity of enemy scientists? Will they perhaps blame their plight on strategic and military blunders by their generals?

If the Germans embrace those reasons as the true cause of their disaster, it will be a sad and fatal thing for Germany and for the world. Men who have never seen a German city intact will be callous about flattening English or American or Russian cities. They may not even realize that they are destroying anything worthwhile, for lack of a normal sense of values. To reestablish the greatness of Germany they are likely to pin their faith on improved military techniques. Such views will lead the Germans straight into the arms of the Prussian militarists to whom defeat is only a glorious opportunity to start a new war game. "Next time it will be different." We know all too well what that will mean.

This case, and others which will be tried in this building, offer a signal opportunity to lay before the German people the true cause of their present misery. The walls and towers and churches of Nuremberg were, indeed, reduced to rubble by Allied bombs, but in a deeper sense Nuremberg had been destroyed a decade earlier, when it became the seat of the annual Nazi Party rallies, a focal point for the moral disintegration in Germany, and the private domain of Julius Streicher. The insane and malignant doctrines that Nuremberg spewed forth account alike for the crimes of these defendants and for the terrible fate of Germany under the Third Reich.

A nation which deliberately infects itself with poison will inevitably sicken and die. These defendants and others turned Germany into an infernal combination of a lunatic asylum and a charnel house. Neither science, nor industry, nor the arts could flourish in such a foul medium. The country could not live at peace and was fatally handicapped for war. I do not think the German people have as yet any conception of how deeply the criminal folly that was Nazism bit into every phase of German life, or of how utterly ravaging the consequences were. It will be our task to make these things clear.

These are the high purposes which justify the establishment of extraordinary courts to hear and determine this case and others of comparable importance. That murder should be punished goes without the saying, but the full performance of our task requires more than the just sentencing of these defendants. Their crimes were the inevitable result of the sinister doctrines which they espoused, and these same doctrines sealed the fate of Germany, shattered Europe, and left the world in ferment. Wherever those doctrines may emerge and prevail, the same terrible consequences will follow. That is why a bold and lucid consummation of these proceedings is of vital importance to all nations. That is why the United States has constituted this Tribunal.

I pass now to the facts of the case in hand. There are 23 defendants in the box. All but three of them — Rudolf Brandt, Sievers, and Brack — are doctors. Of the 20 doctors, all but one — Pokorny — held positions in the medical services of the Third Reich. To understand this case, it is necessary to understand the general structure of these state medical services, and how these services fitted into the overall organization of the Nazi State.

[The material on the organization of the military medical personnel, and where the individual defendants fit into it, has been deleted.]

CRIMES COMMITTED IN THE GUISE OF SCIENTIFIC RESEARCH

I turn now to the main part of the indictment and will outline at this point the prosecution's case relating to those crimes alleged to have been committed in the name of medical or scientific research. The charges with respect to "euthanasia" and the slaughter of tubercular Poles obviously have no relation to research or experimentation and will be dealt with later. What I will cover now comprehends all the experiments charged as war crimes in paragraph 6 and as crimes against humanity in paragraph 11 of the indictment, and the murders committed for so-called anthropological purposes which are charged as war crimes in paragraph 7 and as crimes against humanity in paragraph 12 of the indictment.

Before taking up these experiments one by one, let us look at them as a whole. Are they a heterogeneous list of horrors, or is there a common denominator for the whole group?

A sort of rough pattern is apparent on the face of the indictment. Experiments concerning high altitude, the effect of cold, and the potability of processed sea water have an obvious relation to aeronautical and naval combat and rescue problems. The mustard gas and phosphorous burn experiments, as well as those relating to the healing value of sulfanilamide for wounds, can be related to air raid and battlefield medical problems. It is well known that malaria, epidemic jaundice, and typhus were among the principal diseases which had to be combated by the German Armed Forces and by German authorities in occupied territories. To some degree, the therapeutic pattern outlined above is undoubtedly a valid one, and explains why the Wehrmacht, and especially the German Air Force, participated in these experiments. Fanatically bent upon conquest, utterly ruthless as to the means or instruments to be used in achieving victory, and callous to the sufferings of people whom they regarded as inferior, the German militarists were willing to gather whatever scientific fruit these experiments might yield.

But our proof will show that a quite different and even more sinister objective runs like a red thread through these hideous researches. We will show that in some instances the true object of these experiments was not how to rescue or to cure, but how to destroy and kill. The sterilization experiments were, it is clear, purely destructive in purpose. The prisoners at Buchenwald who were shot with poisoned bullets were not guinea pigs to test an antidote for the poison; their murderers really wanted to know how quickly the poison would kill. This destructive objective is not superficially as apparent in the other experiments, but we will show that it was often there.

Mankind has not heretofore felt the need of a word to denominate the science of how to kill prisoners most rapidly and subjugated people in large numbers. This case and these defendants have created this gruesome question for the lexicographer. For the moment we will christen this macabre science "thanatology," the science of producing death. The thanatological knowledge, derived in part from these experiments, supplied the techniques for genocide, a policy of the Third Reich, exemplified in the "euthanasia" program and in the wide-spread slaughter of Jews, gypsies, Poles, and Russians. This policy of mass extermination could not have been so effectively carried out without the active participation of German medical scientists.

*   *   *

The 20 physicians in the dock range from leaders of German scientific medicine, with excellent international reputations, down to the dregs of the German medical profession. All of them have in common a callous lack of consideration and human regard for, and an unprincipled willingness to abuse their power over the poor, unfortunate, defenseless creatures who had been deprived of their rights by a ruthless and criminal government. All of them violated the Hippocratic commandments which they had solemnly sworn to uphold and abide by, including the fundamental principles never to do harm — "primum non nocere."

Outstanding men of science, distinguished for their scientific ability in Germany and abroad, are the defendants Rostock and Rose. Both exemplify, in their training and practice alike, the highest traditions of German medicine. Rostock headed the Department of Surgery at the University of Berlin and served as dean of its medical school. Rose studied under the famous surgeon, Enderlen, at Heidelberg and then became a distinguished specialist in the fields of public health and tropical diseases. Handloser and Schroeder are outstanding medical administrators. Both of them made their careers in military medicine and reached the peak of their profession. Five more defendants are much younger men who are nevertheless already known as the possessors of considerable scientific ability, or capacity in medical administration. These include the defendants Karl Brandt, Ruff, Beiglboeck, Schaefer, and Becker-Freyseng.

A number of the others such as Romberg and Fischer are well trained, and several of them attained high professional position. But among the remainder few were known as outstanding scientific men. Among them at the foot of the list is Blome who has published his autobiography entitled "Embattled Doctor" in which he sets forth that he eventually decided to become a doctor because a medical career would enable him to become "master over life and death."

*   *   *

I intend to pass very briefly over matters of medical ethics, such as the conditions under which a physician may lawfully perform a medical experiment upon a person who has voluntarily subjected himself to it, or whether experiments may lawfully be performed upon criminals who have been condemned to death. This case does not present such problems. No refined questions confront us here.

None of the victims of the atrocities perpetrated by these defendants were volunteers, and this is true regardless of what these unfortunate people may have said or signed before their tortures began. Most of the victims had not been condemned to death, and those who had been were not criminals, unless it be a crime to be a Jew, or a Pole, or a gypsy, or a Russian prisoner of war.

Whatever book or treatise on medical ethics we may examine, and whatever expert on forensic medicine we may question, will say that it is a fundamental and inescapable obligation of every physician under any known system of law not to perform a dangerous experiment without the subject's consent. In the tyranny that was Nazi Germany, no one could give such a consent to the medical agents of the State; everyone lived in fear and acted under duress. I fervently hope that none of us here in the courtroom will have to suffer in silence while it is said on the part of these defendants that the wretched and helpless people whom they froze and drowned and burned and poisoned were volunteers. If such a shameless lie is spoken here, we need only remember the four girls who were taken from the Ravensbrueck concentration camp and made to lie naked with the frozen and all but dead Jews who survived Dr. Rascher's tank of ice water. One of these women, whose hair and eyes and figure were pleasing to Dr. Rascher, when asked by him why she had volunteered for such a task replied, "rather half a year in a brothel than half a year in a concentration camp."

Were it necessary, one could make a long list of the respects in which the experiments which these defendants performed departed from every known standard of medical ethics. But the gulf between these atrocities and serious research in the healing art is so patent that such a tabulation would be cynical.

We need look no further than the law which the Nazis themselves passed on the 24th of November 1933 for the protection of animals. This law states explicitly that it is designed to prevent cruelty and indifference of man towards animals and to awaken and develop sympathy and understanding for animals as one of the highest moral values of a people. The soul of the German people should abhor the principle of mere utility without consideration of the moral aspects. The law states further that all operations or treatments which are associated with pain or injury, especially experiments involving the use of cold, heat, or infection, are prohibited, and can be permitted only under special exceptional circumstances. Special written authorization by the head of the department is necessary in every case, and experimenters are prohibited from performing experiments according to their own free judgment. Experiments for the purpose of teaching must be reduced to a minimum. Medico-legal tests, vaccinations, withdrawal of blood for diagnostic purposes, and trial of vaccines prepared according to well-established scientific principles are permitted, but the animals have to be killed immediately and painlessly after such experiments. Individual physicians are not permitted to use dogs to increase their surgical skill by such practices. National Socialism regards it as a sacred duty of German science to keep down the number of painful animal experiments to a minimum.

If the principles announced in this law had been followed for human beings as well, this indictment would never have been filed. It is perhaps the deepest shame of the defendants that it probably never even occurred to them that human beings should be treated with at least equal humanity.

*   *   *

I said at the outset of this statement that the Third Reich died of its own poison. This case is a striking demonstration not only of the tremendous degradation of German medical ethics which Nazi doctrine brought about, but of the undermining of the medical art and thwarting of the techniques which the defendants sought to employ. The Nazis have, to a certain extent, succeeded in convincing the peoples of the world that the Nazi system, although ruthless, was absolutely efficient; that although savage, it was completely scientific; that although entirely devoid of humanity, it was highly systematic — that "it got things done." The evidence which this Tribunal will hear will explode this myth. The Nazi methods of investigation were inefficient and unscientific, and their techniques of research were unsystematic.

These experiments revealed nothing which civilized medicine can use. It was, indeed, ascertained that phenol or gasoline injected intravenously will kill a man inexpensively and within 60 seconds. This and a few other "advances" are all in the field of thanatology. There is no doubt that a number of these new methods may be useful to criminals everywhere and there is no doubt that they may be useful to a criminal state. Certain advance in destructive methodology we cannot deny, and indeed from Himmler's standpoint this may well have been the principal objective.

Apart from these deadly fruits, the experiments were not only criminal but a scientific failure. It is indeed as if a just deity had shrouded the solutions which they attempted to reach with murderous means. The moral shortcomings of the defendants and the precipitous ease with which they decided to commit murder in quest of "scientific results", dulled also that scientific hesitancy, that thorough thinking-through, that responsible weighing of every single step which alone can insure scientifically valid results. Even if they had merely been forced to pay as little as two dollars for human experimental subjects, such as American investigators may have to pay for a cat, they might have thought twice before wasting unnecessary numbers, and thought of simpler and better ways to solve their problems. The fact that these investigators had free and unrestricted access to human beings to be experimented upon misled them to the dangerous and fallacious conclusion that the results would thus be better and more quickly obtainable than if they had gone through the labor of preparation, thinking, and meticulous preinvestigation.

A particularly striking example is the sea-water experiment. I believe that three of the accused — Schaefer, Becker-Freyseng, and Beiglboeck — will today admit that this problem could have been solved simply and definitively within the space of one afternoon. On 20 May 1944 when these accused convened to discuss the problem, a thinking chemist could have solved it right in the presence of the assembly within the space of a few hours by the use of nothing more gruesome than a piece of jelly, a semi-permeable membrane and a salt solution, and the German Armed Forces would have had the answer on 21 May 1944. But what happened instead? The vast armies of the disenfranchised slaves were at the beck and call of this sinister assembly; and instead of thinking, they simply relied on their power over human beings rendered rightless by a criminal state and government. What time, effort, and staff did it take to get that machinery in motion! Letters had to be written, physicians, of whom dire shortage existed in the German Armed Forces whose soldiers went poorly attended, had to be taken out of hospital positions and dispatched hundreds of miles away to obtain the answer which should have been known in a few hours, but which thus did not become available to the German Armed Forces until after the completion of the gruesome show, and until 42 people had been subjected to the tortures of the damned, the very tortures which Greek mythology had reserved for Tantalus.

In short, this conspiracy was a ghastly failure as well as a hideous crime. The creeping paralysis of Nazi superstition spread through the German medical profession and, just as it destroyed character and morals, it dulled the mind. Guilt for the oppressions and crimes of the Third Reich is widespread, but it is the guilt of the leaders that is deepest and most culpable. Who could German medicine look to keep the profession true to its traditions and protect it from the ravaging inroads of Nazi pseudo-science? This was the supreme responsibility of the leaders of German medicine — men like Rostock and Rose and Schroeder and Handloser. That is why their guilt is greater than that of any of the other defendants in the dock. They are the men who utterly failed their country and their profession, who showed neither courage nor wisdom nor the vestiges of moral character. It is their failure, together with the failure of the leaders of Germany in other walks of life, that debauched Germany and led to her defeat. It is because of them and others like them that we all live in a stricken world.

THE NUREMBERG DOCTORS' TRIAL,
THE JUDGMENT
(Aug. 19, 1947)

JUDGES HAROLD SEBRING, WALTER BEALS & JOHNSON CRAWFORD

Military Tribunal I was established on 25 October 1946 under General Orders No. 6 issued by command of the United States Military Government for Germany. It was the first of several military tribunals constituted in the United States Zone of Occupation pursuant to Military Government Ordinance No. 7, for the trial of offenses recognized as crimes by Law No. 10 of the Control Council for Germany . . . . The trial was conducted in two languages — English and German. It consumed 139 trial days, including 6 days allocated for final arguments and the personal statements of the defendants. During the 133 trial days used for the presentation of evidence 32 witnesses gave oral evidence for the prosecution and 53 witnesses, including the 23 defendants, gave oral evidence for the defense. In addition, the prosecution put in evidence as exhibits a total of 570 affidavits, reports, and documents; the defense put in a total number of 901 — making a grand total of 1471 documents received in evidence.

. . . .

COUNTS TWO AND THREE

War Crimes and Crimes against Humanity. The second and third counts of the indictment charge the commission of war crimes and crimes against humanity. The counts are identical in content, except for the fact that in count two the acts which are made the basis for the charges are alleged to have been committed on " "civilians and members of the armed forces [of nations] then at war with the German Reich . . . in the exercise of belligerent control", whereas in count three the criminal acts are alleged to have been committed against "German civilians and nationals of other countries." With this distinction observed, both counts will be treated as one and discussed together.

Counts two and three allege, in substance, that between September 1939 and April 1945 all of the defendants "were principals in, accessories to, ordered, abetted, took a consenting part in, and were connected with plans and enterprises involving medical experiments without the subjects' consent . . . in the course of which experiments the defendants committed murders, brutalities, cruelties, tortures, atrocities, and other inhuman acts." It is averred that "such experiments included, but were not limited to" the following:

a) *High-Altitude Experiments.* From about March 1942 to about August 1942 experiments were conducted at the Dachau concentration camp, for the benefit of the German Air Force, to investigate the limits of human endurance and existence at extremely high altitudes. The experiments were carried out in a low-pressure chamber in which the atmospheric conditions and pressures prevailing at high altitude (up to 68,000 feet) could be duplicated. The experimental subjects were placed in the low-pressure chamber and thereafter the simulated altitude therein was raised. Many victims died as a result of these experiments and others suffered grave injury, torture, and ill-treatment. The defendants Karl Brandt, Handloser, Schroeder, Gebhardt, Rudolf Brandt, Mrugowsky, Poppendick, Sievers, Ruff, Romberg, Becker-Freyseng, and Weltz are charged with special responsibility for and participation in these crimes.

b) *Freezing Experiments.* From about August 1942 to about May 1943 experiments were conducted at the Dachau concentration camp, primarily for the benefit of the German Air Force, to investigate the most effective means of treating persons who had been severely chilled or frozen. In one series of experiments the subjects were forced to remain in a tank of ice water for periods up to 3 hours. Extreme rigor developed in a short time. Numerous victims died in the course of these experiments. After the survivors were severely chilled, rewarming was attempted by various means. In another series of experiments, the subjects were kept naked outdoors for many hours at temperatures below freezing . . . . The defendants Karl Brandt, Handloser, Schroeder, Gebhardt, Rudolf Brandt, Mrugowsky, Poppendick, Sievers, Becker-Freyseng, and Weltz are charged with special responsibility for and participation in these crimes.

c) *Malaria Experiments.* From about February 1942 to about April 1945 experiments were conducted at the Dachau concentration camp in order to investigate immunization for and treatment of malaria. Healthy concentration camp inmates were infected by mosquitoes or by injections of extracts of the mucous glands of mosquitoes. After having contracted malaria the subjects were treated with various drugs to test their relative efficacy. Over 1,000 involuntary subjects were used in these experiments. Many of the victims died and others suffered severe pain and permanent disability. The defendants Karl Brandt, Handloser, Rostock, Gebhardt, Blome, Rudolf Brandt, Mrugowsky, Poppendick, and Sievers are charged with special responsibility for and participation in these crimes.

d) *Lost (Mustard) Gas Experiments.* At various times between September 1939 and April 1945 experiments were conducted at Sachsenhausen, Natzweiler, and other concentration camps for the benefit of the German Armed Forces to investigate the most effective treatment of wounds caused by Lost gas. Lost is a poison gas which is commonly known as mustard gas. Wounds deliberately inflicted on the subjects were infected with Lost. Some of the subjects died as a result of these experiments and others suffered intense pain and injury. The defendants Karl Brandt, Handloser, Blome, Rostock, Gebhardt, Rudolf Brandt, and Sievers are charged with special responsibility for and participation in these crimes.

e) *Sulfanilamide Experiments.* From about July 1942 to about September 1943 experiments to investigate the effectiveness of sulfanilamide were conducted at the Ravensbrueck concentration camp for the benefit of the German Armed Forces. Wounds deliberately inflicted on the experimental subjects were infected with bacteria such as streptococcus, gas gangrene, and tetanus. Circulation of blood was interrupted by tying off blood vessels at both ends of the wound to create a condition similar to that of a battlefield wound. Infection was aggravated by forcing wood shavings and ground glass into the wounds. The infection was treated with sulfanilamide and other drugs to determine their effectiveness. Some subjects died as a result of these experiments and others suffered serious injury and intense agony. The defendants Karl Brandt, Handloser, Rostock, Schroeder, Genzken, Gebhardt, Blome, Rudolf Brandt, Mrugowsky, Poppendick, Becker-Freyseng, Oberheuser, and Fischer are charged with special responsibility for and participation in these crimes.

f) *Bone, Muscle, and Nerve Regeneration and Bone Transplantation Experiments.* From about September 1942 to about December 1943 experiments were conducted at the Ravensbrueck concentration camp, for the benefit of the German Armed Forces, to study bone, muscle, and nerve regeneration, and bone transplantation from one person to another. Sections of bones, muscles, and nerves were removed from the subjects. As a result of these operations, many victims suffered intense agony, mutilation, and permanent disability. The defendants Karl Brandt, Handloser, Rostock, Gebhardt, Rudolf Brandt, Oberheuser, and Fischer are charged with special responsibility and participation in these crimes.

g) *Sea-Water Experiments.* From about July 1944 to about September 1944 experiments were conducted at the Dachau Concentration camp, for the benefit of the German Air Force and Navy, to study various methods of making sea water drinkable. The subjects were deprived of all food and given only chemically processed sea water. Such experiments caused great pain and suffering and resulted in serious bodily injury to the victims. The defendants Karl Brandt, Handloser, Rostock, Schroeder, Gebhardt, Rudolf Brandt, Mrugowsky, Poppendick, Sievers, Becker-Freyseng, Schaefer, and Beiglboeck are charged with special responsibility for and participation in these crimes.

h) *Epidemic Jaundice Experiments.* From about June 1943 to about January 1945 experiments were conducted at the Sachsenhausen and Natzweiler concentration camps, for benefit of the German Armed Forces, to investigate the causes of, and inoculations against, epidemic jaundice. Experimental subjects were deliberately infected with epidemic jaundice, some of whom died as a result, and others were caused great pain and suffering. The defendants Karl Brandt, Handloser, Rostock, Schroeder, Gebhardt, Rudolf Brandt, Mrugowsky, Poppendick, Sievers, Rose, and Becker-Freyseng are charged with special responsibility for and participation in these crimes.

i) *Sterilization Experiments.* From about March 1941 to about January 1945 sterilization experiments were conducted at the Auschwitz and Ravensbrueck concentration camps, and other places. The purpose of these experiments was to develop a method of sterilization which would be suitable for sterilizing millions of people with a minimum of time and effort. These experiments were conducted by means of X-ray, surgery, and various drugs. Thousands of victims were sterilized and thereby suffered great mental and physical anguish. The defendants Karl Brandt, Gebhardt, Rudolf Brandt, Mrugowsky, Poppendick, Brack, Pokorny, and Oberheuser are charged with special responsibility for and participation in these crimes.

j) *Spotted Fever (Fleckfieber) Experiments.* From about December 1941 to about February 1945 experiments were conducted at the Buchenwald and Natzweiler concentration camps, for the benefit of the German Armed Forces, to investigate the effectiveness of spotted fever and other vaccines. At Buchenwald, numerous healthy inmates were deliberately infected with spotted fever virus in order to keep the virus alive; over 90 percent of the victims died as a result. Other healthy inmates were used to determine the effectiveness of different spotted fever vaccines and of various chemical substances. In the course of these experiments 75% of the selected number of inmates were vaccinated with one of the vaccines or nourished with one of the chemical substances and, after a period of 3 to 4 weeks, were infected with spotted fever germs. The remaining 25% were infected without any previous protection in order to compare the effectiveness of the vaccines and the chemical substances. As a result, hundreds of the persons experimented upon died. Experiments with yellow fever, smallpox, typhus, paratyphus A and B, cholera, and diphtheria were also conducted. Similar experiments with like results were conducted at Natzweiler concentration camp. The defendants Karl Brandt, Handloser, Rostock, Schroeder, Genzken, Gebhardt, Rudolf Brandt, Mrugowsky, Poppendick, Sievers, Rose, Becker-Freyseng, and Hoven are charged with special responsibility for and participation in these crimes.

k) *Experiments with Poison.* In or about December 1943 and in or about October 1944 experiments were conducted at the Buchenwald concentration camp to investigate the effect of various poisons upon human beings. The poisons were secretly administered to experimental subjects in their food. The victims died as a result of the poison or were killed immediately in order to permit autopsies. In or about September 1944 experimental subjects were shot with poison bullets and suffered torture and death. The defendants Genzken, Gebhardt, Mrugowsky, and Poppendick are charged with special responsibility for and participation in these crimes.

l) *Incendiary Bomb Experiments.* From about November 1943 to about January 1944 experiments were conducted at the Buchenwald concentration camp to test the effect of various pharmaceutical preparations on phosphorus burns. These burns were inflicted on experimental subjects with phosphorus matter taken from incendiary bombs, and caused severe pain, suffering, and serious bodily injury. The defendants Genzken, Gebhardt, Mrugowsky, and Poppendick are charged with special responsibility for and participation in these crimes."

In addition to the medical experiments, the nature and purpose of which have been outlined as alleged, certain of the defendants are charged with criminal activities involving murder, torture, and ill-treatment of non-German nationals as follows:

7) Between June 1943 and September 1944 the defendants Rudolf Brandt and Sievers . . . were principals in, accessories to, ordered, abetted, took a consenting part in, and were connected with plans and enterprises involv-

ing the murder of civilians and members of the armed forces of nations then at war with the German Reich and who were in the custody of the German Reich in exercise of belligerent control. One hundred twelve Jews were selected for the purpose of completing a skeleton collection for the Reich University of Strasbourg. Their photographs and anthropological measurements were taken. Then they were killed. Thereafter, comparison tests, anatomical research, studies regarding race, pathological features of the body, form and size of the brain, and other tests were made. The bodies were sent to Strasbourg and defleshed.

8) Between May 1942 and January 1944 the defendants Blome and Rudolf Brandt . . . were principals in, accessories to, ordered, abetted, took a consenting part in, and were connected with plans and enterprises involving the murder and mistreatment of tens of thousands of Polish nationals who were civilians and members of the armed forces of a nation then at war with the German Reich and who were in the custody of the German Reich in exercise of belligerent control. These people were alleged to be infected with incurable tuberculosis. On the ground of insuring the health and welfare of Germans in Poland, many tubercular Poles were ruthlessly exterminated while others were isolated in death camps with inadequate medical facilities.

9) Between September 1939 and April 1945 the defendants Karl Brandt, Blome, Brack, and Hoven . . . were principals in, accessories to, ordered, abetted, took a consenting part in, and were connected with plans and enterprises involving the execution of the so-called "euthanasia" program of the German Reich in the course of which the defendants herein murdered hundreds of thousands of human beings, including nationals of German-occupied countries. This program involved the systematic and secret execution of the aged, insane, incurably ill, of deformed children, and other persons, by gas, lethal injections, and diverse other means in nursing homes, hospitals, and asylums. Such persons were regarded as "useless eaters" and a burden to the German war machine. The relatives of these victims were informed that they died from natural causes, such as heart failure. German doctors involved in the "euthanasia" program were also sent to the eastern occupied countries to assist in the mass extermination of Jews. . . .

Counts two and three of the indictment conclude with the averment that the crimes and atrocities which have been delineated "constitute violations of international conventions . . . ," the laws and customs of war, the general principles of criminal law as derived from the criminal laws of all civilized nations, the internal penal laws of the countries in which such crimes were committed, and of Article II of Control Council Law No. 10."

Judged by any standard of proof the record clearly shows the commission of war crimes and crimes against humanity substantially as alleged in counts two and three of the indictment. Beginning with the outbreak of World War II criminal medical experiments on non-German nationals, both prisoners of war and civilians, including Jews and "asocial" persons, were carried out on a large scale in Germany and the occupied countries. These experiments were not the isolated and casual acts of individual doctors and scientists working solely on their own responsibility, but were the product of coordinated policy-making and planning at high governmental, military, and Nazi Party levels, conducted as an integral part of the total war effort. They were ordered, sanctioned, permitted, or approved by persons in positions of authority who under all principles of law were under the duty to know about these things and to take steps to terminate or prevent them.

PERMISSIBLE MEDICAL EXPERIMENTS ["THE NUREMBERG CODE"]

The great weight of the evidence before us is to the effect that certain types of medical experiments on human beings, when kept within reasonably well-defined bounds, conform to the ethics of the medical profession generally. The protagonists of the practice of human experimentation justify their views on the basis that such experiments yield results for the good of society that are unprocurable by other methods or means of study. All agree, however, that certain basic principles must be observed in order to satisfy moral, ethical and legal concepts:

1) The voluntary consent of the human subject is absolutely essential. This means that the person involved should have legal capacity to give consent; should be so situated as to be able to exercise free power of choice, without the intervention of any element of force, fraud, deceit, duress, over-reaching, or other ulterior form of constraint or coercion; and should have sufficient knowledge and comprehension of the elements of the subject matter involved as to enable him to make an understanding and enlightened decision. This latter element requires that before the acceptance of an affirmative decision by the experimental subject there should be made known to him the nature, duration, and purpose of the experiment; the method and means by which it is to be conducted; all inconveniences and hazards reasonably to be expected; and the effects upon his health or person which may possibly come from his participation in the experiment. The duty and responsibility for ascertaining the quality of the consent rests upon each individual who initiates, directs or engages in the experiment. It is a personal duty and responsibility which may not be delegated to another with impunity.

2) The experiment should be such as to yield fruitful results for the good of society, unprocurable by other methods or means of study, and not random and unnecessary in nature.

3) The experiment should be so designed and based on the results of animal experimentation and a knowledge of the natural history of the disease or other problem under study that the anticipated results will justify the performance of the experiment.

4) The experiment should be so conducted as to avoid all unnecessary physical and mental suffering and injury.

5) No experiment should be conducted where there is an a priori reason to believe that death or disabling injury will occur; except, perhaps, in those experiments where the experimental physicians also serve as subjects.

6) The degree of risk to be taken should never exceed that determined by the

humanitarian importance of the problem to be solved by the experiment.

7) Proper preparations should be made and adequate facilities provided to protect the experimental subject against even remote possibilities of injury, disability, or death.

8) The experiment should be conducted only by scientifically qualified persons. The highest degree of skill and care should be required through all stages of the experiment of those who conduct or engage in the experiment.

9) During the course of the experiment the human subject should be at liberty to bring the experiment to an end if he has reached the physical or mental state where continuation of the experiment seems to him to be impossible.

10) During the course of the experiment the scientist in charge must be prepared to terminate the experiment at any stage, if he has probably cause to believe, in the exercise of the good faith, superior skill and careful judgment required of him that a continuation of the experiment is likely to result in injury, disability, or death to the experimental subject.

Of the ten principles which have been enumerated our judicial concern, of course, is with those requirements which are purely legal in nature — or which at least are so clearly related to matters legal that they assist us in determining criminal culpability and punishment. To go beyond that point would lead us into a field that would be beyond our sphere of competence. However, the point need not be labored. We find from the evidence that in the medical experiments which have been proved, these ten principles were much more frequently honored in their breach than in their observance. Many of the concentration camp inmates who were the victims of these atrocities were citizens of countries other than the German Reich. They were non-German nationals, including Jews and "asocial persons", both prisoners of war and civilians, who had been imprisoned and forced to submit to the tortures and barbarities without so much as a semblance of trial. In every single instance appearing in the record, subjects were used that did not consent to the experiments; indeed, as to some of the experiments, it is not even contended by the defendants that the subjects occupied the status of volunteers. In no case was the experimental subject at liberty of his own free choice to withdraw from any experiment. In many cases experiments were performed by unqualified persons; were conducted at random for no adequate scientific reason, and under revolting physical conditions. All of the experiments were conducted with unnecessary suffering and injury and but very little, if any, precautions were taken to protect or safeguard the human subjects from the possibilities of injury, disability, or death. In every one of the experiments the subjects experienced extreme pain or torture and in most of them they suffered permanent injury, mutilation, or death, either as a direct result of the experiments or because of lack of adequate follow-up care.

Obviously all of these experiments involving brutalities, tortures, disabling injury, and death were performed in complete disregard of international conventions, the laws and customs of war, the general principles of criminal law as derived from the criminal laws of all civilized nations, and Control Council Law No. 10. Manifestly human experiments under such conditions are contrary to "the principles of the law of nations as they result from the usages established among civilized peoples, from the laws of humanity, and from the dictates of public conscience."

Whether any of the defendants in the dock are guilty of these atrocities is, of course, another question.

Under the Anglo-Saxon system of jurisprudence every defendant in a criminal case is presumed to be innocent of an offense charged until the prosecution, by competent, credible proof, has shown his guilt to the exclusion of every reasonable doubt. And this presumption abides with a defendant through each stage of his trial until such degree of proof has been adduced. A "reasonable doubt" as the name implies is one conformable to reason — a doubt which a reasonable man would entertain. Stated differently, it is that state of a case which, after a full and complete comparison and consideration of all the evidence, would leave an unbiased, unprejudiced, reflective person, charged with the responsibility for decision, in the state of mind that he could not say that he felt an abiding conviction amounting to a moral certainty of the truth of the charge.

If any of the defendants are to be found guilty under counts two or three of the indictment it must be because the evidence has shown beyond a reasonable doubt that such defendant, without regard to nationality or the capacity in which he acted, participated as a principal in, accessory to, ordered, abetted, took a consenting part in, or was connected with plans or enterprises involving the commission of at least some of the medical experiments and other atrocities which are the subject matter of these counts.

NOTES AND QUESTIONS

1. **The doctors' trial and sentences.** The trial known as "The Case Against the Nazi Physicians" was completed on August 20, 1947. 15 of the 23 defendants were found guilty. Seven were found not guilty. One (Poppendick) was acquitted of the charges of having performed medical experiments but was found guilty of SS membership.

Sentence was pronounced the following day. Karl Brandt, Gebhardt, Mrugowsky, Rudolf Brandt, and three nonphysicians — Sievers, Brack, and Hoven — were sentenced to death by hanging. Life imprisonment sentences were imposed on Handloser, Schroeder, Genzken, Rose, and Fischer. Herta Oberheuser, the only woman among the defendants, was sentenced to 20 years, as was Becker-Freysing. Beiglboeck was sentenced to 15 years, Poppendick to 10 years for SS membership. Rostock, Blome, Ruff, Romberg, Weltz, Schaefer, and Pokorny were acquitted and freed. The hangings took place on June 2, 1948. The scene was the prison at Landsberg, in the American zone. Here Hitler had been imprisoned while he wrote MEIN KAMPF. History records that the hangings took 62 minutes. Two black gallows were created in the prison courtyard. Karl Brandt was the only one of the seven who refused religious solace.

The last words of the other murderers were not reported. In any event, seven were hanged, only four of them physicians — seven out of the 23, and out of the many more who, as Dr. Mitscherlich's narrative makes clear, were involved in the Nazi medical crimes. It can never be said that the quality of American mercy had been strained. A. MITSCHERLICH AND F. MIELKE, DOCTORS OF INFAMY 146–148 (1949).

2.   **Murder and torture trial.** Taylor says in his opening that this is a "murder and torture" trial. This is certainly true, but it is much more, as the focus on medical ethics and human experimentation makes clear. Why do you think Taylor decided to go beyond murder and torture and examine the ethics of human experimentation? Do physicians have special obligations not to violate human rights? The "Nuremberg Code" appears at the end of the edited judgment. What is the legal status of the Nuremberg Code? Where does it appear in the International Covenant on Civil and Political Rights? What is the difference between the Nuremberg Code and the Nuremberg Principles (articulated in the IMT)? *See* GEORGE J. ANNAS & MICHAEL A. GRODIN, THE NAZI DOCTORS AND THE NUREMBERG CODE: HUMAN RIGHTS IN HUMAN EXPERIMENTATION (1992). *See also* ULF SCHMIDT, JUSTICE AT NUREMBERG: LEO ALEXANDER AND THE NAZI DOCTORS TRIAL (2004); *Nuremberg Trials Project: A Digital Document Collection* (Harvard Law School Library),http://nuremberg.law.harvard.edu/php/docs_swi.php?DI=1&text=overview.

3.   **Legal status of the Nuremberg code.** Human experimentation without consent has been condemned not only at Nuremberg, but also because it became part of international human rights law when it was specifically prohibited in the International Covenant on Civil and Political Rights and subsequent UN statements on research. In addition, informed consent is at the core of UNESCO's Universal Declaration on Bioethics and Human Rights. *See, e.g.*, George J. Annas, *Globalized Clinical Trials and Informed Consent*, 360 NEW ENGL. J. MED. 2050 (2009). Nevertheless, some leading American medical researchers remain hostile to the doctrine of informed consent, most recently arguing to the US Office of Human Rights Protection that informed consent should either not be necessary or deeply simplified in the case of "standard of care" research. George J. Annas & Catherine Annas, *Legally Blind: The Therapeutic Illusion in the SUPPORT study of Extremely Premature Infants*, 30 J. CONTEMPORARY HEALTH LAW & POLICY 1 (2013).

WORLD HEALTH ASSOCIATION, THE DECLARATION OF HELSINKI
(2013 Version)

First adopted by the 18th WMA General Assembly, Helsinki, Finland, June 1964 and amended nine times since, most recently in Brazil, October 2013.

Preamble

1. The World Medical Association (WMA) has developed the Declaration of Helsinki as a statement of ethical principles for medical research involving human subjects, including research on identifiable human material and data.

The Declaration is intended to be read as a whole and each of its constituent paragraphs should be applied with consideration of all other relevant paragraphs.

2. Consistent with the mandate of the WMA, the Declaration is addressed primarily to physicians. The WMA encourages others who are involved in medical research involving human subjects to adopt these principles.

General Principles

3. The Declaration of Geneva of the WMA binds the physician with the words, "The health of my patient will be my first consideration," and the International Code of Medical Ethics declares that, "A physician shall act in the patient's best interest when providing medical care."

4. It is the duty of the physician to promote and safeguard the health, well-being and rights of patients, including those who are involved in medical research. The physician's knowledge and conscience are dedicated to the fulfilment of this duty.

5. Medical progress is based on research that ultimately must include studies involving human subjects.

6. The primary purpose of medical research involving human subjects is to understand the causes, development and effects of diseases and improve preventive, diagnostic and therapeutic interventions (methods, procedures and treatments). Even the best proven interventions must be evaluated continually through research for their safety, effectiveness, efficiency, accessibility and quality.

7. Medical research is subject to ethical standards that promote and ensure respect for all human subjects and protect their health and rights.

8. While the primary purpose of medical research is to generate new knowledge, this goal can never take precedence over the rights and interests of individual research subjects.

9. It is the duty of physicians who are involved in medical research to protect the life, health, dignity, integrity, right to self-determination, privacy, and confidentiality of personal information of research subjects. The responsibility for the protection of research subjects must always rest with the physician or other health care professionals and never with the research subjects, even though they have given consent.

10. Physicians must consider the ethical, legal and regulatory norms and standards for research involving human subjects in their own countries as well as applicable international norms and standards. No national or international ethical, legal or regulatory requirement should reduce or eliminate any of the protections for research subjects set forth in this Declaration.

11. Medical research should be conducted in a manner that minimises possible harm to the environment.

12. Medical research involving human subjects must be conducted only by individuals with the appropriate ethics and scientific education, training and qualifications. Research on patients or healthy volunteers requires the supervision of a competent and appropriately qualified physician or other health care professional.

13. Groups that are underrepresented in medical research should be provided appropriate access to participation in research.

14. Physicians who combine medical research with medical care should involve their patients in research only to the extent that this is justified by its potential preventive, diagnostic or therapeutic value and if the physician has good reason to believe that participation in the research study will not adversely affect the health of the patients who serve as research subjects.

15. Appropriate compensation and treatment for subjects who are harmed as a result of participating in research must be ensured.

Risks, Burdens and Benefits

16. In medical practice and in medical research, most interventions involve risks and burdens.

Medical research involving human subjects may only be conducted if the importance of the objective outweighs the risks and burdens to the research subjects.

17. All medical research involving human subjects must be preceded by careful assessment of predictable risks and burdens to the individuals and groups involved in the research in comparison with foreseeable benefits to them and to other individuals or groups affected by the condition under investigation.

Measures to minimise the risks must be implemented. The risks must be continuously monitored, assessed and documented by the researcher.

18. Physicians may not be involved in a research study involving human subjects unless they are confident that the risks have been adequately assessed and can be satisfactorily managed.

When the risks are found to outweigh the potential benefits or when there is conclusive proof of definitive outcomes, physicians must assess whether to continue, modify or immediately stop the study.

Vulnerable Groups and Individuals

19. Some groups and individuals are particularly vulnerable and may have an increased likelihood of being wronged or of incurring additional harm.

All vulnerable groups and individuals should receive specifically considered protection.

20. Medical research with a vulnerable group is only justified if the research is responsive to the health needs or priorities of this group and the research cannot be carried out in a non-vulnerable group. In addition, this group should stand to benefit from the knowledge, practices or interventions that result from the research.

Scientific Requirements and Research Protocols

21. Medical research involving human subjects must conform to generally accepted scientific principles, be based on a thorough knowledge of the scientific literature,

other relevant sources of information, and adequate laboratory and, as appropriate, animal experimentation. The welfare of animals used for research must be respected.

22. The design and performance of each research study involving human subjects must be clearly described and justified in a research protocol.

The protocol should contain a statement of the ethical considerations involved and should indicate how the principles in this Declaration have been addressed. The protocol should include information regarding funding, sponsors, institutional affiliations, potential conflicts of interest, incentives for subjects and information regarding provisions for treating and/or compensating subjects who are harmed as a consequence of participation in the research study.

In clinical trials, the protocol must also describe appropriate arrangements for post-trial provisions.

Research Ethics Committees

23. The research protocol must be submitted for consideration, comment, guidance and approval to the concerned research ethics committee before the study begins. This committee must be transparent in its functioning, must be independent of the researcher, the sponsor and any other undue influence and must be duly qualified. It must take into consideration the laws and regulations of the country or countries in which the research is to be performed as well as applicable international norms and standards but these must not be allowed to reduce or eliminate any of the protections for research subjects set forth in this Declaration.

The committee must have the right to monitor ongoing studies. The researcher must provide monitoring information to the committee, especially information about any serious adverse events. No amendment to the protocol may be made without consideration and approval by the committee. After the end of the study, the researchers must submit a final report to the committee containing a summary of the study's findings and conclusions.

Privacy and Confidentiality

24. Every precaution must be taken to protect the privacy of research subjects and the confidentiality of their personal information.

Informed Consent

25. Participation by individuals capable of giving informed consent as subjects in medical research must be voluntary. Although it may be appropriate to consult family members or community leaders, no individual capable of giving informed consent may be enrolled in a research study unless he or she freely agrees.

26. In medical research involving human subjects capable of giving informed consent, each potential subject must be adequately informed of the aims, methods, sources of funding, any possible conflicts of interest, institutional affiliations of the researcher, the anticipated benefits and potential risks of the study and the

discomfort it may entail, post-study provisions and any other relevant aspects of the study. The potential subject must be informed of the right to refuse to participate in the study or to withdraw consent to participate at any time without reprisal. Special attention should be given to the specific information needs of individual potential subjects as well as to the methods used to deliver the information.

After ensuring that the potential subject has understood the information, the physician or another appropriately qualified individual must then seek the potential subject's freely-given informed consent, preferably in writing. If the consent cannot be expressed in writing, the non-written consent must be formally documented and witnessed.

All medical research subjects should be given the option of being informed about the general outcome and results of the study.

27. When seeking informed consent for participation in a research study the physician must be particularly cautious if the potential subject is in a dependent relationship with the physician or may consent under duress. In such situations the informed consent must be sought by an appropriately qualified individual who is completely independent of this relationship.

28. For a potential research subject who is incapable of giving informed consent, the physician must seek informed consent from the legally authorised representative. These individuals must not be included in a research study that has no likelihood of benefit for them unless it is intended to promote the health of the group represented by the potential subject, the research cannot instead be performed with persons capable of providing informed consent, and the research entails only minimal risk and minimal burden.

29. When a potential research subject who is deemed incapable of giving informed consent is able to give assent to decisions about participation in research, the physician must seek that assent in addition to the consent of the legally authorised representative. The potential subject's dissent should be respected.

30. Research involving subjects who are physically or mentally incapable of giving consent, for example, unconscious patients, may be done only if the physical or mental condition that prevents giving informed consent is a necessary characteristic of the research group. In such circumstances the physician must seek informed consent from the legally authorised representative. If no such representative is available and if the research cannot be delayed, the study may proceed without informed consent provided that the specific reasons for involving subjects with a condition that renders them unable to give informed consent have been stated in the research protocol and the study has been approved by a research ethics committee. Consent to remain in the research must be obtained as soon as possible from the subject or a legally authorised representative.

31. The physician must fully inform the patient which aspects of their care are related to the research. The refusal of a patient to participate in a study or the patient's decision to withdraw from the study must never adversely affect the patient-physician relationship.

32. For medical research using identifiable human material or data, such as

research on material or data contained in biobanks or similar repositories, physicians must seek informed consent for its collection, storage and/or reuse. There may be exceptional situations where consent would be impossible or impracticable to obtain for such research. In such situations the research may be done only after consideration and approval of a research ethics committee.

Use of Placebo

33. The benefits, risks, burdens and effectiveness of a new intervention must be tested against those of the best proven intervention(s), except in the following circumstances:

Where no proven intervention exists, the use of placebo, or no intervention, is acceptable; or

Where for compelling and scientifically sound methodological reasons the use of any intervention less effective than the best proven one, the use of placebo, or no intervention is necessary to determine the efficacy or safety of an intervention and the patients who receive any intervention less effective than the best proven one, placebo, or no intervention will not be subject to additional risks of serious or irreversible harm as a result of not receiving the best proven intervention.

Extreme care must be taken to avoid abuse of this option.

Post-Trial Provisions

34. In advance of a clinical trial, sponsors, researchers and host country governments should make provisions for post-trial access for all participants who still need an intervention identified as beneficial in the trial. This information must also be disclosed to participants during the informed consent process.

Research Registration and Publication and Dissemination of Results

35. Every research study involving human subjects must be registered in a publicly accessible database before recruitment of the first subject.

36. Researchers, authors, sponsors, editors and publishers all have ethical obligations with regard to the publication and dissemination of the results of research. Researchers have a duty to make publicly available the results of their research on human subjects and are accountable for the completeness and accuracy of their reports. All parties should adhere to accepted guidelines for ethical reporting. Negative and inconclusive as well as positive results must be published or otherwise made publicly available. Sources of funding, institutional affiliations and conflicts of interest must be declared in the publication. Reports of research not in accordance with the principles of this Declaration should not be accepted for publication.

Unproven Interventions in Clinical Practice

37. In the treatment of an individual patient, where proven interventions do not exist or other known interventions have been ineffective, the physician, after

seeking expert advice, with informed consent from the patient or a legally authorised representative, may use an unproven intervention if in the physician's judgment it offers hope of saving life, re-establishing health or alleviating suffering. This intervention should subsequently be made the object of research, designed to evaluate its safety and efficacy. In all cases, new information must be recorded and, where appropriate, made publicly available.

George J. Annas, *Global Health and Post-9/11 Human Rights,* in HEALTH AND HUMAN RIGHTS IN A CHANGING WORLD 102–113 (Grodin, Tarantola, Annas, & Gruskin, eds., 2013)

After 9/11 it became fashionable to ask, at least in the arena of global health, if human rights had any special relevance anymore. This question is still being asked as the second year of the Obama administration approaches. The president picked Joseph O'Neill's post-9/11 novel Netherland to read shortly after taking office. The novel's narrator, Hans van den Broek, simply refuses to consider many of the questions that I have concentrated on in Worst Case Bioethics. In his words:

> I found myself unable to contribute to conversations about the value of international law or the feasibility of producing a dirty bomb or the constitutional rights of imprisoned enemies or the efficacy of duct tape as a window sealant or the merits of vaccinating the American masses against smallpox or the complexity of weaponizing deadly bacteria or the menace of the neoconservative cabal in the Bush administration, or indeed any of the debates, each apparently vital, that raged everywhere — raged, because the debaters grew heated and angry and contemptuous . . . I had little interest. I didn't really care. In short, I was a political-ethical idiot.

Hans is, of course, not the only one who has lost interest in these topics. Netherland has deservedly been blessed with gushing reviews and a presidential endorsement. Nonetheless, my own choice for pursuing a conversation about "the value of international law" in the context of global health is Falling Man. The conflicting perceptions of the value of international human rights are echoed in the decidedly mixed reviews Don DeLillo's Falling Man, garnered. The novel (like human rights?) has been described by reviewers as "frustratingly disjointed," "masterly polyphonic fizzling," "a terrible disappointment," "setting the standard," and "a display of cumulative brilliance." My own view is that the post-World War II human rights movement in general, and it's much more recent health and human rights application to global health, sets the "standard" and even represents "a display of cumulative brilliance."

DeLillo's last great novel, Underworld, published in 1997, portrays the Cold War and its fallout as well as anything in fiction or nonfiction. Its cover, surely not meant to be purposely prophetic, pictures the twin towers on both the front and back (one a photo positive, the other a negative) with a church steeple and cross in front of them, and a bird of prey flying in their direction. The cover of Falling Man is self-consciously derivative. The front cover is illustrated by a blue sky as seen from above cloud cover; the back cover contains the same cloudscape with the twin towers breaking through. Both books are about our fear and confusion, followed by our death and decay, which we cover up — with more or less success — with consumption and by building massive monuments to ourselves. But Falling Man has more bite than Underworld, no doubt because of the fall of the towers. It is filled, as we are, with loss and self-destruction. Memory loss is its central obsession, but it is also filled with assorted ways and reasons to commit suicide in the midst of plenty. The main character of Falling Man, a survivor from the first tower, is almost universally described by reviewers as a shallow, middle-aged businessman (the typical American?). DeLillo describes his plight at the end of the novel (which ends where it begins, with the main character escaping from the tower, and observing what is happening): "He could not find himself in the things he saw and heard."

Human rights advocates usually don't have a hard time finding themselves, and their general quest is to change the things they see and hear. But they may see more blue sky than threatening clouds on the horizon, and may or may not have faded memories of the horrors of World War II that gave birth to modern human rights. Nonetheless, 9/11 changed the international human rights movement as well. Former Yale Law School Dean Harold Koh, for example, the leading human rights expert in the Obama administration, has perceptively identified four eras of human rights: (1) the Era of Universalism (1941–56), beginning with Roosevelt's Four Freedoms speech (freedom of speech and religion, freedom from want and fear), and containing the founding of the United Nations and the adoption of the UDHR; (2) the Era of Institutionalization (1965–76) when the treaties were adopted and the institutional structures of human rights were formed, mostly at the UN; (3) the Era of Operationalization (1976–89), with the formation of national and regional human rights regimes, constitutional law applications, special reporters, and specialized nongovernmental organizations (NGOs); and finally (4) the Era of Globalization (1989–present). Koh divides the globalization of human rights into two periods: (1989–2001) the Age of Optimism, from the fall of the Berlin Wall to 9/11; and the Age of Pessimism from 9/11 to today. He delineated these eras before the election of Barack Obama, and there is at least the hope that the Obama presidency could mark a turning point in the Age of Pessimism concerning human rights. Nonetheless, reasons for continued pessimism abound.

The United States used 9/11 as a rationale to abandon not only our rhetorical role of global leader in human rights (always contested by some), but also to abandon human rights itself as a professed guide to our own actions, adopting methods we had consistently condemned since World War II, including preemptive war, torture, cruel and humiliating treatment, indefinite detention, disappearances, and grave breaches of the Geneva Conventions. We became a human rights outlaw in promoting the use of torture, and our country is no longer credible as a moral, or even rhetorical, leader in this arena.

This is disheartening. But does it mean that it is also time to abandon the nascent health and human rights movement as a potential fundamental underpinning for global health? I think not. In spite of our recent disgraceful and illegal behavior in the human rights arena labeled "civil and political rights," in the health portion of "economic, social, and cultural rights," as Solly Benatar and Renee Fox have argued, "the United States is the country with the most *potential* for favorably influencing global health trends." (emphasis in original)

HEALTH AND HUMAN RIGHTS

Jonathan Mann is righty identified as the father of the (public) health and human rights movement. As he first noted, it is neither health nor human rights alone that provide the prospect of motivating a global public health movement, but the combination of health and human rights. Not only do negatives in one area exacerbate negatives in the other, positives in both amplify each other.

World War II, arguably the first truly global war, led to a global acknowledgment of the universality of human rights and the responsibility of individuals and governments to promote them. Jonathan Mann also perceptively identified the HIV/AIDS epidemic as the first global epidemic because it is taking place at a time when the world is unified electronically and by swift transportation. Like World War II, this worldwide epidemic requires us to think in new ways and to develop effective methods to treat and prevent disease on a global level. Globalization is a mercantile and ecological fact; it is also a public health reality. The challenge facing medicine and public health, both before and after 9/11, is to develop a global language and a global strategy that can help to improve the health of all of the world's citizens.

To address the HIV/AIDS epidemic it has been necessary to deal directly with a wide range of human rights issues, including discrimination, the rights of women, privacy, and informed consent, as well as education and access to healthcare. Although it is easy to recognize that population-based prevention is required to effectively address the HIV/AIDS epidemic on a global level (as well as, for example, tuberculosis, malaria, and tobacco-related illness), it has been much harder to articulate a global public health ethic, and public health itself has had an extraordinarily difficult time developing its own ethical language. Because of its universality and its emphasis on equality and human dignity, the language of human rights is well suited for public health.

Similarly, Paul Farmer has asked, "What can a focus on health bring to the struggle for human rights?" and answered, "A 'health angle' can promote a broader human rights agenda in unique ways." Using the example of TB in Russian prisons, he noted that he and his colleagues would not have been invited in if they were seen as human rights workers but as physicians with expertise in TB treatment, they were welcomed in the spirit of "pragmatic solidarity" which, Farmer noted, "may in the end lead to penal reform as well."

Health and human rights experts Sofia Gruskin and Daniel Tarantola have made it crystal clear that the health and human rights movement is based on the human rights movement itself, including the corpus of human rights law articulated in international human rights treaties. As such, primary obligations to respect, protect, and fulfill human rights, including the right to health, fall on the governments of those countries that have signed these treaties and have adopted their own domestic laws to operationalize them. Most fundamentally, human rights law is itself founded on the principle of nondiscrimination: All people everywhere should be treated equally. Women and children also merit special protection under the right to health, and their rights are also reinforced by specific treaties, the Convention on the Elimination of Discrimination Against Women (CEDAW), and the Convention on the Rights of the Child (CRC). Gruskin insists that human rights obligations are legal obligations that bind countries, and it is the legal dimension of the health and human rights field that distinguishes it from the more aspirational field of social justice.

Gruskin is, I believe, quite correct. Nonetheless, as a public health advocate, she would likely agree that spending time mining for differences between the human rights and the social justice approaches, rather than seeking commonalities that can lead to public health action, is counterproductive. Human rights is action — and advocacy-oriented, characteristics that also commend it for global public health.

More than ten years ago I was asked to review a conference-generated book entitled Ethics, Equity, and Health for All. The 1997 conference was intended to develop an action plan to promote equity in health and was based on four principles for action: (1) take an inclusive approach to the governance of ethics and human rights in health; (2) give priority to the involvement of countries and groups that are underrepresented in ethics and human rights deliberations; (3) combine shorter- and longer-term efforts to incorporate ethical practice and respect for human rights in the applications of science and technology to health policy and practice; and (4) give priority to the development of human and institutional capacity to ensure sustainability of effort. These principles are reasonable, but the ultimate action plan suggested by the participants, perhaps unsurprisingly, was not. It called primarily for more work to "prepare working definitions of such key terms as ethics, equity, solidarity, [and] human rights, to take account of international . . . and cultural diversity." Writing this article on global health reminded me of the conference, as well as of my initial thoughts about it. Just as books often end by suggesting other books, so conferences have a tendency to end by suggesting more conferences. I wrote at the time:

The conference wound up calling for more conferences. Academic conferences have an important place in health and human rights work, but do we really need more conferences to define "equity, ethics, and human rights" in our world? Aren't the inequalities gross enough and obvious enough to warrant direct attention to actions to deal with the problem itself, rather than to refine the "ethics" of approaching it? Moreover, strong theoretical works already exist that provide astute analyses of the relationships between equity (and ethics) and development. Of special note are two books by Amartya Sen, On Ethics and Economics, and Inequality Reexamined.

Today it is worth asking again, do we really need more conferences (or books?) to define equity, ethics, and human rights before engaging in advocacy and direct health action? I remain skeptical. I think we can conference and write ourselves and the would-be beneficiaries of direct public health action to death. On the other hand, it must be recognized, as Sudhir Anand, Fabienne Peter, and Amartya Sen have suggested in their Public Health, Ethics, and Equity, that "the commitment of public health to social justice and to health equity raises a series of ethical issues which, until recently, have received insufficient attention." Their book however, has not satisfied everyone. Bioethicists Madison Powers and Ruth Faden, for example, suggest that we do need more conferences and books, when they argue that "the foundational moral justification for the social institution of public health is social justice," and that "commentary on ethics and public health is, at best, thin." Nor is their view idiosyncratic.

Jennifer Ruger has argued that although "global health inequalities are wide and growing . . . [and] pose ethical challenges for the global health community . . . we lack a moral framework for dealing with them," and suggests pursuing equality from a theory of justice. Elsewhere, Ruger has suggested that on the specific question of the human right to health, "One would be hard pressed to find a more controversial or nebulous human right than the 'right to health' " (although she has also suggested that a philosophical justification for this right can be provided). Others, including physician-anthropologist and activist Jim Kim, president of Dartmouth College, has argued that the human rights approach to health dispari-ties and inequality is more rhetoric than reality, akin to singing "Kumbaya."

It is easy to be cynical about or disenchanted with human rights. Law professor David Kennedy has catalogued the major critiques of human rights, noting that human rights can be legitimately critiqued for driving out other emancipatory possibilities, for framing problems and solutions too narrowly, for overgeneralizing and being unduly abstract, and for expressing a Western liberalism. Kennedy's list continues: human rights promises more than it can deliver, the human rights bureaucracy is itself part of the problem — it can strengthen bad government, and it can be bad politics in particular contexts. In his words, "The generation that built the human rights movement focused its attention on the ways in which evil people in evil societies could be identified and restrained. More acute now is how good people, well-intentioned people in good societies, can go wrong, can entrench and support the very things they have learned to denounce. Answering this question requires a pragmatic reassessment of our most sacred humanitarian commitments, tactics and tools."

There is a measure of truth in all these observations, and effective action does require defined goals and specific actions to reach them. But as Joseph Kunz observed almost 60 years ago in regard the Universal Declaration of Human Rights, "In the field of human rights . . . it is necessary to avoid the Scylla of a pessimistic cynicism and the Charybdis of mere wishful thinking and superficial optimism." No other language than rights language seems as suitable for global health advocacy. All people have (inherent) human rights by definition, and people with rights can demand change, not just beg for it. And rights matter — and will matter even more as judicial structures to enforce them, like the International Criminal Court, continue to be established and nourished. Values of course underlie rights, but it would be incomprehensible to adopt a "Bill of Values" rather than a "Bill of Rights" to protect people.

In the language of contemporary human rights, governments don't simply have an obligation to act or not to act. Governments have obligations to respect the rights of the people themselves, to protect people in the exercise of their rights, and to promote and fulfill the rights of people. Of course, not all governments can immediately fulfill economic rights, like the right to health, because of financial constraints. International human rights law therefore provides that a government's obligation can be defined as working toward the "progressive realization" of these rights within their resource constraints. Some countries are so limited in their resources that they require assistance from the world community. The novel but potentially powerful right to development speaks to the obligations of the world community to provide that assistance, as do the goals of the UN's Millennium Declaration.

In public health, of course, it is well-recognized that many countries require the support of the world community to deal effectively with epidemic diseases, like SARS and the H1N1 flu, and that such support is in everyone's collective interests. Another development, the globalization of clinical research trials, provides a good example of the conflicting agendas and conflicts of interest that both call for and seek to avoid universal human rights norms.

THE GLOBALIZATION OF CLINICAL TRIALS

The globalization of clinical research trials calls for more effective ethical and legal rules to protect research subjects, as well as to guard the scientific integrity of the research. Nonetheless, as the former editor of the New England Journal of Medicine, Marcia Angell, observed more than a decade ago in this context, "there appears to be a general retreat from the clear principles enunciated in the Nuremberg Code and the Declaration of Helsinki as applied to research in the Third World." The situation has not improved.

During the Bush administration the Food and Drug Administration (FDA) sought to immunize pharmaceutical manufacturers from state lawsuits asserting that FDA-approved drug labels inadequately warned healthcare providers of their risks. This was not the only step the Bush administration's FDA took to aid the pharmaceutical industry by undermining protections for the public. Another involved research trials. Near the end of the Bush administration, the FDA decided that research studies submitted to it for review need no longer follow the Declaration of Helsinki, but instead could follow the less exacting, industry-sponsored, International Conference on Harmonization's Guidelines for Good Clinical Practice.

There is another choice — the human rights choice as articulated in the Nuremberg Code. The Declaration of Helsinki is a statement of research ethics by physicians. But what is the legal status of the Nuremberg Code? Does it, like Helsinki and the Harmonization Guidelines, also represent a collection of bioethics rules that researchers can ignore with impunity? Or has the Nuremberg Code, and especially its uncompromising informed consent requirement, arrived at the status of international human rights norm that must be followed? Just as controversy over the US-sponsored 076 maternal-to-child HIV transmission interruption trials in Africa in the mid-1990s gave rise to a continuing debate about standard of care and benefit obligations, so another mid-1990s research trial in Africa has brought international research rules and the doctrine of informed consent back to center stage.

Four years after it occurred, the Washington Post broke the story of a 1996 medical experiment conducted by Pfizer researchers in Kana, Nigeria, during a meningitis epidemic. The story created a sensation, especially its lead, which described the slow death of a 10-year-old little girl known only as subject 6587-0069. The researchers monitored her dying without modifying her treatment, but simply followed the research protocol designed to test their potential breakthrough antibiotic, Trovan, on children. The Post noted that the story was hardly unique, their investigation having discovered corporation-sponsored experiments in Africa, Asia, Eastern Europe, and Latin America that were "poorly regulated," "dominated by private interests," and that "far too often betray" their promises to research subject and consumers.

Following the expose, the families of the children-subjects in the Kano experiment brought suit against Pfizer in Nigeria, and later in the United States as well, charging Pfizer with conducting medical experiments without informed consent. The lawsuits initially met dogmatic and sometimes zealous resistance by judges in both the United States and Nigeria. Pfizer had successfully argued both that there was no international norm that required the company physicians to obtain informed consent to experimental drugs, and that in any event, any lawsuit against them by the subjects and their families should be tried in Nigerian, not US courts. Pfizer abandoned this latter claim in 2006 when a copy of an internal report by the Nigerian Ministry of Health on the experiment was made public. The report concluded, among other things, that the study violated Nigerian law, the Declaration of Helsinki, and the Convention on the Rights of the Child (ORO). Following the release of the report, the Nigerian government filed both a criminal and a civil suit against Pfizer in Nigeria. Pfizer settled the Nigerian cases in mid-2009 for $75 million.

More important in human rights terms than the Nigeria litigation, is the litigation in the United States, especially the 2009 opinion of the Second Circuit Court of Appeals, which reversed a lower court dismissal of the lawsuit and sent it back for trial. In the area of human rights, the Second Circuit is best known for its 1980 opinion that a physician from Paraguay could sue the inspector general of police of Asuncion, Paraguay, in the United States for the murder and torture of his son in Paraguay under the Alien Tort Statute. The reason, according to the court, was because torture is universally condemned as a violation of international human rights law, and "The torturer has become — like the pirate and the slave holder before him — *hostis humani generis*, an enemy of all mankind." To oversimplify (but not much), at issue in the Pfizer case before the Second Circuit was whether the researcher who experiments on humans without their informed consent violates a substantially similar international human rights law norm.

It is worth underlining that there has never been a trial in this case, and that the facts alleged by the Nigerian families may not be able to be proven in court. Nonetheless, for the purposes of deciding whether they should have their day in an American court, the Second Circuit had to assume the facts as alleged in the complaint are true. These allegations are primarily that, in the midst of a meningitis epidemic in Nigeria, Pfizer dispatched physicians to go to the Kano Infectious Disease Hospital to do a study on 200 sick children to compare the efficacy of their new drug, Trovan, with the FDA-approved antibiotic Rocephin. Trovan had never before been tested on children in its oral form. The experiment was conducted over a two-week period, then the Pfizer team precipitously left. In the court's words, "According to the appellants, the tests caused the deaths of eleven children, five of whom had taken Trovan and six of whom had taken the lowered dose of ceftriaxone, and left many others blind, deaf, paralyzed, or brain-damaged." The central allegation is that "Pfizer, working in partnership with the Nigerian government, failed to secure the informed consent of either the children or their guardians and specifically failed to disclose or explain the experimental nature of the study or the serious risks involved," or the immediate availability of alternative treatment by Médecins sans Frontières (MSF) at the same facility.

The Supreme Court has cautioned lower courts to be conservative in determining whether a particular category of actions contravene "the law of nations" accepted by the "civilized world" as a norm of customary international law. For the Second Circuit to permit this case to proceed it had to conclude that the requirement of informed consent to medical experiments on humans has become a norm of customary international law. The court so concluded because it found the informed consent requirement is sufficiently "(i) universal and obligatory, (ii) specific and definable, and (iii) of mutual concern," to be a customary international law norm that can support a claim under the Alien Tort Statute.

Perhaps of most interest from the global health perspective is that the court found the war crimes trials at Nuremberg, especially the Doctors' Trial, to provide the legal foundation for its conclusion. The major war crimes trial, the International Military Tribunal (IMT), was the only multinational trial at Nuremberg. Nonetheless, the court found that the US military trials that followed the IMT, including the Doctors' Trial, "effectively operated as extensions of the IMT." The Doctors' Trial, of course, produced the 1947 Nuremberg Code in the judgment, the first precept of which is the requirement for voluntary, competent, informed, and understanding consent of the research subject. In the court's words, "The American tribunal's conclusion that action that contravened the Code's first principle constituted a crime against humanity is a lucid indication of the international legal significance of the prohibition on nonconsensual medical experimentation." As important, the Nuremberg consent principle has been widely adopted in international treaties, including the International Covenant on Civil and Political Rights (ICCPR); the Geneva Conventions; and domestic law, as well as in non-binding international ethics codes like the Declaration of Helsinki.

The court found that in addition to being universal, the Nuremberg norm is specific in its requirement (so researchers could understand it), and is of mutual concern among nations. To make this last point the court concluded that promoting global use of essential medicines can help reduce the spread of contagious disease, "which is a significant threat to international peace and stability." Contrariwise, conducting drug trials in other countries without informed consent "fosters distrust and resistance . . . to critical public health initiatives in which pharmaceutical companies play a key role." The example the court cited is the impact of local distrust of international pharmaceutical companies that caused the Kano boycott of the 2004 effort to stem a polio outbreak there that later spread across Africa, making global eradication of polio all the more difficult.

Post-World War II ethical standards of clinical research have not effectively protected subjects or ensured scientific integrity. The Second Circuit's persuasive opinion that the doctrine of informed consent has attained the status of an international human rights norm that can be enforced in the world's courts should help persuade international corporations and researchers alike to take informed consent, and perhaps the other principles of the Nuremberg Code, much more seriously. If so, it will provide a powerful example of the beneficial impact of human rights on the health and welfare of subjects in clinical trials. But could social justice do the job just as well or better? As I have already suggested, I don't think arguing for one approach or the other is terribly fruitful, and that working together is much more likely to promote the publics' health than working separately. In Senator Edward Kennedy's last letter to President Obama on healthcare (the president read from in his September 2009 speech on the subject to a joint session of Congress), for example, Kennedy referenced both "fundamental principles of social justice" and making healthcare "a right and not a privilege" as complimentary rationales for universal access. It is, nonetheless, worth noting that even commentators who seem to believe in social justice alone is the preferable frame for public health action can't help coming back to the health and human rights movement.

SOCIAL JUSTICE AND HUMAN RIGHTS

In their discussion of social justice and public health, Powers and Faden describe what they characterize as "one of the most compelling recent examples of work in public health on behalf of an oppressed group . . . ." The example is the documentation of the rights of women by Physicians for Human Rights (PHR) during pre-9/11 Taliban rule. The authors write, "Research conducted by the group Physicians for Human Rights provides powerful evidence that the denial of basic rights to women resulted not only in horrible injustices with regard to respect, affiliation, and personal security but also with regard to health." Of course, this research project by PHR can be characterized as public health research and as documenting a major injustice to women. But neither characterization accurately describes what PHR itself thought it was doing.

PHR's name could not be more descriptive of their membership and their goals: Physicians for Human Rights. Nor could the subtitle of its Taliban report be any more explicit: The Taliban's War on Women: A Health and Human Rights Crisis in Afghanistan. The first sentence of their report says it again: "This report documents the results of a three-month study of women's health and human rights concerns and conditions in Afghanistan by Physicians for Human Rights." The report continues: "Taliban policies of systematic discrimination against women seriously undermine the health and well-being of Afghan women. Such discrimination and the suffering it causes constitute an affront to the dignity and worth of Afghan women, and humanity as a whole."

PHR's report is extremely powerful and merits the praise it has received. Nonetheless, it is a report by a physician group, not a public health group, and it is a group dedicated to doing health and human rights work, here especially founded on the ICCPR and CEDAW, not engaged in social justice. Although primarily focused on health, the report also noted that "The Taliban's edicts restricting women's rights have had a disastrous impact on Afghan women and girls' access to education, as well as health care. One of the first edicts issued by the regime when it rose to power was to prohibit girls and women from attending school."

Since the beginning of the ongoing post-9/11 war in Afghanistan, conditions for women have marginally improved, but much remains to be done. Leadership in human rights has been since its creation in the hands of a physician, Sima Samar, chair of the Afghan Independent Human Rights Commission. This is the first human rights commission in Afghanistan's history and it has a wide-ranging mandate, including the promotion of health and human rights, especially the health and human rights of women. When this Commission speaks of justice, it means bringing the perpetrators of war crimes in Afghanistan to justice. And when it speaks of health, it does so in the language of human rights, for example in its 2006 report on "Economic and Social Rights in Afghanistan." Of special note is the Commission's recommendation regarding women and children's health: "The Government should prioritize reproductive (prenatal and. postnatal) and child healthcare, according to their obligations under international treaties to which Afghanistan is a party. Afghan women should have universal access to reproductive health care."

It is easy for Americans to criticize the marginalization of human rights and health of women in other countries. But when the health of women in the United States is directly undermined by our government, silence seems the preferred response. Thus, when our Supreme Court ruled that it is constitutionally acceptable for Congress to make it a crime for a physician to use a specific medical procedure that the physician believes is the best one to protect his female patient's health, most commentary focused on abortion politics, rather than the health of women. Few noted that American physicians have never before been prohibited from using a recognized medical procedure, or that prohibiting its use only affected the health of women. The Taliban must have been smiling. As human rights expert Rebecca Cook noted in the broader context of abortion availability globally, "Whether it is discriminatory and socially unconscionable to criminalize a medical procedure that only women need is a question that usually goes not simply unanswered but unasked."

GLOBALIZATION AND HUMAN RIGHTS

American bioethics has had a major positive impact on the way medicine is currently practiced in the United States, especially in the areas of care of dying patients, including advance directives and palliative care, and medical research, including federal regulations to protect research subjects and institutional review boards. It is noteworthy that these accomplishments all came by enacting specific laws related to health. American bioethics has not exhausted what it can usefully accomplish in these spheres, but has of late seen most of its efforts and energy devoted to the interrelated fields of abortion, embryo research, and cloning.

Given the decade-long embryo-centric US activity (Obama's national healthcare plan did produce renewed political interest in discussing "death panels"), I think it is fair to conclude that bioethics is likely to have a stunted future in the real world without a significant reorientation of its focus and direction. I suggest that the most useful reformulation involves recognition and engagement with two interrelated forces reshaping the world and simultaneously providing new frameworks for ethical analysis and action: globalization and public health.

In American Bioethics, I argued that the boundaries between bioethics, health law, and human rights are permeable, and border crossings are common. That these disciplines have often viewed each other with suspicion or simple ignorance tells us only about the past. They are most constructively viewed as integral, symbiotic parts of an organic whole, with a common birthplace: Nuremberg.

Globalization, of course, does not depend upon physicians, ethicists, or lawyers, anymore than it depends upon health law, bioethics, or human rights. It does not even depend primarily upon the actions of governments. Rather, two relatively new players dominate globalization: the transnational corporation, and to a lesser extent, the NGO. Both, I think, can be usefully viewed as new life forms on our planet that are increasingly evolving and changing our environment. A notable health-related example of an NGO is Medecins sans Frontieres (MSF), a humanitarian-human rights organization founded on the belief that human rights transcend national borders and thus human rights workers cannot be constrained by borders but should cross them when necessary. MSF expands medical ethics to include physician action to protect human rights, blending these two fields and treating the law that protects government territorial boundaries as subordinate to the requirements of protecting human rights. Other human rights and health NGOs, like Physicians for Human Rights, view their primary mission as advocating for human rights.

Transnational corporations deserve our attention because of their incredible potential to both help and harm the planet and its people. Corporations have historically seen at least part of their social responsibility as providing charity to the communities in which they have a large presence. They have, however, been quick to argue that this is purely voluntary and that the responsibility to provide direct services to people, including drugs and medical treatment, rests with the government. A nascent movement to articulate the human rights obligations of transnational corporations is now underway, both in the UN and among corporations themselves. It is too soon to tell whether the global recession, which required governments to rescue both large corporations and banks, will lead to a new recognition of the interdependence of governments and corporations, and thus of their complementary obligations to the people of the world.

Prior to the global financial meltdown, John Ruggie, the Special Representative of the Secretary-General on the issue of human rights and transnational corporations released his report on "Business and Human Rights." The report identifies five avenues to introduce human rights law into corporate behavior (in order, from the strongest to the weakest): (1) the state's duty to protect its citizens against non-state actor human rights abuses; (2) corporate responsibility and accountability for international crimes (including the use of slave labor, child soldiers, and the use of torture) under complicity theories; (3) corporate responsibility for other human rights violations under international law (e.g., under the Universal Declaration of Human Rights, although this is currently "not necessarily legal in nature"); (4) "soft law" mechanisms, such as voluntary international agreements, like the Kimberley process, which seeks to prohibit international trade in "conflict diamonds"; and (5) self-regulation, in which at least some of the 77,000 transnational corporations and their 770,000 subsidiaries voluntarily adopt and follow human rights standards in their businesses.

Approximately 3,000 transnational corporations, including some major pharmaceutical companies, have joined the UN's Global Compact and committed themselves to its principles, the first two of which are that corporations should support and respect the protection of internationally proclaimed human rights, and that corporations should make sure that they are not complicit in human rights abuses. In the conclusion to his report, Ruggie makes three points that have special importance to global health: (1) "human rights and the sustainability of globalization are inextricably linked"; (2) corporations can be tried in "courts of public opinion" for human rights violations; and (3) "no single silver bullet can resolve the business and human rights challenge."

In our current climate, where transnational corporations like Pfizer seem intent on fostering protection of intellectual property more than the protection of people, is there any room for optimism? I think there is. This is because it is becoming critical for transnational corporations to respect human rights for their own sakes. As already discussed, for example, transnational corporations are becoming involved in human rights and bioethics because of their desire to do clinical trials around the world. Corporations may want to set their own rules. But most corporations recognize that they must follow generally accepted international norms of informed consent to conduct their clinical trials if they expect to use the results to have their products certified by government regulators. In short, in at least some cases, transnational corporations must adopt and follow human rights norms to accomplish their business goals. In addition, the human rights and bioethics issues that confront corporations continue to expand, and now include patenting, pricing, and access to their products by people who need them to survive or thrive, but who (either individually or through their governments) simply cannot afford them. These are basic human rights issues that have not been addressed by bioethics.

DeLillo would likely think that human rights and transnational corporations make too unlikely a combination to take seriously. In Underground, he saw the transnationals simply taking over from the exhausted Cold War governments. He pictured, for example, waste disposal done in secret by private corporations using underground nuclear explosions. One Kazakhstan company, named Tchaika (meaning seagull, a "nicer name" than rat or pig), is looking for an American broker to recruit US customers:

> They want us to supply the most dangerous waste we can find and they will destroy it for us. Depending on the degree of danger, they will charge their customers — the corporation or government or municipality — between three hundred dollars and twelve hundred dollars per kilo. Tchaika is connected to the commonwealth arms complex, to bomb-design laboratories and the shipping industry. They will pick up waste anywhere in the world, ship it to Kazakhstan, put it in the ground and vaporize it. We will get a broker's fee.

DeLillo may be right. But little progress is likely to be made in global health without the active engagement of the transnational corporations. This could be done either through private-public agreements, or by holding transnationals themselves accountable for not only respecting human rights themselves, but also for protecting and fulfilling them in their spheres of business. In real life, Tchailm, for example, should be legally responsible for all the radiation-caused health consequences of its activities, and should therefore seek to prevent them. The currently contested question, of course, is whether transnationals should have obligations to help fulfill human rights as well, including the right to access to the potentially life-saving drugs whose supply and price they control.

The hero of Netherland, Chuck Ramkisoon, tells Hans that his dream is to bring peace to the planet (or at least New York City) through cricket: "I'm saying that people, all people, Americans, whoever, are at their most civilized when they're playing cricket. What's the first thing that happens when Pakistan and India make peace? They play a cricket match." Chuck is a dreamer, but has an abiding belief in the cornerstone of human rights: All human are fundamentally the same, and will recognize this fact when they get to know each other.

On a grander scale, Tony Blair entitled his thoughts on 9/11 in Foreign Affairs, "A Battle for Global Values." Much in his essay, especially about the continuing wars in Iraq and Afghanistan, is easy to disagree with. But his basic message is sound: We are not in a war that can be won by force of arms. "This is a battle of values [and] we have to show that our values are not Western, still less American or Anglo-Saxon, but values in the common ownership of humanity, universal values that should be the right of the global citizen." A name exists for those universal values that are the "right of the global citizen," and that name is human rights. Blair goes further, noting,

> The challenge now is to ensure that the agenda is not limited to security alone. There is a danger of a division of global politics into "hard" and "soft," with the "hard" efforts going after the terrorists, whereas the "soft" campaign focuses on poverty and injustice. That divide is dangerous because interdependence makes all these issues just that: interdependent. The answer to terrorism is the universal application of global values, and the answer to poverty and injustice is the same. That is why the struggle for global values has to be applied not selectively but to the whole global agenda.

In the sphere of global health, another way to make Blair's point is, as Jonathan Mann put it, health and human rights are inextricably linked.

TABLE OF CASES

[References are to pages]

[References are to pages]

[References are to pages]

[References are to pages]

N

O

[References are to pages]

[References are to pages]

TABLE OF STATUTES

[References are to pages]

[References are to pages]

[References are to pages]

[References are to pages]

INDEX

[References are to sections.]

A

ACQUIRED IMMUNE DEFICIENCY SYNDROME (AIDS)
Generally . . . 5[C]

ADVERTISING
Tobacco . . . 10[D]

AIDS (See ACQUIRED IMMUNE DEFICIENCY SYNDROME (AIDS))

ALCOHOL (See DRUGS AND ALCOHOL)

B

BIOTERRORISM (See EMERGENCY PREPAREDNESS AND BIOTERRORISM)

C

CHRONIC DISEASES
Generally . . . 8[A]
Detection of disease, early . . . 8[C]
Health promotion programs . . . 8[B]
Screening and early detection of disease . . . 8[C]

CIVIL LIABILITY
Generally . . . 11[D]

CONSTITUTIONAL PRINCIPLES
Generally . . . 3[A]
Commerce, power to regulate . . . 3[D]
Federal regulation
    Commerce, power to regulate . . . 3[D]
    Tax and spend, power to . . . 3[E]
Jurisdiction, distinguishing state and federal
    . . . 3[B]
Power to regulate
    Commerce . . . 3[D]
    Tax and spend . . . 3[E]
State residents, state regulation of . . . 3[C]
Tax and spend, power to . . . 3[E]

CONTAGIOUS DISEASES
Generally . . . 5[A]
HIV/AIDS . . . 5[C]
Tuberculosis . . . 5[B]

D

DEATH
Causes . . . 2[A]

DISCRIMINATION
Weight and . . . 9[D]

DISEASES
Chronic (See CHRONIC DISEASES)
Contagious (See CONTAGIOUS DISEASES)

DRUGS AND ALCOHOL
Generally . . . 11[A]
Civil liability . . . 11[D]
Criminal responsibility for intoxication, defining
    . . . 11[B]
Intoxication, defining criminal responsibility for
    . . . 11[B]
Screening . . . 11[C]
Testing and screening . . . 11[C]

E

EMERGENCY PREPAREDNESS AND BIO-TERRORISM
Generally . . . 6[A]
Bioterror preparedness and research . . . 6[H]
Influenza . . . 6[D]
9/11 Investigations . . . 6[B]
Nuclear device explosion, improvised . . . 6[E]
Preparedness and research, bioterror . . . 6[H]
Public health emergency preparedness
    Generally . . . 6[C]
    Administrative aspects . . . 6[C][1]
    Armed forces, use of . . . 6[D][a]
    Fear and security agenda, overreactions and mis-
        use of public health to promote . . . 6[C][2]
    Pandemic preparedness . . . 6[D][a]
    Policy and administrative aspects . . . 6[C][1]
    Security agenda, overreactions and misuse of
        public health to promote fear and . . . 6[C][2]
Research, bioterror . . . 6[H]
Severe acute respiratory syndrome (SARS)
    . . . 6[G]
Smallpox vaccination program . . . 6[F]

EPIDEMICS (See CONTAGIOUS DISEASES)

F

FIREARMS
Generally . . . 12[C]
Appeal, fatal . . . 12[C][1]
Constitutional authority to regulate . . . 12[C][2]
Fatal appeal . . . 12[C][1]
Gun use and ownership, litigation role in determin-
    ing public policy on . . . 12[C][4]
Legislation . . . 12[C][3]
Litigation role in determining public policy on gun
    use and ownership . . . 12[C][4]
Second Amendment to regulate . . . 12[C][2]

FIRST AMENDMENT
Tobacco . . . 10[D]

FOOD
Environment for food and physical activity
    . . . 9[E]

[References are to sections.]

[References are to sections.]